QUALITATIVE
RESEARCH
PRACTICE

QUALITATIVE
RESEARCH
PRACTICE

Edited by
CLIVE SEALE
GIAMPIETRO GOBO
JABER F. GUBRIUM
DAVID SILVERMAN

SAGE Publications
London • Thousand Oaks • New Delhi

Editorial arrangement, Preface, Introduction and Part
introductions © Clive Seale, Giampietro Gobo,
Jaber F. Gubrium, David Silverman 2004
Chapter 1 © Tim Rapley 2004
Chapter 2 © Joanna Bornat 2004
Chapter 3 © Gabriele Rosenthal 2004
Chapter 4 © Phil Macnaghten and Greg Myers 2004
Chapter 5 © Ian Dey 2004
Chapter 6 © Paul Atkinson 2004
Chapter 7 © Molly Andrews, Shelley Day Sclater,
    Corinne Squire, Maria Tamboukou 2004
Chapter 8 © Celia Kitzinger 2004
Chapter 9 © Gavin Kendall and
    Gary Wickham 2004
Chapter 10 © Paul ten Have 2004
Chapter 11 © Anssi Peräkylä 2004
Chapter 12 © Alexa Hepburn and
    Jonathan Potter 2004
Chapter 13 © Ruth Wodak 2004
Chapter 14 © Sara Delamont 2004
Chapter 15 © Anne Ryen 2004
Chapter 16 © Nigel Fielding 2004
Chapter 17 © Les Back 2004
Chapter 18 © Linda S. Mitteness and
    Judith C. Barker 2004

Chapter 19 © James A. Holstein and
    Jaber F. Gubrium 2004
Chapter 20 © Julia Brannen 2004
Chapter 21 © Louise Corti and
    Paul Thompson 2004
Chapter 22 © Malin Åkerström,
    Katarina Jacobsson and
    David Wästerfors 2004
Chapter 23 © Annette Markham 2004
Chapter 24 © Lindsay Prior 2004
Chapter 25 © Sarah Pink 2004
Chapter 26 © Clive Seale 2004
Chapter 27 © Bent Flyvbjerg 2004
Chapter 28 © Giampietro Gobo 2004
Chapter 29 © Robert M. Emerson 2004
Chapter 30 © Udo Kelle 2004
Chapter 31 © Janice M. Morse 2004
Chapter 32 © Gill Ereaut 2004
Chapter 33 © Moira J. Kelly 2004
Chapter 34 © Donna Ladkin 2004
Chapter 35 © Martyn Hammersley 2004
Chapter 36 © Barbara Czarniawska 2004
Chapter 37 © Donileen R. Loseke and
    Spencer E. Cahill 2004
Chapter 38 © Pertti Alasuutari 2004

First published 2004

SAGE Publications Ltd
6 Bonhill Street
London EC2A 4PU

SAGE Publications Inc.
2455 Teller Road
Thousand Oaks, California 91320

SAGE Publications India Pvt Ltd
B-42, Panchsheel Enclave
Post Box 4109
New Delhi 100 017

British Library Cataloguing in Publication data

A catalogue record for this book is available from
the British Library

ISBN 0 7619 4776 0

Library of Congress Control Number 2003103976

Typeset by C&M Digitals (P) Ltd., Chennai, India
Printed in Great Britain by The Cromwell Press Ltd, Trowbridge, Wiltshire

Contents

About the Editors and Contributors

EDITORS

Giampietro Gobo is Professor of Methodology of Social Research at the University of Milan. His research has been focused on qualitative methods and the improvement of survey data collection. His main research topic is on computer-supported cooperative work in call centres. Founder and former chair of the Research Network on Qualitative Methods (European Sociological Association), he is the author of two handbooks on survey data collection and on the ethnographic method, and several articles, including 'Class as metaphor' in *Philosophy of the Social Sciences*.

Jaber F. Gubrium is Professor and Chair of Sociology at the University of Missouri, Columbia. His research focuses on the narrative organization of personal identity, family, the life course, ageing, and adaptations to illness. He is the editor of the *Journal of Aging Studies* and the author or editor of more than twenty books, including *Living and Dying at Murray Manor, Caretakers, Describing Care, Oldtimers and Alzheimer's, Speaking of Life, The New Language of Qualitative Research, The Self We Live By* and *The Handbook of Interview Research*.

Clive Seale is Professor of Sociology at the Department of Human Sciences, Brunel University. His research focuses on topics in medical sociology, including work on the experience of dying and the popular media representation of illness, health and health care. He is the author or editor of numerous books, including *The Year Before Death* (Avebury), *Health and Disease: A Reader* (Open University Press), *Researching Society and Culture* (Sage), *Constructing Death: The Sociology of Dying and Bereavement* (Cambridge University Press), *The Quality of Qualitative Research* (Sage) and *Media and Health* (Sage).

David Silverman is Professor Emeritus in Department of Sociology, Goldsmiths College, University of London. He is the author of two bestselling textbooks, *Doing Qualitative Research* (1999) and *Interpreting Qualitative Data* (second edition, 2001). His research has focused on medical settings (*Communication and Medical Practice,* 1987, and *Discourses of Counselling,* 1997). His main interests are in ethnography and conversation analysis (*Harvey Sacks: Social Science and Conversation Analysis,* 1998).

CONTRIBUTORS

Malin Åkerström is Professor of Sociology at Lund University in Sweden. Her research has focused on medical sociology as well as the sociology of deviance and she is the author or editor of numerous books, including *Betrayal and Betrayers: The Sociology of Treachery* (1991) and *Crooks and Squares: Lifestyles of Thieves and Addicts in Comparison to Conventional People* (1993). She has worked in an inter-actionist ethnographic tradition and published several articles on definitions of violence, on hope, on resentment, and on aspects of time.

Pertti Alasuutari, PhD, is Professor of Sociology and Director of the Research Institute for Social Sciences at the University of Tampere, Finland. His research focuses on topics in cultural and media studies, including everyday life and identity construction, media reception and audiences, cultural dimensions of globalization, and qualitative methodology. He is editor of the *European Journal of Cultural Studies,* and his books include *Desire and Craving: A Cultural Theory of Alcoholism, Researching Culture: Qualitative Method and Cultural Studies, An Invitation to Social Research* and *Rethinking the Media Audience.*

Molly Andrews is Co-director of the Centre for Narrative Research, University of East London. Her research interests include the psychological basis of political com-mitment, psychological challenges posed by societies in transition to democracy, gender and ageing, and counter-narratives. Her recent research has focused on the truth commissions of East Germany and South Africa.

Paul Atkinson is Research Professor in Sociology at Cardiff University, UK. He is Associate Director of the ESRC Research Centre on Social and Economic Aspects of Genomics. His main research interests are the sociology of medical knowledge and the development of qualitative research methods. His publications include *Ethnography: Principles in Practice* (with Martyn Hammersley), *The Clinical Experience, The Ethnographic Imagination, Understanding Ethnographic Texts, Medical Talk and Medical Work, Fighting Familiarity* (with Sara Delamont), *Making Sense of Qualitative Data* (with Amanda Coffey), *Sociological Readings and Re-Readings* and *Interactionism* (with William Housley). Together with Sara Delamont he edits the journal *Qualitative Research.* His recent ethnographic study of an international opera company will be published by AltaMira Press as *Everyday Arias.*

Les Back teaches sociology and urban studies at Goldsmiths College. His initial train-ing was in social anthropology and he has conducted ethnographic fieldwork in the UK in South London and in Birmingham and northern Alabama, USA. His recent books include *Out of Whiteness: Colour, Politics and Culture* (University of Chicago Press, 2002) and *The Changing Face of Football: Racism and Multiculture in the English Game* (Berg, 2001).

Judith C. Barker is a Professor of Medical Anthropology at the University of California, San Francisco. She studies processes by which family and non-kin provide care to community-living older adults, and day-to-day management and experience of chronic illnesses. She is widely published in the anthropological and social geronto-logical literature.

Joanna Bornat is a Senior Lecturer in the School of Health and Social Welfare at the Open University where she writes on courses on ageing and social care. She has been an editor of *Oral History* for over twenty years. She teaches, researches and writes using oral history as a method and has a particular interest in remembering in late life.

Julia Brannen is Professor of the Sociology of the Family, Institute of Education, University of London. She has carried out policy-relevant research for many years within the Institute's Thomas Coram Research Unit. Her research focuses on family sociology including children and young people in families; she has a special interest in methodology and in the interface between work and family life. She is co-founder and co-editor of the *International Journal of Social Research Methodology: Theory and Practice* and (co-)author and (co-)editor of many books. Three recent books include *Connecting Children: Care and Family Life in Later Childhood, Young Europeans, Work and Family Life: Futures in Transition* and *Rethinking Children's Care.*

Spencer E. Cahill is Director and Professor of Interdisciplinary Studies and Professor of Sociology at the University of South Florida. He is a former co-editor of the *Journal of Contemporary Ethnography,* former associate editor of *Symbolic Interaction*, a former advisory editor for *Social Problems*, and a current member of the editorial advisory board for *Sociological Studies of Childhood and Youth.* He has published articles on a variety of topics in such journals as *Social Psychology Quarterly, Sociological Theory* and the *Sociological Quarterly.*

Louise Corti is Head of the Qualitative Data Service (Qualidata) and the Outreach and Training Sections of the UK Data Archive, both based at the University of Essex. She is responsible for the direction and management of these sections for the ESRC/JISC UK Data Access service with the principle aim of providing user-friendly social science data services and support. In the past she has taught sociology, social research methods and statistics, and spent six years working on the design, implementation and analysis of the British Household Panel Study, also based at the University of Essex. She has recently authored a virtual tutorial for social research methods and co-edited the first ever journal issue devoted entirely to the sharing and reuse of qualitative data. She is interested in both qualitative and quantitative aspects of social research, and in the use of data in teaching and learning.

Barbara Czarniawska holds a Skandia Chair of Management Studies at Gothenburg Research Institute, School of Economics and Commercial Law, Gothenburg University, Sweden. She is also a Titular Professor at the European Institute for Advanced Studies in Management, Brussels. Her research focuses on complex organizing processes, most recently big city management. In terms of methodological approach, she combines institutional theory with the narrative approach. She has published in the area of business and public administration in Polish, her native language, as well as in Swedish, Italian and English, her most recent publications being *Narrating the Organization: Dramas of Institutional Identity* (University of Chicago Press, 1997), *A Narrative Approach to Organization Studies* (Sage, 1998), *Writing*

Management (OUP, 1999) and *A Tale of Three Cities* (OUP, 2002). She edited *Good Novels, Better Management* (with Pierre Guillet de Monthoux, Harwood, 1994), *Translating Organizational Change* (with Guje Sevón, de Gruyter, 1996) and *Organizing Metropolitan Space and Discourse* (with Rolf Solli, 2001). Her articles have appeared in *Accounting, Organizations and Society*; *Accounting, Management and Information Technologies*; *Consultation*; *International Studies of Management and Organization*; *Journal of Management Studies*; *Management Communication*; *Management Learning*; *Organization*; *Organization Studies*; *Scandinavian Journal of Management Studies*; and *Studies in Cultures, Organizations and Societies*. She is a member of the Swedish Royal Academy of Sciences and the Swedish Royal Engineering Academy.

Shelley Day Sclater is a Reader in Psychosocial Studies at the Centre for Narrative Research, University of East London. Her research has focused on socio-legal studies of the family and, as co-convenor of the Cambridge Socio-Legal Group, she has co-edited *What is a Parent? A Socio-Legal Analysis* (Hart, 1999) and *Body Lore and Laws* (Hart, 2002). She is author of *Divorce: A Psycho-Social Study* (Ashgate, 1999) and *Families* (Hodder & Stoughton, 2000) and co-editor of *Undercurrents of Divorce* (Dartmouth, 1999) and *Lines of Narrative* (Routledge, 2000). She is writing up research on contact disputes and beginning a new project on self and identity.

Sara Delamont is Reader in Sociology at Cardiff University, UK. She was the first woman to be President of the British Education Research Association, and the first woman to be Dean of Social Sciences at Cardiff. Her research interests are educational ethnography, Mediterranean anthropology and gender. Of her nine single-authored published books, the best known is *Interaction in the Classroom* (1976 and 1983), her favourites are *Knowledgeable Women* (1989) and *Appetites and Identities* (1995). Her most recent books are *Fieldwork in Educational Settings* (2002) and *Feminist Sociology* (2003). She has also published three books with Paul Atkinson and one with Amanda Coffey. She is co-editor of the journal *Qualitative Research,* with Paul Atkinson. With Paul Atkinson, Amanda Coffey, John Lofland and Lyn Lofland she edited the *Handbook of Ethnography.*

Ian Dey is Senior Lecturer in Social Policy in the School of Social and Political Studies at the University of Edinburgh. His research focuses on issues of prejudice and how this is reduced or reinforced in areas of family policy, particularly in relation to family formation. He is currently working on a book on *Reproducing Prejudice.* He developed a software package for qualitative data analysis and two of his books have been concerned with qualitative methods: *Qualitative Data Analysis: A User-Friendly Guide* (1993) and *Grounding Grounded Theory: Guidelines for Qualitative Analysis* (1999).

Robert M. Emerson is Professor of Sociology at the University of California, Los Angeles. From 1983 to 1986 he served as editor of the ethnographic journal, *Urban Life*. His publications on ethnographic and field research methods include an edited collection of readings on ethnography, *Contemporary Field Research* (second edition, Waveland Press, 2000), and *Writing Ethnographic Fieldnotes* (University of Chicago Press, 1995), co-authored with Rachel I. Fretz and Linda L. Shaw. Substantively his work uses qualitative methods to analyse both decision-making practices in institutions of social control, including juvenile courts, psychiatric emergency teams, public schools and prosecutors' offices, and the dynamics of interpersonal troubles and informal social control.

Gill Ereaut is an independent qualitative research consultant. She is co-editor of the series *Qualitative Market Research: Principle and Practice* (Sage, 2002) and author of *Analysis and Interpretation in Qualitative Market Research* (Sage, 2002). With a professional background in qualitative market research, and latterly an engagement with academic qualitative research, she combines commercial practice with writing and training in qualitative methods. Her interests include extending the range of methods used within qualitative commercial research, and promoting communication and exchange between academic and commercial research communities.

Nigel Fielding is Professor of Sociology and Co-director of the Institute of Social Research at the University of Surrey. He has taught field methods and criminology at Surrey since 1978. His research interests are in qualitative methods, new research technologies and criminal justice. He was editor of the *Howard Journal of Criminal Justice* from 1985 to 1998, and co-edits the series *New Technologies for Social Research* (Sage). He has published twelve books, four of them on methodology, and is working on a four-volume set on *Interviewing* (Sage) and a book on courtroom processes in cases of physical violence.

Bent Flyvbjerg is Professor of Planning, Department of Development and Planning at Aalborg University, Denmark. He is the author of numerous publications in twelve languages, most recently *Megaprojects and Risk: An Anatomy of Ambition* (Cambridge, 2003), *Making Social Science Matter* (Cambridge, 2001) and *Rationality and Power* (Chicago, 1998). He is currently doing research on the relationships between power, truth and lying in policy and planning.

Martyn Hammersley is Professor of Educational and Social Research, Faculty of Education and Language Studies, the Open University. He has done research in the sociology of education and has recently been investigating the representation of research in the mass media. However, much of his work has been in the field of methodology. He is the author of several books, including *What's Wrong with Ethnography?*, *The Politics of Social Research*, *Taking Sides in Social Research* and *Educational Research, Policymaking and Practice*.

Alexa Hepburn is Lecturer in Social Psychology at Loughborough University. She has studied school bullying, issues of gender, and violence against children, and interaction on child protection helplines, as well as writing about the relations of the philosophy of Derrida to the theory and practice of social psychology. She has written an integrative survey of critical social psychology, *An Introduction to Critical Social Psychology* (Sage, 2003).

James A. Holstein is Professor of Sociology in the Department of Social and Cultural Sciences at Marquette University. He is the author or editor or numerous books, including *Court-Ordered Insanity, Dispute Domains and Welfare Claims, Reconsidering Social Constructionism* and *Challenges and Choices: Constructionist Perspective on Social Problems*. He is also editor of the journal *Social Problems*. Holstein has collaborated for over a decade with Jaber F. Gubrium to publish a variety of constructionist analyses of everyday life, including *What is Family?, The Self We Live By, Institutional Selves, Inner Lives and Social Worlds, Constructing the Life Course, Aging and Everyday Life* and *Ways of Aging*. They have also collaborated on several methodological ventures, including *The Active Interview, The Handbook of Interview Research, Inside Interviewing, Postmodern Interviewing* and *The New Language of Qualitative Method*.

Katarina Jacobsson is a researcher and lecturer in the Department of Sociology at Lund University, Sweden. In her dissertation, which received an annual dissertation award, she employed a rhetorical and dialogical perspective on ethnographic data from the Swedish deaf world (*A Battle of Words*, 2000; *Conveying the 'Right' Knowledge*, 1999). At present she is engaged in a project on court cases of bribery.

Udo Kelle is a Lecturer in Social Research Methods (qualitative and quantitative) at the University of Vechta, Germany. His main interests cover the methodology and epistemology of research methods. Based on several research projects in the fields of life-course research and the sociology of ageing, he has developed and critically evaluated methods and techniques for social research, methods for typology building and theory construction. His current research and recent publications refer to the integration of qualitative and quantitative methods. He has written and edited a variety of books about methods, including *Computer Aided Qualitative Data Analysis* or *Vom Einzelfall zum Typus*, as well as numerous articles in handbooks and journals.

Moira J. Kelly is Research Fellow at St George's Hospital Medical School, University of London, and Lower Clapton Health Centre, East London. She has worked as a health researcher in palliative care, health promotion, mental health and most recently primary health care. Her publications cover a range of health research topics and methods. Her recently completed PhD is an ethnomethodological analysis of qualitative interview data.

Gavin Kendall is Senior Lecturer in Sociology at Queensland University of Technology, Brisbane, Australia. His research interests are in the areas of political sociology and social theory. He is the author of *State, Government and Globalisation* (2003) with Roger King, *Understanding Culture* (2001) with Gary Wickham, and *Using Foucault's Methods* (1999) with Gary Wickham.

Celia Kitzinger is Professor of Conversation Analysis, Gender and Sexuality in the Department of Sociology at the University of York, UK. Her current research focuses on the mundane construction of the social world through everyday talk in interaction, with a particular interest in the (re)production of normative genders and sexualities.

She is the author or editor of nine books and around eighty articles and chapters on issues of relevance to gender, sexuality and language, including *The Social Construction of Lesbianism* (Sage, 1987), *Heterosexuality* (Sage, 1993, with Sue Wilkinson) and *Lesbian and Gay Psychology* (with Adrian Coyle, Blackwells/BPS Books, 2002). She is currently writing a book on feminism and conversation analysis.

Donna Ladkin, PhD, is a Visiting Fellow at the University of Bath's Centre for Action Research in Professional Practice, where she teaches and supervises MPhil and PhD students. Her main research interests include the processes of conducting research and finding forms for presenting the outcomes of experiential learning.

Donileen R. Loseke is Professor of Sociology at the University of South Florida. She is a previous co-editor of the *Journal of Contemporary Ethnography* and is currently an advisory editor for *Social Problems*. She has served on the publications committees of the Midwest Sociological Society (the *Sociological Quarterly*) and the Society for the Study of Symbolic Interaction (*Symbolic Interaction*). Her books include *The Battered Woman and Shelters* and *Thinking About Social Problems: An Introduction to Constructionist Perspectives*.

Phil Macnaghten is a Lecturer in the Institute for Environment, Philosophy and Public Policy, Lancaster University, where he teaches on the MA in Nature and Culture. He has written extensively on the sociology of environmental issues, including *Contested Natures* (with John Urry). He has designed and conducted a number of focus group studies for environmental NGOs, government agencies, local government agencies and corporate clients, as well as for projects funded by research councils.

Annette Markham is Assistant Professor of Communication at the University of Illinois at Chicago. Her research focuses on the influence of communication technologies on identity, community and culture, the negotiation of identity in computer-mediated contexts, virtual ethnography, and critical interpretative methodologies. She is the author of the book *Life Online: Researching Real Experience in Virtual Space*.

Linda S. Mitteness is a Professor of Medical Anthropology at the University of California, San Francisco. Her research has focused on the experience of chronic illness in mid- and later life, with a smaller emphasis on the role of religion and spirituality in both the experience of illness and in the organization of health services. She teaches qualitative research methods and research ethics.

Janice M. Morse (PhD [Nurs], PhD [Anthro], DNurs [Hon], FAAN) is the Scientific Director of the International Institute for Qualitative Methodology, CiHR Senior Scientist, AHFMR Senior Health Scientist, and Professor, Faculty of Nursing, University of Alberta, and the 1997 Sigma Theta Tau Episteme Laureate. She has published extensively in the areas of comfort, suffering and qualitative methods, and serves as co-editor of the *International Journal of Qualitative Methods* and editor of *Qualitative Health Research*. She has authored, co-authored or edited fourteen books, including *Readme First: A Users Guide to Qualitative Analysis* (2002) with Lyn

Richards, *The Nature of Evidence in Qualitative Inquiry* (2001), *Completing a Qualitative Project: Details and Dialogue* (1997), *Critical Issues in Qualitative Research Methods* (1994), *Qualitative Approaches to Nursing Research* (1985, 1995, with Peggy Anne Field) and *Qualitative Nursing Research: A Contemporary Dialogue* (1989).

Greg Myers is a Senior Lecturer in Linguistics and Modern English Language at Lancaster University. He has written about scientific texts, advertising and (with Phil Macnaghten) environmental rhetoric. He is currently completing a book on the construction of opinions in group discussions.

Anssi Peräkylä is Professor of Social Psychology at the University of Tampere, Finland. His research interests include conversation analysis, doctor–patient communication, psychotherapeutic interaction and emotional communication. He is the author of *AIDS Counselling* (Cambridge University Press, 1995) and several articles in social science and communication journals.

Sarah Pink is a Lecturer in the Department of Social Sciences, Loughborough University, UK. She has worked in Spain, West Africa and England and her research focuses on gender, public performance, media, the home, the senses and visual anthropology. Her research publications include her books *Women and Bullfighting: Gender, Sex and the Consumption of Tradition* (1997) and *Home Truths* (2004). She has a special interest in visual ethnographic research and representation. Her publications in this area include *Doing Visual Ethnography* (2001) and the co-edited volume *Working Images* (2004).

Jonathan Potter is Professor of Discourse Analysis at Loughborough University. He has researched a range of topics including racism, relationship counselling and child protection helplines and has written extensively on meta-theory, theory and methods in the area of discourse analysis, and discursive psychology. His most recent books are *Representing Reality* (Sage, 1996), *Focus Group Practice* (with Claudia Puchta, Sage, 2004) and *Talk and Cognition* (edited with Hedwig te Molder, CUP, 2004).

Lindsay Prior is a Reader in Sociology at Cardiff University. His main interests are in aspects of medical sociology. In conjunction with colleagues at the University of Wales College of Medicine, he is currently working on projects relating to the assessment of cancer genetic risk, the nature of chronic fatigue syndrome, lay understandings of Alzheimer's disease and traumatic brain injury, as well as a study of lay responses to programmes of immunization. His books include *The Social Organisation of Mental Illness* and *The Social Organisation of Death*. His latest book is entitled *Documents in Social Research: Production, Consumption and Exchange.*

Tim Rapley is a Research Associate at the Centre for Health Services Research, University of Newcastle upon Tyne. His current research focuses on innovations in medical knowledge and practice, alcohol and illegal drugs, and the theory and practice of qualitative research.

Gabriele Rosenthal is Professor of Qualitative Methods at the Methodenzentrum Sozialwissenschaften, University of Göttingen. Her research focuses on topics in biographical research and family sociology, including work on transgenerational processes and on traumatization. She is the author and editor of numerous books, including *The Holocaust in Three Generations* (1998).

Anne Ryen is Associate Professor at Agder University College (AUC), Norway. Her research interests are qualitative methodology and fringe benefits in private business. Her recent publications on methodology include *Verneverdig: Barnevern, forskning og metode* (*Child Care, Research and Methodology*) (co-editor), *Det kvalitative intervjuet: Fra vitenskapsteori til feltarbeid* (*The Qualitative Interview: From Philosophy of Science to Fieldwork*), 'Cross-cultural interviewing' in Gubrium and Holstein's *Handbook of Interview Research: Context and Method*, and 'Marking boundaries: culture as category-work', co-authored with David Silverman in *Qualitative Inquiry.*

Corinne Squire is Co-director of the Centre of Narrative Research, University of East London. Her recent publications include *Culture in Psychology* (editor, Routledge, 2000), *Morality USA* (with Ellen Friedman, Minnesota UP, 1998) and *Lines of Narrative* (edited with Molly Andrews, Shelley Day Sclater and Amal Treacher, Routledge, 2000). Her research is on HIV and citizenship in Britain and South Africa, and popular culture and subjectivity.

Maria Tamboukou is Co-director of the Centre of Narrative Research, University of East London. Her research interests and publications are in the sociology of gender and space, the exploration of Foucauldian and Deleuzian analytics and the use of auto/biographies in research. She is the author of *Women, Education and the Self: A Foucauldian Perspective* (Palgrave, 2003) and co-editor with Stephen J. Ball of *Dangerous Encounters: Genealogy and Ethnography* (Peter Lang, 2003).

Paul ten Have has recently retired as an Associate Professor in the Department of Sociology and Anthropology at the University of Amsterdam, where he taught qualitative research methods and related subjects. His substantive interests include doctor–patient interaction, ICT-based (inter)action and practical ecology. He has written numerous articles and some books on qualitative research, conversation analysis and ethnomethodology. His last book is *Doing Conversation Analysis: A Practical Guide* (1999), while a new book, *Qualitative Research Methods: Ethnomethodological Perspectives,* is to appear in 2003.

Paul Thompson is Research Professor in Sociology at the University of Essex. He is Founder of the National Life Story Collection at the British Library National Sound Archive and was the Founding Director of Qualidata from 1994 until 2001. His books include *The Edwardians* (third edition, 1992), *The Voice of the Past* (third edition, 2000), *Living the Fishing* (1983), *I Don't Feel Old* (1990), *The Myths We Live By* (1990) and *Growing Up in Stepfamilies* (1997).

David Wästerfors is a graduate student in the Department of Sociology at Lund University, Sweden. Currently he is working on a dissertation on bribes and corruption, based on stories among Swedish expatriates in Eastern Central Europe (cf. *Tales of Ambivalence*, 2001). In 2000 he was awarded a prize for best essay by the Swedish Research Council for Social Sciences and Humanities.

Gary Wickham is Associate Professor of Sociology at Murdoch University, Perth, Western Australia. His books include *Foucault and Law* (1994), with Alan Hunt; *Using Foucault's Methods* (1999), with Gavin Kendall; *Understanding Culture* (2001), with Gavin Kendall; and *Rethinking Law, Society and Governance: Foucault's Bequest* (2001), edited with George Pavlich.

Ruth Wodak is Professor of Applied Linguistics at the University of Vienna and Director of the Research Centre 'Discourse, Politics, Identity' at the Austrian Academy of Sciences (see www.oeaw.ac.at/wittgenstein for details of recent projects). Her research focuses on discourse analysis, language and/in politics, prejudice and discrimination, and gender studies. She is the author or co-author of more than twenty books and over two hundred articles. Her most recent books published are *Racism at the Top* (2000), with T.A. van Dijk, *Discourse and Discrimination* (2001), with M. Reisigl, *Methods of Critical Discourse Analysis* (2001), with M. Meyer and *The Haider Phenomenon in Austria* (2002), with A. Pelinka. She is editor of the journal *Language and Politics* (with P. Chilton) and the four-book series *Diskursforschung* (Passagen Verlag), *Language and Context* (Lang Verlag, with M. Stegu), *Discourse in Politics, Culture and Society* (with P. Chilton) and *Document Design* (with J. Renkeema).

Preface

This book arose from discussions initiated by Giampietro Gobo with David Silverman and Michael Carmichael of Sage Publications (London). Michael alerted Jay Gubrium and Clive Seale, inviting them to take part and, in September 2000, we formed an editorial team to take the project forward. Though we all met in London in September 2002, the book is a testament to the power of the Internet and e-mail in keeping us in touch with each other, in forging friendships and professional collaboration, and in locating and communicating with the many people around the globe who have contributed chapters to this collection. A book like this would have been almost impossible to put together if we had had to rely on postal services and paper printouts. It certainly would have taken much longer than three years to write and publish. In the story of its production, then, the book is a demonstration of the global nature of the qualitative social research community.

We say a lot, in the introduction to the book, about our conception of the role of methodological debates in informing research practice, so we shall not repeat that here. Suffice to say, we did not just want to write another dull, very large 'handbook' of social research methodology. As you may be aware, the 'handbook' has been an important new concept in academic publishing circles in recent years. This, like such handbooks, is a very big book, but we have decided not to call it a handbook. There is already an excellent volume of this sort on qualitative research in general, currently in its second edition (edited by Norman Denzin and Yvonna Lincoln, the *Handbook of Qualitative Research*, Thousand Oaks, CA: Sage, 2000). This is widely consulted and influential in the field. Our book is in no way conceived as a replacement, alternative or rival to that volume.

This book, then, differs from existing handbooks. Though it is not a 'European' book, it attempts to represent something of the European tradition in qualitative research practice which has been relatively neglected in 'handbook' publications. We should have liked to have included more non-English-speaking authors from outside Europe; maybe one day we shall be able to do so. As it stands, we feel that the contributions reflect some of the best work available in North American, British, European and Australian traditions of qualitative research practice. Thus in its contributions it reflects the global nature of the qualitative research enterprise.

Above all, though, this book is about research *practice*, with methodological discussion being contextualized in the actual conduct of research projects. This, too, we feel distinguishes this book from existing handbooks and indeed from many textbooks on method. There is more that we say about this in our introductory chapter. We hope that this focus on practice will appeal to you as much as it has done to us.

In co-ordinating this book (from London, for practical purposes) the editorial team has benefited greatly from the administrative support of Isabelle Seale (Clive's sister, in case you are curious!), who has been unflaggingly efficient in her organizing role for this large project. We should like to thank her as well as Michael Carmichael and Zoe Elliott of Sage for their hard work and practical and financial support in helping this project come to fruition. This has not been without its stresses for our publishers, and we appreciate the sensitive way in which the various negotiations concerning the book have been conducted.

Additionally, the book has been supported by an international team of advisers (whose names are all listed elsewhere in this book) who have generously contributed their time and expertise in commenting on draft chapters. Contributors, too, have given their services in reviewing others' chapters, and we should like to thank them for this extra service too. We feel that it has helped make the book a more integrated project.

Clive Seale, Giampietro Gobo, Jaber F. Gubrium, David Silverman

Presenting a comprehensive examination of contemporary and traditional varieties of qualitative research practice, each specially commissioned chapter will be an invaluable resource for advanced students and researchers in any discipline.

Qualitative Research Practice starts with the premise that we can best improve our research skills by seeing what researchers actually do in particular projects and by incorporating their procedures and strategies into one's own research practice.

The editors have brought together some of the very best writers and researchers in the social sciences in this important new volume. All the chapters are written by leading, internationally distinguished qualitative researchers who recount and reflect on their own research experiences as well as those of others, past and present, from whom they have learned.

Qualitative Research Practice demonstrates the benefits of using particular methods from the viewpoint of real-life experience. Each contribution teaches us that social research is not only an investigation into the social, but is also a biographical engagement. In an authoritative yet accessible manner, Qualitative Research Practice reveals the special features of this engagement, teaching us that qualitative research is as much a craft and practice as it is a way of knowing.

Qualitative Research Practice is the essential and definitive guide to the major forms of qualitative methods in use today. It will be indispensable reading for anyone interested in the process of doing social research and improving research practice.

Introduction: inside qualitative research

Clive Seale, Giampietro Gobo, Jaber F. Gubrium and David Silverman

Recent years have seen an explosion of texts on qualitative methods. A survey of the Sage catalogue reveals the following chronological distribution of published qualitative methods textbooks:

1980–1987	10
1988–1994	33
1995–2002	more than 130

This excellent trend may hide a danger, represented by the abstraction and hyper-theorization of qualitative research. This is reflected by the tendency of many such texts to give decontextualized rules, advice and general principles.

By contrast, we believe that debates and textbooks about qualitative research are best understood by foregrounding the practical activities of researchers. Learning to do good qualitative research occurs most felicitously by seeing what researchers do in particular projects and incorporating procedures, strategies and 'tricks' (Becker, 1998) into one's own research practice. A pragmatic, researcher-centred perspective is then brought to bear on generalized methodological discussions that are otherwise experienced as some-what abstract and (wrongly in our view) irrelevant. The chapters in this book, therefore, are written by leading research practitioners who recount and reflect on their own research experience as well as that of others from whom they have learned.

If we privilege practice over principles – or at least link them together as principles-in-practice – then these principles of research methodology cannot be allowed to stand on their own, but always must be figured in relation to practice. Every term of reference (for example, sampling, concept formation, generalization, or data collection) needs to be dis-cussed in relation to the empirical world, not any ethereal conceptual space or universe of signs. The best place to turn to for this is the actual practice of working researchers. How is 'testing' done in practice? What does it mean to 'sample' a population? And how do we obtain a sense of the 'population' with whom we are dealing in practice? We do not suggest the rejection of theorizing or conceptualizing in methodological discussions, but rather that principles should never be presented as standing on their own. This clearly means that research practice must be seen as principled or, put another way, that practice has its principles. One of those principles is that principles exist in a world of practice, even as textbook listings. Another one is that the world of research practice is multi-sited and multi-dimensional in its substance and that principles that are not directly tied to at least a sense of that are vacuous. Although we may attend to philosophical debates, our practice does not in the end depend on the outcome of these debates because we are researchers, not philosophers.

It is tempting, when writing generally about qualitative research, to construct a 'progress narrative' of different phases, stages or 'moments' (Denzin and Lincoln, 1994,

2000) corresponding to a rough historical periodization. Such a story might comment on shifts from scientific conceptions of qualitative research to more literary ones, for example. Whatever may be done in the form of caveats and qualifications to reassure readers that no disrespect is directed at 'earlier' approaches, progress narratives have the effect of making it seem that their authors prefer to locate their own research practice within the latest phase. After all, don't we all learn by improving on past practice?

This approach to understanding the vast and various enterprise of qualitative research is, we feel, mistaken. Additionally, as Alasuutari shows in the last chapter of this book, it may have the effect of focusing undue attention on the research practices that have gained popularity in particular global locations, or in particular disciplines. As our own experience in running workshops internationally and participating in international research networks attests, qualitative research is an immensely diverse set of practices, involving an increasingly large subject-disciplinary range. An inevitably incomplete list includes geographers, sociologists, psychologists, anthropologists, educationists, business and management analysts, health-care workers, market researchers, historians, policy analysts, cultural studies experts, communications and media studies scholars, even accountants who, from time to time, identify themselves as 'qualitative researchers'. The great diversity of theoretical approaches, practical problems and local research traditions that people within these disciplines encounter – as well as the different audiences to whom research is addressed – means that any categorization of qualitative research practice into a series of progressive stages is likely to be experienced as unhelpfully ideological. In fact, it is likely to prevent people from learning from each other.

Take the case of those positions broadly associated with postmodernism (Denzin and Lincoln, 2000). These appear to be driven by an anti-methodological tenor that prefers the substance (research topics) to the form (methodology). Such a perspective, born partly in reaction to positivism, waved a flag of the superiority of qualitative research to surveys and experiments and considered methodological principles incapable of achieving a deeper understanding of a fragmented and dislocated culture. However, this research style has not always maintained its promise of achieving a deeper kind of research. The consequences are too often exposed to view: low quality qualitative research and research results that are quite stereotypical and close to common sense.

By contrast, we propose a perspective that places research practice at the centre. Practice involves an engagement with a variety of things and people: research materials (which some like to call 'data'), social theories, philosophical debates, values, methods texts and traditions, reports of other research studies, research participants, research audiences, funders and commissioners, publishers, conference organizers, teachers and examiners, the researcher's own past experience and present hopes. Out of this mix arise particular research inquiries. Sometimes we can learn from these, and if practising researchers are encouraged to write about their inquiries in a methodologically reflective way (though not in a purely confessional manner), we may learn a great deal.

But, it may be objected, where do we stand on the great issues that preoccupy methodologists today? If local research practice lies at the heart of this rather than universal principles, does anything go? How should research practitioners conceive of the larger enterprise of which their particular research project is just a small part? What working framework might guide it and which of the frameworks proposed at present is best? How can we formulate a justification or rationale for the kind of thing that we do when we carry out research that will legitimate it in the eyes of critics? The focus on research practice leading the way means that a thousand flowers can bloom; is this not a recipe for anarchic dissolution unless some general principles can be established?

As we have made clear, we do not reject frameworks, principles and methodological rules, only require that these are contextualized in research practice. In formulating a framework for qualitative research practice, it is important that it be permissive of considerable variety. Not all of the contributors to this book would find it possible to fit their practice within the framework that we prefer and outline in broad terms here. A framework is not helpful if it does not encourage principled choices that have consequences for research practice; it would be a series of empty platitudes without this consequence. And choices imply preferences for some things over others. Much of the rest of this Introduction will provide consideration of these matters, but we would like to be quite firm about this issue of the centrality of research practice before beginning. Anything that we write after this point ought to be considered in this light.

FOUNDATIONS

Placing research practice at the centre of methodological discussion resonates with another position that we hold dear, and this is one that goes some way towards providing a 'framework' for qualitative research practice. This consists of the view that, in doing social research, it is unwise to privilege any particular form or level of social reality over another. During one heyday of American social theory, in the 1950s and 1960s, it was popular to divide social realities into levels (for example, Parsons, 1951). The ostensibly highest level was culture. It was presented as that shared body of beliefs and values that 'surround' our actions, that come to bear on it, if not lead us to articulate who and what we are and what our worlds are composed of. Below this was social structure, which comprised relatively crystallized patterns of social roles and relationships. Beneath this was social interaction and, at the very bottom, at the deepest level of social reality, was experience, with feelings and emotions grounding these foundationally or, in the final analysis, linking us to other living creatures.

It was a neat array of Western categories, organized hierarchically so that cerebral matters were closest to being cosmic, if not divine, and bodily matters basic, if not socially chaotic or explosive. Social theory reflected existentially familiar terrain. From this, it was equally comforting to figure that social theory had many points of departure – from the cultural to the somatic – and that research practice was in principle a matter of seeking fundamental knowledge about which of the levels of social reality was most deterministic in this scheme of things. Thus, some social researchers mounted studies of the influence of culture or social structure on actions and attitudes, while other social researchers felt more comfortable with documenting the determining force of inner life and its somatic linkages on our actions, if not our overarching social worlds. Attitude researchers, for example, were extremely fond of deciphering the opinions and sentiments that they felt could predict an enormous variety of social activities and patterns.

Why should these kinds of categories be so powerful? To answer this question properly, we need to turn away from 'scientific' theorizing and look down, below our feet, as it were, to everyday life. Our world seems to bifurcate between events and structures (often beyond our control) and our personal understandings and inner feelings. Nowhere is this clearer than in media representations of events. Here news stories appear to bridge the gap between fact and emotion by providing 'authentic' accounts from ordinary people forced to confront puzzling events (wars, natural disasters, economic shifts, and so on). So the question 'How was it for you?' becomes a central way of understanding the world, extending beyond news broadcasts to chat shows and the work of the 'psy' professions.

Given this representational milieu, it is hardly surprising that many qualitative researchers, in search of foundations for their practice, buy into this vocabulary. So the media's question 'How was it for you?' has become for many their very own qualitative research instrument and unique selling proposition. For the claim to 'get closer' to 'the individual's point of view' appears to differentiate qualitative research beautifully from those benighted number-crunchers whose concern for mere 'facts' precludes a proper understanding of authentic experiences.

This prevailing position is argued in a recent authoritative work:

> Both qualitative and quantitative researchers are concerned with the individual's point of view. However, quali-
> tative investigators think they can get closer to the actor's perspective through detailed interviewing and
> observation. They argue that quantitative researchers are seldom able to capture their subjects' perspectives
> because they have to rely on more remote, inferential empirical methods and materials. (Denzin and Lincoln,
> 2000: 10)

Denzin and Lincoln's portrayal of what qualitative researchers 'think they can [do]' in
the above quotation is a deadly accurate characterization of much contemporary qualitative research practice. Following this approach, it appears that we can combine the concerns for authentic experience of the 'human interest' reporter and the in-depth
interview methods of the skilled counsellor. In this way, we are tempted to feel that we
may trump the spurious claims of our quantitative colleagues by showing how people
'really' think and feel and, by implication, put others in their place as purveyors of mere
facts. But this orients us away from practice, as well as perpetuating unhelpful stereotypes
about research that uses numbers.

The pragmatic alternative

With their feet firmly planted in the ground, pragmatists have been at considerable odds
with these conventionalized theoretical and procedural perspectives. From the start, the
pragmatist point of departure has been that the social world – whatever its levels or
dimensions – is a matter of practice. Culture and social structure are not just 'there', so
to speak, to be documented for the power of their influence on our thoughts, feelings and
identities. Rather, while there is no question that they figure significantly as categories of
everyday life, they enter into our lives as practical anchors for ordering them in some way
or other. The same goes for our inner thoughts and our ostensibly deepest feelings. For
pragmatists, these are not so much foundational to experience as they are used – quite
effectively at times – to assemble a sense of our everyday lives as grounded, say, in our
deepest feelings.

As such, pragmatists would be loath to seek ultimate knowledge of the social world
from any of these conventionalized realities, whether these be a theoretical construct
such as 'social structure' or the seemingly authentic inner world of the individual. It would
behoove a social researcher focused on the practice of everyday life not to valorize the
emotions, for example, but to investigate the ways that emotions are brought to bear on
our understandings of who and what we are, both in relation to what we apparently are
within and to what we believe we share as members of particular social situations.
Pragmatist sensibilities, in short, are centred in a persistent procedural doubt about what
members of the social world take for granted. Grandly designated conceptual systems,
such as the system of ostensible linkages that embrace our lives from culture and social
structure, at one level, to inner thoughts and feelings, on the other, are topics for investigations, not resources for explaining them.

The real is never abandoned by the pragmatist, but rather sensibly put to the test of
everyday life. When the early American pragmatists William James, George Herbert Mead
and Charles Sanders Peirce urged their scholarly compatriots to turn to the world of
everyday life, to the lives of those who lived them, to gain understanding of human nature
and the social order (see Charles Horton Cooley's 1922 book by the same title), they
were not urging us to abandon the task of understanding the real world, so much as they
urged us to document how reality entered into and figured in our daily lives.

Ludwig Wittgenstein was well aware of this difference and, as a latter-day pragmatist,
turned our attention to the many and varied ways that language related to forms of life. For
instance, in his inquiry into the grounds of certainty, Wittgenstein tried to avoid answers
that were purely philosophical or just common sense. Neither grand theory nor everyday

understandings were appropriate for him, recognizing how difficult it was to find a path that was neither too theoretical nor too concrete. As he wrote: 'It is so difficult to find the *beginning*. Or, better: it is difficult to begin at the beginning. And not to try to go further back' (1972: 62).

As Wittgenstein shows in this book, one way 'to begin at the beginning' is to assemble reminders of when, where and how we say 'I am certain'. Freed from its metaphysical baggage (described by Wittgenstein as a milieu where language 'goes on holiday'), 'certainty' turns out to be a particular kind of 'language game' used (and avoided) in various contexts. For instance, it is difficult to visualize a context in which (without anybody raising any doubt about the matter) I might say 'I am certain that I am in pain'. In our world, pain seems to be part of our personal experience and questions of 'certainty' or 'doubt' about its presence may occur only to third parties (for example, insurance assessors wondering whether we are trying to con them about the effects of an injury).

The neo-pragmatists, such as the ethnomethodologists (e.g. Garfinkel, 1967), put Wittgenstein's invented examples to systematic investigation. Theirs was the task of investigating social practice in relation to the apparently real, with no intention at all of abandoning or dismissing its importance in our lives.

The pragmatist position is anything but an 'anything goes' perspective. It does not throw methodological caution to the winds so much as begin by being cautious about the very things method is assumed to be about. To focus on social practice is not to be unsystematic about methods of procedure but, instead, to put into place self-conscious and systematic methods for addressing the very things that the social and behavioural sciences are presumably about. Rather than being chaotic, pragmatism is, therefore, expressly concerned with investigating the first principle of social worlds, namely, that they are composed of things, parts, linkages and wholes. From this point of departure follows the many and varied methods and procedure that many of the social researchers represented in this book apply in their investigations. It is rigorous from the start – rigorously putting to question the very things that those who lose sight of practice assume to figure significantly in our understanding of social order.

ANTI-FOUNDATIONALISM AS FOUNDATIONALIST

Some recently influential perspectives urge anti-foundationalist principles to be placed at the heart of social research practice. It is important to distinguish such views from our vision, since they may appear at first to be similarly pragmatic, starting as they do from the view that all research knowledge is a matter of local agreement. Paradoxically, this has led to a new form of foundationalism in some circles that we believe to be as unhelpful as the earlier focus on emotions or theoretical constructs.

The position starts from the perception that empiricism is an inadequate basis for research evidence. Facts are never theory- or value-free, so this argument goes. There is, then, no ultimate foundation for research practice. Knowledge claims are no more than 'partial truths' (Clifford and Marcus, 1986). Additionally, language and other kinds of signs are regarded as deriving their meaning from their relation to other signs, rather than from any correspondence with features of the world to which they might refer. Ultimately, this position can be applied to research texts themselves, so that the distinction between fact and fiction breaks down.

Further, the human sciences have an unfortunate history in so far as objectivity, universal truth and science have masked forms of political oppression, achieved in part through systems of knowledge, or discourse, that silence certain voices and privilege others. A considerable degree of introspection on the part of social researchers has been prompted by these views. This has led to a host of confessional narratives in which earlier conceptions of 'reflexivity' (e.g. Gouldner, 1970) have been taken to extremes, or experimental forms of writing that are designed to make aesthetic rather than scientific appeals to audiences. According to this view, if social research has a role, it is to facilitate polyvocality, assist voices that have hitherto been unheard to find an appropriate volume, generate 'catalytic authenticity' (Guba and Lincoln, 1994: 114) and thereby facilitate social change.

These perspectives raise important issues about the role of values in the production of knowledge. It is clear that naïve empiricism or crude realism cannot serve as a foundation for a sophisticated qualitative research practice. Yet serious problems arise if we move from some philosophical doubts about the nature of evidence to a wholesale rejection, especially if this involves importing some alternative set of value-driven foundations that are similarly philosophically suspect. This elevation of epistemological debate and political considerations to the status of deterministic law, to be regarded as a foundational framework for research practice, is to mistake the role of philosophical and political discussion in informing research practice. To put it bluntly, philosophers are able to show that we cannot prove that the sun will rise tomorrow just because it has always done so in the past. In our everyday lives, though, as Wittgenstein shows, we would be unwise to put much energy into this problem; there are the more pressing practical concerns of everyday life to worry about. And social research is a practical concern.

Take, for example, the objection that all 'facts' are constituted by our perceptions. Howard Becker has a relevant point to make here, and it is significant that the force of it is achieved through an example:

> Recognizing the conceptual shaping of our perceptions, it is still true that not everything our concepts would, in principle, let us see actually turns up in what we look at. So we can only 'see' men and women in the Census, because, providing only those two gender categories, it prevents us from seeing the variety of other gender types a different conceptualization would show us. The Census doesn't recognize such complicating categories as 'transgender'. But if we said that the population of the United States, counted the way the Census counts, consisted of fifty percent men and fifty percent women, the Census report could certainly tell us that that story is wrong, We don't accept stories that are not borne out by the facts we have available. (Becker, 1998: 18)

The great conversation that, in practice, is carried out in the world (what some researchers like to call 'common sense'), assumes that facts are 'out there' and can be 'collected' and therefore can constitute 'evidence'. A social research practice that does not go along with this view will, on the whole, fail to enter the world's conversation. This failure to relate in a convincing way to the great issues and concerns of the day is, we feel, increasingly evident in social research texts that take anti-foundationalism to be foundational.

Additionally, the rejection of a correspondence theory of language is also a move against 'common sense' and disables the capacity of such researchers to communicate – even with each other at times. For example, holding on to a view that it is possible to use words in a way to refer to things outside language, we might investigate the ways in which people deploy linguistic skills. This would avoid the mistake made if we refuse to turn rigorously to the investigation of everyday practice and instead jump precipitously into the attempt to explain this. Everyday practice, of course, is the very thing that a pragmatist puts to the test.

WHAT'S WRONG WITH METHODOLOGY?

For these reasons, we believe that any general framework to guide research practice can only be regarded as provisional. Indeed, to sail quite close to the (postmodern) wind, we could even say that any framework can contain only a 'partial truth'. The framework we have outlined should be treated like this. Though some of the contributors to this book would agree with what we have said about an orientation to everyday practices being a potential foundation for qualitative research, not all would go for this. Other frameworks, for example, that of 'subtle realism' (Hammersley, 1992), should be similarly regarded. The best of them (and Hammersley's suggestions come into this category) are *permissive* rather than restrictive.

In order to understand this issue better, we need to distinguish analytically the political (or external) role of methodology from the procedural (or internal) one. In the former case, methodology helps to legitimate and elevate a discipline or practice among other enterprises and social practices. Metaphorically it is the armed wing of science. In the past, experimental methodology and its strict rules had this function. In its procedural role, though, methodology helps to frame a research topic and to guide researchers in concrete terms during the whole process of producing knowledge, especially when they are in trouble.

These two roles or aspects of methodology have often been separated and treated as antithetical. This emerges clearly if we look at the history of 'hard' sciences. For example, on the one hand Galileo (with Bacon) is considered the inventor of experimental method. However, Galileo's rejection of Aristotle's law of gravity was based on conceptual arguments only, because he never did the associated experiment on the tower of Pisa (see Cooper, 1935; Feyerabend, 1975). This experiment is simply a myth. On this matter Galileo was a fudge-maker or liar, because he never did many of the experiments he described accurately in his books. In the same way, Newton, Einstein, Bohr and many others rely many times on experiments that never occurred (see Westfall, 1980). They also manipulate their data to prove their theories. The history of the 'hard' sciences is a continuous, incessant and recursive display of this schizophrenic behaviour: stating strongly overt methodological rules and then secretly disrupting them because, for a number of organizational reasons, it is impractical to apply generalized methodological rules to particular problems.

Traditional methodology is an outcome of a rationalistic view (of which Popper was a leading example), which considers research activities as driven by a set of norms, rules and transparent procedures. In his classic description of Galileo and the telescope, Feyerabend (1975) shows that if methodology and its rationality was the dominant criterion in the acceptance of theory, Galileo should have failed and been considered a bad scientist. Indeed he constructs the telescope but did not know very well how to use it; the public exhibitions where people were invited to look through the telescope were not successful because people 'watched' but did not 'see' what Galileo pointed out; he drew the moon but the drawing was not correct, and so on. The lesson we can learn is that it would be dangerous to give only to methodology and its inner rationality the task of evaluating a theory.

A situated methodology

The perspective we propose therefore tries to solve this schizophrenic attitude and contradictory behaviour by, on the one hand, suggesting a researcher-centred view of the place of methodological rules in guiding research behaviour and, on the other hand, encouraging methodologists to adapt methodology to the research situation. In other words, instead of forcibly applying abstract methodological rules to contingent situations, the research situation is placed in a position of dialogue with methodological rules.

Barry Hindess (1973) stated that methodological perspectives are internally inconsistent and contradictory, bearing only a tenuous connection with what researchers do in practice. This divergence between methodology as professed (or preached) and research as practised alerts us to the social and political functions of methodological claims. To understand this position better, let us see how ethical issues are treated in research.

Professional associations commonly craft ethical codes and guidelines when conducting research. However, such codes 'deal with predictable and planned research, conditions which are not present in fieldwork' (Holdaway, 1982: 66). Consequently a balance must be reached in each research situation. If we consider ethical issues only in the standardized way embraced by codes of professional ethics, there are a number of researcher behaviours that could be considered, in a strict sense, unethical (Gobo, 2001). Among them, covert observation is the best known. To the standardized and rigid conception of research ethics has been opposed the concept of 'situation ethics' (Fletcher, 1966). The latter asserts that, in deciding if a course of research action is morally right or wrong, we need to evaluate several contextual features, such as the aims of the study, the type of social actors observed, the consequences of the researcher's actions, and so on.

In the context of organization studies, another perspective maintains that covert research is ethical when the social actor observed plays a public/civil function or service for users, customers and clients. Policemen, civil servants, doctors, nurses and so on play a public role and are expected to adopt a client-oriented or customer-oriented approach. From this perspective, Rosenhan's (1973) well-known study in psychiatric clinics has some justification. Professional ethical codes for researchers are too often constituted as armchair criticism, distanced from the needs of the research practice. In addition, even if ethical codes aim to be universal, they are a product of a local culture and, as Ryen shows in Chapter 15 (in this volume) about research in Tanzania, are not easily exported outside the original culture.

So we do not neglect the usefulness of methodological rules; instead, we reject top-down rules and prefer bottom-up, user-centred and context-dependent methodological routines and agreements.

SOME PRACTICAL GUIDELINES

It has become popular in recent years to construct guidelines for the evaluation of the quality of qualitative research studies. These often have an educational role, teaching journal editors or research funding bodies, who may have little knowledge of qualitative research, what to look for when assessing a proposal or a report. They may also be designed to help students learning to do qualitative research and they may be useful devices for practising researchers formulating proposals or reports. Used judiciously and with due regard to the local context of the particular research study to which they are applied, they can be helpful devices. In this spirit, then, we offer the following guidelines that may be applied to a variety of qualitative research enterprises in order to enhance their quality. While one might expect all of these to be discussed in a final research report, they could also be things that researchers simply asked of themselves as they proceed about their business. They are organized in two levels and would assist the practical implementation of some of the framework principles we have discussed.

A good qualitative research study is likely to exhibit the following features:

Level 1 – general:

1 Its aim and purpose should be explained and set in the context (e.g. historical, political, disciplinary) in which these arose.
2 The rationale for the design of the inquiry should be explained.
3 The researcher should demonstrate openness to emergent issues.
4 The researcher should seek to be transparent and reflexive about conduct, theoretical perspective and values.
5 The study should provide understanding of context.
6 The study should re-present data or evidence faithfully.
7 A qualitative research study is likely to convey depth, diversity, subtlety and complexity.
8 Data or evidence should be actively and critically interrogated.
9 Claims should be supported by evidence for those claims.
10 Some (but not all) studies may be judged according to their utility or relevance for particular groups of people and particular power relations.

11 Some (but not all) studies may be judged according to whether they provide understanding of subjective meanings (see our comments earlier about the limitations of romantic interpretations that seek for 'authentic' human experience).

12 The study should provide new insights.

Level 2 – specific:

1 The relationship of the study to existing knowledge should be explained.

2 The rationale for a qualitative rather than a quantitative study should be understood.

3 A rationale for sampling should be present and the implications of different approaches to this, and of failures to gain access to certain sources, understood.

4 Negotiations to gain access to sources of evidence and the implications of these for the evidence gathered should be described and assessed.

5 The particular contributions made by different methods for collecting and recording evidence should be understood, and the rationale of the methods chosen be given in the light of this.

6 The rationale for the choice of analytic strategy should be clear, with awareness of the potential of other analytic strategies.

7 Attention should be paid to negative or deviant cases and to alternative explanations.

8 There should be a comprehensive rather than selective examination of data/ evidence.

9 There should be a clear separation between evidence and interpretation of evidence.

10 The language of final reports should be accessible and clear to the intended audiences.

11 The implications of the investigation for broader areas of knowledge and practice (for example, theory, policy, practice) should be explored, and be of significance.

STRUCTURE OF THE BOOK: A PRAGMATIC APPROACH TO METHOD

Just as a focus on people's everyday practices is likely to reward qualitative researchers exploring the social world, so, we feel, an exposition of research practice is likely to reward those who seek methodological guidance. As we hope we have made clear, we believe that methodological principles, while useful, should always be contextualized in the history and outcomes of particular research studies.

Thus most (though not all) of the contributors to this book have adopted a somewhat autobiographical approach to writing that distinguishes this book from generalized methods texts. Many authors told us that they enjoyed writing in this way; it brought what would otherwise be a dry account to life, showing the details of personal involvement and local context that, in research practice, always affect a researcher's capacity to apply generalized methodological principles. In our view, this also makes these chapters both more enjoyable to read and far more 'realistic' than generalized methods texts that may impose an artificial model of the research process. (For example, how many methods primers start with a chapter on how to do a literature review that will lead to the specification of research questions? How many research projects begin, instead, with a bit of interesting 'data'?) At the same time, we have not encouraged a purely autobiographical, personalized mode of writing in the manner of a confession. This is the flip side of the context-free, dry methods text, and can result in a great deal of material that is irrelevant to anyone's research practice. By striking this middle way we hope to have maximized the potential of this text to help its readers learn lessons that can be judiciously applied to their own qualitative research practice. Each part of the book (with the exception of Part 7) is preceded by a short introduction explaining its rationale and its contents in brief, but a short summary is appropriate here.

Part 1 of the book, 'Encountering Method', features researchers using their own experience of particular approaches on particular research projects describing their practice in the context of more general accounts of their preferred methods. Interviewing is perhaps the most widely used method in qualitative research, and it is therefore appropriate to begin with three chapters on different aspects of qualitative interviewing. Chapters on focus groups and grounded theory, also approaches that have captured the imaginations of many qualitative social researchers, are followed by an absorbing account of the application of ethnographic method to the study of performance.

Part 2 turns to analysis. Until recently, there were few methodological guidelines to qualitative data analysis, with the majority of texts focusing on field relations and data collection. With the 'linguistic turn' in human science disciplines, though, there has been a growing awareness that almost anything can be constituted as 'data' and the problem lies not so much in gathering data, but in managing and interrogating it in original ways. A variety of strategies – narrative, feminist, Foucaultian, ethnomethodological, conversational and discourse analytic – are covered. All of these approaches draw on areas of social theory, assisting researchers in seeking ways of seeing that go beyond the taken-for-granted.

Yet field relations remain important for much qualitative research practice, and Part 3 of the book contains chapters that consider various aspects of the relations that commonly preoccupy ethnographers as well as other researchers. Ethical and political issues as well as those concerning the personal safety of the researcher may loom large when researchers 'enter', or perhaps 'constitute', the various fields that they study. Additionally, relations with other researchers, where the context is that of team researcher, may prove crucial in the progress of a project.

Part 4, 'Context and Method', contains chapters that foreground the role of context in the conduct of research, focusing in particular on the uses of a variety of data sources that may not first occur to qualitative researchers oriented largely towards interviewing and ethnography. Visual images, the analysis of documents and Internet resources, the uses of data collected by other researchers or by oneself in the past, and the important role of numerical data in qualitative research are all considered, together with a chapter about shifting analytic contexts.

The authors in Part 5 all consider different aspects of quality and credibility, an issue that has been a particular preoccupation for qualitative reseachers seeking to justify their practices to sceptical, more quantitatively or scientifically oriented audiences, but which is also a general concern of those producing research work. Issues concerning sampling and representativeness are of particular concern to those involved in case-study work, but the issue of quality is far larger than this alone, as the chapters make clear. Many issues of quality are not to be solved by abstract philosophical or methodological debate, but by detailed consideration of particular research practices and decisions on specific research projects.

Without wishing to take on the postmodern or relativist position that judgement depends solely on the perspective of the observer, it is nevertheless true that observers, or 'audiences', of qualitative research vary. Researchers are wise when they notice and take account of this fact. Researchers write proposals so that others can decide whether to fund their work, or they may write in a market research context, where audience expectations are likely to be very different from those of the academic community. Others are concerned with audiences of policy-makers and practitioners, who seek to evaluate their programmes through research studies. Action researchers seek to enter into and change their relationship with an 'audience' too often ignored by social researchers: the 'researched', or the 'participants'. Writing and publishing bring a variety of demands to bear on the capacity of researchers to stimulate audiences, and the teacher–student relationship is also one of audience relations, with qualitative researchers often seeking to pass on their skills to generations of new researchers. All of these aspects are addressed in the chapters in this part of the book.

The book ends with a 'part' that is really a chapter on its own, concerning the globalization of qualitative research by Pertti Alasuutari. We wanted to highlight the importance of this chapter in some way, and debated among ourselves a variety of ways of signalling this, in the end deciding to place it at the end. You might like to read it first, though! In a sense, it deepens understanding of one of the most important rationales for this book: that it should reflect a genuinely international flavour. We wanted this book to involve authors outside the usual Anglo-American 'cartel' (if that is not too strong a word) that tends to dominate the field of qualitative methodology texts. Although all the chapters are written in English, and many by authors in the Anglophone world, we were keen also to represent the rich traditions of qualitative research practice going on in non-English-speaking locations. Alasuutari's chapter will help tell you why this is an important thing to do.

REFERENCES

Becker, H.S. (1998) *Tricks of the Trade: How to Think About Your Research While You're Doing It.* Chicago: University of Chicago Press.

Clifford, J. and Marcus, G.E. (eds) (1986) *Writing Culture: The Poetics and Politics of Ethnography.* Berkeley: University of California Press.

Cooley C.H. (1922) *Human Nature and the Social Order* (revised ed.). New York: Charles Scribner's Sons.

Cooper, L. (1935) *Aristotle, Galileo, and the Tower of Pisa.* Ithaca, NY: Cornell University Press.

Denzin, N.K. and Lincoln, Y.S. (1994) *Handbook of Qualitative Research.* Thousand Oaks, CA: Sage.

Denzin, N.K. and Lincoln, Y.S. (2000) *Handbook of Qualitative Research* (2nd ed.). Thousand Oaks, CA: Sage.

Feyerabend, P. (1975) *Against Method.* London: New Left Review Editions.

Fletcher, J. (1966) *Situation Ethics.* London: SCM Press.

Garfinkel, H. (1967) *Studies in Ethnomethodology.* Englewood Cliffs, NJ: Prentice-Hall.

Gobo, G. (2001) 'Best practices: rituals and rhetorical strategies in the "initial telephone contact"', *Forum: Qualitative Social Research,* 2(1), http://www.qualitative-research.net/fgs-texte/1-01/1-01 gobo-e.htm

Gouldner, A.W. (1970) *The Coming Crisis of Western Sociology.* New York: Basic Books.

Guba, E.G. and Lincoln, Y. S. (1994) 'Competing paradigms in qualitative research', in Denzin, N.K. and Lincoln, Y.S. (eds), *Handbook of Qualitative Research.* Thousand Oaks, CA: Sage, pp. 105–17.

Hammersley, M. (1992) *What's Wrong With Ethnography: Methodological Explorations.* London: Routledge.

Hindess, B. (1973) *The Use of Official Statistics: A Critique of Positivism and Ethnomethodology.* London: Macmillan.

Holdaway, S. (1982). '"An inside job": a case study of covert research on the police', in Martin Bulmer (ed.), *Social Research Ethics: An Examination of the Merits of Covert Participant Observation.* London: Macmillan Press, pp. 59–79.

Parsons, T. (1951) *The Social System.* London: Routledge & Kegan Paul.

Rosenhan D.L. (1973) 'On being sane in insane places', *Science,* 179 (January): 250–7.

Westfall, R.S. (1980) *Never at Rest: A Biography of Isaac Newton.* New York: Cambridge University Press.

Wittgenstein, L. (1972) *On Certainty.* New York: Harper Torchbooks.

Part 1

ENCOUNTERING METHOD

How are qualitative methods to be taught? Are there standard techniques with given advantages and disadvantages that can be learned by rote? Or is qualitative research a kind of craft skill that can only be learned by doing it?

Whichever alternative we choose, we tend to end up in an intellectual dead end. Rote learning is hardly appetizing – even if it is tending to become the default learning method in modern higher education 'factories'. By contrast, craft training seems to imply a one-to-one apprenticeship with a skilled practitioner. While this is appealing, it is hardly a reasonable prospect for mass education (see Hammersley, Chapter 35, this volume).

Part 1 of this book offers a way out of this impasse. Using their own research experience as a model, the authors provide a kind of distance-learning version of craft training. In this sense, encountering method documents a researcher's own experience with using a particular method. And that experience offers you, the reader, an opportunity for your own encounter with method – an encounter that will be enriched as you yourself apply these ideas to the demands and contingencies of your own research studies.

There remains an important qualification to be made. As these chapters show, while methods are important, we must never allow them to rise above their station. Methods are only research techniques. They acquire substantial meaning only in the context of broader decisions involving how we define our research problem, our database, our methods of data analysis and our relationships to those we are studying. These are all methodological matters and choosing a method is only one among them.

Even methodology itself is but a part of a set of much wider issues. Say you have designed a research study using interviews. How are you going to treat your data? Will you view them as containing a set of 'facts' about, say, people's attitudes or experiences? Or will you treat interviewees' utterances as contingent and locally constructed (i.e. with the interviewer) 'versions' of reality? (see Silverman, 2001: 87).

As this example makes clear, analytic choices are embedded in even the most apparently mundane methodological matters. This is because analytic models provide an overall framework for how we look at reality. Even if we would rather do without them, they creep in behind our backs as it were.

So the chapters below also document how our authors themselves came to grips with issues of both method *and* theory. And because the delight (and difficulty) of qualitative research is that there any many, competing analytic models, you can see for yourself what follows when researchers make their (fateful) choices.

In his chapter on qualitative or 'in-depth' interviewing, Tim Rapley take us to the processes by which interviews accomplish their social facts. From recruitment and the formulation of an initial list of questions, to the interaction between interview participants and analysis, Rapley illustrates from his own material the eminently practical contours of the interview enterprise.

Joanna Bornat's chapter on oral history also draws on the interview method. Here, however, the aim is to illustrate and understand historical purposes. Bornat's account of her rich and varied career allows us to see how oral history extends beyond the personal, to include the documentation of community experience.

Gabriele Rosenthal's chapter on biographical method and biographical research traces its origins to early twentieth-century American pragmatist concerns with the 'actor's perspective'. This theme comes forth and resonates throughout the chapter, from suggestions for organizing the biographical interview to a detailed case analysis of one interview subject's life history.

Macnaghten and Myers's chapter is on focus groups. It discusses an aspect that is often neglected: the tension between the moderator and the analyst. The moderator plans and conducts the groups; the analyst draws conclusions from them. There are often tensions between these perspectives, and these tensions affect such practical decisions as the detail of the topic guide, the use of various kinds of visual or verbal prompts, the structure of the sessions or series of sessions, the amount and form of intervention by the moderator, the degree of detail in the transcripts, and the use of the transcript in the analysis. The authors do not try to resolve these tensions, but present them as a dialogue between two perspectives (and the two authors).

Ian Dey's chapter discusses conventional topics in grounded theory methodology, including theoretical sampling, coding strategies and categorization. But it is also a chapter that is innovative and practical in taking the grounded theory analysis of the author's study of trade union activism in unpredictable new directions.

Part I concludes with Paul Atkinson's stimulating and entertaining account of his study of the day-to-day routines involved in producing an opera. Atkinson uses this apparently esoteric topic to depict vividly what is involved in writing an ethnography that endeavours to focus on everyday, mundane practice. As in all these chapters, we move smoothly from the personal to the public, from the local to the general.

REFERENCE

Silverman, D. (2001) *Interpreting Qualitative Methods* (2nd ed.). London: Sage.

1

Interviews

Tim Rapley

I was originally asked to write a chapter on something called 'in-depth interviews'. Now, I knew by that specific term that the editors wanted me to tell a story about something understandable as an 'interview' – a story that describes how two people, often relative strangers, sit down and talk about a specific topic. One of those strangers – an interviewer – introduces the specific topic, then asks a question, the other speaker – an interviewee – gives something hearable as an answer to that specific question, the interviewer listens to the answer and then asks another question ... and so the pattern repeats itself until at some point the interviewer says 'Thank you, that was really helpful/interesting/useful' and then they part company. So far so good – I know what it means to talk about 'interviews'.

Then I came to the term 'in-depth' and I was very aware that they don't want me to talk about interviews that *only* require 'yes-no-maybe' types of answers. But then I got stuck. I knew they wanted a description of a style of interviewing that encourages interviewees to produce 'thick descriptions' – where interviewees are specifically encouraged, by questions and other verbal and non-verbal methods, to produce *elaborated* and *detailed* answers. A doubt emerged; what specifically makes an in-depth interview an 'in-depth interview' compared to the academic literature that names such interviews as: active, biographical, collaborative, conversational, depth, dialogical, focused, guided, informal, life-history, non-directed, open-ended, oral-history, reflexive, semi-structured, etc.? So I decided to write the chapter on *qualitative* interviews, as this term seems to be a useful gloss for the disparate descriptions of the practices of this version of interviewing.

Now, some people may be thinking that I am being pedantic. Others may see those paragraphs above as 'setting the scene' for the argument that follows. My commentary is trying to highlight two things. Firstly that, as Silverman (1993: 19) notes, we are currently part of an '"interview society" in which interviews seem central to making sense of our lives'. The interview – seen in various forms of news interviews, talk shows and documentaries, alongside research interviews – *pervades and produces our contemporary cultural experiences and knowledges of authentic personal, private selves*. The face-to-face interview is presented as enabling a 'special insight' into subjectivity, voice and lived experience (Atkinson and Silverman, 1997). Importantly, we all just know 'at a glance' what it takes to be an interviewer or an interviewee.

Secondly, the sheer range of terms available to encompass the various formats of qualitative interviews begins to outline the trans-disciplinary 'industrial complex' of academic work on interviewing. Interviewing is currently *the* central resource through which contemporary social science engages with issues that concern it (Atkinson and Silverman, 1997). Since the emergence of the classical social survey interview, the interview has been deconstructed and theorized and consequently re-emerged in various guises. Symbolic interactionism sought to 'open' the talk so as to obtain more 'textured' and 'authentic' accounts. Feminist accounts sought to 'unmask' and then 'de-centre' the power balance. Alongside this work emerged an interest in the interview itself as a topic of research (notably Cicourel, 1964) and, following the linguistic turn, the gaze fell to the interviewee's shifting and complex discursive, identity and narrative work.[1]

As my discussion above begins to highlight, qualitative interviewing is, in some senses, both 'simple and self-evident' (Gubrium and Holstein, 2002: 3). It draws on the everyday practices of asking and answering questions and the everyday identities of questioner/answerer and interviewer/interviewee. And I argue below that, contra most of the current literature on 'how to' interview, interviewers don't need massive amounts of detailed technical (and moral) instruction on how to conduct qualitative interviews. This how-to-interview literature, with its concerns with the production of 'neutral and facilitative' or 'rapport building' questions and gestures, is the outcome of specific theoretical concerns about the analytic status of interview data. I argue that interview talk, and hence the 'interview data' that emerges from this, is the product of the local interaction of the speakers. As Gubrium and Holstein note, interviewers 'cannot very well taint knowledge if that knowledge is not conceived as existing in some pure form apart from the circumstances of its production' (2002: 15). Following from this, interviewers don't need to worry excessively about whether their questions and gestures are 'too leading' or 'not empathetic enough'; *they should just get on with interacting with that specific person.*

Interviews are, by their very nature, social encounters where speakers collaborate in producing retrospective (and prospective) *accounts* or *versions* of their past (or future) actions, experiences, feelings and thoughts. As Fontana notes, 'given the irremediably collaborative and constructed nature of the interview, a postmodern sentiment would behove us to pay more attention to the *hows*, that is, to try to understand the biographical, contextual, historical, and institutional elements that are brought to the interview and used by both parties' [author's emphasis] (2002: 166). When it comes to analysing interviews, I argue that *you should analyse what actually happened* – how your interaction produced that trajectory of talk, how specific versions of reality are co-constructed, how specific identities, discourses and narratives are produced.

Prior to offering a textured picture of the range of practices and the processes involved in doing qualitative interviewing, I want to present a very brief outline of debates over the analytic status of interview data.

INTERVIEWING AND THE 'REAL'

Seale (1998), in his overview of qualitative interviewing, identifies the two major traditions on which the analysis of interviews has centred: interview data as a *resource* and interview data as a *topic*. I am aware that such a divide glosses over the myriad of approaches that these terms encapsulates, but, put simply, the story goes something like this:

- *Interview-data-as-resource*: the interview data collected is seen as (more or less) reflecting the interviewees' reality outside the interview.
- *Interview-data-as-topic*: the interview data collected is seen as (more or less) reflecting a reality jointly constructed by the interviewee and interviewer.

The data-as-resource approach has undergone considerable critique from those working in constructionist traditions.[2] Much of this critique stems from highlighting that interviews are *inherently interactional events*, that both speakers mutually monitor each other's talk (and gestures), that the talk is *locally and collaboratively produced*. The critique also centres on the idea that data-as-resource researchers often incorrectly assume that interview-talk is *only* about the official topic of the interview. The talk in an interview may be as much about the person producing themselves as an '*adequate interviewee*', as a '*specific type of person in relation to this specific topic*'. In this sense, interview data may be more a reflection of the social encounter between the interviewer and the interviewee than it is about the actual topic itself. As Dingwall notes, '[t]he interview is an artefact, a joint accomplishment of interviewer and respondent. As such, its relationship to any "real" experience is not merely unknown but in some senses unknowable' (1997: 56).

This leads to considerable analytic attention to view interview-talk as the joint production of *accounts* or *versions* of experiences, emotions, identities, knowledges, opinion, truth, etc. A focus on interview-talk as locally and collaboratively produced does not deny that the talk is reflexively situated in the wider cultural arena (Silverman, 1993). In this sense, interview-talk *speaks to* and *emerges from* the contemporary ways of understanding, experiencing and talking about that specific interview topic. However, these ways of understanding, experiencing and talking about that specific interview topic are contingent on the specific local interactional context and should be analysed, at least initially, from the circumstances of their production.

Confused? Well let me try to offer a brief translation: *Don't rip the words out of context.* Let me now offer a brief demonstration. In a transcript of an interview given below (Excerpt 1, lines 28–36), an interviewee says drugs are meaningful to him by way of the 'fact' that they are *meaningful to everyone* – drugs are 'everywhere', 'so much of it around' and it's 'so much … in the news'. The interviewee's account – that *drugs are an 'inescapable' part of our culture* – is intimately tied to his prior talk, his identity as someone who was trained to conduct drug peer-education and the interviewer's question. The interviewee has already noted that drugs are only 'meaningful to him' as he comes from a 'medical family', so any interest in drugs has *only* entered his life through *legitimate and ordinary* ways.[3] The interviewer then asks whether there was any other 'particular interest' in the fact the training would be about drugs. The interviewee then produces the account that *drugs are an 'inescapable' part of our culture*. So that specific account is intimately tied to that specific interactional context, that the interviewee is arguing that 'I don't do drugs and I didn't become a drug peer-educator because I'm either pro- or anti-drugs' – and 'good' peer-educators should not be overtly pro- or anti-drugs.

Now, that was a (brief) focus on how that account or version was locally accomplished. However, that account – that *drugs are an 'inescapable' part of our culture* – emerges from and is shaped by the broader social context of the *contemporary debate about drugs*. The interviewee, in the very act of drawing on that account, is demonstrating (and reinforcing) that broader social norm. The interviewee is demonstrating *one of the possible ways* that are available to understand, experience and talk about drugs. These can be contrasted with the *other possible ways*, be it in the context of other interviews, government reports, newspapers, etc.

Hopefully, that very brief tour begins to outline the debates over the analytic status of interview data. I will return (again and again) to this debate throughout the chapter. I now want to shift to more 'practical' issues, to offer an account of the process that leads up to the interviews.

RECRUITMENT

The process of finding interviewees and setting up interviews is, as may be obvious, central to the outcomes of the research. Rubin and Rubin (1995) note four key areas around 'recruitment': initially finding a knowledgeable informant, getting a range of views, testing emerging themes with new interviewees, and choosing interviewees to extend results. These are valuable ideals; however, the actual practice can deviate from this

– like many things, recruitment routinely happens on an ad-hoc and chance basis.

For example, in one research project I was involved in I had to interview a range of employers – multinational companies to small one-person firms – to understand their experiences and perceptions of employing women in the construction industry. Initially, just finding knowledgeable informants was problematic. When I contacted large organizations, I was repeatedly passed from one department to the next as no one representative was 'officially' responsible, or felt able to talk 'on the record', for the organization's policy in regard to employing women. In comparison, while out socializing, whenever I discussed my research on 'illegal drug-use', people would often put themselves forward as potential interviewees, sharing part of their 'drug biography' in the process.

As the above examples begin to show, the actual 'problems' of recruitment can vary dramatically. When accessing potential interviewees you have to follow many trails, often relying initially on friends and colleagues and then on contacts given by other interviewees.[4] It is important to *try* and get a range of views on the topic of your research, as those few interviewees who produce 'radically different' or contrasting talk can often be central to modifying your theories. Above all, it is vital to take notes about the recruitment process and to offer it in reports of the research as questions of access and recruitment can be central to understanding the 'outcomes' of the research.[5]

YOUR (INITIAL) LIST OF QUESTIONS

So once you've arranged an interview you have to consider what issues you want to cover with this specific interviewee. Some of the how-to-interview literature discusses taking an interview guide, outline or schedule (e.g. Mason, 1996); some simply talks about interviewers going '[a]rmed with a list of questions' (Warren, 2002: 90). Whatever approach is taken, whether you produce a typed schedule on official headed paper or a handwritten list, it is useful to have something with you, be it 'key' words or written, 'finely crafted', questions.

The actual content of the list of questions is *initially* generated in negotiation with the relevant academic and non-academic literature, alongside your thoughts and hunches about what areas *might* be important to cover in the interview. You need to be aware that the questions you ask can change over the life-cycle of the project. The list of questions I take to interview is always shifting in relation to various influences. They 'mutate' in relation to the specific person I am interviewing – my 'recruitment' conversation on the phone with them, what I've read about them or been told about them. Also, this list is influenced by my conversations with my fellow researchers, what I've read in the recent literature, conferences I've attended, the interviews I've done previously and (increasingly) what the funders and steering group of the research are 'interested in'.

Interestingly, the list of questions can do various things *other than* just help to remind you of questions to ask and, possibly, give some structure to the interaction. They can provide a piece of paper to write down key words interviewees have said as an aide-mémoire for later questions or discussion; help to produce you as an official, competent, interviewer; be something to focus on when the interviewee is 'briefly called away'; help to close the interaction, etc.[6] Above all, irrespective of whether I actually ask any of the questions I have written down, it can come in use for the reasons outlined above (and that inventory is only the start of the ways it is used).

I want to stress that you don't 'have to' use *any* of the questions that you initially prepared. The point is to follow the interviewee's talk, to follow up on and *to work with them* and not strictly delimit the talk to your predetermined agenda. With some interviews I have just asked a 'broad' opening question, with the answer becoming the main source for my questions and our discussions in the rest of the interview. In other interviews I have worked more closely with my schedule – glancing at the list for a suitable 'next question' when I can hear one theme coming to a close and I don't want to follow up on anything more that the interviewee has said.

You don't have to ask the same question in the same way in each interaction. You often cover the same broad themes in different interviews – either through the interviewee or you raising it as a subject for talk. This is a central rationale of qualitative interviewing – *that it enables you to gather contrasting and complementary talk on the same theme or issue.*

BEGINNING THE INTERVIEW

So you've got your list of questions and you try and arrive a little early (but not too early) so as to create the right impression. We don't and can't always arrange interviews in 'private' spaces – the point is to be aware of your immediate environment and how that can and does affect your and the interviewee's talk. For example, when interviewing someone in a coffee shop and we turned to the subject of his sexuality, he began to speak in hushed tones. After the interview he noted that 'This is a small community and I don't want to upset future business clients'. For this interviewee this was a problematic topic to talk about in this *specific* space. So the actual space where you interview someone can sometimes make a difference. Obviously you need to be able to easily interact – to hear one another and be in a space without too much 'outside interaction', be it fellow workers, partners, children. Again, there are no hard-and-fast procedures to follow – just rely on your everyday knowledge and take note of the possible impact of the space on your talk.

I routinely begin by getting out my tape-recorder, re-asking their permission to record and re-explaining issues of confidentiality and anonymity. I also ask the interviewee if they want me to retell the story behind the research project, to remind them of our initial phone conversation where I first introduced the project.

I always try and use a tape-recorder, for some very pragmatic reasons: I want to interact with the interviewee, and I don't want to spend a lot of my time head-down and writing. Also, the tape provides me with a much more detailed record of our *verbal* interaction than any amount of note-taking or reflection could offer. I can replay the tapes, produce transcripts and then selectively draw on these to provide demonstrations of my argument.

The tape-recorder alongside the presence of the interview guide, the initial greetings, and talk about the aims of the research create 'a particular social context for the interview communication' (Warren, 2002: 91). They can work to forecast a specific interactional context, to shift the identities of the speakers to interviewer and interviewee, where the interviewee is produced as 'having something of importance to say'.

A question remains – does the tape-recorder influence the talk? The simple answer is, yes and no. On the brief moments it is mentioned, the how-to literature says things like 'The idea of taping *might* increase nervousness or dissuade frankness' [my emphasis] (Arksey and Knight, 1999: 105) and you '*may* find that [it] inhibits interaction. … The informant *may* feel he or she has to be interesting or dramatic and this *can alter the account*' [my emphasis] (Minichiello et al., 1995: 99). I have found that the tape-recorder is often a topic for discussion before, after and during interviews. Some interviewees want reassurances around how the recording will be made anonymous, who will be able to listen to it. One noted that the recording is 'like a painting, fixed and unchangeable'. Others focus their gaze on the tape-recorder prior to saying something, often implicitly marking it as 'sensitive talk', or others glance at it and say, 'as this is confidential…'. But not all interviewees explicitly orientate to the tape, and for those that do this is only for parts of the interaction.

So there appears to be an issue at stake. For some interviewees the issue is chiefly around trust: will you as a researcher *misuse the information* as this is a 'permanent record' that they could be identified through at a later point (cf. Rubin and Rubin, 1995: 126). This can infer debates about 'authenticity, truth and bias' – that if you build up trust, interviewees will be more 'open and truthful' (cf. Douglas, 1985) – as well as debates around the binary of 'private' and 'public' accounts (Cornwell, 1984). However, I think this is too simplistic a reading of interactions in interviews.

To be sure, interviewees offer 'on and off the record' talk: 'Well, I can say more about [organisation X] after you turn the tape off as well.' It is interesting that *sometimes* different and contrasting talk is produced off-tape. Such off-tape talk is not somehow more 'authentic', it does different work, it emerges from and reflexively creates a different context. It can often construct interviewees as a different type of person, 'Well, *personally* I feel …', that with prior talk 'I-was-speaking-as-a-spokesperson-for-the-company' or 'I-was-being-polite'. Importantly it documents that the prior talk was the product of a specific interactional context (and a specific identity) and that now the context (and identity) has shifted again.[7]

There are *multiple possible* 'influences' on the interaction and the trajectory of the talk – your recruitment conversation, the physical space, your introduction, your status, your gender, etc. – the tape-recorder is another part of that context. However, the central 'influence' is *both* speakers' actual conduct in the interview – your questions, their answers, your comments, your gestures. There is no *ideal* interview. The idea that interviewer/interviewee 'matching' along gendered identities 'automatically' creates a space of rapport and understanding has recently been problematized (see Reinharz and Chase, 2002: 228–33). The overly essentialized authentic subject, of both interviewer and interviewee, along a single and static aged, classed, gendered, racialized or sexualized, etc., category has given way to speakers producing complex, shifting, *subjectivities* (Holstein and Gubrium, 1995, 1997).[8]

As Reinharz and Chase note, '[i]t is crucial that the researcher take account of his or her own and the interviewee's social locations and how they might affect the research relationship' (2002: 233). As I will argue in more detail below, the point is to understand *and* demonstrate which specific subjectivities are relevant at various moments of the interview-interaction.

INTERACTION IN INTERVIEWS

The great majority of methodological discussion about interviewer conduct discusses two ideals-about-interviewer-practices that can be glossed as: *rapport* and *neutrality*. Rapport is something that should be worked 'at/up'. Interviewers, whatever prescriptions they follow, must work to establish 'a suitably relaxed and encouraging relationship. … The interviewer must communicate trust, reassurance and, even, likeableness' (Ackroyd and Hughes, 1992: 108). This is one gloss of the 'ideal' that nearly all interview methods texts share. Put simply, if the interviewee feels comfortable, they will find it easier to talk to you.

The second ideal is 'neutrality'. There are a range of perspectives in regard to interviewer neutrality. Within some methods texts this is held as:

- an *essential* practice (e.g. Ackroyd and Hughes, 1992; Weiss, 1994). If an interviewer is not neutral they will 'unduly bias' the interviewee's story and thus 'contaminate' the data.
- a *bad* practice (e.g. Oakley, 1981; Douglas, 1985). When an interviewer is neutral they create a hierarchical, asymmetrical (and patriarchal) relationship in which the interviewee is treated as a research 'object'. As interviewees offer their own thoughts, ideas or experiences they begin to treat the interviewee as another human being. This cooperative, engaged relationship – centred on mutual self-disclosure – can encourage 'deep disclosure'.

The narrative of *non-neutral* interviewing is dominant in contemporary methodology texts on interviewing. For example, in the conclusion of Fontana and Frey's 'brief journey … through the world of interviewing', they argue:

> 'as we treat the other as human being, we can no longer remain objective, faceless interviewers, but become human beings and must disclose ourselves, learning about ourselves as we try to learn about the other' (1994: 373–4).

So, two strands emerge, one arguing for 'facilitative and neutral' interviewing, the other for 'facilitative and self-disclosing' interviewing. However, there is a third perspective which argues that interviewer neutrality is

- a *misleading* practice (e.g. Holstein and Gubrium, 1995, 1997; Rapley, 2001). '*Doing* neutrality' is *interactionally* possible – interviewers can and do ask non-leading questions and never offer their own thoughts, ideas or experiences. However, actually '*being* neutral' in any conventional sense is actually impossible – interviewers are always active. Interviewers have overarching control, they guide the talk, they promote it through questions, silence and responses tokens (e.g. 'okay') and chiefly *they decide which particular part of the answer to follow up* (cf. Watson and Weinberg, 1982).

This last position, that appeals for interviewer neutrality are misleading, emerges from the constructionist critique of interviewing. As noted above, from this position interviewees' talk is never just a 'reality report', never merely a transparent window on life outside the interview. As Gubrium and Holstein note, both interviewer and interviewee are 'seen as actively and unavoidably engaged in the interactional co-construction of the interview's content' (2002: 15). Interviewers 'cannot very well taint knowledge if that knowledge is not conceived as existing in some pure form apart from the circumstances of its production' (ibid.).

From this perspective, the binary of 'neutrality/mutual self-disclosure' no longer holds. They are no longer polar opposites, but just part of the range of interactional practices that interviewers can, and do, draw on. You do not have to worry if 'that question was far too leading' or wonder whether 'If I'd been more open about my actual feelings on the topic he would have shared a different side of himself'. *Just get on with interacting with that specific person.* Try and explore their thoughts, ideas and experiences on the specific topic and, if you feel it is relevant, offer your thoughts, ideas and experiences for comparison. When it comes to analysing the interviews, *you should analyse what actually happened* – how your interaction produced that trajectory of talk and how specific versions of reality are co-constructed.

The position I am advocating above needs 'unpacking'. Initially, I will show what the various interactional formats of interviewing – 'facilitive and neutral', 'facilitive and self-disclosing', and a more generalized format of 'cooperative work' – can actually look like in practice. I want to compare the interactional practices with the ideals about these approaches and highlight what work each format can achieve. I will then go on to consider in more detail how to analyse interviews as products of 'cooperative work'.

GENTLY NUDGING WITHOUT BIAS

The 'traditional' account of qualitative interviewing goes something like this: 'The interviewer's task is to draw out all relevant responses, to encourage the inarticulate or shy, to be *neutral towards the topic while displaying interest*. Probing needs skill because it can easily lead to bias' [my emphasis] (Fielding and Thomas, 2001: 129). The interviewer should facilitate without overly directing the interviewee's talk. Considerable attention is played to question wording, with the aim of asking non-leading questions and probes (e.g. Berg, 1998; May, 1993). The interviewer's non-verbal work also comes under scrutiny, for example, '[f]rowns on the interviewer's face should indicate lack of understanding, not disapproval!' (Minichiello et al., 1995: 102). As was noted above, such work is concerned to minimize the interviewer's presence, so that they become *neutral* (but interested) *observers*. Let us see an example of this type of conduct in action.

Below is an excerpt from a qualitative interview with a teenager who was trained as a drug peer-educator. I didn't conduct the interview but I transcribed it following some of the conventions of conversation analysis (see below for a discussion of transcription practices). It is *very* typical of the twenty-seven interviews I analysed to discover the lived practices of 'facilitative and neutral' interviewing.[9]

The talk in Excerpt 1 is taken from near the start of the interview. After some ice-breaking questions, the talk shifts to the 'official' topic of the interview – discovering something about Dan's experiences of being a drug peer-educator. They have briefly talked about how Dan heard about the training. We enter the interview as IR asks whether Dan was told that he would have to actually deliver drug-education sessions.

Excerpt 1

1	IR:	°.h° so is it made clear right at that early stage that you
2		could be expected to come back and deliver sessions
3	dan:	Well Yeah he said it is ultimately with you

```
4        and then we'd (.) we discussed it
         seriously
5        individually he spoke to us
6        about i[ t      u ]n and explained
7   IR:          [°°yeah°°]
9   dan: what was really the (.) the set up
         of it and how it was
10       going to be done.
11  IR:  °°(all right) (.) okay.°° .h so can
         you tell me why why did you
12       put yourself forward at that stage
13  dan: erm phh Well it is the sort of thing
         erm (0.4) I like to do
14       and I do I enjoy you know (.)
         learning things I didn't
15       know before and then you know
         teaching it its
16       °things that I do you know° I
         teach a lot of other things
17       as well as drama and so forth so
         um .hh quite used to doing
18       °it° and I come from a medical
         family so er (0.3)
19       [you k]now drugs and so forth we
         do
20  IR:  [m  m]
21  dan: it we discuss quite a lot °and er°
22  IR:  yeah
23  dan: °and it is something it doe- did
         interest me really°
24  IR:  okay=was there any other partic-
         ular interest in the
25       fact that it was drugs I mean is
         that something
26       that is meaningful to you pa[rticularly
         or not
27  dan:                             [°well-°
28       yeah well it is I mean cause >>it's
         everywhere
29       I think is mean- its got to be
         meaningful t- t- to
30       you know<< a greater or lesser
         extent to everyone
31       [because there is so] much of it
         around and
32  IR:  [  °  r  i  g  h  t  °  ]
33  dan: er you know it's good to know
         things as well
34       °I think its er° simply because its
         you know its so much
35  IR:  °mm°
36  dan: °you know in the news° °°and
         everything it's er-°°
```

```
37       (0.4)
38  IR:  so you saY it'[s it's so much
              around  [>and  then  you
              ((continues))
```

The transcript begins to demonstrate the massive amount of *verbal-interactional work* that both speakers are engaged in. I want to make a few observations about IR and Dan's interaction:

- *IR just asks questions.* He doesn't produce any stories about his own experiences, he doesn't compare Dan's experience with that of the others he has interviewed or offer any substantive comment on Dan's answers. You only get something like '°°yeah°°' (7), 'mm' (20), '°right°' (32) which, among other things, works to acknowledge Dan's talk rather than offer an agreement.

- *IR mainly asks follow-up questions.* So, IR asks a question that introduces the topic for discussion (11–12) and Dan produces an answer (13–23) and then IR just produces follow-up questions. By producing follow-up questions (and by allowing Dan space to speak) IR is constantly demonstrating to Dan that he is *trying to work with him*, that he is *trying to understand his story*, *that he is listening* and that *he is interested*. Note also how the questions are asked. We get questions designed as invitations 'so can you tell me' (11) and that are non-leading 'pa[rticularly or not' (26).

- *Dan routinely produces some 'thick descriptions' of his experiences, motivations, and thoughts.* Dan never asks IR any questions, he never works to 'unpack' IRs perspective.[10]

What is really wonderful about IR and Dan's interaction is that in and through their *lived practices* they are reflexively producing some of the *ideals*-about-a-format-of-interviewing. IR works to 'just' follow up on Dan's talk, to facilitate his talk, without asserting his opinions or making any appreciative or critical comments. IR is doing being 'neutral towards the topic while displaying interest' (Fielding and Thomas, 2001: 129) . He is engaged in 'neutral*istic*' conduct *but* he is not 'being neutral' in any conventional sense (cf. Heritage and Greatbatch, 1991).

So, '*being* neutral' is a mythological (and methodological) interviewer stance. This mythology/methodology of interviewer neutrality has the fundamental effect of 'silencing', and in some cases totally banishing, the very active, collaborative work of the interviewer in producing the talk as it is. Equally, this format can assume that Dan is passive. Dan is not just offering *the* truth of his experience; in other interactions, with other questions, other (and Other) truths would emerge.

However, we, as interviewers, can learn a lot from this sequence. It demonstrates some key interactional practices of qualitative interviewing:

- you should ask some questions;
- selectively follow up on specific themes or topics;
- allow interviewees the space to talk at length.

Quite simple ideals but pretty effective at gaining *very detailed and comprehensive talk –* which I take it is a central rationale to qualitative interviewing. Yet, as both speakers are unavoidably co-implicated in producing the talk, interviewers no longer 'have to' ask non-leading questions, they no longer 'have to' withhold their experiences, ideas and thoughts.

Much of the more contemporary literature, irrespective of broader theoretical commitments, argues for an *engaged, active* or *collaborative* format of interviewing. As Denzin notes, 'In the *collaborative or active format*, interviewer and respondent tell a story together. In this format a conversation occurs. Indeed, the identities of interviewer and respondent disappear. Each becomes a storyteller, or the two collaborate in telling a conjoint story' [author's emphasis] (2002: 839). What Denzin describes is very much an (overly) idealized understanding of the possibilities of this interactional format.[11] What he does offer us access to is the interactional directives of this approach: that the interviewer, the previously silent (and silenced) partner, can and *should* now speak. The question is, what should this person now say?

Two specific, and related, trajectories emerge about what action interviewers should take: those advocating 'cooperative *self*-disclosure' (e.g. Douglas, 1985) and those advocating a more generalized strategy of 'cooperative work' (see especially Holstein and Gubrium, 1995). Both formats are intimately related, and often overlap in the literature, but I want to tease apart the differences. First, let us briefly explore interviewing that advocates 'cooperative work'.

INTERVIEWERS AS 'PERSONS'

Collins, reflecting on his own practice, argues:

As the interviewer I am not, I cannot be, merely a passive observer in all this, even though it is primarily the interviewee's life which is under scrutiny. ... As I take less seriously the manuals' advice to maintain a lofty silence, I am increasingly moved to contribute my own stories, to hold them up for contrast or comparison with those of the interviewee. (1998: 7)

Offering the interviewees your own 'stories' can take various forms – your personal experience, your personal opinion or ideas, or the opinion or ideas of other people.

At its broadest level, interviewer self-disclosure just means no longer being 'passive' – no longer censoring your every utterance and gesture for signs of being 'too leading'. You become a *vocal* collaborator in the interaction. Take, for example, my talk in Excerpt 2, below.

Excerpt 2

1	Tim:	I'm quite interested in this idea
2		of the maleness of this context,
3		how that's dealt with. What are
4		the issues about that?
5	Helen:	One of the things that I should
6		say is, whatever the external
7		image is of the industry, I've been
8		here nearly five years now, I'm
9		very aware of these issues and I
10		don't get any of the
11		traditional overt sexual harass-
12		ment, which is great. It's not an
13		issue that comes up. We do
14		sometimes get women feeling
15		that men are not valuing them
16		for their contribution. But I have
17		to say there also, it tends to be
18		the admin rather than the
19		builders. If you asked 98% of my
20		surveyors or women's site
21		mangers, they would say they are
22		treated the same as the men.
23		Their experience is exactly –
24		they don't actually experience
25		sexism. Which a bit of
26		me found really extraordinary,
27		but on another level, to be
28		absolutely honest, they're fairly
29		exceptional women I've got
30		here, they really are. You know,
31		they're quite feisty, they're very
32		confident, they're better, often,
33		than the men.
34	Tim:	I mean that's the story here, you
35		always have to be better than.
36		You're good at your job, well fair
37		enough, you have to be better.

38	Helen:	Yeah, yeah. To be honest, they
39		won't survive if they're not. We
40		do have some women who we
41		take on who are, if they're
42		mediocre it's much they drift
43		down and they go. You've just
44		got to be very good. That's no
45		different, really, to any other sit-
46		uation where they're in a great
47		minority ((continues))

My initial question directs Helen to talk about 'the maleness' of the construction industry. She produces quite a detailed, elaborate response, drawing on various sources of evidence – her professional experience, her professional conversations, her personal awareness and doubts. She argues that 'maleness', in the form of overt sexual harassment, undervaluing women's work and differential treatment, is not that prevalent. She ends this part of her answer by saying that these women 'they're better, often, than the men' (32–33). I then take up that part of Helen's answer, re-positioning this situation as problematic – that women always **have to be better than** (35), that they can't just be 'good'. Helen then marks her agreement 'Yeah, yeah' (38) and then re-positions this as not just specific to the construction industry but rather that it is 'no different … to **any** other situation where [women are] in a great minority' (44–47).

Excerpt 2 is on the one hand quite unremarkable – two speakers producing contrasting positions on a specific topic, and in the process 'debating' a specific issue. However, this is an interview, and I, as the 'interviewer', have offered 'my story', I have disclosed myself as a person, someone who has ideas on this topic. And one of the outcomes of me offering my ideas was some more talk. The point is to *engage* with the interviewee's talk.

At some moments you may offer contrasting *and* complementary ideas to the interviewees or ask leading questions. At other moments, for example in Excerpt 3 below, you may just ask a 'neutralistic' question.

Excerpt 3

Chris:	There's a need for a cultural shift in the way we work, not in just what we do, but in the way we think and our attitudes.
Tim:	What kind of shifts can you see that are needed?
Chris:	What kind of shifts? Well at the moment, as I say, we tend to pass risk

on and pass responsibilities on to other ((continues))

You should be flexible – listen and ask question, offer your ideas and opinions *if you feel it is relevant*. There is another, very specific version of self-disclosure work that we need to see in action – when interviewers offer their *personal-biographical* experiences. Obviously, this is only possible if you have actually had a relevant experience similar to that of the interviewees.

WORKING WITH INTIMATE RECIPROCITY

Johnson argues that, what he labels in-depth interviewing 'differs from other forms because it involves a greater involvement of the interviewer's self. To progressively and incrementally build a mutual sense of cooperative self disclosure and trust the interviewer must offer some form of strict or complementary reciprocity, (2002: 109). Offering 'strict reciprocity' means that interviewers disclose their personal-biographical-emotional experiences. 'Complementary reciprocity' involves the exchange of 'some form of help, assistance, or other form of information' (ibid.). Note that Johnson tells us that you '*must*' engage in reciprocity. Such an extreme view emerges from the idea that by disclosing some aspect of your 'self' interviewees *will* feel more at ease and that this *will* lead to rapport. However, as Reinharz and Chase note, interviewers should not adopt an 'abstract commitment' to it, rather you need to think about 'whether, when, and how much disclosure makes sense' (2002: 288) in reference to each specific interaction.

In order to explore the kind of work interviewer *self*-disclosure can do, look at Excerpt 4 below. It is taken from an interview I conducted with a friend about their illegal drug-use. It has been going on for about an hour, with Adam explaining in detail the various stages of his drug-taking. We enter the interview as Adam explains how he has covered a lot of my questions.

Excerpt 4

1	adam:	there's so much information all I've all I've done is told you the A to Z really
2	tim:	yeah [yeah
3	adam:	[there's loads of places along the way

4	tim:	yeah yeah [yeah yeah
5	adam:	[and you need to think of some questions about what I've said
6	tim:	yeah (1.0) I don't know I mean (1.0) I mean for me I mean this is yeah this is
7		very yeah this is my confession for me um I am that alcoholic but but
8		from my own point of view you know
9	adam:	mm
10	tim:	I I I got to that point where no you know I could you know when you
11		were saying about um I'm not functioning any more as a human being
12	adam:	mm
13	tim:	I'd really got to that point when I wasn't a human being any more that I
14		could recognise [in any
15	adam:	[yeah
16	tim:	way shape or form and I and that was purely my you know
17		addictive personality I don't know whether that exists you know me
18		being um (0.6) just a monster
19	adam:	yeah
20	tim:	you know
21	adam:	not saying no more
22	tim:	yeah yeah yeah basically it got to the point where erm for me it got to
23		like I mean [the end of the line]
24	adam:	[was that all drugs]
25	tim:	all drugs, yeah [other than alcohol and tobacco]
26	adam:	[you never taken anything] ever since
27	tim:	nah nah nah but that was literally to save my sanity [you know
28	adam:	[yeah
29	tim:	it got to that point when my sanity was [( )
30	adam:	[I remember that
31	tim:	yeah do you
32	adam:	yeah I can remember that
33	tim:	yeah yeah
34	adam:	(er) I know lots of people who who sort of have to say it that way I
35		mean that's something that crosses my mind sometimes when I'm totally
36		spannered and I think How can I cope
37	tim:	mm huh
38	adam:	right I know lots of people who or no no not not when I'm totally
39		spannered when when I'm into doing drugs its like over this summer I've
40		not done drugs
41	tim:	mm huh
42	adam:	yeah as I've said I've smoked a spliff ((continues))

From 6, I start to tell my story, 'my confession' (7), in which I compare and contrast my experience with drugs to Adam's. I am not just offering any old story, but a very 'personal' story – when I gave up drugs to 'save my sanity' (27) – a story that does biographical work. As Adam retakes the floor, he initially marks the similarity between my experience to that of some unnamed generalized 'others' that he has known: 'I know: **lots of people** who who sort of have to say it that way' (34). Note how Adam marks that they '**have to** say it that way', in this way he nicely echoes the 'no-choice-but-to-quit' element of my talk. He then goes on to produce his own 'personal sanity' story – 'I mean that's something that crosses my mind sometimes when I'm totally spannered and I think **How can I cope**' (34–6) – which then continues well beyond the excerpt.

Our talk is intimately tied as we:

- Closely follow each other's talk and provide timely responses and follow-up questions.
- Both worked to show 'I-really-got-the-point-of-what-you-are-saying. …' Rather than just *telling* each other that 'I understand', we work to *show* each other that we understand.
- Both 'reflected on' and 'disclosed' our personal/biographical thoughts about and experiences with drugs. We used the language of the self. We both talked about our experiences, feelings, emotions in relation to drugs and produced a specific 'reflective drug-user' identity.

What is central is that we both talked about drugs *in and through* a 'language of personal experiences, feelings, emotions', over, say, a language of biomedicine or legal theory.

There is tension in the how-to literature that advocates mutual *self*-disclosure in the form of disclosing personal/biographical elements of your life. For example, Johnson moves between advocating understanding the *multiple* views and interpretations of interviewees with arguing that in-depth interviewing goes 'beyond common-sense explanations ... and aims to explore the contextual boundaries of that experience or perception, to *uncover what is usually hidden* from ordinary view or reflection or to *penetrate to more reflective understandings* about the nature of that experience' [my emphasis] (2002: 106). There is a discourse of discovering hidden voices that runs close to advocating the *authenticity or truth* of these hidden voices over other voices. As Atkinson and Silverman remind us, the uncritical 'celebration of narratives of personal experience' can 'implicitly reinstate the speaking subject as the privileged hero or heroine of his or her own biography. ... We do not reveal selves by collecting narratives, we create selfhood through narrative and biographical work' (1997: 11–12).

Interviewing can be used as a way to enable previously hidden, or silenced, voices to speak. With my work on women in the construction industry, the interviews literally gave some women the chance to voice something that is very rarely openly acknowledged in the industry: a politics of daily scrutiny around dress and conduct and a politics of inequalities in career progression and pay. I am *not* arguing against interviewers' offering up their own personal stories for contrast and comparison with interviewees' talk. In thinking about my own practice, I don't 'do self-disclosure' just to encourage respondents to be 'more forthcoming' – although that is often an *outcome* of my action. It can encourage more talk – interviewees respond to your talk, they may agree, argue with it or ignore it, but it does routinely continue the discussion in new paths. However, I want to argue that for interviewers and interviewees to engage in 'mutual self-disclosure' *it takes work and does work.*

It can take work, in that both speakers need to talk in a language of their emotions, feeling and experiences. It can do work, 'rapport work' and 'emotion work' and say 'I understand' or 'You're not alone in your experience'. It can produce interviewers as specific types of people in relation to this interaction and this specific topic (cf. Firth and Kitzinger, 1998). It is a specific technology of the interview society that incites a speaker to speak of and for their 'selfhood'. As Gubrium and Holstein note, 'In in-depth interviews, we "do" deep, authentic experiences as much as we "do" opinion offering in the course of the survey interview' (2002: 11).

You may feel, as I do sometimes, that talking about interviewees 'doing rapport work', 'doing emotional work' is a rather sterile, clinical, way to treat people's interactions. It may seem strange that I treat my own personal/biographical drug experience in such a manner. I, above anyone, should know that it 'really happened', that I can take it as 'the authentic truth'. The point is, I am more than aware that there are a multiple number of ways I could, *and routinely do*, describe my experience with drugs. The way I describe it is intimately tied to who I'm speaking to, where I am, the way I feel, what has been said before – in short the local interactional context. But this local interactional context is also intimately embedded in, and emerges from, the broader historico-socio-cultural context.[12]

I only ever offer *versions* of my experience, I can do nothing else. As Rose notes, 'The realities that are fabricated, out of words, texts, devices, techniques, practices, subjects, objects and entities are no less real because they are constructed, for what else could they be?' (1998: 168). As he notes, this does not necessarily lead back to a debate around realism and anti-realism. It does offer me a direction, one in which I take seriously *how* experience (biography, emotion, identity, knowledge, opinion, truth) is produced and negotiated, where I focus on the practical, active, *work* we engage in as part of our everyday life. Part of that practical, active, work of everyday life is doing self-disclosure in interviews.

INTERVIEWING AS MUNDANE INTERACTION

We have finally arrived at the 'format' of interviewing I feel most comfortable with. It involves at its most basic *asking questions and following up on various things that interviewees raise and allowing them the space to talk*. It does not involve extraordinary skill, it involves just trying to interact with that specific person, trying to understand their experience, opinion and ideas.

I want to offer a list of some of the phenomenally mundane interactional 'methods' cooperative interviewing involves:

- Initially introducing a topic for discussion.
- Listening to the answer and then producing follow-up questions (e.g. Excerpt 1).
- Listening to interviewees talk and asking them to unpack certain key terms (e.g. Excerpt 3).
- Listening to interviewees talk and following it up with talk about your own personal

experience (e.g. Excerpt 4) or your personal opinion or ideas (e.g. Excerpt 2) or the opinion or ideas of other people.

- And whilst listening going 'mm', 'yeah', 'yeah, yeah' alongside nodding, laughing, joking, smiling, frowning.[13]

Now that list is by no means exhaustive, but it gives you a flavour of what I see as '*engaged, active* or *collaborative*' interviewing.

However, I am not advocating an 'anything goes policy' in relationship to interviewing. I wouldn't suggest ignoring them, falling asleep or shouting a lot.[14] You have to rely on your own common sense: if you know you often 'daydream' in mid-conversation, just remember to concentrate; if you know you routinely 'talk over people', try and hold back and listen. If you see that interviewees are clearly becoming uncomfortable or very emotional, ask them if they want to take a break or maybe you need to think about ending the interview or switching the topic. Above all, treat them with respect, they are never just 'more data'.

Interviewing is never just 'a conversation', it may be conversation*al*, but you as the interviewer do have some level of control. You routinely decide which bit of talk to follow up, you routinely decide when to open and close various topics and the interaction as a whole. For me, interviewers may choose to produce themselves through their talk and other actions as more 'passive' (facilitative and neutral) or more 'active' (facilitative and self-disclosing, collaborative, active, reflexive or adversarial) or another identity. Whatever ideal about interviewer practices that are locally produced (if they are at all), *no single ideal gains 'better data' than the others*. You cannot escape from the *interactional* nature of interviews. Whatever 'ideals' interviewers practice, their talk is central to the trajectories of the interviewees' talk. As such, it should be analysed in relation to that specific context. However, we are never interacting in a historico-socio-cultural vacuum, we are always *embedded in* and *selectively* and *artfully* draw on broader institutional and organizational contexts. With these last points in mind, I want now to briefly explore how you can analyse interviews.

SOME INTRODUCTORY NOTES ON ANALYSING INTERVIEWS

As should now be obvious from my discussion above, when analysing interviews I follow a broadly 'discursive' approach (see Wetherell,

2001, for various analytic positions under this banner).[15] I'm not trying to establish the 'truth' of interviewees' actions, experiences, feelings and thoughts but rather how specific (and sometimes contradictory) *truths* are produced, sustained and negotiated.

On one level, the process of analysis can seem quite 'routine'. You've got your transcripts in front of you, you read them, re-read. You then note down some interesting themes and may start applying codes, or key words, to the data. You then re-read, apply the constant comparison method (Glaser and Strauss, 1967) and so start to constantly refine your codes. Hopefully, you find a few negative instances (deviant cases), things that make you re-think and then refine your whole analysis (see Seale, 1999). Then you end up with a collection of extracts for each code. You write up what you've found. Now that is one way to describe a process you often go through while doing analysis, or rather, it describes in rather practical terms what you sometimes practically do.

However, I want to offer another description, one that is more layered with some theoretical, methodological *and* practical concerns. First and foremost, analysis *is always an ongoing process* that routinely starts prior to the first interview. As soon as I become interested in a specific topic, I'll start to collect some literature on the topic – both 'academic' and 'non-academic'. This reading, alongside conversations, past experiences and 'bizarre bolts from the blue' (often over a strong coffee), gives me an initial clue as to possible interviewees, interview questions and analytic themes. These sources of knowledge often become analytic themes that I explore with interviewees in interviews. I'll then try and recruit the interviewees, making notes on this process – these notes cover both the successes and the failures, the kinds of accounts people provide for not taking part (again providing more 'data' and more possible questions). Once I've got some interviews lined up, I'll prepare a brief topic guide. In choosing those specific interviewees and in producing that specific topic guide (that is shaped for that specific interviewee), I am already making some specific analytic choices about what types of people, what *voices or identities*, are central to the research (and which ones will remain silenced) alongside what sorts of topics of discussion might be important. I then go to the interview.

During the interview, I often try to raise some of the themes I've been thinking through either by asking interviewees specific questions about them or, sometimes, telling them about my thoughts and letting them comment on them.[16] So in one sense, the actual interview interactions are a space in which I seek to test 'my' analysis of these specific themes by asking interviewees to talk about them. Or to put it another way, *interview interactions are inherently spaces in which both speakers are constantly 'doing analysis' – both speakers are engaged (and collaborating in) 'making meaning' and 'producing knowledge'* (cf. Gubrium and Holstein, 2002: 15; see also Hester and Francis, 1994).

After the interviews I write up my notes on the encounter, noting both pre- and post-tape talk alongside my reactions and observations about the interview itself (another moment of analysis). I then re-think about the trajectory of the research, refine the kinds of themes and ideas I want to think through with interviewees, and go and interview someone else.

In the past, I always used to transcribe the interview tapes myself. In this way, I got to repeatedly listen to the tapes, and so generate, check and refine my analytic hunches whilst simultaneously producing a *textual* version of the interaction that could be used both for further analysis and reports.[17] Increasingly, my tapes have been sent to transcribers, which means I always check the transcript against the tape and add the sort of detail I'm often interested in (pauses, stress, overlapping speech).[18] However, when it comes to sustained periods of analysis, I always prefer to re-listen to the tapes alongside re-reading the transcript. This allows me to get a sense of the interactional, collaborative, work of the speakers. I then try and write up the research (and re-write it, and re-write…).

I've now offered a slightly richer account of the process of analysis – that analysis, in the sense of 'producing knowledge' about a specific topic, is an inherently ongoing accomplishment. Importantly, the interview is a central moment of this analytic work, especially as the interaction itself is a moment of 'knowledge production' – but it is always only part of that analytic work. What remains noticeably absent from my discussion is any detailed, theoretically informed, account of how to analyse these interviews.

HOW I THINK WITH INTERVIEW 'DATA'

To be honest, I don't really want to (and don't feel I can) offer a step-by-step guide on 'how to analyse interviews'. How you analyse interviews is *always* inextricably linked to your specific theoretical interests. And your theoretical interests will, in part, define what sort of questions you ask in interviews, what sort of questions you ask of the 'data', what sort of level of transcription you feel is necessary. So I would prefer it you read my take on 'how I analyse interviews' as just that, a *description of my analytic choices* and not, in any way, a prescription.[19]

I want to return to Excerpt 2, to demonstrate how interviewees and interviewers 'do analysis' and how I, as an academic analyst, try and think about analysing interviews.[20] On one level, Helen's analysis is that in this firm women don't experience overt sexual harassment. However, she does then note, after my re-reading of this (34–37), that what we could call 'covert, institutionalized, sexism' is still prevalent – these women have 'just got to be very good' (43–44), as 'they won't survive if they're not' (38–39). However, we have to view mine and Helen's analysis as *situated,* in that it is intimately tied to the contexts of:

- *The here-and-now interaction.* Both my questions (1–4) and my comment at 34–37 were central to the trajectory of her talk. For example, Helen produces the idea that these women are '**better**, often, than the men' (32–33) as a possible reason why these women '**don't** actually **experience sexism**' (24–25). I then take up this last point in her talk – 'that the story here, you always have to be better' (34–35) – and *re-position this as an example of sexism*: that women 'have to be better than [men]' (35), that they just can't be 'good' (36). Helen *then agrees with this* 'to be honest, they wouldn't survive if they're not' (38–39) and then re-positions this as 'no different' from any situation where women are 'in a great minority' (46–47).
- *This interview interaction.* We both work to produce ourselves as specific types of people in relation to this specific interactional context. As Dingwall notes, interviews are 'a situation [in] which respondents are required to demonstrate their competence in the role in which the interview casts them' (1997: 58). Helen works to produce herself as a *competent interviewee* – able to offer detailed and elaborated descriptions. I work to produce myself as a *competent interviewer* – able to offer timely questions and comments that are appropriate and relevant, that demonstrate I have some knowledge of this topic. Alongside this Helen is also asked to, and does, speak as *an expert in connection with women's employment in her firm*. Note the range of sources of evidence she draws on: her professional experience (5–10), her professional role 'I'm very aware of these

issues' (8–9), other professionals' experiences 'If you asked 98% of my surveyors or women's site managers …' (19–21), and her professional/personal surprise and doubts 'Which a bit of me found really extraordinary' (25–26). In the very process of being interviewed, she actively demonstrates her expertise and knowledge. Intimately connected to this is her role as *a spokesperson of this specific firm*. She works to produce this specific firm as (relatively) free of 'sexism' – and when this firm is cast as potentially 'sexist', this firm's experience is marked as no different from any other situation where women are a great minority (44–47).

- *The broader research project*. My question about the 'maleness' of the industry, and my comment on 'women always having to be better', emerged from my past experiences of working on building sites, my reading around sexism and the interviews I had previously conducted. Also, prior to the tape being turned on, I had outlined that the research project was interested in the 'barriers women face in the construction industry'. Helen answers my question about the 'context of maleness' as a question about the *problems of maleness*: 'traditional overt sexual harassment' (11–12), 'women feeling that men are not valuing them for their contribution' (14–16), 'sexism' (25). In so doing, she orientates to the research project's interests in the 'barriers'. My comment at 34–37 also orientates to and reflexively produces the research project's interest in, and awareness of, current 'barriers women face'.

So even with this brief and relatively fleeting moment, both speakers are engaged in some rather beautiful and artful work. Compare the above analytic work of Helen and Tim with another interview I was involved in.

Excerpt 5

Tim: Okay what do you think, because in the car I said thinking about this industry is institutionally sexist, do you think that is a fair description?

Ben: **Yes of course it is**.

Tim: You say of course, can you tell me why you would say of course then?

Ben: You just have to be on a site for five minutes to know it is, the conversations that go on, the attitudes that go on, I mean it's racist as well. ((continues))

With my initial question, I shift the topic from our previous talk, and introduce something Ben and I originally spoke about while travelling to the space of the interview. For Ben, my description of the industry as institutionally sexist is *just obvious* – 'Yes of course it is'. I then ask Ben to 'unpack' this obviousness. Note how he renders it as obvious – 'You just have to be on a site for five minutes to know it is' – it's just there for anyone to discover in the *everyday activities of the site*, people's 'conversations' and 'attitudes'. So Ben produces himself as the type of person who has knowledge of the sexism in the industry and his entitlement to speak with authority on this is based on his 'ethnographic' experience of the day-to-day activities on building sites.

So how can I as an academic analyst make sense of these situated moments of talk, how can I draw any conclusions? How can I work so that I don't rip this talk about sexism out of context?

On the one hand, you can begin to see that talk about sexism is tied to doing specific work; Helen is not just offering a description of sexism in the company she works for, in and through discussing sexism Helen produces her company as a 'responsible employer' and herself as a 'responsible employee'. Similarly, Ben produces himself as aware of the problems in the industry (and at other moments in the interview as an employer who has tried to overcome these problems). When compared to the thirty-three other interviews I did with people on this topic – including representatives of small firms, housing associations, local authorities and large national employers – I got a huge range of competing and contrasting ways that 'talk about sexism' produces specific biographies, experiences, identities, knowledges, etc. So from one perspective, a way to make sense of the interviews is to focus on the situated ways that 'talk about sexism' enables specific work.

From another perspective, these specific interactional moments reflexively document the contemporary ways of understanding, experiencing and talking about sexism in the construction industry. To be sure, their talk is intimately tied to the contexts of its production – these local interactional contexts. However, in and through producing these local interactional contexts, the speakers draw on and reflexively produce the broader context of 'women experiences in the construction industry'. The speakers are actively and collaboratively producing, sustaining and negotiating contemporary *knowledges* about women's experiences in the construction industry.

As I've stressed above, the 'data', or more preferably talk, you gain in a specific interview *is just one possible version*, a version that is contingent on the specific local interactional context. And we can see how mine and Ben's and mine and Helen's versions, our knowledges, our analysis, are somewhat 'competing'. We have in these two small fragments various truths: *overt* sexual harassment is not a problem, *some* women feel undervalued, women *don't* experience sexism, women *have to be* better than men to survive, *covert* sexism is always a problem where women are in the minority, sexism is an *everyday feature* of the site. Throughout all the interviews – alongside my observations at industry conferences, my reading of the academic and industry writing, informal conversations with people working in the construction industry alongside my experience of working on building sites – sexism is produced as a 'routine truth'. The questions then become: how is it that the contemporary truths of the construction industry are so intimately tied to 'talk about sexism'? How is it that sexism is reproduced as a 'routine truth' of this industry? And how is this 'routine truth' refused and resisted?

SOME CLOSING ASIDES

I want to end this brief encounter on the practices and possibilities of qualitative interviewing by introducing a comment made by Strong (1980), immediately prior to his insightful analysis of interviews with doctors about their treatment of alcoholic patients:

> One further aside. No form of interview study, however devious or informal, can stand as an adequate substitute for observational data. The inferences about actual practice that I or others may draw from those interviews are therefore somewhat illegitimate. My excuses must be that at present we have no better data on the treatment of alcoholic patients and that, more generally, I have at least attempted to ground myself as fully as possible in these few observational studies of medical consultations that have so far been undertaken. Whether all this is a sufficient guide to the specific matter of practice with alcoholics must remain an open question for the moment. (1980: 27–8)

I am inclined to agree with Strong's version. For me, an interview study that *only* uses interviews to understand peoples *lived, situated, practices* seems highly problematic.[21]

The interview may be an economical means, in the sense of time and money, of getting access to an 'issue'. It may also be an economical means of getting access to issues that are not easily available for analysis, to get people to 'think out loud' about certain topics. However, saying this, most topics are 'freely available' for analysis. As Holstein and Gubrium (1995) note, to understand the topic 'family' we do not *need* to interview people or enter people's homes. We can see *how* 'family' is organized, produced and negotiated on the bus, in supermarkets, in newspapers, in talk shows, in legislation, etc. But again we should be sensitive that these – like interviews – are contextually situated practices.

Some may argue that what I'm advocating is 'absurd' – that such work could never gain access to the *individual's* actual thoughts, feelings or experiences. We need to take a slight detour to think through this potential 'reaction'. Mahonny (in Kong et al., 2002: 253) notes in his research diary, whilst reflecting on his 'little empathy' for an interviewee, that '[t]his distancing prevented me from becoming more interactive, which further prevented an expansion of *our* knowledge construction of *his* story' [my emphasis]. This account presents one of the central ironies of qualitative interviewing: that the inherently collaborative interviewer/interviewee interactions can become seen as 'just' about the interviewees' singular or individualized story. A question remains, do we as researchers treat interviewees as *just* individuals? Or do we treat them, at one and the same time, as individuals-*and*-part-of-broader-story-of-the-whole-research? I think this second rendering is more in alignment with a lot of research practice. I feel such work can happen:

- *after the interview*, as we write up the report the 'individual' account becomes part of a broader collection of voices;
- *as part of the interviewing process*, in that we sometimes ask interviewees to speak as a representative of a specific perspective;
- *as part of the interview interaction*, in that we sometimes tell interviewees 'What you've told me is very similar to what I've heard from so and so. ...'

In this sense, as researchers, we don't always orientate to interviewees as 'individuals'.

Similarly, interviewees don't always speak 'as individuals'; they can speak, at various moments, as representatives of institutions or organizations or professions, as members of specific (sub)cultural groups, as members of specific gendered, racialized, sexualized categories, *as well* as thoughtful individuals, feeling individuals, experiencing individuals, etc. As Gubrium and Holstein note, 'Treating subject positions and their associated voices seriously, we might find that an ostensibly single interview could actually be, in practice, an interview with several subjects, whose particular identities may only be partially clear' (2002: 23). So sometimes interviewees talk as (and are reflexively produced as, by interviewers' questions) individuals, at other points they talk as members of 'broader' collectives. So the question remains, if interviewees do not always see themselves, or speak of themselves, as individuals *per se*, why do we, sometimes, insist on interviewing them/writing about them/speaking of them *as* individuals *per se*?

I have one final – more practical – aside which is tied to the practices of conducting interviewing. Nearly twenty years ago, Mishler noted some problems with survey research interviewing: 'In the mainstream tradition, the nature of interviewing as a form of discourse between speakers has been hidden from view by a dense screen of technical procedures' (1986: 7). Unfortunately, some twenty years later, that 'dense screen of technical procedures' has migrated to the very form of interviewing that Mishler was advocating – the qualitative interview. As I see it, interviewers don't need massive amounts of detailed technical (and moral) instruction on how to conduct qualitative interviews. For me, Turkel's (1995, cited in Plummer, 2001: 140) description of how to interview is pretty convincing:

> 'In the one-to-one interview you start level in the unconfidence, in not knowing where you are going. … You do it your own way. You experiment. You try this, you try that. With one person one's best, with another person another. Stay loose, stay flexible'.

ACKNOWLEDGEMENTS

I should like to thank the Economic and Social Research Council and the Social Fund for funding parts of my work. A 'large' thank you must go to all those interviewees who have spoken with me and to those whom I worked alongside on the 'Gender in Construction' Research Project. Thanks also to Ben Gidley and the two anonymous readers who read and commented on this chapter. A final thanks must go to David Silverman; my conversations with him were central to the intellectual trajectory of this chapter.

NOTES

1 Interestingly, by following the trajectory of debates about the appropriate conduct of interviewers and the appropriate way to analyse the products of these face-to-face encounters, you simultaneously follow the trajectory of debates around how to theorize 'the social'.

2 For some 'early' empirical critiques see Baruch (1981), Cuff (1993), Mishler (1986), Potter and Mulkay (1985) and Riessman (1990).

3 He does not connect 'an interest in drugs' to any *other* part of his life, be it friends, school or strangers or a desire to help drug-users.

4 This is often termed 'snowball sampling' (see Seale and Filmer, 1998: 138).

5 For example, the reluctance of people to speak 'on the record' about women being employed in construction and the absence of any representatives responsible for what I was repeatedly told was an 'important issue', reflexively documents the industry-wide *awareness but inaction* with regard to employing women. This discourse – 'awareness but inaction' – was also a central theme in the interviews.

6 For example, I routinely look at the list, while simultaneously offering an on-line commentary on my actions – 'Is there anything else I want to say' – as a preface to closing the 'official' on-tape part of the interaction.

7 It is interesting that the off-tape talk does routinely stay on the topic of the research, often covering new and highly relevant topics. I generally find myself writing up this part of the interaction as soon as I leave the interview.

8 Although see Bourdieu's call for 'social proximity and familiarity' as helping provide ' "nonviolent" communication' (1999: 610) and so reduce distortions and favour 'plain speaking' in interviews. He returns us, again, to an essentialized ideal interview, this time based on 'cultural symmetry'. As I see it, interviewers don't cultural (or professional) asymmetry can be useful. As Carl May (personal communication) noted, being a relative stranger enables you to ask 'stupid questions' which often produce answers that illuminate what the interviewee may take for granted and leave unsaid.

9 For detailed discussion of the various lived practices of facilitative and neutral interviewers see Rapley (2001).

10 In my 'facilitative and neutral interview' data-set, I only have one interview where *the interviewee* (Hal) *asks the interviewer* (IR) *questions* about IR's 'personal' relationship to some of the topics of their talk.

Excerpt A

hal: draw or (like) I mean have you smoked draw (0.5)
IR: °we'll talk about that afterwards.°
hal: no. I'm asking you °now°
IR: °no lets talk about that afterwards°

In this, and other moments when Hal 'breaches' the interview, IR tells Hal that such answers will be given 'afterwards'. This 'afterwards' refers to: *after this interview*. Within this format, the interviewers are not available to answer 'personal' questions relating to the topic of the interview whilst the tape is on.

11 Does the identity of 'interviewer' really disappear? Or does it temporarily, at certain moments, appear, say when opening and closing the interaction, opening and closing specific topics? How do 'interviewees' orientate to these speakers, as 'interviewers' or

some other identity – 'knowledgeable experts', 'novices', 'institutional agents' …? Above all, the identities of the speakers is very much an empirical question.

12 For example, note how I answer Adam's question at 24. I say that I have stopped using 'all drugs, yeah [**other than alcohol and tobacco**]' (25). I redefine my identity from 'ex-drug-user', to 'current drug-user'. In this context, alcohol and tobacco are rendered as 'drugs'. What is hearable as relevant to the category 'drug' is historically situated. Contemporary British pro- and anti-drugs discourse is often centred on debates about whether 'we' are already, through our large consumption of alcohol and tobacco, a nation of 'drug-users'.

13 And despite Minichiello et al. (1995), frowning sometimes to indicate understanding, sometimes to indicate disapproval!

14 Although such a style of interviewing may produce radically different 'data'.

15 I have drawn on various approaches to analyse interviews, including conversation analysis, critical discourse analysis, discourse analysis, membership catergorization analysis and narrative analysis.

16 To make it even more complex, the things I raise are an amalgam of the question I have written, the things I've just been thinking about and, most common of all, questions or comments I think of while interacting with that specific person.

17 There have been calls for 'vigilance', that when researchers produce detailed transcripts, such transcription (and the analytic gaze that ties to it) can help reveal previously unnoticed practices (e.g. Seale and Silverman, 1997; Rapley, 2001). Alongside this – growing from various postmodern angles – is a call for a more explicit and reflexive stance in relation to the inherently representational and interpretative nature of transcription (e.g. Richardson, 2002). The main point is that interview-talk is (re)constructed in the process of transcription as a result of multiple decisions that reflect both very theoretical and pragmatic concerns (see Poland, 2002).

For example, in the excerpts above I have used various styles of presentation: Excerpts 1 and 4 follow some of the conventions of conversation analysis and read more 'as said', whereas Excerpts 2 and 3 read more 'as written'. In part, I choose the specific format of presentation in line with the argument I was making at that specific point: with Excerpts 1 and 4, I wanted to stress the massive amount of verbal interactional work it takes for interviews to happen; with Excerpts 2 and 3, I was more concerned to demonstrate the 'content' of interview talk. The choice of transcription style *for presentation* will always depend on what is necessary for the specific argument and the needs of the research project. For me, the tidying of quotations is appropriate when writing up for publication. Care should be taken that what is removed does not appreciably alter the meaning of what is said. I would also always

recommend that for your main arguments, extracts from interviews should be presented in the context that they occurred, with the question that prompted the talk as well as the talk that follows being offered. In this way, readers can view how the talk was co-constructed in the course of the interview and, thereby, judge the reliability of the analysis.

18 See Poland (2002) for a rich description of the practices (and problems) of transcription and using transcribers.

19 Some discussions I've found useful, and that may help see where my analytic take is coming from, are Riessman's (1990, 2002) perspective on narrative analysis, Baker's (1984, 1997) ethnomethodological account, Kong et al.'s (2002) queering of interviewing, Reinharz and Chase's (2002) feminist overview, alongside the more 'general' discussions of Holstein and Gubrium (1995, 1997), Dingwall (1997) and Silverman (1985, 1993).

20 In fact, the commentaries I have given on all the excerpts begins to demonstrate how interviewees and interviewers 'do analysis', alongside how I try and analyse that work.

21 See especially Dingwall's (1997) call for observational research.

REFERENCES

Ackroyd, S. and Hughes, J (1992) *Data Collection In Context* (2nd ed.). Harlow: Longman Group (original work published in 1981).

Arksey, H. and Knight, P.T. (1999) *Interviewing for Social Scientists*. London: Sage.

Atkinson, P. and Silverman, D. (1997) 'Kundera's *Immortality*: the interview society and the invention of the self', *Qualitative Inquiry*, 3(3): 304–25.

Baker, C.D. (1984) 'The search for adultness: membership work in adolescent-adult talk', *Human Studies*, 7: 301–23.

Baker, C.D. (1997) 'Membership categorization and interview accounts', in D. Silverman (ed.), *Qualitative Research: Theory, Method and Practice*. London: Sage.

Baruch, G. (1981) 'Moral tales: parents' stories of encounters with the health profession', *Sociology of Health and Illness*, 3(3): 275–96.

Berg, B.L. (1998) *Qualitative Research Methods for the Social Sciences* (3rd ed.). Boston: Allyn and Bacon (original work published in 1989).

Bourdieu, P. (1999) *The Weight of the World: Social Suffering in Contemporary Society.* Cambridge: Polity Press.

Cicourel, A. (1964) *Method and Measurement in Sociology*. New York: Free Press.

Collins, P. (1998) 'Negotiating selves: reflections on "unstructured" interviewing', *Sociological Research Online*, 3(3), http://www.socresonline.org.uk/socresonline/3/3/2.html.

Cornwell, J. (1984) *Hard-Earned Lives: Accounts of Health and Illness from East London*. London: Tavistock.

Cuff, E.C. (1993) *Problems of Versions in Everyday Situations*. Lanham, MD: International Institute for Ethnomethodology and Conversation Analysis and University Press of America.

Denzin, N. (2002) 'The cinematic society and the reflexive interview', in J. Gubrium and J. Holstein (eds), *Handbook of Interview Research: Context and Method*. Thousand Oaks, CA: Sage.

Dingwall, R. (1997) 'Accounts, interviews and observations', in G. Miller and R. Dingwall (eds), *Context and Method in Qualitative Research*. London: Sage.

Douglas, J.D. (1985) *Creative Interviewing*. Beverly Hills, CA: Sage.

Fielding, N. and Thomas, H. (2001) 'Qualitative interviewing', in N. Gilbert (ed.), *Researching Social Life* (2nd ed.). London: Sage.

Firth, H. and Kitzinger, C. (1998) '"Emotion work" as a participant's resource: A feminist analysis of young women's talk in interaction', *Sociology*, 32(2): 299–320.

Fontana, A. (2002) 'Postmodern trends in interviewing', in J. Gubrium and J. Holstein (eds), *Handbook of Interview Research: Context and Method*. Thousand Oaks, CA: Sage.

Fontana, A. and Frey, J.H. (1994) 'Interviewing: the art of science', in N.K. Denzin and Y.S. Lincoln (eds), *The Handbook of Qualitative Research*. Thousand Oaks, CA: Sage.

Glaser, B.G. and Strauss, A.L. (1967) *The Discovery of Grounded Theory: Strategies for Qualitative Research*. Chicago: Aldine.

Gubrium, J. and Holstein, J. (2002) 'From individual interview to interview society', in J. Gubrium and J. Holstein (eds), *Handbook of Interview Research: Context and Method*. Thousand Oaks, CA: Sage.

Heritage, J. and Greatbatch, D. (1991) 'On the institutional character of institutional talk: the case of news interviews', in D. Boden and D.H. Zimmerman (eds), *Talk and Social Structure: Studies in Ethnomethodology and Conversation Analysis*. Berkeley, CA: University of California Press.

Hester, S. and Francis D. (1994) 'Doing data: the local organization of a sociological interview', *British Journal of Sociology*, 45: 675–95.

Holstein, J.A. and Gubrium, J.F. (1995) *The Active Interview*. Thousand Oaks, CA: Sage.

Holstein, J. and Gubrium, J. (1997) 'Active interviewing', in D. Silverman (ed.), *Qualitative Research: Theory, Method and Practice*. London: Sage.

Johnson, J.M. (2002) 'In-depth interviewing', in J. Gubrium and J. Holstein (eds), *Handbook of Interview Research: Context and Method*. Thousand Oaks, CA: Sage.

Kong, T.S.K., Mahoney, D. and Plummer, K. (2002) 'Queering the interview', in J. Gubrium and J. Holstein (eds), *Handbook of Interview Research: Context and Method*. Thousand Oaks, CA: Sage.

Mason, J. (1996) *Qualitative Researching*. London: Sage.

May, T. (1993) *Social Research: Issues, Methods and Process*. Buckingham: Open University Press.

Minichiello, V., Aroni, R., Timewell, E. and Alexander, L. (1995) *In-Depth Interviewing: Principles, Techniques, Analysis* (2nd ed.). Sydney: Addison Wesley Longman.

Mishler, E.G. (1986) *Research Interviewing: Context and Narrative*. Cambridge, MA: Harvard University Press.

Oakley, A. (1981) 'Interviewing women: a contradiction in terms?', in H. Roberts (ed.), *Doing Feminist Research*. London: Routledge.

Plummer, K. (2001) *Documents of Life 2: An Invitation to Critical Humanism*. London: Sage.

Poland, B.D. (2002) 'Transcription quality', in J. Gubrium and J. Holstein (eds), *Handbook of Interview Research: Context and Method*. Thousand Oaks, CA: Sage.

Potter, J. and Mulkay, M. (1985) 'Scientists' interview talk: interviews as a technique for revealing participants' interpretative practices', in M. Brenner, J. Brown and D. Canter (eds), *The Research Interview: Uses and Approaches*. London: Academic Press.

Rapley, T.J. (2001) 'The art(fulness) of open-ended interviewing: some considerations on analysing interviews', *Qualitative Research*, 1(3): 303–23.

Reinharz, S. and Chase, S.E. (2002) 'Interviewing women', in J. Gubrium and J. Holstein (eds), *Handbook of Interview Research: Context and Method*. Thousand Oaks, CA: Sage.

Riessman, C.K. (1990) 'Strategic uses of narrative in the presentation of self and illness: a research note', *Social Science and Medicine*, 30(11): 1195–1200.

Riessman, C.K. (2002) 'Analysis of personal narratives', in J. Gubrium and J. Holstein (eds), *Handbook of Interview Research: Context and Method*. Thousand Oaks, CA: Sage.

Richardson, L. (2002) 'Poetic representation of interviews', in J. Gubrium and J. Holstein (eds), *Handbook of Interview Research: Context and Method*. Thousand Oaks, CA: Sage.

Rose, N. (1998) 'Life, reason and history: reading Georges Canguilhem today', *Economy and Society*, 27(2–3): 154–70.

Rubin, H.J. and Rubin, I.S. (1995) *Qualitative Interviewing; The Art of Hearing Data*. Thousand Oaks, CA: Sage.

Seale, C. (1998) 'Qualitative interviewing', in C. Seale (ed.), *Researching Society and Culture*. London: Sage.

Seale, C. (1999) *The Quality of Qualitative Research*. London: Sage.

Seale, C. and Filmer, P. (1998) 'Doing social surveys', in C. Seale (ed.), *Researching Society and Culture*. London: Sage.

Seale, C. and Silverman, D. (1997) 'Ensuring rigour in qualitative research', *European Journal of Public Health*, 7: 379–84.

Silverman, D. (1985) *Qualitative Methodology and Sociology*. Aldershot: Gower.

Silverman, D. (1993) *Interpreting Qualitative Data: Methods for Analysing Talk, Text and Interaction*. London: Sage.

Strong, P.M. (1980) 'Doctors and dirty work – the case of the alcoholic', *Sociology of Health and Illness*, 2: 24–47.

Turkel, S. (1995) *Coming of Age: The Story of Our Century by Those Who've Lived It*. New York: New Press.

Warren, C.A.B. (2002) 'Qualitative interviewing', in J. Gubrium and J. Holstein (eds), *Handbook of Interview Research: Context and Method*. Thousand Oaks, CA: Sage.

Watson, D.R. and Weinberg, T.S. (1982) 'Interviews and the interactional construction of accounts of homosexual identity', *Social Analysis*, 11: 56–78.

Weiss, R.S. (1994) *Learning from Strangers: The Art and Method of Qualitative Interviewing*. New York: Free Press.

Wetherell, M. (2001) 'Themes in discourse research: the case of Diana', in M. Weatherell, S. Taylor and S.J. Yates (eds), *Discourse Theory and Practice: A Reader*. London: Sage, in association with the Open University.

2

Oral history

Joanna Bornat

As an oral historian I greeted the opportunity to draw on my own experience with enthusiasm. Could this be the ultimate in reflexivity? I apply my own method to myself. For once I have the opportunity to hold the floor instead of taking a back seat at the interviewee's performance. But, as an oral historian I also know how complex these interrogative exchanges can be, how much may be revealed, partial, or forgotten, hidden or silenced. How best then to deal with an area of work in which I have lived for getting on for thirty years? I will need to find a way to balance my own engagement and emergent research practice with a detachment that is inclusive of others' experience. Should I reproduce the interrogative characteristic of oral history with an account written in the form of an interview? Lacking the probing insights of another might present problems for the equal presentation of all the different aspects of the self.[1] In fact this will not be my first published reflection on being an oral historian. But then my earlier attempt was a personal reflection on how I had been changed by oral history practice rather than a review of my engagement with the method (Bornat, 1993). This feels like much more of a challenge.

What follows is not a 'how to' manual. Several of these already exist drawing on experience of oral history work and research in different national and cultural settings (Lummis, 1987; Douglas et al., 1988; Finnegan, 1992; Yow, 1994; Ritchie, 1995; Bolitho and Hutchison, 1998; Thompson, 2000; http://www.oralhistory. org.uk). Instead the chapter falls into three sections following a chronology of involvement in oral history as a research method. Each section focuses on an issue that emerged at a particular point in my own development but which, in my opinion, continues to have significance for the practice of oral historians. In tackling each of

these my intention is to illustrate key aspects of a method while highlighting linked debates. The three issues that I identify are: the interview as a social relationship; the transcript and its ownership; and multidisciplinary analysis. The story and the selection are obviously my own. I make no claims as to rights, wrongs or leadership. I simply offer my experience.

As a starting point I provide a description of oral history as I see it today and a delineation of its boundaries with other, cognate, areas of research methodology. Like any other social or historical phenomenon, oral history is a product of shifting paradigms and unbending structures as well as individual initiative and opportunism. In the end I have settled for writing an account that should identify the key issues with which oral historians have engaged but from my own position and perspective. There will be bias, partiality, silence, some revelation and much forgetting, but that is the nature of oral history, and for some people its very interest and significance.

DEFINING AND DELINEATING ORAL HISTORY

The turn to biography in social science (Chamberlayne et al., 2000), coupled with a more open, sometimes grudging, acceptance of the contribution of memory in historical research described by Paul Thompson (2000: ch. 2), has resulted in a proliferation of terms, schools and groupings often used interchangeably, some with a disciplinary base, others attempting to carve out new territory between disciplines. Labels such as oral history, biography, life story, life history, narrative analysis, reminiscence and life review jostle and compete for attention. What is common to all is a focus on the recording and interpretation, by some means or other, of the life experience of individuals. Though there are shared concerns and, to an extent, shared literatures, there are differences, in approach and in methods of data collection and analysis.

One way of grouping these different terms is by reference to their relation to the subject, the informant, interviewee or respondent. Oral history, life history, reminiscence and life review tend to focus on the idea of the interviewee as an active participant in the research process. The conscious and willing participation of the person being interviewed means that the nature and conduct of the interview itself becomes a dominant feature of the research process. Oral history draws on memory and testimony to gain a more complete or different understanding of a past experienced both individually and collectively (Thompson, 2000). Life history takes the individual life and its told history with a view to understanding social processes determined by class, culture and gender, for example drawing on other sources of data, survey-based, documentary, personal, public and private to elaborate the analysis (Bertaux, 1982). The difference between the two is very fine and the two terms are often used interchangeably.

Both oral history and life history, as Ken Plummer argues, draw on 'researched and solicited stories … [that] do not naturalistically occur in everyday life; rather they have to be seduced, coaxed and interrogated out of subjects' (2001: 28). Both oral history and life history share common disciplinary heritages in history and sociology, though the influences of psychology and gerontology are increasingly playing a part (Thompson, 2000; Bornat, 2001).

In contrast, biographical and narrative approaches to life story telling tend to be characterized by analyses that place great emphasis on the deployment of psychoanalytically based theorizing during and after the interview at the stage of data analysis. As Robert Miller suggests, the narrative interview is understood in terms of the individual's conscious and subconscious 'composing and constructing a story the teller can be pleased with' (2000: 12). From this perspective the interview is understood as a social relationship in which 'Questions of fact take second place to understanding the individual's unique and changing perspective' (Miller, 2000: 13). The contribution of the researcher to this process is spelled out by Wendy Hollway and Tony Jefferson:

As researchers … we cannot be detached but must examine our subjective involvement because it will help us to shape the way in which we interpret interview data. This approach is consistent with the emphasis on reflexivity in the interview, but it understands the subjectivity of the interviewer through a model which includes unconscious, conflictual forces rather than simply conscious ones … . (2000: 33).

Such an approach, though it allows for active reconstruction and fluidity in the telling of a story, inevitably draws on the theoretical framework employed in its explanation. Paradoxically, given the focus on subjectivity and theorizing the perception of the individual, it may shift the balance of power away from the teller and towards the interpreter.

Drawing up distinctions and definitions can lead to false boundary construction. It would be wrong to present oral history and life history approaches to interviewing as ignorant of the social relations of the interview or of the varied subjectivities of the interviewee. Luisa Passerini has discussed how 'silences' in workers' accounts of the fascist 1920s in Italy left her baffled until she understood how these pointed to the reality of their daily experience and the need to adjust her own understanding of life at that time (Passerini, 1979). Al Thomson's research with Anzac survivors of the First World War took him into an exploration of the ways in which these very old men had lived with experiences that at times had conflicted with the public account and yet had arrived at a 'composure' that enabled them tell their stories in ways that felt comfortable and recognizable to themselves and to Thomson, their interviewer (Thomson, 1994: 9–12). In a collaborative interview with Linda Lord, a former New England poultry worker, Alicia Rouverol argues that what appears as a 'richly layered, seemingly contradictory narrative' provides a more complete understanding of what losing your job means (Rouverol, 2000). Feminist oral historians and ethnographers helped to shift the focus towards the subject by initiating debates that explored the relationship between interviewer and interviewee, raising questions about shared identity, oppression and ownership as well as voice and perspective (see, e.g., Personal Narratives Group, 1989; Gluck and Patai, 1991; Sangster, 1994; Summerfield, 2000).

Reminiscence and life review are related approaches that at times are used interchangeably with oral history and life history. Where reminiscence is the focus, then the activity of remembering tends to be directed more towards the achievement of an outcome for the speaker or speakers involved. Reminiscence, while it is also a normal part of everyday inner life, when it is encouraged on a group or individual basis seeks to evoke the past with a view to bringing about a change in, for example, mood, social interaction or feelings of self-worth. Life review, as proposed by Robert Butler (1963), is carried out on a one-to-one basis with a professional or practitioner who seeks to help someone to understand and reflect their life as a whole, accepting it in all its aspects, as it has been lived (Bornat, 1994: 3–4). Life review is more of an intervention than a research method. However, it is certainly the case that the life history or oral history interview often has a strong life review aspect within it. Interviewees sometimes express themselves as welcoming the opportunity to reflect and describe new understandings about themselves, others, and events they have experienced.

Life review, subjective reflection, interrogation, recounting and silencing, oral history is in its many aspects, Alessandro Portelli argues, both genre and genres (Portelli, 1997: 4–5). We can say this now, but what about then, when I started?

THE INTERVIEW AS A SOCIAL RELATIONSHIP

The first issue I want to look at is the implication of the interview as a social relationship. Interviewing is the defining method of oral history and awareness of the complexities of intentions and emotions on both sides of the microphone was something that took me a while to acknowledge.

Back in the early 1960s, had I been looking for what I have just described, I would not have found it. Something called oral history existed by name in the USA where Allan Nevins had established an oral history project at Columbia University in 1948. Nevins's aim was to establish a record of the lives of those of significance in US society. This was quite different, as Grele and Thompson both point out, from an initiative some ten years or more earlier, when the Federal Writers' Project and indeed the Chicago School of sociology had been recording and drawing on the life experiences of former black slaves, workers and migrants (Grele, 1996: 64ff.; Thompson, 2000: 65).

In the early 1960s when I was a sociology student there was no sign of any of these developments in any of the courses I followed. I was a student, and also a member of the Communist Party actively engaged in recruiting members, supporting causes and selling the *Daily Worker*. To say that now is to take an intellectual risk just as it was then. To call yourself a Marxist was to invoke ridicule in those Cold War days, but it did mean that you allied yourself in intention if not in practice with challenges to oppression and with a commitment to change at community, national and international levels. It also meant that you were interested in how to make things happen and in theorizing about this.

I mention all this because the rather practical and committed side of my existence as a student was quite separate from what I met up with in most lectures and seminars. My department (Sociology, University of Leeds 1962–5) may or may not have been typical, but the sociology we learned was wholly theoretical in its teaching, even on the methods side. The sociology we learned began with Marx, Weber and Durkheim and then leapt to Parsons and structural functionalism with a brief glance at C. Wright Mills on the way. In parallel we learned about administrative, social and institutional change in what was then the UK together with some social psychology, but were offered no theory that appeared to make sense of all this, apart from Marxism. Parsons, Lipset and Merton read like Cold War rationalizing and US ethnocentrism where class, social conflict and critical analysis were kept in a theoretical bell jar. Our own Marxist academics at Leeds were divided between Trotskyism and the Communist Party and though their lectures are the ones that inevitably inspired me most,[2] I sensed that they were isolated within the teaching group. I might have been saved for sociology if someone had introduced me to the Chicago School.

Methods owed a great deal to positivist thinking and attempts to consolidate the discipline and its outputs as reliable. I see from my lecture notes that the role of methodology in the social sciences was to: provide formal training; increase the social scientist's ability 'to cope with new and unfamiliar developments in his (*sic*) field; to contribute to interdisciplinary work; and organize principles by which knowledge of human affairs can be integrated and codified'. Interviewing was, rightly, given equal prominence with survey design, questionnaires and scaling. We were given detailed guidance on interviewing in a reading by Maccoby and Maccoby. This contrasted standardized and unstandardized techniques but with the caveat that however much we might standardize words and questions, this would not be a basis for comparison since 'the same words mean different things to different people' and 'when one asks a standardized question, one has not standardized the *meaning* [their emphasis] of the question to the correspondent' (1954: 452). I learned that 'the *content* [their emphasis] of the communication ... will be affected by the status relationships'

(1954: 462). Maccoby and Maccoby's overview includes references to Kinsey and Adorno's work as well as other studies that drew out the implications of the interview as a social relationship and awareness of interviewer 'error' (1954: 475). It was all fascinating stuff, but sadly we were given no opportunity to try out the method for ourselves.

My practice took place outside the university lecture room, in discussions on doorsteps, on the street, in the student union and in 'Party' education classes and meetings, with garment workers, engineers, miners, teachers, clerks, typists and other Communist Party activists, including members of the large branch of academics and the 'secret' branch of overseas students whose membership threatened their safety in their own countries. After three years of this divided life I decided that sociology, as I had come to understand it, was not for me. Had I but known it, at the other end of the country a new sociology department set up at the University of Essex had begun with quite a different set of expectations of its students. Peter Townsend's recruitment of a historian, Paul Thompson, and a radical US sociologist, Dorothy Smith, shaped a curriculum that was both historical and practical (Thompson and Bornat, 1994: 44–54). Students were encouraged to engage with current issues and, unheard of at undergraduate level, do their own fieldwork.

None of what I had been exposed to was really an adequate preparation for postgraduate research. I had decided to turn myself into a labour historian and to try to forget about sociology and learn the historian's methods. I knew from my own reading and political life that history as a discipline had become much more interesting. Some historians were apparently keen to make links with sociology (Jordanova, 2000: 67ff.). I had read E.H. Carr (1961) with great enthusiasm for what sounded like a case for the politically and socially committed historian, but more important for me was the output of Marxist and social historians such as E.P. Thompson, G.D.H. and Margaret Cole and Eric Hobsbawm. They had introduced working people into the history curriculum and were not afraid to use terms such as 'class' and 'exploitation'. It felt as if history was more within reach. Indeed, Eric Hobsbawm has recently explained the ascendancy of British Marxism within history in the 1950s and 1960s as being due in part to 'the virtual absence from British intellectual life (outside the London School of Economics) of the sciences of society' (Hobsbawm, 2002: 18). He also gives credit to the Historians' Group of the British Communist Party, 'a body that encouraged academic activities'.[3]

For my topic I settled, after a false start, on the activities of a Yorkshire wool textile trade union between 1880 and 1920. My aim was to find out about the workings of the labour movement in contexts where life was ordinary and less marked by exceptionality. I immersed myself in union minute books, newspapers and official papers. After a while, someone pointed out to me that several of the trade unionists I was interested in were still alive. This was a connection I somehow had failed to make. I have an old notebook, labelled 'Interviews', whose contents show that I did indeed talk to some trade unionists and Communist and Labour activists whose memories went back to 1914 and earlier. However, all the teaching I had apparently absorbed about interviewing methods seems to have left no trace. Now that I was a historian I was more interested in finding out about a past that I was certain was there, intact and to be discovered. It was not the talk or the language of trade unionism I was interested in, nor indeed personal experience, but rather facts about people and events. I consulted these retired experts in much the same way as I engaged with the crumbling pages of the *Yorkshire Factory Times*. I identified issues, elicited responses and took notes. Reflection on the social relationship of the interview and of interviewer bias eluded me. Nor did I appear to be aware of levels and differences of meaning in what I was told. And sadly, the idea that these accounts might be worthy of preservation in their own right simply did not occur to me. All that remains of these encounters are my rather sketchy notes, made at the time. Such as they were, these interviews served my needs as a historian, as I then understood that discipline, offering the world an explanation as to why an industry that employed a large proportion of women in the West Riding of Yorkshire was so weakly unionized. I struggled on with my mountains of documents and with ever-improving skills in note-taking and archive working.

Things were to change after getting married, working on a project investigating race and employment in Bradford, and having two children I went back to my PhD. However, now I was registered at the University of Essex, in the sociology department. It was 1973 and Paul Thompson and colleagues were just completing the first major oral history project in the UK (Thompson, 2000). I was to be introduced to a different way of doing both sociology and history.

It may seem extraordinary that as a professed Marxist (following 1968 I left the Communist Party) it had not occurred to me that the people I was so interested in finding out about might actually have a perspective that was in itself a valid source. With retrospective fairness I would have found it hard, within the discipline of history, to discover examples that might legitimate such an approach. Indeed, the much respected Hobsbawm is still, in 2002, unable to accept sources drawing on memory as having validity:

> I am also struck by a certain flight from the actual past as in the flourishing and fertile field of memory studies that has shot up since about 1980. Here we are concerned not with what was, but with what people think, feel, remember or usually misremember about it. In some ways this can be seen as a development of themes we pioneered, but we explored these things in an entirely different intellectual context. (Hobsbawm, 2002: 19)

The History Workshop Movement that had begun in 1967 (Rowbotham, 2001: 123ff.) provided the intellectual context for many of us at this time. And though many of the texts that Raphael Samuel so wonderfully referenced in his later reviews of the debates about empiricism, labour, culture, theory and people's history (Samuel, 1981: xv–lvi) were an inspiration, I was yet to make up my own mind about the provenance of memory-based sources in academic debate.

My first experience as an oral historian was to dispel any reservations. At Paul Thompson's suggestion I went back to the West Riding and interviewed 21 men and women who had worked in the textile industry before 1921. While I was being presented with data that I could transcribe, manage, analyse and organize, what really led to a long-standing commitment was the process of interviewing. Using an audio cassette recorder that allowed me and the interviewee to relax and simply talk, with the aid of a prepared questionnaire,[4] was astonishingly fresh and revealing. I found myself hearing how people lived with an industry, how it permeated their lives both domestic and industrial. These were not activists but rank-and-file textile workers recalling their young days in the mills. Using the categories of my questionnaire as the basis for my analysis, I generated a whole new set of themes that offered an explanation, in part, as to why a union led by men who were openly committed to equality for women was so unrepresentative in its organization. It seemed that the system of pooling wages in families, though a shared insurance against the uncertainty of employment, did not protect women and young people from marginalization within the workplace and as wage-earners. Union subscriptions were collected in workers' homes and thus a gendered division of domestic labour was carried into the workplace and, by

extension into the union's organization (Bornat, 1980, 1986).

The immediacy of the recall, the sense of speaking directly to the past, completely captivated me. I was entranced by these older men's and women's accounts, their language and forms of expression. This was enough, but what I simply was not prepared for was their expressed enjoyment and commitment in return. I was astonished one day in Slaithwaite, Colne Valley, when an older woman in her sheltered flat thanked me for interviewing her. It simply had not occurred to me that this might be a two-way process in which the interviewee had her own agenda and interest (Bornat, 1993).

What made oral history feel different, and still does, was the sense of working with someone to present a past that was and still is full of meaning. At that stage I was not yet fully aware of the possible dimensions of this process. In those early days, criticisms that oral history was taking a positivist, fact-driven and uncritical approach to memory and the past (Popular Memory Group, 1998) were beginning to be tackled, but if other oral historians were shifting their understanding I was not (Thomson et al., 1994: 33–4).[5] My own political positioning, as a socialist and feminist, provided an essentialist cloak shielding me from complexities within the process. No major epistemological issues arose for me. My understanding of the method was more in the nature of the liberation of truth, the reclaiming of ground by people whose voices were not heard or usually called upon. Oral history in this sense provided me with a new political project in which historians and their subjects could be on the same side. That there might be contestation around the recording and its presentation and 'The confrontation of … different partialities – confrontation as "conflict" and confrontation as "search for unity" – … one of the things which makes oral history interesting' (Portelli, 1991: 58), I was yet to discover.

THE TRANSCRIPT AND ITS OWNERSHIP

Working outside the academy with community groups and individuals to produce local publications, exhibitions, plays, videos and, more recently, multi-media events based on memory and recall was always a likely channel of activity, given that the method involves direct engagement with members of the public and assurances that their accounts, their witness to the past, is a valuable public asset. Working with people to achieve the production of their own accounts of the past presents challenges to the oral historian who feels a commitment to a political or emancipatory role for oral history while at the same time attempting to maintain some kind of critical rigour. Is it possible to work collaboratively with people and retain some form of critical understanding of the past while committed to an emancipatory role for oral history?

A key contribution to such a debate was the collection of papers written by US feminists and edited by Sherna Berger Gluck and Daphne Patai (1991). These are, in the main, a refreshingly honest exploration of methodological dilemmas arising from essentialist and emancipatory assumptions that had tended to mystify the relationship of researcher and researched. Several contributors reflect on experiences where interviewees, other women, challenged their motives and interpretations, where victim or oppressed statuses were not readily assimilated or when generational differences were underacknowledged. Debating with feminists, Martin Hammersley identifies the tension between academic research and practical demands and pressures and argues for an 'institutionalized inquiry' that is independent of particular political or practice objectives. Independence is required, he argues, in order to widen investigations beyond 'relatively narrow and short run concerns' (Hammersley, 1992: 202).

I am not sure whether independent 'institutionalized inquiry' would help wholly to resolve issues of critical rigour and ownership. Indeed, the very heterogeneity and localism of much that can be described as community history would tend to militate against any kind of fixed base or professional specialism. However, recognition of the need for a 'balance between inquiry and the other necessary elements of practice, and appropriate judgement about what it is and is not appropriate to inquire into' (Hammersley, 1992: 202) might well help to support public historians in their dealings with other people's ideas of the past.

In the mid-1980s, at a time when community history projects were burgeoning throughout the UK, I was employed as a lecturer in older people's education by the Inner London Education Authority's Education Resource Unit for Older People (EdROP).[6] As part of my job I was able to answer a request to run an oral history project on the Woodberry Down council estate in Hackney, one of the poorest of London's boroughs. The request came from a social worker, keen to re-establish in their own and others' eyes the historical and social identities of the estate's oldest tenants. Woodberry

Down had at one time been one of the London County Council's show estates. Built directly after the Second World War, it incorporated, when completed, many of the most advanced features of social housing provision, including schools, shops, a library, a health centre and an old people's home, and occupied land next to two reservoirs in what had been regarded as one of north London's most pleasant residential settings. By the late 1980s it was run down with several of the amenities under threat,[7] and the generation of families who were among its first tenants were retired with children in the main living elsewhere.

A colleague and I were the facilitators and as EdROP was able to supply recording and transcribing equipment for what was deemed older adults' learning, we were well resourced. After six months of tape recording with a core group and a few others more loosely associated we had accumulated sufficient material, many hours of recorded interviews, photographs, and documents copied from local archives to produce a display and, by 1989, a book (Woodberry Down Memories Group, 1989). The main narrative was unimpeachably balanced for both older and younger tenants. This was the story of a group of people, and a housing authority with a shared commitment to public housing. They were an ethnically mixed group with members whose backgrounds were Jewish, Italian, Punjabi, Venezuelan and white north London. Their story was one of individual and collective hardship, their own individual deserving status and community harmony. Some were well known on the estate for their past roles as tenant leaders, others were more easily recognized among the church congregation. Most had worked hard to furnish their flats and to provide their children with a start in life that they themselves had been denied. Woodberry Down was very much a part of that better start and their commitment to social housing tenancy apparently complete, even at its most vocally critical.

This is the story that appears in the book. It was the one that the group was most happy with and, in truth, it also appealed to my understanding of social and housing history generally. We spoke with one voice as I mainly restricted my role to one of facilitator rather than investigator. It felt like an emancipatory collaboration drawing on the agency of older people who were willing collaborators in producing a story in which they had a vested interest. Establishing themselves as active and differentiated people and their estate, their public space in the Habermasian sense (Habermas, 1989), as a worthy and politically significant development was their means to critically challenge those contrary voices and accounts that consigned them to the stigmatized and passive status of being old and a council tenant.

I was, however, as were the group, aware of other narratives, missing accounts, conflicting versions. Though my co-worker was black and we made a deliberate target of black pensioners in our publicity, we were never able to recruit an African-Caribbean older tenant as a permanent member of the group. There was, consequently, no story of being a black tenant on an estate with a history of multi-racial and multi-ethnic tenancies. One woman who showed interest was not willing to be recorded, so, given the nature of the book's key source, she remained unrepresented, an interesting issue in itself.

Flats on the Woodberry Down Estate were hard to come by initially. People had to prove need, sharing with parents or in-laws, becoming parents, guaranteed one of the cheaper flats. Among the stories, hidden in asides and comments, there was also mention of graft and favouritism in gaining access to the better flats and maisonettes. These were some of the spoken and hinted-at community stories that were not destined for public consumption.

On a broader political front was the issue of why the estate was built in its particular location. Some visits that I made to the then Greater London Record Office[8] to investigate when the decision to build the estate was taken raised the possibility of gerrymandering in the 1930s, when the estate's development was first mooted. It seemed that Woodberry Down might have played a part in the political manoeuvrings of the the Labour-run London County Council, led by Herbert Morrison. Stoke Newington (later to be absorbed into the London Borough of Hackney) was traditionally Conservative and was unwilling to house 'slum dwellers' from other parts of London (Woodberry Down Memories Group, 1989: 24). Were the first residents deserving recipients of post-war socialist housing policies, or were they the beneficiaries of 1930s struggles to change the political map of London? These are questions that are implicit in the account and that suggest a wider historical and political framework for the reconstitution of this particular community history. My interest in these questions identified me as an outsider to the Woodberry Down group, both professionally and politically. By not pushing them further, was I compromising my own position and critical rigour and so neglecting the 'longer term and/or ... wider perspective' or was I recognizing that such questions might be 'counter-productive from the point of view of practice' (Hammersley, 1992: 202)?

When it came to presenting the account there were to be further compromises. Apart from linking text, provided by me, the bulk of the account was to come from the recorded and transcribed memories of the group. Together we selected those sections that best illustrated people's individual experiences while also providing evidence of what life was like on the estate in the 1940s, 1950s and 1960s. There were photographs too, some personal and some from the local archives. Encouraged by the process, some members of the group chose to write about occasions that were particularly memorable, such as getting the key to their flat. One member of the group, Sid Linder, said he couldn't write anything more than a betting slip; however, when it came to editing in his memories of growing up in the Jewish East End of London and an experience of anti-Semitism in the army in North Africa, he changed his mind and took the transcript away. What he brought back was a much sanitized, in language terms, version of the original, far away from the expressive cadences and turns of speech of the recording and even its subsequent transcription. His preference was for an account that was culturally neutral and grammatically correct, mine was for one that more accurately represented a particular, and historical, form of expression, Jewish East End speech.

How far apart the two versions were is perhaps evident from the following excerpts:

Transcription:

Sid: But I was lucky. I was popular because I was captain of the school. I used to give one of the boys – you have the football this weekend after the football match. The same in the army. I'll tell you something. Some people have never seen a jew. It was one Christmas I was in a big mob and we had a big canteen and we used to invite from other units to come into our canteen Christmas time and a couple of fellas sat here and of course I had my own pals you know, cos beer was rationed you see. So what we used to do – a lot of boys didn't drink so you used to say give me or give my friend, give us tickets and we used to save them and at Christmas we used to have beer. And there was a chap sitting there. We're all enjoying ourselves because some come from Oldham, some came from up north, most of them came from up north and a chap turned round and said for no reason at all I don't like jews he said. I never said nothing but my pal he was a boxer, Billy Simms – so he said to him why don't you like jews he says. He said there's a jew pointing to me. He said go on I don't believe you. So as you know you carry a disc – did you carry a disc?

Les: Well you did in the army.

Sid: I carried a disc and my religion was on it you see. So he said go away from this table see. That's the only incident I had in the army.

Written account:

> I was lucky because I was captain of the school football team and was popular.
>   There was similar prejudice in the army. There were people who had never even seen a Jew. I remember one Christmas in the army canteen sitting with my pals when for no reason at all someone who had joined our table started saying that he did not like Jews. My best pal Billy Simms who was a boxer said, pointing at me, 'He's a Jew'. The other bloke was amazed and said he did not believe it. Billy told him to clear off. That was the only incident I personally had in the army.

A transcript can only be a 'frozen' version of the original oral discourse, as Portelli argues (1991: 279), but the written version is a step much further. Stefan Bohman has pointed out how, although the written and interview versions draw on the author's conserved 'narrative repertoire', the interview 'employs a different language'. He suggests that the spoken language is 'conducive to greater directness and is more vivid' (1986: 17–19). However, there is a danger, the US oral historian Michael Frisch suggests, that carefully reproducing the 'narratives of common people or the working class' will 'magnify precisely the class distance it is one of the promises of oral history to narrow' (1990: 86). Perhaps Sid Linder sensed this possibility more keenly than I did. In the end I climbed down and the written version went into the book. The experience revealed to me how ownership of the finished text is inevitably a negotiated issue and also how transcription is itself open to complexity, being, as Ruth Finnegan suggests, 'a value-laden and disputed process' (1992: 198).[9]

Where do such exchanges and negotiations leave community oral history and the academic? Linda Shopes, a US oral historian, points out the benefits of community oral history for those engaged in the process and its outcomes, yet she

also warns, among other things, against the danger of playing down conflict and the influence of external forces in accounts produced. She calls for a community oral history that is 'problem-centred', thus enabling links to be made between broader structural determinants as well as the identification of more complex issues at a more personal level that might otherwise be glossed over (1984: 153–5).

The challenges she sets are not exclusive to community-based oral history. The experience led me in a more sceptical and reflective direction and to review a previously uncritical commitment to an emancipatory role for oral history. I now had experience of the kinds of compromises involved in work that sought to be collaborative both at the level of the individual and the community and my own position as an academic in this process.

A MULTIDISCIPLINARY ANALYSIS

The burgeoning of activity in biographical and narrative methods across a wide range of disciplines might suggest that there is little to choose between different approaches.[10] In what follows, I want to indicate what I feel makes oral history persistently distinctive and how the method has responded to developments in data analysis. If I have moved in my perceptions of what being an oral historian entails, I am not unusual in this respect; as Penny Summerfield points out, the original impetus to oral history meant 'an emphasis on truth and validity rather than meaning'. More recently there has been a shift towards what she describes as 'greater awareness of the psychic dimensions' (2000: 92). Sensitivity to meaning at different levels has enabled oral historians to identify the significance of silences and subjectivity (Passerini, 1979), fabulation (Portelli, 1988), trauma (Jones, 1998; Langer, 1991) and gendered memory (Chamberlain and Thompson, 1998). What such analysis depends on and what I feel makes oral history a distinctive method is a continuing commitment to multidisciplinarity in its approach to data analysis. To illustrate this point, I am taking an example from research with colleagues into the impact of family change on older people.[11]

As part of a larger research programme we set out to investigate the implications for older people of the coterminosity of two sets of statistics, the ageing of the population and the increase in family change through divorce and separation. By the mid-1990s the proportion of the population over the age of 65 had reached 15 per cent of the population, while in England and Wales, four in every ten marriages were expected to end in divorce (Haskey, 1996; OPCS, 1996).

These statistics raised questions for us about the nature of intergenerational relationships, the care and support of more frail older family members, and issues of inheritance and the sharing of family assets. In designing the research we chose a method, the unstructured life history interview with a sample of 60 interviewees,[12] because we felt this would allow people to use their own language to describe the changes they were experiencing. We were keen to identify meanings attributed to family used over people's lifetimes and also to avoid any fixed notion of what might be happening by use of terms such as 'stepfamily'. The term 'family change' seemed to us more appropriate than the more highly charged language of 'divorce', 'break-up' or 'stepfamily'. We were problem-focused, but in a way that we hoped people would respond to in their own terms and without prejudgement. In all we completed 60 interviews, mainly with people over the age of 50. (For a more detailed account of the project and its methods see Bornat et al., 1998.)

Though we had identified a set of questions, we had no prior theories that we were testing. This is very much an emergent topic for study which, as we began, had only a small literature attached to it, hence the need for an inductive approach that would enable us to develop our understanding and further shape our own ideas as to what might be happening as the data was analysed. The perspectives of those directly involved in family change were important to us. They were actors, with agency and views on what they were experiencing (Miller, 2000: 11). We were keen to enable people to reflect on their own lives over time and to be able to make comparisons, both generational and personal. For these reasons the life history interview presented itself as the ideal instrument.

All the interviews were fully transcribed and analysed using a grounded theory approach (Glaser and Strass, 1967; Gilgun, 1992) that identified underlying themes within the data as well as a focus that emphasized consideration of the language used in relation to family change. Grounded theory tends to be the method of choice for most people working with life history data and oral history data. If the steps in data analysis are made transparent and are explained, it provides the most secure means to guaranteeing a method that, while it deliberately makes use of researcher insight and reflection, guards against allegations of subjectivity and lack of generalizability or theoretical relevance (Wengraf, 2001: 92–5).

What we were presented with at interviews were accounts of family change over a life-time. Recent trends towards divorce had been prefigured by separations explained by war, unemployment, migration, fundamentalist religious practice, evacuation, altogether a wide range of unsettling experiences belying any notion of an original state of family stability prior to the previous thirty years.

Our approach was to read and re-read the whole transcript and to discuss emergent ideas and themes within the context of the whole life as narrated and described in the interview. Ideas and categories were compared and reviewed against the accounts we had collected as we searched for confirmations and contradictions of issues relating to family change by identifying common instances as well as uniquely telling accounts. The value of a life history or oral history approach lies in the opportunity it provides to take the whole life and also wider socio-economic and historical contexts into consideration when analysing the data. We might, for example, see how a particular experience of being a child was later followed up in becoming a parent while at the same time reading up for contextual reasons the social history of the Second World War or the car industry in Luton (where we carried out our fieldwork) and exploring the literature on attachment in later life. Multidisciplinarity meant that the methods of the historian, the gerontologist and the sociologist were brought to bear, and also, significantly, the psychologist, leading to our particular development of 'psychic awareness'.

An understanding of meaning for our oldest interviewees and for those younger people addressing issues of ageing was central to our analysis. The psychologist of old age, Peter Coleman, has argued both that recall of the past is an important contribution to well-being in late life, and that for some older people reminiscence is irrelevant and for others troubling (Coleman, 1986). Others have detected differences in the ways men and women remember, with women's narratives marked by greater diffidence and less assertion, though these differences are not necessarily fixed (Chamberlain and Thompson, 1996). As Coleman et al. (1998) point out, some women report gaining greater confidence in late life and those who survive to a late old age were often striving to express identity themes, particularly relating to family. Bearing in mind differences within and between age cohorts, against the tasks that Erikson (1950), a psychologist, identifies for old age, achieving 'ego integrity', finding meaning in a life story and perhaps accepting the events of a life, the conduct of an interview and its interpretation may have particular age-related features. Reminiscence and oral history with older people has consistently been linked to the significance of identity maintenance or management in the face of significant life changes. The kind of ontological security that Giddens (1991) argues is central to self-identity seems to require strong narrative support in late life, particularly when 'disembodiment' becomes evident with loss of physical powers. At the same time older people may be facing challenges to their ability to exercise choice and control over their lives. Interestingly, despite the increasingly dominant role that older people play in late modernity, demographically speaking, Giddens has little to say about the implications of his ideas for ageing and self-identity, though he does argue that 'A person's identity is not to be found in behaviour nor – important though this is – in the reaction of others, but in the capacity *to keep a particular narrative going*' (1991: 54).

At this point it might help to introduce some excerpts from our interviews to illustrate how the multidisciplinary approach of oral history enabled a more broadly based understanding of family change from the perspective of the older generation:

PL

72, divorced first husband in 1975 (2 children), married a widower in 1981, no children. He died in 1993.

Did you mind her moving? I know you didn't want to say that to her but –

PL: No, but – well, no, not, I mean, I knew, do you see, I was married then to C — , you see, so, you know, and, as I said, it was, that was, you know, if that's what they wanted, I certainly wouldn't stop them. I know, you know, **you miss them, but you can't, once they're married, you just can't – they've got to put their husbands first, and their family first.** And I've got a nice relationship with both my son-in-law and my daughter-in-law, because I never interfere. I'm there if they want me. I don't agree with everything they do. But I've learned to – you don't say anything. And they work it out themselves. And, as I say, I've got a good son-in-law and a good daughter-in-law.

WW

Age 86, she divorced during the Second World War, remarried, widowed, five children from two marriages, daughter and granddaughter also divorced.

WW: Yes, wish they could be the same as us, you know. See but I suppose some parents, they're not all the same, you know. The thing is, parents, they should never interfere with the children when they're married. Because they've got their lives to live, but you're there, when they want you, you're there, and they're there, when we want. **Because they've all got their own little lives, haven't they? – when they're married. And that's how we like it. I mean, I'm on the phone, I can reach any of them and they'll be up here in a minute if I wanted them.** Any of them.

Mr and Mrs S

She married twice to two brothers, two children by first husband who died, daughter divorced, son and daughter married with children.

Mrs S: Because he does permanent nights, yes. So they might stay over the Saturday night. But only perhaps about once a month or six weeks. So, we're not in each other's pockets. But I mean, today, S was able to ring up and ask T — if he could fetch L — from school, because she'd got to take the baby to the clinic for his injections. So I mean, we're near enough for that. And that's good for the grandchildren, I think, and for T — . So, you know, that's handy. So, yes, it is – **I don't like to feel that I hang on to them. But I do like to know that I could get to them if I want, and she could get to me, if she wants me. And also her Dad.**

Excerpts such as these (with key text in bold) suggested that 'You're never too old to be a parent' and that despite changing relationships, longer narratives of family life provided not only a significant source of continuity but also of personal identity. While such observations were supported in the gerontology and sociology literature with Bengtson and Kuypers's notion of 'intergenerational stake' (1971; Giarrusso et al., 1995). However, we could also draw on psychology to show that what we were hearing was the language of attachment in later life (Antonucci, 1994; Bornat et al., 1997) rather than simply the language of calculated investment (Finch and Mason, 1993).

My understanding of oral history is that it works best when approached in multidisciplinary mode. The richness of the data, in terms of the possibilities for levels and contexts of interpretation, suggests a need for access to the methods and theories of more than one discipline and a balanced approach ensures that no one emphasis predominates. We were not seeking an explanation in terms of unconscious motives or emotions, or 'silences' within interviews. Though we speculated, endlessly it sometimes seemed, as to the motives displayed within some accounts, we were not prepared to move into the position of all-seeing interpreters of possible meanings held by our interviewees. We identified certain existential issues and dilemmas relating to death, generativity and personal and social moralities, but theorizing that went beyond, into psychoanalysis, was unattractive on two counts. First, the differing backgrounds and disciplines that we brought to bear – historical, social work, psychological and gerontological – together offered a richer and more broadly structured source of questions and explanations, and second, we wanted, as far as possible, to represent people in their own words and in ways that maintained their own authority as witnesses to, and theorizers about, family change.

CONCLUSION

What have I learned from my experience as an oral historian that I seek to pass on to others interested in the method? From my first encounters it is the recognition of the interview as a social relationship and how this may be drawn on to derive richly individual accounts that would otherwise be hidden or obscured by differences of age, class and gender. From my work with community-based groups I would want to emphasize the need to maintain a problem-focused approach to history-making while acknowledging and supporting ownership rights for participants. Finally, from my experience of working in a more formal, social science context, I see oral history as opening up possibilities for work across discipline boundaries, enriching interpretation through links between past and present, acknowledging situated subjectivities

and demonstrating how individual agency, expressed through language, meaning and memory, interacts with and serves to mediate and moderate the broader structural determinants of society today and in the past. All three aspects for me constitute a good enough 'intellectual context' (Hobsbawm, 2000: 19), true to oral history's original commitment in the 1970s and which encompasses the plurality and subjectivity of researchers and researched now celebrated thirty years later.

NOTES

1 Fiona Williams's (1993) solution to this problem, in an 'interview', was to separate out the personal reflection and chronology of life events in a main narrative, from a footnoted academic commentary.

2 Cliff Slaughter, the anthropologist and leading British Trotskyist, was my tutor and joint author with Norman Dennis and Fernando Henriques of *Coal is Our Life* (1956), a study of a Yorkshire mining community that, as Thompson points out, drew on interviews but neglected the historical context of the village and its people (2000: 90). Griselda Rowntree, like me a member of the Communist Party, came from the London School of Economics to teach us, among other things, the sociology of the family.

3 I perhaps should add that my stepfather, Allan Merson, was a member of the Communist Party History Group, so I was not remote from these influences.

4 I based my list of questions on Paul and Thea Thompson's original questionnaire, which is now presented in the third edition of *The Voice of the Past* as 'A Life-Story Interview Guide'. There it is described as '*not* [his emphasis] a questionnaire, but a schematic outline interviewer's guide for a flexible life-story interview'. In its different formats it has provided a basic tool for oral historians for twenty-five years (Thompson, 2000: 309ff.).

5 The criticisms of the Popular Memory Group (Thomson and Perks, 1998) are still debated. Accusations of empiricism, individual reductionism, objectification of 'the past' and neglect of power relations in the interview are still live. In a rebuttal, Thompson argues that the Popular Memory Group could only argue their case because they were unaware of the influence of subjectivity, in the writing of US and European oral historians such as Grele (1975) and Passerini (1979). However, he does concede: 'I think that we focussed on the objective dimension at the start because we felt we had to show conventional historians and social scientists that our material was not totally invalidated by the vagaries of memory' (1995: 28).

6 The Inner London Education Authority was a grouping of education authorities, covering early years, school and adult education in inner London with a large pooled budget and an enormous staff body of teaching

and support workers. Typical among its many innovative projects and initiatives that drew national attention was EdROP, which was set up in 1985 and lasted until 1990 when the ILEA was abolished by the then Conservative government.

7 In 2002 much of the estate was scheduled for demolition, the library and secondary school had closed as had the residential home for older people, and the social worker and her colleagues who had invited us to run the project were long gone, social services' managers having agreed retrenchment to an office some distance away. With regeneration money it was hoped to rebuild the estate and to preserve some of the more attractive blocks.

8 Now the London Metropolitan Archive.

9 There are legal issues of ownership that anyone undertaking taped interviewing needs to be aware of. EU copyright law gives rights of ownership to the person who gives the interview, which means that use by any other person, the interviewer for example, requires permission in the form of assigning copyright to that person. An example of a form assigning copyright is to be seen at http://www.oralhistory.org.uk.

10 A survey of life history teaching in higher education carried out in 1997–8 demonstrates just how wide a range of disciplines are represented. 1000 questionnaires were sent out and among the 94 replying who reported their teaching of life history were: History, Sociology, English and Literature, Media and Cultural Studies, Women's Studies, Archives and Librarianship, Education, Social Policy, Psychology, Anthropology, Folk Studies, Genealogy, Community History, Engineering, Information Technology, Linguistics, Music, Archaeology, Art, Drama, Historical Geography, Medicine, Medieval Latin, Political Science, Professional Development, Reminiscence Work, Social Science (Thomson, 1998: 31, 58).

11 Bornat, Dimmock, Jones and Peace, 'The impact of family change on older people: the case of stepfamilies', ESRC reference number L31523003. The project was part of the Household and Family Change Programme.

12 A total of 1796 screening questionnaires were sent out during a ten-month period in three electoral wards in Luton. 249 were returned completed. From these, 120 were identified as potential interviewees. All 120 were contacted and this resulted in 49 interviews. The remainder were obtained through contacts made with local groups, bringing the number of people interviewed to 72 (28 men and 44 women). They were characterized in the following way:

i 24 people had lived in a step-household (9 as a child, 7 as the partner of a step-parent, 8 as a step-parent).

ii 21 had experienced the formation of a step-household within their kin group.

iii 18 had experienced the formation of step-relationships (but not step-households) within their kin group.

iv 9 people's lives had been affected by separation but not re-partnering.

REFERENCES

Antonucci, T.C. (1994) 'Attachment in adulthood and aging', in M.B. Sperling and W.H. Berman (eds), *Attachment in Adults: Clinical and Developmental Perspectives*. New York: Guilford Press.

Bengtson, V.L. and Kuypers, J.A. (1971) 'Generational difference and the "developmental stake"', *Aging and Human Development*, 2: 249–60.

Bertaux, D. (1982) 'The life course approach as a challenge to the social sciences', in T.K. Hareven and K.J. Adams (eds), *Ageing and Life Course Transitions: An Interdisciplinary Perspective*. London: Tavistock, pp. 127–50.

Bohman, S. (1986) *The People's Story: On the Collection and Analysis of Autobiographical Materials*, Methodological Questions, No. 3. Stockholm: Nordiska Museet.

Bolitho, A. and Hutchison, M. (1998) *Out of the Ordinary: Inventive Ways of Bringing Communities, their Stories and Audiences to Light*. Murrumbateman: Canberra Stories Group.

Bornat, J. (1980) 'An examination of the General Union of Textile Workers, 1888–1922'. Unpublished PhD thesis, University of Essex.

Bornat, J. (1986) '"What about that lass of yours being in the union?": textile workers and their union in Yorkshire, 1888–1922', in L. Davidoff and B. Westover (eds), *Our Work, Our Lives, Our Words: Women's History and Women's Work*. Basingstoke: Macmillan.

Bornat, J. (1993) 'Presenting', in P. Shakespeare, D. Atkinson and S. French (eds), *Reflecting on Research Practice: Issues in Health and Social Welfare*. Buckingham: Open University Press, pp. 83–94.

Bornat, J. (ed.) (1994) *Reminiscence Reviewed: Perspectives, Evaluations, Achievements*. Buckingham: Open University Press.

Bornat, J. (2001) 'Reminiscence and oral history: parallel universes or shared endeavour?', *Ageing and Society*, 21: 219–41.

Bornat, J., Dimmock, B., Jones, D. and Peace, S. (1997) 'Attachment revisited: the impact of family change on the lives of older people', *Aging Beyond 2000: One World One Future*, 16th Congress of the International Association of Gerontology, Adelaide, Australia, 19–23 August 1997.

Bornat, J., Dimmock, B., Jones, D. and Peace, S. (1998) 'The impact of family change on older people: the case of stepfamilies', in S. McRae (ed.), *Changing Britain: Population and Household Change*. Oxford: Oxford University Press, pp. 248–62.

Butler, R.N. (1963) 'The life review: an interpretation of reminiscence in the aged', *Psychiatry*, 26: 65–73.

Carr, E.H. (1961) *What is history?* Basingstoke, Macmillan.

Chamberlain, M. and Thompson, P. (1998) 'Introduction: genre and narrative in live stories', in M. Chamberlain and P. Thompson (eds), *Narrative and Genre*. London: Routledge, pp. 1–22.

Chamberlayne, P., Bornat, J. and Wengraf, T. (2000) *The Turn to Biographical Methods in Social Science*. London: Routledge.

Coleman, P.G. (1986) *Ageing and Reminiscence Processes: Social and Clinical Implications*. Chichester: John Wiley.

Coleman, P.G., Ivani-Chalian, C. and Robinson, M. (1998) 'The story continues: persistence of life themes in old age', *Ageing and Society*, 18(4): 389–419.

Dennis, N., Henriques, F. and Slaughter, C. (1956) *Coal is Our Life: An Analysis of a Yorkshire Mining Community*. London: Eyre & Spottiswoode.

Douglas, L., Roberts, A. and Thompson, R. (1988) *Oral History: A Handbook*. Sydney: Allen & Unwin.

Erikson, E. (1950) *Childhood and Society*. New York: Norton.

Finch, J. and Mason, J. (1993) *Negotiating Family Responsibilities*. London: Routledge.

Finnegan, R. (1992) *Oral Tradition and the Verbal Arts: A Guide to Research Practice*. London: Routledge.

Frisch, M. (1990) *A Shared Authority: Essays on the Craft and Meaning of Oral and Public History*. Albany: State University of New York Press.

Giarrusso, R., Stallings, M. and Bengtson V.L. (1995) 'The "intergenerational stake" hypothesis revisited: parent-child differences in perceptions of relationship 20 years later', in V.L. Bengtson, K.W. Schaie and L.M. Burton (eds), *Adult Intergenerational Relations: Effects of Social Change*. New York: Springer.

Giddens, A. (1991) *Modernity and Self-Identity: Self and Society in the Late Modern Age*. Cambridge: Polity.

Gilgun, J.F. (1992) 'Definitions, methodologies, and methods in qualitative family research', in J.F. Gilgun, D. Daly and G. Handel (eds), *Qualitative Methods in Family Research*. London: Sage, pp. 22–39.

Glaser, B.G. and Strauss, A.L. (1967) *The Discovery of Grounded Theory: Strategies for Qualitative Research*. New York: Aldine de Gruyter.

Gluck, S.B. and Patai, D. (eds) (1991) *Women's Words: The Feminist Practice of Oral History*. London: Routledge.

Grele, R.J. (1975) *Envelopes of Sound*. Chicago: Precedent Publishing.

Grele, R. (1996) 'Directions for oral history in the United States', in David K. Dunaway and Willa K. Baum (eds), *Oral History: An Interdisciplinary Anthology*. Walnut Creek, CA: AltaMira Press, pp. 62–84.

Habermas, J. (1989) *The Stuctural Transformation of the Public Sphere: An Inquiry into a Category of Bourgeois Society*. Cambridge: MIT and Polity.

Hammersley, M. (1992) 'On feminist methodology', *Sociology*, 26(2): 187–206.

Haskey, J. (1996) 'The proportion of married couples who divorce: past patterns and current prospects', *Population Trends*, 83: 25–36.

Hobsbawm, E. (2002) 'Old Marxist still sorting global fact from fiction', *Times Higher*, 12 July, pp. 18–19.

Hollway, W. and Jefferson, T. (2000) *Doing Qualitative Research Differently*. London: Sage.

Jones, D.W. (1998) 'Distressing histories and unhappy interviewing', *Oral History*, 26(2): 49–56.

Jordanova, L. (2000) *History in Practice*. London: Abacus.

Langer, L.L. (1991) *Holocaust Testimonies: The Ruins of Memory*. New Haven: Yale University Press.

Lummis, T. (1987) *Listening to History: The Authenticity of Oral History*. London: Hutchinson.

Maccoby, E.E. and Maccoby, N. (1954) 'The interview: a tool of social science', in G. Lindzey and G. Allport (eds), *The Handbook of Social Psychology*, Vol. 1. Cambridge, MA: Addison-Wesley, pp. 449–87.

Miller, R.L. (2000) *Researching Life Stories and Family Histories*. London: Sage.

OPCS (Office of Population and Census Surveys) (1996) *Living in Britain: Results from the 1994 General Household Survey*. London: HMSO.

Passerini, L. (1979) 'Work ideology and consensus under Italian fascism', *History Workshop*, 8: 82–108.

Personal Narratives Group (eds) (1989) *Interpreting Women's Lives: Feminist Theory and Personal Narratives*. Bloomington: Indiana University Press.

Plummer, K. (2001) *Documents of Life 2*. London: Sage.

Popular Memory Group (1998) 'Popular memory: theory, politics, method', in R. Perks and A. Thomson (eds), *The Oral History Reader*. London: Routledge, pp. 75–86.

Portelli, A. (1988) 'Uchronic dreams: working class memory and possible worlds', *Oral History*, 16(2): 46–56.

Portelli, A. (1991) 'What makes oral history different', in *The Death of Luigi Trastulli and Other Stories: Form and Meaning in Oral History*. Albany: State University of New York Press, pp. 45–58.

Portelli, A. (1997) *The Battle of Valle Giulia: Oral History and the Art of Dialogue*. Madison: University of Wisconsin Press.

Ritchie, D. (1995) *Doing Oral History*. New York: Twayne.

Rouverol, A. (2000) 'I was content and not content', *Oral History*, 28(2): 66–78.

Rowbotham, S. (2000) *Promise of a Dream: Remembering the Sixties,* London: Penguin.

Samuel R. (1981), 'People's history' (pp. xiv–xxxix) and 'History and theory' (pp. xl–lvi), in R. Samuel (ed.), *People's History and Socialist Theory*. London: Routledge & Kegan Paul.

Sangster, J. (1994) 'Telling our stories: feminist debates and the use of oral history', *Women's History Review*, 3: 5–28.

Shopes, L. (1984) 'Beyond trivia and nostalgia: collaborating in the construction of local history', *International Journal of Oral History*, 5(3): 151–8.

Summerfield, P. (2000) 'Dis/composing the subject: intersubjectivities in oral history', in T. Cosslett, C. Lury and P. Summerfield (eds), *Feminism and Autobiography: Texts, Theories and Methods*. London: Routledge.

Thompson, P. (1995) Letter published in *Oral History*, 23(2): 27–8.

Thompson, P. (2000) *The Voice of the Past* (3rd ed.). Oxford: Oxford University Press (1st ed. 1978).

Thompson, P. and Bornat, J. (1994) 'Myths and memories of an English rising: 1968 at Essex', *Oral History*, 22(2): 44–54.

Thomson, A. (1994) *Anzac Memories: Living with the Legend*. Oxford: Oxford University Press.

Thomson, A. (1998) *Undergraduate Life History Research Projects: Approaches, Issues, Outcomes*. Brighton: Centre for Continuing Education, University of Sussex.

Thomson, A. and Perks, R. (1998) *The Oral History Reader*. London: Routledge.

Thomson, A., Frisch, M. and Hamilton, P. (1994) 'The memory and history debates: some international perspectives', *Oral History*, 22(2): 33–43.

Wengraf, T. (2001) *Qualitative Research Interviewing*. London: Sage.

Williams, F. (1993) 'Thinking: exploring the "I" in ideas', in P. Shakespeare, D. Atkinson and S. French (eds), *Reflecting on Research Practice: Issues in Health and Social Welfare*. Buckingham: Open University Press, pp. 11–24.

Woodberry Down Memories Group (1989) *Woodberry Down Memories: The History of an LCC Housing Estate*. London: ILEA Education Resource Unit for Older People.

Yow, V.R. (1994) *Recording Oral Histories: A Practical Guide for Social Scientists*. London: Sage.

3

Biographical research

Gabriele Rosenthal

It is now more than twenty years since I first came across biographical research in connection with my doctoral thesis. It was a time when this approach was beginning to re-establish itself after half a century, in German sociology in particular but also at the international level. Sociological biographical research began in the 1920s, in association with the migration study *The Polish Peasant in Europe and America* by William Isaac Thomas and Florian Znaniecki (1918–20; 1958) at the University of Chicago. Even then, empirical work was already concentrating on the single case study. Alongside documentary analysis on the migration process, this voluminous work contains only one biography of a Polish migrant, commissioned by the researchers. It was not so much the concrete biographical analysis that made this work so influential for subsequent interpretative sociology and biographical research, but rather the two authors' general methodological comments. One of the most important was their demand that 'social science cannot remain on the surface of social becoming, where certain schools wish to have it float, but must reach the actual human experiences and attitudes which constitute the full, live and active social reality beneath the formal organization of social institutions' (1958: II, 1834).

Biographical research, inspired by this study, blossomed at the Sociology Department in Chicago during the 1920s at the initiative of Ernest W. Burgess and Robert E. Park. Researchers motivated by realization of the necessity of 'getting inside of the actor's perspective' now recognized the advantages of the biographical case study for recording the subjective perspectives of members of various milieus. In the 1970s, sociology increasingly began re-examining the work of the Chicago School, leading to a veritable boom in interpretative biographical research. The first anthology of biographical research was published in Germany in 1978 by Martin Kohli and an international reader by French sociologist Daniel Bertaux[1] followed in 1981. This research tendency is expanding to this day in the various specialist disciplines. In sociology today, biographies are increasingly considered and examined as a social construct of social reality in themselves (Kohli, 1986; Fischer and Kohli, 1987), whereas initially written or narrated biographies were used instrumentally as a source of specific information.

As well as in sociology, biographical research has become especially well established in oral history (Bornat, Chapter 2, this volume; Thompson, 1992; von Plato, 1998) and the educational sciences (Alheit, 1993, 1994; Krüger and Marotzki, 1999). Psychology – where the discipline also began putting down academic roots in the 1920s and 1930s through the work of Charlotte and Karl Bühler and their associates at the Psychological Institute of Vienna University (cf. Bühler, 1933) – has also begun rediscovering the biographical approach. Internationally, the work by Jerome Bruner (1990), George C. Rosenwald and Richard L. Ochberg (1992) and Dan McAdams (1993) – to name but a few – has led to a rediscovery of *verstehende* psychology and above all biographical research operating with narrative methods. Recently the concept of narrative identity has gained more attention and fairly elaborated versions of the concept have been proposed (Holstein and Gubrium, 2000). As Chapter 7 by Molly Andrews et al. (in this volume) clearly shows, this concerns above all 'the potential of narrative to function as a cornerstone of identity formation and maintenance over time'.

My own introduction to biographical research in 1980 came through an interest in social patterns of interpretation that was initially unconnected to biographical approaches. I was studying the patterns of interpretation of a generation whose members were at that time increasingly defining the discourses of the various elites – including professors. My own parents belonged to this generation, the 'Hitler Youth generation' born approximately between 1920 and 1930. I was interested in the question of whether and to what extent the patterns of interpretation internalized under the Nazis had changed in the democratic Federal Republic. As the work progressed, it relatively quickly became clear that I had little chance of understanding their perception and interpretation of social reality and their processes of cognitive transformation unless I was familiar with the history and experiences of the generation – in particular their experiences under the Nazis in the Hitler Youth, during the Second World War, and during the collapse of the Third Reich. Unless I knew their background history, how could I explain why this generation identified so conspicuously with West Germany's economic growth, and why it was at the same time so performance-orientated and so hard on itself and unforgiving of its own weaknesses? On the other hand, much could be understood if one knew the biographical background – their experiences in childhood and adolescence, their concrete experience of youth organization and school. I knew some of this biographical background from the stories told by my parents. For that reason there is a sense in which I have them to thank for my interest in my interview partners' pasts.

So at that point I decided to adopt a life-story approach. At this time, the narrative interview method of Fritz Schütze (1976, 1983) was provoking a great deal of discussion in the field of qualitative research. Following this method, I asked my interviewees to tell me their biographical experiences during childhood and in the years following the collapse of the Third Reich (Rosenthal, 1987, 1989, 1991). Today, many years later, I have reflected on the theory and methodology of my empirical approach at that time, and no longer employ that degree of thematic focus. Instead – like many biographical researchers in Germany – I ask interviewees to tell me their whole life story (see below). This approach – and the associated bracketing of the research question during collection of data and a large part of analysis – involves a significant effort to put aside one's acquired traditional methodological training.

At the outset, for the reconstruction of the life stories of members of the Hitler Youth generation, I drew up an analysis concept where the distinction between life story and life history (i.e., between the narrated personal life as related in conversation or written in the present time and the lived-through life) plays a central role. This means I distinguish between the perspective of the biographer in the past and the perspective of the biographer in the present. This analytical distinction and its methodological realization in analytical steps was in part a result of the theoretical influence of the work of Wolfram Fischer (1982), who demonstrated so clearly the constitution of biographical narrative through the present perspective. It was, however, also a result of my chosen field of research. Narratives concerning National Socialism are characterized in the first place by denials, reinterpretations and formation of myths, so analysis demands that the researcher exercise a permanent methodological doubt and overcome his or her own West German socialization. If one wishes to avoid contributing to the reproduction of myths and denials, one has to pay attention to the difference between the account and the past experience. In my habilitation thesis (Rosenthal, 1995) I went on to develop a gestalt-theoretical-phenomenological concept of the dialectical interrelation between experience, memory and narration, and discussed this distinction as one that must be taken into account in all narrated and written biographies.

BIOGRAPHY-THEORETICAL ASSUMPTIONS

The methodological decision to ask for the whole life story to be told, regardless of the specific research question, is based on fundamental theoretical assumptions. Where we are dealing with questions of social science or history that relate to social phenomena that are tied to people's experiences and have biographical meaning for them, these assumptions lead us to interpret the meaning of these phenomena in the overall context of the biography. The individual assumptions are:

1 In order to understand and explain[2] social and psychological phenomena we have to reconstruct their *genesis* – the process of their creation, reproduction and transformation.
2 In order to understand and explain people's actions it is necessary to find out about both the subjective perspective of the actors and the *courses of action*. We want to find out what they experienced, what meaning they gave their actions at the time, what meaning they assign today, and in what biographically constituted context they place their experiences.

3 In order to be able to understand and explain the statements of an interviewee/biographer[3] about particular topics and experiences in his/her past it is necessary to interpret them as part of the *overall context of his/her current life* and his/her resulting present and future perspective.

So in biographical research we look at the experiences preceding and following the phenomenon in question, and the order in which they occurred. The point is to reconstruct social phenomena in the process of becoming. This applies both to processes of creation and reproduction of established structures and to processes of transformation. When reconstructing a past (the life history) presented in the present of a life narrative (the life story) it must be considered that the presentation of past events is constituted by the present of narrating. The present of the biographer determines the perspective on the past and produces a specific past at times. The present perspective conditions the selection of memories, the temporal and thematic linkage of memories, and the type of representation of the remembered experiences. This means that in the course of a life with its biographical turning points – points of interpretation (Fischer, 1978) that lead to a reinterpretation of the past and present, and also of the future – new remembered pasts arise at each point. This construction of the past out of the present is not, however, to be understood as a construction separate from the respective experienced past. Instead, memory-based narratives of experienced events are also constituted through experiences in the past (Rosenthal, 1995). So narratives of experienced events refer both to the current life and to the past experience. Just as the past is constituted out of the present and the anticipated future, so the present arises out of the past and the future. In this way biographical narratives provide information on the narrator's present as well as about his/her past and perspectives for the future.

The theoretical presumptions discussed above imply particular requirements of the data collection and analysis methods:

1 the requirement to allow insight into the genesis and sequential gestalt of the life history;
2 a proximity to the courses of action and to the experiences, and not only to the present interpretations of the investigated persons; and
3 the reconstruction of their present perspectives and the difference between these present perspectives and the perspectives that were adopted in the past.

In the following I will first present the instrument of the biographical-narrative interview and then discuss the method of biographical case reconstruction using an example case study.

BIOGRAPHICAL-NARRATIVE INTERVIEW

The biographical-narrative interview meets these requirements particularly well. Fritz Schütze (1976, 1983) introduced this interview method in the 1970s; in the meantime it has also become an established interview method in fields other than sociological biography research and has been developed further in terms of an increase in questioning techniques (Rosenthal, 1995: 186–207).

Today most people who pursue this type of research first take into consideration, independent of their social science questions, the entire life story both in terms of its genesis and how it is constructed in the present. That is why when one first conducts interviews and reconstructs life stories, one does not restrict oneself to parts or individual phases of the biography. Observing individual areas of life or individual phases in life in terms of the biography's entire context can take place only after the entire life story's structure or gestalt and the whole life narrative has been taken into consideration.

> **The sequences of a narrative interview are:**
>
> 1 *Period of main narration*
>   Interviewer: initial narrative question
>   Interviewee: main narration or self-structured biographical self-presentation
>   Interviewer: active listening and taking notes
> 2 *Questioning period*
>   (a) internal narrative questions
>   (b) external narrative questions

The initial question

As I indicated above, I started my biographical research with thematically focused narrative interviews. In fact, I conducted my first narrative interview with a completely closed initial question:

> Can you still remember when you first thought about the possibility that Germany might lose World War II? Please tell me about this phase, and your personal

experience of the war, the end of the war, and the years following it, until you felt your life was 'back to normal'.

The answer was: 'Yes, well I have to start much earlier' and the interviewee, who had been a full-time leader of the Nazi youth organization, began to relate her career in the Hitler Youth. She told me how greatly she had identified with National Socialism and her work, and how strongly she had denied all the contradictions between theory and practice. In this biographical self-presentation she attempted to explain to me, but also to herself, why she had been absolutely convinced of the *Endsieg*, the German final victory, right up until the collapse of the Third Reich. This interview was an important lesson for me. In subsequent interviews I changed my initial question and asked my interviewees to talk about their experiences in the Hitler Youth and then about the last years of the war, etc.

Nonetheless, I was still convinced that the interviewees needed a thematic orientation. In my PhD I argued – in opposition to Fritz Schütze – that asking interviewees to tell their life story would be asking too much of them, because they would not know what they should talk about and what they should leave out. I first met Fritz Schütze after publication of this work (Rosenthal, 1987). He had read my criticism of his open method, and simply said: 'Why don't you just try it out with an absolutely open question?' Schütze did not want to argue with me about my objections. Instead, in keeping with the 'grounded theory' approach,[4] he wanted to motivate me to gain an insight through practical experience of my own. I did this, and had to discover that none of the objections drafted at my desk passed the test of empirical practice. Quite to the contrary, an open request to tell his/her life story makes it much easier for the biographer to talk without other considerations and planning. Also, this method opens up new fields and thematic connections to our research question that we had not previously suspected. My failure, in the work on the Hitler Youth, to give sufficient attention to the political attitudes of the parents and their activities in the Nazi Party was an expression of my own blind spots. A subsequent empirical investigation of First World War veterans – the generation of the fathers of Hitler Youth members – made me very aware of the biographical relevance of the background family history (Rosenthal, 1991). This marked the beginning of my interest in multi-generation family studies and in generally integrating the life story in the family history (Rosenthal, 1997, 2002).

The initial question I work with now avoids any thematic restriction. At the beginning of each individual interview, we[5] generally requested the following of the biographer:

> Please tell me/us your family story and your personal life story; I/we am/are interested in your whole life. Anything that occurs to you. You have as much time as you like. We/I won't ask you any questions for now. We/I will just make some notes on the things that we would like to ask you more about later; if we haven't got enough time today, perhaps in a second interview.

In some contexts, however, I recommend working with a more structured form. This relates to situations where an initial question relates to particular research contexts that are not tied to the history of a person. Let us consider, for example, a qualitative study of a particular institution, in which the residents of this institution are interviewed. Here the initial question could be:

> We are interested in your personal experience in this institution. Perhaps you might start by telling your experience when you came to this institution, tell us what you experienced since then until today. You have as much time as you like... (see above).

One intermediate structured form that stands between these two forms of initial question and to an extent offers a compromise between the very open and fairly closed approaches combines the life history with a thematic focus. It reads:

> We are interested in the life stories of people with a chronic disease (or; of people who experienced *perestroika* in Russia), in your personal experience. Please tell me your life story, not just about your illness (not just about the *perestroika* years), but about your whole life story. Anything... (see above).

This form of request is particularly suitable for research contexts (e.g. in my interviews with Holocaust survivors) where we have to state our specific research interest, and where it is not enough simply to refer to an interest in life histories. Furthermore, this allows us to state our topic and ensure that the interviewees speak about it, while still leaving enough room for relating other biographical strands. The subsequent narrative could clearly show what role the illness (or the experience of everyday politics) plays in the biographers' lives, where they link it to other biographical strands, and where they attempt to locate the beginning, for example, of the illness in their life history. Nevertheless, there are reasons to choose the most open form even here if possible. Life stories of chronically ill people who are not initially asked about their illness, and who fail to mention the illness in their self-structured biographical self-presentation, are of particular theoretical interest. This can, for example, be a expression of a difficulty to integrate the illness in the biography.

The main narration and narrative questions

This request to hear the interviewee's life story is generally followed by a long biographical narration (i.e., biographical self-presentation), often lasting for hours. This so-called main narration is at no time interrupted by questions from the interviewers, but instead is only supported by paralinguistic expressions of interest and attentiveness like 'mhm' or, during narrative interruptions, through motivating encouragement to

continue narrating, such as 'And then what happened?', through eye contact, and other gestures of attention. During this phase the interviewer must listen carefully, making notes on the subjects referred to, and noting in particular which parts are not plausible or not told in enough detail. These notes are then used in the second questioning period.

Narrative-generating questions are not posed until the interview's second phase. A narrative question does not mean asking questions about opinions or reasons ('Why did you … ?', 'Why did you do that?', 'Why did you want to … ?'); it instead means encouraging people to talk about phases in their life or particular situations.

Questions are oriented in the following ways:

I Addressing a phase of the interviewee's life.
   'Could you tell me more about the time when you were … (a child, in school, pregnant, etc.)?'
   Or, indicating interest in the process:
   'Could you tell me more about your time in the army, perhaps from the first days until the end of your training?'

2 Addressing a single theme in the interviewee's life by opening a temporal space.
   'Could you tell me more about your parents? Perhaps from your earliest memories until today.'

3 Addressing a specific situation already mentioned in the interview.
   'You mentioned situation X earlier, could you tell me/narrate in more detail, what exactly happened?'

4 Eliciting a narration to clarify an argument already made before.
   'Can you recall a situation when your father behaved in an authoritative way (when you stopped believing in justice, peace, etc.)?'

5 Addressing a non-self-experienced event/phase or transmitted knowledge.
   'Can you remember a situation when somebody talked about this event (how your father died)?'

We first limit ourselves to *internal narrative questions*, meaning questions regarding that which has already been discussed. It is not until the interview's next phase that we orient ourselves according to our own scientific criteria and pose *external narrative questions* regarding topics that interest us and have not yet been mentioned. The internal questions we formulate are based on the notes taken during the main narrative; that means they do not introduce a topic the narrator has not already mentioned. Keeping the narrative-external questions for the last phase of the interview is important so that the interviewer does not impose his/her own relevance system upon the narrator. In the reconstruction of the interview this also simplifies answering such questions as why certain thematic areas or

biographical phases were not covered by the biographer himself or herself. Did he or she assume that these would not interest the interviewer, or did it not fit with the image she or he wants to present, or did he or she find it too embarrassing or too painful to elaborate on this? This can only be clarified in the thematic field analysis (see below).

Since the biographers are first encouraged to give a longer account of their own experiences, they can structure the narration according to the criteria they themselves find relevant and the memory process is supported. Via cognition, feelings or subjects, we listeners also do not experience the narrators at a remove from what they are telling about; it is rather the case that they are embedded in their narrations about biographical experiences. In contrast to argumentations and descriptions, self-lived experiences additionally have the advantage of being closer to what concretely happened and was experienced in the past in the narrated situations. Apart from restaging past situations, telling a story is the *only way to come close to* an integral reproduction of what happened at that time or the past experience's gestalt. However, it is rather the case that argumentations are formulated from the present perspective and from the standpoint of their social desirability. While, in telling about experiences, it is the case that we interact more with our memories than with the listeners, our explanations regarding what we experienced are directed at the interlocutors. If we are able to support the biographers in their narrations without posing any additional questions, and if many memories easily surface in their memory that they can tell about, then what can clearly be seen is how the narrations become more and more detailed, the orientation with respect to the listeners lessens and the physical memories become stronger. While, at the beginning, the biographers perhaps reflect on how they are going to present their life story, on which areas in their life they should talk about, this effort subsides as the narration starts to flow. The narrators increasingly find themselves in a stream of memories; impressions, images, sensual and physical feelings, and components of the remembered situation come up, some of which do not fit in their present situation and which they have not thought about for a long time. The narrations' proximity to the past thus increases in the course of the narration, and perspectives entirely different from the present perspective show themselves, which become clear in the argumentation parts or also in the narrated anecdotes.

BIOGRAPHICAL CASE RECONSTRUCTIONS

The principles: reconstruction and sequentiality

I developed the biographical case reconstruction method presented here over many years in combination with various other methods (Rosenthal, 1993, 1995; Rosenthal and Fischer-Rosenthal, 2000). I – and in the meantime many of my colleagues[6] too – work with a combination of the objective hermeneutics of Ulrich Oevermann et al. (1979, 1987[7]), the text analysis method of Fritz Schütze (1983) and the thematic field analysis of Wolfram Fischer (1982, prompted by

Gurwitsch, 1964). Biographical case reconstructions are characterized – as already mentioned – by the particular attention paid to structural differences between what is experienced and what is narrated.

Biographical case reconstruction shares the reconstructive and sequential approach of other hermeneutic methods. 'Reconstructive' means that the text is not approached with predefined categories – as in content analysis – but rather that the meaning of individual passages is interpreted through the overall context of the interview. 'Sequential' in this context means an approach where the text or small text units are interpreted according to their sequential gestalt, the sequence of their creation. The analysis reconstructs the progressive creation of an interaction or the production of a spoken or written text step by step in small analytical units. In this method, development and testing of hypotheses is based on the abduction procedure introduced by Charles Sander Peirce (Peirce, 1933/1980) where, in contrast to deduction and induction, how the hypothesis is generated is as important as how it will be tested. 'Peirce's theory of abduction is concerned with the reasoning which starts from data and moves towards hypothesis' (Fann, 1970: 5). According to Peirce, the first stage of inquiry is 'to adopt a hypothesis as being suggested by the fact' (para. 6,469). The next stage is 'to trace out its necessary and probable experimental consequences' (para. 7,203) and in the third stage we test the hypothesis by comparing our predictions with the actual results. Both scientific theories and everyday theories have a heuristic value in the development of hypotheses. So unlike in deduction it is not a matter of following and testing a particular theory. Instead a range of concepts are taken as possible explanations of an empirical phenomenon – in other words for forming several possible hypotheses. 'The act of adopting an hypothesis itself, at the instant, may seem like a flash of insight, but afterwards it may be subjected to criticism' (Fann, 1970: 49). In other words: abduction imposes on you to give reasons for your suggestions and to prove them in the concrete individual case.

Just like deduction and induction, the method of abduction comprises three stages of inquiry; only the order of the stages is different. Whereas deduction starts with a theory and induction with a hypothesis, abduction begins by examining an empirical phenomenon. For a sequential analysis this means:

1 *From an empirical phenomenon to all possible hypotheses.* Starting from an empirical

phenomenon in a given unit of empirical data, a general rule is inferred with respect 'to the supposition of a general principle to account for the facts' (Fann, 1970: 10). This step is the actual abductive inference. The important thing is to formulate not only one hypothesis, but all the hypotheses that are possible at the time of consideration and might explain the phenomenon.

2 *From hypothesis to follow-up hypothesis or follow-up phenomenon.* Follow-up phenomena are deduced from the formulated hypotheses, i.e., from this rule other phenomena are inferred that confirm this rule. Or put differently: for each hypothesis a follow-up hypothesis is considered according to what comes next in the text, if this reading proves to be plausible.

3 *The empirical test.* This is where empirical testing is carried out in the sense of inductive inference. The concrete case is investigated for indices to match the deduced follow-up phenomenon. In a sequential procedure this means that the follow-up hypotheses are now contrasted with the text sequences or the empirical data that follow. Some of them gain plausibility whereas others are falsified. The interpretations that cannot be falsified in the process of sequential analysis – that are left over after hypothesis testing has excluded the improbable readings – are then regarded as the most probable.

In biographical case reconstructions, sequential analysis represents a procedure where the temporal structure of both the *narrated* and the *experienced* life history is analysed. Based on the given text, we try to reconstruct the sequential gestalt of the life story presented in the interview and in a subsequent step the sequential gestalt of the experienced life history is also analysed. As well as the question of the sequence and textual sort used by the biographers to present their biographically relevant data, this approach also examines how the individual biographical experiences have layered chronologically in the experienced life history. So in the reconstruction of the life history we try to break down the genesis of the experienced life history and in the analysis of the biographical self-presentation to break down the genesis of the representation in the present, which differs in principle in its thematic and temporal linkages from the chronology of the experiences.

In the approach presented by the author (cf. Rosenthal, 1995) it is crucial to investigate the two levels of narrated and experienced life history in separate analytical steps. That means that

the goal of reconstruction is both the biographical meaning of past experience and the meaning of self-presentation in the present.

The procedure

Biographical case reconstructions of interviews, which are selected for deeper analysis after a global analysis of all interviews according to the model of theoretical sampling (Glaser and Strauss, 1967: 45–78; Gobo, Chapter 28, this volume), are based on a full transcription of the audiotape.

The steps of analysis are:

1 Analysis of the biographical data.
2 Text and thematic field analysis (structure of self-presentation; reconstruction of the life story; narrated life).
3 Reconstruction of the life history (lived life as experienced).
4 Microanalysis of individual text segments.
5 Contrastive comparison of life history and life story.
6 Development of types and contrastive comparison of several cases.

In the following I will first briefly describe these individual steps and then outline the application of the method using an empirical example.

Sequential analysis of biographical data

This step of analysis (see Oevermann et al., 1980) starts by analysing the data that is largely free of interpretation by the biographer (e.g. birth, number of siblings, educational data, establishment of own family, change of place of residence, illness events, etc.) in the temporal sequence of the events in the life course. This data is taken from the transcribed interview as well as from all other available sources (archive material, interviews with other family members, official files such as medical records). The individual biographical datum is initially interpreted independently of the knowledge that the interpreters have from the narrated life story – independently of the further course of the biography. The interpretation of one datum is followed by the next, which tells the interpreters which path the biographer actually took. The interpretation is initially independent of the self-interpretations and accounts in the biographical interview.

This sequential abductive procedure – like the other analytical steps too – demands a degree of methodological discipline, i.e., we always have to bracket out our knowledge of the case. Critics often reject this as unachievable. Experience shows, however, that this is not only possible, but also that we cannot normally memorize either the precise sequence of the data or the fine structure of the corresponding interview passages. Biographical data often gains its significance only after analysis has begun, so when the first data is interpreted it has often not received attention at all or its significance has not been realized. Nonetheless, in this approach great advantages are offered by interpretation in groups where the co-interpreters are not familiar with the interview.

Another critical question directed at this method is why we should consider all the possible interpretations of a datum, when the interviewee made his/her own statements about it thus allowing the meaning to be discovered. Here we can respond that on the one hand the interviewee's self-interpretations are constituted from his/her present, while on the other, as social scientists we strive in particular to reconstruct latent structures of meaning, in other words the meanings to which the interviewee has no access (see Oevermann et al., 1987). Here in particular it is a great advantage to initially avoid looking at the interviewee's self-interpretations and their plausibility, but instead to first investigate other possible interpretations. When we later examine the text with this spectrum of possible interpretations in mind we will be able to find many more possible interpretations between the lines.

The analysis of the biographical data thus serves as preparation for the third step of analysis – the reconstruction of the life history – where we contrast our hypotheses on the individual biographical data with the biographer's statements. However, before we attempt to reveal the past perspectives in the various life phases, it makes sense to first decipher the interviewee's present perspective using text and thematic field analysis. This helps us to adopt a source-critical perspective, so that we avoid satisfying a particular presentation need in the present or naïvely interpreting the perspective reconstituted by the present as a representation of the experience in the past. For example, if we know at the end of analysis that – although she is probably not herself aware of this – the biographer's self-presentation in the thematic field 'I live my life independently and autonomously of my family' serves to avoid talking about family bonding and associated distress, or possibly also the expression of a socially required self-presentation, we are receptive to other interpretations at the level of experienced life history.

Analysing the biographical data *before* the text and thematic field analysis, on the other hand, serves as a contrast for the analysis of the biographical self-presentation. So we can see which biographical data are blown up narratively in the main narration, which are not mentioned at all, and in which temporal order they are presented.

BIOGRAPHICAL DATA OF GALIN'S FAMILY AND LIFE HISTORY Before I turn to this next analytical step, I would like first to demonstrate – at least in outline – the procedure for analysing the biographical data. I use an interview that I conducted in English in Russia in 1992.[8] I called my interviewee Galina.

The first datum with which we begin the analysis is the date of Galina's birth. Here we take into consideration all the information we have – on the level of data – about the family constellation at the time when Galina is born into this setting. In this case it is:

1   Galina was born in 1968 in a small village near Krasnoyarsk, Siberia. She lives together with her paternal grandmother Olga and her great-grandmother Vera – Olga's mother. Galina's parents live and work – after completing university education – in Krasnoyarsk. Her father's family comes from the Ukraine. In the Ukraine Olga was a teacher of Ukrainian language and literature before and during the German occupation. Her political orientation was Ukrainian nationalist. In 1943, after the Red Army reconquered the Ukraine, Olga was imprisoned by the Soviets for alleged collaboration with the Nazis (under Article 58)[9] and was sentenced to ten years' imprisonment and subsequent banishment to Siberia. Her son Vasily – Galina's father – was about five years old when Olga was arrested. In 1956 Olga was rehabilitated.[10]

Looking at this data we build up all the possible resulting hypotheses and deduce from each hypothesis assumptions about the further development of this family system and Galina's personal life history. The main question is: which effects will this family history have on Galina and on her later life? Here we must remember that in 1968 Olga's past was still subject to massive taboos in the social discourse in the Soviet Union. Depending on how openly families deal with this in family dialogue, it will have very different effects on the biography of the granddaughter. Here I can reveal that during her childhood Galina was told nothing of this at the manifest level.

It would be beyond the scope of this chapter to present all the hypotheses I raised in analysing this case. Here I concentrate on two readings concerning the question of Galina's relationship to her grandmother and to her grandmother's past:

1.1 Because Galina grows up with her grandmother and great-grandmother she will probably develop a stronger bond to them than to her parents (Olga will probably take on the mother role). For that reason her past, even if it is passed on only latently, will be of great biographical relevance and will gain increasing significance in Galina's life.

On the basis of this hypothesis we can deduce a number of follow-up hypotheses as to how this could affect her subsequent life course:

1.1a Because of this identification she will, later in her life, grapple with the grandmother's past, in particular with the phases of suffering, and less with her life before her arrest and the time under German occupation.
1.1b In her later life Galina will attempt to deal with this family history in her biographical choices, for example choice of vocation or partner. This hypothesis is based on empirical findings from earlier studies (cf. Rosenthal, 1987).

As counter-hypothesis one could formulate:

1.2 Galina grows up longing for her mother or parents, and dreams of a better life with them in the city. She increasingly develops an aversion to village life with Olga and Vera.

Here, again, several follow-up hypotheses are possible. For example:

1.2a Galina attempts by all means to attract the attention of her parents. One possibility would be to fall ill often or, later, having serious difficulties in school.
1.2b Because she distances herself from the grandmother, when she is an adult she will probably grapple with the grandmother's time before her arrest and perhaps even reject her on grounds of suspicion of

collaboration with the Germans. In this context, in her youth she might also – disassociating from her grandmother – increasingly identify with socialism and become active with the Komsomol youth organization. This might also lead to her not calling into question the legality of Olga's conviction.

After raising all possible hypotheses we turn to the next datum to see how Galina's life history continues. For the sake of brevity I summarize two items of data together here:

2 When Galina is five years old (1973) she moves together with her great-grandmother and grandmother to the region of Bataisk near the Ukrainian border. The parents intend to follow later. One year later they move in with the family.

Again we build up all possible hypotheses one can develop from this data and deduce from each hypothesis assumptions about the further development of this family system and the personal life history of Galina. We can, for example, formulate the following hypothesis:

2.1 Galina finds herself in a serious conflict of loyalty. She will have to ask herself: who is my mother now, who do I look to? Here, in the same way as described in 1, there are various possibilities:
2.1.1 Because of her previous closeness to her grandmother (cf. 1.1) she will reject her mother and continue to orientate on Olga.
2.1.2 She will now be happy to have her mother with her at last (cf. 1.2) and devotes her full attention to her.
2.1.3 She will attempt to escape from the conflict of loyalty and orientates more on her father or great-grandmother.

I will now skip the data on her school career and her career in the Komsomol youth organization, and conclude by examining a very important datum in connection with the family history. Until Galina was thirteen years old, she had no conscious idea of her grandmother's history of imprisonment. At this age she accidentally discovered a hidden document from which she learned that her grandmother had been sentenced to prison in 1943 and was not legally rehabilitated until 1956. Looking only at these data, we can assume that this is an experience of great biographical relevance for Galina. This not only casts doubt on the exact reasons and circumstances of the judgement, but also raises the question of whether the grandmother may have been convicted unjustly. Furthermore, for Galina this discovery is associated with the question of why this past, which also has major implications for her father, has been kept secret from her. Depending on whether or not Galina identifies with her grandmother, she will experience this discovery in very different ways. So here we return to the hypotheses outlined at the outset (1.1a, 1.1b and 1.2). So the question arises as to whether she reacts more empathetically or more critically to her grandmother's history of persecution, or oscillates ambivalently between the two possibilities.

After finishing school, Galina studied history and at the time of the interview she was a lecturer in history. She conducted oral history interviews with a group that had been suppressed and persecuted in the former Soviet Union. Here we can surmise, for example, that this also served as a surrogate way of dealing with the family history.

I will now skip this analytical step and proceed to the text and thematic field analysis, based on the work of Aron Gurwitsch (1964), Wolfram Fischer (1982) and Fritz Schütze (1983).

Text and thematic field analysis

The general goal of this stage of analysis is to find out which mechanisms control selection and organization and the temporal and thematic linkage of the text segments. The underlying assumption is that the narrated life story does not consist of a haphazard series of disconnected events; the narrator's autonomous selection of stories to be related is based on a context of meaning – the biographer's overall interpretation. The narrated life story thus represents a sequence of mutually interrelated themes, which together form a dense network of interconnected cross-references (Fischer, 1982: 168). In the terminology of Aron Gurwitsch, the individual themes are elements of a thematic field. While the *theme* stood in the 'focus of attention', the *thematic field* is 'defined as the totality of those data, co-present with the theme, which are experienced as materially relevant or pertinent to the theme and form the background or horizon out of which the theme emerges as the center' (cf. Gurwitsch, 1964: 4).

Furthermore, the textual sort used by the biographer to present his analysis is crucial for the analysis. These considerations were introduced by Fritz Schütze (1983). Given that each textual sort is able to serve specific referential and communicative functions, one can ask: why did the interviewee choose this sort of text in this sequence and not another sort? The underlying assumption is that 'reality' does not impose the sort of text a speaker uses, but the speaker himself or herself chooses the sort of text for particular reasons (which may or may not be known to himself/herself). The working hypothesis is that these reasons are related to the biographical concept, the lived life, and to the situation of relating his account (including the interviewer's influence) in ways to be found out empirically. From the sort of text and the sequential arrangement one draws conclusions about the narrator and how he/she wants to convey the world. In this analytical step close attention must be paid to the extent to which the selection of textual sort and also the presented themes are due to the process of interaction between interviewee and interviewer. The question of whether the interviewee is orientating more on the relevance system he/she ascribes to the interviewer or more to his/her own biographical relevances is investigated sequence by sequence.

In preparation for the analysis the whole interview text is first sequentialized, that is, briefly summarized in the form of a list of separate units that are divided up according to three criteria. The three main criteria to define the beginning/end of a textual sequence are:

- textual sorts
- thematic shifts and changes
- conversational turn-taking (changes of speaker).

Among the textual sorts we distinguish argumentation, description, and narration with the subcategories report and single stories. A narration refers to a chain of sequences of events of the past, and they are related to each other through a series of temporal and/or causal links. 'The decisive feature distinguishing' a narration 'from narratives is that descriptions present static structures' (Kallmeyer and Schütze, 1977: 201). An argumentation is a sequence of lines of reasoning, theorizing and declaration of general ideas. They show the narrator's general orientation and what he/she thinks of himself/herself and of the world. Let us look now to the first sequences of the sequentialization of the interview with Galina.

This sequencing, which is also used as a kind of table of contents for later analysis, is now itself subjected to a sequential analysis. The question here is no longer the biographical significance of an experience in the past, but instead why the experience is presented this way and not otherwise. In formulating hypotheses we orientate on the sub-questions given in the 'Thematic Field Analysis' panel overleaf.

Sequentialization of the interview with Galina

1/1	initial question:	family history – own life story
1/7	description:	**great-grandma** – father's side
		Ukrainian, old when she died, 92
1/16	argumentation:	she had a very tragic story
		happy childhood stopped by something
		she liked to tell the family story
1/23	report about not-self-	sister of grandfather told the story
	experienced family history	grandfather disappeared without news
		grandmother was in prison after occupation
		ten years in a camp, she never told it
1/37	argumentation:	**mother** told not much about her family – not exciting for her
		met grandparents from mother's side only
		when she was in the third class (11 years old)
1/43	description:	lived with great-grandmother and grandmother
		first language Ukrainian
		small town nearby the town where my parents lived
1/51	condensed situation:	'when I refused to eat'
		grandma told stories about my father in situation
		when he did not eat – about not having enough food
		– father childhood during war
		– father liked to invent words
	evaluation:	'*I liked these stories very much*'
2/18	argumentation:	**past of grandma is not clear**
		this produces a psychological barrier
2/29	**non-verbal asking for turn-taking**	
2/30	I: come to your life story	
2/33	**global evaluation:**	**it is very long and very short**
	description:	born in **Krasnoyarsk** in Siberia

End of main narration is on page 13

Thematic Field Analysis

General questions for developing hypotheses

1 Why is she or he presenting this sequence in such a way?
   why at this place – and in this sequential order
   why in this text sort
   why in this length
   why this topic or content
2 What does the biographer not present? Which biographical data is left out or not elaborated?
3 What it the thematic field? Which themes do not fit in this field?

TEXT AND THEMATIC FIELD ANALYSIS OF GALINA'S INTERVIEW Let us now consider the first sequence in Galina's interview. When asked to tell the story of her family and her life, Galina begins with a description of her great-grandmother, a reference to her ethnic origins and age. At this point we can ask why she starts in this way. Are age and above all ethnic origin perhaps of great relevance for Galina today, especially when the Ukraine became independent just one year before the interview? If this hypothesis (1.1) were true, we would expect that one or both of these themes would be referred to repeatedly later in the interview or be constitutive for the thematic field of this main narration. So here, too, we formulate follow-up hypotheses for a fitting continuation of the text.

Another hypothesis (1.2) is that the great-grandmother is of great biographical relevance for Galina, who will tell a great deal more about her as the interview progresses. We must also consider whether Galina starts with the family's ethnic origins because she assumes that this could be of particular interest to the German interviewer (1.3). A very different hypothesis (1.4) could be that Galina begins with a family member who is less associated with taboo subjects. In other words, she chooses the great-grandmother to begin the family history because she would prefer to avoid speaking about the grandmother's past.

As we see, the second sequence is also devoted to the great-grandmother. It is introduced argumentatively with the story of her suffering. We can ask whether there is a need for legitimization here, and formulate the hypothesis (2.1) that Galina feels the need to present her family history as a story of suffering or victimization in order to justify other elements of the family history. If this hypothesis is true, will she then also introduce the grandmother in this thematic field?

A brief 15-line report follows. We are told that she was told the family's story by the sister of her grandfather, that he went missing in the Second World War, and that the grandmother was imprisoned. The sequence ends with a remark that the grandmother never spoke about this. So at this point we have heard only about the difficult elements of the past (cf. 2.1). As well as the story of suffering, the topic of 'Who spoke about the family history and who did not' is also introduced in this sequence.

This subject becomes even clearer in the following argumentation, telling how the mother told little about her family. After just four lines describing her life with her grandmother and great-grandmother comes a longer sequence (24 lines) dealing with a condensed situation, i.e., a description of a frequently experienced situation where her grandmother told her about her father's childhood. It now becomes clear that one of the major themes of this main narration is 'telling versus silence'. According to Galina's description, the meaning of the silence and the unclarity about the grandmother's past produce a 'psychological barrier'. Here she indirectly accuses the grandmother of having been unable to talk with her about the conviction, and thus with having created this barrier. It is noticeable that Galina requires the interviewer's assistance after this explanation. So we can actually formulate the assumption that this subject also produces a barrier in the text, or blocks the narration of her own life story. This analytical step goes on to show that Galina's self-presentation is constituted by two themes, 'my grandmother's mysterious and secret past' and 'my own life'. These two competing themes make it difficult for her to narrate her own life story and constitute the thematic field 'My own life is burdened and handicapped by the more or less unknown past of my grandmother'. This latent biographical overall interpretation is manifest in the structure of the text. Galina needs the interviewer's help several times in order to switch from talking about the family past to relating her own biography. Galina's present time and future projections are determined by her need to separate herself from this burdening family past and from the corresponding family dynamics. In the interview passages where she then talks about her own life story, she concentrates absolutely on her educational career. The analysis highlights Galina's need to lead her own life more freely and lightly as the dominant topic of her self-presentation. Why, however, does Galina feel this need, or put differently, which biographical experiences have caused this need – which presumes a bond to the family history and that the family exists at all – to arise? So we have to ask in what way Galina is actually bound to the family past. The next analytical step, the *reconstruction of the life history*, can give us an answer.

Reconstruction of the life history and microanalysis

In this step of analysis we return to the biographical significance of individual experiences in the past and above all to the timeline of the life history, its temporal gestalt. We go back to the analysis of the biographical data and contrast it with the biographer's own statements. After approaching the text using text and thematic field analysis with the question of why the biographer presents this in the interview in this way and not differently, we now re-examine the text for traces of past perspectives on the respective events. The hypotheses raised in the first analytical step are falsified or verified by analysing the interview texts, or other new readings are found. To put it in practical terms: following the logic of sequential analysis we move through the biographical experiences in the chronology of the life history, examining at each point the interview passages where the biographer speaks about them. In the process we will also discover further biographical experiences that we had not included in the data analysis. Furthermore we choose several text passages in order to do a *microanalysis of individual text segments*, orientated on the method of objective hermeneutics (Oevermann, 1983). These passages are subjected to a more precise sequential analysis. The goal here is to decipher in particular the text's latent structures of meaning. Paralinguistic peculiarities such as long pauses, slips of the tongue and interruptions, as well as the general impression that the passage contains more meaning than is apparent on first reading, are important criteria for selecting text passages. This analysis also serves to test the hypotheses gained in the previous analytical steps.

GALINA'S LIFE HISTORY In this analytical step it now turns out that in Galina's case, until she was five years old she was very close to her great-grandmother Vera and to a somewhat lesser degree to her grandmother Olga. We had not specifically considered this possibility in the analysis of the biographical data. On the other hand, the text verifies and further differentiates the hypothesis of a closeness to her mother beginning at the age of five. When her parents moved in, the girl experienced growing conflicts of loyalty, especially because her mother and grandmother did not get along well. Galina experienced her mother as the weaker of the two and began to take her side. Today she says that at that time she developed a growing psychological barrier between herself and her grandmother. Here it can be seen that the reasons presented in the present for this psychological barrier – the grandmother's hidden past – is not the only possible one, or that there were other reasons for it in the past. There are also hints that this development in Galina's bonding also has something to do with the time before her fifth birthday and with a conflict-laden relationship between Olga and Vera. There is some evidence for this in the text, and especially in the background family history.

In Galina's life history it is now interesting to see how she experienced the discovery of the well-hidden family secret when she was thirteen years old. At this time, she was already allied with her mother. So we can also assume, in line with our readings in the analysis of the biographical data, that the insight into her grandmother's past did not just lead her to develop empathy for grandmother's past persecution, but also to begin viewing this from a critical perspective. Let us see what she experienced: in an English–Russian dictionary, which Galina wanted to use in learning English, she found the document concerning the rehabilitation of her grandmother, which merely stated that Olga had been convicted under some 'Article 58'. Galina read it and stared at the number of this article:

I was very surprised and I couldn't understand. Why? How? My grandma? I know her and she was convicted

of ... what crime? It was so strange because there was only the number of the article. And with this sheet of paper I ran to my father. (Galina, 1992: 19)

With the help of the interviewer she recalled the fantasies she had had when she first read the rehabilitation card. *'When I read this number I connected her guilt with her second husband'* (Galina, 1992: 21). Her fantasy was that her grandmother had killed her second husband – even though Galina knew that this man, who was divorced from the grandmother before Galina was born, was still alive. How may we interpret this fantasy? First of all, we find here further evidence for a tendency to accuse her grandmother. However, in order to better interpret this fantasy we must at this point conduct a microanalysis of the passage in the text where she speaks about this man. We now look at the text more precisely, line by line, and once again in the sequential order.

Recalling this man whom she had feared, she begins her statement about him as follows:

It is one of the most – er (four-second pause) – frightening recollections from earliest childhood ... .

Here we can ask which frightening experiences Galina actually had with this man. We can assume that these experiences still frighten her today and that her fear perhaps manifested itself again during the four-second pause. If this hypothesis is true there will be evidence of it in the subsequent text, probably at the paralinguistic level. Let us see how the text continues:

it's-, he is-, he is coming-, he is coming

Galina starts to stutter, speaks in the present tense and we practically gain the impression that she is returning to the scene. The hypothesis that it is still frightening for Galina today gains further plausibility. She continues:

and his voice and his- his presence in our home (3) I don't know

In her memory the man is present in the home again. Here, however, Galina hesitates and stops, saying, *'I don't know.'* One possible reading here is that re-experiencing the most frightening recollection is too threatening and is rejected by Galina. The interviewer now responds to her and asks:

When you go back in this situation, he is coming to your home and he is crying loud (3) what can you see?

Galina responds:

Ah- I can't say that eh (2) I (2) I'm lying in my bed in my room and eh, I eh, I am seeing the same low table and that cross and white (2) walls and I just, hear his eh-, very angry voice, very loud. (Galina, 1992: 22)

At the manifest level of the text Galina recounts here and in the following how she feared the ex-husband's visits to her grandmother, and their arguments. However, the text is also open to other readings. We can ask whether the frightened little girl lay in bed hearing scenes of violence between the grandmother and her ex-husband. The text also suggests the possibility that she might herself have become a victim of this man's violence. The hypothesis that she herself experienced violence during childhood gains in plausibility through other text passages. However, even if we cannot prove this on the basis of this text passage, we can at least suppose that Galina's fantasy of her grandmother as the murderer of this man is based on an unfulfilled wish. We may suppose that as a child Galina sometimes wished that her grandmother had been better able to defend herself and her granddaughter against this man.

Now let us return to the situation of her discovery of the document. Galina runs to her father, who tears the document out of her hand. Galina asks what it means and her father says: *'It is about Grandma, it shouldn't be talked about.'* She grabs his arm and tries to take the document back from him, and he hisses at her: *'It's none of your business; don't ask.'* Galina is startled at the violence of his reaction:

> *I was so surprised because I had a very close relationship with my parents, and I discovered that there is something he wants to hide, and I asked my ma and she was just as surprised as I, she said that she didn't know.* (Galina, 1992: 24)

It then turned out that the mother, as she herself related in her interview, also knew nothing of her mother-in-law's conviction and thus also nothing of her husband's childhood. This experience, and the constellation that mother and daughter were excluded from the family's secrecy management, dramatically intensified the bonding between Galina and her mother. Another result is that Galina is unable to find an empathic approach to her grandmother's history of persecution.

The result of Galina's discovery was that she started tormenting herself with questions, and that the psychological distance from her grandmother grew because Galina did not dare to confront her with her questions. And this has remained so until today. As Galina says: *'The story of my grandma is not clear to me. I know only the plot ... and it is a big problem for me that I can't ask.'*

In fact, it is Galina herself who resists learning more about her grandmother's past. Although she is a trained historian, she has never tried to find out exactly what Article 58 was about. We can suppose, on the one hand, that clarifying this past is still too threatening for her, but also that she is unconsciously still avoiding a possible rehabilitation of her grandmother.

Contrastive comparison of life history and life story

The concluding contrastive comparison of life history and life story aims to find possible explanations for the difference between these two levels, i.e., between past and present perspective and for the associated difference in temporality and thematic relevance of narrated life story and experienced life history. In other words, contrasting helps find the rules for the difference between the narrated and the experienced. The question of which biographical experiences have led to a particular presentation in the present is also pertinent here.

In Galina's case the life history level shows a bonding to her mother that strengthened over the years, an increasing accusation against the grandmother (probably based on early childhood experiences where she felt insufficiently protected by her) and an associated, increasing feeling of guilt. At the conscious level in the present this is, however, placed in connection with the grandmother's political past and her silence about it. This family history constellation led to a strong bonding to the family of origin. Galina, however, tries to present herself as leading her life independently of the family history. We may surmise that the need for separation is so strong because she still feels tied to the family and its past.

Development of types and contrastive comparison

The biographical case reconstruction leads, finally, to the development of types. On the basis of reconstruction of individual cases, we aim for theoretical rather than numerical generalization. Generalization from the single case and on the basis of contrastive comparison of several cases are required here (cf. Hildenbrand, 1991; Rosenthal, 1995: 208ff.). Here we do not infer to all cases, but to 'similar cases', as formulated in 1927 by Kurt Lewin in his definition of a law based on Galilean thinking: 'The law is a statement about a type that is characterized by its so-being' (1927/1967: 18), and a type comprises the similar cases. The frequency of occurrence is of absolutely no significance in determining the typical in a case, in the sense used here. The rules that generate it and organize the diversity of its parts are determinant for the type of a case. The effectiveness of these rules is completely independent of how often we find similar systems of rules in social reality.

To develop types, we return to our previously formulated general research question and the explanation of the associated social and psychological phenomena *after* completion of the case reconstruction. If, for example, we are interested in the experience of everyday politics in the former Soviet Union during *perestroika*, we can consider the interviewee's statements on that in the context of his or her whole life. In Galina's case we find an accentuated description of political disinterest and the need *'to separate my life from the life of the state'* (see Rosenthal, 2000). On the basis of our case reconstruction we are now in a position – according to our research question and this one case – to construct a type that not only describes the superficial phenomena (such as an unpolitical attitude) but also explains the biographical course that leads to this presentation or defines the rules that produce this description. Thus we find that Galina's need to separate her own life from her family and the family history is also reflected in her attitude to everyday politics in Russia. We were able to see how the pattern of a need for resolution and at the same time bonding to the family history – which in this case is so closely linked to the social history – constituted itself over the course of this biography. Biographical case reconstructions thus allow the construction of development types that indicate the rules of the genetic process and/ or allow 'How it happened that' narrations (Dausien, 1999: 228) as well as explanations – with respect to both the experienced life history and the narrated life story. In so doing, we are not following the causal relationship and cause-and-effect models borrowed from the natural sciences.

CONCLUSION

The methodological approach of biographical research described in this chapter aims to collect its 'data' by conducting a narrative course of conversation that allows the interviewee's perspectives and subjective relevances to become apparent and to generate texts that give social scientists the opportunity to reconstruct past experience. The procedure of biographical case reconstructions makes a strict distinction between the present perspective of the biographer and his

or her perspectives in the past. The contrastive comparison between life history and life story helps us to trace the rules differentiating the narrated from the experienced – the difference between biographical self-presentation at the time of narration and the experience in the past. In this process the general concern of biographical research is to understand social and psychological phenomena and to explain them in the context of the process of their creation, reproduction and transformation. In this tradition the phenomena on which the research question focuses are examined both from the subjective perspective of the individual and in the overall context of his/her life and the structuring of its processes. This makes it possible to discover the latent and implicit structuring rules. It must be emphasized that the life history, the interpretive review of the past and the manner of presentation of the life story are all constituted through the dialectic of the individual and the social. Biographical research allows us to reconstruct the interrelationship between individual experience and collective framework, so when we reconstruct an individual case we are always aiming to make general statements. Thus the goal of biographical research is not only to understand individual cases in the context of individual life histories, but to gain an understanding of societal realities or of the interrelationship between society and life history (see Rosenthal, 1998).

To conclude, I would like once again to quote two classic researchers, William Isaac Thomas and Florian Znaniecki (1958: II, 1832): 'In analyzing the experiences and attitudes of an individual we always reach data and elementary facts which are not exclusively limited to this individual's personality but can be treated as mere instances of more or less general classes of data or facts, and thus be used for the determination of laws of social becoming.'

Translated by Meredith Dale

NOTES

1 See the overview article by Bertaux and Kohli (1984).
2 Understanding and explaining are understood here in the sense used by Max Weber and Alfred Schuetz. According to Weber's postulate of subjective interpretation, scientific explanations of the social world must refer to the subjective meaning of the actions of human beings and thus explain their actions and the consequences of their actions through the interdependency with the actions of others. Schuetz (1962) is a prominent representative of insisting that sociological constructions should be based on constructs of everyday life.

3 We prefer to use the term 'biographer' instead of the term 'autobiographer' in this context. In our opinion, the latter term does not place adequate emphasis on the social construction of life histories and life stories.

4 As suggested by the title of the work by Glaser and Strauss (1967), *The Discovery of Grounded Theory*, this tradition is concerned with the discovery of theory in the empirical process of research (see Seale, 1999: 87–106).

5 Some interviews were conducted by two interviewers.

6 See also the contributions by Ingrid Miethe and Simone Kreher in Rosenthal (2002), as well as Roswitha Breckner (1998) and Bettina Völter (2002).

7 The English article of 1987 is merely a translated extract from the German article of 1979, which deals in detail with the analysis process.

8 Galina is the granddaughter of a three-generation family in the former Soviet Union, which I reconstructed. For details see Rosenthal (2000).

9 Article 58 of the Criminal Code of the Russian Soviet Socialist Federation deals with high treason. This paragraph was used rather arbitrarily in the Soviet Union.

10 She was one of many who were rehabilitated during the period of political moderation following Khrushchev's 'secret speech' at the Twentieth Party Congress (25 February 1956).

REFERENCES

Alheit, Peter (1993) 'Transitorische Bildungsprozesse: Das "biographische Paradigma" in der Weiterbildung', in W. Mader (ed.), *Weiterbildung und Gesellschaft: Grundlagen wissenschaftlicher und beruflicher Praxis in der Bundesrepublik Deutschland* (2nd expanded ed.). Bremen: Universität Bremen, pp. 343–418.

Alheit, Peter (1994) 'Everyday time and life time: on the problems of healing contradictory experiences of time', *Time and Society*, 3(3): 305–19.

Bertaux, Daniel (1981) (ed.) *Biography and Society*. Beverly Hills, CA: Sage.

Bertaux, Daniel and Kohli, Martin (1984) 'The life story approach: a continental view', *Annual Review of Sociology*, 10: 215–37.

Breckner, Roswitha (1998) 'The biographical-interpretative method: principles and procedures', in *Social Strategies in Risk Societies, Sostris Working Paper 2: Case Study Materials: The Early Retired*. London: Centre for Biography in Social Policy (BISP), University of East London, pp. 91–104.

Bruner, Jerome (1990) *Acts of Meaning*. Cambridge, MA: Harvard University Press, esp. ch. 4, 'Autobiography and self', pp. 99–138.

Bühler, Charlotte (1933) *Der menschliche Lebenslauf als psychologisches Problem*. Leipzig: von S. Hirzel.

Dausien, Bettina (1999) '"Geschlechtsspezifische Sozialisation"—Konstruktiv(istisch)e Ideen zu Karriere und Kritik eines Konzepts', in B. Dausien, M. Herrmann, M. Oechsle et al. (eds), *Erkenntnisprojekt Geschlecht*. Opladen: Leske & Budrich, pp. 217–46.

Fann, K.T. (1970) *Peirce's Theory of Abduction*. The Hague: Nijhoff.

Fischer, Wolfram (1978) 'Struktur und Funktion erzählter Lebensgeschichten', in M. Kohli (ed.), *Soziologie des Lebenslaufs*. Darmstadt/Neuwied: Luchterhand, pp. 311–336

Fischer, Wolfram (1982) *Time and Chronic Illness: A Study on the Social Constitution of Temporality*. Berkeley (published privately) (also habilitation thesis, University of Bielefeld, Faculty of Sociology).

Fischer, Wolfram and Kohli, Martin (1987) 'Biographieforschung', in W. Voges (ed.) *Methoden der Biographie- und Lebenslaufforschung*. Opladen: Leske & Budrich, pp. 25–50.

Glaser, Barney G. and Strauss, Amseln L. (1967) *The Discovery of Grounded Theory*. Chicago: Aldine.

Gurwitsch, Aron (1964) *The Field of Consciousness*. Pittsburgh: Duquesne University Press.

Hildenbrand, Bruno (1991) 'Fallrekonstruktive Forschung', in U. Flick, E. von Kardorff, H. Keupp, L. von Rosenstiel and S. Wolff (eds), *Handbuch für Qualitative Sozialforschung*. Munich: Beltz, pp. 256–9.

Holstein, James A. and Gubrium, Jaber F. (2000). *The Self We Live By: Narrative Identity in a Postmodern World*. New York: Oxford University Press.

Kallmeyer, Werner and Schütze, Fritz (1977) 'Zur Konstitution von Kommunikationsschemata', in D. Wegner (ed.), *Gesprächsanalyse*. Hamburg: Buske, pp. 159–274.

Kohli, Martin (ed.) (1978) *Soziologie des Lebenslaufs*. Darmstadt/Neuwied: Luchterhand.

Kohli, Martin (1986) 'Biographical research in the German language area', in Z. Dulcewski (ed.), *A Commemorative Book in Honor of Florian Znaniecki on the Centenary of his Birth*. Poznan, pp. 91–110.

Kreher, Simone (2002) 'Continuity and change over the generations: trials and tribulations of an East German family', *History of the Family*, 7(2): 183–205.

Krüger, H.H. and Marotzki, W. (eds) (1999) *Handbuch Biographieforschung*. Opladen: Leske & Budrich.

Lewin, Kurt (1927/1967) *Gesetz und Experiment in der Psychologie*. Darmstadt: Wissenschaftliche Buchgesellschaft.

McAdams, Dan (1993) *The Stories We Live By: Personal Myths and the Making of the Self*. London: The Guilford Press.

Miethe, Ingrid (2002) 'East German dissident biographies in the context of family history: interdependence of methodological approach, and empirical results', *History of the Family*, 7(2): 207–24.

Oevermann, U. (1983) 'Zur Sacle: Die Bedeutung von Adornos methodologischem Selbstverständnis für die Begründung einer materialen soziologischen Strukturanalyse', in L. von Friedeburg and J. Habermas (eds), *Adorno-Konferenz 1983*. Frankfurt: Suhrkamp, pp. 234–89.

Oevermann, Ulrich et al. (1979) 'Die Methodologie einer objektiven Hermeneutik und ihre allgemeine forschungslogische Bedeutung in den Sozialwissenschaften', in Hans-Georg Soeffner (ed.), *Interpretative Verfahren in den Sozial- und Textwissenschaften*. Stuttgart: Metzler, pp. 352–434.

Oevermann, Ulrich, et al. (1980) 'Zur Logik der Interpretation von Interviewtexten', in Thomas Heinze, H.W. Klusemann and H.-G. Soeffner (eds), *Interpretationen einer Bildungsgeschichte*. Bensheim: päd extra, pp. 15–69.

Oevermann, Ulrich, Allert, Tilman, Konau, E. and Krambeck, J. (1987) 'Structures of meaning and objective hermeneutics', in V. Meja, D. Misgeld and N. Stehr (eds), *Modern German Sociology*, New York: Columbia University Press.

Peirce, Charles S. (1933/1980) *Collected Papers*, ed. C. Hartshorne and P. Weiss. Cambridge: Belknap.

Plato, Alexander von (1998) 'Erfahrungsgeschichte—von der Etablierung der Oral History', in Gerd Jüttemann and Hans Thomae (eds), *Biographische Methoden in den Humanwissenschaften*. Weinheim: Psychologie Verlags Union, pp. 60–74.

Rosenthal, Gabriele (1987) *'Wenn alles in Scherben fällt ...': Von Leben und Sinnwelt der Kriegsgeneration*. Opladen: Leske & Budrich.

Rosenthal, Gabriele (1989) 'May 8th, 1945: the biographical meaning of a historical event', *International Journal of Oral History*, 10(3): 183–92.

Rosenthal, Gabriele (1991) 'German war memories: narrability and the biographical and social functions of remembering', *Oral History*, 19(2), 34–41.

Rosenthal, Gabriele (1993) 'Reconstruction of life stories', *The Narrative Study of Lives*, 1(1): 59–91.

Rosenthal, Gabriele (1995) *Erlebte und erzählte Lebensgeschichte*. Frankfurt a.M.: Campus.

Rosenthal, Gabriele (ed.) (1998) *The Holocaust in Three Generations: Families of Victims and Perpetrators of the Nazi Regime*. London: Cassell.

Rosenthal, Gabriele (2000) 'Social transformation in the context of familial experience: biographical consequences of a denied past in the Soviet Union', in R. Breckner, D. Kalekin-Fischman and I. Miethe (eds), *Biographies and the Division of Europe*. Opladen: Leske & Budrich, pp. 115–38.

Rosenthal, Gabriele (2002) Guest Editor of *The History of the Family: An International Quarterly*. Stamford: Jai Press. Special issue: *Family History—Life Story*, 7(2).

Rosenthal, Gabriele and Fischer-Rosenthal, Wolfram (2000) 'Analyse narrativ-biographischer Interviews', in U. Flick, E. von Kardorff and I. Steinke (eds), *Qualitative Forschung*. Reinbek: Rowohlt, pp. 456–67; to be published in English by Sage.

Rosenwald, George C. and Ochberg, Richard L. (eds) (1992) *Storied Lives: The Cultural Politics of Self-Understanding*, New Haven: Yale University Press.

Schuetz, Alfred (1962) 'Common-sense and scientific interpretation of human action', in Alfred Schuetz, *Collected Papers*, Vol. 1. The Hague: Nijhoff.

Schütze, Fritz (1976) 'Zur Hervorlockung und Analyse von Erzählungen thematisch relevanter Geschichten im Rahmen soziologischer Feldforschung', in Arbeitsgruppe Bielefelder Soziologen, *Kommunikative Sozialforschung*. Munich: Fink, pp. 159–260.

Schütze, Fritz (1983) 'Biographieforschung und narratives Interview', *Neue Praxis*, 3: 283–93.

Seale, Clive (1999) *The Quality of Qualitative Research*. London: Sage.

Thomas, William I. and Znaniecki, Florian (1958) *The Polish Peasant in Europe and America*, 2 vols (2nd ed.). Champaign, IL: University of Illinois Press (reprint of the 2nd edition of 1928, originally 1918–20).

Thompson, Paul (1992) *The Voice of the Past: Oral History*. New York: Cambridge University Press.

Völter, Bettina (2002) *Judentum und Kommunismus: Deutsche Familiengeschichten in drei Generationen*. Opladen: Leske & Budrich.

4

Focus groups

Phil Macnaghten and Greg Myers

As recently as ten years ago, an academic researcher had to explain, define and justify the seemingly odd research practice of getting eight or so people in a room and making them talk for an overhearing tape-recorder; now everyone, academic and non-academic alike, thinks they know what focus groups are. Focus groups have gone from the specialist knowledge of market researchers and a few innovative academic researchers in such fields as cultural studies and social policy, to wide public notoriety, the topic of television documentaries and the butt of comments about 'focus group fascism' and 'focus groupies' in image-obsessed political and social institutions. But focus groups have also provided data for highly influential studies in a range of social sciences (e.g., Morley, 1980; Burgess et al., 1988a; Liebes and Katz, 1990; Livingstone and Lunt, 1994; Miller et al., 1998; Wodak et al., 1999).

The rapid spread of focus groups corresponds to a new interest, in many social science fields, in shared and tacit beliefs, and in the way these beliefs emerge in interaction with others in a local setting. They are often used in an exploratory way, when researchers are not entirely sure what categories, links and perspectives are relevant. For instance, surveys of public opinion on environmental problems assume that people agree on what constitutes the environment, what the problems are, and their relations to these problems. Focus groups on environmental issues are likely to reveal complex, contradictory and shifting definitions, and different senses of agency.

Of course other qualitative methods might also be used for this exploration. Ethnographies can reveal more about the non-discursive everyday practices that define an issue (Agar and MacDonald, 1995), but they do not necessarily bring out what is not said because it need not be said in this community. One-to-one interviews are more likely to allow for extended narratives, and for more open talk where there are issues of status, conflict and self-presentation (Michell, 1999). But they can also put a great deal of pressure on the relation between interviewer and interviewee; the interviewee can wonder just whom they are talking to. A group can provide prompts to talk, correcting or responding to others, and a plausible audience for that talk that is not just the researcher. So focus groups work best for topics people could talk about to each other in their everyday lives – but don't.

Focus group methods have been set out in a variety of handbooks and introductions (Morgan, 1988; Krueger, 1994; Kitzinger, 1995; Morgan and Krueger, 1998; Wilkinson, 1999), and the classic study by the originators of the method has been reprinted (Merton et al., 1956). Useful short introductions by one of the most innovative of focus group researchers are now available on the web (Kitzinger, 1995). There has been an assessment of the role of focus groups in the development of one field, media studies (Morrison, 1998), and a collection of essays dealing not just with the practicalities, but with methodological and theoretical issues, and especially with relations between the researcher and the participants in the groups (Barbour and Kitzinger, 1999). A study by Puchta and Potter (2003) applies work in conversation analysis and discursive psychology to provide a detailed analysis of interaction from the perspective of the moderator of market research groups. And at last, there is a thoughtful handbook for social science researchers that does more than just give rules, advice and moral support (Bloor et al., 2001). So we will not give yet another general introduction to how to do focus groups. Instead we would like to focus on just one group in one project, and consider two ways of looking at it, that of the moderator actually conducting groups and of the analyst trying to interpret the transcripts.

We are often struck when we work together (Myers and Macnaghten, 1998, 1999) by the productive tensions between our two approaches. For Phil, who has extensive experience planning qualitative research projects and moderating focus groups (Macnaghten et al., 1995; Grove-White et al., 1997, 2000), what matters most comes before and during the two hours spent talking to participants. He pays close attention to the design of the groups, plan of the topic guide, recruitment of participants, facilitation of discussion, and the conceptual scheme that is relevant to this project and this audience. Greg, whose experience is as a discourse analyst (Myers, 1998, 1999, 2000, forthcoming), pays closer attention to what happens after the tape-recorder is turned off and the flip chart folded up: the transcription of the tapes, the analysis of the transcripts, the emergence of an interpretation based on this analysis. Of course Phil also analyses transcripts and Greg also plans topic guides and moderates groups, but our disciplinary hearts are at different stages of the process. To over-simplify somewhat, we might think of two tendencies:

Looking ahead to the focus group	*Looking back at the focus group*
Preparation for the groups	Analysis of the transcripts
Readable transcript	Detailed transcript
Generalization from statements to larger social changes	Understanding of why that statement was made there
Focus on underlying attitudes	Focus on performed interactions
Aims to influence policy and inform theories of social change	Aims to inform methodology and understanding of interaction

As this list suggests, what seems at first to be just a difference of disciplines and roles (and personalities) leads to many of the key practical and theoretical issues in the literature on focus groups. Discussions of the preparation for the groups, the ideal composition of groups, the design of the topic guide and of any exercises, and the ideal degree of intervention, all take up concerns of the moderator. Discussions of the use of transcripts (if the session is transcribed at all), of content coding, interaction analysis and relation to other methods all take up the perspective of the analyst. Marketing and policy research groups may get around some of these questions by arguing that what matter to the client are the speed of reporting and the relevance of the report to decision-making. But in social science research, there will be challenges on such issues as the relation of the researcher to the subjects, the generalizability of any findings, and the reflexivity of the research approach, so the questions cannot be ducked (on other contrasts between social science and market research uses of focus groups, see Puchta and Potter (2003)).

We could say that of course one should pay attention to *all* stages of the research process, from topic guide to publication. But in any particular study, researchers have to make practical choices at each stage, and with each choice they open up some possibilities and close off others. These choices are not just practical matters; they carry implicit theoretical commitments. And in a field as diverse and innovative as focus group research, they cannot be made by reference to some generally agreed code of good practice. We can only try to become more reflexive about the choices we have made and why we made them in a particular study.

PLANNING

We will focus on the most recent of the many commissioned research projects in which Phil has been involved, a series of eight focus groups in August and October 2001 for the UK governmental body Agriculture and Environment Biotechnology Commission (AEBC). The report, *Animal Futures*, is currently available on the web (Macnaghten, 2001), along with a review of the report and a number of other documents from the Commission. As with any study, the background and audience determined many of the choices the researchers made. Phil and his colleagues at the Centre for the Study of Environmental Change (CSEC) had already done a series of focus group studies of related issues such as public responses to genetically modified organisms (GMOs), technological risks, sustainability, recreation and the natural environment. In the case of GMOs, public debate has largely been confined to issues around GM plants, seed companies and crop trials. The client for this study was the Animal Subcommittee of the AEBC, which produced a brief asking for research on how public attitudes and feelings around animals and animal experiments might affect controversies around the genetic modification of animals. With colleagues at CSEC, Phil wrote a proposal responding to the brief, arguing that what AEBC needed was broader research on all the different ways people relate to animals, and in particular the ways their beliefs and values about animals relate to implicit beliefs about what is natural (Macnaghten and Urry, 1999; Franklin, 1998).

Often focus group research takes place in a context of several layers of argument, where people have conflicting beliefs, and where social researchers present different framings of those beliefs. In the case of the 'Animal Futures' groups, there were already survey studies of whether people are for or against animal testing, and for or against GM research and products. These studies, which were summarized in a review of the literature commissioned by the AEBC (Breakwell, 2001), tended to focus on how information about the new technologies affected acceptance or rejection. Phil and his colleagues proposed that the issue might not be whether they are for or against, but the conditions of acceptance or rejection: Do they accept animal testing if it offers help for serious medical problems? Do they reject GM research because of lack of trust of the scientists? These conditions could depend on the ways in which different people relate to animals, whether walking the dog, watching wildlife documentaries, running a small dairy farm, or raising tens of thousands of chickens. The conditions of acceptance might not fit into the categories that policy-makers expected (medical, ethical, commercial, technical …); people might draw their own lines (Kerr et al., 1998), and they might acknowledge their own conflicting, ambivalent, argumentative views (Billig, 1987).The CSEC researchers presented focus groups as an appropriate technique to explore such a complex terrain; as Bloor et al., have argued, focus groups are 'the sociological method of choice' for 'gathering data on group norms' (Bloor et al., 2001: 6). Phil argues that they do this but can do more than this, that through group norms he gains some access to wider processes of attitude formation and social change.

The researchers knew from previous projects that people could hold powerfully ambivalent feelings about such issues as animal experiments. The topic guide they proposed was designed to get them to explore such ambivalences instead of concealing them under yes and no answers. Other research designs might use tasks or exercises to get people talking (Kitzinger, 1990; Bloor et al., 2001). Phil's topic guide has them talking specifically and directly about their relation to animals, and more generally about the ways people interact with animals, before going on to three 3-foot by 4-foot boards to lead into the biotechnology and experimentation issues. The first has pictures to prompt discussion of controversies about treatment of animals; the second and third have statements about the Human Genome Project and animal testing, and about possible uses of genetic modification of animals. It might seem that this crammed the specific topic – animals and biotechnology – into the last thirty minutes of a two-hour session. But the aim was to ground these more specific issues in their everyday experience and understanding of animals. (As it turned out, in some groups, biotechnology was raised earlier as an example by participants, perhaps with reference to such well-publicized cases as 'ear mouse', Dolly the sheep, or xenotransplantation, the development of animals to provide organs for humans (Brown, 1999)).

The planning stage also included booking rooms in which these groups could be held. Handbooks on focus groups recommend some neutral setting (one new handbook has a photo of stackable plastic chairs on its cover), but of course no setting can be neutral, not even one that is blandly decorated with off-white walls, a round table and a one-way mirror. The CSEC group tends to hold its groups in various pubs, or in the living room of the recruiter; each setting has its advantages and disadvantages. A hired room in a pub is convenient for working people on their way home, has lots of room, and chairs that can be rearranged, and pubs are places that people do go to talk. But they can be noisy, and can send the wrong signals; British pubs have strong class and local associations, and an unwary researcher can choose a dart-throwing pub for the *Telegraph*-reading group. A front room may be convenient to local retired people after dinner, or parents coming around after putting the kids to bed, and it can suggest a cosily domestic setting far from university research labs. But the overstuffed chairs in a tight, inflexible arrangement can allow participants to sink out of sight, and can produce dead spots where participants can't see each other. Other researchers try to hold their groups on the participants' home ground, for instance at a day centre the participants attend (Holbrook and Jackson, 1996), or they might take participants out to a relevant site and have them look around. Usually it is the moderator's job, once the chairs are arranged and the flip chart set up, to make do with the setting he or she has, by bringing into the conversation those who have sunk back, getting people to look at boards or cards, or even having them get up and move pictures around on the floor.

Other ways of planning

Of course not all focus groups start with this kind of planning. This particular project was framed in terms of ongoing policy discussions, but other studies may lead to purely academic publications, or the boundary between academic and policy applications may not be so clear. This project was conceived as a small, rather quick stand-alone focus group study; in other longer-term projects the focus groups might be designed to precede, complement or follow up surveys, ethnographies or depth interviews (Morgan, 1993; Agar and MacDonald, 1995; Michell, 1999). The close relation between the researchers at CSEC and the users at AEBC meant that the project could be designed specifically to provide input into the policy process, when it might still have an effect. That also meant that the researchers knew more or less what they were looking for, which is not always the case in exploratory social science research.

One might consider a taxonomy of focus groups in three dimensions: moderator versus participant control; convergent versus divergent outcome; and participants speaking for the group versus speaking as representative of others outside.

- The degree of moderator intervention to keep groups on topic can vary from market research, where responses are usually tightly controlled to remain comparable among many groups, to more loosely moderated academic groups, like those proposed by Jacqueline Burgess and her colleagues (Burgess et al., 1988a, 1988b).
- Some groups and policy consultations aim at generating the widest possible range of responses, so that no voice is left unheard, leaving it to the analysts to select and summarize. Others, such as citizen juries, are designed to present information and force the group to come to some sort of conclusion or agreement.
- Participants can be left as strangers to each other, brought together just for the researcher's purposes, or they can be treated as a group that develops its own aims, norms and relations to one another, whether or not they are drawn from a pre-existing group.

We would place ourselves in the middle of each of these dimensions (which may suggest that we, and other researchers, see the work of the field in terms of how it relates to our practices).

SAMPLING

A quantitative researcher might think that focus group researchers were rather cavalier about traditional demographic categories. Focus group researchers do not aim for a representative sample of a population; they try to generate talk that will extend the range of our thinking about an issue, and to do that they recruit groups that are defined in relation to the particular conceptual framework of the study, a 'theoretical sample' in the terms of Glaser and Strauss (Glaser and Strauss, 1967; Becker, 1998: see also Gobo, Chapter 28, this volume). For instance, in Kitzinger's study of AIDS awareness in the UK (Miller et al., 1998), this meant recruiting, along with many other groups, prison guards, intravenous drug users, families of HIV-positive people, and journalists from African countries who might respond to the popular UK view of AIDS as an African disease. A study of global citizenship (Szerszynski et al., 2000) included both groups that might be expected to see their lives in global terms (media professionals, business executives) and people who might be expected to see their lives in more local terms (owners of small shops, volunteers in local community activities).

In the 'Animal Futures' project we are discussing, this meant recruiting some groups of people who might be expected to have views on GMO animals, such as pet owners and farmers, but also recruiting from some groups whose relations to animals might not be so obvious, such as people who hunt, shoot or fish, or people recruited because they *don't* have pets. There were two groups of farm couples, one for 'intensive farmers', raising thousands of pigs, or hundreds of thousands of chickens, and another for 'extensive farmers' raising sheep or cattle in much smaller numbers. This is an example of a distinction that might not be made in other samples, but one that might be meaningful in relation to the specific topic under study: the researchers thought that farmers who had daily contact with individual, recognizable animals might have different feelings about them from those farmers who dealt with animals as part of an industrial process.

The recruiting criteria also made sure that there would be a demographic range across the groups, so that there would be some groups recruited from ages 25–35, and others from ages 30–50 or 45–70, some would include both men and women while others would be just women, some would be urban, some suburban and some rural, and that different groups would draw on different social classifications (A–B–C1–C2–D). But there was no attempt to have one group for each of the possible combinations, as one would have one cell for each combination in a quantitative study. The aim was not to correlate opinions with these demographic categories, but just to ensure that no obvious group was left out. An addition to the original plan is an example of the kind of thinking behind these categories. After the first six groups had been conducted in Lancashire, the AEBC asked for two more groups in London, matched to two of the North-west groups, just to be sure that the results were not peculiar to one region. (As it turned out, the London groups were not strikingly different.)

Focus groups work better with some categories of participants; almost any report winds up quoting much more from some sessions than from others. It is not true, as some critics have claimed, that they work best with educated, articulate or opinionated participants (a focus group of academics would be a moderator's nightmare). But they do work better with participants who have well-developed routines for talking to each other, which may be why some moderators like particularly working with teenagers, or all-female groups, or retired people. Some participants talk a lot, but talk individually to the moderator, defeating the purpose of the group. Moderators' worst memories are often of a group where participants already saw themselves as representing some group that is under threat in some way, so that the moderator, whatever his or her disclaimers, becomes the representative of outside forces and authorities, and all the matters of procedure, the topic guide, the rules about interruption and overlapping, the tasks, become issues of us and them. Of course researchers need to listen to the views of such highly defensive participants, but focus groups may not be the best way to elicit them.

Most of the participants recruited met for the first time when they came to the focus group; the exceptions were the two groups of farmers – four couples in each – who were recruited through contacts so that they might feel more comfortable. The Wildlife group on which we will focus in this chapter is particularly interesting, because it is fairly heterogeneous in standard demographic terms: 4 male and 4 female, some local and some from elsewhere, some vegetarian and some not, ages from 30 to 50, and occupations such as carer, lawyer, plumber, mother, civil servant, local government officer and shop clerk. What they have in common is that they are all interested in wildlife in some way, and that, as we will see, quickly becomes a bond by which they define themselves as a group.

It might seem that it would be productive – or at least exciting – to bring together people from groups that would take on opposing identities: vegetarian and factory farmer, hunt saboteur and fox hunter, pet owners and people who complain about dog mess. Indeed, such juxtapositions might be the point of deliberative or consultative groups aimed at achieving consensus or giving a representative voice to known positions. But as we have noted, the aim of focus group research is usually the exploration of group norms. It is difficult in the best of circumstances to get a group of strangers to bring out in talk just those assumptions and tensions that they usually leave implicit; when they are faced with familiar and sharply defined positions, it becomes impossible (Becker et al., 1995).

The conventional wisdom in focus group research (and it is just conventional wisdom) is that there has to be some common ground between participants for the differences between participants and tensions within one participant's views to emerge. The homogeneity is of two different kinds, for different reasons. They share some theoretically relevant characteristic (have pets, travelled last year, live near a nuclear plant, have a relative who is HIV-positive, listen to Radio 1) so that they will have something to talk about. But as we have noted, it also helps if they share some ways of talking even before the moderator tries to get them to talk: assumptions about entitlement to speak, ways of disagreeing, ways of conceding, and a sense of humour. Similarities in ways of talking may not correspond to the traditional demographic categories.

Other ways of thinking about sampling

Current approaches in discourse analysis stress the ways people construct identities in interaction (Antaki and Widdicombe, 1998). Focus group research, as a practical matter, proposes categories, persuades the client that these are useful categories, and recruits people in those terms. In this project, some groups referred explicitly to their having an identity; for instance, participants in the Wildlife group referred to the kind of person who might be in the group, as opposed to some imagined others. (We will discuss the form of transcription later in the chapter.)

Phil: well like if you know . it's their terri-
          tory . do you you feel responsible for
          how how you are <u>in</u> their territory?
M: /well you have to be don't you
Karen: /by not treading on their nests and
          that sort of /thing
F: /yeah yeah
F: yeah
Colin: I think that's a perso<u>na</u>lity trait I
          think . you know . as as . as lovers of
          wildlife um . I think you're probably .
          not <u>pi</u>geon-holing because of course
          there's all <u>types</u> of wildlife lo/vers
Phil: /yeah
Colin: but . I think you're talking a person-
          ality trait rather than a wildlife <u>issue</u>
Phil: yeah yeah
Colin: when you see . um people walking
          through the woods um . slurping a
          McDonald's milkshake that they've
          just driven there to-
Phil: yeah
F: mm
Colin: and then throwing it aw<u>ay</u>
M: yeah yeah
Colin: <u>I</u> don't think you can . associate
          wildlife . um uhn fauna flora with
          that <u>per</u>son [laughs]
several: [general laughter]
          [two turns missing]
Iris: they probably wouldn't see it
          <u>any</u>way
Colin: yeah it's it's it's the person I think it's
          the personality trait
Colin: but it <u>may</u> <u>be</u> . the type of person
Phil: mm
Colin: who's attracted to<u>wards</u> wildlife
Phil: mm
Colin: is the sort of person . there may be
          some <u>links</u> there . I wouldn't be
          sur<u>pris</u>ed put it that way (3/7)

These people define themselves as sharing an
interest in wildlife, and values assumed to go
with this interest. They can also refer to this
group identity implicitly, for instance in a joke.
In this group, the round of introductions was
done by asking each participant to tell about 'a
memorable animal'. After they have gone around
once, there is this exchange:

Phil: so when when I asked you . you
          you've all come come up with sort of
          <u>wild</u>life examples . is that right

M: um
M: um
Phil: none of you have thought about . a cat
          or a dog
Colin: well I did initially yeah
Phil: <u>did</u> you?
Colin: yeah . we had- I don't want to bring
          the whole <u>tone</u> down or anything
          [laughter] but uh one of one of one of
          our dogs <u>died</u> a couple of weeks ago
Phil: yeah
Colin: and uh clearly you know the first
          thing <u>you</u> said went into my mind . but
          uh
Phil: yeah
Colin: like like the gentlemen <u>there</u> said uh >
          I should know your name what's your
          name?<
Paul: Paul=
Colin: =Paul . as Paul said . so many . so I
          went for the lion (3/4)

The laughter suggests a shared sense of what is
appropriate for this group. Colin then refers to
the group as a group, assuming he should know
the names already. Other groups may not find it
so easy to define themselves; for instance, 'not
having pets' is not usually a term people use as a
social category. What that group noticed, and
questioned, was that they were all women; Phil
had to explain that the project was not just interested in women, and other groups were mixed.

Some researchers prefer to use existing groups
such as those at a day centre for the elderly, or
colleagues at work (Holbrook and Jackson, 1996;
Miller et al., 1998); in the 'Animal Futures'
study they could have gone to the local RSPCA,
a riding club or a fishing association. This
approach makes it easier to recruit participants,
allows them to be more relaxed, and lets the
group serve as a kind of check on how far someone's statements are consistent with what others
know about them. But some moderators feel that
the familiarity may close off expression of
doubts or differences. And they may not articulate the implicit values that are the point of the
focus group: participants may assume that everyone here knows what they know. The two groups
in the 'Animal Futures' study in which the
people knew each other were the intensive
farmers, for which Phil had to use some contacts
and get friends of a friend. He thought the presence of wives might make the discussions less
adversarial, and might lead the couples to talk
more about interaction with the animals as part
of their everyday routine. One of these was an

odd group, as we will see in the next section, but Phil doesn't think that the participants' knowing each other is the reason for this oddity.

It might seem that the technique most consistent with current thinking on identities would be to run groups over a longer period and let the participants define what the group is. This approach has worked well for Burgess and her colleagues (Burgess et al., 1988a, 1988b). But it does not escape the first question (asked or suppressed) that every participant brings with them to a focus group: 'Why me?' And whatever the dangers for the research of a rigid scheme of categorization of identities, it is useful in planning the groups, because it pushes researchers beyond the voices that are most familiar, most obvious, most articulate, or easiest to recruit.

FACILITATING

Rapley (Chapter 1, this volume) notes that the literature on interviewing has proposed different categories of interview style, reflecting different relations between interviewer and interviewee. Similarly, focus group moderators may be more or less interventionist; they also may have more or less empathy with a particular group, may be more or less identifiable by them as one of theirs, and may contribute more or less of their own personal narratives in the discussion. These styles may even vary between interviewers in the same project, working with the same topic guide. Phil is, by his own admission, a rather interventionist moderator, raising topics directly, calling on some participants and holding off others, cutting off lines of talk that seem unproductive, challenging some apparent contradictions or vagueness. Greg is less interventionist, letting participants talk on even when they wander from the topic guide. This could be the result of his being less experienced, or it could be a reflection of different aims. Phil points out that the terms of reference of an academic article are wider than those of a research project, so a wider range of talk is potentially usable, and discussion can wander more. Either of us can listen to tapes of the other and hear missed or closed-off possibilities, Greg hearing Phil's interruptions, and Phil hearing Greg's failure to bring them back to the topic.

In the Wildlife group, the moderator intervenes by formulating (rephrasing what participants have said in his own words), proposing views to get a response, selecting speakers, and challenging them.

Formulation

Karen: hopefully we're thinking more ab<u>out</u> our animals and trying to

Phil: uh huh

Karen: <u>deal</u> with them in a more humane way

Martin: I think it's more tailored to man's <u>use</u> . uh what sort of mood at the time

Colin: using a more efficient

Karen: yeah fashionable

Martin: really isn't it

Colin: sounds cold and calculating but yeah . agree

Phil: so it seems there are two <u>things</u> going on. There's the kind of you know [writing on flip chart] the cold and calculating . trend yeah that's one trend . and then there's another trend which is . we're actually treating them more humanely . would that be fair . those are the /two kind of things

Amanda: / yeah . there's two sort of thrusts there (3/35)

Proposing views

Phil: What do other people think about that? I mean, in other words what Andrew is saying is that there's nothing wrong with this in principle, all right . It depends on the reasons you're doing it and on the outcomes. But other people might say no, this is just wrong, you know, you shouldn't be messing about with animals in this way. Just on this point what do people think about that?

Speaker selection

[the conversations between Amanda and Phil, Andrea and Ken, go on at the same time]

Amanda: I think you're better doing observations on somebody mind you . if you're looking at the brain and things I suppose it's as easy to examine a monkey's brain isn't it

Phil: yeah

Amanda: rather than a <u>human</u> brain

Ken: no the space ones are necessary

Andrea: but those things like the [[xxx]] experiment

Ken: [[xxx]]

Andrea: in America

Ken: Yeah but they monitor things

Phil: sorry I must say . would . Ken . sorry Ken, one person at a time right [laughs] . otherwise we can't . right . okay so when you think about animals, how many animals do you think are used . let's say in this country and what kinds? [continues] (3/39)

Challenging
[they are talking about a plan to genetically modify mosquitoes so that they can't carry parasites]

Colin: that's one creature I wouldn't mind going extinct

Phil: why why why wouldn't <u>that</u> be scary because you were saying it's scary messing about you don't know what's gonna happen . I mean wouldn't that be the same with mosquitoes?

Amanda: you could save so many people from having malaria

Colin: on the face of it

Amanda: horrible . you know . you're helping people from suffering from diseases (3/56)

The moderator can also do any of these moves more subtly, for instance by giving them backchannel responses ('mm', 'uh huh', 'right') (for more on the moderator's role in interaction, see Puchta and Potter, 2003).

The point of all this intervention is to keep the groups on topic, and to push the topic beyond what has already been said in this and other groups. As we have seen, Phil wanted the talk to go beyond the already familiar statements for or against animal research, for or against biotechnology, and systematically explore the underlying conditions, for instance the relation to medical products, or the deeper sense of what is natural and what is not. He knew from earlier groups that the instrumental uses of animals (as opposed to their affective roles as pets or objects of hunting or wildlife study) tend to be taken for granted, and people tend to close down discussion of such issues and even close off thinking about them. So he had to get groups to acknowledge these tensions, for instance, talking about the discomfort they might feel about the treatment of animals in producing the food that they themselves eat. Despite all this active intervention, the term that Phil often uses for moderating is *empathy*. He sees his aim as getting the people to bring out what is distinctive about their own view, as a group or as individuals.

We have focused here on the moderator's intervention to get the participants to talk. But there are times in which the participants' talk can threaten to derail the interaction. When participants are critical of the researcher (as happened in this project, with a group of intensive farmers), it sometimes helps to make it clear that he or she is not identified with one organization or point of view (though the disclaimers may not work). Moderators sometimes ask participants who are 'expert' (for instance, environmental campaigners, or local officials) to set aside their expertise so that others can speak, or call on silent people, perhaps mentioning a relevant reason for calling on them here. But usually the control of turn-taking is done by more subtle means, by giving continuers ('mm') to one speaker and not another, by keeping their gaze away from the most talkative participants, and by orientating of their body (and particularly shoulders) to a participant who has not been speaking. In extreme cases, the moderator may seize the floor again simply by moving on to the next topic, since it is usually granted that they have control of topic transitions.

Another view of group interaction

As the comparison of the Wildlife transcript and the Intensive Farmers transcript suggests, groups develop different dynamics even when the moderator follows the same topic guide. Participants in the Wildlife group are particularly forward in addressing each other, rather than the moderator. This is a stage most groups get to at some point (Myers, 2000), but this group starts it in the first minutes. There are long stretches when Phil does not intervene much, and they prompt each other. Here they have been taking about the use of animals in medical research, and it is Karen, not the moderator, who poses a question to the others:

Colin: for some people it's the most important issue in their lives

Phil: yeah

Martin: without certain drugs none of us . would be here

Karen: no

Martin: would we possibly

Karen: I think if . I don't know > touchy subject isn't it < but if one was put in the situation where you had a serious illness . and the decision was whether to =

Martin: = save the sheep or you

Karen: well . not so much <u>that</u> but whether to do testing on that . mouse or whatever in order to further . you know

Martin: if it was <u>my</u> life I know which way I'd vote

Iris :   yeah

Karen: well I know . I would . I'm afraid . I'd want my life <u>saved</u> . which is terribly selfish but

Iris: well we <u>are</u> selfish aren't we

M: but

Andrea: but if it works that's it . you don't need to use the animals for that anymore

Phil: what what are the different reasons for using animals for research? (3/37)

All this goes on without much intervention of the moderator, and without there being any pre-existing links or (in this group) strong ties of social identity; it is a group forming itself. This may make it easier to explore group norms, because they become less cautious with each other, more willing to start on unsure ground. But it also means they set up their own sense of interactional norms in the course of the two hours. In the passage just quoted, Martin, Karen and Iris all use tag questions: 'would we ... you know ... aren't we'. Karen categorizes it as 'a touchy subject', a kind of warning that other groups sometimes call 'a matter of opinion', not something everyone is expected to agree on, and she frames this too with a tag question, 'isn't it'. Someone finishes her sentence for her, and she disassociates herself from the volunteered conclusion, 'well, not so much that, but'. Karen characterizes her own preference here as 'terribly selfish'. In every turn, they signal to each other the terms in which the discussion should take place, checking that others are with them, and fencing off potential areas in which they might get bogged down. This careful politeness can provide its own constraints (Kitzinger and Farquhar, 1999).

RECORDING AND TRANSCRIBING

The details of making the groups available for analysis and discussion might seem too trivial to allow for much disagreement, but here too there are important decisions to be made that have theoretical implications. First, Phil and his colleagues chose to record the groups on audiotape, instead of using videotape, which provides much more data for analysis (Bloor et al., 2001; Matoesian and Coldren, 2002) but which can also be more intrusive. They could also have relied on notes instead of transcribing the interaction, but this, while common in market research, is unusual in academic research, because it does not enable the analyst to return to the data and respond to challenges.

The tapes were transcribed by Kate Lamb, of CSEC, who has done many such transcripts, and has become highly skilled at puzzling out overlapping talk and attributing turns to speakers. The conventions Kate has been asked to follow here are simple:

- all words are transcribed, using conventional spelling (not using the spelling to indicate the pronunciation in any way);
- repeated words, broken-off words and back-channel utterances (uh-huh, mm) are ignored;
- uncertain or inaudible passages are indicated;
- there are no indications of pauses, overlaps, stresses, volume, pace or intonation, except in conventional punctuation.

These conventions save transcription time, and make the transcripts readable; the extra features possible in some other transcription systems can make the text nearly unreadable, and can even influence readers' sense of the social status of participants (Ochs, 1979; Coates and Thornborrow, 1999; Bucholtz, 2000; O'Connell and Kowal, 2000).

Other views on transcription

As Guy Cook has pointed out (Cook, 1995), every transcript leaves out something, and the choice is not between selective and unselective representations, but between selections for different purposes. Phil, looking for themes, needs to know what they said, so that he can choose key passages, but he can rely on his memory for some of the feeling of the interaction. A quantitative content analyst needs the accurate and consistent transcription in a simple and readable format; the transcript is then reduced to its coded representation. A discourse analyst needs some of the details that indicate interaction, such as back-channel utterances, pauses, overlaps and stresses. So Greg goes back to the audiotape and adds these in, as he has done for most of the passages in this chapter. He also follows the convention of not inserting capitalization and full stops, because they are part of a process of translating the spoken words into something more like a written sentence. His transcriptions are nothing like as detailed as those used by some conversation analysts (for thoughtful discussions, see Hutchby and Wooffitt, 1998; ten Have, 1999). But it is not simply a matter of the more detail, the better; using a transcript that is more detailed than one needs is like giving a few unnecessary decimal places on one's statistics.

ANALYSING

As Celia Kitzinger (Chapter 8, this volume) has noted in another context, methodological handbooks give much more attention to setting up the research than to analysing the results. Phil's brief project leaves him with about 200,000 words of transcript, even in this basic transcription, the length of two or three PhD dissertations. But only a few writers on focus groups suggest what the researcher might do with the huge amount of data. And it is at this stage that Phil's approach and Greg's differs most sharply, Phil mapping the woods while Greg chops up a tree.

Phil's analysis of the eight 'Animal Futures' transcripts was governed by two facts: he had a brief and he had a deadline, just a few weeks after the last focus groups. This meant that he had to find the key passages quickly, looking for the main themes of his topic guide and his report: different capacities in which animals enter people's lives, conditions for acceptance or rejection of animal testing, and relation of these conditions to new developments in biotechnology. Every time he came across a quotable theme, he marked it with a highlighter, folded down the corner of the page and indexed the page number on the front of the transcript. That way, as he wrote the report, he had eight bundles in front of him, each with a list of possible quotations. While this might seem ad hoc, he was being guided, not just by his reading, but by his own fresh memory of the 16 hours of focus groups. Out of the 200,000 words of data, he chose only about 3700 for the report, but they corresponded to what he saw as central themes, repeated throughout the transcripts, a valid summary, in his view, of the transcripts as a whole. His analysis was admittedly exploratory and open-ended, but he also felt that it got at the underlying dynamics of these discussions, because he came to the analysis with a sense of what the issues and tensions were for these people, and of how the discussions, which he had moderated, had gone.

For the report, Phil chose quotations that made the repeated point simply, briefly and in a striking way. He included some quotations from every group, but some groups, such as Wildlife, were clearly richer for him. For instance, he quotes this passage (as transcribed by Kate Lamb):

Phil: Can I just say, so in what ways do you think these animals are natural?
M: Well, they won't be natural will they?
Paul: They're not natural, they're man made aren't they.
M: They're engineered.
Iris: But we do that now through inter-breeding don't we.
M: But even more so now …
Phil: But that's a point, how is it different from conventional selective breeding?
Martin: It's quicker.
Iris: More precise. (3/57) (Macnaghten, 2001: 27)

He parallels this with another passage from the 'Non-animals' group that he presents as paralleling this one in the way it illustrates 'moral and pragmatic considerations'. Then he goes on to another topic. The short time for analysis meant that he could keep all eight groups in his mind at once, and quote a passage for comparison from another group, while in a larger study over a longer term he might have had to resort to coding systems and software that would essentially do what he was doing with his highlighter and page numbers on the cover sheet.

Other ways of analysing

Greg was not involved in the 'Animal Futures' project, but if he had been, his analysis would have gone in a different direction. While Phil focuses on *what* was said, in relation to certain kinds of arguments about nature, animals and human action, Greg looks at *how* it was said (Myers, forthcoming). So instead of identifying repeated themes, Greg looks for patterns that can indicate what the participants think they are doing here, the relation of the moderator to the participants, and participants to each other, to the topic, and to the conventions of the group. Here is the passage just quoted, as retranscribed by Greg:

Phil: can I can I just say so so in what ways do you think these animals are are natural?
M: (1) well they won't be natural will they=
Paul: =they're not natural they're /man-made aren't they
M: /they'd be . engineered

Paul:	engineered
Iris:	but we do that now through inter-breeding /don't we
M:	/but even <u>more</u> so now /there's all the different applications
Phil:	/but that's a point its it . how is it different from conventional selective breeding?
Iris:	it is /
Martin:	/it's quicker
Phil:	>quicker<
Iris:	more precise
Phil:	>more precise<

Greg might start with the one-second pause and the 'well' in the second turn, which suggests that the speaker is presenting his response as dispreferred, unexpected, because he is rejecting the presupposition of the question that these animals *are* natural. The tag question 'will they' has several possible functions (Eggins and Slade, 1997; West et al., 1997), but here it might be seen as eliciting agreement with this challenge to the question. Paul echoes M, and then M completes Paul's statement, and Paul echoes M again, in the pattern of repetition that is very common in focus groups. The latching of turns (Paul starting without a pause after M's turn) and M's overlapping of Paul's turn, make it into a kind of collaborative statement. Both the next two turns, Iris's and M's, present potential disagreements, and both begin 'but', implying a kind of agree/disagree structure (Pomerantz, 1984; ten Have, 1999). Phil as moderator picks up Iris's comment (which she made a few minutes earlier in the focus group). When Martin answers, Phil echoes him quietly, as if this were one item for a list, not the only possible answer, and Iris, using a parallel form, offers another candidate answer, which Phil also echoes quietly. After the quoted passage, Colin takes this as an opening for a longer turn. These hedges ('well'), tags ('aren't they'), disagreements and repetitions give the rhythm of this group in this interaction. They would help us show how the interaction changes over the course of a group, or how this group is different from that with the Extensive Farmers, or how focus groups differ from other apparently similar kinds of group discussion, such as meetings or dinner-table discussions (Myers, forthcoming).

INTERPRETING

Interpretation, though it is often treated with analysis, can be a rather different stage, one that

began in this case when Phil sat with his annotated transcripts and asked himself, 'So what?' Of course the answer to this question was implicit all along, in the topic guide, sample, facilitation and analysis: it was important to show the range and complexity of human experience and awareness of animals, and to show how these relations would make acceptance or rejection of animal biotechnology conditional, a complex and contradictory issue. For Phil, interpretation is always a matter of placing the particular analysed passages within a framework of current theoretical concerns. The introduction to the passage just quoted ('Can I just say, so in what ways ...) operates as an interpretation telling readers what to make of it for the purposes of his argument.

> [P]eople also appeared to be grasping at a more fundamental difference pertaining to how we, as humans, should be striving towards a relationship in which we interact with nature in a way in which we are only a part of nature, *in a relationship of respect,* and where nature can go on, more or less, regardless of our own actions. The transgression of such boundaries raised both moral and pragmatic considerations. (Macnaghten, 2001: 27)

The dialogue then quoted conveys a specific example of moral considerations: in the passage from the Wildlife group, 'they won't be natural', or in the passage from the Non-animals group, 'If God or whatever meant for cows to do this in the first place it'd be like that already.' The colloquial sound and the detail given by the extended quotations is part of what makes it effective rhetorical support for these more general arguments, but once the main ideas are illustrated, the particular words can be left out of the summaries and bullet points of the report. For Phil, focus groups are microcosms that can stand for wider discussions, real or potential, just as these participants can stand for wider groups.

Other interpretations

For Greg, on the other hand, a focus group transcript is a way of recovering, as far as is now possible, a moment-to-moment situation, and the shifting relations of people in that situation. It can lead beyond this particular group and moment, but only by comparison with interactions in which similar features occur, the way that people disagree in meetings, or raise new topics at a family dinner, or use reported speech in stories. In the passage just quoted, such an analysis might lead to an understanding of how this group works together to bound acceptable opinion, and how they respond differently to the moderator and to other participants. It would be about how they do a focus group, and thus would lead to a more specific account of how focus groups are different from other kinds of talk, and how this group is different from others, and this stage different from earlier and later. Greg's response to the question 'So what?' does not link this talk to attitudes about animals, but to the ways people set up in conversation the possibility of opinions, claims to special knowledge, and ways of dealing with disagreement and still continuing to talk. Focus groups are possible because they are highly constrained occasions (they involve going to an unfamiliar place, at the same time as others, with no aim of one's own, and being led through a discussion on topics one does not usually talk about by a stranger). But they are persuasive because they are seen to be slices of modified ordinary conversation. One task of interpretation is to trace that modification, while also accounting for that sense of ordinariness.

APPLYING

Most social research is about the past; most focus groups are about anticipation, trying to find out what people might do or would say. That is why they are full of hypotheticals and simulations. The researchers are interested in anticipation because someone wants to know how to deal with the projected future. The 'Animal Futures' project would be a success for Phil and his colleagues only if it makes points briefly and forcefully, and in terms of the ongoing debates, so that it can make some mark on the report and recommendations of the AEBC.

As we have seen, the detail of the focus group goes through several reductions before it even reaches the client; Phil interprets and comments on the quotations, then summarizes the interpretations in the introduction to the report. His report is then further interpreted, reduced, and cited in the AEBC report *Animals and Biotechnology*. Here, for example, is one of the bullet points in the section on 'Attitudes to Genetic Biotechnology' that is traceable to his report and to passages of the transcript:

> The research also found that most people regarded the direct genetic modification of animals as both 'new' and 'unnatural'. Although few people rejected the use of technology out of hand, people expressed considerable concern about the pace of developments, the nature of the techniques used, and they anticipated unforeseen mistakes arising from use of the technology. The

researchers found that people commonly were wary of 'going against nature', a term that the researchers considered was key to the distinctiveness of people's concerns about animals and biotechnology. (AEBC, 2002, p. 18)

This clearly does relate to the focus group data we have just discussed: Paul saying 'they're not natural', Martin saying 'it's quicker' and Iris saying 'it's more precise'. But of course a bullet point loses Phil's more complex argument about the tensions in the passage, as well as Greg's points about the particular occasion that led to these statements. The opinions are presented as general statements about 'people', as if they were results of a survey, not of focus groups. Any policy-orientated researcher accepts that their work will be reduced in form when it reaches policy-makers. Phil commented on a draft of this report, and raised issues about how particular points were presented, trying to get in more of his interpretations. The immediate impact of the research depends on this one text; his full report is available on the web page, but it is the Commission report, or the executive summary of the Commission report, that policy-makers would see. Phil wanted to see that the summary, and the summary of the summary, came as close as possible to his longer report.

But this report would not be the only output of the research. Phil has also written an academic paper based on the focus groups (Macnaghten, forthcoming); there the textual impact is likely to be broader but more diffuse. There the frame is not immediate policy decisions, but arguments about the role of the public in decisions about technologies of genetic modification, and especially about the complexity and sophistication of their attitudes towards animals and naturalness. Here is an example of how he uses quotations in which he uses a series of examples from transcripts similar to the one we have just discussed:

> [T]he term shared by nearly all participants was that such applications were 'unnatural' in that they marked a radical departure from nature:
>
> F1 *It's just taking away nature, isn't it?*
> F2 *Mmm, it's not natural.*
> F1 *None of it's natural, no.*
>   (Non-animals group – North-West)
> F1 *I think that's going a bit too far.*
> F2 *It's not letting nature take its course; it's just interfering with nature too much.*
>   (Non-animals group – London)
> F   *It's not right, it's too much messing with nature.*
>   (Pet owners – London)

There appeared to be two dimensions to such responses. On the one hand, people adopted a 'deontological' reaction against the proposed technology as intrinsically a violation of nature and transgressive of so-called natural parameters. On the other hand, people reacted more pragmatically, questioning the apparent 'usefulness' of the putative applications …

What are the quotations doing here? They illustrate the argument, but they also convey, with the colloquial language and the way participants agree, a sense that these are strongly held and widely shared feelings. Then the commentary takes off from these feelings to put them in a more complex framework. Academic focus group studies vary in the amount of space they give to quotations from the data; in some they just provide brief, striking illustrations of the theoretical argument, while in others the main issue is the kind of interaction going on in a group. But in either case, the claim to have something new to say relies at least in part on the sense of authenticity conveyed by the colloquial words on the page, and their contrast with the register of the academic argument going on around them.

LOOKING AHEAD AND LOOKING BACK

It might seem that we have a simple contrast; Phil is a believer in focus groups, extending them to new areas, and Greg is a sceptic, undermining their authority by putting the words back in their situation. But it might be more helpful to see them as representing two perspectives on the focus group process. Phil looks ahead, emphasizing the design, starting with a clear theoretical framework, defining the groups, drafting the topic guide, and facilitating the groups so that he elicits the kinds of discussion that he can use fairly directly in his report. Greg looks back, starting with the analysis of participants' interaction moment to moment, going back to the transcription and tape, and from there to the conditions established by the focus group design. For Phil, the strength of focus group research is that it can get at people's attitudes in all their complexity. For Greg, the strength is that focus groups allow us to account for the situation – the interaction of researcher and participants, the treatment of topics in conversation, the conventions of various forms of group discussions – in a way that other methods, such as surveys or ethnographies, do not.

Each of us can give a devastating critique of the other. In Phil's view, Greg is drawn deeper and deeper into details that, however interesting in themselves, lead away from the overview of issues and attitudes that is, after all, the output of the research. In Greg's view, Phil sometimes takes passages from the transcript without being able to give an account of why the participants said just that just then, or of why Phil chose this bit and not that. Despite these differences in perspective, we manage to collaborate on occasion, because there is a range of phenomena that lie towards the middle of this continuum between seeing the forest and seeing the trees. Phil's theoretical orientation to argument, ambivalence and contradiction directs Greg's attention to ways in which the participants deal with problematic opinions. Greg's emphasis on rhetorical commonplaces in structuring a conversation directs Phil's attention to the form of the repeated, central statements that interest him. Researchers can and do start at either end, with the exploration of complex opinions, or with the odd, hybrid conversational activities that provide the conditions for expressions of opinion in a group. Both kinds of analysis are possible because the data of focus groups are extraordinarily rich.

REFERENCES

AEBC (2002) *Animals and Biotechnology*. London: Agriculture and Environment Biotechnology Commission.

Agar, M. and MacDonald, J. (1995) 'Focus groups and ethnography', *Human Organization*, 54: 78–86.

Antaki, C. and Widdicombe, S. (1998) *Identities in Talk*. London: Sage.

Barbour, R.S. and Kitzinger, J. (eds) (1999) *Developing Focus Group Research: Politics, Theory and Practice*. London: Sage.

Becker, C., Chasin, L., Chasin, R., Herzig, M. and Roth, S. (1995) 'From stuck debate to new conversation: a report from the Public Conversations Project', *Journal of Feminist Family Therapy*, 7: 143–63.

Becker, H.S. (1998) *Tricks of the Trade: How to Think About Your Research While You're Doing It*. Chicago: University of Chicago Press.

Billig, M. (1987) *Arguing and Thinking: A Rhetorical Approach to Social Psychology*. Cambridge: Cambridge University Press.

Bloor, M., Frankland, J., Thomas, M. and Robson, K. (2001) *Focus Groups in Social Research*. London: Sage.

Breakwell, G. (2001) *Research in the UK on Public Attitudes to Biotechnology with Animals*. London: Agriculture and Environment Biotechnology Commission.

Brown, N. (1999) 'Xenotransplantation: normalizing disgust', *Science as Culture*, 8(3): 327–56.

Bucholtz, M. (2000) 'The politics of transcription', *Journal of Pragmatics*, 32: 1439–65.

Burgess, J., Limb, M. and Harrison, C.M. (1988a) 'Exploring environmental values through the medium of small groups: 2. Illustrations of a group at work', *Environment and Planning A*, 20(4): 457–76.

Burgess, J., Limb, M. and Harrison, C.M. (1988b) 'Exploring environmental values through the medium of small groups: 1. Theory and practice', *Environment and Planning A*, 20: 309–26.

Coates, J. and Thornborrow, J. (1999) 'Myths, lies and audiotapes: some thoughts on data transcripts', *Discourse and Society*, 10(4): 594–7.

Cook, G. (1995) 'Theoretical issues: transcribing the untranscribable', in G. Leech, G. Myers and J. Thomas (eds), *Spoken English on Computer*. Harlow: Longman, pp. 35–53.

Eggins, S. and Slade, D. (1997) *Analysing Casual Conversation*. London: Cassell.

Franklin, A. (1999) *Animals and Modern Culture*. London: Sage.

Glaser, B.G. and Strauss, A.L. (1967) *The Discovery of Grounded Theory: Strategies for Qualitative Research*. Chicago: Aldine Publishing.

Grove-White, R., Macnaghten, P., Mayer, S. and Wynne, B. (1997) *Uncertain World*. Lancaster: Centre for the Study of Environmental Change.

Grove-White, R., Macnaghten, P. and Wynne, B. (2000) *Wising Up: The Public and New Technologies*. Lancaster: Centre for the Study of Environmental Change.

Holbrook, B. and Jackson, P. (1996) 'Shopping around: focus group research in North London', *Area*, 28(2): 136–42.

Hutchby, I. and Wooffitt, R. (1998) *Conversation Analysis: Principles, Practices and Applications*. Malden, MA: Polity Press.

Kerr, A., Cunningham-Burley, S. and Amos, A. (1998) 'Drawing the line: an analysis of lay people's discussions about the new genetics', *Public Understanding of Science*, 7: 113–33.

Kitzinger, J. (1990) 'Audience understandings of AIDS media messages: a discussion of methods', *Sociology of Health and Illness*, 12(3): 319–35.

Kitzinger, J. (1995) 'Qualitative research—introducing focus groups', *British Medical Journal*, 311(7000): 299–302.

Kitzinger, J. and Farquhar, C. (1999) 'The analytical potential of "sensitive moments" in focus group discussions', in R.S. Barbour and J. Kitzinger (eds), *Developing Focus Group Research*. London: Sage, pp. 156–72.

Krueger, R. (1994) *Focus Groups: A Practical Guide for Applied Research*. Thousand Oaks, CA: Sage.

Liebes, T. and Katz, E. (1990) *The Export of Meaning: Cross-Cultural Readings of Dallas*. Oxford: Oxford University Press.

Livingstone, S. and Lunt, P. (1994). *Talk on Television: Audience Participation and Public Debate*. London: Routledge.

Macnaghten, P. (2001) *Animal Futures: Public Attitudes and Sensibilities Towards Animals and Biotechnology in Contemporary Britain*. London: Agriculture and Environment Biotechnology Commission.

Macnaghten, P. (forthcoming). 'Animals in their nature', *Sociology*.

Macnaghten, P. and Urry, J. (1998) *Contested Natures*. London: Sage.

Macnaghten, P., Grove-White, R., Jacobs, M. and Wynne, B. (1995) *Public Perceptions and Sustainability in Lancashire: Indicators, Institutions, Perceptions*. Lancaster: Centre for the Study of Environmental Change.

Matoesian, G.M. and Coldren, J.R.C., Jr (2002). 'Language and bodily conduct in focus groups evaluations of legal policy', *Discourse and Society*, 13(4): 469–94.

Merton, R.K., Fiske, M. and Kendall, P.L. (1956) *The Focused Interview: A Manual of Problems and Procedures*. New York and London: Free Press/Collier Macmillan.

Michell, L. (1999) 'Combining focus groups and interviews: telling how it is; telling how it feels', in R.S. Barbour and J. Kitzinger (eds), *Developing Focus Group Research: Politics, Theory and Practice*. London: Sage, pp. 36–46.

Miller, D., Kitzinger, J., Williams, K. and Beharrell, P. (1998) *The Circuit of Mass Communication*. London: Sage.

Morgan, D.L. (1988) *Focus Groups as Qualitative Research*. Thousand Oaks, CA: Sage.

Morgan, D.L. (ed.) (1993) *Successful Focus Groups: Advancing the State of the Art*. London: Sage.

Morgan, D.L. and Krueger, R.A. (1998) *The Focus Group Kit*. Thousand Oaks, CA: Sage.

Morley, D. (1980) *The Nationwide Audience*. London: British Film Institute.

Morrison, D. (1998) *The Search for a Method: Focus Groups and the Development of Mass Communication Research*. Luton: University of Luton Press.

Myers, G. (1998) 'Displaying opinions: topics and disagreement in focus groups', *Language in Society*, 27(1): 85–111.

Myers, G. (1999) 'Functions of reported speech in group discussions', *Applied Linguistics*, 20(3): 376–401.

Myers, G. (2000) 'Becoming a group: face and sociability in moderated discussions', in S. Sarangi and M. Coulthard (eds), *Discourse and Social Life*. Harlow: Pearson Education, pp. 121–37.

Myers, G. (forthcoming) *Matters of Opinion: Dynamics of Talk about Public Issues*. Cambridge: Cambridge University Press.

Myers, G. and Macnaghten, P. (1998) 'Rhetorics of environmental sustainability: commonplaces and places', *Environment and Planning A*, 30(2): 333–53.

Myers, G. and Macnaghten, P. (1999) 'Can focus groups be analysed as talk?', in R.S. Barbour and J. Kitzinger (eds), *Developing Focus Group Research: Politics, Theory and Practice*. London: Sage, pp. 173–85.

Ochs, E. (1979). 'Transcription as theory', in E. Ochs and B. Schieffelin (eds), *Developmental Pragmatics*. New York: Academic Press, pp. 43–72.

O'Connell, D.C. and Kowal, S. (2000) 'Are transcripts reproducible?', *Pragmatics*, 10: 247–69.

Pomerantz, A. (1984) 'Agreeing and disagreeing with assessments: some features of preferred/dispreferred turn shapes', in J.M. Atkinson and J. Heritage (eds), *Structures of Social Action.* Cambridge: Cambridge University Press, pp. 57–101.

Puchta, C. and Potter, J. (2003) *Focus Group Practice.* London: Sage.

Szerszynski, B., Urry, J. and Myers, G. (2000) 'Mediating global citizenship', in J. Smith, (ed.), *The Daily Globe: Environmental Change, the Public, and the Media.* London: Earthscan, pp. 97–114.

ten Have, P. (1999) *Doing Conversation Analysis: A Practical Guide.* Thousand Oaks, CA: Sage.

West, C., Lazar, M.M. and Kramarae, C. (1997) 'Gender in discourse', in T. van Dijk (ed.), *Discourse as Social Interaction.* London: Sage, pp. 119–43.

Wilkinson, S. (1999) 'Focus groups—a feminist method', *Psychology of Women Quarterly*, 23(2): 221–44.

Wodak, R., de Cillia, R., Reisigl, M. and Liebhart, K. (1999) *The Discursive Construction of National Identity.* Edinburgh: Edinburgh University Press.

5

Grounded theory

Ian Dey

Like any cultural artefact, methodologies change and evolve. So it is with grounded theory (Strauss and Corbin, 1994, 1997). The methodology first introduced by Glaser and Strauss (1967) in *The Discovery of Grounded Theory* has since developed in directions its authors did not anticipate and – in the case of Glaser (1992) – did not much approve. Grounded theory began life as an innovative if rather idiosyncratic alternative to existing research methodologies. Now in middle age (as it were) it has achieved the comfortable position of becoming a pervasive and well-established orthodoxy, attracting its own critics in turn (cf. Annells, 1996). Like parents outgrown by their children, its authors have suffered the indignity of being 'corrected' by their offspring (Keddy et al., 1996; Wilson and Hutchinson, 1996). And sadly, what started as a most productive partnership between Glaser and Strauss ended in something akin to acrimonious divorce.

Thus there is no such thing as 'grounded theory' if we mean by that a single, unified methodology, tightly defined and clearly specified. Instead, we have different interpretations of grounded theory – the early version or the late, and the versions according to Glaser (1978), or Strauss (1987), or Strauss and Corbin (1990), among others (e.g. Charmaz, 1990; Kools et al., 1996). Among these various interpretations, fortunately, we can distinguish some questions and themes that they tend to have in common.

In its early days, grounded theory offered first and foremost a vision of how to do theoretically innovative research, from project design right through to writing up. Its authors believed that theory could and should be stimulated through – and 'grounded' by – empirical research, and they set out to show how this could be done. They asked and answered some pretty basic questions about how to do theoretically relevant research:

how to start, how to proceed, how to stop. First of all this requires of the researcher a sensitivity to empirical evidence, a disposition to 'discover' ideas in data without imposing preconceptions. Grounded theory was conceived as a way of generating theory *through* research data rather than testing ideas formulated *in advance of* data collection and analysis. Second, the process of generating ideas through data requires an innovative approach to data selection. Instead of identifying a sample at the outset, grounded theory involves a process of 'theoretical sampling' of successive sites and source, selected to test or refine new ideas as these emerge from the data. Sites and sources are selected flexibly for their theoretical relevance in generating comparisons and extending or refining ideas, rather than for their representational value in allowing generalizations to particular populations. Third, grounded theory relies primarily – but not exclusively – on qualitative data acquired through a variety of methods: mostly observation and unstructured interviews in the initial stages, then more structured forms of data collection as the study becomes more focused. Thus decisions on sampling and data collection develop as the project progresses, informed by and not merely anticipating the results of ongoing data analysis. The process of analysing data, fourthly, centres on 'coding' data into categories for the purpose of comparison. These categories are analytic – not mere labels but conceptualizations of key aspects of the data. And categories are also sensitizing, offering meaningful interpretations of the phenomenon under investigation. Through 'constant comparison' their relations and properties can be identified and refined. Finally, grounded theory offers pointers to how to bring the research to a successful conclusion. Data collection stops when categories reach 'theoretical saturation', that is, when further data no longer prompts new distinctions or refinements to the emerging theory. Data analysis stops when a core category emerges around which the researcher can integrate the analysis and develop a 'story' encapsulating the main themes of the study.

As grounded theory evolved, its prescriptions for design, sampling and data collection became rather eclipsed as its procedures for data analysis became more elaborate. The process of 'coding' data was broken down into different dimensions. Glaser (1978) distinguishes between 'substantive' and 'theoretical' coding. Substantive coding refers to first-order coding closely related to data; theoretical coding involves second-order conceptualizations of how these substantive codes might 'relate to each other as hypotheses to be integrated into the theory' (Glaser, 1978: 55).

But it is the distinctions drawn by Strauss and Corbin (1990) between different phases of coding that have really caught the methodological imagination. They distinguish between three phases of coding: open, axial and selective. Open coding refers to a preliminary process of 'breaking down, examining, comparing, conceptualizing and categorizing data' (Strauss and Corbin, 1990: 61). Axial coding involves 'a set of procedures whereby data are put back together in new ways after open coding, by making connections between categories' (Strauss and Corbin, 1990: 96). And selective coding involves 'selecting the core category, systematically relating it to other categories, and filling in categories that need further refinement and development' (Strauss and Corbin, 1990: 116). Each of these different phases is discussed in detail, providing further guidance on how to conduct data analysis. For example, axial coding is set out in terms of a 'coding paradigm' requiring analysis of the 'conditions, context, action/interactional strategies, and consequences' of the social process being categorized (Strauss and Corbin, 1990: 97). Ironically, this attempt to spell out detailed procedures clearly for a new generation of researchers rather back-fired, for Glaser (1992) argued that data are thereby forced to fit a preconceived paradigm, so losing sight of what he had called 'the myriad of implicit integrative possibilities in the data (1978: 73).

Despite Glaser's critique, the guidelines for data analysis set out by Strauss and Corbin in 1990 proved very popular among a research community still woefully short of clearly articulated guidelines for analysing qualitative data, and already wrestling with the analytic potential of new software to help undertake this task (cf. Tesch, 1990; Kelle, 1995). But the impressive status that the grounded theory has acquired should not blind us to its ambiguities and problems – as I hope to demonstrate through my own encounters with this methodology.

FIRST ENCOUNTERS

I was about to become a rather green undergraduate in sociology when Glaser and Strauss launched grounded theory with such panache in 1967. Their critical assessment of 'armchair sociology' and their valiant if polemical attempt to outline a new method of 'grounding' theory through empirical research made quite a stir at the time. The historical context that gave such an edge to their polemic is now hard to recover, no doubt in some measure thanks to the efforts of Glaser and Strauss themselves to open up new ways of thinking about social research. The academic world they worked in was bifurcated between abstract and formal sociological theories (notably of Talcott Parsons) on the one hand and the 'systematic empiricism' of quantitative sociology – as Willers and Willers (1973) among others were later to decry it – on the other. Sociology in those days was positively 'scientific' in its aspirations (some would say 'pretensions') and its formal theories and dedicated empiricism were fashioned to suit. Of course there were exceptions. But a sociologist such as Erving Goffman, so creative and so adept at constructing theories out of a seam of rich qualitative research experience, remained a perplexing and elusive figure, rather a maverick in the field; and the Chicago School from which Goffman emerged was itself at odds with the dominant professional schools of sociology at the time (Lemert, 1997).

This generally bipolar sociological world, in which theory and empirical research seemed to march almost in parallel universes, may not have been so very different from that of physics, the science it sought to emulate – at least if Leon Lederman's insider account (1993) of particle physics is anything to go by. But the scientific division of labour in physics between theorists on one side and empirical researchers on the other could be attributed to the professionalization of a mature discipline, remarkable for its accumulation of knowledge over the centuries. By comparison, the energies devoted to the social sciences over much the same period – despite always appearing as newcomers, the social sciences also date back at least to the Enlightenment (Herman, 2002) – had produced rather meagre results. For Glaser and Strauss, sociology's 'armchair theorists' represented the epitome of unproductive social science, not least through their distance from or baneful influence on the ambitions and parameters of empirical research. They set out to devise a different relationship between theory and research, one that would liberate theory from the seductive comforts of the armchair and empirical research from the uninspiring and restrictive confines of analysing variables or verifying hypotheses.

This new relationship centred on connecting theory to evidence through engagement with data rather than deduction. Theory was to be 'discovered', not in the cloisters of academia, but in the world beyond. Theory would be stimulated through interaction with that empirical world, not in isolation from it. The metaphor of 'discovery' was pertinent and powerful, implying that research could offer a path to new forms of data and sources of evidence that went beyond the bounds of current preconceptions and prevailing dogmas. The curiosity and excitement of discovery could become a stimulus to generating more productive social theories. These would be more productive, not just through breathing some analytic life into what had become a rather sterile discipline, but also by making that discipline more relevant to the practical world from which it had become abstracted.

When (more by drift than design) I found myself engaged on doctoral research in 1972, I found this clarion call to 'get out there' an evocative one, and events conspired to reinforce it. In a period in which unemployment in Britain was rising sharply to a historic and politically sensitive post-war high, I became interested in how 'ordinary working people' (as I rather patronizingly thought of them at the time) responded to the looming prospects of lay-offs and unemployment. My first inclination, to look at how trade unionists in the local engineering industries had struggled against unemployment during the inter-war years, was frustrated by the usual accidents of space and time: the documentary evidence I sought had been either destroyed or lost. Had the Amalgamated Union of Engineering Workers in Bristol not moved to smaller offices a few years earlier, I might now be writing this chapter as a historian. Instead, and rather by default, I decided to study the contemporary efforts of local trade union activists to challenge a series of redundancies that took place in the Bristol engineering industry in the early 1970s (Dey, 1979).

Although I did not adopt a 'grounded theory' approach, it formed a tacit if unacknowledged influence on my methodological outlook. Without ever trying to follow explicitly the guidelines of grounded theory, I was no doubt influenced at the time by some of its main tenets. For example, the idea of 'theoretical sampling' informed my selection of respondents and issues, the 'constant comparative' method through 'coding' data informed the backbone of my analysis, and my study shared the focus of grounded theory on 'social process', in my case the social process whereby trade union activists tried to resist redundancies. But in retrospect, two broader influences of grounded theory seem more profound.

First of all, as advocated by Glaser and Strauss, I embarked on a study that was intended to generate theory largely through a dialogue with data derived from empirical research. I did not set out to test hypotheses, opting instead to try to develop some ideas about the social process of resisting redundancies through confronting qualitative evidence drawn from a wide range of sources – in-depth interviews, documentary materials and media reports.

I was less confident, even then, in the assertion that such research should and could proceed uncontaminated by preconceptions on the part of the researcher. That I was interested in Marxism at the time may have had something to do with this. Those who read into these words the dogmatic assumptions of a monolithic theoretical orthodoxy might be surprised at the ferment of ideas and arguments that characterized at least some of the many Marxist factions of the day. Newly radicalized by the Vietnam war, this was a generation for which Marxism posed more questions than answers. At any rate, it stimulated my initial interest in the problems of unemployment and the role of trade union activists, and also offered a potentially fertile source of theorizing about redundancy and trade unionism. Or so I hoped.

At the very least, Marxism encouraged a more sympathetic and open engagement with trade union activities, commonly dismissed in the industrial relations theories then prevalent as representing essentially 'sectional' or 'irrational' interests. It also shifted focus from welfare conceived largely in terms of redistribution of goods and services to welfare conceived as a more active and productive process through which people tried to realize their needs and aspirations. Beyond these general orientations, however, Marxism per se had little specific to offer concerning the particular political and social processes through which trade union activists responded to redundancies. This was indeed something of a *tabula rasa*, upon which I hoped to generate some theory (or at least some ideas) through my encounter with the experiences and views of local activists. Thus I shared with grounded theory the ambition of generating theory that would be both stimulated by and grounded in empirical research.

The second influence involved a closer alignment of Marxism and grounded theory, in so far as in both perspectives, theory was orientated to 'praxis' or practical action. In Marxism, of course, praxis is predicated on a grand theory of history, which maps out the general course of events, if not the particular tributaries that contribute to their evolution. Nevertheless, Marxism as I understood it had never had a pat answer to Lenin's question, 'What is to be done?' That had to be figured out according to the context and dynamics of particular conjunctures. In grounded theory, too, there was no grand theory that could be presumed to make predictions in advance of analysis. There were instead 'substantive' theories, which were more immediate, specific and practical in their orientation and anticipated effects. There was also 'formal' theory, to which such substantive theories could contribute by raising up (or perhaps more aptly, stripping down) their conceptualizations to a more abstract level.

Although Glaser and Strauss (1967: 82) claimed that formal theory was produced through the same processes of comparative analysis as substantive theory, the way they linked the two in practice was through a process of conceptual abstraction. Formal theory, then, was neither generated nor grounded quite in the direct and practical manner of substantive theory. To me it seemed a connection between connections, once removed – a fitting occupant of the arid airs of abstracted sociology, perhaps, but not the living, flexible, practical theoretical tool that Glaser and Strauss apparently sought to devise. Where formal theories dealt in abstractions – deviance, power, stigma – substantive theories were more orientated to the pressing practicalities of the here and now.

This practical orientation casts theoretical aspirations in a different light. A theory may be judged not just in terms of its truth, but also its relevance and utility. If the first criterion can at least masquerade as 'universal', with the other criteria we cannot escape the questions: relevant and useful when, and for whom? These questions imply a deeper connection between social science and political values and interests than simply the selection of subjects for study. They connect the conduct of the research project itself – how data is produced and analysed – with the political context in which it is pursued. Along with validity, it requires researchers to take account of the relevance and utility of the knowledge they produce – and the transparency with which they produce it. In the best of all possible worlds, these criteria would coincide; unhappily, researchers must live with the tensions caused when they do not.

THEORETICAL SAMPLING

Though Glaser and Strauss showed a spirited optimism about the prospects of simultaneously pursuing these goals, some awkward compromises were needed to keep the enterprise afloat. Consider 'theoretical sampling' – that is, 'the process of data collection for generating theory whereby the analyst jointly collects, codes and analyzes his data and then decides what data to collect next and where to find them, in order to develop his theory as it emerges' (Glaser and Strauss, 1967: 45).

In my doctoral study, I took an approach rather akin to this flexible and dialectical method of sampling data. First of all I identified an event – a strike against redundancy in a local engineering plant – that seemed to throw into sharp relief the processes of conflict and accommodation through which opposition to redundancy developed. I considered the ways in which the union activists tried to encourage resistance to the redundancy; the problems they encountered in doing so; and the way they adjusted their tactics to changing circumstances as the dispute unfolded. Then I 'sampled' another event, in which opposition to redundancy was expressed, not through strike action, but at the negotiating table instead. Why did union activists adopt this strategy, and how did it affect their ability to negotiate with the company? This episode in turn raised questions about the relationship between union activists and their members, which I pursued by 'sampling' another dispute, this time a redundancy in which the activists tried to take action over redundancies but faced resistance from a recalcitrant membership. The relationship between activists and members in this dispute was mediated by trade union officials. To examine their role more closely I 'sampled' yet another dispute, in which activists and members were united in opposing redundancy, but their efforts were circumvented (activists would say 'sabotaged') by union full-time officials. In all the redundancies I had sampled so far, opposition to redundancies had been led (employers would say 'orchestrated') by a handful of activists operating through their trade union's district committee. To isolate the role of these activists, I then 'sampled' a redundancy in a large well-organized establishment where opposition was largely led by shop stewards and left to those on the shop floor.

Through theoretical sampling, then, one could examine a social process such as resistance to redundancy, first by generating ideas on the basis of initial fieldwork, and then seeking to clarify or amplify these ideas by sampling further settings to provide opportunities for comparison and contrast. Here a strike, there an accommodation. Here activists and members united, there divided. Here union officials playing a key role, there the shop floor. This procedure allowed theory to germinate and grow by continually moving backwards and forwards between ideas and data. Analysis did not follow upon a period of fieldwork, as in the conventional logic of research. Instead, data collection and analysis were interwoven in a seamless dialectic. In a tidy world, the stages of this process would have been clearly demarcated: first sample, then analysis; then next sample, and further analysis, and so on – rather as described above. In practice, the boundaries merged and blurred, so that it was impossible to disentangle the precise points where data collection stopped and data analysis began.

Though akin to theoretical sampling in some respects, my sampling procedure remained within the confines of a particular case and context, whereas for Glaser and Strauss theoretical sampling was intended to generate data (and generalizations) without specific regard to case or context. From this perspective, one looked for comparable or contrasting settings through which to explore the social process under investigation. For example, one might have examined processes of expulsion and resistance in quite different settings, such as those of educational, religious or political organizations. The greater the contrast in settings, the sharper the points of comparison. But the potential gains of such abstracted comparisons are gained by trading off depth of knowledge for breadth of inquiry. My inclination was rather to retain a strong sense of local context – of the individual and idiosyncratic character and bounds of the specific case.

Theoretical sampling was a methodologically bold suggestion, because it freed the researcher from the usual rigours required of producing representative samples. The aim was to sample theoretically stimulating settings, not to generalize from representative samples of populations. This in turn was consistent with a sociological focus on analysing social processes rather than individual attitudes or opinions. But freedom comes at a price. The catalytic virtue of selecting sites to provide new points of comparison for developing theory sits uneasily with the use of sampling to validate and generalize results. However valuable

in generating theory, this procedure has little to offer for its validation. This need not be a problem, where generating theory is conceived as the first step in the long haul of scientific endeavour, to be followed by more rigorous procedures for testing and verification. But if theory is to be relevant, practical and of immediate import, then that rather rules out the long haul. Faced with this awkward problem, Glaser and Strauss (1967: 3–5) fudged the issue. Sometimes they endorsed the long-haul approach, relegating the mundane tasks of validation to others. Sometimes they claimed that theory was validated already, because it was 'grounded' by the very process through which it was generated. And sometimes they dispensed with validation altogether, preferring to emphasize the relevance and utility of theory rather than its accuracy and durability.

CODING DATA

This ambivalence about validation is reflected in the ambiguous treatment of 'coding' in grounded theory. Nowadays, grounded theory has become associated above all with a set of procedures for analysing data, not just producing it. This reflects the influence of computer software for qualitative analysis, which has shifted the methodological focus from how to get good data to how to make good once you have got it. The procedures of grounded theory set out a framework for conducting systematic data analysis. There are several features of this framework that have become very familiar, foremost amongst them the shifts from 'open' through 'axial' to 'selective' coding.

Open coding is 'the process of breaking down, examining, comparing, conceptualizing and categorizing data' (Strauss and Corbin, 1990: 61). Codes are devised which capture and convey meanings, evinced through close examination of and comparisons between different parts of the data. Open coding thereby offers a method of generating ideas by close and detailed inspection of the data. How close is demonstrated in Glaser's injunction to code data 'line by line', asking some very general questions of the data without presuming the analytic relevance of any theoretically derived variables or hypotheses:

What is this data a study of?
What category does this incident indicate?
What is actually happening in the data?

Strauss and Corbin suggest an equally basic repertoire: who, what, when, where, and how?

Such questions seem to imply that categories or codes can be created in direct response to the data, without resorting to or requiring much in the way of mediation by prior theory. The data itself will dictate what categories are there to be 'discovered'. The creative process lies in confrontation with evidence, allowing it to invoke or provoke ideas without any particular preconceptions on the part of the analyst.

This seems to require of the analyst a moment (or better, many moments) of epiphany or revelation, certainly of inspiration. Since analysts are only human, Glaser and Strauss kindly slip in some analytic assistance in the guise of sensitizing concepts. The analyst must come to open coding without preconceptions, but not entirely without ideas. Indeed, the more ideas the better! Analysts can and should draw upon the widest possible range of sources, including a full range of 'coding families' (Glaser, 1978: 81) available within sociology (see Table 5.1), but also ideas from other fields and other disciplines. Acquiring theoretical sensitivity by drawing on an extensive literature outwith the field of study might help to provide the necessary inspiration. Open coding involves generating as many categories as possible in the light of these various possibilities, without prejudging which will prove most valuable at this stage in the analysis.

The emphasis in open coding is on stimulating ideas rather than documenting evidence. It was beyond this point that Glaser and Strauss eventually parted company. Glaser remained wedded to the view that analysis should be shaped through confrontation with data, without preconceptions. One could not prejudge which 'coding family' would be relevant until one became thoroughly engaged with the data. But in the guise of 'axial' coding, Strauss seemed to smuggle in just the kind of 'preconception' that Glaser adamantly opposed. Axial coding was conceived as a method of integrating analysis through connecting categories – by deploying as a general frame of reference the context, conditions, strategies and consequences that characterize interaction. Axial coding in Glaser's view 'privileged' one coding family, that concerned with causality, ahead of others.

Once categories were integrated through axial coding (or perhaps through one of Glaser's other coding families), coding could become increasingly selective. This final phase involved integrating the analysis even further around a 'core' category – that is, a central concept selected to act as a fulcrum around which others can be brought together into a coherent whole. Selection of a core category was required to achieve the 'tight integration and dense development of

Table 5.1 *Selected coding families*

Family	Concepts
Causality	Causes, contexts, contingencies, consequences, covariances and conditions
Process	Stages, phases, progression, etc
Classification	Type, form, kinds, styles, classes, etc
Strategy	Strategies, tactics, mechanisms, etc

Source: Adapted from Glaser (1978: 81).

categories required of a grounded theory' (Strauss and Corbin, 1990: 121). Selective coding could thereby deepen and enrich the analysis, while also forming a framework around which to weave a 'story-line' that conveyed its central import.

Much of this elaboration and formalization of coding procedures (and the disputes it generated) came after I had completed my doctoral analysis. In retrospect, that does not seem to have been much of a handicap. My own attempts at 'coding' data were generally in line with the grounded theory approach, but without anticipating its separation of analysis into distinct phases, its predilection for deriving categories directly from data, or its concept of a 'core' category.

In those days, pre-computer and even pre-photocopy machine, 'coding' involved a laborious process of transcribing bits of data on to cards that could be duplicated and organized under different headings. This was useful, above all, as a way of making comparisons. All aspects of the data pertaining to a particular point could be brought together in one place. This allowed the analysis to develop, both through internal and external comparisons. That is, one could compare all the bits of data under a heading, in order to refine the analysis by identifying similarities and differences; and one could compare the data under that heading as a whole with data categorized under other headings, in order to make connections between them.

For example, I was interested in the underlying conceptual frameworks in terms of which trade union activists perceived and responded to redundancies. How did they conceptualize 'redundancies' and what alternative conceptions did they hold of how firms could manage a period of recession or a process of restructuring? Their conceptions of redundancy depended to some degree on how redundancies were handled. Did firms operate a 'last-in first-out' policy, did they seek 'voluntary' redundancies, did management select employees for redundancy, or some mix of these? For trade union activists these were critical issues, not least because management selection in the name of 'efficiency' could easily target the activists themselves. But they were not their only concerns. Responses to redundancy were also shaped by the kind of alternatives they believed firms could adopt. For example, activists believed that many redundancies could be avoided if overtime was restricted. The control of overtime was a continual bone of contention, bringing union activists into conflict not only with employers but also with other unions, and frequently even with their own members, eager as the latter often were to supplement low incomes with overtime payments. Short-time work was seen by some activists as an immediate and more equitable way than redundancy of spreading the costs of recession. In the longer term, work-sharing in the form of reduced hours was seen by some activists as a better way of distributing the productivity gains of industrial restructuring than increasing incomes for those lucky enough to keep their jobs. Thus one could distinguish a variety of ways of managing redundancies and different underlying conceptions of why they occurred and how they could be prevented.

Such distinctions emerged from the analysis in fits and starts, depending on what data had been collected and analysed to date. A dispute over control of overtime work might point in one direction, a conflict over voluntary redundancy in another. The overall patchwork slowly developed into a more composite picture as further pieces became available. This metaphor – the picture slowly emerging as a patchwork mosaic – is perhaps a more apt way of conveying the process of analysis, since it does not distinguish so sharply between different phases of 'coding'. It allows for multiple points of foci, rather than insisting on a single 'core' category around which all must revolve. Since pictures can tell more than one story, it also allows for a more open-ended, ambiguous and perhaps even contradictory account.

In any case I did not think of the various 'headings' through which I organized and conceptualized my data as 'codes', and the term still makes me uncomfortable. The 'coding' procedures in grounded theory emphasize the direct relationship between observations made and the codes that express them. This is the 'analytic' view, that breaks data down into its constituent parts, only to struggle (through axial or selective coding) to reconnect them. It posits theory as something that emerges *after* categorization, rather than *through* it. Hence the current attraction of software packages that, through sophisticated search and retrieval procedures, allow

one to explore an infinite number of ways of reconnecting codes (cf. Richards and Richards, 1994). This method favours 'interrogating' data over 'interpreting' it. My own headings were more an aid to interpretation, not isolated 'codes' but related concepts connected to and informed by a more complex and holistic account.

Despite the general affinity with a grounded theory approach, evident in both my sampling procedure and my use of categories as a means of managing and conceptualizing data, I did not try to apply grounded theory or even refer to it to justify my own approach. Perhaps this was because of an equally important influence on me at the time – a book by Barry Hindess (1977) on philosophy and methodology in social science. Hindess reviewed various methodological schools of thought, arguing that these various perspectives were not only internally inconsistent and contradictory, but bore only a tenuous relationship with what researchers actually do in practice. This disjunction between perception and practice is of course the very stuff of sociological research – when the subject is not social research itself. The surprise is that sociologists (and social researchers generally) have been so slow to appreciate the ideological and political functions of their own methodological debates. Perhaps Stanislav Andreski's savage critique of the social sciences as sorcery (1972) should be mandatory reading? At any rate, Hindess made me sceptical of grand methodological pretensions, and inclined to see such general prescriptions as a dubious guide to how to do research. Following Hindess, I began to think less in terms of how to *apply* a methodology and more about how it can *inform* (or perhaps obscure) our understanding of the research process.

Much later – three small children later – I developed some software to help analyse qualitative data produced in research projects into employment programmes. Since I was not alone in my desire to escape from the tedious restrictions of pen and ink, others showed interest in my software and (thanks to the enthusiasm and generosity of the late Renata Tesch) I soon found myself presenting the software to international conferences on computer-assisted qualitative data analysis. There I was surprised to find that much of the debate about the role of software in supporting the development of theory in qualitative analysis focused on grounded theory. I was even more surprised to find that colleagues presumed that my own software was predicated on the methodology of a grounded theory approach. Suspicious as ever of the claims of grand methodology, I put this aside even when I set out to write a book about using software (I had my own in mind of course!) to analyse qualitative data (Dey, 1993). Then as now, I thought we might learn more from reflecting on how researchers actually do research, than from the more general accounts and prescriptions. As Clifford Geertz put it: 'If you want to understand what a science is, you should look in the first instance not at its theories or its findings, and certainly not what its apologists say about it; you should look at what the practitioners of it do' (Geertz, 1973: 9).

Nevertheless, practice does not proceed independently of preconceptions about appropriate methods, and I was intrigued by the connections being made between grounded theory and software for qualitative analysis. I set out to explore these in a further book, which unexpectedly turned into an exploration of grounded theory itself as a set of guidelines for qualitative inquiry (Dey, 1999). I wanted to figure out what all the fuss was about.

Since categories figure so centrally in grounded theory, it is worth taking time to tease out the role they play in analysis. An obvious problem arises with the insistence that categories should be fitted to data rather than the other way round. This has invited the criticism that grounded theory is at base a 'positivist' epistemology, in which observations are considered preconceptual and concepts reduced to the sum of the indicators by which they are measured. That Glaser and Strauss (1967: 37–8) emphasized the sensitizing side of categories as well as their analytic purchase suggests a more complex and ambiguous approach, despite Glaser's explicit avowal (1978: 62) of a concept–indicator model. But in any case this is a false dilemma. Data cannot be apprehended as data except through some sort of conceptualization; and concepts themselves – no matter how abstract – have to have some sort of grounding, however derivative, in data to which they refer. Therefore it is not a case of fitting concepts to data, nor of fitting data to concepts, since neither can exist independently of the other.

While Glaser and Strauss seemed to acknowledge this in ascribing to categories a 'sensitizing' as well as an 'analytic' role, it is not clear how these are to be reconciled. In grounded theory, analysis is ultimately predicated on the standard 'concept–indicator' model, in which the meaning of a concept is understood in terms of the set of indicators through which it is observed. This model is rather at odds with other requirements of grounded theory – notably its claim that concepts once generated acquire 'a life of their own' through which they can at once reduce and enrich theory. They reduce because concepts in effect summarize a range of observations; and they enrich because concepts convey connotations that facilitate connections with other concepts.

Perhaps because of its roots in 'naturalistic' inquiry, grounded theory seemed to take for granted the cognitive processes involved in categorization. But how do we develop and use categories in practice? Since categorization is so central, it merits further reflection, which fortunately it has been accorded in other disciplines.

CATEGORIZATION

In cognitive psychology, Harnad (1987) has argued that categories are acquired through identifying and discriminating between a series of positive and negative observations. He shows that at the level of perception, categorization is subject to rules that are ambiguous and subject to continual revision in the face of what he calls 'confusable alternatives'. There is always some further observation that may require an adjustment to our categories if we are to discriminate successfully between one object of perception and another. Categorization is always approximate and provisional, and relative to the vagaries of experience.

Also in psychology, Rosch and Lloyd (1978) have shown that observations are often assigned to categories, not on the basis of rules governing membership but through their affinity with 'prototypes' – that is, on the basis of family resemblance to particularly good exemplars. This makes category membership a matter of degree – not every observation has equal status as an exemplar. A robin is closer than an ostrich to what we categorize as a bird. Category membership is graded, and category boundaries become 'fuzzy' (McNeil and Freiberger, 1994). Assignment to categories is uncertain, and dependent on perceptions of resemblance rather than firm rules that discriminate clearly and consistently between observations.

In linguistics, Lakoff and Johnson (1980) have challenged what they call the 'set-theoretical' model of categorization, in which observations can be assigned unambiguously to categories on the basis of 'requisite inherent properties'; they observe that categorization 'is primarily a means of comprehending the world and as such it must serve that purpose in a sufficiently flexible way' (1980: 122). They argue, moreover, that our concepts are rooted in metaphors: 'our ordinary conceptual system, in terms of which we both think and act, is fundamentally metaphorical in nature' (1980: 3). These metaphors are often extensions from our physical interaction with the world, as for example in the metaphor 'rooted'. The concept of argument itself illustrates the point, since we tend to conceive of arguments metaphorically in terms of fighting, as when one *defends* a *position* from *attack*. Imagine, suggest Lakoff and Johnson, if we thought of argument as a dance rather than a battle.

Lakoff (1987) has argued that categorization ultimately depends on what he calls 'idealized cognitive models'. These are not accurate representations of the world – they are idealized and often metaphorical and holistic in their construction. Categories are never simple representations, since they invariably depend on an underlying cognitive context that informs category judgements and invests them with meaning. For example, the category 'bachelor' depends on an underlying idealized cognitive model that differentiates between married and single – though only within relevant contexts, and in terms of action as well as status. Thus our category judgements are informed by stereotypical expectations (for example, men behaving badly) associated with prototypical examples (usually provided by those accorded celebrity status).

Finally, it is worth recalling that we not only categorize, we also particularize, 'since a category is always distinguished from what is specific or singular' (Pickering, 2001: 29). Categories may help us to classify and order observations, but in our thinking we also have regard to the individual and idiosyncratic as well as shared attributes.

This account of categorization may help to resolve the tensions between the analytic and sensitizing use of categories in the grounded theory approach. It demolishes the pretensions of the concept–indicator model to fixing categories in terms of indicators. The meaning of a category cannot be reduced to a specified set of observations. The sensitizing role of categories, on the other hand, can be understood more fully in terms of the prototypes and cognitive models that invest them with meaning. In short, we are not detached observers who discover meaning through observation. Rather, we attach meanings to observations, in terms of specific contexts and particular purposes. Meaning is created, not 'discovered'.

COMPARISON AND CAUSALITY

When we categorize, we compare like with like, like with unlike. Comparison is at the core of grounded theory, whether comparing bits of data to generate categories, or comparing categories in order to generate connections between them. Comparison is the engine through which we can generate insights, by identifying patterns of similarity or difference within the data. It is no coincidence that Glaser and Strauss described their method as that of 'constant comparison'. But again, it is worth reflecting on the limitations as well as strengths of this mode of thinking.

Comparison is a vital tool in identifying, classifying and ordering data. But these are not the sole purposes of social inquiry. A tool that is well adapted for classification may be less well suited as a means of establishing other forms of connection between observations or categories. Sayer (1992), for example, has distinguished between 'formal' and 'substantive' relations, where the former refers to connections of class and order and the latter to connections of causality. These different forms of connection between concepts are often conflated, most notably in the attempt to reduce causal analysis to the identification of regular patterns of events through correlation. Comparison lies at the heart of Mill's methods of agreement and difference, which provide the logical foundation of this approach. The method of agreement allows us to infer a causal connection where two events regularly coincide, such that whenever A occurs, B occurs. If A precedes B, then A can be identified as the putative cause of B. The method of difference strengthens our inference, where we observe that when A does not occur, neither does B. Both methods assume that where a cause is active, we should be able to observe its effect.

The method of constant comparison exploits this logic by comparing the connections between categories in different settings. In particular it underpins the process of axial coding, whereby the analyst examines the conditions, strategies and consequences of interaction. Suppose we return to my example of resistance to redundancy among trade union activists. What were the conditions for successful resistance? We can try to identify this through a comparison of those cases where opposition succeeded and those where it fell flat. Of course, we need some sense of what counts as success and failure in this context. To simplify, let us simply accept the activists' own definition of success – that redundancies are avoided – without worrying unduly about the criteria employed by other participants in the drama. With this as our 'effect' we can compare different disputes to identify what conditions (and strategies) were common to successful outcomes, and what happens when those were missing.

For example, suppose in one redundancy we observe the following:

	Opposition successful	Opposition unsuccessful
Union officials intervene		×
Union officials do not intervene		

If we find this pattern repeated in other redundancies, we might be tempted to see the intervention of union officials as a factor undermining activist resistance, particularly if we also observe the following pattern in other cases:

	Opposition successful	Opposition unsuccessful
Union officials intervene		
Union officials do not intervene	×	

If, on the other hand, we found cases with values in the other cells (successful opposition where officials intervened, or unsuccessful opposition even where they did not), this might lead us to reject the idea that official intervention undermined resistance. Ideally, we might want a large number of cases, selected at random, with which we can then use statistical analysis to identify whether and how these 'variables' correlate.

But for Glaser and Strauss this was by no means ideal. Though this comparative logic underpinned grounded theory, it was sailing too close to the standard methods of variable analysis for comfort. Why not simply devise a hypothesis (or deduce one from grand theory) and test it through quantitative analysis of survey data? Instead, Glaser and Strauss (1967: 104, 168) rejected the 'inductive' method of establishing 'single causes' as inadequate because it failed to recognize and do justice to the multiple and conjunctural nature of causation. To continue with our example, life becomes complicated (literally) once we recognize that other variables too may affect the success of resistance to redundancy, such as managerial strategies or the strength of union membership on the shop floor. If (as I found) large voluntary severance payments were attractive to many long-service workers, then managements could try to divide opposition by offering a 'voluntary redundancy' strategy and so undermine resistance. This strategy might or might not succeed, depending on other factors, such as the role of other unions, the wage structure of the firm, or the demographic profile of the union's membership. From the simple analysis of single causes, we are quickly plunged into the complexities of multivariate analysis – but without the necessary methodological and statistical tools to do the job.

Though focusing on complex forms of multiple and conjunctural causation, Glaser and Strauss retained a methodology more attuned to isolating single causes. In effect, they retained the method of constant comparison while rejecting the methodological constraints that it required. The 'constant' in 'constant comparison' did not refer to keeping conditions constant to isolate the effects of particular variables. Inconsistencies in the patterns found across different settings could be explained (away) as a result of uncontrolled variation. But without systematic and representative sampling there could be no control of variation. On the basis of correlation between variables, they had no grounds for judging causal connections between categories. Yet through the method of constant comparison they insisted on searching for regular patterns of similarity and difference in the data.

An alternative approach is to think of causality in terms of powers rather than patterns (Sayer, 1992). From this perspective, our sense of causality derives from our interaction with the world – from direct observation of experience rather than inference based on regularity. This is firstly a matter of bodily experience – we know what we know because we are part of the world and we can make things happen (Lakoff, 1987). Later we extend that conception of causation founded on direct experience to other connections between actions and events (Lakoff and Johnson, 1980).

Causation is also a question of intelligibility – of understanding why there is a connection between what we do and what results. For years, it was claimed that red wine provided protection from heart disease; but it was only once the protective function of certain ingredients in wine was understood that a causal connection was established. This connection was identified as a property of the wine (or rather, of particular ingredients within it) and its power to produce certain effects through interaction – that is, when the wine was consumed. Causal analysis in natural science is thus predicated on identifying 'powers' that things have rather than on observing 'patterns' among events, since when exercised these powers may or may not have particular effects, depending on circumstances.

In natural science, circumstances can be controlled (for example, through experimentation) and relationships examined in what is in effect a 'closed' system. In social inquiry in general, it is not possible to achieve such control – the relationship between causes and effects is always contingent. Regularities may therefore be a poor guide to the presence or otherwise of a causal connection. Identifying causal connections is more a matter of understanding 'how things work' by identifying the structure, properties and (inter)actions of those agencies that possess causal powers.

Returning to my union activists, this shifts the focus from comparing events in order to identify patterns (what factors are associated with a success here, or a failure there) to analysing more directly their power to control or influence events. For example, the activists enjoyed some power over local members by virtue of their control of the engineering union's district committee. Within the parameters of national policy, they could devise local strategies and issue directions accordingly. However, the influence that committee once exercised by virtue of the union's provision and regulation of benefits for its unemployed members had been undermined in the post-war period by the nationalization of social security. Nor did the district committee retain the pre-war craft controls it had once enjoyed over access to jobs. The professionalization of industrial relations and the more prominent role of union officials had likewise eroded the democratic authority of the committee. Trade union activism too had shifted its location, during the affluent years of the post-war boom, from the union branch to the shop floor, making the shop steward a more central figure in representation and negotiation. All these factors conspired to undermine the 'power' of union activists to generate opposition to redundancies through the district committee.

DEDUCTION, INDUCTION AND ABDUCTION

Grounded theory is often regarded as an inductive approach, whereby generalizations are produced through analysing a series of cases – though Glaser and Strauss explicitly rejected analytic induction and implicitly disavowed the analysis of cases. Since they were also suspicious of deduction (1967: 3–4), it seems that grounded theory dispenses with procedures that are ubiquitous in and integral to social and scientific inquiry.

Their dismissal of deductive reasoning was consistent with the desire to 'discover' theory rather than test hypotheses deduced from prior knowledge. One problem with this approach is that it requires research always to begin from scratch, instead of using whatever theoretical and conceptual resources that social inquiry has already to hand. The sensitizing role of theory makes some concession to the potential of prior conceptualizations, but it still disallows the more obvious ways in which theory can prompt us to ask questions of data, devise concepts or consider alternative interpretations. It is easier to discount deductive reasoning in theory, however, than to dismiss it in practice. It is clear for example that deductive reasoning underpins the process of theoretical sampling, since this requires the analyst to identify further data against which to 'test' emergent hypotheses. Glaser and Strauss were wary of deduction as a mode of posing questions of data lest it impose a conceptual straitjacket on the generation of theory. But posing questions is not the same as presuming answers.

Glaser and Strauss rejected inductive inference because they were concerned to generate theory rather than to generalize from cases to wider populations. Thus theoretical sampling did not involve representative sampling, such that from a particular sample (of cases) one can generalize to the population from which it is drawn. Instead it was intended to provide contrasting settings through which theoretically fruitful comparisons could be made. In this approach, it is not cases that are sampled, but settings. The focus is on sampling social processes in contrasting settings rather than on sampling particular populations.

If grounded theory nevertheless produces theoretical generalizations about social processes, this prompts the question of whether, when and where these generalizations might apply. This was a question that Glaser and Strauss were inclined to leave to others. In this context, 'others' were likely to be practitioners who could make use of grounded theory to make sense of their own social settings. Whether a grounded theory 'applied' was tested through its practical value and import within particular settings rather than through scientific assessments of its explanatory scope. This did not rule out entirely the accumulation of theoretical knowledge through generalizations, but the pace of social change was in any case liable to render such generalizations redundant. The real test of a theory was therefore whether it 'worked' for practitioners in particular settings. This may seem to give priority to utility above truth, but the truth of a theory was itself grounded in the analyst's ability to 'get by' – that is, to know 'how things work' in the social processes being investigated in the relevant social settings.

Though it involves elements of both deductive and inductive inference, grounded theory clearly privileges neither form of inquiry. It is perhaps more appropriate to see it as a form of abduction. This form of reasoning was first described as 'abduction' by the American philosopher Charles Peirce (Danermark et al., 1997: 88–95), whose philosophy of pragmatism has some affinity with the practical priorities of grounded theory.

In deduction, we start with theory, make an observation and infer a result:

All activists oppose redundancies
These people are activists
These people oppose redundancy

The result follows logically from the preceding premises. By checking to see if this result holds good, we can test the theory from which it is deduced.

In induction, we proceed in the opposite direction. We start with a case, make an observation, and then generalize to a wider population:

These people are activists
These activists oppose redundancy
All activists oppose redundancy

The inductive inference does not follow logically from the premise but it infers beyond it. Thus inductive generalizations are always uncertain, and vulnerable to further observations which may prove inconsistent.

In abduction, we can start with theory, make an observation and draw an inference about that observation consistent with the theory:

Activists oppose redundancy
These people oppose redundancy
These people are activists

Or we can start with an observation, state a theory, and infer a result:

These people oppose redundancy
Activists oppose redundancy
These people are activists

Either way, abduction relates an observation to a theory (or vice versa), and results in an interpretation. Unlike induction, theory in the case of abduction is used together with observation, in order to produce an interpretation of something specific, rather than to infer a generalization.

Unlike deduction, the result does not follow logically from the premises: abduction offers a plausible interpretation rather than producing a logical conclusion.

Using abductive inference is thus a matter of interpreting a phenomenon in terms of some theoretical frame of reference. This can be one of several possible interpretations, depending on the theory we adopt. If it is any good, this theory will offer new insights that help to explain some aspect of the phenomenon under investigation: 'Abduction is to move from a conception of something to a different, possibly more developed or deeper conception of it. This happens through our placing and interpreting the original ideas about the phenomenon in the frame of a new set of ideas' (Danermark et al., 1997: 91).

Following Jensen (1995: 148), Danermark et al. (1997: 91) go on to characterize this mode of reasoning as a process of reconceptualization, whereby we describe, interpret or explain something within a new framework. The frameworks they have in mind are those of grand theory – Durkheim's recontextualization of suicide as social fact, or Marx's recontextualization of human history from a materialist standpoint. In terms of grounded theory, though, the process of 'coding' data can also be usefully considered as a process of recontextualization (cf. Tesch, 1990). In this process, the 'coding' of data (or its reorganization of data under new headings) is not just a matter of attaching labels to particular bits of data for subsequent retrieval and 'interrogation'. It already involves relating selected observations to a theoretical frame of reference (though perhaps not so systematic as to constitute a 'framework') in order to generate new insights. This gives a rather different twist to the logic of 'discovery' in grounded theory. For what is 'discovered' is not so much new facts as new ways of connecting them. Rather like the 'discovery' of America, what is discovered through recontextualization is not so much a new phenomenon per se as a new meaning or interpretation. America became the New World through the 'discovery', not of a continent already well inhabited, but of its new connections with what became the 'old' world.

The relevance of a particular frame of reference is not determined only by its consistency with observations; it also depends on its capacity to generate insights, which taken together can produce a new account of the subject under investigation. 'Taken together' does not imply some cosy consensus, since interpretations may compete with as well as complement each other, and there is plenty of room for ambiguities and contradictions in trying to produce an adequate account. Though the validity of any particular theory can be 'tested' against data, different theories may generate interpretations that are not incompatible but simply different. The problem then is not so much to determine which interpretation is 'true' but which is the most meaningful way of managing the data.

Considered in this way, grounded theory certainly requires creativity, for 'all abduction builds on creativity and imagination' (Danermark et al., 1997: 93). The challenge is to produce accounts that make new connections between things, to see the world differently.

CONCLUSION

Where does this leave us – or rather, me? This is a particularly pertinent question, since I am currently undertaking a project on 'dealing in diversity' (thanks to a grant from the Leverhulme Foundation) which explores the ways in which family policies can exacerbate or reduce prejudice. I have no intention of *applying* grounded theory in this project, but it may nevertheless provide a useful way of *informing* my analysis. Clearly this will not be through the systematic use of the 'coding' procedures that Strauss and Corbin specify in terms of open, axial and selective coding. Though such 'coding' has become increasingly identified as its analytic core, I think there are richer pickings to be gleaned from reflection on the ambitions and ambiguities of a grounded theory approach.

One such ambition is to generate theory that is relevant and practical as well as analytic – what Bent Flyvberg (2001) aptly describes as a 'phronetic' social science. Though Glaser and Strauss never satisfactorily resolved the ambiguity of pursuing both these goals simultaneously, at least they framed theory in ways that appreciated its practical as well as its truth value. Had Glaser and Strauss accepted theory as context-bound rather than aspiring to make it context-free, they might have effected a happier reconciliation between these values.

A second ambition embedded in grounded theory is the generation of theory that offers fresh insights into and interpretations of social processes through comparison and recontextualization. Hence the stress that Glaser and Strauss placed on theoretical sensitivity: on drawing upon a wide range of literature, perspectives and experience to inform the analytic encounter with data. Though obscured somewhat by their war on preconceptions and their faith in discovery from data, the idealized and metaphorical nature of

categorization as revealed in psychological and linguistic studies allows us to restore the balance between the sensitizing and analytic use of concepts.

A further ambition in grounded theory is the development of analysis attuned to the multiple and conjunctural character of causation. Though the generation of theory through 'constant comparison' to identify 'patterns' in the data accepts the limitations of inductive inference based on constant conjunction, at least the aim is to develop a more complex and holistic analysis. But once focus is shifted from identifying patterns to analysing powers, the causal ambitions of grounded theory may be more attainable.

Writing this chapter has impressed upon me, once again, just how intractable are the problems of accounting for what we do as social researchers. Rumour has it that one of the authors of grounded theory themselves remarked (though in private!) on the disjunction between what they prescribed and how they practised. If so, he would certainly have appreciated the challenge addressed in this volume – to reflect on methodology as 'work in progress' rather than an abstract and ossified set of technical prescriptions.

REFERENCES

Andreski, Stanislav (1972) *Social Sciences as Sorcery.* London: Deutsch.

Annells, M. (1996) 'Grounded theory method – philosophical perspectives, paradigm of inquiry, and postmodernism', *Qualitative Health Research*, 6(3): 379–93.

Charmaz, K. (1990) 'Discovering chronic illness: using grounded theory', *Social Science and Medicine*, 30: 1161–72.

Danermark, Berth, Ekström, Mats, Jakobsen, Liselotte and Karlsson, Jan Ch. (1997) *Explaining Society: Critical Realism in the Social Sciences.* London: Routledge.

Dey, Ian (1979) 'A study of the formulation and implementation of policies relating to redundancy and unemployment by the Amalgamated Union of Engineering Workers District Committee, Bristol, 1970–1972'. PhD Thesis, University of Bristol.

Dey, Ian (1993) *Qualitative Data Analysis: A User-Friendly Guide.* London: Routledge.

Dey, Ian (1999) *Grounding Grounded Theory: Guidelines for Qualitative Inquiry.* San Diego, CA: Academic Press.

Flyvberg, Bent (2001) *Making Social Science Matter: Why Social Inquiry Fails and How It Can Succeed Again.* Cambridge: Cambridge University Press.

Geertz, Clifford (1973) *The Interpretation of Culture.* London: Hutchinson.

Glaser, B. (1978) *Theoretical Sensitivity.* Mill Valley, CA: Sociology Press.

Glaser, B. (1992) *Emergence v. Forcing: Basics of Grounded Theory Analysis.* Mill Valley, CA: Sociology Press.

Glaser, B. and Strauss, A. (1967) *The Discovery of Grounded Theory: Strategies for Qualitative Research.* Chicago: Aldine.

Harnad, S. (ed.) (1987) *Categorical Perception: The Groundwork of Cognition.* Cambridge: Cambridge University Press.

Herman, Arthur (2002) *The Scottish Enlightenment: The Scot's Invention of the Modern World.* London: Fourth Estate.

Hindess, Barry (1977) *Philosophy and Methodology in the Social Sciences.* Hassocks, Sussex: Harvester.

Jensen, Klaus Bruhn (1995) *The Social Semiotics of Mass Communication.* London: Sage.

Keddy, B., Sims, S.L. and Stern, P.N. (1996) 'Grounded theory as feminist research methodology', *Journal of Advanced Nursing*, 23(3): 448–53.

Kelle, U. (1995) (ed.) *Computer-Aided Qualitative Data Analysis.* London: Sage.

Kools, S., McCarthy, M., Durham, R. and Robtrecht, L. (1996) 'Dimensional analysis – broadening the conception of grounded theory', *Qualitative Health Research*, 6(3): 312–30.

Lakoff, George (1987) *Women, Fire and Dangerous Things: What Categories Teach About the Human Mind.* Chicago: Chicago University Press.

Lakoff, George and Johnson, Mark (1980) *Metaphors We Live By.* Chicago: University of Chicago Press.

Lederman, Leon (1993) *The God Particle.* London: Quality Paperbacks Direct.

Lemert, Charles (1997) 'Goffman', in Charles Lemert and Ann Brannaman (eds), *The Goffman Reader.* Oxford: Blackwell, pp. ix–xliii.

McNeil, D. and Freiberger, P. (1994) *Fuzzy Logic: The Revolutionary Computer Technology That Is Changing Our World.* New York: Touchstone.

Pickering, Michael (2001) *Stereotyping: The Politics of Representation.* Basingstoke: Palgrave.

Richards, T.J. and Richards, L. (1994) 'Using computers in qualitative research', in N.K. Denzin and Y.S. Lincoln (eds), *Handbook of Qualitative Research.* London: Sage, pp. 445–62.

Rosch, E. and Lloyd, B.B. (eds), *Cognition and Categorization.* Hillsdale, NJ: Erlbaum.

Sayer, A. (1992) *Method in Social Science: A Realist Approach* (2nd ed.). London: Routledge.

Strauss, A. (1987) *Qualitative Analysis for Social Scientists.* Cambridge: Cambridge University Press.

Strauss, A. and Corbin, J. (1990) *Basics of Qualitative Research: Grounded Theory Procedures and Techniques.* London: Sage.

Strauss, A. and Corbin, J. (1994) 'Grounded theory methodology: an overview', in N.K. Denzin and Y.S. Lincoln (eds), *Handbook of Qualitative Research.* London: Sage, pp. 273–85.

Strauss, A. and Corbin, J. (1997) *Grounded Theory in Practice.* London: Sage.

Tesch, Renata (1990) *Qualitative Research: Analysis Types and Software Tools.* London: Falmer.

Willers, D. and Willers, J. (1973) *Systematic Empiricism: Critique of a Pseudoscience.* Englewood Cliffs, NJ: Prentice-Hall.

Wilson, H.S. and Hutchinson, S.A. (1996) 'Methodological mistakes in grounded theory', *Nursing Research*, 45(2): 122–4.

6

Performance and rehearsal: the ethnographer at the opera

Paul Atkinson

INVISIBLE PERFORMANCES

Anna Lisa Tota (1997) has suggested, in a characteristically Italian metaphor, that sociology needs to exorcise itself from the 'evil eye' in which it is held by theatre. She cites De Marinis (1982), who suggests that while the theatre has served sociology quite well, the reverse is not true: there is a marked absence of sociological treatment of the theatre and theatrical spectacle. The worlds of theatre have provided a series of analytic metaphors and analogies for the sociological understanding of everyday life. But there has been remarkably little reciprocal interest in the sociological analysis of theatrical performance. Sociological thought thus finds itself entangled in the web of theatrical imagery, but rarely frees itself to treat theatre and performance as topics of scrutiny in their own right. In particular, there is a collective failure to address the accomplishment of performance in theatrical and other settings.

In some ways, the relative absence of sociological work on the theatre reflects a recurrent imbalance in the sociological examination of culture. Despite the fact that sociology has experienced a remarkable surge of interest in culture, the treatment of 'culture' has been asymmetrical. While all sociologists would insist on an analytic relativism to the point of suspending common-sense values and assumptions concerning 'high' culture and the self-evident importance of different cultural forms, in practice the discipline has displayed a collective inverse snobbery. Popular culture has received much more extensive and systematic attention than so-called serious or high culture. Popular music has received more

sociological attention than 'classical' music; films and musicals have been more studied than opera or the 'straight' theatre. A properly symmetrical treatment of culture would, of course, treat any and all cultural acts and products as equally deserving of sociological analysis. That inverse snobbery is – especially among British practitioners – a reflection of a wider sociological culture that treats the bourgeoisie and the intelligentsia as negative reference-points rather than subjects for empathetic research. The working classes and their cultural forms are, by contrast, invested with inherent value. A similar point can be made about the recent sociological interest in the closely related issues of 'consumption': the consumption of mass culture and goods (the Sony Walkman, Nike branded goods) receives far greater attention than the consumption of art and esoteric culture. Indeed, the so-called 'cultural turn' in the social sciences – important though it has been in some respects – still seems to have left great swathes of cultural production, circulation and consumption virtually untouched by detailed empirical inquiry. Furthermore, a renewed emphasis on cultural consumption has excused a collective failure to examine the social worlds of cultural production as collective work in socially organized settings. It is much easier to comment from the armchair about the postcolonial readings of nature programmes on television, or the representation of extraterrestrials as the 'other' in science fiction, than it is to do the – to my mind – harder work of understanding the often complex sites in which culture gets done (film and television studios, publishing houses, design departments, advertising agencies and so on).

Theatricality and dramaturgy have been subject to sociological reflection in the past.

Elizabeth Burns's analysis of 'theatricality' (Burns, 1972) explores the historical and cultural conventions that define the practices and institutions of the theatre, ranging across different epochs and genres. Notwithstanding her emphasis on performance and interpretation, however, Burns does not ground her analysis in any empirical research on the actual circumstances of performance. Consequently, and ironically, the very essence of 'theatricality' is entirely lost to view. In the absence of any published sociological studies to draw on, Burns would have needed to undertake first-hand field research had she based her analysis on such observations. In a rather similar vein, Georges Gurvitch (1955) provided an outline of a sociology of the theatre – but this was a manifesto for a hypothetical research programme rather than the realization of empirical inquiry. The broad ideas were taken up by Jean Duvignaud (1963, 1965), whose two monographs on the theatre and on the actor trace mainly historical trends in theatrical institutions and the socio-political contexts in which they occur (Tota, 1997: 92). Again, there was a marked absence of detailed analysis of the practicalities of theatrical work and performance.

While the sociology of the theatre remained for many years an underdeveloped research field, the use of dramaturgical ideas was more popular. Erving Goffman's dramaturgical analysis of social encounters (e.g. 1959) was the most famous and the most pervasively influential use of theatrical imagery. His accounts of self-presentation and the ritually delicate nature of the social self were elaborated through an exploration of dramaturgy. Self-presentation is conceived in terms of theatricality; the theatre of the mundane is anatomized in terms of its scenic practices – of props, backstage and frontstage areas, audience evaluations and so on; the social self is conceived of in terms of dramatic self-awareness, and the preservation of control in the face of potential stage-fright. But of course Goffman was in danger of addressing *ignotum per ignotius* – explaining the unknown terrain of everyday life in terms of the even less known domain of the theatre. Theatrical performance itself remained a virtually unexamined resource in Goffman's dramaturgical analysis. (Given the paucity of live professional theatre outside New York and a few other American cities, many of Goffman's original readers might have found theatricality a relatively unknown phenomenon.) In a sense, therefore, Goffman's sociology of everyday life serves to emphasize the continuing neglect of the practices of theatrical life on the part of sociology at large. The development of

Goffman's ideas through his exploration of 'frames' (Goffman, 1974) certainly suggested fruitful directions in which the dramaturgical perspective could be turned back on theatrical encounters themselves: the layerings of rehearsal and performance in Goffman's treatment of reality-construction suggest analyses of the theatre itself, rather than just the metaphoric transfer of ideas from the theatrical domain. Oddly, however, very few researchers have translated Goffman's brilliant insights into practical research on the mundane social accomplishment of theatrical work. The opportunities for ethnographic work are considerable. The processes of improvisation in experimental theatre; the methods of character-construction; the techniques of the body and expressive gesture in acting; the actual 'backstage' life of a theatre company: these and other topics all present themselves for anthropological or sociological treatment.

The relative neglect of the theatrical is all the more ironic given the increasing prominence granted to the notion of 'performance' in the social and cultural sciences. The notion has become prominent among social anthropologists, for instance. The current emphasis on performance among anthropologists represents in part a corrective to the analysis of rituals and other collective observances in terms of their systems of signification. Structuralist and semiotic approaches to ritual had little or nothing to say about rites in action, and had equally little to say about the practical engagement of social actors (Schieffelin, 1998). In addressing the actions of performers themselves, the current anthropological emphasis is also a corrective to analyses of culture that pay exclusive attention to the audiences and the consumption of cultural artifacts.

In general, contemporary social and cultural analysts have stressed the performative quality of social life and its cultural forms. Tulloch (1999) synthesizes research on a variety of topics into a conceptual framework that engages with performative analysis. His own analysis ranges over 'high' and 'low' culture, 'expert' and 'lay' cultural productions. He draws on the literatures of anthropology and theatre studies in stressing the local and situated performance of mundane and expert understandings. The anthropological preoccupation with performativity is brought together in the collection of essays edited by Felicia Hughes-Freeland (1998), with analyses of ritual, dance, spectacles and everyday social encounters. Schieffelin's essay in that edited collection provides a useful overview. He draws on Goffman and the symbolic interactionists to suggest that performance is inherent in human conduct and reality-construction. The only limitation with such accounts is that they treat performance as so pervasive in cultural affairs that there remains little to say specifically about the performing arts or the extraordinary performances of art, music, opera and so on. The specificities of performance and its social organization are in danger of being lost if 'performance' is treated as a fundamental and generic process of social life.

Kirsten Hastrup (1998) is one of the very few anthropologists to have brought such a perspective to bear on the theatre itself. She stresses that she approaches the theatre not as 'art' but as 'life': 'Evidently, it differs from everyday life or there would be no point in making theatre; but the difference is one of condensation. Theatre is a concentrate of action, which is what makes it so (potentially) powerful' (Hastrup, 1998: 30). Hastrup invokes a number of sources to suggest that the theatre is a liminal space and a 'holy' one. The actor has a double identity – enacting himself and herself and the theatrical character simultaneously. The theatrical performance implies a condensation and an extension of everyday action, and a doubling of agency – what Hastrup describes as the 'dilation' of the actor. In the relative absence of studies of the theatre, one is forced to rely more on the reflective accounts of 'insiders', such as Stanislavski (1967; Stanislavski and Rumyantsev, 1998), than on the accounts of ethnographic observers.

Dance is one form of performing art that has attracted the attention of anthropologists, sociologists and others. It has been studied in Western and non-Western cultures. In addition to its intrinsic anthropological interest, the study of dance – more than of any other genre of performance – highlights the embodied character of performing. It thus contributes simultaneously to the documentation of cultural forms and to the analysis of embodiment in diverse cultural contexts (Wulff, 1998a; Buckland, 1999). A substantial proportion of the modest literature on dance is – understandably – preoccupied with methodological problems, especially the notation and recording of dance in the field. Likewise, there is a literature on performing musicians that is relatively modest in volume, if high in quality (e.g. Becker, 1951; Faulkner, 1983; Kingsbury, 1988; Born, 1995).

Notwithstanding the recent cultural turn in sociology and anthropology, then, and notwithstanding the analytic importance attached to notions of performance and performativity, there remains a dearth of ethnographic research on the performing arts in contemporary society. This is true of musical performance, the straight theatre and music-theatre in their various genres. Equally, despite the fact that cultural analysts insist on the necessary symmetry between production and consumption of cultural goods and spectacles, in practice much more attention is paid to cultures of consumption than cultures of production. The sociological study of music is likewise a rather underpopulated field, but does include a small corpus of ethnographic work on the production and consumption of music in everyday lives (see Jones, 1998; DeNora, 2000).

My ethnographic study of an international opera company is intended to go some way towards remedying the current situation. It is based on participant observation in various settings of the Welsh National Opera Company (WNO), with particular emphasis on the processes of rehearsal and performance of specific operas. I have had virtually unlimited access to members of the WNO, including the rehearsal studio and the theatre (backstage and in the wings as well as in the auditorium). The fieldwork was conducted over a period of four years, interspersed with other research and writing commitments. In this chapter I shall try to give a flavour simultaneously of the substance of the ethnography, and also of the fieldwork process. I shall focus my attention here on some of the processes of operatic rehearsal, and on the processes of observation and interpretation.

In the course of this chapter it is not my intention to present a summary account of my ethnographic study of the Welsh National Opera Company. Rather, I want to make some specific observations about the ethnographic enterprise. Having made some preliminary remarks on the topic of cultural performance and production, I shall go on to draw some parallels between the work of the ethnographer and the work of two key people in the opera rehearsal studio – the *repetiteur* and the *producer*. The first helps to capture the theme of repetition. The process of cultural production generates slow, repeated and painstaking progress: the ethnographer needs to take account of and capture the slow processes, even the sheer boredom, of such a process. The second highlights the parallel work of the ethnographer and the theatrical or operatic producer/director. Both are concerned with making sense of intentions and motives in creating or understanding social action. The director is a sort of practical ethnographer. This is a specific example of the analytic – not merely metaphorical – relevance of the dramaturgical to the sociological and vice versa. In contrast to many of the other chapters in this collection, therefore, this is not intended to provide explicit methodological advice on the conduct of ethnographic or other qualitative research. Practical commentary on the conduct of participant observation is to be found in this volume in Sara Delamont's Chapter 14, for instance. Rather, the chapter provides a number of insights into the substantive topic – the everyday work of cultural production in an opera company – and simultaneously into the research process of ethnographic fieldwork. It emphasizes the contribution of ethnographic work to an understanding of the often routine and repetitive forms of social action, and of the quotidian practices of interpretative work that performers (and everyday practical actors) engage in. The discussion extends Goffman's insights, in providing a dramaturgical account of dramaturgical work, but it is not an exclusively Goffmanesque analysis.

If contemporary sociology and anthropology of culture want to engage seriously with the social worlds in which cultural artifacts are enacted and produced, then they need detailed, field-based research that documents the ordinary social activities that go into the making of culture. The theatre, the painter's studio, the concert hall or the opera-house are in principle no different from any other setting of work. The extraordinary outcomes of artistic endeavour are grounded in perfectly ordinary routines, negotiations and work settings (cf. Becker, 1982). The relatively small number of detailed studies of cultural work settings attest to the socially organized practices that underpin the aesthetic and intellectual work of cultural performance (Faulkner, 1983; Kingsbury, 1988; Born, 1995; Wulff, 1998a, 1998b, 2000). It is the distinctive strength and contribution of ethnographic fieldwork that it allows us to understand and document those social practices that are necessary for the collective production of art, culture and performance. The prolonged fieldwork that is characteristic of ethnographic research allows us to document the remarkably detailed and often skilful craft-work that participants bring to bear in the course of creating artifacts or performing works. (The convergence of these two strands of thought in the taken-for-granted phrase *work of art* helps us to remember that the 'works' of an artist or a composer, or indeed the *oeuvre* of a creative or performing artist, are just that – the products of labour.)

THE ETHNOGRAPHER AND THE REPETITEUR

The *repetiteur* is a key member of any operatic company. The repetiteur is a highly accomplished pianist who provides the musical accompaniment for rehearsals in the studio and in the theatre, and for 'music calls' where principal singers rehearse their music privately. (The notion of 'accompaniment' is subtly misleading here: the accompanist for, say, a recital must be prepared to follow the singer, whereas in the opera rehearsal the singers and the pianist must be prepared to follow the musical direction of the conductor.) The ethnographer is a much less obvious participant. Indeed, the sociological or anthropological observer is a very rare bird in any major cultural setting – especially in organizations devoted to the production of 'high' culture. Despite the high profile of opera companies in recent years, and despite the prominence of opera performers among the 'superstars' of global culture, there has been very little work on the everyday life and work of opera companies and their members. My own ethnography is a contribution not only to the study of opera, but also to the sociology or anthropology of the performing arts more generally. In the space of this chapter, I can touch on only some aspects of opera as work, and on the ethnography as work too (see Wellin and Fine, 2001).

The repetiteur is an indispensable, if sometimes unobtrusive member of the music staff, and of any production of any opera. The ethnographer should be unobtrusive as well, but is completely dispensable, a marginal figure doing her or his best to make sense of a multiplicity of musical, dramatic and organizational activities that go into the mundane work of operatic life. I want to suggest some simple phenomena that nevertheless suggest some parallels between the work of the two, before going on to make some more general comments about my work.

The ethnographic work on which I draw has been conducted over a period of time with the Welsh National Opera, based in Cardiff. Here I will not hold up the presentation by giving a detailed account of the company, except to say that it has now been in existence for over fifty years. Based, as I said, in Cardiff, it is a touring company, supported by the Welsh and English Arts Councils. It currently has an annual residency in Belfast as well. Its touring venues include Welsh and English towns and cities. It has an international reputation for the excellence of its musical and production standards, founded on a chorus and orchestra that are highly regarded for the quality of their work.

Repetiteurs have a number of key tasks in the preparation of any opera production. They provide the piano accompaniment for production rehearsals in the rehearsal studio, or in the theatre. They also take 'music calls' with principal singers, coaching them in the technical musical preparation and interpretation of their role. As the title suggests, repetition is a key feature of their everyday work. The dramatic and musical preparation of an opera runs along parallel tracks for much of the time. The producer (a guest producer, not one of the company employees) together with a staff producer and members of the stage-management staff work on production rehearsals, with principal singers and the chorus (when needed). Production rehearsals have piano accompaniment. Meanwhile, the orchestra rehearse in the orchestral studio with the conductor and/or a member of the company's music staff. The chorus, in addition to the production rehearsals, also rehearse their numbers separately, directed by the chorus master, also with piano. The combined forces come together for the first time for two rehearsals, called *Sitzprobe*, that is, 'seated' rehearsals which are exclusively musical rehearsals. The production then moves from the rehearsal studios to the theatre, where there is a further division between production rehearsals and music rehearsals. The former, which are primarily the province of the producer, are again with piano and music stage rehearsals with the full orchestra. The rehearsal cycle culminates in two dress rehearsals – normally complete run-throughs of the entire work. The second 'dress' is before a reduced audience. (This is confined to 'Friends' and patrons of the company in the upper circle seats, the stalls and front circle being the province of the production staff and other company members.) The cycle of rehearsals follows a path from the 'secular' or mundane to the 'sacred'. Rehearsals in the studio are intimate and mundane. Although the work is serious, it is enacted with relative informality, in the everyday surroundings of the rehearsal room; the production staff, music staff and the singers are in close proximity and interaction between them is immediate and informal. As the rehearsals proceed through the cycle, however, the physical and social space between singers, producers and others becomes more distant in physical terms. By the time the production reaches the theatre the physical distance between singers and production staff becomes progressively greater. Singers are in costume, wigs and make-up, and the theatre constructs its own symbolic boundaries between stage, frontstage and backstage areas. The action that was once conducted in the mundane lighting of the rehearsal studio is now defined by stage lighting and a progressively darker auditorium. The stage itself becomes a progressively 'sacred' site, increasingly removed from the 'profane' world of audience and other social actors. The mundane world of the rehearsal studio progressively gives way to the staged theatricality of the theatre itself, and the membrane between backstage and frontstage is reasserted.

Unlike some major international houses (with whom comparison is often made by its members), WNO prides itself on its long and thorough rehearsal period. Normally three operas are produced in a season, a mix of new productions and 'revivals' of previous productions. Revivals receive as much attention as new productions, and as all or many of the cast will be new to it, a revival is treated in many ways like a new production. So singers are not 'shipped in' to perform a role with little or no preparation (as can be the case, for instance, in some major European houses). Extensive preparation time can be a major attraction for singers. For younger singers in particular, WNO provides an excellent site to learn their craft and work thoroughly on a role. It is important for a company like WNO to provide excellent working conditions: they cannot attract singers with very high fees, but many singers are happy to work with them because it offers such an outstanding working environment. (This is not confined to the approach to preparation, it also includes the warmth of its collective ethos, and the excellence of its staff restaurant.)

As I have suggested, the role of the repetiteur draws attention to the theme of repetition. The work of preparing an opera is indeed repetitious. Rehearsals take place over several weeks. For each week there is a careful rehearsal schedule. The working day is normally divided into two three-hour rehearsal periods, from 10.30 to 1.30 and from 2.30 to 5.30 (or thereabouts). Timings are normally adhered to rigorously. There is a 'break' in the middle of each rehearsal period. As there can be three operas in rehearsal at a time, the scheduling of rehearsal times and the availability of staff members, chorus and music staff needs careful planning. For the production rehearsals, the opera is dealt with scene by scene – certainly not necessarily in the running order of the entire work. The personnel involved will depend on the scale of the opera or of the scene in question: a small-scale work obviously differs from a piece with large cast and full chorus. But the general shape of studio rehearsals is fairly stable.

Imagine a modern, large shed-like space. The stage area of Cardiff's New Theatre – where the opera will receive its first performances in the season before going on tour – is laid out with floor tape. The set for the day's act or scene is roughly laid out, with flats in place, and major features of the set – such as raked floors, walkways, stairs – set up. In front of the 'stage' space are trestle tables, which are usually messy and covered in scores, schedules, press cuttings, small props, sweets and personal belongings. In the 'wings' are more props, rehearsal costumes – sometimes but not always worn, so that singers become used to moving and singing with long dresses, hats, cloaks, swords and the like. There is a grand piano, and a music stand for the conductor. In addition to the singers, the personnel include a staff producer and stage-management staff. Depending on the production a language coach may be present, whose task it is to check on the accuracy of pronunciation and inflexion of the Italian, German, French or whatever language the opera is in. Members of the stage crew are on hand to change or re-set the scenery. Depending on the production team, the lighting designer and costume designer may also attend. A choreographer or movement coach may also have been engaged – again, depending on the work being rehearsed and the style of production.

It is common for the rehearsal period to start with the principals who are performing the relevant scene to 'sing through' the music. They do this at the piano; some may consult the vocal score as they do so, others not. Now and throughout the rehearsal singers will not always 'sing out'. In other words, they 'mark', singing without full volume of the supported voice. This is used especially when a singer feels that the voice needs resting or protecting, if they have a cold or feel especially tired. Some singers hardly ever mark, if at all, while others do so much more frequently. The sing through is the first opportunity that the conductor or the repetiteur has that morning or afternoon to make specific observations about details of musical phrasing, pitch (pointing out where a note should be a semitone higher or lower, say) or tempo.

The producer and staff producer then take over proceedings. As they start to work on a scene with the singers, they begin to 'block' the scene, in a way entirely familiar from all theatrical settings. Producer and singers may walk through the scene, or part of it. Often the producer will work closely with them, moving through the set, walking through movements, 'taking the role of the other' for duets and ensembles and so on. When there are large-scale forces to be ordered, this can be a complicated and time-consuming aspect: blocking individual chorus members or sections of the chorus, for instance, can be a demanding exercise.

When the scene has been blocked in this preliminary way, then it is acted and sung with piano. This can be a highly repetitious affair. It can be interrupted for a variety of reasons. The producer will stop and intervene in order to correct or change positions, moves, direction of gaze or gestures. Singers themselves can stop the proceedings – not least if they have 'gone wrong'. They can go wrong musically, with an ill-timed entry, or by losing their place in the music. They can also go wrong dramatically, by forgetting or mistiming an entrance, a move or some other piece of stage business. It is, incidentally, not always the case that the entire process is interrupted by such eventualities. While the scene continues to be sung through, one often sees a dumb show between a principal or chorus member and the producer or staff producer, as singers gesture mutely, querying whether they should be here or there, further upstage or downstage, further towards the wings of centre-stage and so on. There can therefore be a fairly dense traffic of gesture between the 'stage' area and the production staff.

This is a highly repetitious process. Scenes or parts of scenes are repeated in this way. A three-hour rehearsal period can repeatedly go over a section of drama and music that in the final performance will last a few minutes. Moments that will be fleeting in performance can be worked and re-worked in the rehearsal studio. Indeed, the process can be frustrating and tedious. It is frustrating if singers do not or cannot reproduce what the producer has in mind. Not all singers have the same dramaturgical facility. The ability to develop and embody memory for actions is not easy for everyone equally. Producers can get especially frustrated when a singer has something clearly demonstrated to him or her, agrees, says that yes, they see – and then reverts to doing exactly what they were (or were not) doing immediately before they were shown. The repeated stopping and starting of rehearsal to 'correct' failings of performance can make the rehearsal period more tense and fraught than it otherwise might be. The rare event of a singer who has not fully learned the words or the music can be an extreme cause of frustration. The troubles of repetition are not always to be laid at the door of the singers, however. Producers can and do change their mind. Again, this is frustrating for others. It can be especially troublesome when a producer repeatedly re-sets a complicated scene, or calls for repeated entrances and exits by the entire chorus.

Somewhere between the two extremes – of singers' failure and of producers' failure – lies a repeated process of negotiation between producers and performers. The producer, of course, has the *authority* to direct. Indeed, there are two sources of personal authority in play – the producer and the conductor. While I do not elaborate on it here, singers rely on the authority of each. While they are by no means 'cultural dopes' in this setting, singers depend on a *clarity* of direction from both. As I have hinted, the producer who fails to impart clear directions and does not exert her or his directorial control will find respect and response muted. Clarity of musical direction requires the conductor to beat visibly and predictably, in a way that helps the singer to pick her or his way through their vocal entries, to steer a way through difficult rhythms and time-signatures, while being responsive to singers' needs (such as taking breath). Clarity of direction from the producer also needs consistency. While producers' ideas will change and develop as rehearsals proceed, principal singers and chorus members will find wholesale changes of mind irksome. Respect is withheld from producers who seem to change tack gratuitously.

The ethnography of the opera, therefore, needs to capture the slow movement of repetition and progress as the production is negotiated and as it unfolds over the cycles of repetition. The social scientist must be able to appreciate the essential slowness and the detail of what is observed. Indeed, the relative tedium of quotidian activity is part and parcel of the ethnographic enterprise. Experienced researchers know that everyday life, while always 'eventful' in the sense that 'nothing never happens', is not always marked by the overtly exciting, exotic or dramatic (cf. Charlton and Hertz, 1989; Delamont, 2002; Hall, 2000).

To return to the repetiteur, therefore, the music is a constant presence throughout the process. In a sense it is inexorable. It sets stern limits to the possibilities of action. Action and gesture are negotiated and coordinated through the temporal ordering of the music. Social action and dramatic action are constrained by the demands of music. The repetiteur must not 'accompany', in the sense of accommodating to the singers, much less accommodating to the exigencies of dramaturgy. When producers and singers 'find a way' (as they often put it) to solve a particular dramatic need, they must find a way that is feasible within the time available, and that allows singers to be able to sing, breathe and see the conductor. They certainly do not stand stock-still and sing, but the interpersonal negotiation of action is also a musical negotiation of concerted action. As far as possible, therefore, the ethnographer of performance must be sensitive to the delicacies of competing and complementary modes of performance. Action is negotiated within a complex set of spaces: the temporal and technical demands of music; the physical and symbolic space of the set; the dramaturgical significance of gesture, mutual gaze and movement. As the cycle of rehearsal and performance progresses, the staging becomes further marked by lighting (which creates spaces within the set), props, costumes and so on.

Here, then, is a series of themes concerning the ethnography of performance, and the performance of ethnography. The dramaturgical work of the opera studio and the theatre can be understood as a kind of practical ethnography in its own right, while the anthropologist or sociologist tries to make sense of how the participants themselves engage with the work of opera. The 'opera' is not to be found just in the score. It is distributed across a number of texts and sites: the libretto and the score itself, the *mise en scène*, the costumes, wigs and props, the scenery, the production book, the lighting design. The temporal cycles and the physical spaces provide both the resources and the constraints within which the performance is constructed and reconstructed by its participants. The ethnography of the opera, then, is addressed, in part, to an understanding of how these are realized through the mundane work of music theatre. Time is concretely observable through the inexorable cycles of repetition and rehearsal.

In reaching an understanding of the minutely detailed work of rehearsal (and subsequently of performance), there is no alternative to the anthropological-cum-sociological process of protracted engagement with the 'field'. This is not the level of understanding that is gained through one-off interviews, nor yet through the collection of autobiographical narratives of singers and other protagonists. (There are understandings to be gained from such sources, but they are by no means the same.) In the same vein, one cannot otherwise make sense of the interpretative work of the director and his or her performers without detailed attention to the protracted and detailed work through which they collaborate. It is to this that I turn in the next section of the chapter. The engaged observer, in Alfred Schutz's phrase, must 'grow old together' with the participants (Schutz, 1967). Music-theatre is an especially vivid and demanding context for such work: the music of opera provides an inexorable temporarily through which and against which all of the action on stage must be performed. There is little leeway to tamper with the music's temporal flow, especially when the opera is through-composed with a continuous stream of music, as opposed to comprising closed 'numbers' such as arias and ensembles interspersed with spoken dialogue or recitative. Dialogue – whether spoken or sung – gives producers and performers a little more leeway (but even that is precious little given the need to maintain the impulse of music-drama). Likewise, the cycles of rehearsal and performance set their own temporal patterns. The first night of a new production cannot wait until everyone is perfectly comfortable with everything: it must happen on the appointed night, or not at all. (The latter eventuality is not entirely unheard of in the world of opera. In recent times the Royal Opera House had to 'pull' the entire production of Ligeti's opera *Le Grand Macabre* at an advanced stage in the preparations, as the newly reopened house was unable to cope with the technical demands of staging the work.)

The fact that the routine work of cultural production can be repetitive and boring for the participants does not mean that the ethnographic fieldwork is necessarily boring as well. While observers may be entertained briefly by the more exotic and dramatic episodes (and I mention some from the opera later in this chapter), the real analytic significance of much ethnographic work is to be found in the fine-grained detail of the ordinary activities of social actors in specific social worlds. The true intellectual engagement of the ethnographer lies in his or her own craft-work in turning the daily round of observed mundane activities into a coherent and newsworthy account of just how social actors perform their distinctive lives and actions. This is intellectually demanding, in much the same way as performative art is. Indeed, I want to suggest another parallel: outstanding performances and interpretations arise out of mundane work and, in much the same way, the ethnographic report is the outcome of rather ordinary observations of unremarkable activities.

THE PRODUCER AS ETHNOGRAPHER

The process of directing performers is, as we have already seen, a protracted and repetitive one. The producer of a new opera production comes to the rehearsal period with well-elaborated ideas about the opera and its staging. The overall shape of the production is determined before the producer and the cast ever meet. The set, the costumes, the lighting design – these have already been mapped out. Indeed, one of the recurrent activities on the first day of a rehearsal period consists of the producer talking the cast, the staff producer, the stage management group and others from the company through her or (more often) his overall conception of the piece. The degree of elaboration in which this is spelled out varies from producer to producer, but it is an important step in the process whereby a general conception of the piece is translated into the

practical actions of the performers and the material circumstances of sets, props and the use of physical space on the stage. The producer's overall conception of the opera therefore provides a backdrop of expectancies and reference-points. Its realization depends on the detailed negotiation of action, gesture and movement in the rehearsal studio.

The ethnographic observer, therefore, is attentive to the dialogue of words, music and gesture through which the various participants negotiate the staged realization of the opera. The minutiae through which the work is embodied and accomplished are the stuff of performance ethnography. Indeed, the sociological or anthropological observer acts like a kind of meta-ethnographer, for the producer, staff producer and others are themselves engaged in a kind of practical ethnography. They too are preoccupied with the close observation and interpretation of everyday gesture and action. Indeed, one can draw a very specific parallel here. The polymath and opera producer Jonathan Miller (with whom I have spoken briefly about this, although I have never observed him at work) is quite explicit about the 'anthropological' influences on his work in opera. He cites Erving Goffman, whose fine-grained reflections on the mundane rituals of selfhood and the gestures of the encounter provide a reference-point for naturalistic mimesis. There is a certain irony here, of course. Goffman derived his own accounts of everyday life from the dramaturgical metaphor.

Miller's particular use of Goffman aside, there is a more general sense in which the operatic producer (like any other director) is a practical ethnographer. He or she is engaged in the close observation and interpretation of gesture and action. They interpret the principals' actions for themselves and for others. There is, as I have said, a repeated dialogue of gesture and speech between producer and stage. The production staff, moreover, record the action – perhaps not quite as ethnographers might try to, but certainly as practical authors of records of actions. For while the producer and the performers negotiate and sediment the rehearsed, repeated performance, placement and movement are recorded in textual formats by the staff producer. Among her or his other tasks is the creation of the recording book. Production staff have a bound copy of the score, photocopied so that each page of score is faced by a blank folio. The action can thus be recorded in rough outline on the blank sheet, cued and coordinated with the music.

The actions of the performers are frequently 'directed' through two mechanisms: through vocabularies of motive, and through significant gestures. Both of these are themselves part of the stock-in-trade of sociological ethnographers, most notably those steeped in the interactionist sociological traditions. There is, indeed, a reflexive relationship between the work of sociological interpretation and the work of theatrical/operatic direction. Again, these elements of action in opera must be co-coordinated not merely with the overall trajectory of narrative and action on stage, but also with the music. Action in opera does not take place naturalistically in accordance with the real time of interpersonal action, but in accordance with musical time. In contrast to the temporal unfolding of spoken action – for instance as singers walk through a particular scene – operatic action develops through an interaction between narrative and music. The time available, say, to make an entrance, to cross the stage, to 'notice' another performer or to react to another's actions is dictated by the musical structure of the scene. This does not mean that the singers act 'in time to' the music, as if they were engaged in dance or mime; but it does mean that the music places particular constraints on the temporal unfolding of action. The specific ways in which these doings are managed and negotiated differs from one director to another, and it goes beyond the scope of this chapter to discuss these differences in detail. One should note, however, that some directors pay much more attention to what one might gloss as the 'external' appearances of the performance – performers' relative positions, movements within the performing space, stage 'business' with props – while others make much more play of the 'inner' development of characters and the emergence of action from characters' intentions and biographies.

The organization of action often derives from the *attribution of motives*. Sociologists have in the past drawn attention to the problematic nature of motive in interpreting action. C. Wright Mills's classic paper on the subject, for instance, suggests that for the interpretation of everyday practical action, 'motive' is not a psychological state or predisposition, but rather a culturally available and socially shared frame of reference that may be used to render a particular action comprehensible to other (Mills, 1940). What Mills called 'vocabularies of motive' are therefore registers of interpretative frames, used to make sense of actors' practical actions. In the theatre, there is a parallel conceptual task. Much of the action – and the spoken or sung words – are prescribed in the text of a play or an opera. Many aspects of the action are also prescribed, even if they are not at the level of individual movements, gestures, glances and so on. The

practical problem for the performer and the director is, therefore, to try to determine 'Why is this character saying and doing this?', 'What is the character trying to achieve?', or 'What does this tell us about the character's personality, psychological state, or emotions at this particular point?' There is, therefore, a continuous process of attributing motives, not to other performers, but to the fictional characters who inhabit the opera.

The identification of motives or 'intentions' has been a fundamental aspect of theatrical rehearsal and performance in the Western naturalistic tradition. In terms of formal dramaturgical theory it is especially associated with the tradition established by Stanislavski – who directed opera as well as 'straight' theatre in Russia – and whose reflections on the creation of a role remain among the key texts of practical dramaturgical thought (Stanislavski, 1967; Stanislavski and Rumyantsev, 1998). Stanislavski's approach – too readily vulgarized into a rigid system – depended upon an insistence on the concrete. In directing opera, for instance, he urged his singers not to adopt generalized approaches to their characters, but to identify the most specific and concrete of experiences, memories or associations. The actor (singing or not) should thus have a very specific intention at any particular point in the unfolding action or sung number. A director does not have to subscribe to the Stanislavski approach in order to try to find appropriate motives and images to transform material from text to action. One can learn the notes and then the musical interpretation, one can learn the words, and can know the narrative of an opera. But that is not the same as finding an intention and appropriate action at any particular point in the work. The performer needs to establish the appropriate intentional and emotional registers. Equally, the performer cannot merely find her or his own idiosyncratic construction of character or motive. They must be co-coordinated and negotiated with the other performers. Characters' motives and feelings ought to interact, and ought to be congruent with the overall conception of the emplotment of the drama. Some opera producers are deeply committed and immersed in the Stanislavski-inspired tradition, stressing the interior and anterior life of the character, while others are more concerned with the external features of gesture and action. A director from the 'straight' theatre who also produced opera – such as Katie Mitchell who has directed the WNO's *Jenufa* and *Katya Kabanova* – is more likely to stress the biographical and motivational aspects of character. (The latter two works are both by Janáček – a composer whose works have occupied a central place in WNO's repertoire over the years – and have been treated to new productions in recent years.) A more thoroughly 'operatic' director – such as David Pountney, Richard Jones or David Alden – is more likely to stress the 'theatrical' aspects of staging. In the former case, Mitchell would have the opera cast spend the first period of rehearsal doing nothing to music, just exploring the characters, drawing a map of the village where the action is set, constructing a shared history of events that took place long before the action of the opera itself, and creating a rounded biography for each of the characters. While Richard Jones certainly encouraged the male principals to practise playing cards together during rehearsals for Tchaikovsky's *Queen of Spades* – given that the ethos of fate and chance is pervasive while the rules of a particular card game are crucial to the opera – and certainly explored the psychology of the opera's narrative, his everyday directorial work was more focused on the staging of the opera, of realizing his overriding (and far from naturalistic) gothic vision of the piece, 'making pictures' in set-piece scenes, and choreographing the performers' relative positions and movements. Whatever the orientations and methods adopted, however, each director is confronted with essentially similar problems in opera productions.

The process of preparing a role – before rehearsals start, and crucially in the course of the rehearsal period – is, therefore, a matter of constructing and jointly negotiating appropriate characters and motivational frames. It is one of the most important features of the director's work in the rehearsal studio that she or he should help performers to 'find' the intentions. 'Finding' is indeed a recurrent trope that is used by directors. 'Can you find a way to … ?' they ask performers; 'We need to find a way to …' they sometimes say in the course of rehearsal. Consequently, the director is engaged in a recurrent process of attributing motives to characters, suggesting intentions to the performers and searching for analogies whereby to help create the characters and actions. 'Finding' is also a process of more practical activity as well: finding ways to do things convincingly, visibly and within the temporal order of the music and the co-coordinated behaviour of other performers.

This can involve the invocation of all sorts of frames of reference, depending on the director's own personal cultural framings. During the rehearsal period for *Queen of Spades*, for instance, Richard Jones was gripped by the nightly television 'real-life' drama of *Big Brother*. As well as it providing a topic of everyday chatter with other members of the production and stage-management staff, it also provided the occasional frame of reference for the producer to propose psychological or emotional states for characters. In other contexts, 'finding' intentions means a close scrutiny of the text. Libretti are full of words, and those words can be used to key singers' intentions. This may sound entirely obvious, but in practice it is less so. Unless directed to do so, singers do not necessarily take account of the dramatic and psychological possibilities of the detail of words and music. There is always the possibility of entering into a generalized emotional frame rather than engaging directly with the text and with its interpretation. Now there are many contexts in opera where principals do indeed perform 'big numbers' (or indeed entire performances) with little or no reference to the specific dramatic and psychological context. It is not a feature of WNO and its productions, but there are many professional settings where 'star' principals perform their standard version of a part, with little or no account taken of the particular production, set or other performers. In some major houses, star names are flown in with very little rehearsal time. In such contexts, there is little or no opportunity – let alone inclination – for principals to engage in detailed explorations of character and intention. They merely try not to collide with the set, the chorus or their fellow principals. At its worst, such a style of production results in principals doing nothing more than moving rather aimlessly on stage, pausing to deliver their big arias or duets, leaning against convenient features of the stage, and yielding the most broadly generalized of interpretations. Luckily, that is not the style of production that is practised by WNO, which does not operate a 'star' system, and in which even revivals of well-established productions are thoroughly rehearsed and re-created.

FIELDWORK AND PERFORMANCE

Understanding and documenting these processes of cultural production requires ethnographic fieldwork. I have already suggested some parallels between the work of the ethnographer and the work of two actors in the setting – the repetiteur and the director. Both analogies reflect back on the role of the ethnographer. It is important to recognize the slow, unfolding and repetitive nature of the collective action that goes into the rehearsal and performance cycle. One does not appreciate this from the hastily grabbed journalistic impression. The heavily compressed and edited versions of 'behind the scenes' documentaries, such as the TV series *The House* that went backstage at the crisis-hit Royal Opera House, can often create quite false impressions. They highlight the inherently 'dramatic' and emotional episodes, the panics and problems, the failures and the last-minute rescue acts. Of course, such events happen. It would be all too easy to construct a picture of the opera company that focused on those kinds of emotionally heightened and hectic episodes. I could have written a vivid – and more amusing – account that also dwelt primarily on such occasions at the WNO. I could have emphasized the moment when I was watching a performance of Mozart's *La Clemenza di Tito*. The curtain was about to go up for the second half of the evening when Katarina Karnéus – singing Annio, a *travesti* role – rushed back towards me, saying she's forgotten to take on the sword (a problem for a would-be assassin of the emperor) just as Sir Charles Mackerras raised his baton and the curtain indeed went up. I could have lingered on the gallows humour that accompanied the leading tenor's step backwards, off the stage and into the orchestra pit in a theatre rehearsal of *Queen of Spades*. This could have been a double blow for the production, which was not without its practical problems in the rehearsal period, as he was a late replacement for the first choice of tenor who withdrew several weeks into rehearsal. I could elaborate on the spectacular row that took place between a very distinguished international director, the staff producer and the stage management over the health and safety implications of one especially dramatic on-stage death. There are always things that go wrong. 'Never work with children, animals or hydraulics', I was warned. Elaborate stage machinery will often contrive to go wrong: bits of the scene will get stuck instead of going up and down in suitably magical ways. Even if they're not hydraulic, walls can get stuck. Candles and other lights can refuse to go on, or to flicker in the required way. Fires do not light when they should. Doors can always get stuck, or refuse to stay closed. Firearms do not always go off. All of these are the stuff of anecdote and represent the fraught or amusing side of everyday life in the theatre. But they are not the routine stuff of everyday work.

More representative is the day when the chorus have trooped on and off the set of *La Clemenza di Tito*. For the umpteenth time Iannis Kokkos, the producer, wants them to repeat a chorus. There seems no very pressing reason why the scene should be repeated, and he seems to be making but minor changes each time they repeat it. It is towards the end of a long day in the

rehearsal studio. I do not feel that I am learning much more now, and the rehearsal period is nearly over. So I put away my notebook, and make as if to leave the rehearsal studio. I mutter something about needing to pop into the University (which is always a good reason to be elsewhere, whatever fieldwork one is trying to conduct). At this point one of the stage-management staff holds my arm 'We are all bored to tears', she whispers to me, 'and you are going to stay here and watch us being bored!' I did. And while I really cannot pretend that attending rehearsals in the opera company (and other things I have not even mentioned in this chapter) was ever a hardship, it certainly wasn't 'going to the opera' as a treat all the time. Indeed, for the participants and for me, rehearsal and performance are mundane *work*. It can be dull, and is certainly repetitive. A lot of time is spent waiting. A characteristic scene is a group of early-nineteenth-century naval officers (*Billy Budd*) in full uniform sitting around in the bar of the New Theatre in Cardiff playing cards and chatting, and never being called actually to go on stage, because the rehearsal never reaches a scene in which they are required.

Fieldwork is also about trying to capture the intricate details of performance. Carmen is taunting Don José. She is dancing seductively. It is a stage rehearsal. She keeps having to do it again and again. She accompanies herself with 'castanets' made from fragments of a broken plate. She has to keep dashing the plate to the floor and picking up the pieces. She sways over Don José who is lying on the stage. As she dances she slowly and seductively lowers herself over his body. But by dancing slowly and slowly moving her body, she keeps singing too slowly too and falling behind the conductor's beat. She does it over several times, with conductor reminding her 'Don't slow down'. The ethnography of performance needs to capture the work that goes into rehearsing and performing even the most fleeting of occasions such as this. (It also helps to know that the plates should break predictably and safely into conveniently sized pieces because they have been made specially for the purpose by the props department.) In *Peter Grimes*, Grimes himself has to keep practising hauling his boat up the beach. The producer (Peter Stein) wants the boat to be aligned in a very specific way, but the rope and the windlass that helps to pull it up pulls it into a different alignment. They keep doing it over and over again. Stein himself keeps running energetically on to the stage to pull and tug at the boat (which, like the other boats in the production, has been specially built by an East

Anglian boat-builder, although it is lighter than the real thing). At the same time Bulstrode helps Grimes to haul the boat ashore, taking a turn at the capstan. He has to coordinate his movements, pushing towards the audience, and then turning and putting his back into it so that he goes on facing the audience, taking care to step over the taut rope that stretches across the stage between the capstan and the boat. The synchronization of music and action, ensuring that the singer faces out, the combination of naturalism (he really does put effort into heaving on the capstan) with the demands of singing – these are among the fine-grained phenomena wherein action is located in temporal, physical, musical and spatial frames.

Ethnographic fieldwork of the performing arts, then, is about the capacity of the observer to comprehend these performative and interpretative frames. The ethnographer does not have to be an expert in the musicology of opera, nor does one have to be the equivalent of a company's dramaturge (an in-house expert who can research historical and cultural background, visual references, literary sources and other materials), and one does not have to have professional expertise as a director. One's aim is not to usurp or compete with those who are professional experts. Likewise, one is not an amateur critic. The aesthetics of opera and other performing arts are important. But the ethnographer is interested in the local aesthetics that inform the production and the performance and that are the stuff of local reputations and recollections. Unlike the professional critic, the ethnographer is not seeking to evaluate the production or the performance in a more general sense. (Critics of course usually make no mention at all of features of the production that have been laboured over for weeks in the rehearsal room.) On the other hand, the ethnographer cannot perform adequately as a complete outsider. The principle of methodological relativism has sometimes been – quite erroneously – interpreted to imply that anthropological or sociological field researchers approach 'the field' in a state of ignorance or naïvety. This is not true in practice, and total indifference or ignorance would render most fieldwork unsustainable and intolerable. In the case of opera, one cannot make sense of what is going on without a fairly thorough engagement with the genre and its conventions. One cannot in practice spend hours and hours a day, weeks on end, observing and listening to repeated performances of the same scenes, over and over again, if one is completely indifferent on a personal level. Indeed, I find quite the opposite. If I am to make any sense at all of what goes on in the rehearsal studio, the theatre or elsewhere, then I have to have a decent acquaintance with the work being performed. At least this means listening to recordings, reading the libretto, doing background reading and so on. I need to prepare to a much lesser extent than the professionals, but I do prepare in a similar way. I also become intellectually and emotionally engaged with the production itself. You do not have to fall in love with the opera as a work of art in order to care for the production that has taken shape over weeks of painstaking work. Indeed, you do not have to be completely persuaded by the producer's vision of the piece, or its realization in performance, in order to hope that it will 'work' successfully. Within the rehearsal studio and in the theatre, the contrived reality of the staged performance can become the paramount reality for the time being. What matters more than anything else is to get recalcitrant stage machinery or complicated stage business to work, to get the chorus on and off without anyone bumping into the sets or each other, to have a leading lady climb a wall and sing at the same time, to have the tenor crawl across the top of the set and not lose his balance. For the moment, dramaturgical work creates a world of work in which a staged reality is accomplished through the shared work of performers and others. The ethnography of performance documents and embodies the practical action that goes into such collective work. The ethnography documents how aesthetic and dramaturgical judgements are translated into practical behaviour on stage. It shows how the motivational systems of everyday life are invoked in order to make plausible dramaturgical enactments. Above all, the ethnographer engages with the temporary but engrossing social world that is created when performers and others come together to create lasting impressions from ephemeral creations.

ACKNOWLEDGEMENTS

The research on which this chapter is based was supported by a research grant from the Leverhulme Foundation. It was begun during a period of paid research leave from Cardiff University. I am deeply grateful to all members of the Welsh National Opera Company for their support and – above all – their patience while various other projects and obligations have prolonged the completion of the fieldwork and the preparation of publications from my engagement with them.

REFERENCES

Becker, Howard S. (1951) 'The professional dance musician and his audience', *American Journal of Sociology*, 57: 136–44.

Becker, Howard S. (1982) *Art Worlds*. Berkeley: University of California Press.

Born, Georgina (1995) *Rationalizing Culture: IRCAM, Boulez and the Institutionalization of the Avant-Garde*. Berkeley: University of California Press.

Buckland, Theresa J. (ed.) (1999) *Dance in the Field: Theory, Methods and Issues in Dance Ethnography*. London: Macmillan.

Burns, Elizabeth (1972) *Theatricality: A Study of Convention in the Theatre and in Social Life*. New York: Harper & Row.

Charlton, Joy and Hertz, Rosanna (1989) 'Guarding against boredom: security specialists in the US Air Force', *Journal of Contemporary Ethnography* 18: 299–326.

Delamont, Sara (2002) *Fieldwork in Educational Settings: Methods, Pitfalls and Perspectives* (2nd ed.). London: Routledge-Falmer.

De Marinis, M. (1982) *Semiotic del Teatro: L'Analisis testuale dello Spettacolo*. Milan: Bompiani.

DeNora, Tia (2000) *Music in Everyday Life*. Cambridge: Cambridge University Press.

Duvignaud, Jean (1963) *Sociologie du Théâtre*. Paris: Presses Universitaires de France.

Duvignaud, Jean (1965) *L'Acteur*. Paris: Presses Universitaires de France.

Faulkner, Robert (1983) *Music on Demand*. New Brunswick, NJ: Transaction Books.

Goffman, Erving (1959) *The Presentation of Self in Everyday Life*. Garden City, NY: Doubleday.

Goffman, Erving (1974) *Frame Analysis: An Essay on the Organization of Experience*. Boston: Northeastern University Press.

Gurvitch, Georges (1956) 'Sociologie du théâtre', *Les Lettres Nouvelles*, 35: 202–4.

Hall, Thomas (2000) 'At home with the young homeless', *International Journal of Social Research Methodology*, 3: 121–33.

Hastrup, Kirsten (1998) 'Theatre as a site of passage: some reflections on the magic of acting', in F. Hughes-Freeland (ed.), *Ritual, Performance, Media*. London: Routledge, pp. 28–45.

Hughes-Freeland, Felicia (ed.) (1998) *Ritual, Performance, Media*. London: Routledge.

Jones, Stacy Holman (1998) *Kaleidoscope Notes: Writing Women's Music and Organizational Culture*. Walnut Creek, CA: AltaMira Press.

Kingsbury, Henry (1988) *Music, Talent and Performance: A Conservatory Cultural System*. Philadelphia: Temple University Press.

Mills, C. Wright (1940) 'Situated actions and vocabularies of motive', *American Sociological Review*, 3: 439–52.

Schieffelin, Edward L. (1998) 'Problematizing performance', in F. Hughes-Freeland (ed.), *Ritual, Performance, Media*. London: Routledge, pp. 194–207.

Schutz, Alfred (1967) *The Phenomenology of the Social world*. Evanston, IL: Northwestern University Press.

Stanislavski, Constantin. (1967) *On the Art of the Stage*. London: Faber & Faber.

Stanislavski, Constantin and Rumyantsev, Pavel (1998) *Stanislavski on Opera*. London: Routledge.

Tota, Anna Lisa (1997) *Etnografia dell'Arte*. Rome: Logica University Press.

Tulloch, John (1999) *Performing Culture: Stories of Expertise and the Everyday*. London: Sage.

Wellin, Christopher and Fine, Gary Alan (2001) 'Ethnography as work: career socialization, settings and problems', in Paul Atkinson, Amanda Coffey, Sara Delamont, John Lofland and Lyn Lofland (eds), *Handbook of Ethnography*. London: Sage, pp. 323–38

Wulff, Helena (1998a) 'Perspectives towards ballet performance: exploring, repairing and maintaining frames', in F. Hughes-Freeland (ed.), *Ritual, Performance, Media*. London: Routledge, pp. 104–20.

Wulff, Helena (1998b) *Ballet Across Borders*. Oxford: Berg.

Wulff, Helena (2000) 'Access to a closed world: methods for a multilocale study on ballet as a career', in Vered Amit (ed.), *Constructing the Field: Ethnographic Fieldwork in the Contemporary World*. London: Routledge, pp. 147–61.

Part 2

ANALYTIC FRAMEWORKS

The chapters in Part 1 of this book focused on method and merely hinted at the theoretical issues involved in adopting and using different methods. In Part 2, our authors explicitly topicalize theoretical choices in research (and their consequences).

For much of the history of qualitative research, 'theory' has been something of a dirty word. For many early ethnographers, theory was a phenomenon that obsessed social scientists who sat on armchairs in libraries. By contrast, qualitative researchers were instructed to get out of the university and into 'the field'. Here they would simply 'hang out' with the apparently atheoretical remit of faithfully representing subjects' worlds.

Many fine empirical works were generated by this 'naturalistic' thrust. Indeed, naturalism continues to have a strong and justified appeal to many contemporary ethnographers (for an example, see Emerson, Chapter 29, this volume). However, it is now clear to everybody that naturalism does not witness the triumph of research over theory but is just one of many analytic frameworks (see Gubrium and Holstein, 1997). For, without some analytic orientation, one would not recognize the 'field' one was studying, let alone be able to formulate a research problem therein.

So, as philosophers of science have long recognized, theory is the essential background to research. Research cannot be presuppositionless. Without some analytic position there would be no 'facts' to study.

In recent years, however, it is arguable that theory has taken too large a place in our thoughts. Denzin and Lincoln's (2000) influential account of the history of qualitative research seems to have had the unfortunate consequence of making many of us spend too much time choosing the 'moment' into which our current research might properly fit (see Alasuutari, Chapter 38, this volume). Two regrettable off-shoots of this phenomenon may be noted. First, the authors of even the most pedestrian research paper usually now feel that they need to dignify their work by claiming one or another theoretical orientation. Where nothing else comes to mind, theoretical labels are often chosen that bear little relation to the research described. For instance, 'phenomenology' is often the default option used to describe pretty plodding, descriptive research, but there is little indication that the authors have the vaguest idea of what Husserl meant by the term (or of the objections to simply importing a complex philosophical label to very different territory). In such cases, 'theory' can degenerate into mere window-dressing, serving to erect an aura of respectability around a set of rather shoddy wares.

A second consequence of this privileging of theory is seen in the contemporary appeal of the label 'postmodern'. Sometimes this label is used to justify slapdash research in which the maxim 'anything goes' is used not as a complaint but as a recommendation. Sometimes it is associated with absurd claims to originality that turn out merely (and rather poorly) to reinvent the wheel (as in the case of some haphazardly conducted uses of the VCR in 'postmodern' research). And sometimes any sense of the 'field' is lost altogether, as researchers play rather tedious games experimenting with different 'voices' from their armchairs.

As the chapters below show, it is the dialogue between theory and research that is crucial. Echoing C. Wright Mills's (1959) words across half a century, neither Grand Theory nor Abstracted Empiricism will ever cut the mustard.

Chapter 7, written by Molly Andrews, Shelley Day Sclater, Corinne Squire and Maria Tamboukou centres on the authors' 'own stories of [their] relationship with narrative research'. In each instance, we see how autobiography intersects with research material to produce insights into the meaning of researched life stories.

In its critical thrust, Celia Kitzinger's chapter on feminist approaches alerts us to potential views of the relationship between voice, experience and action. The place of essentialism in the feminist project is revisited, along with considerations of the relation of spoken experience to interview material.

In Chapter 9, Gavin Kendall and Gary Wickham show how the apparently obscure theoretical work of Michel Foucault can offer an inspiration for qualitative researchers. Using their own and others' research, they treat the Foucaultian framework as a toolbox that can help us to formulate and study new and fascinating research problems.

Chapter 10 on ethnomethodology, written by Paul ten Have, is a helpful and practical grand tour of the ethnomethodological project, from core notions to breaching experiments, membership, and the use of audio and video records. The lively examples from the author's own work show how deeply practical are members' methods in everyday life.

Conversation analysis (CA) is a key inheritor of Garfinkel's ethnomethodological mantle. In Chapter 11, Anssi Peräkylä shows what follows when we take on board CA's assumptions that talk is structurally organized action.

Using rich examples from his own studies of professional–client encounters, Peräkylä shows that CA is neither esoteric nor trivial but has clear implications for mainstream social science debates about theory, method and practice.

Discourse analysis (DA), in the hands of Alexa Hepburn and Jonathan Potter, is revealed to be a close relation to CA, preferring 'naturally occurring' data and posing similar questions about it. In Chapter 12, Hepburn and Potter use their study of calls to a child protection service to show the analytic and ethical issues that arise at every stage of the research process. As a consequence, DA is depicted as part of a work in process rather than a set of dry theoretical principles.

Finally, in Chapter 13, Ruth Wodak outlines DA's intellectual cousin, critical discourse analysis (CDA). This can be distinguished from DA primarily through the 'critical' focus such analysts bring to bear on relations of power. 'Critical theory' is thus merged with 'discourse analysis' in a research practice in that Wodak's experience investigates and brings to view otherwise hidden dimensions of inequality and domination. Crucially, this is done by socio-linguistic analysis.

The reader will, of course, not expect to find agreement between the authors of these chapters. What they will find, we believe, are glorious diversity and aids to the sluggish imagination.

REFERENCES

Denzin, N. and Lincoln, Y. (2000) *Handbook of Qualitative Research* (2nd ed.). Thousand Oaks, CA: Sage.

Gubrium, J. and Holstein, J. (1997) *The New Language of Qualitative Method*. New York: Oxford University Press.

Mills, C.W. (1959) *The Sociological Imagination*. New York: Oxford University Press.

7

Narrative research

Molly Andrews, Shelley Day Sclater, Corinne Squire and Maria Tamboukou

When we were first asked to contribute a chapter to this volume, we thought this would be a good opportunity for us to bring together our views on narrative research under one umbrella. As Co-directors of the Centre for Narrative Research, we have been involved in ongoing conversations with one another for a long time about narrative theory and method; these conversations have taken on a number of different formats, including an edited book (Andrews et al., 2000). These conversations have not, of course, been only among ourselves, but have also been stimulated by input from the wide array of people who have contributed to the activities of our centre, for instance by giving a presentation in or by attending our speakers' series and/or narrative workshops.

Perhaps it should not have surprised us that when we sat down to plan the chapter, we realized that there was not one but several different stories we wanted to tell, and that each of us had not only different areas of research, but indeed had come to narrative work through quite different paths. We considered trying to find the commonality among us, and to write from this position, but ultimately we came to feel that much would be lost through such a homogenizing process. Even embarking on an attempt to arrive at a robust shared definition of 'narrative' would, we decided, divert us from what was most interesting about the work itself. Rather, we concluded that it was not only admissible but even appropriate that a chapter on narrative in a book on research practice should be organized around our own stories of our relationship with narrative research. For, while we share a general interest in narrative work, this has found very different expression in each of our lives, as the passages below document. But be the topics of interest political engagement, divorce disputes, HIV support networks, or Foucaltian genealogies, our stories are not unconnected to each other. Indeed, we have worked so closely together over a number of years that it would be surprising if we were not present in each others' accounts. Thus, using our own stories as vehicles for exploring more general principles relating to narrative research, the chapter is organized around the themes of life stories and narrative (Andrews), narrative and subjectivity (Day Sclater), narrative genre (Squire) and auto-biographical narratives (Tamboukou).

LIVING COUNTER-NARRATIVES
(Molly Andrews)

In the Introduction to Robert Jay Lifton's deeply thoughtful and moving book about Nazi doctors, he remarks: 'My assumption from the beginning, in keeping with my twenty-five years of research, was that the best way to learn about Nazi doctors was to talk to them' (1986: 6). I have spent the last two decades talking with, and listening to, people telling me stories about their lives. Intuitively, I have always been drawn to stories that lie in tension with the ones that we are socialized to expect; only very recently have I begun to theorize these as 'counter-narratives' (Andrews, 2002a).

My doctoral dissertation was an exploration of lifetime commitment to progressive politics, and for three years I listened to many stories told to me by fifteen women and men between the ages of seventy and ninety, all of whom had been politically active on the left for fifty years or longer (Andrews, 1991). Old age, far from representing the disengagement and depression of which we so often hear, was for these men and women a very full moment in their lives, a continuation of all that they had been fighting for. In fact, I was told, increased age, far from being an excuse to focus in upon the self, had instead the advantage of perspective. Old peace activists were critical to social movements because they were less susceptible to becoming depressed through lack of immediate tangible results. Social historian Peter Laslett comments upon this:

> It could be claimed ... that many more duties of older people go forward in time than is the case in those who are young. This follows from the fact that they owe less to their own individual futures – now comparatively short – and more to the future of others – all others ... . In this the elderly of any society can be said to be the *trustees* of the future. (1989: 196)

As one of my respondents, Eileen, explains to me: 'It's the old people who keep going. I think age brings that perspective.' Trevor Huddleston echoes this sentiment. Speaking in 1987, he tells me: 'I think I've become more revolutionary every year I've lived. And certainly now, because life is so much shorter. I mean I want to get apartheid dead before I'm dead. There's no time to do that.' That he would indeed outlive apartheid, and return to South Africa as the honoured guest of Nelson Mandela, was beyond his greatest dreams. And yet it was something to which he dedicated the whole of his being, and had done so for more than five decades.

Although many of our conversations were not in storied form, some of them were. Elizabeth, for instance, was a great weaver of tales, and would often use dreams to introduce a description of an event or even of a psychological state of mind. At one point in our interviews, Elizabeth describes the mounting pressure on her, as she attempts to balance her responsibilities at home (with four children to look after) with her political commitments. She realizes that if she chooses to participate in a particular protest, she will risk being arrested, being put in prison, and thus unable to attend to her family's needs. At this critical moment, she has a dream:

> I dreamed there was a tray and my hands were underneath holding the tray and I was doing a lot, what with the family and the famine relief and one thing and another. I was doing a lot, and more and more things were piled on this tray, and I said 'Oh Lord, don't put on any more, I can't hold it'. And then I looked under the tray. It wasn't my hands that were holding it, it was sort of symbolic hands, large thick hands that you get on Henry Moore sculptures. And I knew that it wasn't

really me, that what I was doing was right, one was upheld in another dimension somehow... . It was right, and it was go ahead.

With the strength of the insights gleaned from this dream, this 'fictional story' as it were, Elizabeth decides to participate in the protest. In fact her worst fears are realized; she is arrested, and she spends three weeks in a maximum security prison. But she is mentally prepared for this possibility and is able to continue. Elizabeth uses the one story (of her dream) to frame the other; for her, they are deeply integrated into her concept of who she was and who she could become.

I learned much from those conversations, and indeed continue to learn from them. Although the conversations (taped and ultimately transcribed) remain unchanged, I revisit them from time to time, and my understanding of them has evolved as I myself have changed. For me, then, the stories continue to be reinvented as I hear them in different ways. For instance, I recently wrote an article about the stories that these same women and men told me about their mothers (Andrews, 2002b). But I was not a mother at the time when I first heard them. Now, more than fifteen years and two children later, I see in them layers that I did not, and probably could not, have seen before. And so these stories continue to have life, indeed they become new stories, long after they have first been told.

Having completed my PhD, I moved back to the United States, in August 1991, as the Gulf War erupted. Having lived overseas for nearly five years, I had for some time begun to ask myself questions of what it meant to be an American living abroad. Now I wondered what it meant to be an American living in the heart of American militarism during wartime. It was in this context that I developed a project on patriotism (Andrews, 1997b). I was prompted to do so not only by the general context of the war, but by the sight of an American flag that adorned the anti-war 24–7 vigil in downtown Colorado Springs, the most militarized place in the United States and where I was then living. I was curious what this flag meant to those who had planted it there. But American flags were everywhere in Colorado Springs, not only at the peace vigil. What different meanings did this image carry for the many who displayed it?

I interviewed a number of people with contrasting views on the war, most of whom had used the American flag as part of a means for expressing their feelings about the US military involvement. One particular event, 'One Hour for America', featured in many of the accounts that I heard. This event had been organized by some of the residents of Colorado Springs to show support for the war, and had raised a considerable sum of money for families of troops who lived locally. The event, described by Hal, one of the key organizers, was intended as 'a show of patriotism and Americanism' and 'a euphoria of those of us who have served in the military'. The event was held in the downtown area of the city, and attracted thousands. Everywhere one could see, there were American flags, large and small. Some people even had dressed as Old Glory, others as Uncle Sam. Hal describes the 'huge flags, fifty feet by fifty feet, hanging off of the buildings ... what that means to you is freedom.... There's no symbol as strong as that American flag.' He himself 'took three flags down [to the event]. I had them in both hands and I was just one of the crowd.'

But some of the people who had been living at the anti-war vigil decided to attend this event, and their experience of that time was radically different. Mary describes her experience of the 'Love America rally', as she terms it:

> There was so much intense hostility it was incredible ... you could just cut it with a knife ... after the rally itself was over [people] lined up and you could see that they wanted to attack us and the police were there and they were kind of forming this barricade between us and the people at the parade.... It was one of the most depressing moments I've had in a long time ... they just wanted to sing louder and wave their flags faster every time they would look at us and spit.

Despite the fact that anti-war protesters saw themselves as responsible citizens exercising their constitutional right to protest (and on those grounds exhibited the flag at their vigil), this symbol of America was used on occasion as a weapon against them. As one of the peace protesters described to me in his interview:

> There were a couple of times in which people with huge American flags tried to hit us over the head with the actual flag poles and sort of drape the flags over our heads ... there was another time when this pickup truck with some red necks stopped next to the vigil and they harassed us for a while and then they ran around us with their flag in a circle a few times.

And yet, the American flag continued to wave on the grounds of the anti-war vigil. Far from being 'unpatriotic' or 'un-American', the peace protesters saw themselves as making an essential contribution to the democratic process and, as such, doing their duty as 'good citizens'.

The third and final arena that I will use to describe my ongoing engagement with life histories and counter-narratives is that of East Germany. In 1989, many Westerners viewed the acute political upheaval in East and Central Europe as a clear and straightforward victory for capitalism over socialism. The Cold War had ended, and we had won; this seemed to be the interpretation that permeated reporting on these events in Western Europe and the United States. But I was curious how those who lived through those changes regarded what had happened. I decided to go and listen to the stories of those who had been involved in the underground citizens' movement in East Germany (see, e.g., Andrews, 1997a, 1998, 1999, 2000). Contrary to the 'monolithic, mass unquestioning celebration' (Borneman, 1991: 58) portrayed in the Western popular media, many leaders of the East German changes of 1989 experienced deep agony, realizing that they had 'helped give birth to a child that quickly turned into a rather ugly creature' (Sebastian Pflugbeil, quoted in Philipsen, 1993: 161). As autumn turned to winter, they witnessed not the realization but the end of their dreams.

Barbel Bohley, the so-called mother of the revolution, comments upon the capitalist triumphalism that followed the fall of the Berlin Wall:

> It was simply the revolt of the humiliated people. And they did not ask why they revolted, for capitalism or socialism, they were simply fed up to live with this lie.... Most certainly people did not go into the street and shout 'we want capitalism'. Deep down they wanted [to] change the system, change their living conditions ... it was not a victory for capitalism.

Once again, I was confronted with stories that challenged the received narrative in the west. Until I spent time in East Germany, I never knew that in the forty years of the existence of GDR, more than one million people immigrated to East Germany. Instead, one hears only of those who were killed by border guards in their desperate attempts to flee communism. Neither did I know about those East German political dissidents who were involuntarily exiled from their country, forced to spend time very much against their desires in some of the great cities of Western Europe. One such story came to me from Werner Fischer, one of the key leading dissidents of East Germany. It was amusing but also strange to listen to his tale of his months living in London. 'I spent days in bed in London, so that time would pass quicker ... in London, one can study pure capitalism.... I realized that if there is to be a change then it must be within the eastern bloc, there must not be a transition to that system.' Living in the West for six months brought home to Fischer what instinctively he already knew:

> ... I only realized ... when I was in England that my roots were here [in the GDR], that I had become firmly

rooted to this soil, here was the friction that sparked controversy. I did not want to see the GDR disappear. This is how many opposition members express it today: 'better to have a stormy relationship than none at all'.

Fischer tells a revealing story that occurred during his time in London. Describing his relationship with his Stasi interrogator, he tells me:

> ... in a way I quite liked him. In fact, they [the Stasi] chose the interrogators for every opposition member very carefully. They knew our profiles and to whom we would respond ... when I was in custody, he knew everything about me, whilst I knew nothing about him. I could assess him by his appearance; I would notice that he had been to the barber, or that he was married. He had a wedding ring, and he loved wearing a new tie every day. So much so, that when I was in London, I found myself browsing through Harrods' tie department and choosing a tie for him.

The image of Fischer – the man who later would be responsible for overseeing the disbanding of the Stasi – going about in Harrod's, a symbol of capitalist opulence if ever there was one, mentally selecting a tie for his Stasi interrogator, speaks volumes. Here one can experience 'up close' the power of stories, for what Fischer conveys is not only revealing about himself, and his interrogator, and the relationship between them; through this seemingly innocuous detail, one gets a sense of how long the arms of the Stasi really were, and why, even now more than a decade after its abolition, its spirit still haunts the land.

Another image that has stayed with me from my many conversations in East Germany was that told me by Wolfgang Templin, the man once identified by Honecker as 'the number one enemy of the state'. He, like Fischer and Bohley, had been exiled from East Germany, but unlike them, he went to West Germany, where he was still living in 1989. I ask him what he did on the night the Berlin Wall fell. He responds with great warmth: finally, after nearly two years away, he was allowed to come home. Fighting against the crowds pouring into the West, Templin made his way back into East Germany:

> ... the fall of the Wall for me meant that I could go back into the GDR rather than get out of it. And purely physically I experienced this – everybody pushing past me in the opposite direction and me pushing against the stream the other way. I was overjoyed and it was in that mood that I re-entered the GDR... . Two, three weeks later ... my family moved back here.

9 November 1989. The fall of the Berlin Wall. Celebrations, champagne, jubilation. Finally able to return to one's own country. Finally able to return to East Germany. The quintessential counter-narrative.

I do believe that, indeed, we are storied selves (Sarbin, 1986; Bruner, 1990; Rosenwald and Ochberg 1992; McAdams, 1997; Eakin, 1999); that there is a close relationship between the stories we tell and hear and who we are; and that our stories are the cornerstone of our identities (Widdershoven, 1993; Holstein and Gubrium, 1999). But I also think that this is no simple matter, as Shelley Day Sclater discusses below. Critically, our stories are not and can never be wholly personal. Rather, we perceive reality in terms of stories, and ultimately how we construct, interpret, digest and recount for others our own experiences bears a strong relationship to the story-lines that are already 'out there'. As a researcher, what has fascinated me most are those situations in which people fashion stories that challenge – either implicitly or explicitly – those master tales, revealing alternative versions of how those stories we know best might be retold.

NARRATIVE AND SUBJECTVITY
(Shelley Day Sclater)

I spent many years of my life writing stories on behalf of other people. I was a family lawyer – dealing mostly with divorce, 'domestic violence' and 'child care' cases – before I changed focus and came to academia in 1993. Part of my job was to listen to people's stories and write them down – translating them into legal language, emphasizing the parts law wanted to hear, and minimizing (or deleting) the rest. Any lawyer will tell you that making out a good case for a client is a fine art. Legal documents and submissions must include only material that is legally relevant. But, at the same time, the best evidence takes the form of persuasive stories that engage the reader, elicit sympathy and establish the moral rightness of the client's case, while appearing to do nothing other than dispassionately report the 'facts' (see, e.g., Jackson, 1990).

Doing the legal bit was easy enough, once you had some practice, and writing a persuasive tale soon became second nature. What was more difficult – and didn't get much easier as the years went by – was persuading the client that sometimes the issues the client felt to be of vital importance had to be omitted. I discovered that people were wedded, often very deeply so, to their personal narratives and that it was sometimes impossible to prise apart the person from their story, even when judges made it perfectly clear that such-and-such was of no concern to them. This gulf proved to be a major source of stress for many people. It seemed that people needed to tell their stories and, more importantly, they needed to be heard – to have their feelings, and themselves, recognized. And they felt deeply wounded when the law simply refused to participate in any such validation process.

It seemed that people habitually made deep emotional investments in their personal narratives, particularly when their lives had been disrupted by something like divorce. I saw people struggling to cope with various forms of 'family breakdown'. In their stories they attempted to piece together the fragments of their lives and to make sense of what had happened. Those stories were often of desperation, for there were precious few positive cultural scripts available when it came to speaking about divorce. I saw also how little space there was in the legal process for acknowledging feelings of hurt, anger and grief – there was certainly no place at all for recrimination and destructiveness – but as a psychologist I knew that those feelings would not just disappear. I wondered about the role of law in relation to people's coping: in denying these messy feelings, was the legal process helping or was it hindering?

Not long before I left legal practice, interest in 'alternative' forms of dispute resolution crystallized in the UK, and there were attempts to instate mediation as the preferred procedure. My initial reaction was one of interest – here, I thought, was a forum in which feelings could be acknowledged, and stories told and heard; surely everyone would benefit. I did a mediation training course and my illusions were quickly shattered. I discovered that mediation was, fundamentally, about changing people's stories – 'reframing', the process is called. I found it deeply patronizing. And it was 'management' – one of the 'technologies of the self' that Maria Tamboukou, drawing on Foucault's work, talks about – that relied too heavily for my liking on accepted wisdom. The dominant discourses were being offered as templates for the construction of acceptable divorce stories. I began to see mediation as a dangerous proliferation of half-baked psychology being put in the service of social control and Treasury savings.

When I left legal practice and began life as an academic, it seemed natural to pursue research into divorce. A grant from the ESRC enabled me to study people's experiences of different forms of dispute resolution. Part of my mission was to develop a new methodology for divorce work that could take account of psychological dynamics as well as social structures and cultural processes. It was during the long search for such a 'psychosocial' methodology that I encountered 'narrative' in the social sciences – first in the

form of Elliot Mishler's seminal book on research interviewing (Mishler, 1986) and then, quite by chance, Catherine Riessman's little book on 'narrative analysis' (Riessman, 1993). Mark Freeman's *Rewriting the Self* (Freeman, 1993) and Jerome Bruner's *Acts of Meaning* (Bruner, 1990) were two other texts that were particularly significant on my journey as they raised the issue of the 'turn to narrative' as a socio-historical formation. New to academia, it was a relief to find others grappling with the same kinds of preoccupations.

I began my divorce work with a small pilot study in 1995 and wrote it up in several publications (Day Sclater, 1995, 1997, 1998a, 2000). In this early work I was clumsily feeling my way, trying to find the best means to get people to talk at length, always coming up against my own (lawyerish) tendency to ask too many questions, interrupt, guide the direction of talk, take sides, and so on. It was a painful learning process for me; good lawyers don't necessarily make good research interviewers, I soon discovered. By the time I came to look in detail at the 'data' I had collected, vast numbers of questions were lining up in my 'research log'. I was awestruck by the sheer volume of the material I had – and I hardly knew how to begin to 'analyse' it. There was no recipe book for narrative data analysis. But when I started looking at the transcripts, like Riessman (1990), I became interested in the patterns of the narratives that people were telling – 'survivor' stories, mostly – and the kinds of 'selves' that were being claimed in those stories. As I was interested in psychological processes in divorce, I wanted to find ways to focus more specifically on issues of self and identity in personal narratives.

I began 'reading' the personal narratives for the identity claims in the stories. What was immediately striking was the way in which the stories seemed to speak a coherent identity that the subject had had to put together again after the trauma of separation or divorce. Hopper (2001) makes a similar point; selves are foremost among the issues that are contested and negotiated in divorce proceedings. A closer reading of the divorce stories I collected revealed, not coherence and continuity of self, but Humpty-Dumpty-like fragments and partialities – sometimes inconsistent, contradictory even. The appearance of unity and coherence came from the narrative – or, in other words, the autobiographical genre provided a template for a continuing life and a coherent sense of self. What I was seeing were the narratives and 'counter-narratives' in life history work that Molly Andrews describes.

Interestingly, too, the 'personal' narratives were not only 'personal'. Not only did the stories draw on cultural scripts and the kinds of 'genres' that Corinne Squire talks about, but they were also organized around discourses that participants invoked and used for their own ends. Moreover, these stories, and the identities that participants constructed in those stories, took shape in an intersubjective space – in interaction with me as researcher, interviewer and, crucially, as other human subject. In the stories, too, selves were almost invariably fashioned in relation (usually in opposition) to the former partner – the anti-hero in the stories.

My background in psychology and psychoanalysis, and my own experiences on the couch, predisposed me to think psychodynamically about narratives and selves. Much later, this orientation was to make me suspicious about what I recently heard the biographer Victoria Glendinning refer to as the 'lies and silences' of biography, and make me wary of being seduced by narrative (see, e.g., the edited collection by Rhiel and Suchoff, 1996, and Young-Bruehl, 1998). Phillips (1999) also reminds us that Freud was distrustful of biography. For Freud, in telling one story of one's life, we simultaneously avoid telling any number of other stories, involving ourselves in denials, repressions and displacements. I am acutely conscious of these limitations as I tell my own story here. But at the time I was more curious than critical. It seemed a commonplace that selves were constructed in stories (even 'by' stories), but I wanted to know why and how that should be. I found it very helpful at that stage to theorize the storied construction of self using Winnicott's idea of 'potential' space (Day Sclater, 1998b). Stories, I argued, were of the order of 'transitional phenomena' – neither wholly objective, nor wholly subjective – they were creative spaces in which, as in infancy, selves could take shape again and again. I subsequently developed this work with Candida Yates and we explored the idea that narratives, circulating in culture, and taking particular forms, can be either facilitating or constraining for human potential and creativity (see Yates and Day Sclater, 2000).

Thus began my preoccupation with the relationship between narrative and the self, and the problem of how specifically 'psychological' knowledge may be derived from personal narrative accounts. This issue was central in my ESRC-funded project on the Psychology of Divorce Dispute Resolution. This work was written up in several publications (see, e.g., Brown and Day Sclater, 1999; Day Sclater, 1998c, 1999a, 1999b; Day Sclater and Yates, 1999).

Personal narratives were collected during long, unstructured conversations that were modelled on 'life history' work. Psychological well-being was also assessed quantitatively using the General Health Questionnaire (GHQ). What was striking was a distinct lack of fit between the quantitative and the qualitative data we collected; the GHQ indicated deep and enduring psychological distress, but the narratives gave a much more nuanced picture.

Most stories were 'survivor' stories. The majority spoke of the positive rebuilding of lives and selves shattered by divorce, evincing a determination to survive and a growing strength to meet the challenge. These stories challenged prevailing dominant 'divorce as disaster' images. But what was interesting was that these optimistic narratives could co-exist with others that were much less certain and more ambiguous, evincing an ambivalence that I came to see as characteristic of the divorce process. Comparison of the qualitative and the quantitative data helped me to understand divorce as a multilayered process in which the subject marshalled personal, relational and cultural resources to make sense of a past that had become other than it had been before, and to forge a new sense of self. Narrative reconstructions play a central part in that process, as past, present and future are all transformed. Comparison of the two types of data was also an object lesson in the different readings one can make of any 'data'.

A nagging problem was how to derive some specifically 'psychological' data from the narratives. Here we were treading on unfamiliar ground. At about the same time, Wendy Hollway and Tony Jefferson were grappling with a similar problem in their study of fear of crime. Their solution (see Hollway and Jefferson, 2000) was to posit a 'defended' subject and to conduct interviews according to principles of 'free association' such that data analysis then revealed aspects of biographical experience framed in the language of psychoanalysis. Michele Crossley (2000) tackled a similar problem in a different way. She wanted to salvage something of psychology's 'individual' from what she saw as the ravages of postmodern thinking, and she wanted to locate that individual firmly as a 'narrative' subject. Her formulation of a 'narrative psychology' took its place firmly within a social constructionist tradition.

For me, however, these kinds of 'solutions' raised more questions than they answered and more problems than they solved. I began to think that, if there is such a thing as a purely psychological realm of experience, then it was full of tensions, provisos, ambiguities and even contradictions – it was just not possible to 'read off' anything to do with psychology from the narrative interviews. It was tempting to immerse myself in semiotic theory to try to work it out (see, e.g., Silverman, 1983), but the kind of tools I was looking for were not to be found there either. Later I was to come seriously to question whether there was such a thing as a psychological realm of experience, as distinct from the psychological (or social constructionist, or psychoanalytic) discourse we use to think about it.

But I knew that my work could have policy implications and, for that reason, I persisted with the 'psychological' aspect of the analysis. I returned to an old interest – Althusser's idea of 'interpellation' whereby subjects were 'hailed' and thereby constituted 'ideologically' (Althusser, 1971). Davies and Harré's concept of 'discursive positioning' (Davies and Harré, 1990) similarly suggested important links between the social and the individual. But many issues remained: was there anything 'behind' the discursive and narrative choices people made? Why were some identifications more likely than others, some positions more desirable than others? These kinds of issues make some sceptical of the value of narrative. Frosh (1999), for example, asks what is 'outside' discourse, and falls back on an open-ended concept of 'the real'. Craib (2000) goes further and talks about narratives as 'bad faith'.

The question of research ethics also loomed large. The possibility of using the language of psychoanalysis to effect particular readings of the interview transcripts was considered but rejected as potentially going beyond the 'informed consent' that participants give, and potentially neglectful of the jointly produced nature of the narratives. I wanted to avoid a 'realist' take on the unconscious that is implicit in much psychoanalytic discourse. I decided to work, not with the inner worlds of individuals, but with the structures of their stories; psychoanalytic ideas could usefully illuminate dimensions of the stories that might otherwise remain hidden. Read in this way, the stories revealed ambivalences and polarizations that were theorized with reference to Klein's notion of 'splitting' and the vacillations between 'depressive' and 'paranoid-schizoid' positions in the wake of the trauma of divorce. In this way I was able to move from the narratives to say something about the psychological processes in divorce, and the ways in which they were played out in dispute resolution.

I have subsequently embarked on a narrative study of seemingly intractable disputes between divorcing people over their children, funded by the Leverhulme Trust. The project is still ongoing. The focus so far has been on what happens at the limits of law. Litigants who occupy entrenched positions explain their actions in moral terms and the most significant feature of parents' talk is the way in which their negotiations of moral positions take a narrative form. Rights-talk no longer has any currency in family law, but for parents themselves, taking part in a contact dispute is clearly about making or resisting a moral claim. But participation in litigation obliges parents to position themselves in relation to a range of discourses that explicitly exclude 'rights'. Parents' narratives reveal interesting tensions around 'rights' and 'welfare'; verbal performances of the acceptable 'welfare' discourse are common, sitting uneasily alongside other competing discourses, including rights-talk. Disputing parents are adept at reframing their claims to 'rights' as welfare issues.

I am now focusing more on theoretical work, in particular the relations between narrative and subjectivity. I have become quite circumspect about the proposition that selves are narratively constructed. Instead, I want to ask other questions about the nature of subjectivity, and the nature of narrative, and what it means to say that subjectivities and identities are negotiated in stories. I do not want to lose sight of the fact that subjectivities are embodied (see, e.g., Smith, 1993; Curti, 1998) and, after Butler (1990, 1993), gendered and performative. And I want to reassert the importance of material social practice. My current preoccupation is to formulate both 'narrative' and 'subjectivity' in processual terms – narration as embodied practice and subjectivity as many-layered always-becoming in the matrices of culture (see Day Sclater, 2001a, 2001b).

Narrative analysis, for me, is not only a way of finding out about how people frame, remember and report their experiences, but is also a way of generating knowledge that disrupts old certainties and allows us to glimpse something of the complexities of human lives, selves and endeavours. It illuminates not only individual lives but also broader social processes (see Rustin, 2000). Narrative analysis, as an interdisciplinary practice that cuts across the arts, humanities, sciences and social sciences, is also a useful corrective to the reductive tendencies that other analyses, rooted in individual disciplines, can manifest. It opens up some very exciting possibilities for thinking about creativity in relation to research and it provides a very rich source for theory-building – read any stretch of narrative text and remind yourself how many important questions there are still to be asked!

NARRATIVE GENRES
(*Corinne Squire*)

Stories, some researchers say, are rooted in human agency. A story is told *by* someone, although that person may not know everything about the story they are telling. In such accounts, narrative analysis is a kind of compromise between modernism and postmodernism. Stories change over time, and the language of stories constructs our subjectivities; but we are all, nonetheless, active and effective storytellers. In performing narratives we can create new possibilities for identities and actions (Mishler, 1986; Bruner, 1990).

Unsurprisingly, given that HIV threatens physical, personal and social agency, this perspective has been popular in HIV research. The relation of particular stories to the mental and physical health of people with HIV has been explored (Schwartzberg, 1993; Crossley, 1997; Ezzy, 2000). More generally, much research enables people with HIV to tell their own stories, a sort of corrective to the prevailing pathologization of the HIV 'story'. And so when in the mid-1990s I began a longitudinal study in Britain of people's experiences, expectations and requirements of HIV support, I considered doing a biographical analysis of the many stories that people told.

The difficulty with this perspective, for me, is that it understands stories as having, despite their multiplicity, a fixed, human pattern, and frequently claims to know what is a good, healthy story or a bad, maladaptive one. This perspective's emphasis on a purposive, agentic subject is also often at odds with the fragmented, indeterminate subject underlying its more flexible concept of 'stories'. My own findings from the HIV support study, and those of some other HIV researchers (Squire, 1999; Ciambrone, 2001), suggest that the storytelling 'subject' in these cases is a diverse, strategic entity, that stories cannot necessarily be related to universal narrative forms and that it is invidious to judge the psychological value of individuals' stories. People's stories do not always show progressive adaptation over time, for instance. Apparent 'regressions' cannot always be related clearly to health or other life crises. For women living with HIV, as well as people living with the condition in difficult social or political circumstances, for instance as refugees, a story that develops increasingly consistent and coherent notions of identity is exceptional rather than exemplary (Squire, 1999).

There are other ways to read stories. We can, for instance, approach narrative analysis outside of a developmental or teleological frame. We can treat 'story' as an important but culturally variable 'discourse,' that is, a Foucaultian formation of meaning and power with significant but hard-to-determine effects (Parker, 1992). From this perspective, the storyteller is not a unitary self, making holistic sense of his/her life in the telling. Instead, the stories that people tell about themselves are about many selves, each situated in particular contexts, and working strategically to resist those contexts. When analysing the HIV support study interviews, I realized that this analytic frame fitted the stories better than any attempt to turn them into unified biography. When, for instance, Katherine (not her real name), an HIV-positive woman of African origin, told of her current ease with HIV, her 'acceptance' of it, this accepting 'self' was not an independent or stable construct, but a reiterated, strategically resistant moment within a long story about her and her friends' attempts to engage with and then appropriate a medical expertise that defined them as virus carriers. When Katherine told of her new-found empowerment in demanding services, she narrated this 'self' as the resistant coda to a story about social service positionings of her as a 'client'. When she described her desire to break free and do all the things *she* wanted to do, this emergent 'self' was situated, again, as a strategic resistance, within a story of her long-term volunteering and work around HIV (Squire, 1999).

Genre analysis is an emblematic example of the narrative-analytic practice described above. Genres, subtypes of narrative with distinctive structures and contents, are clearly socially and culturally constructed forms. That is why, if you share a genre's cultural matrix, you will know it when you see it (Todorov, 1990). Within Western cultures, some genres – romance, tragedy, comedy and irony – have wide currency (Jacobs, 2000), but genres shift and intermingle all the time. The heterogeneity and fractures within genres also mean that they undermine themselves constantly (Derrida, 1992). Within Western cultures, the term 'genre' has been applied to visual arts that take the everyday as their subject, and to varieties of popular fiction. This indicates the cultural promiscuity that must inform genre analysis, for genres are relatively similar between 'high' and 'low' culture and across media (Todorov, 1990). To address these phenomena, a genre analysis may need to pay attention as much to cultural and media studies as to social science research (for other examples, see Squire, 1994, 1998, 2003).

Within the UK HIV support study, two genres appeared with striking frequency. One was a 'coming-out' story that mirrored lesbian and gay coming-out narratives, moving from uneasy realization of a problem (illness, positive status) through denial, to anger and depression, into an acceptance that often took the initial form of very active engagement with HIV's medical and social context but that later became a more low-level incorporation of HIV within personal and cultural identities. This 'coming-out' story of HIV had been noted by the cultural theorist Cindy Patton (1990); some gay men in the study themselves noted the parallels. Here it was told not just by gay men, but by heterosexual women and men, for whom it seemed to be an accessible and appropriate cultural resource, addressing as it does the relationship of subjectivity to stigma (Squire, 1999). As with lesbian and gay coming-out stories (Sedgewick, 1990), this story did not claim to be closed, to contain everything (Frosh, 1999); it had space for imperfection and abjection. Coming out as lesbian or gay, or as HIV-positive, is never going to be a completed, or a completely comfortable, endeavour. Thus the genre enabled the articulation of an identity that is empowering, but not fixed or imprisoning, through its optimistic yet pragmatic engagement with stigma.

The other genre that appeared with great frequency in the talk of some women with HIV was that of heterosexual romance. It was hard to ignore this genre, since it often took over much of an interview; some women explicitly noted these stories' apparent deviation from the 'support' topic. The romance genre spoke against HIV's fatality, through the living-happily-ever-after and reproductive ideals at which it aimed. Yet these were also specific, *HIV* romances, structured by the limits that the condition places on the genre. Again, HIV romance seemed, for women, a genre with space enough inside it for them to narrate failures, often many and desolate, in their quest for heterosexual love and for their own acceptance of their status, yet to continue their stories after them (Squire, 1999, 2003).

One criticism of genre analysis in the HIV context is that it denies the affective continuities and development of people's stories. Does it, perhaps, fail to connect with the emotional weight of biography, which lies 'under' genre's surface structures? It is undoubtedly true that an HIV diagnosis has deep and long-lasting psychological as well as medical and social implications. However, representation has played a big role in forming personal and political pictures and policies around HIV, and is perceived as important by people living with the condition. It could be argued, consequently, that their uses of

particular genres are highly biographically meaningful. In the study, many interviewees wanted urgently to tell their stories, and the narrative resources available for personal public storytelling were pressing issues. It is important to recognize, too, that a 'life story' is not a universal form, but a genre (Squire, 2000). There are culturally and historically specific rules about how we should autobiographize ourselves, which my study failed deliberately to mobilize, since to do so, to ask people to tell me about their 'lives', would, in this case, have reduced 'life' to 'HIV'. Instead the study asked people about support, and in the process it mobilized the other genres I have mentioned.

Were the genres artefacts of the questions asked? Perhaps the general developmental course of engagement and disengagement with HIV support *produces* a developmental 'coming-out' story. Perhaps chronic illness experience itself impels biographical reconstruction (Bury, 2001). The 'coming-out' subgenre of biography is, however, specific in its engagement with stigma and uncertainty. Again, women interviewees told HIV romances regardless of what questions were being asked. Nor is romance women's preferred biographical genre. HIV romance seemed to be specific to these women's gendered struggles with the physical, reproductive and relationship consequences of seropositivity.

In 2001 I also investigated HIV support in another geographical, economic and political place within the pandemic: townships around Cape Town, South Africa. This study again collected interviews that were full of stories. In Africa, where silence about or 'othering' of HIV (Joffe, 1997) have until recently been political and personal norms, the narrative resources that people have available to them around HIV are, as in the West, key issues (Galavotti et al., 2001). The significance of such resources was magnified for many of these particular research participants by the convergence of their stigmatized HIV-positive status with unemployment, poverty and curtailed education. It seemed in this context that an array of genres were being mobilized to tell HIV stories, as in earlier and more apparently urgent days of the epidemic in the West (Crimp, 1988; Murphy and Poirier, 1993). These genre appropriations were highly persuasive for speakers and those who listened to them. Describing them seemed a relevant research focus at a time when the many voices of people infected and affected by HIV in the country were starting to gain a hearing.

South African interviewees often used a 'talk-show' model of talking about difficult events, telling stories about how they came to accept and disclose their status so that others would benefit, the whole issue would be out in the open, and they could live their lives proudly and positively, in both senses of the word. Sometimes this genre appropriation was explicit; interviewees said there needed to be more talk about HIV, 'like on Ricki [Lake]'. This 'Oprification' genre, and its female identifications, has specific significance when it is adopted, as here, within a nation with some cultural traditions as well as a recent political history around HIV that emphasizes silence – especially for women – and in a situation where HIV-positive status is often accompanied by stigma and disadvantage. In these circumstances, the Oprification disclosure genre might have empowering gendered and social effects. It is important that this genre does not become a coercive model, forcing people to disclose. But it is, like the coming-out genre, an open form. It does not claim to say everything about a person, or to take the same path for every speaker. This incompleteness preserves its emancipatory potential.

Many interviewees also seemed to draw on a religious genre of conversion and witnessing in talking about their initial HIV denial; their later acceptance of their status, which often appeared in the stories as a sudden, life-changing moment; and their evangelical attempts afterwards to help themselves and others live positively with HIV. This religious genre might be expected when faith was so important for the interviewees, many of whom spent large parts of Sunday in worship and some of whom devoted most of their week to religious activities. But it also had the effect of turning stories about HIV, which previously must be silenced or whispered, into literal 'morality tales', ethico-political endeavours.

'Speaking out' is also a kind of nation-building genre in South Africa, one with a long political history. Most recently displayed in the country's saturation with stories from the Truth and Reconciliation Commission (Walker and Unterhalter, 2001), it is more widely exhibited through the increasing volume and multiplicity of voices heard in the country since the end of apartheid, and is foreshadowed in the long preceding struggle for an effective voice for the majority of the population. Nkosi Johnson, the HIV-positive child who told his story to the International AIDS Conference in 2000, spoke as a direct descendant both of the recent TRC storytelling and of that much longer struggle to have your voice heard. Realizing the power of this association, the main South African HIV activist group, the Treatment Action Campaign, placed an image of Johnson, who had recently died, next to the famous picture of Hector Peterson, the thirteen-year-old boy killed in the Soweto uprisings of 1976, on campaign posters.

Interviewees, who also spoke to us in the period just after Johnson's death, occasionally used his public storytelling explicitly as a model for their own speaking out. More generally, speaking out about HIV has become a new field of political activism, the latest move in the trajectory of South Africa's revolutionary political history. But this politicized route to talking about HIV is not easily available to all. The direct and indirect effects of the liberation struggle and the TRC must be set against the still powerful legacy of apartheid, both in creating the economic, educational and political context of the South African epidemic, and more specifically in constraining people's hearing and telling of tales of personal and political resistance to HIV.[1]

Genre is, of course, a co-constructed category. Talking to people with HIV as a white, university-employed, negative-status woman has particular effects on interview data. The situation is further complicated when interviewees are of a different nationality, inhabit communities where English is not usually a first language, and live in informal settlements. In South Africa, too, two-thirds of the interviews were conducted with graduate or undergraduate co-interviewers and translators. While genre is always fluid and negotiable, it is important to recognize that in such circumstances, analysis of what genres are in play must be pursued collaboratively – in this case, with co-interviewers, and by checking with interviewees themselves.

I would suggest that these circumstances of translation and potential research 'colonization' do not make genre analysis impossible, but clarify its limitations (Andrews, 1995). They also point to one further advantage of genre analysis: its accessibility and meaning for research participants. If analyses of their stories are a good means of reflexively engaging interviewees, so too are accounts of the particular kinds of stories they tell, accounts that, moreover, position them – as indeed they are – as creative interpreters and constructors of their places within cultures. In this respect, genre analysis is an exemplary instance of the narrative approach's interest in what people do, representationally, with their lives, how they remake events and experiences into their lived cultures, and at times use this remaking to live differently.

AUTOBIOGRAPHICAL NARRATIVES: A GENEALOGICAL APPROACH
(Maria Tamboukou)

My interest in Foucault coincided with a critical period in my life, when, dislocating myself from familiar spaces and places, I had felt the need to experiment with new modes of thinking and perhaps with new modes of being. It was the early 1990s and I had come to London to make a new start. In following Foucault, I think that I had become passionately interested in a wider shift in the European intellectual landscape: the return of ethics as a primary issue in the philosophical agenda. It is through my particular interest in ethics that I have attempted to excavate the ways people and particularly women have acted upon themselves so as to create a stylistics of life, become ethical subjects, become what they are. It was in the Foucaultian framework that the initial question of a doctoral research project was formulated: What is the present of women in education today? How have we become what we are and what are the possibilities of becoming other?

Drawing on trails of the Foucaultian genealogy, I turned to the past, so that I could trace hidden practices and unnoticed contours intertwined in the conditions that made a cluster of various subject positions available for women teachers to inhabit. Doing genealogy involves focusing on insignificant details, searching in the maze of dispersed grey and dusty documents to trace discontinuities, recurrences and play where traditional research sees continuous development, progress and seriousness. In the process of my inquiries, I have therefore wondered where I should look for those traces, those 'grey meticulous details', the forgotten documents that genealogy is after. This is how I became interested in women teachers' texts of self-representation. Reading their forgotten diaries, letters, autobiographies and memoirs has offered me invaluable experience of genealogical research and has helped me make sense of how 'through autobiographical writing the self is written out of and into its historical context' (Steedman, 1992: 14) and how this very practice of writing is interwoven in a critical *technology of the self*.

In using genealogy as a tool for exploring the female self in education, I stabilized moments in the latest part of the nineteenth century and the earliest part of the twentieth century in the UK as strategically chosen starting points for my inquiries. Women's mass involvement in education has of course been the object of numerous and important historical studies, which have often attempted to find a place for it in a supposedly linear historical development of women's liberation (see Purvis, 1991). However, in the genealogical analysis, this linear development towards progress has been interrogated and problematized. In paying attention to the 'minor' pathways and processes surrounding the historical

highway that has supposedly led women to the public sphere, different story-lines were able to emerge, while dissonances have often disrupted the melody of feminist history. In focusing on the context of the *fin-de-siècle* era, I did not try to recover the woman teacher as a heroic figure of social history. I attempted an analysis of the specification of her emergence in a nexus of signifying genealogical events.

In therefore taking up genealogical analytic trails, I chose to follow lines of life-narratives of the first women who attempted to navigate the difficult ways of forming a new self in the various new educational institutions, both as students and later teachers. These women have often been represented in quite contradictory and often juxtaposing ways: either as lady heroes, the legendary pioneers of women's education, or as agents of oppression, reproducing feminine ideals and middle-class ideologies in the newly opened sphere of women's education (see Prentice and Theobald, 1991). Instead of being confusing, these contradictions have indeed been highly relevant to the genealogical project. As a genealogist of the female subject I was particularly intrigued to look more carefully not only at the surrounding discourses, but also at the discourses of women themselves, their autobiographical narratives through which they made sense of their lives. In bracketing the gaze and discourses of the 'others', I wanted to concentrate on their own processes of subjectification, using the genealogical device of the *technologies of the self*. These *technologies of the self*, according to Foucault, 'permit individuals to effect, by their own means, or with the help of others a certain number of operations on their own bodies, and souls, thoughts, conduct and way of being so as to transform themselves' (Foucault, 1988: 18).

I have argued that the genealogical approach provides the lens for distortions to come to focus, through the examination of autobiographical narratives. It goes without saying, however, that genealogy has not come to operate on deserted and unexplored territories. Various feminist theorists have long argued that recent theoretical debates concerning 'the self' and 'the subject' become particularly interesting when examined in relation to lived and/or written lives, and have stressed the importance of autobiographical narratives in illuminating the conditions of possibility for the female self in education to emerge (Smith and Watson, 1998). However, deviating from the feminist tradition of locating similarities in the textual representation of women teachers' experiences, I have opted for the unveiling of their situated differences, drawing upon feminist theorizations that have seen the female self as multiple, fragmented and incomplete (de Lauretis, 1987). It is within this theoretical cartography that I have found 'a landscape' (Steedman, 1986) for a feminist genealogy drawing on women teachers' autobiographical narratives to be deployed, and it is on some details of this landscape that I will now focus.

Foucault's work has been influential in the theorization of the social nature of spatiality and its interdependent relation with power and subjectivity. Feminist theorists have further explored the role of space and place in the performance of gender and sexuality (Rose, 1993). Drawing on the theoretical encounter between feminism and Foucault, I have examined the ways in which women's longing for some space of their own has been intensely inscribed in their practices of self-representation. Clearly this is not the place to attempt a rigorous genealogy of women teachers' narratives. What follows is a series of vignettes, which trace the emergence of what I have called *technologies of space* (Tamboukou, 1999).

> When my trunk was landed, I was shown my room. This was some twelve feet square on the ground-floor, with one small window flush with the pavement, a narrow bed, a scrap of carpet, a basket chair, one upright chair and a bureau. A fire crackled in the hearth. 'Is this *mine?*' [emphasis in the text] cried I in ecstasy. (Hughes, 1946: 120)

This is an extract from the autobiography of Molly Hughes, a student having just arrived in Cambridge for a new teacher's training college. It seems that well before Virginia Woolf's influential lectures at Girton and Newnham in 1928, where she related women's writing with economic independence and 'a room of one's own' (Woolf, 1945), women teachers had been seriously preoccupied with the deep necessity of acquiring a space where they could think of and for themselves, articulate their intellectual worries, ultimately 'write themselves'. Contrary to prevailing perceptions that women were restricted in the private sphere of the family and sought to enter the public sphere through educating themselves, the genealogical analysis of their autobiographical narratives reveals that women have fought equally strongly to reclaim their right to privacy as well as their right to be public. Their narratives have also revealed that in reclaiming space for themselves, women have imagined themselves in different spaces and not infrequently have sought to fulfil their 'dreams of elsewhere' by travelling:

> Donald, wouldn't you like to go to America, Canada or the great wide west? where perhaps there might be more chance of finding out what manner of being you were? – where there is more room, more freedom, and one is not so hide-bound by conventions – where you could get nearer the soil, and as I said before not be stifled by artificialities and habits and conventions, your own and other peoples'. Oh wouldn't you like it, wouldn't you? Wouldn't you? (Grier, 1937: 34)

This extract comes from a letter written in August 1902 by Winifred Mercier, a woman teacher who later became a leader in the reform of teacher training colleges, to her friend and fellow teacher Jeanne K. Borland, Donald for her friends. While on school holidays, studying for her external London degree and looking after her sick mother, Winifred finds consolation in writing to her beloved friend. Her passionate desire for travel brings together a cluster of practices that are interwoven in the fashioning of women teachers' life-style. Travel is a means of getting away from the 'artificialities and habits and conventions' that are imposed both internally and externally, 'your own and other people's', travel to 'where there is more room, more freedom', in order to seek 'the manner of being you were'.

Women teachers' autobiographical narratives have indeed been inscribed by spatial images, both real and imagined. In reading these narratives, I was intrigued by the multifarious ways that they have tried to work upon themselves in rearranging their space, and giving different dimensions to the unfolding of their lives. Indeed I would argue that technologies of the female self are historically associated with *technologies of space*.

Women teachers' textual narratives have also revealed how by entering the first university-associated colleges, these women lived within the limits of their society, but also beyond them, in yet unrecognized 'different social spaces', which Foucault (1998) has described as *heterotopias*. In Foucault's analyses of space, *heterotopias* contest the real space in which we live, creating transitional spaces and sheltering subjects in crisis. In writing their stories, women have indeed presented their colleges as spaces of 'transition and tension', 'sites outside of society' bringing together 'heterogeneous discourses' – equal opportunities, male educational and ethical values, lady-like behaviour – for the development of young women. Thus, the notion of *heterotopia* has become instrumental in the analyses of women teachers' space narratives (Tamboukou, 1999, 2000). Depicted as *heterotopias*, the pioneering colleges of women's higher education opened up channels to the exploration of the self and gave women access to knowledge, but also to power, 'a pas de deux dance' they had no choice but to follow. In the genealogical analysis of women's narratives, it was not so much the effects of power that were important, but the subjective capacities that were being developed in the attempt to resist the power that had made women what they were. As their narratives reveal, it is no wonder why some of these resisting practices were deployed against the disciplinary arrangement of their space:

> The Mistress's sitting-room and the library, where lectures were given and which was also our common room, were on the ground floor, and the dining-room was in the basement, a bare ugly room with two tables, at one of which we students sat, while the Mistress and her friends sat at the 'High table' alongside. It was at first expected that we should sit in a formal row down one side of our table, lest we should be guilty of the discourtesy of turning our backs upon the 'High'. But this was too much and we rebelled, quietly ignored the rule and insisted upon comfortably facing each other. (Lumsden, 1933: 47)

Women teachers' autobiographical narratives forcefully depict colleges as contested sites, ridden by contradictions and uncertainties. In such a context of controversy, the techniques women used to map their existence would be a nexus of resistance and accommodation practices, inextricably interwoven. It was through these *technologies of resistance* (Tamboukou, 1999) that women began to fashion new forms of subjectivity, always oscillating between what Milan Kundera (1984) would describe as the 'unbearable lightness and heaviness of being', by adopting unstable positions between them.

In making my argument about the role of women's self writings, as *technologies of the female self*, I have drawn on influential feminist analyses of women's strategies for writing the self. These analyses have explored the historical devaluation of women's writings that have both constrained their writing practices and have excluded them from the canon of traditional autobiographical texts. These analyses have further shown how, moving beyond silence, women began making sense of dispersed moments of their existence, and through writing they attempted to describe those moments and articulate them in a narrative system. I have been particularly interested in feminist analyses of women's autobiographies, memoirs, letters and diaries as practices of self-formation, the argument that the female self constitutes itself through writing (Smith and Watson, 1998, 2001). The selves that are inscribed in their autobiographical narratives lack the sense of organic integrity and question the principle of authorial intention that characterizes the male canon of the genre. It is this elusive condition of their textual existence that renders female autobiographical narratives provocative for the genealogist of technologies of the female self.

As already indicated, my particular interest in exploring the *technologies of the self* of women teachers relates to my own experience as a woman teacher, but it goes beyond the 'personal sphere'. Education has been a site of power where freedom has been historically denied to women. It has therefore been a significant locus of resistance. Jana Sawicki (1991) has pointed out that genealogy as resistance opens the way for a 'historical knowledge of struggles', since it uses history to give voice to the marginal and submerged subjects that lie 'hidden from history' and focuses attention on specific situations, thus leading to more concrete analyses of particular struggles. What I have suggested is that women seeking freedom through and within education have attempted not only to disrupt power relations and transcend gendered hierarchical structures, but also to reinvent themselves and live a better life. The genealogical analysis of women teachers' autobiographical narratives has not articulated a closed answer in response to the initial research questions. The Foucaultian toolbox of genealogy has given me the means to pursue my explorations of *technologies of the female self*, in women's practices of self-representation, but has also acted as a source of continuous uncertainty about what I thought had been my 'results' or conclusions. Instead of finding answers, I have rather found new questions that I hope will continue to shake up our perceptions of what we are, what this present of ours is, but also and perhaps most importantly, how we can become other than what we are already.

NOTE

1 I am indebted to Lumka Daniel for many discussions about and insights into the story forms used by people in this study.

REFERENCES

Althusser, Louis (1971) *Lenin and Philosophy and Other Essays*. New York: Basic Books.

Andrews, M. (1991) *Lifetimes of Commitment: Aging, Politics, Psychology.* Cambridge: Cambridge University Press.

Andrews, M. (1995) 'Against good advice: reflections on conducting research in a country where you don't speak the language', *Oral History Review*, 20(1): 75–86.

Andrews, M. (1997a) 'Life review in the context of acute social transition: the case of East Germany', *British Journal of Social Psychology*, 36: 273–90.

Andrews, M. (1997b) 'Fighting for "the finest image we have of her": patriotism and oppositional politics', in Ervin Staub and Daniel Bar Tal (eds), *Patriotism in the Life of Individuals and Nations*. Chicago: Nelson Hall, pp. 271–92.

Andrews, M. (1998) 'Criticism/self-criticism in East Germany: contradictions between theory and practice', *Critical Sociology*, 24(1/2): 130–53.

Andrews, M. (1999) Truth-telling, justice, and forgiveness: a study of East Germany's "Truth Commission"', *International Journal of Politics, Culture and Society*, 13(1): 103–20.

Andrews, M. (2000) 'Text in a changing context: reconstructing lives in East Germany', in Joanna Bornat, Prue Chamberlayne and Tom Wengraf (eds), *The Turn to Biographical Methods in Social Science: Comparative Issues and Examples*. London: Routledge, pp. 181–95.

Andrews, M. (2002a) 'Introduction to special issue: counter-narratives and the power to oppose', *Narrative Inquiry*, 12(1): 1–6.

Andrews, M. (2002b) 'Memories of mother: narrative reconstructions of early maternal influence', *Narrative Inquiry*, 12(1): 7–28.

Andrews, M., Day Sclater, Shelley, Squire, Corinne and Treacher, Amal (eds). (2000) *Lines of Narrative: Psychosocial Perspectives*. London: Routledge.

Borneman, John (1991) *After the Wall: East Meets West in the New Berlin*. New York: Basic Books.

Brown, Joanna and Day Sclater, Shelley (1999) 'Divorce: a psychodynamic perspective', in S. Day Sclater and C. Piper (eds), *Undercurrents of Divorce*. Aldershot: Ashgate, pp. 145–60.

Bruner, Jerome (1990) *Acts of Meaning*. Cambridge, MA: Harvard University Press.

Bury, Mike (2001) 'Illness narratives: fact or fiction?', *Sociology of Health and Illness*, 23(3): 263–85.

Butler, J. (1990) *Gender Trouble*. London: Routledge.

Butler, J. (1990) *Bodies that Matter*. London: Routledge.

Ciambrone, Dierdre (2001) 'Illness and other assaults on self: the relative impacts of HIV/AIDS on women's lives', *Sociology of Health and Illness*, 23: 517–40.

Craib, Ian (2000) 'Narratives as bad faith', in M. Andrews, S. Day Sclater, C. Squire and A. Treacher (eds), *Lines of Narrative: Psychosocial Perspectives*. London: Routledge, pp. 64–74.

Crimp, Douglas (1988) *AIDS: Cultural Analysis/Cultural Activism*. Cambridge, MA: MIT Press.

Crossley, Michele (1997) '"Survivors" and "victims": long-term HIV positive individuals and the ethos of self-empowerment', *Social Science and Medicine*, 45(12): 1863–73

Crossley, Michele (2000) *Introducing Narrative Psychology: Self, Trauma and the Construction of Meaning*. Buckingham: Open University Press.

Curti, Lidia (1998) *Female Stories, Female Bodies: Narrative, Identity and Representation*. Basingstoke: Macmillan.

Davies, Bronwyn and Harré, Rom (1990) 'Positioning: the discursive construction of selves', *Journal for the Theory of Social Behaviour*, 20: 43–63.

Day Sclater, Shelley (1995) 'Theory and method for a psychosocial approach to divorce', *East London Papers*, No. 2. University of East London.

Day Sclater, Shelley (1997) 'Narratives of divorce', *Journal of Social Welfare and Family Law*, 19(4): 423–41.

Day Sclater, Shelley (1998a) 'Nina's story: the construction and transformation of subjectivity in narrative', *Auto/biography*, 6: 67–77.

Day Sclater, Shelley (1998b) 'Creating the self: stories as transitional phenomena', *Auto/biography*, 6: 885–92.

Day Sclater, Shelley (1998c) 'Divorce: coping strategies, conflict and dispute resolution', *Family Law*, 28: 150–2.

Day Sclater, Shelley (1999a) 'Experiences of divorce', in S. Day Sclater and C. Piper (eds), *Undercurrents of Divorce*. Aldershot: Ashgate, pp. 161–82.

Day Sclater, Shelley (1999b) *Divorce: A Psychosocial Study*. Aldershot: Dartmouth.

Day Sclater, Shelley (2000) 'The bubble that burst: Jane's divorce story', *Self, Agency and Society*, 3(1): 44–69.

Day Sclater, Shelley (2001a) 'Narrative subjects and the seductions of narrative', keynote paper presented at the Arts and Narrative Inquiries Conference, Helsinki, January 2001.

Day Sclater, Shelley (2001b) 'What is the subject?', paper presented at the Narrative and Psychology Symposium, British Psychological Society Centenary Conference, Glasgow, March 2001.

Day Sclater, Shelley and Yates, Candida (1999) 'The psycho-politics of post-divorce parenting', in A. Bainham, S. Day Sclater and M. Richards (eds), *What is a Parent? A Socio-Legal Analysis*. Oxford: Hart, pp.135–46.

de Lauretis, T. (1987) *Technologies of Gender: Essays on Theory, Film and Fiction*. Basingstoke: Macmillan Press.

Derrida, Jacques (1992) 'The law of genre', in Derek Attridge (ed.), *Acts of Literature*. London: Routledge.

Eakin, P.J. (1999) *How Our Lives Become Stories: Making Selves*. Ithaca, NY: Cornell University Press.

Ezzy, David (2000) 'Illness narrative: time, hope and HIV', *Social Science and Medicine*, 50: 605–17.

Foucault, Michel (1988) 'Technologies of the self', in L. Martin, H. Gutman and P. Hutton (eds), *Technologies of the Self*. London: Tavistock, pp. 16–49.

Foucault, Michel (1998) 'Different Spaces' (1984), in Rabinow, P. (ed.), *Michel Foucault, Aesthetics, Method, and Epistemology, the essential works of Michel Foucault, 1954–1984*, Vol. II. Harmondsworth: Penguin, pp. 175–85.

Freeman, Mark (1993) *Rewriting the Self: History, Memory, Narrative*. London: Routledge.

Frosh, Stephen (1999) 'What is outside discourse?', *Psychoanalytic Studies*, 1(4): 381–90.

Galavotti, Christine, Pappas-DeLuca, Katina and Lansky, Amy (2001) 'Modeling and reinforcement to combat HIV: the MARCH approach to behavior change', *American Journal of Public Health*, 91(10): 1602–7.

Grier, L. (1937) *The Life of Winifred Mercier*. Oxford: Oxford University Press.

Hollway, Wendy and Jefferson, Tony (2000) *Doing Qualitative Research Differently*. London, Sage.

Holstein, J. and Gubrium, J. (1999) *The self We Live By: Narrative Identity in a Postmodern World*. Oxford: Oxford University Press.

Hopper, Joseph (2001) 'Contested selves in divorce proceedings', in J. Gubrium and J. Holstein (eds), *Institutional Selves*. Oxford: Oxford University Press.

Hughes, M.V. (1946) *A London Girl of the 1880s*. Oxford: Oxford University Press.

Jackson, Bernard (1990) 'Narrative theories and legal discourse', in C. Nash (ed.), *Narrative in Culture: The Uses of Storytelling in the Sciences, Philosophy and Literature*. London: Routledge, pp. 23–50.

Jacobs, Ron (2000) 'Narrative, civil society and public culture', in M. Andrews, S. Sclater, C. Squire and A. Treacher (eds), *Lines of Narrative*. London: Sage, pp. 18–35.

Joffe, Helene (1997) 'The relationship between representationalist and materialist perspectives: AIDS and "the other" ', in Lucy Yardley (ed.), *Material Discourses of Health and Illness*. London: Routledge, pp. 132–49.

Kundera, Milan (1984) *The Unbearable Lightness of Being*. London: Faber & Faber.

Laslett, P. (1989) *A Fresh Map of Life: The Emergence of the Third Age*. London: Weidenfeld & Nicolson.

Lifton, Robert Jay (1986) *The Nazi Doctors: Medical Killing and the Psychology of Genocide*. New York: Basic Books.

Lumsden, L. (1933) *Yellow Leaves: Memories of a Long Life*. Edinburgh: William Blackwood.

McAdams, D.P. (1997) *The Stories We Live By: Personal myths and the making of the self*. New York: Guilford Press.

Mishler, Elliot G. (1986) *Research Interviewing: Context and Narrative*. Cambridge, MA: Harvard University Press.

Murphy, Tim and Poirier, Suzanne (eds) (1993) *Writing AIDS*. New York: Columbia University Press.

Parker, Ian (1992) *Discourse Dynamics*. London: Routledge.

Patton, Cindy (1990) *Inventing AIDS*. London: Routledge.

Philipsen, Dirk (1993) *We Were the People: Voices from East Germany's Revolutionary Autumn of 1989*. Durham, NC: Duke University Press.

Phillips, Adam (1999) *Darwin's Worms*. London: Faber & Faber.

Prentice, A. and Theobald, M. (1991) (eds), *Women Who Taught*. Toronto: University of Toronto Press.

Purvis, J. (1991) *A History of Women's Education in England*. Milton Keynes: Open University Press.

Rhiel, Mary and Suchoff, David (eds) (1996) *The Seductions of Biography*. New York: Routledge.

Riessman, Catherine K. (1990) *Divorce Talk: Women and Men Make Sense of Personal Relationships*. New Brunswick, NJ: Rutgers University Press.

Riessman, Catherine K. (1993) *Narrative Analysis*. London: Sage.

Rose, G. (1993) *Feminism and Geography: The Limits of Geographical Knowledge*. Cambridge: Polity Press.

Rosenwald, G.C. and Ochberg, R. (eds) (1992) *Storied Lives: The Cultural Politics of Self-Understanding*. New Haven: Yale University Press.

Rustin, Michael (2000) 'Reflections on the biographical turn in social science', in P. Chamberlayne, J. Bornat and T. Wengraf (eds), *The Turn to Biographical Methods in Social Science*. London: Routledge, pp. 33–52.

Sarbin, Theodore (ed.) (1986) *Narrative Psychology: The Storied Nature of Human Conduct*. London: Praeger.

Sawicki, J. (1991) *Disciplining Foucault*. London: Routledge.

Schwartzberg, Steven (1993) 'Struggling for meaning: how HIV positive gay men make sense of AIDS', *Professional Psychology: Research and Practice*, 24: 483–90.

Sedgewick, Eve Kofosky (1990) *The Epistemology of the Closet*. London: Harvester Wheatsheaf.

Silverman, Kaya (1983) *The Subject of Semiotics*. New York: Oxford University Press.

Smith, S. (1993) *Subjectivity, Identity and the Body*. Bloomington: Indiana University Press.

Smith, S. and Watson, J. (eds) (1998) *Women, Autobiography, Theory: A Reader.* Madison: University of Wisconsin Press.

Smith, S. and Watson, J. (eds) (2001) *Reading Autobiography: A Guide for Interpreting Life Narratives*. Minneapolis: University of Minnesota Press.

Squire, Corinne (1994) 'Safety, danger and the movies: women's and men's narratives of aggression', *Feminism and Psychology*, 4(4): 547–70.

Squire, Corinne (1998) 'Women and men talk about aggression: an analysis of narrative genre', in K. Henwood, C. Griffin and A. Phoenix (eds), *Standpoints and Differences: Essays in the Practice of Feminist Psychology*. London: Sage, pp. 65–90.

Squire, Corinne (1999) ' "Neighbors who might become friends": selves, genres and citizenship in narratives of HIV', *Sociological Quarterly*, 40(1): 109–37.

Squire, Corinne (2000) 'Situated selves, the coming-out genre and equivalent citizenship in narratives of HIV', in Prue Chamberlayne, Joanna Bornat and Tom Wengraf (eds), *The Turn to Biographical Methods in Social Science*. London: Routledge, pp. 196–213.

Squire, Corinne (2003) 'Can an HIV positive woman find true love? Romance in the stories of women living with HIV', *Feminism and Psychology*, 13(1): 73–100.

Steedman, Carolyn (1986) *Landscape for a Good Woman: a Story of Two Lives*. London: Virago.

Steedman, Carolyn (1992) *Past Tenses: Essays on Writing, Autobiography and History.* London: River Oram Press.

Tamboukou, Maria (1999), 'Spacing herself', *Gender and Education*, 11(2): 125–39.

Tamboukou, Maria (2000), 'Of other spaces: women's colleges at the turn of the century', *Gender, Place and Culture*, 7(3): 247–63.

Todorov, Tzvetan (1990) *Genres in Discourse*. Cambridge: Cambridge University Press.

Walker, Melanie and Unterhalter, Elaine (2001) 'Knowledge, narrative and national reconciliation: race and gender reflections on the South African Truth and Reconciliation Commission', paper presented at the Fourth International Gender and Education Conference, 4–6 April 2001, Institute of Education, London.

Widdershoven, Guy (1993) 'Hermeneutic perspectives on the relationship between narrative and life history', in Ruthellen Josselson and Amia Lieblich (eds), *The Narrative Study of Lives*, vol. 1. London: Sage, pp. 1–20.

Woolf, Virginia (1945) *A Room of One's Own*. Harmondsworth: Penguin.

Yates, Candida and Day Sclater, Shelley (2000) 'Culture, psychology and transitional space', in C. Squire (ed.), *Culture in Psychology*. London: Routledge.

Young-Bruehl, Elisabeth (1998) *Subject to Biography: Psychoanalysis, Feminism and Writing Women's Lives*. Cambridge, MA: Harvard University Press.

8

Feminist approaches

Celia Kitzinger

The reclaiming and validation of women's experience through listening to women's voices has been central to feminism since the second wave of the 1970s. Such ideas constituted the intellectual foundation for the establishment of Women's Studies as a discipline, and for the construction of feminist challenges to conventional forms of Western epistemology (e.g. Smith, 1987, 1992; Harding, 1991). Feminist social scientists argued that men define reality on their own terms, to legitimate *their* experience, *their* own particular version of events, while women's experience, not fitting the male model, is trivialized, denied or distorted. Early second-wave feminism involved, crucially, a reclaiming and naming of women's experience, and a challenge to the male monopoly on truth. The primary research method for achieving this end was taken to be listening to women and hearing what they had to say about their experience.

There have been notable successes with this approach, in that listening to women's accounts of their experience has involved the coining of new terms that have subsequently entered the ordinary language of the culture, and have led to changes in policy and legislation. For example, before the 1970s the label 'sexual harassment' didn't exist. The first recorded use of the term was in May 1975 in New York by a group called Working Women United, which was convened to support a Cornell University administrator, Carmita Wood, who had left her position because of continued sexual invitations and threats from a faculty member. This group held the first reported 'speak out' on sexual harassment, in which women testified publicly about men's use of sexuality in the workplace and commissioned a survey to study the newly identified problem. Lin Farley, a researcher on women and work at Cornell University, described how she was part of a consciousness-raising group in which women talked about their work experience:

> When we had finished, there was an unmistakable pattern to our employment. Something absent in all the literature, something I had never seen although I had observed it many times, was newly exposed. Each one of us had already quit or been fired from a job at least once because we had been made too uncomfortable by the behavior of men. (Farley, 1978: xi)

The term 'sexual harassment' was invented, then, as part of women's speaking out about our experience of the world: 'women were "naming" an experience they had endured in silence for many years' (Bacchi and Jose, 1994: 263). The publication of three books in the late 1970s (Farley, 1978; Backhouse and Cohen, 1979; MacKinnon, 1979) popularized the term 'sexual harassment' and led to a wide range of surveys of the newly identified problem. As a consequence of these, public bodies and institutions in both Britain and North America began to see sexual harassment as a serious cause for concern and to formulate specific codes of practice and grievance procedures to deal with it. Within a decade of the feminist 'invention' of the term, 'sexual harassment' had been formally recognized as a trade union issue, an equal opportunities issue, a civil liberties issue and a human rights concern (Thomas and Kitzinger, 1997).

In many ways, then, the story of sexual harassment is a success story of feminist research. Before the 1970s the label didn't exist and the behaviour it identified was 'just life'. The term 'sexual harassment' was invented as a consequence of listening to women's voices reflecting on women's experience. Over the last two decades, organizations, institutions and national and international legal systems have been forced to take on board concerns initially raised by feminists. The personal experience of women has been recognized in a political context.

With the emergence of feminist social science, researchers generally took the use of women's everyday experiences as a basis for developing research questions and treated women's own reports of that experience as the core topic of empirical inquiry. As Oakley (2000: 47) points out, 'giving voice to the silent has been a dominant feminist metaphor', and one of the earliest collections of feminist social science essays was called *Another Voice* (Millman and Kanter, 1975). The goal of feminist research was conceived in straightforward terms: to listen to women's 'different voice' (Gilligan, 1982) and '[t]o address women's lives and experience *in their own terms*, to create theory grounded in the actual experience and language of women' (DuBois, 1983: 108, emphasis in original).

Listening to women's voices and validating women's experiences remains central to the feminist qualitative research enterprise: a recent feminist methods text lists as a key principle of feminist research a commitment to 'ask research questions which acknowledge and validate women's experiences' (Kirsch, 1999: 4). But understanding what is involved in such listening is, for many of us, no longer so straightforward. As DeVault (1996: 40) says, 'the notion of "women's experience" has been productive for feminist scholarship, but it has also become a richly contested concept'. In this chapter, I explore some of the issues (ethical, political, methodological) underpinning the feminist commitment to 'hearing women's voices' as a route to understanding women's experience.

My focus here is fundamentally practical. For feminism as a political movement outside the academy, consciousness-raising (CR) groups were the forum in which women's experience was talked about, shared and theorized. Within feminist social science research, qualitative data, in particular in-depth interviews, have held 'a prominent place in the history of feminist inquiry' (Rabinowitz and Martin, 2001: 44) and remain 'the chosen method for feminist researchers' (Oakley, 2000: 47) – with focus groups now joining them in popularity (Wilkinson, 1999, 2000a). Interviews and focus groups (like oral histories, narrative autobiographies, and indeed CR groups) are self-report methods, in which participants report on their own experiences, but – unlike ethnographies for example – those experiences are not observed directly by the researcher. Overwhelmingly, however, feminist researchers (like qualitative researchers more generally) use *talk about* experience as evidence for what that experience is

actually like. In the feminist literature, as elsewhere, participants' talk about relationships, behaviours and interactions is treated as an acceptable surrogate for direct observation. I will illustrate what I mean by this in detail in the next section of the chapter.

The use of self-report data raises the important issue of the relationship between the 'voices' of participants and the 'experiences' they report. When we sit down to analyse a pile of interview or focus group data in which women describe their experiences, can we, or should we, as analysts, take everything they say as an accurate reflection of 'what really happened' or even as an accurate record of *their perspective* (or account, or understanding) of 'what really happened'? As feminists we know that women's voices do not always tell 'truths': memories can be fallible, stories can be embroidered, participants may be more interested in creating a good impression than in literal accuracy, speakers contradict themselves and sometimes deliberately lie. From the 'voices' speaking in this research-created context, feminists face the challenge of reconstructing the 'experience' presumed to lie beneath or beyond the talk. This chapter explores the relationship of the data (talk in research interviews) to the conclusions drawn by analysts (about how women think or feel, the kinds of relationships they have, their experience of the world).

I am focusing, then, on the principles underlying data *analysis*. This makes my chapter rather different from most feminist discussions of methods, which focus overwhelmingly on principles of data *collection*. I do not mean to downplay the importance of good techniques and ethical practices in data collection, but they have been amply covered elsewhere and I refer you to these other sources (e.g. Reinharz, 1992; Kirsch, 1999; Rabinowitz and Martin, 2001). By contrast, the principles of qualitative data analysis have been less well covered (the classic feminist text by Reinharz, for example, has nothing at all about data analysis in the chapter on interviewing), and analysis is treated either as a purely technical concern (e.g. which computer package to use) or as an essentially intuitive process inexplicable to anyone who hasn't 'immersed' herself in the data (though see Taylor et al., 1996, for a more detailed discussion of voice-relational analysis).

Nor, again in contrast with many feminist discussions of methods, am I primarily concerned with questions of epistemology or ontology. There are important philosophical issues in the discussion of methodology: on what bases are our knowledge-claims grounded?; is knowledge necessarily gendered (classed, raced, etc.) such that 'objectivity' (what Harding, 1987: 181 calls 'point-of-viewlessness') is neither possible nor desirable?; (how) can feminist and other critical researchers use 'essentialist' or 'positivist' approaches based on notions of natural categories and scientific objectivity?; and what are the costs of abandoning such notions for social constructionist or postmodern approaches emphasizing human flux, discontinuity, relativism and multiple perspectives? (see Kitzinger, 1999, for a discussion of these issues in relation to lesbian and gay scholarship). Although the issues raised in this chapter intersect with those raised in the context of epistemology and ontology, my focus here is a much narrower one. It is this: when we listen to women's voices ('data'), how (as 'feminists' and as 'data analysts') should we hear them?

The rest of this chapter is divided into three sections. In the first, I discuss the feminist concern with hearing women's voices as reports of their experience, and I describe some research that fulfils that goal. As I have indicated above, there are now many criticisms of this approach to analysing data from both positivist and postmodern perspectives and I briefly review these, but suggest, nonetheless, that, for feminists committed to social change, there may be good reasons to set aside these criticisms in pursuit of our pragmatic goals, and I illustrate this with some recent research of my own which, in the interests of immediate feminist concerns, unproblematically treats women's 'voices' as adequate representations of women's experience.

In the second section of the chapter I discuss the kind of data that causes particular problems for this approach – data in which women talk in ways that cannot easily be assimilated into feminist theory. I show how researchers confronted with this kind of data sometimes abandon the notion of a straightforward relationship between 'voice' and 'experience', and actively seek to avoid 'validating' these women's reports – sometimes by excluding them from published reports, sometimes by 'reinterpreting' their words. I understand *why* as feminists we want to do this: it would seem quite wrong unproblematically to report and endorse a woman's claim (for example) that she was sick by virtue of being lesbian, or that she was to blame for having been raped, or that the male behaviour she finds distressing and hurtful isn't 'bad enough' to be sexual harassment. And when feminists analyse the voices of powerful groups (men, heterosexuals, etc.) we routinely abandon the idea that 'voices' offer adequate reports of the world, often treating them instead as self-interested and partial versions. But by implicitly endorsing *some* voices as

offering accurate, truthful or valid ways of understanding experience, while 'explaining away' other voices as merely rationalizations or justifications born of 'false consciousness' or 'patriarchal discourses', we are imposing a heavy (and often unacknowledged) interpretative frame on to our data. This raises ethical and political issues in addition to concerns about the scholarly adequacy of our work, and I discuss these briefly – again with reference to my own research.

Finally, in the third section, I discuss an alternative approach to the relationship between 'voice' and 'experience' that comes from conversation analysis (CA). This is a field that specializes in listening to voices – and listening with great attention to the details both of *what* is said (and not said), and *how* it is said. But whereas most qualitative data analysis treats talk as *a report* of some experience that happened in the past (so that voices offer retrospective accounts of experience of, for example, sexual coercion, or of lesbian oppression), CA treats talk as *constituting* experience at the moment it is uttered.[1] Instead of trying to work out to what extent what someone says maps on to 'what really happened', CA explores how what someone says is itself 'something happening', a kind of action. So, for example, recordings of people actually doing sexual harassment or heterosexism can be analysed for what they tell us about how sexual harassment and heterosexism are done. This is quite different from interviewing people *about* sexual harassment or heterosexism, and then trying to work out what probably happened on the basis of their retrospective accounts. Instead, the conversation analyst works with live instances of the phenomenon under investigation. This approach avoids altogether the problem of the relationship between 'voice' and 'experience': the experience itself is being studied directly, at first hand. I will illustrate this with primary reference to some data analysis of my own.

My own current interest is in the way in which our 'experience' (of sexism, heterosexism, sexual harassment, etc.) is constructed on a moment-by-moment basis in everyday life, and CA offers a very powerful method for exploring such incidents. Some feminist and critical researchers have been very hostile to CA (see Kitzinger, 2000a) and so one of my purposes in this chapter is to show how it can be useful for feminist research. Feminist researchers routinely emphasize, however, that there is no one 'feminist method': the approach you use should be guided by the questions you want to answer, the kinds of answers you expect to find, and the uses to which you want your research to be put. I endorse this position, and want only to offer CA as an addition to the panoply of methods (both qualitative and quantitative) currently used by feminists. I favour methodological pluralism, and continue to use a range of different methods (and to invoke different theoretical frameworks) in different pieces of research. In the conclusion I discuss some of the criteria we might use on any given occasion for selecting methods that fit the questions we are asking and the goals we want to achieve.

'HEARING VOICES' AND 'VALIDATING EXPERIENCE': DESCRIPTIVE INTERVIEWING

In practice, most qualitative feminist social science research equates women's voices with women's experience. That is, the researcher collects data (e.g. from interviews or focus groups) in which women talk about experiences (or that subset of them of interest in the context of any given research project) and treats them as more or less 'accurate' reports of the experiences the women have described. Interviewing, according to this perspective, 'offers researchers access to people's ideas, thoughts, and memories in their own words' (Reinharz, 1992: 19). Access to experience is gained through the talk.

There are at least two major bodies of work that cast doubt on the value of this approach: the positivist and the postmodern. First, positivist social scientists (who still represent the mainstream of the discipline) have shown that a great deal of what people say about their lives and experiences is (either deliberately or inadvertently) at variance with the facts. Discrepancies between objective measures and subjective reports have been well documented (e.g. between the number of beer cans in dustbins and interviewee reports of household beer consumption: Rathje and Hughes, 1975) and people cannot, apparently, be relied upon to report accurately even such an uncontroversial fact as their height (Cherry and Rodgers, 1979). Retrospective accounts are particularly unreliable, being subject to 'conventionalization' (Baddeley, 1979) and influenced by subsequent events and by theories current at the time of interview (Yarrow et al., 1970). People contradict their own words within a single interview session, and talk about their lives in line with culturally constructed implicit theories of self-narration (Neisser, 1994).

Second, postmodernism (including social constructionism and critical discourse analysis)

disputes the possibility of uncovering 'facts', 'realities' or 'truths' behind the talk, and treats as inappropriate any attempt to vet what people say for its 'accuracy', 'reliability' or 'validity' – thereby sidestepping altogether the positivist problems raised above. From this perspective, what women say should not be taken as evidence of their experience, but only as a form of talk – a 'discourse', 'account' or 'repertoire' – that represents a culturally available way of packaging experience. This approach is valuable in so far as it draws attention to the fact that experience is never 'raw', but is embedded in a social web of interpretation and re-interpretation. Women's 'experience' does not spring uncontaminated from an essential inner female way of knowing, but is structured within, and in opposition to, social (heterosexist, patriarchal, etc.) discourses. The cost of this approach for feminism is that it stands in direct contradiction to the feminist claim that women are the experts on our own experience. Instead, we merely animate socially constructed discourses through which our experience is constructed.

Questions about the 'accuracy' or 'truthfulness' of what women say are not of course simply of academic interest. In the 1970s, women's writings about childhood rapes by family members were celebrated as 'a political act of breaking silence in the face of patriarchy' (Brown and Burman, 1997: 8). In the 1990s, the invention of 'false memory syndrome' targeted precisely the 'objectivity' of such retrospective reports (Brown and Burman, 1997). The claim that women's voices offered any kind of unproblematic access to the 'truth' of their experience was challenged both by positivist (experimental) research on memory (which showed that people can produce convincing memories of things that did not happen: Loftus, 1993) and by postmodern claims that memory is socially constructed and that all stories, including autobiographical accounts, are contested versions of events (see Scott, 1997).

In common with other qualitative researchers, feminists have tried to deal with the challenges that have arisen from both positivism and postmodernism, in part through various methodological innovations (e.g. enhanced 'empathy' between interviewer and interviewee to decrease 'social desirability' effects, improved question design, 'triangulation') and in part through making more limited claims about the data (e.g. that they provide evidence for the 'discourses' through which women represent their experience, rather than offering a direct route to that experience itself). Ultimately, however, most feminists (including, as I will show, those who themselves lay claim to a 'post-structuralist' or 'discourse analytic' approach) treat the question of the relationship between what people say and what actually happened as an unavoidable, but minor, technical problem, which – if it cannot be entirely overcome – can be safely overlooked for most practical purposes. The implication seems sometimes to be that in fact we *should* overlook any possible discrepancies as an act of feminist faith in the voices of our female research participants. Despite such challenges, most feminist sociological and psychological research continues to use women's talk about their experiences as relatively straightforward evidence for what those experiences are like.

Lest I sound too critical of feminists for whom this act of faith is the preferred approach, let me be clear that I have taken this approach myself, and that as a feminist and social activist I continue to believe in the importance of this kind of descriptive approach to women's talk, especially for opening up research areas and addressing new issues. It was in part a passion to provide an account of lesbians' experience that led me into becoming a researcher in the first place. In the early 1970s, when, as a teenager, I became involved in my first sexual relationship with a woman, I had never met another lesbian, never seen lesbianism portrayed on television or reported in the press, never heard it mentioned at home or at school, except as a playground taunt. My only source of information was psychology books in the local library from which I learned that I was sick and perverted, that I hadn't resolved my oedipal complex or come to terms with my adult sexuality, that it was phase, a pathological condition caused by faulty parenting, and that I would live the lonely and unfulfilled life of a sexual deviant. I spent four months of my teenage years in a mental hospital being treated by a psychiatrist who tried to convince me that I wasn't really a lesbian. The feminist metaphor of 'voice' captures the sense I had then of being without an adequate language to describe my experience of the world, of being literally 'speechless'. I certainly had no access to the voices or experiences of other lesbians, and an important achievement of lesbian and gay activism and research in the intervening decades has been to 'give voice' to lesbian and gay experience through descriptive interviewing (for recent examples and overviews, see Markowe, 2002; Rivers, 2002; Wilkinson, 2002).

It is still the case that a great many of women's (and, indeed, some men's) experiences have little or no representation in the public domain – or that such representations as do exist are hostile and from the perspective of 'outsiders'. My political commitments lead me, in these cases, to overlook sophisticated methodological doubts and philosophical considerations and to claim the value of descriptive interviewing as a pragmatic strategy for liberation. For example, I recently worked with a talented undergraduate student, Jo Willmott, on women's experience of polycystic ovarian syndrome (PCOS), a diagnosis applied when a woman has ten or more cysts 2 to 8 mm in diameter on her ovaries, resulting in higher levels of androgen production. The resulting symptoms are often described in the literature as having a 'masculinizing' effect and may include infertility or higher risk of miscarriage, hirsutism ('excess' hair growth), menstrual abnormalities, weight gain or obesity, 'maletype' baldness, and acne. Jo had recently been diagnosed with PCOS and had carried out a literature search of her own, the results of which, in many ways, paralleled my own teenage readings on lesbianism. Research on PCOS has overwhelmingly been conducted within a medical or psychiatric framework concerned with establishing levels of psychiatric morbidity in women with the syndrome, and dismissing their concerns about their appearance. The existing literature simply did not reflect Jo's own experience of PCOS, and her research aim was to find out how other women experienced it, and to 'give voice' to those experiences, with particular reference to how women with PCOS negotiate their identities *as women*. The research (Kitzinger and Willmott, 2002) analysed the voices of thirty women with PCOS, and in our analysis of the data we unproblematically took what women said as evidence for what they experienced. When they said they experienced themselves as 'freaks', we chose to believe that they experienced themselves as freaks; when they said they found their own facial and body hair 'upsetting', 'distressing', 'dirty' and 'distasteful', we simply reported their feelings, and quoted voices, like Gita's, as evidence for their feelings: 'I actually used to shave and […] that was so terrible. I felt like really. … Not just being hairy but doing what men do every morning, you know. Not having periods, but shaving and I just felt so much a freak.'

Although we also contextualized the interview extracts in relation to feminist work on the social construction of femininity and the beauty myth, the guiding principle of the research was simply to report what women said, treating it as literally true and representative of their experience, and thereby to break the silence about women's experience of PCOS. The political importance of this for us as feminists was borne out when we received letters and e-mails from women with PCOS thanking us for giving voice to their experience, enabling them, for the first time, to realize that they were not alone: one woman e-mailed to say that she had taken a copy of our article to her doctor as evidence that her feelings about her condition were not abnormal. This represented, for us, a pragmatically successful piece of feminist research, in that it achieved what we wanted it to: giving a voice to women's distressing experiences of PCOS and thereby beginning a process of change.

For the purposes of this research project, Jo and I simply ignored positivist and postmodern doubts about the relationship between 'voice' and 'experience'. Nor did we engage much with issues of how we had analysed the data, presenting our own involvement in the research process as little more than that of amanuenses or conduits for other women's voices. Many other feminists take this position, such as feminist sociologist Barbara Katz Rothman (1996) who describes her research on women's experience of prenatal diagnosis as 'a project in bearing witness'. She says:

> I did think that I could pass through me the grief, anguish, fears, worries, strength and courage that these women showed me, and make that clear and visible to others ... through my voice I represent theirs. I am their representative to the world that reads my words, hears me speak. (Rothman, 1996: 53)

In research reports such as these, authors typically present lengthy extracts that are assumed to 'speak for themselves'. As Hollway (1989: 40) says, 'the value informing the approach is typically that the researchers would not presume to question the truthfulness of the account'. Indeed, in much feminist research, the author states explicitly that she is trying to avoid the imposition of her own meanings or interpretations: that she is simply reporting faithfully what women say to her.

DILEMMAS OF 'EXPERIENCE': CHALLENGING VOICES

One of my concerns about qualitative feminist research is that it often *claims* to be 'representing women's experience' or 'reclaiming women's voices', but is in fact rather selective about what kinds of experiences, and which voices, are endorsed as 'authentic', 'accurate', 'reliable', etc. It has become commonplace for feminists to criticize the early research for falsely universalizing women's experience, pointing out that 'our experience' as women is diverse and sometimes contradictory, a diversity often negated in general statements that falsely construct 'woman' as a unitary category across ethnic, class and sexual identity difference. What is passed off as 'our' experience all too often turns out to be the common and unproblematized knowledge only of white, middle-class, able-bodied, heterosexual Anglo-Americans (see Wilkinson and Kitzinger, 1996). The problem with 'experience' that I want to explore here, though, is not that of inclusiveness (important as this is) but rather the challenge posed to feminist theory by some women's 'experience', and how researchers handle this.

When I initially set out to do research on lesbian experience for my PhD, I quickly realized that I was not willing, as a feminist, simply to report what lesbians said to me when what they said was anti-feminist or even anti-lesbian. Listen, for example, to these lesbians interviewed in the early 1980s:

> I suspect we [lesbians] are in a slightly retarded state. Well 'retarded' is perhaps not quite right. It's a fear, an inability to relate to the opposite sex. There's nothing you can do about it. (Jane, quoted in Kitzinger, 1987: 119)

> Lesbianism is not something you choose; not something anybody in their right mind *would* choose. But if you're stuck with it, then you just have to put up with it, and live your life with as much dignity as you can. Certainly things aren't helped by exhibitionists who run around screaming about their lesbianism and somehow link it to politics, as though you could vote Labour, Conservative or Lesbian. (Lynne, quoted in Kitzinger, 1987: 141)

I found women's voices such as these enormously problematic: they reinforced precisely the 'pathological' model of lesbianism I was trying to challenge in my own work. The same problem arose later, when I was researching sexual harassment (see Thomas and Kitzinger, 1997), when some women I interviewed told me they'd never been sexually harassed and attacked feminist campaigns as unnecessary and unnatural:

> I've never been sexually harassed at work, and I don't think I ever would be. I'm very clear and straightforward in my relationships with my male colleagues, and sex just doesn't enter into it. I don't feel being a woman has ever stood in my way. It's simply irrelevant. (Dorothy, quoted in Kitzinger and Wilkinson, 1997: 567–8)

> I think there's too much fuss about sexual harassment really. I don't mind the odd compliment, you know. It just brightens up the day. There's been a few things at work that the feminists would probably call sexual harassment – men putting an arm around my shoulders, wolf-whistles, that sort of thing. ... It's not natural trying to ban it. It's part of normal relationships between men and women, isn't it. You can't just do away with

sex. I think people who want to ban it must be unsure of their own sexuality. (Eve, quoted in Kitzinger and Wilkinson, 1997: 568)

As a feminist, I do not want merely to act as a conduit for these women's versions of their experiences, nor do I think that simply allowing these women's voices to be heard constitutes feminist research. My own solution, in the book that arose out of the PhD, *The Social Construction of Lesbianism* (Kitzinger, 1987), was to describe as best I could, and in their own words, these women's representations of lesbianism and then to be explicit about my disagreement with them. I wrote:

> I have strong beliefs about which of the identities presented here is the 'best' ... I do not glorify this account by designating it as the most 'well-adjusted' or placing it at the apex of some developmental hierarchy with all other identity accounts trailing behind, indicative of psychological immaturity, but instead argue for my value claims explicitly, and from an overtly political perspective. (Kitzinger, 1987: 93).

This strategy is rare in social science research, and not particularly easy to implement. While I wanted to be honest about my own position, I also worried about abusing my power, as researcher, relative to the participants who had entrusted me with their experiences. After all, they weren't there to argue back.

This problem is pervasive in feminist social science research. Judging from some key absences in the feminist literature, it seems that simply omitting 'difficult' data of this kind must be a very common solution to the problems it poses. So, for example, compared with the many research projects detailing women's reported experiences of sexual harassment, there is virtually nothing about the experience of women who say they've never been sexually harassed and who are frustrated and impatient with feminist definitions of the term (but see Kitzinger and Thomas, 1995; Mott and Condor, 1997). Some researchers have described how they have deliberately censored themselves, choosing not to present data that they thought would be politically damaging: for example, Marie Jahoda (1981) did not publish her work with women students at a prestigious US university who told her that they were there in order to find a husband and were not particularly interested in studying (and see Stanley, 1983: 121 on 'open secrets'): 'things we all know about but almost no feminist ever talks about (apart from behind firmly closed doors'). More often, though, researchers simply remain silent, and these women's voices are not represented, nor their absence alluded to.

When such data are included in published reports, the problems they pose are dealt with by (with varying degrees of explicitness) re-theorizing the relationship between 'voice' and 'experience' such that, while – in general – women can be trusted to 'give voice' to their own experience, these sorts of situations constitute instances in which women's voices are treated as unreliable in some way. The criticisms of positivism and postmodernism about making the leap from 'voice' to 'experience' are sometimes selectively drawn upon in order to discredit the voices of women considered by the researcher to be anti-feminist or non-feminist.

One approach is to treat the voices of women with whom the researcher is in disagreement as fundamentally misguided and as indicative of 'false consciousness', 'male identification', 'developmental immaturity', 'inauthenticity', and so on. If women do not report being oppressed, then this is taken as evidence of the depth of their oppression. Feminist scholar Mary Daly (1988: 47) describes 'patriarchally possessed women' as 'fembots', incapable of moral outrage. Reviewing the feminist literature on cosmetic surgery, Kathy Davis points out the extent to which women who elect to undergo such operations are seen as victims rather than as agents:

> Whether blinded by consumer capitalism, oppressed by patriarchal ideologies, or inscribed within the discourses of femininity, the woman who opts for the 'surgical fix' marches to the beat of a hegemonic system – a system which polices, constrains and inferiorizes her. If she plays the beauty game, she can only do so as 'cultural dope' (Garfinkel, 1967) – as duped victim of false consciousness or as normalized object of disciplinary regimes. (Davis, 1996: 105)

Feminist psychologists typically construct models of consciousness development with anti-feminist views at the bottom, so that increasing developmental maturity is defined as increasing conformity with (one particular version of) feminist ideology. A classic and widely used model of lesbian identity development (Cass, 1984) locates lesbians who believe themselves to be sick at the bottom of a developmental hierarchy: at the top are women who agree with the researcher's own view that lesbianism is just part of who we are as human beings. In a rare, and stimulating, discussion of the problems of this kind of analysis, feminist sociologist Margaret Andersen (1981) describes her work on 'corporate wives' – middle-class women who adopt, and defend, traditional gender roles in marriage. The twenty women she interviewed were well educated (teachers, medical technologists, draughtswomen, etc.), but their careers had become secondary to their marriages, most of them had quit their jobs early on, and they moved frequently as their husbands were transferred from one job to another. They claimed, however, to be content with their situation – and this was, as the author notes, 'in direct contrast to the wealth of research and testimony emerging from the feminist movement which has debunked the conventional image of contentment among traditional wives' (Andersen, 1981: 311). Her initial analysis of these interviews (Andersen, 1979) employed a variant of the 'false consciousness' argument, suggesting that these women's accounts were inauthentic or insincere. In response, her twenty participants (all members of the same newcomers' club in a small US city) organized a collective letter of rebuttal, arguing that women like themselves can, despite the claims of feminist sociologists, find fulfilment as wives and mothers, and accusing Andersen of being jealous of the fact that they did not need to work outside the home due to their husbands' large incomes.

After receiving her participants' collective protest, Margaret Andersen re-analysed her 'corporate wives' talk, suggesting that their contentment should be understood within the context of the privileges they receive from their privileged location within the class system. As she says: 'This argument turns the perspective of false consciousness on its head. Where false consciousness would depict the women as unaware of their true and oppressive conditions, this article suggests that they are keenly aware of their real situation and it is not experienced as oppressive' (Andersen, 1981: 324). In other words, the same women's talk was treated first as evidence of their failure accurately to represent their own experience of gender oppression, and then subsequently as evidence of their experience of class privilege. These may both be fair and reasonable analyses, but they involve (as the author indicates) analytic judgements about the relationship between women's words and women's lives. It is not always clear on what basis such judgements are generally made, or on what principled bases we – as feminists – can make them.

One 'solution' attempted by some feminist researchers has been to share their analyses with their research participants and to publish only those analyses with which their participants are in agreement ('checking with members' or 'participant validation'). This has clear ethical advantages in that it decreases the power difference between researcher and researched and gives the people who contributed the data some control over how it is used. It does not, however, constitute *analysis*. And while researchers whose

participants endorse their analysis sometimes use this as evidence for 'validity', researchers whose participants dislike their analysis rarely suggest that this invalidates their work. Instead they point to exactly the problems I have outlined above: the discrepancy between feminist and non-feminist ways of understanding experience.

Rather than present other women (even anti-feminist women) in an unfavourable light as victims, some researchers use women's talk as evidence that they have arrived at an accurate (i.e., in some sense 'feminist') understanding of social power, but are attempting a non-feminist (or anti-feminist) solution. So, for example, Andrea Dworkin (1983), in her book *Right-Wing Women*, describes how politically reactionary women share feminist concerns about the devaluing of women, and how their insistence on the importance of women in family life is an attempt to elevate and protect women. This bears comparison with my own analysis of women's refusal of the label 'sexual harassment' to describe their own experience:

> The term 'sexual harassment' describes female subordination. When women say, to themselves or to other people, 'I am *not* being sexually harassed', one of the things they are saying is 'I am *not* a victim. I am *not* a subordinated person'. Unable to change the situation they are in, women gain what little power they can by insisting on defining that situation in their own terms. Women who 'make a joke of it' or 'play along' succeed in avoiding the blatant demonstration of their own victimhood: they are 'choosing' what would otherwise be forced upon them. (Kitzinger and Thomas, 1995: 38–9)

Part of my intention in writing the paragraph I've just quoted was to present the best possible case for some women's refusal to see themselves (as I saw them) as victims of sexual harassment. It would have seemed disrespectful to my research participants to write what I probably thought at the time: that they needed their consciousnesses raised about abuses of male power and ought to develop a feminist understanding of sexuality in the workplace. And of course, it's all very well to berate one's research participants for their failure to see the world in feminist terms (and I'd done that in my research on lesbianism: Kitzinger, 1987), but it doesn't change anything. With the 'sexual harassment' research I was trying instead to understand *why* women didn't interpret their experience through a feminist lens, and what the costs and benefits of feminism are for women struggling to make sense of their lives.

The problem with this approach is that it relies heavily on the interpretative skills of the feminist researcher. Women interviewees do not generally say, for example, 'I have an essentially feminist consciousness; I understand the impact of male power in my life; but whereas feminists want to deal with it overtly, by fighting against it, I've decided to gain what power I can by playing along or by acting the part of wife and mother.' This is very much an interpretative gloss (and one with which research participants may well disagree, if asked). Instead of treating women's voices as transparently reflecting women's experiences, it requires the researcher to engage in some kind of (unspecified) transformation of what is said. Such interpretations may be 'right' (valid, useful, interesting), but it is not clear to me now – nor was it then! – how they can be defended or explicated on the basis of the data. In effect, they are not drawn from data analysis at all, but from the researcher's prior theories.

Finally, postmodernism has offered researchers a way of exploiting the contradictions that often arise over the course of an interview. These are said to arise from competing 'discourses' ('accounts', 'narratives', 'repertoires', etc.), some of which are falsely conscious/oppressive and others accurate/liberatory. Instead of treating women's voices as literally representative of their experience, researchers can argue instead that women have access to a range of different 'discourses' (ways of talking about experience), some 'feminist', some 'patriarchal'. According to critical discourse analyst Ian Parker, people 'pick up and reproduce certain discourses about the nature of the self, and they find it difficult to step back and question where those ways of describing the world may have come from, and what interests they may serve' (Parker, 1997: 286). Within this framework, a woman who uses a discourse considered oppressive by the researcher can be described as having, through her talk, 'participated in, and reproduced, her own oppression' (Parker, 1997: 286).

This enables some ways of talking, and some voices (the feminist ones), to be heard as transparently reflecting women's experiences while others (the patriarchal ones) are treated as misrepresentations. Decisions about which talk constitutes a 'discourse', and about which discourses are liberatory and which oppressive, are made on theoretical grounds, and sometimes seem to have only a tenuous connection with the data.

For example, Nicola Gavey (1997) uses a post-structuralist approach (based on Hollway, 1989) in her study of women's experiences of heterosexual coercion. One of her interviewees describes an experience in which she gave in to a man's request for sex because sex is 'no big deal' (Gavey labels this the 'permissive sexuality discourse') and because 'he was sort of desperate to have sex' (which Gavey sees as evidence for the 'male sexual needs discourse'). Nicola Gavey is very critical of both 'discourses', but also anxious to avoid any implication that she is criticizing her interviewee or that the interview is 'falsely conscious' (1997: 60). The former implication is avoided via the post-structuralist reconceptualization of talk as reflecting 'discourses' rather than internal psychological states, so that what is criticized is a socially available discourse, not the individual who avails herself of it. The latter implication is avoided through uncovering contradictory 'positionings' in the talk, which are said to represent a 'battle' between discourse (Gavey, 1997: 60).

An alternative reading of Gavey's work here is that she, a feminist researcher concerned about sexual coercion, has interviewed a woman who represents sexual coercion, at least on this occasion, as 'no big deal'. In other words, the interviewee's analysis of her own experience is different from the analysis Nicola Gavey wants to make of it. Instead of acknowledging that these are two competing interpretations of experience, Gavey – using her power as researcher – scours the transcript for evidence that the interviewee, at some level, agrees with her (or, in post-structuralist language, has access to 'some form of feminist discourse').

In sum, despite the feminist commitment to hearing women's voices and validating women's experience, feminist research often displays considerable ambivalence about these voices and the experiences they claim to represent.

TALK AS ACTION: FEMINIST CONVERSATION ANALYSIS

Feminist researchers, like other qualitative data analysts, have commented that the talk of individual research participants in interviews (and even more so in focus groups) is always a collaborative production. That is, the way people talk about their experiences depends on who they are talking to, what they have been asked, what shared knowledge they think can be assumed, and what kinds of reactions they anticipate and receive. Interviewers are inevitably involved in the co-construction of the words uttered by their interviewees. And yet, with few exceptions, feminist research (like most other kinds) presents its data as the isolated productions of discrete individuals. My own move into a very different (conversation analytic) approach to the relationship between 'voice' and 'experience' began when I started to take seriously the local interactional context in which women's voices were being elicited.

At the time, I was working with a graduate student, Hannah Frith, on women's experiences of sexual refusal and we had become interested in the concept of 'emotion work' (Frith and Kitzinger, 1998; see also Frith and Kitzinger, 1997, 2001). Initially developed and popularized by Arlie Hochschild's classic study, *The Managed Heart* (1983), this is a feminist coinage devised to refer to the work done, disproportionately by women, in dealing with other people's feelings: it includes 'soothing tempers, boosting confidence, fuelling pride, preventing frictions, and mending ego wounds' (Calhoun, 1992: 118). The majority of social scientific studies detailing the prevalence and consequences of 'emotion work' rely on self-report data, extracts from which are used as evidence for analysts' assertions that their research participants do 'emotion work'. The inferential leap from what women *say* (women's voices) to the reality that lies behind the talk (women's experience) is untheorized, and the talk is treated as though it offered a 'transparent' window to an underlying experience. Hannah had collected focus group data in which young women talked about their difficulties in refusing (hetero)sex, and they often gave as a reason for their difficulties their concern about hurting men's feelings ('he could end up getting really upset about it and you really wouldn't want that' or 'the night I finished with him I felt so upset and so guilty that I'd hurt him that I ended up having sex with him'). This kind of data was mirrored in the literature on the gendering of emotion work in heterosexual relationships. For example, Duncombe and Marsden (1993) claim that 'the dominant pattern of our female respondents' experience of coupledom was an asymmetry of emotional response' (1993: 225) and they support this claim with an extract from a group discussion:

> I think I always loved him too much. I didn't really have a 'falling in love' … but I had a deep love for him, but it was all very unequal … . I never felt really very loved and I think that for every one of the sixteen years of my marriage, it was a struggle to make him love me more and to get the relationship equal.

Notice that this extract is presented as an example of how women 'experience' (rather than, for example, 'describe' or 'talk about') coupledom as asymmetrical. In other words, this research participant's description of her marriage is taken as a transparent window through which the analysts are able to see what the marriage was 'really' like. Indeed, later in the same paper, Duncombe and Marsden refer back to this extract with a passing mention of 'the woman who spent sixteen years struggling to make her husband love her' (1993: 236). What she *says* is taken as pretty much accurately reflecting what her marriage was actually like and as revealing the existence of her emotional labour within this marriage. The analysis is brief; the meaning of the data extract is taken to be self-evident and unproblematically to refer to what really happened. Although she is speaking in a group discussion, there is no explanation of why the woman is telling her story at this particular point, how her listeners react, or to which of their expectations and previous statements she may be orienting in telling her story. As I have shown, use of data in this way is absolutely typical of research on emotion work (and, indeed, of feminist qualitative research more generally).

By contrast, Hannah and I tried to understand the voices of women in their local interactional context. Our focus was not on what 'really happened' (i.e., whether or not they actually engaged in 'emotion work' with men) but rather how young women in interaction with other young women *talk about* their own and their male partners' emotions. We showed that whether or not young women 'really' do emotion work when involved in actual sexual negotiations with men, in talking *as though* they do they construct themselves as emotionally stronger than their male partners. Their collaborative depiction of 'what men are like' serves to present men as emotional weaklings who agonize about their own sexual desirability and performance, while young women produce themselves as knowledgeable and sophisticated sexual actors. We showed how the young women in our focus group data worked together to complete each others' sentences, to invent hypothetical and allegedly 'typical' dialogues, and to provide interpretations and glosses of each other's reported experiences, all of which produced them as active agents, knowledgeable about heterosexual relationships and able to take care of delicate male egos. 'Emotion work', we argued, is not simply a concept that analysts apply to their research participants' talk: it is also a resource actively employed by young women in interaction with each other.

As I began to acquire some of the technical skills of CA and started to look at what was happening in focus group and other kinds of group discussion in more detail, I began to see all sorts of actions going on other than simply 'topic talk' – and these other actions gradually became more compelling to me than the topics of discussion that the focus groups were set up to elicit. For example, another graduate student, Virginia Braun, whom I co-supervised with Sue Wilkinson, was carrying out research on women's experience of their vaginas and ran a series of focus groups in which women discussed this – by and large treating the voices in the data as transparently revealing women's actual experiences (Braun and Kitzinger, 2001a, 2001b; Braun and Wilkinson, 2001). But during the course of some of these groups, a few women 'came out' as lesbian or bisexual, i.e. they revealed their sexual identity to others in the group who had not previously known it. The same thing happened in other data collection enterprises run by graduate students and faculty in the department, and soon I had a collection of more than twenty data fragments in which 'coming out' was being done as a live action. The entire literature on 'coming out' is based on interviews or other self-report data in which people *talk about* coming out, and as such it raises all the problems about the relationship between 'voice' and 'experience' that has been discussed here. How do we know that their retrospective account is what it was really like? Are they telling the story of how they came out to their parents, or friends, or colleagues, in a 'slanted' way to impress the interviewer, or to display their own victimization? In fact, these questions about the relationship between 'voices' and 'experience' have led some coming-out researchers to treat reports of coming-out experiences as 'narratives' rather than as representing a lived experiential reality (Plummer, 1995). But by looking at what was going on between people in data collection sessions, I had stumbled across data that I would probably have thought it impossible to collect: real live comings out (see a preliminary analyses of two of these in Kitzinger, 2000a).

This, in turn, led me to some data the analysis of which I want to discuss in more detail. I only have one instance of this, and it is in some ways even more unlikely a 'find' than the live 'coming out' data. It is taken from a focus group run by Sue Wilkinson as part of a research project on women's experience of breast cancer (Wilkinson, 2000a, 2000b). Sue knew I was collecting instances of 'coming out' and remarked casually one evening: 'What a pity it was that I didn't come out in the breast cancer group today or you could have had it for your collection.' At the time, I casually agreed and thought no more about it – and then several months later it dawned on me what she had said. Lesbian and gay life is full of occasions where we don't come out, where we 'pass' as heterosexual – and we feel guilty, resentful or angry about living in the kind of world that makes that commonplace. 'Not coming out' is a highly salient event for many lesbians and gay men on the basis of which

we make ethical and political judgements both about our own behaviour and about the constraints of the world in which we live. Not coming out is one manifestation of 'silencing'. But how do you study something that *didn't* happen? Well, it was on tape, so I asked Sue to find it for me, and here it is. It is transcribed so as to preserve as much as possible of the way in which the talk was produced, both in terms of the relationship of one turn to another (the square brackets indicate overlap, the equals signs mean that there's no space between turns) and in terms of features like emphasis (underscoring), stretched or elongated sounds (colons), volume (capitals for loud, degree sounds around soft talk) and laughter ("huh" is full laughter, (h) shows laughter tokens infiltrating talk). (For a full key to this kind of data transcription, see Chapter 11 by Peräkylä in this volume.) As the fragment opens, Eve is talking about her husband's reaction to her mastectomy. Sue's 'not coming out' is between lines 44 and 46.

Extract I

36	Eve:	I mean he a̲i̲n't sex-<u>mad</u> my 'usband
37		but [I mean] a::ll me:n:
38	Jill:	[No: : : :]
39	Eve:	(0.2) like boobs <u>d</u>on't they.
40		(0.5)
41	Sue:	[°I believe so°]
42	Eve:	[So there you a:re.]=If he didn't- =
43		<u>Wh</u>::y?=Aren't you married¿
44		(0.5)
45	Eve:	hu::h! [h u : h]
46	Sue:	[Di£vo:r]ced£.
47	Eve:	[Di(h)vo(h)rced huh huh]
48	Jill:	[h u h h u h]
49	Eve:	A::h we(h)ll.
50		(0.5)
51	Eve:	°Ah well.° ((sadly))
52		(0.2)
53	Eve:	But m- they <u>do</u>.= I mean it <u>d</u>oes
54		affect 'em a <u>bi</u>:t.=I think. °You
55		know°. But the' get u:[sed to it.]
56	Ann:	[.hhh Yeah I]
		((continues))

From the point of view of a breast cancer researcher interested in women's experience of breast cancer, this interchange is a small aside of no particular significance. But for someone interested in coming out – how it is done, and how it is not done – this is a 'live' instance of 'not coming out' which can be used to understand the operation of normative heterosexuality in action.

A conversation analytic approach to this data fragment reveals that 'not coming out' is here occasioned by having available an interactional slot in which 'coming out' could be but is not done. In other words, it is Eve's question 'Aren't you married?' that makes coming out or not coming out a relevant thing to do. As it happens, Sue did not come out as lesbian in *any* of the focus groups she facilitated with breast cancer patients; but it was only in *this* group, and at this particular moment in this group, that she was relevantly 'not coming out' because nowhere else was she asked questions about her marital status, her sex life, her living arrangements, and so on. It is true that she didn't reveal her sexual identity in any other part of her data only in the sense that she also didn't reveal her class, her ethnicity, her age, her parenthood status, her voting predilections or her preferences in food. By contrast, Eve's question 'Aren't you married?' makes Sue's lesbianism relevant in something of the same way as a question such as 'Don't you like sausages?' would make relevant Sue's vegetarianism. (Technically, Eve's question is a first pair part of an adjacency pair and makes an answer conditionally relevant: see Peräkylä, Chapter 11, this volume, and Heritage, 1984, for more detailed discussion of the technical organization of talk in interaction, especially adjacency pairs and preference/dispreference.)

The answer Sue gives, eventually – after a significant delay (of nearly a second) – 'Divorced' (on line 46), is accurate, but is not the only accurate answer she could have given. It locates her by reference to a past heterosexual marital relationship, and not by reference to her current lesbian relationship. Conversation analysts (e.g. Schegloff, 1972, 1996) have explored in some detail why and how, when there is a range of equally 'accurate' ways of answering a question, people select just one of this array, and what this tells us about the kind of world people take for granted that they share in common. Here, Sue is oriented to normative heterosexuality as the taken-for-granted 'normal' way to be, and she presents herself within that framework.

In fact, normative heterosexuality is apparent earlier in this extract. In talking about her husband – mentioned earlier by name as 'Bill' and referred to as 'my 'usband' in line 36, Eve is presenting herself as heterosexual. It isn't that she is 'coming out' as heterosexual, in the sense that this is an action to which she is oriented. Rather she, like other heterosexuals across my data, treats heterosexuality as the ordinary default way to be. The gender of her partner and their marital status is not treated as anything special: the action that she is engaged in is not 'coming out'

as heterosexual, but launching a telling about her husband's reaction to her mastectomy. Other research and political activism has documented the extent to which we live in a world in which the macro-structures of society – laws about marriage, inheritance, tax, adoption, etc. – presume and reinforce heterosexuality. What we see in this small data fragment (and as I will show, it is replicated over many, many more) is that we also live in a world in which the *micro-structure* of ordinary, everyday interaction – who assumes what about whom, how those assumptions are built into talk – also presumes and reinforces heterosexuality. In a more mundane, routine, and perhaps for that reason more insidious manner, the heterosexual social structure is built and rebuilt through talk by people who are not being overtly homophobic or anti-gay, but who are simply taking for granted a normative heterosexual world, and reconstituting it, moment by moment, in their interactions.

The interactional slot in which Sue does not come out arises, as we have said, as a consequence of Eve's question. But Eve's question is in turn responsive to something earlier in the interaction, at lines 37 and 39. In those lines, a different interactional slot has opened up. Eve has launched her telling about her husband's difficulties with her post-mastectomy body by making a known-by-all-of-us-to-be-true statement about members of the category 'men' (a category of which her husband is commonsensically known to be a member – thereby exonerating him from any personal culpability for his interest in 'boobs'). Her claim that 'all men like boobs don't they' is an instance of what conversation analysts have described as an 'idiomatic' or 'formulaic' statement inviting affiliative responses (Drew and Holt, 1988; Kitzinger, 2000b). In this particular context, she is inviting her recipients, by virtue of being women, to affirm the truth of her statement about men. The interactional slot open at lines 40 and 41, then, is a slot in which agreement or affiliation with shared cultural (heterosexual female) experience is relevant. And here it is relevantly missing.

Sue's (delayed, and quiet) response, 'I believe so' (line 41), disclaims any direct epistemic access to whether or not men like boobs. She withholds affiliation. The relevance of knowing, as women, about what men 'like' sexually, is at least potentially hearable, by a recipient to whom such things matter, as displaying an assumption that all the women present are heterosexual – as an invitation to bond over the presumed-shared knowledge of heterosexual women. In displaying herself not to have direct personal first-hand knowledge, Sue signals some difficulty with or distance from a taken-for-granted (traditional, feminine, married, heterosexual) perspective in a non-specific, but subsequently buildable-upon, manner. Certainly Eve hears it this way and she self-interrupts (in line 43) to offer a candidate account: 'Aren't you married?' In other words, Eve asks her question not out of a dispassionate interest in Sue's marital status, but in order to solve the problem as to why Sue has just distanced herself from this bit of folk wisdom about what all men are like.

Sue's 'answer', then (although it deals with the format of Eve's question), does not really engage with the action Eve is concerned with, and in this sense it is a kind of evasion. Some answer such as 'No, I'm not married because I'm a lesbian and what would I know or care about men's interest in boobs?' would have engaged with Eve's reason for asking her question. It would also, of course, have caused major disruption to the otherwise ongoing activity of the group – activity for which Sue, as the researcher facilitating the group discussion, is responsible. So Sue's turn at line 41 ('I believe so') is a first 'coming out' step in which she is oriented to her lesbianism in contrast with the group's displayed heterosexuality. Her turn at line 46 ('divorced') is a reorientation to her role as researcher responsible for facilitating the group, stepping back from the 'coming out' process she has initiated, and Eve has pursued, and hence 'doing her job'. The cost for lesbians and gay men of 'doing our jobs' across a variety of contexts – that is, of ensuring that our social and professional interactions run off smoothly and unproblematically – is often to suppress our differences from the heterosexuals with whom we are engaging, to allow a heterosexual assumption to continue, so that the actions in which we and they are otherwise engaged can continue without disruption. This little fragment of data displays just that.

In analysing this data, my major resource was not my lesbian feminism – which I have always brought to my data analyses – but rather my more recently acquired knowledge of, and skills in applying, the substantial body of empirical research findings by conversation analysts dealing with the technical features of interaction: features like sequence organization, turn-taking and inter-turn gaps, preference organization, the use of formulaic utterances, and so on. There is nothing inherently 'feminist' (or anti-feminist) about these technical findings; they simply describe some regular organizational patterns in conversational activity. As a lesbian and a feminist I can use the tools of conversation analysis to understand better how the normative social order is constructed in daily interaction.

In pursuing my current interest in how the everyday sexist and heterosexist everyday world is produced and reproduced, live, in situ, there is no particular reason to use interview or focus group data. In fact, these are pretty specialized environments in which people are generally busy 'doing being research participants' or 'doing being researchers'. Of course they sometimes invoke and index their other identities (e.g. as heterosexuals or lesbians) and engage in other interesting activities, but the research focus makes these kinds of data generally less interesting to me than ordinary, naturally occurring conversations in which people are pursuing their own agendas. For example, I have audiotapes of around fifty out-of-hours calls to a locum GP, and one of the features that is immediately apparent is that many of the callers refer to the patient, right at the beginning of the call, using a 'family' reference term such as 'husband' or 'wife' – terms that, of course, are not in any unproblematic sense available for lesbians and gay men in talking about *our* partners. For example:

Extract 2

```
01  Doc:  hello:?
02        (0.4)
03  Clr:  u::h hello.
04        (.)
05        This is Misses W((deleted))
06        (0.9)
07  Doc:  mm hm?
08  Clr:  Um::. (.) My husban::d, (0.2) isn't
09        very we:ll.
```

Extract 3

```
01  Doc:  Hel:lo:,
02  Clr:  Hel:lo, is that' th' doctor¿
03  Doc:  <Yes, Doctor ((deleted)) speaki::ng,
04  Clr:  i:i:Yeah couldja's come an' see my
05        wife please, .h[h
06  Doc:                 [Yes:.
```

Extract 4

```
05  Doc:  Yes it is, Doctor ((deleted))
06        speaking, hh!=
07  Clr:  =Eh: my wife has uh: just fai:nted.
```

This is the sort of behaviour that lesbians and gay men often refer to, ironically, as 'coming out as heterosexual' – although, of course, they are not doing 'coming out' so much as merely getting on with the business of calling the doctor. What we are pointing to in ironically describing their behaviour as 'coming out' is their access to the (heterosexual) kinship terms of the society, and their use of these as a resource in seeking help for a sick partner. Early on in interactions heterosexuals feel free to indicate their heterosexuality, in passing, with no thought, apparently, that they are 'flaunting' their heterosexual relationship, or 'talking about their sex lives', or in any way engaging in the sort of behaviour that when we do it attracts the comment: 'I don't mind gays, but why must they be so blatant?'

The freedom to produce oneself as heterosexual, as Eve does at line 36 in Extract 1 (and Jill has just before this fragment starts), while not being treated as doing anything special, is one manifestation of heterosexual privilege. By contrast Sue, at line 40, is forced either to collude with a heterosexual assumption (that she is the sort of person, i.e., a heterosexual woman, who would know and care about men's liking of boobs) or to disrupt (as it turns out she does) the smooth flow of the conversation by disaffiliating from heteronormativity. For Sue to have come out as lesbian at line 44 or 46 would have been a bombshell dropped into the conversation apparently from nowhere – and would have been, I think, exactly the sort of behaviour that attracts accusations of 'flaunting it'. Conversely, what lesbians and gay men see as the routine reproduction of the heterosexual assumption by people who take for granted their unquestioned right to invoke or allude to their (hetero)sexuality in public, is absolutely not so oriented to by heterosexuals who are just going about their business. What these kinds of data are beginning to reveal, I think, is some fundamental workings of everyday heterosexism, power and oppression. Data like these can help to elucidate how heterosexuality is woven into the warp and weft of ordinary everyday social practices that reflect and constitute the world in which we live. Conversation analysis is about the actions through which the taken-for-granted world is produced: it is not primarily about language or even talk, but about mundane social actions.

CONCLUSION

Women's voices are a key resource for feminist qualitative research – but what we make of these voices, how we understand their relationship to women's 'experience' and women's 'reality', is a complex and contested issue. In this chapter, I have highlighted, in particular, the interpretative leap – from 'voice' to 'experience' – that feminist researchers commonly make in analysing our qualitative data. I have explored a range of

ways in which feminist researchers – including myself – have managed this interpretative leap, and have described both the costs and the benefits of these different approaches.

My own view is that the emphasis on 'voice' has led to an over-reliance on self-report methods, to the detriment of approaches that involve the researcher in direct observation of the phenomenon of interest. So, for example, if 'coming out' is the research topic, data in which research participants *talk about* coming out (or not coming out) as lesbian or gay require the researcher to make an interpretative leap from these retrospective accounts to the experience they purport to represent – with all of the problems associated with such a leap. By contrast, data in which people actually do (or don't) come out as lesbian or gay give the researcher direct access to this topic. They enable her to see coming out (or not coming out) at first hand, as a live action. Not only does this (conversation analytic) approach avoid altogether the problem of the relationship between 'voice' and 'experience' (because experience itself is being studied directly, at first hand), it also enables the feminist researcher to observe everyday acts of (for example, lesbian and gay) oppression, and everyday acts of resistance to such oppression, as they actually happen. While being committed to methodological pluralism, and to achieving the best possible 'fit' between research objectives and research methods, in my view the study of talk as a form of action in its own right offers the feminist researcher unparalleled opportunities for developing insight into the social world.

NOTE

1 Some forms of discourse analysis and narrative analysis also focus on action as it is performed through talk; see Chapter 7 by Andrews et al. and Chapter 12 by Hepburn and Potter (in this volume) for discussion of this.

REFERENCES

Andersen, M.L. (1979) 'Affluence, contentment, and resistance to feminism: the case of the corporate gypsies', in M. Lewis (ed.), *Research in Social Problems and Public Policy*. Greenwich, CT: Johnson Assoc.

Andersen, M.L. (1981) 'Corporate wives: longing for liberation or satisfied with the status quo?', *Urban Life*, 10: 311–27.

Bacchi, C. and Jose, J. (1994) 'Historicising sexual harassment', *Women's History Review*, 3: 263–70.

Backhouse, C. and Cohen, L. (1979) *The Secret Oppression: Sexual Harassment of Working Women*. Toronto: Macmillan.

Baddeley, A. (1979) 'The limitations of human memory: implications for the design of retrospective surveys', in L. Moss and H. Goldstein (eds), *The Recall Method in Social Surveys*. London: University of London Institute of Education.

Braun, V. and Kitzinger, C. (2001a) 'The perfectible vagina: size matters', *Culture, Health and Sexuality*, 3: 263–77.

Braun, V. and Kitzinger, C. (2001b) '"Snatch", "hole" or "honey-pot"? Semantic categories and the problem of nonspecificity in female genital slang', *Journal of Sex Research*, 38: 146–58.

Braun, V. and Wilkinson, S. (2001) 'Socio-cultural representations of the vagina', *Journal of Reproductive and Infant Psychology*, 19: 17–32.

Brown, L. and Burman, E. (1997) Editors' Introduction: 'The delayed memory debate: why feminist voices matter', *Feminism and Psychology*, 7: 7–16.

Calhoun, C. (1992) 'Emotional work', in E.B. Cole and S. Coultrap-McQuin (eds), *Explorations in Feminist Ethics: Theory and Practice*. Indianapolis: Indiana University Press.

Cass, V. (1984) 'Homosexual identity formation: a theoretical model', *Journal of Homosexuality*, 4: 219–21.

Cherry, N. and Rodgers, B. (1979) 'Using a longitudinal study to assess the quality of retrospective data', in L. Moss and H. Goldstein (eds), *The Recall Method in Social Surveys*. London: University of London Institute of Education.

Daly, M. (1988) 'Be-friending: the lust to share happiness', in S. Hoagland and J. Penelope (eds), *For Lesbians Only: A Separatist Anthology*. London: Onlywomen Press.

Davis, K. (1996) 'From objectified body to embodied subject: a biographical approach to cosmetic surgery', in S. Wilkinson (ed.), *Feminist Social Psychologies: International Perspectives*. Buckingham: Open University Press, pp. 104–18.

DeVault, M. (1996) 'Talking back to sociology: distinctive contributions of feminist methodology', *Annual Review of Sociology*, 22: 29–50.

Drew, P. and Holt, E. (1988) 'Complainable matters: the use of idiomatic expressions in making complaints', *Social Problems*, 35(4): 398–416.

DuBois, B. (1983) 'Passionate scholarship: notes on values, knowing and method in feminist social science', in G. Bowles and R.D. Klein (eds), *Theories of Women's Studies*. London: Routledge & Kegan Paul.

Duncombe, J. and Marsden, D. (1993) 'Love and intimacy: the gender division of emotion and "emotion work". A neglected aspect of sociological discussion of heterosexual relationships', *Sociology*, 27: 221–41.

Dworkin, A. (1983) *Right-Wing Women*. London: The Women's Press.

Farley, L. (1978) *Sexual Shakedown: The Sexual Harassment of Women on the Job*. New York: Warner Books.

Frith, H. and Kitzinger, C. (1997) 'Talk about sexual miscommunication', *Women's Studies International Forum*, 20: 517–28.

Frith, H. and Kitzinger, C. (1998) '"Emotion work" as a participant resource: a feminist analysis of young women's talk-in-interaction', *Sociology*, 32: 299–320.

Frith, H. and Kitzinger, C. (2001) 'Reformulating sexual script theory: developing a discursive psychology of sexual negotiation', *Theory and Psychology*, 11: 209–32.

Garfinkel, H. (1967) *Studies in Ethnomethodology*. Englewood Cliffs, NJ: Prentice-Hall.

Gavey, N. (1997) 'Feminist poststructuralism and discourse analysis', in M.M. Gergen and S.N. Davis (eds), *Towards a New Psychology of Gender*. New York: Routledge.

Gilligan, C. (1982) *In a Different Voice*. Cambridge, MA: Harvard University Press.

Harding, S. (1987) 'Epistemological questions', in S. Harding (ed.), *Feminism and Methodology: Social Science Issues*. Milton Keynes: Open University Press, pp. 181–90.

Harding, S. (1991) *Whose Science? Whose Knowledge?* Buckingham: Open University Press.

Heritage, J. (1984) 'Conversation analysis', in *Garfinkel and Ethnomethodology*. Cambridge: Polity Press, ch. 8, pp. 233–80.

Hochschild, A.R. (1983) *The Managed Heart*. Berkeley: University of California Press.

Hollway, W. (1989) *Subjectivity and Method in Psychology: Gender, Meaning and Science*. London: Sage.

Jahoda, M. (1981) 'To publish or not to publish?', *Journal of Social Issues*, 37: 208–20.

Kirsch, G.E. (1999) *Ethical Dilemmas in Feminist Research: The Politics of Location, Interpretation and Publication*. New York: State University of New York Press.

Kitzinger, C. (1987) *The Social Construction of Lesbianism*. London: Sage.

Kitzinger, C. (1999) 'Lesbian and gay psychology: is it critical?', *Annual Review of Critical Psychology*, 1(1): 50–66.

Kitzinger, C. (2000a) 'Doing feminist conversation analysis', *Feminism and Psychology*, 10: 163–93.

Kitzinger, C. (2000b) 'How to resist an idiom', *Research on Language and Social Interaction*, 33: 121–54.

Kitzinger, C. and Thomas, A. (1995) 'Sexual harassment: a discursive approach', in S. Wilkinson and C. Kitzinger (eds), *Feminism and Discourse*. London: Sage.

Kitzinger, C. and Wilkinson, S. (1997) 'Validating women's experience? Dilemmas in feminist research', *Feminism and Psychology*, 7: 566–74.

Kitzinger, C. and Willmott, J. (2002) '"The thief of womanhood": women's experience of polycystic ovarian syndrome', *Social Science and Medicine*, 54: 349–61.

Loftus, E. (1993) 'The reality of repressed memories', *American Psychologist*, 48: 518–37.

MacKinnon, C. (1979) *Sexual Harassment of Working Women*. New Haven, CT: Yale University Press.

Markowe, L.A. (2002) 'Coming out as lesbian', in A. Coyle and C. Kitzinger (eds), *Lesbian and Gay Psychology*. Oxford: Blackwells, pp. 63–80.

Millman, M. and Kanter, R.M. (eds) (1975) *Another Voice: Feminist Perspectives on Social Life and Social Science*. New York: Anchor Books.

Mott, H. and Condor, S. (1997) 'Sexual harassment and the working lives of secretaries', in A. Thomas and C. Kitzinger (eds), *Sexual Harassment: Contemporary Feminist Perspectives*. Buckingham: Open University Press.

Neisser, U. (1994) 'Self-narratives: true and false', in U. Neisser and R. Fivush (eds), *The Remembering Self: Construction and Accuracy in the Self-Narrative*. Cambridge: Cambridge University Press, pp. 1–18.

Oakley, A. (2000) *Experiments in Knowing: Gender and Method in the Social Sciences*. Cambridge: Polity Press.

Parker, I. (1997) 'Discursive psychology', in D. Fox and I. Prilleltensky (eds), *Critical Psychology*. London: Sage, pp. 284–98.

Plummer, K. (1995) *Telling Sexual Stories*. London: Routledge.

Rabinowtiz, V.C. and Martin, D. (2001) 'Choices and consequences: methodological issues in the study of gender', in R.K. Unger (ed.), *Handbook of the Psychology of Women and Gender*. New York: Wiley, pp. 29–52.

Rathje, N. and Hughes, T. (1975) 'A garbage project as a non-reactive approach: garbage in … garbage out?', in H.W. Sinaiko and L.A. Broedling (eds), *Perspectives on Attitude Assessment: Surveys and Their Alternatives*. Manpower and Advisory Services, Technical Report No. 2. Washington, DC: Smithsonian Institute.

Reinharz, S. (1992) *Feminist Methods in Social Research*. Oxford: Oxford University Press.

Rivers, I. (2002) 'Developmental issues for lesbian and gay youth', in A. Coyle and C. Kitzinger (eds), *Lesbian and Gay Psychology*. Oxford: Blackwells, pp. 30–44.

Rothman, B.K. (1996) 'Bearing witness: representing women's experiences of prenatal diagnosis', *Feminism and Psychology*, 6(1): 52–5.

Schegloff, E.A. (1972) 'Notes on a conversational practice: formulating place', in D.N. Sudnow (ed.), *Studies in Social Interaction*. New York: Free Press, pp. 75–119.

Schegloff, E.A. (1996) 'Some practices for referring to persons in talk-in-interaction', in B.A. Fox (ed.), *Studies in Anaphora*. Amsterdam: John Benjamins, pp. 437–85.

Scott, S. (1997) 'Feminists and false memories: a case of postmodern amnesia', *Feminism and Psychology*, 7: 33–8.

Smith, D. (1987) *The Everyday World as Problematic: A Feminist Sociology*. Boston: Northwestern University Press.

Smith, D. (1992) 'Sociology from women's experience: a reaffirmation', *Sociological Theory*, 10: 88–98.

Stanley, L. (1983) 'Open secrets: what they are and what we should do about them', in O. Butler (ed.), *Studies in Sexual Politics*. University of Manchester, pp. 117–39.

Taylor, J.M, Gilligan, C. and Sullivan, A.M (1996) 'Missing voices, changing meanings: developing a voice-centred, relational method and creating an interpretive community', in S. Wilkinson (ed.), *Feminist Social Psychologies: International Perspectives*. Buckingham: Open University Press, pp. 233–57.

Thomas, A. and Kitzinger, C. (1997) 'Sexual harassment: reviewing the field', in A. Thomas and C. Kitzinger (eds), *Sexual Harassment: Contemporary Feminist Perspectives*. Buckingham: Open University Press, pp. 1–18.

Wilkinson, S. (1999) 'Focus groups: a feminist method', *Psychology of Women Quarterly* (special issue on *Innovative Methods in Feminist Research*, Part 2) 23(2): 221–44.

Wilkinson, S. (2000a) 'Feminist research traditions in health psychology: breast cancer research', *Journal of Health Psychology*, 5: 353–66.

Wilkinson, S. (2000b) 'Breast cancer: a feminist perspective', in J. Ussher (ed.), *Women's Health*. Leicester: BPS Books, pp. 230–6.

Wilkinson, S. (2002) 'Lesbian health', in A. Coyle and C. Kitzinger (eds), *Lesbian and Gay Psychology*. Oxford: Blackwells, pp. 117–34

Wilkinson, S. and Kitzinger, C. (eds) (1996) *Representing the Other*. London: Sage.

Yarrow, M.R., Campbell, J.D. and Burton, R.V. (1970) 'Recollections of childhood: a study of the retrospective method', *Monograph of the Society for Research in Child Development*, 35(5).

9

The Foucaultian framework

Gavin Kendall and Gary Wickham

Michel Foucault (1926–1984) produced a body of work that is hard to fit within a singular discipline. His own sense of what he was – a philosopher who used fragments of history to examine and disturb the self-evidence of the human sciences – is a clue to the diagnosis of his work as multidisciplinary. A brief examination of his major works shows that a number of disciplines were objects of his inquiries: psychiatry, psychology, criminology, penology, linguistics, economics, biology, medicine and sexology all received major treatments. In addition, a number of themes – philosophical, historical, ethical and sociological – fascinated Foucault at different points in his life: for example, the nature of the relationship between power and knowledge, the status of the self, truth and truth-telling, and the logic surrounding self-mastery and the government of others. Foucault also found time to make forays into art, music and literature. It is difficult to distil from all this activity a singular Foucaultian framework. To most historians and philosophers, for example, Foucault appears an outsider, and his methods and questions alien. The disciplines that Foucault examined do not seem, in the main, to have reciprocated his interest in them. Foucault has more frequently found a home in the 'meta-disciplines' – the study of studies – and perhaps especially in that branch of sociology that is philosophically nervous about the status of knowledge.

That Foucault's work is diverse, then, we can take as read. What framework can we identify in this diversity, and extract to use as a model for future research? Our approach in this chapter is to do three things. Our first section glosses one of Foucault's areas of interest – the government of self and of others – to examine the strengths and weaknesses of the Foucaultian framework. Our second section tries to reconstruct what

Foucault was trying to do one of his major studies, *The History of Sexuality,* Volume 1: *An Introduction* (Foucault, 1978a). The aim of this section is to uncover the sorts of research questions for which the Foucaultian framework might best be used. In our third section we discuss how, as a writing duo, we became part of an 'intellectual community' that deals in 'Michel Foucault'. The emphasis here is very much on the personal: we offer an account of how this process appeared (and appears) to us. Our aim here is to discover to what sorts of intellectual communities Foucault's work belongs.

GOVERNMENTALITY: A FOUCAULTIAN FRAMEWORK

In the late 1970s, Foucault turned his attention to what he eventually named by a neologism: governmentality. This term covered the idea of 'mentalities of government', as well as 'rationalities of government'. Although Foucault did not develop a full treatment of this area (we have to make do with some rather sketchy remarks in essays and interviews – see especially Foucault, 1978b, 1981, 1989a, 1994), many other scholars have taken up this preliminary work to develop a fully fledged governmentality literature. In a recent, comprehensive book-length survey of the notion of governmentality, Mitchell Dean acknowledges that the 'study of governmentality is continuous with' some aspects of theories of the state (particularly in that it too 'regards the exercise of power and authority as anything but self-evident'), notes that it 'does, however, break with many of the characteristic assumptions of theories of the state' (Dean, 1999: 9), and outlines Foucault's understanding of the basic notion of government as 'the conduct of conduct', especially as it involves thinking about the very act of governing (Dean, 1999: 10–16). He moves on to a definition of the term itself:

> It is possible to distinguish two broad meanings of this term in the literature. The second is a historically specific version of the first. ... In this first sense, the term 'governmentality' suggests what we have just noted. It deals with how we think about governing, with the different mentalities of government. ... The notions of collective mentalities and the idea of a history of mentalities have long been used by sociologists (such as Emile Durkheim and Marcel Mauss) and by the *Annales* school of history in France. ... For such thinkers, a mentality is a collective, relatively bounded unity, and is not readily examined by those who inhabit it. ... The idea of mentalities of government, then, emphasizes the way in which the thought involved in practices of government is collective and relatively taken for granted. ... [This] is to say that the way we think about exercising authority draws upon the theories, ideas, philosophies and forms of knowledge that are part of our social and cultural products. (Dean, 1999: 16)

Dean elaborates the second meaning (the one that is 'a historically specific version of the first') as follows:

> Here, 'governmentality' marks the emergence of a distinctly new form of thinking about and exercising of power in certain societies. ... This form of power is bound up with the discovery of a new reality, the economy, and concerned with a new object, the population. Governmentality emerges in Western European societies in the 'early modern period' when the art of government of the state becomes a distinct activity, and when the forms and knowledge and techniques of the human and social sciences become integral to it. (Dean, 1999: 19)

For his part, the noted Foucaultian socio-legal scholar Pat O'Malley does an extremely good job of introducing the governmentality framework to an audience he assumes to be unfamiliar with it:

> There is a considerable literature exploring and developing this approach. ... Such work has been influenced strongly by the thinking of Michel Foucault ... but has been advanced primarily in recent years by British and Australian scholars. The journal *Economy and Society* has been a principal site for the development of this approach, which is frequently referred to as the 'governmentality' literature. While 'governmentality' refers to a particular technology of government that emerges in the eighteenth century, the term is more generally used to refer to the approach adopted in its study. The approach is characterized by two primary characteristics. The first is a stress on the dispersal of 'government', that is, on the idea that government is not a

> preserve of 'the state' but is carried out at all levels and sites in societies – including the self government of individuals. ... The second is the deployment of an analytic stance that favors 'how' questions over 'why' questions. In other words it favors accounts in terms of how government of a certain kind becomes possible: in what manner it is thought up by planners, using what concepts; how it is intended to be translated into practice, using what combination of means? Only secondarily is it concerned with accounts that seek to *explain* government – in the sense of understanding the nature of government as the effect of other events. (O'Malley, 1998/9: 676, 679n.7)

In speaking of governmentality, we address a body of work which is both Foucault's and his followers'. It is the culmination of a particular reading of Foucault's *oeuvre* coupled with a rejection of standard sociological and political-scientific accounts of power. To a certain extent, 'governmentality' was Foucault's rejoinder to those who found his theory of power useful, but criticized him for his lack of a theory of state power. The governmentality work was Foucault's way of describing how the state could be seen as the result of practices of government, rather than the latter's cause. Some commentators have suggested that Foucault's work on power is an emphasis on micro-processes; it is tempting, then, to imagine that the governmentality work allowed Foucault to weld a theory of macro-processes on to his micro-power theory. However, we suggest that this schema is too easy: first of all, Foucault's work on power is not about micro-social processes – it is about a variety of processes that are local and mobile, but that can operate at any point on the macro/micro continuum. Second, the governmentality approach tends to deal in the same way with mentalities of government whichever end of the macro/micro continuum it considers: the 'conduct of conduct' can be at the individual level (self-government), at the family level (the government of a small group), and at the national level (the king's government of his people and territory). Nonetheless, Foucault's formulation of a governmentality problem space allowed him to look at a novel series of problems – or at least, to examine some familiar problems from a new vantage point.

To reiterate the point we made earlier, governmentality is a kind of meta-analysis. It is not so much a way of doing political science, as a kind of philosophical intervention into the objects of political science. For example, much of the governmentality literature has concerned itself with liberalism: not the liberalism of the political scientists, but the everyday practices of government that liberalism as a mentality/rationality permits and suggests. There have been quite a few attempts, by those who have followed Foucault, to explicate and defend this approach (e.g., as well as Dean, 1999, see Miller and Rose, 1990; Burchell et al., 1991; Rose and Miller, 1992; Barry et al., 1996; Dean and Hindess, 1998; Rose, 1999), though it is enough that we simply note their existence; we do not need to explore them further. The more pressing question is 'How can governmentality help the qualitative researcher?'

Governmentality does not supply tools for qualitative research: rather, it produces a certain attitude or sensitivity towards questions in political science. For example, Kendall (1997) provides a governmentality-inspired analysis of some elements of the government of the Australian colonies in the nineteenth century. While methodologically this piece adopts some standard historical approaches (the collection and analysis of historical archive material in defined territories over a defined historical period; an attempt to be reasonably comprehensive in material surveyed; attention to questions of reliability and validity, and so forth), its use of the governmentality framework forced it to take seriously the mentalities and rationalities of colonial government. In this case, Kendall argued that the usual histories of colonial government, predisposed as they are to demonstrate the self-serving nature of such government, can easily miss the ways in which rationalities of government (in this case, liberalism) informed strategies and programmes that are not necessarily in the best interests of those who govern. In addition, the governmentality focus pushed Kendall to look at government as a problem at the individual, community, national and international levels: governing thus comes to be seen not so much as the imposition of one's will over another, as the insertion of a certain way of thinking and doing within the fabric of everyday life. Governing is revealed to be a fundamentally ethical endeavour.

This mention of ethics will no doubt remind many readers of Max Weber's work, and indeed there are many similarities between Weber and Foucault. The similarities might give us a sense of what the Foucaultian framework is: an approach rather than a methodology, a predisposition to look at certain questions rather than others. Just as the Marxist tends to find most answers in the economy, and the functionalist in the functional or dysfunctional relationship of one part of the social system to another, so the Foucaultian framework emphasizes certain sorts of phenomena. Here we can also see the weakness of this approach: it is sometimes rather one-eyed, and for this reason we suggest that some of the governmentality work has really just reinvented the wheel. More seriously, while Foucault's own work on governmentality amounted to a number of schematic periodizations and distinctions in the history of government, in Foucault's followers this has on occasion turned into using governmentality as a general schema for understanding the history of government. This is a rather perilous approach, since as Hunter (1998) notes, in a powerful set of critical remarks directed at the governmentality approach, Foucault's own remarks tend to downplay the role of theological politics as well as overestimate the extent to which sovereignty disappears from liberal politics. The translation of governmentality into a general schema or a theory of politics is correspondingly fraught with danger.

Our first engagement with Foucault, then, makes it clear that precise methodological tools are not on offer: rather we are given an approach and a series of phenomena to look out for. Hughes and Griffiths (1999) provide an example of how this approach might be translated into an empirical study. Their piece is a straightforward qualitative analysis of changes in patient administration practices in a health service setting. However, because it is informed by the notion of 'governmentality', it sets its sights on the ways in which liberal government is embedded in everyday medical administration, especially through accounting and auditing procedures.

But is there more to the Foucaultian framework than this 'spirit of inquiry'?

FOUCAULT IN ACTION

Kendall and Wickham (1999a: 22ff.) outlined some of the principles that inform 'archaeology', Foucault's term for his methodology. Archaeology is a historical investigation, but one always tempered by scepticism. Just as 'real' archaeologists need time passed for their endeavours to bear any fruit, so the Foucaultian archaeologist needs time passed, not least because Foucaultian archaeology is an approach designed to understand knowledges, practices, relations, etc., that have stabilized, rather than those that are in flux. Foucault himself never did any archaeologies that made their way as far as the twentieth century, even though he usually chose twentieth-century problems to archaeologize. This should be remembered whenever the Foucaultian approach is taken up. So, for example, while the prison is the pressing twentieth-century problem of Foucault's (1977) *Discipline and Punish,* the practices and knowledge Foucault analyses were put together, in the main, in the eighteenth and nineteenth centuries.

A second point is that Foucaultian research in action is problem-based, rather than period-based: in other words, follow your problem back as far as necessary, rather than investigate every element of a specified time period. In all of Foucault's major works, this approach has led to some unexpected rewards (the history of sexuality led Foucault to antique medical texts and dream interpreters; the history of madness led him to leper-houses). It is an approach that has aroused antipathy, not least towards *Madness and Civilization* (Foucault, 1965), yet such criticisms usually stem from the mistaken belief that Foucault was trying to do a 'total' or 'social' history, rather than the analysis of the conditions of possibility for the emergence of knowledges, practices, objects, programmes, etc.

For our most detailed example of the Foucaultian framework in action, we choose one of Foucault's own texts, *The History of Sexuality* Volume 1 (Foucault, 1978a). While Foucault's basic research question in this work seems to be something along the lines of 'How did sexuality come to be the crucial practice for defining the truth of the modern self?', there is some evidence that from as early as the late 1950s, while working on *Madness and Civilization*, Foucault was interested in an archaeology of psychoanalysis, and that to a certain extent *The History of Sexuality* was concerned not just with sexuality but with the modern practice that most closely wedded sexuality and the truth of the self, psychoanalysis. So, while this book touches on some expected resources, especially work by sexologists such as Ellis and Krafft-Ebing, a novel feature of the book is its emphasis on the relation between sexuality and talk (psycho-analysis is, of course, 'the talking cure'). Foucault is always predisposed to seek out dis-continuities, and the major one he spots is in the mid- to late nineteenth century. In a reversal of traditional historical analyses, he produces evidence that the Victorian era, far from being the high point of sexual repression, is an era for the dissemination of knowledge about sexuality, for its tireless examination, for its relentless empirical investigation. The rest of the book does two things: it explores in more detail some of the major areas of sexuality that became the focus of scientific research and popular concern (marriage, masturbation, perversion and hysteria); it also traces this obsession with sex, and with talking and writing about sex, back to a sixteenth-century watershed. For Foucault, the Council of Trent (1546–64) is especially important, since it signals

a change in confessional practice (confession becomes more frequent, more extensive, but also less explicit), a change accompanied by a new conception of the inescapability, the all-pervasiveness, of desire.

No doubt our summary here is familiar; but what can we learn about method from Foucault's approach? First, Foucault pointedly asks 'how' questions, rather than 'why' questions (Kendall and Wickham, 1999a: 21–56). His question, then, is 'How did such-and-such come to exist?', or 'How did such-and such come to have such an important place in our society?' Buried within such an approach is a commitment to construc-tionism (see Hacking, 1999) and a mistrust of anthropological universals. Second, while Foucault does not say a great deal about the selection of his archive, it is clear that his prefer-ence is for what we might call 'programmatic' texts, writings that try to impose a vision or spell out most clearly a new way of conceptualizing a problem. The nineteenth-century sexologists were an obvious resource in this regard, and Foucault makes the judgement that their twentieth-century successors (Masters and Johnson, Hite et al.) are not doing anything especially new. At this point we might note another principle that guides Foucaultian research: look for the novel programmatic statement. With this in mind, we need to keep looking until we find the 'relative beginnings' (Foucault, 1989b: 46) of such state-ments. Similarly, although he regards psycho-analysis as especially significant, he reduces it to a form of confession, and thus decides to keep digging until he finds a paradigm shift in the world of confessing (hence the importance he accords to the Council of Trent).

So far, then, we have seen that Foucaultian research requires: (a) a 'how' question, (b) a decision about an appropriate archive for investi-gation, (c) a preference for programmatic texts, and (d) the commitment to keep digging until one finds the relative beginnings of a practice. We might add at this point that what guides Foucault is an emphasis on what we might term 'discursive history'. By this we mean that Foucault is less concerned with institutions or individuals than he is with knowledge: knowl-edge (such as sexology or psychoanalysis or psy-chiatry) is given a primacy by Foucault, such that 'non-discursive' elements (people, materials, objects) are governed by knowledge. Foucault's approach can be contrasted with some forms of history – those organized around 'great men' or 'the spirit of the age'. Rather, Foucault seeks to make knowledge the stars around which the planets (in this case, humans, institutions, mate-rials, etc.) circle.

To some extent, the Foucaultian framework requires the researcher to write a detective story. We start with a known outcome, but what we need to do is find the precursors that lead to this outcome. The work is about putting together the various pieces of the puzzle so we can see sufficient conditions for the emergence of the problem or issue under investigation. While it can be a dizzying experience to read Foucault – one marvels at the parallels and links that are made across the centuries, and the contrasts that are drawn – the less gifted researcher should not shy away from some of the more conventional procedures of qualitative research to see if a hypothesis will stand up. It is worth trying to generate categories from fragments of data, for example, in a Sacksian or Garfinkelian manner. It is worth counting instances of a phenomenon to see whether a claim to generalizability is supported. It is worth specifying a limited archive for investigation so that a reasonable claim for an exhaustive investigation can be made. To this extent, while it has been fashionable to regard Foucault as representative of a 'postmodern' or a 'post-positivist' movement, it seems to us on the contrary that Foucault is perfectly recuperable within rather traditional and long-established social science approaches. We do not see Foucault as the *enfant terrible* of the social sciences, but as a good modernist (see Osborne, 1998), a rather traditional positivist and neo-Kantian. He is a modernist because his work is an analysis of the 'underbelly' of modernity – to this extent he does not look very different from Marx or Weber. He is a positivist because of his insistence on the analysis of texts and his refusal to go beyond texts into the realm of interpretation, and he is neo-Kantian in his insistence on analysing the 'conditions of possibility' of knowledge.

While we are on this topic, it is important to mention that while Foucault looks for discontinuities, it is interesting to note that he does not find too many of them, and is often forced back through thousands of years to find two or three paradigm shifts. There is a certain conservatism in the Foucaultian framework – or, better, there is a certain scepticism about change. Unfortunately, every generation, it seems, is doomed to believe that they live in a time of major social upheaval, yet Foucault's patient and dogged accounts suggest quite the opposite – that change is a rarity, and that our age is really not so different from one or even two hundred years ago. While much social science research is hell-bent on announcing that the next big thing has arrived, by contrast, the Foucaultian framework is cautious: it does not shy away from demonstrating historical discontinuity, but it is aware that such moments are rare indeed.

BECOMING PART OF THE FOUCAULTIAN INTELLECTUAL COMMUNITY: A KENDALL AND WICKHAM PERSPECTIVE

We decided on writing something Foucaultian together, or at least we decided on the possibility of doing so, very soon after our first meeting, which occurred at the British Sociological Association Conference in Edinburgh in 1988. In those days, such a conference did not feature many papers on Foucault or Foucaultian themes; indeed, they were quite rare (hard to believe now, when they are standard fare at such gatherings). This initial rarity, we must admit, was an important force in forming and binding a community of scholars around the name 'Michel Foucault'. Perhaps this was because, at the time, Foucaultianism – and it was surely then, as now, no more than a loose 'approach' – was felt to represent something of a challenge to the then dominant orthodoxy in sociology. This orthodoxy can fairly be described as Marxist-inspired ameliorativism – the desire for social change, sometimes revolutionary, usually not, but always expressed as 'critique', the call of those whose slogan was something like 'we know something is wrong with "the system" even if most of "the people" do not'. At this stage, one of us had completed a PhD thesis on a Foucaultian theme, while the other was in the process of doing so (Wickham, 1985; Kendall, 1993), and each of us had either published or near-published pieces on Foucaultian topics (Wickham, 1983; 1987a, 1987b; Bevis et al., 1989). So, not only were we aware of the 'secret' pleasures of swimming against the tide of intellectual orthodoxy, we also knew what was involved in taking this as far as the published word. Despite this, and despite the fact that we communicated regularly and met reasonably often, either during Wickham's visits to Britain or Kendall's visits to Australia – we met as often as two academics in different countries who were yet to secure tenured university positions could hope to meet – the best laid plans of mice and Foucaultian scholars …: we didn't get around to submitting anything for publication until 1991.

We built our co-authorship arrangements, and our understanding of what 'the Foucaultian framework' could do, in a series of pieces for the journal *Australian Left Review* (Kendall and

Wickham, 1991a, 1991b, 1992a, 1992b). This journal was at that time experimenting with a young editor with Foucaultian sympathies, David Burchell, in a bid to boost flagging circulation. This was achieved, much to Burchell's credit, but the experiment was not allowed to run its course; the 'old-left' element on the journal's management team, it seemed to us, could not bear the experiment for long and chose eventually to risk letting the journal go under (it did), rather than continue the flirtation with Foucaultianism. This experience not only continued our swim against the tide – it was not much more than a weak current by then (on which, more below) – it also allowed us to assess the extent to which a Foucaultian approach to power and politics could be translated into commentaries on current issues. Our assessment was that such commentaries did not fit well within our Foucaultian framework. We were coming around to the view that if the objects being studied were not given a strong historical dimension, the Foucaultian framework was of no especial value, being little more than an extension of a Marxist or Marxist-inspired approach under a new, French, name.

This methodological emphasis was far from strong in our thinking at this time, but as we also then published a piece with more historical depth (Kendall and Wickham, 1992c), it can at least be called 'a growing influence'. The next few years saw us strengthen this direction in our published work, as we, together (Kendall and Wickham, 1996), and separately (Kendall, 1991, 1997; Wickham, 1992; Hunt and Wickham, 1994; Malpas and Wickham, 1995, 1997; Lewi and Wickham, 1996; Kendall and Michael, 1997, 1998; Collins et al., 1998), further explored the strengths, weaknesses and possibilities of the Foucaultian framework.

Already by the early 1990s it was clear to us, and to others, we presume, that not only was the tide against Foucaultian work no longer strong, it was either on the turn or had turned. The Foucaultian framework no longer felt like a shelter for those who were seeking something other than the Marxist-inspired orthodoxy, a shelter with the warm and fuzzy side of community formation to the fore. Rather, it was beginning to feel more like a large institution, with at least traces of the sort of internal differences that mark the other side of the formation of communities. This feeling certainly did not reach (and has not reached) the fully violent and passionate extreme of this side of the formation of communities, but it was strong enough to produce notice, on our part at least, that the framework was now being taken up by an array of different positions. Feminist, gay, left-political, administrative-governmental, cultural and style-insistent positions, to name just some, were now more evident. Of course, these positions could reasonably be said to have existed all along, very much part of Foucault's multi-faceted self, we might say, guided by his biographers (Eribon, 1991; Macey, 1993; Miller, 1993). However, they were certainly more noticeable, as the 'Foucaultian community' within the 'Foucaultian framework' grew so large as to render problematic the singular form of each of 'community' and 'framework'.

In line with our emergent methodological direction, we began to align ourselves, as participants, more closely to one particular 'community' within the 'Foucaultian community', and to work within one particular 'framework' within the 'Foucaultian framework' – governmentality. We have already introduced the governmentality framework; and in doing so, we introduced the governmentality community. This is to say that our sketch, with its lists of authors, its passing mention of countries (Australia and Britain), its passing mention of the journal *Economy and Society,* provides another pointer to the way in which an intellectual framework is grounded in a set of quite mundane practices and events. We have so far discussed the way in which we, as an authorial team working to advance the Foucaultian framework, far from sitting in some ivory tower and ethereally producing great intellectual insights, slogged away like everybody else – attending conferences, trying to find secure jobs, trying to find time to write pieces, trying to get them published. Through our sketch of governmentality we are adding to this quotidian picture some hints about the quotidian operation of some of the institutions involved. Just as our own intellectual production is much more about 'slogging away' in the daily grind than it is about some secret inspiration, so the conferences, seminars, inter-nation communication, books, journals and suchlike are about the minutiae of daily life. In saying we became members of the governmentality subset of the Foucaultian intellectual community, we are certainly not suggesting we had to undergo some secret initiation ceremony, or pass some secret test. Rather, we are saying we participated, as often as we could, in governmentality conferences around the world, and in the London 'History of the Present' seminars that ran so successfully for a number of years, we read and contributed to *Economy and Society* when we could, and we read and contributed to books that sought to promote the governmentality approach (sometimes we even bought them). In all this, we experienced the vicissitudes of such institutions – the occasional bickering and self-serving common to them all, as well as the camaraderie and good humour they also provide, but no more than this.

Before returning to our 'autobiographical' narrative, we need to say a little more about two of the institutions only pointed to so far. The first is teaching. We mentioned that at the time of our first meeting in 1988 neither of us had secured a permanent academic position. While this situation eventually improved for each of us (Wickham gaining a tenured post at Murdoch University in 1990, Kendall doing so at Lancaster University in 1992 and then, after making the big move to Australia, at Queensland University of Technology in 1995), teaching was a central part of our Foucaultian development on both sides of our tenure-hunt (Wickham held various non-tenured posts at Murdoch from 1985, after a year at Philip Institute of Technology in Melbourne in 1984, Kendall held a temporary post at Lancaster University from 1989 to 1992). The teaching experience helped us to formulate our views, in the way that most scholars report, but it also helped us to present them in what we hoped would be the most telling ways.

For instance, teaching undergraduate and postgraduate students allowed us to monitor closely the intellectual 'tide' we spoke of earlier. When we started teaching, of course, we found ourselves, as it were, seemingly drawn into the role of missionaries among the 'savages of orthodoxy', trying to attract the students away from the orthodoxy of their texts and, it must be added, most of our colleagues. Neither of us felt comfortable in this role. We were quick to see that a missionary zeal would feed into many of the assumptions of the very orthodoxy to which we were opposed. More than this, we were quick to see that the missionary zeal was misplaced: the assumption that the students were somehow automatically of the orthodox faith, in need of 'conversion', was wrong. The students were not wedded to anything at all and were just as happy to learn a Foucaultian approach as they were any other. It was we who had to learn the lesson, not they.

The other institution we wish to further discuss is communication, by which we mean the way in which the participants in any intellectual community around a particular framework communicate with one another. We said earlier that in the formative years of our writing partnership we communicated regularly with each other and kept up with the Foucaultian intellectual community as best we could. We urge our readers to remember that we are talking about the late 1980s and early 1990s. What we are getting at here is that this was B.E. – before e-mail. This communication device has made such a difference to the way we communicate, both with each

other and with the Foucaultian community more widely, that the period B.E. seems like the era of 'hope our pigeons can make the journey' by comparison.

This dramatic change in the means of communication has had a variety of effects. On the one hand, we can now communicate with each other over any distance as quickly as it takes it to reach our computers, speeding up the production of jointly authored work immeasurably. We can also now seek and receive feedback from others just as quickly, and we can participate in e-mail and Internet intellectual exchange sessions (our 'regular' Foucaultian forum is the excellent HoP list run out of Toronto by Engin Isin). On the other hand, there is a set of perhaps less noticeable, but nonetheless crucial, effects that some may see as negative. We will mention just two here. First, there is the problem of feedback overload. As it has become easier to seek instant feedback, so the number of requests, both given and received, has grown exponentially. The swift 'get it out of the way' style of feedback has become more the rule than the exception, something we are each as 'guilty' of as anyone else. Secondly, the rapid increase in the speed and ease of communication has led to a rapid broadening of intellectual communities. While many e-mail lists and websites are 'moderated', no amount of moderation could possibly have stopped this phenomenon. The number of high-quality contributions seems to us to have remained constant, but this means that as a percentage of total contributions they represent a much smaller fraction than they used to. We also suggest that the fracturing or factionalizing of intellectual communities we discussed earlier has been intensified by this development, though we remain silent as to whether this has been a positive or a negative aspect of it.

The autobiography of our writing partnership had, it will be remembered, reached the mid-1990s, with us heading in a more methodological direction, not to mention a more governmentalist direction. Our thinking, in line with our stronger alliance with the 'governmentality' community, and as developed in the publications we produced in the mid-1990s, cited above, was much more a reaction to a growing trend in Foucault-inspired studies than it was some 'natural' aspect of our 'intellectual development'. In other words, we could see the need for a fight and were only too keen to mix it. The Foucault who was starting to dominate cultural studies, and to have quite a role in sociology and other social sciences, was that Foucault who tells people what power is 'really' about, who tells them that power can (and should) be found in the meaning of every situation they come across in their everyday lives, the source of a 'slap it on, any fool can do it' approach to the study of social and cultural objects. This is a Foucault that we cannot abide, a figure so far from the serious and learned scholar we understand to have operated under the name Michel Foucault as to be unrecognizable.

Our determination to promote the scholarly, careful Foucault, at the expense of the one described above, pushed us, with the encouragement of David Silverman, to produce a book on 'our' Foucault, the book released under the title *Using Foucault's Methods* (Kendall and Wickham, 1999a). We cannot speak too highly of Silverman's role in our project. From the tiniest scraps of proposal-like correspondence, he seemed to be able to see what we wanted to do more clearly than we did, and as the editor of the Sage series *Introducing Qualitative Methods,* he was able, and willing (we owe him an overwhelming debt), to do something about it. He encouraged us to submit a formal book proposal and guided it through the various stages to help us secure a contract for the book. We decided, in consultation with him, to write the book in as accessible a style as possible.

This is to say that only one of our goals in *Using Foucault's Methods* was to attack the 'power and meaning', 'slap it on' interpretation of Foucault perpetrated by other writers in the broader Foucaultian community (by this time, we have to admit, this 'broader community' had so fractured into many smaller communities, in the manner described earlier, as to be almost non-existent). More important to us was to reach a student audience, a goal made very important to us by our aforementioned realization that students are not, in the main, the slavish followers of the most simplistic interpretations available, but are quite prepared to engage with the complexities of debates. We tried to address this audience as if only a very small percentage of them needed to be 'de-programmed' before they could understand our position. The main device we employed to achieve this goal was the use of characters, fictitious students who were engaging with Foucault's work at a variety of levels. We allowed just a few of them to be 'slavish followers of the most simplistic interpretations available', but we made sure, unsurprisingly, that the students most sympathetic to our position always won the day. We have been pleased by the largely positive reaction to our strategy, as expressed both in reviews and in strong sales in a very competitive market.

In the few years since the appearance of *Using Foucault's Methods,* we have together produced a Foucault-related chapter in a book of conference proceedings (Kendall and Wickham, 1999b) and, more importantly, one more Foucault-related book together (Kendall and Wickham, 2001), as well as other Foucault-related work separately (Wickham, 2000; Kendall, 2001a, 2001b; Wickham and Pavlich, 2001). Our 2001 book is called *Understanding Culture: Cultural Studies, Order, Ordering.* It pushes our governmentalist Foucaultian line against the power-and-meaning line of Cultural Studies, and as such can be said to continue at least one of the themes of *Using Foucault's Methods.* It is too early yet to judge whether we have had any success with this, though we are all too aware that most things in intellectual life are ever so resistant to change.

Our biographical account here is, perhaps, rather behaviourist. Our point is that intellectual communities are formed around the mundane. They require a number of ballasts if they are to survive: material, technological, intellectual, and so forth. Of course, a similar account could no doubt be produced to describe the emergence of other communities – in this respect the Foucaultian communities and frameworks are nothing special. One interesting point about such biographies does remain to be made. Biographical accounts such as the one above can be understood within the Foucaultian framework. In his work on 'techniques of the self', Foucault (1986) has outlined some of the ways in which human beings work on themselves. He uses a pair of words to describe this process: 'technique' and 'technology'. However, the term used more often by Foucault is 'technique'. This seems to be in marked contrast to the post-Foucaultian literature, which almost exclusively uses the term 'technology', and rarely, if ever, discusses 'techniques'. It seems to us that this is not just a linguistic quibble. Foucault does discriminate between the terms, using the French *'technique'* to refer to a practical instance, while the term *'technologie'* refers to a practical system. In a nutshell, techniques are singular and elemental, while technologies are agglomerations of techniques formed into a logical and systematic whole. When we think of this vocabulary as applied to the object 'the self', a technique of the self is merely a skill or procedure, possibly isolated but possibly integrated with other techniques; a technology of the self, by contrast, is something much more like a Wittgensteinian 'form of life' or a Weberian 'department of existence'. This distinction, then, is important: it seems that Foucault's endeavour was not so much to describe forms of subjectivity as systematized, but as made up of a variety of independent and non-systematic procedures (or techniques). In this usage, then, Foucault is closer to Marcel Mauss (e.g. 1973) than to Weber or Wittgenstein. Mauss described some of the various 'techniques of the body' that are used in different societies at different historical conjunctures, stressing, most importantly, their contingent form; for Mauss, there is no truly or simply human way of walking, eating or swimming, for example. Foucault's account here is also reminiscent of Elias (1978), who dealt with the formation of the person of the Renaissance courtier: the courtier does not build up a coherent form of selfhood based on some *telos,* but merely takes elements from here and there, as they are pleasing. The self is a temporary agglomeration of these 'pleasing ways', but not especially systematic or coherent; it is, rather, emergent and contingent.

In a similar way, our biographical sketch is an attempt to adumbrate some of the sorts of 'technical' procedures by which members of an intellectual community (ourselves as 'Foucaultians') are put together (both intra- and inter-subjectively).

CONCLUSION

Our sketch of our Foucaultian framework might look rather different from what many readers were expecting. We barely mentioned the ubiquity of power relations, techniques of domination, surveillance, the gaze, discipline. While these concepts do appear in Foucault, they are used as specific descriptors of specific historical conjunctions. They are useless as methodological guides, and if we pay too much attention to them, we risk reducing Foucault to a cartoonish mixture of vulgar Marxism and the Orwell of *1984,* made into a sociologist. But this is not our Foucault, and these are not the ingredients for our Foucaultian framework. The framework is a mundane thing and is not brand-spankingly new, but has a sceptical lineage. Membership of intellectual communities that engage in academic work is also built on the quotidian, the mundane, the technical. We have also suggested that the war between Foucault and modernist social science is a phoney war; indeed, the possibilities for synthesis need to be stressed if students are to be taught how to do Foucaultian work; anything else runs the risk of reducing Foucaultian work to individual genius. It is also the case, although we have not explored this issue to a great extent, that the Foucaultian framework and the discipline of history are not ranged in battle against each other. One thing we should like to achieve in this chapter is to build some bridges between

methods; an important task is to contextualize Foucault, and make people see that a Foucaultian approach is not so daunting after all.

ACKNOWLEDGEMENTS

We should like to thank the following for their comments on an earlier draft of this chapter: Amanda Davies, Barbara Czarniawska, Lindsay Prior, David Silverman.

REFERENCES

Barry, A., Osborne, T. and Rose, N. (eds) (1996) *Foucault and Political Reason: Liberalism, Neo-Liberalism and Rationalities of Government.* London: UCL Press.

Bevis, P., Cohen, M. and Kendall, G. (1989) 'Archaeologizing genealogy: Michel Foucault and the economy of austerity', *Economy and Society*, 18(3): 323–45.

Burchell, G., Gordon, C. and Miller, P. (eds) (1991) *The Foucault Effect: Studies in Governmentality.* Brighton: Harvester Wheatsheaf.

Collins, A., Kendall, G. and Michael, M. (1998) 'Resisting a diagnostic technique: the case of reflex anal dilatation', *Sociology of Health and Illness*, 20(1): 1–28.

Dean, M. (1999) *Governmentality: Power and Rule in Modern Society.* London: Sage.

Dean, M. and Hindess, B. (eds) (1998) *Governing Australia: Studies in Contemporary Rationalities of Government.* Melbourne: Cambridge University Press.

Elias, N. (1978) *The Civilizing Process*, Vol. 1: *The History of Manners.* Oxford: Blackwell.

Eribon, D. (1991) *Michel Foucault*, tr. Betsy Wing. Cambridge, MA: Harvard University Press.

Foucault, M. (1965) *Madness and Civilization: A History of Madness in the Age of Reason.* New York: Random House.

Foucault, M. (1977) *Discipline and Punish: The Birth of the Prison.* London: Allen Lane.

Foucault, M. (1978a) *The History of Sexuality*, Vol. 1: *An Introduction.* New York: Pantheon.

Foucault, M. (1978b) 'Governmentality', *I&C*, 6: 5–21.

Foucault, M. (1981) 'Omnes et singulatim: towards a criticism of "political reason"', in S. McMurrin (ed.), *The Tanner Lectures on Human Values,* Vol. 2. Salt Lake City: University of Utah Press, pp. 225–54.

Foucault, M. (1986) *The Care of the Self.* New York: Pantheon.

Foucault, M. (1989a) 'Naissance de la biopolitique', in *Résumé des cours 1970–82.* Paris: Juilliard, pp. 109–19.

Foucault, M. (1989b) 'The archaeology of knowledge', in *Foucault Live: Interviews 1966–84*, tr. John Johnston. New York: Semiotext(e).

Foucault, M. (1994) 'The political technology of individuals', in *Power: Essential Works of Foucault 1954–1984.* London: Penguin, pp. 403–17.

Hacking, I. (1999) *The Social Construction of What?* Cambridge, MA: Harvard University Press.

Hughes, D. and Griffiths, L. (1999) 'On penalties and the *Patients' Charter*: centralism v decentralised governance in the NHS', *Sociology of Health and Illness*, 21(1): 71–94.

Hunt, A. and Wickham, G. (1994) *Foucault and Law: Towards a Sociology of Law as Governance*. London: Pluto.

Hunter, I. (1998) 'Uncivil society: liberal government and the deconfessionalisation of politics', in M. Dean and B. Hindess (eds), *Governing Australia*. Melbourne: Cambridge University Press, pp. 242–64.

Kendall, G. (1991) 'Reading the child reading: literacy and the formation of citizens in England 1750–1850', *History of Education Review*, 20(2): 79–87.

Kendall, G. (1993) 'Literate practices and the production of children: psychological and pre-psychological discourses'. PhD dissertation, University of London.

Kendall, G. (1997) 'Governing at a distance: Anglo-Australian relations 1840–1870', *Australian Journal of Political Science*, 32(2): 223–35.

Kendall, G. (2001a) 'Meaningfulness and normality: detailing the child in the eighteenth century', *History of Education Review*, 30(2): 26–36.

Kendall, G. (2001b) 'From Foucault to Latour and back again: technological, historical nonhumans', *In-between: Essays and Studies in Literary Criticism*, 10(1): 53–64.

Kendall, G. and Michael, M. (1997) 'Politicizing the politics of postmodern social psychology', *Theory and Psychology*, 7(1): 7–30.

Kendall, G. and Michael, M. (1998) 'Thinking the unthought: towards a Moebius strip psychology', *New Ideas in Psychology*, 16(3): 141–57.

Kendall, G. and Wickham, G. (1991a) 'Governing passions I', *Australian Left Review*, 129: 15–19.

Kendall, G. and Wickham, G. (1991b) 'Governing corruption', *Australian Left Review*, 134: 20–2.

Kendall, G. and Wickham, G. (1992a) 'Governing passions II', *Australian Left Review*, 141: 20–3.

Kendall, G. and Wickham, G. (1992b) 'Civic centre', *Australian Left Review*, 143: 20–3.

Kendall, G. and Wickham, G. (1992c) 'Health and the social body', in S. Scott, G. Williams, S. Platt and H. Thomas (eds), *Private Risk and Public Danger*. Aldershot: Avebury Press, pp. 8–18.

Kendall, G. and Wickham, G. (1996) 'Governing the culture of cities: a Foucaultian framework', *Southern Review*, 29(2): 202–19.

Kendall, G. and Wickham, G. (1999a) *Using Foucault's Methods*. London: Sage.

Kendall, G. and Wickham, G. (1999b) 'Lessons from an old millennium: law and regulation in the ancient city', in M. Collis, L. Munro and S. Russell (eds), *Sociology for a New Millennium: Challenges and Prospects*. Melbourne: Monash University Press.

Kendall, G. and Wickham, G. (2001) *Understanding Culture: Cultural Studies, Order, Ordering*. London: Sage.

Lewi, H. and Wickham, G. (1996) 'Modern urban government: a Foucaultian perspective', *Urban Policy and Research*, 14(1): 51–64.

Macey, D. (1993) *The Many Lives of Michel Foucault*. London: Hutchinson.

Malpas, J. and Wickham, G. (1995) 'Governance and failure: on the limits of sociology', *Australian and New Zealand Journal of Sociology*, 31(3): 37–50.

Malpas, J. and Wickham, G. (1997) 'Governance and the world: from Joe DiMaggio to Michel Foucault', *The UTS Review*, 3(2): 91–108.

Mauss, M. (1973) 'Techniques of the body', *Economy and Society*, 2(1): 70–88.

Miller, J. (1993) *The Passion of Michel Foucault*. New York: Harper-Collins.

Miller, P. and Rose, N. (1990) 'Governing economic life', *Economy and Society*, 19(1): 1–31.

O'Malley, P. (1998/99) 'Imagining insurance: risk, thrift and industrial life insurance in Britain', *Connecticut Insurance Law Journal*, 5(2): 676–705.

Osborne, T. (1998) *Aspects of Enlightenment: Social Theory and the Ethics of Truth*. London: University of London Press.

Rose, N. (1999) *Powers of Freedom*. Cambridge: Cambridge University Press.

Rose, N. and Miller, P. (1992) 'Political power beyond the state: problematics of government', *British Journal of Sociology*, 43(2): 172–205.

Wickham, G. (1983) 'Power and power analysis: beyond Foucault?', *Economy and Society*, 12(4): 468–98.

Wickham, G. (1985) 'Problems with power, problems with Foucault'. PhD dissertation, University of Melbourne.

Wickham, G. (ed.) (1987a) *Social Theory and Legal Politics*. Sydney: Local Consumption Publications.

Wickham, G. (1987b) 'Foucault, power, left politics', *Arena*, 78: 146–59.

Wickham, G. (1992) 'Sport, manners, persons, government: Elias, Mauss, Foucault', *Cultural Studies*, 6(2): 219–31.

Wickham, G. (2000) 'Foucault and Gadamer: like apples and oranges passing in the night', *Chicago-Kent Law Review*, 76(2): 101–38.

Wickham, G. and Pavlich, G. (eds) (2001) *Rethinking Law, Society and Governance: Foucault's Bequest*. Oxford: Hart.

10

Ethnomethodology

Paul ten Have

Ethnomethodological studies seek to treat practical activities, practical circumstances, and practical sociological reasoning as topics of empirical studies, and by paying to the most commonplace activities of daily life the attention usually accorded extraordinary events, seek to learn about them as phenomena in their own right.

(Garfinkel, 1967: 1)

Ethnomethodology's standing task is to examine social facts, just in every and any actual case asking for each thing, what makes it accountably just what that social fact is?

(Garfinkel, 2002: 251)

Within the large and heterogeneous family of qualitative social science approaches, 'ethnomethodology' (EM) is a rather strange cousin. While most qualitative researchers try to describe and explain a form of social life as experienced by its participants, ethnomethodologists propose to study the ways in which collectivity members create and maintain a sense of order and intelligibility in social life. In this chapter, I will offer a selective summary account of the emergence, character and development of ethnomethodology as a unique 'alternate sociology'. After an introductory sketch, I will explicate some of ethnomethodology's core notions. The problem of studying common-sense practices will be the theme of my discussion of the ways in which ethnomethodological studies are done, through 'breaching experiments', particular kinds of field studies and the ubiquitous use of audio or video recordings. The chapter ends with some reflections on ways in which ethnomethodology might be combined with or applied to different perspectives on social life, including practical ones.

HAROLD GARFINKEL

Ethnomethodology emerged as a distinctive perspective and style of social research in the teachings and publications of one man, Harold Garfinkel. From a varied set of 'sources of inspiration', including on the one hand most prominently his teacher and PhD supervisor Talcott Parsons, and on other the phenomenological philosophies of Alfred Schutz, Aron Gurwitsch and Edmund Husserl, he has forged a new vision of what social inquiry could be. Taking off from Parsons's synthesization of various classical traditions of sociological theorizing, these have been in a way 'turned on their heads' in ethnomethodology. For the Durkheimian strand in classical sociology, and social research more generally, the ultimate goal is to investigate 'social facts', and their determinants, where 'social facts' have the twin characteristic of being both 'external' and 'constraining' to the actions of individuals. In ethnomethodology, on the other hand – to adapt a phrase from Melvin Pollner (1974) – 'facts are treated as accomplishments', that is, they are seen as being produced in and through members' practical activities. While classical (Durkheimian) sociology is in the business of *explaining* social facts, the effort of ethnomethodology is directed towards an *explication* of their constitution. In Harold Garfinkel's recent book (2002), this interest is presented as a kind of exhumation of a neglected aspect of Durkheim's sociological perspective. In relation to the interests of most qualitative researchers, who want to know the world *as participants see it*, ethnomethodologists prefer to study *how*, by the use of which procedures and methods, *any particular 'world' is produced and perceived.*

Doing ethnomethodological studies requires a deep *familiarity* with the world that is being studied, while at the same time being able to *distance* oneself from its ordinariness, in order to see how it is methodically constituted. Common-sense practices are hard to 'see', because they are so self-evident for their practitioners. One strategy that Garfinkel used to break the spell of ordinariness was to breach the expectancies on which such practices are based. But while these 'breaching experiments' became quite famous or rather infamous, Garfinkel has not limited his efforts to such tricks. The most common way to do ethnomethodological research is to observe naturally occurring situations as closely as possible, which often involves the use of audio or video recordings, but may also depend on quite ordinary ethnographic research practices. There is, however, a marked preference for situations in which ordinary sense-making practices in one way or another seem to run into difficulties, which makes them more amenable for study.

Ethnomethodology's relationship with its 'mother discipline' sociology, and by extension to all 'social science', is rather complex. Both share a deep interest in problems of social order and try to elucidate the organization of social life in all its manifestations. But their general approach is very different. This difference should not in the first place be seen as one of 'research methods', as ordinarily conceived, but as one of *analytic interests*, *problematics* or *conception*. Rather than focusing on issues like the choice between qualitative and quantitative research, the problem is one of research purpose, or the functions that various methods and results have in the argumentation of a research project. Indeed, the observation that ethnomethodological inquiries have a 'qualitative' character does not produce, by itself, a commonality of analytic interests with other kinds of qualitative social research. The purpose of this chapter is to explicate ethnomethodology's interests and problems as these are implicated in its research practices. Before I turn to a discussion of specific practices and examples, however, it may be useful to try to elucidate some of ethnomethodology's core notions, which are often expressed in a rather specific jargon.[1]

CORE NOTIONS

These core notions include member and membership, accomplishment, accounts, accountability and accounting practices, indexicality, indexical expressions, glossing practices and reflexivity. A quote like the following, from the first page of ethnomethodology's foundational book, Harold Garfinkel's *Studies in Ethnomethodology* (1967), already contains most of these jargon terms.

> Ethnomethodological studies analyze everyday activities as members' methods for making those same activities visibly-rational-and-reportable-for-all-practical-purposes, i.e., 'accountable', as organizations of commonplace everyday activities. The reflexivity of that phenomenon is a singular feature of practical actions, of practical circumstances, of common sense knowledge of social structures, and of practical sociological reasoning. By permitting us to locate and examine their occurrence the reflexivity of that phenomenon establishes their study. (Garfinkel, 1967: vii)

The first sentence quoted specifies the special interest of ethnomethodological studies in the ways in which practical actors demonstrate in the *way* they do things *what* they are doing. That is, they somehow provide for the intelligibility of their actions in the very design and execution of those actions. One could say that actors give a 'running commentary' on their actions, if one accepts that this may be non-verbal and if one also accepts that the commentary and the action that is commented on are inseparable. It is this latter feature that Garfinkel points at in the second sentence about 'reflexivity': the accounts refer back to the actions of which they are a part. And finally, because, and in the way they are made intelligible, these practices can be studied.

One should also note the use of the notion 'members' in the first sentence of the quotation. Ethnomethodology is not interested in 'individuals' as such, but in the *competences* involved in being a bona-fide member of a collectivity. As Garfinkel writes in a note:

> I use the term 'competence' to mean the claim that a collectivity member is entitled to exercise that he is capable of managing his everyday affairs without interference. That members can take such claims for granted I refer to by speaking of a person as a 'bona-fide' collectivity member. ... The terms 'collectivity' and 'collectivity member' are intended in strict accord with Talcott Parsons' usage in *The Social System*. ... (Garfinkel, 1967: 57, note 8)

In their 1970 essay, Garfinkel and Sacks (p. 342) write in a similar way that: 'The notion of member is the heart of the matter. We do not use the term to refer to a person. It refers instead to mastery of natural language. ...'

The stress on the properties and usage of 'natural language' in this quotation is related to an early preoccupation of Garfinkel with 'indexical expressions'. These are expressions whose sense depends on the local circumstances in which they are uttered and/or those to which they apply. Expressions like 'you' or 'yesterday' are obvious examples. But, if you think of it, on all occasions, all expressions (and actions) are in fact indexical. Early in the *Studies*, Garfinkel writes about 'the unsatisfied programmatic distinction between and substitutability of objective for indexical expressions' (Garfinkel, 1967: 4–7). In all areas of social life, especially the more formal ones, an enormous effort is made to use objective statements that have a general validity, independent of particular communicative situations. But, Garfinkel maintains, particular conditions of intelligibility are always implicated. Contrary to the generally adhered-to a programme of 'objectivism', Garfinkel seems to suggest that indexicality could be seen as a generally available *resource* for achieving understanding:

> The properties of indexical expressions and indexical actions are ordered properties. These consist of organizationally demonstrable sense, or facticity, or methodic use, or agreement among 'cultural colleagues'. Their ordered properties consist of organizationally demonstrable rational properties of indexical expressions and indexical actions. Those ordered properties are ongoing achievements of the concerted commonplace activities of investigators. The demonstrable rationality of indexical expressions and indexical actions retains over the course of its managed production by members the character of ordinary, familiar, routinized practical circumstances... . I use the term 'ethnomethodology' to refer to the investigation of the rational properties of indexical expressions and other practical actions as contingent ongoing accomplishments of organized artful practices of everyday life. (Garfinkel, 1967: 11)

And in Garfinkel and Sacks's collaborative essay, a similar mission statement can be found:

> The interests of ethnomethodological research are directed to provide, through detailed analyses, that account-able phenomena are through and through practical accomplishments. We shall speak of 'the work' of that accomplishment in order to gain the emphasis for it of an ongoing course of action. The work is done as assemblages of practices whereby speakers in the situated particulars of speech mean something different from what they can say in just so many words, that is, as 'glossing practices'. (Garfinkel and Sacks, 1970: 342)

In other words, ethnomethodological studies are focused on explicating the continuous and endless 'work' by which members of society constitute the intelligibility of the activities that make up that society. Or, to quote one of the more concise definitions of ethnomethodology, the interest is in how actions and accounts are constituted in relation to each other: 'Ethnomethodology can be described briefly as a way to investigate the genealogical relationship between social practices and accounts of those practices' (Lynch, 1993: 1).

Since the publication of *Studies in Ethnomethodology* in 1967, ethnomethodology has developed in various ways, one of the most important being the emergence of conversation analysis (CA) as a related-as-well-as-separate discipline. CA is related to ethnomethodology in its stress on the local achievement of order by the use of socially organized procedures, most notably sequential organization, which can be seen as one of the major ways in which 'indexical expressions' gain their local intelligibility (cf. Maynard and Clayman, 1991; Clayman and Maynard, 1995).

While the core of ethnomethodological preoccupations has stayed the same, a range of new concepts and new fields of application have emerged. Some of Garfinkel's early writings could be read as suggesting that ethnomethodology would be in the business of formulating general rules, statements, practices or procedures used in the constitution of local social orders. The later work, however, clearly stresses the idea that those practices, etc., are too intimately tied to the occasions at which they are being used to be discussed 'independently' of them (Garfinkel, 1991, 1996, 2002). This has been especially clear in ethnomethodological studies of a range of complicated professional activities, as in studies of research laboratories (Lynch, 1985, and many other publications), mathematical proofing (Livingston, 1986) and piano improvisation (Sudnow, 1978, 2001). The general idea is that conventional studies of various specialized kind of work miss the essential 'what' of those activities in favour of traditional sociological features such as 'professionalization', 'status considerations', 'lines of communication', etc. Garfinkel has suggested that in order to be able to study the specifics – the 'quiddity' or 'just whatness' – that make up a particular profession, an investigator should develop a rather deep competence in that type of work. This has been called the 'unique adequacy requirement of methods' (Garfinkel and Wieder, 1992; Garfinkel, 2002). Still later Garfinkel dropped the term 'quiddity' or 'just whatness' in favour of 'haecceity' or 'just thisness', presumably in order to avoid suggestions of a stable 'core' that would define a particular practice (Garfinkel, 1991, 2002). Whatever the fancy terms, the urge is still to study the rational, in the sense of reasonable, properties of indexical expressions and indexical actions. The mission of recent ethnomethodology has been formulated as one of 'respecification' of the classic concepts of Western science and philosophy, such as 'order', 'logic', 'rationality', 'action', etc., *as* members' practices (cf. Garfinkel, 1991, 1996; Lynch, 1993; Lynch and Bogen, 1996). In other words, the grand themes of our intellectual culture are taken up in a fresh way as embodied in local, situated and intelligible practices (Button, 1991).

STUDYING COMMON-SENSE PRACTICES

For ethnomethodology, common-sense practices are the topic of study, but those practices are also, unavoidably, relied on by the researcher her- or himself. Without the use of common-sense, its object of study would be simply unavailable, because it is constituted by the application of common-sense methods. So the problem for ethnomethodology is how common-sense practices and common-sense knowledge can lose their status as an unexamined 'resource', in order to become a 'topic' for analysis. Don Zimmerman and Melvin Pollner (1971) have stated the issues in the following terms:

> In contrast to the perennial argument that sociology belabors the obvious, we propose that sociology has yet to treat the obvious as a phenomenon. We argue that the world of everyday life, while furnishing sociology with its favored topics of inquiry, is seldom a topic in its own right. Instead, the familiar, common-sense world, shared by the sociologist and his subjects alike, is employed as an unexplicated resource for contemporary sociological investigations.
>
> Sociological inquiry is addressed to phenomena recognized and described in common-sense ways (by reliance on the unanalyzed properties of natural language), while at the same time such common-sense recognitions and descriptions are pressed into service as fundamentally unquestioned resources for analyzing the phenomena thus made available for study. Thus, contemporary sociology is characterized by a confounding of topic and resource. (Zimmerman and Pollner, 1971: 80–1)

It is a double-faced problem: on the one hand a problem of minimizing the unexamined use of common sense, and on the other that of maximizing its examinability. This double-sided problem seems to be in principle unsolvable; one is bound to lose either the resource or the topic. So what one has to do is to find practical solutions, which are unavoidably compromises. In an earlier publication (ten Have, 1990), I have suggested a rough typology for these practical solutions.

The first type is especially prominent in Garfinkel's early work (1967). This strategy consists of the close study of sense-making activities in situations where they are especially prominent. Such situations are those in which sharp discrepancies, between on the one hand existing expectations and/or competences, and on the other practical behavioural and/or interpretative tasks, necessitate extraordinary sense-making efforts by members. Such situations may occur naturally – as in the case of a 'transsexual' studied by Garfinkel (1967: 116–85) – or they may be created on purpose, as in the so-called 'breaching' experiments (Garfinkel, 1967: 35–103; also Garfinkel, 2002, on 'tutorial problems').

In order to escape some of the practical and ethical problems generated by such experiments, a different strategy was developed, in which researchers study their own sense-making work by putting themselves in some kind of extraordinary situation. This may be a situation where routine sense-making procedures are bound to fail, or where one has to master a difficult and unknown task, or where one is instructed by a setting's members to see the world in a way that is natural for them but not for oneself. Mehan and Wood (1975: 225–38) use the expression 'becoming the phenomenon', while Schwartz and Jacobs (1979: 247–65) recommend strategies like becoming The Stranger or The Novice. These strategies can be considered variations on the theme that by 'becoming a member', the researcher can gain a more intimate access to the intricacies of 'being a member' than by other investigative means. Out of many possible examples I would like to mention David Sudnow's (1978, 2001) study of learning to play improvised jazz at the piano, and Lawrence Wieder's (1974) study of his being instructed in the use of 'the Convict Code' as a general interpretative and explanatory device in a half-way house for paroled addicts.

While, in these cases, a researcher's own experiences play an important role, in others ethnomethodologists have used more or less ordinary ethnographic fieldwork practices. They have been closely observing situated activities in their natural settings and discussing them with the seasoned practitioners, in order to study the competences involved in the routine performance of these activities. To further this close study, or to be able to study these activities after the fact, recording equipment is often used, but researchers may also rely on traditional note-taking in order to produce their data. Early examples of this kind of study can be found in Garfinkel's (1967) work on juries and coroners, Sudnow's (1967) study of hospital procedures concerning death and dying, and Zimmerman's (1969) study of case-workers in a welfare agency.

In an increasing number of ethnomethodological projects, and in all those belonging to ethnomethodology's close relative conversation analysis (CA), research materials are collected by mechanically recording interactional practices using audio or video equipment. These recordings are then studied directly, but they are also transcribed in a way that limits the use of common-sense procedures to hearing what is being said and noting how is has been said. These transcriptions have a double function: they are used to locate particular phenomena, and they can furthermore be shown to others, or quoted in publications, to support analytic claims made about the recorded practices. Working with recordings and transcripts in CA is discussed in Anssi Peräkylä's contribution to this volume (Chapter 11) (see also Hutchby and Wooffitt, 1998; ten Have, 1999a). The study by Michael Lynch and David Bogen (1996) of the Iran-Contra hearings, to be discussed later, is an example of a non-CA ethnomethodological study based on broadcast video recordings.

In specific projects, these practices may be combined in various ways. Wieder's (1974) study, here cited as exemplifying the second strategy, can also be seen as an example of the third, as his analysis of his own learning of and being instructed in 'seeing' the world of the half-way house in terms of 'the code' is embedded in general ethnographic descriptions. And while CA studies used to rely almost exclusively on recordings and transcripts, in more recent years such analyses are increasingly embedded in and inspired by more ethnographically informed understandings, especially in so-called 'workplace studies' focused on technologically complex environments (cf. Button, 1993; Heath and Luff, 2000; Luff et al., 2000, for examples).

The general idea lying behind these research practices is thus to evade as far as possible the unthinking and unnoticed use of common sense that seems to be inherent in empirical research practices in the social sciences at large. The ethnomethodological critique of these practices comes down to the objection that in so doing one studies idealized and decontextualized 'reconstructions' of social life, made by the research subjects and/or the researcher, instead of that life in its own situated particulars. For that reason, those analyses are called 'constructive' (Garfinkel and Sacks, 1970). So ethnographers may be said to study their own field notes as an unexamined resource for their study of a community's life. Or researchers using interviews study the responses they have recorded as an

unexamined resource for their study of 'underlying' opinions and unobserved activities. In both cases, the situated 'production' of those materials is not given systematic attention in its own right. The theoretical objects of such studies tend to be either individuals or collectivities. In contrast to such a 'methodological individualism' or 'collectivism', ethnomethodology and CA prefer a position that is closer to what Karin Knorr-Cetina (1981, 1988: 22) has called 'methodological situationalism'. She has formulated this position in terms of the then current micro/macro and agency/structure debates: 'I shall call methodological situationalism the principle which demands that descriptively adequate accounts of large-scale social phenomena be grounded in statements about actual social behaviour in concrete situations' (1988: 22).

BREACHING EXPERIMENTS

The aspect of Garfinkel's work that originally was most surprising to outsiders was his use of experimental demonstrations in which covert expectations were 'breached'. Of course people were familiar with a range of experimental set-ups in social psychology, which often involved quite elaborate deceptions, but these were based on a strictly defined cause-and-effect model, and used elaborate 'controls' and quantitative methods to produce reliable results. In contrast to these, the design of Garfinkel's experiments was 'loose' and their effects were not discussed in terms of causes and effects. Furthermore, only some of them were done in a laboratory setting, while many were 'field experiments' given as assignments to his students. And while Garfinkel used the expression 'experiment' and 'experimenter' in his reports, he also stresses their special character as follows:

> A word of reservation. Despite their procedural emphasis, my studies are not properly speaking experimental. They are demonstrations designed, in Herbert Spiegelberg's phrase, as 'aids to a sluggish imagination'. I have found that they produce reflections through which the strangeness of an obstinately familiar world can be detected. (Garfinkel, 1967: 38)

So in terms of their function, these arrangements were 'pedagogical demonstrations', and as such they are part of a larger collection of often ingenious, surprising and at times humorous instructions. The ultimate 'target' of these demonstrations was always the 'incompleteness' of efforts at literal description of real-worldly events or elaborate instructions for action within the world, and thereby of the inevitable 'work' involved in their everyday use. A few examples may clarify how these demonstrations were designed and with what effect.

In the first chapter of his *Studies*, Garfinkel reports on a study of coding practices (pp. 18–24). Two graduate students had to code the contents of clinic folders in terms of a coding sheet designed as part of a study of selection criteria and patient careers. It soon became clear that the coders, in order to code the folder contents to their satisfaction as adequate descriptions of what happened in the clinic, constantly used informal knowledge of clinic procedures. In other words, the instructions contained in the coding sheets were by themselves insufficient to perform the coding task. Coders had to rely on additional reasonings that Garfinkel glosses as '*ad hoc* considerations', which include 'such considerations as, "et cetera", "unless", "let it pass", and "factum valet" (i.e., an action that is otherwise prohibited by a rule is counted correct once it is done)' (pp. 20–1).

In another student assignment, he asked them to write up at the left of a sheet of paper a conversation in which they had participated, adding in a separate column to the right 'what they and their partners understood that they were talking about' (p. 38). He quotes one example and discusses it at some length in two different chapters (pp. 24–31, 38–42):

> Students filled out the left side of the sheet quickly and easily, but found the right side incomparably more difficult. When the assignment was made, many asked how much I wanted them to write. As I progressively imposed accuracy, clarity, and distinctness, the task became increasingly laborious. Finally, when I required that they assume I would know what they had actually talked about only from reading literally what they wrote literally, they gave up with the complaint that the task was impossible. (Garfinkel, 1967: 26)

Both parties to a conversation used and relied on a presupposedly common body of knowledge to 'hear' what was said as making sense, using the progression of successively produced items as 'documents' to be elaborated in a process of discovering what was meant, as an underlying 'pattern'.[2]

> The anticipation that persons *will* understand, the occasionality of expressions, the specific vagueness of references, the retrospective-prospective sense of a present occurrence, waiting for something later in order to see what was meant before, are sanctioned properties of common discourse. (Garfinkel, 1967: 41)

Many of the breaching experiments can be seen as further elaborations of this theme of the 'incompleteness' of literal descriptions and instructions, and the unavoidable use of ad hoc considerations relying on available informal knowledge. Students were, for instance, 'instructed to engage an acquaintance or a friend in an ordinary conversation and, without indicating that what the experimenter was asking was in any way unusual, to insist that the person clarify the sense of his commonplace remarks' (p. 42). Here is one of the examples quoted by Garfinkel:

> The subject was telling the experimenter, a member of the subject's car pool, about having had a flat tire while going to work the previous day.
>
> (S) I had a flat tire.
> (E) What do you mean, you had a flat tire?
>
> She appeared momentarily stunned. Then she answered in a hostile way: 'What do you mean, "What do you mean?" A flat tire is a flat tire. That is what I meant. Nothing special. What a crazy question!' (Garfinkel, 1967: 42)

What was generally observed in these and other breaching experiments was that the 'victims' – as Garfinkel calls them – first tried to 'normalize' the situation, and when this was unsuccessful, reacted with 'astonishment, bewilderment, shock, anxiety, embarrassment, and anger'.

While most of these demonstrations were field experiments with student experimenters, a few were done in a laboratory setting with similar results. In one set-up, subjects were instructed to ask questions about some personal problem in yes/no format and – after they received an answer – record their comments and interpretations, before asking a next question. In fact the choice of an answer as 'yes' or 'no' was based on a table of random numbers. The subjects did not know this and were most of the time able to hear the 'yes' or 'no' as a sensible answer to their question. Garfinkel used this experiment as a demonstration of 'the documentary method of interpretation', which is not so much a specific 'method' of 'interpretative sociology' as one unavoidably used in everyday life as well as in all kinds of sociological inquiry (Garfinkel, 1967: 76–103):

> The method consists of treating an actual appearance as 'the document of', as 'pointing to', as 'standing on behalf of' a presupposed underlying pattern. Not only is the underlying pattern derived from its individual documentary evidences, but the individual documentary evidences, in their turn, are interpreted on the basis of 'what is known' about the underlying pattern. Each is used to elaborate the other. (Garfinkel, 1967: 78)

Taken as a whole, Garfinkel's 'breaching experiments' were explicative devices, pedagogical tricks or tutorials clarifying and demonstrating conceptual issues, rather than research projects as ordinarily perceived. In later periods he has continued to use these and similar devices, but I will not take these up now (cf. Garfinkel, 2002). Such experiments and demonstrations have not become stock-in-trade ways of doing ethnomethodological studies, although in some respects they have influenced the ways in which ethnomethodologists choose research settings and approaches, for instance by investigating settings or experiences in which sense-making was, for some 'natural' reason, especially acute (cf., for instance, Lynch, 1985; Pollner, 1987; Maynard, 1996).

BECOMING A MEMBER

As noted before, breaching expectancies is not the only possibility to make common-sense practices 'visible'. One can observe situations in which such practices are particularly acute for others or for oneself. By placing oneself in a situation in which one encounters particular sense-making difficulties, or by entering such situations for other motives, or even by a whim of fate, one can study how one deals with that situation, as well as how others react to it. In this section, I will discuss some examples of such strategies, both published and unpublished.

To start, I will present some reflections on a learning task, recognizing species of birds by their songs and calls. As part of our membership we know that life forms are being differentiated in multi-layered systems of classification. Plants are seen as basically different from animal forms, mammals as different from birds and insects, etc. Depending on the circumstances of our upbringing and our personal interests, we may learn to make some finer distinctions. At the age of ten, for instance, I could distinguish a number of common bird species, say *Merel* (Blackbird), *Ekster* (Magpie), *Koolmees* (Great Tit), *Roodborst* (Robin), *Huismus* (House Sparrow), *Vink* (Chaffinch), and even some less common ones like *Goudvink* (Bullfinch), which happened to visit our garden at times. I acquired most of this knowledge by looking at the birds and having their names mentioned to me by others. I learned to distinguish the species by sight, acquiring the ability to connect properties of form, colour and behaviour to names. Gradually, I also learned to recognize birds by their songs. The Blackbird was probably among the earliest to be known in this way, as he sang from our rooftop in spring. Seeing a bird you know by sight sing his song is one method of building a repertoire of recognizable bird songs. Over the years I was able to enlarge my repertoire by a variety of means, including having a song I heard 'named' for me by a co-listener, consulting descriptions in field guides and comparing what I had heard outdoors to a specimen song recorded on tape or CD.[3]

According to my experience, the main difficulty in this learning process is to remember the details of what you hear, in order to be able to connect those with a name, on the spot or later. For colours we have names, forms can be described and behaviours characterized, but sounds are more difficult to 'catch'. There are, of course, easy cases, as the *Koekoek* (Cuckoo) who was given his name after his call, a so-called onomatopoeia. There are a number of onomatopoetic bird names, as for instance – in Dutch – *Grutto, Tureluur, Kievit, Kauw* and *Karekiet*. Often the recognizability of the onomatopoeia in the field is not an easy matter. It may take repeated 'connection work' before the sound of, say, the Black-tailed Godwit (*Limosa limosa*) is effectively recognized as *Grutto*. What you do is 'sing' (in your mind) what you hear in the field or on the record, using the Dutch pronunciation of ↑ *grutto* ↑ *grutto* ↑ *grutto*. So in a way you have to learn to hear the sound produced by the bird *as if* it was 'instructed' by the description. In field guides more complicated renderings are given, for instance *rieta-rieta-rieta*, and *gr-wieto* (Peterson et al., 1984). Such renderings could be called 'transcriptions' and they are often given in combination with ordinary descriptions (cf. Jefferson, 1985). Here is an example for the song of the *Kleine Karekiet* (Reed Warbler):

> 'babbelend' in laag tempo, bestaand uit nerveuze, 2–4 keer herhaalde noten (onomatopoëtisch), af en toe onderbroken door imitaties of fluittonen, *trett trett trett TIRri TIRri truu truu TIe tre tre wi-wuu-wu tre tre truu truu TIRri TIRri.* … Tempo af en toe hoger, maar nooit met crescendo van Rietzanger. ['babbling' at a slow tempo, consisting of nervous, 2–4 times repeated notes (onomatopoeic), now and then interrupted by imitations or whistlings, *trett trett trett TIRri TIRri truu truu TIe tre tre wi-wuu-wu tre tre truu truu TIRri TIRri.* … Tempo now and then higher, but never in crescendo like Sedge Warbler.] (Mullarney et al., 2000: 296)

Apart from such published transcriptions and descriptions, birders use a variety of informal tricks to assist their connection work. For instance, two small birds that inhabit the same types of environments and that also sing during the winter, when most others are elsewhere or silent, are the *Roodborst* (Robin) and the

Winterkoning (Wren). The song of the Robin can be described as 'pearling', and a memory-aid for the Wren is to pronounce the Dutch name in the following way: *winterrrrrrrrrrrrrkoning*, with the repeated *rrr*'s representing the rattle-like part that Wrens produced in the middle of their song. So when I hear a 'small' bird in wintertime, I try to fit these two tricks on the sound and make my decision whether it is a Robin or a Wren that I am hearing. Birders exchange such tricks among themselves. The *Grasmus* (Whitethroat, literally 'Grass-sparrow'), for instance, is informally called *Krasmus* ('scratch-sparrow'), after his 'scratchy' song. Once birders have acquired a more solid kind of knowledge of a particular bird's song, they do not need these tricks any more. Experienced birders do what might be called a *Gestalt* recognition: they will need only a small fragment of a song to recognize the bird that produced it, mostly on the basis of the tone-quality of what they hear, together with contextual knowledge of which birds sing where and when. Having that ability for a substantial number of birds is a mark of expert membership. Instead of just enjoying the singing of birds in spring, they hear an ecological soundscape, a natural order.

In this project – and in two others (ten Have, 1999b, 2000), which space considerations forbid me to discuss at any length – I have been using my own experiences to gain access to some rather different kinds of membership competences, in order to be able to study 'from the inside' what is involved in being a birder (or a reader/writer, or a chatter). I did not study myself as an individual, but as a member. It is hard to differentiate, in such projects, the aspects of participation and observation. I would say that here, as in some other ethnomethodological studies in which the researcher relied, at least in part, on 'becoming a member', the conventional label 'participant observation' gains a new significance. To substantiate this point, I will now discuss two episodes from studies by David Goode, in which 'becoming a member' played a crucial part within an overall 'observational' study.

As part of his graduate work, Goode studied children born deaf and blind, who were also retarded and without formal language, due to a rubella infection during pregnancy. This specifically involved the in-depth study of two such children, one hospitalized in a state institution and another living with her parents (Goode, 1994). An important overall theme of these explorations is the continuously emerging observation that the assessment of the capabilities of these children was dependent on the character, format and frequency of the assessor's interaction

with them. In the state hospital, Goode observed that the assessments made by various specialized clinicians were markedly different from those by members of the 'direct-care' staff. The first saw the children only incidentally, for brief periods, and in terms of their practical-professional frameworks, such as medical or educational tests, while the second had to deal with the children every day in a variety of practical contexts. When Goode started to communicate his observation-based ideas that these children might have their own perspective on things and were even 'smart' in their own ways, the very possibility of the children having such capacities tended to be denied by the clinicians and accepted by the direct-care staff. He therefore planned to undertake an intensive study of one child's 'world' through a period of frequent and intense interactions. Most of these interactions with 'Christina' had a playful character in that he could more and more leave his normal seeing/hearing self-evident presuppositions behind and let the child initiate a variety of forms of play. This involved, for instance, the bracketing of the usual functions of various objects, such as musical instruments, to see her use of those object as sensible-for-her, in terms of her perceptual possibilities. In other words, he had to discard a remedial attitude that was so natural for all able seers/hearers when confronted with seemingly bizarre behaviours, since this led inevitably to the application of 'fault-finding procedures'. Here is what he did:

> I decided to *mimic her actions* in order to gain more direct access to what such activities were providing her. I used wax ear stops (placed more securely in the left ear, since Chris has a 'better' right ear than left ear) and gauzed my left eye with a single layer of lightweight gauze to simulate the scar tissue that covers Chris's left eye. I began to imitate Chris's behaviors. ... While the procedure had its obvious inadequacies with respect to my gaining access to Chris's experience of these activities, I did learn a number of interesting things in this way. (Goode, 1994: 33–4)

In this way he could, for instance, understand that she would get some auditory or visual stimulations by moving parts of her body rhythmically in certain positions vis-à-vis particular sources of sound or light. In fact, a lot of her bizarre movements appeared to be 'rational' as effective means of self-stimulation in terms of her particular sensory restrictions. By way of this partial imitation of her conditions and action, Goode was able to gain at least a sense of the significance *in her own terms* of these acts. A major overall condition for these possibilities, however, was that he was free from custodial or pedagogical obligations and therefore free to play with her, allowing her to show him how she was striving for at least some 'primitive' gratifications. By becoming a 'superplaymate' to her, he was able to 'meet her' in ways that staff members could only rarely achieve.

I have tried, in these vignettes of 'becoming a member', to demonstrate some of the benefits for ethnomethodological research of combining researcher practice and observation. It provides a kind of intimate access to the experience that does not seem to be available by other means such as detached observation. In the next section I will deal with some examples of studies in which researcher involvement is less prominent.

USING AUDIO/VIDEO RECORDS

As noted, the use of audio and/or video recordings, and transcriptions made after such recordings, is an essential part of the canonical practice of conversation analysis. And although CA practices have been criticized at times by ethnomethodologists (cf. Bogen, 1999: 83–120), the use of recordings and transcripts has also become prominent in those parts of ethnomethodology that are closer to Garfinkel's core conceptions. As an illustration, I will discuss some aspects of a study by Michael Lynch and David Bogen, *The Spectacle of History: Speech, Text, and Memory at the Iran-Contra Hearings* (1996), in which they use a variety of materials, including prominently public television broadcast recordings. The authors investigate some of the ways in which 'history' is 'produced', by inspecting various scenes from the 1987 hearing by the US Joint House–Senate Select Committee on Secret Military Assistance to Iran and the Nicaragua Opposition. I will discuss just two issues that are raised in this rich study. The first is the epistemological status of the television records and the second the application of the 'respecification' strategy.

In the introduction they write that their aim is to describe 'the production of history', and not to 'deconstruct' it. In fact, a major phenomenon in those hearings was the pervasiveness of 'deconstruction' as a practical activity, as each party tried to undermine the accounts provided by the other. Therefore, 'deconstruction does not identify our own methodological agenda, but instead it is a perspicuous feature of the struggle we describe'. And they continue:

We shall assume an ability to describe and exhibit recognizable features of the video text we have chosen to examine. In this effort we shall inevitably engage in constructive (i.e., productive) practices, such as using the video text as a proxy for the live performances of interrogators and witnesses, and selectively using written transcripts to exhibit recurrent discursive actions. (Lynch and Bogen, 1996: 14)

In other words, they rely on their own ordinary members' competences as any (informed) viewer/hearer of the tapes would, and they concede that their own use of tapes and documents inevitably also involves 'constructive' work, which might be criticized as well by others:

Although it is commonplace in the social sciences to lay out a set of methodological procedures that provide reasonable foundations for the selection and interpretation of data, in this study we trust that readers will be able to discern our methods by reference to what we say about the subject matter. Our methods are organized around, and take many of their initiatives from, the complexity and circumstances of the case at hand. (Lynch and Bogen, 1996: 15)

So again, they present their own, ethnomethodological work on the data as 'ordinary' and intelligible to 'any member'. And then they construct a contrast between this ordinary way of knowing with what are presented as ideals in conventional social science:

Although it is fashionable to attribute latent epistemologies to a text or practice being analyzed, ethnomethodology's approach to practical action and practical reasoning is more in line with the Aristotelian concept of 'phronesis'. Unlike episteme – the geometrical method of deducing proofs from axioms – phronesis takes its departure from the conventional recognizability of a perspicuous case. The presumption is that a community of readers will grasp enough of the details in question, with no need to justify such understanding on ultimate grounds, so that relevant maxims and precedents can be brought to bear on the case and extended to others like it. The failure of such a method to live up to the universal standards of procedure and proof associated with Euclidean geometry carries no necessary stigma. Indeed, it can be argued that science and mathematics do not fully exemplify episteme, and that at the moment of their production all inquiries involve an effort to come to terms with relevant circumstances. (Lynch and Bogen, 1996: 15)

In effect, then, the authors offer a contrast between 'ordinary' understanding practices and 'formal' idealizations concerning proper ways of knowing, which are ascribed to mathematics and the sciences, although they suggest that even inquiries that fall under the latter auspices in actual fact also require 'ordinary' practices of understanding (cf. Lynch, 1985, 1993; Livingston, 1986). So, rather than claiming adherence to a set of formal principles, they, as ethnomethodologists, refer to their co-membership of a 'community of readers' as a good enough basis for the intelligibility of their research materials as well as their own elaborations of those materials:

> Ethnomethodology makes a topic of cases under inquiry in law, medicine, science, and daily life. This does not necessarily place the ethnomethodologist at a metaphysical or epistemological advantage vis-à-vis the practical actions studied, since any analysis of such actions is itself responsible for coming to terms with the circumstantially specific and immanently recognizable features of the case before it. (Lynch and Bogen, 1996: 15)

They are not after some sort of 'deeper' understanding of what happened and they do not try to replace one or another theory of meaning with their own. And neither are they trying to evaluate the truth value of one or another version of 'what happened':

> In view of the fact that so much social-scientific, literary, and philosophical effort has been devoted to getting to the bottom of discourse, our aim of sticking to the surface of the text may strike some readers as curious. It is our view, however, that any deeper readings would have to ignore the complexity and texture of the surface events, and thus they would fail to explicate how an order of activities is achieved as a contingent, moment-by-moment production. (Lynch and Bogen, 1996: 16)

What should again be evident in these remarks is that ethnomethodology takes a very special position vis-à-vis common-sense knowledge and ways of knowing. These constitute an unavoidably used resource, but are *also* the topic of inquiry, to repeat what I have noted earlier referring to Zimmerman and Pollner (1971). We can specify, moreover, two important consequences of this position. The first is that in the 'first phase' of their inquiries, ethnomethodologists' reliance on common-sense methods of knowing puts them in a relation of cultural colleagues with their readers, and therefore they do not need any special warrants for their claims to understanding their materials. The second, however, connected to the second phase of inquiry, necessitates that they take a distance vis-à-vis the differential interests and disputes of common-sense life. So in the case of Lynch and Bogen, they are not in a position to take issue with the disputes they discuss, but rather they study the ways in which these differences are 'produced' in the circumstances in which they occur. The label used to point to this particular kind of distantiation is 'ethnomethodological indifference' (cf. Garfinkel and Sacks, 1970: 345).

The subtitle of the book – *Speech, Text, and Memory at the Iran-Contra Hearings* – already suggests that the authors will discuss how the epistemological status of 'speech', 'text' and 'memory' are treated in the specific context of these events. The hearings themselves consist mainly of 'speech', especially interrogative questions and answers, but in the talking, the participants continuously refer to a variety of documents. Some are shown, quoted or paraphrased in situ, others are referred to in a more indirect manner, especially those that had been shredded. In a chapter on 'The documentary method of interrogation', the authors refer to a dispute between Jacques Derrida and John Searle in which Derrida objects to Searle's stress on speech and its grounding in the intention of the speaker in the speech situation, while he makes the point:

> that a linguistic fragment or text does not lose its intelligibility when divorced from its 'original' situation and authorship. Rather, it becomes an item in (and for) an indefinite series of original, yet intelligible, uses and readings. In this way Derrida argues that writing is autonomous from speech and that its intelligibility cannot be derived from the analysis of speech situations (ideal or otherwise). ... Without taking sides in the debate (and without going deeply into it), we figure that it alerts us to an interesting and taxing problem for participants at the Iran-Contra hearings. (Lynch and Bogen, 1996: 206)

In their ensuing analysis, the authors discuss episodes in which the parties to the interrogation can be seen to 'enact' different positions in this debate, for instance when the interrogator requests confirmations for various details in a text written by the witness, while the latter subtly limits his confirmations to surface details of the text, ostensibly ignoring the fact that he himself was its author. In this way, the strategy of the interrogator to have the witness reveal more than the text says, that is, to let him consult his memories regarding the 'original' situation, fails to have its intended effect. This is but one example out of many of the fruitfulness of the procedure called 'respecification', which they elaborate in the methodological appendix to their book (Lynch and Bogen, 1996: 272–3).

By using records of 'naturally occurring' events, ethnomethodologists can concentrate their analytic attention on the methods that participants have actually used in bringing off these events. In so doing, they are able to exhume interactional details that demonstrably have played a role in the interaction, although they may be hard to discern explicitly when observing the scene in real time. Observing records, and especially studying transcripts, 'fixes' the details of the stream of life and makes them available for a non-participating 'onlooker'. In a way, then, records and transcripts are devices used to enhance the visibility of details in an 'unnatural' way. As such they are part and parcel of the inevitable (?) split between living a natural order and studying it.

CONFRONTATIONS AND APPLICATIONS

I hope that the preceding sections have been able to shed some light on ethnomethodology's ways of doing research in terms of its specific intellectual interests. In short, EM's 'methods' are designed to elucidate the ways in which members of society create and maintain an intelligible lived social order. What may be seen as an open question, however, is how *relevant* EM's methods and findings may be for researchers with different, let us say more conventional, interests.

One way to approach this question is to focus again on the issue of the 'missing what', the ethnomethodological critique of conventional social science approaches that implies that they gloss over the issue of what makes up the specific character of some activity (Garfinkel, 1996). A conventional ethnography may tend to use an onlooker's perspective, which is informed by specifically sociological interests. For instance, William Foot Whyte, in his classic *Street Corner Society*, discusses the activity of bowling as a setting in which the informal hierarchy of the Norton gang was maintained (Whyte, 1955: 14–25). In the methodological appendix published with the second edition, he remarks that at first he had not considered that the bowling events had any importance for his research:

> I had been looking upon Saturday night at the bowling alleys as simply recreation for myself and my friends. I found myself enjoying the bowling so much that now and then I felt a bit guilty about neglecting my research. I was bowling with the men in order to establish a social position that would enable me to interview them and observe important things. But what were these important things? (Whyte, 1955: 320)

In his main analysis, the activity of bowling is 'reduced', it might be said, to its 'social function', in this case maintaining a local ranking system. In an ethnomethodologically informed ethnography, one might try to avoid such a reduction. One could choose to study how bowling was done 'as bowling', 'as recreation', or whatever the local concept might be. Ethnomethodologists try to gain an *inside understanding* of the activities of the members of the local culture. It should be noted, of course, that ethnomethodology's conception of an 'inside understanding' refers to getting a procedural grip on the activities, while other qualitative researchers might want to understand the motivations or perspectives of the relevant actors.

The most frequently used social science strategy to collect data from which to gain an actor-oriented understanding is, of course, to interview people. In contrast to this, interviewing is rarely used as a major data source in ethnomethodology (and it is not mentioned in my overview thus far). This does not mean, of course, that ethnomethodologists do not talk to people or listen to what they have to say, but rather that their general preference for 'naturally occurring events' leads to an overall avoidance of researcher-provoked data, including answers to researchers' questions. When interviews are used at all, they tend to be 'situated' ones, that is, as ongoing talk in an observational situation, used as support for understanding what is going on. Interviews held separately from ongoing activities are indeed quite rare, but when they occur the analysis tends to focus on aspects of 'doing an interview' using concepts from membership categorization analysis (MCA) or conversation analysis (CA). The interest, then, is in 'glossing practices', 'accounting', question/answer sequences, etc., as situated activities.

Finally, I want to consider ways in which ethnomethodology can be 'applied' to practical matters. In a rare essay on this issue, James Heap (1990) takes off from the question why one should undertake any activity, including ethnomethodological (EM) inquiries. This fits into the more general question of how one should live. This is, of course, not a 'scientific' question but a moral one. 'However, [scientific] inquiry can deliver some of what we need to know in order to make reasoned judgements in particular situations about how to act to achieve some end' (p. 39). Therefore, a research enterprise like ethnomethodology might be useful in producing bits of knowledge that may help one in making choices among courses of action. Reflection on why someone should engage in such enterprises, then, requires reflection on the kind of knowledge that it might produce, what kind of 'news' it might deliver. He distinguishes 'two types of news': 'things are not as they appear' and 'X is organized this way'. An often used variant of the former type of warrant is 'others got it wrong as to how things are' (Heap, 1990: 42). In other words, there are two approaches to warranting ethnomethodological studies, one that Heap calls the 'critical news approach' and the other the 'positive news approach'. The first offers a sustained critique of conventional and established conceptions of the organization of social life and of the practical application of knowledge based on such conceptions. What is criticized are especially the individualistic, rationalistic and mentalistic modes of thinking that still dominate most of the human sciences and its practical applications (cf., for instance, Suchman, 1987; Coulter, 1989; Button, 1991, Button et al., 1995).

Whether it is worthwhile to do ethnomethodology depends on the value of the news it produces for an audience, and here Heap differentiates between a professional EM audience and a lay EM audience. What he calls 'straight-ahead EM' is done for a professional EM audience and studies things chosen for their contribution to the development of ethnomethodological knowledge. 'Applied EM', on the other hand, is done for, and reported to, persons or organizations that have a practical interest in the phenomena and activities being studied. Such studies 'may deliver news about the structures of phenomena, and especially about the consequences of those structures for realizing ends and objectives regarded as important outside of ethnomethodology's analytic interests' (Heap, 1990: 44).

In other words, 'pure' EM is analytically motivated and can study *any* activity for what it can add to 'our knowledge of how social order is made possible'. 'Applied EM', on the other hand, is done in the hope that it can deliver some news about the organization of valued activities, which may help to generate ideas as to how things may be done differently. The contrast between 'pure' and 'applied' should not be over-drawn, however:

> There is no reason why straight-ahead EM cannot be done in domains and on topics of importance to non-ethnomethodologists. To render such an EM effort applied, one simply has to draw out the implications, the values of the discovered formal structures of activities or reasoning for those persons having a professional interest in the affairs studied. (Heap, 1990: 44)

What applied EM is all about, ultimately, is to study the *local rationality* of members' practices, i.e. why it makes sense, for participants, locally, in their practical context, to do things as they are done, even if this is at odds with how these practices are planned, evaluated or accounted for 'elsewhere', 'in theory', or at higher hierarchical levels in an organization (cf. ten Have, 1999a: 184–201).

To cite just one example, in a recent paper Jack Whalen and Erik Vinkhuyzen (2000) reported on a study of the work of call-takers in service centres for users' problems with document machines. Their detailed studies revealed, among other things, that the work could be done more efficiently when the database that the call-takers were expected to use was more flexible and when the workers were stimulated to become more knowledgeable about the machines and their problems. Findings and suggestions such as these received a mixed reaction, as the designers and managers working at a distance from the work-site were much more sceptical than the ones closer by. What this study seems to suggest is that ethnomethodology's slogan of 'ethnomethodological indifference' may hide a deeper commitment to bring to light the often neglected local competences and local rationalities involved in concrete practices. In his 1967 book, Garfinkel already had these scornful expressions about people being depicted as a 'cultural dope' by sociologists: 'the man-in-the-sociologist's-society who produces the stable features of the society by acting in compliance with preestablished and legitimate alternatives of action that the common culture provides' (p. 68). And in an elaboration of the contrast between ethnomethodology and what he now calls 'formal analysis', which is equivalent to what was earlier called 'constructive analysis', he writes in his new book: 'Ethnomethodology is not critical of formal analytic investigations. But neither is it the case that EM … has no concern with a remedial expertise and has nothing to promise or deliver. Ethnomethodology *is* applied Ethnomethodology. However, its remedial transactions are distinctive to EM expertise' (Garfinkel, 2002: 114).

Ethnomethodology is now presented as an 'alternate sociology', but its relation to 'formal analysis' is an *asymmetrical* one. That is, while ethnomethodology's approach can be used to study the practices of formal-analytic investigations, it is not possible for a formal-analytic inquiry to uncover the work and phenomena of ethnomethodology's studies (cf. Garfinkel and Wieder, 1992; Garfinkel, 2002: 117).

To conclude, ethnomethodology offers a unique focus on the situated creation and maintenance of social orders. Its research practices mostly have an observational character, with a marked preference for situations in which such orders are in some way problematic for members, which may add to the visibility of order-creating practices. In so doing, ethnomethodological inquiries may be useful to elucidate their interactive and situated character, ordinarily often overlooked as well as taken for granted.

ACKNOWLEDGEMENTS

I would like to express my gratitude for the remarks by Jaber F. Gubrium, Anssi Peräkylä, and especially Douglas W. Maynard on an earlier version of this chapter.

NOTES

1 For more extended explications, see Heritage (1984) for a broad scholarly overview, Sharrock and Anderson (1986) for a concise and sharp discussion of basic issues, Maynard and Clayman (1991) for a consideration of both the unique characteristics as well as the diversity of ethnomethodology, Button (1991) for a collection of essays dealing with ethnomethodological ways of treating some of the classic themes of the human sciences, and Lynch (1993) for pointed and polemical discussions confronting ethnomethodology and the sociology of scientific knowledge. The basic source remains Garfinkel (1967), especially the first three chapters. The new book by Garfinkel (2002) reached me after the present chapter was drafted. It has an extensive introduction by the editor, Ann Rawls, and will be the major source for years to come.

2 These terms are taken from Garfinkel's definition of 'the documentary method of interpretation', quoted later in this section.

3 Cf. Law and Lynch (1988) for a study of birdwatching and the design of field guides as viewing instructions.

REFERENCES

Bogen, David (1999) *Order Without Rules: Critical Theory and the Logic of Conversation*. New York: SUNY Press.

Button, Graham (ed.) (1991) *Ethnomethodology and the Human Sciences*. Cambridge: Cambridge University Press.

Button, Graham (ed.) (1993) *Technology in Working Order: Studies of Work, Interaction and Technology*. London: Routledge.

Button, Graham, Coulter, Jeff, Lee, John R.E. and Sharrock, Wes (1995) *Computers, Minds and Conduct*. Cambridge: Polity Press.

Clayman, Steven E. and Maynard, Douglas W. (1995) 'Ethnomethodology and conversation analysis', in Paul ten Have and George Psathas (eds), *Situated Order: Studies in the Social Organization of Talk and Embodied Activities*. Washington, DC: University Press of America, pp. 1–30.

Coulter, Jeff (1989) *Mind in Action*. Cambridge: Polity Press.

Garfinkel, Harold (1967) *Studies in Ethnomethodology*. Englewood Cliffs, NJ: Prentice-Hall.

Garfinkel, Harold (1991) 'Respecification: evidence for locally produced, naturally accountable phenomena of order*, logic, reason, meaning, method, etc. in and as of the essential haecceity of immortal ordinary society. I. An announcement of studies', in Graham Button (ed.), *Ethnomethodology and the Human Sciences*. Cambridge: Cambridge University Press, pp. 10–19.

Garfinkel, Harold (1996) 'An overview of ethnomethodology's program', *Social Psychology Quarterly*, 59: 5–21.

Garfinkel, Harold (2002) *Ethnomethodology's Program: Working Out Durkheim's Aphorism*, edited and introduced by Anne Rawls. Lanham, MD: Rowman & Littlefield.

Garfinkel, Harold and Sacks, Harvey (1970) 'On formal structures of practical action', in John C. McKinney and Edward A. Tiryakian (eds), *Theoretical Sociology: Perspectives and Developments*. New York: Appleton-Century-Crofts, pp. 338–66.

Garfinkel, Harold, and Wieder, D. Lawrence (1992) 'Two incommensurable, asymmetrically alternate technologies of social analysis', in Graham Watson and Robert M. Seiler (eds), *Text in Context: Studies in Ethnomethodology*. Newbury Park, CA: Sage, pp. 175–206.

Goode, David (1994) *A World Without Words: The Social Construction of Children Born Deaf and Blind*. Philadelphia: Temple University Press.

Heap, James L. (1990) 'Applied ethnomethodology: looking for the local rationality of reading activities', *Human Studies*, 13: 39–72.

Heath, Christian, and Luff, Paul (2000) *Technology in Action*. Cambridge: Cambridge University Press.

Heritage, John (1984) *Garfinkel and Ethnomethodology*. Cambridge: Polity Press.

Hutchby, Ian, and Wooffitt, Robin (1998) *Conversation Analysts: Principles, Practices and Applications*. Cambridge: Polity Press.

Jefferson, Gail (1985) 'An exercise in the transcription and analysis of laughter', in: Teun A. van Dijk (ed.), *Handbook of Discourse Analysis*. London: Academic Press, vol. 3, pp. 25–34.

Knorr-Cetina, Karin (1981) 'Introduction: the microsociological challenge of macro-sociology: towards a reconstruction of social theory and methodology', in K. Knorr-Cetina and A.V. Cicourel (eds) (1981) *Advances in Social Theory and Methodology: Toward an Integration of Micro- and Macro-sociologies*. London: Routledge & Kegan Paul, pp. 1–47.

Knorr-Cetina, Karin (1988) 'The micro-social order: towards a reconception', in N.G. Fielding (ed.), *Actions and Structure: Research Methods and Social Theory*. London: Sage, pp. 21–53.

Law, John and Lynch, Michael (1988) 'Lists, field guides, and the descriptive organization of seeing: birdwatching as an exemplary observational activity', *Human Studies*, 11: 271–304.

Livingston, Eric (1986) *The Ethnomethodological Foundations of Mathematics*. London: Routledge & Kegan Paul.

Luff, Paul, Hindmarsh, Jon and Heath, Christian (eds) (2000) *Workplace Studies: Recovering Work Practice and Informing Systems Design*. Cambridge: Cambridge University Press.

Lynch, Michael (1985) *Art and Artifact in Laboratory Science: A Study of Shop Work and Shop Talk*. London: Routledge & Kegan Paul.

Lynch, Michael (1993) *Scientific Practice and Ordinary Action: Ethnomethodology and Social Studies of Science*. New York: Cambridge University Press.

Lynch, Michael and Bogen, David (1996) *The Spectacle of History: Speech, Text, and Memory at the Iran-Contra Hearings*. Durham, NC: Duke University Press.

Maynard, Douglas W. (1996) 'On "realization" in everyday life: the forecasting of bad news as a social relation', *American Sociological Review,* 61: 109–31.

Maynard, Douglas W. and Clayman, Steven E. (1991) 'The diversity of ethnomethodology', *Annual Review of Sociology*, 17: 385–418.

Mehan, Hugh and Wood, Houston (1975) *The Reality of Ethnomethodology*. New York: Wiley.

Mullarney, Killian, Svenson, Lars, Zetterström, Dan and Grant, Peter J. (2000) *ANWB Vogelgids van Europa*. Den Haag: ANWB.

Peterson, R.T., Mountfort, G. and Hollum, P.A.D. (1984) *Petersons vogelgids*, tr. J. Kist. Amsterdam: Elsevier.

Pollner, Melvin (1974) 'Sociological and common sense models of the labelling process', in R. Turner (ed.), *Ethnomethodology: Selected Readings*. Harmondsworth: Penguin, pp. 27–40.

Pollner, Melvin (1987) *Mundane Reason: Reality in Everyday Life and Sociological Discourse*. Cambridge: Cambridge University Press.

Schwartz, Howard and Jacobs, Jerry (1979) *Qualitative Sociology: A Method to the Madness*. New York: Free Press.

Sharrock, Wes and Anderson, Bob (1986) *The Ethnomethodologists*. Chichester: Ellis Horwood.

Suchman, Lucy (1987) *Plans and Situated Action: The Problem of Human–Machine Communication*. Cambridge: Cambridge University Press.

Sudnow, David (1967) *Passing On: The Social Organization of Dying*. Englewood Cliffs, NJ: Prentice-Hall.

Sudnow, David (1978) *Ways of the Hand: The Organization of Improvised Conduct*. London: Routledge & Kegan Paul.

Sudnow, David (2001) *Ways of the Hand: A Rewritten Account*. Cambridge, MA: MIT Press.

ten Have, Paul (1990) 'Methodological issues in conversation analysis', *Bulletin de Méthodologie Sociologique*, no. 27 (June): 23–51.

ten Have, Paul (1999a) *Doing Conversation Analysis: A Practical Guide*. London: Sage.

ten Have, Paul (1999b) 'Structuring writing for reading: hypertext and the reading body', *Human Studies*, 22: 273–98.

ten Have, Paul (2000) 'Computer-mediated chat: ways of finding chat partners', *M/C – A Journal of Media and Culture*, 4/3. http://www.media-culture.org.au/archive.html#chat

Whalen, Jack and Vinkhuyzen, Eric (2000) 'Expert systems in (inter)action: diagnosing document machine problems over the telephone', in Paul Luff, Jon Hindmarsh and Christian Heath (eds), *Workplace Studies: Recovering Work Practice and Informing Systems Design*. Cambridge: Cambridge University Press, pp. 92–140.

Whyte, W.F. (1955) *Street Corner Society: The Social Structure of an Italian Slum* (2nd ed.). Chicago: University of Chicago Press (originally published 1943).

Wieder, D. Lawrence (1974) *Language and Social Reality: The Case of Telling the Convict Code*. The Hague: Mouton.

Zimmerman, Don H. (1969) 'Record-keeping and the intake process in a public welfare agency', in: S. Wheeler (ed.), *On Record: Files and Dossiers in American Life*. New York: Russell Sage, pp. 319–45.

Zimmerman, Don H. and Pollner, Melvin (1971) 'The everyday world as a phenomenon', in J.D. Douglas (ed.), *Understanding Everyday Life: Towards a Reconstruction of Sociological Knowledge*. London: Routledge & Kegan Paul, pp. 80–103.

11

Conversation analysis

Anssi Peräkylä

My first contact with conversation analysis (CA) was through the criticism that was targeted at this seemingly obscure way of doing social research. An MA-level textbook on phenomenological sociology, published in the early 1970s, described a kind of malformed offspring of phenomenological principles – a particular study that had focused on the mere first five seconds in the openings of telephone calls. This kind of microscopic approach would not help in understanding the social shaping of the experience of human beings, the author argued. Neither was the study of any use in terms of emancipation or social criticism.[1] Later on, as a beginning researcher, I remember having discussions with other qualitatively oriented researchers with whom I agreed that an approach that tries to study the 'mechanics' of social interaction has in fact returned to positivism. And this is weird, we thought, because for us, the study of 'meanings' (which we thought was our main task) required firm rejection of positivistic principles.

A few years later, however, I found myself doing conversation analysis. After having been engaged in ethnographic and interview studies, I joined a research project led by Professor David Silverman, focusing on professional–client interaction in British HIV/AIDS counselling. At that time, AIDS counselling was a newly established professional practice, of the utmost importance both in terms of prevention of the spread of HIV infection and the alleviation of the suffering of HIV-positive patients. As the services had been set up quickly, nobody really knew what was actually done in the counselling sessions. CA offered a way of examining and describing the actions of counsellors and their clients, in much more precise ways than the more traditional qualitative or quantitative approaches could have provided.

In this chapter, I will sketch the historical and theoretical background of conversation analysis. I will also describe the concrete research process – what researchers actually do – in conversation analysis, and present a few examples of CA research results from my own research. Finally, I will discuss the strengths and future challenges of this approach. Throughout the chapter, I hope to show what I found when I started to do conversation analysis, in spite of my initial misgivings, and what motivates me to continue pursuing this research.

HISTORICAL BACKGROUND

Conversation analysis is a method for investigating the structure and process of social interaction between humans. As their data, conversation analytic studies use video or audio recordings made from naturally occurring interaction, i.e. interactions that would take place even if the data collection was not there. As their results, conversation analytic studies offer qualitative (and sometimes quantitative) descriptions of interactional practices (structures underlying all interaction such as turn-taking, and specific actions such as asking questions, receiving news or making assessments).

Conversation analysis was started by Harvey Sacks and his co-workers – most importantly Emanuel Schegloff and Gail Jefferson – at the University of California in the 1960s. At the time of its birth, conversation analysis was something quite different from the rest of social science. Since the early 1950s, the most influential approach in the study of human social interaction had been Robert Bales's interaction process analysis (Bales, 1950; for a comparison between

Bales and Sacks, see Peräkylä, in press). In Bales's approach, the actions of the interactants were categorized using a coding scheme, consisting of twelve different action categories, such as 'shows solidarity', 'gives suggestion', 'asks for orientation', or 'disagrees'. The coding scheme was universally applicable: any interaction could be analysed in terms of these twelve categories. Using this approach, researchers were able to describe the differentiation of the participants' roles in small groups, and to find different phases in the evolvement of interactions. Moreover, the category system was a catalyst for theoretical work on the micro aspects of social organization (e.g. Bales, 1953; Parsons and Bales, 1953).

During the 1950s, two scholars started to develop approaches to social interaction that offered an alternative to the Balesian one. Erving Goffman (e.g. 1955) focused his analytic insights on the moral underpinnings of the interaction process. For example, he explored the various ways in which the participants in interaction maintain, sometimes break and then restore their mutual respect and worthiness, or 'face' (ibid.), and keep up their mutual engagement in the shared reality of conversation (Goffman, 1967). Goffman also adopted a theoretical position that emphasized the relative independence of the structure of social interaction (or the 'interaction order') from both the macro-social and the psychological realities (Goffman, 1983). Harold Garfinkel, on the other hand, became interested in the inferential procedures through which participants to interaction come up with joint understandings of their action and its scene (see Garfinkel, 1967, as a collection of his central articles, and Heritage, 1984, as an accessible account of his ideas). He showed the persistent and practical orientation of the interactants to this primary task of sense-making. For example, they treat all utterances as fragments that point to, or index, unspoken underlying patterns. To take part in a conversation requires continuous inferential work that revolves between the fragmentary spoken utterances and these underlying patterns. (Chapter 10 by ten Have in this volume discusses the work of Garfinkel and his followers.)

Both Goffman and Garfinkel offered a radical challenge to the understanding of social interaction encapsulated in Bales's interaction process analysis. Unlike Bales, they did not use predefined categories in their investigations. Instead, they examined sequences of social interaction case by case, trying to pin down some of the basic orders of social organization that make social interaction possible in the first place. For Goffman, these orders were predominantly moral; for Garfinkel, they involved inferential practices.

Sacks developed conversation analysis in an intellectual environment shaped by Goffman and Garfinkel. He was Goffman's doctoral student (but an independent and a rebellious one in many ways: Schegloff, 1992a) and worked in close collaboration with Garfinkel. In focusing his studies on the intrinsic organization of sequences of tape-recorded interaction, Sacks moved further forward in the direction already indicated in the studies of Goffman and Garfinkel. Like them, Sacks also abandoned the 'coding and counting' approach to interaction. But instead of the moral or inferential underpinnings of social interaction, Sacks started to study the real-time sequential ordering of actions: the rules, patterns and structures in the relations between consecutive actions (Silverman, 1998). Thereby, argues Schegloff (1992a: xviii), Sacks made a radical shift in the perspective of social scientific inquiry into social interaction: instead of treating social interaction as a screen upon which other processes (moral, inferential or others) were projected, Sacks started to study the very structures of the interaction itself.

BASIC THEORETICAL ASSUMPTIONS

Knowing the earlier CA results and understanding the theoretical generalizations based on them is necessary for anyone who wants to start to do conversation analysis. CA has developed through empirical studies that have focused on specific, observable phenomena. So, in the first place, CA is not a theoretical, but a very concretely empirical, enterprise. However, through empirical studies – in an 'inductive' way – a body of theoretical knowledge about the organization of conversation has been accumulated. The actual 'techniques' in doing CA can only be understood and appreciated against the backdrop of these basic theoretical assumptions of CA. In conversation analysis, *methods* of the study of social interaction and *theory* concerning social interaction are very closely intertwined.

In a short chapter, it will not be possible to give an overview of the wide range of empirical studies that have contributed to conversation analysis. However, I will try to sketch some of the basic assumptions concerning the organization of conversation that arise from these studies. There are perhaps three most fundamental assumptions of this kind (cf. Heritage, 1984, ch. 8; Hutchby and Wooffitt, 1998): (1) *talk is action*, (2) *action is structurally organized*, and (3) *talk creates and maintains intersubjective reality*. As theoretical statements, these assumptions would be shared by many 'schools' of social science. The uniqueness of CA, however, is in the way in which it shows how 'action', 'structure' and 'intersubjectivity' are practically achieved and managed in talk and interaction.

Talk is action

As in some other philosophical and social scientific approaches (such as speech act theory: Austin, 1962; Searle, 1969) and discursive psychology (Edwards and Potter, 1992; Edwards, 1997; see also Hepburn and Potter's Chapter 12 in this volume), in conversation analysis talk is understood first and foremost as a vehicle of human action (Schegloff, 1991). The capacity of language to convey ideas is seen as deriving from this more fundamental task. In accomplishing actions, talk is seamlessly intertwined with (other) corporeal means of action, such as gaze and gesture (Goodwin, 1981). In CA, treating talk as action does not involve philosophical considerations, but very concrete research practice. Some CA studies have as their topics the organization of actions that are recognizable as distinct actions even from a vernacular point of view. Thus, conversation analysts have studied, for example, openings (Schegloff, 1968) and closings (Schegloff and Sacks, 1973) of conversations, assessments and ways in which the recipients agree or disagree with them (Pomerantz, 1984; Goodwin and Goodwin, 1992), storytelling (Sacks, 1974; Mandelbaum, 1992), complaints (Drew and Holt, 1988), telling and receiving news (Maynard, 2003) and laughter (Jefferson, 1984; Haakana, 2001). Many CA studies have as their topic actions that are typical in some institutional environment. Examples include diagnosis (Maynard, 1991, 1992; Heath, 1992; ten Have, 1995; Peräkylä, 1998, 2002) and physical examination (Heritage and Stivers, 1999) in medical consultations, questioning and answering practices in cross-examinations (Drew, 1992), ways of managing disagreements in news interviews (Greatbatch, 1992), or advice-giving in a number of different environments (Heritage and Sefi, 1992; Silverman, 1997; Vehviläinen, 2001). Finally, many important conversation analytic studies focus on fundamental aspects of conversational organization that make any action possible. These include turn-taking (Sacks et al., 1974), repair (Schegloff et al., 1977; Schegloff, 1992c) and the general ways in which sequences of action are built (Schegloff, 1995).

Organization of action – be it distinct everyday action such as storytelling, institutional action like diagnosis, or preconditions of all action like turn-taking – lies at the heart of all social life. By focusing its studies on these, conversation analysis has made a special contribution to enrich the foundations of social science.

Action is structurally organized

In the CA view, the practical actions that comprise the heart of social life are thoroughly structured and organized. In pursuing their goals, the actors have to orient themselves to rules and structures that only make their actions possible. These rules and structures concern mostly the relations between actions. Single acts are parts of larger, structurally organized entities. These entities can be called sequences (Schegloff, 1995).

The most basic and important sequence is called 'adjacency pair' (Schegloff and Sacks, 1973). It is a sequence of two actions in which the first action ('first pair part'), performed by one interactant, invites a particular type of second action ('second pair part'), to be performed by another interactant. Typical examples of adjacency pairs include question–answer, greeting–greeting, request–grant/refusal, and invitation–acceptance/declination. The relation between the first and second pair parts is strict and normative: if the second pair part does not come forth, the first speaker can for example repeat the first action, or seek explanations for the fact that the second is missing (Merritt, 1976: 329; Atkinson and Drew, 1979: 52–7).

Adjacency pairs serve often as a core, around which even larger sequences are built (Schegloff, 1995). So, a *pre-expansion* can precede an adjacency pair – for example, in cases where the speaker first asks about the other's plans for the evening, and only thereafter (if it turns out that the other is not otherwise engaged) issues an invitation. An *insert expansion* involves actions that occur between the first and the second pair parts and make possible the production of the latter, e.g. in cases where a speaker requests specification of an offer or request before responding to it. Finally, in *post-expansion*, the speakers produce actions that somehow follow from the basic adjacency pair, the simplest example being the 'OK' or 'thank you' that closes a sequence of a question and an answer, or a request and a grant (Schegloff, 1995).

Adjacency pairs are very frequent in talk and much of our action is organized in terms of them. However, sequential structures are not limited in adjacency pairs. Virtually *all* talk is organized in terms of *sequential implicativeness* (Schegloff and Sacks, 1973; Schegloff, 1979): any current turn at talk (action performed by a speaker) sets the coordinates for the relevant choices for the next turn (Heritage and Atkinson, 1984: 6). Current action never determines the next action, but the next action is always heard and produced as something that occurs at its particular slot in the conversation, i.e., after the current action. In a way, any turn of talk 'renews' the interactants' shared reality, and the next speaker will inevitably speak and act in the world that has thus been renewed.

Talk creates and maintains intersubjective reality

With its analytic interest often focusing on minute details in conversation, and with its insistence on observable evidence for any analytic claims, CA may give an impression of being a rather mechanistic approach (cf. Taylor and Cameron, 1987: 99–107; Alexander, 1988: 243). This was, in fact, the kind of critical position that I shared before really reading any CA studies: CA was considered as an approach that overlooked 'meaning' and 'experience'. My current understanding, however, is that rather than overlooking them, CA offers a tool for studying meaning and experience in a rigorous empirical way. In CA studies, talk and interaction are examined as a site where intersubjective understanding about the participants' intentions is created and maintained (Heritage and Atkinson, 1984: 11). Thereby, CA gives access to the construction of meaning in real time. But, it is important to notice, the conversation analytic 'gaze' focuses exclusively on meanings and understandings that are made public through conversational action, and it remains 'agnostic' regarding people's intra-psychological experience (Heritage, 1984).

The most fundamental level of intersubjective understanding – which, in fact, constitutes the basis for any other type of intersubjective understanding – concerns *the understanding of the preceding turn displayed by the current speaker*. Just as any turn of talk is produced in the context shaped by the previous turn, it also displays its speaker's understanding of that previous turn (Atkinson and Drew, 1979: 48). Thus, in simple cases, in producing a turn of talk that is hearable as an answer, the speaker also shows that she or he understood the preceding turn as a question. Sometimes these choices can be crucial for the unfolding of the interaction and the social relation of its participants, e.g. in cases where a turn of talk is potentially hearable in two ways (as an announcement or a request, or as an informing or

a complaint) and the recipient makes the choice in the next turn (cf. Peräkylä et al., 2002). In case the first speaker considers the understanding concerning his talk, displayed in the second speaker's utterance, as incorrect or problematic, the first speaker has an opportunity to correct this understanding in the 'third position' (Schegloff, 1992c), for example by saying 'I didn't mean to criticize you but just to tell about the problem', or the like.

Another level of intersubjective understanding concerns *the state of the talk* (Heritage and Atkinson, 1984: 10). For example, in completing activities and in initiating new ones, the speakers show their understanding of 'where' or 'at what phase' they are in a conversation. A request cannot be made at any junction, nor can a funny story or sad news be told. Speakers show their orientation to the 'right time' (Erickson and Shultz, 1982: 72) in and through their choices.

An equally important level of intersubjective understanding concerns the *context* of the talk. This is particularly salient in institutional interaction, i.e., in interaction that takes place to fulfil some institutionally ascribed tasks of the participants (e.g. psychotherapy, medical consultation or news interviews) (Drew and Heritage, 1992). The participants' understanding of the institutional context of their talk is documented in their actions. As Schegloff (1991, 1992b) and Drew and Heritage (1992) point out, if the 'institutional context' is relevant for interaction, it can be observed in the details of the participants' actions: in their ways of giving and receiving information, asking and answering questions, presenting arguments, and so on. Conversation analytic research that focuses on institutional interactions explores the exact ways in which the performers of different institutional tasks shape their actions so as to achieve their goals.

RESEARCH PROCESS

I have outlined above, in a rather abstract way, some central principles of conversation analysis. Now I want to move on to a much more concrete level, by giving an account of the research procedure in conversation analysis (for a comprehensive account, see ten Have, 1999). I am going to present this as a linear process consisting of distinct phases. As Hepburn and Potter point out in the following chapter, the actual research work is often much messier: you work simultaneously on many 'phases' and often need to reverse as well as move forward. Nevertheless, a linear account of the research process is useful as a simplified map. It can be used by the researcher to find his or her way from the first contact with data to the written output of research.

By necessity, conversation analytic research starts from the *selection of the research site* – by the researcher choosing what kind of interactions he or she is going to be investigating. By and large, the biggest choice is to be made between 'ordinary conversation' and institutional inter-action. Ordinary conversation means informal, casual conversation without specific institutional goals or tasks. If the research project focuses on this kind of conversation, then it often happens that any site where people talk informally to one another is equally good for research purposes. Many practices of ordinary conversation are ubiquitous in talk, and research material can hence be collected from almost anywhere. In researching institutional interaction, on the other hand, the research questions usually concern par-ticular institutional practices, and the research site has to be chosen accordingly. Even after the basic site (say, medicine, therapy or news inter-views) has been chosen, the researcher has to consider the possible variation in interactional practices at different settings. Practices of, for example, advice-giving are likely to be different in general practice and in more specialized medicine. The researcher has to try and make as well-informed and conscious choices as poss-ible, arising from his/her and his/her sponsors' interest. Another difference is that in getting access to the sites of institutional interaction, quite elaborate official procedures may often need to be undergone, whereas consent to recordings of ordinary conversation may be acquired more straightforwardly.

Tape recording is the second step in the research procedure. In face-to-face interactions, video should be used whenever possible. Even when the actual research topic would not involve any non-vocal aspects, knowing what happens through the gaze, the body movement and the gestures of the participants may be nec-essary to grasp the immediate context and mean-ing of the talk. Telephone conversations, of course, can be recorded only on audio. Modern recording technologies make high-quality recordings possible in many environments (Goodwin, 1992).

Especially in research on institutional interac-tion, *additional information* about the research site, along with the tape recordings, can be of the utmost importance. The conversation analyst may need to make ethnographic observations, conduct interviews or collect questionnaire data. This information is used to contextualize the CA observations, in terms of the larger social system of which the tape-recorded interactions are a part. Even though ethnography, interviews or questionnaires cannot substitute for the tape recordings, they can offer information without which also the understanding of tape-recorded interactions may remain insufficient.

Transcribing the tape recordings is an impor-tant and laborious task. The CA notation was developed by Gail Jefferson (see Appendix and Atkinson and Heritage, 1984, and Drew and Heritage, 1992). This notation includes symbols for a wide variety of vocal and interactional phe-nomena, including pitch variation, prolongation of sounds, amplitude, overlapping speech and silences. Recently, proposals for further specifi-cation of the notation have been made by linguists studying prosody in conversation (see Couper-Kuhlen and Selting, 1996). Computer-ized analysis of, for example, pitch has been introduced along with the traditional notation based on auditive impression.

Using the CA notation requires some skill. To my understanding, anyone can learn it, but advice from a skilled person and some time is needed for training. The 'ear' of the transcriber develops through experience: part of what was first inaudible becomes gradually audible, timing of overlaps becomes more accurate, and so on. If at all possible, it is good to have two persons involved in the transcription of any single inter-action – one actually doing the transcription, and the other one checking and correcting it – because it often happens that one person hears things that the other misses. Having someone correcting one's transcriptions is also an impor-tant learning device.

In some projects, all tape-recorded data are transcribed, and in others, only parts of them. In my own research projects, I have found it worth-while to tape-record as much as possible, and to transcribe only part of the data at the beginning of the research project. In the course of the research, I have become interested in rather spe-cific sequences (such as diagnostic statements in medical consultations), and then I have been able to 'pick up' for transcription these specific sequences from that part of the database that was left untranscribed at the beginning. In other words, the other part of the database has been transcribed only selectively.

Thus far, most conversation analysts have used analogue tape for recording and storing the data, and separate textual document for tran-scription. In recent years, however, computer programs that integrate a digitalized audio or video file and the textual document have gained momentum (for example, WORKBENCH,

CLAN and TRANSANA), and they seem to offer many advantages in terms of simplifying and intensifying the research process.

Unmotivated exploration of the data constitutes the next step in the research process. This is a phase of research where the initial observations regarding the organization of action are made; later, these observations may lead to the actual research results. Exploration of the data involves listening and watching the tapes and examining the transcripts, sometimes focusing on very small segments (e.g. a single utterance) and sometimes on larger entities, trying to explicate the organization of what is happening in the recorded interactions. This can take place as an individual researcher's activity, as pair work, or as a group activity in 'data sessions' where a number (say 3 to 10) of researchers listen to the data and discuss their observations. Intuition is often the point of departure for the examination of data: the chosen segment 'looks like' or 'feels like' something. Intuition is of great value. The examination of the data aims at uncovering the organizational features that give rise to the researcher's initial intuitions. Sometimes it happens that one's initial intuition turns out to be incorrect. In any case, through the exploration of the data, intuition leads to systematic observations and, in the course of the research process, is finally replaced by rigorous analysis. Like many conversation analysts, I find this phase of research extremely rewarding. One easily develops a kind of passion for trying to understand the organization of action in one's data. When other researchers are involved in this (in data sessions), it can also be great fun.

The exploration of data is unmotivated in the sense that the phenomena under consideration are not predefined. Any segment of interaction selected as focus involves numerous orders of organization, which may be discovered through the unmotivated exploration. But the observations that are made do not arise from a void, or from common sense, or from the sheer creativity of the observers. Any observations, including those made by CA researchers, are informed by theories and the observer's preconceptions. Basic theoretical assumptions of CA, arising from previous CA studies, constitute the distinct intellectual resources with the help of which the researchers can make observations that are theoretically valid and differ from what common sense can offer. Therefore, the questions that researchers ask in the unmotivated exploration of data are, in fact, quite disciplined ones. They are of the following kind: 'What is the action in this segment of data?', 'What are the relevant next actions that it gives rise to?', 'How is this action perceived by the other interactants, as shown in their responses to it?', and 'How do the generic organizations of interaction – such as turn-taking, sequence organization and repair organization – figure in and facilitate this action?'

Identification of the phenomena to be examined is possible after the researcher has familiarized him- or herself with the data through the unmotivated exploration of it. Something arises from the data as exciting, challenging, and/or as something that seems to encapsulate seemingly important aspects of social organization or social relations. Usually the phenomenon is a specific practice or a specific kind of sequence. In my own work, such phenomena have included particular types of questions asked by counsellors in AIDS counselling (Peräkylä, 1995), doctors' ways of referring to evidence in their diagnostic statements (Peräkylä, 1998) and, more recently, psychoanalysts' ways of presenting linkages between childhood, current life and the analytic hour (Peräkylä, forthcoming a).

There are basically two ways to proceed at this juncture of research. One is to focus on phenomena that earlier research has in one way or another already covered. Potentially, this is an excellent way of doing research: science needs replication of studies and, moreover, research that starts from an already known phenomenon can show new layers of organization related to that phenomenon. Comparisons between similar practices at different institutional sites are also possible. On the other hand, there is also a danger that the researcher *projects* on his or her data an organization (found from earlier studies) that is not really there, or makes findings that are in themselves valid, but do not in any way transcend what has been found and reported in earlier studies. Therefore, a kind of mastery of doing CA gets manifested in research where genuinely new phenomena – thus far unknown or unanalysed practices or sequences – are identified and examined. One recent example of such a study is found in Heritage and Stivers's (1999) study on 'online commentary' in medical consultations. The practice that they identified was the doctor's 'online' reporting of the findings during a physical examination. This practice had not been discussed in earlier research on medical consultations, and it was hardly mentioned in medical textbooks.

Collection of instances of the phenomenon begins once the researcher has identified the phenomenon or the phenomena that he or she wants to focus on. The researcher now goes through all her transcripts (or a chosen part of them, if the phenomenon is very frequent) and picks up sequences where the object of her interest occurs.

There are CA studies that focus on single instances only; Sacks's (1974) analysis of telling a joke is a classic example. In the long run, however, CA research in general and also individual researchers can only progress through working with collections of cases.

So, in my study of AIDS counselling, I collected all instances of certain types of questions (circular questions, live open supervision questions and hypothetical questions) from my data; in my study of general practice, I collected all instances of diagnostic statements; and in my current work on psychoanalytic sessions, I and my co-researcher Sanna Vehviläinen have collected all interpretative statements from the data transcribed thus far.

The end result of this phase of research is a file – an electronic one, or a hard copy – with a number of instances of the chosen phenomenon (or a few parallel files of different phenomena). It is advisable to be inclusive rather than exclusive when choosing instances for the collection: cases that turn out not to really fit into the collection can always be discarded later, but one cannot easily find anew cases that were discarded at the outset, even if the analysis were later to prove that they would actually have been relevant members of the collection.

Determining the variation of the phenomenon becomes possible as soon as the researcher has created a collection. The researcher examines members of his collection case by case (using the original tape recordings rather than transcripts only). Some cases are examined really intensively – you can spend days with them, and return to them again and again – while others, which seem to replicate some of the structures found in cases subjected to more intensive analysis, are examined only to the degree that their relation to other cases can be defined.

The end result of this stage of the research is a description of the different types of realizations of the sequence or the action under investigation. The results involve typification of some kind – for example, typification of designs in utterances doing the same sort of action or, conversely, typification of different actions performed by similarly shaped utterances. Exactly what kind of things the actual variation involves differs in different studies. I will use my own work as a source of examples.

When investigating doctors' diagnostic statements in general practice, I found that they had three ways of displaying the evidence to patients (Peräkylä, 1998). One involved verbal explication of that evidence, another involved indirect references to evidence through 'evidential' expressions such as 'it seems to be X', and the third one was a plain assertion without any

verbal reference to evidence. Extracts 1 to 3 provide examples:

(1)   (Explicating the evidence)
Dr: As tapping on the vertebrae didn't cause any, ↑pain and there aren't (yet) any actual reflection symptoms in your legs it suggests a muscle h (.hhhh) complication so hhh it's only whether hhh (0,4) you have been exposed to a draft or has it otherwise=
P: =Right,
Dr: .Hh got irritated,

(2)   (Indirect reference to evidence)
Dr: Now there appears to be an (1.0) infection at the contact point of the joint below it in the sac of mucus there in the hip.

(3)   (Plain assertion)
Dr: That's already proper bronchitis.

In my current work on interpretations in psychoanalysis, I have identified a number of techniques through which the analyst displays to the patient the connectedness of the patient's experiences in his or her childhood, in his or her current life, and during the analytic hour. Some of these techniques are used as kind of preparation that takes place before the delivery of the very interpretations, while others are ways of designing the very interpretative utterances (Peräkylä, forthcoming a). And in my earlier work that focused on 'circular questions' in AIDS counselling, I found that a 'full' sequence where such questions were asked consisted of four turns: (1) the counsellor's question to a client concerning the thoughts or feelings of a co-present other client, who was usually a partner or a family member, (2) the client's answer, (3) the counsellor's question concerning these thoughts or feelings to this other client him- or herself, and (4) this other client's answer. In this case, the variation of the phenomenon involved different truncations of this 'standard' sequence: sometimes the counsellor's other question was not there, so that stage 4 followed after stage 2; and in a very few cases, stage 2 was also omitted and stage 4 came right after stage 1.

The core task in the description of the variation of the phenomenon in conversation analytic studies is qualitative: the analyst constructs typifications to pin down the different designs in utterances doing the same sort of action, different actions performed by similarly shaped utterances, or different shapes that a particular sequence can take. In a number of studies, however, the qualitative analysis is followed by a quantitative one. For example, in Clayman and Heritage's (2002) recent study on question design in presidential press conferences in the US, calculations were made to show how the relative proportions of different types of journalistic questions, showing different degrees of 'adversarialness', changed over time. The calculations showed that the journalists have become much less deferential and more aggressive in their treatment of the president.

As conversation analysis is a naturalistic and descriptive approach, much of the researcher's effort is invested in the determination of the variation of the phenomenon. However, the determination of the variation leads seamlessly to another important step in the research procedure, which involves *accounting for the variation*. The researcher examines the data to find out what would account for the variation of the phenomenon. (S)he asks what the different realizations of the phenomenon are used for, and tries to show what interactional consequences these different realizations have. Importantly, when exploring the usages and consequences of the different realizations of the phenomenon, the researcher focuses on the orientations of the participants, as they are displayed in their actions. This is also a rather demanding task where the researcher's perceptivity and creativity are tested.

Again, I would like to use my own recent study as an example. After having outlined the general practitioners' three different ways of displaying the evidence of their diagnostic statements to their patients (see above and Peräkylä, 1998), I explored my data to find out what would account for this variation. Focusing my attention on the context of the delivery of the diagnosis, I found two issues that were associated with the doctors' choices regarding the display of evidence. One was 'inferential distance': it turned out that the doctors used the 'plain assertion' format in cases where the physical examination of the patient, or the examination of the medical documents, was rather straightforward and occurred immediately prior to the delivery of the diagnosis. In these cases, the inferential distance between the diagnosis and its evidence was short. Extract 4 provides an example:

(4) (Expansion of (3))
(Dr has listened to the patient's chest))
Dr: Let's listen from the back. (0.3)
P: .nff
      (9.0) ((P breaths in and out, Dr listens.))
Dr: That's already proper bronchitis.
P: Is it [hh
Dr: [It is.

However, there were other cases where the examination of the patient or the documents was complicated and, hence, opaque for the patient, or there was a temporal gap between the examination and the delivery of the diagnosis. In these cases the inferential distance between the examination and the diagnosis was longer – and the doctors much more frequently explicated the evidence of the diagnosis or referred to it indirectly. For example, in Extract 5, the doctor has just looked at and touched the foot of a patient who complained of a sudden pain in her leg some weeks ago. For a lay participant, the connection between looking at and touching the foot and the negative diagnosis regarding circulation problems is not transparent, and hence the doctor explicates the evidence for his statement (he felt the pulse):

(5) (Explication of evidence)
((The doctor has just examined the patient's foot))
Dr: Okay:. .h fine do put on your,
      (.)
Dr: the pulse [can be felt there in your foot
P: [↑Thank you.
Dr: So, .h there's no, in any case (.) no real circulation problem
      …
      is <involved>.

Thus, it appeared that the doctors' choice of action documented a particular orientation. They treated themselves accountable, vis-à-vis the patient, regarding the evidence of their diagnostic statements: in cases where the patient could have been expected to have difficulties in grasping the direction from which the evidence comes, the doctors showed verbally where it came from.

The other issue that was associated with the doctors' choices regarding the display of evidence was any challenge to the medical authority. In cases where the doctor's diagnosis involved open discrepancy with the views expressed by the patient, and in cases where the doctor indicated uncertainty regarding the diagnosis, explication of evidence and indirect references to it were much more frequent. It appeared that the doctors oriented to an intensified accountability regarding the evidential basis of diagnosis in these kinds of cases.

As for the interactional consequences of the phenomenon, in my study of the delivery of the diagnosis it became apparent that the different turn designs regarding the display of evidence make relevant different types of responses from the patient (Peräkylä, 2002, forthcoming b). Diagnostic utterances where the evidence was displayed often invited the patient to join in the discussion on diagnosis, whereas especially the 'plain assertions' presented the diagnosis as one that would not make relevant the patient's further talk. These orientations were incorporated in the patient's next actions after the doctor's diagnostic utterances.

Accounting for the variation of the phenomenon is a key to understanding both the actors' orientations and the place and 'function' of the phenomenon in the larger context of conversation or institutional interaction. In fact, it may be that any phenomenon can only be understood through attending to variation; as Bateson (1972) suggests, we only observe through attending to differences. In other words, only by examining what brings about the different realizations of the phenomenon (such as different ways of referring to evidence, or different realizations of a sequence of circular questioning) will the researcher understand the phenomenon itself.

The final step in conversation analytic research procedure – a step that in many studies need not be taken at all, but in others is extremely important – involves an effort to *understand the wider implications, for social relations and social structures, of the phenomenon under investigation*. If the preceding step aimed at understanding the place and function of the phenomenon in the larger context of conversation or institutional interaction, this final step widens the scope beyond the actual interaction: the researcher now tries to understand the place and function of the phenomenon in the larger social system.

Especially in research on ordinary (i.e., casual, non-institutional) conversation, this step need not, and in most cases cannot, be taken. The practices investigated by this kind of research are so generic and so omnipresent that it is often neither useful nor possible to define their specific functions for social life. Or we can only say that they are utterly important for *all* social life: turn-taking, for example, regulates all opportunities for verbal action in society. Sometimes, however, somewhat more specific functions of generic practices are useful to discuss: for example, Schegloff (1992c) offers an illuminating discussion on the crucial importance of *repair organization* (conversational devices for dealing with troubles of speaking, hearing or understanding) for the maintenance of intersubjectivity in social life.

In studies focusing on institutional interaction it is more often both possible and useful to define

such functions, also regarding rather specific interactional phenomena. *Gender system* constitutes an overarching institution in society, and many conversation analytic studies have indeed contributed to our understanding of the ways in which specific interactional practices contribute to the maintenance or change of that system. Work by West (1979) and Zimmerman (Zimmerman and West, 1975) on male/female interruptions is widely cited. More recently, Kitzinger (2000) explored the implications of preference organization for the politics of rape prevention, and turn-taking organization for the practices of 'coming out' as gay or lesbian. In a somewhat more linguistic CA study, Tainio (2002) explored how syntactic and semantic properties of utterances are used in the construction of heterosexual identities in elderly couples' talk. Studies like these (for a fresh overview, see McIlvenny, 2002) also amply demonstrate the *critical* potential of conversation analysis. Relations between interactional practices and wider social relations are also addressed in the already mentioned work on presidential press conferences by Clayman and Heritage (2002): they demonstrate the historical change in the US presidential institution and media by examining the evolution of journalistic questioning design. My study on the delivery of diagnosis involves yet another example. The results of this study also seemed to address some issues that were of general social scientific interest.

One quite influential view concerning the relation between doctors and patients emphasizes the doctor's authority. The advocates of this view include, for example, Talcott Parsons (1951), Elliot Freidson (1970) and Andrew Abbott (1988). They point out that the doctor possesses technical and scientific knowledge that enables him to diagnose illnesses, and society has warranted him with the licence to decide about medication and sick leaves, and to perform surgical and other therapeutic procedures. The patient does not have such knowledge and licences. Therefore, these writers point out, the relation between the doctor and the patient is necessarily characterized by the doctor's authority. My conversation analytic research results concerning the display of evidence in diagnostic statements question this view. The doctors in my data oriented systematically to their accountability, vis-à-vis the patient, regarding the evidential basis of their diagnoses. Through the placement and the design of their diagnostic utterances, they ensured that at least some aspects of the evidential basis of the diagnosis are available for the patient. By thus justifying their diagnostic statements through verbal or tacit references to the evidence, the doctors do *not* claim the kind of authority in relation to the patient that has been proposed in the theories cited above.

However, in social science literature there is also another view concerning the relation between doctors and patients. This view emphasizes, often programmatically, the patient's knowledgeability and his or her participation in the diagnostic procedure and the decisions about the treatment. A number of writers, for example in medical anthropology (e.g. Stimson and Webb, 1975; Kleinman, 1980; Helman, 1992), maintain that the patient as well as the doctor has ideas about the nature, the origin and the possible remedies of the patient's ailment. The consultation could and should be an encounter between two differently but equally resourceful agents where they negotiate diagnosis and treatment. In an ideal case, the parties' views will merge. My conversation analytic results are not quite in line with this literature either.

In spite of the doctors' systematic ways of treating themselves as accountable for the evidential basis of the diagnosis, they, as well as the patients, systematically orient themselves to the difference between the doctor's and the patient's ways of reasoning. This orientation is shown, for example, in the patients' ways of responding to the doctors' diagnoses. In ordinary cases, the patients remain silent or produce small acknowledgement tokens in response to the doctors' diagnostic statements (Heath, 1992). Sometimes – especially after diagnostic utterances where the evidence for diagnosis is explicated – they produce more elaborate responses in which they express reservations towards the doctors' diagnosis. Their regular way of questioning the diagnosis is to offer additional observations (discrepant with the diagnosis) that come from their own bodily sensations or other everyday experience. Systematically, they refrain from referring to or discussing the medical evidence that the doctors refer to in their statements (Peräkylä, 2002). Thus, the 'dialogical' model of the doctor–patient relation, referred to above, is at best only half true: conversation analysis shows the limits that the participants themselves put to the degree of negotiation in the doctor–patient relation.

On the whole, the results of my studies on the delivery of diagnosis show the doctors and the patients maintaining a balance between conflicting orientations. At the same time, they orient to the doctors' accountability for the evidential basis of the diagnosis, *and* the doctors' authority in the domain of diagnostic reasoning, *and* the patients' capability to understand some aspects of the diagnostic process. The empirical reality of the doctor–patient relation seems to be much more complex and multi-faceted than the theoretical models of this relation have been able to express. The complexity can be illuminated by rigorous data-driven research, such as conversation analysis.

DISCUSSION

I started this chapter with an account of my first contact with conversation analysis, which was characterized by a quite critical attitude. While being engaged in the studies that I have described in the chapter, my own perception of CA has of course changed. But a scientist should never lose a critical attitude. I will conclude this chapter by first stating the basis of my motivation for continuing to do CA, and by thereafter reviewing the challenges of CA as I see them now.

I think there are two basic reasons for me to keep on doing CA. First, CA offers a way to increase our understanding of the basic, or 'generic', practices of human social interaction. Goffman's (1983) idea of real-time social interaction as a relatively autonomous realm of social organization – independent of both the psychological domain and the macro-social domain – remains a vivid and powerful notion. If one accepts that the interaction order is indeed such a realm of social organization, with its own particular rules, regularities and practices, then one definitely also sees the need for particular research methodology and theory for its investigation. And this is exactly what CA offers. In doing their basic research on the generic practices of social interaction (which are best found in ordinary conversation), conversation analysts come as close to natural science as it is possible in social science: they make systematic observations on the interactional behaviour, in natural settings, of *Homo sapiens*. If this is to be regarded as positivism, then CA *is* positivistic, and, unlike in my student times, I do not see any problem with that. However, CA is also a genuinely *verstehende* approach. The interactional behaviour of humans is always mediated by interpretative processes that are documented in the sequentially organized behaviour itself. CA studies treat these two, behaviour and interpretation, as inseparable.

Second, CA offers a way to observe the workings of central social institutions, such as medicine, law and education, as well as technological systems (Heath and Luff, 2000). Conversation analytic research on institutional interaction gives access to the everyday life shaped by modern social institutions. These institutions encounter individual human beings often (but not exclusively) through social interaction, in consultation rooms, courtrooms, technological working environments, etc. The rules, regularities and practices of social interaction are the medium of this encounter. In the encounter between institutions and individuals, the rules, regularities and practices of social interaction also get modified, in ways that facilitate the workings of the institutions (Drew and Heritage, 1992). In their ongoing research endeavour, conversation analysts explore this modification, in the context of a widening variety of social institutions.

In both these focal areas of CA research – basic practices of human social interaction, and institutional interaction – there are a number of challenges that CA researchers are facing and working with right now. Regarding the former area, three overlapping challenges include the prosody, gesture and affective expression (cf. Hakulinen, 2002). Prosody means the rhythm, the amplitude, the pitch and the voice quality of speech. Research on the ways in which these features of talk are coordinated with and contribute to the basic conversational organization started in the 1990s (see Couper-Kuhlen and Selting, 1996). Researchers are asking, for example, how prosodic features contribute to turn-taking or the constitution of some basic conversational activities such as openings (Schegloff, 1998) or news deliveries (Freese and Maynard, 1998).

Gesture involves another challenge for conversation analysis. For quite a long time, gesture and other aspects of non-verbal communication have been of interest for some conversation analysts (see e.g. Goodwin, 1981; Schegloff, 1984; Heath, 1986). Goodwin (1981) offers a systematic treatise on the interrelations between gaze and turn-taking. However, systematic knowledge on the relations between (other aspects of) gesture and spoken interaction is still lacking. This area of research seems to have attracted more interest in recent years (see, e.g., McNeill, 2000), and we may expect that new findings will be reported in the future.

Affect in interaction involves still another challenge for conversation analytic research focusing on the basic practices of human social interaction. Affect is, indeed, closely intertwined with prosody and gesture: along with the selection of words, prosody and gesture (including facial expression) are central means for the expression of affect. There are a number of individual studies that have touched upon emotionally relevant phenomena, such as troubles-telling (Jefferson, 1988), laughter (Jefferson, 1984; Haakana, 2001), expression of pain (Heath, 1989) or the management of hysterical callers at an emergency centre (Whalen and Zimmerman, 1998), but in this area too, systematic knowledge is still missing. In the near future, we will probably see studies where the means for expression of affect, and their usage in different conversational actions, will be addressed (Peräkylä, in press).

In research on institutional interaction, some of the key challenges include the integration of outcome assessment into CA research designs, and a dialogue between professional practitioners and CA researchers. The central strength of CA is in the *description* of practices and patterns of interaction; CA has, in fact, set a new standard for detailed description of social action in social science. Traditionally, and for good reasons, CA researchers have not asked questions about the outcome or consequences of the interactions that they have studied. The consequences of interaction – such as patient satisfaction and compliance in medicine, or decisions that are made in meetings, or reduction of symptoms in psychotherapy – have simply been something outside the CA business: CA methodology is geared to describe what happens *in* the interaction, and questions concerning the consequences are really something that CA as such cannot handle. However, the outcome of interaction is something that the professionals themselves and the policy-makers are primarily interested in. As CA studies on institutional interaction proliferate, the need to combine conversation analytic description of interaction with outcome measurement becomes increasingly urgent.

Boyd's (1998; see also Heritage et al., 2001) study on medical peer review involves a promising example of this kind of approach. She studied telephone consultations between physicians and the medical representatives of an insurance company. Each consultation yielded a decision concerning the financial coverage of a proposed surgical operation. Boyd showed that the interactional format of the *initiation* of the first topic of the call was a strong predictor of the outcome (the decision concerning the surgery). In other words, the opening of the call set the trajectory for the ensuing review, since as a result of the initiation, the participants were either 'collegially' or 'bureaucratically' aligned, and these alignments led to different decisions. Thereby, the interactional format intervened into the decision-making that was supposed to be based on medical facts only. In the coming years, we will possibly see many more studies where the ways in which the participants' choices in their ways of interacting with one another are linked with the consequences that their interactions have. Studies like that will have a strong potential for making CA relevant for professional practitioners.

Another, related challenge in the study of institutional interaction involves enhancing the dialogue between professional practitioners and CA researchers. In a number of sites studied by conversation analysts (e.g. at therapeutic, medical and educational settings) the practitioners have, as part of their professional knowledge, their own theories and concepts regarding their interactions with the patients (Peräkylä and Vehviläinen, in press, 2003). Various therapeutic and didactic models and concepts of 'patient centred medicine' are examples of this. To a degree, the practitioners describe and assess their work using these models and concepts. The results of conversation analytic research constitute another, often quite different way of talking about the practitioners' work. CA research describes the details of professional practice, while the professionals' own theories and models often offer normative ideals and summarizing descriptions. CA results may sometimes complement (see Peräkylä, 1995, ch. 6) and sometimes correct (Vehviläinen, 1999; Ruusuvuori, 2000) the professionals' own theories. Thus far, however, the CA results and professionals' theories have lived their lives separately, and it remains a future challenge for conversation analysts to create instances for their meeting.

NOTE

1 The research that was criticized was Schegloff's (1968) study on openings of telephone conversations.

REFERENCES

Abbott, Andrew (1988) *The System of Professions: An Essay on the Division of Expert Labor*. Chicago: University of Chicago Press.

Alexander, Jeffrey (1988) *Action and Its Environments: Toward a New Synthesis*. New York: Columbia University Press.

Atkinson, J. Maxwell and Drew, Paul (1979) *Order in Court: The Organization of Verbal Interaction in Judicial Settings*. London: Macmillan.

Atkinson, J. Maxwell and Heritage, John (eds) (1984) *Structures of Social Action: Studies in Conversation Analysis*. Cambridge: Cambridge University Press.

Austin, J.L. (1962) *How to Do Things with Words*. Oxford: Oxford University Press.

Bales, R.F. (1950) *Interaction Process Analysis: A Method for the Study of Small Groups*. Reading, MA: Addison-Wesley.

Bales, R.F. (1953) 'The equilibrium problem in small groups', in T. Parsons, R.F. Bales and E.A. Shils (eds), *Working Papers in the Theory of Action*. Glencoe, IL: Free Press, pp. 43–61.

Bateson, Gregory (1972) *Steps to an Ecology of Mind*. New York: Ballantine.

Boyd, Elizabeth (1998) 'Bureaucratic authority in the "company of equals": the interactional management of medical peer review', *American Sociological Review*, 63: 200–24.

Clayman, Steven E. and Heritage, John (2002) 'Questioning presidents: journalistic deference and adversarialness in the press conferences of Eisenhower and Reagan', *Journal of Communication*, 52(4): 749–75.

Couper-Kuhlen, E and Selting, Margaret (eds) (1996) *Prosody in Conversation*. Cambridge: Cambridge University Press.

Drew, Paul (1992) 'Contested evidence in courtroom cross-examination: the case of a trial for rape', in Paul Drew and John Heritage (eds), *Talk at Work: Interaction in Institutional Settings*. Cambridge: Cambridge University Press, pp. 470–520.

Drew, Paul and Heritage, John (1992) 'Analyzing talk at work: an introduction', in Paul Drew and John Heritage (eds), *Talk at Work: Interaction in Institutional Settings*. Cambridge: Cambridge University Press, pp. 3–65.

Drew, Paul and Holt, Elizabeth (1988) 'Complainable matters: the use of idiomatic expression in making complaints', *Social Problems*, 35: 398–417.

Edwards, Derek (1997) *Discourse and Cognition*. London: Sage.

Edwards, Derek and Potter, Jonathan (1992) *Discursive Psychology*. London: Sage.

Erickson, F. and Shultz, J. (1982) *The Counselor as Gatekeeper: Social Interaction in Interviews*. New York: Academic Press.

Freese, J. and Maynard, D. (1998) 'Prosodic features of bad news and good news in conversation', *Language in Society* 27: 195–219.

Freidson, Elliot (1970) *Professional Dominance*. Chicago: Aldine.

Garfinkel, Harold (1967) *Studies in Ethnomethodology*. Englewood Cliffs, NJ: Prentice-Hall.

Goffman, Erving (1955) 'On face work', *Psychiatry*, 18: 213–31.

Goffman, Erving (1967) 'Alienation from interaction', in Erving, Goffman, *Interaction Ritual: Essays in Face-to-Face Behavior*. New York: Doubleday, pp. 113–36.

Goffman, Erving (1983) 'The interaction order', *American Sociological Review*, 48: 1–17.

Goodwin, Charles (1981) *Conversational Organization: Interaction Between Speakers and Hearers*. New York: Academic Press.

Goodwin, Charles (1992) 'Recording human interaction in natural settings', *Pragmatics*, 2: 181–209.

Goodwin, Charles and Goodwin, Marjorie Harness (1992) 'Assessments and the construction of context', in Alessandro Duranti and Charles Goodwin (eds), *Rethinking Context: Language as Interactive Phenomenon*. Cambridge: Cambridge University Press, pp. 147–90.

Greatbatch, David (1992) 'On the management of disagreement between news interviewees', in Paul Drew and John Heritage (eds), *Talk at Work: Interaction in Institutional Settings*. Cambridge: Cambridge University Press, pp. 268–302.

Haakana, Markku (2001) 'Laughter as a patient's resource: dealing with delicate aspects of medical interaction', *Text*, 21: 187–219.

Hakulinen, Auli (2002) 'Suomalaisen keskustelun-tutkimuksen tila ja rajat' ['The current state and limits of Finnish conversation analysis'], plenary presentation at the First National Conference on Conversation Analysis, Helsinki, January 2002.

Heath, Christian (1986) *Body Movement and Speech in Medical Interaction*. Cambridge: Cambridge University Press.

Heath, Christian (1989) 'Pain talk: the expression of suffering in the medical consultation', *Social Psychology Quarterly*, 52(2): 113–25.

Heath, Christian (1992) 'The delivery and reception of diagnosis in the general-practice consultation', in Paul Drew and John Heritage (eds), *Talk at Work: Interaction in Institutional Settings*. Cambridge: Cambridge University Press, pp. 235–67, 302.

Heath, Christian and Luff, Paul (2000) *Technology in Action*. Cambridge: Cambridge University Press.

Helman, Cecil (1992) *Culture, Health and Illness*. Oxford: Butterworth.

Heritage, John (1984) *Garfinkel and Ethnomethodology*. Cambridge: Polity Press.

Heritage, John and Atkinson, J. Maxwell (1984) Introduction, in J.M. Atkinson and J. Heritage (eds), *Structures of Social Action: Studies in Conversation Analysis*. Cambridge: Cambridge University Press.

Heritage, John and Sefi, Sue (1992) 'Dilemmas of advice: aspects of the delivery and reception of advice in interactions between health visitors and first time mothers', in Paul Drew and John Heritage (eds), *Talk at Work: Interactism in Institutional Settings*. Cambridge: Cambridge University Press: pp. 359–417.

Heritage, John and Stivers, Tanya (1999) 'Online commentary in acute medical visits: a method for shaping patient expectations', *Social Science and Medicine*, 49(11): 1501–17.

Heritage, John, Boyd, Elizabeth and Kleinman, Lawrence (2001) 'Subverting criteria: the role of precedent in decisions to finance surgery', *Sociology of Health and Illness*, 23(5): 701–28.

Hutchby, Ian and Wooffitt, Robin (1998) *Conversation Analysis: Principles, Practices and Applications*. Cambridge: Polity Press.

Jefferson, Gail (1984) 'On the organization of laughter in talk about troubles', in J.M. Atkinson and J. Heritage (eds), *Structures of Social Action: Studies in Conversation Analysis*. Cambridge: Cambridge University Press, pp. 346–69.

Jefferson, Gail (1988) 'On the sequential organization of troubles-talk in ordinary conversation', *Social Problems*, 35(4): 418–41.

Kitzinger, Celia (2000) 'Doing feminist conversation analysis', *Feminism and Psychology*, 10: 163–93.

Kleinman, A. (1980) *Patients and Healers in the Context of Culture*. Berkeley, CA: University of California Press.

McIlvenny, Paul (ed.) (2002) *Talking Gender and Sexuality*. Amsterdam: John Benjamins.

McNeill, David (ed.) (2000) *Language and Gesture*. Cambridge: Cambridge University Press.

Mandelbaum, Jennifer (1992) 'Assigning responsibility in conversational storytelling: the interactional construction of reality', *Text*, 13(2): 247–66.

Maynard, Douglas W. (1991) 'Interaction and asymmetry in clinical discourse', *American Journal of Sociology*, 97: 448–95.

Maynard, Douglas W. (1992) 'On clinicians co-implicating recipients' perspective in the delivery of diagnostic News', in Paul Drew and John Heritage (eds), *Talk at Work: Interaction in Institutional Settings*. Cambridge: Cambridge University Press, pp. 331–58.

Maynard, Douglas W. (2003) *Good News, Bad News: Conversational Order* in *Everyday Talk and Clinical Settings*. Chicago: University of Chicago Press.

Merritt, M. (1976) 'On questions following questions (in service encounters)', *Language in Society*, 5: 315–57.

Parsons, Talcott (1951) *The Social System*. New York: Free Press.

Parsons, Talcott and Bales, Robert F. (1953) 'The dimensions of action-space', in Talcott Parsons, Robert F. Bales and Edward A. Shils (eds), *Working Papers in the Theory of Action*. New York: Free Press, pp. 63–110.

Peräkylä, Anssi (1995) *AIDS Counselling: Institutional Interaction and Clinical Practice*. Cambridge: Cambridge University Press.

Peräkylä, Anssi (1998) 'Authority and accountability: the delivery of diagnosis in primary health care', *Social Psychology Quarterly*, 61(4): 301–20.

Peräkylä, Anssi (2002) 'Agency and authority: extended responses to diagnostic statements in primary care encounters', *Research in Language and Social Interaction*, 35(2): 219–47.

Peräkylä, Anssi (in press) 'Two traditions of interaction research', *British Journal of Social Psychology*.

Peräkylä, Anssi (forthcoming a) 'Making links in psycho-analytic interpretations: a conversation analytical perspective', *Psychotherapy Research*.

Peräkylä, Anssi (forthcoming b) 'Communicating and responding to diagnosis', in J. Heritage and D. Maynard (eds), *Practising Medicine: Structure and Process in Primary Care Encounters*. Cambridge: Cambridge University Press.

Peräkylä, Anssi and Vehviläinen, Sanna (in press, 2003) 'Conversation analysis and the professional stocks of interactional knowledge', *Discourse and Society*, 14.

Peräkylä, Anssi, Lehtinen, Esa, Lindfors, Pirjo, Nikander, Pirjo, Ruusuvuori, Johanna and Tiittula, Liisa (2002) 'Sosiaalisen suhteen rakentuminen vuorovaikutuksessa: erään puhelinkeskustelun analyysi' ['The construction of social relation in interaction: the analysis of a telephone conversation'], *Sosiologia*, 39(1): 18–32.

Pomerantz, A. (1984) 'Agreeing and disagreeing with assessments: some features of preferred/dispreferred turn shapes', in J.M. Atkinson and J. Heritage (eds), *Structures of Social Action: Studies in Conversation Analysis*. Cambridge: Cambridge University Press, pp. 57–101.

Ruusuvuori, Johanna (2000) 'Giving and receiving the reason for the visit in Finnish medical consultations'.

Doctoral dissertation, Department of Sociology and Social Psychology, University of Tampere.

Sacks, Harvey (1974) 'An analysis of the course of a joke's telling in conversation', in R. Bauman and J. Sherzer (eds), *Explorations in the Ethnography of Speaking*. Cambridge: Cambridge University Press, pp. 337–53.

Sacks, Harvey, Schegloff, Emanuel. A. and Jefferson, Gail (1974) 'A simplest systematics for the organization of turn-taking for conversation'. *Language*, 50: 696–735.

Schegloff, Emanuel A. (1968) 'Sequencing in conversational openings', *American Anthropologist*, 70: 1075–95.

Schegloff, Emanuel A. (1979) 'The relevance of repair for syntax-for-conversation', in Givon Talmy (ed.), *Syntax and Semantics 12: Discourse and Syntax*. New York: Academic Press, pp. 261–88.

Schegloff, Emanuel A. (1984) 'On some gestures' relation to talk', in J.M. Atkinson and J. Heritage (eds), *Structures of Social Action: Studies in Conversation Analysis*. Cambridge: Cambridge University Press, pp. 266–96.

Schegloff, Emanuel A. (1991) 'Reflection on talk and social structure', in Deirdre Boden and Don Zimmerman (eds), *Talk and Social Structure*. Cambridge: Polity Press, pp. 44–70.

Schegloff, Emanuel A. (1992a) Introduction, in G. Jefferson (ed.), *Harvey Sacks, Lectures on Conversation*, Vol. 1: *Fall 1964–Spring 1968*. Oxford: Blackwell.

Schegloff, Emanuel A. (1992b) 'On talk and its institutional occasion', in Paul Drew and John Heritage, (eds), *Talk at Work: Interaction in Institutional Settings*. Cambridge: Cambridge University Press, pp. 101–34.

Schegloff, Emanuel A. (1992c) 'Repair after next turn: the last structurally provided defense of intersubjectivity in conversation', *American Journal of Sociology*, 98: 1295–345.

Schegloff, Emanuel A. (1995) *Sequence Organization*. Los Angeles: UCLA Department of Sociology (mimeo).

Schegloff, Emanuel A. (1998) 'Reflections on studying prosody in talk-in-interaction', *Language and Speech*, 41: 235–63.

Schegloff, Emanuel A. and Sacks, Harvey (1973) 'Opening up closings', *Semiotica*, 8: 289–327.

Schegloff, Emanuel A., Jefferson, Gail and Sacks, Harvey (1977) 'The preference for self-correction in the organization of repair in conversation', *Language, 53*: 361–82.

Searle, John R. (1969) *Speech Acts: An essay in the Philosophy of Language*. Cambridge: Cambridge University Press.

Silverman, David (1997) *Discourses of Counselling*. London: Sage.

Silverman, David (1998) *Harvey Sacks: Social Science and Conversation Analysis*. Cambridge: Polity Press.

Stimson, G.V. and Webb, B. (1975) *Going to See the Doctor: The Consultation Process in General Practice*. London: Routledge & Kegan Paul.

Tainio, Liisa (2002) 'Negotiating gender identities and sexual agency in elderly couples' talk', in P. McIlvenny (ed.), *Talking Gender and Sexuality*. Amsterdam: John Benjamins, pp. 181–206.

Taylor, T.J. and Cameron, D. (1987) *Analyzing Conversation: Rules and Units in the Structure of Talk*. Oxford: Pergamon Press.

ten Have, Paul (1995) 'Disposal negotiations in general practice consultations', in Alan Firth (ed.), *The Discourse of Negotiation: Studies of Language in the Workplace*. Oxford: Pergamon, pp. 319–44.

ten Have, Paul (1999) *Doing Conversation Analysis: A Practical Guide*. London: Sage.

Vehviläinen, S. (1999) *Structures of Counselling Interaction: A Conversation Analytic Study on Counselling in Career Guidance Training*. Helsinki: University of Helsinki, Department of Education.

Vehviläinen, S. (2001). 'Evaluative advice in educational counseling: the use of disagreement in the "stepwise entry" to advice', *Research on Language and Social Interaction*, 34(3): 371–98.

West, Candace (1979) 'Against our will: male interruptions of females in cross-sex conversations', *Annals of the New York Academy of Sciences*, 327: 81–97.

Whalen, J. and Zimmerman, D.H. (1998) 'Observations on the display and management of emotion in naturally occurring activities: the case of hysteria in calls to 9-1-1', *Social Psychology Quarterly*, 61(2): 141–59.

Zimmerman, D.H. and West, C. (1975) 'Sex roles, interruptions and silences in conversation', in B. Thorne and N. Henley (eds), *Language and Sex: Difference and Dominance*. Rowley, MA: Newbury House, pp. 105–29.

APPENDIX: THE TRANSCRIPTION SYMBOLS IN CA

[	Starting point of overlapping speech.
]	End point of overlapping speech
(2.4)	Silence measured in seconds
(.)	Pause of less than 0.2 seconds
↑	Upward shift in pitch
↓	Downward shift in pitch
word	Emphasis
wo:rd	Prolongation of sound
°word°	Section of talk produced in lower volume than the surrounding talk
WORD	Section of talk produced in higher volume than the surrounding talk
w#ord#	Creaky voice
£word£	Smile voice
wo(h)rd	Laugh particle inserted within a word
wo-	Cut off in the middle of a word
word<	Abruptly completed word
>word<	Section of talk uttered in a quicker pace than the surrounding talk

<word>	Section of talk uttered in a slower pace than the surrounding talk	?	Raising intonation at the end of an utterance
(word)	Section of talk that is difficult to hear but is likely as transcribed	,	Flat intonation at the end of an utterance
( )	Inaudible word	word.=word	'Rush through' without the normal gap into a new utterance.
.hhh	Inhalation		
hhh	Exhalation	((word))	Transcriber's comments
.	Falling intonation at the end of an utterance		

(Adapted from Drew and Heritage (eds), *Talk at Work*. Cambridge: CUP, 1992.)

12

Discourse analytic practice

Alexa Hepburn and Jonathan Potter

It is an unusually sunny day in summer 2000 and
we are sitting round a table in the small neat
coffee room used by the professionals who field
calls at the London centre for the National
Society for the Prevention of Cruelty to Children
(NSPCC) child protection helpline. There is a
kettle, drinks machine, sink, microwave, water-
cooler and a small bookshelf filled with a varied
range of journals and writings on child abuse and
social work. It is well decorated and new – not
like our departmental coffee rooms! We have
taken up residence for what seems like the whole
of the hot afternoon and we are taking turns talking to a stream of people who are breaking off
from fielding calls to talk to us. We have provisional support from the management team at the
NSPCC to do research on the helpline, but we
need the people who actually work the phones –
the Child Protection Officers or CPOs – to agree.
We have to persuade them that our research is
interesting, that it will not threaten their work,
that we won't be judging them, that they might

find it valuable to take part, and that the NSPCC
might find it useful. We spent a bit of time that
morning deciding what to wear – what gradation
of 'smart casual' sends quite the right 'professional yet informal' message. It feels a little like
being interviewed for a job. Everyone is friendly
and attentive and most say yes, or at least say
they are interested and will think about it. We
spend a bit of time in ones and twos talking
through the technical aspects of recording calls
on to a MiniDisk. How did we get here? How
did/will things develop?

In this chapter we will try to give a different
sense of a research project in the area of 'discourse analysis' (see Box 1). We will try to combine general observations about the nature of this
kind of research and how it can be done with a
feel for the contingent, local, practical nature of
doing research. We will break this into segments
that reflect to some extent the way research of
this kind unfolds. But first, some philosophy and
sociology.

Box 1. Discourse analysis

What is discourse analysis? The answer to this question becomes harder and more complicated every year. Are there seven different types? Or perhaps two broad orientations? Is
discourse treated as a 'thing', as in Continental DA (influenced by Foucault)? In this tradition
you might say you have identified two discourses in a set of interviews about some topic.
Or is discourse a word that constructs language as active: texts and talk in social practice?
Here you are interested in the actions that are done and the practices they contribute to.
These two orientations are not always in tension with one another. For example, some discourse analytic work has been interested in how a range of 'resources' get used in discourse
practices, where these resources might be words, categories, or broader organizations such
as 'interpretative repertoires' (Potter, in press).

Part of the complication has been that different traditions called 'discourse analysis' have
emerged in different disciplinary environments. Often these traditions are structured by, and

against, the basic issues of the parent discipline: how sentences cohere linguistically into discourse; how social organization is made up; how cognition is respecified in interaction. For a sense of the varied intellectual geography of discourse analysis, compare and contrast Phillips and Jorgenson (2002), van Dijk (1996a, 1996b) and Wetherell et al. (2001). Another complication is that a tradition of specifically 'critical' discourse analysis has emerged mainly in linguistics (see Wodak, Chapter 13, this volume); yet in other disciplinary contexts, discourse analysis has often dealt with issues of ideology and asymmetry without the capital C critical preface (see Hepburn, 2003, ch. 7).

One of the reasons for writing about discursive psychology instead of discourse analysis is to avoid some of the terminological confusion that makes discourse analysis a highly ambiguous category.

CONTEXTS OF SCIENTIFIC UNDERSTANDING

When writing about method there are different ways of understanding what the writing is for, and how it characterizes research. On the one hand, there are methodology texts that lay out the logic of research in a way that can be drawn on to justify claims and procedures. On the other, there are writings about the actualities of developing research projects, the practice of qualitative research. This chapter is for a volume with the latter focus. It is worth thinking about this distinction in a bit more detail, and for that it is useful to consider a classic distinction used in the philosophy and sociology of science.

Up to the 1970s the distinction between the *context of justification* and the *context of discovery* was crucial for the way science was understood (Feyerabend, 1975; Mulkay, 1979). It is a subtle distinction. The *context of justification* referred to the way that any particular fact was justifiable by reference to empirical findings, the logic of investigation, the appropriate use of general criteria, theoretical coherence, and so on. At one level, this is the stuff of scientific articles – where reference to findings, methods and so on are run through procedures of peer review before publication. At another level, this is the stuff of philosophers – where discussions of empiricism, progressive research programmes, and so on are part of the discussion of the special nature of scientific knowledge. In contrast, the *context of discovery* refers to all the contingent events and factors that led up to any particular knowledge claim. This is the stuff of psychological and sociological study – the psychodynamics of genius, the social processes that led to the appointment of a particular scientist at a particular institution, the political and funding background that favoured a certain kind of research.

This distinction suited the philosophy of science of the era as it allowed philosophers to consider the way knowledge is justified, without requiring them to perform historical analyses of the detail of what went on in a particular scientific episode. It was the *logic* that counted, and that could be assessed post hoc. Sociologists could be left to sort out the other stuff which was important, but, somehow, not so fundamental. One of the features of the new philosophy of science (Chalmers, 1992) and the sociology of scientific knowledge (SSK; see Ashmore, 1989) was that this distinction started to crumble. In particular, it was concerned to show the contingent, social basis of basic features of justification such as mathematics, replication, criteria for theory choice, and observation. This had two consequences. First, it collapsed the distinction by making it very hard to justify looking at justification abstracted from the contingent and social world, the context of discovery. Second, and more broadly, it suggested a much more complex and rather more fallible view of science. It became harder to keep our understanding of science away from our understanding of everything else. To understand justification properly you need to look carefully at the detailed, practical contingencies of actual research.

There is another twist to this, however. More recent discursive psychology (DP) work on descriptions (Potter, 1996) highlights the way in which descriptions of events are bound up with doing actions, such as providing justification for actions and blaming others. Edwards's studies on relationship counselling show this up beautifully. When a husband and wife each describe what went on at the start of their relationship, the details of what is picked out, how events are sequenced, the moments of vivid detail and broad-brush gloss, work towards why, specifically, the other partner is the one who has the problems and needs the counselling, and should change (Edwards, 1995a, 1997, 1998). Now consider again the context of justification and context of discovery distinction. What SSK did was, in effect, show up the contingency of justification. What DP does is unsettle things the other way. It shows up the way contingency is constructed to do justification. It's a double whammy for the distinction!

How is this relevant here? It highlights the tricky nature of telling the real story of social research, of highlighting the practice. It makes it impossible (well, very hard!) to separate descriptions of practice from issues of justification. Telling a story of contingency almost invariably drifts into a story of justification. That does not mean we are not going to tell a story like that; we are just encouraging a sceptical stance on that story. Put another way, it makes it rather hard to interpret methods writing in social science. What is it for? Is it for guidance in practice? Or is it oriented to offering resources for justification? Is it a repository of claims and axioms that can be reproduced when building the legitimacy of some claim? When methods writings get cited, it is often in the latter way. The hope, of course, is that they *are* used by people to help with their practice, but that this support is less visible.

SOME HISTORY, NATURALLY

What led to our NSPCC research? Where do you start when tackling this question? With childhood, school, an inspirational lecturer, a brilliant book chapter? Let us offer some fragments. I got interested in discourse work and child abuse issues through doing a PhD on Derrida and teacher bullying (that is, bullying of children by teachers, rather than the more familiar kind). (Just a caution about the move into autobiography here: the 'I' (=AH) is a textual convenience, but that does not mean that we are buying the familiar story of authorship and psychology that often goes along with it. It is, to repeat, a textual convenience.) More recently, we both got excited about the possibilities of work beyond interviews and ethnography. We had both analysed a lot of interviews, and AH had done a chunk of ethnography. The excitement was about a naturalistic social science (supported by discursive psychology and rhetoric, inspired by the success of conversation analysis) that would work with records of interaction and address a variety of questions that discourse analysts had used interviews to get at, and also moving beyond those to new questions that emerged from the material (see Box 2).

Box 2.   Interviews and naturalistic data

Discourse analysis has overwhelmingly been done using interview data, particularly that strand of discourse work that developed within social psychology (Billig, 1992; Wetherell and Potter, 1992). Without diminishing the importance of this work, there are a number of virtues of working with naturalistic materials:

1   It does not flood the research setting with the researcher's own categories (embedded in questions, probes, stimuli, vignettes, and so on).

2   It does not put people in the position of disinterested experts on their own and others' practices, thoughts and so on, encouraging them to provide normatively appropriate descriptions (as many interview and questionnaire studies do).

3   It does not leave the researcher to make a range of more or less problematic inferences from the data collection arena to topic (from interviews about counselling, say, to counselling itself) as the topic itself (counselling, perhaps) is directly studied.

4   It opens up a wide variety of novel issues and concerns that are outwith the prior expectations embodied in questionnaires, experimental formats, interviews questions, and so on.

5   It is a rich record of people living their lives, pursuing goals, managing institutional tasks, and so on (Potter, 2002).

One of the reasons often given for studying interviews rather than naturalistic materials is that interviews allow the researcher access to

stuff that is too sensitive to obtain permission to study, or that occurs too rarely to collect realistically. Our experience, however, is that in practice permission can be gained if the right kind of approach is made. One of us (JP) had experience working with Mick Roffe on his PhD on social workers' assessments of parents whose children had been taken into care due to physical or sexual abuse (Roffe, 1996). Mick was able to obtain permission from all involved in this most sensitive of settings to use tape recordings or even video in some cases. One of us (AH) had experience working with Ceri Parsons who started her PhD on gender reassignment. Again, she was able to obtain permission to record first assessment interviews, where applicants were questioned about their reasons for wishing to change gender. Often, the argument is made that material is too sensitive without having tried to obtain permission. Persistence combined with creativity is the order of day here – keep trying new sites and think about how the theme of interest might appear in different settings.

Our NSPCC study also had its origins in PhD work. I (AH) was supervising Sam Bishop who wished to study children's accounts of bullying. She and I spent some time thinking of different settings where issues of bullying emerge – in schools, for example, or families. She and I identified ChildLine as a setting with a lot of potential that fitted both our interests. It is a high-profile service that deals with large numbers of reports of abuse, talking through problems and advising children. After an exchange of letters, we met ChildLine staff to discuss issues of access. Their response was mixed. On the one hand, they were interested in the work and could see a number of possibilities for application. On the other, they were concerned about the assurances of confidentiality in their advertising. They deliberated with their board of directors over possible ways of dealing with these problems, but eventually did not feel able to provide access. However, they were interested enough in the research to offer Sam Bishop access to their ongoing training sessions in peer counselling for school bullying; this is a fascinating research topic in its own right.

On the basis of this experience, I decided to approach the UK's NSPCC. They have a rather different brief from ChildLine. Their role is less centrally to counsel children (although they may do that); rather it is to receive information about abuse and act on it (normally by passing it to the appropriate social services department, sometimes by contacting the police). The letter I sent has evolved through a number of projects. The generic form of this letter is reproduced in Figure 12.1. It is meant to get straight to the worries that potential research participants might have in collaborating with work of this kind. In particular, how are issues of ethics, consent and anonymity going to be managed? What extra work will be involved? How might the work be useful? Implicitly, it is also heading off the idea that the role of the research is to criticize the organization or its individual workers.

Our experience with previous studies is that it is the professionals (the counsellors, social workers, therapists) who are most wary of being researched, although *they* often identify the clients as the ones who have a problem. There are probably a number of reasons for this. Professionals may feel that the adequacy of their work is being questioned. This may be exacerbated by their common feeling that their own performance does not match ideals presented in training materials, or their fantasy of the ideal job. David Silverman (1997) refers to this as the problem of the Divine Orthodoxy. Practitioners are condemned to fail as they are compared to an idealized, normative standard of 'good communication', say, completely removed from actual practice. This was clearly the case with Mick Roffe's social worker participants who worried that their work practices were messy; yet one of the features of his work was to highlight the way apparent disorganization in their practices was a result of their subtle management of a number of concurrent tasks (Roffe, 1996). The letter in Figure 12.1 is designed to address these concerns in an accessible manner.

The next stage in the process of gaining access to the NSPCC was to follow up the letter with a face-to-face interview. The managers at NSPCC were interested and open enough to see what I was like in person. I met the manager of the helpline, John Cameron, the senior researcher, Sue Creighton, and the head of training, Sylvia Tadd, at their London office. I went in with a checklist of their likely concerns to address as well as information about other research projects I had been involved with and the type of academic output I had produced. I was also prepared to address what would be one of the most difficult issues, that of ethics.

There are a number of tensions and complications with ethics in this area. There are different parties to the helpline interaction whose anonymity needs to be protected in different ways and, perhaps, for different reasons. The Child Protection Officers (CPOs) needed to have their identity hidden so that the research did not become confused with issues of promotion and evaluation. My role was research, not staff appraisal. Second, there were the callers; it was crucial that the research did not disrupt the often very delicate reporting process. The first group were easiest in practical terms. And this brings

Dear [Name]

I am writing to ask if you will help me with my research. I am a lecturer in Psychology at Loughborough University. I am studying the process of counselling on telephone help lines, using the recently developed approaches of discourse and conversation analysis.

My aim is to highlight the rich and complex set of discursive and conversational practices that are used by both counsellors and young people. This kind of study has been especially useful in family therapy, social work and relationship counselling, and I have good links with some of the key analysts in this field.

The research will not involve extra work for you or your team in the form of questionnaires or interviews. What would be involved would be some counsellors making records of a small number of sessions using a standard tape recorder. The research will be conducted fully within BPS ethical guidelines – all people involved would need to give their informed consent, and I will ensure unqualified anonymity at all stages of the research. No participants will be identified by name, and all tapes will be transcribed and listened to only by myself and a limited number of research colleagues. For any published output identifying details will be comprehensively anonymized. I have consulted carefully with other researchers who have dealt with sensitive topics of this kind such as relationship counselling talk and social workers' assessments of sexually abusing parents. I have also published a number of articles exploring the issue of school bullying, employing these types of qualitative methods on interview data with teachers and pupils.

I realize that although most people like to help researchers in principle, in practice this involves some extra work in what is already a delicate and demanding job where trust and confidentiality are a premium. What I can offer to counsellors and staff members in return is to share my results with you in the form of a feedback report and workshop. Practitioners in other fields have found the detailed transcriptions of sessions particularly illuminating as they provide an unusually rich record of their interactions, highlighting often unnoticed features. I believe that the detailed analytical points will allow deeper insights into the processes of counselling and other issues of concern to participants. I expect that the research project overall would lead to recommendations for counselling training and strategies, for enhancing existing literature available to counsellors, parents and children, and for informing policy intervention strategies.

Thank you for your time, and I look forward to hearing from you in due course.

Yours sincerely

Figure 12.1   *General permissions letter.*

us back to the start of this chapter and also the point where we started to do the project jointly.

All potential CPOs for the study were briefed about it and given the opportunity to ask questions. They could opt into the research by working with the phone prepared for recording, but there was no pressure to do so. At the start of the project CPOs were typically (and understandably) cautious, and only a few signed up. As time passed and they got to know us, they became more confident that our aim was not to expose their (imagined) inadequacies and more signed up. At time of writing more than twenty CPOs have recorded more than two hundred calls.

The callers raised a trickier ethics issue. We had initially floated the possibility of either a generic or selective recorded message as they called in, noting that the calls might be recorded for research and training, and asking callers to say explicitly if they wanted to opt out of this. Such a message could have provided more detail as necessary. The managers at NSPCC were

(quite appropriately) concerned that this would not allow callers to ask questions about the research that might concern them. They suggested that when CPOs took part in the study they asked the callers at the start of the call if they would mind their call being used for research and training, and assured them of anonymity. This had the disadvantage to us of producing disruption at the delicate point of call opening, although it turned out to be relatively minor in practice. We wrote out an ethics script for the CPOs to use; however, the managers suggested that each CPO develop their own version of this. In practice, this works well as CPOs can tailor it to particular callers (children, say, or people with communication problems). Sometimes the ethics segments of the call are quite brief, sometimes there is an extended set of questions and answers. From our perspective, this approach satisfies our appropriate professional guidelines (laid out by the British Psychological Society) and works for the NSPCC.

TECHNOLOGY, SAMPLING AND QUESTIONS

Some readers will wonder that we are several pages through this chapter and we have talked about a lot of things, but not mentioned research questions yet. To some extent this reflects a move in discourse analysis, and particularly in discursive psychology, to considering a setting or a set of practices rather than starting with a question. This reflects a move from the traditional social science question of 'how does X influence Y?' to the question 'how is X done?' In this case, we are moving away from questions such as 'how does social class influence the incidence of child abuse?' to 'how does reporting abuse get done?', 'how do CPOs deliver appropriate advice?', 'how do they keep highly upset callers on the line long enough to give evidence for police officers or social workers to act?'

There is also a theoretical context for these questions. Discursive psychology is concerned with the role of talk and texts in social practices. However, it also takes a particular theoretical perspective on this topic (Box 3). This focus on action orientation, situation and construction is one of the reasons why work has moved towards study of naturalistic materials (where, however far off the ideal, the attempt is to get at things that would have happened without the intervention of the researcher).

Box 3.   Theoretical principles of discursive psychology

Discursive psychology can be understood as highlighting three core features of discourse (from Potter, 2003):

1   *Action orientation.* Discourse is the primary medium of human action and interaction. Actions are not merely free-standing, but are typically embedded in broader practices. Some are generic (making invitations); some are specific to settings (air traffic control management of flight crew). The idea of action *orientation* discourages the expectation that analysis will discover a one-to-one relation where discrete acts are performed by discrete verbs.

2   *Situation.* Discourse is situated in three senses. First, it is organized sequentially, such that the primary environment of what is said is what has just come before, and this sets up (although does not determine) what comes next. Second, it may be situated institutionally, such that institutional identities (news interviewee, say) and tasks (managing neutrality in news interviews) may be relevant to (although not determine) what takes place. Third, it can be situated rhetorically, such that descriptions may resist actual or potential attempts to counter them as interested.

3   *Construction.* Discourse is constructed and constructive. It is *constructed* in the sense that it is built from various resources (words, of course, but also categories, commonplace ideas, broader explanatory systems). It is *constructive* in the sense that versions of the world, of events and actions, and of people's phenomenological worlds are built and stabilized in talk in the course of actions. A person may account for their absence at a meeting by constructing a version of the city's traffic problems, or of their own faulty cognitive processing.

These broader issues have consequences for the type and quantity of data that we wished to collect and the technology used. In terms of technology, the prime material would be recordings of actual calls. We did not do formal interviews with the CPOs, for example, or ethnography in the call centre. Having said that, we were not trying to *avoid* talking to CPOs or remain *ignorant* of issues to do with work practices, training, organizational structure, and so on. I (AH) have spent a considerable time over two years hanging out with CPOs, chatting to them, and watching them at work. I do not want to call this ethnography or interviews, however. The topic of the research is the business of the calls, the recordings are the prime source for understanding that. The records of calls are the basis for supporting any research claims. What was learned by spending time on site is a resource for understanding, but is analytically secondary. Put simply, we want to avoid claims like the following: it looks like what is going on in this call is X, but our ethnography/interviews shows that it is, in fact, Y. If it is, in fact, a Y, the hanging out may help us get there, but we want to be able to justify the claim with the public material, otherwise we will doubt its veracity. For the most part the recording is a more reliable basis for understanding what happens in the calls than the CPOs' recollections of what happens in the calls, their assertions about what generally goes on, or the researcher's own notes and post hoc reconstructions.

This is a subtle and easily misunderstood point as it can seem counter-intuitive. And it relates to the live debates among discourse workers on the status of context (Schegloff, 1997, 1999; Wetherell, 1998; Billig, 1999). For researchers who see the process of analysis as one that involves contextualizing the study of discourse within a broader analysis of social context (like many in critical discourse analysis), the issue is how this analysis of context will work. In particular, there is a tension between the sorts of analysts' descriptions of context that come from ethnography and the sorts of detailed study of

how descriptions are being used in calls. On a more prosaic level, different CPOs offered different glosses on precisely what their job was and how they acted on the phone. These glosses were insightful and interesting, but we were cautious about using them as a definitive guide to what was happening in the calls.

None of these high-level questions would be very important if we could not make decent records of the calls. We opted to use MiniDisk recorders because of the high-quality digital recordings they produce and because of the length of recording – more than two hours in mono. We set up two workstations in the call centre with MiniDisks, taking a lead directly from the phone socket (various adapters are available from electronics stores for doing this). We produced our own smartly coloured and laminated instruction guide, pared down to the bare essentials, and talked the volunteers through the use of the recorders. Inevitably this was not always sufficient. Over time the CPOs managed to do a wide range of things that messed up recordings. Even after further training and new instructions it is not uncommon to pick up a blank MiniDisk. However, the quality of the recordings makes it all worthwhile.

Box 4.   Digital records

The ideal with discourse research has always been to work with the sound and transcript in parallel. There is a wide recognition of the limitations of transcript alone, particularly in capturing subtleties of intonation and inflection. However, working with cassette tape is a pain. If you are comparing two segments of an interview, say, which are 20 minutes apart, it can take ages pumping the fast forward and reverse keys to find each of them. Or if you want to consider a set of extracts you might be inserting and ejecting cassettes, rewinding (inevitably missing the right place) and winding forward again for a considerable part of the research period. The temptation was always to work with the transcript, which has the enormous virtue of being on paper, which is a wonderfully flexible and transportable medium.

Digital sound and video has changed all that. The recording (whether originally recorded in digital or not) can be recorded into PC software. This turns it into a file that can be copied, edited, listened to, and so on. If it is saved in MP3 it will also be small, at least compared to the original. Video can be saved as MPEG. Both can be burned on to a CD for easy transport. Extracts can be e-mailed between researchers. They can be downloaded from websites in sensible amounts of time, making the provision of recordings alongside paper publications a real possibility. See the journal *DA-Online*, for example, at www.shu.ac.uk/daol/

We use CoolEdit (from www.syntrillium. com) for most sound recording, manipulation and transcription. This software allows you to step through the recording viewing a physical representation of the sound while hearing. This makes timing pauses and noting overlaps much easier. Segments of interest can be cut and pasted just as with text files. It transforms the practice of transcription and analysis, making both much more fluid. Crucially, CoolEdit allows the identifying details such as proper names to be disguised (e.g. by reversing or deleting) and speaker's voice quality can be subtly changed to make them unrecognizable while retaining crucial features of vocal delivery.

How much material should we collect? This was very hard to tell in advance. However, we had some general considerations that guided our collection. First, we were concerned that different individual CPOs might have different styles on the phone. So we wanted to collect calls from different CPOs. Second, we were concerned that different categories of CPOs might be consequential – for example, it might be different reporting sexual abuse to a woman CPO than a man. Third, we were concerned to study some phenomena that turned up only rarely in the calls. For example, we were interested in calls from children reporting abuse, which make up around 10 per cent of the total. Or, to take a more extreme case, we were interested in examples where callers were reporting abuse strongly linked to an ethnic category. The CPOs described these as particularly difficult calls that raised important questions. But we have found them to make up less than 1 per cent of the total. However, by collecting a large amount of material, appreciable instances of rare phenomena can be collected.

TRANSCRIPTION

Transcription is indispensable. However fluidly new technology allows you to use sound and video files, transcript has major advantages: you can write on it, read it in the bath, and publish it in traditional printed journals. The general system developed by Gail Jefferson (and well described in ten Have, 1998, and Hutchby and Wooffitt, 1998) is the de facto standard in discursive psychology and conversation analysis. And for good reason – it has evolved in parallel to thirty years of research considering what features of talk are interactionally live. Where there are deviations from this it is with the use of Jefferson-Lite, particularly in interview studies on critical topics. Such transcript downplays the interactional nature of discourse, and has been more popular with analysts who take a more Foucaultian perspective. Even there, researchers are starting to see the need for high-quality transcript. It is not a matter of being fussy or putting in detail that is not needed, but of having a closer record of what actually went on rather than a record that suggests something else went on!

Having emphasized the importance of quality transcript, there are practical limits. The various funding bids we put in for different parts of this project did not provide the several thousand pounds needed for full transcription of a large

corpus of calls. We decided to use the smaller amount of money to get 'first pass' transcription (without intonation, emphasis, breathing, overlaps, etc.). This raised another difficulty because of the sensitive nature of the material. We opted for a transcription agency that already handled sensitive legal and child protection work for courts and social services. The advantage of an agency like this was speed: they worked from calls burned on to a CD and turned them round in a matter of days. These first-pass transcripts were useful for getting an overall feel of particular calls and to identify broad episodes that might be of interest. They had one feature that made them superior to Jeffersonian transcripts. As they were orthographic, without the words broken up with colons or arrows, they were searchable for particular words or phrases.

There was no getting away from the need for better transcript, however. And there was no alternative to doing it ourselves. We started with a small number of very different calls to have data sessions with and get us into the material. After that the transcription has been bound up with the process of coding and doing particular studies.

CODING AND DEVELOPING A STUDY

Let us return to our problem distinction between context of justification and context of discovery for a moment. We started off with some ways in which the distinction collapsed in on itself, with the justification being grounded in social processes, and the discovery accounts organized to provide justification. Despite the problems, the distinction makes practical sense when trying to describe the process of doing research. What you do does not fit into the sort of neat accounts that appear in methods sections of articles or in philosophical reconstructions of research. Nevertheless, there is a sense to seeing the more chaotic stabs at doing studies being reconstructable in a coherent and justifiable manner. That coherence makes the *logic* of what goes on more accessible to the reader of the article or book. Let us take one example paper from the overall project and try and offer a bit of natural history and a bit of justification.

Soon after we started the NSPCC research, some researchers in the general helpline area got to hear about it, and invited us to write a chapter. It was somewhat too early, and we had hardly done any transcription, let alone analysis. We produced a rough chapter that ended up not

'I'M A BIT CONCERNED' – EARLY ACTIONS AND PSYCHOLOGICAL CONSTRUCTIONS IN A CHILD PROTECTION HELPLINE

ABSTRACT

This paper analyses early actions in 50 calls reporting cases of abuse to a national child protection helpline in the UK (the National Society for the Prevention of Cruelty to Children helpline). It focuses in particular on the early turns in the caller's 'reason for call', and in particular a class of constructions in which the caller describes him or herself as being 'concerned about X' (or similar). Analysis of the corpus of calls suggests concern constructions are canonical early elements of the reason-for-call sequence. Concern constructions (a) are oriented to as a pre-move in the caller's reason for call; (b) project the unpacking of concerns in a way oriented to the NSPCC's institutional role; (c) attend to epistemological asymmetries between caller and call-taker and remove the requirement for disaffiliative next actions such as asking for the basis of claims; (d) provide a way for the Child Protection Officer to take abuse claims seriously while not presupposing their truth; (e) display an appropriate caller stance. These observations are supported by an analysis of deviant cases. The broader implications of this study for the relation between psychology, interaction and institutions are discussed.

Figure 12.2　*Abstract of concerns paper.*

being suitable for the book. However, as is common with these things, the attempt to fulfil a particular brief set off some ideas. It got us particularly interested in issues that arise when callers are giving a first version of the abuse they are reporting, and the way they manage potential problems that arise using psychological descriptions. Our prior interests in problems with cognitive interpretation of mental terms and the delicacy of talking about violent acts were also guiding our early writing. As the study developed, it became more and more focused on the construction of 'concern' and the role such constructions play in reporting abuse (Potter and Hepburn, 2003).

The 'concerns' article evolved into its final state through a series of conference and departmental presentations. The most intensive development was between a presentation in Copenhagen and one a week later in Finland. Those few days were some of the most intensively engaged with the data over the period of the project. The intensive refereeing by people at *Research on Language and Social Interaction* provided the impetus for further refinement. It is very hard to do justice to the complexity of the actual development – the context of discovery in those terms – so let us move to a more cleaned-up context of justification to make the whole thing more accessible. The abstract of the published article is reproduced in Figure 12.2 as a backdrop.

One of the first tasks in doing this study was one of data reduction. With an ever-growing set of calls, some of which lasted more than half an hour, the labour of transcription and analysis is potentially huge. The risk is in losing the specificity of what is going on while trying to encompass too much material. We (eventually) settled on a corpus of fifty openings that reported abuse to a third party. Even producing a corpus as seemingly clear-cut as this was not easy. Various calls that seemed to be reporting abuse turned out (sometimes only after a lot of consideration) to be doing something else (e.g. complaining about social services). The corpus kept shrinking, and new calls had to be pulled in to keep it to size. Various general considerations were also in play in developing this corpus: it should not over-represent any one CPO; it should include both male and female CPOs and callers; it should include child as well as adult callers. We were also influenced by the pragmatic simplicity of working initially with calls that had already been transcribed by the transcription service.

This fifty-call opening corpus was refined. A full Jefferson transcript was produced of each opening. An MP3 sound file of each opening was also produced. This meant that there was a working set of transcripts and recordings focused on openings that could be fluidly analysed.

ANALYSIS AND JUSTIFYING CONCLUSIONS

The temptation when writing about analysis is to focus on the things that are easy to describe.

For example, we did a range of simple counts as an aid to understanding the patterning of the way constructions using the terms 'concerned' and 'concern' were used. At the broadest level, it was interesting to consider how specific to the NSPCC data concern constructions were. To check this we did something very simple, which was to compare prevalence in the NSPCC calls with a corpus of everyday phone calls (collected by Liz Holt). The terms 'concern' and 'concerned' appear an average of 7 times per call in our material, but only 0.3 times per call in the Holt corpus. At a more specific level we were interested in the prevalence of concerns constructions in the call openings, and also how many were initiated by the caller and how many by the CPO. About 60 per cent of openings use concerned constructions; about two-thirds of these were initiated by the caller, and about a third by the CPO.

These counts were certainly interesting, and highlighted some things to follow up. But their implications are not conclusive on their own. Indeed, they are most unclear without considering the specifics of the interaction and how it unfolds. The course of analysis works through developing ideas about what is going on in some materials ('hypotheses' in rather grander methods speak) and exploring them, seeing how far they make sense. Again, the abstract logic of this is rather different from the ad hoc working at it that goes on in practice. When we were doing this analysis we had periods of sitting with a pile of transcripts arguing over what was happening and getting excited about things that seemed to work and depressed about dead ends. We would listen to an extract several times checking whether it made sense with our most recent idea. Often one or other of us would listen to extracts on headphones while scrolling through the transcript. As points of interest (or trouble) came up, we would use the Post-it note facility on the word processor to annotate the transcript file. This is a particularly helpful facility where more than one person is working with a single transcript. Sometimes we needed to go back through the entire fifty transcripts and sound files to check that something that shouldn't be there wasn't there.

This all seems a bit abstract. Let us illustrate it with some of the material. The following is what we came to identify as a canonical call opening. This is a very simple example.

LB neighbour concern

1	CPO:	Hello NSPCC can I
2		help you?
3	Caller:	Good afternoon >I wonder if
4		you could.<
5	CPO:	Yes [certainly,]
6	Caller:	[I'm concerned] about
7		[a-] about a child that lives
8	CPO:	[Yeh]
9	Caller:	next door to me.
10	CPO:	Ri:ght, before you go on
11		can I
12		((ethics script))

We started to call this form of opening 'canonical' in part because of its regular appearance, but, more importantly, because of the standard work it did.

Over the course of analysis we developed a number of ideas about what concerns constructions might be doing in these call openings. First, in line with our interactional focus, we considered the way that concerns constructions work to initiate unpacking. That is, 'I'm concerned about a child that lives next door' prefaces a sequence where the caller details the grounds for this concern. Second, it orients to criss-cross asymmetries in the interaction: the caller knows about the abuse; the CPO knows about child protection, evidence, etc. It treats the actionable status of what is to be reported as not yet established, allowing it to be established in the interaction with the CPO. The other side of this coin is that it heads off a problem that might arise with direct opening announcements ('a child next door has been sexually abused'), which is that the next turn from the CPO would likely be a question about the basis of that knowledge. Third, concerns constructions display the caller's stance to the abuse – it is serious, critical and, well, concerned. They are managing their own stance as reporters (something discursive psychologists have highlighted as particularly important: Edwards and Potter, 1992). Fourth, and perhaps most importantly, concerns constructions allow the CPOs to treat abuse claims as serious without having to assume that they are true, accurate or actionable. The concern opening can evolve into a discussion of specific things in the world – injuries, times, family relationships – or into a discussion of, broadly, the psychology of the caller – their heightened anxieties, confusions or misperceptions.

Box 5. Validating analyses

A range of different validation procedures have been highlighted in discourse analysis and discursive psychology. The following (from Potter, in press) are most important for the style of discursive psychology discussed here:

1 *Participants' orientations.* Any turn of talk is oriented to what came before, and sets up an environment for what comes next. At its simplest, when someone provides an acceptance it provides evidence that what came before was an invitation. If an analyst claims that some conversational move is an indirect invitation, say, we would want to see evidence that the recipient is orienting (even indirectly) to its nature as an invitation. Close attention to this turn-by-turn display of understanding provides one important check on analytic interpretations (Heritage, 1997).

2 *Deviant cases.* Deviant cases play a significant role in the validation of findings. They are often the most analytically and theoretically informative. They can show whether a generalization is robust or breaks down. For example, studies of media interviews show that interviewees rarely treat interviewers as accountable for views expressed in their questions. As Heritage and Greatbatch (1991) have shown, this is the normal (indeed, normative) pattern. There are occasional deviant cases, where a news interviewer is treated as responsible for some view. However, rather than showing that this pattern is not normative, they show up precisely that it *is* normative. Cases of departure can lead to considerable interactional trouble, which interferes with the interviewee making their point (Potter, 1996).

3 *Coherence.* The accumulation of findings from different studies allows new studies to be assessed for their coherence with what comes before. For example, work on the organization of food assessments in mealtime conversations (Wiggins, 2002) builds on, and provides further confirmation of, earlier work on assessments, compliments and news receipts (Heritage, 1984; Pomerantz, 1984). Looked at the other way round, a study that clashed with some of the basic findings in discourse work would be treated with more caution – although if its findings seemed more robust it would be more consequential.

4 *Readers' evaluation.* One of the most fundamental features of discourse research is that its claims are accountable to the detail of the empirical materials, and that the empirical materials are presented in a form that allows readers to make their own checks and judgements. Discourse articles typically present a range of extracts from the transcript alongside the interpretations that have been made of them. This form of validation contrasts with much traditional experimental and content analytic work, where it is rare for anything close to 'raw data' to be included, or for more than one or two illustrative codings to be provided. Sacks's (1992) ideal was to put the reader as far as possible into the same position as the researcher with respect to the materials. Such an ideal is unrealizable, but conversation and discourse analytic work brings it closer than many other analytic approaches.

How did we develop these ideas, and how did we provide support for them with the material? The most important way was to use the way individual calls unfolded, turn-by-turn, and the pattern across the whole the corpus of calls as a resource for checking ideas. There is a lot of detail in the article on this, so let us just take a couple of examples.

One thing that interested us was a class of openings where the caller had not started off with a concerns construction, but the CPO glosses the caller as having concerns. Here is an example.

The extract starts at the point where the CPO has finished running through the ethics script.

WO Abusive friend

1	CPO:	oka:y?=
2	Caller:	=Um: (.) i-its d- really
3		difficult to be honest I
4		know of a (0.2) a e- (.)
5		a young child who- (0.6)
6		h .hh I don't have any
7		solid evidence.
8	CPO:	Ri[: ght.]
9	Caller:	[An' I]'ve not seen
10		any evidence.=
11	CPO:	=Okay well let's have
12		a chat about what
13		your concerns
14		are[: an then we] can
15	Caller:	[R i : g h t]
16	CPO:	deci:de together
17		wh[at the mo]st
18	Caller:	[o k a y.]
19	CPO:	appropriate
20		[course of] action
21	Caller:	[o k a y .]
22	CPO:	might [be.]
23	Caller:	[aha,]

There are a couple of striking things about this example. Particularly interesting is the trouble shown in the caller's opening in lines 2–7. She prefaces her position as 'really difficult'; she identifies a child but breaks off before saying what has happened to him or her, and then notes her lack of evidence. This broad-brush description of the turn understates the trouble we see when looking carefully – note the delays, breathing and false starts, and the insertion of 'really' into 'its difficult', upgrading it. Now consider what the CPO does. Instead of directly addressing individual elements of the caller's opening, she proposes a 'chat about what your concerns are' which will allow the caller and CPO to 'decide together' on a course of action. The informal softened 'chat' (not statement taking, say, or report giving; cf. Antaki, 2000) combined with the egalitarian 'decide together' provide a sympathetic response. Most interesting for us, however, was the concerns construction. In effect, the CPO cleans up the caller's troubled opening, and prepares for a relaxed and collaborative unpacking of 'concerns'.

One of the things that is most productive in analysing discourse is the study of deviant cases. So we paid particular attention to the twenty calls that did not use concerned openings. Did they refute the pattern, and the interactional business that we proposed to account for the pattern? Or did they mark out a range of alternatives and cases that provided further confirmation of the central analysis? We therefore spent nearly as much time on these deviant cases as on the more standard ones. Let us take one class of exceptions to illustrate the style of analysis.

A subset of calls without concerns constructions started with the caller invoking an institutional identity. Here is an example:

JX Health visitor

1		((phone rings))
2	CPO:	Hello NSPCC can
3		I help you?
4	Caller:	↑Hel↓lo: I don't know if I
5		actually got (0.2) the
6		right number I'm a- a
7		health visitor.
8		(0.2)
9		Er[: : m] (.)
10	CPO:	[Yeah,]
11	Caller:	in North Berwick.
12		(0.3)
13	Caller:	. Hhh a::nd >I've
14		actually g-< er:m
15		>I've got a child on
16		my caseload <
17		he's thirtee:n.
18		(0.5)
19	CPO:	Righ[t.]
20	Caller:	[Wh]o er:m (0.3)
21		i:s: (0.3) threatening
22		to kill himse:lf he's
23		being aggressive (0.4)
24		all sorts of real
25		problems.=
26	CPO:	= °Oh dear. °
27		(0.6)
28	CPO:	. Hh can ↑I [jus-]
29	Caller:	[Erm]
30		((ethics script))
31		so you've got a chi:ld
32		on your caseload...

What excited us about this and similar examples was the way the institutional callers did not open with concerns constructions. Rather, they opened with their institutional identity. Note also the detail here – their description of the victim as 'on my caseload' formulates an institutional relationship (this contrasts to neighbour, grandchild and so on that characterize the canonical openings). And this is picked up by the CPO, who repeats the institutional formulation when they get things back on course after the ethics script.

This made perfect sense to us. The institutional callers had much less need to manage their stake and interest with respect to the abused as their interest is institutionally provided for (health visitors are meant to be concerned with the health of children).

They did not have the same requirement to preface asymmetrical unpacking of the abuse report. In the example above, for instance, note the way the caller gives a series of specific descriptions at the outset (e.g. 'he's threatening to kill himself'). The important analytic point is that analysis of these deviant cases did not undermine our initial idea (although it might have!); rather, it provided further confirmation. The business that the professional callers did *not* need to do provided further confirmation of the kinds of business that the lay callers *did* need to do. It provided further confirmation of the value of concern openings *for lay callers*.

Box 6. Discourse analysis, ethnomethodology and conversation analysis

Readers familiar with the work of Harvey Sacks will have noted the similarity between some of the materials and concerns in this analysis and Sacks's earliest work on calls to an Emergency Psychiatric Centre (e.g. the first ten lectures of the Fall 1964–Spring 1965 series). This raises the interesting and rather complicated question of how discourse analysis differs from, and is related to, ethnomethodology and conversation analysis.

Part of the difficulty in answering this question comes from the spread of different approaches that are called discourse analysis (as noted in Box 1). There is also important variation in the way ethnomethodology is understood – particularly between the 'classic' approach of Garfinkel's *Studies in Ethnomethodology* and the more recent programme (Garfinkel, 1967, 2002). In addition, there are differences between Sacks's early work on membership categorization, which has had something of a renaissance recently, and the broader conversation analytic tradition that Sacks developed and inspired (see Silverman, 1998). Within this diversity there is considerable convergence among some strands of discourse analysis, ethnomethodology and conversation analysis.

To simplify this question, five areas of potential divergence between discourse analysis (at least in the tradition presented here), conversation analysis and ethnomethodology can be highlighted:

1 *Construction.* Discourse analysis is a constructionist tradition (as we noted in Box 3). However, it differs from other constructionist traditions in social science in its concrete focus on how versions and descriptions are put together to perform actions. The construction and use of descriptions is taken as topic. It is not clear how far this perspective escapes the kinds of critiques of constructionism developed by ethnomethodologists (Button and Sharrock, 1993; see commentary in Potter, 1996) and conversation analysts. Ethnomethodologists themselves have a long tradition of studying fact construction (e.g. Smith, 1990), and some of Sacks's earliest work was on description (Sacks, 1963). Much of the disagreement here arises from confusion, or is in emphasis rather than on substantive issues. Hutchby and Wooffitt's (1998) introduction to conversation analysis has a chapter on fact construction.

2 *Cognition.* Discourse analysis in this tradition is anti-cognitivist. That is, it rejects the goal of explaining action by reference to underlying cognitive states or entities. Conversation analysts are sometimes ambivalent about the status of cognitive entities (Pomerantz,

1990/1; Schegloff, 1991). Edwards (1995b) has given a reading of Sacks's work that highlights his anti-cognitivism. Ethnomethodologists have sometimes criticized discourse analytic work for being too cognitivist, although the issue at stake seems to be more that of empirical versus conceptual analysis (see Potter and Edwards, 2003). Overall, there are a range of interesting and productive disagreements that are still being worked through by interaction researchers (see papers in te Molder and Potter, in press).

3   *Interviews.* Much of the earlier work in discourse analysis was done using interviews. Indeed, two of the most influential studies (Billig, 1992; Wetherell and Potter, 1992) used interviews to generate most of their data. Conversation analysts and ethnomethodologists have largely rejected interviews as a research tool (although they have been treated as a topic of study). This difference is less pronounced now as discourse researchers have started to accept some of the implications of the critique of interviews (e.g. in Widdicombe and Wooffitt, 1995), and there is an increasing focus on naturalistic materials (as seen in the current chapter).

4   *Resources.* Discourse analysis has had a focus on the resources drawn on in practices as well as the practices themselves. This is seen particularly in early work that studied 'interpretative repertoires' (Potter and Wetherell, 1987). One of the issues at stake is how far such resources can be studied independently of the practices of which they are a part. There is no easy resolution of this. A similar tension is apparent in Sacks's early interest in membership categorization analysis and the later emphasis on sequential analysis. In his introduction to the lectures, Schegloff suggests that the later Sacks is more coherent and is less open to a promiscuous proliferation of interpretations. Nevertheless, the membership categorization tradition continues to be influential (Lepper, 2000).

5   *Epistemology.* Discourse analysis has been strongly influenced by work in the sociology of scientific knowledge, and has often adopted a methodologically relativist position. Indeed, discourse analysts have provided some of the most explicit defences of relativism in recent social science (Edwards et al., 1995). Conversation analysts in particular have tended to take a more robust view of science and knowledge. Ethnomethodological researchers have a position of considerable complexity that is different from CA in some respects, but not one that chimes with the relativist thinking from discourse analysis (Lynch, 1993). There are certainly differences here, although they are mainly at the level of meta-theory. They are unlikely to make a major difference to research practice. Whether a relativist or not, there is still the issue of how to make a coherent choice between different analytic claims, say.

The examples we have given above relate to validation through considering participants' orientations and deviant cases. However, an important part of the process involves readers' evaluations. There are various arenas for this. The various conference presentations we gave offered researchers from a variety of different perspectives the opportunity to suggest different accounts of what was going on in the material (and their effectiveness in doing this is marked by the extent to which the paper changed from its earliest draft). Then the journal referees who considered the submitted paper had the opportunity for the most intensive and consequential read. For example, the editor and referees at *Research in*

Language and Social Interaction provided several pages of detailed comment and some reanalysis. The general point, though, is that in this kind of work the materials under analysis are presented as carefully and completely as is feasible given constraints of space and time. In conference settings we gave out the extracts on handouts and played the sound (suitably anonymized). The submitted article contained a range of examples. This gives the readers the opportunity of not merely being unconvinced by the analysis but finding features that contradict it. This is a different kind of challenge, and a different style of validity from that found in a lot of other areas of social science and psychology.

APPLICATION AND UTILITY

Application and utility are tricky areas. But they are important and often neglected, so they are worth dwelling on at the end of this chapter. We are cautious about the assumption that utility is necessarily a good thing, or is the proper test of good work. The danger is of losing sight of broader political questions about *who* is using the work and for *what*. Some of the most challenging social science is not usable in a clear way; but it might do something else, such as offer a different vision of social organization and social change. In the discourse area, we would see Michael Billig's (1992) *Talking of the Royal Family* as an excellent example of this. It offers an alternative way of understanding conversation, ideology and the way social relations are legitimated.

Our own study might seem to be rather more tightly focused and small-scale than this. Indeed, I (JP) had an interesting discussion with a PhD researcher (Mandi Hodges) who was concerned (!) about its lack of practical use. Let us try to address that. It is quite complicated. Application is often measured against a picture of the application of knowledge that does not work in natural science, let alone social science. Social scientists are often surprised about how difficult it is to chart specific applications from specific advances in the natural or biological sciences (Potter, 1982).

Our study of abuse call openings is very specific and detailed; yet it has a broader theoretical aim, which is to contribute to a body of discursive psychology that is questioning the way cognition is understood in psychology (e.g. Edwards, 1997). This broader intellectual and scientific debate about how persons and psychological stuff should be conceptualized and analysed seems to be fundamental in psychology and social science. The outcome (whatever it is) will be hugely influential not just for specific research, but for the way disciplines such as psychology input into social services, education, organizational life, counselling, and so on. This is a big practical consequence – although this one paper, of course, will not do much on its own. This is a debate being shaped by many participants with different styles of research and positions.

Nevertheless, (with apologies to Mandi) the Mandi Hodges challenge can still be directed at the study. Let us sharpen it up. The suggestion is that the paper seems to be all about talk, and little bits of it at that, but somehow missing the vulnerable children that are the whole point of it all. How might it actually help the NSPCC do their job? Here are some thoughts.

First, and most specifically, the paper helps us understand why certain callers might get into trouble. For example, the one call opening in our corpus that deviates from both the canonical pattern and its standard alternatives was made by a young child. Note the way she announces the nature of the abuse in the opening (line 5); and note that the CPO is then in a position of doing something tricky which is asking for the basis of this knowledge (lines 13–14). Although the NSPCC need this information to be able to follow up on a call like this adequately, it is still easily heard as displaying a sceptical stance to the child.

BN Two 12-year-old girls

1	CPO:	Alright Kath↑ryn (.) .hh so
2		wha-what's goin on:.
3	Caller:	Well .hh what it i:s: (.) is I've
4		got a really close friend an: (.)
5		li:ke hhh (0.3) she's been
6		sexually abu:sed. an (.)
7	CPO:	Mm↓[mm:,]
8	Caller:	[she's] really close to me
9		a-an I just- (0.1) I wanna
10		tell 'er mum but I can't bring
11		myself to do it.
12		(0.4)
13	CPO:	tch.hh so:: ↑how did you find
14		↑out about that.=

The paper provides an analytically grounded account of why problems might appear in calls such as this, and therefore suggests directions for thinking about how CPOs might counter them.

More broadly, discourse studies of this kind aim to explicate the organization of NSPCC calls, and the different sorts of business done by that organization. Understanding this should make a positive input into training. One of the limitations of training for work like that done by the CPOs is that it is often based on idealizations or suppositions about the way interaction works. We found that elsewhere in a study of focus group moderation – the claims in training manuals are often quite different from what we identified as good practice (Puchta and Potter, 2004). One thing we found with this project was that the initial practical input was rather simple. We were able to provide CPOs with a set of digitized and roughly transcribed calls on a CD that they could play in their own PC (stopping and starting, dipping into, and so on). Some of the CPOs found that the facility to reflect on her or his own practice was very helpful. We hope that towards the end of the research we can provide more sophisticated training aids that allow CPOs to step through digitized calls with analytic observations and suggestions about them (e.g. about trouble and its solution). Silverman (1998) has argued that practical input into training of this kind is an important way for the application of interaction research. The aim of these kinds of practical interventions is not to tell the CPOs how to do their job better, but to provide one sort of resource that they can draw on in their training and practice and which is helpful.

ACKNOWLEDGEMENTS

We would like to thank Anssi Peräkylä, David Silverman and Teun van Dijk for helpful comments on an earlier version of this chapter. We would also like to thank all the people at the NSPCC – particularly John Cameron and Ann Johnson, and the various child protection officers – who generously offered time and trust for the research discussed here. This work was supported by a Fellowship from the Leverhulme Trust awarded to the first author.

REFERENCES

Antaki, C. (2000) 'Two rhetorical uses of the description "chat"', *M/C: A Journal of Media and Culture*, 3. http://www.api-network.com/mc/0008/uses.html

Ashmore, M. (1989) *The Reflexive Thesis: Wrighting Sociology of Scientific Knowledge*. Chicago: University of Chicago Press.

Billig, M. (1992) *Talking of the Royal Family*. London: Routledge.

Billig, M. (1999) 'Whose terms? Whose ordinariness? Rhetoric and ideology in conversation analysis', *Discourse and Society*, 10: 543–58.

Button, G. and Sharrock, W. (1993) 'A disagreement over agreement and consensus in constructionist sociology', *Journal for the Theory of Social Behaviour*, 23(1): 1–25.

Chalmers, A. (1992) *What Is This Thing Called Science? An Assessment of the Nature and Status of Science and Its Methods* (2nd ed.). Milton Keynes: Open University Press.

Edwards, D. (1995a) 'Two to tango: script formulations, dispositions, and rhetorical symmetry in relationship troubles talk', *Research on Language and Social Interaction*, 28(4): 319–50.

Edwards, D. (1995b) 'Sacks and psychology', *Theory and Psychology*, 5: 579–96.

Edwards, D. (1997) *Discourse and Cognition*. London: Sage.

Edwards, D. (1998) 'The relevant thing about her: social identity categories in use', in C. Antaki and S. Widdicombe (eds), *Identities in Talk*. London: Sage, pp. 15–33.

Edwards, D. and Potter, J. (1992) *Discursive Psychology*. London: Sage.

Edwards, D., Ashmore, M. and Potter, J. (1995) 'Death and furniture: the rhetoric, politics, and theology of bottom line arguments against relativism', *History of the Human Sciences*, 8: 25–49.

Feyerabend, P. (1975), *Against Method*. London: New Left Books.

Garfinkel, H. (1967) *Studies in Ethnomethodology*. Englewood Cliffs, NJ: Prentice-Hall.

Garfinkel, H. (2002) *Ethnomethodology's Program: Working Out Durkheim's Aphorism*. Lanham, MD; Rowman & Littlefield.

Hepburn, A. (2003). *An Introduction to Critical Social Psychology*. London: Sage.

Heritage, J.C. (1984) 'A change-of-state token and aspects of its sequential placement', in J.M. Atkinson and J. Heritage (eds), *Structures of Social Action: Studies in Conversation Analysis*. Cambridge: Cambridge University Press, pp. 299–346.

Heritage, J.C. (1997) 'Conversation analysis and institutional talk: analysing data', in D. Silverman (ed.), *Qualitative Research: Theory, Method and Practice*. London: Sage, pp. 161–82.

Heritage, J.C. and Greatbatch, D.L. (1991) 'On the institutional character of institutional talk: the case of news interviews', in D. Boden and D.H. Zimmerman (eds), *Talk and Social Structure: Studies in Ethnomethodology and Conversation Analysis*. Oxford: Polity Press, pp. 93–137.

Hutchby, I. and Wooffitt, R. (1998) *Conversation Analysis: Principles, Practices and Applications*. Cambridge: Polity Press.

Lepper, G. (2000) *Categories in Text and Talk*. London: Sage.

Lynch, M. (1993). *Scientific Practice and Ordinary Action: Ethnomethodology and Social Studies of Science*. Cambridge: Cambridge University Press.

Mulkay, M. (1979) *Science and the Sociology of Knowledge*. London: Allen & Unwin.

Phillips, L.J. and Jorgenson, M.W. (2002) *Discourse Analysis as Theory and Method*. London: Sage.

Pomerantz, A.M. (1984) 'Agreeing and disagreeing with assessments: some features of preferred/dispreferred turn shapes', in J.M. Atkinson and J. Heritage (eds), *Structures of Social Action: Studies in Conversation Analysis*. Cambridge: Cambridge University Press, pp. 57–101.

Pomerantz, A. (1990/1) 'Mental concepts in the analysis of social action', *Research on Language and Social Interaction*, 24: 299–310.

Potter, J. (1982) 'Nothing so practical as a good theory: the problematic application of social psychology', in P. Stringer (ed.), *Confronting Social Issues: Applications of Social Psychology*. London: Academic Press, pp. 23–49.

Potter, J. (1996) *Representing Reality: Discourse, Rhetoric and Social Construction*. London: Sage.

Potter, J. (2002) 'Two kinds of natural', *Discourse Studies*, 4: 539–42.

Potter, J. (2003) 'Discourse analysis and discursive psychology', in P.M. Camic, J.E. Rhodes and L. Yardley (eds), *Qualitative Research in Psychology: Expanding Perspectives in Methodology and Design*. Washington, DC: American Psychological Association, pp. 73–94.

Potter, J. (in press) 'Discourse analysis', in M. Hardy and A. Bryman (eds), *Handbook of Data Analysis*. London: Sage.

Potter, J. and Edwards, D. (2003) 'Rethinking cognition: on Coulter, discourse and mind', *Human Studies*, in press.

Potter, J. & Hepburn, A. (2003). ' "I'm a bit concerned" – Early actions and psychological constructions in a child protection helpline', *Research on Language and Social Interaction*, in press.

Potter, J. and Wetherell, M. (1987) *Discourse and Social Psychology: Beyond Attitudes and Behaviour*. London: Sage.

Puchta, C. and Potter, J. (2004) *Focus Group Practice*. London: Sage.

Roffe, M. (1996) 'The social organisation of social work'. PhD thesis, Loughborough University.

Sacks, H. (1963) 'Sociological description', *Berkeley Journal of Sociology*, 8: 1–16.

Sacks, H. (1992) *Lectures on Conversation*, vols I and II, ed. G. Jefferson. Oxford: Basil Blackwell.

Schegloff, E.A. (1991) 'Conversation analysis and socially shared cognition', in L. Resnick, J. Levine and S. Teasley (eds), *Perspectives on Socially Shared Cognition*. Washington, DC: American Psychological Association, pp. 150–71.

Schegloff, E.A. (1997) 'Whose text? Whose context?', *Discourse and Society*, 8: 165–87.

Schegloff, E.A. (1999) '"Schegloff's texts" as "Billig's data": a critical reply', *Discourse and Society*, 10: 558–72.

Silverman, D. (1997) *Discourses of Counselling: HIV Counselling as Social Interaction*. London: Sage.

Silverman, D. (1998) *Harvey Sacks: Social Science and Conversation Analysis*. Oxford: Polity Press

Smith, D. (1990) *Texts, Facts and Femininity: Exploring the Relations of Ruling*. London: Routledge.

te Molder, H. and Potter, J. (eds) (in press) *Talk and Cognition: Discourse, Mind and Social Interaction*. Cambridge: Cambridge University Press.

ten Have, P. (1998) *Doing Conversation Analysis*. London: Sage.

van Dijk, T.A. (1996a) *Discourse as Structure and Process* (vol. 1 of *Discourse Studies: A Multidisciplinary Introduction*). London: Sage.

van Dijk, T.A. (1996b) *Discourse as Social Interaction* (vol. 2 of *Discourse Studies: A Multidisciplinary Introduction*). London: Sage.

Wetherell, M. (1998) 'Positioning and interpretative repertoires: conversation analysis and post-structuralism in dialogue', *Discourse and Society*, 9: 387–412.

Wetherell, M. and Potter, J. (1992) *Mapping the Language of Racism: Discourse and the Legitimation of Exploitation*. Brighton: Harvester/Wheatsheaf; New York: Columbia University Press.

Wetherell, M., Taylor, S. and Yates, S.J. (eds) (2001) *Discourse Theory and Practice: A Reader*. London: Sage.

Widdicombe, S. and Wooffitt, R. (1995) *The Language of Youth Subcultures: Social Identity in Action*. London: Harvester/Wheatsheaf.

Wiggins, S. (2002) 'Talking with your mouth full: gustatory *mmms* and the embodiment of pleasure', *Research on Language and Social Interaction*, 35: 311–36.

13

Critical discourse analysis

Ruth Wodak

In this chapter, I first attempt to provide an overview of some important approaches to critical discourse analysis, as well as a methodology for analysing data from a CDA perspective. Specifically, I will focus on central concepts and terms and present a short summary of the historical development of critical discourse analysis. Owing to problems of space, it will be impossible to illustrate all the different approaches with concrete examples; I will have to refer readers to other research and references where examples are elaborated and discussed.[1] Secondly, I will exemplify important dimensions of our own theory and methodology, the 'discourse-historical approach', and discuss some of the most important issues of applying CDA to specific research questions and text analysis.[2]

The terms 'critical linguistics' (CL) and 'critical discourse analysis' (CDA) are often used interchangeably. In fact, recently the term CDA seems to have been preferred and is being used to denote the theory formerly identified as CL. Thus, I will continue to use CDA exclusively in this chapter (see Anthonissen, 2001, for an extensive discussion of these terms). The roots of CDA lie in concepts of rhetoric, text linguistics and sociolinguistics, as well as in applied linguistics and pragmatics.

'PERSONAL' HISTORY AND THE DEVELOPMENT OF THE 'CDA GROUP'

I myself was educated as a sociolinguist in the 1970s. The relationship between language and society, broadly speaking, became the focus of this new paradigm, quite in opposition to the Chomskyan approach or to other grammar theories (Leodolter, 1975). At that time, many debates were manifest, such as between Jürgen Habermas and Noam Chomsky, or between the quantitative and qualitative paradigms in the social sciences (see Cicourel, 1974). I realized at that time that the study of language, isolated from any context, would not give insights into social processes. Moreover, the interpretation of isolated utterances was usually vague and ambiguous. This turn to the social sciences and away from formal linguistics ultimately led to CDA. However, I have always retained important characteristics of sociolinguistics such as fieldwork and ethnography; moreover the application of multiple methods is relevant when studying discourses as well (see Wodak, 1996a, 1996b).

CDA as a whole network of scholars emerged in the early 1990s, following a small symposium in Amsterdam in January 1991. Through the support of the University of Amsterdam, Teun van Dijk, Norman Fairclough, Gunther Kress, Theo van Leeuwen and I spent two days together, and had the wonderful opportunity to discuss theories and methods of discourse analysis, specifically CDA. The meeting made it possible to confront with each other the very distinct and different approaches that are relevant nowadays. In this process of group formation, differences and sameness were laid out – differences towards other theories and methodologies in discourse analysis (see Titscher et al., 2000), and sameness in a programmatic way, which could frame the differing theoretical approaches of the various schools (see Wodak and Meyer, 2001). Basically, CDA as a school or paradigm is characterized through a programmatic set of principles (see below). Moreover, it is characterized by the common interests in demystifying ideologies and power through the systematic investigation of semiotic data, be they written, spoken or visual. CDA researchers also attempt to make their own perspectives explicit while retaining their respective scientific methodologies.

The start of the CDA network is also marked through the launch of van Dijk's journal *Discourse and Society* (1990) as well as through several books.[3] The Amsterdam meeting determined an institutional start, an attempt both to constitute an exchange programme (Erasmus, for three years)[4] as well as multiple joint projects and collaborations between scholars of different countries and a special issue of *Discourse and Society* (1993), which presented the above-mentioned approaches. Since then new journals have appeared, multiple overviews have been written, and nowadays CDA is an established paradigm in linguistics.

IDEOLOGY, POWER, DISCOURSE AND CRITIQUE

Deconstructing the label of this research programme – I view CDA basically as a research programme, the reasons for which I will explain below – entails that we have to define what CDA means when employing the terms 'critical' and 'discourse'. Most recently, Michael Billig (2003) has clearly pointed to the fact that CDA has become an established academic discipline with the same rituals and institutional practices as all other academic disciplines. Ironically, he asks the question whether this might mean that CDA has become 'uncritical' – or if the use of acronyms such as CDA might serve the same purposes as in other traditional, non-critical disciplines, namely, to exclude outsiders and to mystify the functions and intentions of the research. I cannot answer Billig's questions extensively in this chapter. But I do believe that he points to potentially very fruitful and necessary debates for CDA.

At this point, I would like to stress that CDA has never been and has never attempted to be or to provide one single or specific theory. Neither is one specific methodology characteristic of research in CDA. Quite the contrary, studies in CDA are multifarious, derived from quite different theoretical backgrounds, oriented towards different data and methodologies. Researchers in CDA also rely on a variety of grammatical approaches. The definitions of the terms 'discourse', 'critical', 'ideology', 'power' and so on are also manifold. Thus, any criticism of CDA should always specify which research or researcher they relate to. I myself would suggest

using the notion of a 'school' for CDA, or of a programme, which many researchers find useful and to which they can relate. This programme or set of principles has changed over the years (see Fairclough and Wodak, 1997).

Such a heterogeneous school might be confusing for some; on the other hand, it allows for open discussions and debates, for changes in the aims and goals, and for innovation. In contrast to 'total and closed' theories, such as for example Chomsky's generative transformational grammar or Michael Halliday's systemic functional linguistics, CDA has never had the image of a 'sect' and does not want to have such an image.

The heterogeneity of methodological and theoretical approaches that can be found in this field would tend to confirm van Dijk's point that CDA and CL 'are at most a shared perspective on doing linguistic, semiotic or discourse analysis' (van Dijk, 1993: 253). Below, I summarize some of these principles, which are adhered to by most researchers.

CDA sees 'language as social practice' (Fairclough and Wodak, 1997), and considers the 'context of language use' to be crucial (Benke, 2000; Wodak, 2000):

> CDA sees discourse – language use in speech and writing – as a form of 'social practice'. Describing discourse as social practice implies a dialectical relationship between a particular discursive event and the situation(s), institution(s) and social structure(s), which frame it: The discursive event is shaped by them, but it also shapes them. That is, discourse is socially constitutive as well as socially conditioned – it constitutes situations, objects of knowledge, and the social identities of and relationships between people and groups of people. It is constitutive both in the sense that it helps to sustain and reproduce the social status quo, and in the sense that it contributes to transforming it. Since discourse is so socially consequential, it gives rise to important issues of power. Discursive practices may have major ideological effects – that is, they can help produce and reproduce unequal power relations between (for instance) social classes, women and men, and ethnic/cultural majorities and minorities through the ways in which they represent things and position people. (Fairclough and Wodak, 1997: 258)

Of course, the term 'discourse' is used very differently by different researchers and also in different academic cultures. In the German and Central European context, a distinction is made between 'text' and 'discourse', relating to the tradition in text linguistics as well as to rhetoric (see Vass, 1992; Brünner and Gräfen, 1994; Wodak, 1996a, for summaries). In the English-speaking world, 'discourse' is often used both for written and oral texts (see Schiffrin, 1994). Other researchers distinguish between different levels of abstractness: Lemke (1995) defines 'text' as the concrete realization of abstract forms of knowledge ('discourse'), thus adhering to a more Foucaultian approach (see also Jäger, 2001).

In the discourse-historical approach, we elaborate and link to the socio-cognitive theory of Teun van Dijk (1985, 1993, 1998) and view 'discourse' as a form of knowledge and memory of social practices, whereas 'text' illustrates concrete oral utterances or written documents (Reisigl and Wodak, 2001).

The shared perspective and programme of CDA relate to the term 'critical', which in the work of some 'critical linguists' could be traced to the influence of the Frankfurt School and Jürgen Habermas (Fay, 1987: 203; Thompson, 1988: 71ff.; Anthonissen, 2001). Nowadays this concept is conventionally used in a broader sense, denoting, as Krings argues, the practical linking of 'social and political engagement' with 'a sociologically informed construction of society' (Krings et al., 1973: 808). Hence 'critique' is essentially 'making visible the interconnectedness of things' (Fairclough, 1995: 747; see also Connerton, 1976: 11–39). The reference to the contribution of critical theory to the understanding of CDA and the notions of 'critical' and 'ideology' are of particular importance (see Anthonissen, 2001, for an extensive discussion of this issue).[5]

Critical theories, and thus also CDA, are afforded special standing as guides for human action. They are aimed at producing 'enlightenment and emancipation'. Such theories seek not only to describe and explain, but also to root out a particular kind of delusion. Even with differing concepts of ideology, critical theory seeks to create awareness in agents of their own needs and interests. This was, of course, also taken up by Pierre Bourdieu's concepts of 'violence symbolique' and 'méconnaissance' (Bourdieu, 1989). One of the aims of CDA is to 'demystify' discourses by deciphering ideologies.

In agreement with its critical theory predecessors, CDA emphasizes the need for interdisciplinary work in order to gain a proper understanding of how language functions in constituting and transmitting knowledge, in organizing social institutions or in exercising power (see Graham, 2002; Lemke, 2002; Martin, 2003; van Dijk, 2003).

An important perspective in CDA related to the notion of 'power' is that it is very rare that a text is the work of any one person. In texts discursive differences are negotiated; they are governed by differences in power, which is in part encoded in and determined by discourse and by genre. Therefore texts are often sites of struggle in that they show traces of differing discourses and ideologies contending and struggling for dominance.

Thus, defining features of CDA are its concern with power as a central condition in social life, and its efforts to develop a theory of language, which incorporates this as a major premise. Not only the notion of struggles for power and control, but also the intertextuality and recontextualization of competing discourses in various public spaces and genres, are closely attended to (Iedema, 1997, 1999; Muntigl et al., 2000). Power is about relations of difference, and particularly about the effects of differences in social structures. The constant unity of language and other social matters ensures that language is entwined in social power in a number of ways: language indexes power, expresses power, is involved where there is contention over and a challenge to power. Power does not derive from language, but language can be used to challenge power, to subvert it, to alter distributions of power in the short and the long term. Language provides a finely articulated vehicle for differences in power in hierarchical social structures.

CDA might be defined as fundamentally interested in analysing opaque as well as transparent structural relationships of dominance, discrimination, power and control as manifested in language. In other words, CDA aims to investigate critically social inequality as it is expressed, constituted, legitimized, and so on, by language use (or in discourse). Most critical discourse analysts would thus endorse Habermas's claim that 'language is also a medium of domination and social force. It serves to legitimize relations of organized power. Insofar as the legitimizations of power relations ... are not articulated, ... language is also ideological' (Habermas, 1967: 259).

SOME PRINCIPLES OF CRITICAL DISCOURSE ANALYSIS

1 The approach is interdisciplinary. Problems in our societies are too complex to be studied from a single perspective. This entails different dimensions of interdisciplinarity: the theories draw on neighbouring disciplines and try to integrate these theories. Teamwork consists of different researchers from different traditionally defined disciplines working together. Lastly, the methodologies are also adapted to the data under investigation.

2   The approach is problem-oriented, rather than focused on specific linguistic items. Social problems are the items of research, such as 'racism, identity, social change', which, of course, are and could be studied from manifold perspectives. The CDA dimension – discourse and text analysis – is one of many possible approaches.

3   The theories as well as the methodologies are eclectic, i.e. theories and methods are integrated that are adequate for an understanding and explanation of the object under investigation.

4   The study always incorporates fieldwork and ethnography to explore the object under investigation (study from the inside) as a precondition for any further analysis and theorizing. This approach makes it possible to avoid 'fitting the data to illustrate a theory'. Rather, we deal with bottom-up and top-down approaches at the same time.

5   The approach is abductive: a constant movement back and forth between theory and empirical data is necessary. This is a prerequisite for principle 4.

6   Multiple genres and multiple public spaces are studied, and intertextual and interdiscursive relationships are investigated. Recontextualization is the most important process in connecting these genres as well as topics and arguments (*topoi*). In our postmodern societies, we are dealing with hybrid and innovative genres, as well as with new notions of 'time', 'identity' and 'space'. All these notions have undergone significant change; for example, 'fragmented' identities have replaced the notion of 'holistic identities'.

7   The historical context is always analysed and integrated into the interpretation of discourses and texts. The notion of 'change' (see principle 6) has become inherent in the study of text and discourse.

8   The categories and tools for the analysis are defined in accordance with all these steps and procedures and also with the specific problem under investigation. This entails some eclecticism as well as pragmatism. Different approaches in CDA use different grammatical theories, although many apply systemic functional linguistics in some way or other.

9   Grand theories might serve as a foundation; in the specific analysis, Middle-Range Theories serve the aims better. The problem-oriented approach entails the use and testing of Middle-Range Theories. Grand Theories result in large gaps between structure/context and linguistic realizations (although some gaps must remain unbridgeable).

10   Practice and application are aimed at. The results should be made available to experts in different fields and, as a second step, be applied, with the goal of changing certain discursive and social practices.

MAIN RESEARCH AGENDA

In this section, I provide a short overview of the most important research agenda and theoretical as well as empirical approaches in CDA. All the above-mentioned scholars and schools relate to the principles laid out in the previous section, but with different priorities due to their specific interests.

Language of the New Capitalism

Fairclough (1989) sets out the social theories underpinning CDA, and as in other early critical linguistic work, a variety of textual examples are analysed to illustrate the field, its aims and methods of analysis. Later, Fairclough (1992, 1995) and Chouliaraki and Fairclough (1999) explain and elaborate some advances in CDA, showing not only how the analytical framework for researching language in relation to power and ideology developed, but also how CDA is useful in disclosing the discursive nature of much contemporary social and cultural change. In particular, the language of the mass media is scrutinized as a site of power, of struggle, and also as a site where language is often apparently transparent. Media institutions often purport to be neutral, in that they provide space for public discourse, reflect states of affairs disinterestedly, and give the perceptions and arguments of the newsmakers. Fairclough shows the fallacy of such assumptions, and illustrates the mediating and constructing role of the media with a variety of examples.

Fairclough has also been concerned with the 'language of New Labour' (2000). His most recent work has been centred around the theme of language in New Capitalism – focusing on language/discourse aspects of the contemporary restructuring and 're-scaling' (shift in relations between global, regional, national and local) of capitalism. The book with Lilie Chouliaraki (1999) specifically marked something of a shift in his version of CDA towards a greater centring of social practices, seeing discourse as a moment of social practices dialectically interconnected with other moments. Fairclough has also worked with sociological theorists Bob Jessop and

Andrew Sayer in theorizing language ('semiosis') within a critical realist philosophy of (social) science. Fairclough's grammatical tools relate to Halliday's systemic functional linguistics (1985), as well as to conversation analysis. Rarely does Fairclough undertake fieldwork himself. His examples most frequently illustrate theoretical claims; he has less interest in representative sampling or in the reliability or validity of bodies of data.

Phil Graham elaborates the research on the problems of New Capitalism (Graham, 2002, 2003). The historical investigation of hortatory genres compares the emergence and struggles between Church, 'divine right' monarchs and secular forces over legitimate uses of the sermon form in Western Europe between the tenth and fourteenth centuries with contemporary struggles over genres that are used to motivate people on a mass scale. The main focus of the study is to explore and explain the relationships between new media, new genres, institutions and social change at a macro level. The perspective is primarily historical, political-economic, relational and dynamic. Genres are produced, textured and transformed within institutional contexts over long periods of time. In turn, institutions invest years – in some cases millennia – developing, maintaining and adapting generic forms to changing social conditions in order to maintain or to gain power. Graham believes that at certain times in history, certain genres become very effective for motivating or manipulating large sections of society. Because genres are developed within institutions, and thus within the realms of vested interests, they display inherent axiological biases.

The second project (Graham, 2003) synthesizes perspectives from Marx's political economy, new media theory and critical discourse analysis to investigate relationships between new media, language and social perceptions of value. The corpus for the research is 'new economy' policies with the ostensive purpose of promoting the widespread use of new information and communication technologies (ICTs). The nature of knowledge and its status as a commodity form immediately become problematic. In the tradition of dialectical argumentation, Graham accepts the claims that knowledge can become a dominant commodity form; that a global economy can be built on such forms; and that our new media must, in some fundamental way, underpin the emergence of this new form of political economy. The research problem is therefore formulated as a historical investigation into the relationship between language, new media and social perceptions of value.

The socio-cognitive approach

Teun van Dijk's earlier work in text linguistics and discourse analysis (1977, 1981) manifests the interest he takes in texts and discourses as basic units and social practices. Like other critical linguistic theorists, he traces the origins of linguistic interest in units of language larger than sentences and in text- and context-dependency of meanings. Van Dijk and Kintsch (1983) considered the relevance of discourse to the study of language processing. Their development of a cognitive model of discourse understanding in individuals gradually developed into cognitive models for explaining the construction of meaning at a societal level. Van Dijk turns specifically to media discourse, giving not only his own reflection on communication in the mass media (van Dijk, 1986), but also bringing together the theories and applications of a variety of scholars interested in the production, uses and functions of media discourses (van Dijk, 1985). In critically analysing various kinds of discourses that encode prejudice, van Dijk's interest is in developing a theoretical model that will explain cognitive discourse processing mechanisms (Wodak and van Dijk, 2000).

After his earlier work on discourse and racism, Teun van Dijk generalized his interest in racist ideologies towards a more general, multidisciplinary project on ideology (van Dijk, 1998). In this book, intended as the first of several others on ideology, he develops a new theory of ideology, in terms of an account of the socio-cognitive, societal and discursive dimensions of ideology. He defines ideologies as the axiomatic basis of the social representations of a social group, controlling more specific, socially shared group attitudes and, indirectly, the opinions of the group members, and hence their actions. He especially insists that further work on ideologies needs to explore in greater depth the detailed structures of the mental representation of ideologies and their relations to group attitudes and knowledge. These structures probably reflect the basic properties of the societal position of a group in relation to other groups, and may consist of a social group self-schema with a limited number of characteristic categories, such as the typical actions, aims, norms and resources of a group. The ultimate aim of this long-term project is to provide a detailed theory of the ways in which ideologies are expressed and reproduced by discourse. Most recently, Teun van Dijk has taken up a more detailed study of the role of knowledge in discourse. A third topic in his research is a new approach to the study of context. One of the main arguments of this research is that there is much interest in context and contextualization, but hardly any in theory of context. Van Dijk proposes to define context in terms of context models in episodic memory, that is, in terms of subjective, dynamic representations of the ongoing communicative event and situation. It is these context models that, in van Dijk's view, control all discourse and communication, and especially all dimensions of discourse that adapt it to the current situation – as it is understood by the participants – such as style and rhetoric (van Dijk, 2001).

Multimodality

Recognition of the contribution of all the aspects of the communicative context to text meaning, as well as a growing awareness in media studies generally of the importance of non-verbal aspects of texts, has turned attention to semiotic devices in discourse other than the linguistic ones. In particular, the theory put forward by Kress and van Leeuwen (1996) should be mentioned here, as this provides a useful framework for considering the communicative potential of visual devices in the media (see Anthonissen, 2001; Scollon, 2001). Van Leeuwen studied film and television production as well as Hallidayan linguistics. His principal publications are concerned with topics such as the intonation of disc jockeys and newsreaders, the language of television interviews and newspaper reporting and, more recently, the semiotics of visual communication and music. Van Leeuwen developed a most influential methodological tool: the actor's analysis (1993). This taxonomy allows for the analysis of (both written and oral) data, related to agency in a very differentiated and validated way. The taxonomy has since then been widely applied in data analysis.

Recently, Van Leeuwen has focused on some areas of visual communication, especially the semiotics of handwriting and typography and the question of colour. He is increasingly moving away from using a systemic-functional approach as the single model and feels that it is important for social semiotics to realize that semiotic discourses and methods are linked to semiotic practices, and that grammars are one type of semiotic discourse that is linked to a specific kind of control over specific kinds of semiotic practices. To give an example of a very different type of discourse, histories of art and design focus on the semiotic innovations of specific individuals in their historical contexts, rather than on a synchronous approach to semiotic systems. However, they, too, are linked to the specific ways in which production and consumption is regulated

in that area. It is important for social semiotics to provide models of semiotic practice that are appropriate to the practices they model, and as different semiotic practices are very differently organized, it is not possible to apply a single model to all. All of this is closely related to the role and status of semiotic practices in society, and this is currently undergoing change as a result of the fact that it is increasingly global corporations and semiotic technologies, rather than national institutions, that regulate semiotic production and consumption.

This emphasis on regulatory practices has led to a research approach in three stages, starting with the analysis of a particular category of texts, cultural artefacts or communicative events, then moving to a second set of texts (and/or cultural artefacts and/or communicative events), namely those that seek to regulate the production and consumption of the first set, and finally moving to a third set of texts, namely actual instances of producing or consuming texts (etc.) belonging to the first set. For instance, in a study of baby toys, van Leeuwen and his team analysed the toys and their semiotic potential, as objects-for-use and as cultural icons, then studied discourses seeking to influence how they are used, e.g. relevant sections of parenting books and magazines, toy advertisements, texts on toy packaging, etc., and finally transcribed analysed videos of mothers and babies using these same toys together (Caldas-Coulthard and van Leeuwen, 2001). This type of work leads to a particular relation between discourse analysis, ethnography, history and theory in which these disciplines are no longer contributing to the whole through some kind of indefinable synergy or triangulation, but are complementary in quite specific ways.

Jay Lemke and Ron and Suzie Scollon also have to be mentioned in this context. In the last few years Lemke's work has emphasized multimedia semiotics, multiple time scales and hypertexts/traversals. He extended his earlier work on embedded ideologies in social communication from analysis of verbal text to integration of verbal text with visual images and other presentational media, with a particular focus on evaluative meanings. This work emphasizes the implicit value systems and their connections to institutional and personal identity.

The work on multiple time scales is an extension of earlier work on ecological-social systems as complex dynamic systems with semiotic cultures. It is very important in considering all aspects of social dynamics to consider looking across multiple time scales, i.e., how processes and practices that take place at relatively faster rates are organized within the framework of more slowly changing features of social institutions and cultures. This is a promising practical approach to the so-called micro/macro problem, both theoretically and methodologically (Lemke, 2000, 2001). His newest work has combined both these themes to develop the idea that although we tell our lives as narratives, we experience them as hypertexts. Building on research on the semantic resources of hypertext as a medium, he proposed that postmodern life-styles are increasingly liberated from particular institutional roles and that we tend to move, on multiple time scales, from involvement in one institution to another, creating new kinds of meaning, less bound to fixed genres and registers, as we 'surf' across channels, websites and lived experiences. This is seen as a new historical development, not supplanting institutions, but building up new socio-cultural possibilities on and over them.

In all this work, Lemke uses critical social semiotics as an extension of critical discourse analysis, combined with models of the material base of emergent social phenomena. His concern is with social and cultural change: how it happens, how it is constrained, and the ways in which is it expectedly unpredictable.

The problem that Ron and Suzie Scollon address in recent work is to build a formal theoretical and a practical link between discourse and action. It is an activist position that uses tools and strategies of engaged discourse analysis and thus requires a formal analysis of how its own actions can be accomplished through discourse and its analysis. The problems in developing this framework are that action is always multiple, both in the sense that there are always simultaneous parallel and interacting actions at any moment we choose to analyse, as well as in the sense that these multiple actions operate across differing time scales so that it is not at all clear that we can see 'higher level' actions as simple composites of 'lower level' actions. The linkages are more complex. Jay Lemke's work is, of course, an important resource in looking into this problem.

Ron Scollon's recent work furthers the idea developed in *Mediated Discourse: The Nexus of Practice* (2001), that practice in general is most usefully understood as many separate practices that are linked in a nexus of practice. The relations between discourse and a nexus of practice are many and complex and rarely direct. His current interest is in trying to open up and explicate these linkages through what could be called nexus analysis. This work is now being carried out in two projects. In the first, which Ron and Suzie Scollon have written about in *Discourses*

in Place: Language in the Material World (2002), is a kind of geosemiotics that is the integration of social interactionist theory (including, of course, all forms of spoken discourse), visual semiotics (and significantly including text as fixed and therefore visual forms), and 'place semiotics', especially the built environment. Their interest in this work has been to theorize the link between indexicality in language (and discourse and semiotics more generally) and the indexable in the world. This could also be put as theorizing the link between producers of communications and the material world in which those communications are placed as a necessary element of their semiosis.

Political discourse

National Socialist language became the object of critical philological observations by Viktor Klemperer (Klemperer, 1975). Utz Maas, however, was the first to subject the everyday linguistic practice of National Socialism to an in-depth analysis: he used NS texts to exemplify his approach of '*Lesweisenanalyse*' (Maas, 1984, 1989a, 1989b). His historical 'argumentation analysis', based on the theories of Michel Foucault, demonstrates how discourse is determined by society, i.e. in what may be termed 'a social practice'. In his analysis of language practices during the National Socialist regime between 1932 and 1938 he showed how the discursive practices of society in Germany were impacted by the NS discourse characterized by social-revolutionist undertones. Nazi discourse had superseded almost all forms of language (practices), a fact that made it difficult for an individual who did not want to cherish the tradition of an unworldly Romanticism to use language in a critical-reflective way. Discourse is basically understood as the result of collusion: the conditions of the political, social and linguistic practice impose themselves practically behind the back of the subjects, while the actors do not see through the game (cf. also Bourdieu's 'violence symbolique'). Discourse analysis identifies the rules that make a text, for example, a fascist text. In the same way as grammar characterizes the structure of sentences, discourse rules characterize utterances/texts that are acceptable within a certain practice. The focus is not on National Socialist language per se, but the aim is to record and analyse the spectrum of linguistic relations based on a number of texts dealing with various spheres of life. These texts represent a complicated network of similarities, which overlap and intersect. Therefore it is also important to do justice to the 'polyphony' of texts resulting from the fact that societal contradictions are inscribed into texts. Texts from diverse social and political contexts (cooking recipes, local municipal provisions on agriculture, texts by NS politicians, but also by critics of this ideology, who are ultimately involved in the dominant discourse) are analysed in a sample representative of possible texts of NS discourse.

The method of 'reading analysis' proposed by Maas may be described as a concentric hermeneutic approach to the corpus in five systematic steps: (a) statement of the self-declared content of the text; (b) description of the 'staging' (*Inszenierung*) of the content; (c) analysis of the sense and meaning of the 'staging'; (d) provisional conclusion of the analysis; and (e) development of competing forms of reading (Maas, 1984: 18). In this context it should be stressed that competing readings of texts may result from disclosing the difference between self-declared and latent content. Applications of this method (Titscher et al., 1998: 232) can be found in Januschek's analysis of Jörg Haider's allusions to the NS discourse (Januschek, 1992) and in Sauer's analysis of texts of the Nazi occupation of the Netherlands (Sauer, 1989, 1995).

The Duisburg School of CDA (Jäger and Jäger, 1993; Jäger, 1999) draws on Foucault's notion of discourse. According to Jäger (1999: 116), discourse is 'materiality *sui generis*' and discourse theory is a 'materialistic cultural theory', on the one hand, and Alexej N. Leontjev's 'speech activity theory' (Leontjev, 1984) and Jürgen Link's 'collective symbolism' (Link, 1988), on the other hand. As institutionalized and conventionalized speech modes, discourses express societal power relations, which in turn are influenced by discourses. This 'overall discourse' of society, which could be visualized as a '*diskursives Gewimmel*' (literally, 'discursive swarming'), becomes comprehensible in different discourse strands (composed of discourse fragments from the same subject) at different discourse levels (science, politics, media, and so on). Every discourse is historically embedded, and has repercussions on current and future discourse. In addition to the above levels, the structure of discourse may be dissected into: special discourse versus interdiscourse, discursive events and discursive context, discourse position, overall societal discourse and interwoven discourses, themes, bundles of discourse strands, and history, present and future of discourse strands. DA makes a contribution to (media) impact research, as it analyses the impact of discourse on individual and collective consciousness. Individual discourse fragments that are as characteristic as possible, are selected from the archived material for concrete analysis. Selection is based on a structural analysis of the identified discourse strand. These fragments are analysed in five steps (institutional framework, text 'surface', linguistic-rhetorical means, programmatic-ideological messages, and interpretation), for which a wealth of concrete questions regarding the text is formulated (Jäger, 1999: 175–87). The uniformity of the hegemonic discourse makes it possible that analysis requires only a 'relatively small number of discourse fragments'. Jäger (1999) offers concrete model analyses dealing with everyday racism, the analysis of the 'discourse strand of biopower' in a daily newspaper, and Margret Jäger's analysis of interwoven discourses relating to the 'criticism of patriarchy in immigration discourse'.

Lexicometry

The combination of political science and political philosophy (predominantly under a strong Marxist influence) on the one hand and French linguistics on the other hand is typical of French discourse analysis. Basically, two different approaches may be distinguished. The first is 'political lexicometry', a computer-aided statistical approach to political lexicon, developed at the École Normale Supérieure at Saint-Cloud. A text corpus (e.g. texts of the French Communist Party) is prepared. Texts are then compared on the basis of relative frequency (cf. Bonnafous and Tournier, 1995). One study shows, for example, how the relative frequency of the words '*travailleur*' and '*salarié*' varies significantly between French trade unions, reflecting different political ideologies, and how the frequency changes over time (Groupe de Saint-Cloud, 1982; Bonnafous and Tournier, 1995).

Althusser's ideological theory and Foucault's theory were major points of reference for the second tendency in French discourse analysis, notably the work of Michel Pêcheux (1982). Discourse is the place where language and ideology meet, and discourse analysis is the analysis of ideological dimensions of language use, and of the materialization in language of ideology. Both the words used and the meanings of words vary according to the class struggle position from which they are used – according to the 'discursive formation' they are located within. For instance, the word 'struggle' itself is particularly associated with a working-class political voice, and its meaning in that discursive formation is different from its meanings when used from other positions. Pêcheux's main focus was political discourse in France, especially the relationship between social-democratic and communist discourse within left political discourse. Pêcheux stresses the ideological effects of discursive formations in positioning people as social subjects. Echoing Althusser, he suggests that people are placed in the 'imaginary' position of sources of their discourse, whereas actually their discourse and indeed they themselves are effects of their ideological positioning. The sources and processes of their own positioning are hidden from people. They are typically not aware of speaking/writing from within a particular discursive formation. Moreover, the discursive formations within which people are positioned are themselves shaped by the 'complex whole in dominance' of discursive formations, which Pêcheux calls 'interdiscourse' – but people are not aware of that shaping. Radical change in the way people are positioned in discourse can come only from political revolution.

Pêcheux and his colleagues changed their views on this and other issues in the late 1970s and early 1980s (Maingueneau, 1987; Pêcheux, 1988). The influence of Foucault increased, as did that of Bakhtin. Studies began to emphasize the complex mixing of discursive formations in texts, and the heterogeneity and ambivalence of texts (see, e.g., Courtine, 1981). Some other French researchers investigate detailed rhetorical patterns, for example in the presidential campaigns of 1988 and 1995. The influence of Anglo-Saxon pragmatics is also prominent, and that of the French linguist Benveniste (1996/1974), whose work on 'énonciation' focused on deictic phenomena. In this framework, Achard (1995) produced detailed accounts of the political functioning of a very wide range of text types (see Fairclough and Wodak, 1997, for more details).

THE 'DISCOURSE-HISTORICAL APPROACH'

The study for which the discourse-historical approach was actually developed, first attempted to trace in detail the constitution of an anti-Semitic stereotyped image, or 'Feindbild', as it emerged in public discourse in the 1986 Austrian presidential campaign of Kurt Waldheim (Wodak et al., 1990; Gruber, 1991; Mitten, 1992). In order to be able to study the discourse about the 'Waldheim Affair', 'context' was unravelled into various dimensions. The research team, consisting of six researchers from three different fields (linguistics, psychology and

history), decided in favour of a 'triangulatory approach', which made it possible to focus on the many different genres that were situated in the different political fields of action ('recontextualization') (see Wodak et al., 1990; Wodak, 2001a). The discourse-historical approach has been further elaborated in a number of more recent studies, for example, in a study on racist discrimination against immigrants from Romania and in a study on the discourse about nation and national identity in Austria and in the European Union (Muntigl et al., 2000; Wodak and van Dijk, 2000).

The latter study was concerned with the analysis of the relationships between the discursive construction of national sameness and the discursive construction of difference leading to political and social exclusion of specific out-groups. The findings suggest that discourses about nations and national identities rely on at least four types of discursive macro-strategies. These are constructive strategies (aiming at the construction of national identities), preservative or justificatory strategies (aiming at the conservation and reproduction of national identities or narratives of identity), transformative strategies (aiming at the change of national identities) and destructive strategies (aiming at the dismantling of national identities). Depending on the context – that is to say, on the social field or domain in which the 'discursive events' related to the topic under investigation take place – one or other of the aspects connected with these strategies is brought into prominence.[6] The research on 'Discourse, Politics, Identity' is now located in a research centre at the University of Vienna (see http://www.univie.ac.at/discourse-politics-identity).

Our triangulatory approach is based on a concept of 'context' that takes into account four levels (see Figure 13.1); the first one is descriptive, while the other three levels are part of our theories on context:

- the immediate, language or text internal co-text;
- the intertextual and interdiscursive relationship between utterances, texts, genres and discourses;
- the extralinguistic social/sociological variables and institutional frames of a specific 'context of situation' (Middle-Range Theories);
- the broader socio-political and historical contexts, which the discursive practices are embedded in and related to (Grand Theories).

These levels of context are applied in the analysis of the data and relate to each other. Only by taking the larger context and the co-text of

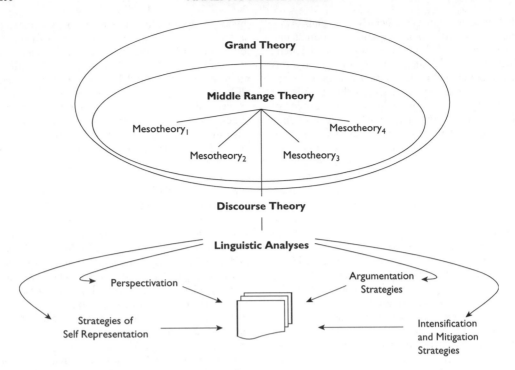

Figure 13.1 *Levels of theories and linguistic analysis.*

utterances into account, is it possible to grasp the intertextuality and interdiscursivity of whole discourses on ethnic groups or on specific persons. Moreover, certain *topoi* are recontextualized from one public domain to the next, but realized through different linguistic devices (Iedema, 1999; Wodak, 2000). A comprehensive analysis should thus relate different approaches and theories from neighbouring disciplines as well. To understand racist, xenophobic or anti-Semitic discourses, it is important to turn to historical, socio-psychological, sociological, psycho-analytic and political claims because the phenomenon is so complex (see Wodak and Reisigl, 1999). In the example below, I cannot summarize all these different, but relevant, theoretical and methodological theories. I will highlight only those that help to understand and explain the specific case study in this chapter, which deals with recent racist discourses and the 'Haider phenomenon' (see also Wodak and Pelinka, 2002). The range of argumentative strategies and insinuations will illustrate new dimensions of the discursive construction of the 'other' in discourse.[7] More importantly, the precise discourse analysis will illustrate how important it might be to integrate several levels of context and a

multi-theoretical approach when analysing political communication.

The specific discourse-analytical approach applied in the four studies referred to is three-dimensional: after (1) having established the specific contents or topics of a specific discourse, (2) the discursive strategies (including argumentation strategies) were investigated. Then (3), the linguistic means (as types) and the specific, context-dependent linguistic realizations (as tokens) were examined (4).

There are several discursive elements and strategies that, in our discourse-analytical view, deserve to receive special attention. We orient ourselves to five constitutive questions:

1   How are persons named and referred to linguistically?
2   What traits, characteristics, qualities and features are attributed to them?
3   By means of what arguments and argumentation schemes do specific persons or social groups try to justify and legitimize the inclusion or exclusion of others?
4   From what perspective or point of view are these labels, attributions and arguments expressed?

Table 13.1 *Discursive strategies for positive self- and negative other-representation*

Strategy	Objectives	Devices
Referential/nomination	Construction of in-groups and out-groups	Membership categorization Biological, naturalizing and depersonalizing Metaphors and metonymies Synecdoches (*pars pro toto, totum pro pars*)
Predication	Labelling social actors more or less positively or negatively, deprecatorily or appreciatively	Stereotypical, evaluative attributions of negative or positive traits Implicit and explicit predicates
Argumentation	Justification of positive or negative attributions	*Topoi* used to justify political inclusion or exclusion, discrimination or preferential treatment
Perspectivation, framing or discourse representation	Expressing involvement; Positioning speaker's point of view	Reporting, description, narration or quotation of events and utterances
Intensification, mitigation	Modifying the epistemic status of a proposition	Intensifying or mitigating the illocutionary force of utterances

5 Are the respective utterances articulated overtly, are they even intensified or are they mitigated?

According to these questions, we are especially interested in five types of discursive strategies, which are all involved in the positive self- and negative other-presentation. We view – and this needs to be emphasized – the discursive construction of '*us*' and '*them*' as the basic fundaments of discourses of identity and difference.

By 'strategy' we generally mean a more or less accurate and more or less intentional plan of practices (including discursive practices) adopted to achieve a particular social, political, psychological or linguistic aim. As far as the discursive strategies are concerned, that is to say, systematic ways of using language, we locate them at different levels of linguistic organization and complexity[8] (see Table 13.1).

In the example below, I will illustrate each level of context and make the sequential analysis transparent, following the categories of analysis that will be defined below. Specifically, we will be concerned with the four levels of context and the linguistic means that relate the contexts to each other. This implies that we have to demonstrate how certain utterances realized through linguistic devices point to extralinguistic contexts, diachronically and synchronically. In our case, we are dealing with xenophobic remarks, which can only be understood by analysing certain rhetorical means, *topoi*, implications and presuppositions as well as insinuations. The impact of such a discourse, however, can only be grasped when relating such meanings to Austrian history and political developments and, most importantly, to the political instrumentalization of anti-foreigner discourses.

Let us now turn to some linguistic terms that are of particular importance for the description of exclusion and discrimination. Often enough, we are concerned with *allusions*. They suggest negative associations without being held responsible for them. The listeners must make the associations in the act of reception (Wodak and de Cillia, 1988: 10). Allusions depend on shared knowledge. The person who alludes to something counts on preparedness for resonance, i.e. on the preparedness of the recipients consciously to call to mind the facts that are alluded to.

In the area of politics, allusions may have the intention, and achieve the result, of devaluing political opponents, without accepting responsibility for what is implicitly said, because this was not, of course, said explicitly: at best an invitation was given to make particular connections. What is not pronounced creates, in the case of allusions, a kind of secrecy, and familiarity suggests something like 'we all know what is meant'. The world of experience or allusion exists, however, in a kind of 'repertoire of collective knowledge'. Allusions frequently rely on *topoi* and linguistic patterns already in play which show a clear meaning content (cf. 'East Coast'; see Mitten, 1992, for discussion), or which point to well-established and perhaps even anti-Semitic stereotypes (such as 'Jewish speculators and crooks'; cf. Wodak and de Cillia, 1988: 15).

Franz Januschek defines 'allusions' in the following way:

In contrast to slogans, allusions require active, thinking and discriminating recipients. Not everyone can understand allusions, and those who do understand them have to do something about it: they have to give meaning to the allusion. The creator of the allusion can thereby renounce responsibility for the meaning that arises: he may distance himself. In other words: allusions can be very short – but they can never be one-sided communicative acts. And, allusions may be understood in a highly explosive way – but always so subtly that they provoke contradiction and cannot be casually filed away in particular drawers. Whereas electoral slogans tend to cause fragmented discourse to break down completely, allusions drive it forward. Under the conditions of fragmentized political communications, they are the linguistic means that relies on the fact that citizens, under these same conditions, generally act intelligently and not merely as puppets for the cleverest manipulators. (Januschek, 1994: 298–301)

In excluding and debasing foreigners, politicians frequently use allusions. By this kind of discourse strategy, they imply certain presuppositions, which many people see as 'common sense beliefs' or 'shared truth'. This is, of course, not a new linguistic strategy in prejudiced discourse. Hence, allusions enable politicians and other speakers to deny the possible meaning attributed to the allusion and refer to the beliefs of the readers or listeners projected into the utterance.

The concept of *presuppositions* is central to linguistic pragmatics. The analysis of presuppositions within speech act theory, which began with John Austin and John Searle, makes it possible to make explicit the implicit assumptions and intertextual relations that underlie text production (see Schiffrin, 1994).

In the case of racist public discourses, frequently no enclosed racist ideological edifice is directly and completely addressed and spelled out. It is rather that an amalgam of ideological tenets is invoked by linguistic 'clues and traces', in order to relate to a particular set of beliefs and a 'discourse space' – irrespective of where the 'roots' of this 'discourse space' may lead.

Now that we have presented some central terms (for further concepts from rhetoric the reader is referred to the very substantial literature on the subject – see note 1), I will apply them to our example. Hence, the very complex relationships between meanings, discourses and contexts should become transparent.

'EVEN BLACK AFRICANS': A SHORT DISCOURSE-HISTORICAL ANALYSIS

The following example[9] is taken from an interview with Jörg Haider, the then leader of the Austrian Freedom Party (FPÖ) (see Wodak and Pelinka, 2002). The interview was printed in the Austrian weekly *Profil* on 24 February 1997, on page 19. The topic was a directive (*Weisung*) issued on 26 November 1996 by the FPÖ politician and now Minister of Finance, Karl-Heinz Grasser, at that time deputy head of the government of the province of Carinthia in Austria and also the highest official (*Landesrat*) in the building and tourist industries in Carinthia. In his directive, Grasser instructed his consultant (*Referenten*) for roadworks to include a regulation in the tender invitations for public building projects that such projects were to be carried out exclusively by indigenous (*heimisch*) workers or by workers from states of the European Union. As a consequence, an intensive public discussion arose, and a strong protest was made against Grasser's proposal of institutionalizing such an 'exclusionary practice'. Finally, Grasser revoked the directive. During the discussion, Jörg Haider was interviewed about the 'Grasser affair'. The journalist from *Profil,* Klaus Dutzler, asked Haider what he, as leader of the FPÖ, was going to recommend to Grasser, his fellow party member and protégé at that time:

> Profil: You will not recommend Karl-Heinz Grasser that he give in?
>
> Haider: We never thought differently and will continue to do so. The indignation, of course, just comes from the side of those like the Carinthian guild master for construction, a socialist, who makes money out of cheap labour from Slovenia and Croatia. And if, today, one goes by one of Hans Peter Haselsteiner´s 'Illbau' building sites, and there, the foreigners, even down to black Africans, cut and carry bricks, then the Austrian construction worker really thinks something. Then one must understand, if there are emotions.

Haider's answer is remarkable in respect of the employed referential strategies, the negative other-presentation by the attributions and predications directed against the different groups of 'them', and the enthymemic argumentation serving the justification of 'emotions' against 'the foreigners, even down to black Africans'.

The social actors mentioned by the journalist are 'Jörg Haider', social-deictically addressed as '*Sie*' (the German formal term of address), and 'Karl-Heinz Grasser'. The social actors mentioned by Haider are – in their sequential appearance – 'we', 'the socialist Carinthian guild master for construction', 'the cheap labour from Slovenia and Croatia', 'the building contractor (and politician of the Austrian party "Liberales Forum") Hans Peter Haselsteiner', 'the foreigners', 'black Africans' and 'the Austrian construction worker'.

There are at least three strategic moves in this short transcript from the interview. The first one is the political self-presentation of the FPÖ as a party that holds firm positions and acts publicly *in unisono*. In this way, Haider woos the voters' favour. According to the question asked by the journalist, one would expect an answer with a transitivity structure in which Haider (as a sayer) would recommend (a verbal and/or mental process in the terms of Halliday, 1994) to Grasser (the receiver or target) that he do something (a proposal). Haider does not meet this expectation. He refuses to present himself explicitly as a leader advising his fellow party member in public (and thereby threatening Grasser's reputation and that of the party). Instead he takes refuge in a referentially ambiguous 'we' (rather than using the expected 'I'), which helps to evade the exclusive referential focus both on Grasser and on himself. The ambivalent 'we' allows different, though not mutually exclusive, interpretations. On the one hand, it can be understood as 'party-we' which is intended to demonstrate a closed, unanimous, fixed position of the whole party on the issue in question. The temporal deixis by past and future tense backs this conjecture. If one knows the history of the FPÖ and the fact that Haider has been an authoritarian party leader since he came into power in 1986, one is tempted to interpret the 'we' as a sort of plural of majesty. This could be applied to prescribe how the party members of the FPÖ are required to think at the moment and in future. Of course, this is a presupposition and an allusion because nothing is said explicitly.

However, after having introduced this ambiguous 'we', which, in addition to having the two functions mentioned above, invites potential FPÖ voters to join Haider's position, Haider then sets out to present the critics of the directive negatively. This is the second strategic move. Haider deliberately chooses two prominent critics (who are also political adversaries) as *partes pro toto* in the groups of critics. He debases the socialist Carinthian guild master (whom he does not identify by proper name) by depicting him as an unsocial, capitalist socialist who exploits 'the cheap labour (*Arbeitskräfte*) from Slovenia and Croatia'. This image of the unsocial capitalist who egoistically wants to profit from wage dumping is also inferentially passed on to the second political opponent mentioned by Haider. We can assume that the reader knows from the Austrian political context that the building contractor, Hans Peter Haselsteiner, is a politician ('inference, presupposition').

Haider's third strategic move is partly embedded in the negative presentation of Hans Peter Haselsteiner. It is realized as an imaginary scenario (with the character of an argumentative example) and aims to justify the 'emotions' of hostility towards foreigners. This move relies on the shift of responsibility, in rhetorical terms, on a *trajectio in alium* that places the blames on Haselsteiner and the socialist Carinthian guild master, instead of on those who have racist 'emotions' and Haider himself (for instigating populism).

Haider's third move contains a blatant racist utterance. Here, the party leader discursively constructs a discriminatory hierarchy of 'foreigners' around the phenotypic feature of skin colour – strictly speaking, around the visible 'deviation' (black) of a specific group of 'foreigners' (i.e. black Africans) from the 'average white Austrian'. Most probably it is no accident that Haider refers to 'black Africans', that is to say, that he explicitly uses the word 'black'. In the context given, the attribute 'black' has an intensifying function. It helps Haider (who, though he explicitly denies it later on in the interview, wants to emotionalize) to carry his black-and-white portrayal to extremes in a literal sense as well. The racist intensification 'even down to black Africans', implies that in Austria, black African workers, because of their most visible 'otherness', are 'an even worse evil' than other 'foreigners', and therefore functions as argumentative 'backing'. Haider seems to intend to construct the greatest possible visual difference between Austrians and 'foreigners'. His utterance can thus be seen as an example of 'differentialist racism' in its literal sense. As their self-appointed spokesman, he asks for understanding for the Austrian workers' 'emotions' in the face of the 'foreign and even black African workers'. At this point, Haider does not argue why 'one' should understand the 'emotions'. He simply relies on the discriminatory prejudice that 'foreigners' take away working places from 'ingroup members'. Furthermore, he relies on the unspoken postulate that 'Austrians', in comparison with 'foreigners', should be privileged with respect to employment.

These argumentation strategies have stayed in public discourses in Austria ever since. The construction of a 'threat by foreigners' as a major *topos* in public discourses because of 'losing jobs' is taking over the debates on EU enlargement as well.

SUMMARY: METHODOLOGICAL STEPS

Of course, it is not possible to provide a really extensive application of the discourse-historical approach and all its categories in one short section. Nevertheless, I would like to summarize the most important procedures to be used in the analysis of specific texts:

- Sample information about the co- and context of the text (social, political, historical, psychological, etc.).
- Once the genre and discourse to which the text belongs have been established, sample more ethnographic information, establish interdiscursivity and intertextuality (texts on similar topics, texts with similar arguments, macro-topics, fields of action, genres).
- From the problem under investigation, formulate precise research questions and explore neighbouring fields for explanatory theories and theoretical aspects.
- Operationalize the research questions into linguistic categories.
- Apply these categories sequentially on to the text while using theoretical approaches to interpret the meanings resulting from the research questions.
- Draw up the context diagram for the specific text and the fields of actions.[10]
- Make an extensive interpretation while returning to the research questions and to the problem under investigation.

These steps are taken several times, always coming and going between text, ethnography, theories and analysis. Most importantly, the decisions that are constantly required in the analysis have to be made explicit and justified. The mediation between theories and empirical analysis, between the social and the text, will never be implemented totally. A gap exists, and hermeneutics and interpretative devices are always needed to bridge the gap.

ACKNOWLEDGEMENTS

This short summary is based on long and extensive discussions with my friends, colleagues and co-researchers as well as students. I would like to mention and thank Rudolf de Cillia, Martin Reisigl, Gertraud Benke, Gilbert Weiss, Bernd Matouschek, Michael Meyer and Richard Mitten, with all of whom I have worked together over the years. Moreover, many ideas have come up with my students. I would like to thank Usama Suleiman, Alexander Pollak, Maria Arduc and Christine Anthonissen for their insights and elaborations. Finally, I would like to thank my peer-group, whom I have written about, and the many colleagues I have not been able to mention here.

NOTES

1 See Wodak and Meyer (2001); Wodak (2002); Titscher et al. (1998, 2000); Reisigl and Wodak (2001); van Dijk (2001); Fairclough and Wodak (1997); Weiss and Wodak (2003); Blommaert and Bulcaen (2000); Anthonissen (2001); Pollak (2002), etc.

2 See also Reisigl and Wodak (2001); Wodak (2001a, 2001b); Wodak and de Cillia (2002a, 2002b).

3 See *Language and Power* by Norman Fairclough (1989), *Language, Power and Ideology* by Ruth Wodak (1989), and *Prejudice in Discourse* by Teun van Dijk (1985).

4 The Erasmus network consisted of a cooperation between Siegfried Jäger (Duisburg), Per Linell (Linköping), Norman Fairclough (Lancaster), Teun van Dijk (Amsterdam), Gunther Kress (London), Theo van Leeuwen (London) and Ruth Wodak (Vienna).

5 In the 1960s, many scholars adopted a more critical perspective in language studies. Among the first was the French scholar Pêcheux (1982), whose approach traced its roots to the work of the Russian theorists Bakhtin (1981) and Volosinov (1973), both of whom had postulated an integration of language and social processes in the 1930s. The term itself was apparently coined by Jacob Mey (1974).

6 For more details see Wodak et al. (1998, 1999); Reisigl (1998); de Cillia et al. (1999); Reisigl and Wodak (2001).

7 The new government in Austria, which brought about the so-called '*Wende*', was installed on 4 February 2000. Immediately after its installation, the other member states of the EU decided on 'measures against the government' because – for the first time in the history of the EU – an extremist right-wing populist party was part of a government (for this debate and its development, see Kopeinig and Kotanko, 2000; Wodak, 2000a; 2000b; Wodak and Pelinka, 2002).

8 All these strategies are illustrated by numerous categories and examples in Reisigl and Wodak (2001, ch. 2).

9 This example is the summary of an extensive analysis in Reisigl and Wodak (2001).

10 See Reisigl and Wodak (2001) for a detailed context analysis and context diagram of the discourse sequence above.

REFERENCES

Achard, P. (1995) 'Formation discursive, dialogisme et sociologie', *Langages*, 117: 82–95.

Anthonissen, C. (2001) 'On the effectivity of media censorship: an analysis of linguistic, paralinguistic and other communicative devices used to defy media restrictions'. Unpublished PhD thesis, University of Vienna.

Bakhtin, M. (1981) *The Dialogic Imagination*. Austin: University of Texas Press.

Benke, G. (2000) 'Diskursanalyse als sozialwissenschaftliche Untersuchungsmethode', *SWS Rundschau*, Nr 2: 140–62.

Benveniste, E. (1966/1974) *Problèmes de linguistique générale*, 2 vols. Paris: Gallimard. Reprinted Bergsdorf, 1983.

Billig, M. (2003) 'Critical, discourse analysis and the rhetoric of critique', in G. Weiss and R. Wodak (eds), *Critical Discourse Analysis: Theory and Interdisciplinarity*. London: Palgrave Macmillan, pp. 35–46.

Blommaert, J. and Bulcaen, C. (2000) 'Critical discourse analysis', *Annual Review of Anthropology*, 29: 447–66.

Bonnafous, S. and Tournier, M. (1995) 'Analyse du discours, lexicométrie, communication et politique', *Mots*, 117: 67–81.

Bourdieu, P. (ed.) (1989) *La noblesse d'état*. Paris: Editions de Minuit.

Brünner, G. and Graefen, G. (eds) (1994) *Texte und Diskurse*. Opladen: Westdeutscher Verlag.

Caldas-Coulthard, C.R. and van Leeuwen, T. (2001) 'Baby's first toys and the discursive constructions of babyhood', special issue of *Folia Linguistica*, XXXV(1–2): 157–82.

Chouliaraki, L. and Fairclough, N. (1999) *Discourse in Late Modernity: Rethinking Critical Discourse Analysis*. Edinburgh: Edinburgh University Press.

Cicourel, A. (1974) *Methode und Messung in der Soziologie*. Frankfurt am Main: Suhrkamp.

Connerton, P. (1976) *How Societies Remember*. Cambridge: Cambridge University Press (1996 reprint).

Courtine, J.-J. (1981) 'Analyse du discours politique', *Langages*, 62.

de Cillia, R., Reisigl, M. and Wodak, R. (1999) 'The discursive construction of national identities', *Discourse and Society*, 10: 149–73.

Fairclough, N. (1989) *Language and Power*. London: Longman.

Fairclough, N. (1992) *Discourse and Social Change*. London: Polity Press.

Fairclough, N. (1995) *Critical Discourse Analysis: The Critical Study of Language* (Language in Social Life Series). Harlow: Longman.

Fairclough, N. (2000) *New Labour, New Language?* London: Routledge.

Fairclough, N. and Wodak, R. (1997) 'Critical discourse analysis', in T.A. van Dijk (ed.), *Introduction to Discourse Analysis*. London: Sage, pp. 258–84.

Fay, B. (1987) *Critical Social Science*. London: Polity Press.

Graham, P. (2002) 'Space and cyberspace: on the enclosure of consciousness', in J. Armitage and J. Roberts (eds), *Living with Cyberspace: Technology and Society in the 21st Century*. London: Athlone Press.

Graham, P. (2003) *The Digital Dark Ages: New Media, New Literacies, and Socio-political Change*. New York: Peter Lang. (For the series *New Literacies and Digital Epistemologies*, ed. C. Lankshear and M. Knobel.) (In press).

Groupe de Saint-Cloud (1982) *La Parole syndicale: étude du vocabulaire confédéral des centrales ouvrières françaises (1971–1976)*. Paris: PUF.

Gruber, H. (1991) *Antisemitismus im Mediendiskurs. Die Affäre 'Waldheim' in der Tagespresse*. Wiesbaden and Opladen: Deutscher Universitätsverlag/Westdeutscher Verlag.

Habermas, J. (1967) *Erkenntnis und Interesse [Knowledge and Interest]*. Frankfurt am Main: Suhrkamp.

Halliday, M.A.K. (1985) *Introduction to Functional Grammar*. London: Edward Arnold.

Halliday, M.A.K. (1994) *Introduction to Functional Grammar* (2nd ed.). London: Edward Arnold.

Iedema, R. (1997) 'Interactional dynamics and social change: planning as morphogenesis'. Unpublished doctoral thesis, University of Sydney.

Iedema, R. and Wodak, R. (1999) 'Introduction: Organizational discourse and practices', *Discourse and Society*, 10: 15–20.

Jäger, S. (1999) *Kritische Diskursanalyse. Eine Einführung*. Duisburg: DISS.

Jäger, S. (2001) 'Discourse and knowledge', in R. Wodak and M. Meyer (eds), *Methods of Critical Discourse Analysis*. London: Sage, pp. 32–62.

Jäger, M. and Jäger, S. (1993) 'Verstrickungen – Der rassistische Diskurs und seine Bedeutung für den politischen Gesamtdiskurs in der Bundesrepublik Deutschland', in S. Jäger and J. Link (eds), *Die vierte Gewalt. Rassismus und die Medien*. Duisburg: DISS, pp. 49–79.

Januschek, F. (1992) 'Rechts-populismus und NS-Anspielungen am Beispiel des österreichischen Politikers Jörg Haider', *DISS-Texte Nr. 15*. Cologne: GNN.

Januschek, F. (1994) 'J. Haider und der rechtspopulistische Diskurs in Österreich', in W. Tributsch (ed.), *Schlagwort Haider*. Vienna: Falter Verlag, pp. 298–301.

Klemperer, V. (1975/1947) *LTI Lingua Tertii Imperii. Die Sprache des Dritten Reiches*. Leipzig: Reclam.

Kopeinig, M. and Kotanko, C. (2000) *Eine europäische Affaire. Der Weisen-Bericht und die Sanktionen gegen Österreich*. Vienna: Czernin.

Kress, G. and van Leeuwen, T. (1996) *Reading Images*. London: Routledge.

Krings, H. et al. (1973) *Handbuch philosophischer Grundbegriffe*. Munich: Kösel.

Lemke, J. (1995) *Textual Politics: Discourse and Social Dynamics*. London: Taylor & Francis.

Lemke, J. (2001) 'Discursive technologies and the social organization of meaning', special Issue of *Folia Linguistica* (ed. R. Wodak), *Critical Discourse Analysis in Postmodern Societies*, XXXV/(1–2): 79–97.

Lemke, J. (2002) 'Multimedia genres for science education and scientific literacy', in M. Schleppegrell and M.C. Colombi (eds), *Developing Advanced Literacy in First and Second Languages*. Mahwah, NJ: Erlbaum, pp. 21–44.

Leodolter, R. (= Wodak) (1975) *Das Sprachverhalten von Angeklagten bei Gericht*. Kronberg/Ts.: Scriptor.

Leontjev, A.N. (1984) 'Der allgemeine Tätigkeitsbegriff', in D. Viehweger (ed.), *Grundfragen einer Theorie der sprachlichen Tätigkeit*. Berlin, pp. 13–30.

Link, J. (1988) 'Über Kollektivsymbolik im politischen Diskurs und ihren Anteil an totalitären Tendenzen', *kultuRRevolution*, 17/18: 47–53.

Maas, U. (1984) *Als der Geist der Gemeinschaft eine Sprache fand. Sprache im Nationalsozialismus.* Opladen: Westdeutscher Verlag.

Maas, U. (1989a) *Sprachpolitik und politische Sprachwissenschaft.* Frankfurt am Main: Suhrkamp.

Maas, U. (1989b) 'Sprache im Nationalsozialismus. Analyse einer Rede eines Studentenfunktionärs', in K. Ehlich (ed.), *Sprache im Faschismus.* Frankfurt am Main: Suhrkamp, pp. 162–97.

Maingueneau, D. (1987) *Nouvelles tendances en analyse du discours.* Paris: Hachette.

Martin, J.R. (2003) 'Voting the "other": reading and writing indigenous Australians', in G. Weiss and R. Wodak (eds), *Critical Discourse Analysis: Theory and Interdisciplinarity.* London: Palgrave Macmillan, pp. 199–219.

Mey, J. (1974) *Pragmatics.* Oxford: Blackwell (1994 reprint).

Mitten, R. (1992) *The Politics of Antisemitic Prejudice: The Waldheim Phenomenon in Austria.* Boulder, CO: Westview Press.

Muntigl, P., Weiss, G. and Wodak, R. (2000) *European Union Discourses on Unemployment: An Interdisciplinary Approach to Employment Policy-Making and Organizational Change.* Amsterdam: Benjamins.

Pêcheux, M. (1982) *Language, Semantics and Ideology* (2nd ed.). London: Macmillan.

Pêcheux, M. (1988) 'Discourse – structure or event', in C. Nelson and L. Grossberg (eds), *Marxism and the Interpretation of Culture.* London: Macmillan.

Pollak, A. (2002) 'Kritische Diskursanalyse und historische Forschung', in B. Ziemann (ed.), *Perspektiven der Historischen Friedensforschung.* Essen: Klartext Verlag, pp. 153–72.

Reisigl, M. (1998) '"50 Jahre Zweite Republik" – Zur diskursiven Konstruktion der österreichischen Identität in politischen Gedenkreden', in O. Panagl (ed.), *Fahnenwörter in der Politik. Kontinuitäten und Brüche.* Vienna: Böhlau, pp. 217–51.

Reisigl, M. and Wodak, R. (2001) *Discourse and Discrimination.* London: Routledge.

Sauer, C. (1989) 'Nazi-Deutsch für Niederländer. Das Konzept der NS-Sprachpolitik in der Deutschen Zeitung in den Niederlanden 1940–1945', in K. Ehlich (ed.), *Sprache im Faschismus.* Frankfurt am Main: Suhrkamp, pp. 237–88.

Sauer, C. (1995) 'Sprachwissenschaft und NS-Faschismus. Lehren aus der sprachwissenschaftlichen Erforschung des Sprachgebrauchs deutscher Nationalsozialisten und Propagandisten für den mittel- und osteuropäischen Umbruch?', in K. Steinke (ed.), *Die Sprache der Diktaturen und Diktatoren.* Heidelberg: Carl Winter, pp. 9–96.

Schiffrin, D. (1994) *Approaches to Discourse.* Oxford: Blackwell.

Scollon, R. (2001) *Mediated Discourse: The Nexus of Practice.* London: Routledge.

Scollon, R. and Scollon, S.W. (2002) *Nexus Analysis: Discourses and the Emerging Internet.* London: Routledge.

Thompson, J.B. (1988) *Critical Hermeneutics* (4th ed.). Cambridge: Cambridge University Press.

Titscher, S., Wodak, R., Meyer, M. and Vetter, E. (1998) *Methoden der Textanalyse.* Wiesbaden: Westdeutscher Verlag.

Titscher, S., Wodak, R., Meyer, M. and Vetter, E. (2000), *Methods of Text and Discourse Analysis.* London: Sage.

van Dijk, T.A. (1977) *Text and Context: Exploration in the Semantics and Pragmatics of Discourse.* Harlow: Longman.

van Dijk, T.A. (1981) *Studies in the Pragmatics of Discourse.* The Hague: Mouton.

van Dijk, T.A. (1985) *Prejudice in Discourse.* Amsterdam: Benjamins.

van Dijk, T.A. (ed.) (1986) *Discourse and Communication: New Approaches to the Analysis of Mass Media Discourse and Communication.* Berlin: de Gruyter.

van Dijk, T.A. (1993) 'Principles of critical discourse analysis', *Discourse and Society*, 4(2): 249–83.

van Dijk, T.A. (1998) *Ideology: A Multidisciplinary Study.* London: Sage.

van Dijk, T.A. (2001) 'Critical discourse analysis', in D. Tannen, D. Schiffrin and H. Hamilton (eds), *Handbook of Discourse Analysis.* Oxford: Blackwell, pp. 352–71.

van Dijk, T.A. (2003) 'The discourse-knowledge interface', in G. Weiss and R. Wodak (eds), *Critical Discourse Analysis: Theory and Interdisciplinarity.* London: Palgrave Macmillan, pp. 85–109.

van Dijk, T.A. and Kintsch, W. (1983) *Strategies of Discourse Comprehension.* New York: Academic Press.

van Leeuwen, T. (1993) 'Language and representation: the recontextualisation of participants, activities and reactions', Thesis, Department of Linguistics, University of Sydney.

Vass, E. (1992) 'Diskursanalyse als interdisziplinäres Forschungsgebiet'. MA thesis, University of Vienna.

Volosinov, V.I. (1973) *Marxism and the Philosophy of Language.* New York: Seminar Press (originally published 1928).

Weiss, G. and Wodak, R. (eds) (2003) *Critical Discourse Analysis: Theory and Interdisciplinarity.* London: Palgrave Macmillan.

Wodak, R. (ed.) (1989) *Language, Power and Ideology.* Amsterdam: Benjamins.

Wodak, R. (1996a) *Disorders in Discourse.* London: Longman.

Wodak, R. (1996b) 'The genesis of racist discourse in Austria since 1989', in C.R. Caldas-Coulthard and M. Coulthard (eds), *Texts and Practices: Readings in Critical Discourse Analysis.* London: Routledge, pp. 107–28.

Wodak, R. (2000) 'Recontextualisation and the transformation of meaning: a critical discourse analysis of decision making in EU-meetings about employment policies', in S. Sarangi and M. Coulthard (eds), *Discourse and Social Life.* Harlow: Pearson Education, pp. 185–206.

Wodak, R. (2000a) Guest editorial: 'The rise of racism – an Austrian or an European Phenomenon', *Discourse and Society*, 11(1): 5–6.

Wodak, R. (2000b) 'From conflict to consensus? The co-construction of a policy paper', in P. Muntigl, G. Weiss and R. Wodak, *European Union Discourses on Unemployment*. Amsterdam: Benjamins, pp. 73–114.

Wodak, R. (2001a) 'What CDA is about – a summary of its history, important concepts and its developments', in R. Wodak and M. Meyer (eds), *Methods of Critical Discourse Analysis*. London: Sage, pp. 1–13.

Wodak, R. (2001b) 'The discourse-historical approach', in R. Wodak and M. Meyer (eds), *Methods of Critical Discourse Analysis*. London: Sage, pp. 63–94.

Wodak, R. (2002) *National and Transnational Identities: European and Other Identities Oriented to Interviews with EU Officials*. Florence (in press).

Wodak, R. and de Cillia, R. (1988) 'Sprache und Antisemitismus'. Vienna: Institut für Wissenschaft und Kunst, *Mitteilungen*, 4.

Wodak, R. and de Cillia, R. (2002a) 'Discourse and politics', in *Handbuch Soziolinguistik*. Berlin: de Gruyter (in press).

Wodak, R. and de Cillia, R. (2002b) 'Sprachliche Identitäten: multikulturelles und multilinguales Erbe und welche Zukunft?', in M. Csaky and P. Stachel (eds), *Orte des Gedächtnisses*. Vienna: Passagen Verlag (in press).

Wodak, R. and Meyer, M. (eds) (2001) *Methods of Critical Discourse Analysis*. London: Sage.

Wodak, R. and Pelinka, A. (2002) 'From Waldheim to Haider – an introduction', in R. Wodak and A. Pelinka (eds), *The Haider Phenomenon*. New Brunswick, NJ: Transaction Press, pp. vii–xxvii.

Wodak, R. and Reisigl, M. (1999) 'Discourse and racism: European perspectives', *Annual Review of Anthropology*, 28: 175–99.

Wodak, R. and van Dijk, T. (eds) (2000) *Racism at the Top*. Klagenfurt: Drava.

Wodak, R., Pelikan, J., Nowak, P., Gruber, H., de Cillia, R. and Mitten, R. (1990) *'Wir sind alle unschuldige Täter!' Diskurshistorische Studien zum Nachkriegsantisemitismus*. Frankfurt am Main: Suhrkamp.

Wodak, R., de Cillia, R., Reisigl, M., Liebhart, K., Hofstätter, K. and Kargl, M. (1998) *Zur diskursiven Konstruktion nationaler Identität*. Frankfurt am Main: Suhrkamp.

Wodak, R., de Cillia, R., Reisigl, M. and Liebhart, K. (1999) *The Discursive Construction of National Identity*. Edinburgh: Edinburgh University Press.

Part 3

FIELD RELATIONS

It is instructive to describe the comparatively limited sociability of interviewing as a background to showcasing the complex social relations of fieldwork. Research based on interviewing obliges interview participants to have rather restricted access to each other. The more structured forms of interviewing specify distinct roles for participants. On the one side is the interviewer, who may also be the principal researcher. Following the usual introductions and the establishment of informed consent, the interviewer presents him- or herself largely in terms of a written interview agenda and, in conventional practice, is careful not to extend the interview's sociability much beyond that. On the other side is the interviewee or respondent. While experiential information of all kinds can be requested of the respondent, meaningful access to this often comes in pre-designated form, either the pre-coded responses presented to the respondent or analytically pre-specified categories of concern with respondents' experience and social worlds. Less structured forms of interviewing relax these restrictions, commonly encouraging interview participants to become acquainted in terms that can extend beyond what is specified in interview schedules.

While the degree of participants' mutual access varies across interviews, it hardly compares with the extent of accessibility commonly present between participants in field research. The sheer extent of involvement by the researcher or fieldworker in his or her subjects' worlds – both in terms of time and space – considerably alters the research encounter. While interviews may extend over an hour, they rarely last longer than two. While interviews often take place somewhere in the respondent's daily world, such as in the home, they rarely extend into the household's nooks and crannies, or accompany the respondent from one location in this world to another. Field research, in contrast, can engage participants in these ways. The fieldworker not only sits down at the respondent's kitchen table, say, turns on the tape recorder, and interviews him or her, but commonly continues the research conversation well after the tape recorder has been turned off. Involvement in terms of time can extend from the early morning hours until well into the night and extend from weekdays into weekends. Indeed, it is not unusual for field researchers to lurk about the field at times – during night shifts, for example – when conventional interviewers have retired to bed for the day. Social space for the fieldworker can take her to households, but also to political rallies, black markets, and locales where danger and emotional distress prevail, not just to the flowing social space and courtesies of the relatively uncharged interview exchange.

The social relations of fieldwork are markedly more complex than those of interviewing. They extend into the daily lives of participants on both sides of the research encounter. Whether the field is tribal territory, a work organization, a health-care setting, a neighbourhood or an urban street corner, the fieldworker engages subjects' lives that extend from their homes, work stations, convalescent beds and front porches, to their neighbours' households, leisure activities, therapeutic regimens, and to cellars and the proverbial smoky backrooms of racketeering. While the imagined moral contours of many of these settings might be clear to researchers at the start and have been prepared for, in time they can present looming horizons of unforeseen actions, expectations and risks. It is not uncommon in fieldwork, for example, for the relatively relaxed and unpretentious atmosphere of subjects' homes to become, with the shifting locales of subjects' daily lives, immersed in unconventional and surprisingly precarious activities. This affects research relations in a way that the conventional sociability of the interview rarely poses for participants. Subjects' lives are open to a research surveillance in fieldwork well beyond what they might agree to in interview research. Open to view can be the full range of circumstances that comprise the day and the night for a particular way of life. These, too, mean that field relations pose a different breed of challenges from those present in interviews.

The chapters of Part 3 present these issues as they occur, unfold, and are dealt with in practice. The authors instruct us in what it means in practice to spend days, weeks, if not months and years in the field, and how this time commitment affects the social relations of the researcher and the researched. Sara Delamont's Chapter 14, comparing the tradition of fieldwork typifying anthropologists, features immersions in lengths of time and social isolation relatively uncommon for sociologists, which result in distinct challenges for participants. In the context of field research, ethical issues can expand precipitously, as lives and their welfare, not just the reciprocities of the interview and a rather limited body of experiential information, can be at stake. As Anne Ryen explains in Chapter 15, ethics link up as much with culture and communication as they present themselves as moral issues to those concerned. Danger, hostility and political sensitivities can emerge to confront research participants in ways that are mostly talked about in interviews, as Nigel Fielding (Chapter 16) and Les Back (Chapter 17) explain in their contributions. Linda Mitteness and Judith Barker show in Chapter 18 how the complexities of field relations can extend to the interaction not only between the lone researcher and the social world in view, but to a whole team of fieldworkers, the challenges and risks of which can geometrically increase the complexities of field relations. It is abundantly clear that the social relations of fieldwork are anything but simply a matter of a suitable research encounter and proper data-collection procedure.

14

Ethnography and participant observation

Sara Delamont

Down the canyon, smoke from meat fires drifted through the cedar and mesquite trees, and if I squinted my eyes in the sun's setting, I could almost pretend that Spanish soldiers in silver chest armour and bladed helmets or a long dead race of hunters were encamped on those hill sides. Or maybe even old compatriots in butternut brown wending their way in and out of history – gallant, Arthurian, their canister-ripped colors unfurled in the roiling smoke, the fatal light in their faces a reminder that the contest is never quite over, the field never quite ours.

James Lee Burke (1993: 344) captures, in the final paragraph of *In the Electric Mist with the Confederate Dead*, all the important things about ethnography. We need to use all our senses: smell, sight, hearing, taste and touch (Stoller, 1989; Wafer, 1991). Smells drift, we have to squint to see in the roiling (i.e., turbid) smoke. Our fieldsite may be among hunter gatherers, or Spanish soldiers. Our contest is never quite over, their field is never quite ours. And, of course, if we were all able to write as well as Burke the social sciences would be much richer. Writing well is particularly important in qualitative research, at all stages from planning to publication. So too is reading: reading wisely and widely throughout the process (Delamont, 2002).

This chapter shows how participant observation is actually done. The processes of conducting observational research will be explained and illustrated with examples from ethnographies. There are three sections. The first section explores what is meant by 'ethnography', 'fieldwork' and 'participant observation', locates these three terms in relation to the wider term 'qualitative research' and clarifies their place in anthropology and sociology. In the second part, ways in which ethnography is done in anthropology and sociology will be contrasted using four fictional researchers. Third, the processes of conducting ethnographic research are explained

with three subsections on watching, recording and reflection. The reflection section will, by definition, include material on how ethnographic research is written and how it is read. The 'watching' section explores the cycle from access negotiations through to exit from the field.

Two bodies of scholarship will be drawn on – anthropology and sociology. Some coverage of the history of the method in each discipline ensures that the pioneers in anthropology such as Boas and Malinowski, Zora Neale Hurston and Camilla Wedgwood on the one hand, and in sociology of the women and men of Chicago on the other, are recognized. From the anthropological side, examples come from the anthropology of Europe (Delamont, 1995). Research conducted on British social anthropologists (Delamont et al., 2000a) is also drawn upon. Interviews were conducted with lecturers and doctoral students in four universities: all universities ('Kingford', 'Southersham', 'Masonbridge' and 'Latchendon') and respondents are protected by pseudonyms. My own background is in anthropology: the British variety taught at Cambridge in the 1960s. I was taught by Edmund Leach (1984, 2001), one of Britain's greatest anthropologists, who introduced structuralism to the UK. After graduation I decided to use anthropological methods in the British educational system, and therefore *faute de mieux* I became a sociologist. In that era, doing fieldwork in the UK made a career as an anthropologist almost impossible (on this point see Jackson, 1987, and Pink, 2000). The interview with Dr Herrick of Masonbridge (Delamont et al., 2000a: 75) reflects on this: 'My PhD was done in Britain, which was extremely unusual at that time in Britain … most people feel who've worked in Britain that that kind of work was not particularly regarded by the British anthropological establishment as proper anthropology … the anthropology of Britain has always been extremely marginal.'

ETHNOGRAPHY, FIELDWORK AND PARTICIPANT OBSERVATION DEFINED

There are three closely related terms – ethnography, fieldwork, participant observation – all of which are part of a wider term, qualitative research. Qualitative research can include many different methods, such as many varieties of interview, documentary work, and the collection of personal constructs and mental maps, as well as observation. The vast majority of the qualitative studies conducted in the past twenty years in disciplines other than anthropology have been based on interviews of one sort or another rather than proper ethnography, as Atkinson (1997), Atkinson and Silverman (1997), Delamont (1997) and Delamont et al. (2000b) have pointed out. This chapter is about proper ethnography, that is, participant observation done during fieldwork.

Participant observation, ethnography and fieldwork are all used interchangeably in the literature, and are therefore synonymous: they can all mean spending long periods watching people, coupled with talking to them about what they are doing, thinking and saying, designed to see how they understand their world. I use ethnography as the most inclusive term, with participant observation and fieldwork being useful descriptions of the data-collection technique and the location of data collection. Fieldwork is the data-collection phase of the research process, especially when researchers leave the university and go out into the world. So a person who sent out postal questionnaires would probably not talk of fieldwork, whereas an investigator doing participant observation, or ethnographic interviewing, in a factory, a hospital, a school or a village in Portugal would do so. The term can cover collecting quantitative data (for example a census) if these data are collected 'in the field', especially during a period of ethnographic observation. We can therefore define the term for this chapter as follows: Fieldwork is the term used in qualitative research to cover the data-collection phase when the investigators leave their desks and go out 'into the field'. 'The field' is metaphorical: it is not a real field, but a setting or a population.

Participant observation is used to cover a mixture of observation and interviewing. In the field the researchers' aim is to understand how the cultures they are studying 'work', that is, to grasp what the world looks like to the people who live in the fishing village, the boarding school or the mining community. The researchers need to discover what 'their' people believe; what they do at work and in their leisure time; what makes them laugh, cry and rage; who they love, hate and fear; and how they choose their friends and endure their relations. This is done by living with the people being studied, watching them work and play, thinking carefully about what is seen, interpreting it and talking to the actors to check the emerging interpretations. The term 'participant' observation does not usually mean real participation: researchers do not usually catch fish, teach classes or dig coal, rather they watch these things being done, and 'help' occasionally. It is important to participate enough to be able to write feelingly about the nature of the work: its pains and pleasures, smells and sounds, physical and mental stresses. However, the researcher cannot actually spend the whole time fishing, teaching or digging coal, because that would prevent both studying other members of the social world and, perhaps more vitally, time spent writing the fieldnotes, thinking about the fieldwork, writing down those thoughts, and systematically testing the initial insights in the setting. So 'participant' does not mean doing what those being observed do, but interacting with them while *they* do it. The researcher may do the same things, but that is *not* a requirement.

In traditional anthropological fieldwork, researchers go to a distant location, possibly in an underdeveloped country the other side of the world, and the fieldwork may last two years or more. In sociological research, the field is more usually visited on a daily basis with researchers returning to their home at night. These are the two main types of fieldwork, which we can gloss as total immersion and partial immersion. In anthropology and some varieties of sociology, researchers have traditionally moved to live at the fieldsite: in the fishing village, in the boarding school, on the housing estate next to the coal mine. In such cases researchers are totally immersed in the culture under study, twenty-four hours a day. Most observational research in sociology and education and the applied disciplines is based on a more partial immersion: researchers eat, sleep and relax at home but spend a large chunk of the twenty-four-hour period in the factory, the hospital or the school. The biggest difference between these is probably the amount of intellectual and emotional support available from academic supervisors or colleagues. In total immersion fieldwork researchers may be very isolated, very lonely, and lose their way. Contact is likely to be by letter, often with a long time-lag between despatch and any advice arriving from home. In both total and partial immersion fieldwork, being fully engaged in another culture is a *sine qua non*. When the research is done, the result is an ethnography: a theorized account of the culture studied with ethnographic methods.

ETHNOGRAPHY IN ANTHROPOLOGY AND SOCIOLOGY

Ethnography has a long history in both social and cultural anthropology and in sociology. Anthropologists still like to claim that they have the exclusive custody of the real, true ethnography (Delamont et al., 2000a) and rely on their use of the method to distinguish themselves rhetorically from other social scientists. As a PhD student at Southersham, Louisa Montoya, told us: 'The qualitative methods used in anthropology are specific to this discipline.' Hirsch and Gellner (2001) feel able to state that while other disciplines may do or claim to do ethnographic fieldwork, the term 'an ethnography' to refer to a monograph 'is confined to anthropological circles' (p.1). In the face of such claims, arguments that there is a convergence between anthropology and other disciplines seem unimpressive. It is true that anthropologists have used ethnography as their main method, and that *no* other technique (experiment, quasi-experiment, survey, observation with pre-specified schedule, questionnaire-based interviews, life history collection, archival or other documentary scrutiny, or narrative analysis) has ever rivalled it. Anthropologists have used some other techniques as subsidiaries to living in a culture full time, but only as subsidiaries (Faubion, 2001; Macdonald, 2001). In the USA, Boas is seen as the pioneer of fieldwork, inspiring disciples including Ruth Benedict and Margaret Mead (see Behar and Gordon, 1995). Zora Neale Hurston's work prefigures much contemporary debate (Hernandez, 1995). In the UK, Malinowski is usually credited with inventing fieldwork, and his disciples included Audrey Richards and Camilla Wedgwood (Leach, 1984; Lutkehaus, 1986).

Sociology has used ethnography as long as anthropology, that is, since the 1890s, but it has often been unfashionable, a minority pursuit. Ethnography has never had the status, and sole domination, in sociology that it had, and has, in anthropology. Ethnography and other qualitative methods were pioneered at Chicago, alongside survey and statistical techniques. Chicago sociology was robustly empirical, and this empiricism spread to other centres of sociology in the USA (Deegan, 1988, 2001). In Chicago, which was the most important sociology department in the world from 1892 until 1935, and still has massive influence, ethnographic methods fell out of fashion in the early 1960s (Platt, 1995; LeCompte, 1998).

Since the mid-1970s there has been a rebirth of qualitative methods in sociology and a rapid growth in their popularity in education, geography, nursing studies and other social sciences (see Atkinson et al., 2001). Journals, textbooks, handbooks and conferences have all developed. This growth has not, however, united sociological and anthropological uses of the method (Delamont and Atkinson, 1995). In the past decade there have been several apocalyptic statements that traditional ethnography is dead. That is simply wrong, but in this chapter there is no space to rehearse the arguments, which are covered elsewhere (Delamont et al., 2000b; Atkinson et al., 2003). Traditional ethnography continues as strongly as ever.

ILLUSTRATING ETHNOGRAPHY IN THE TWO DISCIPLINES

To illustrate sociological versus anthropological ethnography, we can contrast four fictional researchers, starting with Rachel Verinder, an anthropologist, and Lucilla Majoribanks, a sociologist, both doing PhDs at Boarbridge. Doctoral students are used for these fictional episodes because, in practice, the bulk of the ethnographic research done in both disciplines is actually conducted by doctoral students or junior scholars, because senior ones can rarely get time or money to conduct sustained fieldwork themselves. These two fictional characters are based on empirical research on young scholars, the published autobiographical reports on fieldwork, and experience watching young colleagues over thirty years.

Imagine Rachel Verinder has graduated in social anthropology, and has been offered a scholarship to do a PhD at Boarbridge University. She and her thesis supervisor, Dr Selina Goby, decide that Rachel should do research on Galicia, a region in north-western Spain, and the Galician separatist movement. Rachel did A-level Spanish and has spent several holidays there since, and she is interested in Atlantic maritime cultures, the lives of women in fishing communities and regionalist movements in Europe. For nine months Rachel stays in Boarbridge, improving her knowledge of social anthropology, especially the anthropology of Europe and of maritime societies, reading about Galicia and other regions of Spain, and learning the Galician language. Then she packs appropriate clothes and equipment for collecting data, such as a digital camera, minidisk recorder, and lots of notebooks and pens, and sets off from Boarbridge for the ferry to Santander. When she lands in Spain she heads for Galicia, and searches out a fishing village where she will live for the next year or more. She has to try several villages before she finds one that has a bus service to the nearest town, has a family who are prepared to rent her a room, and has fishing boats still working. Rachel's research is similar to that done by Canadian (Rosenberg, 1988), American (Reed-Danahay, 1996), Australian (Just, 2000) and British (Goddard, 1996) anthropologists in Europe over the past thirty years.

Lucilla Majoribanks starts at the same time, and decides with her supervisor, Dr Henry Centum, that she will do an ethnography of students training to be laboratory technicians at a further education (vocational) college. There is a course at a college, 'Midhurst', in Boarbridge, so Lucilla can live 'at home'. She spends about six months reviewing the literature on vocational education, on laboratory technicians, on science and technology education and on qualitative methods. Dr Centum insists that Lucilla writes a draft of her methods chapter, a review of the literature, and a 2000-word paper on her foreshadowed problems, that is, the ideas she expects to develop during the observation. Once her ideas are clear, Lucilla writes to the Principal of Midhurst College, to ask for access both to the institution and to the specific course. He agrees, and despatches her to the staff who teach it; they agree, and she is able to start her data collection with a fresh cohort of students in September, a year after she began to be a student. (Outwith the USA clearance from Human Subject Committees is needed only for medical research.) This will produce a sociological ethnography of an educational institution like those done by American (Raissiguier, 1994; Valli, 1986), Australian (Walker, 1988) and British (Gleeson and Mardle, 1980; Riseborough, 1993) investigators.

Meanwhile in Galicia, Rachel starts her fieldwork. The most important part is living in the village, and watching what goes on. When it is not feasible to join in, she will watch what she is allowed to. Once the villagers have got used to her being around, watching is supplemented with talking. Rachel talks informally to everyone possible, does formal interviews with people,

collecting their family trees and hearing their life stories, plus gathering folk tales and songs, listening to gossip, jokes and legends. A fieldworker is likely to draw maps of the village, of the insides of houses, of the graveyard, diagrams of the seating plans at weddings or funerals, the layout of fishing boats and anything else that has a spatial angle. Rachel will count the number of residents in the village, count the fishing boats, measure the sizes of fields, orchards and pastures, count cows, sheep and pigs, estimate the size of the fishing catch, work out how many tourists come, how many people get the bus each day, how many cars, taxis, motor scooters and even bicycles there are, how many pupils in the school and so on.

It will be important to hear who speaks Galician and who does not, and when Galician and Castilian (Spanish) are used. If Rachel is allowed on a fishing boat she will go, if not she will find out why women are not allowed to sail on them. The lives of the women will probably be easier for her to observe than those of men. If there is separatist political activity, Rachel will try to attend any meetings, meet the activists and discover what is motivating them. Apart from what she can see, and what she can learn by listening and asking, there may also be documents. Rachel might spend days in the provincial capital working on municipal archival material, or in the cathedral or ecclesiastical records, or both. If the Galician regionalist movement has produced newsletters, pamphlets or books, these will all be read. Rachel might get the schoolchildren to write her something, or ask to read letters sent home by villagers living abroad.

While Rachel is in Galicia, Lucilla is doing her ethnography of the students in the vocational college, in Boarbridge. Lucilla can intersperse her data collection with teaching undergraduates, going to seminars, seeing her supervisor every week and using the library. She is only in the field for short periods of some days, does not have to learn a foreign language or eat strange food. She goes to the college nearly every day, sits in the lectures and workshops, writing pages and pages of fieldnotes. She interviews the lecturers, formally and informally, and she hangs out with the students, sometimes going out with them socially. She talks to them in their breaks, and she interviews them formally too.

One difference between Rachel and Lucilla's fieldwork is the *focus* of the research. Lucilla and Dr Centum try to keep very tightly focused on a pre-specified topic: the occupational socialization and student culture of the trainee laboratory technicians (see Coffey and Atkinson, 1994). To gather data on the catering staff, or the fine art appreciation course, or the people taking academic sociology at night school, would be a distraction, a different project, a diversion. If Lucilla drifted, Dr Centum would force her back to 'her' topic. In contrast, Rachel is more likely to settle on a tight focus only on her return to Boarbridge. She has to collect more, because once 'home' she is not, realistically, able to go back. Lucilla, in contrast, can return to consult documents or re-interview participants; and indeed much of what she may need is not 'in the field', but in libraries and offices elsewhere in Boarbridge.

As Rachel goes on living in the village she will find that she has been told different things by different people and she will set out to find out why. As her Galician improves, she will spot that people were lying to her, and find out why they did so. It is common, for example, for villagers to think that outsiders are tax inspectors, CIA agents, spies or other undesirables. As her understanding of the people and the place deepens, Rachel will be able to come up with more and more questions to ask: to cross-check her ideas, to corroborate earlier information, to test her developing hypotheses. She also makes friends and gets involved.

As Lucilla spends more time in Midhurst College of Further Education she discovers that two of the lecturers bitterly resent her presence. One is openly rude, the other keeps suggesting she does not come to his classes because they are 'routine', 'boring' or 'the lads will be using bad language'. This man has terrible discipline problems, which make watching his classes embarrassing. The rude man dislikes the changes in English vocational education that have occurred over the past twenty years. He yearns for the 'old days' when vocational education was dominated by young male apprentices who came in on day release to learn trades. Both these men refuse to be interviewed, and will not talk to her in the common room or dining hall. They see her as the university's spy, or as an informer working for the Principal. The other staff are friendly, and not at all interested in what Lucilla is doing. The students are puzzled by her research: it is not scientific. They are going to get jobs in laboratories in proper subjects like electrical engineering and computer science. Overwhelmingly male, they are tolerant of Lucilla, but suggest she is too scruffy to get a husband and ought to dress more smartly.

At the end of her year or more, Rachel packs up her stuff and returns to Boarbridge. There she sorts out her data and picks a central theme with which to organize them. Using anthropological theory, and organizing her data around that theme, she writes a PhD thesis. Once that is done, she starts to publish articles about 'her' village, and to write a book. That takes a considerable time, so that if Rachel spent 2000 in her village, the book would probably appear in 2005 or so. Jane Cowan, for example, did her main fieldwork in Sohos in the 1983–5 period, got her PhD in 1988, and published her book in 1990. Rachel's career after her PhD should include a lectureship and return to Galicia periodically over the next ten years or so. She might do her next piece of research on Galicians in some other region of Spain (e.g. Catalonia) or working in another country such as Switzerland (Buechler and Buechler, 1981, 1987). She might study a separatist movement in another country.

At the end of her year Lucilla, too, withdraws from Midhurst, although she might still do interviews with the trainees or staff, or meet the trainees when they go out together. She could have decided to re-interview them as a formal follow-up stage of the project. All these are easy because she and her informants are all in Boarbridge. Lucilla too needs to organize her data (although she *should* have been doing this all along, transcribing interviews, and putting her fieldnotes and interview transcripts into AtlasTi as she collected them). Using a sociological theory, she writes her PhD, and then begins to publish papers and ideally a book. This too takes several years. Perhaps she too gets a lectureship, but she is much less likely to revisit Midhurst, or re-study trainee laboratory technicians or even FE: her career would be enhanced by doing her next project on a different topic, perhaps a team of biologists working on mosquito control or stem cells.

If Rachel Verinder is going to be a successful researcher she has to go to her Galician fishing village and come home again to Boarbridge with her data. She is a failure if she hates the staple diet so much that she comes home after a week, saying the villagers are barbarians. However, she is also a failure if she becomes more Galician than the Galicians. If Rachel stops writing her diary, collecting and recording data, and thinking like an anthropologist, and becomes a leading light of the Galician separatist movement, then she has 'gone native'. If Dr Goby visits and finds Rachel leading the protest march on Madrid, or planting a bomb in the police post, or organizing a school boycott, she would have every reason to accuse her of 'going native'. For Lucilla to 'go native' is possible, but more complicated. If she marries one of the students or staff, if she abandons the PhD to train as an FE lecturer, if she decides to retrain as a laboratory technician herself, or become a researcher or officer for the technicians' trade union, then she has gone native. This does sometimes happen with people doing fieldwork in health settings, who abandon sociology to train as a doctor or a nurse, but it is not common in the sociology of education or of science.

Rachel and Lucilla's research and careers look distinct, and are not hard to classify as anthropology and sociology. Rachel will belong to the Association of Social Anthropologists and the American Anthropological Association, publish in the *Journal of the Royal Anthropological Institute* and *American Ethnologist*. Lucilla will belong to the British Sociological Association and the American Sociological Association, and publish in *Sociology* and *Qualitative Studies in Education*. They could be friends, even flatmates or lovers, but they are in different disciplines. They use different theories, and theorists, and have no reason to read or cite each other's work. Because their topics are so separate, this is not surprising. However, the gulf is *not* due to empirical topic, but to disciplinary identity grounded in theoretical differences. Lucilla will never read or cite the anthropology of education either (Atkinson and Delamont, 1980, 1990; Delamont and Atkinson, 1995).

To illustrate the differences further, we can contrast another pair of ethnographers studying urban areas. Imagine that Rachel Verinder starts her PhD alongside a fellow student, Franklin Blake, who is passionately committed to urban anthropology. When Rachel sets off for her Galician village, Franklin packs his bags and heads for Munich, using one of four strategies to find a manageable project. He could choose a neighbourhood, live in it, and treat it as an urban village, like Press (1979) in Seville. He could choose one set of people, such as migrants from a particular place, and make them his focus as Grillo (1985) did in Lyon, and Kenny (1960) did in Madrid. He could choose an institution or organization, such as a hospital or a factory, and treat it as a microcosm of the city. This is frequently done by urban anthropologists in America, such as the contributors to the collections edited by Messerschmidt (1982) and Burawoy and his colleagues (1991). Alternatively, Franklin could choose one category of people, such as members of a trade union, or tour guides, or priests, or practitioners of acupuncture, or antique dealers, and focus on them (e.g. Sheehan, 1993, on Dublin intellectuals). McKevitt's (1991a, 1991b) work in San Giovanni Rotondo focused on devotees of Padre Pio, and McDonogh (1986) focused on elite families in Barcelona.

Munich has migrants from Greece, Italy, Vietnam, Turkey, all the nations of the former Yugoslavia, and Germans who have moved in from rural areas or other cities in Germany. Franklin could therefore choose all sorts of projects for his PhD in Munich, before settling down to use the same range of methods, or a selection of them, as Rachel uses in her fishing village. He could even focus on Bavarian separatists to parallel her Galician regionalists. The fieldwork contexts will be more varied in a big city, depending on the project. McDonogh (1986: xi) describes doing fieldwork at the opera:

> families invited me into another experience of the opera house in the aristocratic loges of the first balcony. The first performance I saw from this vantage was Montserrat Caballe singing *L'Africaine* in her home theatre. The magnificence of that performance highlighted the dualities of my role as participant observer – half attentive to the stage and half attentive to the dramas around me.

Compare that fieldwork setting with Belmonte's (1989: 275) Naples, in a district he calls Fontana del Re, not at all like the opera house in Barcelona:

> the district was notorious in Naples as a dangerous zone, a den of thieves, roughnecks, and prostitutes … a disproportionate number of the inhabitants earned their living collecting cardboard and junk.

Let us assume that Franklin settles on studying the tensions among guestworkers from the former Yugoslavia, and how previously shared identifiers such as Serbo-Croat are unravelling since 1989, a study to parallel Danforth's (1995, 2000) on Greeks and Macedonians in Melbourne.

We can contrast Franklin with a sociologist, Garrett Monmouth, doing an ethnography in Boarbridge itself. He could have decided to focus on one neighbourhood, or one set of people, or one institution or organization. As Boarbridge is a historic city, Garrett might study the tourist industry, or museums, or heritage (Dicks, 2000). If he were more interested in generic urban issues he could focus on perhaps the young homeless (Hall, 2003), bodybuilders using gyms (Monaghan, 1999) or bouncers on the doors of clubs and pubs. However, let us imagine he has decided to focus on refugees from the wars in Yugoslavia, and also discovers the disintegration of the old 'Yugoslavian' identity and the Serbo-Croat language.

The contrast between Franklin's anthropology and Garrett's sociology is just as stark as between Rachel and Lucilla. Franklin is away abroad, working in two other languages, German and Serbo-Croat (or rather Serbian and Croatian). He will not see his supervisor for nine months, merely exchanging letters or e-mails. As

Dr Teague of Southersham said to us: 'I don't feel that one should be poking one's nose into a student's fieldwork ... it can be awkward, embarrassing and annoying for a research student.' Similarly Dr Drummock of Kingford said, 'The student has got to be independent enough to form their own judgement'. Students told us, 'You're not allowed to visit the department when you're in the field. Because you're supposed to be in the field' (Beulah Wyston, Southersham). Franklin will collect a great deal of data and focus on his theoretical theme once 'home' in Boarbridge. Garrett will see his supervisor regularly throughout the fieldwork, and will be told repeatedly by his supervisor to focus on one aspect of the refugees in Boarbridge and not drift off target. Because they have both done PhDs on Serbians and/or Croatians in exile, the two men *might* attend the same seminars or conferences, and even compare findings, but Franklin is likely to go to the same meetings as Rachel, and Garrett to the same ones as Lucilla.

One other clear difference between Rachel and Franklin as anthropologists and Lucilla and Garrett as sociologists will have been their pre-fieldwork training, especially their exposure to methods training. Sociologists in the UK have been much more enthusiastic about compulsory training in research methods, including qualitative techniques, than British anthropologists have. As Dr Trevithick of Southersham told us: 'Participant observation is not, I would say, a research method which can be taught in the classroom and then applied in the field.... It's something you can only learn by doing it.' Dr Fustian of Kingford concurred: 'All this business of training I think is largely spurious. It is something that is learnt by the experience of doing it. It's rather like teaching music. You cannot teach people how to play without a piano. It's only by playing they can learn, and I think fieldwork is like that.'

All four fictional characters could struggle with the issues raised by the 'rhetorical turn' and by postmodernism. In the past fifteen years both anthropology and sociology have been through some turmoil about the ways in which data are analysed and texts written, but the debates are contained within each discipline.

In the next section the general lessons that all four would have learned from their fieldwork are distilled into some general precepts.

ETHNOGRAPHY FROM START TO FINISH

Ethnography is hard work: physically, emotionally and mentally exhausting. The research does not proceed in a straight line, but in a series of loops, because each step leads the researcher to reflect upon, and even revisit, earlier steps. For example, if an observation in a biochemistry lab included one postdoctoral fellow telling the researcher that the senior professor was having an affair with another postdoctoral fellow and allocated her the 'best' projects, that would open up research issues: 'How do projects get allocated?', 'How does gossip in the lab work?', 'What literature is there on women in science?', and so on. Such questions might be dead ends, but a researcher would need to re-read all the fieldnotes and interview transcripts, do a literature search, plan to raise all three topics in future fieldwork, and perhaps revisit any past fieldsites to raise those issues. That example comes from Kevles's (1998) historical reconstruction of the Baltimore case. If he had learned of such an accusation while doing an ethnography he could have followed it up in other labs, other research groups, but because it came up in a history he had no opportunity to pursue the topic further as an ethnographer would do. Because ethnography proceeds in loops, the foreshadowed problems are revisited, the access negotiations reveal key features of the setting used when analysing the data, the analysis returns the scholar to the fieldnotes, and so on *ad infinitum*.

During fieldwork it is vital to sample the setting in a systematic way. A good study focuses on different types of participant, includes observations made at all times of the day (and, perhaps the night), and in all the possible locations. It is not always possible for a researcher to watch the opposite sex, people of very different ages, or push into all the possible settings, but it is necessary to plan to observe systematically wherever possible. In a fishing village the researcher should not only observe fishing, but also net mending, the sales of the catch, boat repair, women's everyday lives, the days of men too old to go out to sea any more, and the experiences of children. Observations should not only encompass the sea, but also the church, the vegetable garden, the school and the fish market. Thinking through all the possible places to observe, the times to observe, the people to watch, and discovering whether or not it is possible and productive to do so, is a central task of good fieldwork (Spradley, 1979).

The beginning, the middle and the end of fieldwork can all be problematic. Autobiographical accounts by anthropologists and sociologists suggest many researchers experience culture shock when conducting their fieldwork; this is rare when researchers gather their data by post while among colleagues. Much of the methods literature also focuses on using the initial culture shock (Geer, 1964) as a particularly fruitful time for insightful data collection. Once accepted by actors at a fieldwork site, researchers have to guard against 'going native': abandoning the researcher perspective and adopting the views of the actors in the setting. Some researchers are reluctant to leave the field even when no further useful insights or data are being gained because actors in the fieldsite have become friends, and the fieldwork comfortable.

Fieldwork in an unfamiliar culture is both harder and easier than fieldwork in one's own familiar society. In an unfamiliar culture everything is strange, and so it is unlikely that the researcher will forget to convey that strangeness. In contrast, researchers studying their own society often fail to report, or to make anthropologically strange, many aspects of the setting. So the French researcher who goes to live in a Brazilian *favela* will have a more frightening, bewildering and confusing experience, but the data will be unfamiliar to her readers in France, and even exotic. The same researcher studying everyday life in France is likely to feel safe, clear-minded and coherent, but to have to work very hard to produce an 'interesting' account of the fieldsite, unless, of course, she becomes embroiled in witchcraft (Favret-Saada, 1980).

One of the biggest problems is that informants often want to help researchers, by showing and telling what they think investigators want to see and hear. Equally, informants may systematically hide things, and tell lies, to protect themselves, their secrets or their privacy. Researchers who prefer fieldwork to the quicker method of interviewing hope to get beyond the informants' impression management, even though sometimes they discover that their informants initially believed them to be spies, tax collectors or loose women (Kenna, 1992).

Foreshadowed problem(s)

Central to good ethnography is an intellectually thoughtful set of foreshadowed problems: ideas that will guide the access negotiations, the initial fieldwork, the early writing of the out-of-the-field diary. These come from reading, from colleagues and mentors, from the core of the discipline. The ethnography is only as good as the ideas the researcher deploys. At the time of writing I am planning an ethnography of opera tourism in Central Europe. The foreshadowed problems include, for example, ideas that people who pay for holidays focused on opera in Prague

and Budapest will also attend opera in the UK, will prefer 'traditional' production values, classic core repertoire works, and appreciate relatively low seat prices. That is, they also go to, for example, Opera North productions in Leeds, prefer the Hebrew slaves in *Nabucco* to look like illustrations from a Ladybird book of the Bible rather than Jews in Dachau, want to see *Tosca* rather than *Der Ferne Klang* or *Die Vögel*, and believe that the two London opera houses, Royal Opera House (ROH) and English National Opera (ENO), cost too much money, as do hotels in London. All these ideas, gleaned from, for example, the correspondence pages of the opera magazines and the brochures of the specialist tour companies, could be blown out of the water by the first period of fieldwork. That would be splendid: it is marvellous when the foreshadowed problems turn out to have been wrong.

This is one difference between team research and an individual project. In a team effort it is necessary to discuss the foreshadowed problems, and share them. The main difference between team ethnographies that ended up with a joint project, such as Strauss et al. (1964), and those that produce an unintegrated collection of individual accounts (e.g. Stake and Easley, 1978) is the pooling of the hypotheses before, during and after the fieldwork. The ORACLE project on primary to secondary transfer (Delamont and Galton, 1986) involved coordinating the fieldwork of seven observers, most of them untrained. In Galton and Delamont (1985) we discussed this as follows:

> The timetable of the ethnographic research allowed us to use the study of the 9–13 schools, in September 1977, as a pilot study for 1978, when the pupils transferred into the 12–18 and 11–14 schools. Thus by 1978 we had a fistful of ideas from the 1977 study which we could use as 'foreshadowed problems' or 'sensitizing concepts' in 1978. Sara Delamont and Maurice Galton were involved in both years, and others only worked in one year, but some of the 1977 lessons were carried forward to 1978.

This was an unusual feature of a school ethnography. We had a chance to think *for a year* between the Ashburton phase of the research and the Bridgehampton and Coalthorpe phase. Our account continues:

> We never believed that ethnographers enter the field open-minded. In the 1977 study of the two 9–13 schools we had a short list of 'foreshadowed problems' derived from our reading of other school studies. These were of two kinds: some vaguely 'theoretical' ideas we had derived from the literature, and some 'common sense' ideas derived more from our members' knowledge. Among the more 'theoretical' ideas we were interested

in utilizing Basil Bernstein's (1971, 1974) ideas on classification and framing and visible and invisible pedagogies, the beginnings of labelling, and the notion of 'coping strategies'. More concretely, we asked all observers to look carefully at pupils' 'adjustment' to their new schools, sibling comparisons, staffroom discussions of pupils, bullying and the schools' responses to it, and to compare 'theory' and 'practice' in such areas as curriculum balance, pupil groupings, allocation of teachers to classes and so on. For example, in Local Authority A we had found that allocation of children to bands at Guy Mannering School was more closely related to the primary school attended than ability or heads' reports, and so we asked the observers in Local Authorities B and C to examine band allocation, class allocation and so forth.

This is a fairly typical list of foreshadowed problems. Some are theoretical at a high level of generalization (visible pedagogy), some are middle-range concepts (coping strategy), some are concrete issues (how are new children allocated to classes?). The big problem with all team research is that each observer is bound to have her own agenda, and they may not all be equally explicit for the researcher herself, or in the fieldnotes or in the out-of-the-field diary and analytic memos. As we commented on the ORACLE project: 'How far the observers took any notice of these "foreshadowed" problems is, in retrospect, unclear – because of the diverse nature of the observers.'

Access and initial encounters

Having done the reading and thinking to develop foreshadowed problems, the good ethnographer negotiates access to one or more fieldsites, making careful notes of all the interactions. Access can be by letters and formal interviews if the fieldsite is a formal organization or a private space such as a family. If the fieldsite is a public place, then access may be a process of hanging out and informal chats. There are many autobiographical accounts of access negotiations (see Delamont, 2002: ch. 6) by sociologists and anthropologists, and the topic is covered in all the textbooks. There are three golden rules. First, every aspect of the processes needs to be meticulously recorded, because vital features of the setting are made visible during the access stages. Second, failed access attempts are 'data', just as successful ones are. Third, the harder it is to gain access, the more likely the work will be rewarding once 'inside' and vice versa: very often deceptively easy access leads to barrier-strewn fieldwork.

Geer (1964) wrote the classic paper on initial encounters, and its insights have not been bettered (see also Atkinson et al., 2003). Given the importance of fighting familiarity (Delamont and Atkinson, 1995; Delamont, 2002), the initial encounter is the best time to see the genuinely unfamiliar and to force oneself to search for the vantage point from which the familiar can be *made* strange.

Data collection

The biggest problem novices find when preparing for ethnographic fieldwork is that the methods books are not explicit enough about what to observe, how to observe and what to write down. It is very hard to describe in words how to observe. Wolcott (1981) has produced an excellent attempt comparing his methods in his anthropological research (in an African beer hall) and his educational projects in the USA. Essentially an ethnographer observes everything she can, writes the most detailed fieldnotes she can, takes time to expand, elaborate and reflect upon them outside the field and/or as soon as time permits, constantly pesters those being observed to explain what they are doing and why, and sweeps up any documents, pictures or ephemera available. The aim is to produce, in Geertz's (1973) classic formulation, a thick description, of the setting and the actors in it, sufficiently rich to enable a reader to live in that setting without unwittingly violating its basic tenets. So if it is absolutely forbidden for women to set foot on fishing boats, or for Turkish children in Munich (Yalcun-Heckmann, 1994) to have fireworks on New Year's Eve, that should be crystal-clear from the eventual publications, which will have been drawn from the observations and interrogations.

Recording

The most important thing researchers have to do is record what they see, usually in fieldnotes but sometimes on tape or film, because anything not recorded is lost. Once recorded, data are safe, although the real work of the research comes with analysing data, interpreting them, and writing them up into accounts for a wider readership. Fieldwork that is never written up is wasted. Reading the autobiographical accounts of both sociologists and anthropologists, it is clear that many ethnographers keep fieldnotes and other kinds of more reflexive records such as an 'out-of-the-field diary' in which theoretical ideas can be rehearsed. In the past decade, scholars have been more prepared to discuss and reflect on how fieldnotes are, and can be, written (Sanjek, 1990; Emerson et al., 1995, 2001). There is no point in observing things and leaving them unrecorded, or in leaving the scribbled notes unelaborated. If interviews are recorded, there is no point in leaving them untranscribed. If photographs are taken, they must be developed, printed and labelled (cf. Pink, Chapter 25, this volume). Film or video, likewise, must have a commentary made while the images are fresh (cf. Pink, ibid.). In anthropological fieldwork, the researcher may need to store data in termite-proof boxes; in all kinds, it is sensible to create duplicates and back-ups as soon as practically possible. The importance of writing, still the most vital form of record-keeping, is explored in Delamont (2002: Chs 4, 8 and 12).

Reflecting

Central to ethnography is the constant and tiring process of reflecting. Reflexivity is the most important characteristic of fieldwork, and of analysis. Hammersley and Atkinson (1995) explore the concept thoroughly. Reflexivity is the way that qualitative researchers strive for reliability and validity, and the development and training of one's reflexive skills and empathies is the keystone of what Coffey (1999) calls *The Ethnographic Self*. Constant exercise of reflexivity should inform all the stages from the foreshadowed problems through the data collection to the eventual writing up (Ellis and Bochner, 1996). One vital stage of the fieldwork, where reflexivity needs to be exercised, is the exit from the fieldsite, which is too often neglected.

Many methods books spend thousands of words on access and initial encounters, while ignoring leaving. Yet the disengagement from the field is just as important as the entry and engagement. Fine (1983), Altheide (1980), Maines et al. (1980), Wulff (2000) and Delamont (2002) all address leaving. A good basic principle is that once the fieldsite feels like home it is time to leave: fieldwork should be uncomfortable. Once it is feeling familiar, it is time to move on.

Analysis

The analytic strategies available to ethnographers have not changed in principle for a century (Strauss, 1987). However, the development of software packages that handle text has changed the practices of analysis and made it much more a matter of public discussion. Useful ways into

the literature on software packages and practices are reported in Weitzman and Miles (1994), Fielding (2001) and Fielding and Lee (2002). Coffey and Atkinson (1996, 2001) address the epistemology of the new technologies. Bryman and Taylor (2003) are entirely devoted to analysis, with several chapters on the analysis of qualitative data. A greater self-consciousness about analysis is inextricably linked to the debates on writing ethnography.

Writing

The ways in which ethnographic data are written have been controversial for the past fifteen years, and the issues are complicated by the vogue for postmodernism. One of the major issues associated with postmodern standpoints concerns the so-called 'crisis of representation' that was especially prominent among social and cultural anthropologists in the 1980s, and permeated other social sciences too in the subsequent years. This supposed crisis threatened the taken-for-granted foundations of social inquiry. The crisis of representation was centred on the appropriate modes of cultural representation or reconstruction. It was, and is, widely recognized that 'the ethnography' has for many decades referred to both the conduct of fieldwork in all its aspects, and the written product of that research such as the monograph. The scholar is thus recognizably engaged in a double process of engagement with the field. First, she or he is engaged in a protracted series of transactions and explorations with informants. In and of themselves, these engagements are far from innocent. The cultures and social realities reported in the course of fieldwork are dependent on the active explorations, and the joint negotiations, that the investigator undertakes in conjunction with her or his hosts and informants. Secondly, there are further acts of interpretation when the scholar acts as author. The discoveries of disciplines like sociology and anthropology are not the revelations of an independent social reality, but are *fictions* – in the sense that they are created and crafted products.

This general perspective was articulated and widely publicized in *Writing Culture* (Clifford and Marcus, 1986). A number of authors explored the textual conventions of cultural anthropology, and through their textual explorations raised more profound questions concerning the ethnographic project. Their reflections included the recognition that ethnographic representation is grounded in conventional modes of representation. These include textual devices and models associated with genres of fiction, as well as styles of non-fiction text, such as travel writing (Clifford, 1988; Atkinson, 1990, 1992). Their concerns were not confined to the purely textual aspects of ethnographic monographs, however. They also focused on the direct relationship between the *authority* of the ethnographic text and the *authorship* of that selfsame text. The conventional ethnographic monograph, it was argued, was a depersonalized document, in which the ethnographer was an invisible but privileged implied narrator. The social world is surveyed and reported from the single, dominant perspective of the ethnographic author, who is elided from the text itself. In other words, the stability of the ethnographic enterprise – an especially enduring characteristic of anthropology for many decades – was held up to question. The authority of the ethnography – as opposed to its subsequent interpretation at the meta-level of comparative ethnology and anthropological theory – had remained relatively stable. The crisis of representation in many ways seemed to offer a more profound challenge than the comings and goings of fashionable theories and debates. It seemed to strike at the very legitimacy of the conventional ethnographic mode of representation, not only in anthropology (Wolcott, 1990; Wolf, 1992).

The textual turn in qualitative research has had its productive side. It has led to a self-conscious attempt on the part of some authors to deploy and develop a variety of textual conventions, to transgress the taken-for-granted boundaries between genres, and thus to match literary styles to analytic interests. Richardson (1994), for instance, makes a case for writing as a mode of analysis in its own right. There are, metaphorically speaking, two kinds of response to the 'crisis of representation' and its associated ideas. The pessimistic view might lead one to regard the ethnographic enterprise as all but impossible. One might lapse into silence. The crisis could easily result in an intellectualized form of writer's block. The more optimistic response would be to recognize literary and rhetorical conventions for what they are, and resolve to use and explore them creatively. In practice many contemporary scholars have taken the optimistic path. If one starts from the recognition that there is no such thing as a perfectly innocent or transparent mode of representation, then it is possible to explore the possibilities of written text – and other representations – in a creative way. One can use them to construct particular kinds of analysis, and to evoke particular kinds of response in one's audience.

CONCLUSION

The chapter started in roiling smoke, and stressed that the contest is never over. It must end in that same smoke. The field is never entirely ours. Ethnographic research is exhausting and fascinating and it is a great privilege to be allowed into other people's social worlds. Despite exaggerated claims that classic methods are outmoded, and classic textual forms extinct, there is plenty of scope for proper ethnography to be done. There are Spanish soldiers, hunter gatherers and Cajun detectives still waiting in the smoke for us to live among them and capture their worlds using ethnographic methods.

ACKNOWLEDGEMENT

Rosemary Jones word processed this paper for me, for which I am grateful.

REFERENCES

Altheide, D. (1980) 'Leaving the newsroom', in W.B. Shaffir, R.A. Stebbins and A. Turowetz (eds), *Fieldwork Experience*. New York: St Martin's Press, pp. 301–10.

Atkinson, P.A. (1990) *The Ethnographic Imagination*. London: Routledge.

Atkinson, P.A. (1992) *Understanding Ethnographic Texts*. London: Sage.

Atkinson, P.A. (1997) 'Narrative turn or blind alley?', *Qualitative Health Research*, 7(3): 325–44.

Atkinson, P.A. and Delamont, S. (1980) 'The two traditions of educational anthropology: sociology and anthropology compared', *British Journal of Sociology of Education*, 1(2): 139–52.

Atkinson, P.A. and Delamont, S. (1990) 'Writing about teachers', *Teaching and Teacher Education*, 6(2): 111–25.

Atkinson, P.A. and Silverman, D. (1997) 'Kundera's *Immortality*: the interview society and the invention of the self', *Qualitative Inquiry*, 3(3): 304–25.

Atkinson, P.A., Delamont, S., Coffey, A., Lofland, J. and Lofland, L. (eds) (2001) *The Handbook of Ethnography*. London: Sage.

Atkinson, P.A., Coffey, A.J. and Delamont, S. (2003) *Key Themes in Qualitative Research*. Walnut Creek, CA: AltaMira Press.

Behar, R. and Gordon, D. (eds) (1995) *Women Writing Culture*. Berkeley: University of California Press.

Belmonte, T. (1989) *The Broken Fountain* (2nd ed.). New York: Columbia University Press (originally published 1983).

Bryman, A. and Taylor M. (eds) (2003) *Handbook of Analysis*. London: Sage.

Buechler, H. and Buechler, J.M. (1981) *Carmen*. Cambridge, MA: Schenkman.

Buechler, H. and Buechler, J.M. (eds) (1987) *Migrants in Europe*. New York: Greenwood Press.

Burawoy, M. (ed.) (1991) *Ethnography Unbound*. Berkeley: University of California Press.

Burke, J.L. (1993) *In the Electric Mist with the Confederate Dead*. London: Phoenix/Orion.

Clifford, J. (1988) *The Predicament of Culture*. Cambridge, MA: Harvard University Press.

Clifford, J. and Marcus, G.E. (eds) (1986) *Writing Culture*. Berkeley: University of California Press.

Coffey, A. (1999) *The Ethnographic Self*. London: Sage.

Coffey, A. and Atkinson, P.A. (eds) (1994) *Occupational Socialisation and Working Lives*. Aldershot: Avebury.

Coffey, A. and Atkinson, P.A. (1996) *Making Sense of Qualitative Data*. Thousand Oaks, CA: Sage.

Coffey, A. and Atkinson, P. (2001) 'Hecate's domain', in C.J. Pole and R.G. Burgess (eds), *Cross-Cultural Case Study*. Oxford: Elsevier, pp. 21–42.

Cowan, J. (1990) *Dance and the Body Politic in Northern Greece*. Princeton, NJ: Princeton University Press.

Danforth, L. (1995) *The Macedonian Conflict*. Princeton, NJ: Princeton University Press.

Danforth, L. (2000) 'How can a woman give birth to one Greek and one Macedonian?', in J.K. Cowan (ed.), *Macedonia*. London: Pluto, pp. 85–103.

Deegan, M.J. (1988) *Jane Addams and the Men of the Chicago School*. New Brunswick, NJ; Transaction Press.

Deegan, M.J. (2001) 'The Chicago School', in P.A. Atkinson et al. (eds), *The Handbook of Ethnography*. London: Sage, pp. 11–25.

Delamont, S. (1995) *Appetites and Identities*. London: Routledge.

Delamont, S. (1997) 'Fuzzy borders and the fifth moment', *British Journal of Sociology of Education*, 18(4): 601–6.

Delamont, S. (2002) *Fieldwork in Educational Settings* (2nd ed.). London: Falmer.

Delamont, S. and Atkinson, P.A. (1995) *Fighting Familiarity*. Cresskill, NJ: Hampton.

Delamont, S. and Galton, M. (1986) *Inside the Secondary Classroom*. London: Routledge.

Delamont, S., Atkinson, P.A. and Parry, O. (2000a) *The Doctoral Experience*. London: Falmer.

Delamont, S., Coffey, A. and Atkinson, P.A. (2000b) 'The twilight years?', *Qualitative Studies in Education*, 13(3): 223–38.

Dicks, B. (2000) *Heritage, Place and Community*. Cardiff: University of Wales Press.

Ellis, C. and Bochner, A.P. (eds) (1996) *Composing Ethnography*. Walnut Creek, CA: AltaMira Press.

Emerson, R.M., Fretz, R.I. and Shaw, L.L. (1995) *Writing Ethnographic Fieldnotes*. Chicago: Chicago University Press.

Emerson, R.M., Fretz, R.I. and Shaw, L.L. (2001). 'Participant observation and fieldnotes', in P. Atkinson et al. (eds), *Handbook of Ethnography*. London: Sage, pp. 352–68.

Faubion, J. (2001) 'Currents of cultural fieldwork', in P.A. Atkinson et al. (eds), *Handbook of Ethnography*. London: Sage, pp. 39–59.

Favret-Saada, J. (1980) *Deadly Words*. Cambridge: Cambridge University Press.

Fielding, N. (2001) 'Computer applications in qualitative research', in P. Atkinson et al. (eds), *Handbook of Ethnography*. London: Sage, pp. 453–67.

Fielding, N. and Lee, R. (2002) 'New patterns in the adoption and use of qualitative software', *Fieldnotes*, 14(2): 197–216.

Fine, G.A. (1983) *Shared Fantasy*. Chicago: Chicago University Press.

Galton, M. and Delamont, S. (1985) 'Speaking with forked tongue? Two styles of observation in the ORACLE project', in R. Burgess (ed.), *Field Methods in the Study of Education*. London: Falmer Books, pp. 163–90.

Geer, B. (1964) 'First days in the field', in P.E. Hammond (ed.), *Sociologists at Work*. New York: Basic Books, pp. 372–98.

Geertz, C. (1973) *The Interpretation of Cultures*. New York: Basic Books.

Gleeson, D. and Mardle, G. (1980) *Further Education or Training*. London: Routledge & Kegan Paul.

Goddard, V.A. (1996) *Gender, Family and Work in Naples*. Oxford: Berg.

Grillo, R. (1985) *Ideologies and Institutions in Urban France*. Cambridge: Cambridge University Press.

Hall, T. (2003) *Better Times Than This: Youth Homelessness in Britain*. London: Pluto Press.

Hammersley, M. and Atkinson, P. (1995) *Ethnography: Principles and Practice* (2nd ed.). London: Routledge.

Hernandez, G. (1995) 'Multiple subjectivities and strategic positionality', in R. Behar and D.A. Gordon (eds), *Women Writing Culture*. Berkeley: University of California Press, pp. 148–65.

Hirsch, E. and Gellner, D.N. (2001) Introduction, in D. Gellner and E. Hirsch (eds), *Inside Organizations*. Oxford: Berg, pp. 1–15.

Jackson, A. (ed.) (1987) *Anthropology at Home*. London: Tavistock.

Just, R. (2000) *A Greek Island Cosmos*. Oxford: James Currey.

Kenna, M. (1992) 'Changing places and altered perspectives', in J. Okely and H. Callaway (eds), *Anthropology and Autobiography*. London: Routledge, pp. 147–62.

Kenny, M. (1960) *A Spanish Tapestry*. London: Cohen & West.

Kevles, D. (1998) *The Baltimore Case: A Trial of Politics, Science and Character*. New York: W.W. Norton.

Leach, E.R. (1984) 'Glimpses of the unmentionable in the history of British social anthropology', *Annual Review of Anthropology*, 13: 1–23.

Leach, E.R. (2001) *Collected Works*, 2 vols. New Haven: Yale University Press.

LeCompte, M. (1998) 'Synonyms and sequences: the development of an intellectual autobiography', in K.B. de Marrais (ed.), *Inside Stories*. Mahwah, NJ: Lawrence Erlbaum, pp. 197–210.

Lutkehaus, N. (1986) 'She was very Cambridge: Camilla Wedgwood and the history of women in British social anthropology', *American Ethnologist*, 13(4): 776–98.

Macdonald, S. (2001) 'British social anthropology', in P.A. Atkinson et al. (eds), *The Handbook of Ethnography*. London: Sage, pp. 60–79.

McDonogh, G. (1986) *The Good Families of Barcelona*. Princeton, NJ: Princeton University Press.

McKevitt, C. (1991a) 'To suffer and never to die', *Journal of Mediterranean Studies*, 1(1): 57–67.

McKevitt, C. (1991b) 'San Giovanni Rotondo and the shrine of Padre Pio', in J. Eade and M. Sallnow (eds), *Contesting the Sacred*. London: Routledge, pp. 77–97.

Maines, D.R., Shaffir, W. and Turowetz, A. (1980) 'Leaving the field in ethnographic research', in W.B. Shaffir, R.A. Stebbins and A. Turowetz (eds), *Fieldwork Experience*. New York: St Martin's Press, pp. 261–80.

Messerschmidt, D. (ed.) (1982) *Anthropologists at Home in North America*. Cambridge: Cambridge University Press.

Monaghan, L. (1999) 'Creating the ' "perfect body" '. *Body and Society*, 5(2–3): 267–90.

Pink, S. (2000) 'Informants who come home', in V. Amit (ed.), *Constructing the Field*. London: Routledge, pp. 96–119.

Platt, J. (1995) 'Research methods and the second Chicago School', in G.A. Fine (ed.), *A Second Chicago School*. Chicago: University of Chicago Press, pp. 82–109.

Press, I. (1979) *The City as Context*. Urbana, IL: Illinois University Press.

Raissiguier, C. (1994) *Becoming Women, Becoming Workers*. New York: State University of New York Press.

Reed-Danahay, D. (1996) *Education and Identity in Rural France*. Cambridge: Cambridge University Press.

Richardson, L. (1994) 'Writing: a method of inquiry', in N.K. Denzin and Y.S. Lincoln (eds), *Handbook of Qualitative Research*. Thousand Oaks, CA: Sage, pp. 516–29.

Riseborough, G. (1993) 'GBH – the Gobbo Barmy Army', in I. Bates and G. Riseborough (eds), *Youth and Inequality*. Buckingham: Open University Press, pp. 160–228.

Rosenberg, H.G. (1988) *A Negotiated World*. Toronto: University of Toronto Press.

Sanjek, R. (ed.) (1990) *Fieldnotes*. Ithaca, NY: Cornell University Press.

Sheehan, E.A. (1993) 'The student culture and the ethnography of Irish intellectuals', in C.B. Brettell (ed.), *When They Read What We Write*. London: Bergin & Garvey, pp. 86–101.

Spradley, J.P. (1979) *The Ethnographic Interview*. New York: Holt, Rinehart & Winston.

Stake, R. and Easley, W. (eds) (1978) *Case Studies in Science Education*. Urbana, IL: CIRCE, University of Illinois.

Stoller, P. (1989) *The Taste of Ethnographic Things*. Philadelphia: University of Pennsylvania Press.

Strauss, A. et al. (1964) *Psychiatric Ideologies and Institutions*. New York: Free Press.

Strauss, A.L. (1987) *Qualitative Analysis for Social Scientists*. Cambridge: Cambridge University Press.

Valli, L. (1986) *Becoming Clerical Workers*. New York: Routledge.

Wafer, J. (1991) *The Taste of Blood: Spirit Possession in Brazilian Candomble*. Philadelphia: University of Pennsylvania Press.

Walker, J.C. (1988) *Louts and Legends*. Sydney: Allen & Unwin.

Weitzman, E.A. and Miles, M.B. (1994) *Computer Programs for Qualitative Data Analysis*. Thousand Oaks, CA: Sage.

Wolcott, H.F. (1981) 'Confessions of a "trained" observer', in T.S. Popkewitz and B.R. Tabachnick (eds), *The Study of Schooling*. New York: Praeger, pp. 247–63.

Wolcott, H.F. (1990) *Writing Up Qualitative Research*, Beverley Hills, CA: Sage.

Wolf, M. (1992) *The Thrice Told Tale*. Stanford: Stanford University Press.

Wulff, H. (2000) 'Access to a closed world', in V. Amit (ed.), *Constructing the Field*. London: Routledge, pp. 147–61.

Yalcun-Heckmann, L. (1994) 'Are fireworks Islamic?', in C. Stewart and R. Shaw (eds), *Syncretism/Anti-Syncretism*. London: Routledge, pp. 178–95.

15

Ethical issues

Anne Ryen

Eke: What do you do (2.0) I mean (1.0) do you never do anything when out travelling? You're always travelling alone.

Anne: I am here to work.

Eke: Yeah, but you can't be working all the time.

Anne: (laughing) That's true. So, what do you offer?

Eke: What do you want?

(Dar es Salaam, Tanzania, February 2001)

Fieldwork is definitely more colourful and challenging than most published versions (for some more personal accounts see Ryen, 2002b). The opening extract is from some after-the-interview talk with one of my male interviewees. Compared to my field experiences both in North and South projects, there is nothing sensational about this extract. The sensation rests with the peculiar situation that the issue of delicate emotions in fieldwork is conspicuous in its absence from methodological textbooks or field reports. Why are these fairly frequent experiences treated as non-data, how do we handle 'field offers', does the effort to get close by building rapport imply that we are cheating, and would it be ethically acceptable (and probably methodologically interesting) to follow up invitations? The outcome of the story in the opening extract does follow later on in the discussion of the ethical dilemmas encountered in my own fieldwork, which will focus on ethics across cultures and online. This illustrates two challenges – ethical practice, and how matters come to be constituted as ethical issues.

Whereas so-called 'private' experiences would earlier either have be seen as purely private experiences or at most as a threat to data, the new constructionist paradigms (Gubrium and Holstein, 1997) have pointed to the challenges of multiple realities and questioned the author's authority (Denzin and Lincoln, 1994). This has motivated reflexivity and made written reflections on field experiences more legitimate. Importantly, we need to look at the interplay between epistemology and methodology or theoretical and empirical work. Through this, according to Erica Haimes, 'social scientists go beyond the specific theoretical and empirical practices to enquire further into the social processes that lie behind the very designation of certain matters as being "ethical issues"' (2002: 89). I will return later to the discussion of the social processes through which these issues become constituted as ethical and on which Zygmunt Bauman claims that 'The foolproof – universal and unshakeably founded – ethical code will never be found' (1993: 2–27). Still, the Western research communities offer national ethics research committees, standard checklists on ethics and research, plus procedures for checking research applications (for examples, see BSA, 2002; ASA, 2002; NESH, 2001). Also, most textbooks on methodology have sections on research ethics (Hammersley and Atkinson, 1983; Kvale, 1996; Silverman, 2001; Ryen, 2002b). Consequently, ethical challenges are expected to be handled in accordance with the official ethical codes and regulatory institutions. However, challenging personal fieldwork experiences still tend to be framed in happy endings, to be put behind the veil of generality or given a backstage position in the footnotes or in the appendices (after all, we are also competing for funding).

Still, fieldwork is constantly ridden by ethical challenges. This is recognized by Gary Alan Fine, who claims that 'The production of good things might not be pretty' (1993: 267) and 'Unresolvable ethical dilemmas are endemic to work' (p. 268). On this ground we should share our dilemmas and our choices with colleagues, still knowing that doing qualitative research often compels us to deviate from idealistic rules and statements of ethical practice. Sometimes you get time for reflection, as in the choice of research design (overt or covert) and data collection (overt or covert tape recording). At other times the context demands instant choices or action as with corruption, erotic offers, or illegal actions or information. Despite conditions of good academic work and acceptable textbook practices (Fine, 1993), we still need to integrate autobiographical experiences with analytic reflections.

According to Steinar Kvale (1996: 10), ethics is not restricted to fieldwork, but refers to all stages in the research process including (field relations and) writing up the report. The main point should be to let autobiographical field experiences prompt analytic reflections. One way is to start by having a look at the elements usually constituting the main issues in research ethics.

THE STANDARD ETHICAL ISSUES

There is no international agreement or regulations of ethical standards in research. This becomes clear for anyone involved in so-called North–South projects. Still, the three main issues frequently raised in the Western ethical research discourse and part of the professional association statements and national research guidelines on ethics are codes and consent, confidentiality and trust (Punch, 1994; Thorne, 1998; Hammersley, 1998). Since they all raise more questions than answers, they are useful to the contemporary discussion of ethical research practice.

Codes and consent

Codes and consent refer in particular to 'informed consent'. This means that research subjects have the right to know that they are being researched, the right to be informed about the nature of the research and the right to withdraw at any time.

The relationship between informed consent and covert research is the ultimate illustration of this ethical dilemma in data collection. The classic debates refer to research in military training (Sullivan et al., 1958), Milgram's obedience experiments (Milgram, 1963), infiltration of religious, political or other groups (Lofland and Lejeune, 1960, on Alcoholics Anonymous, Caudill et al., 1952, on infiltration of a psychiatric ward as a mental patient, and Festinger et al., 1956, on penetration of a small religious sect), dubious sampling techniques as in Laud Humphreys's *Tearoom Trade* (1975, where he reconsiders his decision) and related to the use of deception in social psychological experiments (Bok, 1978: 182–202). Punch (1994) refers to more so-called professional 'misdemeanors' from researchers' fieldwork including Malinowski (1967) and Powdermaker (1966). However, the borderline itself between ethical and unethical fieldwork may also undergo reconsideration (cf. the social processes constituting issues as ethical or not).

In general, deception is only acceptable if discomfort is believed to vanish by itself or is removed by a debriefing process after the study. The debriefing can consist of an honest description of the study once it is over, and of psychological support to cope with the stress or the knowledge gained. As a comment upon disguised observation, Kai Erikson claims that persons can be injured in ways researchers can neither anticipate in advance nor compensate for afterwards (Erikson, 1967). The (disputed?) arguments about the long-term effects on Doc from William Foote Whyte's classic study (1943) may serve as an illustration of this issue. In her discussion, Laurel Richardson (1992) claims that Doc's close relationship with Whyte made it impossible for Doc to go back to his friends. Having been the main informant, he had violated the relationship to his friends on the corner. According to Richardson, it was impossible for Whyte to combine the ethical research codes and the ethical codes in the subculture he studied. The same challenges may apply to studies on intimate behaviour and emotions without the subjects' consent (Thomson, 1975). According to Sissela Bok (1978), the implications may be habitual manipulation and professionally less compunction. Accumulated effects on students may affect the professions and eventually contribute to a more general breakdown in trust between researchers and researched. However, a constant revision and reminding of ethical standards seem to have repressed this. In his differentiation between personal morality and professional ethics (a division opposed by Dingwall, 1980), Erikson (1967) sees the latter as the responsibility we have towards each other and our society and which distinguishes us from journalists and spies.

Robert Dingwall (1980) points to some more dilemmas. The distinction between overt and covert research is often unclear. Ethnographers do not always start out with a clear topic, as is the case also in many interview studies. To avoid bias, researchers often do not want their research subjects to know too much,[1] so the really deep question sometimes remains as to what are they consenting and to what extent are they informed. There is also another reason that may restrict the researcher from giving too much information. This is linked to the vested interest in making the interviewee cooperate, whereas much information may increase the risk of withdrawal. Honesty then refers to levels of overt research and, as pointed to by Sally Thorne (1998) and Gary Alan Fine (1993), the line between 'informed' and 'uninformed' is unclear. Further, in a stratified setting there is a stratified hierarchy of consent where subordinates probably are not as free to withhold consent as are their senior personnel or our gatekeepers in the organization, as in my research on fringe benefits.[2] I am too happy to be accepted to worry too much about hierarchies and authority. Gobo (2001a, 2001b) refers to some further arguments that have been used to legitimize covert research, all sharing a quest for also evaluating contextual elements such as the difference between powerless compared to powerful groups (see also van Dijk, 1987, on covert research linked to ethnic prejudice, and Bulmer, 1982).

Maurice Punch (1994) refers to further problems. 'Informed consent' would mean the end of much 'street-style' ethnography based on accidental happenings. He refers to Hortense Powdermaker (1966), who came face to face with a lynch mob, as an example of activity where it is awkward to obtain consent. This contributes to Punch's conclusion that ethical codes work best as guidelines. In the field ethical dilemmas have to be resolved situationally, and often spontaneously. The general level makes them unable to capture the fine distinctions arising at the level of interaction. A good illustration is represented by his references to how to get data not obtainable in other ways but only by some deception. If the researcher is honest, subjects may hide actions from him or her that they think may be regarded as undesirable. So to obtain honest data, the researcher must be dishonest; or, as Richard G. Mitchells Jr puts it (1993: v), 'secrecy is omnipresent in all research' as all 'researchers choreograph concealment and disclosure'. However, this is not specific to research, but also to frequent elements in daily life interaction.

With a growing tendency to create qualitative databases, archives for storage and retrieval of such material, informed consent is also argued to apply to secondary qualitative research. The direction of a study may evolve over time. A 'process consent' has been recommended to account for this ever-changing field (Thorne, 1998). On the one hand, it is not given that all participants will appreciate secondary use of the material they have provided. On the other hand, secondary analyses will need to rely on interpretations of the original 'informed consent'. The intention is to protect the participant. However, if researchers cannot predict the topics of future research projects based on the databases, how can we demand of lay persons that they possess this knowledge when they originally consent to participation? The same applies to the use of primary qualitative data. Topics may emerge as we analyse data after we have left the interviewee, and not all interviewees are easily traced again. Also, as rich data is published, we cannot hold other researchers back from using them as secondary data in their own publications.

The applicability of informed consent to different kinds of fieldwork is also questionable, as we may tend to perceive 'the field' as a theoretical construct populated by persons sharing certain basic ethical assumptions. This invites reflections on cross-cultural ethics (for challenges in cross-cultural interviews, see Ryen, 2002a). The general ethical correctness of informed consent irrespective of the location of the field may be questionable with reference to the North–South dimension in Third World projects. Written informed consent can be seen as a token of the bureaucratization of Western societies, with its institutionalization of trust into formal bodies of organization, written documentation and well-organized filing systems. In oral societies an invitation to sign formal documents may work as an unintended device to accentuate existing differences rather than building relations in cross-cultural settings (see Ryen, 2002b). It may lead to alienation, it may enforce scepticism and, despite a signature, how could we know if the content was perceived in accordance with all good intentions?[3] The informed consent procedure is built on the taken-for-granted principle that this is to protect subjects and will be perceived as such. This procedure also assumes that former experiences with signed contracts and the symbolism of such documents are positive and thereby ignores that the ethical device may itself also be cultural or contextual. We may also find this scepticism to sign documents in certain Western (sub)cultures. This also refers to the debate in developmental ethics as to whether there is a universal ethics or not (Øyhus, 2000). The fact that different people and different nations have different values becomes an argument for different ethics (Goulet, 1989).

In my own sub-Saharan research, I orally ask my research subjects for a general consent to use the data they give me, but never for any written signatures. Some (high-status) informants have differentiated between information given me as a friend as opposed to data for my research expressed as 'This is only for you, not for your research'. If I have been in doubt, I have simply asked them. One of them put it this way: 'As to the question if you can use the data, yes you can', and another 'I am happy to help you out'. For many poor Third World interviewees, local norms make it difficult to turn down a request from a visitor to be interviewed or they do not know the potential implications of participating in research. Sometimes we have tried to get round this by asking civil servants to sample interviewees for us (depending on topic), a procedure that simply replaces the foreign, Western authority with the local, and thereby introduces us to another ethical dilemma. In a couple of interviews with poor female employees who had been made redundant, the interviewees seemed mentally stressed. Rather than seeing the (oral) informed consent as a licence to go on, I dropped the interviews and took the role of a friend. It is definitely easier for me as a woman to hold the hand of a poor woman compared to a rich businessman (my interviewees in another project). Ethical challenges do not deprive actions of their symbolic value.

This does not imply that I refuse to see ethics as a relevant topic in field research, but rather that in particular written informed consent may work better in some cultures than in others. This accentuates the researcher's responsibility on behalf of the researched to search for practically workable local adaptations of any standard, general ethical guideline.

Confidentiality

The second standard ethical issue refers to confidentiality. We are obliged to protect the participants' identity, places, and the location of the research. However, a substantial number of studies are located in the neighbourhood of the researcher's university, indications can be traced in the list of references, or in a big metropolis (New York, London, Johannesburg), and small communities share the dilemma that they are not easily kept anonymous. The risk is reasonably high that someone will recognize the characteristics of places or persons, especially if the media becomes interested (Dingwall, 1980, illustrates how easily any smart journalist can gain access to confidential information about a sample; see also Picou, 1996).

So how do we know that subjects all want to be treated anonymously? They don't always, and this represents another dilemma. In some cultures there is an established and well-accepted procedure that interviewees' names and titles are given in the appendix (e.g. Tanzania). To deviate from this procedure may be perceived as either confusing or arrogant. This dilemma stems partly from experiences with donor projects such as Western projects in local villages whose aim is to alleviate poverty by offering grants or loans. To be selected for funding demands that your name is put on a list. However, it may be difficult for lay people to differentiate between different categories of projects. Still, this does not rule out the argument of confidentiality, and the researchers' responsibility to protect their research subjects despite the risk of being seen as patriarchal. We find a parallel case in some Western evaluation reports listing the names of organizational members who have been interviewed. Not surprisingly, this has resulted in follow-up meetings between researchers and researched where the demand has been put forward that quotations should be changed or dropped due to the potential consequences to interviewees' careers in small communities. As long as such demands refer to the presentation of data and not to the analyses or conclusions, they may be seen as fair. However, the more deviant and secret the activity, the more the subjects may rightly fear the consequences of private knowledge being disclosed (Punch, 1994: 93), and the greater the responsibility for the researcher to protect them.

This brings us to another topic – 'nonmaleficence' (Thorne, 1998) – meaning that the researcher is obliged to do no harm. Making research subjects into co-researchers as in emancipatory approaches and feminist approaches stressing 'voice' and empowerment (Ladwick and Gore, 1994), and participants' right to negotiate the report (Olesen, 1994), could make confidentiality problematic and unethical. Subjects' voice would be heard, but all the credit given to the researcher, which is counter to the very essence of the concern in feminism.

Using photos from fieldwork can make a story more vivid (as in Rabinow, 1977) and act as proof of the fieldwork, though this practice is scarcely used in Western fieldwork. However, the ethical guideline referring to confidentiality should also apply to photos portraying persons or places if these can lead to the identification of participants who were promised anonymity, irrespective of geographical distance between the field and the researcher's office. Videotaping children at the kindergarten made William

Corsaro (1985) discuss the ethical dilemmas he faced. The researcher simply has to make an ethically acceptable choice.

Trust

Trust refers to the relationship between the researcher and the participants, and to the researcher's responsibility not to 'spoil' the field for others in the sense that potential research subjects become reluctant to research. In this way trust also applies to the report or the discursive practices defining the standards for presenting both the researcher and the work as trustworthy (Fine, 1993). In this way, the three ethical issues of consent, confidentiality and trust are closely linked.

Trust is the traditional magic key to building good field relations, a challenge constantly unfolding during the research process, more so in ethnographic studies than in other kinds of fieldwork. Moreover, in building rapport ethnographers may also rely on impression management (as described by Goffman, 1989), so how do we strike a balance between trust and some kind of deception? In this debate we should also be careful not to enter the field with firm constructions of field relations, in particular a version that constructs the interviewee as powerless. Several researchers report being tested, betrayed, exploited and trapped. If subjects mislead, lie and put up fronts, Jack Douglas (1976) suggests that the same tools should be legitimate for the researcher. If there is no harm, Gary Alan Fine (1993: 275) questions why honesty in practice should be so virtuous as opposed to in theory. Norman K. Denzin and Yvonna S. Lincoln (1994) refer to this stance as the deception model, accepting any method or technique including setting people up, infiltrating settings and deliberately misrepresenting oneself to obtain greater and deeper understanding by simply hiding the truth the way others do too.

As illustrated by Fielding (Chapter 16, this volume), there may be projects where covert research by hiding the truth about our intention may leave us with interesting data. Projects of this kind will most probably be subject to thoroughgoing evaluation from the national or institutional ethical boards or committees. However, there are reasons to assume that experiences from different kinds of fieldwork will influence the researcher's own perception of ethical and non-ethical. Still, these matters may be difficult to convey to others.

Several contemporary areas of study require that the researcher get 'inside', often putting the researcher in a delicate ethical dilemma. Reporting criminal activity would violate access to the subjects' world, whereas not reporting could be seen as accepting the activities, for example. According to Patricia and Peter Adler (2002), the deception studies referred to below and others led to a change in public opinion. In the US this prompted institutional review boards to privilege 'the power of the law and the protection of the institutions sponsoring research (universities) from lawsuits over the informal loyalty between researchers and subjects' (2002: 517). They refer to Mario Brajuha's experiences when he (rightly) refused to give his fieldnotes over to the police after the restaurant he studied burned down (Brajuha and Hollowell, 1986) and to Rik Scarse who also refused to hand over data from his study of animal rights activists (Scarse, 1994). Both these researchers experienced long and expensive court battles and Scarse was also jailed for half a year.[4] Adler and Adler argue that this has resulted in access to certain groups of respondents being curtailed (Hamm and Ferrell, 1998). This points to the importance of historical context to the debate of ethics.

Richard Mitchells Jr (1993) discusses how the researcher is often initially perceived as the naïve sympathizer. If perceived as a potential recruit, she or he may be given special treatment. Being socialized, tested, indoctrinated and taught is a great invitation to the subjects' meaning world. The alternative outcome of apparent cooperation is the researcher ending up as a supplier of goods and services. Mitchells also refer to the paradox of intimacy: 'A high degree of trust achieved early in the investigation may actually curtail researchers' freedom to look and ask' (Mitchells, 1993: 21). This might pose another ethical dilemma, that of not being able to contribute to improving the interviewees' situation. The questions of ethics of involvement and the ethics of detachment have been raised particularly by social action researchers (Fine, 1993). However, you do not operate in a vacuum. Also, other persons in the field make decisions involving yourself or having consequences as to how you are perceived.

Horowitz's (1986) experiences of studying a Chicano gang represent a dilemma referring to both the norms of equality and to sexuality. She reports how having a higher-status role gave her a distance that protected her. She was seen as 'a lady reporter' who deserved respect, and gained access to information never given to the female gang members. Eventually she came to be seen as a peer, but as a female gang member she could also be treated as badly as their girlfriends. Being unable to negotiate a gender identity that would allow her to continue as a researcher forced her to abandon her study. In cultures with a traditional and strong definition of masculinity, female researchers may run into unforeseen problems, as did Eva Moreno (1995) when she tried to negotiate symmetrical relations with her local field assistant. Distance through rank can work to protect you, as shown in Horowitz's case, though it is often perceived as a delicate issue in North–South projects. Still, this may be an important point in practice. As an illustration, I will often hug people I meet, but only shake hands with my driver in Africa. He is a nice, perfect and clever driver, but we spend so much time alone together in the car, also during the evenings, that I see some distance as wise.

Travis Kong, Dan Mahoney and Ken Plummer claim that the link between romance, sexuality and fieldwork has long been one of the silenced questions that is only now being raised (2002: 251), and is closely linked to research ethics. Nevertheless, there are quite a few reports on researchers' own sexual experiences in fieldwork (Rabinow, 1977; Warren, 1988), and a few on actively refraining from such activities in settings that may invite it (for example in Thurnbull, 1986).[5] In her fieldwork in a lesbian community, Esther Newton (1986) makes the erotic dimension explicit, whereas Ralph Bolton (1992) has positively advocated sex with respondents if the topic is to understand sexuality, as in the sex research around AIDS (Kong et al., 2002: 251). Fieldwork is an arena where trust, empathy, rapport and ethics are closely linked. A deep and intense field relation is built on shared understanding, also referring to the researcher's self-presentation through ongoing internal dialogue. Kong et al. (2002: 252–3) see disclosure in gay research as based on trust that the researcher will understand the respondents' lived experiences and co-facilitate interpretation. This is underpinned by their argument that an ethical strategy demands an empathetic, emotional orientation from the interviewer. This may not be specific to gay research, but to all fieldwork, therefore making their argument highly controversial. The issue becomes more delicate in cross-cultural research where the members cannot refer to any communionship of shared identities. In my own research in so-called patriarchal developing societies, the ethical codes on sexuality in fieldwork (don't get too close) have been argued by some of my research subjects to be artificial and alienating. This issue has been raised after I have turned down their offers (irrespective of being attracted or not). Rapport does not imply that we have to comply with research subjects' invitations, but rather that we have to be prepared for handling field practice. Research relations are also intertwined with power relations. The link between fieldwork, sexual invitations and power relations may be more intricate in patriarchal contexts, challenging female researchers in other ways than for male researchers. Reflexivity in this field would gain from less silence and more contextual accounts from research practice.

According to Sherryl Kleinmann and Martha A. Copp (1993), many fieldworkers resort to a linear perspective on empathy – that good feelings should grow over time. They regard feelings as situational. We may like and dislike the same interviewee depending on what she or he says, does or holds back, or we may feel ambivalent. Our feelings may also shift over time, or be complex at the same time – angry and sad. Also, not all research subjects like the researcher. A higher awareness of our feelings towards our interviewees should be related to discussions of the impact on the interview process as they are for opportunity of knowledge construction. Textbook guidelines on rapport, empathy and trust have led many researchers to suppress or ignore his or her feelings, avoid studying particular settings (Adler and Adler, 1987), devote all their energy to liking those studied, and to worry about the recommended ideal of detached concern or distance (Hammersley and Atkinson, 1983).

Criticism of the traditional naturalist interview model has led some feminists to focus on the link between interviews and empowerment (Lather, 1988). According to Donna Eder and Laura Fingerson, reciprocity is one response to power dynamics and can take place on several levels (2002: 185). Conducting multiple interviews with the same interviewee will promote a deeper understanding of their life experiences and lead to empowerment by encouraging self-reflection. Reciprocity can also be materialized as taking something back to the community in which the study takes place or including some form of social action or change (Lather, 1988; Valenzuela, 1999). Lack of reciprocity is definitely an ethical challenge highlighted in cross-cultural projects.

As noted earlier, ethics also relates to the representation of data. In this stage of the research process trust is associated with fidelity, defined by Thorne (1998) as 'the obligation for truth telling', and specifically vulnerable in secondary analyses. This is in line with Steinar Kvale's (1996) claim that loyal written representation of the oral accounts given by the interviewee is an ethical aspect of qualitative research.

What is reported may well be a loyal written representation, but this tells us very little about what has been excluded from the report. That is, selection of data does not refer to the quality of qualitative research only (Seale, 1999; Silverman, 2001), but also to ethics. References to researchers holding back information have been available for decades. Equally, access to subjects' social reality or inner world has been given priority over reporting participation in illegal activities (see references above to Mitchells, 1993; also Polsky, 1962; Lowney, 1984). Another variation of this same dilemma referring to the report is the question of whether there were topics that the researcher chose to avoid. This could be a response to the researcher's uneasiness about moving into a field that could violate the rapport already gained. This is simply done by not probing or using cues to motivate the interviewee to go on despite our observations. It could also be a response to our emotional state where anger may inhibit analysis. If so, this may have severe consequences for what is to be included in the analysis and the report and thereby for the quality of the work. These issues illustrate the interconnection between methodological and ethical issues, and call for methodological reflexivity on the part of the researcher.

Ethics online

Debates in qualitative research have now been supplemented with the differentiation between the 'real' as opposed to the 'virtual' world online. In addition to the ethical dilemmas discussed above, online research also introduces new ethical challenges. How do we relate to research subjects without bodies, what about identities in a world fit for masquerade, are real-time chatrooms like the public square or does conversational chat need written consent to be used in research, have the research subjects now turned into authors and, if so, what are the ethical consequences for researchers? The list is far from extensive. As we do not always start with a clear topic in traditional fieldwork, a parallel exists in online research. Initially, how could we know that an e-mail communication would develop into a close to a one-year online interview (Ryen and Silverman, 2000)? This also visualizes the challenges of traditional ethical committees controlling or evaluating applications for online projects. Online research is a 'researcher-friendly' data-collection method. It makes the criticism accusing qualitative research of being 'armchair research' (Kvale, 1996) relevant and legitimate as access to the 'virtual' field is via your computer. Also, the interviewees themselves send you all data in written form,

facilitating the weak forms of member validation (Seale, 1999). Combined with harsh competition for funding, the interest in this new field will increase, as does the need for developing ethics for online research also (Mann and Stewart, 2000; Ess, 2002a).[6]

Firstly, it has been argued that doing ethical cyberspace research resembles traditional ethical research on human beings (Boehlefeld, 1996). Consequently, the unclear status of Internet data or texts as private or public relates to the traditional ethical practices of getting informed consent, protecting confidentiality and causing no harm. In cases of no strict ethical obligation, as may be argued for listserv archives and e-mail, 'Netiquette' works as a middle ground, defining polite behaviour, inviting a request for permission before quoting. Still, this approach tends to be a simplification because of the variety in online data possibilities[7] and their ambiguous status as private or public.

Secondly, among others, Ess (2003) refers to philosophical ethics and the differentiation between utilitarianism (cf. J.S. Mills), with its concern with consequences based on cost/benefit (or risk/benefit) analyses, and deontological theories (cf. Kant) emphasizing motives.[8] Whereas in the former, harm to the individual may be outweighed by benefit to the group, the latter is concerned with protecting subjects' human rights (self-determination, privacy, informed consent) independent of the consequences. This contrast is reflected in ethical protocols as in the utilitarian US approach compared to the more deontological European (and Scandinavian) approaches.

Thirdly, the dominance of the English and German literature in the field in itself leads to a cultural bias in Internet research and ethics (Waern, 2001). The same could be argued in relation to general research ethics. The absence of explicit ethical codes in some non-Western cultures does not imply that research in these contexts should be devoid of ethical guidelines (Boss, 2001, and Zeuschner, 2001, provide some useful references to cross-cultural approaches to ethics). However, if ethics is cultural it may be problematic or paternalistic to enforce Western standards. Nevertheless, factors such as being unfamiliar with research and the potential implications of participation arguably put a heavier ethical responsibility on the researcher doing research in certain cross-cultural settings. Still, there is no answer to the question of whether research ethics should be universal or relative. This again raises problems concerning how to understand concepts and phenomena such as 'privacy', 'confidentiality' and 'harm' across cultures. To introduce a written informed consent form in oral cultures or in cultures where trust is low is no guarantee that our Western ethical message of care is conveyed (Ryen, 2002b). As already mentioned, a relevant ethical guide in this context should also be to what extent our projects return something to the research subjects or to the community without exchanging the deontological approach for the utilitarian. However, it may be difficult to reciprocate the virtual interviewee and virtual community in the traditional way as they may be impossible to identify and locate in the traditional meaning of the concepts. Still, virtual interviewees could be reciprocated online.

I will illustrate dilemmas in ethical practice from my own experiences in the cross-cultural and the online fields.

BEING OUT THERE CONFRONTING ETHICAL CODES

Doing fieldwork means confronting idealism with practice, in circumstances and situations seldom described in textbooks and in situations that need immediate action or choices. This is the time for realizing that ethical codes cannot be exhaustive. My own projects in both Western and Southern contexts have left me with rich field experiences, none of which I regret, but some certainly more intricate and delicate than others. By sharing some of these, I aim to illustrate the limitations of conventional codes of self-regulation and the ethical dilemmas confronting the fieldworker. The choices we make, both in the field and when writing up experiences, are not entirely theoretical. Fine claims that the person cannot be disentangled from the scholar. 'We have our careers to think of' (Fine, 1993: 283) is most probably one reason for the tendency to see a variety of field experiences as non-data, and exiled to appendices. The balance between privacy and methodological relevance is tricky. Some of my stories are more trivial than others. The answer to the question whether they are ethically correct, depends on the judgement of what it takes to be ethically correct or not.

How do we relate to
information about corruption?

In one of my African projects from Tanzania, we[9] are doing interviews with local businessmen to try to obtain data about bribery and corruption. After the first interviews my co-researcher and I

started discussing how to present the project to potential participants.[10] We tried different presentations of the project, and eventually ended up with what Fine (1993: 276) calls 'Shallow Cover', which is a middle ground announcing the research intent, but still a bit vague in referring to reciprocity in business transactions. Definitely, 'the line between being "informed" and "uninformed" is unclear' (Thorne, 1980: 287). However, since over time we arrange several meetings with each interviewee, rapport and trust become strategic to us (fair or unfair?). As we become more involved, we also get more explicit and less 'shallow'.

This leaves us with another ethical challenge. In a culture where interviewees want to be listed by full name in the report, we may act as imperialists in protecting them from themselves by ensuring that everything is confidential. We see it as our duty to protect Third World research subjects from the hazard of potential consequences of data being disclosed (cf. the deontological stance).[11] If poor businessmen tell us about corrupt civil servants, and their villages were identified in the report, it could lead to local sanctions. Doing research in cultures where 'research', 'confidentiality' and 'data' have no meaning, so to speak, extra ethical responsibility rests with the researcher when doing research on certain groups. In this way we may differentiate the ethical discussion. Doing elite interviews in Western societies, I have experienced interviewees telling me about 'unofficial' practices in their own company, but explicitly saying 'but that is off record' (i.e. to be treated as non-data). It is this familiarity with research that enables the Western interviewees to juggle with stories and relationships.[12] Members of this in-group feel fully capable of evaluating the consequences of whatever is revealed in the interview. As a researcher I have accepted this as non-data, but the stories have still provided me with useful insight.

On the other hand, of course interviewees do lie and put up fronts. One of our East African executive officers being interviewed emphasized that in dealing with applications he based his recommendations solely on the applications and never met the applicants themselves. Later someone else told us that this executive officer had been caught having sex in his office with one of the female applicants. Of course, no one will tell a 'backstage', private story like this to a researcher at their first meeting. Maybe we can get closer to the private stories at our third or fourth meeting. I held back or never disclosed this information to the interviewee, true or not. Of course, it was there in the back of my mind as a background to other questions.

However, having made an ethical choice not to be involved in Third World corruption, one is easily trapped after arrival. During our fieldwork in eastern Tanzania, the local tax inspector insisted on sitting in during the interviews and we only got rid of him by paying him. This is no exception. My local junior colleagues tell me that our strict project budgets have been a problem. They do not leave room for reimbursing the money they take from their own pockets for paying extra to people assisting them in the field. Often you are dependent on assistance from civil servants or others to identify the field and interviewees, and sometimes for transport to remote wards and villages. It is also a dilemma that some insist that you need assistance, seeing the opportunity as one for generating extra income like our local tax inspector. Once I applied for a resident permit;[13] I could get one immediately if I paid a little extra. I refused, so it delayed our fieldwork by two weeks. Later I did pay (too much) on demand to the corrupt official at the airport to make sure I still got on the plane. I already had the ticket. If you get a traffic penalty, it is definitely quicker to bribe the police on the spot compared with being held back at the police station for a whole day. However, there was no way my colleague could know that when the police charged him for not having a warning triangle in the Pajero, it was all fake, including the form. This regulation applies only to bigger cars. Constantly we are reminded that ethical codes are tricky even as guidelines and sometimes we simply get trapped.

Are there ethical limits to balanced relations?

Participating in research is not only voluntary, but often also without compensation. Initially this can be seen as unethical in so far as an interview is regarded as work. Still, research is given an unofficial licence to deviate partly from norms regulating daily interaction. We can ask all possible questions, and we do not compensate in monetary terms. Research subjects not only give of their time, but also share their own private stories or property with us. For a Western consultant the time of an interview definitely has an alternative price in economic terminology. This is a problem I have often faced when interviewing in private companies. I have solved this by enlisting the top manager as gatekeeper, supplied with letters of recommendation from the employers' confederation and labour organizations. My strategy has helped me in doing this, but I still use their scare time. In one study of a company I compensated by offering the interviewees

the chance of a dinner for two at the best restaurant in town.[14] The winner was chosen by drawing lots. The only potential drawback was that I had to convince them that the record of names for the draw was kept separate from the data, and deleted after the winner was chosen. The response was great, but still, not everybody was motivated to join in (see note 3).

I have frequently met expectations that I will reciprocate in one way or another in African settings also. These have been of different kinds, from expecting me to cope with local poverty and offering grants, to gift exchanges and sexual offers. Before interviewing I always explain about the project, clearly recognizing myself in Fine's description of being caught somewhere between the kindly, but not always so honest, researcher (1993: 270 and 174). I am explicit about not having any funds to offer. The problem is that no one refuses to be interviewed. Being asked to participate is for many reasons, very difficult to refuse face to face in a local East African setting. It does not make things easier that interviews are often performed surrounded by people – neighbours, customers or colleagues. The fish trader is interviewed at the fish market, the tailor on a small veranda he has rented sitting with his back to his neighbour, and when the artist invites me to his studio it may be under a big tree. After an interview, interviewees employed in local government may have to give a full account to his or her boss of the interview after we have left. It has been of immense importance to discuss these issues with local colleagues and listen to their recommendations. In sub-Saharan countries, research often gets mixed up with the many Western donor projects that may recently or currently have been in the same area to distribute small grants to local entrepreneurs. Going into poor people's homes, researchers may bring some maize, fruit or school materials for the children as gifts rather than risk offending people with cash. Alternatively, we invite them for a drink in the local café, to get out of the sun. In long-term relations, gift exchanges can be seen as another device to handle the ethical dilemma of getting people's stories for free. However, it is sometimes a dilemma to identify an acceptable gift for our purpose, not too grand and not too poor, both out of respect for our interviewee and worries about our own budget. My colleague also told me a story of how all the local interviewees joined together demanding to be compensated in Tanzanian shillings for their participation. She paid.[15] However, the line between compensation and bribery is unclear, and monetary remuneration is best given after the interview.[16]

A major issue is how to be fair, and what is 'fair enough'? In the short term we definitely differentiate according to the context of our interviews. In the long run it may be problematic if data collection turns into a market process. This is an argument for not putting a price tag on interviews and observations. Field relations turning into economic market transactions will introduce new challenges such as what is fair payment, should we differentiate between interviewees, and will we also get funding for research projects on interviewees with a high market price, and what about the impact on the data? Cash definitely cannot solve all ethical dilemmas. So far I have appreciated that the exchange and intricacy of balancing field relations in time-consuming qualitative research have relied on other mechanisms than the explicit price mechanism. However, this can be seen as an arrogant and unfair attitude. Rather, from an interviewee perspective, it may be seen as unfair that researchers get access to data, the interviewee's property, for free.

Do we need an ethics of flirting?

When interviewing business people about bribery we may invite them for dinner in the evening. Our aim is to find a place they find pleasant and thereby good for building rapport, though it may be ethically tricky that we take rich people to more expensive places than poor people.[17] Still, there are definitely more tricky issues such as ways to build rapport. Flirting is definitely one way of communicating a smooth and relaxed research relationship. Not accepting this may be seen as abandoning one vital resource that female researchers in particular could mobilize in fieldwork. To reject flirting may be perceived as a way of rejecting the masculinity of the male interviewee, and thereby as turning down communicative devices characteristic of building good rapport. Accepting invitations to flirt has made it easier to interview my male interviewees irrelevant of ethnicity – African, Asian or Norwegian – and also to keep up the relationship for more interviews. However, tuning in the communication by including flirt-propelling the interview itself demands a high awareness of the communication process. This implies an alertness to puncture or handle what may have a potential to escalate into more explicit negotiations of gender relations in addition to handling more explicit invitations. First, my experiences from interviews are that constructions of the paired identity as woman–man (see Kong et al., 2002, for references to homosexuality) is one of many more paired identities such as friend–friend or researcher–researched

constructed throughout an interview (see Ryen and Silverman, 2000), and not necessarily a dominating one. Second, I do not accept invitations to very 'private' areas like discos and other people's cars that would accentuate one (delicate) paired identity more than alternative identities, a context that would undermine my say in negotiations or construction of gender in particular in very patriarchal cultures such as the East African. My local male informant has taken on the useful role of 'personal coach' informing me about the landscape. His comment after our third interview with one very successful businessman serves as an illustration: 'Anne, here you must never go alone.' This has put restrictions on data collection. Despite several opportunities to visit this interviewee and his business, I hesitate unless accompanied by my informant. Going alone may have a symbolic meaning not primarily associated with research. This does not deal only with personal (dis)comfort, but also with managing ethical dilemmas in field relations.

An ethical challenge may be argued to exist in the unclear area between flirting and deception (when in accordance with ethical codes we see flirting as a way of building rapport only). This argument may be stronger in cultures of low compared to high contextual languages (Ryen, 2002a). In the latter, one may be better trained in sorting out the finely grained messages also contained in non-linguistic communication. In cross-cultural settings, the roles of researcher versus private person may be perceived as less distinct than is often assumed in ethical research. In the field, arenas and (thereby) roles get blurred. Whereas the African setting may seem to highlight the private person, in particular for female researchers, the focus in Western ethical debate seems to have been on the researcher role (cf. Dingwall's criticism of this division). Finally, one may not be aware of negotiating gender relations. The negotiation may have already been framed by seeing a female researcher travelling by herself, when making appointments to interview men, when using the Western politeness of looking into people's eyes when talking, not to mention the problematic 'When do we have enough rapport before we can relax into friendliness?'.

Here is an illustration from a taped interview after meeting for my third interview with one of my male East African interviewees. The extract is from the dinner out after the interview. Earlier he had shared some reflections with me on our first interview, and I raised this issue again. Among other issues, he had commented that this was his first experience of a white woman spending three hours in the evening (interview time) with a black man. He accepted my request to put on my tape recorder again:

Anne: How did you experience this interview?

Eke: Sometimes you need to be careful about the responses you are giving (3.0). For one thing there is this language barrier. You could say something and it would be interpreted in another way, so you need to be clear [...]

Anne: You remember I asked you to come closer during the interview because of the tape recorder.[18] You later told me that you were thinking 'what will she do if I touch her hand'.

Eke: You're quite right (4.0) frankly speaking. This was my first experience. I could read the signs. I could read the signs, but as you say the cultural barriers eh (2.0). If it were a Tanzanian eh woman or girl I would have been fast or quick in responding (2.0). You see, but with you it was difficult for me to really (4.0) understand what does this (1.0) this signal mean.

Anne: Like what? What signal?

Eke: Like saying eh 'move closer' because I am not audible, that I can't hear properly, because she want me close for the sake of closeness eh was it because it was something else (laughing) ja, so there was lot of questions I was asking myself...

Anne: I remember you were asking me what I was doing when I was alone

Eke: ehe? Yeah, because I (1.0) I mean being a man I know our weakness (both laughing) (Telling two long stories)

Anne: What do you think then, you know when you interview people or if you're interviewed by a woman and you think 'Oh

Eke: mhm

Anne. this is an interesting woman', sexually. What do you think about prosecuting the relation as researcher. Is that ok or is it normal or?]

Eke: [that's quite normal. I mean quite normal in the sense that when you are being interviewed by for example a

woman (3.0). It is just like a normal encounter in a social gathering where you develop some liking and disliking of the other part...

(Dar es Salaam, March 2002)

The extract illustrates that the interviewee sees the interviewer role as just another role like one of many in daily life, so why demarcate this role as subject to special ethical codes compared to non-professional relationships? At the local level, persons meet as individuals and not as theoretical sectioned constructions. This interview 'after the interview' (Warren et al., 2003) can also be seen as negotiating gender, but still experienced as a relaxed talk during evening dinner at an outdoor restaurant, feeling safe with my driver waiting to pick me up. It is also a good illustration that interview relationships are collaboratively accomplished, and further that we as referred negotiate not just one but several relationships during an interview, including interviewer–interviewee, man–woman and friend–friend (for examples, see Ryen and Silverman, 2000). However, according to the ethical codes a research interview is a professional relationship where the professional researcher is the one who succeeds in making the research relationship resemble a friendly, daily life relationship, but without mixing up the private and professional roles. This also applies to practice. I differentiate between how to respond as a private person compared to as a researcher (such as 'no way' compared to 'sorry, I already have an appointment with my colleagues'). If we accept going private, how can we then protect participants from the delicate situations of misunderstandings, power relations and potential cross-cultural communicative dilemmas? Still, maybe we simply lack relevant and updated illustrations. However, if locally constructed man–woman identities in research interviews are but one of several constructions, flirting may be less worrying compared to the alternative (the dominating construction).

Undoubtedly, one can easily identify counter-arguments against making research relations into general relations. Implementing respect of human rights in what may be vulnerable field-work settings, often linked to power,[19] may work to protect both parties. The researcher may use ethical codes as a convenient and accepted explicit argument when needed to negotiate distance, facilitating both presentations of self and other simply due to the code being external. On the other hand, in cross-cultural settings I have also experienced interviewees becoming disengaged and eventually losing interest in participation in further interviews after this strategy. This refers to the complex situated, contextual background of participants' consent to join in our projects.

In general, that outcome of data analyses reflects method talk (see Gubrium and Holstein, 1997) is well described and illustrated by Gubrium and Holstein (1997; see also Frith and Kitzinger, 1998). This signals that we should be careful before drawing conclusions. During fieldwork in a Tanzanian town by the Indian Ocean, Mr Javed, an Asian businessman, invited my Tanzanian colleague and myself out for dinner. He had American Rotary visitors. As this was a pleasant diversion and we were joining in with other guests too, we accepted. Our interviewee remained my neighbour and host throughout the evening, whereas my Tanzanian colleague was assigned a place among the other guests. Later the host leaned over, looked at me, lowered his voice and invited me to a disco, an invitation not unlikely to be seen as private. Most probably I was not invited as a sociologist, so I turned down his offer by referring to our departure the following morning (true by a day). Maybe this was cowardly, but in this way he still could keep face. In case we came back for further fieldwork here it would be strategic to keep good relations. Still, we briefly cleared the air in a nice way when I complimented him on the party before leaving (Ryen, 2002b: 238).

We are there as professionals collecting data, so with reference to the invitation, why do some interviewees get lost in the communication? Well, from another perspective we are being friendly, good listeners, polite, happy to make the interviewee go on and as Western researchers looking into their eyes to confirm our interest in their stories. This may not be easy to sort out, from our interviewee's perspective – as illustrated by Eke's story. Alternatively, we can contextualize the story (Ryen, 2002b: 247–9). We visited Mr Javed's business before lunch to make an appointment for an interview. We met his father and conveyed our errand. He pointed to his son across the production hall who looked at the two women-researchers while smilingly grabbing his golden necklace by his right hand. He nodded; we could come back at 2 p.m. We smiled, left and were back as agreed. He invited us to sit at the couch next to his desk. The couch was deeper than expected, so on my way down I had the feeling of falling so involuntarily that I spontaneously screamed. Trying to hold back in a public setting, my 'Oh' came out close to feminine coquetry. Mr. Javed gave me a smile and poured a soft drink into my glass (his secretary

did so for my colleague). The dinner invitation was after a long and interesting interview. At the dinner table his American guests told a joke relating to Clinton's escapades, causing much laughter. Mr Javed leaned over towards me and said in a low voice: 'Silly story. Every businessman does that.' He was a businessman himself. Seeing this as an extension of our interview I was concerned not to make judgements, so in all the noise from the laughter I ended up with a 'mhmm', nodding my head.

From another perspective I did not dissociate myself from his statement, and by responding to his low-voiced comment I could be seen as accepting a fairly private communication between the two of us. If so, the disco invitation was no longer a typical patriarchal offer, but a result of our ongoing collaborative effort (deliberate or not). Throughout our dialogue from 2 p.m. until midnight we obviously also negotiated gender relations as one of several relations, including researcher–researched. This illustrates that successful rapport is a many-splendoured thing, but also problematic in producing unclear ground. More importantly, it illustrates the social processes through which matters come to be seen as an ethical issue or dilemma. Also, the social processes of labelling, whereby certain matters are designated 'ethical', 'political', etc. (Haimes, 2002: 108), may be more intricate in cross-cultural relations as illustrated in the extracts with Eke. Keeping more 'strict' communication could have been one option. On the other hand, we may then not have received the dinner invitation – an invitation that enlarged our network in this business community. Accepting flirting as a device in building rapport can make communication smoother and may provide further opportunities for data, as here. The ethical dilemma relates to the delicate situation of balancing gender relations, emotions and just passable distance. Flirtation – how, when, how much – is also cultural. This makes the situation even more complicated, as it very often also is related to power, in particular in paternalistic cultures. By joining in orchestrating flirting, I keep greater control compared with being subject to paternalistic flirting. This gives me a better position in the frequent collaborative man–woman negotiations when interviewing. This is also what happened in the introductory extract. By humorously saying, 'What do you offer?', combined with a detaching non-verbal communication, I summed up the situation, made it explicit, but also made it difficult for the interviewee seriously to follow the line. We continued talking as good friends as a good illustration that field relations as paired identities may be more varied throughout an interview than is usually assumed in ethical codes governing research practice. In this way fieldwork is too manifold to produce any ethical code that can cater for all situations, and worries are probably exaggerated.

It can all be summed up in the question of whether or not we need an ethics of flirting. Emotions (not relations) are most probably a rather frequent aspect related to fieldwork, and a rather blank area on our research map,[20] where we would need more research. If 'getting close' is vital either with reference to the quality of data, as in naturalism, or to resistance to paternalism, as in feminism, we should not silence flirting as communication in fieldwork. Also, rather than thinking of flirting as necessarily dominating research relations, it can be one of several ways of communicating in the field. So, rather than an ethics of flirting we may need a sociology of ethics making ethics the subject of sociological research. When the same ethical issues are located in different contexts by different actors, they may accordingly be seen to have different implications and meanings. Doing ethnographic work and elite interviews with male interviewees cross-culturally illustrates the impact of different contexts to different actors. Two matters emerge. These are the variety in the social processes of what comes to be constituted as ethical issues or not, and consequently how this relates to our respective attitudes towards ethical practice (e.g. an ethical issue to me asking for more distance whereas some interviewees see this as a personal relationship inviting reduced distance). The implications for my analysis refer to situating ethics in a socio-historical context, including the possibility of a cross-cultural ethics. According to Haimes, these contexts will raise 'further questions about the framing of ethical debates in certain conceptual terms (such as lying, truth, trust...) and the tendency to ignore or exclude other terms (such as power, politics and authority)' (2002: 111).

Ethics online

Performing a long-lasting online interview, I eventually had to reflect on how to make the interviewee keep up his interest in the communication. We cannot assume the interviewee to be as enthusiastic as the researcher. My interviewee was a busy, aspiring businessman constantly on the road (or in the air) enlarging his business activity. The other potential ethical dilemma I faced in the online field was that of obtaining his permission to publish the data. Whose data? Of course, throughout we also had a light, friendly communication including flirting. Would it be a dilemma meeting in the real field?

My e-mail communication with Sachin, a young university-educated Asian African businessman, started from a brief meeting in the office of another interviewee. He later gave me his e-mail address and we communicated for nearly a year (Ryen, 2002b; Ryen and Silverman, 2000). Early on I invited him to make our communication into an interview, and we negotiated the form of the online interview, thereby building a fairly symmetrical relationship as indicated in one of his responses (extracts copied directly from his e-mails):

Sachin: 'hope this helps you out...theres no
          problem about the questions...and
          i'm glad to help you out for further
          research' (17 November 1998)
Or: 'hope this helps...' (27 December
          1998)

Our online talk about corruption and bribery was at a very general level, leaving me with no ethical dilemmas. However, as our communication evolved, he spent much time on my endless questions (twice a month), and replied with long narratives. Sorting out his businesses, he logged on to answer me whenever possible. Eventually the issue of asymmetry or imbalance became obvious to me. Some feminists link interviews, empowerment and reciprocity. Sachin obviously appreciated our communication where I focused on the qualitative aspects of being an Asian businessman in the East African context. He would send comments like 'its quite unique an experience carrying out meaningful work via the internet...' (22 February 1999). When he later invited me to Kenya to see his businesses, he told me about how he spent the time between our online turn-taking on reflecting on the issues I raised in my questions. When we met I asked him:

Anne: '...how is it to be at the other end of
          my e-mails?'
Sachin: 'Your questions are very new to me.
          I have never thought of them before.
          It takes a long time for me to answer
          them. I have to sort myself out before
          I can write my answers to you. They
          help me to think of these matters. I
          hope you will continue sending me
          question' (in the car, April 1999)

(cited from Mann and Stewart, 2000: 140)

As part of our gift exchange, I received a handwritten letter from his mother[21] where she wrote: 'Sachin have valued your friendship and I am sure the exchange of knowledge will go a long way for his future plans...' (April 1999). Later Sachin asked me for my help in obtaining some relevant information for his businesses. It did take me extra effort to provide this information, but I saw this material as an acceptable exchange for his data most probably contributing to the length of the interview (Ryen, 2002b).

In addition, the interview seemed to contribute to reflexivity on his business experiences and encourage self-reflection.

To allow the possibility for continuing our private e-mails, I suggested to Sachin that each e-mail should consist of two parts, one private and one interview. This worked perfectly. Eventually, the private sections of his e-mail responses also turned out to have wonderful data. My dilemma was that I had told him that I would publish from the interview part only. However, in one publication we ended up also using 'private' data in our draft (Ryen and Silverman, 2000). I explained the situation to Sachin, and was very happy indeed when, close to the deadline for a conference, I obtained his consent. The question is what I would have done without this consent. I had earlier asked Sachin if he wanted me to send him copies of publications. He never responded. I saw his non-response as a sign that my invitation was irrelevant to his business focus and of no interest. He was fully familiar with research and publications, as implicitly indicated by his response to his pseudonym, that of an international cricket player: 'and calling me "SACHIN" is quite an honour..!!!!!!!' (22 February 1999). On those bases I would have drawn the conclusion that it was ethically acceptable to use the data without Sachin's explicit consent apart from extracts of a more private character. His consent was implicit in the sense that I had earlier made it clear that I saw the communication as part of my research. I had promised him that I would be in control of this data, and be the only one to see and select data for co-publications to which I invited. None of these conditions had been violated.

Flirting was used as light remuneration both ways. In spite of our professional and light-hearted relationship, there may have been an expectation on his part that we would continue flirting when we met face to face. We never did. His grandmother's death accentuated the professional relationship. So when kissing him good-bye on both cheeks, he looked at me saying, 'Next time I'll give you one right up front'. There never was a next time. Shortly afterwards Sachin ended his communication.

As demonstrated above, field experiences should be used for analytic reflections. Ethics also reflect epistemological issues and refer both to approaches to fieldwork and to writing the report. As such there is a clear link between ethics and methodology. A presentation of some major qualitative approaches will indicate complexities that also relate to ethical questions, leading to a dialogue between ethical practice and construction of knowledge in research.

VALUES, ETHICS AND PARADIGMS

In general, the obligation to pursue ethical practice towards all parties directly or indirectly involved in the research process, and in the short and long term, involves conflicts. This obligation refers to relatively consistent and permanent values and interests, and more or less fully informed researchers. The *fata morgana* of meeting all these requirements simultaneously is reflected in the above-mentioned debate on Whyte's classical study (see Ryen, 2002b). The myriad of versions and truths refers to the blossoming of new constructionist paradigms. This situation represents a potential for the social sciences to go beyond the specific ethical questions of particular practices, and to contribute beyond mere 'facts'. Reasonably, this multitude is also reflected in research values and ethical stance, as seen in Table 15.1 on values, ethics, field relations and representational practices in some contemporary paradigms of qualitative research. The research paradigms or method talk draw on Gubrium and Holstein (1997). This approach to ethics will provide us with the possibility of seeing the present complexity or multiple perspectives on ethics and ethical practices and, more importantly, offers the possibility of making ethics itself subject to research.

The ontology, epistemology and methodology of each paradigm is well described by Gubrium and Holstein (1997), accentuating the impact of language as to how each method talk constitutes social reality, hence 'method talk'. Naturalism is the paradigm closest to positivism by referring to a stable social reality as expressed by the actor, but departs from positivism in its rejection of one stable external social reality. The other three paradigms all belong to the wide category of constructionist qualitative approaches developed from the 1970s onwards (Denzin and Lincoln, 1994). By their focus on 'how' reality is constructed, ethnomethodologists claim that social reality is locally accomplished by the members in their talk-as-interaction. Emotionalists see

Table 15.1   *Values and ethics in four contemporary qualitative research paradigms*

Aspect	Naturalism	Ethnomethodology[a]	Emotionalism	Postmodernism
Values	Excluded, influence denied	Ethno-indifference	Included–formative[b]	Included–formative[b]
Ethics in general	Extrinsic, tilt towards deception[b]	Extrinsic	Intrinsic, process tilt towards revelation, special problems[b]	Intrinsic, process tilt towards revelation[b]
Field relations	Keep research protocol: don't go native	Natural data, subjects' consent for access to data	'Passionately engrossed'[c]	Researcher authority under attack
Representational practice	Loyal representation of the respondent's version as truth	Non-judgemental attitude	Innovative representations of emotions	Deconstruction, focus on representational practice

[a]Thanks to David Silverman for a previous discussion of this column.
[b]From Guba and Lincoln (1994).
[c]Gubrium and Holstein (1997: 59).

the focus on language as the biggest barrier to grasping social reality by excluding emotions or inner experiences that cannot be expressed. This demands absorption and introspection, whereas postmodernists see the researcher's text as just another representation that needs to be deconstructed. This has profound consequences for values and ethics in each paradigm.

When values are excluded, this reflects the epistemology of the paradigm, whereas values are included in emotionalism in the interest of the powerless and other non-privileged groups whose constructions need to be voiced (Guba and Lincoln, 1994: 114). When ethics are extrinsic to the research process, as in naturalism, ethical field practice is policed by external mechanisms such as codes and committees. When values are intrinsic, one is expected 'to take full account of values and historical situatedness in the inquiry process' (Guba and Lincoln, 1994: 114–15), referring to revelation rather than to deception to get the 'real' story or good consequence as in naturalism. In naturalism, as opposed to in emotionalism and postmodernism, this implies balancing, getting close to but still keeping some distance from the field, to meet the expectation of a loyal representation of interviewee accounts. Ethnomethodologists go for so-called natural data, frequently based on tape recordings, so as to escape relational challenges, but there is still a need for consent to record the tapes. Importantly, they do not make judgements about members' attitudes or actions, but focus on the collaborative constructions. For the postmodernist, representations can be seen as constant loops of deconstruction, whereas emotionalists use innovative representations. Necessarily, the

ethical stance towards research practice varies across paradigms. The most relevant question then is whether existing ethical codes reflect the dominance of a certain ontology and epistemology. If so, what about ethics and ethical practices in the alternative paradigms? Does getting close resemble the deception problem as in naturalism? And how do we know what paradigm will be the one to come up with the representation in the interest of the interviewee? Who should be in the position to decide what is considered good consequences to what person in what situation – perhaps despite potential harm to individual human rights? For some of these questions we can never have definite answers. Still, their value rests with simply being questions raised in the discussion of ethical issues.

CONCLUSION

For the proponents of certain paradigms, certain recommendations are seen as incommensurable as the basic beliefs are contradictable. According to Guba and Lincoln (1994: 115), others are claimed to be reductionist by arguing that all questions of difference can be referred for resolution. Guba and Lincoln argue that a resolution of this dilemma will not emerge until we see a new metaparadigm rendering the existing ones 'not less true, but simply irrelevant' (1994: 116). Ess, however, refers to a pluralist model as a middle ground for resolving apparently different ethical stances. This implies 'a shared agreement on a basic value or norm [...] while different ethical judgements may follow' (Ess, 2002b).[22]

This debate is important and highly relevant to the discussion of ethical practice in research. It raises the issue of universal or relative ethics not only across paradigms, but also across continents and cultures.

By accepting paradigm-specific codes or a pluralist model, we may involuntarily end up with a quasi-postmodern version of 'anything goes', whereas making ethical codes universal is to some extent also deemed to make everybody unhappy. Still, even if we did agree, the complexity and situational of field experiences still have to be handled by persons, or as put by Haimes, 'if we are to understand more clearly how individuals "act ethically" we have to engage in the detailed, contextualized dilemmas' (2002: 105). Ethical issues deal with ethical practice, but ethics is itself a field socially constituted and situated.

ACKNOWLEDGEMENTS

I am grateful to Rosalind Edwards and Giampietro Gobo for their comments on an earlier draft of this chapter.

This chapter draws on material and experiences from my projects in two programmes. The first is the research programme on 'Local Government in Developing Countries' that I am leading at Agder Research, and that is funded by the Norwegian Research Council. The second is the Gender Program that I am leading on the Norwegian side, with Bellah Mahigi as co-leader on the Tanzanian side. The programme is part of the research collaboration between Agder University College, Norway, and Mzumbe University, Tanzania, funded by the Norwegian Agency of Foreign Aid (NORAD).

NOTES

1   For a good and critical discussion of the impact of the introductory text to respondents in surveys, see Holstein and Gubrium (1995).
2   In one of my surveys in a business company, the owner wanted to obtain the names of the few employees who chose not to join in despite his recommendation (command?). With reference to another ethical issue, confidentiality, I did not give him the names.
3   In accordance with deontological ethics, see the following note.
4   Cf. the utilitarian US ethics compared to the deontological European ethics referred to in a later section in this chapter.
5   He describes several occasions from his fieldwork where he refrains from sex in a society where he was expected to engage in sexual relations during certain stages of his stay.

6   Thanks to Charles Ess, chair of the AOIR (Association of Internet Researchers) ethics working committee, for permission to reference this draft.
7   From homepages, Google searches, e-mail as personal exchanges, listservs, chatrooms, etc.
8   Personal communication (2002). Thanks to Charles Ess for sharing his material with me.
9   Thanks to my colleague Nazar Sola, Mzumbe University, for good cooperation.
10 Again, thanks to Nazar Sola, Muzumbe University, for interesting discussions on methodology and culture in cross-cultural settings.
11 Relevant questions could be whether the omnipresence of petty corruption makes it more acceptable, or if the importance of the extra money for supporting the extended family justifies it. Should we differentiate according to the amount of money and the characteristics of the interviewee as in situational ethics? We have a non-judgemental attitude to corruption when interviewing.
12 Thanks to my colleague Arne Olav Øyhus for a good discussion on this issue and for sharing his experience with me during our fieldwork in Bagamoyo, Tanzania.
13 Some years ago we applied for resident permits before going into the Tanzanian field because it made it possible for us to pay the local rent at guesthouses or hotels and thereby save on our project budget. Foreign visitors pay in dollars and at a substantially higher price.
14 Within the tax regulation of maximum value of non-taxable gifts in work relations.
15 Thanks to Bellah Mahigi, Muzumbe University, for sharing this story with me.
16 Here discussed with reference to ethics, not the issue of biased data.
17 Sometimes I feel surrounded by ethical dilemmas in these projects, and simply survive by deciding to 'cool down' and relax. In discussions with my local co-researcher some of my reflections are portrayed as very Western, though I still see them as the basis for my research practice.
18 We were sitting in big chairs in a boardroom and I was afraid the interviewee's distance from the tape recorder might become a problem.
19 Though not always in the way as noted in feminism. Field relations can also be asymmetrical in favour of the interviewee, as when I do elite interviews with businessmen in big companies.
20 The only place where it is legitimately discussed is when related to teaching and supervising students.
21 Sachin's grandmother died just before I arrived, and due to Muslim traditions and death rituals, Sachin had restricted possibilities to take care of a visitor. For this reason, we also had to cancel my meeting and interviews with his parents, hence the letter from his mother.
22 Exemplified by recordings of persons in public spaces without informed consent. Agreeing on the value of persons' expectations, the US CFR argument says that people cannot expect privacy in public

spaces (recording is acceptable), whereas the NESH guidelines (Norway) prohibit such recordings on the basis of the same argument.

REFERENCES

Adler, P.A. and Adler, P. (1987) *Membership Roles in Field Research*. Newbury Park, CA: Sage.

Adler, P.A. and Adler, P. (2002) 'The reluctant respondent', in J.F. Gubrium and J.A. Holstein (eds), *Handbook of Interview Research: Context and Method*. Thousand Oaks, CA: Sage, pp. 515–36.

American Sociological Association (ASA) (2002) *ASA Code of Ethics*. http://www.asanet.org/members/ ecoderev.html

Bauman, Z. (1993) *Postmodern Ethics*. Oxford: Blackwell.

Boehlefeld, S.P. (1996) 'Doing the right thing: the ethical cyberspace research', *The Information Society*, 12(2): 141–52.

Bok, S. (1978) *Lying: Moral Choice in Public and Private Life*. Sussex: The Harvester Press.

Bolton, R. (1992) 'Mapping Terra Incognita: sex research for AIDS prevention – an urgent agenda for the 1990s', in G.H. Herdt and S. Lindebaum (eds), *The Time for AIDS: Social Analysis and Method*. Newbury Park, CA: Sage, pp.124–58.

Boss, J. (2001) *Ethics for Life: An Interdisciplinary and Multicultural Introduction* (2nd ed.). Mountain View, CA: Mayfield Publishing.

Brajuha, M. and Hollowell, L. (1986) 'Legal institution and politics of fieldwork: the impact of the Brajuha case', *Urban Life*, 14: 454–78.

British Sociological Association (BSA) (2002) *BSA Statement of Ethical Practice*. http://www.britsoc.org. uk/about/ethic.htm

Bulmer, M. (ed.) (1982) *Social Research Ethics: An Examination of the Merits of Covert Participant Observation*. London: Macmillan Press.

Caudill, W.C., et al. (1952) 'Social structure and interaction processes in a psychiatric ward', *American Journal of Orthopsychiatry*, 22: 314–34.

Corsaro, W.A. (1985) *Friendship and Peer Culture in the Early Years*. Norwood, NJ: Ablex.

Denzin, N.K. and Lincoln, Y.S. (1994) *Handbook of Qualitative Research*. Thousand Oaks, CA: Sage.

Dingwall, R. (1980) 'Ethics and ethnography', *Sociologcal Review*, 28(4): 871–92.

Douglas, J. (1976) *Investigative Social Research*. Beverly Hills, CA: Sage.

Eder, D. and Fingerson, L. (2002) 'Interviewing children and adolescents', in J.F. Gubrium and J.A. Holstein (eds), *Handbook of Interview Research: Context and Method*. Thousand Oaks, CA: Sage, pp. 181–201.

Erikson, K. (1967) 'A comment to disguised observation in psychology', *Social Problems*, 14: 366–73.

Ess, C. (2002a) 'Ethical decision-making and Internet research'. Recommendation from the AOIR ethics working committee, DraftTHREE. http://www.cddc.vt. edu/aoir/ethics/public/draftthree.html

Ess, C. (2002b) Unpublished manuscript.

Ess, C. (2003) 'Are we there yet? Emerging ethical guidelines for online research', in Shing-Ling Sarina Chen, G. John Hall and M.D. Johns (eds), *Online Social Research: Methods, Issues, and Ethics*. New York: Peter Lang.

Festinger, L., Riecken, H.W. and Schachter, S. (1956) *When Prophecy Fails*. New York: Harper & Row.

Fine, G.A. (1993) 'Ten lies of ethnography: moral dilemmas in field research', *Journal of Contemporary Ethnography*, 22(3): 267–94.

Frith, H. and Kitzinger, C. (1998) '"Emotion work" as a participant resource: a feminist analysis of young women's talk-in-interaction', *Sociology*, 32(2): 299–320.

Gobo, G. (2001a) 'Best practices: rituals and rhetoric strategies in the "initial telephone contact"', *Forum: Qualitative Research*, 2(1), Feb. http://www.qualitative-research.net/fqs-texte/1–01/1–01gobo-e.htm

Gobo, G. (2001b) *Descrivere il mondo. Teoria e pratica del metodo etnografico in sociologia*. Rome: Carocci.

Goffman, E. (1989) 'On field work', *Journal of Contemporary Ethnography*, 18: 123–32.

Goulet, D. (1989) *The Uncertain Promise: Value Conflicts in Technology Transfer*. New York: New Horizon Press.

Guba, E.G. and Lincoln, Y.S. (1994) 'Competing paradigms in qualitative research', in N.K. Denzin and Y.S. Lincoln (eds), *Handbook of Qualitative Research*. Thousand Oaks, CA: Sage, pp. 102–17.

Gubrium, J.F. and Holstein, J.A. (1997) *The New Language of Qualitative Research*. New York: Oxford University Press.

Haimes, E. (2002) 'What can the social sciences contribute to the study of ethics? Theoretical, empirical and substantive considerations', *Bioethics*, 16(2): 89–113.

Hamm, M.S. and Ferell, J. (1998) 'Confession of danger and humanity', in J. Ferell and M.S. Hamm (eds), *Ethnography at the Edge: Crime, Deviance and Field Research*. Boston: Northeastern University Press, pp. 254–72.

Hammersley, M. (1998) *Reading Ethnographic Research*. London: Longman.

Hammersley, M. and Atkinson, P. (1983) *Ethnography: Principles in Practice*. London: Tavistock.

Holstein, J.A. and Gubrium, J.F. (1995) *The Active Interview*. Thousand Oaks, CA: Sage.

Horowitz, R. (1986) 'Remaining an outsider: membership as a threat to research rapport', *Journal of Contemporary Ethnography*, 14: 403–30.

Humphreys, L. (1975) *Tearoom Trade* (enlarged ed.). Chicago: Aldine.

Kleinmann, S. and Copp, M.A. (1993) *Emotions and Fieldwork*. Newbury Park, CA: Sage.

Kong, T.S.K., Mahoney, D. and Plummer, K. (2002) 'Queering the interview', in J.F. Gubrium and J.H. Holstein (eds), *Handbook of Interview Research: Context and Method*. Thousand Oaks, CA: Sage, pp. 239–58.

Kvale, S. (1996) *InterViews: An Introduction to Qualitative Research Interviewing*. Thousand Oaks, CA: Sage.

Ladwick, J.K. and Gore, J.M. (1994) 'Extending power and specifying method within the discourse of activist research', in A. Gitlin (ed.), *Power and Method: Political Activism and Educational Research*. New York: Routledge, pp. 227–38.

Lather, P. (1988) 'Feminist perspectives on empowering the research methodologies', *Women's Studies International Forum*, 11: 569–81.

Lofland, J.F. and Lejeune, R.A. (1960) 'Initial interaction of newcomers in Alcoholics Anonymous: a field experiment in class symbols and socialization', *Social Problems*, 8: 102–11.

Lowney, J. (1984) 'The role of a participant observer in drug abuse field research', *Adolescence*, 19: 425–34.

Malinowski, B. (1967) *A Diary in the Strict Sense of the Term*. London: Routledge Kegan Paul.

Mann, C. and Stewart, F. (2000) *Internet Communication and Qualitative Research: A Handbook for Researching Online*. London: Sage.

Milgram, S. (1963) 'Behavioral study of obedience', *Journal of Abnormal and Social Psychology*, 67: 371–8.

Mitchells Jr, R. (1993) *Secrecy and Fieldwork*. London: Sage.

Moreno, E. (1995) 'Rape in the field: reflection from a survivor', in D. Kulick and M. Wilson (eds), *Taboo: Sex, Identity and Erotic Subjectivity in Anthropological Fieldwork*. London: Routledge, pp. 219–50.

NESH (2001) (National Committee for Research Ethics in the Social Sciences and the Humanities, Norway). 'Guidelines for research ethics in the social sciences, law and humanities', Oslo. http://ww.etikkom.no/NESH/guidelines.htm

Newton, E. (1986) 'My best informant's dress: the erotic equation in fieldwork', *Cultural Anthropology*, 8: 3–23.

Olesen, V. (1994) 'Feminism and models of qualitative research', in Norman K. Denzin and Y.S. Lincoln (eds), *Handbook of Qualitative Research*. Thousand Oaks, CA: Sage, pp. 158–74.

Picou, J.S. (1996) 'Sociology and compelled Disclosure: protecting respondent confidentiality', *Sociological Spectrum*, 16: 209–32.

Polsky, H. (1962) *Cottage Six*. New York, John Wiley.

Powdermaker, H. (1966) *Stranger and Friend: The Way of an Anthropologist*. New York: W.W. Norton.

Punch, M. (1994) 'Politics and ethics in qualitative research', in Norman K. Denzin and Y.S. Lincoln (eds), *Handbook of Qualitative Research*. Thousand Oaks, CA: Sage, pp. 83–97.

Rabinow, P. (1977) *Reflections on Fieldwork in Morocco*. Berkeley: University of California Press.

Richardson, Laurel (1992) 'Thrash on the corner', *Journal of Contemporary Ethnography*, 21(1): 103–19.

Ryen, A. (2002a) 'Cross-cultural interviewing', in J.F. Gubrium and J.H. Holstein (eds), *Handbook of Interview Research: Context and Method*. Thousand Oaks, CA: Sage, pp. 335–54.

Ryen, A. (2002b) *Det kvalitative intervjuet. Fra vitenskapsteori til feltarbeid*. Bergen: Fagbokforlaget.

Ryen, A. and Silverman, D. (2000) 'Marking boundaries: culture as category-work', *Qualitative Inquiry*, 6(9): 107–28.

Scarce, R. (1994) '(No) Trial, but tribulations: when courts and ethnography conflict', *Journal of Contemporary Ethnography*, 23: 123–49.

Seale, C. (1999) *The Quality of Qualitative Research*. London: Sage.

Silverman, D. (2001) *Interpreting Qualitative Data: Methods for Analysing Talk, Text and Interaction*. London: Sage.

Sullivan, M.A., Queen, S.A. and Patrick, R.C. (1958) 'Participant observation as employed in the study of military training program', *American Sociological Review*, 23: 660–7.

Thomson, J.J. (1975) 'The right to privacy', *Philosophy and Public Affairs*, 4: 295–322.

Thorne, B. (1980) '"You still takin' notes": fieldwork and problems of informed consent', *Social Problems*, 27: 284–97.

Thorne, S. (1998) 'Ethical and representational issues in qualitative secondary analysis', *Qualitative Health Research*, 8(4): 547–54.

Thurnbull, C.M. (1986) 'Sex and gender: the role of subjectivity in fieldwork', in T.L. Whitehead and M.E. Conaway (eds), *Self, Sex and Gender in Cross-Cultural Fieldwork*. Urbana: University of Illinois Press, pp. 17–27.

Valenzuela, A. (1999) *Subtractive Schooling: U.S.–Mexican Youth and the Politics of Caring*. Albany: State University of New York Press.

van Dijk, T. A. (1987) *Communicating Racism: Ethnic Prejudice in Thought and Talk*. Newbury Park, CA: Sage.

Waern, Y. (2001) *Ethics in Global Internet Research*. Report from the Department of Communication Studies, Linköping University, No. 3.

Warren, C.A.B. (1988) *Gender Issues in Field Research*. Newbury Park, CA: Sage.

Warren, C.A.B., Barnes-Brus, T., Burgess, H., Wiebold-Lippisch, L., Hackney, J., Harkness, G., Kennedy, V., Dingwall, R., Rosenblatt, P.C., Ryen, A. and Shuy, R. (2003) 'After the interview', *Qualitative Sociology*, 26(1): 93–110.

Whyte, W.F. (1943) *Street Corner Society: The Social Structure of an Italian Slum*. Chicago: University of Chicago Press.

Zeuschner, R.B. (2001) *Classical Ethics: East and West*. Boston: McGraw-Hill.

Øyhus, A.O. (2000) 'The innocent developer: ethics and ox-cultivation. A case-study from the southern Sudan', *Forum for Development Studies*, 2: 236–69.

16

Working in hostile environments

Nigel Fielding

DEFINING HOSTILE ENVIRONMENTS

British diplomats formerly received an allowance when assigned a difficult posting. The city where I spent my teenage years – Washington, D.C. – was such a posting. It wasn't the troublesome natives, though. The embassy crew got the money because of the summer heat and yards-deep winter snows. Washington was a 'hostile environment'. So is the deck of a North Atlantic trawler, the cockpit of a Formula One racing car and the entrance to many British nightclubs after dark. Human cultures recognize hostile environments by paying people 'danger money' to work in them. The irony is that after acclimatization these payments are 'money for old rope'. People who work in hostile environments get used to the conditions. They develop a culture around them. The immediate sense of danger subsides (Pollnac et al., 1995; Winlow et al., 2001).

Researchers work in hostile environments, too. They seldom get paid danger money, though they sometimes get a bit of respect from other researchers. But while they don't get the money, researchers who do this kind of work do develop a culture, like any other group sharing an experience which isn't universal. The culture expresses practices, beliefs and justifications that people sharing the experience are drawn towards, and, like other cultures, it often expresses these things by contrast with the practices, beliefs and justifications held by people who haven't shared the experience. This chapter's purpose is to tell you about some of the working practices, unwritten beliefs and personal justifications of people who research in hostile environments. A particular theme is that research in such settings involves a

dialectic of cooperation and resistance, and the tension between these qualities is a potential analytic resource as well as an important way to gauge the adequacy of the data and monitor threats to the fieldworker's welfare.

Of course, I should have written '*a person* who researches in hostile environments'. Like other qualitative researchers I have an eye for the particular, but it does not stop me generalizing from my own experience. I will support some of my assertions with those published authorities that agree with me, but much of what I say reflects my own circumstances and decisions. I should say what that experience is. My first exposure to researching in hostile environments was also my first experience of field research. I didn't expect hostility. With hair down to my waist and membership of a hard-left political group, I expected to be welcomed as a brother in the US communes I set out to study for my undergraduate dissertation. Arriving in my mother's sports car with an interview schedule that revealed I was almost completely ignorant of the practical realities of communal living, I came to appreciate what feminist methodologists later deemed a 'second wave' feminist insight: shared characteristics do not automatically make for rapport. I learned that nearly any research environment can be hostile if you are incompetent, but also that the emergency repair techniques we use to negotiate awkward situations in ordinary social life can be effective in awkward field situations too.

My PhD's analytic agenda, comparing extremist groups as cases of political deviance, led me back to the field. I discovered that there was no empirical research on the leading party on the British extreme Right, the National Front. It was the early 1970s, with the economy in decline and bitter class conflict. The NF was making headway, and in the two general elections that took place in 1974 it fielded enough candidates to get electoral airtime on national TV. United only by xenophobia, the NF was an uneasy coalition of traditionalist ex-Conservatives, ex-socialists who attributed high unemployment to excessive immigration, straightforward fascists, and 'skinheads' (back then a shaved male head was not a fashion statement but signified a belief in assault as the solution to most social problems). There were frequent violent confrontations with opponents, prominent officials had served prison sentences for violence and weapons-carrying, and the party had active links to Loyalist paramilitary groups in Northern Ireland. As well as the blacks, the Jews and the communists, the party scapegoated sociologists. My study of the NF combined covert and overt observation with interviews, about which more later.

Events at the end of fieldwork and following publication of my research persuaded me that a new research field might be desirable. Before my PhD I had taught at the Metropolitan Police College. It occurred to me – for largely biographical reasons – that one of the things that interested me most was the way people change as they move into new occupations, new relationships and new cultures. After all, I could see how I'd changed, as I moved from a student's critical perspective on 'the system' to a job teaching police recruits. I connected my experience of teaching in police college with my interest in change, and came up with the idea of researching police recruit socialization. Since then I have been engaged in police research. Policing can be a hostile research environment. It must be foremost among working environments that can brutalize its practitioners (constables have told me theirs is 'the only job in which you have to wash your hands *before* you go to the toilet'). It is also hostile in a more straightforward way, as I realized when one tour of observational fieldwork ended with an enraged citizen attempting to use a still plugged-in electric fire to lasso me and the officer I was accompanying.

HOSTILITY TO RESEARCH

Since almost any research environment can be hostile (remembering my blundering non-entry into the world of the commune), we must acknowledge that it isn't only qualitative researchers who negotiate hostile research environments. It is really a matter for anyone who treads 'the field'. Because it was recognized that

if fieldworkers faced obstacles in the field it would affect response rates and data quality, survey research had an early concern with fieldworker safety and security. From this area we derive much of our understanding not just of personal security and access issues but how people respond to being asked about 'sensitive' topics, and how ongoing dealings with sponsors or other interested parties during analysis and publication can be hostile. Since survey research has often dealt with social problems, this literature has been directed to negotiating sensitive topics, ethical safeguards, and protecting the rights and welfare of respondents and researchers.

However, these themes only partially illuminate working in hostile environments. Working in hostile environments should be differentiated from working on sensitive topics. The latter suggests a rather passive respondent group who are getting by quite comfortably until a researcher comes along and upsets them by asking about that class of things that are best left unsaid – drunkenness, drug-taking, masturbation, not wanting to live near people unlike themselves. There is a difference between that and the circumstances we face when the research environment – like the physical environment on the deck of a deep-sea trawler – is actively hostile to one's presence. Hostile research environments are those where the research population is actively resistant to research. It isn't simply indifferent, uninformed, or susceptible to being upset by certain questions or poor technique. It does not want research done, and if research nevertheless takes place, it seeks to control the research and the researcher.

This said, there is great variation among hostile environments. The spectrum covers settings like the National Front, which explicitly repudiates social research, to those such as the police and other occupational groups, some of whose practices are sensitive and in which careless fieldwork can provoke resistance. The latter types of setting are more numerous, where a broadly sympathetic field or setting can become inhospitable in response to specific actions by fieldworkers that are insensitive, irresponsible or unwittingly inappropriate.

Such circumstances pose ethical as well as practical challenges. The highly developed literature on research ethics touches at many points on my concerns (e.g. Homan, 1991). But it seems to me that this literature both reflects something noble – sociology's aspiration to be a moral discipline that falls over backwards to respect its human objects of study – and something less impressive: timidity about entering the more difficult reaches of the social world. It is the latter that has produced a situation where we know a good deal more about the poor – those who are as powerless to resist research as they are to resist every other imposition – than we do about the powerful. Despite years of refinement, no code of ethics can satisfactorily anticipate the messiness of field relations. Those who accept this messiness justify going where their analytic agenda leads by reference to 'situation ethics' (Fielding, 1992). I will discuss situation ethics later, but won't attempt to justify the research topics I have pursued en route.

Rather, I take the view that work in hostile environments is not only a topic for paralysing ethical conundrums but an analytic resource. From work in such circumstances comes distinctive insights. Resistance to research is not only an ethical problem, much less a simply technical one (even if 'recipes' to overcome resistance were available). Resistance to research tells us much about organizations and their members, as Dalton (1959) long ago recognized. Qualitative researchers are familiar with the idea that they are 'the research instrument'. Especially in participant observation, but in intensive interviewing too, understanding flows from interrogating our own field experience. Dalton's discussion of obstacles to access suggests that much can be learned about organizations from who is willing or unwilling to speak to researchers, a theme in several other works of Chicago qualitative sociology by students of Burgess or Hughes (see Fine, 1995).

Obstruction, evasion, refusals and other troubles can in themselves be significant sources of data. Resistance is an important way to understand the culture being researched, and researchers can derive insight into belief systems and other facets of organizational culture from a reflexive stance towards field relations, from being alert to how people interact with them as researchers. Examples abound in elite studies, a fine instance of which is Smigel's (1958) study of Wall Street lawyers. The reasons these powerful professionals gave for why research was out of the question – constant time pressure, corporate clients needing to be assured of confidentiality, and previous research on law having 'gone wrong' – reveal the fetishization of secrecy by which legal elites avoid accountability. Resistance is not, of course, unambiguously an analytic resource. Sometimes researchers may accept that it is legitimate, in which case they should back off.

Like cooperation, resistance is not an invariant quality. Cooperation and resistance are continually renegotiated during fieldwork. In qualitative research we are *always* negotiating access.

Van Maanen (1982: 138) captures the unpredictability well, remarking that

> in the abstract, relations in the field are such that the researcher is provided with trusted information of the sort necessary to both understand and empathize with the observed, but the researcher's presence itself creates little change or disturbance ... concretely, however, such relations wax and wane over the course of a study, approach or exceed the upper and lower limits with different individuals on the scene, and vary according to the practical situation.

Sometimes it is hard to gauge whether refusal represents momentary inconvenience or enduring unwillingness (something survey researchers also ponder; Couper, 1997, found that when people say they are too busy or not interested in the topic they generally are indeed busy or uninterested, and it is seldom worth pressing them).

The signs of resistance or hostility are not necessarily gross. Research participants can use subtle means to regulate data collection and exert influence over data analysis. After all, even our relations with intimates are not entirely explicit or predictable, and the social world is rich in resources with which to deny candour, rescind confidences and excuse missed appointments. When Ostrander (1993) studied a network of wealthy women active in charities she learned much about the way the powerful apparently 'open up' while actually talking past the research question and use such things as invitations to meetings in expensive restaurants to suggest intimacy while engendering a sense of being beholden on the part of the researcher. Ostrander offers tactics useful in meeting these subtle forms of resistance, though none was proof against the discovery that members of her sample sat on the board of the organization from which she was seeking her next job, a discovery that obliged her to delay for several years publication of her book about the research.

That resistance is something we must anticipate, gauging how it may differently affect each element of fieldwork and group of research participants, is illustrated in Silverman's (1997) account of conducting research in a sensitive field of professional practice, HIV counselling. Silverman's conversation-analytic research required precise capture of speech in the setting; recording was essential. 'We ended up with a method of recruitment whereby [HIV] counsellors themselves explained the research to patients (often with the aid of written materials) and invited them to participate ... the audiotapes were simply sent to me by each of the centres for analysis' (Silverman, 1997: 227). Access to clients was ultimately available only on the basis that the practitioners would decide whether to pass on to Silverman any tapes they judged to be usable. As Silverman notes, being in control of the tape recorder had some appeal to the practitioners.

Nespor (1998) encountered innocent resistance to research among primary schoolchildren. His topic simply did not register as important with them and they had nothing to say. Nespor decided to trust the children. He gave them the recorder and let them record what they wished after conducting a classroom project. Though not squarely relating to his topic, some of what they recorded illuminated a dimension of the issue he had not considered. Sometimes, then, resistance is not loss but value-added. As these examples suggest, field research is never something one does *to* research subjects but something one does *with* research subjects. It is co-produced by researcher and subjects. Both our methodological and analytic practice must be sensitive to the fact that, for example, interview data involve co-construction rather than plucking respondents' 'true answer' from them like fruit from the bough (Dean and Whyte, 1958). Anticipating and satisfying subjects' desire to influence the research is not just a matter of smooth field relations or a factor in weighing responses but can help us understand what they find objectionable and why, and contribute fresh analytic themes.

Protecting rights and welfare

Research with the reluctant or obstructive raises concerns about fieldworker security. Before each episode of fieldwork it is sensible to think it through, identifying potential problems and how to respond to them. Where we study those who may be a direct threat to our physical safety and security, the guidelines developed by professional groups in regular contact with dangerous others may be useful. These include going accompanied, and if this is not possible, notifying others where you are, when you aim to return, and times to check in by calling a colleague at intervals. It may also be sensible to meet with research subjects in public places and avoid night-time fieldwork. Social workers, police and benefits staff are trained to recognize signs that the people they are dealing with are becoming threatening, and in counter-measures; it may be worth obtaining such guidance. Professional associations and researchers' organizations also produce such guidance. The methodological literature includes useful treatments of these concerns, particularly from the survey tradition. Surveys tend not to be conducted by the researcher who designs the study but by subcontracted fieldworkers employed by large research organizations alert to their duty of care for employees. Gwiasda et al. (1997) offer practical guidance on safety and security in fieldwork in risky situations, based on their work in high-crime ghettoes.

Every year since 1980 I have sent between 15 and 60 students into the field to conduct observation and interviewing exercises (and my postgraduate students have used these methods more extensively for their dissertations/theses), and it is perhaps reassuring to say that none has suffered physical harm in the course of fieldwork. However, there has been occasional unanticipated resistance. A postgraduate who received permission to observe visitors to a stately home was asked to leave by the senior caretaker because he had been informally interviewing visitors, although she had agreed he could do so. It emerged that the issue was not interviewing but what the respondents had said. All reported that their visit was marred by the policy of keeping rooms in near-darkness to protect antique tapestries. While irrelevant to the student's topic, the overheard criticisms of 'their' stately home had upset the caretakers, who had passed the complaints, with their own view that the visitors were right, to the senior caretaker who had imposed the policy. It revealed an interesting theme concerning the pride the working-class caretakers felt about a property owned by the very rich, but one could not have anticipated that the fieldwork would expose conflict between the staff. One is left with few resources beyond tact and clarity about one's own rights. In this case, it was right for the student to refuse to censor or surrender his fieldnotes, as he had made it clear that the fieldwork involved asking visitors for their impressions.

Resistant fields of study

I have suggested that any setting can prove resistant or hostile to research, but particular research fields do display characteristic qualities. Here I am largely considering settings that are not hostile to research per se but may display resistance to research on particular aspects of their work. Those who study political groups enjoy the advantage that, because such groups seek new adherents, events that would be closed in other organizations are open to scrutiny. Also, politicians talk for a living and are often willing to be interviewed. However, since they strike positions on almost any topic, and ensure that all party representatives espouse it, one tends to hear the same line from every interviewee. Getting genuine engagement with analytically driven topics is not easy. Political organizations are also guarded about the business dimension: party finances, ownership of facilities, the party's backers. They are also cagey about alliances they might form and other tactical aspects of particular electoral scenarios. Researchers should remember that political organizations have massive experience of managing information flows to journalists, and researchers are likely to be seen as a branch of that species.

There are some similarities in researching cults, sects and subcultural groups. While these generally also wish to recruit new members, that is an advantage only if one is prepared to conduct covert participant observation, although it may be possible in an overt study to present the research as an opportunity to tell the 'outside world' what the group is 'really like'. Cults, sects and subcultures may also require converts to have particular characteristics that cannot be faked or fudged, like a particular ethnicity, tangible enjoyment of a particular substance or activity, or willingness to commit criminal acts. Where observation is the preferred method, and whether covert or overt, fieldworkers should be prepared for tests either of their commitment (if passing as a pseudo-member) or of their adherence to conditions of access. Perhaps the best-known problem associated with research on cults arose in Festinger's (1956) study of an end-of-the-world cult. The observers significantly increased the apparent number of the group's believers, strengthening the commitment of genuine members, especially when they learned that some of the new 'converts' were flying in from other cities to participate. One senses that these researchers never fully intended to conduct covert observation, and blundered into a fieldwork relationship that was at the 'fudging' rather than the 'faking' end of the spectrum. It is difficult to tell from the defensive published accounts of the fieldwork whether they experienced much resistance, as opposed to embarrassment, but the study is generally taken as a warning against changing the object of research by the methods used to research it. Very small sects, cults or subcultural groups are probably best studied by interview.

Field research on crime and criminals faces a large obstacle: the behaviours of interest are illegal. This is why 'criminology' is misnamed – it is largely the study of criminal justice, not crime. Nevertheless there is a small but valuable genre of studies of 'active criminals' (ones who are at large; the more numerous studies of criminals in confinement tell us only about unsuccessful criminals, those who have been caught). Naturally most active criminals are resistant to research and the group is therefore an example of one that is generally hostile to fieldwork. The lengths needed to access it are illustrated by Wright and Decker (1994), who persuaded a fringe member of a network of burglars to vouch for them on several conditions, including payment for interviews, interviews conducted in locations decided by respondents, and all data being anonymized and de-contextualized; in other studies, data have been lodged outside national jurisdiction in a country whose laws bar releasing such documents to agents of a foreign government (see Feenan, 2002). Such lengths are justified by the yield of original, high-quality information from studies of criminals at large. I discuss studies of agents and agencies of criminal justice later.

With an increasing range of social institutions playing a regulatory role, research interest has grown in 'informal' social control. Some private-sector regulation is itself dubious, and the profit motive adds another sensitivity that makes for resistance to research. Prior experience of the informal control organization is useful in overcoming it. Indeed, Winlow et al. (2001) suggest it was essential to their study of nightclub bouncers and the people whose behaviour they regulate. Winlow had previously worked as a bouncer and 'looked the part'. The violent and bloody incident forming the article's centrepiece indicates that, as well as looking the part, one must be prepared to play it.

Some argue that the resistance to research that has increasingly been expressed by deprived communities and groups such as asylum-seekers is legitimate and should be respected. They ask why researchers should join other bodies that prosecute their own interests on the backs of the deprived. It is hard to challenge this. Many researchers feel that potential research subjects should have the right to refuse to be researched. Fieldworkers may justify their intention by the good that may come of it. For example, where welfare programmes are at risk because they are abused or ineffective, qualitative research can reveal success stories that disappear in the aggregate of formal programme evaluation methodologies (Ong, 1999). Another response is to pay. Indeed, some deprived communities have formalized a rate set as a percentage of the research budget that is built into the grant application. Researchers proceeding thus should satisfy themselves about the means of distribution into the researched community.

Resistance to research remains less frequent among the powerless than the powerful. Like other resources, privacy flows most directly to the stakeholders in society. Among these are 'the professions'. The concept of social closure was itself developed in the sociology of the professions. Professions have elaborate and effective means to avoid oversight. The insulation from oversight that marks the 'great professions' may, though, be the researcher's best resource. Professionals are aware of the need to grant a measure of accountability if full public oversight is to be avoided. They also often feel their contribution to society is considerable and the world should know about it. Among the professions exercising strong social closure (by which access to professionals and information about their practices is granted only under carefully regulated conditions, prime among which is as a client) are medical and health-related trades, the law, and workers in religion. Elite studies have given rise to an insightful literature on negotiating resistance to research, as discussed earlier. The point to draw out is that research in almost all substantive fields, including that on social institutions having broadly benign functions, will encounter offstage areas and practices that those who inhabit them will prefer to shield from scrutiny.

HOSTILITY IN TWO FIELD STUDIES

I have suggested that neither 'cooperation' nor 'resistance' should be regarded as invariant throughout the fieldwork process, that the means by which these qualities are made manifest to the researcher are not necessarily gross, and that the nature of cooperation or resistance can tell us much analytically. While fieldworkers have long identified the importance of rapport, the several interactions represented by this concept require particularly close attention in fieldwork in hostile environments. I will elaborate these themes in two examples: the first from the National Front research and the second from my community policing research. The National Front research mentioned earlier examined links between extremist politics and political violence, originally comparing extreme Left and extreme Right. However, I soon found there was no empirically based literature on the contemporary extreme Right and the research was refocused on the NF. The community policing research attempted to gauge and document the practical means community officers used to achieve social control sensitive to the community they policed.

The National Front fieldwork

It was fortunate for the National Front research that there were two general elections in 1974. In that time of political turbulence, extremist politics of all hues gained unusual prominence. As the main extreme Right party, the National Front fielded candidates in both general elections, and enjoyed its first party political broadcasts. The NF was a coalition of smaller factions. Significant not in numbers but for their links to the Conservative Party, two factions, the Racial Preservation Society (RPS) and the League of Empire Loyalists (LEL), had particular strength in large South Coast towns like Brighton, where I lived, while membership based on former Labour supporters featured in cities like London, where my PhD was registered.

I conducted my first interviews with branch officers with no definite research design in mind. It seemed best to see whether I could gain access rather than fix a research design ahead of time that might prove unrealistic. The only certainty was that the study would of necessity be qualitative. The NF was virulently hostile to research, and specifically castigated sociology. There was no prospect of getting a membership list and, even if my interests could be expressed in questionnaire items, a general survey would require a large over-sample to collect enough NF voters for statistical analysis. While the status of qualitative method was more subordinate then than now, one warrant for qualitative work was exploratory research, which was what I proposed.

My first interview was successful in the sense that I was not thrown out. Despite my long hair and status as a student sociologist (I presented myself as an undergraduate, thinking this may be less threatening), I was politely received. My respondent warmed somewhat when I deliberately asked a series of questions requiring him to do no more than recite the party ideology. I saw this as a quid pro quo: I would be taken seriously if I took my respondent seriously. It needs to be said that taking my respondent seriously involved not choking with rage or laughter at the expression of views that were both repellent and ludicrous.

Like a police officer's first arrest, this first interview prompted much reflection. I decided that to obtain the information I wanted it was best to avoid antagonizing NF members. If this involved not only reserving my own view but actively misrepresenting it by acquiescing to the views they expressed, I would do so. I had noticed that, when my respondent had delivered himself of a strongly expressed opinion, he momentarily scanned my expression, presumably for signs of condemnation. By simply acknowledging his statement I could encourage him to say more, and these further statements went beyond the recital of standard ideology. It was not hard to offer mildly encouraging or positive acknowledgements because I was familiar with the ideology and current position on contentious policies from party publications.

Another reflection on the first interview was also consequential. The respondent was a candidate for the local council. The interview ranged from the 'big' national issues to the minutiae of local politics. On local matters his views were barely distinguishable from those of mainstream candidates. I was forming an uneasy awareness of the banality of evil, that the danger of extremist politics lies in its ability to cast itself as 'normal', as the real voice of the ordinary people, and that murderous things can be done matter-of-factly. It came to me that it was essential that my research design balanced the interviews with field observation. Reliance on interviews might leave me with a corpus of data that merely invested the ideology in the party literature with the particularities of those I interviewed. I wanted to know how the people who laid claim to this ideology deployed it.

Observation method demanded more complicated decisions regarding my role than those involved in seeking interviews. I wanted to see how the people I was interviewing conducted their party's business in branch activities, and since I would be known to them from the interviews, this could only be done overtly. But my main interest was in political violence, and this was unlikely even to be discussed in the presence of a known observer. I decided to conduct overt observation in branches where I was known from interviews and covert observation in branches and at events where I was not known. Even at a time of lower awareness of fieldworker welfare and security concerns, this was probably foolhardy. I do not commend it as an example, I do not challenge those whose eloquent ethical critiques have condemned what I did, but I do say there was no other way to obtain the data.

There was exhilaration in finding out what the NF's insiders and hardcore opponents knew and I would not gainsay its effect on my motivation. But since I was able to compare what I would have 'known' if I had rested with interviews and what I learned from direct observation and informant testimony, I was also able to assess the 'scientific' justification for what I was doing. The interview response proved consistently misleading about the party's sources of finance, links with paramilitary groups, the way it monitored

its opponents and conducted physical interventions against them.

I have already mentioned that I used what amounts to deception in the front management I adopted during interviews. Once I moved towards overt observation I needed to use the interviews not only to collect data but to negotiate access to branch activities. I needed to observe more than one branch so I could compare the branches where ex-RPS and LEL members predominated with those where ex-Labour supporters predominated. I also wanted to observe branches more than once for reasons of validity. At one branch, my attendance at branch meetings was readily agreed. At another, I sensed during the interview that without an other-than-neutral tack I was not going to get any further than this one interview. For these reasons a change in my approach was necessary.

I decided that I would have to do more than encourage further responses by mildly positive acknowledgements of what was said. I began interjecting statements that implied that I was becoming tantalized and even persuaded by what I was hearing. These statements, which seemed crude and shameless to me, were warmly received. I had arrived at the stance I took in the rest of the overt fieldwork. I would be the researcher-turned-convert. Like Festinger's pseudo-converts, I always fudged exactly where I stood. I was also aware I was under test. However, non-researchers displaying availability-for-conversion are also under test: each event one attends is an earnest of ongoing interest and an occasion for members to work at securing the final commitment. Testing was frequent but not continual; I never felt there was a point of no return and I worked to ensure that members did not think so either.

Cooperation and resistance were thus related to my evolving role. My tactics secured an enhanced but conditional degree of cooperation. Cooperation also varied between different members. I found that it was not hard to get on the wavelength of those that one journalist labelled 'the seaside landladies of the NF'. I had heard some of the views they expressed from my relatives. But these were not the activists in whom I was most interested. Where working-class and young male members predominated, aggressive action was more squarely on the agenda, and my limited experience of this group and lack of interest in football made relations harder to establish.

This hiatus was resolved by a coincidence. As well as the branch fieldwork, I had approached headquarters for interviews with senior officials. Negotiations were slow, being conducted by post

(I wanted a record of our exchanges but, more to the point, as a student I could not afford the telephone). When I was finally granted an interview with a relatively senior official it was tense and largely repeated the too-familiar ideology, interspersed with statements like 'that information is not released' in answer to the more interesting questions. I learned more from observing the interview setting than from the interview (for example, party HQ, an ordinary end-of-terrace house, was encased in corrugated metal, and two-way mirrors protected a weapons safe under the stairs). However, I dutifully wrote down the 'no comments' and my respondent's parade of racist clichés. When I contacted HQ after the interview using the foot-in-door technique that I had stupidly forgotten to ask a few questions and would like to come back, the request was accepted. This time I would be seen by a less elevated official, the National Front Student Association organizer. He turned out to be a sociology graduate and ex-Maoist from Belfast. I would lie if I said other than that we got on extremely well, something that gave me pause at the time and has ever since. Through him I gained an interview with the party's deputy chairman, a meeting with the party leader, and access to a branch actively involved in confronting opponents.[1] I did not inform him that, as well as the overt fieldwork, I was attending other branches and events

I was reaching the final stage of fieldwork when I decided to attend the NF Remembrance Day rally. Branches held their own commemoration at the Cenotaph in London following the official ceremony and then marched to a rally. The event was regarded as the high point of the NF calendar. I had an invitation to attend with the Brighton branch, the day beginning early in the morning and ending in the early hours of the next day as the coach made its final drop-off. A sustained fieldwork occasion like that makes it very apparent that relations with research participants vary from the cooperative to the resistant. Indeed, they varied from the embarrassingly warm to the disturbingly hostile. To show this can be useful analytically, I recount a segment from the morning coach trip.

Sat next to a spry older woman, I was asked how I came to be involved as I did not look like a 'typical National Fronter'. I retailed my line about it having begun as research but having become a personal interest, explaining the NF beliefs that particularly attracted me. When I finished she asked 'Well, what do we believe, dear?' in relation to one of the planks of party belief that I had taken to be most firmly grounded of all. Was this an innocent question?

Perhaps the lady was ex-RPS and did not know the NF policy. Or was it a test? I offered a careful statement of the party line on the topic, concluding that 'When all was said and done Britain is for the British'. The round of applause from the surrounding seats showed me that, witting or not, the lady's question had functioned as a test. When we got off the coach the male activists were deployed to form the edge of the column and point of contact with anti-Nazi protesters. The branch was left without able-bodied men to carry the branch banner. I was asked to carry it, the branch chairman taking the other pole. Analytically the value of this incident came in showing variation in awareness of key party ideology, and in displaying how members achieve a sense of shared purpose and commitment.

As branches arrived at the rally, members milled around behind police cordons waiting for the platform speakers to begin. I stood with the branch committee. I felt something prod into my back and the phrase 'stick 'em up' said in a Belfast accent into my ear. Instinct told me to respond very slowly and treat it lightly. It was the NFSA organizer. He asked whether I was 'here in an objective capacity or just out of interest today'. With the branch group present, I was grateful for the option offered by that construction. He proceeded to offer a connoisseur's critique of the proceedings. This suggested that I had passed another test, by noncommittal statements and because it would have been difficult to interrogate me about my purposes with the branch committee present.

That I was on test that day seemed to be confirmed when the branch broke its journey at an isolated rural pub. The venue was clearly prearranged as we were shown to a back room. A burly branch member who was regarded as the branch's most reliable lynchpin in confrontations with opponents said he would like to talk about branch security. While I was pleased that one of my key interests had come up, it rapidly became clear that the discussion was a barely concealed device to warn me about what happened to people who pretended to affiliation in order to obtain information and then disappear. Particular attention was paid to injuries received by those involved in previous episodes of 'entryism'. I blandly shared in condemning such subterfuge and made further noises about my growing interest in membership. Discussion closed in a dark corner of the room next to an exit well away from the rest of the branch. I was pointedly handed a membership application form and told that after the enjoyable day in which I had participated I would no doubt want to complete the form immediately.

I had always offered to provide NF HQ with a copy of any book I wrote as a result of the research. That the NF wanted to know what I was writing about it became apparent after my thesis was lodged in the university library. The library soon contacted me requesting a further copy, as the middle 200 pages had been cut out. This happened a second time, after which the thesis was withdrawn from public access. Although my book was ready soon after completing the thesis, my publisher's consultations with lawyers took two years, during which the NF referred others wishing to research the party to me. The day the book was published, copies were sent to the NF chairman, deputy chairman, and the NFSA organizer. The deputy chairman was a physically imposing figure who dealt with the practical running of the party while the chairman concentrated on ideology and presenting a statesmanlike image (despite convictions for arms offences). From the chairman I received a polite but cold letter of a few lines some weeks after publication. The evening of publication I received from the deputy chairman a telephone call in which I was threatened with death. The telephone call was marked by alternate bellowing of abuse and bitterly expressed criticism of points in the book. Fortunately I had recently obtained a permanent job and was leaving London, though I did obtain an unlisted telephone number when I moved.

Much of the NF fieldwork had the feel of shadow-boxing. While 'immersion' in the field and intense field relationships feature in the literature about observation method, these were difficult standards when applied to work with a violent racist group. Indeed, the one relationship that came close to these qualities, that with the NFSA organizer, caused me much soul-searching. This sense of shadow-boxing and near-relationships made it hard to gauge the calibre of some of the data. Analytically I did get much of the information I wanted, but some lines of inquiry were closed because of the uncertain status of the data. Cooperation and resistance not only vary but it can be hard for researchers even to tell if they are receiving one or the other. Drawing on her work with US white supremacists, Blee (1998) suggests that in such circumstances we monitor the strategic use of emotion by informants. This can both expose the emotional content of social movements and help us to see how interpretations are jointly shaped in the fieldworker/informant relationship. In this and several other respects there is strong affinity between our respective understandings of fieldwork in extremist political groups, suggesting the enduring character of field relations in such settings.

The police fieldwork

The National Front research contrasts with my second example in having been relatively short-term. While my friends joked about the inevitability of my move from researching racists to researching the police, my interest was not due to the connection with an occupation widely thought to attract authoritarian racists, but precisely because the police I encountered so little fitted the stereotype. Following my appointment to a permanent academic post, and drawing on my pre-doctorate experience lecturing at Hendon Police College, I took the opportunity to explore how people changed when they joined the police. That was in the late 1970s and I have since remained in police research. Long-term presence in a research field makes for different resonances of the cooperative/resistant dimension. There are challenges that could rapidly make it a hostile environment if wrongly handled. A 'long-term research presence' is enabled by careful professional work, of course, but also requires responsiveness to the needs of the research area. It requires skill in seeing how what 'the system' wants can also be made to serve one's own analytic interests.

As well as studies of police socialization I have researched the police investigation of child sexual abuse, community policing, the recruitment of ethnic minority police officers, 'intelligence-led policing', and police efforts to manage the public's fear of crime. The work on community policing combined observation with interviews in an effort to identify factors that promoted successful community policing. We prepared both qualitative fieldnotes and quantitative observation forms, which enabled us to compare the working style of community officers and regular patrol officers, and to assess whether citizens of different ethnicity, status or gender were dealt with differently. We decided that each fieldworker should be attached to one group of officers throughout the fieldwork. I spent a year on fieldwork, so I got to know 'my' officers quite well, not just on patrol but in the canteen and after hours.

One of their number was manning a patrol car when I accompanied him on a night shift from a Friday evening into the early hours of Saturday morning. He had been a participant in the administration of 'street justice' to a black male who had assaulted an undercover female decoy during a bag snatch, which I have discussed in Fielding (1990) as an instance of the need to look at incidents from the participants' perspective to gain a holistic understanding. Earlier in the fieldwork we had discussed the topic and method of the research. Although the research team kept it to a minimum to avoid reminding officers that their work was being observed, we periodically jotted notes in the officers' presence. On this occasion the shift had started quietly, as it was raining. In the late evening we received a call. A man was acting erratically and dodging back and forth from sidewalk to roadway near a major intersection. We found the man easily. He was a heavily built Afro-Caribbean and appeared to be one of the area's large number of vagrants. The constable recognized him. He was 'basically all right' but could be aggressive and hard to handle when drunk. Tonight it looked like he had had 'a skinful'. We approached without blue lamps and parked a few feet behind the man. The constable approached the man, calling him by name in an entirely matter-of-fact tone of voice: 'Hey John, it's not a nice night is it.' The man muttered something, pushed the constable's chest and then hit out at his shoulder. The constable sidestepped the blow and in doing so, steadied John from the waist and, rather as if strolling with a lover, guided him through 180 degrees and into the car. The patrol car was a battered two-door model. Its cramped interior was not designed for maintaining aplomb when steering a 250 lb drunk on to the back seat, but the constable took elaborate and subtle care (not at all attended to by the drunk, who was trying to remember the officer's name) to get him on to the seat without hitting his head on the bodywork.

These manoeuvres were performed with a seamless balletic grace that sticks in my memory as an instance of the unsung but significant portion of policework that is not about verbal or negotiating skill but about body control, hand-holds and balance. To capture the moment I jotted a note, trying to record the movement as well as the few words that were said. The station was nearby so we took the drunk there to sober up in a cell. Back in the car the constable said he had noticed me writing a note and wondered what I had seen that was worth writing down. Officers seldom displayed interest in what we were doing, especially after the initial novelty wore off. This, and the fact that I felt I had a friendly relationship with this officer, made me say that I had taken the note because I was impressed with how he had handled the incident. I added that his movements had struck me as nearing on the graceful and that I felt his skills of coordination had disarmed the man and largely accounted for a surprisingly quick and easy resolution. 'You mean you're writing things down about *me*?!', the constable asked. The tone was one of near-incredulity, but behind it was an unmistakable shading of betrayal. I said that he'd be welcome

to read what I had written. There was nothing to hide and my commentary was the opposite of adverse. 'No, I *don't* bloody want to read it!' I attempted repair by emphasizing that I was seriously impressed by his physical performance. Whether this sounded uncomfortably close to the kind of appreciation a gay man might offer or my flattery was too unctuous I do not know, but the attempted repair failed. The rest of the shift passed in virtual silence. Those who have experienced the deadliness of the early morning hours of a quiet night shift will know that I was being punished.

The episode suggests that cooperation/resistance is a stilted way to express the nature of field relations in long-term fieldwork with small working groups. A sense of relief at being tolerated sometimes excites not only gratitude but a misplaced sense on the part of fieldworkers that they have achieved genuine friendship with those they observe. For all our talk about reflexivity, we are sometimes lazy about taking the role of the other. Perhaps I would not have been shocked by the tone of betrayal the constable expressed if I had troubled to think what it is like to have someone with a notepad staring at you while you do your job, the job on which your mortgage, self-image and friendship network depend. Perhaps if I had bothered seeing it from the constable's perspective I would have recognized how a statement about my 'balletic grace', when I thought all I was doing was stopping a drunken tramp punching me and puking on my wreck of a patrol car, would not only be unbelievably pompous but would highlight the distance between my world and the observer's. Perhaps, indeed, I would remember that these researchers had said they were concentrating on members of the public experiencing community policing interventions rather than watching the officers conducting the interventions and evaluating not only what they did but even how they moved.

For my part I had overestimated how much the officer understood about what we were doing, what type of action our access warranted, and the bounds of our informal relationship. Offering sight of the jotted note was particularly inadvisable. My jotted fieldnotes largely consist of abbreviations and short phrases spoken by field participants that trigger recall when writing full fieldnotes. Even if the constable had read them he would have been unable to see in them the mental picture I had formed. The significance of offering sight of the notes was not that I expected the offer to be accepted or, if accepted, that it would help. Its significance lay in something more primordial than any fieldworker/participant relationship. It was about owning the guilt of betrayal. It was about self-abasement. I had wronged a friend and something should be given to make good the hurt. It did not work. From such circumstances there is no return to normal. The gift relationship lies at the very heart of sociality (Douglas, 1970). When the gift is refused, and there is no other gift to give, the relationship withers.

This was just one field contact and I was just one fieldworker of three. All of us at times felt the bind of personal relationships, particularly when the depth of our contact gave us insight into what lay behind callous, brutal acts of policing, forcing us to consider whether, similarly placed, we could have done any better. Such feelings intrude particularly sharply when 'policy relevance' is criterial. Expensive work like this is seldom funded without some such claim and this encourages the tendency to evaluate rather than simply interpret. Operating with long-term commitment to a substantive field like policing, politics or health gives us another set of interests to negotiate beyond ethical practice, personal feelings and our analytic agenda. It is seldom as crass as pressure to produce a particular analysis or cover up inconvenient data, although this certainly does happen. More insidious, better concealed, and more frequent, is self-censorship.

When a researcher commits to a given field they have to balance the nature of the contribution they wish to make to the discipline against what they have to compromise to operate in that field. That is not something about which principles can be laid down by others. However, one can 'speak truth to power' and survive in one's field, provided one takes the long view. A highly regarded criminal justice researcher conducted in the 1970s a methodologically rigorous study that produced an extremely unflattering picture of a major criminal justice institution. The study refuted government policy in respect of this institution. The researcher was banned from ever entering again a branch of this institution. The researcher turned attention to an unrelated criminal justice institution, making key contributions to that field. Recently the researcher was appointed by the government department dealing with criminal justice to the top national role in respect of a third area of criminal justice, an appointment that has to be approved by a top politician. The point is that the relationship between the policy and research worlds is one marked by competing interests on the part of both policy-makers and researchers (Fielding, 1999). If a controversial researcher is rehabilitated it is because policy-makers have seen an interest in doing so, bearing in mind that a reputation for independence can lend credibility to contested policies and that, since governments change, the thorn in one government's side does not prick for ever.

Since operating in long-term substantive fields that are policy-relevant produces field-specific expertise, and since it is often hard to predict how one's work will be received since one cannot tell which policy faction will predominate in the response to it, it seems best to let integrity decide whether the research environment is hostile or hospitable. But we do need to recognize that all this is out there, affecting our field relations as much as the interpersonal dimensions discussed in my example.

CONCLUSION

The tone of this chapter has run from the jaunty and cavalier to the portentous and perhaps maudlin. It has seemed horribly self-referential in the writing, but we say often enough that in qualitative research the researcher is the research instrument and we must therefore accept being a little more open about our practices than seems comfortable. It is time to extract some ideas from all this autobiography. In terms of practical procedures there are several measures that help protect the fieldworker's physical and mental security and welfare. The heightened sensitivity to the cooperative/hostile dimension of rapport that has been highlighted in this chapter is not just an analytic but a practical resource. Close and reflexive monitoring of reactions to our presence, actions and the topics we raise helps us negotiate the field. It is important to anticipate what challenges may arise so that appropriate precautions are used: a tense situation can be inflamed if respondents realize that fieldworkers regard contact with them as requiring precautions. After each fieldwork event it is worth keeping note of any aspect relating to security or which made the fieldworker uncomfortable; Bruyn's (1966) schema for recording subjective aspects of fieldwork is recommended.

Other security measures are no different from those that people ordinarily take when meeting strangers, with the exception of fieldwork with people engaged in criminal or unethical practices. There thought needs to be given to the legal aspects of holding data in which the authorities have an interest. The sparse case law in this area is based on researchers being analogous to investigative journalists. Conducting research is not a legally acceptable reason to refuse the authorities access to research materials. In the few documented cases, researchers have refused access rather than incriminate their sources, and been sentenced for contempt of court (for a discussion, see Van Maanen, 1982).

In discussing work in hostile research environments I have emphasized the importance of interpersonal skills, especially observation and negotiation. Sensitivity to the others' behavioural display involves monitoring paralinguistic elements as well as verbalizations. The early discussions of interview method made much of its necessary combination with observation, and attention to paralinguistics can be useful both in managing the fieldwork situation and analysing the data. Fieldwork can be seen as a series of negotiations, with the researcher and the researched continually testing the bounds of the relationship. Flexibility is needed, and this means we need to be prepared in difficult research environments to make decisions in the field. We cannot anticipate everything and sometimes we will be asked to do things that give us serious pause. This is why it is important to be clear about our ethical precepts ahead of entry to the field, because when we are in the field they will be tested and our effort will be directed to deciding how to apply them.

I have referred to the utility of play-acting, of being comfortable with playing roles that do not reflect how we are when not in the field. In rehearsing how each fieldwork event may go, we need to consider the demands that may arise which are only solvable by deception, and to decide what degree of deception we are prepared to accept. The practical application of research ethics has less to do with formal codes than with situated practice. Field situations vary so much that blanket injunctions are not helpful, and, in any case, when we think seriously about the methods we use it is difficult to maintain some of the assumptions on which they are founded. For example, we make a distinction between overt and covert observation, but precisely when do sociologists stop observing? If my subject is policing, I may have carefully negotiated with Scotland Yard the threshold above which I would feel obliged to notify superior officers of malpractice rather than use it as data (a quite usual negotiation), but what happens if by chance I witness such an occurrence while walking home after fieldwork? Should I report it? Use it in my analysis? Even if I don't, can I erase it from my awareness so effectively that it won't affect the analysis? Should I approach those I have observed and

tell them I plan to use what they did in my research?

Decisions about what is right (or least wrong) in such instances do not involve pulling the correct principle off the shelf but an awareness of all the principles that must be balanced, a determination of their degree of applicability, and a judgement about their balance. It is similar to the judge's procedure in sentencing: in light of *actus rea* (the thing done) and *mens rea* (the doer's intention), decide the ceiling of penalty attaching to the act, take account of mitigating factors and set the most appropriate penalty. That is the kind of judgement we face in research ethics, not the simple bipolar choice – guilty or not – that we permit the untrained jury. Professional judgement is about the precise application of principles and that is the kind of work that situational ethics requires (Duster et al., 1979). Such ethics rule little out on principle but require a more acute awareness of principles in practice than any code of ethics offers.

One of the hardest judgements is when we consider the gain in knowledge (the 'scientific justification') to warrant means we regard as dubious. What makes it so difficult is that we usually do not know precisely what knowledge will be gained. Agreeing to conceal in one's apartment a stolen gun entrusted to us by a field contact expecting a police search (Polsky, 1971) may enhance our standing with our contact or their contempt for our pliability. Enhanced standing may encourage our contact to share more information with us, but we cannot know if the information will be useful. Refusing to secrete the gun may put us at risk too – declining to do this favour may make our contact indifferent to our security when we operate in their milieu.

For all our care over situational ethics, decisions like this rely at least partly on how our individual personalities respond to risk. Those who enjoy the kind of risk involved in suspending familiar identities have an advantage in working in hostile environments. When deception is involved it may be a matter of degree rather than an absolute, as in cases where one allows others to draw conclusions one does not correct. More than a willingness to use what means are necessary to gather the information we want, working in hostile research environments requires thoughtful planning, anticipating the things that may happen on each fieldwork occasion, interpersonal sensitivity in the field, and flexibility. Above all, it demands awareness that every field decision, including the decision not to go further, must be treated by reference to the *practical* application of ethical *priniciples*.

NOTE

1 There is no implication that the branch or its members precipitated such actions. Details of the circumstances are in Fielding (1981) and Fielding and Fielding (1986).

REFERENCES

Blee, K. (1998) 'White-knuckle research: emotional dynamics in fieldwork with racist activists', *Qualitative Sociology*, 21(4): 381–99.

Bruyn, S.T. (1966) *The Human Perspective in Sociology.* Englewood Cliffs, NJ: Prentice-Hall.

Couper, M. (1997) 'Survey introductions and data quality', *Public Opinion Quarterly*, 61(2): 317–38.

Dalton, M. (1959) *Men Who Manage: Fusions of Feeling and Theory in Administration.* New York: Wiley.

Dean, J. and Whyte, W. (1958) 'How do you know if the informant is telling the truth?', *Human Organization*, 17: 34–8.

Douglas, M. (1970) *Natural Symbols.* London: Barrie.

Duster, T., Matza, D. and Wellman, D. (1979) 'Fieldwork and the protection of human subjects', *American Sociologist*, 14(3): 136–42.

Feenan, D. (2002) 'Legal issues in acquiring information about illegal behaviour through criminological research', *British Journal of Criminology*, 42: 762–81.

Festinger, L. (1956) *When Prophecy Fails.* Minneapolis: University of Minnesota Press.

Fielding, N. (1981) *The National Front.* London: Routledge.

Fielding, N. (1990) 'Mediating the message: the co-production of field research', *American Behavioral Scientist*, 33(5): 608–20.

Fielding, N. (1992) 'Affinity and hostility in research on sensitive topics', in C. Renzetti and R.M. Lee (eds), *Researching Sensitive Topics.* London: Sage, pp. 146–59.

Fielding, N. (1999) 'Research and practice in policing: a view from Europe', *Police Practice and Research*, 1(1): 1–29.

Fielding, N. and Fielding, J. (1986) *Linking Data.* Beverly Hills, CA: Sage.

Fine, G.A. (ed.) (1995) *A Second Chicago School?* Chicago: University of Chicago Press.

Gwiasda, V., Taluc, N. and Popkin, S. (1997) 'Data collection in dangerous neighborhoods' *Evaluation Review*, 21(1): 77–93.

Homan, R. (1991) *Ethics of Social Research.* London: Longman.

Nespor, J. (1998) 'The meanings of research: kids as subjects and kids as inquirers', *Qualitative Inquiry*, 4(3): 369–88.

Ong, P. (ed.) (1999) *Impacts of Affirmative Action.* Los Angeles: AltaMira Press.

Ostrander, S. (1993) 'Surely you're not in this just to be helpful: access, rapport and interviewing in three studies of elites', *Journal of Contemporary Ethnography*, 22: 7–27.

Pollnac, R., Poggie J. and Vandusen, C. (1995) 'Cultural adaptation to danger and the safety of commercial oceanic fishermen', *Human Organization*, 54(2): 355–79.

Polsky, N. (1971) *Hustlers, Beats and Others.* Harmondsworth: Penguin.

Silverman, D. (1997) *Discourses of Counselling,* Appendix 1: 'The history of the research project'. London: Sage.

Smigel, E. (1958) 'Interviewing a legal elite: the Wall Street lawyers', *American Journal of Sociology*, 64: 159–64.

Van Maanen, J. (l982) *Varieties of Qualitative Research.* London: Sage.

Winlow, S., Hobbs, D., Lister, S. and Hadfield, P. (2001) 'Get ready to duck: bouncers and the realities of ethnographic research on violent groups', *British Journal of Criminology*, 41: 536–48.

Wright, R. and Decker, S. (1994) *Burglars on the Job.* Boston: Northeastern University Press.

17

Politics, research and understanding

Les Back

CHARING CROSS STATION, LONDON, 2 APRIL 1998

I arranged to meet Nick Griffin at 5.30 p.m. outside Charing Cross Station in the heart of London. It was a mild grey afternoon, the streets of the capital were covered in the shiny gossamer of rain. Griffin, a key figure in the National Front during the 1970s, was currently active in the British National Party. I didn't know it at the time, but he was a figure of rising importance in the party and ultimately to become its next leader. I had spoken to him on his cell phone earlier that day to confirm the interview. He was in East London canvassing for the forthcoming local elections in the area where, in 1994, fellow BNP member Derek Beakon had become the first member of an extreme right-wing party to be successfully elected. I had approached Griffin for an interview because he was awaiting trial for incitement to racial hatred for his involvement in the production of an extremist tract entitled *The Rune* which included, among other things, articles on Holocaust revisionism, race and criminality, and white nationalism. I wanted to interview him in connection with a research project I was carrying out on nationalist movements and their use of information technology. Although Griffin himself lived in rural Wales, the magazine was produced in Croydon, South London – the place where my family lived and where I had been raised. He was late and I was anxious. I looked up at Nelson's Column and then down at my watch; I would give him another twenty minutes.

My anxiety was compounded by the hostile reaction that my work had received by racists and activists on the far Right. I had attracted the ire of the BNP's magazine *Spearhead*, which cast me as a 'politically correct liberal' and 'mischief

maker' (Thurgood, 1998: 17). Less sophisticatedly, I had also received a string of anonymous hate letters that classified me as a conspiring 'Jew' or a 'race traitor'. The harassment had changed me, not least in respect of the experiential shock engendered from being loathed by strangers as an object – a traitor, a Jew. I should make it clear that I am not Jewish, but it was telling that the authors of the abusive mail I received seemed compelled to read my identity through the cipher of anti-Semitism because it enabled them to make sense of my research and writing. The logic of this seemed to be: 'If you are against racism, you must be a Jew.' George Orwell wrote in 1940 that so much left-wing thought was 'a kind of playing with fire by people who don't even know that fire is hot' (Orwell, 1957: 37). It might also be said that much of the scholarship and academic work on racism suffers from the same syndrome. The experience of being the object of hate altered my comprehension of the exact nature of the white heat of racism and its experiential consequences. Part of the shock was that my family and young children might also become exposed to this bile, a fear that thankfully was never realized.

I was not quite sure what to expect from the imminent encounter with an outspoken advocate of white nationalism. In those minutes that seem to last for ever, it became so clear that the stakes change when one decides to look into the face of racial extremism. For Emmanuel Levinas the notion of the face captures precisely both the fact of human difference and the ethics of communication. For him the ethical challenge is how we coexist while leaving difference and otherness intact and without losing our own integrity. He writes in *Totality and Infinity*:

> The relation between the Other and me, which dawns forth in his expression, issues neither in number nor in

concept. The Other remains infinitely transcendent, infinitely foreign; his face in which his epiphany is produced and which appeals to me breaks with the world that can be common to us, whose virtualities are inscribed in our *nature* and developed in our existence. Speech proceeds from absolute difference. (Levinas, 1969: 194)

But encountering the face *and* the voice of racial nationalism brought into sharp focus the tension between a Levinasian concern to leave the integrity of the Other intact while meeting head-on the pernicious content of much of what was said.

I had no qualms in talking to nationalists and racists over the phone or via the Internet, but somehow having to be in first-hand, real-time dialogue posed a whole series of questions about the ethical terms of such a conversation and the politics of assimilating those who espoused racism into the realm of understanding. In the simulated setting of cyberspace these issues had not felt quite so urgent. I had invented several personae on the Internet in the context of newsgroups and Internet relay chatlines and passed variously as a 'potential recruit' or 'anti-fascist opponent'. Taking on new names and self-invention is entirely normal within this world. Activists often write under pseudonyms. I had also created my own phantom *nom de plume* and used it when contributing articles to anti-fascist periodicals. But in the context of this meeting, and others, I decided that it was important to own my name and to perform a particular kind of masquerade: that of the liberal academic, so much the target of vituperative outpourings in racist publications. A few weeks earlier, I had seen Griffin during the initial hearings of his case at Harrow Crown Court, on the outskirts of London. On that occasion he arrived with a group of young male followers or protectors. If I am honest with myself, I was afraid that he would appear on this occasion with a similar group, and they would not only know my name but also find out what I looked like. I waited.

As Nick Griffin entered the car park in front of the station I identified him not from his face but from his walk. I had seen many pictures of him leading National Front marches and he had a loping stride that was immediately recognizable. I moved towards him, he was alone, and we greeted each other and shook hands. The thing that was immediately striking about Griffin was how ordinary he looked in the context of the ebb and flow of London life at rush hour. He was dressed in a blue jacket, a white open-necked shirt and khaki trousers. He was unremarkable in most respects, except for the fact that he had lost the sight of one eye during an accident and he had a false eye. There was nothing to signal that this was a man on the margins of the political spectrum. Born in Barnet, North London, he had grown up in a political household of parents who were right-wing Tories. His family moved to rural Suffolk when he was nine where he completed his schooling. He went to his first National Front meeting in Norwich in his early teenage years and went on to form a group in Ipswich.

As we walked along the Strand we exchanged pleasantries. He suggested that we conduct the interview in a nearby restaurant. I asked him about the court case and why he had elected to defend himself. He told me that the barrister allocated to his case had suggested that he plead guilty, which he found unacceptable. It transpired that Griffin had some knowledge of the legal system. A graduate of Cambridge University, he had studied law during his final year and had been awarded a second-class honours degree. During his time there he had also earned a 'blue' representing the university as a featherweight boxer. He told me later that one of his great sporting idols was Mohammed Ali. During his time at Cambridge he had also become politically involved with the National Front, gaining notoriety among the student body as a vocal supporter of the extreme Right.

These details were surprising in many respects, but the overwhelming impression was how familiar Griffin seemed. He had done his homework on me, but not in a way that I expected. As we walked he told me: 'I know about you; you're an expert in multiculturalism, aren't you? I did a search of your publications, very interesting.' At that point I wasn't completely sure who was researching whom. In another ironic twist, Griffin suggested that we conduct the interview in a Mexican restaurant in Covent Garden called Chi-Chi's. It was just a short walk away. The restaurant's manageress that night was a young black woman who greeted us warmly. It seemed so incongruous. Here I was in the company of a white nationalist – in the midst of his prosecution for incitement to racial hatred – in a Mexican restaurant of his choice, being shown to our table by a young black woman. As Griffin tucked into his Tostados salad, the conversation ranged over a variety of topics from Holocaust denial to his defence of 'white culture'.

In the course of a long interview lasting close to two hours, the tone of the conversation ranged from the convivial discourse of 'educated men', to moments when our political incommensurabilities were laid bare. 'If you take out the political road and ban any political expression of white feeling or racial nationalism – call it what you will – then there are several thousand people who are sufficiently dedicated in *my* language – fanatical in *your* language – [and] they will think – if there is no possibility of a political road then they will think "we must use some other road". Then there will be serious racial trouble', he warned. His defence of revolutionary racial nationalism was that it posed a 'safer option' and an alternative to the threat of white terrorism. We might have been speaking different political languages, but this encounter was also about uncomfortable resemblances – what Levinas refers to as the 'virtualities' of social life: we were approximately the same age, graduates, loving fathers. These uncomfortable congruences undercut any simple separation between anthropologist and ethnographic subject or between the liberal and fascist.

I want to return to this encounter throughout as a way of opening up issues relating to the ethical stakes and political and methodological issues. In both Europe and the United States, there has been a long-standing debate about the politics of 'race relations' research (Ladner, 1973; Staples, 1976; CCCS, 1982; Keith, 1992; Harris and James, 1993), in large part this has focused on the ways in which white sociologists have misrepresented minority communities and also been complicit in producing social research that is little more than surveillance. Here I want to focus on the issues that are at stake when one refocuses the sociological view to examine the perpetrators of racism. In some respects these issues are specific to this highly politicized area of research. However, there are areas of wider relevance that are significant to the concerns of this volume as a whole. There has been some concern to connect sociology to the process of empowering research participants, but how is this different when you are studying people who use ideologies like racism to empower themselves? Also, in circumstances such as those described above, what should we do as researchers when we encounter views that are politically and morally offensive? How are our own biographies and social positions implicated in the research act and in the process of understanding and analysis?

One suggestion that emerged within the debate about racism and research is the question of whether the interviewer and research participant should be matched in terms of their ethnicity or 'racial background'. More worryingly, it seems that, particularly within the United States, many researchers have embraced the opportunity to explore whiteness as if it was somehow a less ethically problematic form of investigation to enter into because it does not involve the mediation of racial or cultural difference. I want to suggest that while the issue of 'matching' recognizes that the research act involves a social encounter, the nature of that encounter is not necessarily elucidated simply by creating a real or imagined equivalence in social profile. My starting point is that we need to recognize that social identities are at play in the research encounter. These identities are not fixed or stable, and what is important is to try to explicate the quality of each encounter rather than assuming that authentic communication occurs only when the social backgrounds of researcher and researched are identical.

I want to argue for the necessity of connecting the investigation of social injustices like racism with a broader commitment for ameliorating and dismantling systems of white supremacy, while cautioning against striking hyper-political postures or what might be called 'political inflation' in academic rhetoric. This raises broader questions about the nature of the relationship between sociology and values. In 1918, Max Weber commented famously that 'politics is out of place in the lecture-room' (Weber, 1948: 145). Weber rightly guarded against the possibility of sociology becoming merely political propaganda: 'the prophet and the demagogue do not belong on the academic platform' (ibid.: 146). However, writing about highly politicized issues like racism in itself means being drawn in political alignments. In this sense, there is no neutral place for Weber's cool-headed scientist to stand, what Chris Rojek and Bryan Turner have recently proposed in their notion of 'engaged detachment' (Rojek and Turner, 2000: 643).

There has been much debate in sociology about the issue of partisanship (Gouldner, 1971; Hammersely, 2000). Howard Becker summed up this problem in his classic essay 'Whose side are we on'? For Becker the resolution is to embrace that necessity of creating hierarchies of credibility and developing a critical view: 'Whatever side we are on, we must use our techniques impartially enough that a belief to which we are especially sympathetic could be proved untrue. We must always inspect our work carefully enough to know whether our techniques and theories are open to allow that possibility' (Becker, 1967: 246). It is this combination of dialogue and critical judgement that is the chief concern of this chapter.

I want to focus on two related questions: How are the ethics of investigating racial power implicated in these strange acquaintances – necessitated by the research act itself – and the desire to understand the advocates of intolerance and racism? What issues does this extreme case, where one is almost literally researching political opponents, raise in relation to wider concerns of sociological practice and in particular the place from which we make interpretations and strive for understanding?

ANTHROPOLOGICAL EPISODES

George Marcus has argued that, in the aftermath of recent critiques of ethnography, the classic observational objective 'eye' needs to be supplanted with the personal 'I' of the ethnographer (Marcus, 1994: 41). Beyond this he identifies the need to make a shift from analytic exegesis towards dialogue between anthropologist and the research participants. But what would this look like with regard to entering into an ethnographic dialogue with people who espouse xenophobia and racism? Much of the debate around dialogic fieldwork in postmodern anthropology seems predicated upon a very particular imbalance across the horizon of investigation, namely, the European anthropological 'I' and the 'they' of postcolonial subjects of former empire. What difference would it make if we situate the debate around dialogic fieldwork in the context of an encounter with a member of a white supremacist organization? Are the commitments of polyphony the same if one is sharing ethnographic authority with an outspoken advocate of Holocaust denial?

It is here that Taylor's notion of *perspicuous contrast* becomes useful in that it offers the possibility of combining critique with dialogue. He writes:

> It will almost always be the case that the adequate language in which we can understand another society is not our language of understanding, or theirs, but rather what one could call a language of perspicuous contrast. This would be a language in which we could formulate both their way of life and ours as alternative possibilities in relation to some human constants in both. ... Such a language of contrast might show their language of understanding to be distorted or inadequate in some respects, or it might show ours to be so ... . (Taylor, 1985: 125)

As Levinas points out, 'to see is ... always to see on the horizon' (Levinas, 1969: 191), but the task of interpretation following Gadamer is a matter of the 'fusion of horizons' (Gadamer, 1975: 358).

This point is picked up by Clifford Geertz in his extraordinary essay 'The Uses of Diversity'. Criticizing both the ethnocentrism displayed in Lévi-Strauss's later writings and philosopher Richard Rorty's cultural self-centredness, Geertz argues for a model of cross-cultural understanding that focuses on the space between Self and Other. For him the question of understanding is about an ethics of:

> Learning to grasp what we cannot understand. ... Comprehending that which is, in some manner or form, alien to us and likely to remain so, without either smoothing it over with vacant murmurs of common humanity, disarming it with to-each-his-own indifferentism, or dismissing it as charming, lovely even, but inconsequent, is a skill we have to arduously learn and having learnt it, always very imperfectly, to work continuously to keep alive; it is not a connatural capacity, like depth perception or the sense of balance, upon which we can complacently rely. (Geertz, 1994: 465)

Implicitly, for both Taylor and Geertz, their argument against ethnocentrism is laced with assumptions about the integrity of the ethnographic subject and an appeal to give voice to what appears alien to us. It is telling that Richard Rorty, in his answer to Geertz, points to the limits of 'wet liberalism' and the dilemma posed when 'the alien' is a racist, fascist or political fundamentalist: 'When we bourgeois liberals find ourselves reacting to the Nazi and the fundamentalist with indignation and contempt – we have to think twice. For we are exemplifying the attitude we claim to despise. We would rather die than be ethnocentric, but ethnocentrism is precisely the conviction that one would die than share certain beliefs' (Rorty, 1991: 203).

These are thorny questions and push the ethics of understanding to its limits. The resolution proposed here is to insist both on the possibility of simultaneous dialogue and critique; to attempt to grasp an 'alien turn of mind' that disrupts the ethnographer's preconceptions, while at the same time critically to evaluate the taken-for-granted predispositions of the communities under study. A mutual destabilization is thus produced on both sides of the ethnographic divide. Clifford Geertz pushes this approach further to suggest that the understanding of sameness and difference operates *both* where people share the same culture or patterns of subjectification – in our cases, those interpellated as 'white' – and also in the context of cross-cultural communication. He writes: 'Foreignness does not start at the water's edge but at the skin's. The sort of idea that both anthropologists since Malinowski and philosophers since Wittgenstein are likely to entertain that, say, Shi'ias, being other, present a problem, but, say, soccer fans, being part of us, do not, or at least not the same sort, is merely wrong' (Geertz, 1994: 458). Geertz shows the importance of avoiding the syndrome of seeing the problem of Otherness only in distant cultures.

It is equally misguided to make the 'soccer fan' into an incorrigible Other. Rather, we should insist on an ethics of interpretation that can both identify what is alien and other – i.e. the 'soccer fan', or the 'BNP member' – and yet at the same time hold on to the possibility of a semblance of a shared likeness.

Geertz's invocation of the soccer fan conveniently provides the link with the example I want to use to illustrate what an ethics of interpretation might look like following this approach. In 1996 I followed a trial of two white soccer fans. On being refused entry to a match the two soccer fans had gone to a local pub with a group of other friends. They followed the fortunes of their team on the teletext and started to drink heavily. Their team lost 2–0 and, disgruntled, they left the pub, itself just a short walk from the stadium. They were looking for opposition fans to confront as a way of compensating for the collective loss of honour engendered by the humiliating defeat by a local rival team. After a few abortive skirmishes they came upon a young black man waiting for a bus. They attacked him. But the lone black man fought the group off, to the extent that the white group started to walk away. The black man picked up a brick and followed his assailants up the street, since he wanted to make sure that they were going to leave him be. The police arrived and arrested all the young men, including the black person who had been attacked.

After a few days the police dropped their inquiries into the behaviour of the black man and focused attention on the group of white men. Of a group of six to eight youths, only two were prosecuted. I observed the trial at its various stages and, over a period of months, I got to know the families of the assailants. The two young men – Paul and Ken – were from different backgrounds. Paul had been involved in petty crime and had a series of convictions for violence. Ken, on the other hand, had no prior convictions. He was from a respectable working-class family and, at the time of his arrest, was in full-time employment and had a girlfriend whom he planned to marry. Neither of the two men had been involved in organized racist politics or associated with racist youth cultures. Their racism was of the quotidian variety.

The role of racism in the attack took up a good deal of the trial. Ken's barrister made much of the fact that Ken's sister was black, his family had adopted her at a young age and they had grown up together. Ken's sister appeared in court as a character witness and denied the accusation that Ken was a racist. The prosecution lawyer produced a policewoman as a witness. She had sat in the back of the police van with Ken after his arrest and read out what he had said, a mixture of drunken rant and resentful racism. The black victim of the assault also came and gave evidence, describing the racist epithets and insults directed at him during the incident. In the aftermath of his testimony I sat in the court restaurant with Ken's mother and stepfather. 'When that boy who'd been attacked gave his evidence he just sat there smiling, didn't he?' she said. There was no attempt to dismiss what Ken had done or explain it away. Ken's stepfather replied, 'Well, there's no getting around it – what they did to that boy was wrong and Ken's going to have face that. There's nothing we can do about it, what's done is done.' This was not a family of committed racists. They displayed no more racism and no less tolerance than any other white working-class family in South London that I had encountered, including my own.

The jury found the two young men guilty. As they stood up for sentencing, Paul's face was expressionless as if this was almost routine. Ken was visibly shaken. He stood with his hands clasped together in front of him, he looked at them and held his head down. The judge said that the seriousness of the offence meant that it would be a custodial sentence: 'I will be taking the racial character of your crimes into consideration.' He sentenced Paul first to two years imprisonment. Then, turning to Ken, he told him that he would be sentenced to eighteen months in prison. As Ken heard the news, his bottom lip started to quiver. There was a terrible fear written on his face. Dazed, he looked back at his parents and his girlfriend for a brief moment. Then the court guard led him away to the cells to begin his sentence.

Ken's expression at that moment haunted me for days afterwards. It was the face of complete dread. From that moment, this very ordinary young man would have the distinction of a criminal record for violent racism. What does it mean to empathize with perpetrators in this way? I think that moment affected me so deeply because I could almost see myself in his situation, it almost felt like part of me was standing in the dock with him. My family background was almost identical to Ken's, I had been socialized into commensurable amounts of working-class racism and understood equally the ritual embodiment of such territorial masculinities. Yet, at the same time, the account of his rant against black people in the back of the police van was deeply disturbing. Although this group had not been looking to attack a black person out of blind hate, it was their racism that identified a young black man standing at bus stop as a substitute target for violent attack in the absence of fans from the rival team. It was in this space, replete with ambivalent tensions, that I was forming my interpretation and my analysis of this particular incident of racist violence. Thus, by building on the interpretative schema of Charles Taylor and Clifford Geertz, what I am arguing for is a reflexive interpretative reading that arises within the space between what is familiar and that which is alien.

WHITE ON WHITE? RESEARCH, POLITICS AND THE SPECTRUM OF THE GREY ZONE

Is it the implication of this argument that 'white people' are in the best position to conduct the ethnography of whiteness? Am I thus reinforcing the Manichean intellectual division of labour that I set out to argue against at the beginning of this chapter? I want to make it clear that such a conclusion is *not* the logical consequence of this argument. Rather, I want to suggest that the dialectic of difference and similarity embodied in this interpretative view is appropriate, regardless of the positionality of the researcher. What may vary are the experiential materials that the interpreter utilizes in each case. Beyond the philosophical dimensions of this process it is all too easy to assume that people who are identified as white will not 'confess' to racialized subjectivities, or their commitment to racism if confronted by persons who are not included in the category. I have heard this line of argument deployed, but what is strange about this logic is the way it inverts the debate about the relationship between race and research. Part of the defence that 'white' researchers have made against the charge that they cannot adequately relate to black or ethnic minority interviewees, is the claim that dialogue in the research encounter is complex and demonstrates a variety of social features (i.e. gender, sexuality, class, age, etc.) none of which can be adequately accounted for through a notion of 'race matching'. However, it is alarming that a similar logic is not necessarily articulated when it is the other way around. The presumption that 'whites will not talk' to a black or minority researcher does not tally with the experience of writers who have conducted such an inquiry.

Raphael S. Ezekiel interviewed followers and leaders in the militant racist movement in America in researching his book *The Racist Mind*. He did participant observation at rallies and at the movement's social gatherings. He reflected:

I have dealt openly and honestly with these people, making it clear that I am Jewish, a leftist opposed to racism, a professor at the University of Michigan. I have told them, honestly, that I think people build lives that make sense to them, and that my goal is to understand the sense the person's life makes to that person. I tape-recorded conversations so that the person's own words can be used. I listen much more than I talk. I try to ask searching questions. I try to encourage the respondent to give me a full picture of his life. I show him, periodically, how our basic beliefs differ and explore with him the bases of those beliefs. Occasionally I explain myself with passion; if I already know the respondent, I learn a lot from confrontation. Communication rests on my candor, their interest in being heard, my deep interest in understanding the phenomenon, and my background in a particularly racist culture. (Ezekiel, 1995: xix–xx)

The fact that Ezekiel identified himself as Jewish appeared to have little bearing on the willingness or otherwise of the neo-Nazis to be involved in the research. Indeed, it is exactly the combination of difference and human likeness that informs his interpretative scheme. This can be summed up in the clash between (a) the white supremacists' desire to be heard; (b) Ezekiel's interest in what makes them alien; and (c) his experience of belonging to a social group for which the people he is trying to understand profess a hatred. It is precisely in the processing of such confrontations that he develops an understanding through the 'language of perspicuous contrast'.

This experience also resonates with the ethnographic work on a male skinhead gang that I conducted in 1994 with my colleague Anoop Nayak. Anoop grew up in a predominantly white district of Liverpool, although his parents were from India. We worked jointly with this group of boys on a video project that aimed to give them a space to express their views around race and other issues. The discussion groups took place in a local youth club. The group of boys – which included two black members – claimed not to feel inhibited in any sense by Anoop's presence. On several occasions, members of the group went into tirades about 'Pakis that stink' and Asians who 'walk about with towels round their heads' despite the fact that Anoop was sitting in the room contradicting all their assertions by his very presence. The group listened to and answered Anoop's questions, as they did mine. But it was interesting that the boys never turned their hostility towards Anoop and in many respects were much more antagonistic to me. On one occasion Anoop couldn't be present at the video session because of a prior commitment. I went ahead and conducted the session anyway.

There was much discussion about why Anoop wasn't at the session. 'Did we scare 'im off?' one of the boys asked.

The session was focused on showing the video footage we had shot with the group. We had hoped that this would have provided a context to open up some critical dialogue around what they had said in previous weeks. However, watching the video only provided another context in which to celebrate their racism. After the video had been shown, a member of the group called Robbie came back and asked if we could do another session. I said that we could and then he said, 'Yeah what you should do is bring some Pakis down and we can have a debate. We can listen to what they got to say and we'll tell 'em what we think.' He paused for a moment and then said excitedly, 'Bring some big, dirty smelly Paki down and we can have an argument!' What is telling about this incident in terms of the issue of research practice was that for Robbie, this monstrous image of Asian otherness was necessary in order for him to inflate his own 'white selfhood' to the level of an equal opposite. This not only demonstrates the interlocked process whereby white identity is expressed through the construction of a contrasting racial otherness, but it also shows that the articulation of whiteness and racism is perfectly congruent with a situation where the audience is seen to be Other. As I said goodbye to the group I asked them, 'Does it make a difference when Anoop is here? Would have you said the same things you said to me tonight if he had been here?' Without hesitation Robbie replied, 'No, it wouldn't make any difference! You've asked us to tell you what we think and that is what we did!'

It follows that one should be sceptical about the degree to which 'racial matching' automatically guarantees reliable accounts of white racial subjectification. Establishing a kind of 'white on white' methodology, to use Ruth Frankenberg's characterization (Frankenberg, 1993: 23), need not in itself guarantee that participants will identify and confide in the researcher. Having things 'in common' is not necessarily the prerequisite for insightful dialogue in this case in relationship to the social construction of whiteness. Frankenberg, in her innovative empirical study of race and racism in white women's personal histories, points to the tension between declaring her anti-racist political position and other moments where she 'colluded in keeping it [racial consciousness] repressed' (ibid.: 40). Frankenberg makes a strong and compelling argument against the research persona as the 'neutral observer'. Rightly, she points to the fact that all positions, especially those that invoke

'objectivity' and 'science', are committed. However, she developed a model of dialogic research in which she revealed her disagreement at the same time as opening up opportunities for empathy and the possibility of accord. She writes: 'Central to my dialogical method were the ways in which I offered information both about myself as inscribed within racism and about my analysis of racism as systematic as well as personal. In effect, I broke the silence of the blank-faced interviewer in order to facilitate the breaking of silence on race by a diverse range of white women' (ibid.: 35). Ruth Frankenberg's research illustrates the tension between a commitment to women's empowerment through research (see also Oakley, 1981; Harding, 1987) and the possible collusion in a shared whiteness that both concealed and normalized white supremacy. The tangled combinations of privilege and subjugation make a simplistic notion of empowerment untenable. Put simply, white supremacy always empowers and critical investigation should aim to find ways of dismantling that privilege.

For 'white people', class and gender disadvantage is thus complicated by the advantage that whiteness confers. Such ambivalences between adversity and supremacy make a vanguardist notion of empowerment through research difficult to sustain. More broadly, Judith Stacey has argued that there are endemic tensions between feminism and ethnography. Her experience of field research placed her in 'situations of inauthenticity, dissimilitude, and potential, perhaps inevitable betrayal. ... Perhaps even more than ethnographic process, the published ethnography represents an intervention into the lives and relationships of its subjects' (Stacey, 1988: 25). But equally, should we aspire to empowerment in research when the ethnographic subjects are privileged by their 'race'? In this sense the empowerment of research participants in the investigation of whiteness is a contradiction in terms. More broadly, I think this insight might also qualify broader application of models of social research that are framed within an aspiration to emancipate or empower the research participants.

The research process itself can be the context in which lines of political difference are drawn between researcher and researched. Rather than empowerment this is about confrontation, as was profoundly manifested in my encounter with Nick Griffin described at the beginning of this chapter. In the course of our meal I mentioned that it was 'interesting' that he had developed links with black separatist organizations, particularly in America. 'Why should that be interesting as opposed to inevitable?' he said abruptly. 'As not just nationalists but racial nationalists you can respect and understand the same views. You know precisely how someone else feels, even if they are a different colour. It doesn't make any difference, if they have these same views.' With the tone of irritation growing in his voice, he concluded, 'Ultimately, I've probably got more in common with *them* than I have with *you*! They don't want their kids or grandchildren growing up half-caste. It is anathema to them as it is to me.'

These claims were not merely rhetorical. During the 1980s the National Front established links with a number of American Black Separatist organizations in the Nation of Islam and the Pan-African International Movement (PAIN). Indeed, in his trial that followed in late April 1998, Osiris Akkebala of PAIN gave evidence as a defence witness for Griffin. His expenses paid by the British National Party, Akkebala made a spectacular entrance at the trial. Dressed in a colourful African dashiki he stood up in the court and said, to the delight of the public gallery packed with BNP supporters:

> Well it is not offensive to me as a black man to hear a white man indicate his proudness about his race. I think that is just a natural state of mind to be in. I know it is an international conception that anyone who advocates race separation and race pride walks hand in hand with racism. That I deny vehemently. I am not a racist. I am a true advocate of racial separation and it is not possible at this moment for me nor [*sic*] you to be a racist if you really understand the true definition of the term itself.

In his final question, Nick Griffin directed Akkebala's attention to the cover of the *Rune* magazine:

> [Nick Griffin:] The combination of the noose on the front and words such as 'White unity, final victory, capital work' in this piece, the prosecution said is a coded call to hang black people like the KKK, the Ku Klux Klan. Can you comment on this?

> [Osiris Akkebala:] Well, I read the White Survival Piece and the only thing I would change here is the word 'white' and replace it with 'black', and the noose, in its shape, the rope, it is not offensive to me at all. …

After the day's proceedings Akkebala and Griffin posed for press pictures outside the court (George, 1998). To assume that I – as a white researcher – would have privileged access to Griffin's confidence, is to elide the political chasm that existed between us. Also, it is important to make visible the fraternity that exists between racial nationalists regardless of their shade. These strange alliances also disrupt the

idea that anti-racist virtue can be attributed in crude black-and-white terms.

A further question is, what status should be given to the accounts of white perpetrators of racism? The group with whom Anoop and I had worked was on the peripheries of violent racism. They often had their own self-exonerating accounts of their involvement in racist conflicts. Nick Griffin, equally, was keen to exculpate racial nationalists, whom he cast as innocent victims: 'As a revolutionary I decided a long time ago not to take the easy road, it's not easy, you don't choose to be in nationalist politics for an easy life. It's grief, being harassed, being trapped, being prosecuted and running the risk of being put in prison for your political beliefs. So you don't do that if you want an easy life.' There is a strong current of victimology in far-right discourse. But beyond just describing their accounts, how do we develop an interpretative framework to evaluate and analyse them? As Judith Stacy points out: 'As author an ethnographer cannot (and, I believe, should not) escape tasks of interpretation, evaluation and judgement' (Stacey, 1988: 26). So what kind of credence should we give the accounts of perpetrators in order to assess and weigh them and ultimately use them to subvert and dismantle the structures of white supremacism?

This issue of the status of perpetrator accounts has been particularly key in the historiography of Nazism and the Holocaust. Daniel Jonah Goldhagen, author of the controversial *Hitler's Willing Executioners*, argued that such accounts should always be ruled out of consideration. In the methodological appendix to his voluminous study of the complicity of ordinary Germans in the persecution and extermination of the Jews, he writes: 'Attempting to explain the Germans' actions, indeed just writing a history of this period, by relying on their self-exonerating testimony would be akin to writing a history of criminality in America by relying on the statements of criminals as given to police, prosecutors, and before courts. Most criminals assert that they have been wrongly accused of the crimes' (Goldhagen, 1996: 471). For him such accounts are always compromised by the perpetrators' guilt so that to accept them without corroboration 'will lead one down many false paths, paths that preclude one from ever finding one's way back to the truth' (ibid.: 472).

Goldhagen's book is in large measure a response to Christopher Browning's study of the same period entitled *Ordinary Men* (Browning, 1992), from which Goldhagen attempts to distance himself on virtually every issue, even when there is actually clear agreement between the two historians. One of Goldhagen's lines of criticism is that Browning's study is flawed because he gives too much credence to the testimony of the perpetrators. Browning's response, first published in the newspaper *Die Zeit* in the middle of the furore caused by Goldhagen's book in Germany, is interesting because it picks up on the issue of the status of perpetrator accounts. Browning argues that always to rule out on principle testimony that is deemed to be self-exculpatory impoverishes the interpretative range of any study of perpetration. For him it is a matter of explicating those perpetrator accounts that possess the 'feel' of plausibility. He offers an example of the testimony of one of the reserve policemen interrogated in 1964. Initially, this person denied having any involvement in the 'Jew hunts' and executions. Browning characterizes this as a classic case of perpetrator denial. Then, two days later, the same man reappeared uninvited and recounted in graphic details his involvement in executions. In his testimony he claims he abhorred the killing, which made him physically sick. Browning concludes:

> He then went on to explain his unusual return to the office of the investigators. 'I showed up here again today, to be rid of what I just said .... The reason for my return was to unburden my conscience.' This is the kind of testimony that Goldhagen's methodology excludes, and the result is a kind of 'methodological determinism', screening out much that could give some texture and differentiation to a portrayal of the German killers.... (Browning, 1998: 64)

This attention to plausibility in racial narratives, while at the same time remaining sensitive to self-exculpating elements, is an appropriate bearing to bring to the issue of the validity and interpretation of accounts. Revisiting my encounter with Nick Griffin, it seems clear to me now that we were partners in a dance of deceit that was to some degree mutual though tacitly agreed. I presented myself as an academic, but Griffin made it clear that he knew I had been a public advocate of multiculturalism and no 'neutral observer'. He, on the other hand, fashioned what he wanted me to hear, no doubt aiming to present an image of racial nationalism that would confound conventional wisdom. The task of a reflexive interpretative analysis is to establish the plausibility of each account, while remaining attentive to the discursive and rhetorical moves utilized to both enunciate and legitimate a particular view of the world. Critical insight was produced where common ground was established, or equally in moments when our respective world-views came into direct confrontation.

Finally, I want to end this section by reflecting on what is at stake when we, as researchers, expand our moral imagination to incorporate the racist into the realm of understanding. I want to make a case for the role of ethnography in bearing witness to forms of injustice, in this particular case ideological and everyday racism, that is neither a matter of asserting an anti-racist moral high ground, nor disclosing collusion with the very thing we aim to abolish. The challenge is to think beyond such an either/or logic, refusing both a vanguardist position and the confessional narcissism of apologia.

It is here that the work and thought of Primo Levi offers a way out of such forms of ethical simplification. Levi, an Italian chemist and non-religious Jew, was transported to the Nazi death camps at the end of 1943. His books combine personal testimony of the genocide (Levi, 1979) with allegorical and analytical reflection (Levi, 1985, 1989). As Murray Baumgarten has commented, his thought demonstrates a 'special combination of accurate observation, rigorous analysis, clear reasoning, linguistic sensitivity, imaginative conception [and] *multicultural understanding ...*' (my emphasis) (Baumgarten, 1998: 115). Levi's last book *The Drowned and the Saved* was written just before he committed suicide in 1987. In it he points to a series of issues relating to the ethics and politics of understanding terror. In keeping with the sagacity of Levi's method, I want to be clear that I am not suggesting that interrogating whiteness is somehow the same as bearing witness to the Nazi genocide. Rather, my point is that there are lessons to be learned from this specific genocidal moment, in particular with regard to what it means to replicate the quest to understand the contemporary imitators of the Nazis.

Levi writes in *The Drowned and the Saved* that the true witnesses of the terror of the Holocaust are not the survivors. Rather, those in full possession of its appalling exactness are the drowned, those who died. The survivors – the saved – speak in their stead, they are witnesses by proxy. Levi describes how the Nazis, through the camp system, reduced the humanity of the victims, so that the prisoners were assimilated into a system of brutality. This integration compromised the victims: 'It is naïve, absurd, and historically false to believe that an infernal system such as National Socialism was, sanctifies its victims: on the contrary, it degrades them, it makes them similar to itself, and this all the more when they are available, blank, and lack a political or moral armature' (Levi, 1989: 25). The Nazis established hierarchies among the prisoners that set apart the functionaries, the 'Special Squads' and, most debased of all, the 'crematoria ravens'. The spectrum of complicity not only included the German perpetrators and those bystanders who said and did nothing; it also implicated the victims. The result was a 'grey zone, with ill-defined outlines which both separate and join the two camps of masters and servants. It possesses an incredibly complicated internal structure, and contains within itself enough to confuse our need to judge' (ibid.: 27). It is within this context that Levi invites us to understand the phenomenon of survivor guilt and the high incidence of suicide among the 'saved'.

The functionaries were not all collaborators, and Levi talks about the 'camouflaged opponents' who recorded the truth of what was going on in the Lagers. Their 'privilege' gave them access to secret information. The SS delegated responsibility for the implementation of the massacre to the prisoners themselves. The tasks of the Special Squads, who numbered between 700 and 1000, was to do the dirty work of genocide. They were the bearers of the terrible truth and they were regularly killed to hide it. But some members kept diaries, 'feverishly written for future memory and buried with extreme care near the crematoria in Auschwitz' (ibid.: 35). Levi demonstrated that for a minority it was because of their location in the 'grey zone' that they became record-keepers, witnesses and scribes and privy to an accursed truth.

Fellow Auschwitz prisoner and philosopher Jean Améry writes: 'Nowhere else in the world did reality have as much effective power as in the camp, nowhere else was reality so real' (Améry, 1980: 19). Améry was born in Vienna in 1912 into a family that was mainly Jewish, although he was assimilated completely into the culture of the Austro-Hungarian Empire. In the Lager everywhere he turned in his mind for solace and strength belonged to the enemy – be it Beethoven, Dante or Nietzsche. The problem for him, as a Jewish intellectual of German education and cultural sensibility, was that the brutal reality of the camp meant the end of metaphysics, philosophy and aesthetics:

> In the camp the intellect in its totality declared itself to be incompetent. As a tool for solving the tasks put to us it admitted defeat. However, and this is a very essential point, it could be used for *its own abolishment*, and that in itself was something. For it was not the case that the intellectual – if he had not already been destroyed physically – had now become unintellectual or incapable of thinking. On the contrary, only rarely did thinking grant itself a respite. But it nullified itself when at almost every step it ran into its uncrossable borders. The axes of its traditional frames of reference then shattered. Beauty: that was an illusion. Knowledge: that turned out to be a game with ideas. Death veiled itself in all its inscrutability. (Améry, 1980: 19)

For Améry, the Lager did not make people more mature ethically, rather it erected an uncrossable border in understanding: '… we were not even left with the feeling that we must regret its departure' (ibid.: 20).

Améry committed suicide in 1978. In *The Drowned and the Saved*, Primo Levi dedicated a whole chapter to the issue of the position of intellectuals in concentration camps, a posthumous dialogue with Améry. 'To argue with a dead man is embarrassing and not very loyal', he wrote (Levi, 1989: 102). But this 'obligatory step', as he referred to it, was necessary. Levi develops in this essay other ways of looking at intellectual activity under the heel of Nazi terror. The chemist in the Lager – unlike the philosopher – set about interpreting and analysing:

> … from my trade I contracted the habit that can be variously judged and defined at will as human or inhuman – the habit of remaining indifferent to the individuals that chance brings before me. They are human beings, but also 'samples', specimens in a sealed envelope to be identified, analysed and weighed. Now, the sample book that Auschwitz had placed open before me was rich, varied and strange; made up of friends, neutrals and enemies, yet in any case food for my curiosity which some people, then and later, have judged as detached. … I know that this 'naturalistic' attitude does not derive only or even necessarily from chemistry, but in my case it did come from chemistry. (ibid.: 114)

Levi is equivocal about whether he was or was not an intellectual in Auschwitz, but he is sure that experience made him so afterwards. For him 'the Lager was a university; it taught us to look around and to measure men' (ibid.). In Levi's writing we find not the sensibilities of a metaphysician of the mind and its limits, but a proto-ethnographer of human frailty and brutality.

Levi writes in *The Drowned and the Saved* about his relationship with the German translator of his Auschwitz memoir *If This Is a Man*. He recounts both his initial scepticism and the complete faith that he later developed with the man who would bring his book to a German-speaking audience. In one of its most revealing passages, he describes a recurrent argument that developed over the nature of the translation. The barks of the German guards were imprinted on Levi's aural memory. Levi was not a fluent German speaker, like many other non-German prisoners he often just understood the violence in the feral shouts of the SS. He wanted these sounds to be faithfully reproduced in the German edition of the book. His translator maintained that the language Levi recollected was not good German and that post-war readers would not understand. Levi insisted: 'I was driven by a scruple of super-realism' (ibid.: 141). In a situation where reality was more real, Levi reached for a realism with greater acoustic life and aural brilliance. All of these elements – naturalistic method and realism – are the hallmarks of a putative ethnographer, but this an ethnography of witness, of survival. But at the heart of Levi's writing there is an uneasiness. He too is positioned in the spectrum of the grey zone. As Paul Gilroy has said, his suicide casts a shadow over his written work. For Gilroy, at the heart of Primo Levi's work is a tension between, on the one hand, his desire to understand the Nazi terror and its German perpetrators, and, on the other, the personal consequences of this brutality for Levi as a Holocaust survivor. Levi gives us a wealth of evidence and insight, but this dialectic is left unresolved.

There are two lessons that I want to take from this with regard to the encounter within a research context with today's imitators of fascism. The first is a commitment to Primo Levi's model of garnering evidence and his acute interpretative view. The second is to argue that there is a contemporary equivalent to Levi's 'grey zone' and that the ethnographer is, perhaps inevitably, drawn into its spectrum. This occurred to me very powerfully during Nick Griffin's trial, which took place in Harrow Crown Court just a few weeks after we had dinner in Covent Garden. I watched the trial unfold and sat in the public gallery packed with BNP members and journalists. On the second day Griffin called the notorious French Holocaust denier, Robert Faurisson, a former professor of literature at the University of Lyon-2. He had also given evidence at both trials of the notorious Holocaust denier, Ernst Zundel, in Canada (see Lipstadt, 1993: 160–1) Griffin had told me during his interview that he had met Faurisson while on his honeymoon in France. Faurisson, on the surface a harmless old man, took the stand. An older male BNP supporter clapped loudly and cheered, 'He's a courageous man!'

Faurisson told the court he was a specialist in 'the criticism of texts and documents and in the investigation of meaning and counter meaning'. The judge had tried to keep Faurisson from commenting on the status of the revisionist claims made in *The Rune*, the pamphlet for which Griffin was being prosecuted. However, Faurisson continued to tell of his 'research' into the gas chambers. He asserted that he had found no hole for the Zyklon B gas to pass into the gas chamber. The judge seemed slightly bewildered but Faurisson continued unabated. 'It is quite simple', he said in his broken English laced with French accent, 'no holes, no Holocaust!' There was a stunned silence as those words filled the

room. It was punctured only by the murmurs of agreement from Griffin's supporters. After his testimony several people approached Faurisson and shook his hand. He then entered the public gallery and came and sat down next to me.

I took the opportunity to speak to him. I introduced myself as an English academic and he was instantly willing to talk. We walked out into the foyer of the court and I conducted an interview with him. He talked for about forty-five minutes and I scribbled down what he said. At one point Faurisson showed me an album of photographs taken after being physically assaulted by opponents. He offered the picture of his face swollen by having acid thrown into it as a kind of talisman. About halfway through, the old BNP supporter who had applauded when Faurisson took the stand came over and handed me a leaflet assuming that I was a sympathizer. My heart sank. I felt as if I had crossed a line. The interview finished and Faurisson got up. I stayed behind to check and correct my notes while his words were still echoing in my mind. About fifteen minutes passed. I packed up my bag and left the empty court. As I passed through the exit doors, Griffin and his supporters were standing in front of the building talking. He saw me and approached holding out his hand. I shook it. He was enthusiastic and clearly pleased with the day's proceedings. Faurisson had managed to air in open court his revisionist views on the Holocaust. The Frenchman approached, stood and listened, then he took my notepad and scribbled something down. He handed it back to me; it read:

A 'Nazi'? No: a Palestinian.
My writings are the stones of my Intifada.
I am living in an occupied country
With a special apartheid law: the Lex Faurissonia.

I read it and Faurisson explained, 'There is one thing that I didn't tell you. Revisionism can be fun.' 'Fun', Griffin repeated laughing, 'you get beaten up for it.' Faurisson continued, 'It's not great fun, but it is fun.' I felt an enormous sense of doubt as to what I was doing there. It is obvious that Griffin and the BNP crave publicity and I was giving him precisely what he wanted – attention. I felt exhausted and drained from watching the trial. I really didn't want to have any more to do with these people. But here I was standing with a world-famous Holocaust denier and prominent associate of the British National Party. I had entered the 'zone of grey consciences' (Levi, 1987: 171).

On my way home that night I kept hearing Faurisson's words: 'No holes, no Holocaust! No holes, no Holocaust!' It was the eve of the fiftieth anniversary of the State of Israel. That night, Pete, an old school friend whom I'd grown up with in South London, phoned me unexpectedly. He was not Jewish but had married a Jewish woman and was living in Israel with his two children. My friend's tone was poignant: 'It's hard, mate, everyone here is enjoying the celebration but I am separated from everyone in England and I don't completely belong here either.' We talked and laughed about old times. 'It's weird', he said, 'but I start to see what independence means through the eyes of my children.' It was fantastic to speak to a dear friend, but I couldn't get out of my mind that just a few hours earlier I had been talking to a man who claimed the gas chambers never existed. Faurisson invoked the cause of the Palestinians as a way of claiming minority status and to claim that he was a victim. This opportunistic gesture elided the conditions and injustices of the Palestinians in Israel. The political point of entering into this world is to identify and counter the anti-Semitism. It is also a matter of being opposed to any politics of blood and soil that would deny social justice to the Palestinians.

Perhaps the approach I have described here necessitates a kind of ethical ambivalence. The fact that people like Griffin and Faurisson seem so ordinary and prosaic is what should be disturbing. Hannah Arendt summed this up well in her chilling phrase 'the banality of evil' (Arendt, 1963: 231). To admit to this is risky. Such an admission does not sit well with the tendency in our political culture to define whites as either chaste 'anti-racist angels' or rotten to the core 'racist devils'. But such a dualism conceals much of the complexity in the argument developed here. Finally, I want to suggest that the critical engagement should not aspire to resolve the tension created across the desire to understand. This is applicable beyond the specific interrogation of cultures of racism because it invites a disruption on both side of the divide between speaker and interpreter.

REFLECTIVE ENGAGEMENT, CRITICAL JUDGEMENT

To present white racists as humans is not to approve their ideas or their actions. But to picture them only in stereotype is to foolishly deny ourselves knowledge. Effective action to combat racism requires honest inquiry. (Ezekiel, 1995: xxxv)

Throughout this chapter it has been argued that there is limited utility in caricaturing racists as monsters. This is precisely the point that Raphael

Ezekiel makes in the above quotation. I have argued against the application of crude contrasts and suggested a reflexive interpretative view in which understanding is established through 'a language of perspicuous contrast'. Such a mode of interpretation is potentially more disturbing since it invites new insight precisely because it is not predicated on stereotypes or political demonology. Kathleen Blee writes of similar challenges in her extraordinary study of women's involvement in the Ku Klux Klan:

I was prepared to hate and fear my informants. My own commitment to progressive politics prepared me to find these people strange, even repellent. I expected no rapport, no shared assumptions, and no commonality of thought or experience. What I found was more disturbing. Many of the people I interviewed were interesting, intelligent, and well informed. Despite my predictions that we would experience each other as completely foreign, in fact I shared the assumptions and opinions of my informants on a number of topics (excluding, of course, race, religions, and most political topics). (Blee, 1991: 6)

It is this combination of difference and likeness that I want to propose not only in relation to the hermeneutics of whiteness but also as a model for ethnographic interpretation and understanding. Such a position seeks to avoid the perils of political credentialism and the rhetoric of empowerment, while at the same time escaping the pale solipsism of confessing collusion. Following Levinas, through communicating with the Other we enter a relationship with him or her but this does not necessarily lead to a dependence. In *The Periodic Table,* Primo Levi makes it clear that there can be no absolution for those who perpetuate intolerance, only judgement. This is an adversary who 'perseveres in his desire to inflict suffering, it is certain that one must not forgive him: one can try to salvage him, one can (one must!) discuss with him, but it is our duty to judge him, not to forgive him' (Levi, 1985: 222–3). The investigation of racism must be coupled with a commitment to achieving social justice through understanding how racism functions and therefore how it can be dismantled. This brings me back to my dinner with Nick Griffin in London's Covent Garden.

As we left the restaurant Griffin asked me which way I was heading. I told him I was walking back to Charing Cross. 'Where do you live, do you live near Goldsmiths?' he asked. I balked at the question. The hate mail and harassment I'd received had been sent to my office. I didn't want 'them' to find out the location of my home. So I lied and told him that I lived outside London in the countryside of Kent. He immediately seized on this: 'Oh, I bet there's a lot of multiculturalism out there!' He smiled as if to say, 'Yes, you liberals champion the cause of "the ethnics" but don't want to live with them.' I changed the subject: 'What about your wife, isn't she worried that you might go to prison?' The charges against him meant that he could get a prison sentence of six months. Up to this point Griffin had just shrugged off this suggestion or made light of it. It was almost like a game, a form of public school rebelliousness in which he was breaking the housemaster's rules. But he sobered as he talked about his wife and family. 'Yes, she is worried because we have four children to bring up. It will be no fun if I am not around. My wife is a nurse and while she works shifts I usually work from home with my publishing and writing and take care of the children.'

When we arrived at Charing Cross we said our goodbyes and I thanked him for his openness. He went down to the Underground and I walked into the mainline station to catch a train to my home in South London. I found myself feeling a kind of depressed pointlessness. Griffin's martyrdom to a cause that quite clearly has no moral or pragmatic foundation seemed so futile. It was a strange feeling because in many ways it wasn't an unpleasant experience to meet and talk to Nick Griffin. I sat on a train full of people of all shades. The faces in the train were evidence of the fact of multiculture. Griffin demonstrated all of the standards and codes of civility of his class and his education. It wasn't as if he was spitting racist bile and threatening behaviour, it was all very genteel, a kind of racial nationalism with an Oxbridge face and polite bourgeois manners. The experience of meeting him left me feeling a strange combination of disgust and ease.

It is precisely this sense of disorientation that I want to propose as an interpretative position from which ethnography – even of one's political enemies – should be conducted. It was important to have met him and it was important to have looked into his eyes and hear him articulate his sickening views about the Holocaust, race and crime, and the incompatibility of the 'white tribes' with 'immigrants' and 'coloured people'. This was not the rampant ugly face of fascism, although I am sure he could, in the right circumstances, lapse into the demotic racism of the gutter. At his trial a policewoman reported a telephone conversation she overheard in which Griffin said to an unknown caller: 'It's all right at least there are no Pakis or Jews', referring to the officers searching his house. But that night in Covent Garden I encountered racism with a genteel, well-mannered and articulate voice. The ethics of such an inquiry must confront the fact that bearing witness to whiteness also involves being placed on the spectrum of the grey zone. This can never and should never be resolved. It is the comfortless condition of looking into the face of racism and seeing a trace of oneself reflected in its eye.

I want to end by suggesting that confronting these questions is in fact part of the politics of doing this kind of work. After the initial publication of this chapter, reactions were varied. Some questioned why I had focused on one case – i.e. Nick Griffin, a notorious right-wing extremist – as the key dialogue. 'Isn't this giving pernicious views a platform?' 'Doesn't it reinforce the idea that racism is about marginal and extreme people?' My response was to say that my intention was quite the contrary. To insist on the ordinariness of these so-called extreme cases calls into question the colouring of respectable norms. It also calls into question the enduring political orthodoxy that organizes racism into some bodies – either political deviants or working-class – and out of the genteel circles of public life, be they on the Left or the Right of the political spectrum. Theodor W. Adorno warned that 'Every debate about the ideals of education is trivial and inconsequential compared to this single ideal: never again Auschwitz. It was the barbarism all education strives against' (Adorno, 1998: 191). The politics of understanding the features of contemporary racism and the imitators and apologists of Nazism is dedicated to this aim. Critical thinking can play a modest part here, in the commitment to see at the intersection of horizons and contrasting values. It involves critical judgement while remaining open to counter-intuitive possibilities that challenge both our interpretations and our political beliefs.

Hyper-political posturing is not necessarily politics. More than a few self-professed 'political intellectuals' – of all ages – indulge in pieties of this sort on the conference circuit. Such histrionics mask difficult matters of substance. As political tools books are fairly weak instruments of change, regardless of the current talk about the relationship between knowledge and power. Primo Levi once wrote that 'It is a matter of practical observation that a book or a story, whether its intentions be good or bad, are essentially inert and innocuous objects. … Their intrinsic weakness is aggravated by the fact that today all writing is smothered in a few months by a mob of other writings which push up behind it' (Levi, 1991: 157). Perhaps the desperate academic invocations of 'political intent' are a response to the inherent weakness identified so eloquently here. Academic 'prophets' and 'demagogues' – to cite Max Weber's telling phrase – may take comfort from playing to the colloquium gallery.

I want to suggest, in contrast, that the political value of sociological work lies in being open to unsettling dialogues with humility. This is not a good way to produce a stirring manifesto, but it perhaps has the merit of greater honesty with regard to the truths that are touched, if not wholly grasped, through sociological endeavour.

It does not, however, follow that this means a retreat from political issues and towards detachment and neutrality. In this sense, Rojek and Turner's notion of 'engaged detachment' (Rojek and Turner, 2000) is not only a literal contradiction but also confused and obfuscating. The kind of orientation I want to propose with regard to the project of understanding and political contestation might be described as *reflective engagement,* i.e. a political intervention that realizes the limits of writing and the complexities of dialogue and listening. The urgency and speed of politics mean that the window of opportunity for making an intervention will not wait for a beautifully crafted monograph three years after the fact. Making public interventions and aspiring to be a public intellectual involves embracing a wide range of writing genres alongside academic forms. It includes writing letters to newspapers, journalism, and essays for popular and political journals. Some might conclude that proximity to research participants and empirical dialogue always runs the risk of the researcher's judgement being clouded and duped through over-familiarity. Part of the politics of doing the work I have discussed in this chapter is to subject odious and pernicious views to critical evaluation, deconstruction and analysis: it is not merely a matter of reproducing them. I would suggest that familiarity, rather than militating against criticism, involves the deepening of critical judgement.

What does this amount to? What, if any, lessons follow from the discussion offered here. Well, the first and most fundamental point is to be careful about the risks involved when venturing into the public sphere and openly criticizing groups that may have the power to harass and harm you. In the information age researchers are not the only ones with inquiring eyes, you may need protection from those who look back through the research lens at the researcher. Second, there are gains to be had from getting close in ethnographic terms to the thing one is trying to describe and understand. This encounter not only involves confronting unsettling voices, it may produce a disruption in the language and categories of our understanding and interpretation. Third, there is real merit in using the invitation to sociology to enrich the stories we tell about our world, ourselves and our times. John Berger once wrote that writers, storytellers, and by extension sociologists, are 'death's secretaries'

(Berger, 1991: 31). By this I think he meant that writing is about keeping a record and producing a kind of register of life. Regardless of the epistemological melancholy and self-mutilating doubt abroad in today's social science faculties, the tradition of drawing and transcribing *life passed in living* is a noble one to be cherished. This also includes an account of our place in the story we are telling. Finally, I think it is incumbent on us – where possible – to show the people we have listened to what we have written about them, even if it means having to present them with severe criticism. This brings me back to my initial point of departure and that meeting with Nick Griffin on a grey afternoon in London.

I thought long and hard about what I should do as the publication date of *Out of Whiteness* – which included an early version of this chapter – approached. In the period between our initial meeting in 1998 and publication, Griffin's fortunes had changed dramatically. He emerged as the chairman of the British National Party and in the general election of 2001 he stood for parliament in a constituency in northern England called Oldham West and Royton, polling 16.4 per cent of the vote, while elsewhere in Oldham East and in Burnley the BNP took 11 per cent of the vote. In total the BNP secured 12,000 votes in Oldham and one news report claimed that 50 per cent of the voters in one working-class ward had voted BNP. In the aftermath of these events he received considerable media attention both in print and on television. During the intervening years he had gone from an obscure figure – although an acknowledged key player in racist politics – to the most visible face of British extremism. I had given the assurance at the beginning of our correspondence that I would show him any written material in which he was cited. In early 2002 I sent Griffin a proof photocopy of the passages where he was mentioned and Primo Levi's book *The Drowned and the Saved*. I received no reply.

ACKNOWLEDGEMENT

This essay was first published in V. Ware and L. Back, *Out of Whiteness: Color, Politics, and Culture* (Chicago: University of Chicago Press, 2001). It is reproduced here in an amended and updated form.

REFERENCES

Adorno, T.W. (1998) *Critical Models: Interventions and Catchwords.* New York: Columbia University Press.

Améry, J. (1980) *At the Mind's Limit: Contemplations by a Survivor on Auschwitz and Its Realities.* Bloomington: Indiana University Press.

Arendt, H. (1963) *Eichmann in Jerusalem: A Report on the Banality of Evil.* New York: Viking Press.

Baumgarten, M. (1998) 'Primo Levi's periodic art: survival in Auschwitz and the meaningfulness of everyday life', in R. Rohrlich (ed.), *Resisting the Holocaust.* Oxford: Berg, pp. 115–32.

Becker, H. (1967) 'Whose side are we on?', *Social Problems*, 14 (Winter): 239–47.

Berger, J. (1991) *And Our Faces, My Heart, Brief as Photos.* New York: Vintage International.

Blee, K.M. (1991) *Women of the Klan: Racism and Gender in the 1920s.* Berkeley: University of California Press.

Browning, C.R. (1992) *Ordinary Men: Reserve Police Battalion 101 and the Final Solution in Poland.* New York: Harper Collins.

Browning, C.R. (1998) 'Ordinary men or ordinary Germans', in R.R. Shandley (ed.), *Unwilling Germans: The Goldhagen Debate.* Minneapolis: University of Minnesota, pp. 55–73.

Centre for Contemporary Cultural Studies (CCCS) (ed.) (1982) *Empire Strikes Back: Race and Racism in 70s Britain.* London: Hutchinson.

Ezekiel, R.S. (1995) *The Racist Mind: Portraits of American Neo-Nazis and Klansmen.* New York: Penguin Books.

Frankenberg, R. (1993) *White Women, Race Matters: The Social Construction of Whiteness.* London: Routledge.

Gadamer, H. (1975) *Truth and Method.* London: Sheed & Ward.

Geertz, C. (1994) 'The uses of diversity', in R. Borofsky (ed.), *Assessing Cultural Anthropology.* New York: McGraw-Hill, pp. 454–67.

George, P. (1998) 'Black leaders fly in to help racist activist', *Daily Telegraph*, 10 May: 12.

Goldhagen, D.J. (1996) *Hitler's Willing Executioners: Ordinary Germans and the Holocaust.* London: Abacus.

Gouldner, A.W. (1971) *The Coming Crisis of Western Sociology.* London: Heinemann.

Hammersley, M. (2000) *Taking Sides in Social Research: Essays on Partisanship and Bias.* London: Routledge.

Harding, S. (1987) *Feminism and Methodology.* Bloomington: Indiana University Press; Milton Keynes: Open University Press.

Harris, C. and James, W. (eds) (1993) *Inside Babylon: The Caribbean Diaspora in Britain.* London: Verso.

Keith, M. (1992) 'Angry writing: (re)presenting the unethical world of the ethnographer', *Society and Space*, 10: 551–68.

Ladner, J. (ed.) (1973) *The Death of White Sociology.* New York: Vintage Books.

Levi, P. (1979) *If This Is a Man* and *The Truce.* London: Abacus.

Levi, P. (1985) *The Periodic Table.* London: Abacus.

Levi, P. (1987) *Moments of Reprieve.* London: Abacus.

Levi, P. (1989) *The Drowned and the Saved.* London: Abacus.

Levi, P. (1991) *Other People's Trades.* London: Abacus.

Levinas, E. (1969) *Totality and Infinity: An Essay on Exteriority.* Pittsburgh: Duquesne University Press.

Lipstadt, D. (1993) *Denying the Holocaust: The Growing Assault on Truth and Memory.* Harmondsworth: Plume.

Marcus, G.E. (1994) 'After the critique of ethnography: faith, hope and charity, but the greatest of these is charity', in R. Borofsky (ed.), *Assessing Cultural Anthropology.* New York: McGraw-Hill, pp. 40–52.

Oakley, A. (1981) 'Interviewing women: a contradiction in terms', in H. Roberts (ed.), *Doing Feminist Research.* London: Routledge & Kegan Paul, pp. 30–61.

Orwell, G. (1957) *Inside the Whale and Other Essays.* Harmondsworth: Penguin Books.

Rojek, C. and Turner, B. (2000) 'Decorative sociology: towards a critique of the cultural turn', *Sociological Review*, 3: 629–648.

Rorty, R. (1991) 'On ethnocentrism: a reply to Clifford Geertz', in R. Rorty, *Objectivity, Relativism, and Truth: Philosophical Papers*, vol. 1. Cambridge: Cambridge University Press, pp. 203–10.

Stacey, J. (1988) 'Can there be a feminist ethnography', *Women's Studies International Forum*, 11(1): 21–7.

Staples, R. (1976) *Introduction to Black Sociology.* New York: McGraw-Hill.

Taylor, C. (1985) *Philosophy and the Human Sciences: Philosophical Papers 2.* Cambridge: Cambridge University Press.

Thurgood, J. (1998) 'Ungoodthink: race busy bodies in big flap', *Spearhead*, 347 (January): 17.

Weber, M. (1948) 'Science as a vocation', in H.H. Gerth and C.W. Mills (eds), *From Max Weber: Essays in Sociology.* London: Routledge & Kegan Paul, pp. 129–56.

18

Collaborative and team research

Linda S. Mitteness and Judith C. Barker

The founding figures of the social sciences are all remembered as individuals – from Weber, Durkheim, and Marx through Boas, Malinowski, Parsons, etc. These ancestors appear in our shorthand to have worked as solitary scholars in individual settings. Even today, when naming leading figures in the fields of anthropology and sociology, the names come as individuals – Foucault, Bourdieu, and so forth.[1] When we move to the mid-range theorists, the names are still individuals, even though there are a number of significant co-authored works. Well-known exceptions to this 'rule' may be the collaborations between Glaser and Strauss or between Margaret Mead and Gregory Bateson – and these both broke up! Is there something about the qualitative social sciences that works against collaborative work? Is creative scholarship by nature solitary?

While many of the social forms of the academy work against collaboration, significant contemporary changes in the larger society are encouraging collaborative work. Here we explore some of the social factors that influence ways of doing collaborative work, tracing first the historical roots of collaboration, then outlining our perspective on some factors that foster or constrain collaborative work, on to describing a variety of types of collaboration and their strengths and weaknesses. Finally, we make some recommendations, based on our experience and the literature in this area, about what makes research teams work and offer suggestions about practical and theoretical implications of the wider practice of collaborative work in the qualitative social sciences.

SOCIAL FORCES INFLUENCING COLLABORATION

The 'ideal' of the solitary scholar is not limited to the social sciences. The natural sciences and humanities have much longer traditions of consideration of scholarly work as a fundamentally solitary activity. The eccentric wild-haired man, locked in his laboratory or library, disconnected from the basic rules of social interaction as he pursued his lonely intellectual calling, is a fondly held stereotype about academics, whether absent-minded professors or mad scientists. Even the 'real world' of academia involves a variety of stereotypes about solo scholarship. These stereotypes help form some of the constraints on collaboration.

Collaboration in the natural sciences

If we look at the natural sciences, we see some interesting patterns regarding collaborative work. At one extreme, high-energy physicists often publish papers that have 200 or more authors and collaborative teams regularly have 50–500 members (Teruya, 1999). The common explanation for these substantial collaborations is that the tools needed to do the research (e.g. linear accelerators) are extremely expensive and rare, the experiments are difficult and expensive to mount, and the skills required are diverse – all factors leading to large team efforts (Austin and Baldwin, 1991; Teruya, 1999). At the same time, theoretical physics, which is largely mathematically based, requiring computer resources and a library, but comparatively little in the way of equipment and money, is much more often done by sole scholars or small groups of two to three people. Qualitative social science collaboration is often more like that in theoretical physics, rarely getting beyond five members on any one project or the sub-projects in a series of related endeavors.

In the biological and medical domains, the frontiers of scholarship in the twenty-first century lie between disciplines. This phenomenon has led to the creation of new interdisciplinary ways of training and of organizing research programs. Increasingly, the tradition of organizing academic life into quasi-autonomous departments, with research and teaching done with an intradepartmental focus, has proved to be more of an intellectual barrier than a logical necessity. As a result, most research universities have seen a proliferation of 'centers' of various sorts. Today, the organizational structure of any research-based university looks less like a tree than a confused spider-web, as centers and institutes appear in response to needs to support these emergent interdisciplinary and collaborative ventures.

History of collaboration in the social and behavioral sciences

The behavioral and social sciences jumped on the collaboration bandwagon relatively early, for example, when the Institute for Social Relations was formed at Yale University in 1931 and the Department of Social Relations at Harvard University in 1946, the latter founded by Talcott Parsons. They were joined by a variety of 'Human Development' programs that attempted to foster multidisciplinary and interdisciplinary scholarship. However, the collaborative efforts begun at that time were always controversial and many no longer exist. Their limited success, we believe, was not based on any fundamental lack of need for such collaborative ventures. It was rooted in the fact that the disciplines of psychology, sociology, and anthropology, to name three of the basic fields involved, often lack a common worldview and common language that the older sciences now largely enjoy. The so-called 'bench' or 'natural' sciences share, without much need for discussion, a view of the fundamental physics, chemistry, mathematics, and even biological ideas upon which they base their work. The social sciences lack that advantage, partially because of the history of their development. While psychology, sociology, and anthropology all trace their roots back to philosophy, they have constructed their histories with different ancestors. While sociology and anthropology share a common lineage, tracing their origins to Marx, Durkheim, and Weber, psychology traces its roots to Wundt, James, and Freud. (Of course, Freud appears in all three fields, moving in and out of favor.) These lineal differences are the roots of contemporary theoretical divergences and methodological differences. While many cross-disciplinary collaborations among these fields do work effectively, they all require some basic agreement about the way the world works, the theoretical models that underpin the research, the goals of the research endeavor, and ways of approaching the research process.

The persistence of ideas of solo scholarship

Our image of the 'traditional' way of doing qualitative research is that a solitary scholar finds an important research question and engages in research where he or she does it all independently, from formulation, to fieldwork, to analysis and writing. The doctoral dissertation in social science still lauds this model – we train people to be solitary investigators, to demonstrate their ability in solo work, and then we launch them into a world where, increasingly, collaboration is demanded of them. In contrast, the biological and physical sciences more deliberately train their students from the very beginning to be members of teams.[2] There are two mythic components of this 'solo' idea that are relevant for our discussion. First, for some people, underlying the conviction of the value of doing it yourself is an assumption that what goes on in qualitative analysis is so cognitively interpretive, interior, and bound up with the researcher as instrument, that a research team or research collaboration is an oxymoron. This stance is supported theoretically by a variety of interpretive 'postmodern'-isms and newer styles of writing ethnography, including some post-colonial, post-feminist, and post-othering work.

The other myth involved in the image of the solitary researcher is that all the important work is done by this one scholarly person, and that while there may be intermittent consultation with others, the actual work is done by the sole investigator. Thus the spouse who accompanies one on the fieldtrip and types the fieldnotes or edits the manuscripts, and the graduate students who code endless interview transcripts, are not really collaborating in the research effort, but are tools for achieving one's aims. The key informant who gets one into a fieldsite, translates for all interactions, and mediates with community leaders is simply a helper or an employee, not a collaborator. Of late, there has been an effort to acknowledge the vital contributions of these team members (e.g. Werner, 1998; Lassiter, 2001).

In the contemporary academic arena, we see four social forces that constrain opportunities for meaningful collaboration and four that foster such collaboration. Some of these forces have been discussed by other authors, while others stem from our own observations.

Constraints on collaboration

REWARD STRUCTURES The most commonly cited constraint on research collaboration, one that appears to be a problem across disciplines, is the structure of rewards in the academic setting. Promotion and tenure reviews at most universities and in most social science disciplines still count single-authored papers and books as being of more value than multiple-authored works (Hafernik et al., 1997; Teruya, 1999). Even in disciplines where collaborative research is the norm rather than the exception, junior researchers are often advised to quickly carve out a piece of a research project so that it can be identified as their own creative contribution. Many assistant professors are advised to save the collaborative instinct for when they become senior scholars. First-authored papers are routinely counted by committees that review vitae for promotion. In our institution, as in many, a promotion packet that contains multiple-authored works must be accompanied by a note about who made what contribution to the most important papers selected for inclusion in the promotion packet. When a search committee for a faculty position sees a packet where virtually every paper is written with the same co-author, then the question arises about who really might be 'the brains' of this duo – to ensure that the university hires the right person. While administrators of universities, especially research universities that are strong in the biological or health sciences and technology, are highly cognizant of the special characteristics of the contemporary collaborative research landscape, changing the culture of evaluating the performance of individuals is a difficult and long-range process.

INSTITUTIONAL ORGANIZATION A second major constraint on collaborative research is the structure of the institutions in which research is done. Whether we are working in universities, research institutes, public agencies, or consulting firms, the structures of administrative organization usually precede the research collaborations (except when a research collaboration becomes seriously entrepreneurial, as in many contemporary biotechnology endeavors). Universities are usually organized into schools and departments. Faculty have their primary appointments in particular departments. Departments are generally organized around disciplinary structures that have histories that go back generations. In theory, then, faculty have more intellectual interests in common with others within their home department than those in different departments. Collaborations are presumed to grow out of those common interests. However, the changing faces of knowledge, whether in the natural or social sciences or humanities, increasingly means that departmental boundaries are irrelevant (at best) or impediments (at worst) to the work being done. Thus collaborative research often does not fit well within a single department. The consequences are petty in an intellectual sense but nonetheless important: if two people in different departments are equal partners in an outstanding research effort, which department gets to claim the indirect costs[3] or the credit for fostering cutting-edge innovations? This dilemma, while mundane, is extremely important to the institution's administrators, and is regularly a subject of discussion as collaborative projects get underway.

It would seem that intellectual community is a basic value of the academic world and certainly a precursor to collaborative or team research. One might expect that it would be easier to create intellectual community among people within the same disciplines than among people from diverse disciplinary backgrounds. However, we have seen (and been members of) departments that struggle to find common ground, and equally have been members of multidisciplinary groups where intellectual community was clearly present, because of some shared vision of the world and goals, despite the fact that the participants came from widely differing disciplines. Academic researchers need to have meaningful intellectual community within which to work. Of course, creating intellectual community is no mean feat, either within or between departments. Damrosch (1995) echoes our own experience when reporting that many faculty find multiple reasons for a lack of a community of scholars within a department, creating a world where each faculty member becomes a 'community of one' with highly individuated sets of research interests. This is a profoundly discouraging part of academic life – but something that can be effectively countered when meaningful, enriching collaborations do form.

TIME A third constraint on research collaboration is temporal. In our experience, it takes a considerable investment of time to make any research collaboration effective. The time that needs to be spent is not just time for developing ideas, writing grant proposals, conducting the research, and writing for publication – the most important time investment is much more intangible. Time spent getting to know how the other member or members of the team think is most crucial. Of course, the time spent in creating team cohesiveness (or colloquially, getting a team to 'gel') is less if the team members have worked together before or know each other well.

But often new teams are formed among people who know each other's work and have common interests, but are essentially strangers, or established teams have to incorporate new members. This requires an investment in wide-ranging discussions of ethical stances, pet peeves, intellectual roots and idiosyncrasies, interpretations of the literature, analytic strategies, and even of politics, sports, music, and food preferences. While one reviewer of this chapter suggested that this has made little difference in his experience of research, we and other readers have repeatedly found that table fellowship engenders trust, openness and deeper knowledge – of who is the astute observer and manager of details, who is the synthesizer across disparate domains, who stays task-focused, who soothes over potential troublesome issues, who balks or bridles at what, and when. Baba (2001) provides a fascinating account of how globally distributed teams in business need to develop this intersubjectivity. She suggests, but does not provide instances of, the importance of this for social science teams as well. Unless the collaborators know each other well at a personal as well as meaningful level, the collaboration is almost inevitably headed for trouble at some point (as we will describe later). The constraint is that nobody has time – one defining characteristic of life in the twenty-first century is that everyone is overworked and short of time. The reason many of us are willing to make this temporal investment is that we can 'win' something at the end – perhaps not faster research, but deeper, more satisfying analyses, faster progress toward important research goals, and intellectual community.

DISCIPLINARY VALUES AND PREJUDICES A fourth constraint on research collaboration for qualitative social scientists is disciplinary. Despite the richness of the tradition of collaborative research, in both European and American schools of anthropology and sociology, there are still significant prejudices against collaboration (Erickson and Stull, 1998). The strength of these prejudices probably varies by location and discipline. We propose that the prejudice against collaborative work may be stronger in the 'pure' than in the 'applied' forms of the qualitative social sciences. To partially test this, at least in the field of anthropology, we looked at four years (1998–2001) of articles in each of three journals, one in applied anthropology and two in general anthropology. During this period the *Journal of the Royal Anthropological Institute* (a British anthropology journal) published 113 papers, of which 91 percent were single authored, 8 percent had two authors, and only

1 percent had three or more authors. The *American Anthropologist* (published by the American Anthropological Association) published 148 papers, of which 75 percent were single authored, 16 percent had two authors, and only 9 percent had three or more authors. The applied journal, *Human Organization* (the journal of the Society for Applied Anthropology), published 190 papers, of which 64 percent were single authored, 18 percent had two authors, and 17 percent had three or more authors. These multi-authored papers represent an important facet, that of writing partnerships, but only a portion of them are based on complete research collaborations.

Forces fostering collaboration

Social forces inside and outside academia are certainly not all lined up against collaboration. In fact, there are very powerful forces encouraging collaborative research. Of the four factors that we see fostering collaboration, two are related to the financing of research, one is connected to the research 'problems' attractive to researchers, and the last is technological.

FUNDING AGENCIES The first financial factor that fosters research collaboration is based in the activities of funding agencies. The financial sources of research have always had a significant impact on issues or problems studied. From the days of the British colonial government providing funds to anthropologists (e.g. Evans-Pritchard) to the funding agendas of the US National Institutes of Health (NIH), money has driven research. This is not because researchers are craven corrupters of the faith, but because it costs money to do research and the organizations that provide the money have a vested interest in making suggestions about how the money will be spent. While a few funding agencies still ascribe to a lone investigator model of social science research, the vast majority of funding agencies recognize that the problems in their domain often demand the skills of collaborative teams or groups of researchers. The NIH, the National Science Foundation, the Social Science Research Council, the Ford and Rockefeller Foundations, and their British and European counterparts, all fund research that involves collaboration. In fact, requests for proposals from most agencies are increasingly calling for research that involves skills that are broader than any single investigator can master.

Why do we have this new focus on collaboration? Is knowledge really more complex? Is this an effort of social scientists to follow the practices of the natural sciences? Is it fashion? In quantitative social sciences, complex collaborations build because specialist knowledge is needed for certain statistical analyses or because particular individuals have access to certain datasets or have specialized expertise in a particular analytic practice. In qualitative social science we are increasingly doing work that expands beyond single communities, requiring varied expertise. We are now often doing work that is larger in scope than 'traditional' qualitative research, quintessentially regarded as ethnographic research in small or at least geographically bounded communities. Sometimes our research questions demand researchers with differing skills. The important thing is whether or not more insightful research results – a hypothesis neither tested to date nor probably really testable.

INSTITUTIONAL DEMANDS The second financial factor that fosters research collaboration is the fact that in most academic research universities, the institution increasingly demands that faculty obtain outside funds to cover part or all of their salaries. As local institutional support for researcher salaries decreases, the need for extramural funding increases. Our home institution is perhaps an extreme case – only 11 percent of the faculty on this health sciences campus receive a major portion of their salary from university funds. The rest are supported by research monies or by clinical revenues. Even tenured faculty are expected to bring in at least 50 percent of their salaries from outside sources. In doing so they further the research endeavor by hiring additional faculty with the 'savings' from those tenured salaries that have been released. While this practice creates a lively and productive research environment, it also creates very strong pressures to divide one's efforts across multiple collaborative enterprises. Only at the very junior ranks can a single research grant cover all or most of one's salary, so as one becomes more senior, the need becomes stronger to be a collaborator on two to five or more projects.

But this mode of funding leads to consequential changes in the modes and meanings of collaboration, as the researcher's energy inevitably becomes less focused on a single project and more widely spread across a variety of (often bureaucratic) tasks. This also results in senior qualitative investigators being more a sort of technical consultant than a key player, spending less and less time doing hands-on data collection and day-to-day analysis and more and more time on grant administration and management of team members' activities. All of which have serious

and deleterious consequences for theory development and methodological innovation in qualitative research. It too often seems that just as one begins to really master the intricacies of participant observation or qualitative interviewing or an analytic technique, one is forced to move on to doing ever more burdensome bureaucratic tasks instead of employing those hard-earned skills in 'the field'.

THE TRANSLATIONAL IMPERATIVE A third, more substantive social change that has taken place in the last twenty-five years fosters collaborative research. All of the sciences, both natural and social, are facing the need for stronger interrelationships between basic science and the applications of that science, for 'translation' across this divide. The most fundamental of biological sciences find that their research is enhanced by interactions with clinical researchers. Similarly, social scientists increasingly find themselves working closely with more applied versions of their disciplines and with clinical and social service providers in other disciplines. Even the most interpretive or hermeneutic branches of the social sciences find important reasons to broaden their collaborative scope to include those formerly known as the 'subjects' of research, incorporating them now as co-researchers (Byrne-Armstrong, 2001).

These changes are partially induced by the funding context for research, which has changed to be much more outcome-oriented than it was thirty years ago. However, much of this change is equally driven by factors internal to the disciplines and emergent new knowledge. Regardless of the impetus, as soon as research questions come not solely from the scholarly project of the researcher, but are responsive to concerns outside the theoretical project, collaboration or team research becomes not only desirable but almost inevitable. While a qualitative researcher may take on an assignment from an agency and still be a sole investigator, there are considerable advantages to doing community-based research, where the person with the research skills collaborates deeply with the community or agency that wants certain questions answered. This is a very particular and complex kind of team research.

TECHNOLOGY The final factor that we identify as fostering collaborative research is technological. For the last several years, debate has raged about whether qualitative data analysis software fundamentally changes the research process (e.g. Richards and Richards, 1994; Harrisson, 1995; Hesse-Biber, 1995; Wall, 1995; Smith and Hesse-Biber, 1996). We argue that, in fact, the technological influences on research practices are much broader than the issue of qualitative data analysis software. These influences can be traced at least to the development of affordable photocopying machines and tape recorders. Personal computers, facsimile (fax) machines, e-mail, and qualitative analysis software only accelerated the trend. What all of these have in common is speed, transparency, and connection. Research materials are much easier to prepare in forms that are readily manipulable and accessible by other people. Those research materials are easier to distribute and discussions about research issues are much less expensive than in the days of letters and telephone conversations.

The instantaneousness of fax and e-mail also allows the contraction of space as well as time – people can be geographically, even globally, dispersed and still work together effectively and efficiently (see Baba, 2001, for a discussion of globally dispersed business teams). We have one colleague in Europe who sends us an e-mail message in the morning and if we haven't responded by afternoon he telephones to scold us – completely disregarding the fourteen hour difference in time of day. As people learn new ways of working together, technology continues to develop in new ways that further change the way people work. Consider the development of the 'track changes' function in word-processing software or the progressive changes in the scope of services that qualitative data analysis software provides.

There is one arena where we do believe that technological developments in qualitative software have had a significant troublesome influence. The last few years have seen qualitative research methods translated into just another tool in the toolbox of applied social sciences, such as epidemiology and public health. Increasingly, people who have not been trained in the theoretical underpinnings of the varied disciplines that use qualitative approaches have come to see these methods as useful. From our observations of those who come to us for consultation and advice, it appears that the existence of qualitative data analysis software has deluded some researchers (especially but not exclusively those in applied or service realms) into the notion that qualitative analysis can be divorced from a theoretical foundation especially derived from social science. Qualitative software is equated with statistical analysis software – where raw data are inserted into the computer and 'results' emerge. Of course, this is just as delusional for statistical analysis as it is for qualitative analysis, for all analysis requires interpretation based on a thorough understanding of the theory and assumptions underlying the study. This delusion wreaks all kinds of havoc, including poorly designed and executed qualitative research, under-theorized research, sample sizes that are impractically large, analyses that are devoid of much insight or originality, and grave disappointment at the end of projects. We would wager that there are many unpublished studies, and unfortunately a few published studies, that demonstrate our point.

DIMENSIONS OF TEAMWORK

These social forces that underpin contemporary team research in the qualitative social sciences have resulted in a variety of patterns of teamwork. There is no one best model for being a team. It is instructive, however, to examine some of the dimensions or characteristics of teams that are prevalent.

Collaborations differ from solo efforts along two distinct dimensions: size and organization. Two-person teams are often quite different from three- or more person teams, if for no other reason than the complexity of managing interactions. Organizational issues that cross-cut size include hierarchy, complementarity of skills, dispersion over time or place, multidimensional relationships among team members, and the nature of the intellectual work.

Collaborative research is clearly not a single thing – there are many ways of working together. In order to get to a point where we can discuss what makes for effective collaboration, we need first to discuss more explicitly the varieties of approaches to collaboration that exist in the qualitative social sciences. To such an end, we reflected on teams we have participated in or heard about, explored collaborative work that we have read, and informally interviewed a highly selected group of colleagues who have participated in collaborations that are quite different from anything we have done ourselves. The result of this highly idiosyncratic endeavor is a typology of teamwork, which we offer as a starting point for discussion of the variety of ways that social scientists collaborate with each other. We have participated in most but not all of these types of collaborative efforts, and discuss our own experiences in the next section.

First, a comment on terminology: some authors make a distinction between collaborations and team research, with collaborations involving equal intellectual endeavors and teams being hierarchically organized groups where not all members have equal intellectual investment or power. Austin and Baldwin (1991) go as far as to define true collaboration as including characteristics such as: work being done among equals; characterized by choice; ongoing; interactive; involving the creation of ideas; and implying an equality of investment of time and effort. While these distinctions are important, we are not sure that the issue is clear enough that some groups of researchers clearly can be called teams while others are collaborations. We think that the only good judges of whether a group is a team or collaboration are the participants. We tend to use the term 'team' where we see hierarchy as being probably important and 'collaboration' where we believe equals are working in a shared way, but sometimes we use the terms interchangeably to emphasize the heuristic rather than existential nature of this distinction. It is important to note that we are not talking here about writing partners, but about research partners, where the entire process of research, not just the product, results from the work of more than one person.

Project size

While it is not a requirement, team and collaborative research tends to involve relatively large projects, i.e. those that have large samples, more than one type of respondent, complex recruitment procedures, multiple investigators overseeing sub-projects, many goals or disciplinary perspectives, more than one research site, or long duration with repeated contacts with informants (Mitteness and Barker, 1994: 85). In such circumstances, qualitative research is usually not solely descriptive or ethnographic in approach, but is often concerned with hypothesis testing, random sampling or stratification, investigation of the range of diversity of a phenomenon, longitudinal design, or study of subgroup variation (Mitteness and Barker, 1994: 84). Large projects often generate the need for teams composed of people with varying backgrounds and expertise, training and commitment, and with distinct roles in the project. Many teams incorporate students as well as faculty or specialist researchers and so become learning/teaching sites as well as research endeavors. Roth (1966) and Mitteness and Barker (1994: 93–6) refer to role and task specialization and the nitty-gritty of managing such projects.

Hierarchy

As implied above, many ostensibly solitary research endeavors are really hierarchically organized efforts, with research assistants working for money or course credit and lead investigators working for scholarly credit as well as income. The essential characteristic of a hierarchical team is that one person (or a small group of people) is responsible for the instigation of the project and its intellectual directions, while other research activities may be dispersed among other team members, who may or may not have a strong investment in the project. Hierarchical team research has a long history in the social sciences; for example, *The American Soldier* (Stouffer et al., 1949a and 1949b) and *Frustration and Aggression* (Dollard et al., 1939), while not qualitative studies, did have qualitative components. The variety of hierarchical teams ranges from lead investigators with a group of research assistants to large-scale, geographically dispersed projects such as the Whitings' *Six Cultures* study (Whiting, 1963; Whiting and Whiting, 1975) or 'Project AGE' led by Chris Fry and Jennie Keith (Keith et al., 1994). These latter studies involved several fieldwork projects that were designed and led by a core group of leaders, with experienced fieldworkers at each site. We describe these as hierarchical teams because the central vision for the studies was held by the core leaders and may or may not have been equally shared by all the field investigators. Hierarchies are encountered among some two-person teams (e.g. the researcher and a single assistant), but most multiple-person teams have some element of hierarchy in their organization, perhaps more at some times in their existence than at other times (e.g. data collection versus data analysis periods), often most clearly signaled in authorship positions, as we discuss later.

Complementarity

Research partners often bring very different methodological or theoretical skills to the formulation and execution of the research work, and the resulting project builds upon each set of skills to create something quite different than either could or would do alone. Many two-person teams are brought together initially because of their complementary skills or interests. Complementary teams can be between people who are both qualitative researchers (e.g. Holstein and Gubrium, 2000), although frequently team members can also bridge qualitative and quantitative paradigms (e.g. Arcury and Quandt, 1998). The latter are usually extremely complicated studies to conduct because of the often unspoken but significant differences in disciplinary language and worldview that can sometimes impede effective communication. However, people who are working in complementary teams find that the complementarity of perspectives provides some of the most exciting intellectual work that participants experience in their professional lives.

Dispersion

There is a selective but significant tradition within anthropology, of ethnographers returning to the same fieldsite many times over the course of decades (Foster et al., 1979). Often, these fieldworkers may begin their research as solo or partner investigators, but eventually take on one or a series of collaborators to work in the same site (e.g. Scudder and Colson, 1979; Kemper and Royce, 1997). Some of these are simultaneous collaborative efforts, with both fieldworkers working in the field at the same time. At other times there is a less equal presence in the field, but the initial or senior investigator 'sponsors' the more junior investigators and so an asynchronous team develops. One of the complications of such long collaborations is that changing constellations of fieldworkers are accompanied by social and historical changes in the fieldsite itself.

Globally dispersed teams are even more extreme instances of dispersion over space. The Whitings' *Six Cultures* study is a classic example, from an era when it was much more difficult to keep in touch with teams dispersed across multiple continents, from India to Africa to the US (Whiting, 1963; Whiting and Whiting, 1975). 'Project AGE' is a more recent example (Keith et al., 1994) that attempted to answer a set of core questions about aging and identity in six widely differing societies. There are a number of international health projects that not only have globally distributed teams but span a variety of public health, epidemiological, and anthropological disciplines. These widely dispersed teams face issues of developing and maintaining similar and therefore more easily comparable research protocols and data collection and analysis strategies (Keith, 1994). Even in this day of instantaneous communication via telephone, cell phone, fax, or e-mail, there are significant differences in the capacity of various sites to sustain this technology. Success in these circumstances requires the initial forging and subsequent maintenance of common procedural strategies as well as a degree of flexibility and equanimity in the face of adversity. Each team member must have a clear understanding of what is essential as opposed to simply desirable for accomplishing the study's goals (Mitteness and Barker, 1994: 86). Keith (1994) discusses the need to document, standardize, collate, and organize notes,

codes, analyses, etc., when a complex study is done by a team.

Multidimensional relationships

There are at least two types of multidimensional relationships that can be present in qualitative research teams: collaborations between people who are romantically linked, and the more common collaborations between faculty and their students. Both kinds of relationships are complicated by the presence of issues and demands that are central to the relationship but not part of the research.

PARTNERS   There is a long, but somewhat hidden, tradition of scholarly work done jointly by marital partners or domestic partners. In some fieldwork settings, the ability to split fieldwork tasks along gender lines greatly strengthens the depth of the ethnographic work (see Fernea, 1965, 1975; Firth, 1972; Benedict and Benedict, 1982; Turner, 1987). These collaborations differ from other types of collaborations in several ways, as Gottlieb (1995) and Kennedy (1995) have so effectively discussed. Doing research in the context of a personal relationship is emotionally and procedurally complicated – and the complications probably differ for each relationship. There are also structural complications. In the old days, formal institutional policies around 'nepotism' led to academic positions being offered to only one member of such a partnership, usually the husband. The social changes of the last thirty years have to a large extent transformed those policies, but there are still significant formal and informal institutional barriers to partner collaborations, ranging from the difficulties of finding two comparable positions in the same geographic area, to administrative assumptions that one partner is more important or more central to the research than the other. Such problems are familiar to many academic couples, whether they collaborate in their research or not, but are accentuated when they are collaborators.

FACULTY–STUDENT TEAMS   There is a power dynamic in all multidimensional research relationships, but the dynamic plays out in different ways when the collaboration concerns faculty and students. Faculty and student teams offer particular complications precisely because students can never reach a point of equality or dominance in the team, however fleeting that point may be (see Roth, 1966; Foster et al., 1979: 393). Because of the power differences between the two participants, the issues of trust and credit are complicated in ways that two peers would not experience. Students often learn the craft of research by apprenticeship; only a student who has graduated, become a journeyman, can match the authority of the master craftsman.

Faculty work with students for any of several reasons. It is often expected that faculty will employ students as research assistants, will offer students 'hands-on' experiential learning. Students are often relatively inexpensive to hire and readily available. Students are sometimes easier to train in research procedures than some non-student research assistants. Faculty often find that working with students keeps them up to date with a burgeoning literature. Students work with faculty for several quite different reasons. They need money to get through school, experience with research methods, letters of recommendation for later employment, or simply an opportunity to do larger research than they could do on their own. Sometimes the funding situation is such that the faculty member has access to research funds that are unavailable to the student.

The imbalance in these reasons for working together creates significant problems. We have found that it is essential for students and faculty to recognize the issues that are bringing them together and discuss each party's expectations of the collaboration. Even so, misunderstandings can happen. Yet, when things go well, the results can be more than either person would have been able to do independently (see Herskovits and Mitteness, 1994, for an example).

'Thelma and Louise' collaborations

Sometimes collaborative teams exist for the sake of convenience, but sometimes research partners goad each other to take risks and work in new ways. We call this the 'Thelma and Louise'[4] collaboration. While this may or may not be common in qualitative research collaborations, it probably is quite common in writing partnerships. When one does find oneself in a collaborative research venture, there can be an aura of excitement and adventure about it that makes this rather flippant label appropriate. Partners challenge one another to stretch their boundaries. An example is the reanalysis of an existing dataset focused on service needs to produce work on homelessness (Kramer and Barker, 1996) and alcohol use among American Indian elders (Barker and Kramer, 1996). This type of team probably is limited to small groups, perhaps only to two-person teams. These teams are likely to be difficult to recognize from the outside – for who but the participants can really say that working

together helped them do more than they would have been able to individually?

We identify this type of collaboration because personally it is the most valuable characteristic of our work together. As we look back on the work we have done, we see that we are a complementary team – we differ dramatically in our disciplinary background (LSM was initially trained in human development and JCB in social anthropology). In the arena of medical anthropology, we have each separately and jointly been drawn into working on a variety of different topics with quite distinctly different disciplinary collaborators – from the fields of neurology, internal medicine, geriatrics, dentistry, nursing, alcohol and substance use, health communication, HIV/AIDS, sexuality, sociology, and religious studies, to name but a few. Despite this complementarity, we have also constructed hierarchical teams, since most of the studies we have done have been relatively large (e.g. Wolfsen, et al., 1993; Barker et al., 1994; Mitteness and Barker, 1995). We have had extensive experience with multidimensional teams, because of our personal relationship, and because we have worked with many students from different backgrounds over the years (e.g. Herskovits and Mitteness, 1994; Mitteness et al., 1995; Barker et al., 1998a, 1998b; Barker and Saechao, 2000). Our partnerships have led us to do work that individually we would not have done and to expand the horizons of and approaches used in the individual projects we have undertaken. Because of our collaborative work, LSM has been pushed theoretically, to include social science theory along with that from training in psychology and human development, while JCB has been pushed methodologically, to include and appreciate the contributions quantitative approaches can make to understanding. JCB would not have been a central contributor to the anthropology of aging if LSM had not encouraged her. LSM would have spent her entire career in aging if JCB had not pushed her to other arenas. While the collaborative nature of these pushes does not always appear in print, they are major parts of the fabric of our research together.

WHAT MAKES TEAMS WORK?

Team or collaborative research is not always a success. In fact, there are many ways for these modes of research to fail. Failures can happen through any combination of a number of (often only partly controllable) factors, from having an inadequately formulated basic idea through 'poor chemistry' of team members to financial constraints or work overload. Some failures are just incompletely mobilized or tentative explorations of collaborative intent, some are just juxtaposed ideas from disparate disciplines with little epistemological, theoretical, or applied linkages, some are such treasured ideas – 'property' – of a key player that true exchange of ideas and development of novel procedures cannot take place. Most collaborations falter, however, because of insufficient attention to the crucial aspects of the collaborative process. There are three arenas where special attention must be provided in order for team or collaborative research to be a successful and satisfying experience. First, the relationships among the participants need to be carefully constructed and monitored. Second, the design and practices of the research itself need to be effective. Third, the contexts of the research need to be supportive.

Relationships in teams

The construction and maintenance of an effective research team has several important components. These include team members having significant knowledge of each other, developing a common language, establishing trust and mutual respect, constructing patterns of formal and informal leadership, providing support for one another, and establishing non-destructive means of sanctioning one another when things go awry. While most of these components appear to be important in any kind of team research, they take on special significance and relevance to the content or results of the team effort for qualitative researchers because so much of the success of qualitative research depends on the researchers as the primary tools of the research effort.

KNOWLEDGE AND SOCIAL LOCATION When individuals are brought together to create a team, time needs to be spent on getting to know one another. This is not a naïve community-building effort, but rather a crucial task.

Merchant (2001) and Zurita (2001) have bravely offered a detailed case study of the problems that can arise when the research topic is differently difficult for the researchers on a team. Merchant is a white woman, an assistant professor at the time she hired Zurita, a Latina graduate student, to be a research associate on an intensive study of the experiences of Mexican immigrant students in a rural white school district. They both describe the processes of 'missing the mark with each other' as they did fieldwork together.

This was a setting where at least three factors worked to make their experiences different. First, at the fieldsite (a school), the teachers and students responded to them differently because of their differing ethnicities and ages. Second, their own perspectives on research differed in a significant way. Merchant was comfortable with an academic approach that sought to describe and understand a situation. Zurita was more interested in an action orientation or advocacy research. Third, as evidence of discrimination against the school's Mexican immigrant students increased, Zurita not only wanted to intervene, but was having to deal with the emotional and cognitive issues around her own life experience of discrimination. Merchant couldn't really understand or see this as effectively as she would have liked.

The profound message of their experience is that the social locations and life experiences of researchers on a collaborative team can vary significantly – they can be so different that their understandings of and social interactions in the field can be wildly different. If such differences can be made apparent to the team and become the subject of analysis in their own right, they can be very revealing of the process the team is attempting to study. While this can be valuable for analytic purposes, it is very stressful and difficult to recognize – we often do not understand just how differently located we are, even when we seem to know each other very well.

COMMON LANGUAGE A special case of the need to establish effective communication and common goals is the case of multidisciplinary teamwork. Where the people involved come from different disciplines, significant potential for fundamental misunderstandings exists (Clair et al., 2003; Li et al., 2003). Perhaps we have all been involved in research design discussions where it soon becomes apparent that the gulf in training, expertise, worldview, ethical stance, etc., is so significant that the participants have to train each other about fundamental issues. In order to succeed, at least three things are required of every participant in these multidisciplinary efforts: (1) each person needs to respect the other perspective(s), (2) each person must want to engage in the intellectual mission of cross-fertilization, and (3) each person needs certainty about where and how his or her discipline can contribute in innovative and important ways to move the research beyond the usual limits of each discipline.

While multidisciplinary teams are complex, within-discipline theoretical or ideological divides are often harder to bridge than between-discipline ones. Within the qualitative paradigm that is so dependent on the specific theoretical and epistemological leanings of researchers it seems that it is sometimes easier to respect other disciplines than to embrace the legitimacy of varying approaches within one's own field of study.

Another perspective on the issue of trust and respect, of 'knowing each other', is offered by Byrne-Armstrong (2001), who talks about several efforts to do co-research – by which she means collaborative research that is 'with people, rather than on them'. In each case, the original research plan was designed by one person (Byrne-Armstrong) and people with relevant interests were drawn into it, not conceptualized as research subjects or informants, but rather as 'co-researchers'. Not surprisingly, conflicts inevitably arose as the unacknowledged power differences surfaced to disrupt the research process. Byrne-Armstrong concludes that 'collaboration can occur only if we move away from researching to find truth, whether it is on people (positivism), or with people (co-research), and move towards joining with people in conversation to examine the taken-for-granted assumptions and practices informing any research context' (p. 110). While ideologies of equality may be attractive, we have never seen instances where people of vastly different educational backgrounds, investments in the study, and research experience have been able to overcome issues of hierarchy and operate as equals throughout every portion of a research effort. We suggest that researchers need to get over the idea that a common ground is ever more than fleeting. Social hierarchies exist and are not mitigated by ideological stances to the contrary. Active attention to and sensitive maintenance of trust, respect, rapport, and open dialogue go a long way to reducing the deleterious potential inherent in social hierarchies.

Yet another aspect of knowing each other involves clarification of and commitment to a set of common goals for the project. In addition, individual goals need to be commonly recognized and compatible. There needs to be regular and effective communication and the rewards of the research need to be carefully anticipated. Both potential and actual rewards need to be examined. Failure to engage in frank discussion and negotiation of the end products of the research (e.g. books, papers, intervention programs) can tear a team apart, especially if inexperienced researchers are involved or there is a great power differential between the project leader and the others. These issues express themselves differently for different types of teams. Two-person collaborators may find it easier to co-construct the goals of a research project than do hierarchical teams or larger complementary groups. However, this does not mean that two people who work together do not need to explicitly clarify their common and individual goals, or work at communication. The intensity of two-person collaborations may mean that communication needs are more personal, hence more emotionally intense, than for larger groups of researchers.

TRUST AND MUTUAL RESPECT   Through discussions with a variety of qualitative researchers who have worked in collaborations, the universal recommendation is that there needs to be an environment of mutual respect for differences in approach, knowledge, background, and skills. Participants in a collaborative project need to be able to trust each other, to be certain of and respect each other's skills and competence, to know the way each person on the project thinks. Ideally, multidisciplinary team members should have some basic knowledge of the other discipline's views and approaches in order to establish rapport and trust, not to say understanding.

Each of us has had the experience of being invited to join a multidisciplinary team to design a project where endless meetings have resulted in complete failure because people never got to the point where they could understand each other or where trust or mutual respect were assured. Such episodes are very draining of energy and enormously discouraging. It is fundamentally true that for collaborations to be successful there needs to be a significant investment of time at the beginning for people to begin to relate to each other, not just as intellectuals, but as people. This is as true of hierarchical teams as it is of any other kind of collaboration. Too often, the leader of a team thinks that mutual respect and understanding have been accomplished when they have not or where it is assumed that this is a one-time issue rather than an ongoing and necessary process. Inevitably, then, trouble appears down the road. While we may think this is an issue particular to qualitative research, Teruya (1999) found that physicists were equally likely to emphasize the importance of trust for effective collaboration. Trust and respect cannot be taken for granted, but need to be continually monitored and reinforced, to ensure that the good relationships among the researchers are sustained throughout the process of the research. Teams where the participants know, trust, and respect each other are fun, exciting, stimulating, supportive, and productive.

Trust and respect need not be quiet virtues. Indeed, some of the most successful and productive teams we have encountered frequently engaged in noisy, passionate, table-thumping disagreements. But because fundamental trust and respect and good emotional leadership was present, these vociferous exchanges are tiffs resulting in crucial clarifications and progress rather than ruptures leading to the incipient dissolution of the team or to project failure.

FORMAL AND INFORMAL LEADERSHIP Leadership within a team comes in two distinct but equally vital modes. First, the formal leadership hierarchy based on seniority, initiative in developing the research agenda or obtaining funding, undertaking specific responsibilities, and so forth. These leaders are explicitly designated, as the Principal Investigator, or the 'boss', and are widely recognized both within and outside the team as having the ultimate decision-making capacity and responsibility for the scientific, ethical, and fiscal conduct and integrity of the study.

And second, informal leadership that develops out of personality, interaction style, or specific interests (both research- and non-research based). In established collaborations, the team 'clown', 'curmudgeon', 'optimist', 'skeptic', or 'techno-wizard' are easily identified and comprise important roles that never appear on any organizational chart. While informal leadership roles undoubtedly exist in every kind of team, their presence and influence is probably less acknowledged, less consciously manipulated in quantitative research teams. For qualitative collaborations, these informal roles and leadership styles enable team members to know and to calibrate the fundamental instruments of their research – i.e. themselves.

The formally designated team leader is not the only person who can provide the necessary leadership. Taking charge and trying new approaches and new ideas can be any team member's prerogative. With sufficient trust and respect on the part of all, novel or divergent forays in the research process can be very fruitful. For instance, many years ago we were engaged in a study of social relations among nursing-home residents. Most of the other participants in the team were young adults who had never had significant experience in skilled nursing facilities. During training for the observational part of the study, we noticed that in any practice session, we were not all seeing the same thing. While one of us was trying to tinker with the procedures to make the observations easier to do, and another of us was planning endless practice sessions, a third member of the group just began going to the skilled nursing facility with her four-year-old son and visiting the residents. Soon the rest of us

joined in. She had the insight and leadership to realize that we needed to know the people behind the social positions if we were ever going to do decent work in that setting. When we stepped back from 'visiting' to do observations, the reliability of those observations was significantly enhanced.

The issues around relationship creation and maintenance are quite different for two-person collaborations and for larger teams. While a dyad is a particularly intense way to work, larger groups really need to understand the necessities of the small group process. Parsons and Bales (1955) talked about small groups having yet another kind of informal leadership crucial to success – teams (small groups) must have both instrumental and emotional leadership. These leaders are not consciously chosen or formally designated but rather result from the ways in which intersubjectivity is collectively construed, enacted, and managed within any small group. Successful collaborative research efforts that we have engaged in involving more than two people have demonstrated the need for – and efficacy of – both kinds of leadership. Any one individual is not able to fulfill both leadership roles at the same moment, but may demonstrate both at different times: on occasion, for example, being the person who calls the group back to talking about informant recruitment issues (instrumental leadership) yet a few minutes later raising ethical concerns over proposed consent procedures (emotional leadership). Both leadership styles are vital, but they are truly distinct. They can rotate or move from person to person depending on the task or on the situation. Trust and respect among members of the team are much easier to develop when there is capable instrumental and emotional leadership – the absence or ineffectiveness of either will undermine the relationships within the team in no time at all.

Often teams will consciously value instrumental leadership, which is clearly aimed at getting things done, but undervalue or dismiss emotional leadership. Pinn (2001) makes a side comment about the 'gendered ethical concern to make everything all right', which highlights the devaluing of emotional leadership. It also raises the question of gender and ethnic composition of a team and their varying styles of providing and responding to instrumental and emotional leadership. We do not consider emotional leadership to be simply smoothing things over or reducing tension in the group. Qualitative research is a demanding enterprise, with emotional content – whether it is a fieldwork moment that is particularly difficult or tensions within the research team – that must be managed, understood, and used analytically to explore the topic under consideration. Teams need to have emotions, express them, discuss them, and recognize their impact on the 'researcher as instrument' that is so specifically characteristic of qualitative research. Emotional debriefing is as vital to teamwork as technical discussions about research design, coding, or analysis.

SUPPORT SYSTEMS Emotional leadership is not the same as emotional support, though both are important. A few papers have appeared in recent years describing some of the difficulties that may ensue when emotional issues have not been adequately addressed within a team and emotional support has gone awry. Gilbert (2001), for instance, does psychodynamic research on grief processes. Thus her interview data are usually very intense. She reports both negative and positive effects of these intense interviews on her research associates, both those who code data and those who transcribe interviews. The lead researcher in her study had more experience with the phenomenon being studied, and had greater ability to use intellectual defenses to manage what otherwise might be overwhelming material. It is easy to forget that not all other members of the research team may have such resources. The leader may be the last to recognize that her research materials are causing significant distress. While hierarchy and experience are issues here, so are time pressures and the idiosyncrasies of life stories. Sometimes the team leader is the least connected to the emotional character of the materials; sometimes student participants have little empathy. Whatever the situation, it is incumbent on the team to address such issues as they arise.

In our experience, this is an ongoing important issue and one that is partly addressed by having portions of team meetings devoted to discussions of the emotional and other difficulties in the material or procedures, usually accompanied by the consumption of tea and cookies or, all too often, chocolate. Discussions go back and forth between jokes and serious comments about and grappling with the underlying distressing issues. Jokes are usually self-deprecating comments about the research procedures or evocative labels given to particularly memorable, difficult, or unpleasant informants. These help the team wrestle analytically with emotional responses. I doubt we will ever forget 'Legs Marie', a gregarious but demented and malodorous older woman with uncontrollable urinary incontinence and weeping sores on her legs, who greatly enjoyed talking with us. Understanding why we so disliked encountering her and what we did to avoid

her, gave us considerable insight into the processes of stigmatization and social extrusion occurring to her on a daily basis. Pain is managed through laughter. But mirth is not the only solution to these issues – each team finds its own safety valves.

SANCTIONING SYSTEMS Just as in other parts of life, research team members are not always well behaved. Sometimes they are tardy or sloppy in completing tasks, are disrespectful to other team members, are constantly complaining about the research procedures, or are just plain reluctant to undertake some assigned activities. Team members can have things happen in their personal lives that distract from work, or be grumpy, upset, resentful, or inattentive to the research for a variety of non-work as well as work-related reasons.

The team's patience and tolerance for inappropriate or disruptive behavior will eventually become exhausted and it will rein in the errant or offending member. Usually this is done through the informal positive and negative sanctioning methods available to all small groups, i.e. through expressing sympathy and emotional support, by offering help, through the recounting of cautionary tales about possible undesirable outcomes of uncorrected misbehavior, or, when things get really vexing, through teasing and gossip. The latter are often particularly effective as they draw on knowledge of the person's likes and dislikes, values and stances, derived during times of shared fellowship over meals, at team meetings and debriefings. If informal sanctions prove ineffective, then the principal investigator might have to step in with an official warning to the offender or, even, withdrawal of funds. The ability to accomplish social control informally (or if need be formally) without inducing lasting rancor or dissent is an important indicator of the emotional health of the team.

If, as occasionally happens, a team member or sub-project leader should become locked into a power struggle with the principal investigator, attempting to wrest control away from officially designated leader(s), it usually proves extremely difficult to mobilize effective sanctions, whether formal or informal. More often than not, such situations destroy collaborations, tearing at team members' loyalties and diverting energy and attention away from the research. It is not easy to predict when or why such a situation will arise. However, we would suggest it will most likely arise from personality clashes, inability to give up control, fundamental lack of respect for other team members or different disciplinary perspectives, or, rarely, demonstrated incompetence on the part of the formally designated leader. In circumstances involving this level of intra-team conflict (except, perhaps, the last), it is probably best for everybody, research team, informants, and funders, if the project is actively terminated.

Effective design and procedures

Any collaborative research effort has some specific design and procedural demands.

COMMUNICATION: TIME AND TRACKING The first such demand continues the theme of communication: there needs to be substantial time built into the project for team members to talk to each other on a regular basis. This is both the most essential design element and, inevitably, the hardest to meet. Frankly, we're terrible at this. There just never seems to be enough time – but we never stop trying to make enough time.

Team meetings need to begin early in the development of the project and they need to be considered not just as opportunities for mundane or routine exchange of information, but part of the analytic process. Just as we recommend that fieldworkers keep fieldnotes and a personal journal, team meetings need to result in notes that are both content and process oriented. In reality, there simply is not enough time in any project to have enough meetings and to record those meetings adequately. Yet the brilliant ideas that move the analysis forward often emerge not in the organized part of the meeting, but in the chance comment, the amusing anecdote, or the crabby exchange. Audio taping team meetings helps prevent loss of the brilliant moment, as long as one does not commit the project to transcription of any but the most crucial aspects of the tapes. We recommend that as any project begins, each team member begin a journal of ideas, thoughts, and musings and that those journals be the basis of the discussion at regular team meetings, with another journal of meetings being written to complement the individual journals. Fortunately, qualitative data analysis programs, such as NVivo (Qualitative Solutions and Research, Pty Ltd, 1999, 2002), now have merge functions to allow all these disparate notes to be incorporated into the analysis.

ATTENTION TO SCALE The third significant design characteristic of productive collaborations is careful attention to scale. It is so easy to think that collaborative research necessarily involves large projects, but this is a baseless assumption. Qualitative studies need to be as large as necessary to answer the research question, but no larger (Mitteness and Barker, 1994). Unfortunately, except for consensus analysis, there is no formal power analysis that can predict the appropriate size study. Instead, at the design stage one makes considered judgments based on past experience. Then, during the research process, analytic demands should tell the team when the study is large enough – when sufficient analytic scope has been reached, when theoretical saturation is reached, or whatever criterion for scale is most appropriate to the project.

INTERSUBJECTIVE CONGRUENCE It is vitally important that teams establish or adopt a common and accepted code of ethics and moral practices. Early in their existence, teams must develop intersubjective congruence on these issues. Nothing destroys a team or a project's integrity faster than to have different standards of acceptability about how to treat human research participants, how to respect confidentiality, how to avoid fabricating or falsifying data, how to fairly and equitably manage the work, or how to address and resolve difficulties with team mates. In other words, the same standards of honesty, integrity and decency must underpin the actions of all team members. These issues are not entirely straightforward. In any project there is the potential for variation in how participants interpret one or more of these issues. As with authorship, ethical issues need timely, frank, prolonged, and repeated discussion throughout the research process as issues arise.

While congruence in some areas is necessary, there is also room for divergent goals. This requires some humility and respect for the worldviews and procedures of people who have quite different perspectives or training, but are collaborators. This is particularly important in the context of multidisciplinary research and with respect to the increasingly popular 'campus–community partnerships'. Working with the non-academic sector introduces another level of discourse as teams negotiate their way around disparate politics, economics, and service goals. Tension between the desire to 'get something done' and the 'need to understand what is happening' requires careful management. As our research endeavors more often require us to work with people whose skills and ultimate goals are quite unlike our own, it is imperative that we not look at the world with a methodologically or theoretically 'ethnocentric' perspective.

For instance, we are currently engaged in a study of the cultural meanings of risk among older residents of San Francisco, as expressed in their decision-making about whether or not to make home safety modifications. We were invited to do this study by colleagues at the local Department of Public Health (DPH), who have a safety education program for seniors. They were finding that a surprising number of older people refuse simple environmental modifications, such as installing grab bars, removing throw rugs, and repairing hand railings. Since DPH's concern is to reduce injuries, they wanted to better understand what was going on as people refused these seemingly innocuous interventions. Our research team includes two anthropologists, two master's-level research associates, and two health educators from DPH. The health educators do not care about theory-building and we are less than enchanted with individual-focused interventions. So we meet in a middle ground and we continually remind ourselves at team meetings that we all have valid goals, but those goals are quite different. Even so, frustration can mount as we academics insist on documentation of what happened during intervention episodes and as the health educators insist on more attention being paid to providing services rather than analyzing the processes by which services came about.

TRANSPARENCY OF COMMUNICATION Over and over, the theme of transparency of communications arises in discussions of both successful and troublesome collaborations. Transparency of communications and research procedures, while difficult to achieve completely, is an essential underlying value to every activity within a research team. If all members of the team understand what is going on both within the group and in themselves and are willing to talk about it, the potential for misunderstanding, obstruction, or outright collapse of the effort is greatly reduced. Communication is a responsibility of the formal team leaders, equally as important as the research design or data analysis procedures.

Supportive contexts for research

INSTITUTIONS There are also contextual issues that make for more or less successful collaborations. Institutional settings that devalue collaboration are major hindrances. Sometimes this devaluation is real and sometimes it is handed down as mythic knowledge, which turns out to be wrong. In either case, such devaluation keeps many people from collaborative projects. We work in a setting where our primary affiliations are with a medical school where collaborative efforts are everyday stuff and fully accepted. But we also have linkages to a department of anthropology on a liberal arts campus. Our graduate students are continually given mixed messages: from the liberal arts campus they see by both word and deed that the only way to do research is by oneself; from our example and the example of other research collaborations in our unit, they see that collaborative work is creative, fulfilling, and productive. So students usually come up with an elaborate explanatory schema to rationalize these different perspectives.

JUSTICE Another significant issue is that of justice – all parties to the collaboration need to be treated fairly by the academic or other employer. Injustices can happen at the micro level, where the leader(s) of a team pay their staff inadequately (or force them to part-time work in order to avoid paying benefits) or fail to acknowledge their contributions appropriately. Injustice can also happen at the institutional level, where formal or informal policies do not allow for appropriate credit to be distributed among members of collaborations – such as the case of the department where 'tradition' says that undergraduate students cannot be co-authors but graduate students may be offered co-authorship, even when the undergraduate made meaningful contributions worthy of recognition.

AUTHORSHIP Authorship is such an important problem in collaborative research that it deserves special mention, especially as it serves to solidify and signal not only successful research but also particular hierarchical relationships within a team. In the past fifteen years, the scientific communities have had extensive discussion on authorship dilemmas. There are two issues: credit and responsibility. When a paper or book is prepared for publication, only one person can be first author – so explicit communication about priorities and creative ways of dividing the work and the credit are essential. The lingua franca of academic scholarship is authorship – to be denied authorship or to be relegated to a position in a list of authors that one feels does not represent one's true contribution is a devastating experience. Editors of journals are concerned about who will be assigned the responsibility for the correctness of the research report. This issue has arisen of late because of the range of findings of fraud and fabrication in biomedical research where many papers that have been withdrawn due to findings of misconduct have a number of authors who knew nothing about the problems of the study (Rennie and Flanagin, 1994; Smith, 1997b; Northridge, 1998; Council of Science Editors, 2003). Recent research on authorship practices suggests that editors and researchers differ significantly in their evaluation of what constitutes authorship, with researchers much more willing to consider the practical tasks of research as being worthy of authorship consideration (Bhopal et al., 1997). Authorship dilemmas and their resolution are generally not discussed in the qualitative research literature, despite the importance of the issue.

There are many approaches to solving 'authorship' problems. Some medical journals are moving from authorship paradigms to 'contributorship' approaches – where the contribution of each person in the byline is specified in a note at the end of the paper (Smith, 1997a; Northridge, 1998). Our practice and recommendation is to have the authorship discussion before the research begins (parallel to initial design discussions), not just when starting data collection or later. We believe that to claim authorship implies that one has been intellectually involved in several phases of the research. We specify this by suggesting that authorship is appropriate when a person has been involved in three or more of the following: design of the study, writing grant proposals and obtaining funding, development of background materials, collection of data, coding and data analysis, writing reports and manuscripts, and reviewing or revising papers for publication. Other people may develop other definitions of what constitutes an authorship-level contribution.

In any case, the important thing is to think these things through before doing the research. By proactively discussing what the requirements of authorship are and having every participant lay on the table where their primary authorship interests lie, potential conflicts can be recognized and resolved before personal enmity sets in. Open lines of communication throughout the research process are vital. The team must be able to talk openly and frankly about issues without fear of reprisal, demotion, job loss, or punishment. We have learned this lesson the hard way. Very early in our careers, one of us worked on a project that we thought was collaborative, and in our naïveté, no discussions were held about authorship. When it came time to publish a book that would summarize this important study, it became apparent that only the formally designated leader would be an author. This was devastating news. It soured relationships and bogged down the entire project for years. Much later, on a different project, a different scenario developed. Our research team agreed to write a co-authored book but this could not be accomplished during the period the study was funded. As the principal team members were all supported solely by research funds or 'soft money', they moved on to new projects. This, along with a variety of other personal and institutional reasons, meant the book never materialized. We still feel guilty, but someday....

We not only have discussions about authorship, we document the group's decisions and all parties keep a record. At the same time, we recognize that things change as research progresses. The person who planned to be a primary collaborator suddenly gets a job across the country and withdraws. The research assistant moves from having a very limited role in the study to being a formative contributor to major analytic projects. In these cases, and others where circumstances change, the initial agreements about authorship need to change. The most important part of this process is voicing one's investment, mutually recognizing each other's goals, building flexibility into the process, and establishing commonly accepted criteria for making these basic decisions.

FINAL MUSINGS

In the qualitative paradigm, there are two theoretical implications of the move to collaborative research. The first is the need for ever more tight and coherent explication of the linkages among epistemology, theory, and method. Especially when teams are working in complementary modes, it is crucial that these linkages be carefully analyzed and understood by all participants. While different components of the project can come from quite different theoretical perspectives, each piece needs to be coherent in and of itself. As team researchers become more comfortable making theory–method links, the coherence of their work and its fit into and contribution to the literature increases.

A second implication of collaboration for social science theory-building is that different types of teams will result in different emphases in theoretical or methodological innovation. We expect that complementary teams will tend to push the theory envelope while multidisciplinary ones will tend to generate new and different forms of methodological rigor in qualitative research. But our hunch might be wrong. Along with several other aspects of team and collaborative research, this is an issue worthy of study.

There is an old expression among American social scientists about the 'lone wolf' fieldworker, who does research independently. Many of our colleagues have fruitfully followed this tradition and we honor their contributions. When the frustrations and bureaucratic exigencies of team research get us down, we too on occasion nostalgically hanker after this mode of research.

The irony is that wolves hunt in packs, not as lone animals. And packs survive and thrive precisely because of the extended territory they can cover and the enhanced interaction between members. We are convinced that the riches of the scholarly research life are partially expressed in this irony – we idolize the solitary, but actually receive the greatest rewards from the collaborative. Just as we have had to learn to explicate qualitative methods, so we need to explore the strengths and weaknesses of various ways of working together. This requires some reflection and some systematic effort. Every collaborative effort has the potential to build a stimulating intellectual community, to create vibrant, innovative investigations that extend the range and ensure the well-being of our disciplines as well as enhance their contributions to the scholarly enterprise.

ACKNOWLEDGEMENTS

We wish to thank the colleagues with whom we have shared teamwork, those who have talked to us about their experiences, and those who have served as role models for us as we explored the complicated terrain of collaboration. We have learned much from them all, but especially from a small group of scholars who have told us of their experiences, including Christine Fry, Madelyn Iris, Lyn Richards, and Geoffrey Hunt.

NOTES

1　The inaccuracy of this shorthand is illustrated by Oakes and Vidich's analysis of the correspondence between C. Wright Mills and Hans Gerth, where debates about authorship and credit were clearly contentious (Oakes and Vidich, 1999).

2　We by no means suggest here that the educational model of the natural sciences has no flaws or that it should serve as a direct model for social science education.

3　Indirect costs are also known as 'overhead costs' or 'facilities and administration costs', those funds that are awarded by a funding agency to a research institution for reimbursement for research costs that are not easily separated from other costs. For instance, the cost of electricity to power computers used by a research project is an indirect cost while the cost of the personal computer on the research assistant's desk is generally considered to be a direct cost, if the computer is used entirely for the research project being funded.

4　Taken, somewhat facetiously, from the 1990 movie of the same name, where two women embark on a cross-country trip that evolves from vacation to crime spree.

REFERENCES

Arcury, T.A. and Quandt, S.A. (1998) 'Occupational and environmental health risks in farm labor,' *Human Organization,* 57(3): 331–4.

Austin, A.E. and Baldwin, R.G. (1991) 'Faculty collaboration: enhancing the quality of scholarship and teaching' (ASHE_ERIC Higher Education Report No. 7). Washington, DC: The George Washington University.

Baba, M. (2001) 'The globally distributed team: learning to work in a new way, for corporations and anthropologists alike', *Practicing Anthropology*, 23(4): 2–6.

Barker, J.C. and Kramer, B.J. (1996) 'Alcohol consumption among older urban American Indians', *Journal of Studies on Alcohol*, 57: 119–24.

Barker, J.C. and Saechao, K. (2000) 'A demographic survey of Iu-Mien in West Coast States of the U.S., 1993', *Journal of Immigrant Health*, 2: 31– 42.

Barker, J.C., Mitteness, L.S. and Wolfsen, C.R. (1994) 'Smoking and adulthood: risky business in a nursing home', *Journal of Aging Studies,* 8: 309–26.

Barker, J.C., Battle, R.S., Cummings, G.L. and Bancroft, K.N. (1998a) 'Condoms and consequences: HIV/AIDS education and African-American women', *Human Organization*, 57: 273–83.

Barker, J.C., Morrow, J. and Mitteness, L.S. (1998b) 'Gender, informal social support networks, and elderly urban African-Americans', *Journal of Aging Studies*, 12: 199–222.

Benedict, B. and Benedict, M. (1982) *Men, Women and Money in Seychelles: Two Views*. Berkeley: University of California Press.

Bhopal, R., Rankin, J., McColl, E., Thomas, L., Kaner, E., Stacy, R., Pearson, P., Vernon, B. and Rodgers, H. (1997) 'The vexed question of authorship: views of researchers in a British medical faculty', *British Medical Journal,* 314: 1009–12.

Byrne-Armstrong, H. (2001) 'Whose show is it? The contradictions of collaboration', in H. Byrne-Armstrong, J. Higgs and D. Horsfall (eds), *Critical Moments in Qualitative Research*. Oxford: Butterworth-Heinemann, pp. 106–14.

Clair, S., Teng, W., Stopka, T., Li, J. and Salaheen, H. (2003) 'Experiences of non-anthropologists in an anthropologically driven research center', *Practicing Anthropology*, 25(3): 12–16.

Council of Science Editors (2003) 'Services: Selected References in Authorship'. http://www.councilscienceeditors.org/services.

Damrosch, D. (1995) *We Scholars: Changing the Culture of the University*. Cambridge, MA: Harvard University Press.

Dollard, J., Miller, N., Doob, L.W. and Mowrer, O.H. (1939) *Frustration and Aggression*. New Haven, CT: Yale University Press.

Erickson, K.C. and Stull, D.D. (1998) *Doing Team Ethnography: Warnings and Advice* (Qualitative Research Methods Series, vol. 42). Thousand Oaks, CA: Sage.

Fernea, E.W. (1965) *Guests of the Sheik: An Ethnography of an Iraqi Village*. New York: Doubleday.

Fernea, E.W. (1975) *A Street in Marrakech: A Personal Encounter with the Lives of Moroccan Women*. New York: Doubleday.

Firth, R. (1972) 'From wife to anthropologist', in S. Kimball and J.B. Watson (eds), *Crossing Cultural Boundaries: The Anthropological Experience*. San Francisco: Chandler, pp. 10–32.

Foster, G., Scudder, T., Colson, E. and Van Kemper, R. (eds), (1979) *Long-Term Field Research in Social Anthropology*. New York: Academic Press, pp. 227–54.

Gilbert, K. (2001) 'Collateral damage? Indirect exposure of staff members to the emotions of qualitative research', in K. Gilbert (ed.), *The Emotional Nature of Qualitative Research*. Boca Raton, FL: CRC Press, pp. 147–61.

Gottlieb, A. (1995) 'Beyond the lonely anthropologist: collaboration in research and writing', *American Anthropologist*, 97(1): 21–5.

Hafernik, J.J., Messerschmitt, D.S. and Vandrick, S. (1997) 'Collaborative research: why and how?', *Educational Researcher*, 26(9): 31–5.

Harrisson, D. (1995) 'Qualitative research and utilization of the NUDIST program', *Society/Société*, 19(2): 15–17.

Herskovits, E.J. and Mitteness, L.S. (1994) 'Transgressions and sickness in old age', *Journal of Aging Studies*, 8(3): 327–40.

Hesse-Biber, S. (1995) 'Unleashing Frankenstein's monster? The use of computers in qualitative research', *Studies in Qualitative Methodology*, 5: 25–41.

Holstein, J.A. and Gubrium, J.F. (2000) *The Self We Live By: Narrative Identity in a Postmodern World*. New York : Oxford University Press.

Keith, J. (1994) 'Consequences for research procedure', in J.F. Gubrium and A. Sankar (eds), *Qualitative Methods in Aging Research*. Thousand Oaks, CA: Sage, pp. 105–22.

Keith, J., Fry, C.L., Glascock, A.P., Ikels, C., Dickerson-Putman, J., Harpending, H.C. and Draper, P. (1994) *The Aging Experience: Diversity and Commonality Across Cultures*. Thousand Oaks, CA: Sage.

Kemper, R.V. and Royce, A.P. (1997) 'Ethical issues for social anthropologists: a North American perspective on long-term research in Mexico', *Human Organization*, 56(4): 479–83.

Kennedy, E.L. (1995) 'In pursuit of connection: reflections on collaborative work', *American Anthropologist*, 97(1): 26–33.

Kramer, B.J and Barker, J.C. (1996) 'Homelessness among older American Indians, Los Angeles, 1987–1989'. *Human Organization*, 55: 396–408.

Lassiter, L.E. (2001) 'From "Reading over the shoulders of natives" to "Reading alongside natives," literally: toward a collaborative and reciprocal ethnography', *Journal of Anthropological Research*, 57(2): 137–49.

Li, J., Shaw, S., Singer, M. and Clair, S. (2003) 'The tensions of unity: Challenges of community-centered research', *Practicing Anthropology*, 25(3): 8–11.

Merchant, B.M. (2001) 'Negotiating the boundaries and sometimes missing the mark: a White researcher and a Mexican American research assistant', in B.M. Merchant and A.I. Willis (eds), *Multiple and Intersecting Identities in Qualitative Research*. Mahwah, NJ: Lawrence Erlbaum, pp. 1–18.

Mitteness, L.S. and Barker, J.C. (1994) 'Managing large projects', in J.F. Gubrium and A. Sankar (eds), *Qualitative Methods in Aging Research*. Thousand Oaks, CA: Sage, pp. 82–104.

Mitteness, L.S. and Barker, J.C. (1995) 'Stigmatizing a "normal" condition: urinary incontinence in late life' *Medical Anthropology Quarterly*, 9: 189–211.

Mitteness, L.S., Barker, J.C. and Finlayson, E. (1995) 'Residential managers' experience of urinary incontinence in elderly tenants', *Journal of Applied Gerontology*, 14: 408–25.

Northridge, M. (1998) 'Annotation: new rules for authorship in the journal: your contributions are recognized – and published!', *American Journal of Public Health*, 88: 733–4.

Oakes, G. and Vidich, A.J. (1999) *Collaboration, Reputation, and Ethics in American Academic Life*. Urbana: University of Illinois Press.

Parsons, T. and Bales, R.F. (1955) *Family, Socialization and Interaction Process*. Glencoe, IL: Free Press.

Pinn, J. (2001) 'Crises of representation', in H. Byrne-Armstrong, J. Higgs and D. Horsfall (eds), *Critical Moments in Qualitative Research*. Oxford: Butterworth-Heinemann, pp. 185–98.

Qualitative Solutions and Research, Pty Ltd (1999, 2002) NVivo (Qualitative Data Analysis Software). Melbourne, Australia.

Rennie, D. and Flanagin, A. (1994) 'Authorship! Authorship! Ghosts, guests and grafters, and the two-sided coin', *Journal of the American Medical Association*, 271: 469–71.

Richards, T.J. and Richards, L. (1994) 'Using computers in qualitative research', in N.K. Denzin and Y.S. Lincoln (eds), *Handbook of Qualitative Research*. Thousand Oaks, CA: Sage, pp. 445–62.

Roth, J. (1966) 'Hired hand research', *American Sociologist*, 1(4): 190–6.

Scudder, T. and Colson, E.F. (1979) 'Long-term research in Gwembe Valley, Zambia', in G. Foster et al. (eds), *Long-Term Field Research in Social Anthropology*. New York: Academic Press, pp. 227–54.

Smith, B.A. and Hesse-Biber, S. (1996) 'Users' experiences with qualitative data analysis software: neither Frankenstein's monster nor muse', *Social Science Computer Review*, 14(4): 423–32.

Smith, R. (1997a) 'Authorship is dying: long live contributorship. The BMJ will publish lists of contributors and guarantors to original articles', *British Medical Journal*, 315: 696.

Smith, R. (1997b) 'Authorship: time for a paradigm shift? The authorship system is broken and may need a radical solution', *British Medical Journal*, 314: 992.

Stouffer, S.A., Suchman, E.A., DeVinney, L.C., Star, S.A., and Williams, R.M. Jr., (1949a) *The American Soldier*, Volume 1: *Adjustment During Army Life*. Princeton, NJ: Princeton University Press.

Stouffer, S.A., Lumsdaine, A.A. Lumsdaine, M.H., Williams R.M., Jr., Smith, M.B., Jains, I.L., Star, S.A., and Cottrell, L.S., Jr. (1949b) *The American Soldier, Volume 2: Combat and Its Aftermath*. Princeton, NJ: Princeton University Press.

Teruya, C.N. (1999) 'Faculty research collaboration: the invisible model of knowledge production'. PhD dissertation, University of California, Los Angeles.

Turner, E. (1987) *The Spirit and the Drum: A Memoir of Africa*. Tucson: University of Arizona Press.

Wall, E. (1995) 'The problem with NUDISTs', *Society/Société*, 19(1): 13–14.

Werner, O. (1998) 'Referencing native consultants', *CAM: The Cultural Anthropology Methods Journal*, 10(2): 29–30.

Whiting, B.B. (ed.) (1963) *Six Cultures: Studies of Child Rearing*. New York: Wiley.

Whiting, B.B. and Whiting, J.W.M. (1975) *Children of Six Cultures: A Psychocultural Analysis*. Cambridge, MA: Harvard University Press.

Wolfsen, C.R., Barker, J.C. and Mitteness, L.S. (1993) 'Constipation in the daily life of frail elderly', *Archives of Family Medicine*, 2: 853–8.

Zurita, M. (2001) 'La mojada y el coyote: experiences of a wetback researcher', in B.M. Merchant and A.I. Willis (eds), *Multiple and Intersecting Identities in Qualitative Research*. Mahwah, NJ: Lawrence Erlbaum, pp. 19–32.

Part 4

CONTEXT AND METHOD

Qualitative researchers apply many strategies to investigate the shifting contexts of experience. There is no uniform set of research procedures. While survey researchers, for example, limit themselves to questionnaires and face-to-face interviews, qualitative researchers not only interview their respondents, but also take inspiration from the varied ways their subjects represent themselves to each other across time and social space. If we were to take a lead from survey researchers, we would guess, for instance, that people represented their experiences rather narrowly, through relatively formalized speech exchanges. The proverbial alien from another planet might conclude from this that social researchers – being as human as their subjects are – merely reflect the methods of procedure found in subjects' worlds, which researchers then use to represent those worlds.

What is ironic about this is that the interview as a method of procedure and a representational practice is relatively new in human experience, emerging as a formal research procedure in the twentieth century. Qualitative researchers, indeed, often find that standardized interviews, and face-to-face interviewing in general, seem to be rather confined means of working up the shifting details of social worlds and uncovering patterns in them. Speaking of life is only one way that experience is communicated. Indeed, being offered the opportunity to speak again in several follow-up interviews may in its reflexive thrust be a method of procedure qualitatively distinct from the common one-shot interview, which is not prompted in relation to an earlier or later speech opportunity. Reinterviewing provides for recall, the possibility of mulling over earlier expressions of opinion, and the resulting comparative context for communicating meaning. While reinterviewing of various kinds is part of the stock-in-trade of qualitative reseachers, how often do conventional interview researchers replay sections of earlier interviews with respondents or provide subjects with additional interviews on a topic as a basis for considering the unfolding meaning of an experience?

If everyday life were limited to one-shot communications of meaning, it would appear strange indeed, bereft of the possibilities that derive from changing one's mind, considering what transpired earlier, and orientations to future occasions when one anticipates being given the opportunity to re-express oneself. Yet, in broad outline, this is precisely the kind of methodological practice that survey researchers, in particular, commonly apply in their investigations. The result is that everyday life is bereft of its shifting contexts, and limited instead to the formalized context of an interview occasion. Indeed, the shifting contexts of the formal interview itself, which can construct countless moral environments for participants, is overshadowed by the data-gathering and analytic momentum of homogenized research agendas.

The authors of the various chapters of Part 4 move in a different direction, typical of qualitative researchers. While none takes a general account of the wide range of 'methods of procedure' that their subjects use in communicating information about their lives to others, they do make use of a similar variety. We might guess, for example, that in everyday life people not only respond to individual questions about their attitudes, feelings and actions, but that they leave traces of these matters in how they decorate their homes, the outside appearance of their houses, what they own, what they wear, and how they care for themselves, among a spectrum of material ways of presenting themselves to each other. We might suppose that they also write about who they are and what others they are concerned about are or should be. We might consider that the way they arrange these things in time and space is also a way of representing themselves. These suppositions inspire the parallel methods of procedure that qualitative researchers apply in representing the lives, experiences and social worlds they study. The variety, if observed by our proverbial alien, would lead him or her to perhaps conclude that human experience is more richly variegated and fleeting than it is otherwise construed in research practice.

Material methods of procedure are not all that qualitative researchers borrow from the representational arsenal of their subjects. Qualitative researchers also look to the working symbolic spaces that constitute and comprise meaning in everyday life. Some try to alter these in situ, as ethnomethodologist Harold Garfinkel's (1967) famous 'breaching' experiments aimed to do, applying the same method of procedure in this regard that members do in everyday life. Others zero in on the naturally occurring rhythms of shifting contexts and take various angles of vision on these, as a means of grasping those meanings, how they are organized, and why they relate to each other as they do at different times and in various places. Whether intrusive or unobtrusive, these are methods that take up contextuality not merely as a feature of meaning, but as a means by which social researchers themselves can prompt or uncover interpretative activity.

Paralleling these representational practices, the authors of Part 4 apply a broad range of methods of research. James Holstein and Jaber Gubrium (Chapter 19) take the lead with a discussion of how shifts in analytic context – working it up, down, and across, as they put it – can uncover richer veins of meaning than keeping a single analytic context in place. Julia Brannen (Chapter 20) provides a helpful discussion of how a combination of qualitative and quantitative methods and research material can expand one's analytic horizons, offering complementary explanatory support for each other. Louise Corti and Paul Thompson (Chapter 21) take us to archived traces of experiences and social worlds to show how repeated examination can uncover diverse senses of the messages they contain. Malin Åkerström, Katarina Jacobsson and David Wästerfors (Chapter 22) also take us to written material, but in this case material originally collected by researchers themselves, informing us that shifting analytic contexts can cast new light on experiences cast earlier in rather different terms. Annette Markham (Chapter 23) turns us to the Internet as a research context, showing how its representational practices shape meaning and our resulting understanding of the experiences conveyed. Lindsay Prior (Chapter 24) returns us to documents, but this time in the context of discourse and institutional practice, illustrating how the analytic acumen of qualitative research extends across systems of knowledge and the minutest details of communication. Last, but not least, Sarah Pink (Chapter 25) reminds us that spoken and written modalities do not exhaust our representational practices. As she explains, sights and visual methods can literally reveal experience and social worlds in ways that other methods cannot, providing yet another gamut of contexts for meaning and understanding. Taken together, the chapters of Part 4 indicate that context and method are anything but separate domains of research practice.

REFERENCE

Garfinkel, H. (1967) *Studies in Ethnomethodology*. Englewood Cliffs, NJ: Prentice-Hall.

19

Context: working it up, down, and across

James A. Holstein and Jaber F. Gubrium

'There was some nice things I brought. ...
Brought them from the rocketship.'

What should we make of this utterance? What is
going on in this spate of talk about a spaceship?
What might it mean? These are certainly challenging questions, both for social researchers and
for lay persons. And the answer that nearly anyone would give is, 'It depends'.

Suppose Jon is riding a municipal bus downtown, quietly minding his own business. In the
usual course of events, a stranger takes a seat
next to Jon. The stranger is speaking quietly, but
to whom it's not clear. The talk becomes more
animated as the stranger now launches a narrative of what appear to be his afternoon exploits.
The story gets a little confusing as the stranger's
accounts begin flirting with the bizarre. 'I just
got these new shoes. ... There was some nice
things I brought. ... Brought them from the rocketship.' Now this is too much for Jon: 'This
guy's freakin' crazy', he concludes as he decides
to get off the bus a stop early.

The inference that the stranger on the bus is
'crazy', 'insane', 'delusional', or otherwise
psychiatrically disturbed seems reasonable under
the circumstances. But what if one were to hear
the very same utterance in a different setting.
Suppose, for example, that Maya works for the
National Aeronautics and Space Administration
at the John F. Kennedy Space Center in Cape
Canaveral, Florida. When she arrives home after
work on a Friday evening, Maya opens her brief-
case to surprise her two young sons with a few
treasures she carried home from work: 'There
was some nice things I brought. ... Brought them
from the rocketship.' The boys are excited and
Mom's a local heroine, bestowing 'souvenirs'
that she scavenged from a bin of items that
were going to be jettisoned from the recently

returned space shuttle. Mom is evidently far
from being 'crazy'.

Of course the circumstantial possibilities for
how the rocketship reference might be construed
are virtually endless. Uttered by a child in an
amusement park, it could be a simple explanation of where a new-found baseball cap had
come from. It could be equally comprehensible
as a punch line for a joke, or as dialog from an
action movie. The 'it depends' quality of meaning is simply another way of highlighting the
importance of context in the interpretive process.
Words, utterances, actions, perceptions, and cog-
nitions all depend on context for their intelligibility, substance, and understanding (see, among
others, Wittgenstein, 1953; Garfinkel, 1967;
Heritage, 1984). Accordingly, 'I brought them
from the rocketship' derives different meaning
and carries different implications depending on
the context of its telling, hearing, and use. It's a
thoroughly 'indexical' expression (Garfinkel,
1967).

A CONTEXTUAL QUANDARY

Context has been a central concern in qualitative
inquiry from the start. Whether it is construed in
terms of 'distal' factors such as culture, socio-
economic status, or social structure, or more
'proximal' conditions such as interactional settings or sequences, context has been the stock-in-
trade of researchers who seek to describe and
explain social action and organization. Broadly
speaking, sociology itself is dedicated to understanding the myriad effects of social context on
lived experience.

Consider, for example, how context figures
into possible explanations that could be offered

for the rocketship reference as it actually occurred in a courtroom study. One of the authors (Holstein) was conducting an observational study of a Southern California courtroom when a person on the witness stand matter-of-factly stated that 'There was some nice things I brought. … Brought them from the rocketship.' The announcement seemed to have major consequences for the proceedings, but various aspects of the social context can be differently implicated in how the statement came to be understood. Let us look initially at how context, in perhaps its most readily available form, could be used to understand what was going on.

'Metropolitan Court' is a special venue, reserved for cases relating to mental health laws. Holstein was there to study involuntary commitment hearings (see Holstein, 1993). In these cases, a 'candidate patient' appeared before a judge, who would determine if the candidate patient should be remanded to an in-patient psychiatric facility and receive treatment for mental illness. Candidate patients were afforded the services of an attorney (usually a public defender), the state's interests were represented by an assistant district attorney, and a mental health professional – usually a psychiatrist – delivered testimony concerning the candidate patient's mental health. In the rocketship case, Lisa Sellers was being interrogated by the district attorney, when, after a series of rather innocuous questions seemingly exploring Sellers's reality orientation, Sellers blurted out that she had brought some nice things from the 'rocketship'. A few minutes later the judge ordered her involuntary commitment to a state mental hospital.

Now, under the circumstances, particular aspects of social context might easily be invoked to understand the immense consequences of this utterance. In the context of everyday life in contemporary Western society, rocketship travel is merely fanciful, if not impossible. To speak of being on a rocketship is implausible, and most people hearing such a statement would attribute it to the speaker's faulty 'reality orientation'. In the context of mental illness, we might readily explain such a disjuncture between Sellers's claim and our understanding of everyday possibilities by framing her version of the world as being the product of mental derangement (see Coulter, 1975; Pollner, 1987). Typically, we would say this was delusional ideation and talk.

Such an explanation, however, would rely upon taken-for-granted aspects of cultural context. Further, we would assume that a person deemed to be in this 'state of mind' would be a likely candidate for psychiatric treatment. When such speech appeared in an involuntary commitment hearing, we would presume that it would result in commitment and psychiatric treatment. But the terms for such an understanding would emanate from cultural assumptions about mental illness and the role of involuntary commitment in dealing with the mentally ill. Still, this would not specify the practice of applying cultural knowledge under the circumstances, nor would the use of such cultural understandings be consciously acknowledged.

This situation, and the context (or contexts, as we will later argue) in which it developed, are even more complex than that. First, Lisa Sellers, like all other candidate patients appearing in Metropolitan Court, had been diagnosed as psychiatrically disordered. Moments before she began discussing the rocketship, a psychiatrist had testified that Sellers was seriously mentally ill. Indeed, like all candidate patients appearing in Metropolitan Court, Sellers had long diagnostic and treatment histories. So, if being mentally ill wasn't distinctive, what distinguished Lisa Sellers's case for commitment?

Many candidate patients make bizarre or 'incredible' statements but they aren't committed. It is unlikely that the specific reference to rocketship travel – as opposed to some other form of delusional talk – was the deciding factor. After all, Metropolitan Court is only about 15 minutes from Hollywood. Claims about rocket travel and other technological marvels within the entertainment industry aren't that unusual. And 30 miles south of Metropolitan Court – in Disneyland – millions of people have actually been on a rocketship of one sort or another as part of the Disney fantasy experience. Accounts of such experiences don't call one's sanity into question. And yet, after Sellers's testimony, the judge specifically referred to the rocketship announcement in his account for deciding to commit her.

Qualitative researchers might turn to still other contextual features of the situation to explain the judge's decision. Among these might be the myriad 'structural' variables that sociologists like to reveal as 'working behind the scenes', so to speak, to influence and constrain individual behavior. For example, during the 1960s and 1970s, proponents of the so-called labeling perspective produced a substantial literature arguing that structural attributes like gender, age, social class, and socioeconomic status significantly influenced the outcomes of involuntary commitment hearings (see Holstein, 1993). After all, Lisa Sellers was an apparently poor, black woman. The invisible hand of social forces might have imperceptibly shaped the judge's decision. But, once again, such an explanation would rely, in an unexplicated fashion, on knowledge about social structural context. And as it so happens, gender, race, or economics per se didn't seem to be related systematically to hearing outcomes in Metropolitan Court (but see Holstein, 1993, for discussion of how they were related).

Clearly, context can come into interpretive play in seemingly endless ways. It is essential to any understanding of social behavior, yet it is not uniformly consulted or used in social analysis. Perhaps the vision of a static set of influential circumstances – a set of variables that surround persons, actions, or situations – is not the most analytically astute way of construing context. Its multiple manifestations and varying influences suggest that context is a fluid, socially emergent constellation of contingent factors that are 'worked up' – not just encountered – in the course of everyday interaction.

The events we have described merely scratch the surface of the interpretive possibilities for making sense of what was going on in Metropolitan Court, all of which depend on context in one way or another. For a comprehensive understanding of the practical organization and meaning of social actions, one needs to methodically and rigorously examine the myriad ways that context is actively incorporated into interpretive practice. Most importantly, one needs to examine how context is brought to bear on the experiences of everyday life – how it is made salient, pertinent, and operational (Gubrium and Holstein, 1997; Schegloff, 1997). To the extent that we treat context as a more-or-less invisible force working 'behind people's backs', qualitative analysis will be undermined by reliance upon unspecified, deterministic explanatory resources. Instead, our own research experience has taught us to look at how context actually manifests its presence – how it works – in lived experience. In our view, should qualitative analysts call upon social context to explain social action, they must consider social context as it is relevant to the experience of the social participants under consideration (Gubrium and Holstein, 1997; Schegloff, 1991, 1997).

Moreover, the fact that we can easily specify multiple dimensions of context – diverse manifestations of context – should sensitize us to the emergent, elastic nature of context. It is never fixed, but instead is actively brought to bear in the ongoing course of social life. In our view, context is best treated as an interpretive resource rather than a deterministic condition. Moreover, if we take the position that everyday realties are socially constructed, it is imperative that we account for social context both as a circumstance of social construction, and as a social construction itself. As research practice has taught us, the respective *whats* of social construction and the *hows* of socially constructive activity are reflexively related (Garfinkel, 1967; Gubrium and Holstein, 2000a).

APPROACHING CONTEXT

Given that 'it depends', how does one deal analytically with social context? A key point is to avoid the presumption that context is an objective set of circumstances that stands apart from, and works its magic over, social actors who, as a result, are cast as 'interpretive (contextual) dopes'. We would be better served to look at how context is used by actors themselves. But, because context is experienced as part of a full-blown, lived reality, it is virtually impossible to delineate where, when, or how its manifestations begin and end. One might, for example, approach context from either the 'top' or the 'bottom', so to speak. From the top, for instance, institutionally based knowledge and discourse might provide a broad, yet elastic, context for understanding activities and their consequences within the institutional purview. (Of course, this begs the question of just how far or near that purview extends.) Alternatively, from the bottom, the communicative exchanges of situations provide emerging contexts for meaning that is constantly emerging through chains of actions and events. Either approach has its advantages and challenges.

As Harvey Sacks (1992) and others have suggested (see Garfinkel, 1967; Schegloff, 1997; Silverman, 1998), context is never a settled matter, so we must look at how participants in interaction continue to co-produce the very context they inhabit through that very interaction. Similarly, Paul Drew and John Heritage (1992: 21) argue that context is 'inherently locally produced, incrementally developed, and … transformable at any moment'. The upshot of this perspective is to carefully describe and analyze the construction of social context in conversational interaction – 'turn by responsive turn' – from the bottom working up. It is equally plausible to start at the top and 'work down' to explore the significant distal contexts of social interaction as well (see Smith, 1987; Mehan, 1991). This would mean starting with cultural or institutional meanings, for example, and looking to see how they are formulated then imported to, and used in, the scenes of consequential social interaction.

While these approaches are commonly presented as distinct analytic strategies, our research experience strongly suggests that neither the bottom-up nor top-down approach suffices as a comprehensive explanatory framework. This is because, in the practice of everyday life, at least two primary sources of context – talk-in-interaction and culture and institutions – are always at play. It is important to emphasize that these different approaches are not set in stone. We use bottom-up and top-down metaphorically, as ways of designating points of departure for analysis. Because of the reflexive relation between top and bottom in practice, we must pay keen and continuous attention to, and resist, their possible reification. The approaches provide different perspectives on the practice of everyday life. It is everyday life that is focal, not a figurative but analytically useful top nor a figurative but analytically useful bottom.

Working from the bottom up

One approach to understanding context is to start at the interactional level of social order to show how context is built up in the sequential environment of conversation. This provides a 'ground floor' look at the interactions that constitute social realities. It requires the researcher to examine the details of everyday interaction to understand how the social context of any activity is accomplished in situ in real time

Let us return to our previous rocketship example, this time examining Lisa Sellers's courtroom interaction more closely. Drawing upon a conversation analytic perspective (Sacks, 1992; Sacks et al., 1974; see Heritage, 1984; Silverman, 1998), we will investigate the moment-by-moment, turn-by-turn exchange between Lisa Sellers and an assistant district attorney, which produced the interactional context that invited Lisa's rocketship revelation. This became the context the judge used to justify her commitment. Recall that Sellers was called to the witness stand by a representative of the district attorney's (DA) office to testify about her state of mind and current living circumstances.

The interrogation began with a series of fourteen direct questions (e.g. What's your name? Where are we right now? Where do you live? What day of the week is it?) to which Sellers responded with brief answers. This series comprised fourteen straightforward question–answer pairs. There were no notable pauses at the end of questions and answers (i.e. possible speakership transition points), nor were there any intrusions or interruptions of one party by the other. At the end of this sequence, the DA took a different tack:

1	DA:	How do you like summer out here, Lisa?
2	LS:	It's OK.
3	DA:	How long have you lived here?
4	LS:	Since I moved from Houston
5		((Silence)) [Note: if unspecified, time is 1 to 3 seconds]
6	LS:	About three years ago
7	DA:	Tell me about why you came here.
8	LS:	I just came
9		((Silence))
10	LS:	You know, I wanted to see the stars, Hollywood.
11		((Silence))
12	DA:	Uh huh
13	LS:	I didn't have no money.
14		((Silence))
15	LS:	I'd like to get a good place to live.
16		((Silence 5 seconds))
17	DA:	Go on. ((spoken simultaneously with onset of the next utterance))
18	LS:	There was some nice things I brought
19		((Silence))
20	DA:	Uh huh
21	LS:	Brought them from the rocketship.
22	DA:	Oh really?
23	LS:	They was just some things I had.
24	DA:	From the rocketship?
25	LS:	Right.
26	DA:	Were you on it?
27	LS:	Yeah.
28	DA:	Tell me about this rocketship, Lisa.

The sequence culminates in Sellers's rocketship reference, with the DA avidly following up. But Sellers didn't simply blurt out this 'delusional' statement, as if mechanically reproduced from some distant location. Rather, it developed out of the faltering conversation that Sellers tried valiantly to salvage. Close examination permits us to understand how the rocketship utterance and its resulting context came into play.

At the beginning of the extracted exchange, the DA changes the question and answer pattern – the sequence of question–answer adjacency pairs – that seems to have emerged as the normative expectation for the interrogation. After the previous series of questions that were answerable with short, factual replies, in line 1, the DA now asks an open-ended question. In his next turn (line 3), he returns to a more straightforward question, but when Sellers produces a candidate answer (line 4), the DA declines to take the next turn at talk. A silence emerges following line 4, where a question from the DA may have been expected. The gap in talk is eventually terminated (line 6) by Sellers's elaboration of her prior utterance.

In line 7, the DA solicits further talk, but this time it is not in the form of a question. Instead, it is a very general prompt for Sellers to provide more information. The adequacy of a response to this kind of request, however, is more indeterminate than for a direct question. In a sense, the DA puts himself in the position to decide when his request for information is adequately fulfilled. The adequacy and completeness of Sellers's response will thus depend, in part, on how the DA acknowledges it.

At line 9, the DA doesn't respond to Sellers's candidate answer at the first possible opportunity. When silence develops, Sellers elaborates on her previous answer (line 10). The DA fails to respond to this utterance as well, and another noteworthy silence ensues. Such silences signal conversational difficulties, troubles that implicate the prior speaker, who may attempt remedial action (Maynard, 1980). Sellers did just that by reclaiming speakership and embellishing a prior utterance on several occasions (lines 6, 10, 15, and 17). In each instance, she filled silences with her own talk.

Several times, then, in the course of this conversation, the DA's refusal to take a turn at talk provokes Sellers to continue her own turns. At line 12, the DA encourages this practice by offering a minimal acknowledgment (Uh huh), which implies that an extended turn at talk is in progress and is not yet complete (Schegloff, 1982). He uses this brief turn to subtly prompt Sellers to continue, which she does (lines 13 and 15). Her responses, however, meet only with silence. At line 17, the DA explicitly encourages Sellers to 'Go on', which she does by changing the line of talk to focus on 'some nice things [she] brought' (line 18). The DA again refuses speakership (line 19), then offers a minimal prompt (line 20), to which Sellers finally replies with 'Brought them from the rocketship' (line 21). Now this elicits a strong display of interest from the DA ('Oh really?' – line 22), who then actively resumes questioning Sellers about the rocketship. At this point the give and take of questions and answers is re-established and the interrogation moved on without notable gaps, pauses, or silences.

The DA's 'Oh really?' is a compelling display of interest. In the difficult conversational environment that had emerged, it provided a virtual beacon toward which Sellers might orient her talk. Put differently, it signals that the prior utterance was noteworthy, even newsworthy. 'Oh really?' shows that the DA is especially interested

in what Sellers has to say at this juncture; it indicates a significant 'change of state' (Heritage, 1984) – in this instance from a state of apparent indifference to one of keen interest. Responding to this, Sellers elaborates 'on point', formulating a new, more 'successful' line of talk – with 'success' being defined in terms of the ability to re-establish and sustain a viable and dynamic question–answer sequence. In vernacular terms, the rocketship statement and its aftermath helped Sellers keep up her end of the conversation.

To understand the role of context in conversation analytic terms, we would focus on the ways in which the sequential context of the conversation provided grounds for what was said, by whom, at what juncture. The answer to the 'why that now?' question (Schegloff, 1997) should be available to both the conversational actor and the analyst in the emerging context of situated talk. In this instance, Sellers found herself in a nonresponsive conversational environment. In the face of repeated emerging silences that might be accountably attributed to her, Sellers responded so as to fill the silence by resuming speakership at possible speakership transition points where her conversational partner – the DA – declined to speak. In effect, Sellers was fulfilling perceived normative responsibilities for the ongoing exchange by producing extended utterances to close conversational gaps.

In a sense, Lisa Sellers did what any competent conversationalist might do; she engaged in practices commonly followed in similar conversational circumstances. When her rocketship disclosure drew the DA back into the conversation, Sellers once again followed competent practice by pursuing a productive line of talk centered around the rocketship. She *used* the rocketship reference to put an end to conversational difficulties and elaborated it to sustain a thriving line of talk. Again, in more vernacular terms, she competently fulfilled her conversational responsibilities, but, in the process, betrayed another sort of competence. Only close examination of the way the sequential context of conversation was worked up could afford such an explanation.

Working from the top down

The judge in the commitment hearing we have been examining eventually ordered Lisa Sellers to be committed for psychiatric treatment, citing her delusional talk in his account. It is tempting, then, to highlight the delectable irony that Lisa Sellers was found to be 'incompetent' by virtue of the very conversational *competence* that allowed her to capably sustain a conversation under very trying interactional circumstances. But to focus on this irony would unduly limit our understanding of what competence could possibly be.

It would be overly simplistic to say that competence was simply a matter of interactional dexterity. Emphasizing such proficiency would obscure the importance of meaning to social action and experience. This would be just as big a mistake as simply assuming that the presumed delusional meaning of the rocketship utterance was prima-facie evidence of mental and social incompetence. Understanding *what* was said is no less, or no more, important than *how* it was said in explaining the utterance.

Indeed, our experience tells us that *what* was said and *how* it was said are reflexively related so that one cannot be fully understood without reference to the other. An understanding of how Lisa Sellers competently managed the courtroom conversation described above cannot adequately explain why her rocketship disclosure drew the keen interest and attention of her conversational partner as well as everyone else in the courtroom – including the judge. *What* she said was extremely consequential. In our view, the question of why the disclosure drew her partner's keen interest cannot be answered by focusing exclusively on how a conversation unfolds, but must take into account what was at stake in the matter. (See Gubrium and Holstein, 1997, for a discussion of *how–what* reflexivity as a basis for addressing *why* questions.) To understand the impact of this statement, we need to examine an interactional context of another sort, one that is more expansive than the sequential environment of the situation at hand. To approach context from this perspective, we need to start at a location more distant from the interaction in question.

Recall from the discussion above that full emergence of the rocketship disclosure hinged, at least in part, on the significant noticing implied by the DA's 'Oh really?' Such a noticing might accomplish several things in addition to cueing the DA's conversational partner into a topic of interest to the DA. It might also call attention to the 'faulted' quality of the utterance, suggesting the need for repair. It could be heard as an expression of surprise or disbelief. As such, it might even be heard as a call for elaboration that could dispel implied doubts by altering, repairing, retracting, or reframing the problematic utterance. To understand which, if any, of these were actually the case, one would need additional insight into the content or meaning attached to the rocketship utterance.

Such insight would need to come from outside the spate of talk we have just examined. Indeed,

it might emanate, in part, from some very distant aspects of the context in which Lisa Sellers's statement is embedded. Understanding the role of such distal aspects of context requires ethnographic and perhaps even historical/archeological/genealogical sensibilities (see Foucault, 1965; Sheridan, 1980). If social interaction is accomplished through *discursive practices* it is made meaningful and consequences specified by *discourses-in-practice* (Gubrium and Holstein, 2000a, 2000b; Holstein and Gubrium, 2000).

In what way, for instance, are we to understand the fact that the judge accountably committed Lisa Sellers to psychiatric treatment based, at least in part, on the rocketship disclosure? At one level, we would need to understand the cultural and socio-historical context that provides both commonsense and technical meaning to concepts such as mental illness, delusion, psychiatry, treatment, and other discursive building-blocks of prevailing orientations to mental and interactional competence. Common sense might tell us that rocketship travel by lay persons is unlikely, hence its description is apt to be delusional, but qualitative researchers are usually wary of relying upon such unexplicated analytic resources. A more rigorous analysis might include a history of the discourse of insanity such as Michel Foucault's *Madness and Civilization* (1965), for example.

Still, as we noted above, many candidate patients in Metropolitan Court are found to be delusional and all are diagnosed as mentally ill. So, once again, why is the rocketship disclosure so consequential? Another part of the answer might be found in the 'local culture' (Gubrium and Holstein, 1997) of Metropolitan Court. This is accessible through ethnographic observation of the courthouse setting, which was precisely Holstein's (1993) aim in observing the courtroom for over three years. (He also carefully read Carol Warren's 1980 study of the same setting.) He was attempting to understand a *what* matter that was not as contextually encompassing or distant as Foucault's understanding of the discourse of mental illness. Instead he sought a more localized understanding of what it meant to be in need of involuntary commitment.

Observation of the setting and its activities, conversations and informal interviews with courtroom personnel, and even closer scrutiny of selected spates of courtroom talk, yielded a discursive ethnography of the everyday workings of Metropolitan Court. One of the study's central observations was that parties to commitment hearings routinely consider whether or not the candidate patient can establish viable living arrangements outside the hospital that can contain the havoc – both internal and to the community – associated with mental illness (Holstein, 1993). While judgment of psychiatric disorder is necessary, civil commitment doesn't depend on psychiatric diagnosis or symptomatology as much as on decision-makers' pragmatic assessments of the *tenability* of a candidate patient's proposed community living situation. This tenability is discursively constituted in terms of the following factors: (1) the person's ability to provide for, gain access to, and properly utilize life's basic necessities, including food, clothing, and shelter; (2) the willing presence of someone in the vicinity who will serve competently as a 'caretaker' and see to the well-being of the released candidate patient; and (3) the candidate patient's cooperation with a community-based treatment and/or custody regime. In the conspicuous absence of any of these, social and psychiatric disturbances are considered inevitable and commitment is likely to be ordered (Holstein, 1993).

With this background knowledge – supplied by ethnographic observation – we are in a better position to make sense of the judge's decision. Only moments after Sellers brought the rocketship into the scene, the judge found Sellers 'gravely disabled' and ordered her commitment. In his account for the decision, he argued that Sellers was clearly delusional and that her delusions compromised her ability to carry out the most basic tasks of daily life. He noted that she wasn't able to keep her delusions in check even though she clearly knew that she was literally 'on trial' for her freedom. If she couldn't keep her mental illness from spilling forth under these circumstances, how could the court expect her to do so if she was released and not closely monitored? Given that there was no one available to keep an eye on her 24 hours a day, the judge argued, he had no recourse but to order Sellers's hospitalization.

In effect, the judge had called upon a locally known and shared version of the technical designation 'gravely disabled' to warrant his decision to commit. If an observer were to casually look in on a few cases at Metropolitan Court, he or she would likely be baffled at the seeming inconsistency and arbitrariness in the application of the law. Indeed, attorneys and judges who were temporarily assigned to Metropolitan Court sometimes experienced a sort of professional vertigo as they found it difficult to recognize laws as they were situationally formulated and used. They found working within the local culture to be akin to following Alice in Wonderland down the rabbit hole.

Knowing the working meaning-making context of the court, however, provides an interpretive schema within which the particulars of individual cases can make local sense. (See Garfinkel, 1967, for a general discussion of the documentary method of interpretation, or Holstein, 1987, for a local demonstration of the documentary method.) In this case, Sellers's mention of the rocketship was not cited as evidence of delusions per se. It was taken for granted that she was, at times, delusional. Within the local context, however, the delusional statement was taken to be a practical marker of Sellers's inability to function in consequential social situations. The emergence of delusional talk was evidence of grave disability not because it revealed psychiatric problems, but because it portended social troubles. In effect, the judge argued that Sellers was unable to keep her delusions in check when the chips were down. Only knowledge of the local culture of decision-making knowledge gleaned more or less from the top down makes this understanding possible.

The upshot of our consideration of the local and broader *whats* of these courtroom proceedings and the *hows* of their emergence in talk-in-interaction, can go a long way – but not all the way – toward explaining how Lisa Sellers came to make and sustain the rocketship revelation. One could not deduce the consequences of the production of this and subsequent utterances unless one knew something about the local and broader substantive contexts of the utterance that elicited the 'Oh really?' response from the DA. The point we would like to emphasize here is that the meaning of Lisa Sellers's words played an important role in the outcome of her situation. *What* she said is as important as *how* she said it – not more or less.

We stress that neither is more important than the other. Because the two are *reflexive*, they are, in effect, mutually constitutive. To look at one and ignore the other is to miss the full picture. To say that conversational or interactional context is more consequential or foundational than situational, institutional, or cultural context – or vice versa – is to miss our central point altogether. That point, phrased differently, is that proximal and distal aspects of social context are always reflexively at play, and to emphasize one and diminish the importance of the other is to obviate the possibility of understanding the way context comes to bear on social experience. This, of course, would undermine any nuanced understanding of the phenomena of interest.

CONTEXTUAL ALTERNATIVES

The 'it depends' factor in understanding social action and experience is remarkably complex.

Because context can be consequential in both its conversational and cultural manifestations, we can turn to these *how* and *what* contingencies to help discern how meaningful interaction transpires. But there is a limit to this, since the practical reflexivity of 'it depends' in relation to contextual matters makes it virtually impossible to pin down exactly what a particular context might be at any particular moment, or how it might be used to make sense of everyday experience.

Conversation analysts tell us that context is continually emergent; each conversational action helps build a new context to which subsequent actions will respond (Heritage, 1984). Cultural and institutional contexts are similarly variable – either in their local conversational manifestation or their slightly more distant capacity as 'conditions of possibility' (Foucault, 1979). Specific sites tend to promote particular conditions of possibility, so contextual variability may be practically circumscribed to a certain extent. At the same time, however, the purview of any particular organization or institution is a situated achievement. All told, this leaves us with some sense of the possible directions social interaction might take, but it clearly doesn't allow us to anticipate or predict with certainty how interaction will unfold. Context simply isn't that determinant.

If we are to gain further analytic purchase on the role of context, we need to be constantly aware of the locally unarticulated contextual alternatives that can come into play at other times and places. While *how* and *what* questions turn us to the communicative mechanisms by which particular forms of everyday life are accomplished, these do not necessarily direct us in specific ways to the contextual alternatives that, from the top down, might inform particular sites of social interaction. For this, we might well raise two other types of questions – questions of *when* and *where* – while keeping in mind that *when* and *where*, empirically, are working features of everyday life. It is important to avoid the danger of treating analytic possibilities as empirical fact.

When questions would direct us to patterns or points in time at which distinct contexts come into play in particular settings. That is, any concrete setting might have distinct cultural and institutional contours at particular times. *Where* questions encourage us to seek out the various ways that a particular form of everyday life, such as commitment hearings or family gatherings, are organized in their meaning-making activities. Developing comparative strategies would broaden our knowledge of the 'it depends' quality of context by working *across* social settings to make visible how alternative forms of meaning-making are accomplished.

Working in relation to **when**

The *when* question became especially pertinent for one of the authors (Gubrium) as he and David Buckholdt conducted an ethnographic study of the everyday organization of inappropriate behavior in a residential treatment center for emotionally disturbed children named 'Cedarview' (Buckholdt and Gubrium, 1979). Initially, they attended to how emotional disturbance was discursively constructed in relation to what was locally available for assigning meaning to talk and interaction. *How* and *what* questions directed them to both talk-in-interaction and institutional meaning-making. Occasionally, however, when fieldwork extended beyond normal business hours, the pertinence of the *when* question loomed in significance. It became clear that the conduct and consequence of social interaction from 9 a.m. to 5 p.m. was not the same as at other times.

Cedarview was privately operated and under contract with local public schools and county welfare departments to improve children's learning skills, behavior management, and emotional control. At the time fieldwork was conducted, the public school's multidisciplinary assessment teams designated the children enrolled at Cedarview as emotionally disturbed. This officially transformed a variety of rather nebulous misbehaviors into something more concrete and pathological, yet treatable. When teachers, principals, and others generally felt these children to be too difficult to manage in the classroom, they were officially classified and subsequently remanded to residential centers such as Cedarview for therapy. Currently, the complex of behaviors and disturbances that were identified to single out children in need of treatment would likely be called attention deficit hyperactivity disorder (ADHD).

Cedarview's treatment program was based on behavioral programming, centered on an elaborate token economy. The children collected tokens for appropriate behaviors, which they could redeem for valued items at a facility store. They also could trade tokens for a variety of privileges, such as participating in extracurricular activities. The token economy was linked with a complex assessment system and treatment regimen in which targeted misconduct – such as 'swearing behavior', 'teasing behavior', and 'off-task fantasizing' – were measured before treatment (called 'baselining') and at intervals during treatment (called 'postbaselining'). The token economy, assessment system, and treatment program were major components of the prevailing therapeutic discourse and the local technology of behavior construction and modification.

To provide a sense of how the assessment system worked in practice during regular business hours, consider an episode of baselining surrounding one child, Maurice Clay's, teasing behavior. During their observations, staff members focused especially on the child's body and much less on what the child expressed in speech. This was their way of 'staying out of the children's minds', as a consulting behavioral psychologist once advised at a psychiatric staffing meeting. Staff members regarded the child's body as a well-articulated surface of signs that could reveal children's disturbances.

Maurice was to be baselined while in special education teacher Sally Meath's classroom. Before the children arrived, two staff members – Joe Julian and Francine O'Brien – informed Meath about the assessment and took their places in the observation room at the back of the classroom. All classrooms at Cedarview had observation rooms, outfitted with sound equipment and one-way mirrors. When an observation room was darkened and the classroom was full of light, the one-way mirror was transparent only from the inside out. Savvy children, however, occasionally cupped their hands around their eyes immediately in front of the mirror, attempting to peak through the glass to see if anyone was watching, reversing the proverbial panopticon in place.

To start, Gubrium (the observer) joined the assessment team in the observation room and together they waited for the children to take their seats and settle down before the baselining began. Julian and O'Brien were to tally how many times Maurice teased (exhibited teasing behavior) in a predesignated time period. The following conversation, reconstructed from fieldnotes, soon unfolded. Note the extent to which Maurice's body figured in quantifying pertinent features of the conduct under consideration. This and other conversation extracts were part of the focus at the time on the *whats* and *hows* of context in the assessment process.

Observer: Who are you baselining today?
Julian: Maurice Clay. I'm getting his teasing behavior.
Observer: What's teasing behavior?
Julian: Look at these categories [hands rating sheet to the observer]. It's considered teasing if he hits, touches, makes faces or negative comments, or does any name-calling during work time.

Julian and O'Brien soon turned to the classroom. There was a long pause as they centered their attention on Maurice. Julian eventually expressed his disappointment that 'nothin'' was happening and that, instead, Maurice was fantasizing. This prompted the following exchange:

Julian: Damn! I should have done fantasizing this week and teasing last week. He was teasing a lot then, but nothin' now. Just look at him staring into space – that's fantasizing if I ever saw it.
Observer: How do we know what fantasizing is?
Julian: Good point. I guess I really couldn't count staring into space like that. We only count verbal stuff for that. He may be staring into space, but is really thinking about his work. Who knows? So we only count verbal stuff like when he talks about Mr Greaso, Spiderman, or Super-what's-his name.

Notice how a possible shift in attention from teasing to fantasizing behavior provided working rules for interpreting Maurice's body to signify a different form of misbehavior. Concurrently, the institutional discourse of behavior deficits, treatment, and progress was artfully crafted in the colorful terms of what Julian took to be locally understood. This shift in context gave fantasizing extemporaneous meaning, figuring it in immediately recognizable ways, while still adhering to the institutional assumptions about behavioral embodiment. The *whats* in which Julian and O'Brien were interested – emotional disturbances – were reproduced through skillful rule formation in talk-in-interaction. Documenting *how* this was done made visible the various ways that staff members constructed meaning according to a distinct therapeutic culture.

Such episodes of assessment and the language of disturbance and treatment were observed and heard time and again during the fieldwork: in observation rooms, within classrooms proper, in counseling sessions, in psychiatric staffings, and in behavioral assessment training sessions. The documentation of related practices became a body of growing evidence about the institutional construction of identities by way of the discourse of disturbance. Observation of the *hows* and *whats* of the setting increasingly convinced the researchers that Cedarview staffers were skillfully and systematically constructing the subjects they needed to do their work. Cedarview, in short, was a setting that, through its elaborate constructive technology, was both producing and transforming emotionally disturbed children.

The pertinence of possible *when* questions wasn't obvious at first. As is typical in organizational fieldwork, Gubrium and Buckholdt assumed that they were gathering data on the *hows* and *whats* of emotional disturbance that operated round the clock. They assumed that the children, once constructed as emotionally disturbed and assessed accordingly, were viewed in these terms throughout their stay at Cedarview. What Joe Julian and Francine O'Brien were 'doing with words' in the observation room of the preceding extracts was what they and others did with words at Cedarview in general.

In time, however, the researchers came upon a simple phrase used by the children that had remarkable significance for contextual alternatives. They began to notice that around midafternoon on Fridays, children would respond to staff members' comments about their disturbances and the consequences of inappropriate behaviors with some version of the phrase, 'Oh, come on, it's the weekend'. Staff didn't dismiss the usage and clearly didn't respond as forcefully to the conduct in question in terms of the institutional discourse that we had assumed to be generally in place. Staff members knew that, in just a matter of hours, they would be absent until Monday and couldn't effectively enforce the behavior modification program in the same way they might have during the week, or earlier in the day on Fridays. The children, in turn, knew that there would be a skeleton staff in place over the weekend, most of whose members were merely custodial, not the behavioral programming specialists who ran the show during regular business hours.

Use of and responses to the phrase 'come on, it's the weekend' were accompanied by a range of comments and reactions not typical of weekdays. For their part, the children tended not to care as much about the consequences of verbal and behavioral indiscretions. It wasn't that the staff didn't respond to them with consequences, but staff responses were couched less in behavioral terms than they were in the vocabulary of informal persuasion and interpersonal accommodation. For example, in response to a 'Oh, come on, it's the weekend', a staff member once remarked, 'Okay, if you're going to be that way about it, don't count on me to shoot baskets with you tomorrow'. The institutional language of disturbance and behavioral treatment wasn't fully in effect from about mid-Fridays until Monday morning; it was replaced by a more casual

language and expectations for relationships that allowed staffers and the children to deal with each for the duration of the weekend. This is not to say that the discourse of disturbance disappeared, but rather that an alternative context, expressed in a different, more personalized language, was brought into play by both the children and the staff.

Recognizing the effects of *when* on how the setting was understood suggested that 'it depends' not only on what meanings presumably were in place and how those meanings and variations on them were articulated, but also that *how* and especially *what* were circumscribed in time. While the *hows* of the matter might be figured to be unimpeded by time, because the machinery of conversation cuts across time borders, it was found that even in this regard Cedarview staff members were more alert to the details of children's conversational expression during regular business hours than otherwise. While staff were oriented mainly to bodily signs as strong behaviorists, they also tuned in to long pauses, interruptions, and other features of children's conversations as possible indicators of misdeed, insolence, and other forms of disturbed behavior, but this was less evident after hours. At the very least, when such conversational events were noticed after hours, they weren't as readily construed as signs of disturbance. Instead they more commonly were figured to be problems of daily living. In this way, the *hows* of the matter came under the contextual purview of an interpersonal weekend; the normal institutional discourse went on holiday, so to speak. What Joe Julian and Francine O'Brien deftly did with words during the weekday when Gubrium and Buckholdt observed them was probably not what they would have done on the weekend. In their glibber moments, the researchers began to say that at Cedarview, as at other places like it, emotional disturbance starts at around 9 a.m. Monday mornings and comes to an end on Friday afternoons. It didn't actually punch a time clock, but, in effect, the language of disturbance worked a five-day week.

Working in relation to **where**

If time at Cedarview became an important contextual alternative, Gubrium's (1986) field study of support groups for the home caregivers of Alzheimer's disease (AD) sufferers showed how much alternative support group settings could figure in meaning-making. Gubrium's observations found that support groups that formed in varied settings, developed distinct local cultures of understanding regarding the caregiving experience. Some were highly structured and others rather loose and fluid. These *wheres*, which varied in place rather than time, colored both the *whats* and *hows* of what went on in the caregiving groups.

A comparison of the local cultures of contrasting support groups illustrates this contextual effect. First, consider Dee's support group, which was facilitated by two experienced caregivers. The group shared a fairly common set of understandings that govern AD support groups. The perspective centered on the notion that the typical AD caregiving experience has a normal course of development. This 'life course' was conveyed in terms of the burdens of the so-called 36-hour day that caregiving allegedly entails; it resembled Elisabeth Kübler-Ross's (1969) stage model of the dying process. In this group, members take it for granted that caregivers initially orient to the sufferer's recovery; the caregiver's own needs are ignored and caregivers devote 36-hour days to the care receiver. While caregivers eventually acknowledge the general inevitability of the sufferer's decline, they refuse to believe it applies to their own afflicted family member and enter a stage of denial. Caregivers may feel guilty that they are not doing enough for the afflicted member or that they occasionally inadvertently place their own welfare ahead of the care receiver. As domestic life goes from bad to worse, with no hope for recovery for the sufferer and no relief in sight for the caregiver, caregivers enter a stage of depression. Soon, it is hoped, caregivers move on to the final stages, when they realize that there is more at stake in caregiving than the affliction. In this stage, as the caregivers take stock of the personal and familial impact of the disease, they recognize the inevitability of full dementia. Their attention then centers on institutionalization or nursing home placement 'for the sake of all concerned'.

Dee's group shared this understanding, which was especially evident when group members resisted viewing what they were 'going through' in these stage-like terms. As the following extract from a group meeting shows, group members were held accountable to the local culture of the group even when they felt its experiential stages didn't apply to them. The extract follows an extended discussion between Anne, Ruth, and Belle about how similar the course of their care experiences have been. They discuss their troubles in terms of familiar stages, which finally lead them to recognize the limits of caregiver responsibility. Anne and Ruth are the group's facilitators and the discussion soon centers on Dee's contrasting experience. (We should note that some group members, such as Belle and Dora, continue to participate in support giving after they have institutionalized their afflicted family member.)

Dee: I don't know, Belle. Sure, I can see what happened, why you decided to start looking for a place [nursing home] for Harold [Belle's demented husband]. I guess if I was in your shoes, I wouldn't fight it anymore either. You do have to start thinking about how you feel inside and what's happening to your family. ...

Dora: [To Dee]. Well then, dear, what's your problem? We're all in this together. You're no different, you just think you are. I was like you once. [Elaborates] I did everything. I had no time to think. It was get this, do that, and take care of Ben [her husband] 24 hours a day. Well, I learned the hard way and nearly put myself in the hospital. Ben's on the waiting list [for nursing home placement] at Pine Crest. God help me, it won't come too soon.

Belle: I don't think I'm ready for that yet, but I know I'll have to pretty soon. I know it's coming. It's only a matter of time.

Dee: I don't think it's that simple, Belle.

Anne: Oh, come on, Dee. That's what it is in a nutshell. You have to start thinking about yourself. [Elaborates] Look at you. You're all worn down and I'll bet you're feeling lonely and depressed.

Dee: No, that's what I was trying to explain last time. I'm really not lonely. I'm. ...

Ruth: You're denying. We all try to deny it.

Ruth's final comment – which takes issue with Dee's alleged feelings – became a springboard for elaborating the group's stage model of the caregiving experience. Following this extracted part of the conversation, there was an extended discussion of denial, its workings, and how the stage model applies to several caregivers, including Dee. Participants concretized and embellished the model out of their individual experiences in a 'documentary method of interpretation' (Garfinkel, 1967), mutually reaffirming empirically that the caregiving experience comes in stages. The local care culture was reflexively constituted in the process – what 'everyone' said was what they all knew and shared.

Dee was faced with the challenge of accounting for why her experience was different, which she took up by arguing that she had no other family members to worry about who deserved her care as much as her husband did. As she succinctly put it, 'Gordon's my family', implying that she had no one else to think about. Indeed, at one point, Dee explained that if she had had other family members – say, children in her care – 'I'd probably be going through all the phases of this thing'. This account, which also affirmed the group's shared understanding of the caregiving experience, seemed to pass muster for a while, but the group soon reasserted the need to get through all the stages so as to overcome the personal and familial travails of denial.

Other support groups, in different settings, had strikingly different caregiving cultures. They had little or no prevailing view of a normal course of development for the caregiving experience. In these groups, meetings consisted mostly of shared thoughts and feelings about previous weeks' home happenings. Answer to questions of personal responsibility in home care were considered in terms of continuous interpersonal comparison, unmediated by an overarching sense of 'what we all know'.

These contrasting *wheres* of context occasionally presented themselves to members as interpretive choices. This was particularly telling one evening when a member of one of the support groups with no prevailing view of the caregiving experience referred with irritation to the group 'across town' that she used to attend. This caregiver had become quite dissatisfied with her previous group. As she explained, that group was always telling her what she was going through. She indicated that whenever anyone felt differently or figured that they were moving in a direction at odds with that of other members, the group accused the deviant member of 'denying'. She even exasperatedly noted that she could hardly take a breath or pause without some group member jumping in or otherwise interrupting her with the locally prevailing opinion on the caregiving experience – thus directly implicating even the local *hows* of the matter. She eventually commented that she was glad to now be attending a group that would listen to her and not make her feel guilty for saying the wrong things. This caregiver, in effect, made a contextual choice. She selected an interpretive context in which she would be held accountable in a way more acceptable to her. In choosing where she attended a support group, she affected the understandings to which she would be subject, as well as the communicative regime that articulated it.

CONCLUSION

As we have seen, context can be worked up from the conversational ground floor. It can also work on situated interaction from a distance, implicating culture, time, place, and other everyday contingencies. Qualitative researchers should always be aware of this as they, themselves, work up, down, and across context as an object of analysis. The overall lesson is that context is a complex phenomenon; appeals to context in qualitative analysis raise complex issues and should not be taken for granted. We conclude this chapter by highlighting several related points.

First, qualitative researchers must be careful about the analytic and empirical horizons that they open up under the rubric of context. As our examples have demonstrated, there isn't a lone, immutable realm of circumstances that might confidently be called *the* context of any particular action or interaction. Context cannot be singularly defined. As Charles Goodwin and Alessandro Duranti have argued, it isn't possible 'to give a single, precise, technical definition of context, and eventually we may have to accept that such a definition may not be possible' (1992: 2). The lack of a singular definition of context should not dissuade qualitative researchers from examining the effects and ramifications of social context, but it compels us to clearly specify those factors that we will draw under this rubric.

As they specify and employ context as an analytic topic or referent, qualitative researchers should appeal to context only by way of its empirical manifestations. Too often, analysts make overtures to social context – often as an independent variable – with no empirical warrant whatsoever. Social structure, social class, social integration, social disorganization, and other overarching constructs are commonly invoked without empirical specification or description of just what these social 'things' might amount to in the situation being examined. While a singular definition of context may not be possible, those empirical manifestations that one chooses to consider must be demonstrated if context is to be brought on board in service to analysis. This requires the analyst to demonstrate empirically the linkage between action and contextual effects.

For those interested in studying social structures, traces of those structures and their linkages should be made apparent as they bear upon locally situated activity. Those studying talk-in-interaction must acknowledge the extra-situational empirical sources of meaning that necessarily inform situated interaction – in particular, the larger *whats* that impel us to talk in particular ways and that present distinct consequences for doing so. Context cannot simply be invoked by fiat or presumed from the details of social interaction. It must be described and analyzed as it is more or less recognized by, or related to, members and their activities (Gubrium and Holstein, 1997; Schegloff, 1997).

Even as context is empirically documented, qualitative researchers should be careful not to reify or 'freeze' it into a static entity. As we have illustrated from our own work, context is emergent, variable, and highly elastic. Of course, it must be stopped in its tracks momentarily to allow for description and analysis. Still, the analyst should never assume that a particular aspect of context will operate the same way in other circumstances or that social actors will appeal to, or use, context in precisely the same fashion all of the time. Context is better understood as an occasioned phenomenon, built up (or down) across the real-time, situational circumstances in question.

Qualitative researchers should also be wary of conferring determinative powers upon aspects of context. Sociologists, for example, are fond of attributing causal power to social structure, but are less adept at specifying how social structures actually manifest themselves in everyday life. Some qualitative analysts, for example, are prone to suggest that particular aspects of context – such as the material conditions of economic or class relations – automatically, or through a rather nebulous process such as 'habitus', form characteristic social outcomes (see, e.g., Bourdieu, 1977).

Our caution stems from orienting to context as a practical accomplishment. As such, context is unlikely to have the opportunity, let alone the deterministic power, to operate independently from everyday life. As context is built up, down, or across its venues, it is actively consulted and used, in effect specifying the 'conditions of possibility' (Foucault, 1979) that become a compelling force in social interaction.

Finally, by employing a metaphor of context that resiliently stretches from far to near, from top or bottom, and across time and social space, we have avoided suggestions of foundationalism. We have tried to remain agnostic about the point of departure that should be taken or the emphasis that should be given to either communication, situation, or culture in the analysis of context. Working from the bottom up, from the top down, or across contexts should be a matter of preference and research interest, not a dictate of dogma. Being doctrinaire is simply too costly in explanatory payoff.

To insist on starting at the top – at the level of culture, say – and working down toward interaction risks needlessly overlooking the detailed elements of conversational context that help explain how, and even why, particular actions take place when and where they do (Schegloff, 1997). Put strongly, 'Invoking social structure at the outset can systematically distract from, even blind us to, details of [organized social conduct] in the world' (Schegloff, 1991: 61). An insistence on looking primarily at the 'big picture' can virtually shut down attention to the actual and integral dynamics of social interaction. This amounts to an inexcusable loss of data (Maynard, 2003) that should discomfit qualitative researchers.

On the other hand, to insist on starting with, and attending primarily to, the sequential development of conversation can lead researchers to bury themselves in the procedural *hows* of interaction at the risk of providing little or no sense of the consequences of forms of talk or choices that speakers have in the matter. In doing so, researchers may fail to acknowledge the extent to which interpretive resources are hung on sequential scaffoldings in order to make (speech) acts meaningful in terms that members, as well as analysts, understand. Some have even suggested that devoting too much attention to the minutiae of sequential development leads analysts to miss the forest of meaningful social life for the trees of adjacency pairs and repair sequences.

Our recommendation is that the point of departure – or even the primary emphasis – is not as important as the ultimate product of the analysis. Qualitative researchers have wasted too much time and effort talking and writing past one another about the necessity of one point of departure or another (see, e.g., Schegloff, 1997, 1999a, 1999b; Billig, 1999a, 1999b). It would seem far more productive to devote our attention to finding rigorous ways of examining social context and the ways that the *hows* and the *whats* (as well as the *whens* and *wheres*) of interaction reflexively constitute that which can be situationally construed as consequential social context. Recently, Douglas Maynard (2003), for example, has attempted to develop conversation analysis in relation to social context by clearly indicating the ways in which he will incorporate select aspects of more distal context into his close examination of sequential context. In doing so, he specifies several ways in which he can exploit a 'limited affinity' between conversation analysis and ethnography. This allows his 'from the bottom up' approach to specifically acknowledge when the analyst is drawing upon resources beyond the sequential context under consideration. The approach is more open to the complexities of context than many conversation analysts have been in their insistence on starting at, and concentrating on, the conversational bottom of interaction.

Not wanting to privilege any particular point of departure, elsewhere we have outlined a more inclusive perspective for studying social life in context, outlining a procedure we have called 'analytic bracketing' (Gubrium and Holstein, 1997, 2000a). In this approach, the qualitative researcher alternately orients to everyday realities as both the *products* of members' reality-constructing procedures and as *resources* from which realities are constituted. At one moment, the analyst may be more-or-less indifferent to the structures of everyday life in order to document their production through discursive practice (e.g. talk-in-interaction). In the next analytic move, he or she brackets discursive practice in order to assess the local availability, timing, distribution, and/or regulation of resources for reality construction. This places particular activities or circumstances in the foreground at one moment, while assigning others to the analytic (and contextual) background. Following this, at the next analytic step, the positions are reversed, with the backgrounded phenomenon moving to the foreground. In this way, the ever-changing sense of social context can be accommodated by the alternating analytic perspectives.

Analytic bracketing thus amounts to an orienting procedure for flexibly attending to the *whats, hows, whens,* and *wheres* of social life in order to assemble both a contextually scenic and a contextually constructive picture of everyday life. Either constitutive interactional sequential environments or available discursive resources become the provisional phenomenon of interest, while the other is temporarily consigned to the analytic periphery. In a sense, the constant interplay in the analysis mirrors the lived interplay between social interaction, its immediate interactional environment, and its more distant going concerns (Hughes, 1984).

Because talk-in-interaction and discourses-in-practice are mutually constitutive, one cannot argue that analysis should begin or end with either one, although one is surely entitled to preferences and predilections. Some prefer to begin closer to the top. Dorothy Smith and her colleagues (see Smith, 1987, 1999; DeVault and McCoy, 2002), for example, advocate beginning where people are located within the institutional landscapes of everyday life. Conversely, conversation analysts insist on beginning at the bottom with discursive practice. Wherever one starts, neither the cultural and institutional facets of discourse nor its interpolations in social interaction predetermines the other. If we set aside the need for an indisputable resolution to this question, we can designate a reasonably useful point of departure and proceed from there to specify the research phenomenon and its context in relation to our research interests.

Ultimately, there is no pressing need to decide, once and for all, the most appropriate framework for dealing with context. Qualitative inquiry would be better served if researchers made principled choices regarding their analytic vantage points, and acknowledged their priorities, predilections, and challenges. Casting context as overarching forces working to constrain action can prevent the analyst from seeing the nearly invisible structures that provide the very scaffolding of everyday life. Focusing too hard on these structures, can prevent qualitative researchers from acknowledging social conditions that are virtually staring them in the face. Both positions on how to characterize context will benefit from viewing context as something that can be worked up, down, and across in the interest of comprehensive qualitative inquiry.

REFERENCES

Billig, Michael (1999a) 'Whose terms? Whose ordinariness? Rhetoric and ideology in conversation analysis', *Discourse and Society*, 10: 543–58.

Billig, Michael (1999b) 'Conversation analysis and the claims of naivety', *Discourse and Society*, 10: 572–6.

Bourdieu, Pierre (1977) *Outline of a Theory of Practice*. Cambridge: Cambridge University Press.

Buckholdt, David R. and Gubrium, Jaber F. (1979) *Caretakers: Treating Emotionally Disturbed Children*. Beverly Hills, CA: Sage.

Coulter, Jeff (1975) 'Perceptual accounts and interpretive asymmetries', *Sociology*, 9: 385–96.

DeVault, Marjorie L. and McCoy, Liza (2002) 'Institutional ethnography: using interviews to investigate ruling relations', in J.F. Gubrium and J.A. Holstein (eds), *Handbook of Interview Research*. Thousand Oaks, CA: Sage, pp. 751–76.

Drew, Paul and Heritage, John (eds) (1992) *Talk at Work*. Cambridge: Cambridge University Press.

Foucault, Michel (1965) *Madness and Civilization: A History of Insanity in the Age of Reason*. New York: Vintage Books.

Foucault, Michel (1979) *Discipline and Punish*. New York: Vintage Books.

Garfinkel, Harold (1967) *Studies in Ethnomethodology*. Englewood Cliffs, NJ: Prentice-Hall.

Goodwin, Charles and Duranti, Alessandro (1992) 'Rethinking context', in A. Duranti and C. Goodwin (eds), *Rethinking Context: Language as an Interactive Phenomenon*. Cambridge: Cambridge University Press, pp. 1–42.

Gubrium, Jaber F. (1986) *Oldtimers and Alzheimer's: The Descriptive Organization of Senility*. Greenwich, CT: JAI Press.

Gubrium, Jaber F. and Holstein, James A. (1997) *The New Language of Qualitative Method*. New York: Oxford University Press.

Gubrium, Jaber F. and Holstein, James A. (2000a) 'Analyzing interpretive practice', in N. Denzin and Y. Lincoln (eds), *Handbook of Qualitative Research*, (2nd ed.). Thousand Oaks, CA: Sage, pp. 487–508.

Gubrium, Jaber F. and Holstein, James A. (2000b) *Institutional Selves: Troubled Identities in a Postmodern World*. New York: Oxford University Press.

Heritage, John (1984) *Garfinkel and Ethnomethodology*. Cambridge: Polity Press.

Holstein, James A. (1987) 'Mental illness assumptions in civil commitment proceedings', *Journal of Contemporary Ethnography*, 16: 147–75.

Holstein, James A. (1993) *Court-Ordered Insanity: Interpretive Practice and Involuntary Commitment*. Hawthorne, NY: Aldine de Gruyter.

Holstein, James A. and Gubrium, Jaber F. (2000) *The Self We Live By: Narrative Identity in a Postmodern World*. New York: Oxford University Press.

Hughes, Everett C. (1984) 'Going concerns: the study of American institutions', in D. Riesman and H. Becker (eds), *The Sociological Eye*. New Brunswick, NJ: Transaction Books, pp. 52–64.

Kübler-Ross, Elisabeth (1969) *On Death and Dying*. New York: Macmillan.

Maynard, Douglas W. (1980) 'Placement of topic changes in conversation', *Semiotica*, 30: 263–90.

Maynard, Douglas W. (2003) *Bad News, Good News: Conversational Order in Everyday Talk and Clinical Settings*. Chicago: University of Chicago Press.

Mehan, Hugh. (1991) 'The school's work of sorting students', in D. Zimmerman and D. Boden (eds), *Talk and Social Structure*. Cambridge: Polity Press, pp. 71–90.

Pollner, Melvin (1987) *Mundane Reason*. Cambridge: Cambridge University Press.

Sacks, Harvey (1992) *Lectures on Conversation*, vols I and II. Oxford: Blackwell.

Sacks, Harvey, Schegloff, Emanuel and Jefferson, Gale (1974) 'A simplest systematics for the organization of turn-taking for conversation', *Language*, 50: 696–735.

Schegloff, Emanuel A. (1982) 'Discourse as an interactional achievement: some uses of "uh huh" and other things that come between sentences', in D. Tannen (ed.), *Georgetown University Roundtable on Language and Linguistics*. Washington, DC: Georgetown University Press, pp. 71–93.

Schegloff, Emanuel A. (1991) 'Reflections on talk and social structure', in D. Boden and D. Zimmerman (eds), *Talk and Social Structure*. Cambridge: Polity Press, pp. 44–70.

Schegloff, Emanuel A. (1997) 'Whose text? Whose context?', *Discourse and Society*, 8: 165–87.

Schegloff, Emanuel A. (1999a) ' "Schegloff's text as Billig's data": a critical reply', *Discourse and Society*, 10: 558–72.

Schegloff, Emanuel A. (1999b) 'Naivete vs. sophistication or discipline vs. self-indulgence: a rejoinder to Billig', *Discourse and Society*, 10: 577–82.

Sheridan, Alan (1980) *The Will to Truth*. New York: Tavistock.

Silverman, David (1998) *Harvey Sacks: Conversation Analysis and Social Science*. New York: Oxford University Press.

Smith, Dorothy E. (1987) *The Everyday World as Problematic*. Boston: Northeastern University Press.

Smith, Dorothy E. (1999) *Writing the Social*. Toronto: University of Toronto Press.

Warren, Carol A.B. (1980) *The Court of Last Resort*. Chicago: University of Chicago Press.

Wittgenstein, Ludwig (1953) *Philosophical Investigations*. New York: Macmillan.

20

Working qualitatively and quantitatively

Julia Brannen

Qualitative and quantitative research have been represented as two fundamentally different paradigms through which to study the social world. These paradigms act as lightning conductors to which sets of epistemological assumptions, theoretical approaches and methods are attracted and that are treated as incompatible across paradigms (Bryman, 2001: 445) These paradigmatic claims resurface throughout the history of the social sciences and seem set to continue in the future since, on the one hand, qualitative approaches embrace even greater reflexivity, and on the other hand, quantitative research adopts ever more complex statistical techniques.

At the same time, there are pressures towards convergence that suggest a move away from the separate paradigms model. One pressure towards convergence arises from the ways in which boundaries around social science disciplines are being eroded (Bernstein, 2000). Erosion occurs in the context of increased demands from research funders for researchers to be more responsive to the needs of policy-makers and the potential range of different interest groups seeking to 'use' research. Such pressures influence both the questions posed in the research and also the ways researchers write up research for those audiences. The theoretical aspect of research that is underpinned by disciplinary specialisms is thereby weakened. The declining importance of theoretical concerns is accompanied by the downplaying of methodological concerns – that is, fundamental questions concerning what data 'are' and how knowledge is generated. The aim of methodology is well described by Kaplan in the 1960s: 'to describe and analyse [these] methods, throwing light on their limitations and resources, clarifying their presuppositions and consequences. ... In sum the aim of methodology is to help us to *understand* [emphasis in the

original], in the broadest possible terms, not the products of scientific enquiry but the process itself' (Kaplan, 1964: 23). Instead growing importance is given to research methods, that is, to the techniques employed in the collection and manipulation of data. In this context, research practice becomes chiefly a technical matter concerning the application of skills. While the trend towards greater methodological competence and skill is to be welcomed, there is a risk that learning to conduct research will be reduced to the 'transfer of skills' if this process becomes divorced from the wider processes of enculturation into the social sciences. In that sense the separate paradigms approach may be a healthy sign that theory and method are still matters for scientific debate.

PARADIGMS OR RESEARCH STRATEGIES

Before turning to the practice of research, I do not propose to rehearse once again the epistemological arguments that qualitative and quantitative approaches are fundamentally different (see, e.g., Bryman, 1988, 2001, and Hammersley, 1992, for a discussion of the problems in making such assumptions). I shall simply highlight the dichotomies that are typically proposed and the arguments that have been put forward to suggest that the notion of different paradigms defies the ways in which research is carried out in practice. According to Hammersley (1992), the following distinctions are said to make qualitative and quantitative research unsuitable bedfellows: (1) that qualitative research uses words while quantitative research uses numbers; (2) that the former focuses on meanings while the latter is concerned with behaviour; (3) that the former relies on an inductive logic of inquiry while the latter utilizes the hypothetic-deductive method; (4) that qualitative research lacks quantitative research's power to generalize.

There is, as Hammersley (1992) has argued, a lack of robustness in these distinctions. The association of qualitative research with words rather than numbers is simplistic and is closely related to the issue of meaning, the logic of inquiry and the question of generalizability. Choice of research design and method is in practice likely to depend upon the nature of the research problem or problems. For example, how important is it within a research inquiry to be able to estimate the frequency of a particular defined phenomenon according to other pre-defined variables and to be able to generalize those frequencies and their associations to a parent population (issues: (1) quantification and (4) generalizability)? How important is it to be able to describe a particular social process or to create a typology of different modes of relationship? How far is it the study's aim to test a hypothesis and how far to generate new hypotheses (issue 3)? How important is it to find out how people think about a particular social phenomenon (issue 2) or how important is it to know which people have a particular view concerning particular representations of the phenomenon? It is of course entirely feasible to have more than one aim within the same research investigation. The aims and questions posed by many research investigations are varied and cannot be addressed by a single research approach or strategy. In such a case, a study may employ a variety of samples, methods of data collection and types of analysis to address different research questions or aspects of a research question. A multi-method approach is thus likely to be called for in many types of investigation. Moreover, some researchers prefer to 'triangulate' their approach by using a variety of methods to study the same phenomenon (Webb et al., 1966).

My own view is that ontological and epistemological assumptions and theoretical considerations are relevant to the choice of research method. However, there is no necessary linkage between assumptions on the one hand, and methodological approaches on the other. One ontological/epistemological stance may lead to very different kinds of methods; for example, researchers who adopt a realist stance may adopt either qualitative or quantitative methods, or both. While the choice of methods may be shaped in the context of inquiry – the research design phase – they need again to be questioned in the context of justification when the data

are analysed and interpreted. As Smith and Heshusius (1986) suggest, in the context of justification the resulting datasets cannot be linked together unproblematically. It is at this phase that ontological, epistemological and theoretical issues raise their heads, that is, when we reflect on different kinds of 'truth' and 'validity'. Different types of data need to be seen as constituted by the assumptions and methods that elicit them. In this perspective, qualitative and quantitative data need to be treated as broadly *complementary*, though not necessarily as compatible, rather than as adding up to some rounded reality, as advocated by exponents of triangulation (Denzin, 1970).

In rejecting the logic of the paradigms argument, the dichotomy between qualitative and quantitative research has been rejected on the grounds that research is complex and diversified *in practice* (Hammersley, 1992, 1996; Bryman, 1988, 1992, 2001). This is not, however, to argue against the value of elaborating and debating different epistemological and theoretical approaches to the study of social phenomena or to argue that every social inquiry necessarily requires a range of different methods. However, as I shall indicate in discussing some of my own research practice, even social inquiries with a single theoretical focus and method may require that the researchers contextualize their research in relation to others' research and other datasets. In such cases it is likely that these data will have been generated by different methods and assumptions which will need to be addressed in making comparisons with one's own findings.

Although the distinctions often asserted between qualitative and quantitative research emerge as less robust under closer examination, none the less clear differences exist between qualitative and quantitative *researchers*. Indeed the differences look set to widen in some respects among researchers of both persuasions. There are also different fashions *among* qualitative and quantitative researchers, each with their attendant risks. For example, the current turn to reflexivity in qualitative research in respect of the focus upon the researcher risks neglecting research participants. By contrast, in some current versions of participatory research, there is the opposite risk whereby researchers attribute to their research participants a monopoly over meaning. There is a danger here of downplaying the interpretative role of the researcher. As qualitative researchers, we seek to understand the perspectives of the Other, but our explanations for patterns of social action often lie outside those that the informants themselves provide (Hammersley, 1989).

Moreover research questions and the ways in which they are operationalized in decisions concerning research design and choice of methods are shaped by the biographies of researchers. Those who pursue only one method or approach, while they may rationalize what they do in terms of what they see to be fundamental distinctions of ontology, epistemology or theory, may well develop particular expertise or preferences for particular approaches. This in turn may mean that they lack the time and inclination to extend their skills and interests in other directions (Brannen, 1992).

Research practice is also shaped by the different types of working environments that researchers inhabit – academia, independent research organizations, government and other policy environments – and the different employment contracts that researchers hold, for example fixed-term contracts or tenured academic status. Research biographies and research environments are moreover shaped in particular historical contexts. As Janet Finch argued in the mid-1980s, a preference in British government for quantitative evidence was long established in contrast to more pluralistic methodological preferences of US governments in the same period (Finch 1986). The importance placed upon research evidence and upon evidence of particular kinds is subject to changes in political climates and persuasions.

WAYS OF COMBINING QUALITATIVE AND QUANTITATIVE DATA

It is a matter of empirical investigation whether multi-method research is on the increase in different political and policy contexts as well as within social science research generally, though it seems to be so. As I shall indicate, to answer this question raises definitional issues, namely, how broadly or narrowly one defines the term 'multi-method research'. However, it is clear that researchers often pursue a variety of aims when they seek to combine different methods or types of data within a single research project.

Bryman (2001) discusses the combination of qualitative and quantitative data in terms of the 'strategies' researchers develop towards managing the research process. In developing a concept of 'multi-strategy research', Bryman discusses a classification created by Morgan (1988), which applies two criteria in distinguishing the ways in which qualitative and quantitative research are

combined: (a) the *importance* given to qualitative and quantitative approaches in the research investigation, and (b) the *time ordering* or sequencing of the approaches. Bryman suggests that such distinctions are not always possible in practice because they rely on being able to identify the dominance of one approach (Bryman, 2001: 448). Hammersley (1996) suggests a tripartite classification of the ways in which researchers employ different types of data in the processes of *interpreting* their data:

(a) Triangulation, where one type of data (usually quantitative) is used to *corroborate* another type of data (typically qualitative), as when theoretical insights are derived from one type of data which are also put to the test on another dataset.

(b) Facilitation, where collecting one type of data *facilitates* the collection of another type of data; for example, when qualitative interviewing methods are first employed in preliminary pilot work in order to help design a large-scale pre-coded survey.

(c) Complementarity, when two different sets of data are employed to address different but *complementary* aspects of an investigation; for example, qualitative data are used to understand social processes while quantitative data are employed to examine associations and their statistical generalizability to parent populations.

My own view is that in general it is preferable to treat qualitative and quantitative data as *complementary*, though not necessarily at ontological, epistemological and theoretical levels (Smith and Heshusius, 1986). Each dataset needs to be interpreted in relation to both the conceptualization of the research question and the method by which it was generated and, as I shall go on to argue, their role and status in the research process. Different types of data cannot be unproblematically added together in the context of justification to constitute a single truth or rounded reality.

THE FOCUS OF THE CHAPTER

In this chapter, I shall suggest that the purposes to which qualitative and quantitative data are put within different social investigations vary. Drawing upon my own research experience and practice, I shall argue that the importance and purpose of working qualitatively and quantitatively need to be understood in relation to their introduction into and status within the research process. When researchers work with different types of data within the same research project, the way in which they use these data will vary according to the *phase or aspect* of the research in which the researcher brings the different datasets into play. I shall illustrate the ways in which qualitative and quantitative data are employed in respect of different phases of the research process.

Before moving to this discussion, I shall first suggest that decisions about methodological approaches need to be understood more broadly within the context of the development of a research career. Research careers are shaped by the funding and organization of research, which need to be located and understood in a historical context. In order to indicate how my own preferences for and orientations towards particular methodological approaches developed over the course of my research career, I shall briefly relate part of my own research biography, first by placing it within a broader historical context. I shall identify some of the main influences that are shaping research careers today and those that directed me towards an engagement with both qualitative and quantitative data. As I shall suggest, these changes in terms of the funding and policy environment and within academe itself are fuelling the growth of both qualitative and quantitative researchers and they are moving social science research in more generic, less discipline-based directions, and are prioritizing the acquisition of multiple research skills. Such trends are likely to encourage, rather than work against, the practice of mixing methods.

RESEARCH CAREERS IN HISTORICAL CONTEXT

Over the period 1992–2002, demand for research has grown in Britain, especially from government, which has sought to make 'evidence-based policy'. The types of research required by major funders (government, research councils and charitable foundations) have also diversified, with increased demand for practical rather than scientific research (see Hammersley, 2000, for a discussion of this distinction). The effect of this demand is to weaken the power of disciplines over the organization and procedures of research as I have already intimated. Emphasis by those who fund research is moreover placed on making scientific research more accountable to funders and more accessible to users in terms of the representation of the research findings. Contractual relationships between funders and researchers are today increasingly specified while funded research is almost always required to be relevant to policy (with only a few notable exceptions). Indeed, in 1993 Britain's Economic and Social Research Council (ESRC) was required by government to provide trained social scientists to meet the needs of users and beneficiaries, thereby contributing to 'the economic competitiveness of the UK, the effectiveness of public services and the quality of life' (Marshall, 2002). In this endeavour, researchers today are required to communicate in 'double speak': in the specialized languages that define their fields (rather than disciplines) and in a generic language that addresses audiences of 'research users'. This emphasis on presentation seems likely moreover to increase the importance of qualitative data and its prominence in the way research is represented.

Both in Britain and in the US, as governments are put under increasing pressure to account for and formally evaluate their expenditure, there is a whole industry devoted to evaluation research. Increasingly, such research utilizes both qualitative and quantitative methods. There has also been a huge growth in researchers of different kinds, including increased demand for qualitative researchers. In the US, the demand for qualitative research has been caught up in the wider politics of interest groups who have argued that the benefits of government programmes to the poor did not show up in many quantitative studies (Ong, 1999). A similar debate seems set to take place in the UK. For example, the New Labour government currently evaluates its New Deals (employment programmes to encourage labour market participation among underemployed groups) chiefly by examining the numbers moving into work through these programmes. Yet the period of the employment programmes' introduction has coincided with a tight labour market, making it difficult to disentangle the causes of the rise in employment that is occurring both in the general population as well as among the clients of the programmes. In so far as the effects of the employment programmes need to be assessed in terms of their effects upon clients' employment orientations, and developments in their occupational trajectories and longer-term employability, other kinds of methods (i.e., qualitative research methods) are likely to be required as well.

The impetus for the expansion in research has come also from the institutional context of university funding. (Funding provided by government to British universities is allocated on the basis of qualitative and quantitative assessments of research productivity – the Research Assessment Exercise, RAE.) This has required that academics and researchers expand their reach into the growing markets of funded research. Such pressures apply across the board, bringing many new recruits, for example from the humanities, into funded research, especially into qualitative research. Those who are in more senior positions have to spend more time raising research funding and when they are successful they typically have to manage and work on several research projects simultaneously. Moreover, while in the past researchers may have spent long periods in their research careers working under the tutelage of more experienced researchers, there is pressure on today's researchers, especially those on the middle rungs of the research ladder, to find their own funding and to design and direct their own investigations, perhaps in some cases making them run before they can walk. Even when supervised by more senior researchers, those who are less senior are often given greater autonomy in practice than they might have been given formerly, since today's senior researchers are engaged much more in research management and in directing a number of research projects at the same time.

The pressures of research markets and the marketization of British universities in the 1990s and 2000s are themselves driving the increased demand for and emphasis upon the development of explicit models of institutional research training. However, an unintended consequence may be that the largely implicit models of research apprenticeship that prevailed throughout the 1960s and 1970s are being undermined. In the 1970s (when I was starting out on a research career in the UK), it was common for those seeking a career as a contract researcher to work as a research assistant with greater responsibility for data collection and data management than for research design, data analysis and writing. A rather ad hoc pattern of research apprenticeship operated in Britain at the time in which few researchers had higher degrees (certainly not PhDs) and few had taken formal courses in philosophy of science and research methodology at master's degree level. Researchers' orientations were largely discipline-based. In terms of their institutional status and employment conditions, there was a clear distinction between two groups: university teachers who tended to generate the funding and direct the research; and contract researchers who were dedicated to working on projects (on a part-time or full-time basis). This latter group of contract researchers, unlike their academic counterparts, had few other responsibilities. Moreover, in being largely trained on the job and less highly qualified than the academics, they were accorded lower status within the university. They were also typically female, a situation that has changed little at least in the UK.

Over the past twenty or so years, credentialism has grown among the researcher community (as among the general population), with increased emphasis on researcher enculturation through master's courses that offer generic research training across a broad range of social science disciplines. The arrival of a skills-based economy in which training has superseded notions of apprenticeship is as influential in research as elsewhere in the labour market. This has led to a demand from social science funding councils that research degrees should have an explicit research training component; in Britain, in the past ten to fifteen years, we have seen a steady expansion of master's degrees and other courses dedicated to research training. However, these changes have brought benefits also. One such benefit is that students on research-based master's courses have been introduced to both qualitative and quantitative methods, whereas in the past they have been less exposed to opportunities that open up the possibility of more varied research trajectories on the one hand and a range of different kinds of methods on the other.

SOME AUTOBIOGRAPHY

In the mid-1970s, following the completion of a master's course in social research (at the University of Surrey) that was the first of its kind in Britain, I embarked on a research career. Towards the end of the 1970s when I was seeking employment as a contract researcher, employment opportunities for new researchers were often located in large teams. The studies were large or medium scale while their methods were quantitative/statistical. My own research career did not begin in this way, since in my first funded research project I carried out a small-scale intensive study and took the main responsibility for the study from its design to its writing up (Brannen and Collard, 1982). However, as the study came to completion I decided that my next career move was to gain experience of working on a larger project and as part of a large research team. The next study I worked on was longitudinal. It was highly qualitative in its method of data collection. By contrast, in the analysis phase, the qualitative data were all coded according to a complex set of rating scales while statistical analysis techniques were employed in their manipulation. Together with my earlier research experience, this provided me with an opportunity to develop an interest in qualitative interviewing.

In my next employment, I was afforded the opportunity to build a qualitative element into a longitudinal study that was largely designed to be quantitative. After the study ended I was fortunate in being offered an opportunity to reflect on the ways I had worked with both qualitative and quantitative data. I was awarded a grant by the original funder (a government department) to write a paper on combining approaches for policy-makers and also asked to organize a seminar for government-funded researchers to discuss different ways of combining approaches and their advantages and disadvantages (Brannen, 1992). Following the dissemination of the paper within government, I was asked to convene a meeting with a very senior government scientist to expound on the merits of qualitative research.

If I had been interviewed then about my own preferences concerning research strategies or the direction of my research career, I doubt that I would have suggested any burning interest in working with both qualitative and quantitative data. As a sociologist who had also studied social anthropology at undergraduate level I was, however, attracted to particular kinds of research questions that related to meanings, understandings and rationalities. At the same time, ethno-methodological approaches, which were fashionable at the time, held little attraction for me. More fundamental at that time were political issues, which took me in two directions. First, arising out of a political interest in gender inequalities in the 1970s, I was concerned to make women and their perspectives more visible in social science research. Second, I wanted to understand how women interpreted their lives in the context of the structured inequalities in women's access to power and resources. The latter concern took me down a qualitative route and the endeavour to understand agency and actors' perspectives, while the former concern led me to an interest in social structure and to an examination of statistical indicators of women's inequality. In making sense of women's social worlds, my concern therefore was to connect micro and macro levels. My interest was more political than theoretical; I considered that the knowledge that research generated should help in the process of bringing about social change, notably in the lives of women and men.

It was also the case that my political interest in the women's movement and my emerging theoretical interest in gender influenced *the kinds* of research projects in which I sought employment as a contract researcher in the late 1970s and early 1980s. Theoretical and methodological orientations were secondary concerns, at least at the point of taking a job.

In my own case, I would argue that while a predisposition towards qualitative methods and an interest in particular issues related to feminism were very important to the development of my research career, other factors were also relevant. In terms of my own research biography, they include: the broad-based research training I undertook, which supplied me with credentials and introduced me to and gave me much practice in both qualitative and quantitative methods; and a political concern to link micro-level understandings (of women's perspectives) to broad structural patterns. It is interesting to reflect that many feminists have preferred to see themselves as wedded to qualitative approaches. In addition, my research career and interest in both qualitative and quantitative approaches took place in the wider research context related to the growth in research funding, the institutionalization of research training, the changing job market in research, and a growing recognition on the part of funders of the value and legitimacy of qualitative research.

WORKING QUALITATIVELY AND QUANTITATIVELY IN PRACTICE

In the rest of the chapter, I shall discuss some of the different methodological strategies that I have employed in the course of my research career relating to the use of both qualitative and quantitative data. I shall examine the different considerations that shaped the choice of a particular combination of approaches as well as the ways in which the combination was applied in practice. In the following discussion of four research studies on which I have worked, I shall identify the priority given to and the sequencing of both the qualitative and quantitative aspects of the research methodology. I shall suggest, according to the argument proposed earlier, that in each case the different datasets were employed largely to complement one another rather than as corroborating evidence for one another. There were, however, instances when similar data were collected using different research methods and which *offered* the possibility for corroboration, though this was not the prime intention for collecting them. In two of the projects that I shall discuss, one dataset was clearly designed also to facilitate the next phase of the study. I shall argue that an important part of the story of mixing methods concerns the ways in which the qualitative and quantitative elements of the research were introduced into different *phases of the research process*: the research design phase; the fieldwork phase; and the phase of interpretation and contextualization. As

I shall also suggest, these phases can also be distinguished in relation to (a) the context of inquiry (research design strategies), in which methods are chosen to address substantive and theoretical questions; and (b) the context of justification, in which data are discussed in relation to the methods, assumptions and theories by which they are constituted.

The research design phase

In the first two studies to which I shall make reference, the two datasets were clearly specified in the research design phase as distinct and separate parts of the investigation, each of which was as valid in its own right. The two parts of the study were also linked in terms of the sampling strategy. The first study I shall refer to as 'Young people, health and family life' (Brannen et al., 1994), while the second focused on children's concepts of care and their contribution to family life – referred to as 'Children's concepts of care' (Brannen et al., 2000). The first phase in both studies was a large-scale self-completion questionnaire survey of school-based populations – in one case of young people aged 16 years and another of children aged 11. The second phase of the studies involved subsamples of particular groups of children and their parents, selected on specified criteria and drawn from the first phase of the studies (with a total sample size of 64 and 63 children in each case). This second phase was an interview study using a semi-structured interview schedule.[1]

The research aims underlying the collection of the two datasets were distinctively different. They addressed different types of research question and were designed to generate data analyses that complemented one another.

Research aims

Young people, health and family life study: 'The schools survey was used to provide quantitative data concerning young people's health related behaviour and backgrounds. …In the household study we sought to explore the negotiation of social relationships and transactions concerning health.' (Brannen et al., 1994: 8–9)

Children's concepts of care study: 'Our methodological approach in the study involved the following research strategy. We sought to combine an extensive approach to understand the ways in which children's views and practices were distributed across a wide range of children in the community, with an intensive approach in which we sought to elicit the perspectives of particular groups of children. We included a range of methods which took account of children's interests and competencies, while being attentive to the sensitive nature of family life and family change. We included mothers' views of children's experiences since mothers were key figures in children's family lives but also because mothers could provide important contextual material.' (Brannen et al., 2000: 12–13)

Moreover, it was also the case that the second (qualitative) phase depended upon the first quantitative phase and that the interview cases were embedded within school-based surveys located in particular social milieux that we also sought to describe. The surveys provided contextual information about the populations of children and young people who had been selected.

A second purpose of the first phase of the two studies also to do with research design was to provide a sampling frame for a second phase – the interview studies conducted with children and young people and their parents (separately). Gaining access to young people and children via the schools was essential not only for the school-based questionnaire surveys but also to accessing particular subgroups for the interview studies.

(The questionnaires were not anonymized but contained codes that were linked to children's names; this enabled us later to identify and contact those groups whom we wished to select for the interview study.) Access required careful negotiation but also some reciprocity on the part of the researchers towards the schools. We sought to make a trade-off: by providing the school with quantitative data drawn from the questionnaire survey phase relating to the particular school, we hoped this would help us to gain access to the qualitative sample. The questionnaire surveys were therefore designed and carried out with this additional purpose in mind.

As others have argued (Thompson, 2003), the case to be made for attaching qualitative subsamples to statistically derived samples, for example national cohort studies, is a strong one. It benefits qualitative researchers by providing the chance to make controlled comparisons outside their own typically small samples and to test their hypotheses on other samples drawn from larger, statistically representative samples. It also benefits quantitative researchers by enabling them to come to grips better within their sampling base as well as their interpretations of informants' behaviour.

Thus in the two studies, both quantitative and qualitative data had a particular importance. We used each dataset rather differently in the writing up of the study. We also drew upon different methods of representation in presenting the different types of analysis, with survey data typically represented in the form of percentages and tables and so on. This mode of presentation is more economical than that which typifies qualitative analysis. Presenting qualitative material typically involves creating typologies and demonstrating their validity and substance, with references frequently made to informants' verbatim accounts taken from the original transcripts. Certainly the analysis of the qualitative phase of these two studies took up more space in the two books we wrote. However, it was not our intention to give the qualitative evidence more weight in the overall analysis. Rather, the evidence was presented in the form that best suited it.

Although, as I have said, the two phases of the research were designed to fulfil different purposes and were quite discrete, none the less there was some overlap in the data collected by each. While the main intention was not to corroborate the data by using different methods, we did not ignore the opportunity to compare the different datasets. The surveys and the interview studies were separated in time so that not only was the method different but any changes in children's or young people's accounts given in relation to each research method could also be caused by actual change occurring over time. Children and young people in each study were asked to report in their survey questionnaires on their household circumstances, and again mothers and children were asked similar questions in their interviews. Some differences in these reports we were able to attribute to actual changes in household living patterns. However, in one of the studies, 'Young people's health and family life', young people's reports of their health emerged as rosier in their face-to-face interview encounters than in their questionnaire surveys; this occurred even though there was little evidence from young people's accounts (or those of their parents) that their health had changed in the intervening period. Similar differences have been found between

responses to self-administered questionnaires and in-depth interviews, especially on sensitive subjects, for example in a study of women's experiences of motherhood and child health (Oakley, 1992). In these cases different methods were used for different purposes that related to the context of inquiry. The resulting data were examined in relation to their methods in the context of justification.

The fieldwork phase

At a critical phase of my research career, mentioned earlier, I was able to help to change the direction of a research project. The research investigation focused on women's return to employment following maternity leave and their children's experience of different kinds of day care. The initial broad aims of the study, as set out in the original research proposal submitted before I joined the study, were 'to describe the histories and experiences of the mothers and children; to assess their welfare and development, including the type and stability of nonparental care... a variety of [quantitative] methods to be used, including interviews, observations and developmental assessments' (Brannen and Moss, 1991: 18). In effect, the study was initially conceptualized in quantitative terms to examine the effects of maternal employment on women and children. In terms of the methodological approach envisaged in the original proposal, 'The original proposal assumed that the project would be entirely oriented to a quantitative approach with statistical methods of analysis' (ibid.).

The impetus for the methodological changes was both theoretical and political or, as we wrote rather vaguely in our book *Managing Mothers,* to do with 'changed perspectives' (Brannen and Moss, 1991: 17). Moreover, the study was part of a government-funded programme of work that stretched over a six-year period. There was therefore considerable scope in time and material resource terms for the development of the conceptual focus and the research methodology.

In terms of conceptual focus, an important shift took place, that is, away from a focus upon mothers to a focus upon the household. In exploring the reasons why mothers were employed (or not) in children's early years, we also sought to understand the contribution fathers made and the ways in which mothers viewed men's breadwinning and their contribution to fatherhood, care work and domestic labour. However, we did not have the resources to interview the fathers directly while observation of parent–child relationships largely continued to focus on mothers. We thereby sought to problematize the theoretical assumptions that had thus far underpinned the existing mainly psychological research literature on 'working mothers'; these studies took mother care as the desired norm and assumed that non-maternal care was bad for children.[2]

The changes in conceptual perspectives were translated into changes in the study's design and methodology, in particular in the method of interviewing and a new set of aims that underpinned the collection of the qualitative material. The result was an interview schedule that combined structured questions (the responses to which were categorized according to pre-defined codes) with unstructured interview questions and flexible probes (the responses to which were transcribed and later subjected to qualitative analysis).[3] Since many of the original aims of the investigation remained in place, we were still committed to collecting in structured ways a whole range of data. However, the interviewers were required to collect such data while seeming to adopt a flexible, in-depth mode of interviewing in which the research participants were encouraged to speak at length and to introduce and articulate their own concerns. It is matter of note that this combined interviewing approach was so successful that when we decided to return to a structured interview approach with some of the sample at a later contact point in the study (see below), we found that the women were reluctant to do so and continued to respond in the way they had done in the earlier semi-structured interviews.

The implications of the changes in conceptual focus meant that a qualitative component was added to the study in which we were concerned to examine in an open-ended, exploratory way how mothers made sense of their situations and responsibilities and the ways in which they and their households actively organized and construed employment and parenthood. Moreover, since the return to employment in children's early years was unusual in Britain at that time and the dominant ideology favoured full-time motherhood, it was likely that women would experience ambivalent feelings about returning to work as well as being subject to the conflicting demands of home and work. The development of a methodology that allowed for the expression of contradictory views and feelings was therefore an important development for a study with this particular focus. As we described in *Managing Mothers,* the methodology produced both narrative accounts of women's experience of motherhood and returning to work (through semi-structured interviewing approaches) and

general evaluations of their situations (through more structured questions). These different types of data illuminated broader theoretical concerns, as we wrote in *Managing Mothers*: 'the interpenetration of ideology and practice ... the mechanisms by which women reproduce and integrate contradictory elements of their beliefs, actions and the situations in which they find themselves ... beliefs and practices ... [that are] part and parcel of larger ideological debates concerning gender roles and the practice of everyday life' (Brannen and Moss, 1991: 7).

Thus attention to the ways in which different types of data (generated by researchers' ways of questioning and by the ways respondents choose to frame their accounts) contradict each other, is a fruitful direction to follow. We gave a further example where the coded data on women's responses to a direct question concerning satisfaction with their partner's contribution to the dual-earner life-style appeared to suggest that women experienced little dissatisfaction. Yet we also found that in many cases they reported the fathers' contributions to be (at best) subsidiary and that most women also professed a belief in equal sharing when both parents with a young child were working full-time. We wrote:

> Examination of the qualitative analysis of women's comments suggested a more complex conclusion. In many cases a good deal of criticism or ambivalence was expressed, especially when women recounted particular incidents. Critical comments, however, were often retracted or qualified in response to direct global questions concerning satisfaction with husbands' participation ... the strategy adopted was to examine the contexts in which women's responses were located, together with a content analysis of responses. In this way the contradictions were confronted, and the processes identified by which dissatisfaction was played down or explained away. (Brannen and Moss, 1991: 20)

The changes to the study's conceptual focus and fieldwork methods had far-reaching consequences in terms of resources of time and money since we were committed to interviewing the mothers at four points over their first three years of motherhood. (We later decided at contacts three and four to do a structured interview with those women who were no longer employed full-time and the complete 2½-hour interview to the 66 women who were still in full-time employment.) Moreover, with the changes to the fieldwork method, it had been necessary to train the research team in what to them was a wholly different interviewing approach. It required a high level of commitment on the part of the interviewers since the interviews took longer and were less mechanistic, requiring greater flexibility, concentration and listening skills. Moreover, in addition to being required to code the structured data (after the interview), the interviewers were also now involved in a considerable amount of transcription which had to be done by hand on to the interview schedules. The researchers also had to take account of the research concepts, which were referenced on the interview schedule in relation to each interview question, and were required to cross-reference different parts of the transcribed interview where the material referred to concepts that were not highlighted or expected in relation to the particular interview question. Since this is a classic scenario for coder error (Crittenden and Hill, 1971), a great deal of time resources were devoted by the senior members of the research team to listening to the interview tapes, and to checking the transcribed material against the coding on the interview schedules.

Thus, in this study, the context of inquiry, i.e., the data-collection phase of the research process, was a focus for the integration of quantitative and qualitative approaches into the investigation. They were integrated via a single research instrument. In analysing the two datasets, we analysed all the coded data using SPSS and we carried out a full content analysis of the transcribed data for a subset of the sample (70 women at three contact points). For particular analyses, other interviews were also considered. In the context of justification, i.e. in writing about the analysis process in our book, *Managing Mothers*, we suggested that the two datasets had different purposes and uses. We noted particular ways in which the different datasets made a contribution and the benefits that would have been lost had we not included the qualitative component:

> The quantitative data proved particularly useful to establish patterns of behaviour, both cross-sectionally and over time – for example occupational mobility, the sharing of domestic work and social network contact. In general the data analysed qualitatively proved useful in the identification of conceptual issues; the qualitative data fleshed out the coded responses, elaborating already encapsulated in the codes [concepts] or added new meanings. For example, examination of the way in which women described decisions concerning the return to employment led to an understanding that those who did not return did not regard it as a decision at all, while those who intended a return saw it as an individual rather than a household decision. If the issues had simply been addressed quantitatively, such insights would have been lost. (Brannen and Moss, 1991: 19)

In writing up the material, we suggested that the three ways discussed by Hammersley (1996) of combining qualitative and quantitative data were present in our own analysis. We also suggested that some ways were more significant than others. In particular we indicated that one approach – whereby qualitative material is used to corroborate results derived from quantitative analysis – was less significant. More important in our own analysis was a second approach, namely to use the quantitative data to facilitate the qualitative analysis. The example referred to above concerning women's apparent satisfaction with fathers' contributions to the dual-earner life-style can be seen as an example of this; in this case, coded responses to single structured questions were subjected to further analysis of the qualitative narrative accounts which revealed significant contradictions. A third approach – the complementarity approach – is also evident, namely whereby both data analyses are given similar weight in the analysis and presentation of the material since both proceed as separate but parallel exercises. In this case, the two data analyses are seen to address different but associated questions. Again, we gave examples in *Managing Mothers* of this way of using our different types of data (Brannen and Moss, 1991).

In general we think that this particular investigation, which involved working in two different ways simultaneously within what was in effect one dataset, highlights the problems as well as the advantages of working both qualitatively and quantitatively. Tensions arise between the different theoretical interests and around the allocation of resources. There is the particular methodological tension between carrying out an analysis across a large number of cases and carrying out a qualitative, in-depth analysis of particular cases. This tension is particularly difficult to manage in a longitudinal study with several contact points as well as a large number of substantive issues to be addressed at each contact point and the requirement of repeating the same questions at subsequent contact points. We know that much more analytical work might have been done to understand how, in particular cases and sub-groups in the study, different dimensions and factors come together in particular ways (Platt, 1988). Such an approach would have required a process of analytic induction (see Bryman, 2001). Ideally, such case-by-case analysis proceeds during the course of the fieldwork and not post hoc (Lindesmith, 1947). In this particular investigation, to have proceeded along a path of analytic induction in which theory is developed and refined on a case-by-case analysis was not possible. For one thing, a large amount of resources (funding) had been invested in the quantitative approach so that we were committed to generating a large amount of quantitative analysis, including a range of outcome variables, for example relating to mothers' well-being. The tensions between the different levels and types of analysis were managed at the analysis phase of the research and the result was inevitably a compromise.

This way of combining qualitative and quantitative data within one fieldwork instrument was unusual in the way it came about. Moreover, in today's marketized research world, with tightly specified research contracts and considerable demands upon researchers to meet users' requirements, such an evolutionary approach would be unlikely to occur. It happened under particular conditions: in a historical period when funding was less marketized and when it was possible for researchers to have more control over the nature and direction of their research. It happened in a particular kind of investigation in which ideological orthodoxies had been influential in determining the initial formulation of the research questions (and were moreover the reason why the research was funded – in the late 1970s – in the first place!). It took place among a particular group of researchers at a particular point in their research careers and with a particular interdisciplinary mix of sociology, social policy and psychology.

However, combining approaches in this way was generative. Intellectually it was challenging in bringing different perspectives together upon a topic (maternal employment) that in the British context had been framed, both in social scientific and policy discourses, according to a particular ideology (full-time motherhood). In particular, the combined approach served theoretically to confront the contradictions in, and to highlight the fragmented and multi-faceted nature of, human consciousness. It was generative methodologically in expanding the skills and competences of researchers in both data collection and data analysis. It brought out the best of both approaches as well as the tensions between them. It highlighted the importance of spelling out clearly the concepts researchers bring from their own intellectual backgrounds and the taken-for-granted assumptions that we as human beings bring to our research. It underlined the importance of posing exacting as well as open-ended questions to our informants, notably in respect of issues to which we seek specific answers. It counselled us against the risks of precision for its own sake (Sell, 2000).

Interpretation and contextualization

In this third aspect of the research process, the phase of interpretation and contextualization of the data analysis, working qualitatively and quantitatively did not involve collecting both types of empirical data. In the late 1990s I was engaged in a cross-national study with researchers from five countries on a study of young people's views of work and family life with respect to their futures (Brannen et al., 2002). The project, which I shall refer to as 'Young Europeans, work and family', was largely designed as small-scale qualitative research; no primary extensive empirical data were collected by the research team. The data-collection method involved a qualitative approach: focus groups and individual interviews with different groups of young people aged 18 to 30, selected according to life-course phase relating to education and employment and also according to educational and occupational level. In interpreting the cross-national data, we engaged, as all researchers must, in processes of contextualization. We located our small-scale studies of particular groups in relation to their structural and institutional contexts in each country. In particular, we had recourse to the official statistics in each of our five countries and examined our results in the context of other research evidence. (In some research, it is also possible to carry out secondary analysis of large-scale datasets in order to gain appropriate comparison groups for one's own study.)

Interpretation occurs at *all* phases of the research process, not only at the writing-up stage. Layder's review of the issues concerning interpretation is helpful here (Layder, 1998). In discussing the linkages that researchers need to make in studying the micro-world of interpersonal relations, the stuff of many qualitative investigations, he argues that it is important methodologically *not* to separate the links between agency and structure. 'The whole point of a focus on the relations between agency and structure in research is to underline their simultaneous implications in each other – to trace their actual interpenetrations and linkages – and not to abandon this task because of a methodological "problem"'. (Layder, 1998: 14). Part of the solution for Layder lies in attending to the epistemological status of the concepts employed in the investigation – the ways in which they refer to different aspects of social reality. In particular, he draws attention to what he terms 'bridging concepts' which forge links between the actor and systemic/institutional/structural levels. For example, the concept of social network acts as a bridging concept and a useful methodological tool; I have fruitfully employed this concept in some of the studies I have worked on and referred to earlier.

Consideration ought to be given also to the use of data external to the particular research project. In methodological texts there is surprisingly little attention given to this issue. Indeed it is only when the issue of working across different countries is addressed that contextualization is deserving of separate attention (see Hantrais, 1999, for a review of the issues to be addressed in contextualizing cross-national research). It may well be that this matter is ignored because contextualizing one's own research is typically compartmentalized in a separate phase of the research process, namely in the literature review in which researchers are not routinely expected to discuss issues of methodology.

In 'Young Europeans, work and family', we employed qualitative methods only in the collection of primary data. In writing up the research comparatively we made reference to secondary data sources concerning trend data and public policies in our respective countries. We also paid attention to the ways in which our respective social scientific and common-sense languages affected our understandings of what we were doing methodologically, in terms of the research design and data-collection phases as well as in the data analysis (Smithson and Brannen, 2002). For example, at one point it was necessary to revisit our research design in order to create greater sample compatibility; this arose because of our realization of definitional problems concerning the choice of particular groups upon which the study focused.

There was moreover a larger methodological issue to be decided at the design stage of the study concerning the appropriate choice of comparison groups. We were careful in our choice of groups to take account of the life course of young people but also their opportunity structures. Such decisions were based upon contextualization in terms of the structural patterns that shaped the lives of young people in the different countries (based on published evidence) and upon theoretical concerns. By selecting groups of young people appropriately and by taking care in the choice of groups to be compared in the analyses, we thereby hoped to reduce the risk of much qualitative inquiry, which is to focus too single-mindedly upon discourse and to move beyond a purely thematic analysis which is so common in the analysis of such material.

In writing a social scientific book (we also wrote a report: Lewis et al., 1998), the way in which we interpreted the qualitative data was rooted in particular theoretical frameworks that different team members applied. There were clear differences of theoretical perspective between the different researchers in the cross-national team. In writing a collaborative book we have sought to clarify these different theoretical perspectives rather than to paper them over, as is common presentational practice in much cross-national research. An example here is in order. The psychologists among us engaged with the concept of psychological contract and sense of entitlement as frameworks for interpreting how young people's expectations of employers were changing (Lewis et al., 2002a, 2002b). In other chapters, the sociologists problematized the methodological strategy of focusing only upon the discourses generated in young people's focus groups and sought to make the structural constraints upon young people's lives visible in the analysis. One way of doing this was to problematize theoretical perspectives that have dominated youth research in recent years, notably individualization theory (Nilsen and Brannen, 2002). A methodological strategy was to take account of the silences in young people's discourses. For while some young Norwegians in the study, for example, displayed a 'confident planning mentality' about their future lives as parents and workers, they failed to suggest how such feelings of mastery and independence are premised upon the support of a strong welfare state (Nilsen et al., 2002).

CONCLUSION

In this chapter I have related something of my own research practice and experience over a number of years in which I have drawn upon both qualitative and quantitative data in different ways within the same investigation, for different purposes and to different effect. I have suggested that the impetus to work qualitatively and quantitatively can be understood with reference to researchers' own careers as they are made in particular historical conditions and as they relate to a range of issues, including the nature of the research questions in the social inquiry, researchers' preferences and skills, and the circumstances and fashions of research funding and research organization.

Through a consideration of four studies I have illustrated the ways in which different types of methods and data enter into and figure in the research process. Moreover I have also suggested that considerations bringing qualitative and quantitative data together may be different in relation to (a) the context of inquiry and (b) the context of justification. In two studies, I suggested that different methods figured in the context of inquiry – the research design phase. Two phases of the research were designed with very different purposes in mind. The first phase (a self-completion questionnaire survey) was intended to facilitate the second phase (an interview study) by providing a sampling frame and so helping to negotiate and provide access to cases in the qualitative phase. In addition, two datasets were generated which were considered in the phase of justification. Since each addressed particular research questions and was based on particular epistemological assumptions, we analysed the data in respect of these. In writing up the two datasets, however, we largely employed them to complement one another. I also noted the benefits of the general principle of locating qualitative research samples within larger representative samples, a practice that offers a two-way benefit for both the qualitative and quantitative data related to understanding sampling biases and issues of contextualization and interpretation.

With reference to a third study, I gave an account of the way in which a large research programme designed to employ quantitative methods was developed in order to make way for a qualitative component. The incorporation of a qualitative component in the phase of developing the fieldwork method involved turning a structured interview into a seamless combination of structured and semi-structured questions. The redesigned research instrument brought into play new research questions and also new types of analysis posing challenges for the context of justification. The opportunity for development within this particular study was generative both theoretically and methodologically for the research team as well as producing new substantive insights.

In a fourth study, I turned to a broader aspect of the research process, namely the interpretation and contextualization of a small study in relation to the literature and other data sources. I discussed how in a small-scale qualitative inquiry the researchers sought to contextualize their analyses with reference to secondary sources of quantitative data drawn from national statistical sources, other datasets and a range of theories. I noted that the methodology literature has failed to scrutinize such ways of combining qualitative and quantitative data except when the research investigation is cross-national, as was the case in this study. This third research exemplar, like the third, also focused on the context of justification.

On the basis of these reflections upon research methodology and practice, I would reiterate the point that multi-method research involves a range of research strategies and research designs. A multi-method strategy may enter into one or more phases of the research process: the organization of the project; sampling; data-collection methods; data analysis; and contextualization. I have suggested that to understand the employment and value of qualitative and quantitative data it is further necessary to distinguish between the context in which researchers design research for particular purposes and with particular questions, and also the phase in which we make sense of our data and recontextualize them in relation to ontological, epistemological and theoretical assumptions. In including issues of contextualization and interpretation, I am suggesting that it may be necessary to expand further the definition of multi-method research. Such a broad definition of multi-method research would thereby encompass the very different types of activity involved in creating and making sense of data.

If the generation of knowledge is understood with reference to the procedures and processes involved in doing research as well as to the ideas that underpin the framing of the research questions, then the issue of two competing paradigms of qualitative and quantitative research recedes into the background. Rather what is foregrounded is the purposes of social inquiry. As Kaplan has suggested in the reference I quoted at the beginning of the chapter, the aim of methodology is to help us to *understand*, in the broadest possible terms, not only the products of scientific inquiry but the process itself. A multi-method strategy should be adopted to serve particular theoretical, methodological and practical purposes. Such a strategy is not a tool kit or a technical fix. Nor should it be seen as a belt-and-braces approach. Multi-method research is not necessarily better research. Rather it is an approach employed to address the questions posed in a research investigation. The resulting data are analysed and interpreted in relation to the methods and assumptions by which they were generated.

As with all practices, research practice is shaped by fashions relating to time and place – the types of research careers that we forge for ourselves in particular historical contexts and the factors that shape these. In a context in which social science disciplines appear to be breaching their boundaries, when policy-driven or policy-relevant research is in the ascendant, and in which research training is being institutionalized, working both qualitatively and quantitatively looks to be increasingly popular. The popularity of the multi-method approach may either inspire new debate or be greeted by silence.

NOTES

1 In the 'Children's concepts of care' study, the interview phase also drew upon other methods including vignettes, genealogies and social network maps.

2 We conceptualized women's paid work in the labour market and their gender roles in the household and family life as a relationship between the public and private rather than as 'separate spheres'. Instead of seeing mothers as being caught psychologically between 'dual roles', we assumed that the tensions were also structural.

3 In the 'Children's concepts of care' study, we also integrated several different methods into the in-depth interview, including the use of vignettes to explore children's rationalities of care, and the mapping of family relationships and significant others. The organization of the interview around structured methods in conjunction with a flexible interviewing approach worked well with this group of children. Indeed, it may be argued that in-depth interviews in which onus is put on to children to respond to adult questions and to elaborate their often brief answers may be burdensome to children but also may have an inhibiting effect in relation to the elaboration of standpoints and meanings.

REFERENCES

Bernstein, B. (2000) *Pedagogy, Symbolic Control and Identity: Theory, Research, Critique*. Lanham, MD: Rowan & Littlefield.

Brannen, J. (1992) *Mixing Methods: Qualitative and Quantitative Research*. London: Gower (reprinted).

Brannen, J. and Collard, C. (1982) *Marriages in Trouble: Seeking Help for Marital Problems*. London: Unwin Hyman.

Brannen, J. and Moss, P. (1991) *Managing Mothers: Dual Earner Households After Maternity Leave*. London: Unwin Hyman.

Brannen, J., Dodd, K., Oakley, A. and Storey, P. (1994) *Young People, Health, and Family Life*. Buckingham: Open University Press.

Brannen, J., Heptinstall, E. and Bhopal, K. (2000) *Connecting Children: Care and Family Life in Later Childhood*. London: Routledge Falmer.

Brannen, J., Nilsen, A., Lewis, S. and Smithson, J. (eds) (2002) *Young Europeans, Work and Family Life: Futures in Transition*. London: Routledge.

Bryman, A. (1988) *Quality and Quantity in Social Research*. London: Unwin Hyman.

Bryman, A. (1992) 'Quantitative and qualitative research: further reflections on their integration', in J. Brannen (ed.), *Mixing Methods: Qualitative and Quantitative Research*. London: Gower (reprinted), pp. 57–81.

Bryman, A. (2001) *Social Research Methods*. Oxford: Oxford University Press.

Crittenden, K. and Hill, R. (1971) 'Coding reliability and validity of interview data', *American Sociological Review*, 36: 1073–80.

Denzin, N. (1970) *The Research Act in Sociology*. London: Butterworths.

Finch, J. (1986) *Research and Policy: The Uses of Qualitative Methods in Social and Educational Research*. Lewes: Falmer Press.

Hammersley, M. (1989) *The Dilemma of Qualitative Method: Herbert Blumer and the Chicago Tradition*. London: Routledge.

Hammersley, M. (1992) 'Deconstructing the qualitative-quantitative divide', in J. Brannen (ed.), *Mixing Methods: Qualitative and Quantitative Research*. London: Gower (reprinted), pp. 39–57.

Hammersley, M. (1996) 'The relationship between qualitative and quantitative research: paradigm loyalty versus methodological eclecticism', in J.T.E. Richardson (ed.), *Handbook of Research Methods for Psychology and the Social Sciences*. Leicester: BPS Books, pp. 159–79.

Hammersley, M. (2000) 'Varieties of social research', *International Journal of Social Research Methodology: Theory and Practice*, 3(3): 221–31.

Hantrais, L. (1999) 'Contextualisation in cross-national comparative research', *International Journal of Social Research Methodology: Theory and Practice*, 2(2): 93–109.

Kaplan, A. (1964) *The Conduct of Enquiry: Methodology for Behavioral Science*. San Francisco: Chandler.

Layder, D. (1998) *Sociological Practice: Linking Theory and Social Research*. London: Sage.

Lewis, S., Smithson, J., Brannen. J, das Dores Guerreiro, M., Kugelberg, C., Nilsen, A. and O'Connor, P. (1998) *Futures on Hold: Young Europeans Talk About Work and Family*. Manchester: IOD Research Group.

Lewis, S., Smithson, J. and Kugelberg, C. (2002a) 'Into work: job insecurity and changing psychological contracts?', in J. Brannen, A. Nilsen, S. Lewis and J. Smithson (eds), *Young Europeans, Work and Family Life: Futures in Transition*. London: Routledge, pp. 68–89.

Lewis, S., Smithson. J. and das Dores Guerreiro, M. (2002b) 'Into parenthood: young people's sense of entitlement to support for the reconciliation of employment and family life', in J. Brannen, A. Nilsen, S. Lewis and J. Smithson (eds), *Young Europeans, Work and Family Life: Futures in Transition*. London: Routledge, pp. 140–62.

Lindesmith, A.R. (1947) *Opiate Addiction*. Bloomington, IN: Principia Press.

Marshall, G. (2002) Presentation given as Chief Executive of the Economic and Social Research Council. London: Institute of Education.

Morgan, D.L. (1988) 'Practical strategies for combining qualitative and quantitative methods: applications for health research', *Qualitative Health Research*, 8: 362–76.

Nilsen, A. and Brannen, J. (2002) 'Theorising the individual-structure dynamic', in J. Brannen, A. Nilsen, S. Lewis and J. Smithson (eds), *Young Europeans, Work and Family Life: Futures in Transition*. London: Routledge, pp. 30–48.

Nilsen, A, das Dores Guerreiro, M. and Brannen, J. (2002) '"Most choices involve money": different pathways to adulthood', in J. Brannen, A. Nilsen, S. Lewis and J. Smithson (eds), *Young Europeans, Work and Family Life: Futures in Transition*. London: Routledge, pp. 162–85.

Oakley, A. (1992) *Social Support and Motherhood: The Natural History of a Research Project*. Oxford: Blackwell.

Ong, P. (ed.) (1999) *Impacts of Affirmative Action*. Los Angeles: AltaMira Press.

Platt, J. (1988) 'What can case studies do?', *Studies in Qualitative Methodology*, 1: 1–20.

Sell, H. (2000) 'Exactness and precision', *International Journal of Social Research Methodology: Theory and Practice*, 3(2): 135–57.

Smith, K.K. and Heshusius, L. (1986) Closing down the conversation: the end of the quantitative-qualitative debate among educational inquirers', *Educational Researcher*, 15: 4–11.

Smithson, J. and Brannen, J. (2002) 'Qualitative methodology in cross-national research', in J. Brannen, A. Nilsen, S. Lewis and J. Smithson (eds), *Young Europeans, Work and Family Life: Futures in Transition*. London: Routledge, pp. 11–30.

Thompson, P. (2003) 'Researching family and social mobility with two eyes: some experiences of the interaction between qualitative and quantitative data', *International Journal of Social Research Methodology: Theory and Practice*, in press.

Webb, E.J., Campbell, D.T., Schwartz, R.D. and Sechrest, L. (1966) *Unobtrusive Methods: Nonreactive Methods in the Social Sciences*. Chicago: Rand McNally.

21

Secondary analysis of archived data

Louise Corti and Paul Thompson

Archived qualitative data are a rich and unique, yet too often unexploited, source of research material. They offer information that can be reanalysed, reworked, and compared with contemporary data. In time, too, archived research materials can prove to be a significant part of our cultural heritage and become resources for historical as well as contemporary research. In this chapter we explore the methodological, ethical and theoretical considerations relating to the secondary analysis of such qualitative data.

There is a well-established tradition in social science of reanalysing quantitative data. Nor is there any logical intellectual reason why this should not be so for qualitative data. However, among qualitative researchers there is no similar research culture encouraging the reanalysis of data collected by other researchers. Until very recently there has been a striking lack of discussion of the issues involved and very little published 'evidence' of the benefits and limitations of such an approach. In this chapter we outline some ways of reusing data, and discuss their strengths and weaknesses, drawing on various examples including a case study by Paul Thompson. Thompson's reflections of his own personal experiences of reanalysing data from his pioneering oral history study conducted in the 1970s, provide the reader with first-hand evidence of both the difficulties and gains that resulted. It was these early experiences of reuse that led Thompson to establish the National Life Story Collection at the British Library, and then ESRC's national archiving centre for qualitative data, Qualidata.

Finally, we summarize the ways archived qualitative research data are best presented so as to be of maximum potential use to other researchers. Experience is drawn from two qualitative data services, Qualidata in the UK and the Murray Research Center in the US. We discuss the organization, preparation and documentation of data, and also legal and ethical issues.

DEFINING QUALITATIVE DATA AND THE IMPLICATIONS FOR REUSE

Qualitative data are collected across a range of social science disciplines, often with varying techniques or emphasis, but typically aiming to capture lived experiences of the social world and the meanings people give these experiences from their own perspectives. Often a diversity of methods and tools rather than a single one are encompassed. The types of data collected vary with the aims of the study and the nature of the sample. Samples are most often small, but may rise to 500 or more informants. Such data include interviews – whether in-depth or unstructured, individual or group discussion – fieldwork diaries and observation notes, structured and unstructured diaries, personal documents, or photographs. Thus any one study may yield a wide range of data types for archiving. Moreover most of these types of data may be created in a variety of formats: digital, paper (typed and handwritten), audio, video and photographic.

In Britain the decades since 1950 witnessed an unprecedented flowering of social research: in the growth of its influence, in the spread of its themes, and in the development of its methods – both quantitative and qualitative. From the 1960s into the 1970s sociology was not only an exceptionally popular subject with students, but was also given more national research resources than at any time before or since. This enabled social researchers to carry out studies of a thoroughness unlikely ever to be equalled.

Just one example is Peter Townsend's in-depth investigation into the nature and status of older people's institutions in post-war Britain. The publication resulting from this research, *The Last Refuge* (1962), was considered a pioneering piece of research when it was published and attracted much publicity for its focus on an important and hitherto neglected area of policy, and also for its methodology and its policy recommendations. But Townsend's meticulously preserved fieldwork descriptions of old people's institutions and accompanying interviews, now archived and available to researchers at the University of Essex, are in the long run equally significant: not only a unique historical record, but equally a rich, multi-layered resource for institutional research that seeks to explore the meaning and nature of institutional life across both micro and macro levels of analysis (Charlesworth and Fink, 2001).

Clearly the scope and format of data usually determine its potential for secondary analysis. For example, data from a research study that collected, recorded and transcribed a hundred in-depth interviews and documented detailed fieldnotes, particularly when based on a clear sampling strategy, are much more likely to be useful than a set of handwritten interview notes from twenty brief semi-structured interviews. But as with all archived material, sometimes the most striking discoveries come from re-examining material that hitherto has not been thought worth researchers' attention. Thus Zeitlyn argues that field photographs and more recent recordings by camcorders are among the most prolific, largest and least exploited resources produced by anthropology (Zeitlyn, 2000).

The availability of qualitative data for reuse

From the early days of social research onwards there have always been a minority of researchers who deliberately chose to publish their interview data. Classic instances run from Henry Mayhew's interviews with the London poor in the mid-nineteenth century through to the much more sustained life-story genre in North American anthropology (from Leo Simmons to Oscar Lewis and Sidney Mintz) and the two briefer waves of life-story research in Chicago sociology (as in the work of Clifford Shaw and Helen Hughes) (Thompson, 2000). Some of these – such as the Chicago sociologists – also deliberately archived their interviews. There are also exceptionally large archives of ethnographic research data in Scandinavia. But in the UK, such researchers have remained a minority. This

is partly because of the defensive position that qualitative social research has had in relation to the much better-funded tradition of quantitative social research, in which informants' words disappear behind statistical findings and speculations. But it is also because even qualitative researchers can be more interested in offering their own interpretations in their papers, articles and books addressed to academia, rather than presenting their original sources for others to evaluate.

Thus, not surprisingly, if we take a look across the world in an attempt to identify qualitative data sources that could be openly consulted, we immediately encounter problems. The first is the absence in most countries of any national effort to either gather together or draw attention to existing research sources. The second is the lack of infrastructures and also of agreed practical procedures for preparing, storing and disseminating qualitative data. Throughout the world there are innumerable archives that collect (mainly historical) qualitative material, as well as a large number of sound archives and ethnographic archives, but there are few common descriptive standards, access to many collections is poor, and there are no integrated resource discovery tools.

One of the earliest and perhaps best-known sources in Britain is the collection of papers resulting from the 1930s social research organization, Mass-Observation. These were established as a notably well-organized and accessible public archive at the University of Sussex in the early 1970s, and since then have attracted a notably high number of researchers (Sheridan, 2000). More typically, other data collections that were retained were stored as in-house research resources, such as the Berkeley and Oakland cohorts collected from the 1920s to the 1990s at the Institute for Human Development at Berkeley. It has also been not unusual for the papers of eminent scholars, sometimes representing a lifetime's research, to be transferred on retirement to their local university archives. Such papers may include not only primary research data, but also administrative documents about the research, such as grant proposals and correspondence. A collection may also contain 'secondary' sources utilized for a particular research study, such as newspaper clippings and organizational or medical records. University archives may sometimes retain broader evidence of theoretical or intellectual processes in the institution, for example the development of ideas within a key social science department, as was used by Platt for her account of the Chicago School of Sociology (Platt, 1996). More generally, however, attempts to archive qualitative research material were both rare and unsystematic.

It was only from the late 1980s that any sustained concern with archiving qualitative research data began to develop. Paul Thompson had earlier seen the importance of archiving the material from his national study of 'Family Life and Work Experience before 1918' (Thompson, 1975), a unique and unrepeatable set of 444 interviews with men and women born before 1906. These interviews were kept in a special room within the Sociology Department at Essex, and as a result became the basis of a series of books and articles by visiting scholars. But this was an informal archive with no secure future, and this led him to be concerned about the lack of any national archival facilities for in-depth interviews. The National Sound Archive had only just been established, and was then without an oral history section, focusing mainly on music and nature.

In 1987 Paul Thompson, with the support of Asa Briggs, set up the National Life Story Collection as an independent charitable trust within the British Library National Sound Archive, and at the same time the NSA appointed Rob Perks as its first oral history curator. The result has been a dramatic improvement in the archival situation. On the one hand, NLSC has been generating new life-story history projects creating public research resources, such as the recording projects on artists and sculptors jointly with the Tate Gallery, on Holocaust survivors, on the financial elite of the City of London (Courtney and Thompson, 1996), on the book trade, the Post Office, North Sea oil workers, and on workers at British Steel (Dein and Perks, 1993). On the other hand, NSA has become a national repository for the tape recordings from social research interviews. It is this cross-disciplinary approach that is unusual, for across the world the oral history community now has a professional interest in preserving tape recordings gathered from oral history interviewing projects, and indeed in the US this archiving goes back, for example at Columbia University Library and at the Bancroft Library at Berkeley, for over forty years. In Europe more recent oral history archives across Europe include in Germany the oral history archive of 'German Memory' based in Hagen, which comprises some 1500 life-history interview recordings with witnesses of time periods from East and West Germany (Leh, 2000); and in Hungary, the 1956 Institute holds oral history interviews, trial records and photographs dealing with research relating to the 1956 Hungarian Revolution, its development and subsequent effects (Lux, 2000).

Since the 1990s new technology has led to new possibilities for sharing qualitative data, especially through online resources and databases. For example in anthropology, Paul Stirling's longitudinal research on two Turkish villages between 1949 and 1994 has been electronically archived. The resource consists of over thirty volumes of fieldnotes, and a selection of his other field materials, including photographs, video and audio tapes (Zeitlyn, 2000). Of the many approaches to digitization, we see three as particularly promising. First, web-based multimedia samplers of key qualitative materials can provide 'edited highlights' to illustrate the potential of the collection for research and teaching. Second, thematic sets of interviews, across topic or time, can be drawn together by interweaving raw data collections and related methodological information into an intellectual and substantive framework. Finally, the mark-up of textual documents enables a range of data types and formats to be accessed via the Web, as demonstrated by the 'Edwardians Online' project, undertaken by Qualidata (Barker, 2002).

Other examples come from the field of sociolinguistics. Since 1990 the Institute of Psychology at the University of Zürich has archived video-based interview narratives from psychotherapy sessions in order to investigate the linguistic structures within psychotherapeutic communication. The collection includes digitized audio-visual data, patient card files, transcripts of therapy sessions, extracted narratives, research publications and student research papers that are integrated into a central database (the JAKOB database) to make it accessible for research purposes (Luder et al., 2000). Equally, there are corpora of speech that are archived. The Spoken Language Corpus of Swedish at Göteborg University (Allwood et al., 2000) is a growing corpus of audio-visual spoken language samples from several languages taken from naturalistically occurring interactions from as long ago as the early 1980s. The goal of the corpus is to capture differences in pronunciation, vocabulary, grammar and communicative functions.

Towards national archiving

Nevertheless in Britain, as indeed in most Western countries, until recently no infrastructure existed for the systematic archiving and dissemination of qualitative data from social science research. The Economic and Social Research Council (ESRC; then SSRC) had already recognized from very early on, in 1967, the value in retaining the most significant machine-readable data from the empirical research that it funded by establishing a Data Archive. Since the 1970s, social science data archives across the world have typically acquired a significant range of data relating to society, both historical and contemporary, from sources including surveys, censuses, registers and aggregate statistics. Equally, these centres of expertise have established networks of data services for the social sciences which foster cooperation on key archival strategies, procedures and technologies.

Thus crucial survey data can be reanalysed by other researchers, and the money spent on research has become not only an immediate outlay but an investment for the future. There was, however, a significant gap in this policy in that qualitative data were rarely acquired, even when much interview data became transcribed in word-processed form. When a small pilot study commissioned by the ESRC was carried out by Paul Thompson in 1991 (Thompson, 1991), it was revealed that 90 per cent of qualitative research data was either already lost, or at risk, in researchers' homes or offices. However, the 10 per cent 'archived' was found not to have the basic requirements of an archive, such as physical security, public access, reasonable catalogues, with recorded material or listening facilities. It was further calculated that it would have cost at least £20 million to create a resource on the scale of that at risk. For the older British sociological material, moreover, the risk was acute, and the need for action especially urgent. This was borne out by the very recent destruction of research data on the classic British community studies of Banbury (Stacey, 1974); on race and conflict in Sparkbrook (Rex and Moore, 1967); and the unique longitudinal study on child-rearing, consisting of over 3000 interviews recorded over thirty years by John and Elizabeth Newson (1963, 1976) – all lost after the retirement of these researchers.

In 1994, with support from the ESRC, the first UK qualitative data archiving project on a national scale was established at the University of Essex. Its first task was a rescue operation aiming to seek out the most significant material created by research from the past fifty years. The second was to work with the ESRC to implement a Datasets Policy (ESRC, 2002) to ensure that for current and future projects the unnecessary waste of the past did not continue. Qualidata was not set up as an archive itself, but as a clearing house and an action unit, its role being to locate and evaluate research data, catalogue it, organize its transfer to suitable archives across the UK, publicize its existence to researchers, and encourage reuse of the collections (Corti et al., 1995; Thompson and Corti, 1998).

Qualidata established procedures for sorting, processing and listing both raw data and accompanying documentation (metadata); systematically describing studies for web-based resource discovery systems; for establishing appropriate access; and for training in the reuse of qualitative data (Corti, 2000). By 2002, Qualidata had acquired, processed and catalogued some 140 datasets, and catalogued a further 150 already housed in archives across the UK. Surviving 'classic studies' data from key researchers were also rescued, including well-known British single projects such as John Goldthorpe et al.'s *The Affluent Worker* (1968); Stan Cohen's *Folk Devils and Moral Panics* (1971); and the entire life's work of pioneering UK researchers such as Peter Townsend's *Family Life of Old People* (1957), *The Last Refuge* (1962), and *Poverty in the United Kingdom* (1979), and Paul Thompson's life-history interview studies of *The Edwardians* (1975) and *Families, Social Mobility and Ageing: An Intergenerational Approach* (Thompson and Bertaux, 1993).

From 2001, Qualidata began a new life as a specialist unit housed within the UK Data Archive (UKDA) at the University of Essex, with a focus on acquiring and distributing digital data. Qualidata's emphasis on providing quick and easy access to data has led to the development of the 'Edwardians Online' project (Barker, 2002), an online resource that offers thematic access to a collection of oral history interviews with people who lived in Edwardian Britain. The multi-media resource integrates the original text transcripts, digital sound-bites of the original audio tapes, background material concerning the original research study, and details of publications based on secondary studies of the interview texts. This resource has provided a model for the digitization and interactive online provision of 'classic collections' based on qualitative data for research and teaching resources.

In the US, there is also a centre that has been systematically gathering qualitative as well as quantitative research data in order to make it available to other social science researchers. Founded in 1976, the Murray Research Center: a Center for the Study of Lives is a national repository for social and behavioural science data on human development and social change, with special emphasis on the lives of American women (James and Sorensen, 2000). The archive holds more than 270 datasets with a wide range of topics, samples and designs. Many of these studies include in-depth interviews or surveys with some open-ended questions. The Center holds a major collection of longitudinal studies of mental health, including Glueck and Glueck's

(1968) crime causation study, some material from the Institute of Human Development, and Lewis Terman's (1954) life-cycle study of children of high ability. In the area of racial and ethnic diversity, an important study is Brunswick's (1980) Harlem longitudinal study.

Finally, over the past few years there have been a number of other initiatives across the world that have sought to establish national archiving projects for qualitative research data. At the time of writing, a small-scale Czech Archive of Qualitative Data has been recently established at Masaryk University; proposals are being prepared in Germany and Switzerland for qualitative archival resource centres; and national (survey-based) Social Science Data Archives in Finland, the Netherlands, Denmark and Canada are conducting feasibility work for extending the scope of their own collecting.

This build-up of qualitative data resources has thus encouraged the uptake of secondary analysis. It also reflects some of the efforts invested in promoting or repackaging data collections to meet researchers' needs. And as resources grow, so experiences of secondary research have begun to find their place in the academic domain.

APPROACHES TO REUSING QUALITATIVE DATA

The reuse of qualitative data provides an opportunity to study the raw materials of recent or earlier research to gain both methodological and substantive insights. Because new data are usually expensive to collect, using existing sources may cut costs as well as avoiding duplication of effort. Nevertheless there has been a noticeable silence on this issue among the qualitative research community. While there are a large number of published texts describing different styles of qualitative interviewing (e.g. Burgess, 1982), and fewer on how to analyse and interpret interview material (Plummer, 1983; Silverman, 2000), there are none that have appraised the secondary analysis of qualitative data. Methodological handbooks recommend that newcomers to the qualitative method should undertake a fieldwork project to gain experience of data gathering, data analysis and writing up, yet rarely introduce the concept of exploring existing data sources to answer a research question. Surprisingly, even when a historical perspective is explicit, earlier qualitative research data have not been considered as a source (Marwick, 1970). Approaches to reusing survey data, on the other hand, are well documented with guidance on both theoretical and practical approaches to the method.

The ways in which qualitative data can be reused have much in common with those familiar for the secondary analysis of survey data, yet there are different and perhaps more challenging intellectual and practical problems for the user to consider. Here we identify six approaches to reusing data. We discuss these in relation both to theoretical issues recently raised about reanalysis, and to the actual experiences of researchers.[1] Issues relating to the practical and perceived barriers to secondary analysis follow this discussion.

Description

The first use of qualitative data is descriptive, and the possibilities here are very wide, encompassing both the contemporary and historical attitudes and behaviour of individuals, groups and organizations, or societies. Thus when David Kynaston came to write the final volume – from 1945 until 2000 – of his authoritative series, *The City of London* (2001), he was able to draw on the 'City Lives' interviews archived in the National Life Story Collection. These were first used by Cathy Courtney and Paul Thompson for their book *City Lives* (1996). Kynaston describes the original interviews as 'invaluable', 'a treasure house' for his own volume: 'City men have never been great talkers.... The interviewers proved extraordinarily effective at getting even normally taciturn subjects to speak candidly.' The interviews were especially vivid in showing attitudes, such as the importance of 'trust', the consequent perfunctoriness of checks on behaviour, the beliefs in nepotism and in using insider knowledge, and the reluctance to 'go American' and introduce new practices (Kynaston, 2002).

In the same way, any significant data created now, will in time become a potential historical resource. The oral testimonies of ordinary men and women can complement official and public sources such as newspapers or government reports. Such evidence can also be used to document individual lives – including those of significant researchers – in a biographical approach. Similarly, Sheridan (2000) notes how Mass-Observation material has been used not only to provide historical evidence, but also to examine the role of Mass-Observation itself in the social, political and cultural milieu of the 1930s and 1940s. Researchers wishing to reuse material in these ways need first to evaluate the evidence, examine its provenance, and weigh up the veracity of the sources – in short, to be prepared to adopt the practice of social historians.

*Comparative research, restudy
or follow-up study*

Secondly, qualitative data can be compared with other data sources or be used to provide comparison over time.

The cumulative building up of knowledge in the social sciences has been incremental, resting on the foundations of earlier findings, and hence interpretation has often depended upon comparisons: with other contexts, other periods of time, other social groups, and other cultures. Comparison is most effective when there are sufficient data to enable convincing re-evaluations. It is fortunate that many social scientists grasped this relatively early. For example, in Britain the original returns of the population census were kept as public records, and have proved an invaluable basis for consultation in recent years. Similarly, Sidney and Beatrice Webb (1894), on completing their pioneering study of British trade unionism, archived their fieldnotes from their national sample of interviews, which remain the principal source of information on trade unionism in the late nineteenth century.

Early classic restudies include Seebohm Rowntree's (1901) three surveys of poverty in York, Llewellyn Smith's (1930–5) repeat of Charles Booth's (1891–1902) famous poverty survey in London, or the Lynds' studies of *Middletown* (1929, 1937). In anthropology, perhaps the best-known instance is the controversial restudy and reinterpretation by Oscar Lewis (1963) of Redfield's (1930) research on the village of Tepotzlan in Mexico.

Comparison brings greater power to answer scientific questions, for example when a dataset can be combined with data beyond its own sample or geographical limitations. An example of a comparative study from the US Murray Research Center cited by James and Sorensen (2000) is provided by Stewart and Healy (1989). These researchers combined five archived datasets to create a multi-cohort study using coded questionnaire data and open-ended material for developing constructs such as employment patterns, careers, role models, internal conflicts and world-views. The pooled cohort data spanned some forty years dating from the First World War to the 1960s baby boom. Using this rich combined sample, the authors showed how both social pathways and personality development differed by cohort, influenced by events and social changes such as the impact of the Vietnam War or trends in female employment.

Equally, samples from original studies that have been preserved can be followed up. Sometimes this is because the original longitudinal study is still ongoing but can be redirected, as with Glen Elder's *Children of the Great Depression* (1974), based on both new fieldwork and a reorganization of the earlier interviews and participant observant of the Berkeley and Oakland cohorts recorded from the 1920s onwards. Alternatively, sometimes the sample from a one-off study can be recontacted, allowing the new investigators to redesign the outcome measures, so that a study that was not longitudinal becomes so (James and Sorensen, 2000). Most often, however, the original data will simply be reanalysed. One such example, using data archived at the Murray Research Center, is Franz et al.'s (1991) follow-up of Sears, Maccoby and Levin's (1957) *Patterns of Child Rearing* study. In 1951, mothers of five-year-old children in the Boston area were interviewed about their own and their husband's parenting practices. The children from this sample were re-interviewed at later stages into adulthood. The resulting longitudinal data spanning some fifty years were reanalysed with a focus on predictors of types of adjustment.

Follow-up studies typically require ethical approval. In addition, particularly in the health field, original investigators are often keen to become collaborators, rather than just being cited as the original data collectors (Corti and Wright, 2002).

Reanalysis or secondary analysis

Reanalysing qualitative data, as with the secondary analysis of survey data, allows both for reinterpretations and also for new questions of the data. New themes can be studied. For example, childhood sexual abuse was not brought to public attention until the early 1980s, long after many of today's important longitudinal studies were launched (James and Sorensen, 2000). Charlesworth and Fink (2001) draw upon research material from *The Last Refuge* (1962), Peter Townsend's study of institutional care, to illustrate the potential that his archived data hold for the analysis of such diverse topics as the power dynamics within institutions, the spatial organization of the workplace and the relationship between research and policy.

Similarly, new angles can be applied or new methods employed that may not have been possible at the time of the original data analysis. Sometimes new analytical tools can spotlight sections of data that were previously ignored. In this volume, Åkerström, Jacobsson and Wästerfors (Chapter 22) argue for the significance of 'continuous analytic digging', allowing themselves the opportunity to revisit and reanalyse material, even if already written up. In general, the more in-depth the material, the less likely that it has already been fully exploited. Finally, theoretical sampling, as proposed by Strauss and Corbin (1990), can also be applied to the data sample itself (e.g. Szabo and Strang, 1997).

There are relatively few published examples of experiences of reanalysis of data in the UK. Fielding and Fielding (2000) present an insightful account of their work on revisiting Stan Cohen and Laurie Taylor's (1972) original analysis of long-term imprisonment of men in maximum security prisons published as *Psychological Survival*. They argue for the ethical and practical advantages of reanalysis of existing data in their field:

> secondary analysis has a particular role in qualitative research, addressing sensitive topics or hard to reach populations, because researchers can best respect subjects' sensitivities, and accommodate restricted access to research populations, by extracting the maximum from those studies which are able to negotiate these obstacles. Secondary analysis can protect the sensitivities of subjects and gatekeepers by ensuring they are not over-researched, and can position further enquiries so that they ask what is pertinent to the state of analytic development, building on, rather than simply repeating, previous enquiries. (Fielding and Fielding, 2000: 678)

In their findings, Fielding and Fielding further state how the reanalysis offered 'a means to extract further analysis purchase from research on a group seldom exposed to fieldwork' (2000: 688).

In the US, the Murray Research Center offers some excellent examples of reanalysis. These demonstrate, from a variety of disciplinary perspectives, the ways in which qualitative data can be 'radically restructured' for new research. Creative approaches include seldom used methods such as creating new prospective studies out of existing ones and using multiple datasets for multi-cohort designs. The availability of raw data, such as transcripts of in-depth interviews, observations and responses to tests, are especially valuable in enabling the application of different perspectives and new scoring procedures to the original data (James and Sorensen, 2000).

In the field of psychology, Elaine May (1988) reanalysed a study by Kelly on long-term personality development among married persons. While Kelly had originally mainly used psychological test assessment, May shifted her focus to the respondents' own testimonies. In these they 'wrote about their lives, the decisions they made concerning their careers and children, the quality of their marriages, their family values, their sexual relationships, their physical and emotional

health, and their major hopes and worries. In these open-ended responses, freed from Kelly's categories and concerns, they poured out their stories' (May, 1988: 12). May combined these testimonies with other documentary sources to write about how the Cold War period affected aspects of family life, thereby challenging the assumptions of the happy housewife of the 1950s and suggesting some of the causes for disruption in family life over the following decades. James and Sorensen highlight how 'quotations from the Kelly data, sprinkled liberally throughout each chapter, illuminate and validate her claims in ways that closed-ended answers to the survey questions never could' (2000: para 46)

A second example from a US-based criminological study concerned the restructuring and recoding of data. Laub and Sampson (1998) applied event history analysis techniques, not yet formulated in the 1960s, to data from a longitudinal study, *Unraveling Juvenile Delinquency* (Gluek and Gluek, 1968). The sources included case records, interviews with the respondents and their families, teachers, criminal justice officials, employers, and correspondence relating to family and school experiences, employment and the military service. Laub and Sampson recoded a wide variety of materials into a longitudinal framework for studying, very successfully, criminal careers.

Research design and methodological advancement

Data can be used to help design a new study or develop a methodology or research tool by studying the sampling methods, data-collection and fieldwork strategies and interview guides of earlier research. The Mass-Observation archive has been used to explore the process of researching, including methods at both the collecting and interpretation stage, and ethical issues (Sheridan, 2000). Paul Thompson refers below to the stimulation of drawing on interview guides designed by earlier researchers in a similar field.

There is a growing emphasis on publishing the details of a study's methods in books and reports, but often the details offered are too brief. Of course earlier research may be equally valuable as a warning of potential dangers and pitfalls, of what to avoid as much as what to follow. Perhaps the most dramatic instance of this was the publication of Malinowski's fieldwork diaries (1967), peppered with the racist and sexist assumptions that helped to shape his social observation. Researchers' own research notes, fieldwork diaries or memos can both offer much insight into the history and development of the research, and also help inform new thinking.

Verification

Archived data can be scrutinized with scientific rigour to support or challenge a set of findings or to appraise the method. Generally, qualitative researchers are not used to making their findings accountable, and some may feel vulnerable about others seeing their data, leaving themselves open to criticism. But the practice of opening data for inspection may lead to better and more transparent research. On the other hand, even where archived data are already available for research findings to be verified, there is as yet no evidence of this actually happening.

Hammersley (1997) identifies the benefits and weaknesses of using 'replication' to check findings. True scientific replication, he argues, is not possible as studies generally do not have equal social phenomena. Even restudies suffer from differences in time and the researchers' subjective perspectives. Well-documented and 'complete' datasets can help the scrutinizer to reconstruct the evidence by retracing the original analytic steps. However, it is unlikely that the research process could ever be made fully explicit, primarily because the path of qualitative analysis is never linear, and is almost certainly likely to involve a degree of trial and error in the pursuit of interesting lines of investigation. A researcher report is not simply a representation of data peppered with narrative and interpretation, but is in itself a social and literary construction (Kvale, 1996).

Fielding and Fielding (2000) suggest that qualitative software may help the process of verification. Retention of the original coding frames means that these can be reapplied by another investigator, providing us with a type of audit tool.

Teaching and learning

Older 'classic' studies in the social sciences and more contemporary focused sets of transcripts along with supporting documentation can provide valuable material for social science teaching, both in research methods and in substantive areas. Students can learn many fundamental aspects of qualitative research, and the theoretical and methodological strategies that helped to create chosen datasets, while also gaining first-hand experience of critically reanalysing and comparing data from well-known sources.

A good example of the learning potential of such datasets is provided by the Katherine Buildings study undertaken by Peter Townsend in the late 1950s, and now archived by Qualidata. This unpublished study of social change is itself a restudy. It focused on the inhabitants of Katharine Buildings in Stepney, London, established in 1885 as an experiment in improving working-class housing conditions. Townsend's study includes his analysis of the original ledgers and notes kept by the managers of the Buildings, archived at the London School of Economics, who included the young Beatrice Potter (Webb), and his own interviews with residents, some of whom were descendants of the original inhabitants. The questionnaires, with many open-ended questions, provide a unique picture of a working-class community in transition. Using these materials in a learning environment, students can examine data collected using sociological and anthropological research methods, and can compare these with earlier historical data collected in the late nineteenth century. Training exercises can take up aspects of long-term social change, such as the kinship patterns recorded in both Townsend's interview material, questionnaires and notes, and Webb's detailed notes on the tenants (Qualidata, 1999). Students can also be encouraged to examine the methods used and the research outcomes, and to consider whether they may have approached the research differently.

Learning about the work of researchers who have made a significant impact in their field allows young researchers to take the best practice elements from this work and further develop them in their own research work (cf. Zeitlyn, 2000).

DIFFICULTIES IN REUSING DATA

We have demonstrated earlier that the practice of secondary analysis of qualitative data is not a commonplace research activity. Why has there been a reluctance to draw on material created by other researchers? Is it that it is a problem of the implicit nature of qualitative data collection and analysis? Or is it a question of lack of time to become fully acquainted with research materials created by someone else? How constraining is informed consent? And what about scientific verification – is there an insecurity about the exposure of one's own research practice?

The recent, though sparse, literature points to a number of key concerns regarding the practice of reusing qualitative data. However, in discussing the issues directly with qualitative researchers, it appears that the views are by no means homogenous. In fact, when asked what, if any, barriers existed to further exploitation of data by a secondary analyst, responses varied from overt support for sharing one's own data to vehement displeasure at the thought of being asked to share a 'possession' considered to be of personal value (Corti et al., 1995; Corti, 2000; Fink, 2000).

Here we identify the key issues that present themselves as difficulties in both reusing and sharing data, and discuss possible measures for overcoming them.

Ethical and consent considerations

The prime anxiety of most researchers relates to questions of confidentiality and agreements made at the time of fieldwork. Such concerns about confidentiality have been discussed in detail in other papers (Corti et al., 2000), and a number of guidelines for researchers on the ethical and legal issues surrounding informed consent, confidentiality and copyright with respect to reusing data have now been published (e.g. Qualidata, 1998; ESRC, 1999; Oral History Society, 2002).

Archived data should always conform to ethical and legal guidelines with respect to the preservation of anonymity when this has been requested by informants or guaranteed to them. There are various ways of achieving this, ranging from fully anonymizing the original data – which in some cases would seriously damage its value – to obtaining legal undertakings to protect informants' anonymity from any researcher allowed to consult the dataset.

Finally, tied up with ethical considerations is that of the copyright ownership, by the interviewee, of the words they have spoken. Under the 1998 UK Copyrights, Designs and Patents Acts, copying work, such as citing large extracts in a research publication, is considered to be an infringement unless it is within the context of 'fair dealing'. For other future researchers to be able to exploit their data fully, it is essential for investigators to obtain from informants in writing a transfer of copyright, or permission to archive for other future research use (Qualidata, 1998).

Representation, coverage and context of the research and fieldwork

In the process of analysing and coding data, researchers use their own personal knowledge and experiences as tools to make sense of the material, which may be indefinable and cannot

be easily documented. A pertinent question we must consider, then, is whether data can be effectively used by someone who has not been involved in the original study. How much of the jigsaw can be missing yet leave the puzzle still worth attempting?

Mauthner et al. (1998) argue that 'data are the product of the reflexive relationship between the researcher and researched, constrained and informed by biographical, historical, political, theoretical and epistemological contingencies' (1998: 742). The researcher's own reflexivity enhances the raw data gathered and stimulates the formulation of new hypotheses in the field. Additionally, in-depth interviewing or observation requires a full advance preparation, with the researcher becoming familiar with the context of a respondent's community, generation, work, and personal and family life. Some researchers thus believe that qualitative data cannot be used sensibly without the accumulated background knowledge and tacit understanding that the original investigator had acquired – understanding commonly not written down but held in the researcher's head. Thus the original context can never be truly reconstructed. The complexity, quirks, or lack of adequate documentation of data may thus be major difficulties in reanalysis, particularly when no input from the original investigating team is possible (Corti and Wright, 2002). The loss of the essential contextual experience of 'being there' and the lack of being able to engage in reflexive interpretation may then be viewed as a barrier to reuse. Even when revisiting one's own data, the problem of loss of context may apply. Mauthner et al. (1998) highlight how their own 'ability to interpret their own data may also decline over time as memories wane; changes in personal situation and new knowledge that they have gained since the primary study may also influence their reinterpretation of the data'.

However, the loss of context in archived data should not be seen as an insurmountable barrier to reuse. Indeed, there are very common and accepted instances where research data is used in a 'second-hand' sense by investigators themselves. For example, principal investigators writing up the final analysis may not have been directly engaged in fieldwork, having employed research staff to collect data. Similarly, for those working in research teams sharing one's own experiences of the fieldwork and its context are essential, but never total. In both instances, the analysers or authors must rely on fieldworkers and co-workers documenting detailed notes about the project and communicating them. However, documentation of the research process can help recover a degree of context, and while it cannot compete with 'being there', fieldnotes, letters and memos documenting the research can serve to help aid the original fieldwork experience. Audio-visual recordings of interviews can also enhance the capacity to reuse data without having actually collected them.

A further issue concerning representation of the interview is the nature or method of transcription. Ways of transcribing interviews vary enormously between disciplines and individuals. As such, transcriptions are usually a subjective interpretation of the real-life original. While sociologists typically want to capture the words, conversation analysts and socio-linguistics are more concerned with documenting the paralinguistic features of speech, such as pauses, laughter, tears, and so on. In terms of maximizing the potential of a qualitative dataset for reuse, then, the ideal scenario is to retain original audio recordings. Jacobsson, in this volume (Chapter 22), demonstrates the problem of transcription very clearly in her description of revisiting her own collection. Her original interview transcriptions were highly edited, so that in order to pursue her new line of inquiry, she needed to go back and re-transcribe parts of the data – to consider the nuances of hesitancy, embarrassment and defensiveness previously unobserved. This illustration demonstrates the value of retaining audio material for archival collections of qualitative data.

Finally, the parts of a collection that find their way into an archive, either personal or public, may not represent the original collection in its entirety. Research collections are vulnerable to erosion or fragmentation, both from natural causes – like accidental loss or damage – or man-made reasons such as a policy of deliberate weeding or disposal for lack of sufficient storage space. Particularly sensitive interviews may have been destroyed, sometimes at the behest of the interviewee. In short, material is judged to be worthy of preservation by the originator as well as the archivist. It is therefore important for archivists to document, where possible, what data is missing and why.

Hammersley summarizes these points concisely: 'the data collected by different researchers will be structured by various purposes and conceptions of what is relevant. As a result, users of archives are likely to find that some of the data or information required for their purposes is not available' (Hammersley, 1997: 139). Hence reusers of data will need to use their own judgement in assessing the quality of the material. Nor should we forget that the practice of research in other disciplines, such as social

history, is fully based on interpreting evidence created by other witnesses.

Unfamiliarity with the method

Because most qualitative researchers are unused to consulting data collected by other people, their concept of 'secondary analysis' is still typically associated with the 'number crunching' of survey datasets. By contrast, the positive experiences of researchers who have gone back to their own data or have embarked upon new investigations on archived data testify how fruitful the effort can be (Fielding and Fielding, 2000; Åkerström et al., Chapter 22, this volume). We would therefore assume that with time the inhibition of unfamiliarity with reanalysis will become much less relevant than it is today.

Lack of infrastructure for data-sharing

One of the barriers to reusing data in the past, and indeed in many countries still, has been the lack of an infrastructure to enable access to the rich research data collected in the academic community. While in some disciplines professional networks enable high-quality data to be shared on an informal basis, the preservation of these sources is not ensured, nor does it allow equal access for all researchers. The growing establishment of national data-sharing policies is helping to secure data and provide access and support for reuse, although the stock of data archived still rests on willingness to share by the original investigators.

Documenting data to the high standard required to render it easily accessible, however, can be a huge task, particularly without specific funding to support this. Investigators who have constructed large-scale or perhaps long-running studies may be daunted by the prospect of transforming their data into a widely usable resource. If qualitative data are to be shared, the infrastructure needs to be in place to offer guidance, support and adequate funding from the start of the project to enable the documentation and archiving of its data.

The question of public investment in archiving is an issue that is often mooted by research investigators. A significant tension between investment in data preparation for archiving and new data collection and primary research, in a world in which scientific budgets are limited, must be recognized. Indeed, where a prospective data policy exists, such as for the Economic and Social Research Council in the UK and the National Science Foundation in the US, resources for archiving can compete with those for new research. Many researchers see the need for a policy to determine relative levels of investment in data preparation and documentation according to different types of datasets and for different end uses. For example, for large-scale or longitudinal studies the not insignificant costs of good project housekeeping, high-quality data documentation, anonymization and sample maintenance are valued as good investments. With smaller studies, however, most of the needs for making future archiving possible can also be viewed as useful for the research itself, as a form of structuring and good housekeeping.

Misinterpretation

Concerns about misinterpretation of data may arise from fear of selective and opportunistic interpretation in reanalysis. Researchers conducting longitudinal programmes feel particularly vulnerable due to the potentially negative impact of bad publicity on sample attrition. Finally, there is a concern surrounding the misuse of politically sensitive occupational or environmental data by pressure groups, industry or the press (Corti and Wright, 2002). While journalistic misinterpretation is harder to control, most instances have in practice ensued from publication by the original researchers rather than from archiving. Straightforward misinterpretation by other academics is not often a problem. Much more typical, and usually after a considerable time-lag, is a serious critique of the original study. But this is precisely how intellectual understanding advances. And paradoxically, at the same time it may give the original study new attention and esteem, both because of the controversy generated, and because the criticism itself recognizes the original as a worthwhile target.

Threat to intellectual property rights

Some researchers have voiced concern over the loss of their control over data or their intellectual property rights when data become publicly archived. Many wish to complete working on the data before it can be offered to the wider community. In the medical field, there is a perception that investigators may not get their names on secondary research papers as collaborators if the datasets were accessed through an independent archive (Corti and Wright, 2002). Keeping data in-house and restricting access is thus one way of preserving intellectual capital.

Other researchers consider their data as private property, and seem almost bonded to their own ethnographic fieldwork notebooks or interviews. Anthropologists may have built a career around studying one particular remote region, and the data generated over the course of a professional career will be seen as unique, as a stock of intellectual capital that he or she can exploit through their lifetime.

PERSONAL REFLECTIONS OF REUSING DATA: AN ACCOUNT BY PAUL THOMPSON

Having put forward a number of approaches to reusing existing qualitative data, and discussed the potential benefits of and difficulties in reanalysis, in this section we observe the reflections of an experienced researcher who has reused data. Did he reuse data to answer substantive questions or for methodological purposes? How useful were the data sources he drew upon? Were they rich enough for him to pursue his line of inquiry? Following Thompson's testimony, we assess these issues.

I have worked in sociology for over thirty years, but my first research in the early 1960s was as a social historian, and I still keep some of the influence of that early experience. Historians were and are still essentially jackdaws, scavengers: they use other people's detritus rather than create their own data. At that time historians got no training of any kind in research methods, but two things were always clear. First, you should be willing to make the best use you could of whatever sources you could find, whether in public archives, or in business offices, or in private house attics or sheds. And second, you should search for unknown new sources, for finding a significant new source was the biggest scoop you could make.

My thesis was about the labour movement in London, and I was also writing about architectural history as a sideline. I certainly had my own high moments of discovery. I still have vivid memories of an old socialist bringing out precious minute books from his garden shed in a North London suburb; or of cold winter days in the grimy unlit cellar of a Birmingham glassworks, reading packets of letters from the 1850s, unopened for a century, in the fading daylight. One certainly had to be prepared to suffer in the cause, of course much less drastically than an anthropologist, but I do remember eating squashed flies in a cut bread sandwich offered to me by a Yorkshire vicar whose son was keeping a chicken farm on the glebe (the parish priest's land) next to the vicarage – and it paid off, because within an hour he had lent me another precious bundle of forgotten correspondence.

As it turned out, one of the best sets of already archived sources for my labour movement thesis turned out to be in the library of the London School of Economics. The core was the deposit by LSE's founders, Sidney and Beatrice Webb, pioneers of British social science, of their own papers covering their lifetime's personal activity, politics and research work. Beatrice Webb had the foresight to keep her handwritten notes of the large number of interviews that she carried out with union leaders from the 1880s for their classic pioneering study of British trade unionism (Webb, 1894). These notes provided me with unique information, by far the best source on the earlier development of trade unionism in the capital. I did not realize the full significance of this experience at the time, or recognize how the systematic quality of this material and the thoroughness of its scope were consequences of its being research data: for me, it was simply a very good source. But I did not forget Beatrice Webb's example, and it was one of the early influences that set me on the path to Qualidata.

First experiences of archiving and reusing interviews: early twentieth-century family relationships

Most of my research in the last thirty years has focused on family relationships, how they change, and how they relate to the economy and the community. Soon after I came to Essex, initially as a social historian, Peter Townsend, the first Professor of Sociology at Essex, with whom I taught a course on social policy and social change, suggested to me that it might be worthwhile to interview older people for my research. And to help convince me, he showed me bunches of extracts from the interviews he had recorded himself for his first major book, *The Family Life of Old People* (Townsend, 1957). I remember in particular the vivid material on changing funeral customs. So here was a second experience of reuse. And it is good to know that those same interviews, along with the whole data from Peter Townsend 's lifetime of research, very likely the most in-depth documentation that will ever be collected of the conditions and experience of old age and poverty in Britain, a unique and unrepeatable set of qualitative research material, have now been archived by Qualidata in the National Archive of Social Policy and Social Change at the University of Essex.

Initially, however, the influence of these interviews led me towards my first important experience of creating my own research material through interviewing. Commissioned to write a social history of Britain in the early twentieth century, I wanted to write about the themes that a sociologist would have then highlighted for a portrait of contemporary Britain, including gender issues, childhood, youth culture, the informal culture of work and family leisure, sexuality and marriage. As a result of receiving a generous grant from the new Social Science Research Council in 1970, our research team were able to carry out some 450 interviews right across Britain with a quota sample of men and women born between the 1870s and 1906.

These interviews provided the basis for a large part of my book *The Edwardians* (Thompson, 1975). In practice it proved impossible to use the whole set, because there was much too much information to absorb. Nor was there appropriate software to help us: we sorted out the transcripts into themes using scissors and staples. I used the interviews not only in detail for cross-analysis, for example of childrearing practices such as punishment by parents, but also as a set of in-depth family portraits to illustrate the whole range of the social spectrum, from a landowning family at one extreme to a Welsh West Indian boarding house or an impoverished London labourer's home at the other; and two final portraits of women, a London socialist and a struggling Stoke pottery worker, as examples of the contrasting dynamics of social change, conscious and unconscious.

We developed our interviewing method for this project initially from sociological influences. Right from the start we always used an interview guide, but equally importantly, we used it with a light touch, flexibly, giving as much space as possible to the informant to talk freely. It was only later on that we learnt that a comparable practice using the memories of the old – but without samples or interview guides, and then mainly focusing on 'great men' – had evolved in the USA under the title 'oral history'. But by the later 1970s there had sprung up not only an international oral history movement, but also a parallel movement among life-story sociologists launched by Daniel Bertaux from France. This first project for *The Edwardians* was closer to oral history, in that we only collected detailed evidence from informants about their lives up to 1918, which was the period I needed for my book. In retrospect, I feel that this was a serious mistake, because the potential value of the interviews, for example for studying social mobility or intergenerational influences, would have been far greater if they had also covered the missing fifty years up to the present. It would have been better to have done fewer but fuller interviews. All my later projects have used full life-story interviews, and I believe that this is the form not only most likely to reveal insights to the original researcher, but also for subsequent users.

It was, however, clear to us from very early on that we were collecting a unique set of interviews of great potential value to others, and so we set up an informal archive in the department. The interviews were read over the next twenty years by large numbers of both students and outside researchers, and the result was a far larger number of publications by others than we could have ever achieved on our own – at least five times the output from the research. These include, for example, Standish Meacham's *A Life Apart*, David Crouch and Colin Ward's *The Allotment* on working-class culture; substantial parts of Charles More's *Skill and the English Working Class* and Michael Childs's *Labour's Apprentices* on work; and John Gillis, *For Better, For Worse,* on marriage, as well as articles on class by Patrick Joyce and Richard Trainor, on social mobility by David Vincent, and on women and the family by Ellen Ross.

Although in recent years the most important users have been other researchers, I have also had the experience of reusing my own material from a new perspective for a later project. This was the research on the experience of ageing, funded as part of the Economic and Social Research Council's Ageing Initiative which I carried out in the late 1980s, leading to the publication of *I Don't Feel Old* (Thompson et al., 1990). We also collected a substantial new dataset for this, interviewing up to three generations in a national sample of 'the Hundred Families' (Thompson and Bertaux, 1993), a very rich source which, to my surprise, has not attracted reusers in the way that the set for *The Edwardians* does, although providing just the same type of information for the period since 1920. However, combining information from the earlier dataset with the new evidence undoubtedly gave us added strengths.

A key issue for the new project was how relationships between grandparents and grandchildren were changing over the longer timespan. So the first advantage of the older material was that it went back twenty or more years further, with recollections of grandparents by informants born as far back as the 1880s. This meant that I was able to write a whole chapter in *I Don't Feel Old*, 'At the Edge of Living Memory', on the experience of ageing in an earlier generation, through the point of view of grandchildren. A second advantage was more accidental. When I was researching for *The Edwardians*, I had not been interested in grandparenting as such, so that the interview guide did not include any questions about this topic. But the consequence was that the material on grandparents that did appear in the interviews was spontaneous, because people just wanted to tell us about them. With the later research, by contrast, we deliberately drew them out. So we could compare how far the two forms of interview brought in similar material – and reassuringly, it was indeed broadly similar. We were also able to evaluate from the earlier interviews, I think more clearly because they were more spontaneous, for how many people was a grandparent really significant?

Being able to estimate the earlier significance of grandparents was one important gain from having an alternative dataset to reuse. We were also able to draw a good picture of older people's occupations and other sources of income in the late nineteenth century, a point on which contemporary statistics are not at all reliable. And we gained a lot of information too about mutual help, exchanges of help each way between the generations, the extent of influence of grandparents, and the varying ways in which grandchildren helped them in later life. None of this would have been possible if we had not kept the material, and we undoubtedly learnt a lot from it in new ways.

Commentary on Paul Thompson's experience

Like Jacobsson's account of recycling data in this volume (Chapter 22), Thompson's own experiences of attempting reanalysis of one's own data offer us first-hand insight into some of the real issues encountered.

In his early days as a young researcher, Thompson was heavily influenced by famous social research pioneers, such as the Webbs and Peter Townsend, both of whom had collected highly detailed notes from fieldwork. But his first experience of reusing research materials was for historical and descriptive purposes, to provide information on the development of the London labour and socialist movement.

His desire to consult existing sources of data later on in his career arose from this first-hand experience of using archives as a social historian, and from the belief that rich data, such as the life-story material he began to collect, should be made available to others.

Some years down the track, now as an experienced researcher, Thompson hoped to study social mobility and intergenerational influences using a set of interviews he had already collected himself. This hope was thwarted due to the fact that he did not have access to critical information – the latter half of the interviewees' lives that he could have collected at the time of interviewing. This oversight caused him to review his own data-collection strategy for subsequent studies, and he advocated for all future studies the use of full life-story interviews. Here we see evidence of a fundamental development of methodology.

The second occurrence of reuse reported by Thompson concerned a new interest in a topic not specifically covered in the original set of interviews. Mentions of grandparenting, however, turned out to be richly sprinkled among the interviews. As a consequence the data could be reanalysed with this new focus in mind.

QUALITATIVE DATA: ITS LONGEVITY, AND WHAT TO PRESERVE TO ENSURE MAXIMUM REUSE

Creating a national stock of qualitative research resources requires that the collections acquired are suitable for informed use and meet the demand from researchers. National qualitative data archives such as Qualidata and the Murray Research Center have acquisitions policies to ensure that all materials deposited meet certain criteria: that data are documented to a minimum standard, are in appropriate formats, are complete, and that confidentiality, data protection and copyright issues have been addressed. Priorities must also be assigned to data, so that the inflow of data meets the resources available for processing. Potential studies are thus always evaluated from a long-range perspective to predict their future value. Priorities focus on:

- the historical value of the study;
- data complementary to existing data holdings;
- data that have further analytic potential than the original investigation, i.e. have not been exhaustively analysed;
- data based on large-scale national samples;
- data that are longitudinal in design;
- the possibility of further follow-up of the sample;
- mixed methods data;
- studies that include a wide range of measures.

Data format

The format and mark-up of data also determine the usefulness of a collection: for example, whether a study is available digitally, and how the text has been described and marked up. Recommended strategies for the preparation, storage and dissemination of qualitative data are published elsewhere (Corti, 2002). There is a debate about the long-term value of coded data, mainly because the coding process is subjective, often geared towards specific themes, and therefore may not be applicable to the secondary analyst's topic of investigation. For larger studies, however, there is a stronger case for retaining coded data, in order to aid searching within voluminous bodies of text. Indeed, the 'Edwardians Online' project (Barker, 2002) has followed the structure of the existing coding to provide navigation through the huge bulk of text – some 50,000 pages of interview transcript.

CONCLUSION

In this chapter we set out to demonstrate how existing sources of qualitative data can be reused. Firstly, this is because secondary analysis makes more effective use of material that is costly to collect; secondly, it enables further exploration of the data from a new perspective; thirdly, it enables comparative research to be carried out in a number of contexts (e.g. geographically, over time, cross-culturally); and last, it allows for verification of the original study.

In many ways these methods parallel those that are used and documented for the secondary analysis of survey data: comparative research; replication or restudy; asking new questions of old data; the strengthening of scientific inquiry through the open discussion of methods; help in new research designs; and providing resources for training in research and substantive learning.

We have shown that there are important gains to be made from reanalysis. At the start of a research project, it can be invaluable in providing a sense of the topics that can be successfully covered in interviewing, and therefore make the pilot stage of the new project both more effective and also much swifter. At a later stage a comparable interview set may also provide a crucial wider sample base for testing the interpretations that are emerging. Finally, by making research data available to reanalysis by others, the investigator may multiply the outcomes from this initial research through the publications of others from the same material.

Equally there are methodological and practical difficulties in reusing data, which include understanding the coverage and context of the research; ethical and consent considerations; unfamiliarity with the method; and the general lack of suitable data available.

Over the last five years we have witnessed a new culture of the secondary use of qualitative data, which has been largely born out of data-sharing policies, such as in the UK. This new culture needs to be nurtured by acquiring relevant data and documenting and presenting it in user-friendly ways. Qualitative data services can help fulfil this role by encouraging a culture of sharing in research practice and enabling support; developing appropriate collection priorities; creating digital resources for teaching and research; and by offering support and outreach activities such as training. It is also significant from the experiences of two well-established centres, the Mass-Observation archive in Britain and the Murray Research Center in the US, and also by the major ethnological archives in Scandinavia, that a particularly effective model is to combine archiving with in-house research on the data held: this generates both relevant acquisitions and a high level of use by researchers. Finally, looking into the future, innovative online data access and analysis tools are very likely to both encourage and facilitate the reuse of qualitative data.

NOTE

1 In 1999 Qualidata conducted a national survey of academics and researchers to ascertain what kind of data resources researchers wished for, receiving over 550 valid responses from a wide range of user communities. 92 per cent wanted to see datasets in a digital and accessible format that could be used for both research and teaching purposes. The highest demand was for qualitative data on health, criminology and social policy (Corti and Thompson, 2000).

REFERENCES

Allwood, J., Björnberg, M., Grönqvist, L., Ahlsén, E. and Ottesjö, C. (2000) 'The spoken language corpus at the Department of Linguistics, Göteborg University', *Forum: Qualitative Sozialforschung/Forum: Qualitative Social Research* [online journal], 1(3) (December). Available at: http://qualitative-research.net/fqs/fqs-eng.htm

Barker, E. (2002) *The Edwardians Online Pilot Resource.* Qualidata, UK Data Archive.

Booth, C. (1891–1902) *Life and Labour of the People in London.* London: Williams & Norgate; Macmillan.

Brunswick, A.F. (1980) 'Health stability and change: a study of urban black youth', *American Journal of Public Health*, 70: 504–13.

Burgess, R.G. (ed.) (1982) *Field Research: A Sourcebook and Field Manual.* London: Unwin Hyman.

Charlesworth, J. and Fink, J. (2001) 'Historians and social science research data: the Peter Townsend Collection', *History Workshop Journal*, 51: 206–19.

Cohen, S. (1971) *Folk Devils and Moral Panics: The Creation of the Mods and Rockers.* Oxford: Basil Blackwell.

Cohen, S. and Taylor, L. (1972) *Psychological Survival: The Effects of Long-Term Imprisonment.* London: Allen Lane.

Corti, L. (2000) 'Progress and problems of preserving and providing access to qualitative data for social research – the international picture of an emerging culture', *Forum: Qualitative Social Research* [online journal], 1(3).

Corti, L. (2002) *Qualitative Data Processing Guidelines.* Qualidata, UK Data Archive.

Corti, L. and Thompson, P. (2000) *Annual Report of Qualidata to the ESRC.* University of Essex.

Corti, L. and Wright, M. (2002) *Consultants' Report to the Medical Research Council on the MRC Population Data Archiving and Access Project.* UK Data Archive, University of Essex.

Corti, L., Foster, J. and Thompson, P. (1995) 'Archiving qualitative research data', *Social Research Update,* No. 10. Department of Sociology, University of Surrey.

Corti, L., Day, A. and Backhouse, G. (2000) 'Confidentiality and informed consent: issues for consideration in the preservation of and provision of access to qualitative data archives', *Forum: Qualitative Social Research* [online journal], 1(3).

Courtney, C. and Thompson, P. (1996) *City Lives.* London: Methuen.

Dein, A. and Perks, R. (eds) (1993) *Lives in Steel: Audio Compilation.* London: British Library.

Elder, G.H. (1974) *Children of the Great Depression: Social Change in Life Experience.* Chicago: University of Chicago Press.

ESRC (1999) *Guidelines on Copyright and Confidentiality: Legal Issues for Social Science Researchers.* Swindon: ESRC.

ESRC (2002) *ESRC Datasets Policy.* Swindon: ESRC.

Fielding, N. and Fielding, J. (2000) 'Resistance and adaptation to criminal identity: using secondary analysis to evaluate classic studies of crime and deviance', *Sociology,* 34(4): 671–89.

Fink, A.S. (2000) 'The role of the researcher in qualitative research', *Forum: Qualitative Social Research* [online journal], 1(3).

Franz, C., McClelland, D. and Weinberger, J. (1991) 'Childhood antecedents of conventional social accomplishment in midlife adults: a 36-year prospective study', *Journal of Personality and Social Psychology,* 60(4): 586–95.

Glueck, S. and Glueck, E. (1968) *Delinquents and Nondelinquents in Perspective.* Cambridge, MA: Harvard University Press.

Goldthorpe, J., Lockwood, D., Bechhofer, F. and Platt, J. (1968) *The Affluent Worker: Industrial Attitudes and Behaviour.* Cambridge: Cambridge University Press.

Hammersley, M. (1997) 'Qualitative data archiving: some reflections on its prospects and problems', *Sociology,* 31(1): 131–42.

James, J. and Sorensen, A. (2000) 'Archiving longitudinal data for future research: why qualitative data add to a study's usefulness', *Forum: Qualitative Social Research* [online journal], 1(3).

Kvale, S. (1996) *Interviews: An Introduction to Qualitative Research Interviewing.* Thousand Oaks, CA: Sage.

Kynaston, D. (2001) *The City of London,* Vol. IV: *A Club No More, 1945–2000.* London: Pimlico.

Kynaston, D. (2002) 'Three taps on the nose', *National Life Story Collection Newsletter,* 8: 1–2.

Laub, J. and Sampson, R. (1998) 'Integrating quantitative and qualitative data', in J. Giele and G. Elder, Jr (eds), *Methods of Life Course Research.* Thousand Oaks, CA: Sage, pp. 213–30.

Leh, A. (2000) 'Problems of archiving oral history interviews: the example of the archive German memory', *Forum: Qualitative Social Research* [online journal], 1(3).

Lewis, O. (1963) *Tepotzlan Restudied: Life in a Mexican Village.* Urbana: University of Illinois Press.

Llewellyn Smith, H. (1937–5) *The New Survey of London Life and Labour.* London: P.S. King.

Luder, M., Neukom, M. and Thomann, B. (2000) 'The JAKOB database: psychodynamic psychotherapy research at the University of Zürich', *Forum: Qualitative Social Research* [online journal], 1(3).

Lux, Z. (2000) 'Computerized support for research and publication in contemporary history', *Forum: Qualitative Social Research* [online journal], 1(3).

Lynd, R.S. and Lynd, H. (1929) *Middletown: A Study in American Culture.* New York: Harcourt, Brace.

Lynd, R.S. and Lynd, H. (1937) *Middletown in Transition: A Study in Cultural Conflicts.* New York: Harcourt, Brace.

Malinowski, B. (1967) *A Diary in the Strictest Sense.* London: Routledge & Kegan Paul.

Marwick, A. (1970) *The Nature of History.* London: Macmillan.

Mauthner, N., Parry, O. and Backett-Milburn, K. (1998) 'The data are out there, or are they? Implications for archiving and revisiting qualitative data', *Sociology,* 32(4): 733–45.

May, E.T. (1988) *Homeward Bound: American Families in the Cold War Era.* New York: Basic Books.

Newson, J. and Newson, E. (1963) *Infant Care in an Urban Community.* London: Allen & Unwin.

Newson, J. and Newson, E. (1976) *Seven Years Old in the Home Environment.* London: Allen & Unwin.

Oral History Society (2002) *Oral History Society Ethical Guidelines.* London: Oral History Society.

Platt, J. (1996) *A History of Sociological Research Methods in America, 1920–1960.* Cambridge: Cambridge University Press.

Plummer, K. (1983) *Documents of Life: An Introduction to the Problems and Literature of a Humanistic Method.* London: Unwin Hyman.

Qualidata (1998) *Legal and Ethical Issues in Interviewing.* Qualidata website www.qualidata.essex.ac.uk

Qualidata (1999) *Teaching Pack, The Last Refuge: A Qualitative Research Study by Peter Townsend.* University of Essex.

Redfield, R. (1930) *Tepotzlan: A Mexican Village; a Study of Folklife.* Chicago: University of Chicago Press.

Rex, J. and Moore, R. (1967) *Race, Community and Conflict*. Oxford: Oxford University Press.

Rowntree, B.S. (1901) *Poverty, a Study of Town Life*. London: Macmillan.

Sears, R., Maccoby, E. and Levin, H. (1957) *Patterns of Child Rearing*. Stanford, CA: Stanford University Press.

Sheridan, D. (2000) 'Reviewing Mass-Observation: the archive and its researchers thirty years on', *Forum: Qualitative Social Research* [online journal], 1(3).

Silverman, D. (2000) *Doing Qualitative Research: A Practical Handbook*. London: Sage.

Stacey, M. (1974) 'The myth of community studies', in C. Bell and H. Newby (eds), *The Sociology of Community*. London: Frank Cass, pp. 13–26.

Stewart, A. and Healy, J. (1989) 'Linking individual development and social changes', *American Psychologist*, 44(1): 37–42.

Strauss, A.L. and Corbin, J. (1990) *Basics of Qualitative Research: Grounded Theory Procedures and Techniques*. Newbury Park, CA: Sage.

Szabo, V. and Strang, V.R. (1997) 'Secondary analysis of qualitative data', *Advances in Nursing Science*, 20(2): 66–74.

Terman, L.M. (1954) 'Scientists and non-scientists in a group of 800 gifted men', *Psychological Monographs: General and Applied*, 68(7): (whole issue No. 378): 1–44.

Thompson, P. (1975) *The Edwardians: The Remaking of British Society*. London: Weidenfeld & Nicolson.

Thompson, P. (1991) *Pilot Study of Archiving Qualitative Data: Report to ESRC*. Department of Sociology, University of Essex.

Thompson, P. (2000) *The Voice of the Past* (3rd revised ed. 1st ed. 1978). Oxford: Oxford University Press.

Thompson, P. and Bertaux, D. (eds) (1993) *Between Generations*. Oxford: Oxford University Press.

Thompson, P. and Corti, L. (1998) 'Are you sitting on your qualitative data? Qualidata's mission', *Social Research Methodology: Theory and Practice*, 1(1): 85–90.

Thompson, P., Itzin, C. and Abendstern, M. (1990) *I Don't Feel Old: The Experience of Ageing*. Oxford: Oxford University Press.

Townsend, P. (1957) *The Family Life of Old People*. London: Routledge.

Townsend, P. (1962) *The Last Refuge: A Survey of Residential Institutions and Homes for the Aged in England and Wales*. London: Routledge.

Townsend, P. (1979) *Poverty in the United Kingdom: A Survey of Household Resources and Standards of Living*. London: Penguin Books.

Webb, S. and Webb, B. (1894, revised ed. 1920) *History of Trade Unionism*. London: Longmans, Green.

Zeitlyn, D. (2000) 'Archiving anthropology', *Forum: Qualitative Social Research* [online journal], 1(3).

22

Reanalysis of previously collected material

Malin Åkerström, Katarina Jacobsson
and David Wästerfors

A common and relatively fixed view portrays field research in a linear, steplike fashion (Gubrium, 1991: 132). We are taught to gain access to a field, collect data, analyse them and write things down – in that order. The 'writing up' is seen as a final statement; a specific report, article or book counts as the end in the production of research. In this chapter, on the other hand, we argue for the significance of continuous analytical exploration. Instead of discarding material that has been collected earlier on the simple grounds that it has already been written up, we maintain the importance of allowing ourselves to revisit and reanalyse it. In their chapter on secondary analysis of archived qualitative data, Corti and Thompson (Chapter 21, this volume) make the same argument but concentrate on revisiting others' material rather than – as in our case – one's own.

We want to counter an oft-repeated worry among graduate students and colleagues that their data once used cannot be used again, or that their data are getting old. A return to dusty material from the past, we argue, may not only be fruitful but also intellectually stimulating and fun. These positive values derive from an explorative potential that may be found particularly through long-term familiarity with material. Despite this potential, 'we rarely go back to try out radically alternative versions to see where they might lead' (Atkinson, 1992: 452).

Recycling data is nothing new or out of the ordinary.[1] Most ethnographers do it, perhaps using 'key incidents' to illustrate a new analytical point, as Emerson discusses in this volume (Chapter 29). In a way, recycling is a matter of degree. It can take the form of a distillation process where one theme guides a search through older material gathered in other settings

than the one studied at the time (see e.g. Emerson et al., 1995: 176–7). Here we will address a more drastic recycling: applying a new perspective or grid to the material.

Two cases in which the researcher actually did go back serve as the focal point in this chapter. The first one is a study of a single interview picked from a research project carried out twenty years ago. One of us recently used this tiny piece of material in a Swedish anthology, thereby epitomizing and exemplifying its specific theme: victims who do not want to present themselves as such (Åkerström, 2001). The second case is a major work in which one of us reinterpreted the whole material from her previously analysed and published study. In so doing, she developed a tailored discursive perspective in order to reconsider a certain field: the Swedish deaf world (Jacobsson, 2000). Using these two cases as points of departures, an interview revisited and a field reanalysed, we want to display and discuss the explorative potential of recycling data.

The following text is organized into three parts. The first two parts contain our empirical cases, written in the first person singular. In the third part we discuss our cases in more general terms and outline some conclusions.

REVISITING DATA: GIVING VOICE TO ANNIE

The researcher's narrative

Shortly after finishing my dissertation (Åkerström, 1983/1985), in which I analysed criminal life-styles, I was asked to conduct a study on violence and threats in prisons.

Although I was slightly tired of the field, the offer promised some freedom in relation to the duties I was fulfilling at the Swedish National Council for Crime Prevention. In contrast to the autonomous conditions as a graduate student, this bureaucracy expected its employees to be present at the office, to partake in coffee breaks and to demonstrate interest in the contemporary debates on criminal policy. The task I was now offered, on the other hand, gave me a chance to work on my own.

As a result, three graduate students in sociology and myself roamed the country for prisons during 1983 and 1984. The Swedish Correctional Authorities required that both inmates and staff, men and women, were interviewed at various prisons. In the end the study covered 145 persons.

Retrospectively, I remember only a few of the inmates. There was one woman, though, who was hard to forget. I have named her Annie. She presented herself in much the same ways as the male criminals I had studied in my previous project: entrepreneurial, self-contained, independent. In short, she did not express herself in ways that invoked pity. This was rare among the women inmates we talked to, maybe not because of their gender, but perhaps because this study focused on conflicts *in* prison.

Annie, unlike the others, insisted on talking a lot about life *outside* prison, a topic that might offer more opportunities for declarations of agency and independence. She also told me about her former violent relationship with a man. She could thus have matched the typical construction of 'battered women', who according to researchers at the time were supposed to be 'oversocialized into feminine identity', 'bewildered and helpless', 'immature and lacking clear self-identities' and 'overwhelmingly passive and unable to act on their own behalf' (Loseke and Cahill, 1984). However, none of these labels could be attached to Annie, in fact reverse labels would have fitted better. Annie also made an impression on me by countering her rather tough language with a certain appearance. She entered the visitor's room smiling and carrying a sponge cake, announcing she had baked it that morning. Her general appearance was that of a rather ordinary, confident, healthy young woman, around 26–28 years old. Our meeting had some 'cozy' and conventional elements to it, as if ignoring the environment in which it took place. We talked, laughed and had coffee, cake and cigarettes.

The reasons why Annie was stuck in my mind had much to do with her defiance of the common understanding of criminal women in general, and of female drug addicts and 'battered women' in particular. Occasionally I have also thought about my interview with her as an unsolved

analytical problem. I felt that I had not done justice to it. More exactly, I used some parts but not in order to focus on what seemed special about the interview as a whole. The only extract included in my original report was placed in a discussion on how snitches were detected. When talking about drug dealings, many interviewees described how other prisoners read and evaluated their 'papers', that is, court records and police reports:

> Different strategies are developed to protect oneself from snitches. Sending for court records in order to judge whether inmates are trustworthy becomes important in this context as well:
>
> > 'This thing with court records?'
> > 'Yeah, that's what you do. We send for court records. ... But things like that improve when there aren't any drugs. [Annie was serving time at Österåker, known as a drug-free prison.] Cause we don't have to look out for anyone – [...]. So we can accept each other, without asking. It must be good for the prison. ... At Hinseberg [another prison] it's more common 'cause there's stuff you're afraid they'll [the prison staff] get to know about. And then it becomes something else. Here, we don't have that problem. We don't ask each other; it's never talked about.'

> And a male inmate from Tidaholm [another prison] has the same point of view about the use of 'papers'. ... (Text and then a quote used as illustration.) (Åkerström, 1985: 116–17, translated)

Three stylistic and methodological features may be pointed out as emblematic in this extract. First, the report is written as a 'realist tale' (van Maanen, 1988). Formulations such as 'Different strategies are developed to protect oneself from snitches' indicate an attempt to analyse the inmates' conflicts as they manifested themselves in prison. However, I was aware that interviews were not an uncomplicated source. I did not solely interpret the answers in a naïve way, as clear-cut evidence of a reality 'out there', but also as indicating values and norms of a prison culture. Nevertheless, my analytical framework emphasized content more than form, the 'whats' rather than the 'hows' (Gubrium and Holstein, 1997: 38–56).

Second, the analysis was based on fragmentation of the transcripts into categories and instances. As Atkinson (1992) testifies, the conventional idea of the time when working with qualitative material was that of cutting extracts of one's interviews or fieldnotes into shorter fractions in order to illustrate different themes and categories, or variations within a theme or category. Consequently, the inmates' talk was more or less routinely disintegrated and distributed under several headings, creating concise and persuading 'excerpt-commentary units' (Emerson et al., 1995: 182) and thereby favouring certain lines of interpretation but obstructing others.

Third, our project operated under an expectancy of having numerous interviews. Textually representing and illustrating a subject presumed the use of many cases. As apparent in the extract above, I quickly introduced another interviewee after Annie's statement in order to expand and back up this passage with further empirical support. In a report of this kind, one was not supposed to linger on a single person's deliberations.

This way of analysis did not articulate the impression Annie made on me. I showed the interview to a colleague, Ann-Mari Sellerberg, who suggested I should write something about the whole piece since she thought it would be a pity to cut it up in the traditional way. I agreed in principle but shrugged it off, mainly because I did not know how to do it. The thing that came to my mind was a case study. In criminology, there are several such minor classics as Shaw's *The Jack-Roller* (1930/1968), Sutherland's *The Professional Thief* (1937) and Klockars's *The Professional Fence* (1974), but they have all known a great deal more about their subjects. Klockars, for instance, interviewed and observed Vincent's dealings as a fence for fifteen months. In contrast to the vast and rich empirical material in these works, I had my one and only interview.

Apart from seeing funding of the project as nearly impossible, an observation study was out of the question for practical reasons. I had a small baby at that time, and moreover, I have never felt like mingling day and night with thieves and addicts. It was not even certain that Annie and her friends would have wanted me around. I also remember reflecting on the difficulties that the new material might bring. New interviews usually expose new aspects, or other ways of presenting experiences or ways of life. If I conducted more interviews, in which other and possibly contrasting aspects of Annie's life might be displayed, how would I as a researcher be able to account for that? After all, my curiosity and research idea were built upon this first and peculiar interview.

Eventually, almost twenty years later, I did write an article based on my interview with Annie (Åkerström, 2001). Looking at the material anew, it struck me as full of stories, stories that formed a major narrative. Annie's trajectory in her telling involved a persistent theme of independence, now possible for me to articulate

analytically in terms of a narratively constructed identity. This way of seeing my data permitted me to look for form(s) of telling about experience instead of the content to which language refers (Bruner, 1990; Hydén, 1997: 50; Riessman, 2002: 697). Furthermore, my worries that new interviews would contain different stories immediately turned into something beside the point. Analysts in the narrative genre take it for granted that there is not *one* story that can be told about a specific event, phenomenon, life, etc. (Hydén, 1997: 52). In fact they draw on and explore this distinctive character of storytelling, defending the idea that particular and even exceptional narratives may also be worth studying in their own right.

Annie's narrative

Choosing the name Annie was no coincidence. Essential points in her narrative have similarities to Irving Berlin's well-known *Annie Get Your Gun*. Annie Oakley is the girl who rides, throws a lasso and shoots better than the one she loves, Frank. Their mutual attraction is surrounded by challenges; one of the best-known songs in the musical goes 'Anything you can do, I can do better'. In the end Annie lets Frank win in order to save their relationship. The analogy should not be pushed too far; our Annie is not better at fighting, and her story does not end with her giving way to male vanity. The point of the analogy is that her narrative theme is identical to one of the themes in the musical: female independence. This theme is carved out in opposition to what it *could* have been: a story of victimhood.

With the help of the 'narrative turn' in social science,[2] I could see how Annie's telling not only reflected her as an individual but also responded to a major social discourse, typical of the time. Her stories illustrate how such a discourse can be tackled. As Riessman (2002: 697) notes in her reflections on her study of divorce: '...the [narrative] approach illuminates the intersection of biography, history, and society. The "personal troubles" that participants represent in their narratives ... tell us a great deal about social and historical processes.'

The way Annie talked and how she expressed herself now became as important as what she said. I began to look for 'accounts' (Scott and Lyman, 1968; Buttny, 1993), but also more precise language forms that she used in order to dramatize and authenticate her experiences. A new analytical grid was outlined in which the verbalizations of 'I', 'you' or 'we' were important, the employment of passive or active subjects, the use of historical present, 'active voicing' (Wooffitt, 1992), etc. These were devices that I hardly could have used at the time of my report since much of my familiarity with them as analytical entries developed later on.

With this new grid I could see how Annie talked about violence and conflicts in a way that placed her in a collective of veteran criminals, distinguished through a We-and-Them dichotomy: the experienced versus the less experienced. Right from the start Annie presents herself as a member of the former, by way of *en passant* comments such as 'we belong to these "recidivists", you know'. She employs 'you' (*man* in Swedish): 'those who are a bit younger look up to you 'cause you've done so much time'. When qualifying this membership in detail, as when talking about buying drugs on credit, she straightforwardly presents herself as I:

Annie: I have quite a solid reputation in these circles, of making money on the outside.
Malin: Isn't it unusual that one is allowed to be in debt for that much money?
Annie: Well, that depends on *who* you are.

Annie's choice of pronouns served as one of my analytical keys. Scholars interested in language use have shown how people may employ the Swedish indefinite pronoun *man* ('you'/'one') not only to generalize experiences but also to ascribe packages of thoughts and feelings to those who implicitly are included in this pronoun (Adelswärd, 1997: 224; Pillsbury, 1998[3]). In this way Annie refers to experienced female criminals as a particular 'tribe', and herself as its unquestionable member. In other parts of the interview, Annie developed her use of this image of experienced female criminals in order to correct the discourse by which such women are usually portrayed:

Many of us become the one who.... In the end, I got tougher penalties than my man even though we were sentenced for the same crime. That's not that common either. I was considered as the driving force behind the crimes.... which was true. So the court has changed their view of us women a bit. But the myth is still alive. This thing with criminal women, that they must be prostitutes. It's totally wrong, 'cause we criminal women we've chosen you know....

In my previous study, I would not have regarded Annie's words as sufficient in themselves. Instead, I would have looked for a group, a collective or a culture that I could report about, on the basis of several interviews. In so doing, established ideas in criminology could have been contrasted with a discovery of some 'true criminal women' who were claiming responsibility, independence and competence. With a narrative perspective it was sufficient to see how Annie chose to present herself in terms of not being an appendage to men – a presentation she confirms with 'evidence' (the changed view of the court, the penalty). She also opens up a dialogue with 'the myth' of criminal women and engages in an explicit effort to discredit it. In this way Annie can be seen as actually fulfilling some of the sociological work I previously thought I had to do, although in her specific style: defining a group and giving it a voice.

Early in the interview Annie tells about a biographic 'turning point' (Mishler, 1999) when talking about how she felt abandoned when her first boyfriend was sent to prison. She states that she told herself: 'never again, never will I be dependent on a man'. This statement seems to work as Annie's general stance in defining who she is or has become. The continuity of this theme corresponds to a description of how Annie interprets what others would call 'wife battering'. Shortly after the discussion quoted above we start talking about her former husband. I comment on the fact that some people understand female criminals as 'dependent on guys and that's why they hang on'. Annie's response turns this idea upside down:

Annie: No (laugh) ... my last marriage crashed because of my independence. I crushed my husband by being more ambitious than him, by having better contacts than he had, by, yeah. ...
Malin: He was also into... ?
Annie: Oh yeah, he's been in these circles longer than I have ... he also belongs to the old-timers who see girls as a kind of appendage. He almost killed me because of that. I was mentally stronger too. I swallowed him, you know, with my mouth and my way of being. ...

Here the violence is dramatized as a result of a distinct confrontation: between a modern, independent woman and a man's traditional, old-fashioned views of how a woman should be. This is Annie, maybe not better at shooting or throwing a lasso, but earning more from crime than her man: 'It was almost like a competition between me and my former husband. If he went out and made five thousand bucks, I went out and made ten (laugh).'

Scholars who have noticed how violence can be talked about in either an active or a passive form provided further tools. People often use the latter when trying not to attribute violence to an acting subject, for instance 'there was a fight' (Coates et al., 1994). Others have noted how connotations of unilateral action are implied in the wording. As Emerson (1994) notes when analysing the construction of victims in a judicial setting, 'fight' might be avoided as this conveys a mutuality, which does not fit the associations of 'victims'. With this point of departure, I could look for how Annie put across that she was *not* a victim. In her stories, violence is described as markedly interactional, almost something of a dance. Her experience is conveyed with a playful flavour, in spite of the drastic character of its content:

In the end it was scary, you know … it ended with him pouring petrol on me and trying to set me on fire. We almost killed each other. I hit him with my car (laugh) so he ended up at the intensive ward. … He broke my eyebrows and my teeth and … I had bruises almost all the time. – if you can take a punch then maybe it would've stopped with that. But I can't take a punch; I hit back you know, even when I know that I'll be beaten up. I can't handle that thing.

'Annie' was my way of naming her. Still, the very person behind this pseudonym might actually have been acquainted with Annie Oakley. Figures in popular culture form social types that are generally available. This is not to say that the woman I interviewed in prison in any simple way imitated or identified with the lasso-throwing heroine in Irving Berlin's musical. Rather, this figure, or someone like her, can be seen as being part of our social landscape of types, and consequently also part of a possible and accessible cultural script when presenting oneself (Narayan and George, 2002). Annie Oakley or other figures from history, fiction or real life may serve as rhetorically loaded examples inspiring the way one formulates one's life story.[4] Whereas my former study contextualized the inmates' talk in terms of criminals' life-styles or prison culture, thereby analytically relying on features in a concrete field to understand my material, I now found the case of Annie more suitable to contextualize with the help of broader cultural terms. There is a larger story (cf. Chase, 1995: 177ff.) by which Annie's narrative style is inversely shaped, through open confrontation and silent circumvention. Theoretically this contextualization presumes two things: that culture

is seen as potentially manifest in particular practices in everyday life, and that a speaker who verbally reports and reflects on such practices is seen as engaged in a social action, telling, that is worth studying in itself (Chase, 1995: 25).

In this way it is not hard to look upon Annie as engaged in a counter-project in which the narrator's self is formulated not in accordance with but in contrast to a dominating cultural model. As Riessman (1993: 3) points out, people's storytelling may be especially relevant when their experiences represent 'a breach between ideal and real, self and society'. For me this breach became a topic that Annie put into words, more clearly now than twenty years ago. I came to see her as presenting her preferred identity at odds with others' expectations but also as giving voice to criminal women against images of subordination and against a common discourse of 'battered women'. Above and beyond relating her own story, she sketches an image of the 'Annies' in this world, saying: this is how women can be, too.

REANALYSING DATA: BRINGING IN DISCOURSE TO THE SWEDISH DEAF WORLD

A background

My initial interest in deaf issues concerned how the 'right' way to educate and treat deaf people and deafness was constructed, particularly in relation to people holding 'erroneous' opinions. At the time, a 'deaf culture perspective' was officially accepted and supported in Sweden, mainly promoted by the deaf movement and significant occupational groups. The emergence of a new category had recently provided a challenge to this perspective: children with cochlear implants. This new surgery, which gives a deaf person the capability to experience sound with the help of electrical signals, has given rise to strong protests in the deaf movement and in some professional circles, particularly teachers. Their fear was that greater priority would be given to speech than to sign language.

Informal social control was my key concept when studying this conflict. I tried to identify various forms of control within the deaf world that aimed at teaching and guarding a preferred way of relating to deaf people and sign language in response to cochlear implantation. My work resulted in a study called *Social Control Within the World of the Deaf* (Jacobsson, 1997, translated title). A few years later I reinterpreted practically the same material and wrote a second study: *A Battle of Words – Competing Truths in the Deaf World* (Jacobsson, 2000, translated title).

Triggers to recycle

How did it happen that I wrote two different studies based on the same set of data? One answer can be found in practical and financial circumstances. During my first years as a graduate student I learned that I would improve my chances of a financed assignment if I passed an exam (comparable to an American PhD) prior to the Swedish PhD. I decided to go for this strategic move. However, after finishing my first study I considered myself virtually done with the field. I was even bored with it. All my ideas were now formulated and published. My new assignment gave me only another eighteen months to finish my dissertation. To collect more data from the same field could have been an alternative. My specific problem, though, was that I already had a large amount of data, some would perhaps say too large. Several years of research in this field had generated around 1500 pages of transcripts from about sixty extensive interviews, a pile of fieldnotes and a huge quantity of documents. New data would not necessarily have generated new ideas. What I needed was a new analytical angle that could rearrange my material in an exciting way.

Retrospectively, this new angle can be traced back to my first analysis of the Swedish deaf world. Now and then I stumbled across a sidetrack that did not fit into my original frame of analysis. As in the case of Malin Åkerström's interview with 'Annie', it involved a shift from focusing on *what* people say to *how* they say it. Several times I had touched upon the fact that different interviewees used nearly identical formulations, sometimes as if at a given signal. At times they expressed themselves 'sloppily', in a disjointed manner, as if expecting me to share their local knowledge, and therefore did not bother to elaborate in detail. At other times the interviewees leapt to defend themselves although there was no suggestion of noticeable criticism. Despite my early interest in these phenomena, it was not by coincidence that they were left behind in my first study. I was not familiar with any analytical or theoretical tools that could make them understandable in a coherent and systematic way. Still, these 'leftovers' in my material bothered me and encouraged me to further inquiry.

Searching for a new sociological vocabulary, I turned to scholars focusing on language use (e.g. Adelswärd and Säljö, 1994) and discourse analysis (e.g. Potter, 1996) as well as scholars inspired by ethnomethodology (e.g. Holstein, 1992; Gubrium and Holstein, 1997). Through the literature I became acquainted with Mikhail Bakhtin, whose texts turned out to be the major key and trigger for analysing my material anew.

I found that Bakhtin (1981, 1986/1999) seemed to capture the very same dialogic phenomena that I was now discerning in my material. On several occasions during the interviews, and especially while analysing them, it seemed to me as if the interviewees were answering questions I had never asked. Why did a mother state that her cochlear implant operated child 'definitely should be allowed to be a child and play like everybody else'? I had never questioned their right to play. After a while it became clear that the mother was responding to criticism raised by opponents of the implantation. A common argument among them is that the special training that must follow the operation is too demanding for a child. Another mother, negative to the implantation, formulates the criticism like this: 'How will they have time to just be children and play?' It made more sense to look upon these rejoinders as constituting a dialogue between the two mothers rather than (merely) a dialogue with me as an interviewer. Both mothers are educated in the deaf culture discourse; the latter is using it and the former is replying to it. As interviewees they are consequently addressing this particular discourse whereas I am serving as their 'audience'. With the help of Bakhtin I could understand dialogues like this as concrete instances of how others' words are borrowed and replied to in speakers' utterances, that is to say, as instances of the dialogical character of language.

Saturation as a topic

From the very beginning, members of the deaf world presented arguments and descriptions that soon became familiar to me. Advocates of the established deaf culture perspective expressed themselves in terms very similar to the magazines for deaf and hard-of-hearing people. After a while I experienced this repetitive talk as tedious. At first, I recognized my growing sense of boredom as an indication of my data being theoretically saturated (Glaser and Strauss, 1967: 61). I believed I had reached the saturation point beyond which nothing new or unpredictable would turn up (Alasuutari, 1995: 59). This is the time where textbooks on method instruct you to stop your inquiries.

For me, though, this point served as a starting point. I realized that I could make use of this 'saturation' by turning it into a topic in itself.[5] The concept of discourse seemed to represent the most accurate way of describing this. I came to look upon the actors in the studied field as using shared discursive resources to explain and account for the constitution of the Swedish deaf world. A discourse provides them with prefabricated phrases, topics, argumentations, interpretative frameworks and narrative forms, which are maintained, reinforced and even challenged through recitation, allusion and repetition. In this way the fact that interviewees said the same thing over and over again was no longer a source of frustration but a phenomenon that called for explanation and interpretation. From now on I started to read my transcripts and listen to my taped interviews as if a third party was present: the deaf culture discourse.

In my original study I was guided by an interest in actors who held opinions at odds with socially established truths. I paid less attention to how the 'righteous' described their view of deaf people and sign language in general. As a consequence I also failed to notice the interviewees' possibility of using certain terms in order to indicate that they subscribed to the established discourse. My new interest did not only focus on *how* that happened but also *when*. I found that 'discourse activation' occurs at specific topical shifts, for instance when a speaker is correcting others' opinions or declaring his or her personal beliefs. It also took place when speakers start to discuss historical changes within the deaf world.

The extract below may serve as an example. In the first run I considered it useless since the interviewee, a teacher for the deaf, only retells the official story of developments in deaf education – a story I had heard several times earlier. In the second turn I focused on how the teacher employed the deaf culture discourse, which turned the sequence into something more compelling:

Katarina: Have you seen any changes in your profession?

Teacher: Yes. You know I got into this during the biggest changes (K: mhm) and historically you know it was like (.) the 50s and the 60s, then we had the strongest (.) oralistic period we've had in education for the deaf. (K: mhm.) And then when (.) the turning point started at the end of the 60s, when the deaf themselves through their organizations could represent you know (2.0) got eh, (2.0) had influence in the parliament, they had somebody, a couple of politicians that- hearing (K: mhm) who were presiding.

Katarina: Which organization was it?

Teacher: SDR [the Swedish Deaf Association]. There they got representatives that could present their views. Plus the fact that there was a teacher in Stockholm who (.) started to do research on this and people at the university who also started to get some results. Taken all together this gave an impact so that you accepted that (.) all deaf people could | not | be the same as hearing people. Cause that is what they, when the development of hearing aids took place in the 50s (3.0) then they made like (.) successful (.) results with some you know. *All* the deaf could learn how to speak. They weren't allowed to use signs.

(Jacobsson, 2000: 84–5, translated)

The teacher's account is a collection of locally well-known landmarks, expressions and interpretations. He is expressing himself in terms very similar to fragments in official books and texts about education for the deaf: the trends that dominated different decades, the importance of linguistic research, the statement that 'all deaf people could not be the same as hearing people'. Whereas my initial question concerned whether the teacher as an individual had experienced changes in his profession ('have *you* … ?'), his answer consists of a general account of a period in which he had not even begun teaching. Additionally, my question was about changes in his *profession*. His answer, in contrast, deals with political and educational changes for the deaf, not teachers for the deaf.

In my first study I did not take the teacher's account into consideration. I was trained to capture interviewees' own experiences rather than their reliance on official or formal accounts. When writing my second study, however, my changed analytical lenses allowed me to point at members' choice to prefer a collective story instead of a story about one's own experiences. In cultures such as this, characterized by distinct and crystallized narrative structures that define what to tell and how to tell it, it may be hard for a researcher to acquire a personal story (cf. Tiljander Dahlström, 1998: 14). To request such a story may almost routinely be interpreted as a request for the collective story since that one is rated as more accurate, relevant and meaningful. Gubrium and Holstein (2002: 21–2) tell, for instance, of a doctoral student who interviewed pharmacists using drugs. The interviewees had participated in recovery groups and it was obvious that they incorporated the groups' ways of describing drug abuse into their 'own' stories.

When focusing on the wording in my second study I could also see how the teacher indicates his activation of the deaf culture discourse, using the opening phrase 'and historically you know…'. A more detailed transcript gives the opportunity to see how he retells the collective story with the aid of minor but distinguishable modification in style and rhythm. The words 'could | not | be' in the phrase 'all deaf people could not be the same as hearing people' is for instance uttered in staccato (clearly separated) which makes it sound firm and undeniable.

Interviews as conversation

My changed analytical view involved a new way of looking at interviews. I began to consider the interview talk itself as the focal point for analysis rather than regarding the interviewee as an informant. This redefinition was not unproblematic; it necessarily meant that my own speech was drawn into the analysis. Initially, that felt weird to the point of embarrassment. When re-listening to the tapes it was clear that I often expressed myself in less flattering ways: imprecise, blurry and even clumsy. But above all, I had great difficulties in analysing (or even seeing) my own contribution to the conversation. Using another person's interviews turned out to be one way to overcome this.

A colleague of mine had conducted several interviews with professionals in the deaf world in a study on her own (Ryding, 1999) interviews that I now had access to. In contrast to an established view, which states that the analysis of interviews is enhanced if they are collected by the researcher rather than someone else (see e.g. Charmaz, 2001: 340), I found this kind of secondary data helpful (cf. Silverman, 2001: 120–1). By listening to Anna Ryding's tapes as well as reading her transcripts and treating them as conversations I could later on reproduce that kind of reading and listening in regard to my own interviews. A minor temporal distance was also helpful. Between my first and my second study I was on parental leave for one year. When returning to my data they were older and therefore, paradoxically, somewhat new. As Atkinson (1992: 460) notes when going back to his old fieldnotes, 'one comes to them "cold"'.

Having decided to view my data as conversations, I learned that some scholars, for instance conversational analysts, are sceptical about using interviews as primary material. 'Naturally occurring talk' is preferred. An interview, on the other hand, is considered as a special form of interaction that cannot be generalized in regard to other contexts (Leppänen, 1997: 17–18). Ethnographers, who were also important for my focus, also downgrade interviews, arguing that they fail to show interactional production of meaning and instead tend to highlight cognitive production. Interview talk is not situated in everyday interactions but 'decontextualized' from such interactions (Emerson et al., 1995: 140). In other words I found myself trapped with material that from the very beginning was marked as worthless in doing the kind of analysis that I wanted to do, namely, stating something about the deaf culture in general.

By now, however, I was convinced that I had found something substantial in this material, which made the project worth pursuing. I did this by (1) slightly questioning the concept of 'naturally occurring talk' and (2) maintaining that the talk in these particular interviews had relevance outside the interviews too. For the former I used Potter (1996: 149), who argues that 'naturally occurring talk' is not a straightforward discovered object but a theoretical and analytical stance on conversational interaction, possible to take no matter what material one is working with. For the latter, I used my fieldnotes and documents that supported the claim that members are actively using deaf cultural arguments and descriptions in far more settings than just during interviews. Similarly, in his study of a half-way house, Wieder (1988: 131) stressed that members' habit of 'telling the code' was not just performed to him as a researcher, but also a significant interactional event between staff and residents.

Creating 'new' material by elaborating transcripts

Since some of my own speech was highly edited in my original tapes it was necessary to go back and retranscribe parts of them. During this work, I found a wide range of significant utterances that at the outset I had transcribed rather sketchily. When filling in details and nuances I actually turned my well-known interviews into a different set of data. The extract below is taken from my first transcription of an interview with a home instructor (a teacher who regularly makes visits to families with deaf children). My question goes like this:

Katarina: One thing I wondered, I cannot think of a better way to say it, but, can you make a distinction between 'good' and 'bad' parents? I'm not saying that-

(Jacobsson, 1997: 109, translated)

When relistening to the tape and transcribing it again the question came out like this:

Katarina: [commenting on previous answer] No problem, no (.) no (.). No. (2.0) eh (6.0) [looks down at interview guide] well you know. (1.0) Sometimes I write things that makes me wonder what I am really doing- one thing I was thinking about is, I cannot think of (laughs a bit) a better way to say it but can you see:: can you see like differences between 'good' and 'bad' parents (.) so, how m- do you get what I mean (laughs a bit) of course I'm not saying that-

(Jacobsson, 2000: 105–6, translated)

It was not just a consequence of embarrassment that made me shorten this vague and defensive question in my first transcript. It was also a consequence of my focus being not on the conversation but rather on the content of the interviewee's subsequent rejoinders. The interview continued:

Home instructor: No, I see- I was about to say that it sounds awful (laughs).

Katarina: Yes (laughs) yeah, but (.) I don't know what to say. Right or wrong attitude or- cau- often you have- I suspect that (.) you have a (1.0) well, you have that of course, a firm view (H: yes) about what's good for this child (H: yes) and if one acts in a different way or (.) or this thing

with (.) yeah a parent who (.) like (.) really is at odds with (H: yes) or downgrades sign language and things like that. (H: mm) I suspect that's what you would call a less good parent? (1.0) You know (2.0)

Home instructor: Not coming to terms with one's situation (K: uhu) enough you could say, (K: uhu) it sounds a bit- 'cause it's all the time it- it's a matter of, (K: uhu) where am I in the crisis? (K: uhu) Often you know it's we- 'cause all parents want the best possible for their children (K: uhu) and if you're blocked, you can't see 'cause it's such a different world that is opening up for them (K: uhu) and I think it's important to feel fear for that. They have to go through this (K: uhu) 'cause it's nothing you can just accept right away (K: no) I don't think so. (ibid.)

Earlier I was interested in this passage in order to identify how the interviewee accounted for parents who do not follow her instructions. I interpreted her 'crisis model' in terms of a theory of deviance. Parents who are newcomers in this world and therefore do not know the expected way of conduct are at first met by patience and hopefulness. The experts explained that they will ultimately 'come to terms with the situation' once they have gone through their 'crisis', which is assumed to follow the diagnoses. My new transcript, however, made it possible to discern other aspects. It exemplifies 'incompatible descriptions', displaying a coercive aspect of this discourse. This is not only manifested in the interviewees' answers but also in my questions as well as in our speech collaboration. My attempt to talk about parents in explicitly moral terms is intrinsically problematic: it is hard to accomplish because of its incongruity with the prevailing discourse that is drawn upon in the conversation. This 'disrupted talk' (Chase, 1995), emerging through a clash with the terms that the home instructor prefers, is only noticeable in my second and detailed version of the transcript. So is our mutual effort to gradually replace my moral terms with therapeutic ones in order to find our way back to discursively safe ground. With my 'uhus' and my 'no' (so-called continuers) inserted in the home instructor's answer, I am supporting her version no less than eight times.

Although the concept of discourse may seem hard to employ because of its abstract and all-encompassing flavour, returning to my 'old' material with this concept at hand allowed me to explore how a detailed study of speech can be made sociologically relevant, no matter what field is being studied (cf. Fairclough, 1995; Fairclough and Chouliaraki, 1999). By raising the deaf world to this relevance, expressing its features of conflicts and tensions in specific yet general terms, I simultaneously lowered 'discourse' to a specific field, thereby emphasizing its down-to-earth aspect. Along with other closely related concepts, such as Bakhtin's 'dialogism' and Potter's (1996) 'rhetorical constructions', discourse was in this way materializing by the use of my data. The project of understanding the Swedish deaf world turned into a matter of unfolding not only its practices of social control in a general sense but also a detailed version of this control, expressed through a continuous battle of words.

DISCUSSION

When describing our recycled studies above, we implicitly tend to depict the researcher as a pragmatic sculptor of knowledge (cf. Davies, 1996: 239). Faced with the task of presenting a new piece of art, she takes a stroll in her private storage of materials, selects some already used blocks and then tries to figure out what tools can turn them into something yet unseen. Our cases also demonstrate, however, that this is only part of the truth. A body of material is not automatically easy to define, a set of tools not always directly found or unproblematically tried out, and one's tools and material are far from mutually isolated. Thus, if the researcher resembles a sculptor, this sculptor seems to be a peculiar one, using tools that are meshed with the material and material that is meshed with the artist. With regard to this blurring of methodological demarcations, we will discuss the weaknesses, virtues and possible practical management of recycling data a little further.

Defining a body of material

To select data to recycle is clearly a question of choosing precisely what pieces to reuse. In that choice, new tools can spotlight parts previously left behind. The parts that were used from the interview with Annie were selected not just because of their characteristics per se but also since they seemed interpretable from a narrative perspective. In a similar way the extracts that were recycled in the deaf world study were to some extent selected because of their potential to fit into a discourse perspective. Not equally clear, though, is the fact that a recycling study in a more general sense redefines its material. The second deaf world study, for instance, was highly dependent upon a new way of looking at interviews, guiding the researcher's concrete reworking of it: her retranscriptions.

To redefine material may have an even more practical side, noticeable if we add a few details not mentioned above. Owing to promises of confidentiality, the tape with Annie's talk was erased, as were some tapes in the deaf world study. Although not obstructing their respective projects, these circumstances undoubtedly made the original documentation less than optimal. We might find a lesson in this. If data are to be recycled they should, in at least some respect, be documented so that they can be redefined. It is probably not sufficient to say that the optimal documentation always lies in a high level of details, even if that is true in our cases, which both involve a zooming in on subtle features. Another recycling project can very well involve the opposite: looking at broader pictures instead of minor ones, employing a naturalistic perspective to replace a narrative or discursive, etc. If one maintains that it is possible to multiply the ways in which one's data are put into words, as well as one's initial sorting of them according to relevance, one also maintains the conditions for multiplying them analytically. The significance of such a lesson depends on the typically continuing changes of one's research interests.

Finding tools

Qualitative material is commonly so rich that most of it is left unanalysed. Some of it may be used to the point where you cannot get any further (at least for the moment). But much of the material may simply be reported, 'written up' to please grant-givers or the like, or just filed away for possible future use. Then you may stumble over an article or a concept, discover a new thinker or rediscover a classic that helps you to get a handle on your data. Most researchers probably have a few sketchy manuscripts in their desk waiting for such analytical explanations. Finding tools is therefore a vital part of the work in any recycling process.

In the light of our cases, finding new analytical tools is also a matter of separation: old tools have to be abandoned as new ones are tried out. The reason is well known and often recited. We look at our material through lenses that we are accustomed to, even trained, to take for granted. We routinely acknowledge this when stating that we have preconceptions, that we are committed to one of today's 'idioms of qualitative inquiry' (Gubrium and Holstein, 1997) or 'imageries' (Becker, 1998). In both our cases, the original way the researcher looked upon her data implied an aspiration for immersion (Emerson et al., 1995: 232), to take 'the role of the other'. When trying out another perspective, involving an emphasis on forms of talk rather than contents, both researchers found themselves struggling to get rid of this ambition while replacing it with new ones.

Finding new tools may be as much a result of hard work (doing your reading) as well as luck or 'coincidence', in the way Becker (1998) discusses it. Neither of these two circumstances, though, was hardly necessary in order to discover 'the language turn' in social sciences. To avoid being influenced by such a broad shift would even have been difficult. A commentator on one of its species, narrative studies, has remarked that researchers in many fields appear to be 'in the grip of a kind of "narrative mania"' (Freeman, 1994: 201).

Elapsed time – asset and obstacle

Time is often an issue for scholars who have done and argued for reanalysing or revisiting old material (Becker, 1986: 103; Rosaldo, 1993: 7). As Katz (1997) has argued, ethnographers need warrants. Warrants to recycle qualitative data are perhaps more specific since they must have a temporal aspect, aimed at contemporary ideals of never looking back and never revising one's statements. Even though some local conventions among scholars certainly value revisions and refinement, such warrants may be crucial.[6]

In our cases the researchers' wrestling with such a 'time norm' was more or less prevalent. Both had a feeling that 'going back' to past material stands in opposition to 'moving forward', and that the latter is an ideal. Slightly simplifying, this might be looked upon as partly a consequence of one's surroundings, partly a consequence of one's own standpoint. The fact that it is harder to obtain funding for secondary analyses than for primary ones is the most evident indication of a surrounding world pushing for studies on new material. To search continuously for new arenas for expressing oneself is a celebrated value; 'being on the move' may count as a sign of success and prosperity (Zerubavel, 1987; Bauman, 1998). Of course, collecting new data can be done at the same time as revisiting and reanalysing old data. As Silverman (2001: 120–1) points out, borrowing other people's previously collected material can serve to kickstart one's analysis at an early stage of a project, for instance a dissertation, as well as kickstart one's confidence in analysing. Nevertheless, in most academic worlds there is no denying the perils of only using old data. Digging at the same spot can easily be translated into being perceived as narrow, typified with phrases like 'it's that old project of his' or 'is she still writing on that ancient stuff?' This, on the other hand, might be the case even if a researcher hunts for new material but sticks to an original analytical framework, although such inflexibility more often seems to be understood in terms of good character – being consistent and committed.

A related unwillingness to recycle data may be fostered by ascribing to the data a specific sense of one's past. The fact that a social scientist's material is usually just papers and letters does not diminish the potential of emotional loading. One graduate student described how she felt sick to the point of vomiting when she returned to her old fieldnotes after some years of looking after children. Full of coffee stains, scribbled notes and exclamation marks she now wondered about, these notes represented great involvement and aspirations, never fulfilled. To start rereading such notes, identified with a lack of movement through time, may feel like entering a private time-warp.

In many cases, however, the time distances may also be a resource. Revisiting the interview with Annie was exciting partly because of its age; it endowed the project a certain feeling of solving an important riddle. Returning to and reanalysing the Swedish deaf world was in a similar way conducted by playing with time. For instance, the new focus on the researcher's own talk in the interviews became more comfortable because of a distance in time, a distance that helped the study to produce something new. In our first case the time difference made it easier to focus on something that did not fit into the pattern since the broader picture no longer occupied the researcher. In our second case the time difference facilitated a new look on the very pattern (repetitive talk per se).

CONCLUDING REMARKS: TWOFOLD EXPLORATIONS

In order to conclude this chapter we would like to linger on what we perceive as the double nature of recycling studies. They seem neither fully concentrated on new analytical tools or literature nor on new data or new field studies. Rather, they are something in between.

An ambivalent aspect in using literature can be clarified through the deaf world study, in which Mikhail Bakhtin served as one of the thinkers. His texts helped the analysis in both a practical and a moral way, not only in identifying dialogizations in interview talk but also in being an authority to lean on stylistically. The latter was not a straightforward matter, however. The researcher soon learned that Bakhtin was no exception to the rule that almost every classic figure nourishes a small community of supporters (for instance, the 11th International Bakhtin Conference took place in 2003). Without doubt these experts know the man and his work far more thoroughly than an empirical sociologist who just had read some of his texts. Daring to use Bakhtin, and not, as Becker (1986: 135–49) puts it, being 'terrorized by the literature', the researcher had to state to herself and others that she did not intend to become another Bakhtin expert. Rather it was a matter of using his thinking to locate analytical tools to understand the material at hand. As other studies exemplify, Bakhtinian concepts such as 'dialogism' and 'voices' can be seen as productive tools in almost any interview study, if used in an eclectic way (Wästerfors, 2001).

There appears to be a subtle balance between on the one hand positioning oneself, calmly and informatively, in relation to a previously untried sociological tradition, and on the other hand becoming captivated by this new positioning and unable to leave it. The latter might be a notable trap not only when recycling data but possibly in all empirical studies. After all, an untried analytical track may be attractive as such. In our recycling studies it was not only the allure of finding new results that motivated the researchers but also the very use of new analytical tools. Although such use is always difficult, because of one's amateur status and because of the difficulty of being both empirically and theoretically oriented, it may still trigger a study. In fact, 'being difficult' is an important trigger; it indicates that the work is neither undemanding nor impossible.

In our cases the new perspectives (Bakhtin's 'dialogue', 'rhetoric'', 'discourse', 'narrative', the use of pronouns, and 'identity performance') in themselves came to constitute arenas to be explored by the respective researcher. From this point of view, scholarly literature *in practice* seems to play an important part when going back to material that has been collected earlier, since the researcher's very familiarity with this material may allow her to try out what she has subsequently read. The literature is addressed via a body of material, saying: this is how an empirical sociologist may think of this theory or that kind of analysis.

Consequently, researchers in a recycling study may feel that their exploration has two directions. Their analytical tools are revealing something essential in the material *and* the material is showing something essential in the tools. Although never completely merging, one might say that it is the researcher's self-ascribed task to consider it possible to rhetorically tie these two pragmatic entities to each other: seeing the analytical tools in the material and the other way round. In so doing the tools may also become a kind of material and the material a kind of tool. This task is huge and never-ending, itself an instance of social life. As Rosaldo (1993: 8) argues, 'all interpretations are provisional; they are made by positioned subjects who are prepared to know certain things and not others'. Ethnographers' analyses, Rosaldo argues, are therefore always incomplete.

Recycling data may serve as one way to acknowledge what Rosaldo points out. If the provisional and incomplete character of qualitative studies is to be recognized, it can be done not only in principle but also in practice.

NOTES

1 Much research in conversation analysis, for instance, is carried out by renewed analysis of not only one's own but others' material as well. Furthermore, the creation of open and accessible qualitative databases that Corti and Thompson (Chapter 21, this volume) discuss promises to make such renewed analyses more common.

2 See Riessman (2002: 696) for a brief examination of the contributors to 'the narrative turn'.

3 Pillsbury (1998) writes about the use of English 'you' instead of 'I'.

4 Catherine Riessman has explored similar connections between performed identities in interviews (in narratives of men facing multiple sclerosis) and ideals exemplified by popular figures (Seminar, 18 October 2001, Department of Sociology, Lund University).

5 Becker (1998: 95–8) makes a somewhat similar point when encouraging field researchers to turn their sense of 'nothing's happening' into a topic, i.e., what is happening when nothing's happening?

6 Such scholarly conventions, even though they do not necessarily consist of drastic revisions of standpoint or perspective, include for instance the process whereby a report or an unpublished manuscript is distilled into an article. Subsequently a rewriting process may be

generated by academic journals' system of reviewers, when – and if – the author is asked to 'revise or resubmit'.

REFERENCES

Adelswärd, Viveka (1997) 'Berättelser från älgpassen', in Lars-Christer Hydén and Margareta Hydén (eds), *Att studera berättelser.* Stockholm: Liber, pp. 198–235.

Adelswärd, Viveka and Säljö, Roger (1994) 'Becoming a conscientious objector: the use of arms and institutional accounting practices', in W. de Graaf and R. Maier (eds), *Sociogenesis Reexamined.* New York: Springer, pp. 205–17.

Åkerström, Malin (1983/1985) *Crooks and Squares: Lifestyles of Thieves and Addicts in Comparison to Conventional People.* New Brunswick, NJ: Transaction.

Åkerström, Malin (1985) *Våld och hot bland intagna i kriminalvårdsanstalt.* Kriminalvårdsstyrelsen, Forskningsgruppen, Norrköping. Rapport 1985: 2.

Åkerström, Malin (2001) 'Annie – en motberättelse', in M. Åkerström and I. Sahlin (eds), *Det motspänstiga offret.* Lund: Studentlitteratur, pp. 265–81.

Alasuutari, Pertti (1995) *Researching Culture: Qualitative Method and Cultural Studies.* London: Sage.

Atkinson, Paul (1992) 'The ethnography of a medical setting: reading, writing and rhetoric', *Qualitative Health Research*, 2(4): 451–74.

Bakhtin, Mikhail M. (1981) *The Dialogic Imagination. Four Essays by M.M. Bakhtin,* ed. Michael Holquist, tr. Michael Holquist and Caryl Emerson. Austin: University of Texas Press.

Bakhtin, Mikhail M. (1986/1999) *Speech Genres and Other Late Essays*, ed. Caryl Emerson and Michael Holquist. Austin: University of Texas Press.

Bauman, Zygmunt (1998) *Globalization: The Human Consequences.* Cambridge: Polity Press.

Becker, Howard (1986) *Writing for Social Scientists.* Chicago: University of Chicago Press.

Becker, Howard (1998) *Tricks of the Trade: How to Think About Your Research While You're Doing It.* Chicago: University of Chicago Press.

Bruner, Jerome (1990) *Acts of Meaning.* Cambridge, MA: Harvard University Press.

Buttny, Richard (1993) *Social Accountability in Communication.* London: Sage.

Charmaz, Kathy (2001) 'Grounded theory', in Robert M. Emerson (ed.), *Contemporary Field Research* (2nd ed.). Prospect Heights, IL: Waveland Press.

Chase, Susan E. (1995) *Ambiguous Empowerment: The Work Narratives of Women School Superintendents.* Amherst: University of Massachusetts Press.

Coates, L., Bavelas, J. and Gibson, J. (1994) 'Anomalous language in sexual assault trial judgments', *Discourse and Society*, 5(2): 189–206.

Davies, Karen (1996) *Önskningar och realiteter: om flexibilitet, tyst kunskap och omsorgsrationalitet i barnomsorgen.* Stockholm: Carlsson.

Emerson, Robert M. (1994) 'Constructing serious violence and its victims: processing a domestic violence restraining order', in Gale Miller and James A. Holstein (eds), *Perspectives on Social Problems.* Greenwich, CT: JAI Press, pp. 3–28.

Emerson, Robert M., Fretz, Rachel I. and Shaw, Linda L. (1995) *Writing Ethnographic Fieldnotes.* Chicago: University of Chicago Press.

Fairclough, Norman (1995) *Critical Discourse Analysis: The Critical Study of Language.* London: Longman.

Fairclough, Norman and Chouliaraki, Lilie (1999) *Discourse in Late Modernity: Rethinking Critical Discourse Analysis.* Edinburgh: Edinburgh University Press.

Freeman, M. (1994) 'Living to tell about it', *New Ideas in Psychology*, 12: 201–8.

Glaser, Barney G. and Strauss, Anselm L. (1967) *The Discovery of Grounded Theory: Strategies for Qualitative Research.* New York: Aldine.

Gubrium, Jaber F. (1991) 'Recognizing and analyzing local cultures', in William B. Shaffir and Robert A. Stebbins (eds), *Experiencing Fieldwork: An Inside View of Qualitative Research.* London: Sage, pp. 131–41.

Gubrium, Jaber F. and Holstein, James A. (1997) *New Language of Qualitative Method.* New York: Oxford University Press.

Gubrium, Jaber F. and Holstein, James A. (eds) (2002) *Handbook of Interview Research: Context and Method.* London: Sage.

Holstein, James A. (1992) 'Producing people: descriptive practice in human service work', in G. Miller (ed.), *Current Research on Occupations and Professions*, vol. 7. Greenwich, CT: JAI Press, pp. 23–39.

Hydén, Lars-Christer (1997) 'Illness and narrative', *Sociology of Health and Illness*, 19: 48–69.

Jacobsson, Katarina (1997) *Social kontroll i dövvärlden.* Lic. avh. Lund: Sociologiska institutionen, Lunds universitet, 1997: 1.

Jacobsson, Katarina (2000) *Retoriska strider – konkurrerande sanningar i dövvärlden.* Akad. avh. Lund: Palmkrons förlag.

Katz, Jack (1997) 'Ethnography's warrants', *Sociological Methods and Research*, 25(4): 391–423.

Klockars, Carl B. (1974) *The Professional Fence.* New York: Free Press.

Leppänen, Vesa (1997) *Inledning till den etnometodologiska samtalsanalysen.* Lund: Sociologiska institutionen, Lunds universitet. Research Report 1997: 3.

Loseke, Donileen and Cahill, Spencer (1984) 'The social construction of deviance: experts on battered women', *Social Problems,* 31: 296–310.

Mishler, Elliot G. (1999) *Storylines: Craftartists' Narratives of Identity.* Cambridge, MA: Harvard University Press.

Narayan, Kirin and George, Kenneth M. (2002) 'Personal and folk narrative as cultural representation', in Jaber F. Gubrium and James A. Holstein (eds), *Handbook of Interview Research: Context and Method.* London: Sage, pp. 815–31.

Pillsbury, Gerald (1998) 'First-person singular and plural: strategies for managing ego- and sociocentrism in four basketball teams', *Journal of Contemporary Ethnography*, 26: 450–78.

Potter, Jonathan (1996) *Representing Reality: Discourse, Rhetoric and Social Construction*. London: Sage.

Riessman, Catherine Kohler (1993) *Narrative Analysis*. Qualitative Research Methods Series, vol. 30. Newbury Park, CA: Sage.

Riessman, Catherine (2002) 'Analysis of personal narratives', in Jaber F. Gubrium and James A. Holstein (eds), *Handbook of Interview Research: Context and Method*. London: Sage, pp. 695–710.

Rosaldo, Renato (1993) *Culture and Truth: The Remaking of Social Analysis*. Boston: Beacon Press.

Ryding, Anna (1999) *Föräldrakunskap: Olika tolkningar. Institutioners varierande vetande och former för familjestöd till föräldrar med döva barn*. Lund: Sociologiska institutionen, Lunds universitet. Research Reports, Program in Medical Sociology (1999: 1).

Scott, Marvin B. and Lyman, Stanford M. (1968) 'Accounts', *American Sociological Review*, 33: 46–52.

Shaw, Clifford R. (1930/1968) *The Jack-Roller: A Delinquent Boy's Own Story*. Chicago: University of Chicago Press.

Silverman, David (2001) *Doing Qualitative Research: A Practical Handbook*. London: Sage.

Sutherland, Edwin H. (1937) *The Professional Thief: By a Professional Thief* [Chic Conwell]; annotated and interpreted by Edwin H. Sutherland. Chicago: University of Chicago Press.

Tiljander Dahlström, Åsa (1998) 'The performance of displacement – life histories in the Tibetan diaspora'. Paper. Uppsala: Kulturantropologiska avdelningen, Uppsala universitet.

van Maanen, J. (1988) *Tales of the Field*. Chicago: University of Chicago Press.

Wästerfors, David (2001) 'Tales of ambivalence: stories of acceptance and rejection among Swedish expatriates in Poland'. CFE Working Paper No. 16. Lund: Centre for European Studies at Lund University. www.cfe.lu.se/CFEWP/CFEPaper16.pdf/

Wieder, D.L. (1988) *Language and Social Reality*. Lanham, MD: University Press of America.

Wooffitt, R. (1992) *Telling Tales of the Unexpected: The Organization of Factual Discourse*. London: Harvester Wheatsheaf.

Zerubavel, Eviatar (1987) 'The language of time: toward a semiotics of temporality', *Sociological Quarterly*, 28: 343–56.

23

The Internet as research context

Annette N. Markham

Computer-mediated communication is not just a tool; it is at once technology, medium and engine of social relations. It not only structures social relations, it is the space within which the relations occur and the tool that individuals use to enter that space.

Steven G. Jones, *Cybersociety*

What I know of the Internet is like filling a thimble full of water, and saying I hold the ocean in my hands.

Sheol, study participant

Conducting qualitative research in the unfamiliar field is challenging. Via the Internet, the unfamiliarity of the field can be complicated by the fact that the field is negotiated versus geographic; interviewing is often, and perhaps preferably, an anonymous exchange of text messages. On the Internet, using acronyms, odd spelling conventions, or referring to personae using pronouns like splat, h**, or spivak is equivalent to learning the language of the culture you're visiting. To make it even more strange, you may be sitting on your couch for much of the fieldwork, traveling to multiple cultural venues through your laptop, and interviewing text beings you'll never see in the flesh. I find it fascinating. Others, I'm sure, would shake their heads and gladly trade computer and couch for pencil, notebook, two chairs, and good old-fashioned conversation.

The goal of this chapter is to illustrate several methodological quandaries, apparent in any research context but particularly highlighted by Internet contexts. Using various excerpts from my research journals, I discuss my own encounters with study participants in the virtual field, primarily in interview settings, to exemplify these quandaries, provide a sense of my lived experience as both researcher and Internet user, and to display the significance of the researcher's choices on the outcome of the ethnographically informed project. To give the reader an idea of how users make sense of the Internet, as well as possibilities for studying in this swiftly growing area, I also offer a general framework for how the Internet is conceptualized.

```
>I ache everywhere.
I've been talking with people for hours,
but my jaw is sore because I haven't spoken.
I feel like my voice is migrating to the tips of my fingers,
which means my brain doesn't have to translate so much.
I suppose this is a good thing...
but I'm a bit troubled by what is happening to my conversational skills.
beginning to prefer fragments
and all lowercase
have trouble completing sente-
I dreamed that I was having a conversation with someone
and I could see the letters
--courier font, probably size 12--
streaming out of my gaping and silent mouth.
Sentences hung for a moment in the air and then wafted up to the ceiling,
.........where they dissolved.
I resent my body's intrusion on my life online,
```

and my online life's impact on my body.
***
Sometimes I will take a deep breath and realize
I haven't been breathing......
then I'll feel giddy with the rushing intake of air.
Sometimes I blink,
and realize I must not have blinked in a long time, because it feels so good.
Then I'll close my eyes for awhile,
enjoying the sensation of not staring
bug-eyed
at the glare of the computer screen.
After a few hours online, my body is screaming with pain.
If I don't chew gum, I'll clench my teeth.
If I don't talk, my throat gets raw and sore.
My hands take the most punishment. They ache and throb
because I forget to stop typing.
So why can't I stop?
I lose track of time, and four, five, six hours will pass
before I realize I haven't stood up, leaned back,
or even taken a sip of water.
I haven't had hot coffee in months;
it's always cold before I remember to drink it.
My body hurts.
Yet I'm actively participating in life online.
I chat with people,
With all the windows open
In one, my mom and I get to be together
In another, I feel the breeze as I walk down the avenue,
and pick up a frisbee
to throw it to my interviewee, Beth Ann.
In a third, I'm in a chatroom and just met dominOh!, whom I hope to interview.
In this window, I'm writing research notes.
At the same time that I'm engaging in these activities,
my eyeballs are drying out,
I don't speak a word,
and no part of my body is moving at all except my hands.
In a way, I resent the
encroachment
of my body into my life here.
This frightens me, sort of....
***

In 1995, I started meeting people who spent a lot of time interacting with others on the Internet. I also started hearing stories in the popular media warning us about an emerging disorder called Internet Addiction. In a conversation with a colleague, I learned that he spent almost half his waking hours interacting with others on the Internet. I couldn't imagine what would engage these people for so many hours of every single day. As a researcher, I couldn't resist the opportunity to talk with them. I knew that if I really wanted to understand these people and their online lives, I would have to go online, too. I figured out how to use different interaction programs, closed myself in my office, dialed up

an Internet connection, and got started. What I thought would be a short-term project using the Internet for structured and semi-structured interviewing turned into a two-year, exhausting, exhilarating exploration of the lives of a dozen individuals who lived online. As any good ethnographer would, I had gone to live with them.

The excerpt from my research journal above is representative of how I felt during my stint in this virtual field. I spent much of my time sitting in an office chair focusing on a point about 18 inches from my nose. Yet the point of focus rarely felt only 18 inches away; I was miles and worlds away, right here in a cozy online chatroom, talking to a scientist from Sweden, another researcher in South America, or an American college student living somewhere between the Atlantic Ocean and the Pacific.

The stories told to me by the people I met formed the backbone of my book *Life Online*, and, to a large extent, my professional research life. The issues I confronted while talking with them as a researcher have become the issues I grapple with every day in the classes I teach and my continuing research. Since that first study, I have moved to a different office and learned to look away from the screen every once in a while to spare my vision, but the lessons I learned in conducting this research have never left me.

There is an elegant simplicity to the idea of studying Internet contexts as a social scientist: collecting, analyzing, and interpreting data to build theory and knowledge of this network of social potential. But from the point of one who works in this virtual field, the apparent simplicity is an abstraction fraught with multilayered complexity and paradox as one faces the actuality of trying to know anything about the other, online.

What does it mean to interview someone for almost two hours before realizing (s)he is not the gender the researcher thought (s)he was? Does that say more about the researcher or the participant, and how should an ethnographer account for this in both research design and practice?

What do you do when 500 people respond to your request for interviews, when you imagined you would get about 20?

How do you draw a sensible boundary around the ethnographic context when the culture you're studying is a collective living in 55 different countries around the globe and the basic frame of the society is constituted by a network of e-mail messages rather than persons generally located in the same physical space?

How does the researcher extract him or herself from the culture under study when every word he or she types actively contributes to the ongoing formation of the cultural boundaries?

The dilemmas associated with doing Internet research often arise in the midst of a study, unanticipated and unaccounted for by even the most careful research design. Inductive and explorative, the potential of the Internet as a tool or context for research is still emerging, particularly as technologies for interaction change. As I illustrate the complexities of using text to interview, interpret, and represent others in the research report, I hope to encourage researchers to maintain close sensitivity to the context; constantly critiquing one's own role in co-constructing the cultural spaces of inquiry, and mindfully attending to the premises guiding and shaping the interpretation and presentation of the object of analysis.

WHAT DO WE MEAN BY THE TERM *THE INTERNET*?

Now that the dust has settled in the frenetic race to explore, settle, colonize, buy, build, control, and study the Internet, we have the opportunity for calmer, more experienced reflection. Many of us are still wondering what it all means. Others of us have set our sights on what comes next. Regardless of differences in methodological approaches and objects of analysis, most qualitative researchers who consider themselves part of the growing interdisciplinary field of Internet Studies agree that the concept we label *The Internet* is, both in practice and theory, a multiplicity of cultural phenomena not limited to either a monolithic entity or a universal set of experiences. The term sustains itself through its ambiguity; surfers, netizens, consumers, and researchers can and do interpret it freely, deriving and applying meaning of the concept in countless ways.

We have a vast range of choices for delineating and studying the Internet. Even as I argue that the term Internet is not easily encapsulated by a solid set of experiences or approaches, I offer a general framework describing how people experience the Internet as well as how we investigate it in the social sciences and humanities. In an earlier work (Markham, 1998) I posit the argument that users experience computer-mediated communication alternately or simultaneously as *tool*, *place*, or *way of being*. Extended from computer-mediated communication to the Internet (however one defines it), this framework comprises a useful heuristic.

One can usefully conceptualize the Internet as a *tool* for retrieving or transmitting information and connecting with others. As a medium, the Internet can be seen as a research resource. In my own work, I view the Internet as an umbrella term for those social spaces constituted and mediated through computer-mediated interactions. As such, the Internet can be seen as a *place* or a research context. If one conceptualizes the Internet as a *way of being*, the focus shifts away from looking at the Internet as a tool or a cultural space and moves toward the ephemeral territory of exploring the ways individuals in a computer-mediated society construct and experience themselves and others because of or through Internet communication. As everyday life becomes more and more inundated with communication technologies, it is appropriate to focus a critical, analytic gaze on how individuals construct and negotiate their lives in an information-saturated environment.

The Internet engages most users at multiple conceptual levels. The extent to which we have mixed metaphors when talking about the Internet (highway, frontier, community, net, web) implies both a complex understanding and an effort to understand through a sensible if changing linguistic frame. The fact that we shift terminology frequently may indicate a familiarity with jargon. For instance, we talk about going *there*, doing research *there*, going to work *there*, and so on. Even when we use these descriptors, we may not visualize ourselves as being any specific place any more than when we are on the phone. We commonly talk about *being* online or on the Internet, but we do not seem to mean this literally.

Shifting terminology can, however, indicate shifting meanings and shifting experiences. The change from conceptualizing the Internet as a tool to a place can emerge through the design of the interface, the level of engagement in the activity, the length of time we've been online, the depth of the involvement, and so forth. The deeper distinctions between considering the Internet a place and a way of being seems to depend on the extent to which one integrates technology into one's concept of being as well as one's concept of social construction.

Internet as tool

The most common frame used to describe the Internet is that of tool. As such, the Internet is a network of electronic connections, a communication medium, a conduit that allows information to flow from one place to another. Utilized in the framework of a *tool,* the Internet can extend one's reach, expand the senses, and complicate traditional notions of time and space. Whether we're saving time by shopping online, spending time surfing the latest film reviews, collapsing physical distance to chat with a group of friends in three different countries, or increasing psychological distance by using e-mail rather than walking across the hall, Internet communication is altering the fundamental processes by which we get things done.

In very basic terms, a researcher can elect to study the tool itself, social interactions afforded by this tool, or use the tool to aid in the research project, all depending on the specific research project, the form of the research questions, the researcher's epistemological stance, and the researcher's methodological preferences. Research in the past decade has delved deeply into the first and second areas; we have learned a great deal about how these connections are made possible, what types of interaction are possible, and what the effects are on individuals, groups, corporate processes and structures, and so forth.

The impact of the Internet in everyday life is both predictable and surprising as individuals, communities, and even nations adopt this technology and use it in their own creative ways (see Miller and Slater, 2000, for an example of the Internet in Trinidad).

The third area is of more recent concern. As Mann and Stewart (2000) note, we have only begun to imagine the ways computer-mediated communication can be used to augment our traditional qualitative methods. Mann and Stewart's book, in fact, is arguably the first attempt to comprehensively lay out principles and practices for qualitative research using Internet communication as a resource. This work notably shifts our focus from considering research *of* the Internet to research *using* the Internet as a tool. Instantaneous transmission, high-speed connections, and inexpensive networks provide access to participants and cultural phenomena beyond our local reach; software eases the difficulties of transcription and augments our capacity to access, sort, and code data. Organizational and community artifacts are readily available for easy download, storage, and analysis. Online interviews can be synchronous or not, designed and timed to satisfy the needs of both participants and researchers. Observation in ethnographic settings can be less obtrusive.

Of course, as Marshall McLuhan, Neil Postman, and other media skeptics note, all technologies come with a double edge. The potential to enhance is accompanied by the potential to remove, disable, or diminish. This fact should not stop one from using this tool, but it should be reason for reflection and flexibility.

For example, instantaneous worldwide networks provide a connection to the context or participant that is not physical but virtual; studying them at a distance, often via text-based computer-mediated communication, I no longer have access to many of the nonverbal cues I normally rely on during data collection in the field. Although many text-based cues have been invented to simulate embodied nonverbals (Baym, 1998; Witmer and Katzman, 1998), for many users these emoticons or verbal expressions may not completely satisfy one's need for embodied knowledge. In my own experience, the absence of the body does not make the interaction less real, or the 'knowing of other' impossible, but it forces an adjustment of perspective; I must be keenly aware of my preconceptions. I must alter research design, strategies, and tactics based on the fact that Internet communication removes previously assumed embodied cues that contribute vital information utilized in understanding what is meant by what is uttered.

Internet communication allows me to collect, archive, and analyze greater quantities of social texts. At the same time, it may also compel me to fall into the delicate trap of continuing to collect data simply because I can and not because I should. There is a growing trend to collect larger and larger datasets for qualitative analysis of Internet communication. While I am as yet unwilling to conclude that this is a good trend, I am quite willing to point out that trends can morph subtly into normative rules. It is worth remembering that larger datasets can require more time and possibly the use of more data analysis aiding software solutions, neither of which may be optimal for all types of qualitative research projects.

Additionally, online interviewing diminishes the difficulties of scheduling and distance because we can meet our subjects in real time or we can exchange messages over time, each from respective locales. The removal of bodies from an interview changes the nature of the interaction from orality to textuality, which is not a minor shift. In addition, there are other problematic issues encountered by researchers. Interviewing in text requires different pacing. It also requires deliberate attention to providing written examples of conversational markers such as smiling or laughing at a story being told, indicating confusion, or subtly prompting more information without verbally interrupting the respondent. Interviewing via text may be more suitable for people who type fast, who are accustomed to the medium, and, depending on the research question, whose personalities come through in the text as clearly as they would face to face. Interviewing online requires constant rethinking of the definitions of the terms 'real' and 'authentic'. It tests our notions of trust and brings new forms of stereotyping to the foreground, such as spelling ability, sentence construction, and depth of vocabulary, not to mention the tendency to assume by default that the other with whom we are interacting is white and educated (Nakamura, 1995; Poster, 1998; Kolko, 2000).

Observing people's behaviors in computer-mediated communication contexts is certainly less obtrusive, in that a researcher can lurk and not be noticed. Participant observation is also easier, in that joining groups is not difficult. Yet both these capacities afforded by the Internet must be balanced carefully with ethical considerations. Some public groups perceive their interaction to be private and can be surprised and angered by intruding researchers (Bromseth, 2002). Other groups know their communication is public but nonetheless do not want to be studied (Gajjala, 2002; Hudson and Bruckman, 2002). Confidentiality is almost impossible to preserve with the sophistication of search engines (Mann, 2002). Ethical issues have sparked much debate and disagreement among experts and remain a vital issue for each researcher to consider (see, e.g., the ethics committee of the Association of Internet Researchers and their associated statement, 2002).

As a tool, medium, or conduit, the Internet can be viewed as a portal through which we access and interact with information and other people. For many users, the Internet is more than this; it also has dimension and meaning as a location for interaction.

Internet as place

As the quote by Steve Jones at the beginning of this chapter articulates, the Internet is not only a conduit that facilitates the swift and planet-wide flow of information, it comprises the cultural spaces in which meaningful human interactions occur. There, in a described, imagined, or perceived *place*, one can spend time wandering, navigating, and otherwise exploring. One can converse, come to know and love, insult [flame], and otherwise interact with others one meets there. Although computer-mediated social spaces have no literal physical substance, they can be perceived as having dimension, comprising meaningful, structured places where things happen that have genuine consequences. In this frame, the Internet is not so much a prosthetic for the senses but a separate environment where the self can travel and exist.

Conceptualized as a place, the Internet becomes a research context, a sociocultural milieu that can and should be studied in context. Using basic terms, one can study the space itself, the interactions within these places, and the relationships and communities formed through the interactions.

Just as the context is defined in multiple ways, the boundaries of the culture are sketched not just by the preconfigured design or programmed parameters of interaction but by the interactions of participants. Borders are thus negotiated processes (Hine, 2000) rather than well-defined, static, or geographic. Also, as I have noted previously (Markham, 1998), the researcher's engagement with people in these contexts influences directly the structure and border of culture quite significantly. The researcher's presence and influence presents problematic issues in all arenas of ethnographic inquiry but is accentuated by the highly negotiable feature of boundary in computer-mediated contexts.

As the field grows steadier in its sensibilities and approaches, we learn that computer-mediated environments are both like and unlike physical cultures. These spaces of interaction can draw on or transcend traditional ways of being with others, reify traditional or create new stereotypes, democratize or marginalize. These spaces, like the humans constituting and occupying them, are like any social space we see and study in physical environments; I argue that the primary distinctiveness of the Internet lies in the capacity for anonymity and the unique way this technology reconfigures time and space. It has as much potential and limitation as our imagination.

Suffice it to say, the contexts of Internet-facilitated relationships, communities, and cultures are as multiple as the members. Consequently, research of these spaces by anthropologists, sociologists, and scholars from multiple related disciplines is both vast and varied. As the surge to capitalize on this new arena for research slows, our methods of approaching and studying these contexts will improve.

Internet as way of being

The reality of the Internet as a social space is beginning to be taken for granted in this academic field of inquiry. We also acknowledge and, for the most part, laud the idea that Internet communication can be a very influential mediator/moderator of human experiences. Through the design, control, and play of information in online contexts, personalized worlds can be created, organized, and enacted. Though the Internet is quite literally a network of computers, the outcome is a fuzzy mapping of imagined geographies, perceived physicalities, and transcendent forms. As a means for reinscribing, reconfiguring, or otherwise shifting identity, body and self's connection with other, the Internet becomes, for some, a way of being.

This third frame involves a more integrated sense of the Internet as a part of the self. Within this frame, users may not focus on the technology used or occupied but rather on the expression and negotiation of self and other with or through Internet technologies. Users who have integrated Internet technologies into their lives to a high degree can be seen to incorporate the Internet as a way of being. Users might spend much of their time as computer-mediated beings, adopting alternative or additional personae in various text and graphic online environments, seeking transcendence from embodiment or a different embodiment, protection from embodied others, or an eventual merge of mind and body with machine. On the other hand, there are those users whose embodied connection to the

technology is powerfully evident, such as those who broadcast daily activities as public display via webcams or even those who feel best when the Internet is practically attached to the body via mobile communication technologies.

Interestingly though, while we might have a sense of 'being there', both the 'being' and the 'there', as Novak points out, are user-controlled variables. Objects and bodies are but 'collections of attributes … assembled for temporary use, only to be automatically dismantled again when their usefulness is over' (1991: 235). In other words, we can create and destroy our various identities and selves at will in cyberspace; our identities can be perceived as having continuous malleability and transformative potential. Of course, this potential is intertextual; Internet beings dialogically and recursively constitute each other simultaneously or alternately as author and audience, performer and stage, marking and marked.

From this perspective, computer-mediated communication is both process and product, medium and outcome. Online identities and associated cultural contexts are multitudes of ever-evolving, self-referential sets of texts, influencing and being influenced by readers and writers and the individuals' willingness to treat these texts and the associated social structure constructs as real. Within this frame, the focus of research might be to reconsider and reconceptualize certain taken-for-granted aspects of being human with others, to explore the intersections of individual, technology, and identity, and to examine closely how Internet technologies are woven into a participant's life experience.

The boundaries between these three frames of tool, place, and way of being are permeable, if not artificial. One can conceptualize and experience the Internet as both tool and place, use the Internet as a tool while integrating it as a gestalt, or land in various categories depending on the time of day, type of technology, person with whom one is interacting, and any other number of factors. Rather than a taxonomy, model, or theory, this framework is simply one way of making sense of experiences of the Internet as well as the complex growing field of Internet research.

The remainder of the chapter describes in more depth specific issues one might face when moving from the theoretical to the practical, tactical engagement as a researcher within the cultural phenomenon of the Internet. I focus here on my experiences interacting with users solely within Internet contexts to illustrate that within even this single area, many design and interpretive challenges must be confronted and negotiated.

INTERVIEWING TEXT-TO-TEXT: ENABLING AND CONSTRAINING FEATURES FOR RESEARCHERS

How much of good conversation is based on reading the other person's face? How much of good storytelling relies on the nodding head, strategic pauses, chuckles, gasps, or raised eyebrows?

Online interviewing, at the most basic level, involves the exchange of texts. Through this exchange, the qualitative researcher is hoping to glean something meaningful about organizational members' lived experience, attempting to draw out examples, stories, or descriptions that will speak to the depths of experience, the meaning of relationships, and the understanding of identity. Engaging others in conversation may always involve a great deal of patience, careful listening, and constant interpretation, but face to face, conversational knowing is, for the most part, taken for granted. We humans, as a rule, trust our senses, particularly vision. We generally believe in the universality of nonverbal communication and have developed an amazing faith in the naïve notion not only that our messages are understood perfectly by others, but that we truly know what others mean by what they say. Here, I shall provide some examples in my own research when my interactions with participants confronted me with the reality that conversation is an accomplishment, revealed many of my tendencies to categorize, stereotype, and otherwise encapsulate participants, and highlighted the dilemmas of filtering and editing the words and possibly the being of the participants of our studies. These dilemmas are not restricted to Internet contexts; indeed, the examples I provide highlight the need in any study for ethical reflection on the choices one makes throughout the collection, analysis, and presentation of those people we study.

Talking with participants: the conscious accomplishment of conversation

```
Beth-ANN smiles

Markham nods understandingly

Beth-ANN says "I think I like it this
way because I can just type what
commes to mind and not have to think
about it as much thinkgs seem to be
communicated better through my fin-
gers then my voice."
```

I tried my best not to type something back immediately, because I had been running over Beth's sentences constantly since we started the interview. I just couldn't stop myself; long pauses between messages often got interpreted as a dropped connection. My participants and I frequently interjected the anxious question 'Are you still there?' if the pause in our conversation grew longer than 15 seconds. Sure enough, Beth eventually continued:

```
Beth-ANN says "that's why I like
being on here so much."
```

I asked:

```
Markham asks "do you think that talk-
ing with your fingers better than
your voice is the major difference
between RL and online communication?"
```

And then, as an afterthought, I added:

```
Markham asks "for you, I mean?"
```

Beth wrote:

```
Beth-ANN says "I use the Internet for
a lot of things even now to find
information, chat, look for things
just use it for everything but I
haven't brought anything off the
Internet yet."
```

I wondered if Beth meant to type 'bought' instead of 'brought'. I typed, 'What do you mean by brought off…' I considered for a moment, and then erased the message. My colleague Bill had just knocked on my office door and was feeling very scattered. Better to buy myself some time, I thought, and wrote a different message:

```
Markham asks "Beth, can you hang on a
minute while I use the restroom?"
```

Beth said:

```
Beth-ANN says "yes it is because I can
type what i'm feeling better then I
can voice my;m"
```

A few seconds passed, then Beth continued:

```
Beth-ANN says "feelings it just comes
a little easier seeing things to answer
then hearing and having to answer I
like to worrk with my hands alot."
```

Hmmm…good thing I hadn't pressed on with the question of 'bought' versus 'brought'; as usual, I was racing ahead of Beth and she was plodding along, answering questions in the order I asked them.

```
Beth-ANN exclaims "yes I can!"
```

Ah-ha. She means, Yes, she'll wait while I'm in the restroom. I quickly typed:

```
Markham exclaims "thanks! back in a
flash!"

Beth-ANN says "ok taht's cool"
```

I sighed with relief, leaning back in my chair to pay attention to the physical person who had just walked into my office.

'Hi, Bill.' I motioned distractedly to a chair. My colleague had dropped by to check on the progress of the interview. We chatted for about a minute about the blessings and banes of multi-tasking when I noticed a message had appeared on the screen from Beth:

```
You sense that Beth-ANN is looking
for you in Hut X

Beth pages, "is a girl who's inter-
viewing me and it's on here that she's
interviewing"
```

I quickly sent the message:

```
Markham says "hi again"
```

followed quickly by a smiley emoticon:

```
Markham :-)
```

Beth replied:

```
Beth-ANN says "hi. your back. that's
cool."

Beth-ANN smiles

Markham smiles back
```

Before e-mail, instant messaging, and other forms of computer-mediated communication became ubiquitous in my life (and the lives of everyone I know), I found these media awkward and unwieldy tools for conversation. Interviewing in these media was even more challenging, in that it forced me to become aware of and monitor my own interaction tendencies. Indeed, it might be better to say simply that interviewing via the Internet highlights the fact that interviewing, in general, is difficult. Text-based online interaction requires active reflection on and management of very basic elements of conversation, such as taking turns at the appropriate time, nodding, or mm-hmm-ing to imply, 'Go on, I'm listening.' Online, I couldn't give a questioning glance or wrinkle my forehead or frown slightly to let the other person know I didn't understand what they were getting at. I couldn't smile, chuckle, or laugh sponta-neously. Indeed, if I wanted to react (without interrupting the flow of the story) to something I found amusing, funny, striking, or in some other way noteworthy, I had to type something such as 'emote smiles' or 'emote grimaces understand-ingly'. Then a message would appear on their

screen that read 'markham smiles' or 'markham grimaces understandingly'.

Each time I felt compelled to react 'nonver-bally' to statements the participants made, I had to decide whether or not to risk disrupting their thoughts to let them know I was listening and was engaged in the conversation by verbally signifying a nonverbal behavior. This issue became less trou-blesome as the interviews progressed and I became more adroit with this activity, but not less salient.

Synchronous interviewing online took about twice as long as face to face. I didn't anticipate this and had to make many adjustments throughout the process to accommodate different participants' writing style and speed. For example, Beth would answer each question in order, constant and steady, even if I interrupted with other clarification ques-tions. Sheol, another participant, seemed to be as scattered as I, able to leap back and forth between topics in short phrases and disjunctive ideas.

I wrote to Beth:

```
Markham asks "what do you do mostly
when you are online? Where do you go?"
Beth-ANN says "I'm usually on the MOO
when I'm in my room. But I go all over
the place I have lots of bookmarks on
my computer.

Markham asks "mostly the moo? or do
you irc too?"

Beth-ANN says "I just love to look
aroud at everything and anything
aplus my teacher my English professor
likes us to search for things in class
for projects and stuff she's an
Internet junky too."
```

Considering this an interesting label to give her professor, I asked:

```
Markham asks "What do you mean by
'internet junky?'"
```

Beth continued her response:

```
Beth-ANN says "I love the Internet and
my professor likes it that I like thae
Internet because she says it's the wave
of the future and there are not enough
women on the Internet. The Internet is
a place we can make the most impact"
```

The conversation seems disjunctive because our pacing was not synchronized. I had to learn to slow down to give participants enough time to respond fully to the questions. When I was inter-viewing Beth, I would ask a question and wait for what seemed like a long time for her to respond. Sometimes, if I didn't see writing on the screen shortly (don't ask me how I define 'shortly' ... I'm sure the actual passage of time was much shorter than the multiple minutes I imagined), I would wonder if she had received the message. Then I would wonder if she was still there. Then, to make sure she was there, I would send the same message again or another message asking if she got the first one. At other times, after Beth would send a message, I would ask the next question (a logical enough conversational move, I thought), and Beth's response would be a continuation of her previous message.

In effect, I interrupted almost every story she tried to tell. She would be warming up to the question, getting started on an in-depth answer, and I would abruptly ask a different question. I couldn't help myself. In my discomfort with what I thought was silence, I felt compelled to fill the blank void with more writing. Meanwhile, Beth was chatting away ... I just couldn't see/hear it yet.

Two considerations are important at this point. Constant interruption of the participant's talk can have a significant impact on the flow and content of ideas. Yet interruption is a primary mode of interaction in text-based spaces and therefore is a necessary skill to be practiced by researchers. The disjunctive, fragmented, and nonlinear character of text-based computer-mediated synchronous conversation no longer seems acutely strange for many users because they have grown accustomed to it. As researchers using this form of communication, we must attend to the details, acknowledge the possibilities and limitations, and be both practiced and flexible to adapt to each situation as it arises.

For example, because I continually interrupted Beth, I perceived her ideas to be cut off. To solve this problem, I forced myself to focus on other things. I started writing a research journal at the same time so that she had time to respond in peace. Learning to be patient was crucial for another reason as well. If I asked a question, got a complete response, and still remained silent, she would often fill the empty space with more depth regarding her previous answer or another related story that occurred to her during the silent period. Most interviewers learn to do this in face-to-face contexts, but here it took concentrated effort *not* to type. At the time of this interview, to cope with my own inability to manage this highly fragmented and nonlinear format, I developed the strategy of literally sitting on my hands, which gave Beth time to catch up with my questions and kept the conversation more sensible for me. I wouldn't call this a practiced art, just a desperate strategy at the time. Still, it highlights the necessity when working in a computer-mediated environment to develop keen sensibilities about how the interaction works and practice strategies that prompt without interrupting talk in this space.

Another example illustrates the importance of working with rather than against the disjunctive and text-only form of the interaction. I realized that small talk was both extremely time-consuming and essential to the conversations. Often, side conversations became intimately interwoven into the series of answers to questions I had constructed prior to the interview.

All interviews have elements of small talk, comic relief, or subtle shifts in new conversational directions; these features allow the participant to relax, encourage a conversational mode, and allow the conversation to guide the questions rather than the other way around. These elements are so natural in face-to-face contexts, they often remain unnoticed. In particular, the nonverbal features of interaction can be communicated without interrupting, acknowledged even as the recipient continues his or her statement. For the interviewer, these taken-for-granted elements of communication are unobtrusive yet vital means to encourage, prompt, shift, verify, validate, confirm, question, and so forth. In a textual environment, however, even clarifying a participant's response took time to write and several messages back and forth to complete. In short, the basic elements of good conversation seem to steal precious time from what I had been taught was the heart of the interview, the set of protocol questions. Flexible adaptation allows one to make better use of the situation as well as the predetermined questions. In my interview with Beth, dismissing the protocol and shifting to an unstructured interview was necessary to remain sensitive to the context.

In general, interviewing online took more planning, more time, and more self-control than I thought it would. There is, however, a significant tactical advantage of online interviewing: time to devise and deploy dynamic, context-driven follow-up questions. In the act of interviewing online, I could see the story unfolding and the response developing textually as the participant sent message segments. This meant I could attend to the message more than once. I could re-read what the participant had just sent, and while she was composing her next message, I could discern appropriate follow-up questions.

This is both a tactical and strategic improvement to interview techniques. The process becomes more granular in nature, observable in time steps. Not only do I have more time to consider the direction of the discussion, or scroll back to previous comments, I can adjust the form of the question in mid-utterance. For example, with Sheol I could ask a closed-ended follow-up question, 'Are you an addict?' or, after seeing it in text, consider carefully what I really wanted to know, and edit my own text to ask an open-ended question that allowed Sheol to set the parameters: 'What would define "addict"?' In another instance, I started with the question, 'Why did you start using the Internet?' and changed it to 'What drew you to the Net?' because even as I was writing the question, what I was reading in Sheol's answer scrolling up on my screen led me to ask the question in what I perceived would be a more provocative manner. These actual questions vary only slightly, but as any interviewer knows, the form of the question is vital for facilitating a participant's response.

Having response and interaction lag time is beneficial for another reason as well: it provides valuable processing time for consciously formulating overall interview direction, depth, and flow. Within the synchronous time frame of an interview, I could pretend I had been interrupted by the phone or other people (which I learned by actually being interrupted by the phone or people who didn't realize I was conducting an interview while sitting at my keyboard). Contrived interruptions gave me time to ponder and reapproach issues that were emerging.

Considering authenticity: how much do one's texts represent the real person?

At a recent conference, a journal editor indicated that he believed I should interview participants offline as well as online to get a 'more holistic picture of who they really are'. This is not the first time I have delved into the debate that surrounds the issue of authenticity and whether or not one must devise methods that will establish the real identity of the participant, a process that, for many researchers, requires offline interviewing. The debate raises fundamental questions about knowing, truth, and our beliefs about reality. The question often asked about participants in online contexts is 'Who are they, really?' By this, one often means, who are they, as I can see, verify, and know them in a body? Asked from a slightly different perspective, one might ask: How much do we rely on our bodies and the bodies of participants to establish presence and know other? Is this reliance warranted or desirable? Will our picture of other, in person, make our understanding of them more whole? More directly: does the embodiment of a participant gauge their authenticity?

The answer is, as with most of life's important questions, 'it depends'. It depends not only on the question one is seeking to address but also on the researcher's underlying epistemological assumptions. If one is simply using the Internet to expand one's reach to participants and interviewing them online is merely a convenience, one may want seriously to consider the extent to which people can and do express themselves well, truly, or fully in text. But if one is studying Internet contexts as cultural formations or social interaction in computer-mediated communication contexts, the inclusion of embodied ways of knowing may be unwarranted and even counterproductive.

Let us take my research participant named Sheol. Online, Sheol's texts were eloquent, albeit horribly misspelled, full of poetic expression and a genuine love of life and Shakespearean language. Conversing with Sheol was a delicate balance of interviewing and flirtatious play with language. I have no way of knowing if he would have engaged in these same behaviors offline. At the time, I insisted that I should not interview any of my participants offline; my goal in that project was not to compare but simply interpret the richness of experience. Even if my goal were comparison of online and offline contexts of performance and interaction, I am unwilling to conclude that interviewing both on and offline would satisfactorily accomplish the goal.

Christine Hine argues that we should question seriously our desire to seek authenticity in these contexts, as any degree of authenticity is negotiated and situated: 'A search for truly authentic knowledge about people or phenomena is doomed to be ultimately irresolvable' (Hine, 2000: 49). Still, researchers are plagued by questions of authenticity; we desire trust in our interviews with participants, often believing that if we know each other truly, in some authentic sense, we will know who they really are.

As qualitative researchers, we have neither fully explained nor adequately examined the function of text, practically and aesthetically, in the performance of self, perception of self and other, and sustenance of relationship. Does the form of the text matter? To what extent does an online persona's text represent the embodied being? Is the text merely a tool for interaction?

My overall goal as a researcher has been to utilize symbolic interactionist principles and interpretive ethnography practices to analyze and build knowledge of how people interact and negotiate identity and culture via the Internet. Of paramount concern during the research project is the design, exchange, and interpretation of text messages, for this is where the building blocks of culture reside. Online, culture is literally constructed discursively. Sensemaking is wrapped up in the text more obviously than in physical spaces because other mediating factors are perceived as absent.

Yet, even as I emphasize text and truly believe in the totality of intertextuality as the means by which we construct, maintain, and resist social structures, my training as a cultural researcher is embedded in embodied theory and practice. I am socialized to rely on and privilege the five senses, as most social scientists are. Having grown up in the wilds of Idaho, knowledge through the body is sometimes a matter of survival. Natural biologist Diane Ackerman describes vividly this reliance on traditional bodied senses as the means for knowledge:

> We live on the leash of our senses. Although they enlarge us, they also limit and restrain us, but how beautifully. ... To understand, we have to use our heads, meaning our minds. ... Most people think of the mind as being located in the head, but findings suggest that the mind doesn't really dwell in the brain but travels the whole body on caravans of hormone and enzyme, busily making sense of the compound wonders we catalogue as touch, taste, smell, hearing, vision. (Ackerman, 1991: 2–5, *passim*)

Should one interview Internet users in person as well as in text so one can know what the other senses say they are? Would this make them more authentic or make my study more valid? These questions are both instinctive and pragmatic. To dismiss them as mere logistical issues, however, is to overlook the ethical consequences of this fundamental research design decision. Although there are no easy answers, the process demands ongoing reflexive consideration of the issues within the context of each individual research project.

```
When I am online,
I restrict some of the senses that would typically help me make sense
of this place, Other, and the context.
I cannot see the body of others,
but I can get
a verisimilitude of them
as they describe themselves to me.
Of course, all I have
is their description of themselves.
I must, therefore, trust their vision of themselves,
rather than using my own sensibilities
and stereotypes
to interpret what they look like
....to me.

...but I'm still using my stereotypes and presuppositions and experiences to
filter them into something I can recognize.....

This is only fair.
After all, they chose this context
to mingle, and chose word play
as a way for Other to know the Self.
Yet....
....I also cannot hear their voices
or the sounds of the worlds where they sit.
It's a lonely place for my ears.....
I only hear the sound of
my own fingers
tapping
the
keyboard....
...or the humming of the air conditioner in the background.
I can't smell or taste the air they must be breathing
as we interact.
Does this really make a difference?
....Maybe.
```

This is not a new problem, of course. But in Internet ethnography, the problem is salient because the existence of both the researcher and the researched within the research context is solely text; a fact that emphasizes the already complicated features of 'being with', not to mention the problem of being compelled, by our disciplines, to verify, validate, or otherwise authenticate one's sensemaking of the participants, of the perceived place, and of the shared context. One might reply that this is impossible in any study, and I would agree. This doesn't completely remove the trained desire to distinguish between the authentic and the apparent and to find consistency and reality using one's eyes and ears as well as one's mind.

Considering textuality: how much does the form of one's texts matter?

To give this abstraction more shape, let me offer two examples. One is the use of poetic form by academic authors. In a chapter of a handbook on qualitative research methods, for example, how would a typical reader make sense of an author who used poetry to make claims about matters of social and scientific importance? How would the use of poetic forms or fonts or unconventional grammar and punctuation influence your perception of the author, the supposed scholar? If the text is primarily comprised of traditional scholarly texts, the poetic chapter would seem out of context, perhaps even dismissible at an initial glance. If the reader is trying to move beyond the content of the chapter to understand something about the author, paralinguistic cues provide vital data for the reader. One could glean a great deal of information from the length of line, use of tense, word clusters, degree of formality, active versus passive voice, and flow of thought created through particular punctuation choices.

In this framework, the complexity of understanding *other* is in some ways inseparable from the texts presented. On one hand, we might consider the exercise one of futility as the reader may not be able to discern the degree to which language use is deliberate or unintentional, and therefore to what extent it represents the author's intended, true, or perceived sense of self. On the other hand, whether intentional or accidental, communicative behaviors reveal important aspects of a person's identity, which makes the interpretive exercise quite fruitful. If there could be a third hand, I would mention the underpinning, consistent fact: the interpretation will always be the reader's. Moreover, the analysis may represent the reader as much as or more than the intended object of the reader's gaze.

A second example illustrates the elusiveness of the subject as a concrete knowable entity and highlights key complications inherent in any interpretive activity, online or offline.

Sheol is a self-described 'heavy user' of the Internet and a 'budding hacker' interviewed in an anonymous text-based synchronous chatroom. Sheol's interview is marked by frequent and intense inclusion of emoticons and punctuation to accent the content, such as LOL, exclamation marks!!!, and smiley faces :-)

```
<Sheol> *LOL* This is way cool!! I
have never been asked for an inter-
view before:)

<Sheol> I am intrested in talking
to:) Could you be more spesific about
what questions you will ask? Just let
me know when you want to talk, and I
will try to accomidate! :)

<Sheol> On the net you can be who or
what ever you want to be. That is the
trap! when you want your cyberlife to
be your real life. That's what
hapened to me.

<Sheol> I became a very popular (I
know that sounds conseeded) figuar on
the line I called home. I am ruled by
the right side of my brain so I liked
the diea of being that personality.

<Sheol> My cyberfriends and I liked
to roleplay ... we went on fantastic
adventurs over the net. The only
limit was our imagineations. Not any-
thing like in the real world!! I am
shy by nature...I am also a big fan
of Shahspear langue. I can use that
style of speaking, and not be shy
about on the net:)
```

Of immediate interest and concern to me as a qualitative researcher conducting close textual analysis is the form that envelops the content. I could elect to bracket or set aside the form and focus only on the content. However, the goal of my research in this case is to explore how people experience the Internet and how their identities are presented and negotiated. To ignore the form in this interview could be seen as a poor choice, given the well-founded premise that nonverbal behaviors function discursively in the presentation of self, negotiation of identity, and eventual symbolic construction of culture. Yet, multiple dilemmas can plague the Internet researcher:

How much does text represent the reality of the person? Put more personally, how much would I want to be bound by what I wrote at any particular time? How might the findings shift if I focus on form versus content? How much are my own preconceptions and stereotypes influencing how I make sense of this data?

One of the first problems impeding the interpretation of this interview is that I do not know Sheol *in culture*. I am interviewing from the outside, therefore it remains difficult to assess the intention of Sheol's use of graphic accents. It is also difficult to assess the meaning in any accurate sense, because the interaction is abstracted from the typical context of Sheol's online existence. More directly, Sheol is not participating in online culture, Sheol is participating in an online *interview*.

Should I base any of my interpretation on Sheol's grammar? As the researcher, I have numerous choices. I have many more choices than Sheol does, in terms of creating cultural knowledge about how people interact in cyberspace. Reflection on each research decision as well as the premises undergirding the choices I make is crucial if I am to preserve Sheol's dignity as a human being and his autonomy as a human subject in my research. The interview yields fruitful insight about Sheol's discursive practices and sensemaking practices. Throughout our interactions, Sheol appeared unconcerned with how the writing appeared and unaware of how the construction of text might mediate identity for others. Although Sheol mentions spelling once, Sheol never tried to change it or correct errors.

I, on the other hand, could not ignore Sheol's presentation of self through the text, both content and form. I am a creature of my upbringing; the number of social labels I mentally attached to Sheol during our interviews probably came close to the number of spelling errors I found – a number that was considerable. This is not a tangential point. It illustrates a potentially irresistible tendency to leap to conclusions and make hasty judgments about people. The interpretive lens is not separable from the researcher's frame of reference and history, but researchers often deemphasize or totally ignore this limitation under the protective guise of scientific tradition.

In order to preserve the integrity of the online interview project, it is essential that the researcher address these issues. For example, for two hours of the interview, Sheol was *female* (stereotypical gendered language style was very evident in tags, qualifiers, expressions of emotion, and heavy use of graphic accents). Sheol was *young* (spelling was phonetic, attention to language misuse was not at all evident). Sheol was perhaps *not very intelligent* (multiple spelling errors,

unreadable messages, apparent lack of ability to be a real hacker). Sheol was, of course, *Caucasian* (default characteristic because of mainstream cultural assumptions about use of the Internet as well as the tendency to make the online other look more like the self). Additionally, and solely based on the interpreter's frame of reference, Sheol was heterosexual, middle-class, and American.

It is essential to expose these assumptive interpretations to detailed examination. In this case, each interpretation I was making about the subject based on the text had to be reviewed. Conclusions could not be driven by my own social and academic conditioning. Even so, one must acknowledge that caution may improve and justify interpretive decisions in some cases but not others. As much as one understands the qualitative researcher's right and responsibility to build knowledge through interpretation, this example highlights the extent to which the very existence of the online persona being studied is comprised solely by the pixels on a computer screen. Therefore, the choices we make to attend to, ignore, or edit these pixels have real consequences for the persons whose manifestations are being altered beyond and outside their control. If a subject types solely in lowercase and uses peculiar spelling, the researcher's correction of grammar may inappropriately ignore and thus misrepresent a participant's deliberate presentation of self. If someone spells atroshiously or uniQueLY and the researcher corrects it in the research report for readability, alteration of a person's desired online identity may be the price of smooth reading.

On the other hand, a participant's exclusive use of lowercase may be simply a time-saving device. A new keyboard, carpal tunnel syndrome, a broken finger, or a project due tomorrow for the boss may prompt typographic errors that the participant ordinarily would avoid. Our interpretation of certain data as meaningful or dismissal of other data as meaningless may be well founded or absolutely unwarranted depending on any number of underlying factors, only some of which are comprehensible. The methodological dilemma is to be sensitive to the context, to figure out what the most suitable interpretive path is, and to remain epistemologically consistent. Of course, in my own experience, this is easier said than done, as the following segment illustrates.

Considering anonymity and identity: how reliable is a shifting subject?

Complicating the issue of authenticity, the online persona may be much more fluid and changeable than we imagine. Anonymity in text-based environments gives one more choices and control in the presentation of self, whether or not the presentation is perceived as intended.

The best example of this developed quite unexpectedly in an online course I was teaching. We had met online for six weeks, never meeting face to face, as the participants were both local and distant. We had met in various online environments to assess the impact of each technology on our participation in class as well as the development of individual identity and overall sense of community. One night my students and I met in Internet Relay Chat (IRC), a synchronous anonymous chatting environment. At the request of the students leading class discussion, we adopted colors as our names. I thought I would be satisfied with 'Forest Green', but I got bored, and switched it. As I changed my 'nick', this message appeared on everyone's screens:

```
*** Forest green is now known as
"GhostlyGreen"
```

For me, GhostlyGreen was satisfactory for a while. After all, it was very close to Halloween. But I was feeling playful – finally, I could experience a classroom environment in which I was not immediately identified and characterized as Annette or Dr Markham.

```
*** GhostlyGreen is now known as
babypuke
```

Much better. I acted out my 'color identity' – made rude comments, interrupted other participants, and such. Still, I thought, rather gross. It wasn't really 'me'. I continued my spectrum of development:

```
*** babypuke is now known as
"RottenJackOrange"
```

This still did not quite feel right, and I was in an obnoxious student mood, so I shifted my nickname again:

```
*** RottenJackOrange is now known as
oatmeal"
```

I oozed and squelched while the rest of the class attempted to carry on a scholarly conversation. Occasionally they would get into the playful mood and walk around me, get their shoes stuck in my porridge-ness. One student threatened another, using me as the potential weapon. We all had a good laugh about that, which disrupted the class even more. Finally and wisely, the students running class discussion decided it was time to reveal the actual identities behind the colors.

As I watched various students reveal themselves, I saw IndigoBlu turn to AMarkham:

```
*** IndigoBlu is now known as
AMarkham
```

I had never chosen IndigoBlu as my color identity. I thought to myself, someone's playing a good game. So I went along with it and after all the other students had presumably revealed their actual names, I unmasked as if I were the only unnamed student remaining:

```
*** oatmeal is now known as DennisL.
```

For the remainder of the class, almost two hours, the rest of the students believed he was the professor and responded to him as if he were me. I played the role of student. They believed I was a student.

What does this example tell us? Importantly, this example reiterates the symbolic interactionist concept that identity is negotiated (Blumer, 1969). It seems to support the idea that we all wear masks and adopt roles that eventually come to represent our authentic self (Goffman, 1959). This example can also illustrate Turkle's notion that we have fragmented selves in Internet contexts (Turkle, 1995). Basically, it tells me that titles can mean everything or nothing in the moment of the interaction, implying a negotiation of reality based on discourse as much as perception of one's title. Anonymous Internet-based interactions facilitate knowledge of self and other that is interwoven with naming and perception, and yet is fundamentally grounded in the exchange of texts.

Authenticity, in this case, is found as much in the perception of participants as in the body/title attached to the name. Richard MacKinnon (1995: 119) aptly points out that in cyberspace, the phrase 'I think, therefore I am' is woefully inadequate. It is not even enough to say 'I type, therefore I am'. In cyberspace, the more appropriate phrase is 'I am perceived, therefore I am'. MacKinnon means this in a literal sense, where one's texts must be both seen and acknowledged for one's existence to be meaningful in context. Read in a different sense, perception is the defining point for reality, making authenticity either a label defined by other or, at most, negotiated by the participants in context. This notion has significant methodological impact.

I return to the question I hear in so many classes and conferences, when students want to study the Internet as social space but feel uncomfortable about the issue of authenticity, embodiment, and reality: 'Does it matter that people may be different than who they appear to be?'

Given the example above and the multiplicity of experience in anonymous Internet-facilitated environments, this is not the most useful question. The flexible negotiation of identity in a text-based social space seems to require a different set of questions for the ethically sensitive researcher:

- 'As researchers and members of various communities and cultures, what do we use to construct a sense of who the Other really is?'
- 'In what ways do our methods of comprehending online others either disavow or validate multiplicitious, polyvocal, ever-shifting constructions of identity?'
- 'To what extent do we acknowledge our own participation in the construction of the subject of inquiry?'

As pioneers on the research frontier of qualitative Internet studies, we must continually address what I call the embodiment dysfunction. When we rely on our embodied sensibilities of knowing, we are not necessarily getting a better or more 'accurate' picture of the subjects of our studies; we may be simply reflecting our own comfort zones of research. Critical reflection on the product of our gaze can reveal some of these comfort zones for introspection and interrogation.

Considering the shape I give them: why do they all look like me?

To what extent do we transform the subjects of our research into images of ourselves? With what effect? Every time I study online social interactions and conduct interviews online, I visualize the participants. I always give them a body. Before I became very reflexive about my practices and premises, my imagination wasn't that great; they all ended up looking like friends of mine.

In my first study using exclusively online interviews, Beth Ann and Sheol were very young, based on their typing and spelling ability. Melissa was in her forties because she spoke clearly, seemed comfortable with herself, and was so sensible in her attitude toward the Internet. Matthew was old, or in any case, old*er*, because he told me he had children. Teri was short, dark-haired, wore lots of either black or pink, and had a New York accent because she typed fast and I knew she was attending school there. In my mind's eye, Beth Ann had straight brown hair that extended a little past her shoulders. She had translucent creamy-white skin and downcast eyes. Sheol never combed his hair. They were all some variation of Caucasian. They were all middle-class.

When I teach in distance learning environments, my students seem white to me. I think they speak middle-America English with very little accent if they have an anonymous name. If they use the name that corresponds with their enrolled identity, I adjust my image based on what I think the name represents. I didn't realize I was making these judgments until my editor pointed out the absence of discussion about absence of race or socioeconomic markers for self-identification. It was not the focus of my study so I had not asked about race. Participants never mentioned it. I had been so preoccupied with my research focus and *their* presentation of self through their texts, yet I had been equally unreflexive of my own filters of interpretation. This is typical of the way many people make sense of another who is known only via the text. This fact illustrates how much we rely on and use our own parameters to categorizes others into something we can comfortably address. Scholarly discussion of race and the Internet, particularly of how the Internet has been created and perceived naïvely as a raceless space, is growing (Kendall, 1998; Poster, 1998; Kolko et al., 2000). These discussions will help researchers better reflect on the spaces studied as well as the assumptions made during the collection and interpretation phases of the project.

Ironically, although I have always been aware of and critical of others' perceptions of me and my physical embodiment, I rarely reflected on this when I began studying Internet culture. I assumed others would perceive me as I constructed myself via the text. At times, I used sentence structures and terminology that I thought would mark me a scholar. Other times, I modified my voice to give the impression that I was young, streetwise, hacker-friendly. I did this glibly and without guile. I knew that I was engaging in impression management, but isn't that what we do all the time anyway? If it loosens up the participant and helps them tell good stories, then I believed I had been a productive researcher.

Mediation of the self via the computer becomes a problematic proposition. As a middle-class white female, I am privileged to have relative invisibility in most physical contexts. Still, Internet technology beguiles one into thinking that one has a high degree of control over the presentation of one's own self. More succinctly, in my early forays in online research, I assumed that everyone I met would interpret me as I chose to convey myself – a naïve and somewhat ironic misperception, since one finding of my study was that one's identity for others is not a user-controlled variable, but a negotiation.

It didn't occur to me I would appear to them differently than I appear to myself when I look in the mirror every morning. If I had stopped to consider the image of me looking through the screen and seeing someone else, I might have wondered at their possible perceptions of me. But to many users, the Internet as a medium for being with others is under the user's control. Users believe they can see and know others, but remain comfortable in the perception that they can control the way others see them. Another way to look at this is to consider that for the most part, users believe they see others truly and also believe they control what others see/know of themselves, whereas actually, both parties see only the words of the other, superimposed by their own reflections on the screen. Hence, while early discussions of Internet contexts lauded the capacity of ultimate freedom in the presentation of self (Benedikt, 1991), more recent thought acknowledges that all presentation is a much more complicated negotiation between people whose interpretive frameworks are fraught with their own preconceptions.

The Internet provides a unique space for the construction of identity in that it offers anonymity and an exclusively discursive environment. The difficulty of interviewing in this space is that our expectations remain rooted in embodied ways of collecting, analyzing, and interpreting information. Our methods are still more suitable for research in physically proximal contexts. Moreover, although the technology of the Internet has afforded us greater reach to participants and provided a space for researchers to interact with participants in creative ways, our epistemological frameworks don't yet fit. It is necessary not only to accommodate the features of computer-mediated communication into our basic assumptions, but also to rework the very premises we use to make sense of the world.

I hope to have complicated the simple and elegant project of studying identity formation or knowing and presenting the other in Internet contexts. I have many questions but few answers. In the end, however, our goal as qualitative researchers remains; we strive to understand other in context, analyze some of what it means, and, when we think we know something, present this knowledge to colleagues. Rommetveit (1980) reminds us that what we know is more often a shared faith rather than any actual understanding of what is meant by what is said.

In whatever ways we utilize the potential of Internet-mediated communication to facilitate our social inquiry – as a tool, a place, or a way of being – ethically sensitive approaches are complicated, even impeded, by methods. Depending on the academic discipline we find ourselves working within, we will be encouraged to varying degrees to oversimplify the complexity of human experience, transforming the mysteries of life into discrete variables that are easily measured. This is done for admirable reasons and by no means am I recommending a complete dismissal of traditional means of collecting and analyzing data. At the same time, Internet contexts prompt us to reconsider the foundations of our methods and compel us to assess the extent to which our methods are measuring what we think they are, or getting at what we have always assumed they did. This is not an inconsequential point. Through the Internet, identities, relationships, and social structures can be constituted solely through the exchange of texts. This is unique in that we have the opportunity to observe how written discourse functions to construct meaning and how textual dialogue can form the basis of cultural understanding. The taken-for-granted methods we use to make sense of participants in our research projects may need to be thoroughly reexamined in light of our growing comprehension of how intertextuality happens, literally.

How can this be accomplished? Give careful reflection to the outcome of interpretation and critical examination of the extent to which the interpretation reflects one's own biases versus the experiences of the participants. Even within a contemporary framework of sociological inquiry, whereby the distinction between the researcher and researched is problematized, the researcher's role is acknowledged, and bias is accepted as a fundamental fact of interpretation, our obligation to the participant remains. Here, I do not offer a set of prescriptives. Rather, I raise essential questions and reflect on my own practices, which may help researchers see the utility of such questioning in their own works.

ACKNOWLEDGEMENTS

The author would like to thank Rebecca de Wind Mattingly and Margaret Gonzales for their helpful input in the creation of this chapter.

REFERENCES

Ackerman, D. (1991) *The Natural History of the Senses*. New York: Random House.

Association of Internet Researchers (2002) 'Ethical decision making and internet research'. Retrieved 1 December 2002 from http://www.aoir.org/reports/ ethics.pdf

Baym, N. (1998) 'The emergence of on-line community', in S. Jones (ed.), *Cybersociety 2.0*. Thousand Oaks, CA: Sage, pp. 138–63.

Benedikt, M. (1991) *Cyberspace: First Steps*. Cambridge, MA: MIT Press.

Blumer, H. (1969) *Symbolic Interactionism*. Englewood Cliffs, NJ: Prentice-Hall.

Bromseth, J. (2002) 'Public places ... private activities?', in A. Morrison (ed.), *Researching ICTs in Context*. Oslo: Intermedia Report 3/2002, Unipub forlag, pp. 44–72. Retrieved 1 December 2002, from http://www. intermedia.uio.no/publikasjoner/rapport_3/

Gajjala, R. (2002) 'An interrupted postcolonial/feminist cyberethnography: complicity and resistance in the "cyberfield"', *Feminist Media Studies*, 2(2): 177–93.

Goffman, E. (1959) *The Presentation of Self in Everyday Life*. New York: Anchor Press.

Hine, C. (2000) *Virtual Ethnography*. London: Sage.

Hudson, J.M. and Bruckman, A. (2002). 'IRC Français: the creation of an Internet based SLA community', *Computer Assisted Language Learning*, 15(2): 109–34.

Jones, S.G. (1995) 'Understanding community in the information age', in S.G. Jones (ed.), *Cybersociety: Computer-Mediated Communication and Community*. Thousand Oaks, CA: Sage, pp. 10–35.

Kendall, L. (1998) 'Meaning and identity in "cyberspace": the performance of gender, class and race online', *Symbolic Interaction*, 21(2): 129–53.

Kolko, B.E. (2000) 'Erasing @race: going white in the (inter)face', in B.E. Kolko, L. Nakamura and G.B. Rodman (eds), *Race in Cyberspace*. New York: Routledge, pp. 117–31.

Kolko, B.E., Nakamura, L. and Rodman, G.B. (eds) (2000) *Race in Cyberspace*. New York: Routledge.

MacKinnon, R.C. (1995) 'Searching for the Leviathan in usenet', in S.G. Jones (ed.), *Cybersociety: Computer-Mediated Communication and Community*. Thousand Oaks, CA: Sage, pp. 112–37.

Mann, C. (2002) 'Generating data online: ethical concerns and challenges for the C21 researcher'. Keynote address, Nordic conference on internet research ethics, Trondheim, Norway, June 2002.

Mann, C. and Stewart, F. (2000) *Internet Communication and Qualitative Research: A Handbook for Researching Online*. London: Sage.

Markham, A. (1998) *Life Online: Researching Real Experience in Virtual Space*. Walnut Creek, CA: AltaMira Press.

Miller, D. and Slater, D. (2000) *The Internet: An Ethnographic Approach*. New York: New York University Press.

Nakamura, L. (1995) 'Race in/for cyberspace: identity tourism and racial passing on the Internet', *Works and Days*, 13(1–2): 181–93.

Novak, M. (1991) 'Liquid architectures in cyberspace', in M. Benedikt (ed.), *Cyberspace: First Steps*. Cambridge, MA: MIT Press, pp. 225–54.

Poster, M. (1998) 'Virtual ethnicity: tribal identity in an age of global communications', in S.G. Jones (ed.), *Cybersociety 2.0*. Thousand Oaks, CA: Sage, pp. 184–211.

Rommetveit, R. (1980) 'On "meanings" of acts and what is meant and made known by what is said in a pluralistic social world', in M. Brenner (ed.), *The Structure Of Action*. Oxford: Basil Blackwell, pp. 108–49.

Turkle, S. (1995) *Life on the Screen: Identity in the Age of the Internet*. New York: Simon & Schuster.

Witmer, D.F. and Katzman, S.L. (1998) 'Smile when you say that: graphic accents as gender markers in computer-mediated communication', in S. Rafaeli, F. Sudweeks and M.L. McLaughlin (eds), *Network and Netplay: Virtual Groups on the Internet*. Boston: AAAI/MIT Press, pp. 3–11.

24

Documents

Lindsay Prior

Documents? There never were any. There are no written orders, no ordnance maps, cryptographs, leaflets, proclamations, newspapers, letters. The custom of writing memoirs and diaries does not exist (most frequently there is simply no paper). There is no tradition of writing histories. Most importantly – who would do this? (Kapuściński, 2001: 4)

Kapuściński is speaking of life in southern Sudan in the last decade of the twentieth century. He is speaking of life in a war zone; of life among peoples such as the Dinka and the Nuer – peoples who had been closely studied during the middle part of the last century by anthropologists such as Evans-Pritchard (1940) and Lienhardt (1961). He is also speaking of a world that is lost – precisely because there is no documentation to hold it in place. Without documents there are no traces. Things remain invisible and events remain unrecorded. The only resource is word-of-mouth accounts. It was in such worlds that anthropology was developed. So it is, perhaps, understandable that the research acts of the anthropologist turned on matters of observation, and the recording of speech and behaviours. For how could one use documents in the absence of paper? Naturally, in the modern affluent world – the world in which we live – documentation is central. The written order forms a cornerstone of modern life. It is a point that was emphasized during the early 1900s by Max Weber in his analysis of that quintessential organizational form of the twentieth century: bureaucracy (see Weber, 1979). Yet, in modern social science, the written trace continues to be neglected. There are few studies concerned directly, rather than merely tangentially, with the use of documentation in contemporary life and even fewer texts devoted to the problem of research on forms of documentation. For analysis of speech, on the other hand, the range of materials is expansive – as other chapters in this volume demonstrate. This is so even though the analysis of speech has, necessarily, to be mediated through text; that is, via a transcription (see, e.g., Silverman, 1996: 254). In that light it would be an interesting research exercise in itself to look at the emergence of the various social scientific tools and techniques that have been used to translate talk into text – though that is not the task of this chapter.

There is, of course, no obvious way to account for the differing fortunes of speech and writing in social scientific research. Perhaps the neglect of the role of writing in contemporary life serves as something of a pointer towards a fundamental blind spot in Western culture. Such an undervaluing of the written, as opposed to the spoken word, has of course been remarked upon elsewhere. Thus, the anthropologist Jack Goody (1968, 1977) has frequently referred to writing as a rich, yet neglected, field for research studies, while Ong (1982) has sought to underline the ways in which the influence of writing – as against 'orality' – has been underestimated in Western scholarship. More fundamentally, the philosopher Jacques Derrida (see Howells, 1998) has emphasized, on a number of occasions, how the written word has always been considered subsidiary and secondary to the spoken word in the philosophical corpus of the West. Yet the subordinate role of writing to speech is far from deserved, and in this chapter I hope to demonstrate just how that is so.

Documentation is not coterminous with text, of course, for not all documents involve written traces. Nor is it possible to state in any *a priori* manner what a document might be. For, as I have pointed out elsewhere (Prior, 2003), documents are situated products and as such can take many forms (Ong, 1982, considers an important distinction between print and writing in this respect). Hence, architectural drawings (Prior, 1988, 1992), books, paintings, gravestone inscriptions, film, World Wide Web pages, bus tickets, shopping lists and tapestries can all fall into the category of 'document' – depending on the use that is made of such artefacts. Furthermore, documents enter into episodes of social interaction in a dual manner. In the first place, they enter as receptacles of content, and in the second they enter as functioning agents in their own right. Social researchers can approach the study of documents from either direction. In this chapter, however, I am going to forgo the study of document content in favour of an emphasis on the study of documents as agents. In particular, I am going to suggest that the study of the processes of document production and consumption (or use) provide two sturdy pillars around which interesting and essential research programmes can be built and developed. Naturally, in the hurly-burly of ordinary everyday activity, issues of production and consumption become entwined, and it is not always easy to distinguish clearly between the one process and the other. Nor is it necessarily easy to place the study of documents 'up front' when one is engaged in social research.

In what follows I am going to reflect upon sites of research where either the production or the consumption of documents has loomed large. They are sites in which I have worked and studied – government bureaucracies, medical clinics and hospitals. Looking back on my work in such sites, I suspect that I tended to regard documentation as somehow peripheral to the nature of the research process (although I always acknowledged the presence of documents and documentation). Perhaps this was because, as with so many others, I felt that real data were only to be found in talk and interaction. Only with time and practice did I come to realize the significance of inscription in organizational settings. In any event, in the following sections I am going to examine something about how documents are produced, how they are used, and how they are exchanged and circulated in various kinds of work setting, my overriding aim being to study the manipulation of documents in action.

PRODUCING DOCUMENTS: MANUFACTURING FACTS

It is something of a paradox that one of the most useful and malleable of quantitative measures that is called upon to assess the 'health' of populations

is the death rate – or, more accurately, the mortality rate. Thus, the rate (per thousand born) of babies of who die in the first year of life (the infant mortality rate), for example, has long been used by agencies in the advanced industrial societies as a key measure of both the health and quality of life of a population. Health agencies are, of course, also interested in what people die from as well as how many people die at any given age. Thus, the World Health Organization (WHO) publishes, on an annual basis, a manual of world health statistics (e.g. WHO, 1998). The latter provides data on both the numbers of people who die in any one country during a given year, and also on the cause of death of the individuals concerned. In that respect the manual exists as a resource for social scientific or epidemiological study. One can lift it off the library shelf and consult it for facts about mortality, or health, or, if one wishes, transpose and integrate the data into a measure of the 'quality of life' in Nigeria, Canada, the Ukraine or the United States. Furthermore, and where required, the facts within the manual can be plotted on graphs, slotted into tables, or correlated one with another to reveal trends and patterns (see Unwin et al., 1997, for a review of possibilities). Yet, as with many reports of this kind, it is often more revealing to look not so much at what can be derived from the document, but at the building blocks of the document itself – at how the report was put together in the first place. It is a line of inquiry that I learned rather by accident, and the document that I was originally encouraged to deconstruct was an Annual Report on Births, Deaths and Marriages.

The foundation stones of reports – such as the WHO report – are often designed and set at some distance from the final product. In the WHO case this is so in both a bureaucratic and a geographical sense. For example, one rather important 'stone' for the production of the report is the death certificate (Prior, 2001). The latter has many functions – and, as with all documents, those functions tend to alter according to the occasion of use. In most Western societies a medical practitioner completes the certificate on the death of an individual, and it forms an occasion to explain why a person died. (It lists a culturally acceptable 'cause of death'.) Such certificates are then processed through a series of local, regional and national agencies so as to compile a picture of mortality in any given country. It is from the national pictures that the international (WHO) picture is derived. To illustrate key procedures, I am going to begin with the concept of a cause of death and move upward. My aim is to show how facts about death (and life) are routinely manufactured in state bureaucracies, and how studying decision-making procedures in such settings can reveal a great deal about the nature of human culture.

We should be aware that deciding on the cause of death of any individual is not a simple task (Prior, 1989; Bloor, 1991). This is partly because people commonly die of many things at one and the same time, and it is not always easy to disentangle one cause from another. A serious infection of the lung, for example, may accompany a growth in the airways, leading to eventual heart failure. A minor wound may encourage the development of septicaemia, or whatever. In addition, we have to be aware that the physiological 'causes' of death are not always easy to determine in the absence of autopsy. For instance, brain tumours are particularly difficult to diagnose at death without an autopsy and it would be impossible to determine the precise nature of a lung infection without recourse to laboratory analysis. Despite this, only a minority of people is ever autopsied. Indeed, in many cases the physician or coroner or other individual who certifies a death may not consider it worthwhile to find out exactly why a person died. Often all that is important is to determine whether the individual died 'naturally' – as part of a plausible series of events – or from foul play. Further, and even if one feels able to overlook the aforementioned (technical) obstacles, one is faced with the fact that, in the discourse of Western medicine, only some causes of death are regarded as legitimate in the first place. In that context, readers may be delighted to note that one is simply not allowed to die of either 'old age' or 'poverty'. More significantly, the exclusion of such causes suggests that modern Western societies have very specific vocabularies of causation as far as matters relating to death are concerned, and a distinct image of what can and cannot cause a death.

So what can one die of? The answer to that question is buried (if that is not an entirely inappropriate metaphor) in another WHO manual. This latter is called The *International Statistical Classification of Diseases and Related Health Problems* (WHO, 1992). It is often referred to in an abbreviated form as the ICD. The current edition of the manual is the tenth, and so the abbreviation is, more accurately, ICD-10. ICD-10 provides a list of all currently accepted causes of death, and they are classified into 'chapters'. Thus, there are chapters relating to diseases and disorders of the respiratory system, the circulatory system, the nervous system, and so on. In different decades different diseases and causes of death are added and deleted from the manual.

HIV/AIDS is an obvious example of an addition and it appears as a cause of death only in ICD-10, while 'old age' as a cause of death was eliminated in ICD-6. In all cases, of course, the conceptual architecture in terms of which death is comprehended is structured around the human body (Foucault, 1973: 3)

As well as containing a long list of medical causes of death, the ICD also contains rules about which causes of death are more important than others, so that when a person dies of many conditions, the people responsible for coding the data on which the health statistics depend, 'know' which cause to select as *the* cause of death. Thus, diseases of the heart, for example, commonly take precedence over diseases of any other organ, and cancers take precedence over infections and so on. These rules also change from decade to decade. Thus, during the early part of the twentieth century diseases of the liver and lung took precedence over disease of the heart (see Prior, 1989).

In the context in which it is here considered, ICD-10 is an excellent example of what we might call a generative document. It contains both the conceptual structure in terms of which any explanations have to be built, and, in addition, rules for the building process. Generative documents come in various forms. The ICD is, perhaps, one of the most important for getting to grips with professional, 'expert', understandings of physical health and illness and serves, in many ways, as a window into Western culture (Bowker and Star, 1999). A related publication – the *Diagnostic and Statistical Manual of Mental Disorders* (American Psychiatric Association, 2000) or DSM IV – is available for the classification of psychiatric (mental) conditions. One might say that the DSM provides the conceptual architecture in terms of which Western culture comprehends disorders of the mind.

It is already clear then that the WHO *World Health Statistics Annual* (1998) that was mentioned at the start of this section is a secondary document, its production dependent on the existence of pre-given items. First, there is a conceptual structure, developed over decades and reflecting fundamental assumptions about the nature of disease, death and the human body. It is best encapsulated in the ICD. Next there are national statistics. These latter sum up all the individual details of people who have died from HIV/AIDS, or lung cancer, or pneumonia, or road accidents, or whatever, and form the basis for the published tables. The national statistics, in turn, are produced partly on the basis of the death certificates of individuals, and partly on the basis of the ICD rules and codes. So, producing a report on mortality clearly requires the development and exploitation of a conceptual (theoretical) as well as a technical and organizational structure. Indeed, to understand the fundamentals of the WHO Annual, we probably need, once again, to step down a couple of notches. To that end it would be as well for us to focus on a single topic within the WHO publication. Any topic – such as the provision of heart disease statistics, cancer statistics or AIDS statistics – would serve our purpose. Here, however, I intend to focus on a set of numbers that are reported upon at the foot of each of the national tables, namely, suicide statistics.

Accounts of suicide

Suicide is a sad and depressing business for all those involved in its discovery. It is rarely clear, however, whether any given death is as a result of deliberate intent on behalf of the deceased or not. People are found dead. They are found under the wheels of vehicles, and by the side of rail tracks. They are found lying face down in rivers in the late afternoon. They are found in hotel bedrooms with plastic bags over their head. They are found at home, dead in bed, shot through the head, or in fume-filled garages. Yet others are washed up on beaches. But few people leave written or verbal declarations of any intent to kill themselves (and even if they have, such notes must be treated with caution). Consequently, 'suicide' is always something of a problematic category. Indeed, suicidal intent and motives have always to be read into the circumstances and events in question.

In the days when I worked in the state bureaucracy that dealt with the matters of which we speak (called the Registrar General's Office), I was of course aware that such matters of imputation had already been studied in a variety of circumstances (Garfinkel, 1967; Cicourel, 1968). I was also aware that a number of sociologists had attempted to trace the procedures through which suicide verdicts were arrived at. For example, following the work of Douglas (1967), J.M. Atkinson (1978) had focused on the reasoning processes of English coroners with respect to suicide, while Taylor (1982) had investigated the organizational processing of deaths of people who had 'jumped' in front of London's trains. I was not especially interested in the ways that a sudden death was translated into a suicide. Yet I encountered something of the process without searching for it.

My focus was on how the people who coded death certificates (that is, the people who turned words into numbers that computers could manipulate) made sense of what they were doing. Somewhat inevitably, some death certificates referred to individuals who may have died from self-inflicted procedures. What follows are descriptions of some of the puzzling deaths that the coders had to deal with. The summaries are transcripts of the coroner's 'findings' that flowed through the Registrar's Office. I have altered some of the personal details so as to disguise the identities of the deceased and I have added a few details [in brackets] to assist with the reading.

Case 1

Married male. Age 28. Unemployed.

Cause of death: Poisoning by alcohol, Valium and Dalmane.

In 1989 the deceased had been attacked and had received head injuries. After that he suffered from headaches for which he took tablets. He spent the night of 9 June alone, in his sister's house. When the deceased failed to return home, his brother-in-law went to the house where the deceased had stayed, and forced an entry. He found the deceased lying dead on the floor of the sitting room. There were 367 mg of alcohol per 100 ml in his blood. Its effects had been increased by the use of the drugs Valium and Dalmane.

Case 2

Married female. Age 58. No occupation.

Cause of death: Poisoning by Maprotiline.

The deceased suffered from depression for five years for which she had received hospital outpatient treatment. On 20 June 1990 her husband was admitted to hospital with a chest complaint and she visited him there on 23 June. Later that day she was visited at home by her grandson. The next day she failed to pay her customary visit to her daughter. Consequently her daughter called at her mother's house and asked the police to force an entry to the house at about 16.00. She found her mother dead in bed with several empty packets of Ludiomil [an anti-depressant] nearby.

Case 3

Married male. Age 40. Salesman.

Cause of death: Alcohol and chloral hydrate poisoning.

The deceased had a ten-year history of depression. He had recently received [psychiatric] hospital treatment for his condition. At hospital he had been prescribed 'Noctec' [the source of the chloral hydrate] to help him sleep. In the past he had often taken overdoses of prescribed drugs when in a low and confused state. He had also been reckless in taking pills with alcohol. On 17 May he returned home after drinking, but was not drunk. He went to bed at 21.00 and took four 'Noctec' tablets. He was found dead the following morning.

These three accounts of death were written by coroners; the words within square brackets are mine. The accounts are of considerable interest in themselves, and not least for the manner in which they seek to describe the salient history of an event and thereby single out some issues for mention while ignoring others. (On the notion of an 'account', see Scott and Lyman, 1968.) For example, psychiatric histories, dates and times are mentioned, and so too are family relationships. On the other hand the financial background of the individuals or, say, their religious beliefs are not mentioned. (Note how the use and application of terms such as 'history of depression', 'substance abuse', 'reckless in taking pills', and so on, form potentially useful examples of Sacks's membership categorization devices: see sacks, 1992; Silverman, 1998.)

In each of these accounts there is supposed to be sufficient information to enable any reasonable observer to form a judgement as to whether the deceased intended to kill him or herself, or whether their death was accidental or even homicidal. In that sense, such accounts function as what we might call meaning-making devices.

Only one of the above deaths was coded as a suicide (the second). The other two were coded as accidental deaths. And it would be natural to think that these decisions were arrived at by detailed and considerable deliberation of a jury or some such, and that the accounts provided above are only summary statements that emerged from more complex analyses carried on elsewhere. There is something to that claim, but the only information that the person coding the data had on these events was as above. That is to say, the individual who was required to translate the narrative details (above) into the WHO category of 'suicide' had little else to go on. So the coder had to read into descriptions such as these her own personal images of what a suicidal person might or might not do. It would, of course be useful if the coder had used simple rules about the decision-making process – such as, for example, any mention of a psychiatric history to be taken as being suggestive of a suicide. Once again, however, it was not evidently so. The decision-making process was, and remains, a messy and often incoherent one. Indeed, as Garfinkel (1967) had indicated, no matter how rule-bound a coding system may be, the rules have always and in every case to be interpreted by the coder afresh. Garfinkel referred to such a process as 'ad hocing' – in this case, interpreting the information at hand in a manner that enabled the coder to finish his or her task. The study of ad hocing procedures forms a potentially rich terrain for research into the construction of documents (see, e.g., Benson and Hughes, 1983; Reiner, 1996). For we do know that when we ask people (such as coders) to explain their reasoning, they can and do point towards rule-based systems.

The significance of these detailed and somewhat concentrated deliberations is that the WHO suicide statistics referred to earlier are, ultimately, assembled on the basis of such procedures. Indeed, the examples that I have drawn upon are taken from work conducted in Belfast, and so it is on the basis of such accounts that the official statistics for the town and the associated region are constructed. It is, however, important to realize that suicide decisions have not always been executed in this manner. In fact, during the period 1968–82 there were a series of major changes in the law concerning who could and could not bring in a verdict of 'suicide' (Prior, 1989). After 1982 verdicts of suicide, accident and homicide were abolished and so, in the strict legal sense, there are no suicide verdicts in Northern Ireland at all. Deaths are categorized as suicide for the sole purpose of providing mortality statistics.

A number of important lessons concerning the research process can now be derived from our deliberations. First, that the procedures through which events in the world are categorized and enumerated constitute an important 'topic' for research in its own right. Most social scientists, of course, prefer to gloss over these considerations and use social and economic statistics as a 'resource' – as if they reflected facts in the world unmediated by organizational processes. (On the distinction between 'topic' and 'resource', see Zimmerman and Pollner, 1971.) We have seen that there are good reasons for refuting such an argument. In fact, the claims that we have made above could be applied with equal force and fervour to the construction of crime statistics, cost of living statistics, birth statistics, marriage statistics, business statistics, and any other realm of enumeration that one might care to study. (For an early example of official statistics studied as 'topic', see Kitsuse and Cicourel, 1963.) Second, we have noted how the day-to-day activities of those who manufacture documents work within well-established frameworks of relevance and order, such as are contained in generative documents. The latter are documents that provide the conceptual framework in terms of which the world is reported upon. In the above cases that framework was encoded in the ICD. Whatever the framework, however, it is essential to underline the fact that our original document – the WHO *Health Statistics Annual* – is akin to a rather large Chinese box. Open the lid and we find other boxes within: boxes containing conceptual frames, boxes that contain operational rules, and boxes that contain situated organizational decisions. The WHO Annual in that respect serves as little more than a wrapper. It provides an image of a unified and independent object (document) while, in fact, hiding a vast machinery of manufacture. The WHO Annual is not alone in this respect, and one essential (though rarely executed) task of the social researcher bent on collecting 'facts about society' should, therefore, involve removing the dust jackets of the documentary material that he or she encounters, and asking a number of simple questions, namely: How exactly, and by whom, was this document assembled? Who was intended to read it, and for what purpose? (For another example of how to deconstruct a statistical report see Prior, 2003: ch. 2.)

Examining the rule-based procedures of people who make decisions and who thereby manufacture things and facts and statuses is, then, a rather important research topic and one that can be executed in most organizational settings. In my next example, however, I am going to focus on how documents function rather than how they are produced.

DOCUMENTS IN ORGANIZATIONAL LIFE

In his discussion of a psychiatric record, Hak (1992) provides an example as to how a professional psychiatrist translates items of patient talk and observed behaviour into a written record. In so doing the psychiatrist – as note-taker – highlights the essential details of a patient's conversation, codes them into professional language (of delusions, hallucinations, diagnostic terms, etc.) and makes suggestions for future action (entry into a psychiatric unit or whatever). In Figure 24.1 we can see similar processes at work. The figure is a facsimile of a page of nursing assessment notes that I came across in a UK psychiatric hospital in the late 1980s. It is clear from the notes that the members of the nursing staff were concerned to categorize their patients in a variety of ways. The latter included a one-word diagnosis of the patient's condition, an assessment of 'activities of daily living' (ADL) skills, brief notes concerning the level of cooperation and hygiene exhibited by the patient, and so forth. These assessments were based on conversations and interchanges between nurses and patients and among nurses alone. It is important to recall that the patients/clients – as with all human

beings – commonly indulged in a wide array of activities and behaviours. For example, patients would talk to themselves, watch television, lend each other cigarettes, shout, laugh, go to work in the hospital workshops, and so forth. Yet of such a myriad array of activity only a few are ever highlighted. Thus, in the case of the first-named patient, it is their 'schizophrenia', their poor ADL skills, their temper tantrums and quarrelsome behaviour that is highlighted. This selectivity of focus would become even more evident were one to examine other kinds of patient records. Thus, in the hospital to which I am referring there were also psychiatric records (called 'charts') and social work records kept on each patient. The former were maintained by the medically trained psychiatrists and contained other kinds of information, such as data on whether the patients exhibited any 'first rank symptoms' (of schizophrenia), their medication and its effects, their 'history', items about family life, patient delusions, and so forth. In fact the psychiatric records looked very much like those alluded to and reported upon by Hak (1992). Social work records were also made up for each of the patients. These paid relatively little attention to medical diagnoses and the effects of medication and referred more often to the stability and maturity of the patient vis-à-vis relationships with others, the nature and level of their state benefits and the like. Considerable reference to the whereabouts, behaviours and opinions of other family members was also made within social work files. Access to such records and the 'right' to make entries in such records were more or less restricted to the members of the individual professional groupings. In that respect the text in each document served, in part, to mark out the realm and expertise of the various parties – in much the same way as did the various form of script in Tambiah's Thai village (see Tambiah, 1968). Thus social work talk belonged in social work records, psychiatric talk belonged in medical records, and nurse talk belonged in nursing records.

Recorded observations on patients/clients were, then, highly selective. In the case of public service agency files, such records often define the human beings to whom they refer in specific and particular ways. In so doing they call upon and activate a whole series of what we referred to above as membership categorization devices (Sacks, 1992). How a particular device comes to be associated with any individual and how that categorization might be used and called upon to account for and explain an individual's behaviour in specific circumstances can form the occasion for important and fundamental sociological research.

Patient	Admissions	Diagnosis	Problems/Constraints	Medication	Plans	Assets
Name: Dob 11/12/36 **Admin area:** East **Dr:** Yellow **Ward:** Blue	**No. of adm.** = 1 **Date of last adm.** 17/06/1962	Schizophrenia	Long time in hospital Temper tantrums & bad language Activities of daily living poor Recently quarrelsome with ASB	Gavison tabs bd Trifluoperazine 2mg bd Vit BPc 1 tab mane	Maintain	
Name: Dob 23/02/53 North **Dr:** Green **Ward:** Blue	**No. of adm.** = 5 **Date of last adm.** 29/09/1987	Paranoid Schizophrenia	Loner. Poor motivation Wishes to stay in hospital Failed RA (stay in residential accommodation) Injury to right hip	Piroxican 30 mg nocte Ranitidine 150 mg nocte Vit BPC am	Move to community	ADL skills good
Name: Dob 3/07/58 West **Dr:** Green **Ward:** Blue	**No. of adm.** = 3 **Date of last adm.** 17/05/1988	Schizophrenia Low IQ	Poverty of thought Withdrawn ADL skills limited Childish and naïve in manner Mother has encouraged Dependence over the years But is now opting out Poor road safety	Benxtropine 2 mg mane Thioridizine 75mg tid Senna 2 tabs nocte	ADL activities	Pleasant & co-operative Hygiene good
Name: Dob 10/08/60 West **Dr:** Green **Ward:** Blue	**No. of adm.** = 6 **Date of last adm.** 10/03/1988	Dependent Personality	Multiple somatic complaints Resistant to suggestions Poor compliance tends to opt out Poor response to antidepressant therapy Poor attendance at OT unit Poor Hearing	Thyroxine 0.1 mg mane Nifedipine 10 mg bd Thioridizine 50 mg bd	Maintain	ADL good

Figure 24.1 Facsimile of a ward-based nursing assessment record (UK psychiatric hospital, 1989).

In my work on the psychiatric hospital referred to above, I was primarily interested in how patients came to be classified in different ways through routine procedures (see Prior, 1993). Naturally, the use of notes and records forms only one support for the identification system that surrounds patients. Everyday conversation and casual interchanges form another, and in any organization there will always be a constant interchange between talk and text. Thus I provided in my 1993 study a short extract of an exchange between nurses in the ward office concerning the issue as to what was wrong with X. Thus,

Nurse 1:   Does anyone know what's supposed to be wrong with X?
           [Blank looks and silence meet the question]
Nurse 2:   Schizophrenia, I suppose.
Nurse 1:   Hmm. I've never seen any sign of it.
Nurse 3:   Well, he's on chlorpromazine, so he must be schizophrenic.

The membership categorization device (Sacks, 1992) of 'schizophrenic' recorded in the notes is, then, sustained and underlined in this case by means of a casual conversation – and especially the reference to X's medication. (The use of medication to define a specific psychiatric disorder, rather than the other way around, is not uncommon in psychiatry.) If, however, there were any real doubt about 'what was wrong with X', it would be the notes that would carry the day. So the researcher who wishes to concentrate on the use of documents in action has to be constantly aware as to how the written record is tied into and anchored within other aspects of organizational life such as conversations at the nursing station. Nevertheless, it is only when assessments are written down and can be pointed to, that they are used to form a foundation on which routine social actions are built. Thus medical professionals can and do use 'the files' as a warrant for their actions in relation to their patients – showing how what they do to patients is warranted by the information on the record(s). Indeed, in the context of psychiatry, Barrett (1996: 107) has underlined how 'clinical writing' not only describes the treatment of patients, it also constitutes the treatment.

In a wider context, Bowker and Star (1999) and Young (1995) have also pointed out how (documented) nomenclatures of disease are routinely tied into the financial accounting mechanisms of hospital life. So, psychiatrists routinely draw down a diagnostic category from the DSM, 'fit' it to a given patient, and then justify what

was done for and to the patient/client in the light of the category (this, in the full knowledge that categories and patients rarely make a 1: 1 fit). Indeed, the naming of diseases and disorders in modern medical systems (using the ICD and the DSM) is often used more for purposes of financial reimbursement (to and from insurance companies), and other accounting and monitoring purposes, than they are for forming accurate descriptions of a given patient's condition.

Arguing along a similar path, Zerubavel (1979: 45) indicated some years ago how notes written up by medical and nursing professionals were 'among the main criteria used by their supervisors to evaluate their clinical competence', as well as forming the primary mechanism through which continuous supervision of patients was maintained. In fact, Zerubavel's study highlights the centrality of documents as charts, graphs and records of all kinds in underpinning the routine social organization of hospital life. Thus, he noted how printed schedules were used to organize the patient/staff day; how printouts of various kinds were routinely used to monitor patients, and notes written so as indicate how the 'hospital' cared for its clients. (In US hospitals, of course, patient records are, as we have already indicated, also used as a hook on which to hang financial costs and transactions.)

This capacity of medical records to mediate social relationships of all kinds has been further researched by Berg (1996, 1997), who points out how hospital patients are both structured through records and accessed through records. One important feature of patient existence that is emphasized by Berg is the manner in which medical records are used so as to keep the case (and the patient) 'on track'. Such structuring of patient trajectories through records is achieved in numerous ways, planning and monitoring being two of them. In this respect it is of interest to note the column headed 'Plans' in Figure 24.1. In the context of these records the most important plans concerned whether or not the patient was ready for life in the community. (My own hospital study was executed at that rather important cusp where psychiatric patients were being moved out of hospitals and into 'the community'.) In most cases, the patients were to be 'maintained' (kept in the hospital ward). The detail hardly concerns us here. What is important to note is that records of this type always contain some rules for action. Other rules for action are contained in the column relating to medication. Latour (1987) has used the term 'action at a distance' to indicate how decisions written down in one context and setting can carry implications for action in future settings. And it is indeed the case that records often contain instructions for future organizational activity.

There is one final point that perhaps needs emphasis. For it is clear that people not only maintain records so as to legitimize action or to claim warrant for their actions, or, indeed, to classify events, objects, processes and others in the everyday world, but that they often use records to sustain micro-interactions. In this respect the following extract is worth studying. It was obtained in a fatigue clinic during 1999. The physician (denoted by D) usually had difficulty in telling his patients (denoted by P) that, despite extensive test procedures, no evident physical pathology could be found to account for their 'being ill'. An alternative explanation raised the possibility that psychological states might be implicated in their condition – a suggestion that few of the patients welcomed. In this extract the physician is attempting to 'talk to his notes' and thereby use them as a key prop to his consulting strategy. (Incidentally, the patient referred to below was seated in a wheelchair at the time of the interchange.)

57 D [reading notes containing test results]:
   MRI scan tells us that you haven't
   got M.S ... Blood tests, fine ...
   antibodies ... fine/
58 P65: /What is it then?
59 D: Well, we've checked out the central
   nervous system and there's nothing
   untoward there. Maybe we ought to
   check out the peripheral system.
   [Returns to his notes, reading
   apparently to himself whilst the
   patient talks to her husband]

70 D: You were treated for depression in
   um/
71 P65: /The doctor [i.e., the Primary Care
   Practitioner], he just kept on saying
72 I was depressed.
73 D: And were you?
74 P65: I'm housebound, I can't get out of
   bed in the mornings ... I have
75 to climb the stairs on my bum ...

I have explored the wider implications of these kinds of conversations in Banks and Prior (2001). Here I am mainly interested in drawing attention to the use of written documents as an ally in face-to-face interactions. On a wider front, I am also seeking to highlight how documents are involved in the construction of human identities and characteristics. To pursue that argument further, I am going to turn to an examination of another kind of clinic.

MAKING THINGS VISIBLE

In his *Art and Artifact in Laboratory Science*, Lynch (1985: 153) points out how 'Documents are integrally a part of the work of doing science'. Documents serve not simply as a source of ideas and information but also as an integral component of bench work itself (in the form of notes, recipes, instructions, and so forth). One type of document that appears prominently in Lynch's study is the pencil and paper diagram. In most cases such diagrams portray structural aspects of a particular part of rat brain (the hippocampus). Such drawings are themselves based on other images – derived, for example, from laboratory slides of sliced sections of rat brain, and electron-microscope enlargements of brain tissue, the preparation of slides, the staining or 'labelling' of tissue and the microscopic enlargements serving to make the hippocampus and its functioning processes visible. In the interaction between organic materials, technical processes and human activity, of course, the possibility arises that some of the things that are visible are not 'natural'. In the language of the lab scientist, these latter are referred to as artefacts. For example, it may be that the staining process or the cutting process alluded to above, produces marks, blotches, appearances that are a product of the experimental interventions rather than ordinary features of the hippocampus. Exactly how lab scientists distinguished between artefactual and natural effects was one of the issues that Lynch set to examining. This was especially difficult in those cases where the artefact was an absence rather than a presence – that is, in those cases where something that should have appeared on a slide or an enlargement failed to appear.

This relationship between organic matter, pencil and paper images, electron-microscope images, staining techniques and so forth is central to the production of many kinds of fact. As other science analysts have indicated (Latour and Woolgar, 1979; Myers, 1990; Fujimura, 1996; Rapp, 2000), the world of nature is never immediately visible but has to be made and manufactured in order to be seen; Rapp (2000) refers to 'imagistic knowledge' in this context. Among the procedures for making things visible, photographic imaging techniques have an important place. (Since the completion of Lynch's work, of course, other imaging strategies and technologies have come to the fore, some of which will be mentioned below.) The graphic image thus presents only one of many ways of reading or seeing 'things'. Indeed, as the following example illustrates, the same 'thing' can usually be seen or read in many different ways, some of which are graphical and some of which are, shall we say, numerical, and some of which are behavioural. The relationship between ways, of seeing (documenting) things and forms of professional practice constitutes a potentially important field for social scientific research (see, e.g., Keating and Cambrosio, 2000). In the first part of the discussion that follows we shall focus on ways of documenting what is known to be a common form of disease in older people – Alzheimer's.

Alzheimer's disease is a well-known form of dementia. The key features of dementia are memory loss, confusion, and mood and behavioural disturbance. In most cases people simply lose the ordinary skills of daily living. Dementia is most frequently found in older people (it affects around 20 per cent of people aged 80 years or more), but in rare cases it can occur in people of half that age. At the time of writing, and in the literature of the UK Alzheimer's Disease Society, the disorder is described as follows:

> Alzheimer's is a physical disease which attacks brain cells (where we store memory) and brain nerves and transmitters (which carry instructions around the brain). Production of a chemical messenger acetylcholine is disrupted, nerve ends are attacked and cells die. The brain shrinks as gaps develop in the temporal lobe and hippocampus, important for receiving and storing new information. The ability to remember, speak, think and make decisions is disrupted. After death, tangles and plaques made from protein fragments, dying cells and nerve ends are discovered in the brain. This confirms the diagnosis. (http://www.alzheimers.org.uk)

The Alzheimer's Disease Society literature also lists a range of specialists who can be involved in the diagnosis and the management of the disease; these include psychiatrists, neuro-psychiatrists, psychologists, nurses and social workers. The list is in itself instructive because it suggests that what the disease 'is' is likely to differ according to the forms of professional practice that surround it. In particular, it seems likely that different professional groupings have different images of the disease in practice. Note that, according to the passage above, the 'disease' can only be confirmed at autopsy – that is, after death. (In fact one could, if one wished, analyse the extract above as content – looking at the metaphors that are used and the relationships between the items that are referenced – though that is not the route to be followed here.)

Making Alzheimer's visible in living people (as opposed to making it visible in the dead brain) is a difficult process and, as with so many things, it can be done in different ways. Thus diagnosing people on what are called clinical grounds is possible and desirable, but clinical diagnosis and diagnosis at autopsy do not always match. Thus it is sometimes said that clinical diagnosis is only up to 80–90 per cent 'accurate' – a point that serves to highlight how different forms of visibility provide different answers to our problems.

Clinically, the condition is determined by examining how the patient behaves and talks and reacts. In fact, clinicians usually refer to three realms of evidence in the determination of a diagnosis. These are the symptoms that the patient brings to the consultation (say, a report of 'not feeling right'); the signs that the doctor discovers in the patient (such as memory loss and confusion); and evidence available from investigations (such as brain scans). So there is always an ensemble of traces – of visibilities and translations – used to determine whether a person is or is not dementing (Harding and Palfrey, 1997), and in the early stages of the disorder the decision may be far from clear-cut. (There is a sense in which the diagnosis is always and forever matter for negotiation.)

Even were we to concentrate solely on visual data – from brain scans – we would still be faced with alternative pictures of what is apparently the same disease. Thus, there are several types of brain scan available. For example, CT or CAT (computerized axial tomography) scans are a way of taking pictures of the brain using X-rays and a computer. MRI (magnetic resonance imaging) scans also use a computer to create an image of the brain but, instead of X-rays, they use radio signals produced by the body in response to the effects of a very strong magnet contained within the scanner. SPECT (single photon emission computerized tomography) scans look at the blood flow through the brain rather than at its structure, while electroencephalography (EEG) traces would provide yet another means of imaging brain dysfunction. Indeed, each type of scan provides different kinds of visibility and evidence for brain 'pathology', though none of them on their own would suffice to provide a diagnosis of Alzheimer's. Indeed more important than the evidence derived from scans would be evidence gathered from an examination of a patient's routine behaviour. Most important of all, we can say that there are radically different performances (Mol, 1999, 2000) of Alzheimer's: neurological, psychological and behavioural. How the one form is translated and then meshed into the other is a matter of interest in itself, though here we shall focus simply on the role of documentation in providing translations.

As an adjunct to a doctor looking at and talking to the patient, it is possible for him or her to use a standardized set of questions in the shape of what is usually referred to as an outcome measure. (Note how the very term 'outcome' gives emphasis to the notion of performance.) Outcome measures usually take the form of a series of observations or questions about behaviour, the answers to which can be scored. For example, in looking at dementia, an outcome measure is likely to include questions about whether a person forgets names, and dates, and events; about whether they lose their way around familiar places, or lose things; or whether they have lost ordinary daily skills – of dressing, washing and self-care. To each question there is attached a numerical score. Scores can then be added up and the results can be translated in terms of a numerical scale (say, from zero to 100) so as to form a judgement about the presence or absence of Alzheimer's. (For an example of such a measure, see the references to the Mini Mental State Examination on http://www.alzheimers.org.uk.)

As just stated, Alzheimer's usually affects older people. In some families, however, it can have what is called an 'early onset', that is to say, it can appear in people aged from 35 to 60 years. So, for example, there are about 17,000 affected people in this age group within the UK. One group of people who tend to suffer from an early onset of Alzheimer's are those with Down's syndrome. Down's syndrome is a genetic disorder that usually results in people having learning difficulties. In conjunction with the learning difficulties, there is often a characteristic facial appearance. (More often than not, it is the facial appearance that people focus on. One might say that that is how the syndrome is made visible in lay culture.) Naturally, the severity of the learning difficulties and the accentuation of the facial features vary considerably in the Down's population.

Autopsy studies have shown brain changes (neuropathology) similar to that of Alzheimer's disease in almost all adults with Down's syndrome over the age of 40 years. It is an observation that is supported by neuroimaging findings – of the type derived from the scanning procedures noted above. Neuroimaging is a relatively new kind of technology. As a form of documentation it provides us with new translations of what Down's syndrome is. In the absence of neuroimages, however, professionals tend to restrict themselves to looking at the behavioural dimensions of the disorder. Yet, by looking at behaviour, dementia can be diagnosed in only around 9 per cent of adults with Down's syndrome aged 40–49 years, and around 55 per cent of those aged 60–69 years. In short, although one might

be able to 'see' the presence of Alzheimer's disease in a human brain (if one had the tools), one cannot easily detect it in daily life.

In a sociological sense, therefore, we might say that there are at least three different sites in which Alzheimer's can be made visible – namely, in the autopsy room, in the neuro-imaging suite and in the clinic. Different forms of text and visual image are associated with the different kinds of setting, and one of the tasks of the social scientific researcher should be to examine how the various forms of documentary evidence available to human actors is woven into specific forms of translation. This is because what the disease 'is' changes according to the availability of the images. Or, to put things another way, the visibility of the disease is dependent on the use of different kinds of inscription device (Latour, 1987) by different kinds of professional.

As we have stated, one important set of such devices are the outcome measures. Unfortunately, there are various kinds of such measures – and they in turn give different images of the disorder. For example, one such instrument is the 'Mini Mental State Examination' (MMSE) (Folstein et al., 1975). Another is the 'Dementia Questionnaire for Mentally Retarded Persons' (DMR) (Evenhuis, 1992). Yet a third is the 'Dementia Scale for Down's Syndrome' (DSDS) (Gedye, 1995). In one clinical study where all three measures were applied to a rather mixed group of people, it became evident that of 30 subjects who had an MMSE score of less than 24 (which is taken to be the usual cut-off for the detection of possible dementia), 23 did not have a diagnosis of dementia according to any other criteria. In other words, the instrument produced dementia where it was not otherwise evident; indeed, it seemingly overestimated prevalence by about 75 per cent.

So the upshot of all this is that the outcome measures very often give different answers to the same basic question, 'Is this person dementing?' In so far as that is the case, we might say that whether a living person has Alzheimer's or not is often a matter of documentation rather than of biology. It is documents that make the disorder visible, and it is documents that define its severity. (In fact, one of my current projects is aimed at devising a new outcome measure that takes account of how relatives recognize the onset of Alzheimer's in their Down's syndrome dependants.) In terms of situated social scientific inquiries, of course, it would be crucial to note how the various means for making Alzheimer's visible are called upon and manipulated by different kinds of people, and how those tools are used in different kinds of organizational setting – hospitals, care homes, day centres, and so forth.

It is, perhaps, odd that investigations into the role of documentation in defining and specifying things in the world are not more common. For my own part I find that attention to the manner in which documents function in everyday work practices always pays dividends. Furthermore, the ways in which documents are manipulated and referred to, often serve to underpin the nature of the division of labour in organizations – and to mark out the boundaries of different forms of expertise. In this regard, the paper by Prior et al. (2002) as to how forms of genetic risk are made visible, provides further examples of these rather important processes. I am going to end this chapter, however, by moving away from a focus on the ways in which documents are produced and consumed (function), and switch instead to a focus on the manner in which documents circulate.

CIRCUITS OF COMMUNICATION

In modern cultural studies there exists a concept of the cultural circuit (du Gay et al., 1997). The circuit supposedly incorporates 'moments' of production and consumption as well as of representation, regulation and identity. The image of a circuit is, in part, chosen to illustrate the dynamic and interlinked nature of the ways in which cultural products are appropriated and produced in the modern world. Documents can be considered likewise. Yet, somewhat oddly, there is one important theme that is entirely absent from the 'circuit' that is discussed and analysed by the cultural studies cohort. It is the theme of circulation itself.

The circulation and exchange of goods and services has often formed a major topic of investigation by anthropologists. It was in that context, for example, that Malinowski, in his *Argonauts of the Western Pacific*, examined the sociology of the Kula. As Malinowski, pointed out, 'The Kula is a form of exchange' (1922: 81). It was a form of exchange, involving bracelets and necklaces, carried on by peoples among a ring of islands in Melanesia.

In writing about the Kula, Malinowski sought to develop insights about social life in general. Thus, he noted that the Kula system was not primary to economic life, but rather to social life. In so doing, he was emphasizing the fact that the exchange process cemented social partnerships, rather than economic relations. His insights were built upon throughout the twentieth century, and were later developed into what has been called social exchange theory (Ekeh, 1974). Our interest in Malinowski's analysis is that we can consider documents and their exchange and circulation in much the same way as Malinowski considered necklaces and shells.

For example, in the modern world the exchange of greeting cards is a commonplace event. Birthdays, weddings, and even deaths form occasions where people send cards to one another. People also buy and send cards to those who are ill – 'Get well soon cards'. But to whom, exactly, do people send such cards? And what do the patterns tell us about social life? In a rather fascinating study, Weiner et al. (1999) looked at the distribution of such cards among hospital patients suffering from two different types of disorder. The first were medical disorders (for example, heart diseases and diabetes) and the second were serious psychiatric disorders. What they noted was that although both sets of patients were hospitalized (for more than three days), the medical patients were far more likely to get visits, gifts and 'get well soon' cards than were the psychiatric patients. Such a pattern of gift exchange, suggested the authors, tells us something fundamental about how we view psychiatric illness and psychiatric patients in our society. (The authors argue that psychiatric patients are commonly regarded as not being 'really' ill, and even when they are so regarded it is often thought to be their own fault – so sympathy is in short supply.) Although it was not part of the planned investigation, the hospital researchers could have gone further, and used the cards to do something more. They could have used the exchange of cards to trace patterns of a social network.

The exchange of communications, such as cards, between individuals not only facilitates the flow of information, but also marks out channels and boundaries of social influence. For example, Figure 24.2 is a network graph. It represents a trace of information exchange events among a small group of primary care practitioners in Wales. The lines represent connections between people who seek 'advice and information' from one another. Thus, by viewing the graph it is possible to see clearly the existence of groups of people who seemingly consult each other a lot, possibly because they work closely together – in the same building. For instance, individuals referred to as numbers 25, 26, 27, 28 and 29 evidently belong together, as do the GPs numbered 17–22. It is also possible to see that some people are contacted considerably (numbers 29 and 34, for example) while others look relatively isolated (numbers 61, 32 and 42).

Such a pattern of contact and communication is traceable in other ways – say by asking people about their e-mail contacts, or text-messaging contacts. And what the results of such questioning

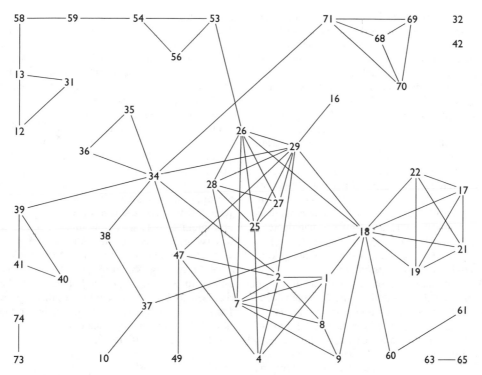

Figure 24.2 *Information contacts among primary care professionals in South Wales.*

show is not simply evidence about who contacts whom, but also evidence of social power and social influence. For example, in the study concerning the GP contacts discussed here, it was possible to link the patterns in the graph to other information about the GPs, so as to understand why the patterns were as they were. Professional factors, ethnic factors and gender factors all seemingly structured the patterns of contact and communication. And although the graph in Figure 24.2 represents an image of verbal communication, it could, in theory, be extended to represent an image of communication via the use of written documents.

In his conversations with Latour, Serres (1995: 161) refers to objects that trace or 'make visible the relations that constitute the group through which it passes, like the token in a children's game'. The term that Serres uses to refer to such objects is 'quasi-object' – a term chosen to emphasize the fact that the world cannot be simply divided into objects and humans, for objects and people belong in an ensemble that is often difficult to unravel. For example, in the GP network just referred to, one of the questions being studied related to the dissemination of innovations, in particular, the dissemination of

knowledge about new drugs (pharmaceuticals) such as Viagra. At a distance it might seem that it is easy to distinguish between such an object and the human influences upon it. Yet in practice it is not. For what the drug (Viagra) is, is fashioned by what is said about it, by patterns of use, and by patterns of reception. The technology that is represented by the drug is thereby wrapped up in a whole series of relationships and networks. To understand the technology we need to follow the thing (document) through its social channels. And all the while the circulation of communications about the document will serve to mark out the boundaries of social groupings and social relationships – as in Figure 24.2.

CONCLUSIONS

During the late 1980s when I was researching into the affairs of psychiatric hospitals, I visited the Northern Ireland Public Records Office (PRONI) for some data on the hospital in which I was working. An office such as PRONI serves as a depository for records gathered over many centuries from prisons, hospitals, schools, businesses, and indeed any organization that leaves written traces of its activities. Records are invariably indexed, and as far as researchers are concerned, they cannot be accessed without an index number. I recall that one day while I was waiting for some documents on a psychiatric hospital to be delivered to my desk, I picked up the index for police records – out of mere curiosity. The index was instructive. For, if I remember correctly, it was lodged in a couple of large, bound, volumes. Yet on opening the index I was surprised to see that almost all but the title pages of the volumes were blank. Reams and reams of bound white paper were all that was visible. The primary reason for the absence of such detail was that secrecy ruled OK, and someone had decided that the public should not even be allowed to know what exact police records were being kept at PRONI, still less access them.

This tiny narrative of secrecy and thwarted curiosity serves to underline the fact that documents are never inert. Indeed, they frequently serve as active agents in schemes of human interaction – agents to be recruited, manipulated, scorned or hidden. We should never forget that people burn, suppress and forge documents as well as read them precisely because documents can often become agents in their own right. It is for that reason that the ways in which documents are manufactured, how they are used and how they function in organizational settings should figure as key questions in the research process. Unfortunately, they are questions that are rarely addressed.

In this chapter I have tried to demonstrate how documents stand in a dual relation to episodes of human interaction. In the first place documents have content. Such content requires analysis, and there are various techniques that can be used to analyse content. I have described my own methods in Prior (2003). Secondly, documents enter into the stream of interaction as agents (with functions) – and it this second form of relationship that I have focused on here. Thus, I have indicated how documents can function so as to structure identities, circumstances, and 'facts about society'. Hence, in my first example I drew upon work executed in the office of the Registrar General (where death certificates are processed). The task there was not so much to look at what the document contained but at how it was put together – at how the rules and principles of composition were called upon, and the ways in which the raw materials were woven into a final 'report'. In my second example I drew upon work executed in a psychiatric hospital. There the task was to examine the ways in which documents functioned to define the nature of the patient, and specify the

role of the psychiatric nurse (and to show how documents were called upon in the work process as a whole). For my third example I drew upon some current work on Alzheimer's disease. My task there was to demonstrate how documents, in the form of outcome and diagnostic measures, could make things (diseases) visible, and thereby manageable. My final example drew on some data from an investigation concerned with GP prescribing. The task there was to indicate how documents might circulate, and in circulating inscribe the boundaries of a social network.

As I stated in the introduction, in all of my research settings documentation was central. Yet while I was in those settings I often regarded talk and interaction as somehow more real and more deserving of attention than the paperwork that was lying around and about me. Nevertheless, if I were nowadays asked to give just one piece of advice to the novice researcher, it would be as follows: look at the documentation, not merely for its content but more at how it is produced, how it functions in episodes of daily interaction, and how, exactly, it circulates.

REFERENCES

American Psychiatric Association. (2000) *Diagnostic and Statistical Manual of Mental Disorders. DSM-IV-TR.* Washington, DC: American Psychiatric Association.

Atkinson, J.M. (1978) *Discovering Suicide.* London: Macmillan.

Banks, J. and Prior, L. (2001) 'Doing things with illness: the micro-politics of the CFS clinic', *Social Science and Medicine*, 52(1): 11–23.

Barrett, R. (1996) *The Psychiatric Team and the Social Definition of Schizophrenia: An Anthropological Study of Person and Illness.* Cambridge: Cambridge University Press.

Benson, D. and Hughes, J.A. (1983) *The Perspective of Ethnomethodology.* London: Longman.

Berg, M. (1996) 'Practices of reading and writing: the constitutive role of the patient record in medical work', *Sociology of Health and Illness*, 18(4): 499–524.

Berg, M. (1997) *Rationalizing Medical Work: Decision-Support Techniques and Medical Practices.* Cambridge, MA: MIT Press.

Bloor, M. (1991) 'A minor office: the variable and socially constructed character of death certification in a Scottish city', *Journal of Health and Social Behaviour*, 32(3): 273–87.

Bowker, G.C. and Star, S.L. (1999) *Sorting Things Out: Classification and Its Consequences.* Cambridge, MA: MIT Press.

Cicourel, A.V. (1968) *The Social Organization of Juvenile Justice.* New York: John Wiley.

Douglas, J.D. (1967) *The Social Meanings of Suicide.* Princeton, NJ: Princeton University Press.

du Gay, P., Hall, S., Janes, L., Mackay, H. and Negus, K. (1997) *Doing Cultural Studies: The Story of the Sony Walkman*. London: Sage.

Ekeh, P. (1974) *Social Exchange Theory*. London. Heinemann.

Evans-Pritchard, E.E. (1940) *The Nuer: A Description of the Modes of the Livelihood and Political Institutions of a Nilotic People'*. Oxford: Clarendon Press.

Evenhuis, H.M. (1992) 'Evaluation of a screening instrument for dementia in ageing mentally retarded persons', *Journal of Intellectual Disability Research*, 36: 337–47.

Folstein M.F., Folstein, S.E. and McHugh, P.R. (1975) 'Mini Mental State. A practical method for grading the cognitive state of patients for the clinician', *Journal of Psychiatric Research*, 12: 189–98.

Foucault, M. (1973) *The Birth of the Clinic*, tr. A.M. Sheridan. London: Tavistock.

Fujimura, J.H. (1996) *Crafting Science: A Sociohistory of the Quest for the Genetics of Cancer*. Cambridge: MA: Harvard University Press.

Garfinkel, H. (1967) *Studies in Ethnomethodology*. Englewood Cliffs, NJ: Prentice-Hall.

Gedye, A. (1995) *Dementia Scale for Down Syndrome. Manual*. Vancouver, BC: Gedye Research and Consulting.

Goody, J. (1968) *Literacy in Traditional Societies*. Cambridge: Cambridge University Press.

Goody, J. (1977) *The Domestication of the Savage Mind*. Cambridge: Cambridge University Press.

Hak, T. (1992) 'Psychiatric records as transformations of other texts', in G. Watson and R.M. Seiler (eds), *Text in Context: Contributions to Ethnomethodology*. London: Sage, pp. 138–55.

Harding, N. and Palfrey, C. (1997) *The Social Construction of Dementia: Confused Professionals?* London: Jessica Kingsley.

Howells, C. (1998) *Derrida. Deconstruction: From Phenomenology to Ethics*. Cambridge: Polity Press.

Kapuściński, R. (2001) 'Death in Sudan', tr. K. Glowczewska. *New York Review of Books*, 48(7): 4–6.

Keating, P. and Cambrosio, A. (2000) '"Real compared to what?" Diagnosing leukemias and lymphomas', in M. Lock, A. Young and A. Cambrosio (eds), *Living and Working with the New Medical Technologies: Intersections of Inquiry*. Cambridge: Cambridge University Press, pp. 103–34.

Kitsuse, J.I. and Cicourel, A. (1963) 'A note on the use of official statistics', *Social Problems*, 11(2): 131–9.

Latour, B. (1987) *Science in Action: How to Follow Engineers and Scientists Through Society*. Buckingham: Open University Press.

Latour, B. and Woolgar, S. (1979) *Laboratory Life: The Social Construction of Scientific Facts*. London: Sage.

Lienhardt, G. (1961) *Divinity and Experience: The Religion of the Dinka*. Oxford: Oxford University Press.

Lynch, M. (1985) *Art and Artifact in Laboratory Science: A Study of Shop Work and Shop Talk in a Research Laboratory*. London: Routledge & Kegan Paul.

Malinowski, B. (1922) *Argonauts of the Western Pacific*. London: Routledge.

Mol, A. (1999) 'Ontological politics: a word and some questions', in J. Law and J. Hassard (eds), *Actor Network Theory and After*. Oxford: Blackwell, pp. 74–89.

Mol, A. (2000) 'Pathology and the clinic: an ethnographic presentation of two atheroscleroses', in M. Lock, A. Young and A. Cambrosio (eds), *Living and Working with the New Medical Technologies: Intersections of Inquiry*. Cambridge: Cambridge University Press, pp. 82–102.

Myers, G. (1990) *Writing Biology: Texts in the Construction of Scientific Knowledge*. London: University of Wisconsin Press.

Ong, W. (1982) *Orality and Literacy: The Technologizing of the Word*. London: Methuen.

Prior, L. (1988), 'The architecture of the hospital: a study in spatial organisation and medical knowledge', *British Journal of Sociology*, 39: 86–115.

Prior, L. (1989) *The Social Organization of Death*. Basingstoke: Macmillan.

Prior, L. (1992) 'The local space of medical knowledge: disease, illness and hospital architecture', in J. Lachmund and G. Stollberg (eds), *The Social Construction of Illness*. Stuttgart: Franz Steiner Verlag, pp. 67–84.

Prior, L. (1993) *The Social Organization of Mental Illness*. London and Newbury Park, CA: Sage.

Prior, L. (2001) 'Death certificate', in O. Learman and G. Howarth (eds), *Encyclopaedia of Death and Dying*. London: Routledge, pp. 136–7.

Prior, L. (2003) *Using Documents in Social Research*. London: Sage.

Prior, L., Wood, F., Gray, J., Pill, R. and Hughes, D. (2002) 'Making risk visible: the role of images in the assessment of genetic risk', *Health, Risk and Society*, 4(3): 241–58.

Rapp, R. (2000) *Testing Women, Testing the Fetus: The Social Impact of Amniocentesis in America*. New York: Routledge.

Reiner, R. (1996) 'The case of the missing crimes', in R. Levitas and M. Guy (eds), *Interpreting Official Statistics*. London: Routledge.

Sacks, H. (1992) *Lectures of Conversation*, 2 vols. Oxford: Blackwell.

Scott, M.B. and Lyman, S.M. (1968) 'Accounts', *American Sociological Review*, 33: 46–62.

Serres, M. (1995) *Conversations on Science, Culture and Time*, with Bruno Latour, tr. R. Lapidus. Ann Arbor: University of Michigan Press.

Silverman, D. (ed.) (1996) *Qualitative Research: Theory, Method and Practice*. London: Sage.

Silverman, D. (1998) *Harvey Sacks: Social Science and Conversation Analysis*. Cambridge: Polity Press.

Tambiah, S.J. (1968) 'Literacy in a Buddhist village in north-east Thailand', in J. Goody (ed.), *Literacy in Traditional Societies*. Cambridge: Cambridge University Press, pp. 86–131.

Taylor, S. (1982) *Durkheim and the Study of Suicide*. London: Macmillan.

Unwin, N., Carr, S. and Leeson, J. (1997) *An Introductory Study Guide to Public Health and Epidemiology*. Buckingham: Open University Press.

Weber, M. (1979) *Economy and Society*, 2 vols, ed. G. Roth and C. Wittich. Berkeley: University of California Press.

Weiner A, Wessely, S. and Lewis, G. (1999) '"You don't give me flowers anymore": an analysis of gift-giving to medical and psychiatric inpatients', *Social Psychiatry and Psychiatric Epidemiology*, 34: 136–40.

World Health Organization (1998) *World Health Statistics Annual, 1996.* Geneva: WHO.

World Health Organization (1992) *International Statistical Classification of Diseases and Related Health Problems* 10th Revision. London: HMSO, 3 vols.

Young, A. (1995) *The Harmony of Illusions: Inventing Post-traumatic Stress Disorder*. Princeton, NJ: Princeton University Press.

Zerubavel, E. (1979) *Patterns of Time in Hospital Life: A Sociological Perspective.* London: University of Chicago Press.

Zimmerman, D.H. and Pollner, M. (1971) 'The everyday world as a phenomenon', in J.D. Douglas (ed.), *Understanding Everyday Life*. London: Routledge & Kegan Paul, pp. 80–103.

25

Visual methods

Sarah Pink

Sarah: *You've got a radio.*

Virginia: Yes, well that was an inheritance from my friend from Canada [who returned this year]. But I actually find that really handy in a morning, it kind of gets me going. I put the radio on when I'm having a shower ... then once I've come back up here after I've had my breakfast in a morning, I switch that one on and it gets me going, you know, a music station as opposed to Radio 4. I might listen to Radio 4 downstairs when I'm having breakfast, but you know, by the time I get up here I want to really wake up. I know I've got to wake up cos I'm on my way to work

Sarah: *What about when you're cleaning, do you use it then?*

Virginia: Yes, I do actually, quite often. Actually I don't have to do it, I don't have it on as much as I used to. I used to have it on all the time but work, mosquito aah, but I do, yes, I'll put music on for the cleaning and stuff. Bloody mosquitoes, they're horrible.

Sarah: *Do you choose specific music for the mood?*

Virginia: Yes, yes I do. I suppose I listen to classical if I'm feeling a bit melancholy. And some sort of other, I don't know, pop bands... stuff like that, but then I will choose more, you know, different sort of types more – I'm sorry I'm just being

distracted by this mosquito. It's sort of having a go at you. Yes, I will listen to more sort of upbeat music if I'm, perhaps if I'm cleaning and stuff, and if I want to get ready for work or do whatever, then yes, it's got to be more upbeat music. You're going to be eaten alive, girl.

As I interviewed Virginia about her bathroom I recorded our experience using a small domestic digital video camera. Dodging the English summer mosquitoes in 1999, our exploration of the visual content of this room prompted our discussion of the objects she kept there and the everyday practices she associated with them. Using video encouraged my informants to play their music to me, demonstrate how their home technologies functioned, and tell me the biographical and everyday stories they invested in the photographs and pictures on their walls, their furniture, ornaments and the structure of their homes. Using visual methods allows us to extend our research to incorporate knowledge that is not accessible verbally (see also MacDougall, 1997: 292). This adds significantly to both the knowledge that a researcher can generate when actually in the field and the options that she or he has later to represent the results of this work to others. Using video in my research about the home allowed me to probe my informants about the activities, knowledge and emotions that they associated with the visual aspects of their homes. Later I was able to analyse these video recordings to interpret the narratives, objects and performances that were represented on them as well as the transcribed verbal dialogue between myself and the people I interviewed. Finally, to represent the findings of my work I was able to use the videos of those informants who agreed to allow me to screen parts of their tapes in public in presentations and to develop CD ROM hypermedia projects that combine visual still and moving images and written texts.

I had already learned about the benefits of making the visual part of my research in Spain in 1992–4 where I did research about the position of women in the local bullfighting culture. In this research, using photography as an integral part of my study, I was both an ethnographer and a local amateur bullfight photographer, photographing performances, practice sessions at the bullfighting school, social events and activities at the bullfight clubs and museums and other local festivities. The bullfight, like many of the activities we study, is a visual and embodied performance. I soon learned that photography was so embedded in the way that it was understood locally that there were aspects of this event that could only be discussed photographically. For example, it is said that to be able to anticipate and photograph a performance well a bullfight photographer ought to have the skilled knowledge of the performance almost equal to that of the bullfighter himself. By asking my informants to comment on my own photographs I was able to gauge their thoughts about my own process of learning about the performance that was progressing, and at the same time receive their judgements of the woman bullfighter I had photographed. As visual knowledge about the bullfight was so important to the local world I was working in, my photography also offered me a means of producing materials that I could later use to represent aspects of this knowledge in my book *Women and Bullfighting* (Pink, 1997), without having to attempt the almost impossible task of translating it into words.

INTRODUCTION

Visual anthropology, accompanied by visual sociology, is a leading subdiscipline in the development of visual research. Key texts in the historical development of visual anthropology include Bateson and Mead's *Balinese Character* (1942) and Collier's *Visual Anthropology: Photography as Research Method* (1967), although these works have now been extensively critiqued and should be read in conjunction with the more recent work cited below. In visual sociology, Becker's (1974) work on 'Photography and Sociology' is a key early text. Since 2000 a number of new books and articles on visual research and representation in qualitative

research have been published. These originate in various social science disciplines, including anthropology (Banks, 2001; Pink, 2001b, 2003; Ruby, 2000; Pink et al., forthcoming, 2004), sociology (Emmisson and Smith, 2000), cultural geography (Rose, 2001), queer studies (Holliday, 2001), psychology and health studies (Radley and Taylor, 2003) and incorporating multidisciplinary approaches (van Leeuwen and Jewitt, 2000). Certain concerns, shared by these disciplines, are reflected in the recent texts: the analysis of existing visual images, covered well by Rose (2001); the visual observation of objects, spaces, activities and behaviours (Emmison and Smith, 2000); and the wider field of the visual in ethnography (Pink, 2001a; Banks, 2001), which covers a range of methods of visual research and representation and is critical of purely observational approaches such as that proposed by Emmison and Smith (2000). This literature has established new themes within the emergent field of visual methods (see Pink, 2001b). In particular, writers such as Ruby (2000), Banks (2001), Rose (2001) and Pink (2001a) emphasize a reflexive and collaborative approach. They call for attention to the materiality of visual images, the relationship between the image producer, the image itself and its viewer, and the ambiguity of visual meanings.

There are many ways of introducing photography and video into qualitative projects. These might include: the analysis of existing photographs and videos (such as family albums or home movies, in magazines, newspapers or news programmes, or in sports or other special interest clubs); using photographs as prompts or topics for discussion in interviews, focus groups or informal conversations with informants (sometimes called 'photo elicitation' and covered in detail by Harper, 2002); asking informants to produce photographs or video along certain themes and questions to discuss and analyse later; or the researcher producing photographs and video in collaboration with informants during participant observation or interviewing. In this chapter I focus on the latter. However, these different methods are often linked. For example, when I take photographs or video I often discuss these images with informants later, or when I am video recording an interview my informants will often discuss existing photographs with me.

My interest in visual research began as a student at the University of Kent (UK) in the 1980s when I began to explore uses of photography in an undergraduate methods course and to analyse museum archive photographs in my dissertation. An MA at the Granada Centre for

Visual Anthropology in Manchester taught me ethnographic video-making skills and theory of visual anthropology, which were to inform much of my subsequent research. Since then I have used photography and video in research about migration from Northern Ireland, women bullfighters in Spain (Pink, 1997), carnival and textile production in West Africa, and gender and home in England and Spain (Pink, forthcoming, 2004). Each project required and inspired a different mixture of visual technologies and methods of visual research and representation, ranging from using photographs in books and articles, to videos and multimedia projects that combine still and moving images and written texts presented on CD ROM.

In this chapter I draw from these experiences to outline the process of doing ethnography with a camera. Every qualitative visual research project is different, presenting new problems and dilemmas (which can usually be resolved!), inspiration and ideas. Visual research is a creative process, requiring researchers to respond creatively to their own research situation with well-informed innovations and adaptations to existing methods.

PLANNING VISUAL RESEARCH

Deciding which visual media and methods best suit a research project

Different media and methods are best suited to different research projects and contexts. Descriptions of existing projects exist in the texts mentioned above as well as the journals *Visual Anthropology, Visual Anthropology Review* and *Visual Sociology* (now *Visual Studies*); a browse through these publications can provide the individual researcher with both an idea of the scope of visual methods and media and ideas for one's own project. Sometimes it is impossible to be sure which technologies and methods are appropriate until one has started work on a project. For example, when I set out to do research about the bullfight in southern Spain I had planned to video record performances and informants' days out at the bullfight extensively. I then proposed to ask my informants to view and comment on videos of themselves and other people. However, once I arrived in the city of Córdoba where I did fieldwork, I found that in the early 1990s very few of my informants used video to produce their own records of the bullfight or the fiestas and meetings associated with it. Instead there was a thriving local culture of amateur and semi-professional bullfight photography. As a

participant observer it seemed wholly appropriate that I slip into this local pattern of photographic activity. My plans for video were better achieved using photography, allowing me to carry much more portable equipment (in the early 1990s video cameras were large and cumbersome), to participate and share in an activity my informants already practised, and to show and discuss my photographs with informants easily on the spot in bars, cafés and bullfighting clubs rather than organizing video screenings.

Planning my research in the 'strange' context of the Spanish bullfighting world from England, it had been impossible to know which technologies would be best suited to my work. In contrast, when in 1999 I began research into gender and domestic life in England, I could confidently plan my video research in advance. My research partners had already undertaken a pilot study, videoing informants in their homes, demonstrating that the method we planned to use would produce the materials we were interested in and that informants would feel comfortable and even enjoy the video interview process. In this instance, working in my own culture with a tested method, I could anticipate which equipment should be purchased for the project and how it would be used throughout. I describe this work more fully below.

The examples above contrast the use of photography and video in different projects. Some projects call for a combination of media and methods. For example, in 2000 I undertook a project about women's hairstyling. This involved working with informants in their homes, out shopping and in their workplaces. We were sure we could video informants in their homes. However, our use of video and photography outside the home had to be negotiated on a case-by-case basis depending on what different shops and workplaces would permit. In some locations visual research was impossible. Photography was not allowed in offices where personal and confidential data was stored, or in institutions like hospitals. Some shop managers gave on-the-spot permission to photograph or video, others required written applications, necessitating advance planning. Planning and selection of equipment may rest on a series of factors such as: the appropriateness of using different media in specific cultural and personal contexts; the privacy of others associated with the research context; institutional rules and regulations; the possibility of carrying out a pilot study to determine appropriateness beforehand; and the extent to which a project can be planed in detail in advance or if, as with much qualitative research, it will unfold in the field. Visual researchers should always keep an open mind about developing new methods and switching technology during the research.

Budgets, equipment and deadlines: resolving practical dilemmas

Although project funding applications often require concrete methods planning and a budget, ironically visual research projects can produce many surprises. Visual materials frequently inspire new ideas about the presentation of the results of the research. For example, I initially planned to produce video and photographic essays based on my research in Spain and West Africa. Shortly after the research I was offered the opportunity to produce these texts on CD ROM as part of a multimedia project funded by the University of Derby while I was a lecturer there. Each project combined written, photographic and video materials that worked better as combined multimedia texts than as simply photo or video essays. Nevertheless, innovative visual representations of visual research can be costly. I have heard many tales from ethnographic filmmakers who still have undeveloped film footage from projects they undertook years ago because, although they had been able to buy the film, their project budget did not stretch to developing it. Thinking through possibilities and their costs at the budgeting stage and during fieldwork can help avoid such frustrating scenarios. This should include careful budgeting for camera equipment, batteries or other power sources, film and tapes, computing equipment, editing facilities for video making, developing, printing, digitalizing and reproduction costs and any technical support or training that might be needed to work with this equipment either before or after the research has been completed. When I later came to plan my video research into domestic lives in England and Spain I was in a position to anticipate the research methods, and to draw from my previous experiences to plan how this work would be represented in advance. My initial proposal included the production of a CD ROM, and included a budget for the digitalization of the videotapes.

Equipment should also be carefully chosen according to the demands and budgetary limitations of each project. The range of visual technology now available is immense, ranging from disposable stills cameras, basic video and stills cameras, domestic and professional digital cameras, to cameras that will both photograph and video. Visual technologies are constantly changing and developing, therefore I shall not review particular models but make some basic suggestions.

First, the most expensive and latest equipment is not always the most appropriate. Researchers should consider their proposed research context and the quality of the visual results required for the project. In some contexts expensive cameras are out of place and a researcher might be better served with a stills camera that is recognizable to her or his informants. In my experience, in some situations when one is videoing a public event a large and imposing professional video camera can help one gain access to prime locations from which to film and view. In other contexts such cameras are intimidating and a small domestic model may be more appropriate. To interview people in their homes I used a small domestic digital video camera with a fold-out screen. In this context this camera had two advantages. First, its small size made it easier for me to video in the often confined spaces of the smaller rooms of my informants' houses. Second, the camera was new on the market, but known to many informants as the latest model in domestic video technology. Most were curious to ask about it, examine and hold it, helping to make them feel relaxed with the camera.

When their use is appropriate, the more costly digital stills and video cameras have some clear advantages. Because both have screens on which recently shot still images and video footage can be viewed, researchers can play back images to informants on the spot. This can serve to generate trust and sharing in the research process and instant feedback about the images as well as allowing researchers to check that appropriate visual materials are being produced and review the materials immediately rather than waiting for images to be printed or viewed on a video player. Working with digital media can cut out the cost and cumbersome process of tape transfer, using VHS players and waiting for developing. Video footage and still images can now be loaded directly from most contemporary digital cameras on to home computing equipment, allowing researchers to work directly with still and moving images and written texts on the same screen.

Permissions and ownership of materials

Permission to film or video will vary between research contexts, cultures and locations. It is polite, not to mention ethical, to ask people's permission before photographing or videoing them, and to explain to them the purpose of your doing so. In projects where one is working in private or restricted rather than public space, such as the home or a workplace, then clear rules can be established regarding what is permissible. When I carried out a series of forty interviews using video with informants in their homes, I asked each informant to sign a form agreeing to take part in the study and to the confidentiality of the materials I would produce. Later when I produced visual projects about the study, I wrote to my informants asking if they would allow me to use their images in my visual projects and to confirm if they would like to re-view and approve the images I selected before these were screened publicly. In fact half of the informants approached agreed to allow me to use their video interviews. However, before I have allowed any of this work to be released into the public domain I have asked these informants to inspect and comment on the way I have represented them in multimedia projects. Working this way, I intended to ensure that both my informants and I were comfortable with the way they were represented. This method can also offer useful feedback – informants do not always agree with our analyses of them and their comments can provide important new insights that allow us to reflect on our own subjectivity and methods of interpretation as well as those of our academic disciplines.

The extent to which permissions are needed to video or photograph public events will vary and should be checked in each new location. For example, in Spain I did not need to seek permission to photograph at bullfights or public bullfight events or speeches. However, in some contexts it is necessary to purchase an official permit to photograph, and at any rate even if one has purchased an official permit, whenever possible it is still polite to ask private individuals if they mind being photographed. In the case of performers who are already subject to press and other photography throughout their presence at the event, in my experience of the bullfight it is general practice that the audience members and their fans will photograph them both during and before and after their performances.

In some projects researchers collaborate with other bodies and organizations or with informants themselves to produce visual and other research materials, and ownership of video and photographs produced during the project might be shared. In these cases it is useful to establish a written agreement regarding the ownership and rights of use over these materials at the outset of the project.

Rights and permission are also bound up with ethical issues and agreements. Ethical considerations are raised when relevant throughout this chapter. However, researchers are advised to consider the new ethical questions raised by visual methods in the context of the ethical codes of conduct and legal issues surrounding the specific disciplines they are working in.

Designing interviews and participant observation with photography and video: balancing the visual and verbal

Although we often refer to visual research methods, in fact it would be difficult to define any research method as purely visual (or purely verbal for that matter). In fact the new emphasis on visual methods really serves to bring the visual and visual media and technologies to the fore in the research process, and to recognize and analyse the role of images in qualitative enquiry. When we do visual research, be it a video or photographic interview or participant observation at a celebration, we are actually mixing the visual with other perhaps more established qualitative methods. However, in doing so we should not treat the visual as an add-on, but as an integrated aspect of the experience of interviewing or interacting with informants. When we interview or simply converse with people they frequently make visual references to both present and absent visual images, sometimes fetching their photograph albums or guiding us to their photographic wall-displays, thus weaving these photographs into their verbal narrative to create new meanings in the conversation.

To demonstrate this, I often ask students to think back to their first weeks in the university hall of residence, a period of intense socializing, meeting new people and significantly learning about them and their lives. It is at such times in modern Western cultures that we might make great use of photographs to tell new friends about our families and lives at home. Video and photographic interviews are especially suitable for both encouraging and recording this type of behaviour. Visual interviews allow informants to tell us about their lives using not only words, but also visual images, gestures and body movements. When I interviewed informants in their homes they often enacted or performed certain ideas or activities they wanted to express, they led me to and talked me through their photographic collections, the paintings they had on their walls, their ornaments and their furniture. In doing so they were telling me stories about themselves, their lives and their experiences. For example, as Christine talked me through the paintings in her dining room I learned about her family and friends, her shopping and her passion for horses:

Christine: The paintings, my brother bought this one for me in America and I've just, it's just come back framed. I'm very pleased with that.

Sarah: *What was it that you liked about it in particular?*

Christine: I think a painting is a very personal choice, something you feel you can live with. It will remind me of my holiday there and I just liked the style of the painting, it was very soft I'd like to be there looking at it now.

Sarah: *And what about the others?*

Christine: The hunting scene I bought at a novice show this year because I'm obviously interested in horses. I just thought that was quite pleasant.

Sarah: *You just enjoy shopping then?*

Christine: I enjoy spending my money yes. I try to work hard and play hard. This painting a friend of mine, who's obviously a very good artist, did. This is a horse that I had for a long time. Obviously in my younger days when I did the trials and it's nice to have the picture.

Each painting raised a new topic that could have been followed up in more depth as the interview progressed. Therefore when designing such projects, writing interview outlines and checklists it is useful to leave space for the unexpected in terms of visual input, to remind oneself to probe about images and to encourage informants to show them. Using video and photography also help informants to make explicit links between visual and verbal knowledge that they wish to convey; for instance, my informants often told me to 'make sure you get that on video' or to take a photograph of a particular object, activity or moment.

Integrating the visual into an interview expands the series of prompts that one might have noted down on a written checklist for the interview. To this are added the unforeseen visual prompts that form part of the physical environment of the interview. As such the visual becomes not only the subject of research but an element in its design, varying and constantly updated as the researcher moves between different research contexts.

DOING VISUAL RESEARCH

Getting started: finding informants

Inevitably the only people who participate in visual research are people who are willing to be photographed and/or videoed for a research project. To include people who are unwilling,

photographing or filming them secretly would be unethical. Researchers who are obsessively worried about the representativeness of their sample should make concessions that balance the added advantages of visual methods with the influence their use will have over the sample. In my own experience, different types of project require different methods of recruiting informants. Participant observation allows us to find informants 'on the spot'. Their consent to participate in a visual project is contextual; for example, an individual may allow me to interview and video or photograph him or her while attending a bullfight, but would not consent to a photographic or video interview in his or her home. At public events one might produce ad hoc photographs or video interviews according to one's interaction with different people. Attending a public lecture given by a Spanish bullfighter in Spain I was able to video her activities after the lecture, signing autographs for her fans and having her photo taken with them. At my informants' requests I took photographs of them with the woman bullfighter, sometimes with their camera and sometimes with my own.

Before embarking on a large video or photographic project it is advisable to carry out a small pilot study to ensure that you will be able to find people who are willing to participate in such a study. In some cases making payments to informants and/or guaranteeing them total confidentiality can encourage people to participate. However, in such cases the final uses of the visual materials for the representation of the work can be very limited. While with careful writing anonymity can be guaranteed in written projects, representing the visual knowledge that is produced though research might require revealing the identity of informants. Such decisions should be carefully weighed up alongside the ethical issues they raise and in relation to discipline-specific ethical codes of conduct since, as I shall argue in the final sections of this chapter, visual and written texts work together to represent different types of knowledge, and usually visual knowledge cannot be directly or adequately translated into written words.

One of the greatest anxieties that a researcher can experience during fieldwork is the question of 'Will I be able to get any informants?'! Usually the answer is yes, although this may be of little comfort when one is lying awake at night wondering if at last someone will say 'yes' the following day. When recruiting informants for visual research projects, an important issue is trust. When interviewed on video or photographed alongside tape-recorded interviews, people make themselves identifiable and vulnerable, they might make comments during the interview that they would not normally make in public, or make comments about a friend or relative that they would not like to be known to that person. There are several ways to generate this trust. As I noted above, offering anonymity is one possibility. In one video research project I used this strategy. We needed informants to fulfil a particular sample requirement within a short space of time. The informants were recruited through an experienced market research recruitment agency and were paid for the four hours of work they gave to the project. The interviews produced excellent in-depth visual and verbal materials. However, this meant sacrificing the possibility of visual representation and limiting the ways the materials could be used.

In my opinion the best way forward is to develop a collaborative relationship with informants whereby they become involved in decision-making about the way the interview materials are used. For my research about gender and home I recruited my informants according to a target sample but using personal networks. I began with people I already knew and after interviewing them asked them if they could recommend me to other people who fell within the categories I needed for my sample. During the interviews I usually showed my informants the first few minutes of video that I had recorded before continuing so that they would feel confident about the way I was filming them. Some also spent over half an hour viewing sections of the hour-long tapes at the end of the interview. Many said they had enjoyed the interview experience, some finding it amusing, and some finding they had learned new things about themselves while discussing their homes and lives with me. They were happy to recommend me to others and in this way I was soon able to achieve the full sample I sought.

Being a reflexive visual researcher

I noted above that some of my informants commented on how much they had learned about themselves through their interviews with me. It is also crucial that visual researchers should be self-aware, or *reflexive*. Reflexivity has become something of a buzz-word in recent qualitative methodology literature. However (see Pink, 2001a), it should be taken seriously rather than just engaged in as a token measure. The knowledge that is produced through any qualitative research encounter (visual or not) should be understood as the product of a specific interaction between researcher and informant(s). Our informants tell and show us what they do *because* they are in a research situation with us as individuals; this encounter and the knowledge produced through it can never be objective. Therefore it is essential that we attempt to understand the subjectivities through which our research materials are produced. When doing research this means being aware of how our own experiences, knowledge and stand-points inform our behaviour with and interpretation of our informants. It involves not just analysing our informants but our fieldwork relationships.

My experience of interviewing each of my informants was different. When I was working with informants in their homes with video we were focusing on a very personal and intimate space of their lives, in a way that I tried not to make intrusive, but that inevitably intruded beyond the normal limits of their privacy as I asked to see and video record the clothes in their wardrobes and the contents of their fridges. In each situation I felt enveloped in some way by my informant's life and the objects that belonged to it as their stories unfolded through their homes. Usually this was a positive experience. I often left feeling inspired by the way my informants had created their homes and lives, and grateful for their frankness and willingness to work with me. Sometimes I felt saddened by some of the experiences they described to me. Such reflexivity is not only an important means of helping researchers to understand the materials they are producing and the way these have been affected by the subjectivities of themselves and their informants. It is also a key element of the way we represent our visual research and enable others to understand the status of the knowledge we have created.

Understanding the meaning of the camera in your particular research setting

For the visual researcher it is not only the relationship between researcher and informants that requires a reflexive focus, but also the role of the camera in that relationship. This raises a series of questions. For instance, how does the type of camera one uses and the way it is used contribute to the way informants see and judge the researcher? As I have noted above, if possible equipment should be carefully selected to suit each research setting. When I was doing participant observation in the bullfighting world in Spain I used a Pentax camera similar in quality and function to the cameras used by my informants. I needed a camera that could use fast film to be able to participate in their hobby of photographing the bullfight, using black and white film. I doubt my work would have been taken seriously had I used a small automatic camera because such equipment was associated with snapshotters rather than serious amateur photographers of the bullfight. Choice of camera can thus impact on the knowledge that a particular research situation produces.

I noted above how a small domestic digital video camera was an appropriate technology for video research in the home. In public contexts informants tend also to associate different types of camera with different activities, again showing how the technology and how it is interpreted impacts on the type of knowledge each research situation produces. As a student I found that working in Britain using a larger professional-looking camera with a sound recordist can attract ad hoc interviews with informants who wish to express their opinions in what they perceive as a public medium. Visual researchers should also seek any particular local or cultural meanings associated with video or photography that should be accounted for. Local understandings of media and visual representations also provide important background to our understandings of how informants perform in front of the camera. We should research local media and other narratives that informants might adopt when a camera is introduced into a research situation.

Introducing the camera: finding the right moment

There is never an essentially 'right' moment to introduce the camera. Usually it varies according to the circumstances of each project, and is often incorporated in the agreement between a researcher and those who are to be photographed or videoed. In some projects photography and video begin from the outset. In others they might be introduced later once the researcher has established her or his relationship with informants without the camera. Personally I prefer to develop some contact with informants before photographing or videoing them. In my work in the home I spent up to half an hour chatting with and interviewing each informant before taking out my video camera. I usually introduced the camera to my informants as an interesting new technology. Rather than recording them directly, I let them hold it and examine it and explained how it functioned. When one is working in one's own culture it is usually easier to judge, or ask, when it would be appropriate to video or

photograph. To determine when, where, how and whom one should start photographing or videoing in other contexts may require some sensitivity and local research. For example, making oneself aware of local uses of these technologies, studying local exhibitions, private displays and family and personal collections of photography will offer insights into the visual culture in which one is working and give a sense of how and where a researcher's photography might fit in.

Working with informants: collaborative aspects of visual research

Without the collaboration of my informants my research about the home would have been impossible. As Banks points out (2001: 19), because anthropologists and sociologists have to negotiate with their informants to produce knowledge anyway, most research is collaborative. A collaborative approach contrasts with the purely observational approach that strives to produce objective data through unobtrusive methods, as recommended by Emmison and Smith (2000). Their observational method concentrates on analysing anything that can be seen – from objects to social interaction and body posture. It avoids most other contact between researcher and subject. Emmison and Smith find covert research more convenient because it evades the 'usual problems of normative responding' (2000: 110). Unlike Banks (2001) and myself (Pink, 2001b), they are not interested in how knowledge is produced through the intersubjectivity of encounters between the researcher and the social and material world that she or he is investigating. Such covert research allows researchers to observe unobtrusively and thus more fully 'control' their research situation. However, it has the disadvantage that it cannot account for the voices, views and feelings of its subjects and therefore can tell us little about their identities, experiences and values.

To research the relationship between my informants' homes and self-identities I developed an approach that reflected more closely Banks's idea of negotiation. Rather than simply observing their activities in their homes, I depended upon my informants to show me their homes and their lives in them, using the physical environment of the home itself as a series of prompts to encourage informants to elaborate certain themes. The following extract and stills are my video interview with Mario who at the time was in his late twenties. He worked as the president of a Student Union whilst developing his freelance writing career. Here Mario is showing me around his room, telling me about how he feels this space expresses his present and past life stages, relationships, interests, ambitions and personality:

Sarah: *Okay and what about this, this is where you actually sit and do your work is it?*

Mario: Yes this is the hub of my brain. TV and video, I don't really use it very very much I've just got it. This is my pride and absolute joy, my computer, which I've called The Daddy because it's great and the printer and things like that. Now I write in notebooks a lot and then type it up on the computer and I use this just to bounce things on, bits of writing work, freelance writing projects I'm working on I stick up there. Because again not only is it very useful to have it, because I tend to forget about things so it's good to have it actually on show, but also this says to me I am a working freelance writer. It creates that environment which I enjoy very much. This is, normally I have a picture of my girlfriend there but as you can see I dropped it through the printer and as it was printing it fell off and she wasn't very happy so that's my girlfriend. She doesn't always look like that but she is very pretty. And I think she looks like this cat. I think the resemblance is stunning and so I can't have this picture, I'll put it up somewhere else in a minute actually, a bit later on but in the meantime I'll put that there because that reminds me of my girlfriend. So when she rings me on the phone I look at that and think of her, which she's not very pleased about as you can imagine. And then it's just paraphernalia, lots and lots and lots of books and stuff shoved in because the space here isn't very much and just a few videos on the top there but various bits and pieces shoved here and there. So my stereo which desperately needs a clean which I must sort out very soon and CDs. I've got lots of CDs and lots of things like that. And then my books. This is my reading list, this is the things, apart from these things

here that's what I'm trying to read. A book on the desert on the top you see and these are all books I'm saving and trying to get through and read and also an overspill on the floor.

Here Mario took the lead in describing his life to me, and I later picked up on the themes and details he raised for follow-up questions. The existing visual environment of his room facilitated these descriptions and contributed to the development of the interview. In other projects I have worked with informants to photograph events and activities. To research a 'day in the life of' a set of women informants I spent a day with each woman at her workplace. I tape-recorded short interviews with her throughout the day and photographed places, events, interactions and activities that we determined as important in her day. Such methods can be adapted and used less formally in participant observation. For example, working in the bull-fighting world in Spain I accompanied informants to bullfights. My informants would tell me which parts and moments of the performance to photograph, partly to express their knowledge about how a bullfight should be photographed, and because they were interested in guiding my photography because they wanted copies of my photographs. In doing so they taught me about their personal knowledge of the bullfight and showed me visually which images were important to them.

By working with informants to produce images that are meaningful for them we can gain insights into their visual cultures and into what is important to them as individuals living in particular localities. This means being sensitive to the visual, paying attention to the visual in informants' lives, and the uses they make of images as well as listening and sometimes tape-recording, but not producing exclusively visual materials. For example, it was evident that the visual symbols and objects Mario used to create his working environment in his room held special meaning for him, validating his professional identity. He also described the images and photos he had displayed on his wall:

Mario: As I say I'm really into favourites and icons and things, I directed that play when I was a student. It went down very well. It was very good so that's a bit of pride for me. Eric Cantona, as you can see from the duvet, is a big hero of mine, he's a big icon of mine and so's John Malkovich. That's just a nice photo call, a nice bit of photography. Happy pictures of me. I've got quite a hassle over self image but I'd broken up with an old girlfriend and I moved in here because I had to and I moved out of rooms with her and I just thought sod it I'll put on the wall lots of happy memories of me so I've just got lots of happy memories of me doing something odd, in front of someone famous in Europe or wherever so I've got Hungary, Sweden, France, Malta all sorts up there so that's me doing all that.

Like many interviewees, Mario used images and photographs to construct identity and memory. I noted the visual images he showed and the words he used to describe them to develop ideas about how he represented and saw himself, his wider personal ambitions, and how these aspects of his identity fitted with his everyday life and practices. Using video to explore Mario's home and his life in it created a situation in which our interview included references to visual objects, displays and images. My analysis of these images and how he described them formed the basis of my understanding of how his self-identity and home were mutually created. The videotapes thus had a dual function. They represent visual records of the spoken words, photographs and visual appearance of his room. However, they are simultaneously a representation of the research encounter, produced through a unique interview situation; anything that is understood from them is therefore the product of a subjective interaction between the researcher and the informant.

Such attention to the visual can be applied to a wide range of public and intimate research contexts. For example, my research into bullfighting culture in Spain included a study of the photographic displays and exhibitions found in bullfighting bars. Here, as I have described elsewhere (Pink, 1997), the members of bullfighting clubs used photographs, paintings and prints to construct visual histories of their local bullfighting world. In creating their various different versions of local history these clubs were also attempting to define the present but emphasizing particular lineages of bullfighters and the relationships between them. Other examples might include the analysis of family albums, personal collections of photography and memorabilia.

UNDERSTANDING AND ANALYSING VISUAL RESEARCH

The relationship between research and analysis

In many qualitative projects, and particularly projects that use ethnographic methods, it is difficult to separate research and analysis. Analysis is often ongoing as research proceeds and researchers develop understandings of informants and their social and cultural worlds, even if this involves no formal or overt analytical methods. This might include reflexive analysis of the process and relationships through which knowledge is being produced, viewing of photographs and videotapes as a basis from which to develop further questions for the research and for informants, analysis of local visual documents that one has borrowed, especially those that one might not be able to copy or take away for future analysis (for example, I have done this with materials such as personal photograph collections or home movies). The analysis of such materials will then feed back into research, enriching the knowledge base upon which the project can proceed and inspiring new questions.

What are visual research materials?

Visual research materials serve a range of different functions within qualitative research: as visual records/data; as representations of research experiences; and as material artefacts/material culture. In my view none of these three definitions can be understood as independent from the others. The meanings of visual materials are contingent on all three aspects of their identity. To a certain extent research photos and video can be seen as visual records, their content can be analysed using formal or informal methods of image analysis (see Rose, 2001, for a discussion of the various forms such analysis might take). However, in order to understand what these tapes or photos are images of, we should account for the research context they were taken in. Such qualitative research materials are representations of the research experience: they are not objective visual records but subjective representations produced by the researcher in collaboration with informants and other individuals involved. Moreover, people in research photographs are only ever people in images; they are not real people or events transported out of the fieldwork context for our analysis. It is on this basis that visual research materials should be analysed. Photographs and videos do not tell us the whole story about either our own or our informants' experiences; instead, like our written notes, they are subjective representations of reality.

As recent work in visual anthropology has emphasized, along with the idea that visual images are products of our own subjectivity, the meanings of visual images are neither objective nor fixed. The meanings of visual images are ambiguous and we cannot assume that a photograph or video recording produced during our research will always have the same meaning. It will be given different meanings according to the subjectivity of the person viewing and interpreting it. This is also important when using images in published work (see below). At the analysis stage researchers should be aware of how and why we interpret our research images ourselves: how do we build our interpretations of images, and on what experiences, knowledge and uses of the image are these based? Recent writing in visual anthropology has also reminded us that photographs are material objects (Edwards, 1999; Banks, 2001; Pink, 2001a). As such their meanings are as arbitrary as those of other objects of material culture; they may be given new uses and new meanings as they move into different contexts.

Visual materials are inextricably linked with and comprehensible in terms of other research materials, such as diaries, fieldnotes and interview transcripts. Analysis should not separate these different materials, rather we should seek the links between them. As I suggest below, these links can be made at the stage of ordering, storing and cataloguing research materials using manual or digital methods.

Storing and cataloguing visual materials

There are no hard-and-fast rules regarding how to organize research materials. This depends on factors such as: types and quantities of materials; type of analysis and methods that will be applied to them; and whether the research is teamwork or undertaken by a single researcher. Different methods and degrees of detail of storage and cataloguing will be appropriate in these various situations. For example, as a single researcher working on an in-depth study of women and bullfighting, I was the only person who consulted my research materials. I organized my fieldwork photographs into sets according to the events at which I produced them. I did not keep lists and logs of the 200 or so images and their contents. As the researcher who produced them I had good enough knowledge of each of my folders, the photographic themes and content to locate and select relevant images for further analysis as necessary. In my fieldwork diaries I had detailed notes of the contexts in which the photographs were taken and the relationships involved in these. My diaries also charted my analysis of my visual materials and experiences as they developed throughout the research. Therefore I could cross-reference the thematically organized diary notes and the visual materials. Because I was working alone, it was not necessary that these linkages should be accessible to other researchers.

In contrast, for my video research about the home I was the researcher responsible for the project, writing up and analysis, but the project was designed so that I could share materials with research partners and so that they could apply further analysis or examine materials indicated in my report. I shared electronic and printed versions of all the interview transcripts and digitalized and VHS copies of all the videotapes with my research partners. Thus I could reference precise logged points on the digitalized videos stored on CD ROM and make quotations easily accessible through the search function in Word files when referencing from interview transcripts. Without using a time-consuming and complex logging procedure, I made both visual and verbal data accessible. Electronic methods also allow convenient sharing of data. For example, if one is working in a research team a video clip, photograph or written text file can be shared by the group by e-mail or placed on a protected Intranet site enabling all researchers in the team to comment or contribute to analysis.

Until recently, most visual researchers may have had little use for computer applications of the organization of their photographic prints, informants' drawings, 35 mm film and/or VHS videotapes. However, like other technologies, computer-assisted qualitative data analysis software (CAQDAS) is fast developing new capacities and some new packages also store and analyse video materials. For some projects it is worth using specialized software to log and store digital materials, and Coffey et al. (1996) have suggested that CAQDAS that has hypermedia component might be useful for ethnographers as a multilinear device that can include visual images and written text and that will serve as an analytical as well as a representational device.

Programs such as Atlas-ti and Nudist offer facilities for coding, storing and retrieval of video, still images, sound and written files. However, comparing Atlas/ti with Nudist software, Barry advises that 'Not every piece of software will be relevant to every task and researchers will often be able to achieve their ends using non-technology solutions or simple word processing cut and paste'. Barry encourages potential users of such software to get to know the different programs and their capacities, so that they will know when it might be appropriate to use them. Such software should not used as a matter of principle, but she advises that 'the individual researcher' should 'take responsibility for deciding how useful the software will be for them, which package they should use, and how they will integrate this into their existing analysis methods' (Barry, 1998: 2.11–2.12).

It is also important to recognize the limits of such software and to combine their use with other methods. Barry notes that qualitative data analysis software has been criticized for providing only a simplistic analysis or not allowing researchers to gain a good overview of their materials. She argues that such views misunderstand how qualitative researchers ought to use qualitative data analysis software, pointing out that in her own research she uses Nudist 'as just one tool in my analysis armory, as it only helps me to do part of the work of analysis', and other methods are used to complement this (Barry, 1998: 2.7). The advantage of such software is that one can organize and interlink complex sets of materials, easing retrieval and sharing of data. However, when deciding whether to use these programs, one should weigh up the cost of the financial outlay and time investment in both learning to use the software as well as in logging and inputting data involved in these procedures against the benefits for specific projects. Often researchers find they can invent their own digital systems of data storage that are specifically suited to the requirements of their own projects by using simple word-processing files, a basic photo editor and video editor. The software required for this is not costly and the files can be ordered and accessed and linked through hyperlinks.

Plans to use digital storage systems should be made if possible at the outset of the project, allowing purchase of appropriate hardware and software. Non-digital videotapes can be transferred into electronic files; however, this can be costly and should be budgeted for in advance. Printed photographs can be scanned or digital copies can be ordered when they are developed.

REPRESENTING VISUAL RESEARCH

Integrating the visual into research publications

The written word is an effective medium for presenting the findings of theoretical and empirical research and should by no means be devalued in favour of the visual. Nevertheless the visual should not be a mere add-on, supplement to or illustration for the written word. Instead, by combining the visual and the verbal in the same texts as appropriate, each may represent the ideas, experiences and knowledge that it best communicates.

Several genres of representation that combine the visual and the verbal are becoming established in the social sciences. The main genres I discuss here are: written essays that include photographs; the photo-essay; the video essay; ethnographic video; and hypermedia texts. Other alternatives include public exhibition and performance.

Photographs and written text

Written texts (books and articles) that include photographs are the most common use of photography in social science representation. Often, photographs are used as captioned illustrations of examples referred to in the written text, as in Figure 25.1(a).

Such uses of photography provide limited knowledge and understanding beyond being visual 'evidence' of the examples described in the written text. An alternative approach would be to change the caption to give the photograph meaning not solely in relation to its visual content, but to make it comprehensible in terms of my own fieldwork experience and learning and my informants' understandings of both the photograph and of women performers. The longer caption, as in Figure 25.1(b), would situate the photograph more deeply in the research context.

This second use of the photograph and caption might be suited to a photograph in a written essay. Alternatively a series of images, captions and theoretical paragraphs such as this might together create a photo-essay with a more equal balance between words and images. In a photo-essay one seeks to create relationships between the knowledge represented in photographs and texts, and to juxtapose photographs so they have implications for the meanings represented by each other.

Figure 25.1(a) *A woman bullfighter performing with the cape.*

Figure 25.1(b) *I took this photograph in January 1993 from my seat in the audience when the woman bullfighter Cristina Sanchez performed in a town called Valdemorillo, near Madrid in Spain. This was one of her early public performances and there was some resistance to the idea of women bullfighters, demonstrated by men shouting comments such as 'women belong in the kitchen' and 'she's got a nice bum'. Later I showed this and my other photographs to my informants in Córdoba. They commented on how my photography was progressing – I had managed to capture some of the key moments of the bullfight. They were especially interested in this photograph for what they could learn about Cristina's physiological capacities; they commented that as a woman performer her arms were too weak to work well with the cape and that this was evidenced by the way she was holding it.*

For example, the first photograph could be followed by the following photograph and caption (Figure 25.2), which would introduce certain anthropological and sociological themes: family and kinship in bullfighting culture, the public life of the performer, and local heritage. These themes would be developed in theoretical paragraphs. By introducing the context the photographs were taken in, and how they were interpreted during fieldwork, the relationship between image and text allows reflexivity, acknowledging that these photographs are not objective recordings, but the outcomes of subjective and intersubjective situations, and open to a variety of different interpretations. As I have noted above, there are many forms the photo-essay might take. An excellent source from which begin to study the different possibilities is the journal *Visual Studies* (formerly *Visual Sociology*), where numerous photo-essays have been published in recent years.

The video essay

An obvious difference between video and photography is that photographs can be included in printed texts but videos cannot. The most conventional form of representing qualitative research in video has been ethnographic film-making. Usually using an observational film style, ethnographic film-makers normally seek to represent something of the perspectives, lives and experiences of the subjects of their films, using little voice-over narration and allowing anthropological themes to emerge from the film. Detailed discussion of ethnographic film-making can be found in the work of Loizos (1992) or Barbash and Taylor (1997). Ethnographic films are usually visually appealing, interesting, and provide condensed and in-depth insights into the lives and experiences of other people. They play an important role in social science, but have recently been critiqued in favour of the 'video essay' (see, Ruby, 2000; MacDougall, 2001). This is a response to the limitations of ethnographic film, which is often expensive to produce and driven by the standards of television production rather than the requirements of academic disciplines. A video essay might be longer than a conventional ethnographic film and supply a different range of knowledge, possibly including theoretical components. They will certainly be useful, particularly for specialist academic or user audiences. However, video essays maintain the linear format of film and cannot be interactive; in my view a more appropriate complement to ethnographic film is ethnographic hypermedia.

Figure 25.2 *In March 1993 the Director of Museums (centre right) in Córdoba, where I was based, invited Cristina Sanchez (centre left) to give a lecture at the bullfighting museum. Her father (far left), who was also a bullfighter and worked in Cristina's team as a banderillero, accompanied her that day as he had throughout her career at the bullfighting school and in her training. I took this photograph in the Callejón de las Flores, one of Córdoba's key tourist sights pictured framed here in a style most typical of local postcards with the tower of the famous mezquita (mosque) in the background. During the morning before the lecture we toured the mesquita, the old part of the city and the local bullfighting bars and clubs. A local bullfight journalist (far right) interviewed Cristina. My own role was to photograph the event for all concerned.*

Ethnographic hypermedia

The use of hypermedia to organize and interlink visual and written research materials was discussed above. It also offers an exciting new medium for the representation of research findings that combines written words and still and moving images, using other facilities not available in print or video, such as multilinearity, hyperlinks, colour and novel text layouts. Anthropologists such as David Zeitlyn and Mike Fischer (see www.lucy.ukc.ac.uk) and Jay Ruby (see www.temple.edu/anthro.ruby) are increasingly using hypermedia in online projects. Sociologists are also beginning to engage with hypermedia as a method of ethnographic representation (see, e.g., Mason and Dicks, 2001). Others are developing such projects on CD ROM and DVD which at

present has greater capacity to store and retrieve video clips, e.g. Rod Coover (see Coover, forthcoming, 2004), Peter Biella (see Biella, 1997) and myself (see Pink, forthcoming, 2004).

When deciding which format to use, ethical issues also come to the fore. Researchers should consider if it would be appropriate to publish video of others online (even with their consent). Here, by way of example, I complete the story of my video research in the home to discuss how I developed *Gender at Home,* a multimedia hypermedia project stored on CD ROM. In this research, knowledge was produced both using video and in-depth interviews. The idea of doing visual research is not to later translate images into words, indeed sometimes they might not be translatable (see Pink, 2001b). Instead, here I wanted to make full use of images and words and to combine them in a text that aimed to represent how my informants spoke about, showed me and experienced their homes. Detail of the theoretical and representational issues that informed the planning and construction of this project is discussed elsewhere (see Pink, forthcoming). Here I explain the structure and content of the work. In *Gender at Home* I included written theoretical narratives and narratives that combine images and words to represent the research materials and experience. These were viewed for approval by the informants who had participated in the study. The uniquely multilinear, multimedia and interactive qualities of hypermedia allowed me to achieve this. As the flow chart in Figure 25.3 shows, each of the links on the page shown above connects to either a purely written text or a text that combines still and moving images and words in the same page.

As such I aimed the text to meet some of the demands currently put on visual and written publications in social science research: that the text should be reflexive (using video to reveal the research process through which visual and written knowledge was produced), ethical and collaborative (in the selection of the medium and requesting informants' approval), and should engage with the theoretical and methodological concerns of its discipline (using written texts to discuss theoretical issues and drawing from the concerns of recent debates in ethnographic representation to inform the development of the whole hypermedia project) (see Pink, forthcoming, where the ideas behind this are discussed in detail). Many new opportunities exist for combing visual and written materials in hypermedia. This evolving area offers new styles, formats and possibilities that are currently emerging and can be viewed on some of the websites noted above.

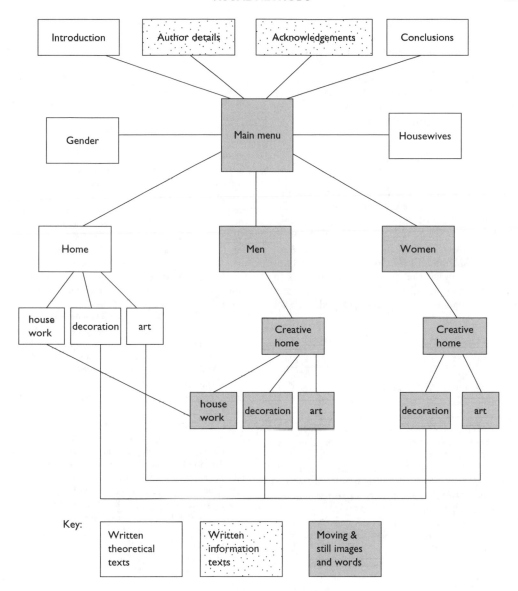

Figure 25.3 *Gender at Home: map of project.*

SUMMING UP

Every visual research project will flow in its own way and each researcher will be confronted with personal dilemmas and opportunities throughout this process. It would be impossible to issue a 'how to' guide to visual research. As I have described, choices of equipment, fieldwork methods, and styles and media of representation must be carefully developed for each unique research context and as an integral element of each project.

In this chapter I have followed the visual research process from planning to representation based on my experiences of working with visual media over the last decade. However, it is impossible to examine all the intricacies of research, theoretical perspectives, issues and possibilities it raises in a single chapter. For a broader, more historical and detailed discussion of photography, video and hypermedia in the ethnographic process, I would direct readers to Marcus Banks's *Visual Methods in Social Research* (2001) and my book *Doing Visual Ethnography* (2001b), in which some of the arguments I make, and the examples from my Spanish fieldwork I mention, are developed in more detail. For a discussion of more recent literature and innovations in theory and methods of visual research, including art, drawing, video and digital media in the social sciences, I recommend *Working Images* (Pink et al., forthcoming, 2004), and the *Visualising Ethnography* website.

ACKNOWLEDGEMENTS

The research projects I have discussed in this chapter would not have been possible without the generous support of the following organizations. Fieldwork in Spain was made possible by an ESRC research studentship, fieldwork in West Africa by sabbatical leave from the University of Derby. The video and photographic projects in the home were funded by Unilever Consumer Research, and in most part developed with Dr Katie Deverell.

REFERENCES

Banks, M. (2001) *Visual Methods in Social Research.* London: Sage.

Barbash, I. and Taylor, L. (1997) *Cross Cultural Filmmaking: a Handbook for Making Documentary and Ethnographic Films and Video.* London: University of California Press.

Barry, C. (1998) 'Choosing qualitative data analysis software: Atlas/ti and Nudist compared', *Sociological Research Online,* 3(3), <http://www.socresonline.org.uk/socresonline/3/3/4.html>.

Bateson, G. and Mead, M. (1942) *Balinese Character: A Photographic Analysis.* New York: New York Academy of the Sciences.

Becker, H.S. (1974) 'Photography and sociology', *Studies in the Anthropology of Visual Communication,* 1: 3–26.

Biella, P. (1997) 'Mama Kone's possession: scene from an interactive ethnography', *Visual Anthropology Review,* 12(2): 59–95.

Coffey, A., Holbrook, B. and Atkinson, P. (1996) 'Qualitative data analysis: technologies and representations', *Sociological Research Online,* 1(1), <http://www.socresonline.org.uk/socresonline/1/1/4.html>.

Collier, J. (1967) *Visual Anthropology: Photography as Research Method.* Albuquerque: University of New Mexico Press.

Coover, R. (forthcoming, 2004) 'The representation of cultures in digital media', in S. Pink, L. Kurti and A.I. Afonso (eds), *Working Images.* London: Routledge.

Edwards, E. (1999) 'Photographs as objects of memory', in M. Kwint, C. Breward and J. Aynsley (eds), *Material Memories.* Oxford: Berg, pp. 221–36.

Emmison, M. and Smith, P. (2000) *Researching the Visual.* London: Sage.

Harper, D. (2002) 'Talking about pictures: a case for photo-elicitation', *Visual Studies,* 17(1): 13–26.

Holliday, R. (2000) 'We've been framed: visualising methodology', *Sociological Review,* 48(4): 503–22.

Loizos, P. (1992) *Innovation in Ethnographic Film.* Manchester: Manchester University Press.

MacDougall, D. (1997) 'The visual in anthropology', in M. Banks and H. Morphy (eds), *Rethinking Visual Anthropology.* London: New Haven Press, pp. 276–95.

MacDougall, D. (2001) 'Renewing ethnographic film: is digital video changing the genre?', *Anthropology Today,* 17(3): 15–21.

Mason, B. and Dicks, B. (2001) 'Going beyond the code: the production of hypermedia ethnography', *Social Science Computer Review,* 9(4): 445–57.

Pink, S. (1997) *Women and Bullfighting: Gender, Sex and the Consumption of Tradition.* Oxford: Berg.

Pink, S. (2001a) 'More visualising, more methodologies: on video, reflexivity and qualitative research', *Sociological Review,* 49(4): 586–99.

Pink, S. (2001b) *Doing Visual Ethnography: Images, Media and Representation in Research.* London: Sage.

Pink, S. (2003) 'Representing the sensory home: ethnographic experience and ethnographic hypermedia', in G. Bloustein (ed.), *En-visioning Ethnography: Exploring the Complexity of the Visual Methods in Ethnographic Research (special issue), Social Analysis,* 47(3).

Pink, S. (forthcoming, 2004) *Home Truths,* Oxford: Berg.

Pink, S. (forthcoming) 'Visualising ethnography: transforming the anthropological vision?', to be published in a collection from the *Visible Evidence* seminar.

Pink, S., Kurti, L. and Afonso, A.I. (eds) (forthcoming, 2004) *Working Images.* London: Routledge.

Radley, A. and Taylor, D. (2003) 'Images of recovery: a photo-elicitation study on the hospital ward', *Qualitative Health Research,* 13(1): 77–99.

Rose, G. (2001) *Visual Methodologies.* London: Sage.

Ruby, J. (2000) *Picturing Culture: Explorations of Film and Anthropology.* Chicago: University of Chicago Press.

van Leeuwen, T. and Jewitt, C. (2000) *Handbook of Visual Analysis.* London: Sage.

Websites

Experience Rich Anthropology. Accessible at <http://www.era.anthropology.ac.uk/index.html> date of last visit 13.12.01

Ruby, J. *Maintaining Diversity.* Accessible at http://www.viscom.or.kr/ date of last visit 13.12.01

Visualising Ethnography http://www.lboro.ac.uk/departments/ss/newwisite/visualisingethnography.htm

Part 5

QUALITY AND CREDIBILITY

The quality and credibility of qualitative research has been often questioned. Generally speaking, quality refers to the transparency of the whole research process; credibility pertains to the validation of findings and results. For a long time these issues have also been associated with discussions of the *reliability* (of methods) and *validity* (of data). Many qualitative researchers have wanted to dismiss these as merely 'positivist' concerns. However, there also has been movement in other directions: on the one hand, these two concepts have become detached from the label of positivism and imported into qualitative paradigms (for example by Kirk and Miller, 1986; Hammersley, 1990, 1992; Silverman, 1993, 2000; Seale, 1999). On the other hand, new concepts have been proposed in order to deal differently with these issues:

- *completeness* of descriptions (Miles et al., 1994: 279);
- *saturation* of categories (Glaser and Strauss, 1967);
- *authenticity* as certification of the researcher's presence in the setting;
- *ecological validity* (Cicourel, 1996);
- *consistency*, 'with which instances are assigned to the same category by different observers or by the same observer on different occasions' (Hammersley, 1992: 67);
- *credibility* as a bridge between a researcher's interpretation and 'reality' (Agar, 1986; Hammersley, 1990: 57, 61; Miles et al., 1994: 279);
- *plausibility* as the consistency between the researcher's findings and theories accepted by the scientific community.

The result of this movement of ideas has been a reframing of quality and credibility issues through qualitative research language.

What is often left after epistemological and methodological debates about the nature of data as treated by positivism, critical realism, constructionism, relativism and postmodernism is a practical approach (Gobo, 2001). In other words, an abstract and philosophical treatment is not always useful for dealing with issues of quality and credibility. For example, a realist theory of truth could be appropriate for some properties of the social world that are constructed by bureaucratic processes. Properties applicable to individuals (such as citizenship, place of birth and residence, educational degrees, ownership of driving license, having voted, police record, and so on) are recorded officially. This record may be conceived as not merely registering these properties, but *constructing* the status of the person (see Marradi, 1990: 81). Although a respondent can lie to the interviewer about his or her attitudes or political opinions without fear of being found out, properties such as citizenship, educational qualifications or the other matters listed above can be checked by the researcher in official records. This rather practical perspective on the truth of accounts can help us escape from many sterile and inconclusive debates.

In this section there are chapters that deal with quality and credibility in a practical way. In Chapter 26, Clive Seale shows how quality can be achieved by comparing two studies of the mass media coverage of illness. From the comparison we can learn better ways of doing research, which Seale conceives as consisting of an 'inner' dialogue with quality that precedes the 'outer' dialogue that a research report may generate once published. Taking this concern with quality further, Chapters 27 and 28, by Bent Flyvbjerg and Giampietro Gobo, respectively, are devoted to one of the most frequent accusations against the knowledge produced by qualitative studies: that this is not generalizable. These chapters outline both theoretical and practical arguments for an alternative approach to this issue.

Chapter 29, on working with 'key incidents' by Robert M. Emerson, turns to issues of quality in data analysis. Emerson outlines the role that can be played by an intensive focus on particular incidents in field data in the course of naturalistic and ethnographic projects. Such key incidents are often chosen because they crystallize many themes that have emerged in the course of reviewing the fieldnotes of other, perhaps less rich, incidents. In arguing this, Emerson conveys the emergent nature of qualitative analysis particularly effectively. Continuing the concern with analysis, Chapter 30, by Udo Kelle, assesses the contribution made to rigour by computer software for qualitative data analysis. In presenting this discussion, Kelle is prompted to reflect on the nature of 'coding' in qualitative research, and in scholarship in general.

REFERENCES

Agar, Michael H. (1986) *Speaking of Ethnography*. London: Sage.

Cicourel, A.V. (1996) 'Ecological validity and "white room effects": The interaction of cognitive and cultural models in the pragmatic analysis of elicited narratives from children', *Pragmatics and Cognition*, 4(2): 221–64.

Glaser, Barney G. and Strauss, Anselm L. (1967) *The Discovery of Grounded Theory: Strategies for Qualitative Research*. Chicago: Aldine.

Gobo, Giampietro (2001) 'Best practices: rituals and rhetorical strategies in the "initial telephone contact"', *Forum: Qualitative Social Research*, 2(1), http://www.qualitative-research.net/fqs-texte/1-01/1-01gobo-e.htm.

Hammersley, M. (1990) *Reading Ethnographic Research: A Critical Guide*. London: Longmans.

Hammersley, M. (1992) *What's Wrong with Ethnography: Methodological Explorations*. London: Routledge.

Kirk, J. and Miller, M. (1986) *Reliability and Validity in Qualitative Research*, Qualitative Research Methods Series, vol. 1. London: Sage.

Marradi, Alberto (1990), "Fedeltà di un dato, affidabilità di una definizione operativa", *Rassegna Italiana di Sociologia*, XXXI(1): 54–96.

Miles, Matthew B. and Huberman, Michael A. (1994) *Qualitative Data Analysis: An Expanded Sourcebook*. Thousand Oaks, CA: Sage.

Seale, Clive (1999) *The Quality of Qualitative Research*. London: Sage.

Silverman, David (1993) *Interpreting Qualitative Data: Methods for Analysing Talk, Text and Interaction*. London: Sage.

Silverman, David (2000) *Doing Qualitative Research: A Practical Handbook*. London: Sage.

26

Quality in qualitative research

Clive Seale

In periods when fields are without secure foundations, practice becomes the engine of innovation.

(Marcus and Fischer, 1986: 166)

One of the most important things that one learns as a practising social researcher is that different things impress different audiences. In my career, for example, I have had to attend to the priorities of the medical research community, and the somewhat different ones of the sociological community. I have learned that health service research journals catering for the medical community often like to see a firm separation between literature review, methods and findings, appealing to a conception of social research as science. Sociology journals, on the other hand, often prefer to see a looser division between these areas. Here, it is best to include in the methods section considerable quantities of generalized methodological discussion, involving references to philosophers and social theorists, so that the report can announce to the reader its literary, or at least post-scientific, credentials. The chapters in this volume by Loseke and Cahill (Chapter 37) and Czarniawska (Chapter 36) attest to the changing expectations of the audiences of research writing.

The insight that the criteria for a good performance vary according to the audience is of course no different from the lesson we all have to learn in life. Howard Becker (1964) put this well when he wrote in a piece on 'Personal change in adult life':

The person, as he moves in and out of a variety of social situations, learns the requirements of continuing in each situation and of success in it. If he has a strong desire to continue, the ability to assess accurately what is required, and can deliver the required performance, the individual turns himself into the kind of person the situation demands. (Becker, 1964: 44)

Taken seriously as a philosophy of life, this lacks integrity and could lead to a degree of cynicism about higher ideals. Becker was perhaps aware of this, as he noted that sometimes people develop a quality that he calls 'commitment' that can involve resistance to the demands of local audiences.

Social researchers nowadays are increasingly confronted with tensions between commitment to ideals of rigorous practice and the more 'Machiavellian' possibilities of writing what will please different audiences. This is because of developments in the philosophy of social science that have left research practitioners unprotected by the epistemological guarantees that once provided a secure defence of their enterprise as a high-minded and neutral search for truth. Some, in searching for new ideals (Guba and Lincoln, 1989, 1994; Lincoln and Denzin, 1994; Smith and Deemer, 2000), seek to substitute moral values and political positions as guarantors of standards: promoting dialogue, emancipating the oppressed, empowering the weak become the purposes of social research. But the epistemological relativism that these writers often claim stands in marked contrast to their political absolutism My view is that such attempts to resolve the problem of criteria by resort to political values are frighteningly weak – the kind of thing that, as European history has shown, can be swept away in a few nights of concentrated book-burning. I am also impressed by the general observation that one person's liberation may be another's oppression, and that 'emancipatory' positions too often involve closed minds.

Something bigger is required to justify social research, that is not tied to a particular political ideology. Commitment to the revelation of truth always had that 'big' quality. Maybe all we have got now is a general sense of the value of careful scholarship, commitment to rigorous argument, attending to the links between claims and evidence, consideration of all viewpoints before taking a stance, asking and answering important rather than trivial research questions. Perhaps the very fragility of these ideals in the face of power is what makes it worth devoting one's life to their support (Weber, 1948). The hope that these are our ideals could be what gives the general public a reason for trusting researchers more than politicians.

More positively, I believe there is a lot to be said for a more local conception of social research as a craft skill, rather than a realization of philosophical or political schemes. The craft of social research can be informed but ought not to be over-determined by social theories and political values, the skilled practitioner constructing things (research reports, talks to audiences, advice for policy-makers, practitioners and others planning practical endeavours) whose quality can be judged by a relevant research community devoted to practising, developing and teaching those skills. Hopefully these products will attract the attention of people outside the research community so that, like some new school of artistic practice achieving renown outside its own narrow community, novel and enlightening perceptions of 'reality' are generated that, incidentally, are likely to disrupt the fixed categories of power-brokers. Learning how to produce good-quality work, then, becomes a matter of honing practical research skills in the service of creativity, partly through engagement with methodological debate, partly through witnessing the work of more skilled practitioners (through reading their research reports, or studying with them). But above all, good-quality work results from doing a research project, learning from the things that did and did not work, and then doing another, better one, that more fully integrates the creativity and craft skills of the researcher, and so on until a fully confident research style is developed. The issue of constructing abstract, universally applicable criteria for judging whether work is of good quality can happily remain unresolved for such a craftsperson, who is nevertheless continually preoccupied with issues of quality more locally conceived, relevant to the particular research project at hand.

Another way of putting this is in terms of an 'inner' and 'outer' dialogue that a social researcher must conduct (the parallels with Campbell and Stanley's (1966) conception of external and internal validity are deliberate). The outer dialogue concerns the external relations of a research project – its relevance to practical and political projects, its consequences, uses and overall purpose. The inner dialogue concerns its internal logic (for example, the adequacy of links between claims and evidence). A craftsperson ought to be concerned with the outer dialogue for which a study is being prepared, else he or she becomes a socially irresponsible technician, but cannot allow these to overshadow the inner dialogue. The quality of the inner dialogue of a research project can be enhanced if the researcher learns how to draw on philosophy, social theory and methodology in developing practical research skills. I shall consider each of these in turn before showing how researchers can also draw on the example of other researchers to improve the quality of their work.

LEARNING FROM PHILOSOPHY

A conventional history of developments in the philosophy of social science charts a course from crude realism and empiricism, through neo-realist or subtle realist attempts to preserve some degree of separation between knowing subject and the object of research, ending with varieties of post-foundationalist, relativistic thinking in which such separation is unfeasible and the very enterprise of research as discovery is called into question. Thus Smith and Deemer (2000) structure their account, focusing on the work of Hammersley in particular to represent the neo-realist position. According to this story, the foundation of empiricist social science in unmediated perception of reality, so that facts were deemed to be 'out there', knowable through the sensory equipment of the researcher, was discredited by Thomas Kuhn and others some years ago. Hammersley (1990) is characterized as following Karl Popper in accepting the view that facts are never neutral, always have a constructed quality, being generated to an unknowable extent from the preconceived values and theories of the researcher. Thus the apparently simple fact that an eraser was 'thrown' across a room by a child might seem neutral, but if the word 'tossed' were substituted to describe the action, the fact becomes different. How then can Hammersley (and Popper) retain a separation between facts and theories, description and interpretation, pursuing the view that social science proceeds through refutation of theoretical propositions by facts, if those same facts are already preconstituted by theory?

One might argue that the theory that helps constitute the facts is probably going to be a different one from that which is being tested, making the comparison at least interesting. Howard

Becker (again) offers a useful way in which social researchers can side-step the philosophical point and usefully continue to compare theories and 'facts' in a passage in which he advises how to tell 'scientific stories':

> ... the story must be congruent with the facts we have found out. I suppose there's also an argument about what it would mean for stories and facts to be congruent. Thomas Kuhn taught us that ... there aren't any 'facts' independent of the ideas we use to describe them. That's true, but irrelevant here. Recognizing the conceptual shaping of our perceptions, it is still true that not everything our concepts would, in principle, let us see actually turns up in what we look at. So we can only 'see' men and women in the Census, because, providing only those two gender categories, it prevents us from seeing the variety of other gender types a different conceptualization would show us. The Census doesn't recognize such complicating categories as 'transgender'. But if we said that the population of the United States, counted the way the Census counts, consisted of fifty percent men and fifty percent women, the Census report could certainly tell us that that story is wrong. We don't accept stories that are not borne out by the facts we have available. (Becker, 1998: 18)

Ignoring this side-step for the moment, the next stage in the story about how philosophers of science have changed is to say that we must all learn to live with relativism, in a world in which there are no absolute foundations for knowledge. Yet, as Smith and Deemer argue, this is not to say that 'anything goes', for at the heart of post-foundationalist research practice lies a moral commitment. This involves attention to a wide variety of viewpoints, openness to dialogue about research decisions rather than shoulder-shrugging dismissal of debate, commitment to expanding one's views beyond current prejudices, and recognition that all truths are partial, spoken from a particular standpoint. Additionally, there is the value-driven view that good-quality social research should be committed to promoting 'social justice, community, diversity, civic discourse, and caring' (Lincoln, 1995: 277–8). Smith and Deemer get into a difficult tangle here, considering the subject of a hypothetical research report containing racist messages, this fact alone, in their view, justifying its suppression.

Up until the bit about unwavering commitment to social justice providing new foundations for researchers which, if interpreted too enthusiastically, contains the potential for oppression, I can live with the relativist position. As someone once said in relation to the philosophical problem of induction, ordinary people do not worry about whether the sun will rise tomorrow, even though philosophers have concluded that there is no logical reason to believe that it must do so just because it has done so every morning up until now. Similarly, I do not think social researchers wanting to produce good-quality work need to be over-concerned with the problem of philosophical foundations, or the lack of them, since the practical task of doing a research project does not require these things to be resolved at the philosophical level. Neither should they be too worried about political correctness, since this can get in the way of creativity just as much as the blind methodological rule-following of the (mythical) positivist.

More constructively, we might ask what researchers can learn from philosophical debate. I think we ought to hold on to the insights of both relativists and subtle realists. Incommensurability at some higher level of logic does not mean that one side has nothing to offer and the other has it all. Factuality may be a fiction, but it appears to be a useful one, and attention to how (constructed) facts relate to (constructed) claims and theories is a widely recognized hallmark of good-quality research. This is because it is the way most people who are not social researchers currently think about the world, and to participate in this widespread language game researchers have to accept its underlying rules if they want to communicate. At the same time, attention to the political context of research, and the role that research knowledge can play in the relief of suffering, seems desirable too. The journey that can be taken through these debates offers practising social researchers valuable perspectives, of considerable help in crafting the next research project.

LEARNING FROM SOCIAL THEORY

The second great area of abstract discourse from which researchers can learn how to construct good-quality work is that of social theory. This position, however, must be immediately qualified by saying that social theorizing also contains the capacity to ruin the research enterprise, so this is very much a two-edged thing.

A great deal of research work goes on, even after Mills's (1959) identification of the problem of 'abstracted empiricism', in an apparently 'atheoretical' fashion. The original charge made by qualitative researchers against the quantitative 'positivist' orthodoxy was, of course, that such researchers proceeded as if their work were theory-free, yet theories and values were implied all the time in the framing of research questions, leading to a loss of critical edge. Thus researchers studying 'juvenile delinquency' (Hirschi and Selvin, 1967) simply by choosing that term to describe the phenomena of interest were applying a very particular and questionable category system; by choosing psychological and social variables to explain the 'causes' of delinquency, the researchers implied an essentialist and deterministic theory of human nature, disturbingly in tune with dominant policy-makers' discourses on youth culture as a social problem. A researcher working from a different theoretical perspective, an 'emotionalist' perhaps (to use the term in the sense of Gubrium and Holstein's, 1997), might have inquired into the perceptions and feelings of the 'delinquents' themselves, and accepted participants' own terms for the behaviour under study. An ethnomethodologist might have investigated how the category of 'delinquent' came to be constructed in interaction, perhaps by looking at court proceedings. A Marxist might have attended to the meaning of delinquent acts as 'resistance' to power. A feminist researcher might have paid more attention to the gendered nature of delinquency, asking research questions from the same 'critical plane' (Harding, 1987: 11) as the 'delinquents' themselves. A poststructuralist discourse analyst might have examined the official construction of delinquency and its causes, perhaps by analysing official documents, media discussions or the research reports of quantitatively minded researchers in order to detect the way in which these promote certain versions at the expense of others.

Clearly, then, social theory can direct the attention of a researcher to some things rather than others, having the advantage of promoting conceptualizations of phenomena that differ from those in common currency in public debates, policy-making circles, and the perceptions of welfare practitioners and others in authority. This is what distinguishes social research from journalism, and gives it an advantage in terms of insight and originality, so it is clearly a general aspect of the quality of social research work.

Yet social theory can also overwhelm the enterprise of social research, encouraging an attitude of mind that is dismissive of the laborious task of constructing careful arguments with adequate supporting evidence and due attention to alternatives. Instead, there arises a superficially impressive mode of discourse that favours complexity and indeterminacy of meaning, ultimately involving little of conclusive weight, often requiring the learning of a fashionable specialist language that serves as much to obscure meanings as to reveal them. Such was the situation faced by Glaser and Strauss in the 1960s

when Parsonian structural functionalism appeared dominant in American sociology, constituting a kind of 'theoretical capitalis(m)' (1967: 10). In revolt against these tendencies, which threatened to relegate qualitative researchers to the role of assistants to social survey workers (who themselves often did little more than verify the hypotheses of grand theorists), Glaser and Strauss famously proposed their scheme for discovering grounded theory. This sought to place the prestigious activity of theorizing in the hands of qualitative researchers who enthusiastically embraced the new, liberating creed. In fact, grounded theory was to become so popular as a legitimizing label that it is nowadays often applied to work that contains no theory at all, using common-sense categories to analyse material in a journalistic style (see Silverman, 1998, 2000).

Nowadays, however, there is a new kind of threat from the excessive dominance of social theory to the quality (and status) of social research work. Students feel obliged to 'theorize' their work, putting energy into ambitious reviews of literature at the expense of applying research skills. Because contemporary social theory and constructionist philosophy of social science have become merged, an illusion has been created that a clever argument will always win the day. 'Facts' are trapped in inverted commas, and no longer enter the intellectual fray without shaming footnotes explaining their dubious provenance. This does not just undermine the quality of social research, it undermines its capacity to exist, and it contributes to the marginalization of the human sciences from constructive participation in public discourse.

LEARNING FROM METHODOLOGY

The contrast between following rules of method and applying the creative, interpretative insights of the scholar has been drawn out rather effectively (if a little unfairly to the methodologist) by Billig (1988). He contrasts dependence on methodological procedures with the 'individual quirkiness' (1988: 200) of the scholar. Through wide reading, creative connections are made by the scholar between different texts, which may include research materials of the sort that methodologists call 'data', such as a political speech. The rule-follower, on the other hand, imagines that the work of interpretation can be given over to non-human procedures. Whereas the scholar analysing a right-wing political speech might trace the intellectual history of conspiracy theory, in which the speech is then located, the methodologist feeds the speech into a computer program to count (reliably) the number of times the word 'conspiracy' occurs. The sensible scholar is sensitive to the fact that a speaker against conspiracy theory would use the word frequently; the foolish methodologist would conclude that frequency reflects the speaker's commitment to the idea. The scholar looks at the context of words; the methodologist is in danger of supplying an obviously incorrect interpretation because of inattention to meaning.

Behind this portrayal (atrocity story?) is an obvious stereotype of quantitative and qualitative approaches to textual analysis. A standard text on quantitative content analysis, for example, begins with the statement 'There is no simple right way to do content analysis' (Weber, 1990: 13), and later points out that 'Words ... classified together need to possess similar connotations in order for the classification to have semantic validity' (1990: 21). But Billig's general point is helpful nevertheless. We have to think about our research while we are doing it if work of good quality is to be produced (Becker, 1998); blindly following methodological rules can close things down and lead to accounts that don't hold up under criticism. I, though, am more hopeful than Billig about the potential for methodology in improving quality. It can do this if researchers learn to read methodological writings as moments of scholarly reflection in a research career that, for the writer, encapsulate some research skills that the writer has learned. These skills may or may not be useful outside their original research context, and readers have to exercise powers of judgement – just like a scholar – when deciding whether to incorporate the ideas into their own practice. Thus the reading of methodology (and going on methods courses) becomes a 'time-out' in a brain gymnasium for social researchers, in which research practitioners engage in quality-strengthening exercises.

I also differ from Billig in my view of quantitative method, since I believe this method, and perhaps more particularly the methodological reflections that arise from it, have a great deal to offer qualitative researchers. When the original methodological writings of the quantitative social research tradition are encountered (rather than experienced through watered-down accounts in textbooks), it becomes clear that these thinkers were profoundly 'scholarly' in Billig's sense, promoting a thoughtful, fallibilistic style of research. Thus Cook and Campbell (1979) in their advice on designing experiments and quasi-experiments note: 'When we use the terms valid

and invalid in the rest of this book, they should always be understood to be prefaced by the modifiers "approximately" or "tentatively"' (Cook and Campbell, 1979: 37). Later, they point out that 'It is our inescapable predicament that we cannot prove a theory' (1979: 22). Their practical advice on research design derives from earlier work by Campbell and Stanley (1966) in which the construction of arguments using numbers was conceived as a process of assessing threats to the validity of arguments, and then designing (always provisional) solutions to these threats through such procedures as creating a control group, or statistically controlling for confounding variables (see, e.g., Rosenberg, 1968). Campbell and Stanley showed validity in the quantitative tradition to be a matter that could never be finally settled by the blind application of some technical procedure. Mishler has explained this very well, in a passage that also points out the importance of the local research context in applying methodological principles:

> Campbell and Stanley [understood] that validity assessments are not assured by following procedures but depend on investigators' judgements of the relative importance of the different 'threats'.... [N]o general, abstract rules can be provided for assessing overall levels of validity. ... These evaluations [of threats] depend, irremediably, on the whole range of linguistic practices, social norms and contexts, assumptions and traditions that the rules had been designed to eliminate ... 'rules' for proper research are not universally applicable [and] are modified by pragmatic considerations. ... (Mishler, 1990: 418)

In fact, the use of the 'threats' requires an imaginative effort by the researcher to enter the minds of potential critics, conducting thought experiments to identify what, in the context of qualitative research, has been identified variously as the 'deviant case' or the 'negative instance' (Becker, 1970; Peräkylä, 1997), accounting for which improves the richness of the eventual account. All of these devices encourage a desirable methodological awareness, setting up an internal dialogue that ensures research findings are presented to their public in as good order as is possible, so that external debate about them can begin at a higher level than might otherwise be the case.

Thus methodological procedures assist an inner dialogue of the researcher that is designed eventually to be continued in a dialogue with an external audience as part of a general commitment to fallibilistic, open-minded debate about the merits of research-based propositions. This commitment to dialogue bears many points of similarity with the ethical dialogic commitments of many contemporary qualitative research practitioners: 'One of the principal lessons of postfoundational epistemology is that we must learn to live with uncertainty, with the absence of final vindication. ... Contingency, fallibilism, dialogue, and deliberation mark our way of being in the world' (Schwandt, 1996: 59).

However, a commitment to producing an external dialogue with users of research is weak when it is not accompanied by advice on how to set up a preceding inner dialogue, a subject that is prone to be neglected if confidence in method- ological procedures has been undermined by philosophical doubts. The application of rigor- ously self-critical research procedures ensures that a research inquiry engages with public debate in a more sophisticated state than com- monly available knowledge, thus having greater potential to move that debate on, should that be what is required. Schwandt, being influenced by anti-methodological arguments, takes the view that it is wrong to insist on the necessity of 'regulative norms for removing doubt and set- tling disputes about what is correct or incorrect, true or false' (1996: 59), associating these with an unhelpfully confrontational relationship with 'parties to the research encounter' (1996: 68). In my view this fails to distinguish between differ- ent audiences of research reports, whose interests may range from opposition to happy alignment. Some of the best research studies are celebrated precisely because – to use the language of foun- dational epistemology for a moment – they demonstrate that the views prevailing in some important party to the research encounter are quite wrong. The ideal that one is seeking after truth is a helpful mental device, just as is the practice of distinguishing facts from theories and description from interpretation, since these things make research possible, and make good- quality research more likely. As Weinberg has observed: 'Though we must forgo the chimera of a fixed gold standard for truth, we need not there- fore distrust that on any actual occasion of dis- pute there will be resources at hand, sufficient for all practical purposes, to determine the most ade- quate among competing accounts' (Weinberg, 2002: 13). Methodology, then, can be understood as helping to provide such resources.

LEARNING FROM PRACTICE

Good methodological writing is the result of thought about research practice, and researchers are in the lucky position of being able to learn from others' practice as well as their own. This can be done by reading others' research reports and seeing what mistakes or clever things may have been done, but may also be possible through reading methodological writing (like the present chapter), as long as plenty of examples are given. Collections of good examples exist in the methodological literature (e.g. Becker, 1998; Seale, 1999) and can be consulted for a fuller account than can be given here. Here I shall con- centrate on an extended example, discussing some of the things done in two research studies that examined the portrayal of cancer in the mass media. It is helpful to be asking three broad ques- tions in assessing the quality of these studies, which I take from Martyn Hammersley (1992). Firstly, we can ask how important or relevant the topic is for some community. Secondly, we can ask whether the claims made are plausible given our existing knowledge about the subject. Thirdly, we can ask whether the credibility of the claims is supported by sufficient evidence. It is, of course, this last point that is the most crucial in determining quality, being the 'inner' dialogue that the researcher must conduct.

The first study

The first study is by Deborah Lupton (1994) on 'Femininity, responsibility, and the technological imperative: discourses on breast cancer in the Australian press'. Analysing three years of Australian newspaper and magazine stories, comprising 960 items, she concludes two things. Firstly, a medical perspective is dominant. Thus, 'hegemonic discourses supporting the institution of medicine are reproduced in a forum such as the popular press' (1994: 83), her analysis demonstrating 'the press's valorization of medical technology, medical practitioners, public health rhetoric, and medical research to the exclusion of the needs, wants, and feelings of women in the general population' (1994: 83).

Secondly, press discourse places women in a double bind. On the one hand, 'Breast cancer [is presented as] retribution for the rejection of motherhood and the traditional feminine role in favor of material success in the working world' (1994: 86). This is done through stories empha- sizing the potential breast cancer risk associated with taking the contraceptive pill, and the protec- tive effect of early childbirth. On the other hand, traditional 'passive' femininity is stigmatized in stories about how an 'active' or 'fighting' atti- tude is more likely to beat the disease. Triumph narratives of 'how I beat breast cancer' are a popular genre. Lupton observes that 'Press accounts served thus to blame women regardless of which role they chose to take: early motherhood seemed protective, but not feminine passiveness; careerism and material achievement were dangerous, but assertiveness was protective' (1994: 78).

Clearly this is an important public issue, relevant to the concerns of both women and health promoters. Studies of the media reporting of breast cancer were rare in 1994, so the study was breaking new ground. On these criteria of quality the topic is relevant and important. Lupton's work on media reporting of this and other health issues has made a significant contribution to critical sociological analysis and practical intervention in this field (e.g. Chapman and Lupton, 1994), previously dominated by the rather narrow perspectives of health educators (see Seale, 2003, for a review). One might say, then, that this piece has considerable potential for a productive external dialogue with research audiences and users. The quality of the inner dialogue, though, is less adequate. We can begin to see the reasons for this in her statements about her methodological orientation, explained in an early passage in the report: '[My] critical analysis ... takes a specifically political stance, revealing how linguistic processes construct and privilege certain definitions and meanings and the processes by which certain interests, norms, values, and opinions receive attention over others. Emphasis is placed on the subtextual rather than the surface meaning of texts' (Lupton, 1994: 73).

On the one hand, this might announce a capacity to see things that less 'critical' researchers would not see. On the other hand, it could be an author giving herself permission to prioritize her political convictions over careful examination of the material. Which way this goes can be evaluated by a critical assessment of links between claims and evidence, as well as how the claims fit with other knowledge about the subject (which in this case has developed since Lupton's study). These reveal flaws.

The first of these is caused by her reluctance to count phenomena, meaning that she is open to the common charge made of qualitative research that the author only presents instances of data that support the claims being made, suppressing negative instances. Thus Lupton states that 'several news items' (1994: 75) linked reproductive choices to breast cancer, and medical treatments and mammography were publicized more than 'other, less invasive ways of dealing with breast cancer' (1994: 79), such as breast self-examination. However, she presents no counts to quantify the precise meaning of 'several' and 'more' and no count of deviant cases where these things were not done in news reports. Such

counting, where it occurs in qualitative research, is usually based on a carefully developed coding or 'indexing' scheme that directs the attention of the analyst to the representation of all instances of data in the research report and helps focus on instances that are hard to index or fit into coding categories. Such a scheme is not mentioned in the report.

Secondly, Lupton's claims involve speculation about the impact of these representations on women, saying that 'Such dramatic headlines and details could only serve to arouse anxiety in women ...' (1994: 78). Yet she presents no audience study of the meaning of the press reports for women. While she acknowledges this towards the end of the piece (calling them 'speculations' and arguing for the importance of audience research), the relevant passages in the body of the report contain no such qualification.

Thirdly, some contradictions are evident in the analysis. She says on the one hand that 'women suffering from breast cancer were rendered largely invisible and passive in this macho medicalized rhetoric' (1994: 81). Yet on the other hand the press (women's magazines in particular) 'were particularly fond of personalizing stories about women's experiences of breast cancer in terms of their triumph over the scourge' (1994: 81). Partly to deal with this contradiction, Lupton claims that such active, triumphant women are presented in the press as 'living examples of the victory of medical intervention' (1994: 84), citing (just two) items in which women were reported as having been saved by both orthodox medical intervention and personal determination.

Here, we can turn to evidence from other studies (done after Lupton's) that contradict this link. These considerations relate to the plausibility of Lupton's analysis in the context of other investigations of the same topic. Closest to Lupton's study in terms of location and time period is a study by McKay and Bonner (1999), who present an analysis of personal narratives of breast cancer in Australian women's magazines between 1994 and 1996, noting that, unlike Lupton's reading of these as linked to an oppressive medical discourse, 'The expansion of the genre may be seen as part of recent contestations over the right of patients to be publicly heard within biomedical discourse' (1999: 564). These authors found that stories of personal recovery often stressed the role played by women's inner resources and local family or community support, downplaying the role of orthodox medical efforts or pharmaceutical treatments. In fact, 'the quality of medical advice included in [the stories] was devalued' (1999: 568) and the authors take the view that the sensationalized reporting of medical misadventures found in these stories could lead to excessive distrust of medicine rather than the 'valorization' that Lupton claims. Contradicting Lupton's view that press discourse excludes the needs, wants and feelings of women, these authors conclude (though also without any evidence from audience studies) that the magazines operate 'as an integral part of so many women's lives … giving coherence and meaning to illness … a means through which … women can benefit' (1999: 570).

My own work on this topic (Seale, 2002), based on an analysis of newspaper stories appearing in 1999 in the world's English-language press (though excluding Australia), compared the stories of women and men with cancer, and found many points of agreement with McKay and Bonner's findings. Breast cancer stories, in particular, were frequently heroic narratives of successful struggle against disease, containing significant components of opposition to orthodox medical authority, often indicated by a celebration of the role played by alternative or complementary therapies in promoting recovery. Reports frequently involved claims that the power of the human spirit to triumph over disease is ignored by conventional medical practitioners. Significant gender differences in these portrayals occurred, with women presented as highly skilled in emotional expression and self-transformation, able to draw on a community of other women and fellow sufferers from the disease. Men, on the other hand, were portrayed using conventional masculine stereotypes, finding it difficult to talk about feelings or get support from other men, drawing on pre-existing strengths of character and generalized masculine 'toughness' to get them through the disease. It seemed to me, therefore, that men were being portrayed as lacking in power. The women in the reports appeared to have quite extraordinary powers.

Another discrepancy with existing evidence are her claims about the alliance of interests between organized medicine and the media. In fact, these two institutions have a history of considerable distrust, as studies of the production of medical soap operas in the US have shown (Turow, 1989). Karpf's (1988) history of relations between the BBC and health professional interests also demonstrates the variable extent to which medical and media interests have been aligned, and the frequency with which they have in fact clashed. This is papered over in Lupton's analysis, in favour of a depiction of institutional conspiracy.

Lupton's study, then, scores highly on the criterion of relevance, but falls down badly on those of credibility and plausibility, largely because links between claims and evidence are not well made. In the terms used by Glaser and Strauss (1967), the account is inadequately 'saturated', something that is 'easily spotted, since the theory associated with it is usually thin and not well integrated, and has too many obvious unexplained exceptions' (1967: 63). Underlying this is the influence of the researcher's pre-existing value position, which has led to a presentation that is biased. There is a weak commitment to the separation of facts and their interpretation, resting presumably on a rejection of this distinction at the philosophical level. A reluctance to support qualitative insights with counting or coding, or to deepen the analysis through consideration of negative instances, stems from the author's rejection of content analysis in favour of critical discourse analysis (see also Lupton, 1999). This appears to give her permission to dispense with the kind of self-critical fallibilism that lies at the heart of the advice on research design and data analysis given by writers like Becker, or Campbell and Stanley (reviewed earlier). Studies done since Lupton's, producing claims diametrically opposed to hers, make it easy to demonstrate the flaws in her methodological procedures.

The second study

We can see how worthwhile the goal of objectivity may be to pursue (whether or not philosophers ever agree on whether it is a feasible thing at an abstract level) by seeing a research study that is demonstrably more credible than Lupton's, but is nevertheless highly relevant to the gender politics that concern Lupton. Because its inner dialogue is in better shape, it is more likely to enter into a productive external dialogue with its audiences. This is a study of a similar topic, this time focusing on media representations of inherited breast cancer, done by Lesley Henderson and Jenny Kitzinger (1999). It is a qualitative study, supported by counting.

Like Lupton, these researchers studied three years of press reports (this time from UK media), gathering 708 of these for analysis. They also studied broadcast media over a shorter period. Unlike Lupton, though, these authors also looked at the production and audience reception of the messages they analysed, interviewing 40 journalists and other media producers and running focus groups with 143 women, among whom were some with personal involvement with breast cancer. Statements about the intentions of message producers, their relationships with sources (such as medical interests) as well as the way in which these messages were interpreted by audiences, could therefore be based on evidence rather than speculation.

In their reporting of media representations, qualitative extracts from news reports were selected on the basis of a systematically applied coding scheme that assigned instances of data to categories according to consistent definitional rules, category assignment being checked by more than one researcher in an attempt to produce a reliable and valid foundation for analysis. This is a procedure developed originally by quantitative content analysts in pursuit of objectivity and replicability, an approach we have seen to be stigmatized by Billig and Lupton for its presumed association with incorrect epistemological views. This procedure allowed a precise count of the risk factors mentioned in press reports, demonstrating the high profile given to genetic factors and inheritance in the causation of breast cancer when compared with other causes that are arguably more important in epidemiological terms. Thus in 152 press reports from the three-year sample in which a risk factor was mentioned, 51 of these involved mention of its genetic cause, more than any other factor apart from age and considerably more frequently than pregnancy or the pill (the factors highlighted by Lupton). The authors were also able to demonstrate that a high proportion of these mentions were in the context of 'human interest' rather than 'hard news' reports, and from their focus group data could show that such human interest stories (for example, a soap opera character or a celebrity with breast cancer) were more influential on audiences than hard news stories about, say, scientific discoveries.

Unlike Lupton, who assumed that newspapers simply reflected medical interests, Henderson and Kitzinger were able to demonstrate significant discrepancies between medical and journalistic interests because they had gathered evidence about journalists' motives, and could demonstrate how these differed from the motives of public health professionals. Breast cancer genetics stories fit in with a populist agenda, as one journalist explained:

> It [breast cancer] is incredibly newsworthy. It will virtually walk into a paper compared to trying to write about other forms of cancer of arguably greater social consequences. ... You only have to go up to the news desk and say 'There is something about breast cancer' and they will say 'We will have it' and 'Go and do it'. (Journalist, quoted in Henderson and Kitzinger, 1999: 569)

Henderson and Kitzinger record their view that public health interests are, in fact, ill served

by this news agenda: 'This is all good news for the media, but the implications may be less welcome for those seeking to promote public understanding of cancer or genetics' (1999: 570). They explain the source of this concern not with speculation about the effects of media representations on audiences, but with evidence. In their focus groups, participants recorded a high level of interest and memory of 'human interest' stories about this topic, many of which featured women who had had prophylactic mastectomies in order to prevent the potential occurrence of this cancer. Although a fuller analysis of audience responses is not given in the paper, being planned for a later publication, there is clearly considerable potential for sensationalistic media presentations to have an adverse influence on women's decision-making and result in a lot of unnecessary surgical mutilation. Thus the findings point to issues that are highly relevant to the political agenda that concerned Lupton.

The authors demonstrate no bias towards a pre-existing set of beliefs, although their choice of research question and topic is one that is likely to have relevance for an understanding of how women's experience is influenced in modern society. They demonstrate no preconceived commitment to either qualitative or quantitative method, being both willing and skilled in their deployment of both where appropriate. They pay considerable attention to the links between claims and evidence and demonstrate an interest in potentially disconfirming evidence (as might have been revealed, for example, had they found that breast cancer genetics was not a risk mentioned particularly frequently in the press, or had they found a widespread alienation from, or resistance to, media messages among audience members). The result is a study that is highly persuasive and begins its life as a public document in good shape for external dialogue.

CONCLUSION

In this chapter I have argued that good-quality research does not depend on the adoption of a particular philosophical or theoretical position, or on the commitment to particular political goals. Consideration of all of these things is relevant for research practice, but it is a mistake to allow any one of them to over-determine practice. For example, a theoretical position can help a researcher perceive things that a common-sense view would ignore; a theoretical position can equally screen out other ways of seeing. Harding (1987) has shown how a self-consciously political position can lead to better research questions than relying on the ones set by people in power, but Lupton's study shows, equally, how this may overwhelm inner dialogue. Social research, in fact, possesses a unique practical logic of its own, relatively autonomous from other spheres, though usefully drawing on these for strength from time to time. This is something I have experienced, and seen others experience.

I have also seen a lot of things that worry me as a research practitioner and teacher of social researchers. One of my biggest worries, and this is reflected in the topics I have chosen to write about in the chapter, is the rejection by some qualitative researchers of the lessons that can be learned for contemporary qualitative research practice from the example and methodological writings of scientifically minded, and quantitatively competent, researchers. Because of the weakening of philosophical justifications that used to be assumed to underpin such scientific practice, social theoretical and political conceptions of the research process have become increasingly dominant, involving stigmatizing and inaccurate depictions of other traditions. This can lead to a lack of respect for the 'otherness' of the material we like to call data and an excessive 'valorization' of partial views (often those based on values that the researcher brings to the project) that determine analytic claims. In a past era I might have been on the side of those developing anti-scientific qualitative alternatives to what was then the dominant orthodoxy that devalued these. Now, however, the anti-science voice is itself an orthodoxy, based on the foundation mythology of qualitative researchers, whose rhetorical force is now spent, whose assumptions need to be challenged, so that some skills that social researchers once knew about can be re-learned.

One of the things that stops me worrying, though, is the knowledge that skilful, good-quality social research studies keep surfacing, their authors having learned their trade through a very widespread kind of apprenticeship system, in which witnessing and reflecting on others' practices leads to their incorporation into their own studies. Naturally, the continued health of the research community that supports this 'trade' depends on a host of political and institutional factors that support, financially and morally, the value of free, open debate. I hope this chapter assists in strengthening your confidence and commitment to this mode of learning, and to social inquiry through research practice.

ACKNOWLEDGEMENTS

1 As well as the assistance of other members of the editorial team of this book, I am grateful for the helpful comments of Thomas Eberle, Martyn Hammersley, Donna Ladkin and Darin Weinberg.

REFERENCES

Becker, H.S. (1964) 'Personal change in adult life', *Sociometry*, 27: 40–53.

Becker, H.S. (1970) 'Fieldwork evidence', in H.S. Becker (ed.), *Sociological Work: Method and Substance*. Chicago: Aldine, pp. 39–62.

Becker, H.S. (1998) *Tricks of the Trade: How to Think About Your Research While You're Doing It*. Chicago: University of Chicago Press.

Billig, M. (1988) 'Methodology and scholarship in understanding ideological explanation', in C. Antaki (ed.), *Analysing Everyday Explanation*. London: Sage, pp. 199–215.

Campbell, D.T. and Stanley, J.C. (1966) *Experimental and Quasi-Experimental Design for Research*. Chicago: Rand McNally.

Chapman, S. and Lupton, D. (1994) *The Fight for Public Health: Principles and Practice of Media Advocacy*. London: British Medical Journal Publishing Group.

Cook, T.D. and Campbell, D.T. (1979) *Quasi-Experimentation: Design and Analysis Issues for Field Settings*. Chicago: Rand McNally.

Glaser, B.G. and Strauss, A.L. (1967) *The Discovery of Grounded Theory: Strategies for Qualitative Research*. Chicago: Aldine.

Guba, E.G. and Lincoln, Y.S. (1989) *Fourth Generation Evaluation*. Newbury Park, CA: Sage.

Guba, E.G. and Lincoln, Y.S. (1994) 'Competing paradigms in qualitative research', in N.K. Denzin and Y.S. Lincoln (eds), *Handbook of Qualitative Research*. Thousand Oaks, CA: Sage, pp. 105–17.

Gubrium, J.F. and Holstein, J.A. (1997) *The New Language of Qualitative Method*. Oxford and New York: Oxford University Press.

Hammersley, M. (1990) *Reading Ethnographic Research: A Critical Guide*. London: Longman.

Hammersley, M. (1992) *What's Wrong With Ethnography: Methodological Explorations*. London: Routledge.

Harding, S. (1987) *Feminism and Methodology*. Bloomington: Indiana University Press; Buckingham: Open University Press.

Henderson, L. and Kitzinger, J. (1999) 'The human drama of genetics: "hard" and "soft" media representations of inherited breast cancer', *Sociology of Health and Illness*, 21(5): 560–78.

Hirschi, T. and Selvin, H.C. (1967) *Delinquency Research: An Appraisal of Analytic Methods*. New York: Free Press/Collier-Macmillan.

Karpf, A. (1988) *Doctoring the Media: The Reporting of Health and Medicine*. London: Routledge.

Lincoln, Y.S. (1995) 'Emerging criteria for quality in qualitative and interpretive inquiry', *Qualitative Inquiry,* 1: 275–89.

Lincoln, Y.S. and Denzin, N.K. (1994) 'The fifth moment', in N.K. Denzin and Y.S. Lincoln (eds), *Handbook of Qualitative Research*. Thousand Oaks, CA: Sage, pp. 575–86.

Lupton, D. (1994) 'Femininity, responsibility, and the technological imperative: discourses on breast cancer in the Australian press', *International Journal of Health Services,* 24(1): 73–89.

Lupton, D. (1999) 'Editorial: health, illness and medicine in the media', *Health*, 3(3): 259–62.

McKay, S. and Bonner, F. (1999) 'Telling stories: breast cancer pathographies in Australian women's magazines', *Women's Studies International Forum*, 22(5): 563–71.

Marcus, G. and Fischer, R. (1986) *Anthropology as Cultural Critique*. Chicago: University of Chicago Press.

Mills, C.W. (1959) *The Sociological Imagination*. Oxford: Oxford University Press.

Mishler, E.G. (1990) 'Validation in inquiry-guided research: the role of exemplars in narrative studies', *Harvard Educational Review*, 60(4): 415–42.

Peräkylä, A. (1997) 'Reliability and validity in research based on tapes and transcripts', in D. Silverman (ed.), *Qualitative Research: Theory, Method and Practice*. London: Sage, pp. 201–20.

Rosenberg, M. (1968) *The Logic of Survey Analysis*. New York: Basic Books.

Schwandt, T.A. (1996) 'Farewell to criteriology', *Qualitative Inquiry*, 2(1): 58–72.

Seale, C.F. (1999) *The Quality of Qualitative Research*. London: Sage.

Seale, C.F. (2002) 'Cancer heroics: a study of news reports with particular reference to gender', *Sociology*, 36(1): 107–26.

Seale, C.F. (2003) *Media and Health*. London: Sage.

Silverman, D. (1998) 'The quality of qualitative health research', *Social Sciences in Health*, 8(1): 104–18.

Silverman, D. (2000) *Doing Qualitative Research: A Practical Handbook*. London: Sage.

Smith, J.K. and Deemer, D.K. (2000) 'The problem of criteria in the age of relativism', in N.K. Denzin and Y.S. Lincoln (eds), *Handbook of Qualitative Research* (2nd ed.). Thousand Oaks, CA: Sage, pp. 877–96.

Turow, J. (1989) *Playing Doctor: Television, Storytelling, and Medical Power*. Oxford and New York: Oxford University Press.

Weber, M. (1948) 'Science as a vocation', from H.H. Gerth and C.W. Mills (eds and trans.), *From Max Weber: Essays in Sociology* (1991 reprint by Routledge), pp. 129–57.

Weber, R.P. (1990) *Basic Content Analysis* (2nd ed.). Newbury Park, CA: Sage.

Weinberg, D. (2002) *Qualitative Research Methods*. Oxford: Blackwell.

27

Five misunderstandings about case-study research

Bent Flyvbjerg

When I first became interested in in-depth case-study research, I was trying to understand how power and rationality shape each other and form the urban environments in which we live (Flyvbjerg, 1998). It was clear to me that in order to understand a complex issue like this, in-depth case-study research was necessary. It was equally clear, however, that my teachers and colleagues kept dissuading me from employing this particular research methodology.

'You cannot generalize from a single case', some would say, 'and social science is about generalizing.' Others would argue that the case study may be well suited for pilot studies but not for full-fledged research schemes. Others again would comment that the case study is subjective, giving too much scope for the researcher's own interpretations. Thus the validity of case studies would be wanting, they argued.

At first, I did not know how to respond to such claims, which clearly formed the conventional wisdom about case-study research. I decided therefore to find out where the claims come from and whether they are correct. This chapter contains what I discovered.

THE CONVENTIONAL WISDOM ABOUT CASE-STUDY RESEARCH

Looking up 'case study' in the *Dictionary of Sociology* as a beginning, I found the following in full citation:

> *Case Study*. The detailed examination of a single example of a class of phenomena, a case study cannot provide reliable information about the broader class, but it

may be useful in the preliminary stages of an investigation since it provides hypotheses, which may be tested systematically with a larger number of cases. (Abercrombie et al., 1984: 34)[1]

This description is indicative of the conventional wisdom of case-study research, which, if not directly wrong, is so oversimplified as to be grossly misleading. It is correct that the case study is a 'detailed examination of a single example', but as we will see below it is not true that a case study 'cannot provide reliable information about the broader class'. It is also correct that a case study *can* be used 'in the preliminary stages of an investigation' to generate hypotheses, but it is misleading to see the case study as a pilot method to be used only in preparing the real study's larger surveys, systematic hypotheses testing, and theory-building.

According to the conventional view, a case and a case study cannot be of value in and of themselves; they need to be linked to hypotheses, following the well-known hypothetico-deductive model of explanation. Mattei Dogan and Dominique Pelassy (1990: 121) put it like this: 'one can validly explain a particular case only on the basis of general hypotheses. All the rest is uncontrollable, and so of no use' (see also Diamond, 1996: 6). Similarly, the early Donald Campbell did not mince words when he relegated single-case studies to the methodological trash heap:

> [S]uch studies have such a total absence of control as to be of almost no scientific value. ... Any appearance of absolute knowledge, or intrinsic knowledge about singular isolated objects, is found to be illusory upon analysis. ... It seems well-nigh unethical at the present time to allow, as theses or dissertations in education,

case studies of this nature (i.e., involving a single group observed at one time only). (Campbell and Stanley, 1966: 6–7)

If you read such criticism of a certain methodology enough times, or if you hear your thesis advisers repeat it, you begin to believe it may be true. This is what happened to me, and it made me uncertain about case-study methodology. As I continued my research, however, I found out that Campbell had later made a 180-degree turn in his views of the case study and had become one of the strongest proponents of this method. I eventually found, with the help of Campbell's later works and other works like them, that the problems with the conventional wisdom about case-study research can be summarized in five misunderstandings or oversimplifications about the nature of such research:

Misunderstanding no. 1. General, theoretical (context-independent) knowledge is more valuable than concrete, practical (context-dependent) knowledge.

Misunderstanding no. 2. One cannot generalize on the basis of an individual case; therefore, the case study cannot contribute to scientific development.

Misunderstanding no. 3. The case study is most useful for generating hypotheses, that is, in the first stage of a total research process, while other methods are more suitable for hypotheses testing and theory-building.

Misunderstanding no. 4. The case study contains a bias towards verification, that is, a tendency to confirm the researcher's preconceived notions.

Misunderstanding no. 5. It is often difficult to summarize and develop general propositions and theories on the basis of specific case studies.

These five misunderstandings indicate that it is theory, reliability and validity that are at issue; in other words, the very status of the case study as a scientific method. In what follows, I shall focus on these five misunderstandings and correct them one by one. First, however, I shall outline the role of cases in human learning.

THE ROLE OF CASES IN HUMAN LEARNING

In order to understand why the conventional view of case-study research is problematic, we need to grasp the role of cases and theory in human learning. Here two points can be made. First, the case study produces the type of context-dependent knowledge that research on learning shows to be necessary to allow people to develop from rule-based beginners to virtuoso experts. Second, in the study of human affairs, there appears to exist only context-dependent knowledge, which thus presently rules out the possibility of epistemic theoretical construction. The full argument behind these two points can be found in Flyvbjerg (2001: chs 2–4). For reasons of space, I can only give an outline of the argument here. At the outset, however, we can assert that if the two points are correct, it will have radical consequences for the conventional view of the case study in research and teaching. This view would then be problematic.

Phenomenological studies of human learning indicate that for adults there exists a qualitative leap in their learning process from the rule-governed use of analytical rationality in beginners to the fluid performance of tacit skills in what Pierre Bourdieu (1977) calls virtuosos and Hubert and Stuart Dreyfus (1986) true human experts. Here we may note that most people are experts in a number of everyday social, technical and intellectual skills like giving a gift, riding a bicycle or interpreting images on a television screen, while only few reach the level of true expertise for more specialized skills like playing chess, composing a symphony or flying a fighter jet.

Common to all experts, however, is that they operate on the basis of intimate knowledge of several thousand concrete cases in their areas of expertise. Context-dependent knowledge and experience are at the very heart of expert activity. Such knowledge and expertise also lie at the centre of the case study as a research and teaching method; or, to put it more generally still, as a method of learning. Phenomenological studies of the learning process therefore emphasize the importance of this and similar methods: it is only because of experience with cases that one can at all move from being a beginner to being an expert. If people were exclusively trained in context-independent knowledge and rules, that is, the kind of knowledge that forms the basis of textbooks and computers, they would remain at the beginner's level in the learning process. This is the limitation of analytical rationality: it is inadequate for the best results in the exercise of a profession, as student, researcher or practitioner.

In a teaching situation, well-chosen case studies can help the student achieve competence, while context-independent facts and rules will bring the student just to the beginner's level. Only a few institutions of higher learning have taken the consequence of this. Harvard University is one of them. Here both teaching and research in the professional schools are modelled to a wide extent on the understanding that case knowledge is central to human learning (Cragg, 1940; Christensen and Hansen, 1987).

At one stage in my research, I was invited to Harvard to learn about case methodology 'in action'. During my stay, it became clear to me that if I was going to aspire to become an expert in my field of expertise, and if I wanted to be an effective help to my students in their learning processes, I would need to master case methodology in research and teaching. My stay at Harvard also became a major step forward in shedding my uncertainties about the conventional wisdom about cases and case studies. At Harvard I found the literature and people who effectively argued, 'Forget the conventional wisdom, go ahead and do a case study'. I figured if it is good enough for Harvard, it is good enough for me, and I suggest others might reason like this, including whole institutions of learning. There is much to gain, for instance, by transforming the lecture format still dominant in most universities to one of case learning (Christensen and Hansen, 1987).

It is not that rule-based knowledge should be discounted: it is important in every area and especially to novices. But to make rule-based knowledge the highest goal of learning is regressive. There is a need for both approaches. The highest levels in the learning process, that is, virtuosity and true expertise, are reached only via a person's own experiences as practitioner of the relevant skills. Therefore, beyond using the case method and other experiential methods for teaching, the best that teachers can do for students in professional programmes is to help them achieve real practical experience; for example, via placement arrangements, internships, summer jobs, and the like.

For researchers, the closeness of the case study to real-life situations and its multiple wealth of details are important in two respects. First, it is important for the development of a nuanced view of reality, including the view that human behaviour cannot be meaningfully understood as simply the rule-governed acts found at the lowest levels of the learning process, and in much theory. Second, cases are important for researchers' own learning processes in developing the skills needed to do good research. If researchers wish to develop their own skills to a high level, then concrete, context-dependent experience is just as central for them as to professionals learning any other specific skills. Concrete experiences can be achieved via continued proximity to the studied reality and via feedback from those under study. Great distance to the object of study and lack of feedback easily lead to a stultified learning process, which in research can lead to ritual academic blind alleys, where the effect and usefulness of research becomes unclear and untested. As a research method, the case study can be an effective remedy against this tendency.

The second main point in connection with the learning process is that there does not and probably cannot exist predictive theory in social science. Social science has not succeeded in producing general, context-independent theory and has thus in the final instance nothing else to offer than concrete, context-dependent knowledge. And the case study is especially well suited to produce this knowledge. In his later work, Donald Campbell (1975: 179) arrives at a similar conclusion, explaining how his work has undergone 'an extreme oscillation away from my earlier dogmatic disparagement of case studies', which was described above. In a logic that in many ways resembles that of the phenomenology of human learning, Campbell now explains:

> After all, man is, in his ordinary way, a very competent knower, and qualitative common-sense knowing is not replaced by quantitative knowing. ... This is not to say that such common-sense naturalistic observation is objective, dependable, or unbiased. But it is all that we have. It is the only route to knowledge – noisy, fallible, and biased though it be. (Campbell, 1975: 179, 191)

Campbell is not the only example of a researcher who has altered his views about the value of the case study. Hans Eysenck (1976: 9), who originally did not regard the case study as anything other than a method of producing anecdotes, later realized that 'sometimes we simply have to keep our eyes open and look carefully at individual cases – not in the hope of proving anything, but rather in the hope of learning something!' Proof is hard to come by in social science because of the absence of 'hard' theory, whereas learning is certainly possible. More recently, similar views have been expressed by Charles Ragin, Howard Becker and their colleagues in explorations of what the case study is and can be in social inquiry (Ragin and Becker, 1992).

As for predictive theory, universals and scientism, the study of human affairs is thus at an eternal beginning. In essence, we have only specific cases and context-dependent knowledge. The first of the five misunderstandings about the case study – that general theoretical (context-independent) knowledge is more valuable than concrete, practical (context-dependent) knowledge – can therefore be revised as follows:

Predictive theories and universals cannot be found in the study of human affairs. Concrete, context-dependent knowledge is therefore more valuable than the vain search for predictive theories and universals.

CASES AS 'BLACK SWANS'

The view that one cannot generalize on the basis of a single case is usually considered to be devastating to the case study as a scientific method. This second misunderstanding about the case study is typical among proponents of the natural science ideal within the social sciences. Yet even researchers who are not normally associated with this ideal may be found to have this viewpoint. According to Anthony Giddens, for example,

> Research which is geared primarily to hermeneutic problems may be of generalized importance in so far as it serves to elucidate the nature of agents' knowledge-ability, and thereby their reasons for action, across a wide range of action-contexts. Pieces of ethnographic research like … say, the traditional small-scale community research of fieldwork anthropology – are not in themselves generalizing studies. But they can easily become so if carried out in some numbers, so that judgements of their typicality can justifiably be made. (Giddens, 1984: 328)

It is correct that one can generalize in the ways Giddens describes, and that often this is both appropriate and valuable. But it would be incorrect to assert that this is the only way to work, just as it is incorrect to conclude that one cannot generalize from a single case. It depends upon the case one is speaking of, and how it is chosen. This applies to the natural sciences as well as to the study of human affairs (see also Platt, 1992; Ragin and Becker, 1992).

For example, Galileo's rejection of Aristotle's law of gravity was not based upon observations 'across a wide range', and the observations were not 'carried out in some numbers'. The rejection consisted primarily of a conceptual experiment and later of a practical one. These experiments, with the benefit of hindsight, are self-evident. Nevertheless, Aristotle's view of gravity dominated scientific inquiry for nearly two thousand years before it was falsified. In his experimental thinking, Galileo reasoned as follows: if two objects with the same weight are released from the same height at the same time, they will hit the ground simultaneously, having fallen at the same speed. If the two objects are then stuck together into one, this object will have double the weight and will according to the Aristotelian view therefore fall faster than the two individual objects.

This conclusion operated in a counter-intuitive way for Galileo. The only way to avoid the contradiction was to eliminate weight as a determinant factor for acceleration in free fall. And that was what Galileo did. Historians of science continue to discuss whether Galileo actually conducted the famous experiment from the leaning tower of Pisa, or whether it is simply a myth. In any event, Galileo's experimentalism did not involve a large random sample of trials of objects falling from a wide range of randomly selected heights under varying wind conditions, and so on, as would be demanded by the thinking of the early Campbell and Giddens. Rather, it was a matter of a single experiment, that is, a case study, if any experiment was conducted at all. (On the relation between case studies, experiments and generalization, see Wilson, 1987; Lee, 1989; Griffin et al., 1991; Bailey, 1992.) Galileo's view continued to be subjected to doubt, however, and the Aristotelian view was not finally rejected until half a century later, with the invention of the air pump. The air pump made it possible to conduct the ultimate experiment, known by every pupil, whereby a coin or a piece of lead inside a vacuum tube falls with the same speed as a feather. After this experiment, Aristotle's view could be maintained no longer. What is especially worth noting in our discussion, however, is that the matter was settled by an individual case due to the clever choice of the extremes of metal and feather. One might call it a critical case: for if Galileo's thesis held for these materials, it could be expected to be valid for all or a large range of materials. Random and large samples were at no time part of the picture. Most creative scientists simply do not work this way with this type of problem.

Carefully chosen experiments, cases and experience were also critical to the development of the physics of Newton, Einstein and Bohr, just as the case study occupied a central place in the works of Darwin, Marx and Freud. In social science, too, the strategic choice of case may greatly add to the generalizability of a case study. In their classic study of the 'affluent worker', John Goldthorpe et al. (1968–9) deliberately looked for a case that was as favourable as possible to the thesis that the working class, having reached middle-class status, was dissolving into a society without class identity and related conflict (see also Wieviorka, 1992). If the thesis could be proved false in the favourable case, then it would most likely be false for intermediate cases. Luton, a prosperous industrial centre with companies known for high wages and social stability – fertile ground for middle-class identity – was selected as a case, and through intensive fieldwork the researchers discovered that even here an autonomous working-class culture prevailed, lending general credence to the thesis of the persistence of class identity. Below we will discuss more systematically this type of strategic sampling.

As regards the relationship between case studies, large samples and discoveries, W.I.B. Beveridge (1951; here quoted from Kuper and Kuper, 1985: 95) observed immediately prior to the breakthrough of the quantitative revolution in the social sciences: '[M]ore discoveries have arisen from intense observation than from statistics applied to large groups.' This does not mean that the case study is always appropriate or relevant as a research method, or that large random samples are without value (see also the Conclusions below). The choice of method should clearly depend on the problem under study and its circumstances.

Finally, it should be mentioned that formal generalization, be it on the basis of large samples or single cases, is considerably overrated as the main source of scientific progress. Economist Mark Blaug (1980) – a self-declared adherent to the hypothetico-deductive model of science – has demonstrated that while economists typically pay lip service to the hypothetico-deductive model and to generalization, they rarely practise what they preach in actual research. More generally, Thomas Kuhn has shown that the most important precondition for science is that researchers possess a wide range of practical skills for carrying out scientific work. Generalization is just one of these. In Germanic languages, the term 'science' (*Wissenschaft*) means literally 'to gain knowledge'. And formal generalization is only one of many ways by which people gain and accumulate knowledge. That knowledge cannot be formally generalized does not mean that it cannot enter into the collective process of knowledge accumulation in a given field or in a society. A purely descriptive, phenomenological case study without any attempt to generalize can certainly be of value in this process and has often helped cut a path towards scientific innovation. This is not to criticize attempts at formal generalization, for such attempts are essential and effective means of scientific development. It is only to emphasize the limitations, which follows when formal generalization becomes the only legitimate method of scientific inquiry.

The balanced view of the role of the case study in attempting to generalize by testing hypotheses has been formulated by Eckstein:

[C]omparative and case studies are alternative means to the end of testing theories, choices between which

must be largely governed by arbitrary or practical, rather than logical, considerations. … [I]t is impossible to take seriously the position that case study is suspect because problem-prone and comparative study deserving of benefit of doubt because problem-free. (Eckstein, 1975: 116, 131, emphasis in original; see also Barzelay, 1993: 305ff.)

Eckstein here uses the term 'theory' in its 'hard' sense, that is, comprising explanation and prediction. This makes Eckstein's dismissal of the view that case studies cannot be used for testing theories or for generalization stronger than my own view, which is here restricted to the testing of 'theory' in the 'soft' sense, that is, testing propositions or hypotheses. Eckstein shows that if predictive theories existed in social science, then the case study could be used to test these theories just as well as other methods.

More recently, John Walton (1992: 129) has similarly observed that 'case studies are likely to produce the best theory'. Eckstein observes, however, the striking lack of genuine theories within his own field, political science, but apparently fails to see why this is so:

Aiming at the disciplined application of theories to cases forces one to state theories more rigorously than might otherwise be done – provided that the application is truly 'disciplined,' i.e., designed to show that valid theory compels a particular case interpretation and rules out others. As already stated, this, unfortunately, is rare (if it occurs at all) in political study. One reason is the lack of compelling theories. (Walton, 1975: 103–4)

The case study is ideal for generalizing using the type of test that Karl Popper called 'falsification', which in social science forms part of critical reflexivity. Falsification is one of the most rigorous tests to which a scientific proposition can be subjected: if just one observation does not fit with the proposition, it is considered not valid generally and must therefore be either revised or rejected. Popper himself used the now famous example of 'All swans are white', and proposed that just one observation of a single black swan would falsify this proposition and in this way have general significance and stimulate further investigations and theory-building. The case study is well suited for identifying 'black swans' because of its in-depth approach: what appears to be 'white' often turns out on closer examination to be 'black'.

Finding black swans was an experience with which I became thoroughly familiar when I did my first in-depth case study, of urban politics and planning in the city of Aalborg, Denmark (Flyvbjerg, 1998). For instance, at university I had been trained in the neoclassical model of 'economic man', competition and free markets.

As I dug into what happened behind closed doors in Aalborg, I found that economic man does not live here. The local business community were power-mongers who were busy negotiating illicit deals with politicians and administrators on how to block competition and the free market and create special privileges for themselves. The neoclassical model was effectively falsified by what I saw in Aalborg. Similarly, the model of representative democracy, which on the surface of things appears to apply, and by law is supposed to apply in Aalborg and Denmark, was strangely absent in the deep detail of the case. Here I found a highly undemocratic, semi-institutionalized way of making decisions, where leaders of the business community and of the city government had formed a secret council, which in actual fact replaced the democratically elected city council as the place where important decisions on urban politics and planning were made. My colleagues in third-world nations, who appear to hold fewer illusions about markets and democracy than academics in the first world, get a good laugh when I tell my Aalborg stories. They see that, after all, we in the North are not so different; we are third-world in some ways too.

We shall return to falsification in discussing the fourth misunderstanding of the case study below. For the present, however, we can correct the second misunderstanding – that one cannot generalize on the basis of a single case and that the case study cannot contribute to scientific development – so that it now reads:

One can often generalize on the basis of a single case, and the case study may be central to scientific development via generalization as supplement or alternative to other methods. But formal generalization is overvalued as a source of scientific development, whereas 'the force of example' is underestimated.

STRATEGIES FOR CASE SELECTION

The third misunderstanding about the case study is that the case method is claimed to be most useful for generating hypotheses in the first steps of a total research process, while hypothesis-testing and theory-building is best carried out by other methods later in the process. This misunderstanding derives from the previous misunderstanding that one cannot generalize on the basis of individual cases. And since this misunderstanding has been revised as above, we can now correct the third misunderstanding as follows:

The case study is useful for both generating and testing of hypotheses but is not limited to these research activities alone.

Eckstein – contravening the conventional wisdom in this area – goes so far as to argue that case studies are better for testing hypotheses than for producing them. Case studies, Eckstein (1975: 80) asserts, 'are valuable at all stages of the theory-building process, but most valuable at that stage of theory-building where least value is generally attached to them: the stage at which candidate theories are tested'. Testing of hypotheses relates directly to the question of 'generalizability', and this in turn relates to the question of case selection.

Here generalizability of case studies can be increased by the strategic selection of cases (on the selection of cases, see further Rosch, 1978; Ragin, 1992). When the objective is to achieve the greatest possible amount of information on a given problem or phenomenon, a representative case or a random sample may not be the most appropriate strategy. This is because the typical or average case is often not the richest in information. Atypical or extreme cases often reveal more information because they activate more actors and more basic mechanisms in the situation studied. In addition, from both an understanding-oriented and an action-oriented perspective, it is often more important to clarify the deeper causes behind a given problem and its consequences than to describe the symptoms of the problem and how frequently they occur. Random samples emphasizing representativeness will seldom be able to produce this kind of insight; it is more appropriate to select some few cases chosen for their validity.

Table 27.1 summarizes various forms of sampling. The *extreme case* can be well suited for getting a point across in an especially dramatic way, which often occurs for well-known case studies such as Freud's 'Wolf-Man' and Foucault's 'Panopticon'. In contrast, a *critical case* can be defined as having strategic importance in relation to the general problem. For example, an occupational medicine clinic wanted to investigate whether people working with organic solvents suffered brain damage. Instead of choosing a representative sample among all those enterprises in the clinic's area that used organic solvents, the clinic strategically located a single workplace where all safety regulations on cleanliness, air quality and the like had been fulfilled. This model enterprise became a critical case: if brain damage related to organic solvents could be found at this particular facility, then it was likely that the same problem would exist at

Table 27.1 *Strategies for the selection of samples and cases*

Type of selection	purpose
A. Random selection	To avoid systematic biases in the sample. The sample's size is decisive for generalization.
1 Random sample	To achieve a representative sample that allows for generalization for the entire population.
2 Stratified sample	To generalize for specially selected sub-groups within the population.
B. Information-oriented selection	To maximize the utility of information from small samples and single cases. Cases are selected on the basis of expectations about their information content.
1 Extreme/deviant cases	To obtain information on unusual cases, which can be especially problematic or especially good in a more closely defined sense.
2 Maximum variation cases	To obtain information about the significance of various circumstances for case process and outcome, e.g. three to four cases that are very different on one dimension: size, form of organization, location, budget, etc.
3 Critical cases	To achieve information that permits logical deductions of the type, 'if this is (not) valid for this case, then it applies to all (no) cases'.
4 Paradigmatic cases	To develop a metaphor or establish a school for the domain that the case concerns.

other enterprises that were less careful with safety regulations for organic solvents. Via this type of strategic choice, one can save both time and money in researching a given problem. Another example of critical case selection is the above-mentioned strategic selection of lead and feather for the test of whether different objects fall with equal velocity. The selection of materials provided the possibility to formulate a generalization characteristic of critical cases, a generalization of the sort, 'If it is valid for this case, it is valid for all (or many) cases'. In its negative form, the generalization would be, 'If it is not valid for this case, then it is not valid for any (or only few) cases'.

How does one identify critical cases? This question is more difficult to answer than the question of what constitutes a critical case. Locating a critical case requires experience, and no universal methodological principles exist by which one can with certainty identify a critical case. The only general advice that can be given is that when looking for critical cases, it is a good idea to look for either 'most likely' or 'least likely' cases, that is, cases that are likely to either clearly confirm or irrefutably falsify propositions and hypotheses. This is what I thought I was doing when planning the Aalborg case study mentioned above (Flyvbjerg, 1998). I was mistaken, however, but to my chagrin I did not

realize this until I was halfway through the research process. Initially, I conceived of Aalborg as a 'most likely' critical case in the following manner: if rationality and urban planning were weak in the face of power in Aalborg, then, most likely, they would be weak anywhere, at least in Denmark, because in Aalborg the rational paradigm of planning stood stronger than anywhere else. Eventually I realized that this logic was flawed, because my research of local relations of power showed that one of the most influential 'faces of power' in Aalborg, the Chamber of Industry and Commerce, was substantially stronger than their equivalents elsewhere. This had not been clear at the outset because much less research existed on local power relations than research on local planning. Therefore, instead of a critical case, unwittingly I ended up with an extreme case in the sense that both rationality and power were unusually strong in Aalborg, and my case study became a study of what happens when strong rationality meets strong power in the arena of urban politics and planning. But this selection of Aalborg as an extreme case happened to me, I did not deliberately choose it. It was a frustrating experience when it happened, especially during those several months from when I realized I did not have a critical case until it became clear that all was not lost because I had something else. As a case researcher charting new terrain one must be prepared for such incidents, I believe.

A model example of a 'least likely' case is Robert Michels's (1962) classical study of oligarchy in organizations. By choosing a horizontally structured grass-roots organization with strong democratic ideals – that is, a type of organization with an especially low probability of being oligarchical – Michels could test the universality of the oligarchy thesis, that is, 'If this organization is oligarchic, so are most others'. A corresponding model example of a 'most likely' case is W.F. Whyte's (1943) study of a Boston slum neighbourhood, which according to existing theory should have exhibited social disorganization, but in fact showed quite the opposite (see also the articles on Whyte's study in *Journal of Contemporary Ethnography*, 21(1), 1992).

Cases of the 'most likely' type are especially well suited to falsification of propositions, while 'least likely' cases are most appropriate to tests of verification. It should be remarked that a most likely case for one proposition is the least likely for its negation. For example, Whyte's slum neighbourhood could be seen as a least likely case for a hypothesis concerning the universality of social organization. Hence, the identification of a case as most or least likely is linked to the design of the study, as well as to the specific properties of the actual case.

A final strategy for the selection of cases is choice of the *paradigmatic case*. Thomas Kuhn has shown that the basic skills, or background practices, of natural scientists are organized in terms of 'exemplars', the role of which can be studied by historians of science. Similarly, scholars like Clifford Geertz and Michel Foucault have often organized their research around specific cultural paradigms: a paradigm for Geertz lay for instance in the 'deep play' of the Balinese cockfight, while for Foucault, European prisons and the 'Panopticon' are examples. Both instances are examples of paradigmatic cases, that is, cases that highlight more general characteristics of the societies in question. Kuhn has shown that scientific paradigms cannot be expressed as rules or theories. There exists no predictive theory for how predictive theory comes about. A scientific activity is acknowledged or rejected as good science by how close it is to one or more exemplars, that is, practical prototypes of good scientific work. A paradigmatic case of how scientists do science is precisely such a prototype. It operates as a reference point and may function as a focus for the founding of schools of thought.

As with the critical case, we may ask, 'How does one identify a paradigmatic case?' How does one determine whether a given case has metaphorical and prototypical value? These questions are even more difficult to answer than for the critical case, precisely because the paradigmatic case transcends any sort of rule-based criteria. No standard exists for the paradigmatic case because it sets the standard. Hubert and Stuart Dreyfus see paradigmatic cases and case studies as central to human learning. In an interview with Hubert Dreyfus (author's files), I therefore asked what constitutes a paradigmatic case and how it can be identified. Dreyfus replied:

> Heidegger says, you recognize a paradigm case because it shines, but I'm afraid that is not much help. You just have to be intuitive. We all can tell what is a better or worse case – of a Cézanne painting, for instance. But I can't think there could be any rules for deciding what makes Cézannne a paradigmatic modern painter. ... [I]t is a big problem in a democratic society where people are supposed to justify what their intuitions are. In fact, nobody really can justify what their intuition is. So you have to make up reasons, but it won't be the real reasons.

One may agree with Dreyfus that intuition is central to identifying paradigmatic cases, but one may disagree that it is a problem to have to justify one's intuitions. Ethnomethodological studies of scientific practice have demonstrated that all variety of such practice relies on taken-for-granted procedures that feel largely intuitive. However, those intuitive decisions are accountable, in the sense of being sensible to other practitioners or often explicable if not immediately sensible. That would frequently seem to be the case with the selection of paradigmatic cases. We may select such cases on the basis of taken-for-granted, intuitive procedures but are often called upon to account for that selection. That account must be sensible to other members of the scholarly communities of which we are part. This may even be argued to be a general characteristic of scholarship, scientific or otherwise, and not unique to the selection of paradigmatic social scientific case studies. For instance, it is usually insufficient to justify an application for research funds by stating that one's intuition says that a particular research should be carried out. A research council ideally operates as society's test of whether the researcher can account, in collectively acceptable ways, for his or her intuitive choice, even though intuition may be the real, or most important, reason why the researcher wants to execute the project.

It is not possible consistently, or even frequently, to determine in advance whether or not a given case – Geertz's cockfights in Bali, for instance – is paradigmatic. Besides the strategic choice of case, the execution of the case study will certainly play a role, as will the reactions to the study by the research community, the group studied and, possibly, a broader public. The value of the case study will depend on the validity claims that researchers can place on their study, and the status these claims obtain in dialogue with other validity claims in the discourse to which the study is a contribution. Like other good craftsmen, all that researchers can do is use their experience and intuition to assess whether they believe a given case is interesting in a paradigmatic context, and whether they can provide collectively acceptable reasons for the choice of case.

Finally, concerning considerations of strategy in the choice of cases, it should be mentioned that the various strategies of selection are not necessarily mutually exclusive. For example, a case can be simultaneously extreme, critical and paradigmatic. The interpretation of such a case can provide a unique wealth of information, because one obtains various perspectives and conclusions on the case according to whether it is viewed and interpreted as one or another type of case.

DO CASE STUDIES CONTAIN A SUBJECTIVE BIAS?

The fourth of the five misunderstandings about case-study research is that the method maintains a bias towards verification, understood as a tendency to confirm the researcher's preconceived notions, so that the study therefore becomes of doubtful scientific value. Diamond (1996: 6), for example, holds this view. He observes that the case study suffers from what he calls a 'crippling drawback', because it does not apply 'scientific methods', by which Diamond understands methods useful for 'curbing one's tendencies to stamp one's pre-existing interpretations on data as they accumulate'.

Francis Bacon (1853: xlvi) saw this bias towards verification not simply as a phenomenon related to the case study in particular, but as a fundamental human characteristic. Bacon expressed it like this:

> The human understanding from its peculiar nature, easily supposes a greater degree of order and equality in things than it really finds. When any proposition has been laid down, the human understanding forces everything else to add fresh support and confirmation. It is the peculiar and perpetual error of the human understanding to be more moved and excited by affirmatives than negatives.

Bacon certainly touches upon a fundamental problem here, a problem that all researchers must deal with in some way. Charles Darwin (1958: 123), in his autobiography, describes the method he developed in order to avoid the bias towards verification:

> I had … during many years followed a golden rule, namely, that whenever a published fact, a new observation or thought came across me, which was opposed to my general results, to make a memorandum of it without fail and at once; for I had found by experience that such facts and thoughts were far more apt to escape from the memory than favorable ones. Owing to this habit, very few objections were raised against my views, which I had not at least noticed and attempted to answer.

The bias towards verification is general, but the alleged deficiency of the case study and other qualitative methods is that they ostensibly allow more room for the researcher's subjective and arbitrary judgement than other methods: they are often seen as less rigorous than are quantitative, hypothetico-deductive methods. Even if such criticism is useful, because it sensitizes us to an important issue, experienced case researchers cannot help but see the critique as demonstrating a lack of knowledge of what is involved in case-study research. Donald Campbell and others have shown that the critique is fallacious, because the case study has its own rigour, different to be sure, but no less strict than the rigour of quantitative methods. The advantage of the case study is that it can 'close in' on real-life situations and test views directly in relation to phenomena as they unfold in practice.

According to Campbell, Ragin, Geertz, Wieviorka, Flyvbjerg and others, researchers who have conducted intensive, in-depth case studies typically report that their preconceived views, assumptions, concepts and hypotheses were wrong and that the case material has compelled them to revise their hypotheses on essential points. The case study forces upon the researcher the type of falsifications described above. Ragin (1992: 225) calls this a 'special feature of small-N research', and goes on to explain that criticizing single-case studies for being inferior to multiple-case studies is misguided, since even single-case studies 'are multiple in most research efforts because ideas and evidence may be linked in many different ways'.

Geertz (1995: 119) says about the fieldwork involved in most in-depth case studies that 'The Field' itself is a 'powerful disciplinary force: assertive, demanding, even coercive'. Like any such force, it can be underestimated, but it cannot be evaded. 'It is too insistent for that', says

Geertz. That he is speaking of a general phenomenon can be seen by simply examining case studies, as Eckstein (1975), Campbell (1975) and Wieviorka (1992) have done. Campbell discusses the causes of this phenomenon in the following passage:

> In a case study done by an alert social scientist who has thorough local acquaintance, the theory he uses to explain the focal difference also generates prediction or expectations on dozens of other aspects of the culture, and he does not retain the theory unless most of these are also confirmed. … Experiences of social scientists confirm this. Even in a single qualitative case study, the conscientious social scientist often finds no explanation that seems satisfactory. Such an outcome would be impossible if the caricature of the single case study … were correct – there would instead be a surfeit of subjectively compelling explanations. (Campbell, 1975: 181–2)

According to the experiences cited above, it is falsification and not verification that characterizes the case study. Moreover, the question of subjectivism and bias towards verification applies to all methods, not just to the case study and other qualitative methods. For example, the element of arbitrary subjectivism will be significant in the choice of categories and variables for a quantitative or structural investigation, such as a structured questionnaire to be used across a large sample of cases. And the probability is high that (1) this subjectivism survives without being thoroughly corrected during the study and (2) that it may affect the results, quite simply because the quantitative/structural researcher does not get as close to those under study as does the case-study researcher and therefore is less likely to be corrected by the study objects 'talking back'. According to Ragin:

> this feature explains why small-N qualitative research is most often at the forefront of theoretical development. When N's are large, there are few opportunities for revising a casing [that is, the delimitation of a case]. At the start of the analysis, cases are decomposed into variables, and almost the entire dialogue of ideas and evidence occurs through variables. One implication of this discussion is that to the extent that large-N research can be sensitized to the diversity and potential heterogeneity of the cases included in an analysis, large-N research may play a more important part in the advancement of social science theory. (Ragin, 1992: 225; see also Ragin, 1987: 164–71)

Here, too, this difference between large samples and single cases can be understood in terms of the phenomenology for human learning discussed above. If one thus assumes that the goal of the researcher's work is to understand and learn about the phenomena being studied, then research is simply a form of learning. If one assumes that research, like other learning processes, can be described by the phenomenology for human learning, it then becomes clear that the most advanced form of understanding is achieved when researchers place themselves within the context being studied. Only in this way can researchers understand the viewpoints and the behaviour that characterizes social actors. Relevant to this point, Giddens states that valid descriptions of social activities presume that researchers possess those skills necessary to participate in the activities described: 'I have accepted that it is right to say that the condition of generating descriptions of social activity is being able in principle to participate in it. It involves "mutual knowledge", shared by observer and participants whose action constitutes and reconstitutes the social world' (Giddens, 1982: 15).

From this point of view, the proximity to reality that the case study entails, and the learning process that it generates for the researcher, will often constitute a prerequisite for advanced understanding. In this context, one begins to understand Beveridge's conclusion that there are more discoveries stemming from the type of intense observation made possible by the case study than from statistics applied to large groups. With the point of departure in the learning process, we understand why the researcher who conducts a case study often ends up by casting off preconceived notions and theories. Such activity is quite simply a central element in learning and in the achievement of new insight. More simple forms of understanding must yield to more complex ones as one moves from beginner to expert.

On this basis, the fourth misunderstanding – that the case study supposedly contains a bias towards verification, understood as a tendency to confirm the researcher's preconceived ideas – is revised as follows:

> *The case study contains no greater bias towards verification of the researcher's preconceived notions than other methods of inquiry. On the contrary, experience indicates that the case study contains a greater bias towards falsification of preconceived notions than towards verification.*

THE IRREDUCIBLE QUALITY OF GOOD CASE NARRATIVES

Case studies often contain a substantial element of narrative. Good narratives typically approach the complexities and contradictions of real life. Accordingly, such narratives may be difficult or impossible to summarize into neat scientific formulae, general propositions, and theories (Roth, 1989; Benhabib, 1990; Rouse, 1990; White, 1990; Mitchell and Charmaz, 1996). This tends to be seen by critics of the case study as a drawback. To the case-study researcher, however, a particularly 'thick' and hard-to-summarize narrative is not a problem. Rather, it is often a sign that the study has uncovered a particularly rich problematic. The question, therefore, is whether the summarizing and generalization, which the critics see as an ideal, is always desirable. Nietzsche (1974: 335 [§ 373]) is clear in his answer to this question. 'Above all,' he says about doing science, 'one should not wish to divest existence of its *rich ambiguity*' (emphasis in original).

In doing the Aalborg study, I tried to capture the rich ambiguity of politics and planning in a modern democracy. I did this by focusing in depth on the particular events that made up the case and on the minutiae that made up the events. Working with minutiae is time-consuming, and I must concede that during the several years when I was toiling in the archives, doing interviews, making observations, talking with my informants, writing, and getting feedback, a nagging question kept resurfacing in my mind. This is a question bound to haunt many carrying out in-depth, dense case studies: 'Who will want to learn about a case like this, and in this kind of *detail*?' I wanted the Aalborg case study to be particularly dense because I wished to test the thesis that the most interesting phenomena in politics and planning, and those of most general import, would be found in the most minute and most concrete of details. Or to put the matter differently, I wanted to see whether the dualisms general–specific and abstract–concrete would metamorphose and vanish if I went into sufficiently deep detail. Richard Rorty has perceptively observed that the way to re-enchant the world is to stick to the concrete. Nietzsche similarly advocates a focus on 'little things'. Both Rorty and Nietzsche seem right to me. I saw the Aalborg case as being made up of the type of concrete, little things they talk about. Indeed, I saw the case itself as such a thing, what Nietzsche calls a discreet and apparently insignificant truth, which, when closely examined, would reveal itself to be pregnant with paradigms, metaphors and general significance. That was my thesis, but theses can be wrong and case studies may fail. I was genuinely relieved when, eventually, the strategy of focusing on minutiae proved to be worth the effort.

Lisa Peattie (2001: 260) explicitly warns against summarizing dense case studies: 'It is simply that the very value of the case study, the contextual and interpenetrating nature of forces, is lost when one tries to sum up in large and mutually exclusive concepts.' The dense case study, according to Peattie, is more useful for the practitioner and more interesting for social theory than either factual 'findings' or the high-level generalizations of theory.

The opposite of summing up and 'closing' a case study is to keep it open. Here I have found the following two strategies to work particularly well in ensuring such openness. First, when writing up a case study, I demur from the role of omniscient narrator and summarizer. Instead, I tell the story in its diversity, allowing the story to unfold from the many-sided, complex and sometimes conflicting stories that the actors in the case have told me. Second, I avoid linking the case with the theories of any one academic specialization. Instead I relate the case to broader philosophical positions that cut across specializations. In this way I try to leave scope for readers of different backgrounds to make different interpretations and draw diverse conclusions regarding the question of what the case is a case of. The goal is not to make the case study be all things to all people. The goal is to allow the study to be different things to different people. I try to achieve this by describing the case with so many facets – like life itself – that different readers may be attracted, or repelled, by different things in the case. Readers are not pointed down any one theoretical path or given the impression that truth might lie at the end of such a path. Readers will have to discover their own path and truth inside the case. Thus, in addition to the interpretations of case actors and case narrators, readers are invited to decide the meaning of the case and to interrogate actors' and narrators' interpretations in order to answer that categorical question of any case study:'What is this case a case of?'

Case stories written like this can neither be briefly recounted nor summarized in a few main results. The case story is itself the result. It is a 'virtual reality', so to speak. For the reader willing to enter this reality and explore it inside and out, the payback is meant to be a sensitivity to the issues at hand that cannot be obtained from theory. Students can safely be let loose in this kind of reality, which provides a useful training ground with insights into real-life practices that academic teaching often does not provide.

If we return briefly to the phenomenology for human learning, we may understand why summarizing case studies is not always useful and may sometimes be counterproductive. Knowledge at the beginner's level consists precisely in the reduced formulas that characterize theories, while true expertise is based on intimate experience with thousands of individual cases and on the ability to discriminate between situations, with all their nuances of difference, without distilling them into formulas or standard cases. The problem is analogous to the inability of heuristic, computer-based expert systems to approach the level of virtuoso human experts, even when the systems are compared with the experts who have conceived the rules upon which these systems operate. This is because the experts do not use rules but operate on the basis of detailed case experience. This is *real* expertise. The rules for expert systems are formulated only because the systems require it; rules are characteristic of expert *systems*, but not of real human *experts*.

In the same way, one might say that the rule formulation that takes place when researchers summarize their work into theories is characteristic of the culture of research, of researchers, and of theoretical activity, but such rules are not necessarily part of the studied reality constituted by Bourdieu's (1977: 8, 15) 'virtuoso social actors'. Something essential may be lost by this summarizing – namely the possibility to understand virtuoso social acting, which, as Bourdieu has shown, cannot be distilled into theoretical formulas – and it is precisely their fear of losing this 'something', that makes case researchers cautious about summarizing their studies. Case researchers thus tend to be sceptical about erasing phenomenological detail in favour of conceptual closure.

Ludwig Wittgenstein shared this scepticism. According to Gasking and Jackson, Wittgenstein used the following metaphor when he described his use of the case-study approach in philosophy:

> In teaching you philosophy I'm like a guide showing you how to find your way round London. I have to take you through the city from north to south, from east to west, from Euston to the Embankment and from Piccadilly to the Marble Arch. After I have taken you many journeys through the city, in all sorts of directions, we shall have passed through any given street a number of times – each time traversing the street as part of a different journey. At the end of this you will know London; you will be able to find your way about like a born Londoner. Of course, a good guide will take you through the more important streets more often than he takes you down side streets; a bad guide will do the opposite. In philosophy I'm a rather bad guide. (Gasking and Jackson, 1967: 51)

This approach implies exploring phenomena first-hand instead of reading maps of them. Actual practices are studied before their rules,

and one is not satisfied by learning only about those parts of practices that are open to public scrutiny; what Erving Goffman (1963) calls the 'backstage' of social phenomena must be investigated, too, like the side streets that Wittgenstein talks about.

With respect to intervention in social and political affairs, Abbott (1992: 79) has rightly observed that a social science expressed in terms of typical case narratives would provide 'far better access for policy intervention than the present social science of variables'. MacIntyre (1984: 216) similarly says, 'I can only answer the question "What am I to do?" if I can answer the prior question "Of what story or stories do I find myself a part?"' Several observers have noted that narrative is an ancient method and perhaps our most fundamental form for making sense of experience (Novak, 1975: 175; Mattingly, 1991: 237; see also Arendt, 1958; Ricoeur, 1984; Carr, 1986; Abbott, 1992; Fehn et al., 1992; Rasmussen, 1995; Bal, 1997).

To MacIntyre (1984: 214, 216), the human being is a 'story-telling animal', and the notion of a history is as fundamental a notion as the notion of an action. In a similar vein, Mattingly (1991: 237) points out that narratives not only give meaningful form to experiences we have already lived through. They also provide us a forward glance, helping us to anticipate situations even before we encounter them, allowing us to envision alternative futures. Narrative inquiries do not – indeed, cannot – start from explicit theoretical assumptions. Instead, they begin with an interest in a particular phenomenon that is best understood narratively. Narrative inquiries then develop descriptions and interpretations of the phenomenon from the perspective of participants, researchers and others.

Labov and Waletzky (1966: 37–9) write that when a good narrative is over 'it should be unthinkable for a bystander to say, "So what"?' Every good narrator is continually warding off this question. A narrative that lacks a moral that can be independently and briefly stated, is not necessarily pointless. And a narrative is not successful just because it allows a brief moral. A successful narrative does not allow the question to be raised at all. The narrative has already supplied the answer before the question is asked. The narrative itself is the answer (Nehamas, 1985: 163–4).

A reformulation of the fifth misunderstanding, which states that it is often difficult to summarize specific case studies into general propositions and theories, thus reads as follows:

It is correct that summarizing case studies is often difficult, especially as concerns case process. It is less correct as regards case outcomes. The problems in summarizing case studies, however, are due more often to the properties of the reality studied than to the case study as a research method. Often it is not desirable to summarize and generalize case studies. Good studies should be read as narratives in their entirety.

It must again be emphasized that, despite the difficulty or undesirability of summarizing case studies, the case-study method in general can certainly contribute to the cumulative development of knowledge; for example, in using the principles to test propositions described above under the second and third misunderstandings.

CONCLUSIONS

Today, when students and colleagues present me with the conventional wisdom about case-study research – for instance, that one cannot generalize on the basis of a single case or that case studies are arbitrary and subjective – I know what to answer. By and large, the conventional wisdom is wrong or misleading. For the reasons given above, the case study is a necessary and sufficient method for certain important research tasks in the social sciences, and it is a method that holds up well when compared to other methods in the gamut of social science research methodology.

Let me reiterate, however, that this conclusion, and the revision of the five misunderstandings described above, should not be interpreted as a rejection of research that focuses on large random samples or entire populations; for example, questionnaire surveys with related quantitative analysis. This type of research is also essential for the development of social science; for example, in understanding the degree to which certain phenomena are present in a given group or how they vary across cases. The advantage of large samples is breadth, while their problem is one of depth. For the case study, the situation is the reverse. Both approaches are necessary for a sound development of social science.

Here as elsewhere, the sharp separation often seen in the literature between qualitative and quantitative methods is a spurious one. The separation is an unfortunate artefact of power relations and time constraints in graduate training; it is not a logical consequence of what graduates and scholars need to know to do their studies and do them well. In my interpretation, good social science is opposed to an either/or and stands for a both/and on the question of qualitative versus quantitative methods. Good social science is problem-driven and not methodology-driven, in

the sense that it employs those methods that for a given problematic best help answer the research questions at hand. More often than not, a combination of qualitative and quantitative methods will do the task best. Fortunately, there seems currently to be a general relaxation in the old and unproductive separation of qualitative and quantitative methods.

This being said, it should nevertheless be added that the balance between case studies and large samples is currently biased in favour of the latter in social science, so biased that it puts case studies at a disadvantage within most disciplines. In this connection, it is worth repeating the insight of Thomas Kuhn that a discipline without a large number of thoroughly executed case studies is a discipline without systematic production of exemplars, and that a discipline without exemplars is an ineffective one. In social science, more good case studies could help remedy this situation.

NOTE

1   The quotation is from the original first edition of the dictionary (1984). In the third edition (1994), a second paragraph has been added about the case study. The entry is still highly unbalanced, however, and still promotes the mistaken view that the case study is hardly a methodology in its own right, but is best seen as subordinate to investigations of larger samples.

REFERENCES

Abbott, Andrew (1992) 'What do cases do? Some notes on activity in sociological analysis', in Charles C. Ragin and Howard S. Becker (eds), *What is a Case? Exploring the Foundations of Social Inquiry*. Cambridge: Cambridge University Press, pp. 53–82.

Abercrombie, Nicolas, Hill, Stephen and Turner, Bryan S. (1984) *Dictionary of Sociology*. Harmondsworth: Penguin.

Arendt, Hannah (1958) *The Human Condition*. Chicago: University of Chicago Press.

Bacon, Francis (1853) *Novum Organum*, in *The Physical and Metaphysical Works of Lord Bacon*, book 1. London: H.G. Bohn.

Bailey, Mary Timney (1992) 'Do physicists use case studies? Thoughts on public administration research', *Public Administration Review*, 52(1): 47–54.

Bal, Mieke (1997) *Narratology: Introduction to the Theory of Narrative* (2nd ed.). Toronto: University of Toronto Press.

Barzelay, Michael (1993) 'The single case study as intellectually ambitious inquiry', *Journal of Public Administration Research and Theory*, 3(3): 305–18.

Benhabib, Seyla (1990) 'Hannah Arendt and the redemptive power of narrative', *Social Research*, 57(1): 167–96.

Beveridge, W.I.B. (1951) *The Art of Scientific Investigation*. London: William Heinemann.

Blaug, Mark (1980) *The Methodology of Economics: Or How Economists Explain*. Cambridge: Cambridge University Press.

Bourdieu, Pierre (1977) *Outline of a Theory of Practice*. Cambridge: Cambridge University Press.

Campbell, Donald T. (1975) 'Degrees of freedom and the case study', *Comparative Political Studies*, 8(1): 178–91.

Campbell, Donald T. and Stanley, J.C. (1966) *Experimental and Quasi-Experimental Designs for Research*. Chicago: Rand McNally.

Carr, D. (1986) *Time, Narrative, and History*. Bloomington: Indiana University Press.

Christensen, C. Roland and Hansen, Abby J. (eds) (1987) *Teaching and the Case Method*. Boston: Harvard Business School Press.

Cragg, Charles I. (1940) 'Because wisdom can't be told', *Harvard Alumni Bulletin*. Harvard Business School Reprint 451-005, pp. 1–6.

Darwin, Charles (1958) *The Autobiography of Charles Darwin*. New York: Norton.

Diamond, Jared (1996) 'The roots of radicalism', *The New York Review of Books*, 14 November, pp. 4–6.

Dogan, Mattei and Pelassy, Dominique (1990) *How To Compare Nations: Strategies in Comparative Politics* (2nd ed.). London: Chatham House.

Dreyfus, Hubert, Dreyfus, Stuart with Athanasiou, Thomas (1986) *Mind Over Machine: The Power of Human Intuition and Expertise in the Era of the Computer*. New York: Free Press.

Eckstein, Harry (1975) 'Case study and theory in political science', in Fred J. Greenstein and Nelson W. Polsby (eds), *Handbook of Political Science*, vol. 7. Reading, MA.: Addison-Wesley, pp. 79–137.

Eysenck, H.J. (1976) 'Introduction', in H.J. Eysenck (ed.), *Case Studies in Behaviour Therapy*. London: Routledge & Kegan Paul.

Fehn, Ann, Hoestery, Ingeborg and Tatar, Maria (eds) (1992) *Neverending Stories: Toward a Critical Narratology*. Princeton, NJ: Princeton University Press.

Flyvbjerg, Bent (1998) *Rationality and Power: Democracy in Practice*. Chicago: University of Chicago Press.

Flyvbjerg, Bent (2001) *Making Social Science Matter: Why Social Inquiry Fails and How It Can Succeed Again*. Cambridge: Cambridge University Press.

Gasking, D.A.T. and Jackson, A.C. (1967) 'Wittgenstein as a teacher', in K.T. Fann (ed.), *Ludwig Wittgenstein: The Man and His Philosophy*. Sussex: Harvester Press, pp. 49–55.

Geertz, Clifford (1995) *After the Fact: Two Countries, Four Decades, One Anthropologist*. Cambridge, MA: Harvard University Press.

Giddens, Anthony (1982) *Profiles and Critiques in Social Theory*. Berkeley: University of California Press.

Giddens, Anthony (1984) *The Constitution of Society: Outline of the Theory of Structuration*. Cambridge: Polity Press.

Goffman, Erving (1963) *Behavior in Public Places: Notes on the Social Organization of Gatherings*. New York: Free Press.

Goldthorpe, John, Lockwood, David, Beckhofer, Franck and Platt, Jennifer (1968–9) *The Affluent Worker*, vols 1–3. Cambridge: Cambridge University Press.

Griffin, Larry J., Botsko, Christopher, Wahl, Ana-Maria and Isaac, Larry W. (1991) 'Theoretical generality, case particularity: qualitative comparative analysis of trade union growth and decline', in Charles C. Ragin (ed.), *Issues and Alternatives in Comparative Social Research*. Leiden: E.J. Brill, pp. 110–36.

Kuper, Adam and Kuper, Jessica (eds) (1985) *The Social Science Encyclopedia*. London: Routledge & Kegan Paul.

Labov, William and Waletzky, Joshua (1966) 'Narrative analysis: oral versions of personal experience', in *Essays on the Verbal and Visual Arts: Proceedings of the American Ethnological Society*. Seattle: American Ethnological Society, pp. 12–44.

Lee, Allen S. (1989) 'Case studies as natural experiments', *Human Relations,* 42(2): 117–37.

MacIntyre, Alasdair (1984) *After Virtue: A Study in Moral Theory* (2nd ed.). Notre Dame, IN: University of Notre Dame Press.

Mattingly, Cheryl (1991) 'Narrative reflections on practical actions: two learning experiments in reflective story-telling', in Donald A. Schön (ed.), *The Reflective Turn: Case Studies in and on Educational Practice*. New York: Teachers College Press, pp. 235–57.

Michels, Robert (1962) *Political Parties: A Study of the Oligarchical Tendencies of Modern Democracy*. New York: Collier Books.

Mitchell, Richard G. Jr and Charmaz, Kathy (1996) 'Telling tales, writing stories: postmodernist visions and realist images in ethnographic writing', *Journal of Contemporary Ethnography*, 25(1): 144–66.

Nehamas, Alexander (1985) *Nietzsche: Life as Literature*. Cambridge, MA: Harvard University Press.

Nietzsche, Friedrich (1974) *The Gay Science*. New York: Vintage Books.

Novak, M. (1975) '"Story" and experience', in J.B. Wiggins (ed.), *Religion as Story*. Lanham, MD: University Press of America.

Peattie, Lisa (2001) 'Theorizing planning: some comments on Flyvbjerg's *Rationality and Power*', *International Planning Studies*, 6(3): 257–62.

Platt, Jennifer (1992) '"Case study" in American method-ological thought', *Current Sociology*, 40(1): 17–48.

Ragin, Charles C. (1987) *The Comparative Method: Moving Beyond Qualitative and Quantitative Strategies*. Berkeley: University of California Press.

Ragin, Charles C. (1992) '"Casing" and the process of social inquiry', in Charles C. Ragin and Howard S. Becker (eds), *What is a Case? Exploring the Foundations of Social Inquiry*. Cambridge: Cambridge University Press, pp. 217–26.

Ragin, Charles C. and Becker, Howard S. (eds) (1992) *What is a Case? Exploring the Foundations of Social Inquiry*. Cambridge: Cambridge University Press.

Rasmussen, David (1995) 'Rethinking subjectivity: narrative identity and the self', *Philosophy and Social Criticism*, 21(5–6): 159–72.

Ricoeur, Paul (1984) *Time and Narrative*. Chicago: University of Chicago Press.

Rosch, Eleanor (1978) 'Principles of categorization', in Eleanor Rosch and Barbara B. Lloyd (eds), *Cognition and Categorization*. Killsdale, NJ: Lawrence Erlbaum, pp. 27–48.

Roth, Paul A. (1989) 'How narratives explain', *Social Research*, 56(2): 449–78.

Rouse, Joseph (1990) 'The narrative reconstruction of science', *Inquiry*, 33(2): 179–96.

Walton, John (1992) 'Making the theoretical case', in Charles C. Ragin and Howard S. Becker (eds), *What is a Case? Exploring the Foundations of Social Inquiry*. Cambridge: Cambridge University Press, pp. 121–37.

White, Hayden (1990) *The Content of the Form: Narrative Discourse and Historical Representation*. Baltimore: Johns Hopkins University Press.

Whyte, W.F. (1943) *Street Corner Society: The Social Structure of an Italian Slum*. Chicago: University of Chicago Press.

Wieviorka, Michel (1992) 'Case studies: history or sociology?' in Charles C. Ragin and Howard S. Becker (eds), *What is a Case? Exploring the Foundations of Social Inquiry*. Cambridge: Cambridge University Press, pp. 159–72.

Wilson, Barbara (1987) 'Single-case experimental designs in neuro-psychological rehabilitation', *Journal of Clinical and Experimental Neuropsychology*, 9(5): 527–44.

28

Sampling, representativeness and generalizability

Giampietro Gobo

Sampling in qualitative research has had a hard time. On the one hand, it has been long neglected by many qualitative researchers as a mere positivistic worry; on the other hand, it has been undervalued by survey researchers because of the use of non-probability methods. Qualitative researchers often maintain that qualitative research does not need to sample or to consider seriously sampling issues, arguing that the most theoretically significant and important studies in field research (accomplished by Gouldner, Dalton, Becker, Goffman, Garfinkel, Cicourel, Sudnow and so on) were based on opportunistic samples. This argument may lead to the idea that thinking about issues of sampling, representativeness and generalizability is a waste of time. However, defining sampling units clearly before choosing cases is essential in order to avoid messy and empirically shallow research. As a matter of fact, in contemporary organizational research the problem of representativeness is a constant and growing concern of many researchers. In addition, traditional qualitative researchers often forget that sampling is an unavoidable consideration because it is, first of all, an everyday life activity deeply rooted in thought, language and practice.

On the other hand, survey researchers have often disqualified qualitative research because it is based on non-probability samples. Their reasoning, expressed in numerous research methods texts, lies in the following logic:

1 *only surveys and polls use representative samples;*
2 *to be representative a sample needs to be drawn up using probability methods;*
3 *as qualitative research is based on non-probability samples, its samples are not representative;*

4 *only findings from a representative sample are automatically generalizable to the population;*
5 *(therefore) representativeness leads to generalizability;*
6 *if research is not carried out on a representative sample, its findings are not generalizable;*
7 *findings of qualitative researchers are not generalizable.*

These sentences have become such commonplaces that they form an undisputed part of most researchers' background assumptions. However, survey researchers do not realize that in social science (as I shall show later) probability samples are achieved very rarely because of a number of theoretical and practical reasons (such as the nature of social or cultural objects, the lack of a population list for most variables, the phenomenon of non-response, and so on). This implies that it is in survey research as well that issues of sampling, representativeness and generalizability need to be reframed in a new perspective.

For decades, field and survey researchers avoided each other and failed to respect the scientific credentials of their respective works. However, recently a conciliatory offer has been made by some qualitative researchers, legitimating both ways of doing research by stating that there are two kinds of generalizations: a generalization about a specific group or population (which aims at estimating the distribution in a population) and a generalization about the nature of a process. Sampling requirements are completely different in the two cases. The former generalization, which is implemented in a survey or a poll, is based on statistical logic; the latter, applied in field research, is based on the notion of 'theoretical sampling' (Glaser and Strauss, 1967).

To make clearer the difference between these two kinds of generalization, some authors have called the second one 'transferability' (Guba, 1981), 'analytical generalization' (Yin, 1984), 'extrapolation' (Alasuutari, 1995) and 'moderate generalization' (Williams, 2002). While this offer was welcome and undoubtedly wise from a political point of view, it seems not to solve completely the theoretical and practical problems involved in notions of representativeness and generalizability.

In this chapter I shall try to follow an alternative path, in search of more adequate answers to the two main linked questions usually raised in social research:

1   How do we know to which extent our cases (sample) are representative of all members of the population from which the cases were selected?
2   Can we generalize from a few cases (a sample) to a population without following a purely statistical logic?

To understand this complex matter, several progressive analytical steps will be followed. First, some (misleading) commonplaces on which statistical sampling is grounded will be deconstructed, showing how probability samples are rarely achievable in survey research. Second, the theoretical legitimacy of non-probability samples will be described. As a matter of fact, experiments (reckoned by many scientists as the best possible examples of scientific procedure) are not based on probability samples. Third, the research practice of disciplines (such as palaeontology, ethology, biology, astronomy, anthropology, cognitive science, linguistics, and so on) whose scientific work is based on few cases, will be considered to see if we can learn something useful for qualitative social research.

In order to answer the first question, we need to go back to the core problem of representativeness: the variance of the phenomenon under study. In social studies representativeness is often a practical matter, hardly ever an outcome of automatic (statistical) procedures, which are often useless (as well as difficult to implement) because in social research we look at the social significance of samples instead of a statistical logic.

In order to answer the second question as listed above, we need to distinguish two analytically different problems that are usually confused with one another: the representativeness of *samples* and the generalizability of *findings*. Offering these issues as two sides of the same coin neglects the existing social space between these two activities. In the social process that starts with the creation of a representative sample and ends with the generalization of findings, the researchers' activity is constantly driven by biases and organizational obstacles.

Issues of sampling, representativeness and generalizability need to be faced in a practical way, quite differently from the abstract way usually suggested in textbooks where methodological principles and rules stand on their own with only a weak relation to practice. On the contrary, it is necessary to approach the whole question of sampling sequentially because it is misleading to plan the whole strategy before starting. In order to obtain representativeness, the sampling plan needs to exist in dialogue with field incidents, contingencies and discoveries.

Some of these issues will be discussed through an (invented) dialogue between a teacher and a class. The content of this conversation is a collection of questions, doubts, observations and objections that I encountered several times when teaching research methods over a long period of time.

Setting: a professor (P) with students (S) in a class

P: Today we'll talk about how to sample.
S1:   Are we going to taste some wine?
Class: ha ha ha (*laughing*)
P: What? … Oh yeah, I get it. If I think it over … in fact it's not a silly joke … it has some truth.

          I told you in earlier weeks that there are many links between ordinary language and scientific language, or between common sense and scientific knowledge. This is just another case.

SAMPLING IN EVERYDAY LIFE

P: Before becoming a scientific procedure sampling probably was, and still is, a practical activity of daily life: the cook takes one macaroni out of the pot to know if the pasta is ready to be served; the buyer tastes to choose a wine or a cheese; the teacher asks a student some questions to assess his or her knowledge on the whole syllabus. In everyday life social actors sample constantly. If we refer to traditional classifications of knowledge (see Frege, 1892; Peirce, 1902; Gomperz, 1905; Ogden and Richards, 1923; Morris, 1938; Whorf, 1956; Popper, 1972; Marradi, 1994), which divide it in three worlds (see Figure 28.1), we notice that there are sampling activities in all three worlds.

With regard to thought, cognitive psychologists Kahneman and Tversky showed that human beings use particular ways of reasoning called 'heuristics'. One of these is the *heuristic of representativeness* (Kahneman and Tversky, 1972; Tversky and Kahneman, 1974), that is, people's tendency to generalize based upon a few observed characteristics or events. With regard to the world of language, the same function is performed, as Becker (1998) has stated, by 'synecdoche, a rhetorical figure in which we use a part for something to refer the listener or reader to the whole it belongs to' (1998: 67). Finally, in the world of action the representative function is performed by the sample. The seller shows a sample of cloth to the customer; in a paint shop the buyer skims through the catalogue of shading colours in order to choose a paint.

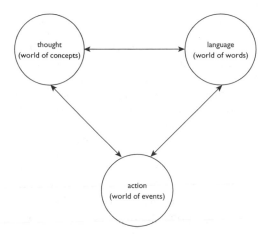

Figure 28.1   *The three worlds of knowledge.*

FROM EVERYDAY LIFE TO SCIENCE

P: Yes, please (*seeing a student with a raised hand*).
S2:   But we don't know if they are representative … it could be a fake or damaged piece of cloth.
P: Wait, wait … you are going too fast. Before arriving at this point we first need to define a sample.

After having specified a population, the researcher decides if he or she will collect information on all its individuals (complete enumeration) or on a sub-set only (sample). So the sample is just a subset of cases. Nevertheless, it might also be one case only. Various scientific disciplines use one case as sample: geologists with a fossil or a fragment of stone, palaeontologists with fragments of skull, bones or a skeleton, archaeologists with ornaments

or grave goods specimens, and so on. As Becker states:

> Archeologists and paleontologists have this problem to solve when they uncover the remnants of a now-vanished society. They find some bones, but not a whole skeleton; they find some cooking equipment, but not the whole kitchen; they find some garbage, but not the stuff of which the garbage is the remains. They know that they are lucky to have found the little they have, because the world is not organized to make life easy for archeologists. So they don't complain about having lousy data. (Becker, 1998: 70–1)

S2:   Yes, but still they do not know if these samples are representative …
P: This concerns the *nature* of the outcome (the sample) and the associated process for obtaining it, not the outcome itself. We'll face this issue in a few minutes. For now the only thing you have to remember is that *the process or procedure employed to select cases (e.g. a random one) has nothing to do with the concept of sampling itself.* They are two separate issues.

SAMPLING IN SOCIAL SCIENCE

P: One important question is that of why we sample.

Sampling was not always dominant in social sciences. Once it was common to select the whole population of residents (a census), car owners, magazine subscribers, people in the phone directory, and so on. The main problem of this method was not the difficulty of reaching the whole population, but the difficulty of obtaining feedback because many of them did not send back mailed questionnaires.[1] However, at that time researchers trusted in the 'law of large numbers', that is, if you have collected a great number of cases (it doesn't matter how big is the related population) you are all right and do not have to worry. However, today we can state that those studies were not, in a strict sense, studies of populations but of … samples, that is, sub-sets formed by people who participated through their answers.

S1:   So what's new about the proposal about sampling from the statisticians George Gallup and Elmo Roper, the two 'bad guys' who forecast correctly the 1936 US presidential election? Samples were, even though unconsciously and against researchers' intentions, used also before 1936!

P: Yes and no. You are right in pointing out that the change was not from the population method to the sampling method. However, the change was in the *nature* of samples. In the population studies, samples were always an *output* of the failure of recruiting participants; in the subsequent studies, samples were a rational and deliberate *input*. Researchers wanted to 'rule the game' (that is, to decide who to contact and how many) instead of waiting for participants to decide whether to answer a mailed questionnaire.

S1:   That's it?

P: No, of course. There were other major advantages to this new method of recruiting participants, such as lower costs, saved time, and fewer human resources needed to contact them. However, in the whole business there is one enormous disadvantage, which troubled statisticians for long time: a sample will always be a sub-set of a population.

S2:   What does that mean?

P: It means that a sample always has a drawback. The idea of a sample was born from the material impossibility of examining the whole population (see Pinto, 1964: 623; Galtung, 1967: 51; Perrone, 1977: 71). Also, Popper's refutability and falsification principles are based on such a recognition of the impossibility of the ideal of checking and controlling all members of a specified population. We wish we could do it but we cannot. Also, when this is needed, as in a census, some residents are always missing. For example, the 1990 US census failed to include about 10 million residents and double counted about 6 million others – for a total net undercount of 4 million people.[2] So for the 2000 census the US Census Bureau decided to use scientifically proven statistical methods to account for non-respondents. A paradox!

S3:   How can we overcome this problem?

P: There is no way to get out of it even though natural scientists believe that it is possible through the idea of the representativeness of a sample.

S1:   Thank God! Finally we arrive at the point of representativeness…

P: Yes, but you will have many surprises.
      The sampling procedures in use in social sciences come from biology. This was made possible by the positivistic climate of the beginning of the twentieth century when social disciplines, in order to be scientific, imported language and procedures from natural sciences. It was a bad period and its consequences unfortunately are still present. Anyway the first problem, long and well debated, arises from this emulation of natural science. Many authors have observed that biology or physics differ from social science in the nature of their units of analysis (Goode and Hatt, 1952: 327): a Russian chemist has no doubt that his or her atom of nitrogen acts in the same way as the atom of nitrogen of his or her Japanese or French colleague; however, no human being is similar to another one. So the presupposition of homogeneity, on which sampling in natural science is based, does not work in social

science because individuals are not interchangeable in the same way as atoms of nitrogen or little balls in a box.

S2: Is that all?

S3: It is an old criticism based on an abstract argument and has been solved anyway by survey researers!

P: I will show later on that these problems have never been solved but only swept under the carpet. For the next few minutes I want to stay on the abstract level, as you said, because statistical principles are abstract and there are many other theoretical pitfalls in treating social sciences as if these were a branch of mechanics.

DO SURVEYS AND POLLS USE REPRESENTATIVE SAMPLES?

P: We previously made the important distinction between a representative sample and a sample. Let us go back to the cook, the buyer and the teacher.

They focus on a part to infer information about the whole because they think that the part (the sample) is representative of the whole (the population). While one macaroni drawn from the boiling pot may look like the others, answering some questions correctly does not necessarily mean the student knows the whole syllabus. As a matter of fact it is crucial to differentiate between a representative sample (a sub-set that is a *miniature* of the population) and a sample (a sub-set of cases the researcher focuses on during any research). While one macaroni is a representative sample, the student's answers might be only a sample.

Strictly speaking, using representative samples is plausible if there is no doubt that they mirror the characteristics of the population.

S3: Let us say that researchers aim at obtaining generalizable findings: how can they be sure that the sample they are focusing on is also representative?

P: There are two different ways (or criteria) to check this: inductive and deductive. But ... before describing those I need to make a digression ...

S1: Oh boy! How long it is taking to see the end of this tunnel!

P: Hey hey hey ... It's not my fault if in the past methodologists have complicated things instead of solving them.

My digression relates to the concept of probability. In many textbooks of methodology it has been written that for a sample to be representative it needs to be based on probability methods. On this basis they have disqualified qualitative research.

Usually such textbooks distinguish between probability samples (simple random, systematic, proportional stratified, non-proportional stratified, multistage cluster) and non-probability samples (haphazard or convenience, purposive sampling, snowball) used by qualitative research. As for the latter, Bailey (1978: 115) says that the evident drawback of non-probability sampling is that, as the researcher does not know each subject's probability of being selected, usually she or he cannot state that his or her sample is representative of the population. This reduces the possibility of generalizing the findings beyond the sample in use; non-probability sampling can only be adequate if the researcher does not aim at generalizing his or her findings beyond the sample.

S3: It seems to me quite reasonable what Bailey said.

P: Yes, it could be ... but only if it is possible in practice to work also with a probability sample. Let's see an example. You did this calculation several times in maths or statistics classes: when rolling a dice, what is the probability of the number two appearing in one throw only?

S2: One in six.

P: Right! To make this calculation you need to know in advance the whole range of alternatives, that is, the *population* of the number of the die. In social science it is the same. Firstly, in a simple random sample, to know the probability if each person really has the same probability of being included in the sample the researcher has to know this probability (no matter whether each individual will be chosen or discarded). Secondly, to make sure someone is not missed during the selection, the researcher needs a complete list of the population, that is, to know exactly the number of cases within the population.

The first drawback: the list of population

According to statistical criteria, we now realize we cannot go on without the complete population list. It means that in order to know if the sample actually mirrors the characteristics of the population, 'you need to know empirically (for these characteristics) both the sample and the population' (Marradi, 1989: 53). As Bailey (1978: 108–14) says, random selection is possible if we have accurate information about the distribution of the statuses among the characteristics of the population, which we try to re-create proportionally in the sample using probability criteria.

As a matter of fact, finding a complete population list is often difficult and sometimes impossible because the list is not available, so that simple random sampling is seldom applied in surveys. At registry offices, at town halls or in electoral registers, complete lists of the population are available, but they record only a small number of characteristics, mainly socio-demographic. For most of the sub-sets of population or the characteristics sociology is interested in (emotions, attitudes or behaviours), these lists are not available. As Corbetta points out: 'how can we obtain a random sample of unemployed people … if we do not have the whole list of unemployed people?' (1999: 332). Many unemployed people register for work at employment agencies, yet not all of them have registered. Thus:

> a population list is not available for most of studies of special groups of people. Let us think about studies of blue collar workers, the unemployed, people who work at home, artists, immigrants, housewives, pensioners, sports team supporters, churchgoers, members of political movements, volunteers who do social work, elderly people who live alone, cohabitants and so on. (Corbetta, 1999: 333)[3]

TROUBLE WITH SYSTEMATIC SAMPLING

Survey researchers say that the alternative to simple random sampling is *systematic sampling*.

It consists of choosing an individual (even without a population list) at pre-set k intervals, obtaining random samples. There is only one condition: the whole population must be gathered in one place only, so that the researcher can choose at regular intervals the individuals who will be included in the sample. This procedure is in widespread use in areas such as the quality control of handmade products, exit polls, market research, and surveys of visitors to museums, cinemas and theatres. Even this is quite difficult as in social sciences it is not always possible to gather all the individuals with the characteristic (or characteristics) observed in one place to select them. Therefore, when there is no population list (or an equivalent that allows the researcher to reach the whole population theoretically), we have to give up using probability sampling procedures. As a matter of fact, each individual of the population cannot have the same probability of being selected.

The significance of this argument is even greater when we think of other more dynamic units: as we do not know how characteristics concerning emotions, attitudes, opinions and behaviour are distributed in the population, aiming at statistical representativeness of samples is technically groundless. Is there a population list on authoritative or unselfish behaviour?

The argument in favour of the implementation of probability sampling in social sciences is theoretically weak because it works only when the population is known.[4] But what do we do when the population is infinite or unknown?

Three problems in statistical sampling theory

Statisticians state that probability sampling is applied only when the size of the population is unknown. The method helps to find quantitative estimates (parameters) that are unknown in the population and to determine the sample size, even though we do not know the magnitude of the population. It estimates the variance of a variable (for example churchgoers) in the population. This method comes from classical statistics and is based on sampling theory, involving the theorem of the central limit. However, in social sciences the application of this method involves problems.

SAMPLE SIZE ASSOCIATED WITH THE NUMBER OF VARIABLES First, such a sample size is valid only when doing a univariate analysis (an analysis focused on one variable only). If we want to carry out a bivariate (two variables) or multivariate (three or more variables) analysis, to determine the sample size we should make a calculation that takes account of each variable. The sample is therefore bound to increase, otherwise when analysing the data some cells might lack cases. However, according to Sudman (1983: 157), this occurs often: while it is rare that published studies have an insufficient sample if considered in their totality, in multivariate analysis samples have to be subdivided and in most of such subdivisions samples are inadequate (see also Capecchi, 1972: 50–1).

THE PROBLEM OF THE NON-TRANSFERABILITY OF THE LOGIC OF REPRESENTATIVENESS   Secondly, following the previous argument, representativeness has to be achieved on each variable of the research. Capecchi (1972: 50–1) exemplified clearly that in an interview with 80 questions (consequently with 80 variables), representativeness has to be achieved for each of them. However, if we follow the statistical method recommended in sampling theory we would need an enormous sample. But nobody does it. What survey researchers really do (in order to construct a sample that claims to be a miniature of the population) is to estimate the variance of a few variables only, usually socio-demographic ones (such as gender, age, education, political vote, residency and a few others) of which we know truly the population parameters from previous censuses. But what about the remaining 70 or so variables regarding attitudes, behaviours, feelings where we do not know their distribution in the population? As stated by Marradi (1989: 60), representativeness cannot be transferred from one variable to another.

Let us look at a trivial example: if survey researchers aim to study sexual behaviour (a variable whose distribution in the population is unknown), they usually construct a (claimed) representative sample based upon the 'gender' variable, that is, they choose some men and some women. They calculate the variance of sexual behaviour by looking at the two values (male and female) of the gender variable. But this is not *behaviour*; it is gender! In other words, we cannot study behaviour indirectly through a representative sample constructed on the basis of the gender variable. Indeed, the category 'sexual behaviour' has at least six sub-categories: heterosexual, homosexual, bisexual, abstinence, mostly heterosexual and mostly homosexual. The idea according to which a sample that is representative of some socio-demographic characteristics is automatically representative of psychological features (or behaviours or opinions) is highly problematic.

SOCIETY IS NOT RANDOM   Another assumption of statistics is that cases are distributed at random in the population. However, as Gilli (1971: 230ff.) reminds us, society is not random. There is no evidence that the sampling assumptions underlying natural sciences (i.e. that cases are interchangeable because they are *equal* and *distributed at random* in the population) works well in social sciences. On the contrary, in society almost nothing is at random: for example, there are social inequalities affecting people's position in the population.

Probability sampling equalizes the chance of every case, including the odd ones, turning up. This seems, sociologically speaking, nonsense because not every person has the same relevance in society. We need a probability sample if we study a topic such as the political vote, where everybody counts: one head, one vote. However, when we study political behaviours not everybody counts in the same way: leaders, some politicians and their advisers, lobbies, minorities, financial supporters count more than voters. If we study black minorities, we do not consider Martin Luther King or Malcolm X to be on the same level as others; however, random sampling does this. More than thirty years ago Capecchi said: 'we can state without any doubt that no national or regional sociological research based on interviews has ever used a representative sample that follows the rigorous consequences of statistical logic' (1972: 53).

THE PHENOMENON OF NON-RESPONSE

Following the logic of statistical theory it would seem that, at least, polls on a few socio-demographic variables might be done with representative samples. If this is true in theory, practice shows that another drawback always lies in wait: non-response. As Marradi points out:

> the concept of random selection is theoretically very simple and, thanks to the ideal-typical image of the box, quite clear to public opinion. However this clarity is misleading ... human beings differ from balls in the box on two features: they are not at the researcher's hand ... and they are free to decide not to answer. (1989: 78)

We have to take into account the gap (which varies according to the research project) between the *initial* sample (all the individuals about whom we want to collect information) and the *final* sample (the cases we managed to get information on): 'the two sets may correspond but usually a part of objects of the first sample is not gathered' (Gasperoni and Marradi, 1996: 628).

The phenomenon of non-response is composed of three different aspects:

1   Lack of contact with the person who had been selected (because she or he has moved, is unknown at that address, not there at the moment, ill, a prisoner, dead, or for other reasons).
2   Refusal to be interviewed.
3   Refusal to fill in the whole questionnaire if there are questions considered too sensitive by the respondent. In Italy these missing answers may vary from 5 per cent up to 60 per cent, especially on questions concerning income (Gobo, 1997: 177).

Usually there is about a 30 per cent non-response with peaks of 50–60 per cent. This would not be a serious problem if the 70 per cent taking part in the poll were similar to the people who refused; in this case the representativeness of the sample would not be jeopardized. But in practice quite the reverse often occurs: those who refuse to take part in the poll are not a random sub-set of the sample (Marradi, 1989: 73–6). As Kish (1965: 558) states, replacing non-responses is often a mistake because substitutes are like those who accepted to be interviewed rather than those who refused to answer. Non-responses may have systematically different statistical distributions compared to interviewed people concerning their main socio-demographic characteristics (Castellano and Herzel, 1971, 302; Marradi, 1989; Brehm, 1993: 17). Non-response makes non-random a sample chosen at random. This brings about serious distortions of the univariate characteristic values such as mean and variance and of bivariate and multivariate coefficients.

However, survey researchers have found a remedy: weighting. As a matter of fact, in order to obtain a representative sample, some criteria have been developed to weight the answers of the interviewed people who, on some socio-demographic characteristics, are similar to those who have not been reached by interviewers or have refused the interview. However, this process seems too artificial and quite arbitrary (Pitrone, 1984: 149–50; Marradi, 1989: 68–78). Indeed, statisticians avoid it and suggest doing the analysis on actually collected data only.

If according to survey methodologists Converse and Schuman (1974: 40) the 20 per cent is a reasonable amount of missing data and does not jeopardize the representativeness of the sample, it has to be stressed that we are far from working on representative samples. As survey methodologists Groves and Lyberg (1988: 191) pointed out, non-response error threatens the survey's unique characteristic compared

to other research methods: the statistical inference from sample to population. If the sample strays from the probability model, nothing can be said about its general representativeness, that is about the fact that it truly reproduces all the characteristics of the population.

REPRESENTATIVENESS IN QUALITATIVE RESEARCH

S3:   This detailed argument leads to a sort of nihilism because it seems impossible to do research with representative samples …

P: Don't be too pessimistic. The aim was only to show that the criticisms by survey methodologists of qualitative research are exaggerated because in most of their studies not even probability samples are what they are claimed to be. In addition, I rejected the forced choice, as some scholars portray it, between an (approximately) random sample and a totally subjective one, or between a partial probability sample and a sample whose representativeness we cannot be sure of. This false dilemma does not take into account an alternative path, which can be developed by thinking radically differently about the problem of representativeness in social science …

S2:   In which way?

P: First, admitting that the most important studies in qualitative research, which produced significant theories, were based on non-probability samples: Gouldner (1954) observed one small gypsum extraction and refining factory located close to his university, so this was a haphazard sample; Dalton (1959) did a study at Milo and Fruhling, two companies in a highly industrialized area in the US; Becker (1951) studied many dance musicians; anthropologist De Martino (1961) observed 21 people suffering from tarantism disease; ethnomethodologists Sudnow (1967) and Cicourel (1968) observed two hospitals and two police districts respectively; Goffman (1963) analysed various interactions between various people.

S3:   Does this mean that thinking about issues of sampling, representativeness and generalizability is a waste of time?

P: That is a good point! Many qualitative researchers think as you.

However, defining the sampling unit clearly (which comes before choosing the cases and thus picking the sample) is important in order to avoid messy and empirically shallow research. During their analysis of some Finnish studies of 'artists', Mitchell and Karttunen (1991) noticed different findings according to the definition of artist employed by the researchers. Some studies included in the category 'artist' only those who defined themselves as artists; in other cases, only those who created durable works of art were included; in other cases, only those who were considered artists by the whole community; and in yet other studies, those who were registered by artists' associations. A comparison is therefore nonsense.

S1: So we need to sample with accuracy ...

P: Yes, and fortunately the problem of representativeness is a constant and growing concern of many young qualitative researchers.

S4: But how do we know the extent to which our cases (the sample) are representative of all members of the population from which the cases are selected?

S5: Can we generalize from cases-study findings to a population without following a purely statistical logic?

P: You have raised two important questions that until now have not been solved by qualitative methodologists.

First of all, in order to produce persuasive answers, we need to keep these two questions separate. Putting them together belongs to an old way of framing the problem. Methodologists too often equate representativeness and generalizability, forgetting that the former characterizes *samples* only and the latter concerns *findings*. We shall see this clearly later.

SAMPLING UNITS

P: Let us start with sampling units and then look at their representativeness.

In sociology and political science the main trend is choosing clearly defined and easily detectable individual or collective units: persons, households, groups, associations, movements, parties, institutions, organizations, regions and states. The consistency of these collective subjects is not very real. In practice, members of these groups are interviewed individually: the head of the family, the human resources manager, the statistical department manager, and so on. This means that the *sampling* unit is different from the *observational* unit (i.e. the respondent). Only a focus group can (at least in part) preserve the integrity of the collective subject. On the other hand, as Galtung (1967: 37) stated, choosing individuals implies an atomistic view of society, whose structural elements are taken for granted or reckoned to be mirrored in the individual (which means neglecting the sociological tradition that gives priority to relations instead of individuals).

S1: What is the alternative?

P: Other, more dynamic units are wrongly neglected:

- beliefs, attitudes, stereotypes, opinions;
- emotions, motivations;
- behaviours, social relations, meetings, interactions, ceremonies, rituals, networks;
- cultural products (such as pictures, paintings, movies, theatre plays, television programmes);
- rules and social conventions;
- documents and texts (historical, literary, journalistic);
- situations and events (wars, elections).

The researcher should focus her or his investigation on these kinds of units, not only because social processes are more easily detectable and observable, but also because these units allow a more direct and deeper analysis of the observed characteristics. When Corsaro, for instance, tried to analyse systematically children's behaviour in kindergartens, the unit he chose was 'the interactive episode'. He defined this as 'sequences of behavior which begin with two actors in an ecological area and their try/tries to reach a shared meaning of an ongoing or starting activity. The episodes end with a physical movement of the actors who leave the area where the behavior had started' (Corsaro, 1985: 24), disappearing from the stage. Corsaro emphasizes that the most important thing is not his definition (which may be questionable) but the need to create and employ explicitly units based on the researcher's theoretical and practical aims.

SOCIAL VERSUS STATISTICAL POPULATIONS

P: After having chosen the sampling unit we turn to the representativeness of samples. In order to evaluate this, it is crucial to distinguish between logical versus social universes.

S1:   What is this?

P: The former belongs to statistics, the latter to social sciences. The consequence is that the former aims at statistical significance, the latter aims at the social significance or the sociological relevance of the population. As Goode and Hatt (1952: 339) pointed out, if in a study of marriage you extract a sample from the 'universe of marriages that happened in New York in the last ten years', from a statistical point of view this procedure is correct because for statistics the actual reality of such a universe is irrelevant. However, from a sociological view this is nonsense because such a universe simply doesn't exist, it doesn't have any social substance, it isn't a collective subject as a social movement or an organization. It is a researcher's invention only.

S2:   So how can we proceed?

P: First, you look at the variance of the phenomenon under the study. If it is high, you need many cases in order to include in your sample each category or class of your phenomenon. If its variance is low you need few cases; sometimes one case could be enough ...

S1:   I can scarcely believe my ears ...

P: The conversation analyst Harvey Sacks (1992, vol. 1: 485, quoted in Silverman, 2000: 109) reminds us of anthropologist and linguist Benjamin Lee Whorf, who managed to reconstruct Navajo grammar by interviewing extensively only one native Indian speaker. Usually grammars have low variance. It would probably have been different if he wanted to study how Navajos bring up children or how they have fun. In his famous study, anthropologist Clifford Geertz (1972) attended 57 cockfights and ethnologist Ernesto De Martino (1961) observed 21 people (socially labelled as) suffering from tarantism disease. They selected a sample with so many or so few cases probably because this reflected the variance. This is the only very important rule for selecting the sample, and it is a pity that many qualitative and quantitative researchers seem to forget it.

S2:   Can you give us another example?

P: Let us take my recent study of call centres. In Italy it has been estimated (this means that nobody knows the real number) that there were 1020 call centres in 2000. I was interested in 'customer relationship management' (the sampling unit) done by call takers in order to solve clients' requests. What is the variance of this sampling unit? If I followed the traditional way of sampling, focusing on the call centre as organization, I would have selected three types of call centres: *private* or marketing oriented; *public*, as for example medical emergency dispatch centres; and *non-profit*. However, if I am interested in 'customer relationship management' practices, to make a representative sample one has to consider their variance in the population instead of the variance of call centres. In other words, the reference is not the variance of the call centre but the variance of 'customer relationship management' practices within call centres. Reviewing literature, talking with experts and doing ethnographic research, I found that there are mainly four types of such practices based on the nature and structure of tasks: counselling, marketing, interviewing and advertising. In addition, looking closely at each of them, while the three latter seem to have low variance, counselling has a higher variance due to the nature of counselling itself, which ranges over different kinds of assistance: technical, medical, psychotherapeutic, and so on.

S1: This is quite complicated.

P: Yes, but it is a good way to obtain representativeness. I did not have enough resources to select four samples; I could study only one type of practice using this approach. This meant that when attempting to generalize the findings, one will be conscious about the extent to which the sample is representative. In addition, this is a way of getting away from many sociological stereotypes. We sample leftists versus rightists to know what they think about immigrants. Why not do the reverse? Sample attitudes about immigrants and then look at where leftists and rightists are located. This procedure avoids the effects of conventional theories.

S3: Maybe I am too stupid with statistics but I still cannot believe that a few cases, even selected with the accuracy you describe, can make a representative sample …

P: There is some evidence for it. At the end of the 1980s I did a study of interviewing, particularly on rituals and rhetorical strategies used by one interviewer in his telephone contacts in order to obtain the consent for the interview, with ten Italian respondents (Gobo, 1990, 2001). I tape-recorded the verbal exchanges and analysed them. Some years later I read a similar study conducted in the US by Maynard and Schaeffer (1999) and I found in it more or less the same patterns. This happened not because I was lucky but because interviewers receive a similar training and use in their work similar cognitive artefacts (scripts and questionnaires).

PERVASIVENESS OF SOME SOCIAL PHENOMENA

P: As I have already said, the precision of a sample, its being an accurate miniature of the universe, is better when the population from which it is drawn is *homogeneous*, and it is lower when it is more *heterogeneous*. This is the key issue for legitimating qualitative research sampling.

We already know that an inductive procedure used to check the correspondence between sample and population is almost impossible for practical reasons.

S4: So we have to change procedure and follow the deductive one.

P: This implies thinking through whether the social phenomenon under study is pervasive. In other words, we may expect there are not *significant* differences between the population and the sample. For this reason a few cases, mirroring a pervasive phenomenon in society, may be enough if its population is quite homogeneous. Following this reasoning is perfectly acceptable in many qualitative studies. For example, anthropologist Vincent Crapanzano (1980) studied Moroccan social relations through the experience, of Tuhami, a furnace-workman. Anthropologist Marcel Griaule (1948) reconstructed the cosmology of the Dogon, a population from Mali, questioning a small group of informants only; Bourdieu's book (1993) on professions is based on 50 interviews with policewomen, temporary workers, attorneys, blue-collar workers, civil servants and the unemployed. In general, biographical method relies on this methodological assumption (Javeau, 1987: 176ff.). Referring to conversation analysis, Harvey Sacks (1984: 22, quoted in Silverman, 2000: 109) has provocatively argued: 'tap into whomsoever, wheresoever and we get much the same things'.

STUDYING SIMILARITY OR DIFFERENCE?

Because probability sampling has many theoretical problems and is also almost impossible to apply in social research, the only practical and sensible way is to work with non-probability samples. We have two broad criteria in building a non-probability sample depending on a researcher's interest: looking at similarities or differences among cases. The former criterion maximizes the probability of extracting odd cases, but focuses on their similarities. The latter selects only odd (deviant) cases.

In the 1700s in biology there was a great controversy about this, associated with the two fundamental aims of natural history: disposition and denomination. This controversy has been marvellously described by Foucault (1966: 150–79). To accomplish these two tasks, naturalists of that time used one of two different and opposite techniques: the System (Linnaeus) and the Method (Buffon, Adanson, Bonnet). On the one hand, Carolus Linnaeus's taxonomic technique was concerned with finding similarities among animals and plants; on the other hand Buffon, criticizing Linnaeus, maintained that our general ideas

> are relative to a continuous scale of objects of which we can clearly perceive only the middle rungs and the extremities increasingly flee from and escape our considerations.... The more we increase the number of divisions in the productions of nature, the closer we shall approach to the true, since nothing really exists in nature except *individuals*, and since genera, orders, and classes exist only in our imagination. (Quoted in Foucault, 1966, 146–7)

Bonnet seems no less resolute:

> There are no leaps in nature: everything in it is graduated, shaded. If there were an empty space between any two beings, what reason would there be for proceeding from the one to another? Above and below every human being we find other beings that are close to him by some characters and differentiated from him by others.

It is therefore always possible to discover 'intermediate organisms', such as the polyp between the animal and the vegetable, the flying squirrel between the bird and the quadruped, the monkey between the quadruped and the man. Consequently, our divisions into species and classes 'are purely nominal'; they represent no more than 'means relative to our needs and to the limitations of our knowledge' (1764, quoted in Foucault, 1966: 147).

This historical digression is epistemologically important, as in social research these two methods have been largely used. Most studies and associated samples follow the former criterion in search of dominant characteristics of pervasive phenomena: biographical method, conversation and discourse analysis, organizational ethnography, and so on. However, there are some important studies that have focused on deviant cases in order to understand standard behaviour [e.g. Goffman (1961) on ceremonies and rituals in psychiatric clinics; Cicourel and Boese (1972) on deaf children's interpersonal communications; Garfinkel (1967) on achievement of sex status in an 'intersexed' person; Pollner and McDonald-Wikler (1985) on interactions in a family with a mentally retarded child] or to explore subculture or emergent or avant-garde phenomena that could become dominant or significant in the future [e.g. Festinger, et al. (1956) on Jehovah's Witnesses; Becker (1963) on marijuana smokers; Hebdige (1979) on style groups such as mods, punks and skinheads; Fielding (1981) on right-wing political movements]. The deviant case can be used also as a proof of refutability and falsification of a well-known and received theory, as Rosenhan (1973) did against the psychiatric theory that locates mental disease in a person's head, or De Martino (1961) did against the medical theory that considered the tarantism syndrome as being caused by the sting of a spider. The latter procedure (widespread in palaeontology) does not consider to what extent the study's finding is distributed in the population, but only notes that the phenomenon exists and must therefore be reviewed and understood theoretically.

THEORETICAL SAMPLING

Theoretical sampling concerns both. The expression was coined by Glaser and Strauss (1967), and refined by Schatzman and Strauss (1973), Strauss (1987) and Strauss and Corbin (1990). In the following refinements the notion has been expanded, producing different versions and loosening it from its initial meaning. Theoretical sampling means 'sampling on the basis of concepts that have proven theoretical relevance to the evolving theory. [Relevance means] that concepts are deemed to be significant because they are repeatedly present or notably absent when comparing incident after incident, and are of sufficient importance to be given the status of categories' (Strauss and Corbin, 1990: 176). In addition, as Mason writes, 'theoretical sampling is concerned with constructing a sample which is meaningful theoretically because it builds in certain characteristics or criteria which help to develop and test your theory and explanation' (1996: 94).

Theoretical sampling was and still is a tremendously important way of reasoning in order to select cases for your sample. However, at least in its first versions, it does not explicitly and clearly take account of the problem of representativeness, but simply avoids it. In such a useful concept there is nevertheless no suggestion on how to consider the representativeness of selected categories. The selection of cases is driven only by their relevance for the phenomena under study and not by the need for representativeness. How, then, should we address Denzin's concern that 'the researcher has to show that these units, compared to all other similar phenomena, are representative' (1971: 232), recently pointed out also by Becker (1998: 67)? For past generations of qualitative researchers the notion of theoretical sampling (beyond being extremely useful) was also pedagogically harmful because (wrongly) it was received as a slogan and an implicit invitation not to care about representativeness.

PRACTICAL ADVICE ON SAMPLING

What are the criteria for selecting cases in order to construct a representative sample in social research? Some criteria have been already described, but I shall summarize them together here even though there is not a precise logical itinerary because methodological principles and rules do not have to stand on their own, having only a weak relation to practice. On the contrary, it is necessary to approach the whole question of sampling sequentially and it would be misleading to plan the whole strategy before starting. In order to obtain representativeness, the sampling plan needs to be set in dialogue with field incidents, contingencies and discoveries. Here is an example of changing or adding to the sampling plan on the basis of something the researcher learns in the field:

> Blanche Geer and I were studying college students. At a certain point, we became interested in student 'leaders', students who were heads of major organizations at the university (there were several hundred of them). We wanted to know how they became leaders and how they exercised their powers. So we made a list of the major organizations (which we could do because we had been there for a year and knew what those were, which we would not have known when we began) and interviewed twenty each of men and women student leaders. And got a great result – it turned out that the men got their positions through enterprise and hustling, while the women were typically appointed by someone from the university! (Becker, 13 July 2002, personal communication)

Afterwards consistency must be reached in the sampling reasoning, not through just applying procedural steps. The reasoning could be as follows:

(1) The researcher usually starts from his or her research questions. Dalton's ones were:

> Why did grievers and managers form cross-cliques? Why were staff personnel ambivalent toward line officers? Why was there disruptive conflict between Maintenance and Operation? If people were awarded posts because of specific fitness, why the disparity between their given and exercised influence? Why among executives on the same formal level, were some distressed and some not? And why were there such sharp differences in viewpoint and moral concern about given events? What was the meaning of double talk about success as dependent on knowing people rather than on possessing administrative skills? Why and how were 'control' staffs and official guardians variously compromised? What was behind the contradictory policy and practices associated with the use of company materials and services? Thus the guiding question embracing all others was: what orders the schism and ties between official and unofficial action? (Dalton, 1959: 274)

Research questions contain concepts and categories (behaviours, attitudes and so on) the researcher is interested in studying.

(2) Then she or he carries out *primary* (or 'provisional' and 'open',[5] following Strauss and Corbin, 1990: 193) sampling in order to collect cases in accordance with concepts.

(3) Because not every concept can be directly studied, in crafting the provisional sample she or he reasons about some aspects:

(a) specificity (focusing on precise social activities, with clear contours as a ritual or a ceremony);

(b) degree of openness of the field (open or closed places);

(c) intrusiveness (the will to reduce the researcher's visibility);

(d) institutional accessibility (free-entry versus limited-entry situations *within* the organizations);

(e) significance (frequent and high organizational relevance of social activities).

(4) It is recommended to sample types of actions or events, '**incidents** and not persons per se!' (Strauss and Corbin, 1990: 177, bold in the original text), in contrast with the common habit of sampling bodies and of seeking information from these bodies about behaviour and events that are never observed directly (Cicourel, 1996). This important recommendation has two reasons: first, we do not want to replicate the survey sampling mistake about the transferability of ideas about representativeness; second, the same person can engage in several activities. For example, Dalton (1959), exploring power struggles in companies, found five 'types of cliques': vertical (symbiotic and parasitic), horizontal (defensive and aggressive) and random. If we

sample individuals we will notice that they stay in more than one clique according to the situation, intentions and so on. If we look at activities, everything is simpler.

(5) Until now in social research four main types of sampling have been invented: purposive, quota, emblematic and snowball. We will see more of these later. In selecting cases you need to pay attention to the variance of concept in order to include in the sample different voices or cases.

(6) During the study the researcher will certainly refine his or her ideas, categories and concepts, or come up with new ones. The important thing is to make connections among them, thus formulating working hypotheses. Even if some qualitative researchers believe that field research is carried out without hypotheses, making hypotheses is as much an everyday life activity as comparing, sampling, making inference, finding causes, and so on. A hypothesis is a conjectural statement or assertion about the relation between two or more properties. Not every hypothesis is testable; indeed the most interesting ones often aren't. However, if we want to persuade the reader we need to formulate them in a testable way.

(7) When the researcher has set up some hypotheses, then she or he restarts sampling in order to collect systematically cases that relate each hypothesis, trying to make his or her analysis consistent. Strauss and Corbin call this second sampling 'relational and variational: it is associated with axial coding. It aims to maximize the finding of differences at the dimensional level' (1990: 176). The authors frame the research process as a funnel-shape: through three better and better focused steps (open, axial and selective) the researcher clarifies his or her statements because 'consistency here means gathering data systematically on each category' (Strauss and Corbin, 1990: 178). When the researcher finds an interesting aspect she or he would always have to control for it if this finding happens in other samples (Perrone, 1977: 27).

(8) To guarantee representativeness she or he needs to collect cases on recurrent behaviour at different moments. As the researcher cannot observe the population 24 hours a day, she or he has to decide at what time and where she or he will observe the population (Schatzman and Strauss, 1973: 39–41; Corsaro, 1985: 28–32). Social practices always recur in certain places and at certain times of the day. If the researcher knows all the different rituals of the organization observed she or he can draw a representative sample. We do not aim to know the distribution of such behaviours (how many times), a purpose that surveys cannot succeed in, as we saw, but

only if they are quite recurrent and significant in the organization under study. In addition, 'our concern is with representativeness of concepts' (Strauss and Corbin, 1990: 190).

(9) The researcher can sample new incidents or she or he can review incidents already collected: 'Theoretical sampling is cumulative. This is because concepts and their relationships also accumulate through the interplay of data collection and analysis ... until theoretical saturation of each category is reached' (Strauss and Corbin, 1990: 178, 188).

(10) This interplay between sampling and testing hypotheses is needed because

(a) representative samples are not predicted in advance but found, constructed and discovered gradually in the field;

(b) it reflects the researcher's experience, previous studies and literature regarding the topic. In other words, the researcher will know the variance of a phenomenon cumulatively, study by study;

(c) representative samples are used to justify the researcher's statements.

STRATEGIES OF SAMPLING

There are four important sampling procedures in qualitative research.

Purposive sampling

Purposive sampling consists of detecting cases within extreme situations as for certain characteristics or cases within a wide range of situations in order to maximize variation, that is, to have all the possible situations. We can choose two different elementary schools where, thanks to the press, to previous studies or interviews or personal experiences, we know we can find two extreme situations: in the first school there are enormous integration difficulties among natives and immigrants, while in the latter there are virtually none. We can also pick three schools: the first with huge integration difficulties, the second with average difficulties, and the third with rare cases. In the 1930s and 1940s the American anthropologist W. Lloyd Warner (1898–1970) and his team of colleagues and students carried out some studies on various communities in the United States. When he had to choose the samples, he decided to select different communities whose social structure mirrored some important features of American society. Four communities (called by assumed names) were chosen: a city in Massachusetts (Yankee City) ruled by traditions on which he wrote five volumes; a lone Mississippi county (Deep South, 1941);[6] a Chicago black district (Bronzetown, 1945),[7] and a city in the Midwest (Jonesville, 1949).[8]

Quota sampling

Quota sampling is employed for objects that contain a wide range of statuses. The population is divided up into as many sub-sets as the characteristics we want to observe and the proportion of each sub-set in the sample is the same as in the population. This sampling method is in widespread use in market research and polls and is usually associated with the use of questionnaires. Curiously, even though it is not a probability sample, it is largely employed in quantitative research because it helps obtain good findings while cutting down on costs. Even though statisticians do not consider it to be scientific, because cases are not selected at random but by a human being (always the bearer of some bias), in the last few decades quota samples have been shown to produce findings as precise (and sometimes even more precise) as probability samples.[9] A good example of this sampling method (with nonproportional quotas) applied to ethnographic research is Jankowski's (1991) study of criminal gangs. He observed for ten years 37 different gangs selected according to their ethnicity, size and members' age in Los Angeles, New York and Boston.

Another example is Gouldner's (1954) research. At that time the gypsum company employed approximately 225 people. In his methodological appendix he reported that his team did 174 interviews, that is, almost all of the population (precisely 77 per cent of it): 132 of 174 interviews were done with a 'representative sample' of blue-collar workers in the company. Gouldner used quota sampling stratified by age, rank and tasks. Then he did another representative sample of 92 blue-collar workers who were given a questionnaire.

The emblematic case

The emblematic case may have up to three features: average (the typical provincial hospital, the organization of a typical mountain-village town hall), excellence (a well-known car-manufacturing firm) and emerging (or avantgarde, such as recent juvenile phenomena). Middletown, the two famous studies carried out

by Robert S. and Helen M. Lynd (1929, 1937), is a pioneer attempt to study a typical American community applying social anthropology methods. The households chosen were 'typically' American and not statistically representative ones. Other examples are two studies that Gouldner (1954) carried out between 1948 and 1951 in a small gypsum extraction and refining factory, Dalton's research (1959) at Milo and Fruhling, two companies in a highly industrialized area in the US, and, as a covert observer, Kanter's (1977) observations of a company with high technological density for five years. As particular elements are more easily detectable through comparison, during each study it is advisable to observe at least two cases.

Snowball sampling

Snowball sampling means picking some subjects who feature the necessary characteristics and, through their recommendations, finding other subjects with the same characteristics. The research of Whyte (1943) may be an example: thanks to Doc, a young unemployed man who attended the social service, the author gradually managed to get in touch with the network of his acquaintances, the people and the groups belonging to the 'street corner society'. If snowball sampling respects some criteria, it may also be included in probability sampling (see TenHouten et al., 1971).

As we can see, most samples used in qualitative research are still linked to a traditional style of constructing samples, i.e., sampling individuals instead of concepts.

REPRESENTATIVENESS AND GENERALIZABILITY

P: We have arrived at the last issue: the relationship between representativeness and generalizability. Even here there are some commonplaces left to be deconstructed:

1   only findings from a representative sample are automatically generalizable to the population;

2   (therefore) representativeness leads to generalizability;

3   if a study is not carried out on a representative sample, its findings are not generalizable;

4   findings of qualitative studies are not generalizable.

In the methodological literature, generalizability is usually considered a direct and automatic consequence of representativeness.

S1:   Why is it not?

P: Let us take another example. Why, sometimes, do pre-electoral polls fail? As their samples are statistically representative, generalization should be automatic and predict correctly the (probability of) results.

S4:   If polls fail it means that their samples weren't representative!

P: This is a trick. Do you mean that representativeness is evaluated only after the result? It seems to me quite tautological, a kind of statistical Darwinism whereby success reframes the past. What about two different polling agencies working with the same statistically representative sample and producing different results?

Too often we forget that between the representativeness of a sample and the generalizability of its findings there is a number of activities that depend on at least eight different domains: the trustworthiness of operational definition, the trustworthiness of operationalization, the reliability of method, the suitability of conceptualization, the researcher's accuracy, his or her degree of success with field relations (people can lie), and data and interpretation validity (data analysis error – see Groves, 1989). These aspects and their associated mistakes (called *measurement error*) may jeopardize the equivalence between representativeness and generalizability. And it happens quite frequently in any research study.

S4:   So we are not certain …

P: The only way is to check. However, in social research the generalizability of findings is quite problematic because it is objectively very difficult to check to see if, at the end of the study, the findings from a sample actually mirror the rest of the population. To do such a thing we would have to check the population anew by a census. This seldom occurs; an example is given by polls on voting intentions: the research is carried out on a representative sample and then, thanks to the findings of the ballot (a census of votes), we can check the generalizability of the data drawn from the sample. Nevertheless, as we saw before, success or failure of forecasts could not depend only on the representativeness of the sample. There are other factors, which have nothing to do with the method, that might have an impact on the success of the forecasts: chance, luck, artificial manipulations during data processing (weights), …

S1:   Lack of new political parties.

P: Right! Indeed, pre-electoral polls usually show a difference when a new party enters the electoral competition for the first time. This failure happens because sampling is always based on the previous census (the past election), not on the present situation. So forecasts may be unsuccessful even though statistically representative samples are employed. This means that, if findings deriving from samples may be eliminated by the findings of the elections, it is always advisable to check the population: theoretically, without the confirmation given by the elections, all findings might be valid. Without this control we would never be able to know which different data published by polling agencies mirror the population. Unfortunately, there is no similar census on most of the topics sociological research is interested in.

GENERALIZABILITY IN STATISTICS

P: Let us see briefly how generalization in statistics works. This is called *inference*. It is an academic issue since we have already seen that in most surveys there aren't statistically representative samples. To estimate the probability that the finding (e.g. an existing relation between variable A and variable B) drawn from your sample is also in the population, you are helped by some statistical tests. There are many statistical tests for controlling hypotheses. The best known is chi-square. However, if you do a study of a whole population (e.g. all of the 300 students in the Research Methods class instead of just some), you do not need such a test and an inspection cross-tab by cross-tab is needed. In other words, statistical tests of significance are used only when you want to infer from a sample to the whole population. In the past there was a long controversy about the appropriateness of applying statistical significance tests in social sciences (see Morrison and Henkel, 1971). The main criticisms, well known by survey methodologists, are:

1 the arbitrariness of the probability threshold of 0.05 below which the null hypothesis is rejected;
2 the associated crudeness of this dichotomous decision, without any gradation, in order to accept or refuse the probability of the null hypothesis being valid for the population;
3 the statistical test assumes a rigorously random sample, otherwise the procedure is nonsense. However, as we have already seen, this is quite difficult to obtain in social research;
4 the chi-square is heavily affected by sample size: it increases in significance when sample size increases! With very large samples even small trends will appear significant.

So statistical tests are of modest usefulness in social research. They can be helpfully used only as orienting criteria for the researcher's decision-making.

S3: In addition, chi-square is a significance test only …

P: Right. It tells if a relation is likely to *exist in the population* only. It doesn't say anything about the *strength* of this relationship. You need other tests, associated to the nature of your variables (nominal, ordinal, interval and so on), such as phi, Cramer's V, Pearson's C, and so on. However, they are rarely used. Generally speaking, all these issues have been neglected with the consequence that many survey researchers still venerate

these tests and many field researchers are still afraid.

ARE QUALITATIVE RESEARCHERS' FINDINGS NOT GENERALIZABLE?

S1: So methodologists who say that qualitative studies are not generalizable should be more careful because survey studies also have many troubles with generalization?

P: You got the point: statistical inference in social studies is quite problematic. Unfortunately this hasn't been pointed out by most qualitative methodologists, who (on this issue) accepted the received view. For example, Strauss and Corbin state:

> in terms of making generalization to a larger population, **we are not attempting to generalize as such but to specify** … the condition under which our phenomena exist, the action/interaction that pertains to them, and the associated outcomes or consequences. This means that our theoretical formulation applies to these situations or circumstances but **to no others**. (1990: 191, bold in the original text)

S3: They refer to a kind of 'internal generalization' …

P: Yes. And a similar position is held by Lincoln and Guba (1985: 20–21), Hammersley (1992: 186ff.) and many others. The underlying idea is that there are two kinds of generalizations: a generalization about a specific group or population (applied in surveys and polls) and a generalization about the nature of a process (applied in field research). Consequently sampling requirements are completely different in the two cases. The latter is based on the notion of 'theoretical sampling'. To make clearer the difference between these two kinds of generalization, some authors have called the second one 'transferability' (Guba, 1981; Lincoln and Guba, 1985: 77, 217),[10] 'naturalist generalization' (Stake, 1983: 282), 'analytical generalization' (Yin, 1984: 31), 'extrapolation' (Alasuutari, 1995: 157) and 'moderate generalization' (Williams, 2002). These proposals are politically wise because they try to give qualitative research scientific legitimation; however, they do not solve adequately the theoretical and practical problems involved in the notions of representativeness and generalizability.

We might ask: if a qualitative researcher's findings are not generalizable, why does she or he carry out a study? What is the point, for instance, for an ethnographer spending months planning a study, weeks negotiating access to the field, months observing social actors' behaviour, days organizing and analysing ethnographic notes and, finally, writing a research report if then she or he is told that the findings are only applicable to his or her community/organization/group (the sample) and not to many/all cases of the population? This is masochism!

Besides, this was not the way in which the studies done by Goffman, Gouldner, Whyte and so on were received. No one would remember them for the findings of one setting only.

S2: What is the trick then?

P: The logical mistake is in confusing the representativeness of the case with the representativeness of its characteristics observed by the ethnographer. Even though the case may be a firm, we should take into account the relationship among employees, the psychological and relational effects of a new work organization, the power relationships between chiefs and subordinates, and so on. So the sample is a compound of such characteristics, and is not just the firm. For this reason I consider it misleading to use the widespread expression 'case study' and also damaging to the image of qualitative research. As a matter of fact, to use Mason's words 'you may have sampled people but what you really want to compare are their experiences' (1996: 96). It is what Gouldner (1954) did: he sampled blue-collar workers to discover their values, motivations and so on.

And Becker, writing about the cognitive process of generalization, stated: 'in every city there is a body of social

practices – forms of marriage, or work, or habitation – which don't change much, even though the people who perform them are continually replaced through the ordinary demographic process of birth, death, immigration, and emigration' (2000: 6).

S4: Yes, but we do not know the distribution in the population.

P: But nobody can know this; neither can statistics help you. You can quantify or correctly estimate the distribution only for characteristics already counted in a census. How many of them are there in social research? So the only method (as far as I know) is by evaluating the social pervasiveness of your concepts under study.

As Alberoni and his colleagues wrote in their Introduction about a study carried out on 108 political activists of the Italian Communist Party and the Christian Democratic Party:

if we want to know, for instance, how many activists there are of both parties in the whole country coming from families of the Catholic or Communist tradition, [this] study is useless; quite the reverse, if we want to show that family background is important in determining if a citizen will be an activist in the Communist rather than in the Christian Democratic party, this research can give the right answer. If we want to find out what are and what have been the percentages of the different 'types' of activists ... in both parties, the study is useless, while if we want to show these types exist the study gives a certain answer. ... The study does not aim at giving a quantitative objective description of Italian activism but can help in understanding some of its essential aspects, basic motivations, crucial experiences and typical situations which gave birth to Italian activism and help to keep it alive. (Alberoni et al., 1967: 13)

Alberoni was too afraid of the predictable quantitative criticism.

A NEW CONCEPT OF GENERALIZABILITY FOR QUALITATIVE RESEARCH?

In this chapter I have documented the need for a new, bottom-up, socially informed and practically driven theory of sampling, representativeness and generalization. This theory goes back and remains faithful to the original central problem of representativeness as theorized by statisticians: the variance of the phenomenon under study. The variance is the only worry the researcher needs to take into consideration.

The concept of generalizability now introduced is based on the idea of social representativeness, which goes beyond the limits of statistical representativeness. The aim is to observe extensively the relations between variables, not only to assess (which is always a quite problematic task) the number of persons who feature one characteristic. Therefore, generalizability is mainly a practically and contingent outcome related to the variance of the research topic; in other words it is a function of the invariance (regularities) of the phenomenon, not a standard or automatic algorithm of a statistical rule.

This is a reason why the findings of the studies of Goffman on social embarrassment, deference and demeanour, Sacks and his colleagues on telephone conversation machinery, Whyte (1943) on social organization and leadership in a group, Gouldner (1954) on bureaucracy in medium enterprises, Cicourel (1968) on the description of a typical juvenile offender, van Dijk (1983) on the cognitive processes of racial prejudice, and Norman (1988) on accidents in the use of technology in everyday life, and so on, have always been considered generalizable.

In qualitative research, generalizability concerns general structures rather than single social practices, which are only an example of this structure. The ethnographer does not generalize one case or event that, as Max Weber pointed out, cannot recur but its main structural aspects that can be noticed in other cases or events of the same kind or class. For example, in the conclusions of his study of the relationship between a psychotherapist and a patient suffering from AIDS, Peräkylä says:

> The results were not generalizable as descriptions of what other counselors or other professionals do with their clients; but they were generalizable as descriptions of what any counselor or other professional, with his or her clients, *can* do, given that he or she has the same array of interactional competencies as the participants of the AIDS counseling session have. (Peräkylä, 1997: 216, quoted in Silverman, 2000: 109)

Something similar happens in film and radio production with noise sampling. The squeak of the door (which gives us the shivers when we watch a thriller or a horror) does not represent all squeaks of doors but we associate it with them. We do not think about the differences between that squeak and the one made by our front door; we notice the similarities only. They are two

different ways of thinking, and most social sciences aim at finding such patterns.

While the verbal expressions of an interactive exchange may vary, exchange based on the question–answer pattern features a formal trans-institutional (even though not universal) structure. While maybe to lay a page of a newspaper on the floor and declare one's sovereignty over it (Goffman, 1961) is a behaviour observed in one psychiatric clinic only, the need to have a private space and control of territory has been reported many times, though in different forms. However, the extension of this structure must be well organized. On the other hand, as Rositi states, we may reasonably doubt the generalizability of findings of 'studies of 1000–2000 cases which claim to sample the whole population. We have to wonder if we should prefer such samples with such aims.... Studies with samples of 100–200 conversational interviews, structured to "describe" variables rather than a population, are definitely more suitable for a new model of studying society' (1993: 198).

ACNOWLEDGEMENT

I wish to thank Howard Becker, Aaron Cicourel, two anonymous referees and the editors for helpful comments and suggestions.

NOTES

1 Incidentally I emphasize that this remains a problem even for studies based on samples.
2 See http://www.census.gov/dmd/www/samfaq.htm
3 The author also writes: 'the situation is slightly better where the unit is a group because an aggregate of individuals is usually institutionalized (schools, universities, companies, hospitals, commercial activities); however, the situation becomes more complicated for unofficial structures: private language or computer courses, sport, leisure and cultural associations, charities, amateur theatre groups, bowling clubs, pensioners' recreation groups and so on' (Corbetta, 1999: 333).
4 Even among those who seem to accept the legitimacy of inferential procedure, there are authors who have doubts about it, such as Isidor Chain (1963: 512), who states that we are never sure that findings on sample can be applied to population unless we also simultaneously do a census.
5 As Strauss and Corbin (1990: 176) explain: 'open sampling is associated with open coding. Openness rather than specificity guides the sampling choices'. Open sampling can be done purposively (e.g. pp. 183–4) or systematically (e.g. p. 184) or occurs fortuitously (e.g. pp. 182–3). It includes on-site sampling.
6 Cf. Davis et al. (1941).

7 Cf. Drake and Cayton (1945).

8 Cf. Warner (1949).

9 As Barisione and Mannheimer write: 'The experience in public opinion surveys has showed that quota samples are on the average reliable; as a matter of fact their results do not differ from results obtained with random samples of the same size more than two random samples differ between them' (1999: 54). This is another case when experience and practice predominate over abstract statistical principles (1999: 54).

10 According to the authors the expression 'transferability' does not stand for a researcher's inference process but a choice of the reader, who may transfer this information to other situations on the base of a solid thick description provided by the researcher (Lincoln and Guba, 1985: 362).

REFERENCES

Alasuutari, Pertti (1995) *Researching Culture*, London: Sage.

Alberoni, Francesco, et al. (1967) *L'attivista di partito*. Bologna: Il Mulino.

Bailey, Kenneth D. (1978) *Methods in Social Research*. New York: Free Press.

Barisione, M. and Mannheimer, R. (1999) *I sondaggi*. Bologna: Il Mulino.

Becker, Howard (1951) 'The professional dance musician and his audience', *American Journal of Sociology*, 57.

Becker, Howard (1963), *Ousiders*. Glencoe, IL: Free Press.

Becker, Howard (1998), *Tricks of the Trade*. Chicago: University of Chicago Press.

Becker, Howard (2000) 'Italo Calvino as urbanologist', *L'Année Sociologique*.

Bourdieu, Pierre, et al. (1993) *La misère du monde*. Paris: Editions du Seuil.

Brehm, John (1993) *The Phantom Respondents: Opinion Surveys and Political Representation*. Ann Arbor: University of Michigan Press.

Capecchi, Vittorio (1972) 'Struttura e tecniche della ricerca', in Pietro Rossi (ed.), *Ricerca sociologica e ruolo del sociologo*. Bologna: Il Mulino.

Castellano, V. and Herzel, A. (1971) *Elementi di teoria dei campioni*. Rome: Ilardi.

Chain, Isidor (1963) 'An introduction to sampling', in C. Selltiz and M. Jahoda (eds), *Research Methods in Social Relations*. New York: Holt & Rinehart, pp. 509–45.

Cicourel, Aaron Victor (1968) *The Social Organization of Juvenile Justice*. New York: Wiley.

Cicourel, Aaron Victor (1996) 'Ecological validity and "white room effects" ', *Pragmatics and Cognition*, 4(2): 221–64.

Cicourel, Aaron Victor and Boese, R. (1972) 'Sign language acquisition and the teaching of deaf children', in Dell Hymes et al. (ed.), *The Functions of Language: An Anthropological Approach and Psychological Approach*. New York: Teachers College Press.

Converse, Jean Marie and Schuman, Howard (1974) *Conversations at Random*. New York: Wiley.

Corbetta, Piergiorgio (1999) *Metodologia e tecniche della ricerca sociale*. Bologna: Il Mulino. Translated as *Social Research*. London: Sage, 2001.

Corsaro, William A. (1985) *Friendship and Peer Culture in the Early Years*, Norwood, NJ: Ablex.

Crapanzano, Vincent (1980) *Tuhami, Portrait of a Moroccan*. Chicago: University of Chicago Press.

Dalton, Melvin (1959) *Men Who Manage*. New York: Wiley.

Davis, Allison, Gardner, Burleigh B. and Gardner, Mary R. (1941) *Deep South*. Chicago: University of Chicago Press.

De Martino, Ernesto (1961) *La terra del rimorso*. Milan: Il Saggiatore.

Denzin, Norman K. (1971) 'Symbolic interactionism and ethomethodology', in Jack D. Douglas (ed.), *Understanding Everyday Life*. London: Routledge & Kegan Paul.

Drake, St Clair and Cayton, Roscoe Horace (1945) *Black Metropolis*. New York, Harcourt Brace.

Festinger, L., Henry, H.W. and Schachter, S. (1956) *When Prophecy Fails*. Minneapolis: University of Minnesota Press.

Fielding, Nigel (1981) *The National Front*. London: Routledge & Kegan Paul.

Foucault M. (1966) *Les mots et les choses*. Paris: Gallimard. Translated as *The Order of Things*. New York: Vintage Books, 1973.

Frege, G.F.L. (1892) 'Über Sinn und Bedeutung', *Zeitschrift für Philosophie und philosophische Kritik*.

Galtung, John (1967) *Theory and Methods of Social Research*. Oslo: Universitets Forlaget.

Garfinkel, Harold (1967) *Studies in Ethnomethodology*. Englewood Cliffs, NJ: Prentice-Hall.

Gasperoni, Giancarlo and Marradi, Alberto (1996) 'Metodo e tecniche delle scienze sociali', in *Enciclopedia delle scienze sociali*. Rome: Istituto della Enciclopedia Italiana, vol. 5, pp. 624–43.

Geertz, Clifford (1972) 'Deep play: notes on the Balinese cockfight', *Dedalus*, 101: 1–37.

Gilli, Gian Antonio (1971) *Come si fa ricerca*. Milan: Mondadori.

Glaser, Barney G. and Strauss, Anselm L. (1967) *The Discovery of Grounded Theory*. Chicago: Aldine.

Gobo, Giampietro (1990), '*The first call: rituals and rhetorical strategies in the first telephone call with Italian respondents*'. Paper presented at Annual Meeting of the ASA, Washington, DC, 11–15 August.

Gobo, Giampietro (1997) *Le risposte e il loro contesto*. Milan: Angeli.

Gobo, Giampietro (2001) 'Best practices: rituals and rhetorical strategies in the "initial telephone contact" ', *Forum: Qualitative Social Research*, 2(1), http://www.qualitative-research.net/fqs-texte/1–01/1–01gobo-e.htm

Goffman, Erving (1961) *Asylums*. New York: Doubleday.

Goffman, Erving (1963) *Behavior in Public Places*. Glencoe, IL: Free Press.

Gomperz, H. (1905) *Weltanschauungslehre*, vol. I: *Methodologie*, Jena: Diederichs.

Goode, William, and Hatt, Paul K. (1952) *Methods in Social Research*. New York: McGraw-Hill.

Gouldner, Alvin G. (1954) *Patterns of Industrial Bureaucracy*. New York: Free Press.

Griaule, Marcel (1948) *Dieu d'eau: entretiens avec Ogotemmêli*. Paris: Editions du Chêne.

Groves, Robert M. (1989) *Survey Errors and Survey Costs*. New York: Wiley.

Groves, Robert M. and Lyberg, L.E. (1988) 'An overview of nonresponse issues in telephone surveys', in Robert M. Groves et al. (eds), *Telephone Survey Methodology*. New York: Wiley.

Guba, Egon G. (1981) 'Criteria for assessing the trustworthiness of naturalistic inquiries', *Educational Communication and Technology Journal*, 29: 75–92.

Hammersley, Martyn (1992) *What's Wrong with Ethnography?* London: Routledge.

Hebdige, Dick (1979) *Subculture: The meaning of Style*. London and New York: Routledge.

Jankowski, Martín Sánchez (1991) *Islands in the Street*. Berkeley: University of California Press.

Javeau, C. (1987) 'Analisi dei singolare e sociologia', in Roberto Cipriani (ed.), *La metodologia delle storie di vita*. Rome: Euroma-La Goliardica.

Kahneman, Danny and Tversky, Amos (1972) 'Subjective probability: a judgment of representativeness', *Cognitive Psychology*, 3: 430–54.

Kanter, Rosabeth Moss (1977) *Men and Women of the Corporation*. New York: Basic Books.

Kish, L. (1965) *Survey Sampling*. New York: Wiley.

Lincoln, Yvonna S. and Guba, Egon G. (1985) *Naturalist Inquiry*. Beverly Hills, CA: Sage.

Lynd, Robert S. and Lynd, Helen M. (1929) *Middletown*. New York: Harcourt, Brace.

Lynd, Robert S. and Lynd, Helen M.(1937) *Middletown in Transition*. New York: Harcourt, Brace.

Marradi, Alberto (1989) 'Casualità e rappresentatività di un campione: contributo a una sociologia del linguaggio scientifico', in Renato Mannheimer (ed.), *I sondaggi elettorali e le scienze politiche*. Milan: Angeli, pp. 51–133.

Marradi, Alberto (1994) 'Referenti, pensiero e linguaggio: una questione rilevante per gli indicatori', *Sociologia e Ricerca Sociale*, 43: 137–207.

Mason, Jennifer (1996) *Qualitative Researching*. Newbury Park, CA: Sage.

Maynard, Douglas W. and Schaeffer, Nora Cate (1999) 'Keeping the gate', *Sociological Methods and Research*, 1: 34–79.

Mitchell, Ritva and Karttunen, Sari (1991) 'Perché e come definire un artista?', *Rassegna Italiana di Sociologia*, 32(3): 349–64.

Morris, Charles W. (1938) *Foundations of the Theory of Signs*. Chicago: University of Chicago Press.

Morrison, D.D. and Henkel, R.E. (1971) *The Significance Tests Controversy: A Reader*. Chicago: Aldine.

Norman, Donald A. (1988) *The Psychology of Everyday Things*. New York: Basic Books.

Ogden, C.K. and Richards, I.A. (1923) *The Meaning of Meaning*. London: Routledge & Kegan Paul.

Peirce, Charles S. (1902) 'Sign', in J.M. Baldwin (ed.), *Dictionary of Philosophy and Psychology*, vol. II. New York: Macmillan.

Peräkylä, Anssi (1997) 'Reliability and validity in research based upon transcripts', in David Silverman (ed.), *Qualitative Research*. London: Sage, pp. 201–19.

Perrone, Luca (1977) *Metodi quantitativi della ricerca sociale*. Milan: Feltrinelli.

Pinto, Roger (1964) *Méthodes des sciences sociales*. Paris: Dalloz.

Pitrone, Maria Concetta (1984) *Il sondaggio*. Milan: Angeli.

Pollner, Melvin and McDonald-Wikler, L. (1985) 'The social construction of unreality', *Family Process*, 24: 241–54.

Popper, Karl R. (1972) *Objective Knowledge*. Oxford: Oxford University Press.

Rosenhan, David L. (1973) 'On being sane in insane places', *Science*, 179: 250–8.

Rositi, Franco (1993) 'Strutture di senso e strutture di dati', *Rassegna Italiana di Sociologia*, 2: 177–200.

Sacks, Harvey (1984) 'On doing "being ordinary" ', in J.M. Atkinson and J. Heritage (eds), *Structures of Social Action*. Cambridge: Cambridge University Press, pp. 513–29.

Sacks, Harvey (1992) *Lectures on Conversation*, vol. 1. Oxford: Blackwell.

Schatzman, Leonard and Strauss, Anselm L. (1973) *Field Research*. Englewood Cliffs, NJ: Prentice-Hall.

Silverman, David (2000) *Doing Qualitative Research*. London: Sage.

Stake, Robert (1983) 'The case study method in social enquiry', in G. Madaus, M. Scriven and D. Stufflebean (eds), *Evaluation Models*. Boston: Kluwer-Nijhoff, pp. 279–86.

Strauss, Anselm (1987) *Qualitative Analysis for Social Scientists*. Cambridge: Cambridge University Press.

Strauss, Anselm and Corbin, Juliet (1990) *Basics of Qualitative Research*. London: Sage.

Sudman, Seymour (1983) 'Applied sampling', in P.H. Rossi, G.D. Wright and A.B. Anderson (eds), *Handbook of Survey Research*. San Diego: Academic Press.

Sudnow, David (1967) *Passing On*. Englewood Cliffs, NJ: Prentice-Hall.

TenHouten, Warren, Stern, John, and TenHouten, Diana (1971) 'Political leadership in poor communities: application of two sampling methodologies', in P. Orleans and W.R. Ellis Jr (eds), *Race, Change and Urban Society*, vol. V. Beverly Hills, CA: Sage.

Tversky, Amos and Kahneman, Danny (1974) 'Judgment under uncertainty: heuristics and biases', *Science*, 185: 1123–31.

van Dijk, Teun Adrian (1983), 'Cognitive and conversational strategies in the ethnic prejudice', *Text*, 3(4): 375–404.

Warner, L. William (1949) *Democracy in Jonesville*. New York: Harper & Row.

Whorf, Benjamin Lee (1956) *Language, Thought, and Reality*. Cambridge, MA: MIT Press.

Whyte, William Foote (1943). *Street Corner Society*. Chicago: University of Chicago Press.

Williams, Malcolm (2002) 'Generalization in interpretive research', in Tim May (ed.), *Qualitative Research in Action*. London: Sage.

Yin, Robert K. (1984) *Case Study Research*. Thousand Oaks, CA: Sage.

29

Working with 'key incidents'

Robert M. Emerson

Emphasizing their ties to the classic Chicago School fieldwork tradition, many sociological field researchers characterize their approach as 'naturalistic'. Naturalistic approaches seek to provide 'rich descriptions of people and interaction as they exist and unfold in their native habitats' (Gubrium and Holstein, 1997: 6), to limit the role of received theory to that of 'sensitizing concepts' (Blumer, 1969) and to minimize the use of preconceived theory and conceptual categories (Schatzman and Strauss, 1973), and above all, to remain 'loyal to the phenomenon' under study (Matza, 1969). Using the term 'naturalism' to characterize this style of fieldwork has the advantage of foregrounding a number of its distinctive qualities, as Lofland and Lofland (1995: 7) emphasize:

it suggests an appropriate linkage to *naturalist* as that word is used in field biology. From the realms of philosophical discourse, it has acquired the connotation of minimizing the presuppositions with which one approaches the empirical world – a laudable resonance indeed. Moreover, as a literary genre, *naturalism* involves a close and searching description of the mundane details of everyday life.

Although classic naturalistic ethnography faces a number of contemporary challenges to its core tenets, particularly to its underlying methodological stance of treating field research as a matter of entering social settings framed as 'geographic fields of experience' in order to understand and convey 'their worlds' and 'their stories', it nonetheless remains 'a cornerstone of qualitative sociology' (Gubrium and Holstein, 1997: 19).

Prioritizing description, minimizing a priori theorizing, and remaining loyal to the phenomena under study have generated distinctively qualitative approaches to theory and analysis. As Glaser and Strauss (1967) insisted early on, the analysis of field data is not a matter of hypothesis testing aimed at establishing the relation between a few key variables decided in advance, nor of applying received theory to observed events and processes. Rather, naturalism requires ethnographers to develop theoretical propositions *during or after* immersion in the field, so that analyses are *grounded* in observations and data derived from these first-hand experiences. Naturalistic ethnographers view theory as 'grounded' when it departs from and incorporates what those studied actually say and do, referencing local routines and dramas in something like their own terms. Similarly, they characterize theory as 'grounded' when it derives from and is built on close, careful consideration of detailed data, usually fieldnotes and informal interviews.

The primary strategies recommended by ethnographers for grounding analyses in observation and data have, until this point, relied on distinctively conceptual approaches, notably analytic induction and grounded theory. In this chapter I want to explore a complementary way of grounding ethnographic analyses, a strategy that honors and grows out of field researchers' working sense that their analyses are touched off by and tied to particular in-the-field events or observations that stimulate or implicate original lines of inquiry and conceptualization. I shall term events or observations that come to be used in this way *key incidents*. Key incidents suggest and direct analysis in ways that ultimately help to open up significant, often complex lines of conceptual development. In this chapter I shall initially review current naturalistic approaches to grounding analysis and examine some instances and general features of key incidents. Then, using materials from my own fieldwork on juvenile courts and psychiatric emergency teams, I shall trace in detail the natural history of grounded analyses tied to two distinctive types of key incidents, extreme cases and interactional disjunctures.

THE USE OF KEY INCIDENTS IN GROUNDED ANALYSES

As previously noted, naturalistic analysis is necessarily open-ended and emergent, tied to and deriving from specific pieces of what has been seen, heard, and recorded. Of course, fieldworkers never start without concepts,[1] but they will inevitably abandon some initial concepts, significantly modify others, and develop and elaborate new and often unanticipated concepts, all as the result of close consideration of first-hand observation and data. In this respect, field researchers not only fit their analyses to critical features of what they study, but also modify what they are studying and the kinds of data collected so that the data bear on and advance these emerging analyses. Thus naturalistic analysis involves not strict induction (if such is possible), but rather 'retroduction' (Bulmer, 1979; Katz, 1983), employing procedures that are 'simultaneously deductive and inductive' (Lofland, 1976: 66). As Becker has characterized this process (1998: 211–12):

> analysts in this style typically assemble all the data that bear on a given topic and see what statement they can make that will take account of all that material, what generalizations best encompasses what is there. If some of the data do not support a generalization, the analyst tries to reframe the generalization, complicating it to take account of the stubborn fact; alternatively, the analyst tries to create a new class of phenomena that differs from the one the datum was originally assigned to, which can have its own explanatory generalization.

Naturalistic retroduction – moving back and forth between observations and theory, modifying original theoretical statements to fit observations, and seeking observations relevant to the emerging theory – introduces distinctive complications into the analytic process. Observation and data collection are not systematically guided by a predetermined, fixed analytic focus, although different foci may 'emerge' as fieldwork proceeds.[2] Indeed, many fieldworkers frequently write detailed fieldnotes with no explicit, or at least articulated, notion of their immediate or future analytic import; they seek to record closely observed accounts of actions and talk that they intuitively experience as striking or surprising, or that members react to or otherwise mark as meaningful or significant, in this sense focusing on what they see and hear in the field, not on theoretical significance. As a result fieldnotes accumulate cresively, according to insights and commitments that shift and change over the course of the study. These processes fundamentally shape the fieldnote corpus upon which the field researcher relies for analysis:

> Fieldnotes grow through gradual accretion, adding one day's writing to the next's. The ethnographer writes particular fieldnotes in ways that are not pre-determined or pre-specified; hence fieldnotes are not collections or samples in the way that audio recordings can be, i.e., decided in advance according to set criteria. Choosing what to write down is not a process of sampling according to some fixed-in-advance principle. Rather it is both intuitive, reflecting the ethnographer's changing sense of what might possibly be made interesting or important to future readers, and empathetic, reflecting the ethnographer's sense of what is interesting or important to the people he is observing. (Emerson et al., 1995: 10–11)

Fieldwork analyses characteristically address a massive corpus of data collected for a variety of different, often unarticulated purposes. How, then, can the naturalistic ethnographer produce some sort of analytic order out of what is often a literal mess of data?

A first answer from naturalistically inclined fieldworkers is to urge grounding analysis in these observations and data. But this maxim provides only in-principle guidelines about how to actually approach the analysis of field data. As a practical matter, how is a naturalistic fieldworker enmeshed in a complex field situation and confronting a mass of loosely related data to produce an analysis 'grounded in observation and data'?

Contemporary ethnographers frequently advocate theoretically focused strategies for grounding analysis in observation and data. Analytic induction and grounded theory provide the two most widely known such strategies. Analytic induction explicates *a distinctive logic for data analysis*. The field researcher seeks to develop a rough formulation of the phenomenon to be explained and an initial hypothesis explaining the phenomenon. Examining a data set item by item, the fieldworker seeks to provide a 'perfect' explanation, that is, one that 'applies to every case that fits the definition of the phenomenon to be explained' (Becker, 1998: 195). This can be achieved either by modifying the hypothesized explanatory factors, or by redefining the phenomenon to be explained, in order to exclude as irrelevant cases that do not fit. By looking at every case, and by deliberately searching for and incorporating negative cases into the analysis, analytic induction 'abstracts from a given concrete case the features that are essential, and generalizes them' (Bulmer, 1979: 661).[3]

Grounded theory takes a somewhat different tack, offering *a set of practical procedures that advance and facilitate analysis*. Starting with 'detailed, intensive, microscopic examination of the data in order to bring out the amazing complexity of what lies in, behind, and beyond those data' (Strauss, 1987: 10), grounded theorists urge developing analyses through the use of two specific procedures: First, *coding*, the line-by-line reading of the data in order to identify and name theoretical categories, a process that is keyed to and focused on the data themselves, but that also draws upon the analyst's theoretical sensitivities and broader life experiences.[4] Second, *memoing*, sustained writing that identifies the properties, dimensions, and subdimensions of selected analytic categories by systematically asking about conditions, interactions, strategies and tactics, and consequences (Strauss, 1987: 27–8).[5]

But even these more concrete, theory-focused strategies provide only partial answers and limited guidance to the problem of actually how to ground analysis in observation and data. For example, both analytic induction and grounded theory emphasize the use of *comparison* to propel theoretical development, the former by insisting on the need to identify and incorporate (or exclude) *negative cases*, the latter in advocating *constant comparison* – looking for variations and contrasts in the data – as the key to developing and specifying the relations between theoretical categories. In both cases, comparison requires identifying and considering data that contradict tentative analytic claims; both approaches, then, refuse to 'write disconfirming evidence off as some sort of dismissable variation, … [rather] addressing it as evidence that has to be theoretically accounted for and included as part of the story' (Becker, 1998: 210). But in practice, how does the ethnographer identify appropriate negative cases and relevant comparisons? Negative cases require relatively specific hypotheses; how are these developed? 'Constant comparison' is extremely open; how do fieldworkers determine when comparison is needed and what comprises an appropriate or relevant comparison?

Furthermore, even the more procedural focus of the grounded theory approach offers only partial and incomplete help for the practitioner in developing naturalistic analyses. Coding and memoing are useful ways for pursuing and developing analysis from data, but do not provide a set of guidelines or a model for actually carrying out analysis. While there are suggestions and recommendations at various places about how to proceed – e.g. types of questions to ask of data to generate grounded analytic code

categories – many key issues remain unspecified. For example, given the multitude of codings that can be produced, how do fieldworkers decide which ones are important or worth pursuing and which should be dropped? How do fieldworkers determine when and where to seek out comparison cases? How carefully and closely do conflicting cases have to be considered? How do fieldworkers go about reworking and combining several separate memoed strands of analysis into a single integrated memo?

Certainly, delineating a systematic logic of inquiry or regular procedures for analyzing data are valuable ways of encouraging and facilitating naturalistic analysis. But such theory-focused approaches leave aside entirely the actual experience of many ethnographers, the frequent sense that *their eventual analyses were strongly shaped by particularly telling or revealing incidents or events that they observed and recorded*. Such key incidents involve particular observations that play a central role in identifying and opening up new analytic issues and broader lines of theoretical development. Examining the nature and use of such key incidents can fruitfully complement theory-focused strategies for grounding analysis in observation and data.

An exemplar of a key incident, one used to generate several of the core analyses in the classic *Boys in White* (Becker et al., 1961), is found in Becker's (1993) account of how he came to learn about and understand medical students' use of the term 'crock'. During his first week of fieldwork on medical student training in the University of Kansas Medical Center, operating with only the most general theoretical guidelines ('that these kids came in at one end and 4 years later come out at the other end and that something certainly must have happened to them in between'; 1993: 28), Becker reports the following observation:

> One morning as we made rounds, we saw a very talkative patient, who had multiple complaints to tell the doctor about – all sorts of aches, pains, and unusual events. I could see that no one was taking her very seriously, and on the way out, one of the students said, 'Boy, she's really a crock!' (1993: 31)

Becker's immediate reaction was not a 'lightning bolt of intuition', but a sense of interest and intrigue at the use of such a term:

> I understood this, in part, as shorthand for 'crock of shit'. It was obviously invidious. But what was he talking about. What was wrong with her having all those complaints? Wasn't that interesting? (1993: 31)

He followed up by asking this medical student 'what's a crock?', eventually eliciting the answer that a crock was a patient with a psychosomatic illness. But when another patient diagnosed as psychosomatic was not classified as a crock because 'he really has an ulcer', Becker continued exploring medical students' use of the term, and gradually came to a more precise definition: a crock was 'a patient who had multiple complaints but no discernible physical pathology' (1993: 32). This definition led Becker to consider *why* medical students devalued such patients, and eventually to specify the central features of the concept of 'medical student culture' that organizes *Boys in White*. At the core of this culture lay student emphasis on learning the practice of medicine less through 'book knowledge' and more by means of 'clinical experience'. That is, medical students valued and sought out 'actual experience in dealing with patients and disease' as the key to learning to be an effective physician. Since the only experience they gained from 'crocks' was talking to them to calm them down, they felt they learned nothing medically important from such cases.

On one level Becker appears to have been initially provoked by this key incident because of the 'invidiousness' of the term 'crock' and the associated disinterest in the patient's actual complaints. But the observation also took on interest because of the theoretical possibilities he sensed and identified in it. This incident drew his interest and attention not simply because of the 'invidious' character of the term 'crock', but also because of his theoretical proclivity to view invidious terms as revealing more about those who invoked them than about those to whom they were applied. As Becker describes his analytic reaction to hearing the term 'crock':

> To put it most pretentiously, when members of one status category make invidious distinctions among the members of another status category with whom they regularly deal, the distinction will reflect the interests of the members of the first category in the relationship. More specifically, perhaps less forbiddingly, the invidious distinctions that students made between classes of patients would show what interests they were trying to maximize in that relationship, what they hoped to get out of it. (1993: 31)

Thus, once Becker had worked out how medical students used the term, he took up the question of why students devalued crocks, of 'what interest of theirs was compromised by a patient with many complaints and no pathology?' (1993: 32). The concept of 'clinical experience' came to highlight students' distinctive interest in encountering and learning first-hand 'the sights, sounds, and smells of disease in a living person' (1993: 33).

Becker's account of coming upon and digging out the meanings and implications of the term 'crock' highlights several important features of key incidents. First, key incidents need be neither highly dramatic nor deeply significant or highly memorable to those studied. The student Becker originally heard characterizing a patient as a 'crock' was nonplused at his follow-up question, 'what's a crock?'; talk about crocks was recurrent and unremarkable, part of the taken-for-granted daily concerns of these medical students. Second, key incidents need not transform analytic sensitivity and orientation in an immediate, dramatic fashion; as in Becker's case, such incidents may provide not flashes of insight, but niggling prods of interest and possibility. And finally, key incidents are not self-explicating, but have to be nurtured and mined; often initially opaque and uncertain in meaning and implication, they provide starting points and pushes for more empirical inquiry and comparison, not clear-cut analytic claims and propositions.

A strategic focus on key incidents shares common ground with Katz's (2001) examination of 'luminous description', as both approaches explore how the actions, talk, and concerns of the observed may play significant roles in developing grounded analyses of social life. As Katz argues, ethnographers' characterizations of pieces of their own or another's observations as 'rich', 'powerful', or 'vivid' do not point simply to the detailed and subtle *descriptive* qualities of such data. Rather, such data provoke movement from description to analysis, from 'showing *how* social life takes the shapes that it does' to 'making a convincing argument about *why* social life works as it does' (2001: 447, emphasis added). Katz then examines specific pieces of data characterized as 'revealing', 'vivid', 'poignant', 'paradoxical', 'strategic', and 'situated'. Such evaluations, he contends, reflect readers' 'initially unreflective appreciation of some data passages as particularly effective' (2001: 446), appreciations that ethnographers can self-consciously explore, extend, and elaborate into different kinds of grounded analyses. In similar fashion, key incidents involve fieldnote accounts of some specific event or interaction that allow fieldworkers to recognize and open up new lines of inquiry and analysis.

Clearly, key incidents may involve dramatic events or activities, and hence will not be viewed as mundane, routine, and ordinary by those participating in them. Observers in juvenile courts, for example, will encounter dramatic, 'serious' cases involving violence and media publicity and make pivotal use of these cases in subsequent analyses of court decision-making (as in the distinction between 'first-resort' responses to 'serious' cases and 'last-resort' handling of some routine, minor cases; Emerson, 1981). Similarly, Fantasia (1988: 75–120) relied upon observations of two spontaneous, wildcat strikes several months apart at a steel-casting factory to explore and analyze worker dissatisfaction with and resistance to standard union–management grievance procedures.

Such out-of-the-ordinary, dramatic, or 'critical' key incidents raise the question of what other substantive types of key incidents are evident in the ethnographic literature. Again, seizing on an 'invidious' term like 'crock' inevitably directs attention to contrastive positive terms – in Becker's case, to those sorts of patients considered desirable by medical students. These interesting cases involved patients who were characterized as 'really sick' with a detectable 'pathology', particularly one that was relatively new to students (Becker et al., 1961: 327ff.). In this sense, talk about indigenous 'members' types' and 'typologies' (Emerson et al., 1995: 119–22) provides another general category of key incident.

In this chapter, I shall examine two further types of possible key incidents – *extreme cases* and *interactional disjunctures* – in order to explore the pragmatics and uses of key incidents in naturalistic analysis. I take these key incidents from my own work, starting with the original fieldnotes and then examining the sequence of theoretical uses to which I put them. In so doing I seek to provide natural histories of the analytic paths taken in field research,[6] offering case studies of my use of two different types of key incidents to work up and elaborate analyses tightly focused on local activities and indigenous meanings.

AN 'EXTREME CASE': ANALYZING A 'SOCIOPATH' IN JUVENILE COURT

At an early point in my fieldwork in an eastern juvenile court, I was sitting with the chief judge in his chambers chatting about his day in the courtroom. As he talked he referred to a case that he had heard that morning but that I had not observed. My original fieldnote (with only the name of the clinic psychiatrist changed) read as follows:

'This little girl today, she's hopeless!' This girl has been in before and defaulted last week when her case came up. She was in for prostitution, and was examined [at the psychiatric clinic associated with the juvenile court]. Dr. James [said] that it was the first 100% sociopath she'd seen. 'Absolutely no conscience. She could not have

cared less about being in here. We couldn't do a thing for her. … The best you can hope for in a case like that is to put it on probation and let it go. That's all you can do. She['s] completely indifferent about it.' Girl is not ready for psychiatric treatment, as she would not cooperate. Girl was originally from North Carolina (but is white). She was arrested at the age of 14 for fornication. Moved to [eastern city] and was married at 17. 'Her husband left and she went out on the street.' Specialized in Chinatown, walking the streets 'propositioning Chinamen' until caught by the vice squad.

I followed this case closely over the next several months, interviewing the probation officer and psychiatrist about their dealings with and evaluations of the girl, reviewing the psychiatric evaluation and her court file, and continuing to talk to the judge about subsequent developments in the case. When I began to turn explicitly to analyzing my data, this case became a rich source of ideas and concerns. But my analytic interest in the case shifted and developed over time, eventually moving through three distinct phases: (1) 'sociopath' as a court assessment of an extreme form of 'moral character'; (2) 'letting a hopeless case go' as a process of 'making do'; and (3) 'last resorts' and disjunctures between assessment and decision outcome.

The specification of 'labeling' as assessments of 'moral character'

Initially I was taken with this case simply because the youth was described as a 'sociopath'. The year before, in writing my dissertation proposal, I had been directed to the then new statements of labeling theory of Becker (1963), Kitsuse (1962), and Erikson (1962). As a result my proposal had evolved into a study of 'the labeling process in juvenile court'. My assumption had been not only that juvenile court staff 'labeled' some youth 'delinquent' and not others, but also that this labeling would occur with adjudication, i.e. that labeling would involve decisions that some youth had actually committed acts that would be offenses if committed by adults, and that other youth had not committed such acts. It was quickly apparent, however, that few youth were ever found 'not delinquent', and that court staff routinely assumed that accused youth had in fact committed the acts alleged against them. Somewhat at a loss as to just where and how I was going to find 'labeling', I began to pay close attention to how court staff described, characterized, and evaluated youth in their everyday talk.

Against this background, I was excited by coming across a case that court staff saw as a 'sociopath'. I had selected the juvenile court as research setting in part because of an interest in the interface between law and psychiatry, and had read some of the existing literature on psychopaths and sociopaths, including work by William and Joan McCord (1956). Drawing on Sutherland's (1950) classic article on the diffusion of sexual psychopath laws, I had quickly adopted a 'labeling' perspective on this psychiatric category: to hear a youth diagnosed as a 'sociopath' was to encounter a judgment that this youth was completely and irretrievably 'bad' or 'criminal'. This impressed me as an unusually clear-cut and unequivocal evaluation, unlike the more nuanced or ambiguous assessments of youth commonly rendered by court and clinic personnel.

In this respect, the 'extreme' quality of the term 'sociopath' proved important in my initial analyses in my dissertation, as I came to identify the key to juvenile court 'labeling' in its assessment of the 'moral character' of accused youth. As I eventually developed this general argument (Emerson, 1968: 248):

> ... at later stages of court involvement attention shifts away from the behavior patterns and circumstances which led to the identification of trouble and toward judgments and inferences more directly concerned with the nature of the delinquent actor involved. Thus the direction of the delinquent's subsequent career within the Juvenile Court hinges on the kind of answer found by Court staff to the question: What kind of youth are we dealing with in this case? This process occurs through inquiry into a dimension of the youth's background, personality and future potential that will be conceptualized as 'moral character'[7].

Armed with a clearly 'invidious' type of moral character, I asked what other sorts of moral character court staff recognized, eventually characterizing 'sociopath' as the extreme form of *criminal* moral character, and contrasting it with two other types, *normal* and *disturbed* character. Furthermore, I argued that the different types of moral character corresponded with different court responses to cases:

> ... the very categories of kinds of actors – in terms of kinds of moral character – are shaped by the alternative courses of action open to the Court. ... In this way, the three classes or kinds of moral character recognized by the Court – normal, criminal, or disturbed – correspond to the following general courses or responses which the Court may try to implement: (1) routine handling of the case (generally probation and the relatively minor obligations and checks contingent upon it); (2) restraint or incarceration; (3) special care and handling. (Emerson, 1968: 260)

Here court assessments of criminal and disturbed character appeared particularly significant, since these judgments often entailed decisions to intervene actively and consequentially. Thus

> ... the Court primarily deals with and responds to cases in terms of abnormal character. If such character is firmly established the Court comes to feel that something drastic must be done with the case, and it becomes largely an academic question of how and why the delinquent got to be that way. (Emerson, 1968: 256)

But throughout, my theoretical interest in 'sociopath' lay not simply in the extremely negative judgment of moral character it exemplified, but also in the firmness and finality of this assessment. This fixed, unquestioned discrediting of the sociopath rendered concern with the causes of this condition irrelevant: 'If a case is "hopeless", i.e., totally identified as irretrievably criminal or sick, if character is firmly and solidly shaped, what matters is not how it came to be shaped, but rather how it is presently to be dealt with and controlled' (1968: 257). In contrast, in most cases assessments of moral character were tentative, much 'less clear-cut' and more 'ambiguous'. In these cases

> ... some delinquent behavior is apparent, but it is not of a particularly serious sort, [and] the court faces real difficulties in reviewing and coming to terms with these cases. It must grapple with contradictory indications of a 'real' potential for delinquency. ... [It] must weigh information and material capable of different and conflicting interpretation and meaning in order to determine whether or not special action is required. (Emerson, 1968: 249)

Finally, I sought to identify other dimensions of difference between these categories of moral character in the typical motives attributed to delinquent actors, the degree of intentionality linked to their behavior, and their 'reformability'. The sociopath exemplified the kinds of motives attributed to the criminal-like delinquent: 'The criminal-like delinquent is compelled by "evil" motives, acting ruthlessly to realize his own illegal ends, disregarding all social and legal conventions and feeling little or no compassion in the process' (Emerson, 1968: 261). Similarly, the sociopath exemplified delinquents seen as completely lacking in 'reform potential', a quality I supported by citing a somewhat edited version of the original fieldnote:

> The criminal-like delinquent is perceived as irrevocably committed to delinquent and criminal behavior. Essential to this perception is the perceived lack of any likelihood or possibility of change (reform) in the child. Delinquent activity is not a passing or temporary phase of growing up, but an established condition. The youth

is seen as set in his criminal-like ways, needing only time and experience to blossom forth as a full-fledged adult criminal, one for whom, as a probation officer notes, 'Springdale (the maximum security prison) is the only place.'

This lack of any potential for change or rehabilitation is clearly revealed in the Court's assessment of cases as 'hopeless':

> The Judge commented on a seventeen-year-old white girl in Court for prostitution, a girl the Clinic called 'a 100% sociopath': 'This little girl today, she's hopeless. ... Absolutely no conscience. She could not have cared less about being in here. We couldn't do a thing for her. ... The best you can hope for in a case like that is to put it *on probation and let it go.* That's all you can do. She's completely indifferent about it.' (Emerson, 1968: 262)

In sum, my initial analytic concern lay in using the case of the sociopath as the prototype of a delinquent of 'bad' or 'criminal' moral character. But at the same time I departed from this incident to consider other dimensions or features of such assessments: how fixed or established (as opposed to provisional) such judgments were, the types of motives attributed to this and other sorts of moral character, and the inference of 'hopelessness' and intractability to any and all treatment/rehabilitative possibilities.

'Letting a hopeless case go' as 'making do'

While completing the dissertation in the fall of 1967, I moved to Berkeley where I had a two-year Russell Sage Foundation postdoctoral position at the Center for the Study of Law and Society. During my first year there I met with Egon Bittner, then at the Langley Porter Institute at UCSF, to talk about my dissertation. At one point Bittner commented on the pervasive tendency of the court staff to 'make do', i.e. not to always make the most aggressive or seemingly most 'appropriate' response to delinquent youth, but rather to take measures that were practically feasible, minimizing the use of court resources and court personnel time and effort.[8] Bittner's comments led me to see the 'sociopath' case in a new light as I worked on revising the dissertation for publication as a book. I was astonished that I had missed the significance of the judge's comments about the 'hopeless' quality of the case and having 'to let it go'. Going back over my fieldnotes, I now keyed on interview comments by a probation officer (PO) that I had by and large previously ignored. The following two excerpts now gained importance as revealing specific court practices for 'making do':

(1) The PO commented on how many resources were wasted on cases that did not respond. I brought up the case of the 'sociopath': 'You mean like with that girl this morning?' 'Yes, she's a sociopath.' Now living in X, which is small town rather than urban. 'I told her, look, if you can keep from breaking any law until June [it's now April], and come to see me every month exactly when I say, your record will be cleared in June.'

'Garland (public defender) let me down on her. I told him, here, you do something, you're her lawyer. When I recommend six months probation, you suggest something more lenient and that it be cut to three months. But he just sat there when I recommended six months and didn't say a thing.' (Implication: because he did this I am saddled with a hopeless case for another three months.)

(2) In talking about a delinquent girl recommended for psychiatric placement by the clinic, the PO insisted that realistically no local residential facility would take her, and that the best you could expect was for the girl to get a job and hold it. The PO then immediately mentioned Joyce, who had reported on time today. Question about where her baby was, Joyce saying she had it but police reported otherwise. PO retold story of how public defender 'forgot his lines', prolonging probation past June. PO continued: 'I'm not supposed to do much with it', since the girl was 17. Joyce was then supposed to go her own way of (vice?) and crime and get picked up by the police as an adult, instead of [being] called on her probation as a juvenile. For this reason PO was not digging into truth on the baby, or into her suspicions that her husband was involved in crime of some sort because he had no means of support.

These pieces of data posed a contradiction for my central argument regarding moral character. In that I had claimed that criminally assessed moral character leads to (or at least is linked with) particularly restrictive responses – restraint or incarceration – I had an obvious exception here. This sociopath represented the 'worst' criminal-like character, yet the judge was talking not about incarceration but about 'letting it go'. Yet in the dissertation I had not explicitly framed this datum as a 'negative case'; for example, this footnote followed the fieldnote excerpt of the quote above:

> It should be pointed out that in this case incarceration is not considered necessary in a 'hopeless' cases because of lack of dangerousness. This in turn is related to the fact that the delinquent involved is a girl, and hence inherently less of a threat than a hopelessly delinquent boy. *Thus in general dangerousness is always an element in hopelessness, and hence in abnormal character.* (Emerson, 1968: 313, emphasis added)

In retrospect I had clearly fudged an obvious contradiction: I recognized that the judge felt he could 'let it go' because he perceived no threat or danger from the youth's future behavior; but I treated this as a statistical aberration, as a more or less chance variation for the more common pattern in which 'hopeless' cases are also 'dangerous' cases.

In this respect, I needed the concept of 'making do' to see something rational (in pragmatic terms) and patterned here, rather than simply an instance of organizational laxity and hence insignificant variation. This reframing allowed me to recognize contradiction, indeed to see this as a 'negative case'. Consider the final analysis included in the book (Emerson, 1969: 99):

> Finally, case outcomes may not exactly reflect judgments of moral character because of the juvenile court's inclination to 'make do', i.e., to exert only the minimally adequate effort and resources toward dealing with cases. The effects of 'making do' are particularly striking where a delinquent comes to be regarded as hopelessly criminal *yet not dangerous* in character. In such circumstances, despite criminal character, the court perceives no need for restraint and incarceration. Its concern is then merely to mark time until the youth passes into the jurisdiction of adult authorities. For example:
>
> > [fieldnote on the judge discussing the 'hopeless' case of the '100% sociopath', as in the earlier passage]
>
> In practice, however, only girls of criminal-like character are considered so unthreatening as to permit this kind of response.

In sum, recognizing 'making do' as a feature of juvenile court decision-making provided a way not only of explaining why assessments of moral character did not necessarily directly and linearly 'determine' case outcomes, but also and more fundamentally, of seeing the court's 'let it go' response as a contradiction to the basic thrust of the moral character argument. I was thus led to recast moral character not as the determinant of case outcomes, but as an assessment shaping the court's sense of 'what should be done', leaving open the possibility that what was actually done could be shaped by a number of practical contingencies and the court's own commonsense reasoning about what would happen with particular cases. Thus, in addition to different ways of 'making do', the book also considers instances of differential court responses to cases assessed similarly in terms of moral character.

From disjunctures between assessments and decision outcomes to 'last resorts'

I made yet another analysis of the case of Joyce some years later in analyzing the structure of 'last-resort' decisions (Emerson, 1981). Last-resort decisions were those accounted for by establishing that all normal or conventional remedies had been tried and had failed, such that a decision outcome normally regarded as faulted or even outright harmful emerged as the 'only alternative'. My thinking about last-resort decisions had been stimulated by court talk about Joyce, particularly by staff's clear recognition of the disjuncture between their extremely negative assessment of her character and extreme 'leniency' of their actual response. This led me to review my juvenile court data looking for other instances of disjunctures between assessed moral character and case outcomes; indeed, the core of the last-resort analysis emerged from the mirror image of Joyce's case, a case in which a youth was incarcerated despite court staff assessment that he was basically normal in character (Emerson, 1969: 97–8; 1981: 8).

But in addition, Joyce as a case of 'making do' became critical for specifying a further feature of last-resort decision rationales. As I developed this argument:

> Even if it has been shown that all normal remedies have been tried and have unequivocally failed,...several further conditions may have to be met before last-resort sanctions will legitimately be granted. First, the control agent may have to show that it is not possible simply to reinstitute some prior normal remedy; that is, the agent must show that some escalation in response is necessary. ... [Here] those controlling access to last-resort sanctions may entertain the possibility of reemploying some prior normal remedy rather than invoking the dubiously valued last resort. In juvenile court, for example, a delinquent facing incarceration may ultimately be kept 'on the streets' on probation precisely because court staff continue to see incarceration as an avoidable outcome. This action may be taken reluctantly and pessimistically (i.e., without believing that a response that has failed in the past will work now) and is pervaded by a sense of 'making do'. A successful last-resort request will thus require some showing that it is now *necessary* to invoke that last-resort sanction. (Emerson, 1981: 15–16)

In conclusion, I have examined the analytic unpacking of an 'extreme case' in the context of a specific juvenile court. This key incident, initially involving talk about a 'sociopath', was extreme in several respects. This was a locally unique event, the only case of a pure sociopath I encountered in juvenile court, and the first in the judge's experience; extreme formulations pervaded the judge's account – 'hopeless', '100% sociopath', 'absolutely no conscience', etc.; and the judgment of moral character was both totally and deeply negative and marked by unusual clarity and definitiveness. The analytic potential of extreme cases, then, may lie exactly in these exceptional, exaggerated qualities, qualities that accentuate and make visible features and processes that appear in hazier, more partial form in routine cases.

INTERACTIONAL DISJUNCTURES: ANALYZING THE DYNAMICS OF PSYCHIATRIC EMERGENCY TEAM INTERVENTION

In 1973 Mel Pollner and I began fieldwork in Los Angeles on psychiatric emergency teams (PET teams), two-person mobile units going out into the community in response to calls for crisis intervention and/or mental hospital evaluation. Two theoretical concerns foreshadowed this field research: first, we viewed PET teams as (psychiatric) third parties intervening in and making decisions about how to handle messy interpersonal troubles;[9] second, we anticipated PET would regularly confront and have to disentangle 'reality disjunctures' – contradictory experiences of or claims about 'reality' (Pollner, 1975) – as matters of practical decision-making. However, our initial substantive publications on PET dealt with different issues, issues that we had not anticipated: the grounding for and significance of PET's understanding of its own work as 'dirty work', and the logics and practices for selecting candidate calls for field visits (Emerson and Pollner, 1976, 1978). Yet we retained our original interests in how PET approached and dealt with interpersonal messes and reality conflicts, over the years developing and elaborating analyses of some of the critical processes of in-the-field decision-making (Pollner, 1976; Emerson, 1989).

I observed the following case during our second week of fieldwork. While in some ways uneventful and devoid of the high-drama qualities PET cases could exhibit, this case came to play a key role in framing our analysis of these issues.

A. Going out

In the PET office there are three slips recording calls on Chris Alford. The first, called in by his mother, herself a board and care home resident, describes the following 'problem': 'Has attacked mother in B & C home. Walks around in rain w no shoes on and in tee shirt. Has threatened to kill mother if she puts him away.' [Names of two public mental hospitals; box for 'previous psychiatric hospitalization' checked 'yes'.]

Shelly, an experienced psych tech who is coordinating PET today, comments that they have had nine calls just this morning on this guy, including one from a city councilman who knows the father. When Ted, a social worker, arrives for the 1 p.m. shift, she tells him: 'Ted, I don't usually ask this. If this guy is sick or isn't sick, please do something!' Ted agrees to go out that afternoon with Rosanne, another psych tech. While he is temporarily out of the office, Shelly fields another call from the mother, and after hanging up, tells those in the office: 'I'll bet you he isn't even that bad. … It's just a bunch of anxious people, that's all. That's what it sounds like to me.'

I accompany the team to the apartment building. The father is not there to meet us as arranged, but Ted proceeds anyway. On the way in he checks with the wife of the apartment manager, who lives on the first floor, and asks: Can we come down and use your phone if we have to? The woman readily agrees, and as we start up the stairs asks: 'You all come to get him?' Ted: 'We came to talk to him.'

B. The encounter

Upstairs we find the right apartment and knock. A thin young black man cracks open the door and sticks his head out. Ted checks to confirm that he is Chris Alford, then explains that we are from Mental Health and would like to talk with him. Chris nods his agreement, but makes no move to open the door. Ted asks: Can we come in? Chris, looking at the two PET workers and me, responds: 'How many does it take to talk?' Ted replies that it will only take about five minutes, and makes a move toward the door, which Chris now opens, allowing all of us to move into his small one-room apartment. Rosanne sits in the only chair, the rest of us remain standing. Ted begins by asking: 'How've you been?' Chris does not reply at first, but then answers 'Ok' when Ted repeats the question. Ted: How long since you got out of the hospital? Chris: A long time. Ted: How long? A couple years. Did they give you medicine? Yes. Have you been taking it? Part of the time. Does it help you? Yes. Ted then continued, Chris, we've had calls that you've been bothering people. Chris: I haven't been bothering nobody. Ted: We've had calls that you have. No. What about your mother? Did you threaten her? I have trouble hearing the soft-spoken man as he recounts talking to his mother and poking her on the chest to emphasize a point; she then got upset and said he hit her. A silence ensues, as Ted seems at a loss about what to ask next, and turns to Rosanne and me, asking if we have any questions. We do not, and after a somewhat embarrassed but brief silence, Ted concludes, 'Thank you. That's all.'

C. Aftermath

We leave the room and go downstairs. On our way out to the car the apartment manager's wife intercepts us to say that the father wants to talk with us on the phone. In their apartment, Ted's side of the conversation includes the following: '... We did an evaluation. We cannot hospitalize. [pause] I understand how you feel, sir. But we can't break the law. [pause] Sir, we didn't observe any of this behavior when we saw him. We can't do anything here. We have to go by the law.' He then reviews the specific criteria required by the Lanterman-Petris-Short (LPS) act – danger to self, danger to others, gravely disabled – regulating involuntary mental hospital commitment.

Driving back to the clinic, Rosanne comments: 'To me he looks like he been smoking weed.' He seemed a little spaced out to me. Ted responds that he seemed a little crazy, but he wasn't bothering anyone. Rosanne reiterates this theme: 'He's got a right to be crazy.' He's not hurting anyone, no reason to put him in the hospital. A bit later Ted characterizes Chris as harmless, kind of into his own world, but not looking to hurt anyone, then exclaiming: 'a harmless, little impotent schizy kid!'

This brief, single incident touched off and grounded a number of different analytic riffs, both immediately and in the long term. These included: (1) PET typically confronted 'candidate patients' (Holstein, 1993) rather than confirmed patients, and often was literally in the business of 'creating patients' in the face of silence, denial, and non-participation. (2) Candidate patients who were encountered without an in-person complainant – typically those who lived alone rather than with some significant other – were thereby protected (somewhat) against unwanted disclosure of discrediting information, decreasing their chances of being hospitalized against their will. (3) Decisions to hospitalize (or not), while informed by and sensitive to the California legal criteria of danger to self, danger to others, or grave disability, were practical, contingent, and emergent matters, keyed more to assessments of the tenability or manageability of candidate patients' actual living situations than to mental condition or psychiatric diagnosis.

Overcoming silence, minimalization, and denial to create psychiatric patients

Very little seemed to happen in the interaction between candidate patient and PET in this encounter. The former offered minimal responses, denying any upset and problems, but providing an alternative version of the episode with his mother that diminished its alleged 'violent' character. Indeed, in the field I had been impressed by the stumbling, disjunctive quality of the interaction, commenting immediately after the above fieldnote: 'The talk with Chris seemed awkward; Ted soon seemed to run out of things to ask or say, and when neither Rosanne or I picked up the

ball, seemed to have no other easy option but to leave.' As a result, Ted elicited little new 'evidence' to use in making his evaluation and hospitalization decision. Again as I wrote in my immediate impressions: 'Initially Ted seemed ambivalent about Chris's evaluation, commenting that he hadn't seen much. ... [But by the time we were back in the car], his view of Chris quickly seemed to become consolidated, less ambiguous. No more mention of a brief evaluation. Rather he seemed committed to the position that this was an "impotent, schizy kid", by implication not falling within the LPS guidelines.'

And upon continued reflection, we were struck by how effectively resistant this candidate patient was to PET's overtures to talk about his circumstances, how difficult it seemed for the PET workers to come up with next questions, and how inconclusively the encounter ended. It appeared that PET had been denied access to any meaningful display of this candidate patient's thoughts and feelings, and hence was unable to come up with any relatively firm psychological assessment. As an observer I walked out feeling that the man may have been hallucinating or even deeply psychotic, but that interactional disjunctures with the PET team prevented any revelation of what was going on with him.

In subsequent work, we explored the implications of this subtle, undramatic incident by viewing it as a situation in which a candidate patient had quietly but effectively refused to assume the role of 'patient'. We developed this line of analysis by considering the differences between the psychiatric patient who comes to an outpatient, office appointment, and the circumstances PET workers regularly faced in confronting people who had not necessarily agreed to conduct themselves as patients. To quote at length from our initial analysis of these issues in an unpublished paper (Pollner, 1976: 21–3):

> In the vast majority of cases, certain fundamental aspects of psychiatrist-patient interaction may be taken for granted by the office psychiatrist. ... For example, the patient will be prepared to display himself and his mind, to honor and allow the psychiatrist to have questioning concerns, to maintain a certain level of civility, etc. In a variety of ways, the voluntary patient is one who will allow himself to be governed by the understanding that this relationship is one in which 'I am patient – you are expert' prevails as guiding maxims. ...
>
> PET teams which respond to calls from the community for aid/evaluation are denied the benefits of the 'pre-understanding' usually guaranteed the office practitioners. ... For example, having been called by neighbors, relatives – that is, persons other than the client himself – PET teams come to their clients from out of the blue. Typically, the persons who are the objects of

PET visits are the last to know about the visit: often their first indication of a PET visit is provided by a knock on the door. Thus PET is an unexpected visitor – and, moreover, a visitor who not all of the Pettees (i.e., those visited by PET) would care to have calling at that moment or at all. Thus, PET often finds itself in an interaction in which its relation to the Pettee is yet to be established at some rather fundamental level. That is, the definition of who is acting in what capacity with what rights, etc. is, at best, a unilaterally sustained version. From the point of view of the Pettee, PET's appearance is anything from and including relief, the denouement of an ongoing family 'trouble' situation, the moment of betrayal, invasion, of fear, of deep puzzlement, of utter astonishment, anger, etc.

A not uncommon response to PET is no response. That is, a person will not respond to any of PET's solicitations or questions: they stare at or beyond PET. From a Pettee's point of view the silence may be serving a number of interactional functions. For example, we all know the ways in which it is not wise to talk to strangers and PET members are almost always strangers. We know as well the ways in which it is sometimes wise not to dignify a question with a reply, and Pettees are often asked questions which are quite undignified in what they imply about the Pettee's competence and ability to manage his own affairs. We know further that the 'direct cut' can be a marvelously effective albeit brute way of signaling that another's presence is deeply undesirable. There are a variety of ways in which the silence becomes an interactional way to dismiss or discount an illegitimate accosting. We are reminded here of Jay Haley's remarks some years ago that if one is to avoid defining a relation he must exhibit the features characteristic of schizophrenia.

In sum, our initial take on this interactionally awkward encounter keyed on muted candidate-patient resistance, not only to PET's presence but also to the allocation of roles that its presence implicitly and explicitly proposed. We developed this line of analysis in subsequent work, looking systematically at how PET initiated contact with unknown candidate patients, paying close attention to PET's on-the-doorstep explanations of who they were and what they wanted as truncated practices for trying to recruit or create 'patients' (Emerson, 1989).

'Living alone' and lack of an immediate complainant as insulation from psychiatric intervention

As we reflected on Chris Alford's encounter with PET, we also began to notice how he had been 'protected' exactly because he lived alone, and because his primary complainant (his mother) was not present to challenge his claims

or to provide alternative, discrediting versions of events in his life. In this sense, we came to see this situation as that of a 'candidate patient seen alone', retrospectively finding new import in other observations in which the caller/complainant was present for the field visit and came to align with the PET teams in undermining the candidate patient's claims that there was 'no problem'. This line of analysis interested us in part because of the deep emotional impact made by the first extended PET case we had observed. In this case, in a process exemplifying Goffman's (1961) 'betrayal funnel', a husband overrode his young wife's attempts at silence and withdrawal, leading to involuntary hospitalization. Consider the following portions of our fieldnotes on this case:

A. First encounter

We go out with a PET team composed of psych techs, Shelly and Renee, to evaluate Rosemary, a young mother of a four-year-old child whose husband had called earlier, very 'agitated' and 'panicky', asking PET to call the police and the hospital. As we drove to the apartment Renee noted that the husband had reported of his wife: 'She's doing bizarre things. ... She burnt herself. She rants and raves. She smashed her car into another.'

We arrive at the apartment building and ring the doorbell for #2. There is no response. The PET workers chastise themselves for not having called the husband, who works five minutes away, to come meet them, and begin trying to locate a phone elsewhere in the building to now make this call. As they are doing so, a young woman wearing a blue quilted jacket and dark slacks, comes up the stairs to #2, takes out her keys and opens the door. The two PET workers immediately approach her, with Shelly introducing herself by name, adding: 'We'd like to talk with you.' Woman: 'Why?' S: 'Because we've heard you've been having problems.' Woman: 'What problems?' S: 'I'd rather not talk about it out here in public.' The woman said nothing in response, but remained blocking the doorway, first gazing rather blankly at the two PET workers and the two fieldworkers (we were standing on the stairs leading up to the apartment), then staring at each of us in turn, moving from one face to the next with the same kind of confused, deliberating look. ...

Eventually Shelly and Renee gave up and left, telling Rosemary they would return tomorrow. In the car Shelly commented that Rosemary was 'obviously hallucinating. She's very paranoid. ... She was listening to every sound. ... She's sick! She's in mortal terror!' They would hospitalize her, but: 'We don't have time today.' (It was now almost 4 p.m.) 'We'll get the husband and come tomorrow.' Shelly also reported: 'I asked her how she felt. She said she didn't know. I said obviously she wasn't feeling well. ... I told her we could help her feel better.' At another point, 'she said she didn't understand anything that was going on'. She talked about calling her husband. But then she said, no, 'he wants to put me away'.

B. Second encounter

The next day the same PET workers went to meet the husband at the apartment at 1:30, planning to commit Rosemary to the psychiatric ward of a nearby, highly regarded hospital. This time the husband opens the door and leads the four of us into a small living room. While their four year old son continues to play with his toys on the living room floor, Rosemary moves toward us from the adjoining dining area. Almost the same beginning as yesterday: 'We want to talk to you Rosemary.' 'Why?' 'We've heard you have problems.' 'I don't have any problems.' This sequence seems to cycle a few times with some minor variations, with Rosemary responding 'What kind of problems?', pacing and seeming to stay as far away from the PET presence in the living room as possible. Eventually the husband, who has taken a seat at the dining room table, tells Rosemary: 'Sit down and talk. These people want to help you.' But Rosemary continues to mix pacing with standing against the dining room wall.

One PET worker then asks her how long she has been feeling like this. No answer, but a sort of grimace. The question and lack of response is repeated. Shelly then turns to the husband and asks when he first noticed this. About two years ago. No, recently. About two weeks ago. And he then begins to recite a list of problems, beginning with: 'Her mother's three thousand miles away and she said this morning that her mother lived right next door. She lives in New York state.' And, she doesn't know all kinds of things; this morning she didn't know who I was. Rosemary: I knew it. Husband: You see! She didn't know my name (i.e., know she doesn't even know she didn't know). Shelly asks: What's his name Rosemary. Rosemary: I know what he *says* his name is.

Husband then talks about yet another problem: 'She walks and walks all the time. You see what she is doing now? She does that at two in the morning. Three in the morning. I work, I have to sleep and she is walking all the time. I'm getting an ulcer from this. I put her in front of TV to watch and she walks back and forth. When we eat, she walks. And this morning she talks like a baby. I don't understand what she says, it's meaningless. And she laughs.'

In this case, even after their first, more or less aborted encounter at the front door, PET was convinced that the candidate patient was seriously disoriented and in dire need of psychiatric hospitalization.[10] But when confronted alone, her resistance and silence stymied full elicitation of her psychological and behavioral peculiarities. In contrast, setting up the situation to encounter Rosemary with her husband allowed PET to rely on his interventions and informings in the face of her silences and efforts not to participate. Thus, we came to view these two encounters as almost a controlled experiment in which the candidate patient had more or less successfully minimized any display of mind and interaction when confronting PET while alone, but had been deeply exposed and discredited when encountered in the presence of an intimate other.

The contingencies of decisions to hospitalize (or not): LPS, tenability, and 'craziness plus'

Finally, we began to consider the different outcomes of these two cases: in the first, seemingly certain hospitalization, prefigured by accounts of violent behavior, multiple, persistent complainants, and prior hospitalizations, did not come to pass; in the second, PET's commitment to hospitalization never seemed to waver, despite the lack of any overtly 'dangerous' or threatening behavior. How to account for these different, unexpected outcomes?

First, we had seen a number of cases in which PET workers paid minimal attention to the presence or absence of indications of mental illness, but rather became preoccupied with determining the anticipatable, disruptive ramifications of mental illness in that actual living situation. Thus, PET was not necessarily concerned with mental illness 'per se', but rather often displayed an orientation to the 'tenability' or manageability of candidate patients' life circumstances (Emerson, 1989). Chris's situation both exemplified and helped us recognize this pattern. Even his meager display of mind was adequate for PET's practical purposes with assessing mental condition not in the abstract but in the context of tenability. In person he seemed quiet and passive; he lived alone so that whatever he did at home would trouble no one; and the only reported complaint came from his mother, who lived elsewhere and could be presumed not to make frequent contact. Indeed, as a practical matter, his living situation was tenable, even if he were psychotic.

This understanding of PET concern with tenability had important implications for analyzing PET decisons to recommend involuntary hospitalization generally. In most instances, PET sought to hospitalize when the candidate patient not only acted in a disturbed fashion, but also engaged in acts that created a potentially unmanageable or untenable living situation. In this sense hospitalization generally required 'craziness plus' (Emerson, 1989: 221):

PET did not ordinarily assume that because someone was seriously mentally ill they should be treated in a mental hospital. Hospitalization became *necessary* when that disturbance could be seen as getting out of hand, as prefiguring unmanageable or uncontrollable situations and happenings. In this sense, PET tended to hospitalize not simply those they found to be seriously crazy, but rather those who had what can be called '*craziness plus*'; that is, serious disturbance plus factors indicating that the situation would become seriously and consequentially unmanageable without hospitalization. ... In several cases PET did not hospitalize blatantly paranoid and presumably dangerous patients, accounting for this action by pointing to the ways in which the patient's living situations could absorb or circumscribe anticipatible harmful behavior growing out of the paranoid state.

But secondly, what about the situation of Rosemary? PET did show some concern with untenability in this case, as a wife with a young child was seemingly not providing minimally adequate and safe care.[11] But more critical here were the different attitudes PET displayed toward chronic as opposed to first-time, 'acute' patients. While hospitalization served no purpose and was avoided where possible for chronic patients, it was a different story with acute patients: here aggressive intervention, including hospitalization, was felt to provide a helpful, effective response. To quote from an article examining these issues (Emerson and Pollner, 1976: 247): 'As one social worker remarked with regard to the "occasional acute case" that PET came across: "There we can do something. Things begin to happen. Things begin to straighten out."' Rosemary provided our prototypical acute case, a candidate patient whose problems could be positively and successfully treated by the therapeutic options, including hospitalization, to which PET had access.

In conclusion, we had come away from our observation of the Chris Alford case with a general, unarticulated impression of a PET intervention stymied, of an interaction that stuttered and petered out, in the face of silence, denial, and minimal participation by the candidate patient. Key incidents involving such interactional disjunctures can help highlight points of strain and tension in the perspectives and concerns different parties bring to and pursue during face-to-face encounters. Exploring the different facets and ramifications of this moment of interactional difficulty led us to problematize the very notion of 'patient' in PET work, and to explore the routine processes whereby PET sought to 'create' patients in encounters that began when they knocked on the doors of reportedly troubled strangers (Emerson, 1989).

CONCLUSION

Naturalistic analysis proceeds by exploring and elaborating the implications of 'key incidents' in fieldnote accounts of specific events or interactions. Key incidents are not necessarily dramatic matters, significant or noteworthy for those involved. Rather a key incident attracts a particular field researcher's immediate interest, even if what occurred was mundane and ordinary to participants. This 'interest' is not a full-blown, clearly articulated theoretical claim, but a more intuitive, theoretically sensitive conviction that something intriguing has just taken place. In the case of my juvenile court research, as in Becker's medical school research, the use of strange or unusual terms – 'sociopath' and 'crock' respectively – proved subtly intriguing. In studying PET, a feeling of awkwardness and disjuncture as the team tried unsuccessfully to talk to and draw out a candidate patient drew my attention. Clearly the researcher provides the 'interest' that makes incidents 'key', but this is more an intuitive sense of analytic possibility than an explicit theoretical proposition.

Key incidents tend to be empirically 'rich', incorporating first-hand data preserving the complex reality of social life and suffused with many seemingly trivial details and unanticipated topics. While his initial account of hearing about 'crocks' is bare bones, Becker clearly followed up and collected a rich variety of materials about when and how medical students used the term. Similarly, the fieldnote accounts I have presented reveal multiple concerns and dimensions. The judge's talk not only referenced a 'sociopath', but also the terms of this psychiatric diagnosis, the sense of a 'hopeless' case, and the practical logic of having to 'let it go'. The second case study not only drew upon description of the face-to-face contact between PET team and candidate patient, but also provided background and context – the stream of demands to 'do something', neighbors' expectations that the young man was to be hospitalized.

Since key incidents are (or can be made) empirically rich and multi-stranded, the process of drawing out their analytic implications will often involve a gradual clarification and unpacking of one dimension, then another, then yet another. For key incidents have the potential to point toward a number of different analytic issues, and these issues may be best developed one by one over time, as the ethnographer identifies and works through the implications of different lines of theorizing. Before delineating the nature and dimensions of moral character, for example, I was not in a strong position to take up the implications of the judge's and probation officer's 'let it go' stance toward this particular case. Similarly, to explain the varied conditions under which PET came to seek involuntary hospitalization first required recognizing and then specifying the conditions under which they failed to convert candidate patients into real patients.

That different analytic issues evoke and require different comparisons within the data also promotes the step-by-step framing and elaboration of different analytic issues from key incidents. Working with key incidents proceeds by generating a sequence of shifting and more finely tuned comparisons. For example, my analysis of PET work moved from comparison of Chris Alford to other cases of those who passively resisted PET overtures, to comparisons of cases of very active resistance, and then to differences in the ways PET teams planned for and first managed contact with candidate patients. The first juvenile court comparisons were between 'sociopath' and other cases involving extremely negative assessments of moral character, then with cases where such assessments were tentative and uncertain. Having completed these lines of analysis, I was in a position to identify and compare cases where assessments of moral character and decision outcomes appeared disjointed.

If working with key incidents involves constant but graduated, shifting, issue-by-issue comparisons, it also reveals underlying complexities in the identification and use of negative cases. It is not only a matter of having to formulate a specific hypothesis before we can identify a relevant negative case, but of recognizing something as a contradiction in the first place. In my juvenile court analyses, I initially did not conceive of the court's insistence on handling the case of a '100% sociopath' by 'letting it go' as a fundamental contradiction of the relationship between negative assessments of moral character and decision outcomes I had posited; 'letting it go' looked like simple laxity and indifference, it seemed a legally irrational stance without pattern or order, hence some sort of random variation. Seeing it as a negative case required additional analytic resources from the idea of 'making do'. 'Making do' allowed me to appreciate that 'letting it go' was not some surreptitious practice hidden on the margins, but something court staff openly and recurrently talked about in this case and others. 'Making do' reframed 'letting it go'

as an instance of the practical working rationality common to most frontline agents of social control. And once recognized as a distinctive feature of court activity, its relevance as a negative case became clear. In this sense, negative cases do not always jump out at us, but may be framed and elicited by our own analytic work.

NOTES

1   In their early work Glaser and Strauss (1967: 33) did urge fieldworkers to enter research settings as nearly tabula rasa as possible, 'without any preconceived theory that dictates ... relevancies in concepts and hypotheses'. But most grounded theorists now reject this 'tabula rasa' imagery. Charmaz (2001: 337) in particular denies that analytic categories 'inhere in the data and may even leap out at the researcher', insisting that such categories are products of 'the interaction between the observer and observed'. Thus initial theoretical concerns should be viewed as sensitizing concepts in Blumer's sense, serving only as *points of departure* to look at data, to listen to interviewees and to think analytically about the data' (Charmaz, 2001: 337, emphasis in original).

2   Some ethnographers try to minimize such complications by insisting that data collection and analysis should proceed simultaneously. Strauss (1987: 26–7), for example, advocates beginning analysis 'with the very first, second, or third interview or after the first day or two of fieldwork, ... [so that] the next interviews and observations become informed by analytic questions and hypotheses about categories and their relationships'. In practice, field researchers certainly make decisions about some analytic priorities and foci as they are actively collecting data (Lofland and Lofland, 1995, talk about first 'focusing data', then 'analyzing data'); but few are able to work out full-blown, more elaborated analyses until considering the data corpus as a whole.

3   Contemporary proponents of analytic induction now generally understand the search for perfect explanation not as a goal in itself but as a pragmatic research strategy for conceptual refinement (Ragin, 1994: 98). Thus Katz (1983: 133) maintains: 'The test is not whether a final state of perfect explanation has been achieved but the *distance* that has been traveled over negative cases and through subsequent qualifications from an initial state of knowledge.'

4   Here in particular there are definite points of tension between grounded theory's priority on generating theory and the often more descriptive emphases of ethnography, a tension Glaser and Strauss (1971: 183) accented in contrasting their model of the researcher as primarily 'an active sampler of theoretically relevant data' with that of 'an ethnographer trying to get the fullest data on a group'.

5   In his recent work, Becker (1998) offers another approach and resource, inventorying a range of fruitful

analytic 'tricks' – that is, 'ways of thinking' that allow the fieldworker 'to turn things around, to see things differently, in order to create new problems for research, new possibilities for comparing cases and inventing new categories, and the like'.

6 This effort extends the naturalistic fieldwork tradition of providing natural histories of in-the-field research activities – what Sanjek (1990: 398–400) has termed 'the ethnographer's path' – to include detailed case studies of how ethnographers actually go about developing 'grounded', context-sensitive analyses (see Emerson, 2001: 304–6). Analytic induction provides a number of exemplars of such case studies (Cressey, 1953; Lindesmith, 1968; Katz, 1982), since most studies using this approach have provided some fairly detailed account of the step-by-step development of the analysis.

7 Here follows a footnote attributing the term 'moral character' to Carl Werthman (1964), specifically quoting this sentence: 'Judgments about moral character are based on knowledge of a person's fundamental *attitude* toward the authority of the moral order.' Linkages to the concepts of 'total identity' (Garfinkel, 1956) and 'moral career' (Goffman, 1961) are also cited.

8 Although he did not explicitly use the term, in his work on police patrol decision-making Bittner highlighted the pervasiveness of and conditions for such 'making do', particularly in the practices of 'the restricted relevance of culpability' on skid-row (1967a) and 'restitution of control' and 'psychiatric first aid' in handling the mentally ill (1967b).

9 I was developing a general analysis of interpersonal troubles and the consolidating consequences of third-party intervention published a few years later in Emerson and Messinger (1977).

10 Despite the seeming certainty of this diagnostic evaluation and of making a hospital commitment, PET was very aware of the possibilities of caller exaggeration and 'overreaction' in reporting another's psychiatric problems, as became strikingly evident in the Chris Alford case. As a consequence, any initial 'diagnosis', based as in this case on congruence between a caller's report and what had been observed directly (albeit in truncated fashion) about the candidate patient, held only 'until further notice', i.e. unless and until no contradictory information emerged. These concerns surfaced during the drive out on the second day, when Shelly explained that they would rather not hospitalize under these circumstances; 'we don't like to go into someone's home when there's a husband or mother not there.' Renee added that one reason for this was to make sure that it wasn't one of those folie à deux things we talked about yesterday on the ride home; 'we see if it's the patient's fault.'

11 Thus we were thinking of this case in the following analysis: 'hospitalization might occur in situations where serious disturbance was not really at issue. In homes in which a young child was present, for example, PET workers were inclined to hospitalize much more readily than in home situations without

such children, often pointing to the high vulnerability of the youngster to harm by the parent' (Emerson, 1989: 221).

REFERENCES

Becker, Howard S. (1963) *Outsiders: Studies in the Sociology of Deviance.* New York: Free Press.

Becker, Howard S. (1993) 'How I learned what a crock was', *Journal of Contemporary Ethnography*, 22: 28–35.

Becker, Howard S. (1998) *Tricks of the Trade: How to Think About Your Research While You're Doing It.* Chicago: University of Chicago Press.

Becker, Howard S., Hughes, Everett C., Geer, Blanche and Strauss, Anselm L. (1961) *Boys in White: Student Culture in Medical School.* Chicago: University of Chicago Press.

Bittner, Egon (1967a) 'The police on skid-row: a study of peace-keeping', *American Sociological Review*, 32: 700–15.

Bittner, Egon (1967b) 'Police discretion in emergency apprehension of mentally ill persons', *Social Problems*, 14: 278–92.

Blumer, Herbert (1969) *Symbolic Interactionism: Perspective and Method.* Englewood Cliffs, NJ: Prentice-Hall.

Bulmer, Martin (1979) 'Concepts in the analysis of qualitative data: a symposium', *Sociological Review*, 27: 651–77.

Charmaz, Kathy (2001) 'Grounded Theory', in Robert M. Emerson (ed.), *Contemporary Field Research: Perspectives and Formulations.* Prospect Heights, IL: Waveland, pp. 335–52.

Cressey, Donald R. (1953) *Other People's Money: A Study in the Social Psychology of Embezzlement.* Glencoe, IL: Free Press.

Emerson, Robert M. (1968) 'The juvenile court: labeling and institutional careers'. Unpublished PhD dissertation, Brandeis University, Waltham, MA.

Emerson, Robert M. (1969) *Judging Delinquents: Context and Process in Juvenile Court.* Chicago: Aldine.

Emerson, Robert M. (1981) 'On last resorts', *American Journal of Sociology*, 87: 1–22.

Emerson, Robert M. (1989) 'Tenability and troubles: The construction of accommodative relations by psychiatric emergency teams', in James A. Holstein and Gale Miller (eds), *Perspectives on Social Problems*, vol. 1. Greenwich, CT: JAI Press, pp. 215–37.

Emerson, Robert M. (2001) *Contemporary Field Research: Perspectives and Formulations* (2nd ed.). Prospect Heights, IL: Waveland Press.

Emerson, Robert M. and Messinger, Sheldon L. (1977) 'The micro-politics of trouble', *Social Problems*, 25: 121–34.

Emerson, Robert M. and Pollner, Melvin (1976) 'Dirty work designations: their features and consequences in a psychiatric setting', *Social Problems*, 23: 243–55.

Emerson, Robert M. and Pollner, Melvin (1978) 'Policies and practices of psychiatric case selection', *Sociology of Work and Occupations*, 5: 75–96.

Emerson, Robert M., Fretz, Rachel I. and Shaw, Linda L. (1995) *Writing Ethnographic Fieldnotes*. Chicago: University of Chicago Press.

Erikson, Kai T. (1962) 'Notes on the sociology of deviance', *Social Problems*, 9: 307–14.

Fantasia, Rick (1988) *Cultures of Solidarity: Consciousness, Action and Contemporary American Workers*. Berkeley: University of California Press.

Garfinkel, Harold (1956) 'Conditions of successful degradation ceremonies', *American Journal of Sociology*, 61: 420–4.

Glaser, Barney G. and Strauss, Anselm L. (1967) *The Discovery of Grounded Theory: Strategies for Qualitative Research*. Chicago: Aldine.

Glaser, Barney G. and Strauss, Anselm L. (1971) *Status Passage*. Chicago: Aldine.

Goffman, Erving (1961) *Asylums: Essays on the Social Situation of Mental Patients and Other Inmates*. Garden City, NY: Doubleday.

Gubrium, Jaber F. and Holstein, James A. (1997) *The New Language of Qualitative Method*. New York: Oxford University Press.

Holstein, James A. (1993) *Court-Ordered Insanity: Interpretive Practice and Involuntary Commitment*. New York: Aldine de Gruyter.

Katz, Jack (1982) *Poor People's Lawyers in Transition*. New Brunswick, NJ: Rutgers University Press.

Katz, Jack (1983) 'A theory of qualitative methodology', in Robert M. Emerson (ed.), *Contemporary Field Research*. Boston: Little, Brown, pp. 127–48.

Katz, Jack (2001) 'From how to why: on luminous description and causal inference in ethnography (Part 1)', *Ethnography*, 2: 443–73.

Kitsuse, John I. (1962) 'Societal reactions to deviant behavior: problems of theory and method', *Social Problems*, 9: 247–56.

Lindesmith, Alfred R. (1968) *Addiction and Opiates*. Chicago: Aldine.

Lofland, John (1976) *Doing Social Life: The Qualitative Study of Human Interaction in Natural Settings*. New York: Wiley.

Lofland, John and Lofland, Lyn H. (1995) *Analyzing Social Settings: A Guide to Qualitative Observation and Analysis* (3rd ed.). Belmont, CA: Wadsworth.

McCord, William and McCord, Joan (1956) *Psychopathy and Delinquency*. New York: Grune & Stratton.

Matza, David (1969) *Becoming Deviant*. Englewood Cliffs, NJ: Prentice-Hall.

Pollner, Melvin (1975) ' "The very coinage of your brain": the anatomy of reality disjunctures', *Philosophy of the Social Sciences*, 5: 411–30.

Pollner, Melvin (1976) 'The micro-politics of psychiatric emergencies'. Unpublished manuscript.

Ragin, Charles C. (1994) *Constructing Social Research: The Unity and Diversity of Method*. Thousand Oaks, CA: Pine Forge Press.

Sanjek, Roger (1990) 'On ethnographic validity', in R. Sanjek (ed.), *Fieldnotes: The Making of Anthropology*. Ithaca, NY: Cornell University Press, pp. 385–418.

Schatzman, Leonard and Strauss, Anselm L. (1973) *Field Research: Strategies for a Natural Sociology*. Englewood Cliffs, NJ: Prentice-Hall.

Strauss, Anselm L. (1987) *Qualitative Analysis for Social Scientists*. New York: Cambridge University Press.

Sutherland, Edwin H. (1950) 'The diffusion of sexual psychopath laws', *American Journal of Sociology*, 56: 142–8.

Werthman, Carl (1964) 'Delinquency and authority'. Unpublished Master's Thesis, Department of Sociology, University of California, Berkeley.

30

Computer-assisted qualitative data analysis

Udo Kelle

Computer use in qualitative research can now look back on a history of two decades. Nowadays more than twenty different software packages are available that can assist qualitative researchers in their work with textual data, and some of these programs (like NVivo, ATLAS/ti or MAXQda) are widely applied. The field of 'computer-assisted qualitative data analysis' (sometimes referred to by the acronym 'CAQDAS') now represents a well-established field in the domain of qualitative methodology, with its own 'networking projects', conferences and several discussion lists on the Internet.

From its beginning this development was accompanied by a lively debate about the potential methodological merits and dangers of computer use in qualitative research, with discussants expressing great optimism as well as concerned warnings. Whereas enthusiastic proponents of CAQDAS emphasized the great efficiency gains provided by the mechanization of cumbersome tasks of data organization and the various possibilities to implement new strategies of data analysis with the help of the computer (cf. Conrad and Reinarz, 1984), critics have often expressed their concerns about a potential alienation between researchers and their data and the enforcement of analysis strategies that go against the methodological and theoretical orientations qualitative researchers see as the hallmark of their work (cf. Agar, 1991; Seidel, 1991; Lonkila, 1995; Coffey et al., 1996).

Like many other controversies in the field of social research methodology, the debate is overburdened with rather abstract concepts and ideas. In the following I shall make an attempt to discuss different aspects of computer use not from a general methodological or epistemological perspective but from research practice, by drawing on my own experiences as a researcher and a methodological consultant for research projects. Thereby it will be shown that the evaluation of arguments in the methodological debates mentioned above requires a thorough discussion and evaluation of often used folklore techniques of data organization and data management. Such techniques, whose methodological significance is often underestimated and even neglected in the technical literature, are not neutral technical tools but have a far-reaching impact on the research process and its results. Despite the often discussed danger of alienating researchers from their data, the invention of CAQDAS had the great advantage that the use of this technology requires the explication of data management strategies that help to think about their methodological and epistemological significance. Thereby, the use of computers for the management of qualitative data draws our special methodological attention to the process of 'coding' and 'indexing' of the materials researchers bring home from their research fields.

In the first section of this chapter I shall discuss how code-and-retrieve facilities provided by almost every CAQDAS package can make visible a problem often hidden if manual methods are used – the problem of finding adequate categories and concepts for structuring data. In the second section it will be shown how this issue relates to the demanding methodological problem of defining the role of theory and the researcher's previous knowledge in the research process. The final section will relate these considerations to sophisticated tools for theory building and hypothesis testing nowadays provided by almost all the available CAQDAS packages.

THE COMPUTER AS A DEVICE FOR THE CODING OF 'QUALITATIVE DATA'

My first contact with CAQDAS dates back to the time when I started my first appointment as a research assistant at the Methodology Unit of the newly founded Sociological *Sonderforschungsbereich* (Special Collaborative Centre) at the University of Bremen. *Sonderforschungsbereiche* (normally abbreviated Sfb) are funded by the German National Research Council, *Deutsche Forschungsgemeinschaft*, which is the largest funding body in the field of basic research in Germany. Unlike former sociological Sfbs, the Sfb in Bremen laid a strong emphasis on qualitative research: most of its research projects not only analysed standardized large-scale datasets by means of statistical methods but also conducted extensive qualitative studies. At that time the 'paradigm wars' fought in the 1970s and the 1980s had calmed down and qualitative research had gained some acceptance in the sociological community outside those small circles of phenomenologists, constructivists and interactionists who had started the qualitative movement. But since the methodological mainstream in German sociology of the late 1980s was clearly quantitative, qualitative methods still suffered from the suspicion of being journalistic and impressionistic. Consequently, the qualitative studies of the Sfb were scrutinized by a suspicious review board. At the same time many researchers who proposed qualitative methods still saw themselves as partisans fighting for the acceptance of the members' views and perspectives in empirical sociology. Among them were many 'paradigm warriors' (Tashakkori and Teddlie, 1998) who had adopted the qualitative perspective as a firm epistemological and theoretical standpoint and shared a strict rejection of any form of standardization. But apart from that, a great heterogeneity of research styles and analysis methods could be found.

The passion of the qualitative community for abstract methodological considerations and concepts, together with the heterogeneity of research methods in qualitative praxis, caused some difficulties for many members of the Sfb's junior staff doing their first research project. Looking at the literature available about qualitative research in the late 1980s, one could find sophisticated arguments about the theoretical and epistemological underpinnings of qualitative methods. More technical works contained hints and advice concerning fieldwork and interviewing methods. But it was rather difficult to obtain concrete guidance about how to analyse the materials researchers had brought from their field.

Nowadays we are accustomed to refer to such materials as 'data', but we should keep in mind that this notion was initially borrowed from the quantitative research tradition. Furthermore, its application to qualitative work is itself a result of far-reaching structural changes in social research: the mode of inquiry employed by the founding parents of qualitative methods (the early ethnographers and cultural anthropologists) meant gaining an intimate personal knowledge of the research domain by living there for a certain time, by observing conversations and events, and by conducting numerous more or less informal conversations with people with different social roles. The researchers' understanding of the social processes, as well as the descriptions and explanations they formulated to account for these processes, were a result of personal experiences and the expertise they had brought with them and developed further during their research. Thus the acceptance of insights coming from this kind of field research was highly dependent on the confidence researchers enjoyed from their audience.

But this strong and ineliminable element of subjectivity also raised suspicions and reservations among many members of the sociological community. The tape recorder, used for qualitative interviewing since the 1960s (for the critical aspects of this development see Douglas, 1976: 32), turned out to be a powerful tool in transforming the unique and non-recurring encounter between 'researcher' and 'member' to a methodically controlled production of 'data': bits and pieces of information that could in principle be subject to re-examination. The tape recorder thus gave birth to 'qualitative interviewing' as a special method of data collection and thus helped to adopt an otherwise informal style of inquiry to a standard model of research. Furthermore, this model allowed for the employment of bureaucratic procedures necessary for research funding and grant applications: researchers applying for grants were now able to satisfy review boards and authorities by detailed reports about how and where they were going to 'collect data', about their strategies of 'sampling' and the expected size of the 'qualitative sample', and about when and how data were to be 'analysed'.

Simultaneously the term 'qualitative analysis' (or 'qualitative data analysis') became popular, a term uncommon in the works of the early ethnographers or the qualitative studies of the Chicago School from the 1920s until the 1960s. Although the term was frequently used in the 1970s, it was not until 1984 that a textbook about 'Qualitative Data Analysis' became available. This book, written by Matthew Miles and Michael Huberman, was subtitled 'A Sourcebook of New Methods' and drew heavily on examples from funded and evaluation research. The authors considered 'data overload' to be one of the most crucial problems of the qualitative research process and elaborated in much detail on one specific method to cope with this problem: the 'coding' of data, a technique first described in an article by Howard Becker and Blanche Geer in 1960 and extensively discussed by Barney Glaser and Anselm Strauss in their often cited monograph *The Discovery of Grounded Theory* (1967). The understanding of 'qualitative coding' that was made popular by Glaser and Strauss was used throughout the subsequent literature. Following this understanding the coding of qualitative data means relating chunks of data (which usually means text passages of field protocols or transcribed interviews) to categories that the researcher had either previously developed or that he or she develops ad hoc. 'The analyst starts by coding each incident in his data into as many categories of analysis as possible, as categories emerge or as data emerge that fit in an existing category' (Glaser and Strauss, 1967: 105). As with the terms 'data', 'interview' and 'sample', the word 'coding' was also borrowed from the quantitative stream of social research, namely from the tradition of qualitative content analysis. But unlike in classical content analysis the purpose of qualitative coding is not to extract quantifiable information from unstructured textual data, but to develop (theoretical) concepts and categories from the data.

Especially for the more pragmatically oriented among the researchers in the Bremen Sfb, 'coding data' seemed to be a feasible way to deal with the large amounts of transcribed interviews. By constructing detailed qualitative sampling plans and in their efforts to meet reviewers' real and anticipated expectancies, some empirical projects had conducted numerous (in one case up to ninety) in-depth interviews summing up to thousands of pages of transcribed texts. Members of research staff looking for ways to manage these data in many cases encountered serious difficulties in their efforts to apply coding strategies mentioned in the literature. Junior researchers and novices in qualitative methods in particular found it extremely hard to develop a pragmatic strategy of analysis by means of developing code categories from the data that could be related to text segments. Soon it became obvious that the limited number of writings about techniques of qualitative data analysis (at that time especially Glaser and Strauss, 1967, and Miles and Huberman, 1984) often did not provide sufficient

information for researchers looking for concrete coding rules and guidelines. Unlike standard textbooks for quantitative research, the technical literature about qualitative methods rarely described the research process in a stepwise manner as a series of procedures that followed a set of well-defined rules. One reason for that is that the process of qualitative data analysis is open to all kinds of different decisions about how to code, what to code and where to draw the codes from. Furthermore, qualitative analysis does not consist of a limited number of well-described and documented textbook techniques. Instead it represents a heterogeneous field of diverse research styles and strategies of inquiry. Methodological rules applied by different schools of thought are often not explicated but form a folklore of research passed on verbally from teachers to pupils.

Junior researchers and novices in the field of qualitative research who are not trained in the context of a certain tradition often experience serious uncertainties as to whether the terms they develop in the ongoing analysis deserve to be regarded as 'real' or 'good' code categories. Hence they may find it difficult to develop code categories that could adequately describe, condense and summarize the data. This problem can be further aggravated through methodological concepts maintaining the necessity not to dissolve the perspectives of the research subjects. This stance found its expression in the often quoted advice to let categories and concepts 'emerge' from the data instead of forcing them on the data (Glaser and Strauss, 1967; Glaser, 1992). But despite great sympathies for the members' views and high-flying aspirations concerning the construction of empirically well-grounded categories, it often happens that nothing emerges from the data. Researchers who do not succeed in finding categories that do not only account for a single incident but are applicable to other pieces of data often try to dig further into the data; they turn to methods of fine-grained hermeneutic interpretation.

In the German sociological community of the 1980s a methodological approach of that kind had attracted some attention, although it remained largely unnoticed on the international scene. A group of sociologists at the University of Frankfurt (Oevermann et al., 1979) had coined the term *Objektive Hermeneutik* for a method of interpreting textual data, whereby different interpretations ('*Lesarten*') are developed in a team of researchers who mutually criticize their *Lesarten*. The analysis of the textual data in a strict sequential manner allows for the exclusion and modification of interpretations. Thereby the different *Lesarten* are regarded as preliminary hypotheses that in principle can be falsified by further empirical material.[1] This method had the enormous advantage of providing an explicit rule-governed procedure. Nevertheless, following these rules can make text interpretation an extremely tedious and time-consuming enterprise, which is only feasible with small amounts of text. Oevermann advises analysts to stick stubbornly to their critique of interpretations in order to avoid the premature acceptance of insufficient interpretations. Oevermann's group usually needed several days (sometimes weeks) and numerous sessions for the interpretation of a single text passage. Since the method stimulates thinking about the data in theoretical terms, it helps to overcome the kind of obsessive descriptivism that can arise from exaggerated demands to let the data or the research subjects 'speak for themselves'. Nevertheless, it may aggravate the problem of data overload by leading to a proliferation of competing interpretations. Researchers may easily drown in the data while defending stubbornly their interpretations and, given the theoretical heterogeneity of qualitative approaches, this can be accompanied by intense debates about the correct methodology underpinned by various theoretical and epistemological arguments.

At the Sfb, however, pressures of research funding were pushing towards quicker solutions: one year before the end of the first project term many researchers felt that too many months had passed with futile methodological discussions. The idea came up that the use of computers could provide a way out of the trouble by offering possibilities to facilitate and accelerate the time-consuming analysis of the interview transcripts. As a member of the Sfb's methodology division, I was asked to support some research projects in their search for possibilities to abridge and limit the excessive analysis of the qualitative material. At that time, software for handling textual data had been available for at least twenty years: in 1966 the GENERAL INQUIRER was introduced (Stone et al., 1966), a program to calculate the frequencies of occurrences or co-occurrences of words. But such developments attracted only a limited group of experts interested in quantitative content analysis, a method based on frequency counts of words using a content-analysis lexicon. The majority of qualitative researchers were reluctant to integrate computers into their work. This reflected on the one hand the distance of these scholars from the mainstream methodology of quantitative research where, during the 1960s and 1970s, the computer had become an important device for data analysis. On the other hand, the demand for a machine for the automatic

processing and manipulation of symbols was not very great within a research tradition that emphasized the context-relatedness of symbolic interaction. The idea that 'the operation called *Verstehen*' (Abel, 1948) is not merely a technical operation but a holistic process highly dependent on the stocks of (partly implicit) background knowledge on which the interpreter can draw, is almost paradigmatic for the qualitative research tradition. But computers require exact and precisely stated rules, which are completely context-free and contain no ambiguities (cf. Dreyfus, 1972; Dreyfus and Dreyfus, 1986; Winograd and Flores, 1986). For the same reasons, quantitative content analysis had provoked criticism for being too atomistic and oversimplistic to really capture the semantic content of texts (Kracauer, 1952/53: 632) long before the GENERAL INQUIRER was invented.

It took more than ten years to let the idea emerge in the qualitative community that computers, although they maybe inappropriate for the *analysis* of texts, can be still helpful for the *organization* and *management* of textual data. The development of this idea was clearly a result of an important shift in information technology. In the era of the mainframe the use of computers required special training and was accompanied by high costs in terms of financial and personal resources. Computers, were mainly seen as calculators performing arithmetic operations. But with the advent of the personal computer, many social researchers had discovered the possibilities of word processors and database management systems for the easy storage and retrieval of text. In the late 1980s several qualitative researchers invented independently from each other straightforward techniques of indexing textual data with the help of word processors like MS-Word; thereby code words were simply inserted into the text and an index could be automatically produced by using the word processor's index functions. By drawing on this index a researcher could easily use the information about the page numbers where certain topics were mentioned in transcribed interviews or field protocols.[2]

Such indexing techniques corresponded to a great extent to the coding techniques described by Glaser and Strauss (1967: 106) or by Miles and Huberman (1984: 54ff.). Another frequently used technique of data organization, however, was as awkward to realize with word processors as with manual methods. Before word processors came into use, drawing together all text passages relating to the same topic required that the researcher had to 'cut up field notes, transcripts and other materials and place data relating to each coding category in a separate file folder or manila envelope' (Taylor and Bogdan, 1984: 136; see also Lofland and Lofland, 1984: 134), or on index cards (Miles and Huberman, 1984: 66). Using a word-processing program for cutting and pasting has hardly any advantage over manual methods. Also the employment of standard database systems for the purpose of coding and comparing text segments imposes certain restrictions on this task. In comparison to word processors, standard database software offers extended possibilities for data organization,[3] but it requires the definition of a fixed record structure before entering the data. This makes it difficult if not impossible to change the coding scheme and thus to develop theoretical categories during the ongoing analysis.

From the perspective of information technology the most reasonable way to apply a flexible coding scheme on an already existing corpus of non-formatted textual data would be the attachment of *pointers* or *addresses* of text segments to codes defined by the user. Since this represents a way of handling textual data rarely used in other contexts, special software programs had to be designed that helped with the *coding* and *retrieval* of text segments, that is, the attachment of codes to text segments and the searching for and displaying of all text segments from a defined set of documents to which the same code has been assigned.

The first software packages that were designed for such a purpose, such as QUALPRO, TEXTBASE ALPHA, TAP or THE ETHNOGRAPH,[4] were developed in the 1980s in specific qualitative research projects. Once their developers had realized that such software may also be helpful to others, they offered them to a broader scientific community. The majority of the available programs were distributed by a small company, 'Qualitative Research Management', which also offered consultation to research projects in utilizing the software. The founder of the company, Renate Tesch, who also published a widely read monograph about computer use in qualitative research (Tesch, 1990), was rather successful in disseminating the different software packages and propagating their use in international conferences on social and educational sciences. However, at the Sfb the attempt to implement one of the existing code-and-retrieve programs into research processes almost immediately led to a division of the teams into two camps: one group, which mainly consisted of senior researchers or research team leaders who had only limited interests in debates about methodological issues (which in their opinion had already wasted too much of the disposable time), showed great interest and a positive attitude towards the software. These researchers were interested in achieving research results quickly even if this would lead to sacrifices concerning 'methodological correctness'. The other group, who wished to stick to the fundamentals of qualitative research, namely the principles of thorough and fine-grained analysis and of the development and emergence of categories from the data, heavily opposed the invention of code-and-retrieve software.

In practice, difficulties and conflicts mainly arose around coding: the search for and the definition of the adequate coding categories became extremely tedious and a subject of sometimes numerous and endless team sessions. The declared purpose to let codes emerge from the data quickly led to an enduring proliferation of the number of coding categories, which in one case made the whole coding process insurmountable. Another group of researchers described this process of code proliferation in a methodological self-reflection:

> Especially the application of an *open coding* strategy recommended by Glaser and Strauss – the text is read line by line and coded ad hoc – proved to be unexpectedly awkward and time-consuming. That was related to the fact that we were doing our utmost to pay attention to the respondents' perspectives. In any case we wanted to avoid the overlooking of important aspects that may lie behind apparently irrelevant information. Our attempts to analyse the data were governed by the idea that we should address the text tabula rasa and by the fear of structuring data too much on the basis of our previous knowledge. Consequently every word in the data was credited with high significance. These uncertainties were not eased by advice from the corresponding literature that open coding means a 'preliminary breaking down of data' and that the emerging concepts will prove their usefulness in the ongoing analysis. Furthermore, in the beginning we had the understanding that 'everything counts' and 'everything is important' – every marginal incident and phenomenon was coded, recorded in numerous memos and extensively discussed. This led to an insurmountable mass of data. ... (cf. Kelle et al., 2003, translation by UK)

In their empirical studies of CAQDAS users, Lee and Fielding describe similar experiences: in several reported cases the coding process proliferated. Users reported: '*We were regularly coding 8, 10, 12 codes per line, it was just so complex*' (1995: 38). Coding can obviously block the whole process of analysis and may lead to serious frustration among the researchers and even to resentments concerning computer-aided coding and retrieval (1995: 36; see also Holbrook and Butcher, 1996). At the Sfb at least one of the projects working with CAQDAS stopped its use for a long time. The interesting fact about this was that the research team emphasized in its research report that CAQDAS had proved to be of no use for the purposes of the project since it required the application of a pre-defined code scheme. This statement overtly contradicted the developer's claims concerning the flexibility of the software, which should allow for the definition and alteration of the coding scheme during the coding process.

Before assuming that the research team had simply failed to grasp fully how to handle the software technically, one should keep in mind that the danger of 'forcing' predefined code categories on the data is a *topos* frequently used in the methodological literature (see, e.g., Glaser, 1992). Furthermore, since the advent of software for aiding qualitative analysis, many qualitative researchers, developers of such software among them, have felt unease about the prospect that the computer could alienate the researcher from their data and enforce analytic strategies that go against the methodological and theoretical orientations qualitative researchers see as the hallmark of their work (see, e.g., Agar, 1991; or Seidel, 1991; Seidel and Kelle, 1995). In an early publication, Lee and Fielding (1991: 8) linked this fear of the computer taking over the analysis to an often used literary archetype expressed in Shelley's famous Victorian novel *Frankenstein. Or: the Modern Prometheus.* In their analysis of debates in an Internet forum for CAQDAS users, Holbrook and Butcher (1996) had addressed the same problem as the 'straightjacket issue'. In a series of articles in the Internet journal *Sociological Research Online*, the thesis was extensively discussed that the increasing use of CAQDAS could lead researchers to adopt a new orthodoxy of qualitative analysis (Coffey et al., 1996; Lee and Fielding, 1996; Kelle, 1997). The use of coding techniques, in particular, was suspected of leading to the dominance of a specific methodology, namely grounded theory (Lonkila, 1995; Coffey et al., 1996).

Several authors have argued that these concerns lack solid empirical ground. Lee and Fielding (1996), for instance, inspected the *Social Science Citation Index* for studies citing John Seidel's descriptive writings on THE ETHNOGRAPH (Seidel and Clark, 1984; Seidel, 1985, 1988), 'a package often thought to be avowedly oriented to grounded theory' (Lee and Fielding, 1996: 3.2). Less than a third of these studies cited a work associated with the grounded theory tradition. Many of the concerns of the computer 'taking over analysis' and alienating the researcher from the data and from his or her epistemological and theoretical roots seem to be overemphasized, if one takes into account that the use of indexes (or

'registers', or 'concordances') represents an age-old technique of data management used in all hermeneutic sciences for centuries (cf. Kelle, 1997: 2.3f.): in history, philology and theology coding and retrieval gained a great methodological importance for hermeneutic analysis of text long before the invention of computer software for the management of textual data. The theory about the origin of the four gospels that is nowadays most widely accepted, for instance, was developed in the nineteenth century on the basis of manual code-and-retrieve techniques that are called 'synopses' in biblical exegesis. Also other techniques of CAQDAS, e.g. the principles of 'hyperlinks', had been widely known and applied for hundreds of years, which can be easily proved by opening any King James Bible where 'links' (or 'cross-references') to other text passages are displayed on every page.

If one takes into account that coding, indexing, cross-referencing and the synoptical comparison of text segments represent a very flexible technology for working with great amounts of text, one has good reasons to assume that the CAQDAS technology did not introduce new methodological problems to qualitative data analysis but made visible already existing difficulties by forcing the researcher to be explicit about certain steps of analysis that were regularly performed in a more implicit manner with manual methods. The most important problems that are made visible by the necessity to explicitly 'code' the data concern the relation between data and theory in qualitative analysis and the role of the researcher's previous theoretical knowledge in the coding process. This issue will be discussed in the following section.

THE CONSTRUCTION OF CODING SCHEMES AND THE ROLE OF THE RESEARCHER'S PREVIOUS THEORETICAL KNOWLEDGE

The most crucial questions that arise during coding, namely '*Which terms can be used as codes?*' and '*To which phenomena shall the codes refer?*', often raise no diffulties for experienced researchers. Among novices, however, questions of this kind may provoke endless (and fruitless) discussions. Such problems would be quickly solved if a predefined category scheme is used for coding. But many qualitative researchers rightly feel that this may violate some of the most fundamental methodological principles of the qualitative paradigm: by using already formulated concepts and hypotheses, the discovery of yet unknown structures and patterns of meaning can be restrained rather than facilitated. In order not to neglect and overlook the member's views in the domain under study, qualitative researchers should always be cautious not to force preconceived concepts, hypotheses and theories on the data. Unfortunately, this fact has also inspired a popular methodological myth claiming that qualitative researchers should approach their empirical field without any theoretical concepts whatsoever. This myth has been nurtured by some methodological ideas contained in Glaser and Strauss's earliest methodological writings. In their *Discovery* book, Glaser and Strauss encouraged researchers 'literally to ignore the literature of theory and fact on the area under study, in order to assure that the emergence of categories will not be contaminated. ...' (1967: 37). Most ironically, this stance represents one of the main roots of modern positivism. Early empiricist philosophers such as Bacon and Locke were the first to put forward the idea that the only legitimate theories were those that could be inductively derived by simple generalization from observable data. However, one of the most widely accepted insights of contemporary epistemology and cognitive psychology is the fact that 'there are and can be no sensations unimpregnated by expectations' (Lakatos, 1982: 15). Consequently, qualitative researchers who investigate a certain form of social life cannot drop their own lens and conceptual networks or they would no longer be able to observe and describe meaningful events, but would be confronted with fragmented phenomena (Kelle, 1995, 1998: 38). The problems discussed in the previous section of researchers who literally drown in the data clearly illustrate the practical aspects of such epistemological principles: to free oneself from any theoretical preconception whatsoever can hardly be considered a useful methodological rule for the analysis of qualitative data.

Glaser and Strauss did not overlook this problem, however, since in their *Discovery* book they also maintained that the researcher 'does not approach reality as a tabula rasa' (1967: 3). Furthermore, according to Glaser and Strauss the qualitative researcher must have a 'perspective that will help [him] see relevant data and abstract significant categories from his scrutiny of the data' (ibid.). This ability, called 'theoretical sensitivity', creates 'theory that exists within a sociologist' which 'can be used in generating his specific theory': 'A discovered, grounded theory, then will tend to combine mostly concepts and hypotheses that have emerged from the data with some existing ones that are clearly useful'

(1967: 46). Thus the *Discovery* book contains two different concepts concerning the relation between data and theory with conflicting implications: on the one hand the idea was stressed that theoretical concepts 'emerge' from the data if the researcher approaches the empirical field with no preconceived theories or hypotheses; on the other hand the researcher is advised to use also his or her previous theoretical knowledge to identify theoretically relevant phenomena in the data.[5]

Novices usually experience far more difficulties than experienced researchers in realizing theoretically significant phenomena and structures in the data and in talking in theoretical terms about empirical facts. Consequently they often find it hard to code data with theoretical sensitivity, which means in practice that they have much greater problems in defining codes ad hoc that 'fit' the data. This leads to the question whether theoretically sensible coding is merely a gift of charismatic researchers or whether certain aspects of it can be made explicit, for instance by determining relevant 'theoretical codes' before the data are coded. Can it be justified to divert from the methodologically correct way of 'open coding' and to use a partly predefined coding scheme?

To solve this problem, it may be helpful to draw on a concept that plays an important role in Popperian methodology: the concept of *falsifiability* or *empirical content*. In quantitative research this concept is normally used to identify sound scientific hypotheses: only clear-cut and precisely formulated propositions with empirical content are regarded as adequate hypotheses in this methodological framework. Concepts and hypotheses that lack empirical content and thus cannot be falsified are considered as highly problematic in hypothetico-deductive research since they cannot be tested with the help of empirical data. Such concepts, however, may play a very useful role if the goal of empirical research is not the testing of predefined hypotheses but the empirically grounded generation of theories, since concepts with low empirical content do not force data into a Procrustean bed but can be related to a great variety of empirical phenomena. Their lack of empirical content gives them flexibility so that a variety of empirical phenomena can be described with their help. Although such concepts cannot be tested empirically, they may be used in the research process as *heuristic concepts* that represent the already mentioned lenses through which the researcher perceives facts and phenomena in the field under scrutiny.

Two different types of coding categories represent heuristic concepts and may be used to define an initial coding scheme that can be supplemented, refined and modified in the ongoing process of empirical analysis:

1   A variety of *theoretical concepts*, definitions and categories drawn from 'grand theories' in the social sciences are too broad and abstract to deduce directly empirically contentful propositions,[6] but may, regardless of how empirically contentless and vague they are, serve as heuristic tools for the construction of empirically grounded theories. A concept like 'role expectations' may serve as a good example of that. The proposition that individuals act in accordance with role expectations does not contain a lot of information by itself. This concept may, however, be useful in formulating a variety of research questions for the investigation of different substantive fields: do role expectations play an important role in the empirical domain under study? What kind of role expectations can be found? By which means do empirical actors try to meet them? Do certain actors develop strategies to avoid the fulfilment of role expectations? Are such strategies revealed by other actors in the investigated field?, etc. Concepts from so-called 'utility theory' may serve as another good example: at the core of utility theory is the idea that human actors will choose the action that seems the most adequate for the achievement of a desired goal from a set of given action alternatives. Without specifying *which* goals the actors pursue and *which* actions they consider to be adequate, such a proposition has no empirical content. The theory is like an 'empty sack' (cf. Simon, 1985), if one does not specify further auxiliary assumptions.[7] Instead of allowing for the development of precise hypotheses, utility theory may provide researchers with useful research questions and heuristic codes: qualitative researchers may, for instance, code text segments that refer to the potential *costs* and *benefits* that certain actions may have for the actors, they may code segments that relate to the *intentions* and *goals* of the research subjects or to the *means* they use to reach their goals, etc. In this manner researchers may draw on a wide variety of abstract notions from different theoretical traditions to structure the data. Especially at the beginning of the analysis process, however, special attention should be paid to whether a chosen code can serve for heuristic purposes or whether it 'forces' the data. Therefore it may be extremely helpful always to pose the question 'Does the chosen code exclude certain phenomena from being analysed?'

2   A second type of coding categories, which do not force data but allow for the discovery of previously unknown relations and categories, are categories that relate to general *topics of interest* covered in the data material. Such *topic-oriented codes* can often be easily found by drawing on general common-sense knowledge or on specific local knowledge of the investigated field. Code categories like 'school', 'work' or 'family' represent simple examples of that. Topic-oriented codes may be far more complex than this. However, one should always ask the question, as with heuristic theoretical concepts, whether a certain code can serve for heuristic purposes or whether it excludes relevant phenomena from examination.

A heuristic coding scheme for the structuring of qualitative data may contain both general theoretical concepts drawn from grand theories and topic-oriented codes drawn from stocks of everyday knowledge. Thereby, the initial coding scheme must not contain empirically contentful concepts but should consist of terms that relate to all different kinds of social phenomena. Thus, heuristic coding categories drawn from general theories or from everyday knowledge may fit various kinds of social reality, and it is not necessary to know something concrete about the investigated domain in order to use these concepts.

The coding scheme presented in Figure 30.1, which was used for the analysis of semi-structured interviews with school leavers who were asked about their future plans when entering vocational training courses (Heinz et al., 1998; Kelle and Zinn, 1998), combines the different types of codes mentioned above. The main coding categories represent topic-oriented codes: in the interviews all text passages were coded where the interviewees talked for instance about experiences in their jobs, about relevant institutions, about their families, etc. These codes were combined with concepts relating to a general theory of action used in the research project; the decision processes described by the interviewees were structured according to the following three categories: (1) *aspirations,* which represent the respondents' preferences that were used to account for occupational options, (2) *realizations,* which consist of the actual steps of action that were taken to fulfil realizations, and (3) *evaluations,* which were the respondents' assessments of the relations between aspirations, conditions and consequences of action. These categories represent the sub-codes (1.1–1.3, 5.1–5.3, 8.1–8.3) shown in Figure 30.1.

1	**job and profession**
1.1	job and profession/aspirations
1.2	Job and profession/realizations
1.3	job and profession/evaluations
	(...)
5	**cohabitation**
5.1	cohabitation/aspirations
5.2	cohabitation/realizations
5.3	cohabitation/evaluations
8	**children**
8.1	children/aspirations
8.2	children/realizations
8.3	children/evaluations

Figure 30.1 *An extract from a coding scheme.*

In some research contexts and for answering specific research questions, it may be useful to code qualitative data not only with the help of heuristic concepts of the kind discussed above, that is, by using concepts with limited empirical content drawn from grand theories or general topics of interest. In certain situations the application of more precise or empirically contentful sociological terms like 'social class', 'stigma' or 'doing gender' will be helpful to break up the data. But this also brings about the danger that theoretical terms are forced on the data, which means that the perspectives and relevances of the research subjects are dissolved by the researchers' preconceived concepts. A methodologically important question arises from that: how can concepts that contain too much empirical content and thus exclude relevant empirical phenomena from scrutiny be differentiated from concepts that are open enough to serve as heuristic tools?

In many cases this question can be answered only if the empirical data used are taken into account, as the following example shows: in a study about care work in families, semi-structured qualitative interviews were carried out with respondents caring for their frail and helpless elderly parents or relatives. The main purpose was to identify typical situations and events that triggered a major change in the care arrangement, thus for example leading to a situation where the caregivers were no longer able to provide help at home and the parent or relative had to move to a care home. Besides this, the analysis aimed to identify conditions and reasons for establishing the care relation between the providers of care and the elderly care receiver. For this purpose a heuristic framework was used based on concepts drawn from decision theory, which comprised the categories 'situation that leads to taking over the role of caregiver',

'decision for caregiving', 'aspects of care work', 'consequences of care arrangement' and 'caregiver's resources'. When coding the data it soon became apparent that the category 'decision for caregiving' was not adequate to describe the situation most of the interviewees had experienced. Respondents often did not describe the development of the care relation as if it had been a certain point in time when they or their family were confronted with a 'decision' to take over the role of a caregiver. Instead, minimal signs of growing weakness and increasing helplessness set in motion a slow process in which the care receiver required more and more help from the caregiver, who often did not realize for quite a long time that a relation of strong dependency and obligation was evolving. Respondents sometimes used notions like 'slipping into' the care relation or reported that the care relation 'somehow evolved'. Some respondents who took over the main responsibility also described feelings of becoming 'trapped' in that process. Hence the term 'decision for care giving', which was deduced from a framework of a theory of purposive and intentional action, failed to grasp real social processes in the domain under investigation and had to be supplemented by another category 'habituation of care giving', developed from the material.

During the process of structuring textual material through coding, many researchers find it hard to appreciate the benefits of computer-aided analysis. Coding is often experienced as tedious and often as frustrating, especially since it delays the most exciting part of the project in which the analyst tries to make sense of the data by constructing 'meaningful patterns of facts' (Jorgenson, 1989; 107). However, coding of the data is only the preliminary for the computer-aided retrieval of text passages. Retrieval techniques represent the central technological innovation of qualitative data management made possible by the computer, which greatly facilitates and accelerates the already mentioned age-old techniques of synoptical comparison of text passages. Whereas the manual compilation of text segments for an index-based text synopsis of interviews or field protocols may last many hours, a computer-based text retrieval will yield its results in less than seconds. That makes it possible to conduct various synopses within one research project in order to identify similarities and differences, patterns and structures, within text passages coded with a variety of different codes. In this way the possibilities of synoptical analyses may be enhanced to a great extent. The actual analysis, however, is clearly the task of the human interpreter who carefully inspects and analyses the text segments in order to identify those aspects (or 'dimensions') that can serve as criteria for a comparison. The result of this process (sometimes addressed in the literature as 'dimensionalizing', see, e.g., Strauss, 1987; Strauss and Corbin, 1990: 69ff.) is the development of new categories, which can be integrated in the developing code scheme: often they serve as subcategories of the coding categories that formed the initial coding scheme.

This process maybe further illustrated with another example. In a research project about men's attitudes towards their spouses' labour market participation (Braemer, 1994), lengthy open interviews with 60- to 70-year-old men were conducted. In these interviews a variety of normative aspects of marriage and family were stressed. The evaluation of the behaviour of their own children with respect to cohabitation and marriage turned out to be an important issue for the interviewees. As a first step of analysis, the textual material was structured according to the topic (among others) 'cohabitation among people of the younger generation'. Thereafter all text passages where this issue was mentioned were compared in order to identify similarities and differences. Take these three passages as an example:

> I mean, that was … how we found us, how we lived together after that, the marriage and how we lived together when we married, somehow, I liked it more. As it is today, I mean, I mean that this is not good today. It is not ideal, how they are together or not … I don't know, that's nothing for me. (Case 60)

> Well, I mean, if one moves together in one apartment, … one should marry, or be at least engaged at the beginning. That has perhaps something to do with morality, since we were educated that way. Morals have become a little bit loose today. … (Case 98)

> Well, I like it that one obviously does not live, so to speak, under that strong pressure [to get married] today, and the children can do it today in different ways. … But there is also some regret, that it is a little bit too loose today. … (Case 46)

All three text passages display a certain similarity: declining moral standards in the younger generation are regretted. The interviewees also expressed some uncertainty and sometimes a defensive position concerning their own moral values (often using phrases like 'perhaps, I don't know…'). But there are also important differences between the three cases: case 46 and case 98 both show general disapproval of the kind of cohabitation they think the younger generation prefer, but case 46 is more or less ambivalent. These three passages can be regarded as specimens

of two different types that can also be found in the utterances of other respondents. Two new subcodes were defined to account for these two types: 'ambivalence' (case 46) and 'disapproval' (cases 60 and 98). Within the category 'disapproval' one can differentiate between respondents with a more defensive (case 60) and a more offensive position (case 98). This example, of course, shows only the start of the process, and these categories were not constructed exclusively on the basis of these three cases, but further validated with additional data material. In fact, the qualitative data material in this project showed a variety of moral arguments that led to the development of more different coding categories.

It is this comparison that becomes the basis of the construction of concepts, types and categories that form the building blocks of an emerging theory. Thus the 'flesh' of empirically contentful concepts found in the empirical research field is added to the theoretical axis or 'skeleton' of heuristic coding concepts. Such addition of flesh to the bones of a heuristic skeleton then leads to an increase in the empirical content of the whole body during the ongoing process of qualitative analysis, allowing for the formulation of more concrete and empirically contentful statements, hypotheses and theories.

ADVANCED TECHNOLOGIES IN CAQDAS AND THEIR LIMITS

The construction of theories and their further testing has attracted a lot of attention in the developing CAQDAS community, in the writings surrounding CAQDAS and in the e-mail discussion groups devoted to debates about CAQDAS use. After the first, sometimes rather awkward and user-unfriendly versions of software for aiding coding and retrieval were improved and more and more complex functions were added (which helped, for example, with the recording of memos or with the construction of more complicated coding schemes), a strong tendency among the developers of such software could be found to advertise the capacities of their programs for 'theory building' supported by complex facilities for coding and retrieval. As has been described before, the first code-and-retrieve programs linked codes to text segments by using pointers. Similar data structures can be employed to define linkages between codes themselves. These linkages can also be used to display the logical relations between codes and the structure of an emerging theory, as in the example shown in Figure 30.2: text segments

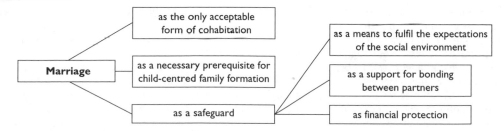

Figure 30.2 *A hierarchical coding scheme.*

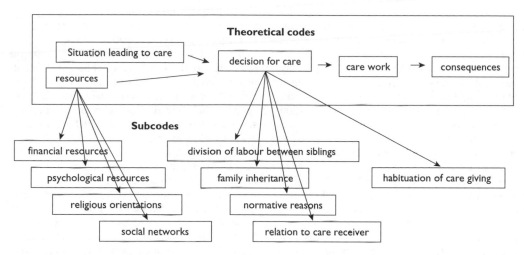

Figure 30.3 *Complex relations within a coding scheme.*

where interviewees talked about the role of marriage in their lives were coded with subcodes according to whether the idea was expressed that being married is the *only acceptable form of cohabitation*, or whether marriage was viewed by the respondents as the *prerequisite for child-centred family formation*, or whether marriage was regarded as a kind of *safeguard*. In text passages coded with the subcode 'marriage as a safeguard' three different arguments could be found: marriage was seen as (1) offering financial protection, (2) providing a support for the bonding between the partners, or (3) a means to fulfil the expectations of their social environment (parents, relatives, etc.).

Almost all programs for computer-aided qualitative analysis nowadays support the definition of relations between categories, although most of them allow only for hierarchical tree structures as in the previous example. That means that it is usually not possible also to define relations between subcodes themselves. An exception is the programme ATLAS/ti, which provides extremely flexible tools that allow the user to define all possible forms of linkages between the 'objects' of his or her qualitative database (that means text segments, categories and subcategories, and memos). These tools support the construction of complex networks of these objects, making it possible, for instance, to display different forms of relations and structures in the developing category scheme. Figure 30.3 gives an example of how hierarchical relations and causal relations between codes and subcodes may be integrated in this way.

Furthermore, a variety of complex retrieval functions were developed and integrated in several of the software packages, which can be used to retrieve information according to whether certain codes co-occur in the text (see Hesse-Biber and Dupuis, 1995; Huber, 1995; Richards and Richards, 1994: 447f.). Such tools were sometimes referred to as instruments of 'hypothesis testing': using these functions a researcher who has for instance coded his or her data with codes for 'critical life events' and 'emotional disturbances' may put forward the hypothesis that critical life events are always or frequently accompanied by emotional disturbances. The hypothesis can then be transformed into a query about all co-occurrences of text segments coded as 'critical life event' with segments coded as 'emotional disturbances' (cf. Huber, 1995).

However, writings proposing such concepts of 'qualitative hypothesis testing' usually pay only limited attention to the specific nature of qualitative codes and qualitative coding. The transfer of technical terms borrowed from a different methodological tradition to qualitative research may result in serious misunderstandings and methodological artefacts if the specific context in which these terms are employed is not adequately taken into account. Like the terms 'data' and 'data analysis', the notion 'hypothesis' stems from the context of hypothetico-deductive experimental research, where it denotes empirically contentful statements about the relations between certain variables or categories. In this framework the testing of hypotheses means the application of *exact rules* which leads to a decision on whether the hypothesis can be accepted or rejected. There are essential methodological prerequisites for the employment of such rules: in the above example it would be of the utmost importance that it is possible to decide whether a given observed event is a case of a 'critical life event' or an 'emotional disturbance' or not. Consequently, the concepts or categories used in the hypothesis must be *mutually exclusive*; that is, it must be possible to decide whether a certain life event is 'critical' or 'non-critical', and whether a given person is 'emotionally disturbed' or 'not disturbed'. In other words, codes must represent clearly defined empirical events. But, as Charmaz points out:

> Qualitative coding is not the same as quantitative coding. The term itself provides a case in point in which the language may obscure meaning and method. Quantitative coding requires preconceived, logically deduced codes into which the data are placed. Qualitative coding, in contrast, means creating categories from interpretation of the data. Rather than relying on preconceived categories and standardized procedures, qualitative coding has its own distinctive structure, logic and purpose. (Charmaz, 1983: 111)

The qualitative codes described above, codes derived from general theoretical concepts, or codes referring to topics of interests, do serve the purpose of breaking up the data. Such codes do not denote clearly defined facts but represent 'perspectives' of the researcher rather than clearcut empirically contentful variables or categories. The authors of earlier writings about qualitative coding were still aware of this important difference between qualitative and quantitative

coding, which often became obscured in later texts: in qualitative research the coding of textual data does not serve to condense relevant information and to decide whether a certain person or event falls under a certain class of events or persons, but simply to make sure 'that all relevant data can be brought to bear on a point' (cf. Becker and Geer, 1960: 280). A qualitative researcher may be interested in coding text segments with the code 'critical life event' not so as to denote the fact that the interviewee has experienced a clearly defined event that belongs to the greater class of 'critical live events', but to show that this text segment has (possibly in a broad and general sense) a relation to the concept of critical life events. Qualitative codes, in particular such codes that are used to break up the data, are usually not 'factual codes' that denote the existence or absence of certain facts, but 'referential codes'; they serve as 'signposts' that support the identification of relevant text passages and help to make them available for further interpretation and analysis (cf. Seidel and Kelle, 1995). In most cases referential codes are not very useful for the testing of statements about the exact relation between two defined variables.

Consequently the kind of hypothesis examination that may be conducted with the help of referential codes is something quite different from 'hypothesis testing' in quantitative, experimental research. If all segments where the interviewees talk about 'critical life events' and those passages where 'emotions' are mentioned are coded with the respective codes, the coded text segments may be retrieved to explore the emotional significance of life events. The reason for such a search could be a theoretical assumption or 'hypothesis' about a possible relation between life events and emotions. However, the term hypothesis has to be understood here differently than in hypothetico-deductive, quantitative research. In quantitative research, hypotheses should be highly specified and definite propositions about certain facts, whereas hypotheses of the first kind, when they first come into a researcher's mind, represent tentative and imprecise, sometimes very vague conjectures about possible relationships. Instead of precise descriptions and propositions concerning well-defined relations between certain variables, they are rather hypotheses about what *kind* of propositions, descriptions or explanations will be useful in further analysis. They are insights that 'whatever specific claim the successful H[ypothesis] will make, it will nonetheless be an hypothesis of one kind rather than another' (Hanson, 1971: 291). The notion of hypothesis testing would be rather misleading here, if one understands it as an attempt to falsify an empirically contentful statement. But a hypothesis of this kind can lead to the development of falsifiable statements, for example if one finds that interviewees with specific life events also talk about specific (negative) emotions. This process is of course not hypothesis testing in the traditional sense, that means the application of a set of precisely defined rules that are intended to help the researcher with the decision whether a certain statement is true or false.

Consequently, strategies for 'hypothesis testing' that can be employed using elaborated retrieval techniques offered by certain CAQDAS packages can be applied in two completely different ways. The search for co-occurring codes can be used as a *heuristic device*: the objective then is to retrieve the original text to which the co-occurring codes had been attached. In this case the researcher investigates the meaning of a certain co-occurrence by a thorough analysis of the original text, and the interpretative analysis of interview texts forms the basis for the clarification and modification of the researchers' initial (possibly very general or vague) assumptions. Alternatively, if the analysis of the qualitative data material has fairly progressed and researchers have already developed empirically contentful hypotheses, the mere fact of co-occurring codes in the text may itself be regarded as evidence or counter-evidence for a certain hypothesis. Researchers may then formulate their hypotheses in the form of a series of 'if/then' statements of the kind 'If code A AND code B AND code C are present in a certain document or text segment, THEN the hypothesis has to be accepted'. Here, the primary goal is not to retrieve text but to use the information represented by the codes themselves as a basis for decision-making. Similar to statistical significance testing, the decision-making process is strictly rule-governed.

However, there are certain methodological requirements and limitations to such a strategy: the *prerequisite of independent testing* requires that a hypothesis is not tested with the empirical material from which it is developed. Furthermore, the hypotheses must be empirically testable; that means they must be precise enough and have empirical content. Finally, the codes that are used for hypothesis testing must represent distinct and objectively verifiable facts whose presence could be ascertained independently from a specific context. Additionally, the analyst would have to ensure that the codes are applied consistently and in a reliable manner to the raw data. In particular, one has to make sure that the coding is inclusive and exhaustive,

which means that every incident that is represented by a certain code category has been actually coded. Consequently, if a researcher starts with a '*text-based*' strategy of analysis with the help of referential codes and then switches to a '*code-based*' analysis that requires factual coding of the data, it would, in most cases, be necessary (1) to *reformulate the coding scheme* and (2) to *recode material*. However, this means that one would have to apply a method of text analysis called 'quantitative content analysis', which is already well known and discussed extensively in the literature since the 1950s.

This also applies to methods proposed in the literature for an advanced code-based analysis other than qualitative hypothesis testing, namely to the method of typology building with the help of certain statistical methods (e.g. cluster analysis) proposed by Kuckartz (1995) and the method of 'qualitative comparative analysis' based on the application of Boolean logic developed by Ragin (1987, 1995). Such methods always presuppose factual coding, which means that researchers must have precise concepts and hypotheses at hand about the potential relation of certain events before coding the data. In this case a research logic representing a hypothetico-deductive approach (which is remote from the logic of interpretative inquiry) is applied, and the researchers have to take precautionary measures that such a combination of different research logics will not lead to confusion, to the misinterpretation of data and results and to serious artefacts.

However, up to now not many research teams have exposed themselves to the dangers of code-based analysis described above which may lead to 'reifying the code and losing the phenomenon' (Seidel and Kelle, 1995). In the ongoing discussions in the 1990s it became apparent that enhanced strategies for hypothesis testing, quantitatively oriented typology construction and 'qualitative comparative analysis' were only seldom applied by CAQDAS users. Several discussions on the Qual-software mailing list (qual-software@mailbase.ac.uk) as well as investigations among qualitative researchers (Dotzler, 1995) demonstrated that in practice many users of computer software restrict themselves to ordinary coding and retrieval and do not exploit the various possibilities of computer-aided 'theory building'.[8]

The alleged significance of facilities for theory building and hypothesis testing in several CAQDAS packages and writings about CAQDAS may rather reflect the necessities of academic careers and scientific software marketing than methodological requirements. Unlike scientific publishing, the development and selling of scientific software carries the promise of reasonable economic returns. The great interest and obvious demand that was answered by CAQDAS in the early 1990s not only inspired high-flying aspirations of developing new, more rigorous methods of qualitative research but also set in motion a race between developers to include as many features as possible in the newest versions of their programs. Thus the offering of 'software for theory building' became a part of marketing strategies. Strong economic competition fuelled the use of misleading metaphors and concepts, among them the idea that techniques of complex retrieval within a data archive can be treated as methods of 'hypothesis testing'. For some qualitative researchers the use of such metaphors produced ideas of a far-reaching mechanization of qualitative analysis that led to exaggerated enthusiasm as well as to ungrounded fears of a 'Frankenstein's monster technology'.

As observers of the scene realized as early as the mid-1990s, neither the high-flying expectations nor the concerns were fully justified (cf. Lee and Fielding, 1995; Kelle, 1997). Many of the fears of the computer taking over analysis as well as concerns of a new methodological orthodoxy emerging from computer use, do not so much reflect the basic capabilities of software for the management of qualitative data, which helps the researcher with the necessary but analytically mundane tasks of ordering the data material. By supporting the construction of archiving systems based on complex coding schemes, software packages for computer-aided qualitative data analysis represent extremely useful clerical tools that free up the mind for analytic operations that are otherwise swamped by clerical work. By using retrieval facilities researchers can perform synoptical comparisons with the data or can examine theoretical assumptions by the inspection of the raw data – tasks that often must remain undone for lack of time if only mechanical methods are available. In this way, CAQDAS allows the exploitation of qualitative data more fully. But this is achieved not through the development of computer-aided analytic techniques unfamiliar to qualitative researchers but through the mechanization of clerical tasks used in the hermeneutic sciences for hundreds of years. To be clear about this issue we should address these programs as software for 'data administration and archiving' rather than as tools for 'data analysis'.

CONCLUSION

The invention of computer-aided techniques has clearly influenced and changed long-established practices in qualitative research. In many research projects, code-and-retrieve techniques have been proved to be straightforward tools to cope with data overload. However, since their use requires the time-consuming coding of data, it may also increase the workload of research projects. In a certain respect CAQDAS may be seen as a further step in the rationalization or even 'industrialization' of qualitative research work, a process that had already started with the adoption of models of the research process initially developed in the quantitative tradition, conceptualizing research as a process of collection and subsequent analysis of 'data'. One of the dangers arising from this is that qualitative research work loses much of the adventurous and unpredictable nature that inspired the works of the early ethnographers, allowing for fascinating insights into yet unknown social life worlds. By utilizing great masses of data collected much more systematically than in those early days, qualitative researchers may also produce more trivial and uninteresting results.

On the contrary, a crucial benefit of CAQDAS lies in helping to clarify analytic strategies that formerly represented an implicit folklore of research. The use of specific software forces the researcher to be more explicit about the categories that are developed in the ongoing research process. This can lead to the clarification and reconsideration of important methodological issues, in particular problems discussed in this chapter surrounding the relation between theory and data. Thus CAQDAS helps to gain a clearer understanding of qualitative theory building as a process starting with a heuristic framework consisting of concepts with low empirical content. Structuring the material with the help of such a framework is the prerequisite for a systematic comparison of empirical incidents in the data that transforms common-sense concepts or abstract theoretical concepts into empirically contentful categories, propositions and middle-range theories.

In this process of theory building, CAQDAS also helps with the systematic use of the complete evidence available in the data much better than any mechanical system of data organization. If the data are methodically coded with the help of software, researchers will find evidence and counter-evidence more easily. This clearly reduces the temptation to build far-reaching theoretical assumptions on some quickly and arbitrarily collected quotations from the material. But although such an increase in accountability and transparency induced by a new technology may impress funding bodies, it should not be forgotten that the validity of data, methods and research results always remains to a certain extent a matter of trust, regardless of the research methodology the researchers are committed to.

By helping to reflect on the nature of theory and on the role of hypotheses in the qualitative research process, CAQDAS has inspired several methodological debates in the 1990s. An important function of future discussions concerning computer use in qualitative research will be to demystify methodological concepts. Certainly the best way to succeed with this will be a 'rational reconstruction' of the actual processes of data management and data analysis by drawing on practical examples from research practice.

NOTES

1　The idea that interpretations can be 'falsified' is rooted in Oevermann's strict structuralist approach, which has provoked a number of critical comments (see, e.g., Reichertz, 1986; Bude, 1987; Kelle, 1997: 180–5).

2　Since such methods proved to be a data organization tool that suffices for many research contexts, they are still in use despite the invention of sophisticated CAQDAS programs (cf. Nideroest, 2002).

3　It allows, for example, to sort text segments according to many different criteria simultaneously.

4　Of these programs, only THE ETHNOGRAPH has been developed further and adapted to current operating systems such as Windows 95.

5　Much of Glaser's and Strauss's later methodological work can be understood as attempts to develop further the concept of theoretical sensitivity in order to reconcile these prima facie divergent ideas. Thereby Strauss proposes the use of a general theory of action to build an *axis* of the emerging theory (Strauss, 1987: 27f.; Strauss and Corbin, 1990: 99ff.). Glaser, although he heavily opposed this idea (Glaser, 1992), had proposed a similar concept previously: 'theoretical codes' that the researcher has at his or her disposal should be used to conceptualize how events and incidents in the data 'may relate to each other as hypotheses to be integrated into a theory' (Glaser, 1978: 72). Thus the controversy between Glaser and Strauss boils down to the question whether the researcher uses a well-defined 'coding paradigm' and always looks systematically for 'causal conditions', 'phenomena', 'context', 'intervening conditions', 'action strategies' and 'consequences' in the data (Strauss and Corbin, 1990: 99), or whether he or she should employ theoretical codes ad hoc, thereby drawing on a huge fund of 'coding families' (Glaser, 1978: 72–80). In the research teams mentioned above, those who opted for a pragmatic approach towards coding clearly favoured the 'paradigm model' of Strauss and Corbin. Others who emphasized the dangers of neglecting the perspectives of the research subjects in the coding process shared Glaser's position.

6　Herbert Blumer had coined the term '*sensitizing concepts*' to describe theoretical concepts that 'lack precise reference and have no bench marks which allow a clear-cut identification of a specific instance' (Blumer, 1954: 7). Sensitizing concepts are useful tools for descriptions but not for predictions, since their lack of empirical content permits researchers to apply them to a wide array of phenomena: a great variety of social events, for instance, may be described in terms of 'role-taking' or 'power relations'.

7　Think, for instance, of Blumer's definition of 'Symbolic Interactionism': 'Symbolic Interactionism sees meaning as social products, as creations that are formed in and through the defining activities of people as they interact' (Blumer, 1969: 5). Any attempt to deduce from it logically an empirical statement that can, in principle, 'falsify' the theory would fail or provoke endless philosophical discussions about the meaning of terms like 'interaction', 'meaning', etc.

8　Software developers have sometimes bemoaned this as a sign of the technological conservatism of users who utilize only a small part of the possibilities offered by the software (cf. Fielding, 1993).

REFERENCES

Abel, Th. (1948) 'The operation called *Verstehen*', *American Journal of Sociology*, 54: 211–18.

Agar, M. (1991) 'The right brain strikes back', in: N.G. Fielding and R.M. Lee (eds), *Using Computers in Qualitative Research*. Newbury Park: CA: Sage, pp. 181–94.

Becker, H. and Geer, B. (1960) 'Participant observation: the analysis of qualitative field data', in R.N. Adams and J.J. Preiss (eds), *Human Organization Research: Field Relations and Techniques*. Homewood, IL: Dorsey Press, pp. 267–89.

Blumer, Herbert (1954) 'What is wrong with Social Theory?', *American Sociological Review*, 19: 3–10.

Blumer, Herbert (1969) *Symbolic Interactionism: Perspective and Method*. Englewood Cliffs, NJ: Prentice-Hall.

Braemer, G. (1994) 'Wandel im Selbstbild des Familienernährers? Reflexionen über vierzig Jahre Ehe-, Erwerbs- und Familienleben'. Working Paper No. 29, Sonderforschungsbereich 186, Bremen.

Bude, H. (1987) *Deutsche Karrieren. Lebenskonstruktionen sozialer Aufsteiger aus der Flakhelfergeneration*. Frankfurt am Main: Suhrkamp.

Charmaz, K. (1983) 'The grounded theory method: an explication and interpretation', in R.M. Emerson, (ed.), *Contemporary Field Research: A Collection of Writings*. Prospect Heights, IL: Waveland Press, pp. 109–26.

Coffey, A., Holbrook, B. and Atkinson, P. (1996) 'Qualitative data analysis: technologies and representations, *Sociological Research Online* [Online Journal], 1(1), http://www.socresonline.org.uk/1/1/4.html#top [11/11/02].

Conrad, P. and Reinarz, S. (1984) 'Qualitative computing: approaches and issues', *Qualitative Sociology*, 7: 34–60.

Dotzler, H. (1995) 'Using software for interpretive text analysis: results from interviews with research teams'. Paper presented at the conference SoftStat '95; The Eighth Conference on the Scientific Use of Statistical Software, 26–30 March, Heidelberg, Germany.

Douglas, J. (1976) *Investigative Social Research*. London: Sage.

Dreyfus, H.L. (1972) *What Computers Can't Do: A Critique of Artificial Reason*. New York: Harper & Row.

Dreyfus, S.E. and Dreyfus, H.L. (1986) *Mind over Machine: The Power of Human Intuition and Expertise in the Era of the Computer*. Oxford: Blackwell.

Glaser, Barney (1978) *Theoretical Sensitivity: Advances in the Methodology of Grounded Theory*. Mill Valley, CA: Sociology Press.

Glaser, B.G. (1992) *Emergence vs. Forcing: Basics of Grounded Theory Analysis*. Mill Valley, CA: Sociology Press.

Glaser, B.G. and Strauss, A.L. (1967) *The Discovery of Grounded Theory: Strategies for Qualitative Research*. Chicago: Aldine.

Fielding, N. (1993) 'Qualitative data analysis with a computer: recent developments', *Social Research Update* [Online Journal], March, http://www.soc.surrey.ac.uk/sru/SRU1.html [11/11/02].

Hanson, N. (1971) 'The idea of a logic of discovery', in S. Toulmin (ed.), *What I Do Not Believe and Other Essays*. Dordrecht: Reidel, pp. 288–300.

Heinz, W.R., Kelle, U., Witzel, A. and Zinn, J. (1998) 'Vocational training and career development in Germany: results from a longitudinal study', *International Journal of Behavioral Development*, 1: 77–101.

Hesse-Biber, S. and Dupuis, P. (1995) 'Hypothesis testing in computer-aided qualitative data analysis', in U. Kelle (ed.), *Computer-Aided Qualitative Data Analysis: Theory, Methods and Practice*. London: Sage, pp. 129–35.

Holbrook, Allyson and Butcher, Lyndon (1996) 'Uses of qualitative data analysis software in educational research: the literature, the hard questions and some specific research applications', *Australian Educational Researcher*, 23(3): 55–76.

Huber, G. (1995) 'Qualitative hypothesis examination and theory building', in U. Kelle (ed.), *Computer-Aided Qualitative Data Analysis: Theory, Methods and Practice*. London: Sage, pp. 136–57.

Jorgenson, D.L. (1989) *Participant Observation: A Methodology for Human Studies*. Newbury Park, CA: Sage.

Kelle, U. (ed.) (1995) *Computer-Aided Qualitative Data Analysis: Theory, Methods and Practice*. London: Sage.

Kelle, U. (1997) 'Theory building in qualitative research and computer programs for the management of textual data, *Sociological Research Online* [Online Journal], 2(2), http://www.socresonline.org.uk/socresonline/2/2/1.html [11/11/02].

Kelle, U. (1998) *Empirisch begründete Theoriebildung. Zur Logik und Methodologie interpretativer Sozialforschung* (2nd ed.). Weinheim: DSV.

Kelle, U. and Zinn, J. (1998) 'School-to-work transition and occupational careers – results from a longitudinal study in Germany', in T. Lange (ed.), *Understanding the School-to-Work Transition*. New York: Nova Science Publishers, pp. 71–91.

Kelle, U., Marx, J., Pengel, S., Uhlhorn, K. and Witt, I. (2003) 'Die Rolle theoretischer Heuristiken im qualitativen Forschungsprozess – ein Werkstattbericht', in H.-U. Otto, G. Oelerich and H.-G. Micheel (eds), *Empirische Forschung. Sozialarbeit – Sozialpädagogik – Soziale Probleme*. Neuwied and Kriftel: Luchterhand, pp. 112–30.

Kracauer, S. (1952/53) 'The challenge of qualitative content analysis', *Public Opinion Quarterly*, 16: 631–42.

Kuckartz, U. (1995) 'Case-oriented quantification', in U. Kelle (ed.), *Computer-Aided Qualitative Data Analysis: Theory, Methods and Practice*. London: Sage, pp. 158–66.

Lakatos, I. (1982) *The Methodology of Scientific Research Programmes. Philosophical Papers*, vol. 1. Cambridge: Cambridge University Press.

Lee, R.M. and Fielding, N.G. (1991) 'Computing for qualitative research: options, problems and potential', in N.G. Fielding and R.M. Lee (eds), *Using Computers in Qualitative Research*. London: Sage, pp. 1–13.

Lee, R.M. and Fielding, N.G. (1995) 'User's experiences of qualitative data analysis software', in: U. Kelle (ed.), *Computer-Aided Qualitative Data Analysis: Theory, Methods and Practice*. London: Sage, pp. 29–40.

Lee, R.M. and Fielding, N.G. (1996) 'Qualitative data analysis: representations of a technology. A comment on Coffey, Holbrook and Atkinson', *Sociological Research Online* [Online Journal], 1(4), http://www.socresonline.org.uk/socresonline/1/4/lf.html [11/11/02].

Lofland, J. and Lofland, L.H. (1984) *Analyzing Social Settings: A Guide to Qualitative Observation and Analysis*. Belmont, CA: Wadsworth.

Lonkila, M. (1995) 'Grounded theory as an emerging paradigm for computer-assisted qualitative data analysis', in: U. Kelle (ed.), *Computer-Aided Qualitative Data Analysis: Theory, Methods and Practice*. London: Sage, pp. 41–51.

Miles, M.B. and Huberman, A.M. (1984) *Qualitative Data Analysis: A Sourcebook of New Methods*. Newbury Park, CA: Sage.

Nideroest, B. (2002) 'Die technikunterstützte Analyse von qualitativen Daten mit Word', *Forum: Qualitative Sozialforschung/Forum: Qualitative Social Research* [Online Journal], 3(2), http://www.qualitative-research.net/fqs/fqs.htm [17/10/02].

Oevermann, U., Allert, T., Konau, E. and Krambeck, J. (1979) 'Die Methodologie einer "objektiven Hermeneutik" und ihre allgemeine forschungslogische Bedeutung in den Sozialwissenschaften', in H.-G. Soeffner (ed.) *Interpretative Verfahren in den Sozial- und Textwissenschaften*. Stuttgart: Metzler, pp. 352–434.

Ragin, C. (1987) *The Comparative Method: Moving Beyond Qualitative and Quantitative Strategies*. Berkeley: University of California Press.

Ragin, C. (1995) 'Using qualitative comparative analysis to study configurations', in U. Kelle (ed.), *Computer-Aided Qualitative Data Analysis: Theory, Methods and Practice*. London: Sage, pp. 170–89.

Reichertz, J. (1986) *Probleme qualitativer Sozialforschung*. Frankfurt and New York: Campus.

Richards, T.J. and Richards, L. (1994) 'Using computers in qualitative research', in N.K. Denzin, and Y.S. Lincoln (eds), *Handbook of Qualitative Research*. Thousand Oaks, CA: Sage, pp. 445–62.

Seidel, J.V. (1985) *The Ethnograph Verson 2.0 User's Manual*. Littleton, CO: Qualis Research Associates.

Seidel, J.V. (1988) *The Ethnograph Verson 3.0 User's Manual*. Littleton, CO: Qualis Research Associates.

Seidel, J.V. (1991) 'Method and madness in the application of computer technology to qualitative data analysis', in: R.M. Lee and N.G. Fielding (eds), *Using Computers in Qualitative Research*. London: Sage, pp. 107–16.

Seidel, J.V. and Clark, J.A. (1984) 'THE ETHNOGRAPH: a computer program for the analysis of qualitative data', *Qualitative Sociology*, 7: 110–25.

Seidel, J.V. and Kelle, U. (1995) 'Different functions of coding in the analysis of textual data', in U. Kelle (ed.), *Computer-Aided Qualitative Data Analysis: Theory, Methods and Practice*. London: Sage, pp. 52–61.

Simon, H.A. (1985) 'Human nature in politics: the dialogue of psychology with political science', *American Political Science Review*, 79: 293–304.

Stone, P.J., Dunphy, D.C., Smith, M.S. and Ogilvie, D.M. (1966) *The GENERAL INQUIRER: A Computer Approach to Content Analysis*. Cambridge, MA: MIT Press.

Strauss, A.L. (1987) *Qualitative Analysis for Social Scientists*. Cambridge: Cambridge University Press.

Strauss, A. and Corbin, J. (1990) *Basics of Qualitative Research: Grounded Theory Procedures and Techniques*. Thousand Oaks, CA: Sage.

Tashakkori, A. and Teddlie, Ch. (1998) *Mixed Methodology: Combining Qualitative and Quantitative Approaches* (Applied Social Research Methods Series, vol. 46). Thousand Oaks, CA: Sage.

Taylor, S.J. and Bogdan, R. (1984) *Introduction to Qualitative Research Methods: The Search for Meanings*. New York: Wiley.

Tesch, R. (1990) *Qualitative Analysis: Analysis Types and Software Tools*. London: Falmer Press.

Winograd, T. and Flores, F. (1986) *Understanding Computers and Cognition*. Chicago: Ablex.

Part 6

AUDIENCES AND APPLICATIONS

After the 1970s the reader gained a central role in the human sciences. Semiotics, literary criticism, structuralist poetics, reception theory, textual linguistics and so on have renewed our interest in audiences. In the social sciences, this movement has culminated with the well-known book edited by anthropologists Clifford and Marcus (1986) which marked the return of the reader. Audiences have always been one of the most important elements in the whole research process because hypotheses, the selection of findings and the communication of the results are often inserted into a virtual dialogue with an audience imagined by the researcher. The audience plays a central role even before research starts as one plans a research proposal. As Barry A. Turner (1988: 112) stated, the main motivation for Glaser and Strauss (1967) in writing their famous book on grounded theory was a political one: to make available to students and researchers a methodological textbook to be quoted in their proposals when applying for research funding to institutions which at that time were usually prejudiced against qualitative research.

The essays collected in Part 6 show how to deal practically with the audience and outline the wide range of applications of qualitative research. During the 1990s applied qualitative research has been acknowledged as a powerful instrument for analysing the kind of social practices that interest research funding bodies. Qualitative research has become required in many applied fields (such as management, business, clinical research, action research, education, nursing, administration, health, workplace studies, human–computer interaction,

marketing, evaluation research, knowledge management, and so on), sometimes because its capacity to describe behaviours, to explain processes and to propose practical remedies is seen to be greater than much quantitative research.

In Chapter 31, Janice M. Morse deals with preparing and evaluating qualitative research proposals. Writing a successful proposal requires sensitivity to the expectations (and blind spots) of particular audiences, and is at least as skilful a performance as writing a final report. Particularly with qualitative research, which is often somewhat exploratory, it is hard to indicate ahead of time how a project will go – yet in a research proposal an importance audience must be persuaded to trust in the researcher sufficiently to allocate funds. Morse's chapter contains a number of suggestions to help in this.

Chapter 32 is devoted to qualitative market research: Gill Ereaut, an experienced market researcher who has also 'crossed over' into academic qualitative research from time to time, is well positioned to point out the special contribution that this form of research practice makes. Because of its institutional context, qualitative market research has developed features of its own, including a lively oral culture of research training. Ereaut's chapter shows how both academic and market researchers can learn important skills from each other.

Chapter 33, by Moira J. Kelly, deals with qualitative evaluation research. Using a wide range of studies, including her own work on health promotion, she shows the practical value of qualitative studies to a variety of audiences. This value derives in no small part from the ability of good qualitative research to identify social processes unavailable to quantitative work. Then, in Chapter 34, Donna Ladkin shows some of the problems and benefits in doing action research. Relations with the funding agencies, interactions with participants and exchanges between the members of the research team are treated in a practical and reflexive way.

Chapter 35, by Martyn Hammersley, analyses the teaching of qualitative method, an important but often neglected aspect of the role of many research practitioners. Hammersley examines the difficulties in training researchers in what he says can be seen as largely a craft skill (though he outlines competing conceptions of this as well). In this sense, his chapter resonates with the emphasis by other authors in this book, on the relation between research and biography. Hammersley's position can be compared with what we say in the introductory chapter to this book, where it is argued that biography should illuminate methodological principles (in practice) rather than replace them.

Barbara Czarniawska, in Chapter 36, makes a strong case for more self-reflective social scientific writing, illustrating the variety of ways in which writers of research use literary devices and figures of speech. An awareness of these, Czarniawska believes, helps in developing more varied writing skills, as well as assisting readers to make critical judgements of texts. Finally, in Chapter 37, Donileen R. Loseke and Spencer E. Cahill, former editors of the *Journal of Contemporary Ethnography*, offer an inside view of the processes involved in publishing qualitative manuscripts. Like the authors of other chapters in this part of the book, Loseke and Cahill offer numerous tricks of the trade to follow in making publication of papers more likely.

REFERENCES

Clifford, J. and Marcus, G.E. (eds) (1986) *Writing Cultures: Poetics and Politics of Ethnography*. Berkeley: University of California Press.

Glaser, B.G. and Strauss, A.L. (1967) *The Discovery of Grounded Theory: Strategies for Qualitative Research*. Chicago: Aldine.

Turner, Barry A. (1988) 'Connoisseurship in the study of organizational cultures', in A. Bryman (ed.), *Doing Research in Organizations*. London: Routledge & Kegan Paul, pp. 108–23.

31

Preparing and evaluating qualitative research proposals

Janice M. Morse

The purpose of preparing a research proposal is to place the researcher in the best position for successfully doing research. If the researcher is a student, it allows the committee to assess that the student is best prepared to carry out the project. It provides the ethics review committee with a document to evaluate so that they may be assured that harm resulting from the research is unlikely and minimized. Most importantly, it provides the researcher with the opportunity to intrigue the granting agency that this is an interesting and important problem that will likely yield important results, that the researcher is competent to carry out the research, and that the project is worthy of funding.

Qualitative proposals differ from quantitative proposals, yet there are few examples in the literature to use as models.[1] While the quantitative proposal may be considered contractual, the unknown course of qualitative inquiry and the unforeseen (and often unpredictable) outcomes mean that it should only be regarded as a *guide* to approach the proposed problem. In qualitative inquiry, not only the outcome but also the *course* of inquiry is dictated by the findings. Qualitative proposals should not be considered to be unchangeable. Indeed, if the researcher is not getting the type of data needed, if the methods are shown to be 'not feasible' in the chosen setting, or if, in retrospect, the questions appear poorly stated and 'off base', then the problems encountered must be documented and the proposal (and research design) altered to fit the actual research conditions. Such flexibility is not an option with quantitative work, where altering the hypotheses to fit the data would be considered a questionable practice at best. But an equivalent sin in qualitative inquiry is forcing data or twisting categories to fit the proposed questions, theoretical frame, or anticipated results.

Thus, in qualitative inquiry, there is less dependence on the procedures outlined in the proposal per se and the relationship between the initial proposal and the eventual outcome of the projects, than there is in the quantitative proposals where 'what you see is what you get'. But this is not to suggest that, in qualitative inquiry, preparing the proposal is not an important step in the process of doing research. It is very much so, and can be considered a phase of research on its own. During proposal preparation, the researcher becomes fully acquainted with the literature, becomes versatile in alternative methodological approaches to the research problem, and becomes aware of possible ethical problems. He or she may also, at this point, become practiced in approaching participants, the use of equipment, conducting interviews and observations, and data analytic techniques. Once completed, the proposal provides a means for obtaining programmatic approval, for negotiating entry and obtaining administrative approval to conduct the research, for obtaining funding, and for documenting, negotiating, and building the research team, as well as a guide for conducting the research. In short, it provides direction from which the research starts.

In this chapter, I shall outline the process of preparing a qualitative proposal – from conceptualization through to writing and pre-submission review – and outline the processes of review, including how the review committee evaluates and recognizes its potential. This chapter is based on my experience of more than twenty-five years of conducting qualitative research, from submitting more proposals than I care to count that were soundly rejected (for reasons fair or foul!). It comes from having more than thirty projects funded to more than $3 million, from years of supervising students and post-doctoral students, and from more than twenty years experience of reviewing proposals for granting agencies from the US, Canada, Britain, the Netherlands, Australia, New Zealand, and South Africa.

PREPARING THE PROPOSAL

The armchair walkthrough

One of the most important steps in proposal writing is the preparatory conceptualizing to determine the type of project to be undertaken, the intensive groundwork necessary for determining the direction that the proposal will take, and determining the characteristics of the participants required and the setting in which to conduct the research. This armchair walkthrough is also needed for identifying the necessary components to ensure feasibility and rigor for the project (Morse and Richards, 2002). Such decisions do not mean that the researcher rigidly adheres to the plan, or continues to use the procedures outlined in the proposal, if they are clearly not feasible in practice. Rather, the proposal provides an outline of the project, allowing it to be approved by the institute or agency and enabling it to be funded. For the student, it provides a contract between him or her and the supervisory committee. In short, it places the researcher in the best possible position to commence researching, but need not chart a course that cannot be altered.

All research begins with an idea. The fact that the idea is the most creative and important part of conducting research – and must fall at the beginning – places rather terrifying pressure on new researchers. They ask themselves: How do I know that this is a 'good' idea? Is it new? Is it interesting? Is it one worthy of spending years of my life? Is it feasible? Possible to study? and, If *I* have thought of it, how is it that no one else has? Some degree of assurance can be gleaned at the beginning of a project by conducting a thorough review of the literature, by discussing your idea with your advisor and colleagues, and even by contacting researchers who are working in that particular area. But with qualitative research – I emphasize this as one of the most significant differences between a qualitative and a quantitative proposal – a researcher cannot prepare a proposal that will definitively outline the steps and strategies of the research process, so that the results of the project will be promised or predicted. At best, the qualitative researcher can prepare a proposal that states: *This is an interesting topic worthy of investigation; this is what we know and don't know about this question; this is how I will go about looking at this area; and, it is important to know about this area because of thus and so, and the results of my study will enable us to move forward in this way or that way.* The proposal may even list problems with current theory or approaches to the topic, and argue that a certain area needs to be reexamined.

Thus, before the writing of the proposal actually begins, a great deal of thinking takes place. Occasionally a student is lucky and finds an advisor with a research program in place, with researchable questions available, as is common in the hard sciences. But unfortunately this advantage is the exception rather than the rule in social science, in which it is more common for the student to be expected to develop their own question.

IDENTIFYING A QUESTION If a researcher feels put on the spot, and cannot think of a question or even decide what they are interested in, feelings of panic may supersede constructive thinking. If this happens, I recommend that the researcher do some self-reflection, asking: What topics do I often find myself thinking about? What literature catches my eye in the library? What papers have I enjoyed writing? Or in practice, what areas or problems do I find most intriguing?

Once the general subject area is identified, go to the library and pull the literature pertaining to that topic. If it is an area that is new to you, then begin with textbooks or review articles that will provide an overview before seeking the more specific and narrow research articles. This helps you to narrow your interest and topic even further. Next, sort the research articles according to knowledge revealed, at the same time making a 'we know that …' list, and a list of assumptions. The assumptions on which an article is based are often overt – the authors explicitly present their theoretical stance and aspects of the topic they are accepting or taking for granted, while at other times they are less obvious. It may be necessary to read between the lines, thinking to yourself: *if* the author asked this question, *then* she or he must think thus and so.

Once you feel competent about the literature surrounding your topic, step back and think broadly about the areas that interest you most. Your research question will be identified because you feel that some area is thin and under-explored, is suspect or not well grounded;

perhaps the theory that underlies the information is wrong, or you may simply find a gap that needs to be explored. Keep track of the reasons for selecting your question, for you will need this information to justify your question in the literature review in your proposal. In fact, many researchers begin writing the literature review portion of the proposal at this point.

IDENTIFYING THE METHOD   Once the topic is identified, the next phase of the armchair walk-through is to consider the possible methods for answering your question, and develop a research design that will best answer the question. Furthermore, each alternative may require a different setting to gather optimally the most appropriate data. Basically, some qualitative methods best elicit meaning (phenomenology: see van Manen, 1997), some are more suited than others to explore processes (grounded theory: see Glaser, 1978; Strauss, 1987), and some a better fit to analyze everyday life as it occurs (e.g. ethnography: see Agar, 1996). Some methods provide a particular frame (such as observational methods: see Spradley, 1980) that may be micro-analytic (video analyses: see Morse and Bottorff, 1990) or macro-analytic (participant observation: see Spradley, 1979). These issues are addressed by planning. Ask yourself, 'If I asked this question, then I would need to use this qualitative method, and I would need to conduct the research in this setting, with these particularly types of participants. On the other hand, if I were interested in these aspects, then I would need to ... thus and so.' Envision each alternative and outline the research process. Issues of design should also be addressed. For example, if it is a comparative question, consider which two groups would reveal the greatest differences, and in what setting would they provide the best data. How would I get access?

The decisions made at this time are crucial for the success of the study. For example, I once wanted to study nurses' efforts in comforting patients in hospitals. The rule of thumb for good qualitative research is that the concepts should be studied at the place where they are maximized – that is, researchers must study the best and clearest examples, rather than the average incident. If the phenomenon one is studying is clear, smaller samples are required, fewer data are needed, one can identify the characteristics of the phenomenon more readily, and the results are more definite, the researcher more certain. Therefore, to study comfort, I needed to find a situation in the hospital in which the participants are distressed and in need of comfort, in pain, able to move and respond to the pain, and which should not be transient. Two areas fit this description: labour and delivery, or the emergency department. Because obstetrics usually lacks the stress of life and death, I selected the emergency department. Again, because little work had been done in the area, I chose to begin with participant observation so that I could first describe the types of comforting (see Morse, 1992).

To compare the alternative approaches for researching a topic, you may outline each option in a table. In separate columns, list each question, the method, setting and participants required, research techniques, analytic strategies, and the types of results that each method would produce. An example of such an approach is illustrated in Denzin and Lincoln's *Handbook of Qualitative Research* (1994) (see Morse, 1994: 209–19).

PRELIMINARY INPUT   Often, at this phase, before actually preparing the proposal, researchers prepare a 'concept' memo – a two-page outline of the proposed project for initial input from their advisors or to obtain input from a granting agency. This memo contains all the elements of a full proposal, but in outline form. In essence, it provides others with notification of your research plans, so that they may express interest, veto it, or suggest modifications to your plans before you have too much effort invested in the research ideas.

If you are planning to submit your proposal for external funding, identify the agency at this point, and obtain the agency's guidelines for submission. These can usually be obtained from the agency website (see Table 31.1 for a partial list). Note the deadlines for submission, for some agencies accept applications only one to three times per year. Once you have the deadline, *work backwards*, establishing your own timeline to complete and submit your proposal. Allow two weeks for approvals to be obtained from your university, time to obtain ethics approvals and access to research sites, three weeks for internal review, and at least three months for writing/conceptualizing. Agencies tend to have their own special forms and format for the components of the proposal, and it is important to conform strictly to their guidelines, or you may find that your proposal, after all that work, will not be accepted for consideration. Most agencies have very strict rules about page length, even type size, and the number of copies to be submitted. They have firm instructions about the order of the components of the research process, the presentation of the researcher's vitae, and so forth. They have firm regulations about what budget items are allowable, the duration of funding, and

Table 31.1   *Selection of funding agencies*

Country	Disciplines	Agency/Internet URL
Australia	Health and medical research	National Health and Medical Research Council
		http://www.health.gov.au/nhmrc/
	Multidisciplinary/social sciences	Australian Research Council
		http://www.arc.gov.au/ncgp/
	Education	Commonwealth Department of Education Science and Training
		http://www.detya.gov.au/highered/research/index.htm
Canada	Health and medical research	Canadian Institutes for Health Research
		http://www.cihr-irsc.gc.ca/
	Multidisciplinary/social sciences/education	Social Sciences and Humanities Research Council
		http://www.sshrc.ca/
Europe	Health and medical research	Medical Research Council
		http://www.mrc.ac.uk/
	Multidisciplinary/social sciences	Economic and Social Research Council
		http://www.esrc.ac.uk/
		Economic and Social Research Council/European Research Centre
		http://www.lboro.ac.uk/departments/eu/funding_opportunities.html
	Education/social sciences	UK Research Office
		http://www.ukro.ac.uk/
USA	Health and medical research	National Institutes of Health
		http://grants1.nih.gov/grants/index.cfm
	Multidisciplinary/social sciences	The American Council of Learned Societies
		http://www.acls.org/mor-intr.htm
	Education	US Department of Education
		http://www.ed.gov/index.jsp

budget limitations. Read this information now, to ensure that your project is a good fit with the agency and that you will meet all their requirements and deadlines.

How do you know that you will need to apply for funding? All research requires *something*, and qualitative research can actually be quite expensive. Minimally, you need a tape recorder, tapes, and perhaps someone to help you to transcribe the tapes. You need a computer, software, and perhaps a printer. You may need cameras, film, a VCR, and so forth. You need paper and money for copying, so that even if your research is 'self-funded' you should be aware of these costs before embarking on the project. There are many small grants (usually under US $5000) to assist graduate students with their research, so that it is uncommon that research is conducted without a research grant.

WRITING THE PROPOSAL

Some guides to writing a qualitative research proposal have been published, and are listed in Table 31.2. How you prepare your proposal depends on the requirements of your advisory committee (if you are a student), the agency from which you are requesting funds, and

perhaps even your institution's requirements for its ethics committee. But we sometimes forget that the proposal should be prepared for one's self, as a plan for conducting the research, and something to keep the research project on track. Fortunately, once the proposal is written in one format, if it is necessary to revise the formats for other purposes or bodies, this is not an onerous task. Graduate students should discuss proposal requirements and expectations with their supervisors. Because of the uncertain nature of qualitative research (discussed at the beginning of this chapter), some supervisors require only a 2–3-page summary, others require 10–20 pages, and yet others ask the student to prepare the first three chapters of the dissertation – the introduction, literature review and methods chapter.

Recall, when writing the proposal, that in addition to guiding your research, the proposal is a document to interest, entice, and persuade others that this is an excellent idea. In that sense it is a political document. Although the ideas must be presented comprehensively and fairly, they are structured so that you are building your case that studying this problem is necessary, urgent, and important. Importantly, the proposal must be internally consistent, with matching components: the questions must have supporting literature, the methods must answer the question, the data and

Table 31.2 *Additional resources for writing a qualitative proposal*

Proposal preparation

Campbell, L. (1994) Lois Campbell's list of guidelines for qualitative research studies. http://www.qsr.com.au/resource/proposal.txt

Connelly, L.M. and Yoder, L.H. (2000) 'Improving qualitative proposals: common problem areas', *Clinical Nurse Specialist*, 14(2): 69–74.

Heath, A.W. (1997) 'The proposal in qualitative research', *The Qualitative Report*, 3(1). http://www.nova.edu/ssss/QR/QR3-1/heath.html

Mackay, J.A. (no date) A template for Chapter 3 in a qualitative dissertation proposal. http://www.unocoe.unomaha.edu/mackay/qualitative.html

Morse, J.M. (1994) 'Designing qualitative research', in Y. Lincoln and N. Denzin (eds), *Handbook of Qualitative Inquiry*. Menlo Park, CA: Sage, pp. 220–35.

Morse, J.M. and Richards, L. (2002) *Readme First for a Users Guide to Qualitative Methods*. Thousand Oaks, CA: Sage.

Ratcliff, D. (no date) Issues that should be addressed in a qualitative research proposal. http://don.ratcliff.net/qual/prologuide.html

Swenson, M.M. (1996) 'Essential elements in a qualitative dissertation proposal', *Journal of Nurse Education*, 35(4): 188–90.

The Grants Information Center, University of Wisconsin, Madison, has a useful list of Internet resources for proposal preparation. http://www.library.wisc.edu/libraries/Memorial/grants/proposal.htm

Obtaining funding

Brink, P.J. (1990) 'Dialogue: the granting game', in J.M. Morse (ed.), *Qualitative Nursing Research: A Contemporary Dialogue*. Newbury Park, CA: Sage.

Cheek, J. (2000) 'An untold story? Doing funded qualitative research', in N.K. Denzin and Y.S. Lincoln (eds), *Handbook of Qualitative Research* (2nd ed.). Thousand Oaks, CA: Sage, pp. 401–20.

Cohen, M.Z., Knafl, K. and Dzurec, L.C. (1993) 'Grant writing for qualitative research', *Image: Journal of Nursing Scholarship*, 25(2): 151–6.

Morse, J.M. (1991a) 'On the evaluation of qualitative proposals', *Qualitative Health Research*, 1(3): 283–6.

Morse, J.M. (1991b) 'On funding qualitative proposals' (Editorial), *Qualitative Health Research*, 1(2): 147–51.

Munhall, P.L. (2001) 'Institutional review of qualitative research proposals: a task of no small consequence', in *Nursing Research: A qualitative perspective* (3rd ed.). Sudbury, MA: Jones & Bartlett, pp. 551–64.

Office of Behavioral and Social Sciences Research (2001) *Qualitative Methods in Health Research: Opportunities and Considerations in Application and Review*. Washington, DC: National Institutes of Health.

Tripp-Reimer, T. and Cohen, M.Z. (1991) 'Funding strategies for qualitative research', in J. Morse (ed.), *Qualitative Nursing Research: A Contemporary Dialogue*. Newbury Park, CA: Sage, pp. 243–56.

the analysis must provide information that will enable the questions to be answered, analytic techniques must facilitate the type of results and theory required, and all necessary components must be accounted for in the budget and the timeline must be adequate to account to the work plan.

Components of the proposal

All proposals have the following components:

Title: Proposal titles are usually descriptive, and longer than titles of articles, although some agencies may restrict the length by *numbers of characters* (for instance, the National Institutes of Health restrict to 56 characters, including spaces). Titles are placed on the cover page, along with the all the identifying information (principal investigator and other investigators, institutions, and contact addresses and phone numbers). If the agency provides forms, then these substitute for front pages.

Abstract: This is a summary of the entire project, usually about half a page in length. Because this must reflect your project, and because you may make some changes in design during the writing phase, write it last, once the proposal is almost completed.

Lay abstract: This is a revision of the abstract, but written in lay terms, often using grade 8 (about Form 3) reading level. This is often requested by the funding agency, and is used in press releases, brochures, and other materials, should your proposal receive funding.

Body of the proposal: The *Introduction* is a short (1–2 page) introduction to the proposal. In it, the researcher introduces the research problems and its importance, and may define any special terms that will be used in the proposal.

Literature review: The literature review sets the stage for your project. In essence, the literature review justifies the need for your study, provides the background information so that the reviewers understand the significance of the problem, and creates a logical argument leading to your research question. By the time the reviewer has read the review, he or she should not only be well informed about the topic, but also be convinced that you are competent and capable of conducting the study.

The skill, therefore, in writing the review is to be able to synthesize a great deal of information in the amount of space allocated in the funding agency's guidelines. A common mistake is to write sequentially about the work of individual researchers, rather than initially providing a broad overview of the background work, and comprehensively documenting these statements with pertinent citations. Detail is provided only about those studies most relevant to your project, and discussion of these closely related studies will show the reviewer how your work – and answering your research question – will extend knowledge and reveal the significance of the implications of your project.

Methods: The use of qualitative methods must be justified: Why are you choosing this approach? The method selected must place the researcher in a position to obtain the type of data that will best reveal the phenomenon and can be analyzed readily to reveal the type of results you are anticipating. This fit is important. Many researchers, for instance, attempt to elicit data by outlining descriptions from participants (that is, by using interview methods) when the phenomenon could be more accurately described by observing it directly. This fit between research question, data collection, and analysis is crucial.

In the proposal, the description of the methods must be clear and simple enough to be intelligible to those who have no knowledge of qualitative methods, yet sophisticated enough for those who are knowledgeable of qualitative methods to understand that the approach is the most prudent and appropriate, and also see that you have a strong understanding of the methods.

Budget: The budget is one of the easiest parts of the proposal to prepare, yet one that is often not given adequate attention by researchers. Yet it is the part of the proposal that is of most concern to the funding agency, because this is how much the project will cost them! If budgeting to pay research assistants to help with the interviewing, for example, you must allow not only for the length of time that the interview is expected to take, but also for the set-up and travel time. The time allowed for transcription ranges from four to eight times the length of the interview, depending on the type of transcription, with conversation analysis taking much longer than a verbatim transcription. Also often underestimated is the amount of time required for conceptualizing and

writing – and without these, the project is less than it should be! A good rule of thumb is that every project will take twice as long as the investigator initially anticipates. Equipment and supplies are usually straightforward and easily justified.

Timeline: Closely related to adequate allowance for conceptualization is the anticipated timeline. As noted in the previous sections, estimate the amount of time you think the project will take, and then double it!

Checking and evaluating the proposal

Before deciding that your proposal is finished, put the proposal in the best shape possible by reviewing it yourself. A good proposal must be polished, with no errors. Have the proposal edited professionally, and double-check the budget. Are all items accounted for? Allowed as expenditures by the agency? Is the proposal complete and all requested information provided? Are supporting materials, such as letters of permissions and ethics approvals, included? Check the proposal for clarity and comprehensiveness: Is the proposal intelligible to someone not familiar with qualitative inquiry? Are all the assumptions explained, the terms defined, procedures clear? Is the proposal sufficiently broad in scope to allow for true exploration of the phenomenon, and not rigidly constraining? And finally, is the proposal a 'good read'? Does it excite and interest the reader, and persuade the reader of the significance of the research?

If your research is being submitted for funding, obtain a copy of the criteria that the committee uses for its review. As I discuss later, some committees appear to use criteria that are suited to a quantitative proposal rather than to a qualitative inquiry. At this time, prepare your proposal defensively. For instance, if the criteria state that the hypothesis will be evaluated, explain in your proposal why a hypothesis is inappropriate. If the criteria ask for a random sample or power test, explain why you have made your design decisions, and why randomization would be inappropriate and how it would invalidate your research. It may be unfair that you have to educate the committee in your application, but if you want to be funded from that agency, I do not know of any alternative course of action.

INTERNAL REVIEW

One of the most important steps before submitting the proposal is to have the proposal reviewed by colleagues who have not been associated with the development of the proposal. Invite several colleagues to review your proposal – both those who are and are not qualitative researchers and who are and are not familiar with the topic. If possible, give them a copy of the review criteria used by the agency to which the application is being submitted. Some researchers not only provide colleagues with the criteria and ask for a written review and comments, but may also want to hold a mock review panel meeting. They appoint a chair, and the investigator is an observer to the process, unable to ask questions or defend the work. The discussion may be recorded so that the investigator then has the opportunity to revise the proposal to meet the concerns of a 'representative' review panel. While this seems time-consuming, such preparation greatly enhances the chances of successful approval for funding.

Once the proposal is perfect in the eyes of the investigator and his or her colleagues, and is to be submitted to an agency for funding, then the necessary number of copies are made and the proposal submitted. Agencies usually acknowledge the receipt of a proposal, so that if you do not hear from the agency within a short time following submission, contact the agency to make certain they have received it! We shall now discuss how proposals are evaluated by the funding agency.

PROPOSAL EVALUATION

Review committees are usually composed of a relatively heterogeneous group of scientists; that is, one may find that the committee is made up of established scientists from any area (and this is particularly the case in health research), so a committee voting on your proposal may have members who are quantitative researchers and are not only unfamiliar with the methods you have described, but also know nothing about your topic. However, assignment for primary review is usually given to someone familiar with your topic and someone familiar with your methods; thus, the main assessment of your work will be done by researchers who are competent in your area, and these researchers will prepare a review – an assessment – on which the rest of the committee will base their decision.

One major problem with the evaluation of qualitative proposals by committees on which the majority of members are quantitative researchers, who are used to reviewing quantitative proposals, is that the qualitative proposal is quite different from the quantitative proposal.

The quantitative proposal is more definite and contractual: the hypothesis to be tested is clearly stated, the procedures for conducting the research and analyzing the data clearly detailed, and the implications of the research clearly predicted. By comparison, the qualitative proposal appears unclear, indecisive, and the outcomes unknown. But recall, this uncertainty is the nature of qualitative inquiry; it is also its strength and its significance. Qualitative inquiry investigates basic research – problems about which little is known – and does not test hypotheses.

Unfortunately, some evaluation committees, in their attempts to be fair and even-handed in their evaluation, use very detailed and specific criteria developed for the evaluation of quantitative proposals. I say 'unfortunately' because the majority of the researchers on these committees, and the applications they review, are quantitative and the criteria they develop fit only quantitative and not qualitative inquiry. These committees use inappropriate criteria for qualitative inquiry, evaluating, for instance, the hypothesis or type of experimental design.[2] Hopefully, as previously discussed, if your application is being submitted to such a committee, the researcher will have included additional rationale to justify his or her decisions.

How should a qualitative proposal be evaluated?

In qualitative inquiry the first criteria to be examined should be the researcher's skills, followed by the worthiness and relevance of the research question, and the rigor of the methods. Finally, the committee will question the feasibility of the research – not only the possibility of successfully completing the work, but also the adequacy of time you have allocated for completion and the amount of funding you have requested.

INVESTIGATOR CAPABILITY   In qualitative proposals, the most important evaluation criterion is the quality of the researcher. As it is the researcher who solves the problem, not instruments or questionnaires or statistical tests of significance, the researcher is the 'tool' for the investigation. The applicant should have listed their background and skills. Further, competence should be evident in the writing itself – by seeking and explicating an excellent research problem and identifying an interesting and clearly stated question, by analyzing the literature to demonstrate that a qualitative approach is needed, and by competently describing not only the methods, but how the method will be used to tackle the problem and to answer the question. The researcher will have described the checks and balances in the research project, to show throughout the research process how rigor will be maintained, how reliable data will be obtained, and how the validity of the results will be ensured.

What about the researcher's skills? For an established researcher, the review committee's task is easy – they simply review the researcher's track record. If this record is solid and reveals a good funding record, completed projects and publications, then the committee assumes that this study will also be completed, and funding is awarded. If this is your first project, then the task of demonstrating your competence is more difficult. Perhaps you could list courses and workshops you have taken, conferences you have attended, and projects in which you have worked as a research assistant. If you are a student, be certain to provide information about the track record of your advisor, committee, and/or consultants, who will be advising you during the course of the study, and funding will be awarded assuming your project will be well supervised.

Methodological versatility is a plus, for the uncertain course of qualitative inquiry often means that the proposed strategies must be evaluated and perhaps changed during the course of the inquiry, once the phenomenon is better understood or if the investigator discovers that she or he is not getting 'good' data.

THE RELEVANCE OF THE RESEARCH Relevance refers to the potential contribution of the research – the worthiness of the research question and the possible impact of the results to the discipline and to social science in general.

Assessing the *relevance* of the research questions is a critical component for evaluation, for if answering the research question will not add to the literature, then the study is not worth funding. The reviewers must be convinced that the project is vital for the advancement of their disciplinary goals. Thus proposal writing, while objective, balanced, and realistic, is also a political endeavor. Ideally, the qualitative proposal should, to use Glaser's (1978) term, 'grab' everyone's attention. It must intrigue even those reviewers who are from another discipline, who have little knowledge of the area, and who are not familiar with the disciplinary focus, assumptions, and theoretical needs that this proposal will address.

The topic must make a significant contribution to discipline topic and practice. Contrary to Glaser's (1978, 1992) recommendations, excellent researchers should explore the literature broadly at the planning stage, for in order to be funded, the proposal must be logically, accurately,

and wisely argued. The literature review should address the *need* to answer the question. To do that, the literature review must be complete and comprehensive, it must be a theoretical/conceptual analysis, and it must place the present study in the theoretical context of the literature.

In light of this, affecting the *rigor* of the proposed research, the literature review must be comprehensive, addressing all major relevant studies. The applicant must have synthesized the material so that it is a 'good read'. Some applicants submit tables listing all relevant studies, and this is a useful method to inform the committee that you have done your homework, are familiar with the literature, and confident in your claims. The analysis of the literature should include analysis of the relevant concepts and theories, and an excellent critical analysis of these concepts and theories may be publishable, making a contribution in its own right.

A conceptual framework, dictating which variables will be examined or even coded, is usually not used in qualitative inquiry as it violates principles of analytic induction, hence threatening validity (Huberman and Miles, 1994). In addition, it is important that if philosophical underpinnings are used, they must be made explicit. The researcher often has a philosophical agenda, such as using a feminist perspective or critical theory, and, if used, this must be explained. Often these perspectives have been integrated into the methods, such as critical ethnography (Reason, 1994) or feminist grounded theory (Wuest and Merritt-Gray, 2001), but this is not always the case.

Finally, the excellent literature review 'funnels' the reader from the general to the specific, so that by the time the review committee reaches the questions or problem statement, they have been sold on the idea itself. This does not mean that the qualitative researcher selectively ignores information that does not help build the case; rather, such information is countered in the argument. The argument then ends with a convincingly significant and clearly stated problem statement or question.

The *feasibility* of the problem or question is evaluated by considering if the proposal is doable. Is it an appropriate scope? Projects that are designed too broadly will take too long to achieve any degree of depth and to saturate data, and will become unmanageable; projects that are defined by a question that is too narrow will not answer the question adequately. The evaluation of feasibility of a question is tricky, but one that must be addressed by the investigator.

Occasionally, qualitative research is contentious because it threatens to undermine the status quo. Someone's research career may have been built on the very concepts that the qualitative applicant is proposing to reopen; the applicant must be able to produce adequate evidence that the presently used conceptualization is suspect, possibly flawed, and worthy of reexamination, even though it has been defined consistently in a certain way. Committees generally have mechanisms for members who would be in conflict with such an application to withdraw from the discussion of the proposals. Yet it is these proposals (and subsequent publications) that instigate corrections and paradigm shifts, and may prove to be a risk well worth taking for the committee. One such example is the work by Hupcey (1998) reconceptualizing social support, criticizing the looseness of the way the concept was used in research. She noted that researchers did not attend to the direction of the support, the timing or pacing of the reciprocal relationship, negative or positive support, or to whom the reciprocity was targeted, arguing that present measures of quality and satisfaction of social support were inadequate.

Infrequently, a 'black hole' proposal will be presented to the committee. In health care, for instance, we have many phenomena for which we have no language and little knowledge, yet exploration of these topics is important for understanding our practice. Often these areas have been unexplored because of the emotional cost to the investigator, and it is easier for the caregiver not to know. For instance: How do patients maintain control during states of agony? How do surgeons learn to cut through skin? How do we control or block the effects of the excruciating pain of a patient, or control the contagion of suffering? Investigation must start somewhere. In these cases, the committee must consciously support the *investigator* and the *idea*, rather than the mechanics of the research design, and the applicant should have provided the committee with enough information to support the proposal confidently knowing that the investigator is skilled enough to achieve the proposed goals.

ISSUES OF RIGOR Rigor refers to the adequacy and appropriateness of the method and solidity of the research design to address the questions proposed. *Rigor* is evaluated according to how well the proposal meets methodological standards for qualitative inquiry. Does the proposal describe how the interviews and observations will be conducted? What other data will be sought for the analysis? One of the problems in reviewing the proposal is the researcher's uncertainty about the course of the inquiry. Is the researcher aware of unanticipated findings and open, responsive, and flexible to possibly incorporating unexpected

findings into the design? Will the design permit comparisons? Longitudinal exploration of phenomena? And so forth?

Issues of *rigor* include how data will be coded and analyzed, congruent with the method proposed. If computer software is used, is the investigator skilled in its use, and aware of its limitations? Does the investigator have plans for the verification of data? How will the emerging categories and themes be evaluated for saturation? What level of explanation/abstraction will be sought? How will concepts be developed and theory constructed?

FEASIBILITY *Feasibility* refers to the ability of the researcher to conduct the research, the resources available and requested, and evidence of access to the setting and participants, including ethical concerns for protecting the rights of human subjects. In other words, feasibility refers to the probability that the project can and will be completed as described.

The scope of inquiry should be considered in light of the design, again to assess *feasibility*. Any proposed components of multi-method or mixed design to obtain different perspectives of the phenomenon, the level of abstraction or theory sought, and the skill and abilities of the investigator, should also be evaluated, asking if the project seems practical and possible.

If qualitative inquiry is to be good, it is expensive. Collecting interview data, transcribing it, and analyzing the text is slow and time-consuming. Investigators may use 'rules of thumb' when estimating their budget. For instance, basic transcription usually takes four times as long as the recording (or eight times as long for transcript preparation for conversation analysis), and these calculations should be presented in the budget.

The quandary of 'how many subjects?' and 'how much data?' can only be approximated at the proposal stage, but realistically, for purposes of determining the budget, needs to be estimated. Qualitative researchers calculate the proposed sample size by evaluating the scope of the project and the expected variation in data, the duration of data collection (one-time versus longitudinal design), the number of participants needed in other studies to reach saturation, plus including a contingency allowance for lost interviews due to equipment failure or poor participants and to allow expansion into unanticipated areas of interest.

Feasibility of a project is also evaluated by examining the *time* the principal investigator and research team has allocated to the research project. Is it an adequate timeframe to complete the work? Budget is also examined: if a budget appears excessive and is not well justified, it will be cut back by the committee.

HUMAN SUBJECTS   The final part of the review is to ensure that the rights of human subjects have been protected. This usually ensures that the risks of participating in the research are not greater than everyday life, that participants are informed and consent to participating in the research, and that they have the opportunity to withdraw from the research. University committees, as well as review committees responsible for the site hosting the study, usually provide with the proposal written certification that they have reviewed and approved of the study. Nevertheless, it is the responsibility of the review committee also to review the proposal for ethical concerns. It is these issues, if concerns are raised, that will prevent the study from going ahead and interfere with the *feasibility* of the study.

Qualitative inquiry is usually considered low risk. Investigators must take precautions to protect the identity of participants, or if identities are revealed (as in video research), ensure that the participants are aware and have provided additional consent for the tapes to be shown publicly. While anonymity may be respected, confidentiality is not. Committees, as well as researchers, must be aware that qualitative traditions of publishing quotations in the text of manuscripts violates promises of confidentiality (Corbin and Morse, 2003). If the committee desires that the design be modified to protect human subjects, depending on the nature and extent of the changes, this may interfere with *rigor*.

OTHER   Every funding agency has its own quirks and unique requirements, and the onus is on the investigator to ensure that these are met. For instance, applications to the American National Institutes of Health will be asked to report on the expected gender ratio in the sample, to ensure that women are not excluded. They also insist that the investigator report on the minority composition of the proposed sample, to ensure that minorities will be included. Applicants are also required to explain if children will be included, and, if not, to justify their exclusion. Many funding agencies require a plan for dissemination of findings, and will even provide funding for the principal investigator to attend conferences to present the findings, and perhaps funds for publication.

Scoring, approving, and ranking proposals

Once the proposal has been presented to the committee, questions answered, and concerns discussed by the committee, the proposal is scored. All members vote, and the mean score determines the ranking of the proposal among all the proposals reviewed by that group, and whether or not it is approved for funding.

BEGINNING YOUR PROJECT

The approval and funding of the project means that an investigator may actually commence the project! After the long delays, and waiting through the period of uncertainty during evaluation, starting may come as a shock, now you actually have to work on the project. Start-up is often slow – assembling, hiring, and training the research team and 'getting in' to the research setting often takes much longer than the principal investigator has anticipated, so that many research projects are delayed, even before they really get going.

Recognizing the uncertainty in funding qualitative inquiry

I began this chapter by outlining the difficulties for the funding agencies in funding research that was not contractual – which had an uncertain course and poorly defined outcome. While all research is, to some extent, a process of discovery, this is maximized with qualitative inquiry. One way to prevent unpleasant surprises at the final report stage is for the agency to request annual reports, and for the investigator to contact the agency if major decisions are made that substantially alter the course of the project.

Sometimes qualitative researchers report that they were originally asking the wrong research question, and during inquiry must rethink and rephrase the original question. Although such information makes the funding agency uneasy, it is essential for the validity of the final study. For instance, Norris (1991), while exploring the experience of mothers consenting to their adolescent daughter having an abortion, came to realize in the course of the study that the abortion itself was a part of the larger process of protecting their daughters from pregnancy. To delineate the emerging analysis with the single event of 'consenting for the abortion' would have truncated the results and made the findings less rich and less significant. Thus, committees must recognize that occasionally the expected outcomes from a funded study may not be exactly what they get. The onus is on the investigator to communicate frequently with the research staff at the agency, and to keep them informed with regular progress reports.[3]

CONCLUSIONS

Preparing a qualitative proposal requires extensive planning and consideration of alternatives, decisions that may or may not be carried through, flexibility, versatility, and patience. Proposals – by definition a technical document – must also be written at a level such that someone unfamiliar with qualitative inquiry can understand the rationale for the decisions and consider the work to be 'good science'. The applicant must also entice the funding agency into recognizing the significance of inquiry into the topic and the possible importance of possible results, yet also the importance of flexibility of the inquiry. This appears a difficult task, but is one that is not impossible. Excellent qualitative inquiry begins with a solid proposal.

NOTES

1 Two published examples are Tripp-Reimer (1986) and Morse (1996), and a recent special issue of *Qualitative Health Research*, 13(6). It is appropriate to request a copy of a proposal from a funded investigator, or to request a copy of a funded proposal from the granting agency.
2 For instance, some review criteria are based on the Cochrane criteria (Sackett, 1993). According to the Cochrane criteria, qualitative research is the weakest design, ranking it at Level 5, with 'opinion'.
3 While external funding may inherently influence findings, it is important that the agency be acknowledged in all presentations and communications, as well as to the participants (Cheek, 2000).

REFERENCES

Agar, M.H. (1996) *The Professional Stranger.* San Diego: Academic Press.
Cheek, J. (2000) 'An untold story? Doing funded qualitative research', in N.K. Denzin and Y.S. Lincoln (eds), *Handbook of Qualitative Research* (2nd ed.). Thousand Oaks, CA: Sage, pp. 401–20.
Corbin, J. and Morse, J.M. (2003) 'The unstructured interactive interview: issues of reciprocity and risks', *Qualitative Inquiry*, 9(3): 335–54.

Denzin, N.K. and Lincoln, Y.S. (1994) *Handbook of Qualitative Research.* Thousand Oaks, CA: Sage.
Glaser, B.G. (1978) *Theoretical Sensitivity.* Mill Valley, CA: Sociology Press.
Glaser, B.G. (1992) *Basics of Grounded Theory Analysis.* Mill Valley, CA: Sociology Press.
Huberman, A.M. and Miles, M.B. (1994) 'Data management and analysis methods', in N.K. Denzin and Y.S. Lincoln (eds), *Handbook of Qualitative Research.* Thousand Oaks, CA: Sage, pp. 428–44.
Hupcey, J. (1998) 'Clarifying the social support theory-research linkage', *Journal of Advanced Nursing*, 27: 1231–41.
Morse, J.M. (1992) 'Comfort: the refocusing of nursing care', *Clinical Nursing Research*, 1: 91–113.
Morse, J.M. (1994) 'Designing qualitative research', in Y. Lincoln and N. Denzin (eds), *Handbook of Qualitative Inquiry.* Menlo Park, CA: Sage, pp. 220–35.
Morse, J.M. (1996) 'The qualitative proposal', in J.M. Morse and P.A. Field, *Nursing Research: The Application of Qualitative Approaches.* Cheltenham: Stanley Thornes, pp. 160–96.
Morse, J.M. and Bottorff, J.L. (1990) 'The use of ethology in clinical nursing research', *Advances in Nursing Science*, 12(3): 53–64.
Morse, J.M. and Richards, L. (2002) *Readme First for a Users Guide to Qualitative Analysis.* Thousand Oaks, CA, Sage.
Norris, J. (1991) 'Mothers' involvement with their adolescent daughters' abortions', in J.M. Morse and J.L. Johnson (eds), *The Illness Experience: Dimensions of Suffering.* Newbury Park, CA: Sage, pp. 210–36.
Reason, P. (1994) 'Three approaches to participative inquiry', in Y. Lincoln and N. Denzin (eds), *Handbook of Qualitative Inquiry.* Menlo Park, CA: Sage, pp. 324–39.
Sackett, D.L. (1993) 'Rules of evidence and clinical recommendation', *Canadian Journal of Cardiology*, 9(6): 487–9.
Spradley, J.P. (1979) *The Ethnographic Interview.* New York: Holt, Rinehart & Winston.
Spradley, J.P. (1980) *Participant Observation.* New York: Wiley.
Strauss, A.L. (1987) *Qualitative Analysis for Social Scientists.* New York: Cambridge University Press.
Tripp-Reimer, T. (1986) 'The Heritage Health Project: a research proposal submitted to the Division of Nursing', *Western Journal of Nursing Research*, 8: 207–28.
Van Manen, M. (1997) *Researching the Lived Experience.* London, Ontario: Althouse.
Wuest, J. and Merritt-Gray, M. (2001) 'Feminist grounded theory revisited: practical issues and new understandings', in R.S. Schreiber and P.N. Stern (eds), *Using Grounded Theory in Nursing.* New York: Springer, pp. 159–76.

32

Qualitative market research

Gill Ereaut

Qualitative researchers of all kinds may sometimes carry out work for commercial or fee-paying organizations. However, this chapter describes the form of commercial research known as *qualitative market research*, a thriving arm of the market research industry; this constitutes a highly adapted species of qualitative method. It concerns the practice of professional research specialists who, having no academic affiliation, make their living carrying out qualitative research projects directly for businesses and other commissioning organizations, including those in the public sector. The presence of this chapter alongside so many others concerned with academic or social research might create a degree of puzzlement or even unease. The commercial and academic research worlds have, on the face of it, little to offer each other; they are perhaps fundamentally divided by their objectives, methods, standards and politics. Acknowledging this context, I aim in this chapter to do a number of things:

- to give a more complete picture of qualitative market research than I believe has been generally available outside the industry, highlighting important differences in philosophy and practice between Europe and the US;
- to offer a framework for making sense of key differences between qualitative practice in market research and in academia;[1] and
- to suggest that, despite their different aims and traditions, greater mutual understanding and exchange of knowledge between commercial and non-commercial qualitative research communities might be of benefit to both.

Many readers will know very little of qualitative market research and for them this chapter will serve to introduce the field. Others, though, may have already formed a view about it. They have heard that qualitative market researchers work on relatively small projects and to very tight time-scales, that they must always serve the needs of their clients, and that they are notoriously fond of, even reliant on, one method – the 'focus group'. It is possible to dismiss market research because clearly it does not – cannot – conform to accepted standards for academic qualitative research, in so far as such consensus exists. I do not intend to offer a defence of commercial practice in these terms, but to describe and explain it so it may be understood on its own terms.

Garfinkel and Bittner's work on clinical records offers a useful parallel (Garfinkel, 1967).[2] They set out to explore why psychiatric clinical records, such as those accessed for research purposes by social researchers, are often so frustratingly inadequate for these purposes. Their conclusion is that the records are not 'bad', but in fact reflect the social, organizational and contractual processes and priorities of the clinic. In effect, they have to fulfil quite different objectives to those of the social researchers trying to use them, and make good sense in this context. In the same way, I imagine the practices of commercial qualitative research could look limited or perplexing from the outside (and, as in any field, there is always room for improvement), but they work well and make perfect sense to participants. Like the record-keeping procedures studied by Garfinkel and Bittner, qualitative market research practices are not random, nor a product of the ignorance or perversity of those involved, but are specifically adapted to the social, organizational and contractual processes and priorities of that business. In this sense, I shall present qualitative market research not as an odd or underdeveloped variety of qualitative practice, but as a uniquely adapted species. It is one evolved under and adapted to particular conditions, and has developed for several decades in isolation from what an academic audience might regard as 'qualitative research'.

THE ACADEMIC–COMMERCIAL DIVIDE: A VIEW FROM THE BRIDGE

I write this chapter from a somewhat liminal position between commercial and academic research communities. I joined the market research industry after graduating in psychology in London in 1980; there was a huge boom in qualitative market research within the UK during the late 1970s and 1980s and the sector has enjoyed growth and increasing status since this time.[3] After employment in a number of agencies, I set up what became a thriving qualitative research consultancy. Following seventeen years in practice, however, I returned to academia and took an MA in sociology, again in London; here I discovered the wealth of substantive and methodological writing about qualitative research in the social sciences. Typical among commercial researchers, I was quite unfamiliar with this academic qualitative literature and with the growth in qualitative research in academia. At the same time, I realized that my teachers – among them eminent qualitative methodologists – and my fellow students knew next to nothing about 'my' version of qualitative practice. I was surprised by this gap; here were two hard-working, thoughtful qualitative research communities, often grappling with similar problems, but apparently occupying parallel universes and showing little awareness or understanding of each other.[4]

Why should this have been the case? Catterall (2001) traces the history of today's qualitative market research practice and its relationship to academia. In the US in the early decades of the twentieth century, as qualitative market research was developing, there was indeed a 'productive interchange of ideas between the academic and commercial research worlds', involving respected academics such as Paul Lazarsfeld and Burleigh Gardner (Catterall, 2001: 36). Catterall suggests that commercial practice may also have been connected to academia in France and Italy; at least it remains overtly linked to theory and philosophy (2001: 204). However, this was and is not the situation in Britain. Here, from the early days of qualitative market research, she notes that practitioners 'could not call upon local academic support for their emerging work. Ignored by academia, [they] were left to their own devices and to develop their work subjected only to an internal market research industry critique' (2001: 47).

So, certainly in the UK, academic and commercial research communities have developed qualitative methods in parallel, against the dominance of quantitative methods. During this time, academics have had little cause to look closely at commercial practice; similarly, it has not been professionally necessary for commercial researchers to know anything of academic qualitative research. Academics from marketing and consumer research disciplines do sometimes examine qualitative market research practice (e.g. Colwell, 1990; Gabriel, 1990; Catterall, 2001), but such attention seems relatively rare – and is even rarer outside these disciplines. It is also true, though, that academics have not easily been able to examine commercial qualitative research, especially European practice, because until recently it has been the subject of a very sparse literature. Commercial confidentiality constrains the publication of substantive findings, while formal development and publication of methodological theory has not been professionally required of commercial researchers. There is now interest on both sides in ending the academic/commercial estrangement and changes are occurring, at least in the UK, that might facilitate this. As a commercial research community, we have begun the task of systematically exploring and codifying our own practice, in the process making it available to those outside the business. From my own conviction that there would be benefit in making current practice explicit came a Sage series (Ereaut et al., 2002); before this there were limited textual resources for practitioners themselves and very little access for academics to details of everyday commercial practice.[5] There is also now more interest within the business in engaging with academic methodological thinking.

A DESCRIPTION OF PRACTICE

This section gives a brief description of common practice, concentrating on qualitative market research in the UK.[6] It begins, though, by highlighting some important differences between broadly European and US traditions.

International contexts

Commercial qualitative research differs markedly in key respects between Europe and the US. There have long been two distinctly different styles or traditions of practice, reflecting quite different epistemological assumptions and quite different uses of the group interview format (Cooper, 1989; Goodyear, 1998; Imms and Ereaut, 2002). Both European and US traditions have tended to favour interview- and group-based methods, but there the similarity ends. Both styles do exist on both sides of the Atlantic, and some in the industry argue that the difference between them is diminishing, but the legacy of each remains. Practice in other parts of the world tends towards one or other of these styles, depending on the relative influence of European or US client organizations as they extend across global economies (Cooper and Patterson, 1995; McDonald and King, 1996). There is evidence that in some areas researchers are fluent in both these styles and apply them as appropriate to the nationality of a client (Goodyear, 1998). There are certain immediately visible differences in research conventions; for example, a US 'focus group' will comprise between ten and twelve respondents, while in the European tradition this is considered far too many to be productive and, in the UK, the conventional maximum for a 'group discussion' is seven or eight. More fundamentally, there are clear differences in what is treated as valid data and in the role ascribed to the researcher.

In the US style of qualitative market research, the greatest value tends to be placed on what is actually said by respondents. Alongside this, group process or interaction effects are regarded as contamination and will thus be minimized by moderation practices and/or be ignored in analysis. Often in the US the researcher's role is primarily one of group moderator – asking, in a skilled and professional manner, the list of questions that has been supplied by or agreed with the client, probing and clarifying where necessary but with limited deviation from this agreed scheme. Use is often made of flipcharts or similar to summarize what has been said. Regularly, all of the groups will be viewed as they happen by representatives of the client organization. This viewing experience, and the discussion between the client team and the moderator immediately after it, is seen as the core of the research. The groups are seen to have revealed 'authentic' responses and these are taken and used as they stand. There might be little in the way of formal analysis before clients take action based on what they have seen and heard, though a later report may explore issues in more depth (Langer, 2001).

The European tradition, in contrast, gives the researcher a wide-ranging role as qualitative investigator, with considerable freedom to explore the client's issue or problem as she or he sees fit within the general parameters of the project, and to amend the research approach throughout the group or the project. Groups are not run to a formula. The group is treated as a flexible frame or vehicle producing rich, complex data and within which many research approaches may be taken, both between and within projects. Most importantly, especially in the UK and France, highly interpretative approaches are taken that 'read around' what is said by individuals and in which other forms of data such as the non-verbal and the interactive are actively sought. In this model, too, the researcher has a key interpretative role and client decisions are usually deferred until the researcher has analysed, interpreted and reported fully on the project. Certain social psychological concepts are deeply engrained in ideas of good practice in handling interviewing and group dynamics (Chrzanowska, 2002), though in other respects practice long ago moved beyond reliance on psychological concepts such as 'attitudes' and 'motivations' (Chandler and Owen, 1989; Ereaut, 2002). Aspects of group process and the interactive nature of the event are an essential part of what is analysed. It is absolutely not the case, as stated by Myers (1998), that these are ignored (see Catterall and Maclaran, 1997; Ereaut, 2002).

Interviewing remains the dominant field method within qualitative market research, but there is now significant use of observational and ethnographic approaches. Interestingly, there is again variation between the US and, for example, the UK (Catterall, 2001). In the US, where 'focus group research' is quite programmatic, this has strengthened the development of ethnography as a distinct alternative, to be conducted within specialist ethnography agencies (Denny, 1995; Mariampolski, 1999). In the UK, where qualitative market research thinking is already more flexible and fluid, field methods such as ethnography are more likely to be integrated into the repertoires of existing qualitative suppliers (Desai, 2002).

The confusion of US and European styles among clients and in the wider world has been actively resisted, not least through many British practitioners' attempts (ultimately, it seems, unsuccessful) to retain their usual term 'group discussion' in the face of widespread adoption of the US-originated term 'focus group'

(Imms, 1999). The potential for conflation remains, however, and this is a point I wish to emphasize. Much of the published work referring to or drawing on market research methods with which academics are likely to be familiar emanates from the US (e.g. Fern, 1983; Morgan, 1997; Morgan and Krueger, 1997) and may not reflect this difference of practice, or accurately represent the interpretative European tradition. The remainder of this section describes key aspects of practice in the UK.

The functions of qualitative market research

The applications of qualitative market research have expanded rapidly over the past few decades and clients now include not just commercial businesses (manufacturers, retailers, advertising agencies, marketing agencies) but not-for-profit organizations (including charities, educational institutions, political parties) and public-sector bodies (Marks, 2000).

Although preliminary qualitative work sometimes informs later quantitative investigation, qualitative market research is by no means limited to this role (cf. Gofton, 1998). The integration of qualitatively and quantitatively derived knowledge is an important task for organizations (Smith and Fletcher, 2001), and qualitative/quantitative hybrid projects are common, but qualitative market research has long enjoyed a quite independent role and status. In practice, it directly influences organizational decision-making, as 'a form of informational flow from the market that is complementary [to quantified research] yet unique, irreplaceable and standing on its own' (Vineall, quoted in McDonald and King, 1996: 167).

The kinds of problem addressed and the kinds of knowledge provided by qualitative market research are probably more varied and more complex than is generally recognized. Very few projects in my experience amount to the simple collection of attitudes, opinions, or even 'group reactions to stimuli' (Bloor et al., 2001: 17). Today's clients demand and get far more than this. Qualitative market research is a form of specialized knowledge production, tackling increasingly challenging client demands for diagnosis (how things are and why they might be this way), prognosis (how things could be different and what might bring this about) and creativity (generating creative problem solutions or innovative thinking) (Imms and Ereaut, 2002). Fulfilling these demands often means using expressed attitudes and responses to stimuli as important sources of qualitative data, but many other forms

of data are also generated and used (see, e.g., Gordon, 1999; Chandler and Owen, 2002; Chrzanowska, 2002). Importantly, too, useful knowledge for clients is rarely provided by relaying simple research findings, but relies on complex activities of analysis, interpretation and professional judgement on the part of the researcher (Ereaut, 2002; Lillis, 2002).

A typical project

A 'typical' project is hard to define; projects vary greatly in their scope and objectives. They may be highly strategic (in what general areas should this food manufacturer be investing and innovating?) or firmly tactical (which of these yoghurt pack designs best meets its design and marketing objectives?). They may be wide in scope, covering many countries and/or many discrete groups of people, or rather narrow. They might begin from a position of little prior knowledge of a field or activity, or (more usually) they are designed to develop, refine or challenge the client's existing knowledge in a field. Many projects are highly focused on a specific aspect of a consumer product – my own experience includes looking in microscopic detail at diverse everyday objects such as pasta sauces, antihistamines, mobile phones and teabags. But other projects are broader and more exploratory; I have for example explored the nature of the fear of flying for a major airline and also looked very generally for a credit card company at young women's relationships with credit and finance. Another project for a food manufacturer examined popular images, meanings and constructions of 'the family', and yet another for the same client compared the use, meaning and role within food culture of microwave ovens in the UK and the US.

Larger organizations generally have specialist research buyers acting as brokers between suppliers and internal users of market research. Most often, then, the client organization itself identifies a specific need for qualitative research and approaches specialist qualitative researchers or agencies. Projects may be put to formal tender, especially in public-sector work, but often they are not. After a briefing meeting, the researcher(s) may write a proposal outlining a suggested approach, particularly for larger projects and/or those in the public sector. However, it is often the case that there is a high level of mutual knowledge and trust between clients and researchers who work together often, and a project will simply proceed with minimal documentation, perhaps just a confirmatory e-mail. Most research designs are interview-based and involve group discussions (these are now widely known as 'focus groups', though British researchers generally prefer the former term) and/or individual or 'depth' interviews.

The research sample agreed between client and researcher is usually recruited through a specialist qualitative recruitment agency employing freelance recruiters who identify and gather eligible respondents. In the UK, many interviews and group discussions are conducted in the recruiter's home and are routinely audio tape-recorded; however, use of specialized viewing facilities, with one-way mirrors and audio/video recording equipment, is becoming common. In the US, and in much of continental Europe, qualitative market research is almost always conducted in such facilities. The existence of a developed and efficient support infrastructure is an important feature of commercial practice and allows the business to operate with high volumes and fast turnaround times. Apart from making use of specialist recruiters and viewing facilities, researchers have access if they wish to fast high-quality transcription services and will often enjoy ample administrative support. This leaves them to concentrate on the key tasks of problem analysis, fieldwork, data analysis and interpretation, and applying the research to the client's issues.

Many UK domestic (i.e., single-country) projects comprise between four and ten group discussions, each of one and a half to two hours' duration and each involving six to eight respondents (though group duration and number of participants might vary for specific purposes and individual interviews might form part or all of the sample: see Chrzanowska, 2002; Imms and Ereaut, 2002). The face-to-face fieldwork is carried out and analysed by the researchers who were briefed directly by the client, sometimes with two or more researchers working as a team. A period of formal analysis precedes the 'debrief', a meeting at which the researchers present and discuss with the client their findings, interpretations, conclusions and recommendations for action. This debrief typically takes place within two weeks of the end of fieldwork and a project of average size will thus last around four to six weeks, although this might vary from less than a week to several months. The debrief is often followed by the preparation of a full written report, but this can be replaced by a summary document, perhaps when relevant client action is to be taken immediately and a full report will be superfluous and wasteful. This decision depends on the nature of the project and the client's preferences (Lillis, 2002). Data analysis in commercial research is often carried

out within short time periods and, unlike in academia, is not generally open to critical scrutiny by those outside the project. However, in my experience (and certainly in accepted best practice) analysis is treated as a serious matter. It is certainly not normally limited to the use of researchers' scribbled notes, nor done by a 'report writer' collecting information from a number of group facilitators, as suggested by Bloor et al. (2001: 4). Rather, it is ordinarily regarded as a crucial and intensive activity that must be carried out by researchers themselves, usually working from tapes and/or transcripts (Ereaut, 2002).

The 'group' in market research: multiple forms, multiple functions

The prevalence of groups in commercial research (whether they are termed 'group discussions' or 'focus groups') is quite well known, but the real nature and variability of these groups is not recognized outside the industry. The market research group is far from being a consistent or standard entity.

First, as stated earlier, the UK 'group discussion' and the US 'focus group' in their typical forms are not at all the same thing. The differences in philosophy and in practice between these two approaches have already been discussed; those looking at the ways in which the group interview is or can be used more widely in other forms of qualitative research can now, I hope, consider both models.

Second, it is not the case that because the basic group format is standard, the use made of it, or its content, is also standard. Barbour and Kitzinger imply that market research groups are predominantly 'formulaic' (1999: 1), but this may reflect only the US model, or partial knowledge of the business. In my experience, market research practitioners in the UK make highly flexible use of groups and have constantly evolved fresh approaches within this form over the past decades. This perception is supported by the empirical work of Catterall, who comments (using the term 'focus group' but referring primarily to UK practice) that 'market research focus groups are simultaneously concrete and ambiguous. The focus group is sufficiently concrete to be easily communicable to clients and also sufficiently ambiguous to absorb much of the diversity in commercial research practice at any one time as well as changes over time' (2001: 164).

Groups are routinely used for very diverse purposes and are carefully designed to give access to quite different things, depending on the client's objectives. So they might well be used for collecting 'attitudes', 'opinions' or 'responses to stimuli', but their use is by no means limited to this (cf. Bloor et al., 2001). They are also widely used to uncover group norms, shared cultural meanings and definitions; to explore complex and emotional issues or decisions; to enable collaborative exploration of a problem or field between clients and respondents; to facilitate creative idea generation, and so on. Although conscious awareness of epistemological models is not high among practitioners, in practice the group discussion has been made to absorb a number of such frameworks (Chandler and Owen, 1989; Ereaut, 2002).

Because qualitative market researchers have traditionally addressed very varied research questions through a single data-collection method, they have devised or adapted many techniques to make the most of this method. So straightforward questioning forms only a part of the moderator's investigative repertoire. Verbal and non-verbal tasks and activities – all of which are fed back into and become an integral part of the discussion itself – are also primary tools (see Gordon and Langmaid, 1988; Chandler and Owen, 2002; Chrzanowska, 2002; Wardle, 2002). In this way, the group format has been made into a powerful and flexible research approach, applicable to a wide range of research problems.

Apart from being variable in content, market research groups in the UK are also set up and managed in diverse and purposeful ways. Options include varying the number of respondents or duration of groups, designing recruitment to set up homogeneity or conflict within groups, using different locations, reconvening, or setting tasks. Often what is wanted is unprompted discussion, but in other cases respondents are given focusing or even 'disruptive' tasks to perform for a few days before coming to the group. They might be asked to keep a diary of a relevant activity, to refrain from an everyday activity such as cleaning the lavatory or watching TV, or to avoid their regular brand of some product. This gives participants a perspective on the meaning to themselves of that issue, activity or brand which can then be explored in the group, greatly enhancing the researcher's understanding. Similarly, groups may be conducted in relevant locations (say in a retail store or public house, or on board an aircraft mid-flight) so that the environment itself is part of the discussion. There have been other kinds of experimentation, such as conducting simultaneous groups. Here, for example, one group discussion is conducted with children and another simultaneously with their mothers as they observe this first group through a one-way mirror (or older people might watch and discuss a group of younger people talking about ageing). More radically, researchers have experimented with 'unmoderated' groups (Yelland and Varty, 1997). Market researchers acknowledge that the research group is not a naturally occurring social environment, and on the whole do not treat it as such or try to make it seem so. Rather, they actively exploit the strengths and opportunities offered by group working to obtain depth of understanding of an issue or field, from a range of individuals, in a cost- and time-efficient way.

Finally, although groups and interviews remain central to the qualitative market research repertoire, the situation is changing. The methodological orthodoxy was shaken up somewhat by the entry of semiotic and cultural analysis into the British and French markets in the 1980s. The acceptance of such overtly 'theoretical' and non-interviewing methods was initially held back in the UK by naturalized assumptions within the industry about what constituted 'qualitative market research', but they are now well established. A second wave is evident in the growing adoption into commercial research of ethnographic and observational approaches (Desai, 2002). These changes will potentially shift the emphasis regarding what is being bought and sold in qualitative market research, away from 'groups and depths' and towards problem-solving and analytic skill (Ereaut and Imms, 2002).

The nature of the industry

Qualitative market researchers themselves are typically graduates; there was at one time a bias towards psychologists but this no longer applies. Formal qualitative research qualification or previous research experience is not necessary, since qualitative market research is treated as a craft skill needing apprenticeship and on-the-job training. Although some short training courses are available, there is no definitive education programme. As already noted, there is also no accepted canon; little of the knowledge residing within the industry has, until recently, been formalized and made explicit.

There are generally long-term relationships between clients and suppliers and an established researcher's previous experience is highly valued. Despite the existence of a few large agency suppliers, qualitative market research remains a field in which individual researchers are valued for their skill and experience and there are very many small agencies and freelance research consultants. Clients are very particular about *who* carries out their qualitative work, recognizing in practice the intertwining of research and researcher characteristic of all qualitative inquiry. This means that personal reputations matter more than company size and that even individual freelancers routinely conduct important projects for large client organizations.

In today's market, qualitative market researchers have to deliver high-quality thinking that is not only insightful, sensitive and creative interpretation of what emerged from the field, but which is also sharply applied to the client's problem, clearly communicated, on time, and to budget. This offers a series of practical, professional and intellectual challenges that many relish. Commercial researchers usually work on several projects at once and will conduct and analyse on average two or three group discussions or their equivalent per week, often in the evenings (though a full office-hours working day is also expected by clients and employers). There is also much travelling to do, often to distinctly unglamorous places. One must live a chameleon-like existence, performing the 'face work' required, say, to interview groups of young down-market beer drinkers one week, but also to present conclusions authoritatively to the board of directors at the brewery the next. With increasing use of research facilities (with one-way mirrors that allow groups to be viewed by several observers), researchers must regularly manage a roomful of clients, and the 'performance' aspect of the event, as well as concentrate on the respondents and the research itself.

Qualitative market research is a service industry so the client's needs must be met and there are always pressures, especially on time; but it is also engaging, challenging and often fun. It involves long hours and very hard work, but is, by most standards, well paid. It also allows those who have established a professional reputation to work independently and flexibly if they wish; it is no coincidence that this is a largely female industry where career breaks and part-time or flexible working, even at the most senior levels, are common.

MAKING SENSE OF QUALITATIVE MARKET RESEARCH PRACTICE

The conditions and professional norms within which qualitative market research operates contribute to its distinctive nature. Here I examine a number of such features that may help make sense of its working practices, especially to those more familiar with other forms of qualitative research.

The dual role of the qualitative market researcher

The fact that commercial researchers work to someone else's objectives, for a fee, is an obvious but fundamental condition of commercial qualitative practice and has important implications. It is not that qualitative market researchers attempt to do the same kind of work as academic or social researchers, simply being funded to do so by different kinds of agencies. Rather, the positioning of qualitative market research as a paid-for ad hoc business *service* entails particular responsibilities, requires distinct skills, and brings into play certain kinds of evaluative standards. In effect, the commercial researcher must do very specific things in order to be a good researcher in this context and he or she must always perform a 'dual role' (Imms and Ereaut, 2002).

First, market researchers have a professional commitment to research as an investigative activity, within which the researcher strives to remain neutral.[7] Commercial practitioners seek to be at all times independent of their clients, embracing ideas of rigorous independent research and ethical practice. Research that is by these standards bad research – that which simply tells clients what they want to hear, which only perpetuates the researcher's pet theories, which is dishonest, or which allows any other kind of serious bias – cannot be good commercial research, not least because it is actually of no use to clients. But market researchers have another equally demanding obligation – they have a professional role as providers of business advice to their clients. This means they must not only conduct impartial research, but they must *also* be 'on the client's side' and ultimately translate this research for the benefit of the client. In practice, this means they must extract *useful and relevant* knowledge from every research project, knowledge that provides maximum benefit and value for money to a commissioning organization. A piece of research that does not address the client's issues and deliver relevant knowledge, no matter how good on other measures, is also not good commercial research (Lillis, 2002).

This puts market researchers in a position of tension; they must always balance the demands of doing impartial and careful research with the equal demands of delivering relevance to the client – and deal with any conflicts that arise. On the subject of project design, for example, this often means making radical compromises against an 'ideal' design to allow for timing or cost imperatives, because meeting these imperatives is part of making the research relevant to the client. It is the researcher's professional duty and skill to understand the nature of the compromises being made, to alert the client to their possible implications, and to make allowance for them as far as possible in delivering conclusions and recommendations based on the research.

The requirement to deliver findings (to funding bodies and others) in a way that can be *used* is, I am told, increasingly relevant to academic researchers, too. But the emphasis is perhaps different: while it is still possible to do good and valuable academic research that is not applied, this is simply not true in commercial research, which only exists in order to be applied. The tension between ensuring the impartiality and rigour of the research and ensuring its relevance to client issues is visible within the structure of the industry itself (Imms and Ereaut, 2002). That is, nearly all commercial qualitative research is carried out by individuals or agencies who are not directly employed by client organizations, but it is carried out in the context of long-term client–researcher relationships. These relationships are rarely formalized but are enacted and reaffirmed with each new project that is commissioned. In this way, researchers preserve their independence, but gain enough understanding of particular client organizations to make sure their research is relevant, and to build collective cumulative knowledge of fields and markets. Clients, in turn, have research suppliers who understand and care about their businesses, but who maintain the distance seen as essential to conducting useful, impartial research.[8]

Qualitative market research as a product within a market

I shall argue here that qualitative market research practice is both constrained *and* liberated by being linked to a market, not to academic standards and requirements, and that this is visible in its practice.

Many things can be regarded as market-imposed constraints within commercial research (though again these are perhaps increasingly familiar to academics). Practitioners do not choose the topics they research, although most will have the opportunity to develop clients in fields they find interesting. There are undoubtedly restrictions on working practices imposed by the commercial environment. Especially,

compressed time-scales within business are a perennial and increasing problem, particularly where time for analysis is concerned (Ereaut, 2002; Lillis, 2002). Methodological norms centre on 'doing groups' and it can be hard to persuade clients to try unfamiliar research approaches. Occasionally there is pressure to standardize methods even further in international cross-cultural research. With the global extension of US marketing culture, too, European researchers are sometimes obliged to adopt an alien (and to their mind limiting) US-style research approach.

The popularity of groups in commercial research certainly reflects their tested value and effectiveness, but their prevalence as a field method may also reflect market conditions. That is, making a service business out of qualitative research means reconciling the open-ended nature of qualitative inquiry with the commercial push towards definable processes, products and systems. Qualitative research in general is characterized by flexibility, open-endedness and sensitivity to context. Deep understanding or 'thick description' (Geertz, 1973) of a social unit, a phenomenon or an activity is a typical objective; ideally as much fieldwork and analysis as necessary will be done, of whatever nature is required, and for as long as it takes, to meet this objective. This ideal will always be constrained by realities such as funding, but real flexibility and long time-scales are undoubtedly more achievable in some forms of academic research than in commercial practice. Client organizations are not only usually working to short time-scales, but both buyers and suppliers have to specify and agree, for management and accounting purposes, exactly what is being bought. This includes agreeing time-scales for delivery and, significantly, an appropriate chargeable unit of service. The apparently concrete, visible and countable unit of the group discussion neatly provides just such a unit, greatly facilitating the commoditization of such a slippery entity as qualitative research. I must stress that this is patently *not* the only reason for the use of the group, which has undoubtedly proved a flexible and fruitful business research tool (Imms and Ereaut, 2002), but it puts an additional real-life context on this methodological decision.

While the market imposes some constraints on commercial researchers, it seems to me that in other respects it also brings certain freedoms. In practical terms, clients expect to pay within a project fee for researchers to use the support infrastructure described earlier, so commercial researchers do not generally suffer the frustrations of inadequate funding for administration and support that increasingly apply within academia. The primacy of market assessment, rather than peer-group assessment, brings other benefits. That is, it is obvious even to anti-qualitative critics that clients would not continue to buy qualitative market research if they did not find it meaningful and useful, but they do, and in increasing numbers. Clients also generally know that they need specifically *qualitative* research before approaching a specialist supplier. So these researchers rarely have to justify their use of qualitative methods to a hostile or uninformed third party, a challenge that it seems their academic counterparts often encounter. There is also less opportunity to become 'lost' or bogged down in a project as sometimes described in academic qualitative research (Marshall, 2000). Operating within a market, working constantly to tight deadlines and on specific problems, engenders a degree of focus and clarity of purpose in research that many enjoy.

Finally, being methodologically accountable to a commercial client and to the standards of the industry, rather than working under the different constraints imposed by academic norms, offers researchers certain intellectual freedoms and opportunities. At least in the UK, commercial researchers have considerable room to invent and experiment. A research proposal is judged primarily on how far it seems likely to tackle the problem creatively, to produce relevant and useful findings, and to give value for money for the client, rather than on any other formal criteria.

Once a project is under way, again there is no one to please or be accountable to methodologically except the client, who by this stage is usually more interested in useful outcomes than the detail of method, and trusts the researcher to be dealing with that. This means one can follow one's instincts as a researcher without fear of censure, for example extending the scope, nature and energy of a discussion by inventing tasks, games or exercises either before the event or on the spot. I have asked participants to draw in colour and abstract form the last headache they had, and asked others to write a mock obituary for a favourite but failing brand. These and many other such tasks (which respondents then discuss in the group) are common approaches in commercial research (Gordon, 1999; Chandler and Owen, 2002; Chrzanowska, 2002; Wardle, 2002). I have spontaneously rearranged chairs mid-group to allow respondents to demonstrate and further explore the frustrations of the aircraft-seating environment they had just been talking about (the territorial 'battle of the elbows' and other indignities). A researcher with

a tough problem to crack might throw away the topic guide mid-group and try a radically different line of inquiry; or indeed (as is routine) adopt research approaches drawn from several different theoretical frameworks within the same project. If new tactics prove useful they can be adopted and developed for this and future projects; if not, they can be dropped. There is rarely need to account for, justify or pre-test any such experimentation. Similarly, in analysis and interpretation there is no paradigmatic restriction – it is quite normal to mix paradigms, using apparently incommensurate models drawn from psychology, anthropology, semiotics, sociology or anywhere else to frame and understand a set of research data (Catterall, 2001; Ereaut, 2002). This theoretical eclecticism is discussed further in a later section.

In looking at the market as an environment for practice, I would however add that in the area of ethics commercial researchers do sometimes act in an apparently uncommercial way. There are agreed professional codes of ethical conduct going beyond statutory protection, covering respondent anonymity, freedom from harm and informed consent.[9] These recognize the need to protect research subjects from abuses of the client's and researcher's power. Ensuring compliance with these codes is the responsibility of the researcher and this can mean denying a potential client organization something it wants and is prepared to pay for. Such requests include, for example, using 'research' activities to build a database of prospective customers; in genuine market research, clients are never allowed access to the names or personal details of respondents. Although there are grey areas within these codes and some problems of enforcement, all researchers occasionally refuse contracts or client requests on ethical grounds (see Imms and Ereaut, 2002).

The importance of experience: expertise through practice

It is hard to overstate the importance attached to practitioner experience by researchers and clients alike. And commercial researchers do have a great deal of practical experience; Gordon and Langmaid estimated that they had between them conducted over 8000 groups (1988: 50), while Judith Wardle calculates that over a period of around twenty years she has had 'qualitative conversations' with approaching 19,000 people (2002: biography). These researchers, while experienced, are not atypical, but I am told that few academic researchers would acquire this level of hands-on practice. Without the obligation to teach students, or to write for an external audience, market researchers' focus is primarily on doing research; even those running agencies remain active researchers or risk losing professional credibility. Practitioners are thus repeatedly exposed to the processes of problem definition, project design, fieldwork, analysis and interpretation and they accumulate a great deal of practical skill and substantive knowledge.

Cumulative experience is important to qualitative market research in a number of ways. First, commercial researchers develop highly refined interviewing and group moderating expertise, skills that it is commonly held can be learned only through practice. The business expects high levels of proficiency, especially in group moderation.[10] It is believed to take at least two years 'live' experience, working at a rate of around two or three groups per week, for a new researcher to be competent in basic research skills. Client-oriented abilities – understanding client needs and objectives, knowing how the research findings might be used, and how to make the best of a less than ideal situation – take longer to acquire and again are achieved largely through supervised practice. The same applies to analysis and interpretation: junior researchers, working alongside more experienced colleagues, witness and gradually absorb the processes through which data are analysed, interpretations made and conclusions drawn. This is a particularly subtle part of the research process and is known to be difficult to train, but simply going through this activity again and again is seen as the best means by which tacit knowledge may be transferred from more experienced to less experienced researchers.

Apart from the acquisition of these craft skills, practitioners in the commercial field must accumulate two other kinds of knowledge through experience. First, they develop a sensitivity to how people typically act and respond in a market research situation, an important benchmark against which they assess the practical validity of specific research findings (Ereaut, 2002). Second, researchers usually develop specialized substantive knowledge of a number of markets, activities or aspects of everyday life. Researchers tend to work regularly for loyal clients, thus accumulating empirically based understanding of particular sub-groups, fields or activities (such as youth culture, or domestic finance, or feeding a family). This, too, is used as a validity check on the conclusions drawn from a particular project. A third benchmark for validity assessment is the prior knowledge residing in the client organization. Even if the research topic is new to the researcher, clients are very rarely starting from scratch in an area. The key role for both researchers and clients of prior knowledge in validating small-scale research, and the way this avoids becoming a self-fulfilling prophesy, is discussed by Smith and Fletcher (2001). Significantly, while each individual piece of research will have its own immediate objectives, only seldom will a single project be expected to provide a definitive and comprehensive picture of a field. More usually its purpose will be to address a specific question in the context of, and to contribute to, the client's ongoing project of knowledge accumulation and use. In this sense, even the smallest-scale commercial research project adds to a cumulative body of knowledge; unlike academic work, however, this knowledge is not publicly available or subject to peer review.

Objectives, outcomes and theory

Creating theory or contributing to a body of scientific knowledge beyond that relevant to the client is not a primary purpose of qualitative market research; again, this is obvious but is worth stating. In practice, producing good research according to the measures of the business itself is of far more importance to researchers and clients than engaging in theoretical debate. Commercial research by definition addresses organizational and not academic objectives and its products are thus measured by how well they meet these objectives. In this context, research that is effective for a client in resolving a problem, answering a puzzle, or helping to guide a decision is good and successful research. (This is not to say that anything goes or that pleasing the client is the only measure of value or quality. It is implicit in the commercial contract between client and researcher that the research conclusions will, as far as possible, accurately and sensitively reflect the group, phenomenon or activity researched; that they will not have allowed avoidable bias or influence; and that they will have taken due account of all available sources to assess the validity of the findings: see Ereaut, 2002, for further discussion of quality in market research.) However, none of this means that qualitative market research is completely atheoretical (Silverman, 1993: 23). It is useful to discuss three forms of theoretical thinking in the context of qualitative market research: methodological theory, theory as an intellectual resource, and 'emergent' theory.

There is now more interest within the industry in understanding the implications of epistemology and methodological theory, but these have not been issues of central concern to practising commercial researchers. Before the creation of our Sage series (Ereaut et al., 2002) only a few practitioners cared to consider such questions (Chandler and Owen, 1989; Valentine and Evans, 1993; Valentine, 1995). Academic qualitative methodology is not highly visible to commercial researchers and is imagined within the industry to be both obscure and irrelevant to commercial practice (Catterall, 2001). I have personally found many texts thought-provoking and potentially relevant (including, for example, Patton, 1990; Mason, 1996; Silverman, 1997; Barbour and Kitzinger, 1999; Seale, 1999; May, 2002), but in my experience academic methodology does require a process of determined translation to make it usable within a market research context.

The sustained distance between academia and the average practitioner is also important in understanding that the qualitative methods used commercially in the UK have largely evolved quite separately from the canon of academic methodological writing. An experienced practitioner driven by the need to address a client's problem creatively may thus invent for themselves a method or way of working, without knowing it in fact exists in a recognized and named form in academic qualitative arenas. For example, I have long been using in commercial research what I only now recognize, through new-found familiarity with the literature, as a version of discourse analysis. This 'feral' practice might well be *refined* by exposure to formal and explicit theory, moving it from unconscious to conscious competence, but it has not relied on it, nor necessarily been derived from it.

The second way in which theory is relevant to qualitative market research is as an intellectual resource. Although unfamiliar with methodological theory, British commercial researchers are certainly interested in other forms of theoretical thinking and they make eclectic, almost magpie-like, use of established models and concepts drawn from a wide range of sources. These sources include (but are not limited to) psychology, anthropology, sociology, consumer theory and marketing theory. To commercial researchers with a problem to solve, any kind of conceptual or theoretical thinking might trigger a key insight into their data. Again, theoretical eclecticism is not unknown within academia, but my impression is that it is taken to an extreme in commercial fields; it is also distinctive in being essentially non-paradigmatic. Various intellectual tools and models are selected that are suggested in some way by the data or seem best

suited to the task in hand, and this may mean mixing quite separate approaches within one project. In a single study about chocolate bars, for example, psychoanalytic concepts might be suggested by individual responses to the product and be used to help interpret them; using ideas from social psychology or neuro-linguistic programming (NLP) might draw meaning from the interaction within the group; and thinking semiotically could help unravel respondent comments about packaging and retail display. All of this thinking is integrated into the total picture and sense made of the project and presented to the client.

One might regard this pick-and-mix use of theory as intelligent and creative, or as wanton and reprehensible, but it is an essential characteristic of commercial practice in the UK. As Catterall notes, it positions the commercial researcher as a kind of 'bricoleur theorist' (2001: 228), producing what Denzin and Lincoln describe as 'a pieced-together set of representations that are fitted to the specifics of a complex situation' (2000: 4). Denzin and Lincoln also observe that 'The combination of multiple methodological practices, empirical materials, perspectives, and observers in a single study is best understood, then, as a strategy that adds rigor, breadth, complexity, richness and depth to any inquiry' (2000: 5). In commercial qualitative research, we have far to go in adopting a true bricolage of field method, but we already work with wide-ranging ideas about what can be accessed via a group discussion, and a highly eclectic approach to interpretative and theoretical perspectives. More about theoretical eclecticism within market research can be found in Barker et al. (2001), Ereaut (2002) and Chrzanowska (2002).

The third form of theoretical thinking relevant to qualitative market research is 'emergent' theory – the conceptual view or understanding of a phenomenon, group or activity that emerges from empirical work. In commercial research the fundamental requirement is to deliver usable research to clients and, as noted before, contribution to wider scientific theory is not a primary aim. However, being practical or applied does not mean producing reports or interpretations that are simple or superficial, or that are concrete and literal. Conceptualizations or theories – of problems, product fields or relevant sub-groups – are of far wider use to clients than specific respondent comments and are thus, at least in the UK model of research, essential to the outcome of many projects. The three levels of qualitative data transformation proposed by Wolcott (1994) are helpful here. Analysis at his first level, 'description', is often very useful – in our case, descriptions of activities, behaviours and expressed attitudes as reported or observed in interviews and groups. These will form an important backbone to some projects, especially if a field is new to the client. But research that remains only at this level is called 'reportage' within the UK market research business, a highly pejorative term. Wolcott's next category is 'analysis' – his term for thematic analysis. Again, themes and patterns can be very useful to clients and are a common part of commercial work. However, analyses that operate at his final level – 'interpretation' – are also vital to what is considered good commercial research. These conceptual analyses – 'theories' – are produced at the level of the individual project (where a study may offer, for example, a model of the relationships between banks and their customers), but are also the product of researcher experience. As I have already noted, repeated investigation allows researchers to develop general theories concerning the nature and dynamics of certain fields. This is not 'high' social theory, but it is empirically based social theory of a kind and is an important resource for researcher and client alike. In academic marketing and consumer research fields such emergent theory has sometimes been taken and used as the basis of further theoretical development (Mick, 1996; McEnally and de Chernatony, 1999).

Publication, reputation and professional credibility

Here again commercial qualitative research shows a marked difference from the academic world. Providing perceptive, intelligent and useful outcomes for clients is paramount to professional credibility in this field, not publication. This, along with the need to protect the commercial confidentiality of substantive findings, is a key reason for the lack of published work in this area. A qualitative market researcher's reputation is built primarily on word-of-mouth recommendation passed from client to client (agencies do also acquire high professional standing, but often this is attached to one or more key individuals within the company). Professional reputation is reflected in the volume and quality of the work offered to researchers, and the prestige of the clients who offer it. Speaking at seminars or courses, or writing papers for industry journals or conferences, are activities likely to enhance a reputation, but are not seen as a key measure of it. This is especially so for British qualitative practitioners, who tend to see the Market Research Society and its journal and annual conference – major outlets for papers – as organized predominantly by and for quantitative researchers. There is no imperative to publish and when business is brisk there is little time or incentive to do so. These criteria for professional credibility and reputation have important implications, especially for the way in which expert knowledge is communicated within and outside the industry. As already noted, knowledge is passed on primarily through the apprenticeship and direct training of practitioners. Although this is in the process of changing, qualitative market research is a business dominated by expert but tacit knowledge.

COMMERCIAL AND ACADEMIC QUALITATIVE RESEARCH COMMUNITIES: POSSIBILITIES FOR EXCHANGE

While acknowledging again the diversity of qualitative practice within both academic and commercial fields, I shall make some general observations about possible exchange between these research communities. First, what might commercial researchers draw from academic practice? Wholesale adoption of academic approaches within market research would be, I believe, unnecessary and professionally inappropriate. Qualitative market researchers would nevertheless find much of relevance in aspects of academic qualitative practice, an awareness of which I am actively engaged in encouraging within our business. We would certainly benefit from being more reflexive, from making explicit the taken-for-granted foundations of good practice and from exploring alternative perspectives. We would gain, in my view, from seeing 'our' version of qualitative research as part of a broader qualitative research world, allowing greater methodological awareness and experimentation.

For the final part of this chapter, I shall briefly consider ways in which commercial practice could be of interest and use to academic researchers. In order to use commercial practice, however, those outside the business would first need to know and understand it better. My observation is that qualitative market research is normally either ignored or criticized within much of academia, but also that the real nature of practice is not understood. References to market research, when they appear, often display erroneous assumptions or partial knowledge. For example, writers state or imply, wrongly, that market researchers always work with (or reduce things to) simple problems, that clients are satisfied with straightforward or superficial analyses, or that qualitative methods are simply the 'latest fashion' in market research (Silverman, 1993; Gofton, 1998; Fielding and Lee, 2002). General statements are made about analytic procedures in market research that just do not fit with common practice across the industry (Myers, 1998; Bloor et al., 2001). I am told informally that academics imagine commercial researchers take a naïve realist stance towards data and use basic and outdated epistemological notions; again, this generalization is incorrect (Chandler and Owen, 1989; Thorpe, 2003). Other criticisms of market research I encounter anecdotally in academia ('weak', 'poor', 'shortcuts', 'simplistic') also do not recognize that the defined objectives of qualitative market research affect practice in a legitimate way.[11]

The fact that many academics work with partial knowledge and ungrounded assumptions about market research is not surprising, since practitioners have been slow to write about what they actually do. However, many of these assumptions will be challenged by the detail of practice becoming available. I reiterate that many different models of qualitative research exist within market research, including the basic (and indeed sometimes formulaic) collection of 'attitudes' and 'opinions' but commonly extending to highly creative and interpretative qualitative investigation. Awareness of the range and complexity of commercial practice might encourage those outside to explore and perhaps selectively use the knowledge residing within it, particularly in its more sophisticated forms. Better understanding of commercial practice will not of course prevent its rejection by some on political or ideological grounds, but it would allow more informed judgement and perhaps some useful exchange.

So what benefit might academics gain from looking at commercial research? Methodologists might simply find it interesting to examine what is a significant application of qualitative research method. Understanding how and why this practice operates as it does provides another perspective on qualitative method as a whole. Beyond this, though, researchers might draw on commercial practice more directly in a number of ways.

Using commercial researchers' experience as a resource

Academic researchers could tap and adapt for their own purposes some of the experience-based knowledge of commercial researchers. There is, for example, a wealth of learning about constructing qualitative sample structures and research group compositions that 'work' on the ground (Imms and Ereaut, 2002). There is also a great deal of knowledge about interviewing and group discussion moderation (Chrzanowska, 2002). Barbour and Kitzinger (1999) rightly argue that social scientists must develop their own adaptations of 'focus group' method and not simply adopt those of market research. However, it is my view that the range of method that exists in market research is far wider than they assume, and would offer genuinely useful approaches and perspectives for many social researchers (see also Catterall, 1998). As academic interest in 'focus groups' grows, this seems a resource too obviously of potential use to ignore.

As I argued earlier, qualitative market researchers have been somewhat tied to the group interview format, while also being unhindered by theoretical orthodoxy. They have thus been in a position to exercise great inventiveness regarding what can be done with groups, building an extensive toolbox of focusing and enabling techniques and a wide repertoire of alternatives to straightforward discussion. Jennifer Mason (2002) has recently called for more tools and techniques to access the non-verbal in qualitative interviewing; these already exist in abundance within commercial practice (see, e.g., Gordon and Langmaid, 1988; Gordon, 1999; Chandler and Owen, 2002; Chrzanowska, 2002; Wardle, 2002).

The degree to which commercial researchers creatively and purposively play around with the composition, location and working methods of groups, and the way they mix paradigms in analysis, might also offer something to those pursuing 'bricolage' in their own research. Although the process of codifying this knowledge has begun, much of it remains the tacit wisdom of experienced researchers and can only be seen clearly in its application to specific problems. It might thus be best shared by collaborative working and writing between academic and commercial researchers, a route I have myself begun to explore.

Accessing knowledge of consumer culture

There is increasing academic interest in consumption and consumer culture, reflected in the plethora of research, publication and funding in this field, across many disciplines (see, e.g., Miller, 1995). Substantive market research findings must always remain confidential to the commissioning client and are anyway likely to be too specific to be of real academic value. However, qualitative market researchers' solid empirical knowledge of consumption practices and their place in everyday life, gained over myriad projects and multiple fields, might be made accessible to academic researchers, if appropriate channels can be established.

Applying commercial skills to non-commercial work

Perhaps more contentiously, academics might on occasion adapt certain of the commercial skills of their market research colleagues. I am told repeatedly that academics are under increasing pressure to 'deliver' – to deliver to funding bodies and to academic research review inspectors, as well as to their community of peers. This pressure can involve tightened budgets and reduced time available for research, as well as the requirement to produce presentations or summaries for different groups. Whatever the rights and wrongs of this situation, the framework of practice and the strategies developed within commercial qualitative research – handling client–supplier relationships, dealing with pressures of time and cost, delivering focused and usable research outcomes – could conceivably be applied within an academic environment. Recently working collaboratively on an academic funding proposal, my academic colleagues and I were interested to see how a commercial 'focusing' strategy proved very useful in this context.

Qualitative market research as a topic

Qualitative market research itself presents an object for investigation, not just by marketing academics but by social scientists. At a general level, commercial researchers operate as 'cultural intermediaries' (Bourdieu, 1984), mediating and negotiating meaning between the public on the one hand and powerful organizations such as manufacturers, advertisers and governments on the other. Understanding how this process works is potentially of interest and concern to social scientists, for example in how businesses and other institutions are involved in shaping the social meaning of foods (Murcott, 1999). At a more detailed level, qualitative market research itself can be examined as a micro-social process. For example, using Conversation Analysis, one can look at the market research interview or group as semi-formal institutional discourse

(Drew and Heritage, 1992; Myers, 1998; Puchta and Potter, 2003).

Qualitative market research as a career path for students

Finally, qualitative market research is of practical interest to academics since it represents a potential career path for those students of qualitative method or social science who enjoy research but who do not wish to remain within academia. Individuals with academic qualitative research training or experience would still be expected to learn through apprenticeship the specific skills and knowledge required for commercial research, but grounding in the theoretical and practical issues of qualitative method would certainly be of value in a prospective commercial researcher. Better formal and informal contact between academic institutions and the qualitative market research industry would of course facilitate such a flow.

CONCLUSION

The wide community of academic and social qualitative researchers has had access only to a partial view of qualitative market research practice, and this means that there is little awareness of the nature and variety of practice within this field. It especially means that important differences between Europe and the US are not recognized, above all regarding the nature of the research group interview. Apart from addressing these knowledge gaps, necessarily briefly, I have offered a framework for understanding why qualitative market research practice operates as it does, outlining some of the structural conditions and professional norms within which it works. It has been my argument throughout that this practice constitutes a highly adapted species of qualitative research, not an unintelligible or deficient one.

There has been great distance between the worlds of academic or social research and commercial research, but this situation is changing and the opportunities for fruitful exchange, for those with an appetite for it, are expanding. This context for making sense of key differences between qualitative market research and academic qualitative practice is offered as an opening bid in what I hope will become a productive dialogue between these communities.

ACKNOWLEDGEMENTS

I should like to acknowledge the invaluable contribution of Mike Imms and Miriam Catterall to the development of many of the ideas represented here, and to thank colleagues who helpfully read and commented on earlier drafts: Chris Barnham, Philly Desai, Nigel Fielding, Anne Murcott and Nick Tanner.

NOTES

1　There is significant variability in qualitative practice within both academic and commercial fields. In order to make certain points of comparison clear, however, I have assumed a rather idealized version of academic qualitative research, focusing on basic rather than applied forms (though arguably the latter would have more in common with aspects of commercial practice). Similarly, I have not fully represented the range of commercial research activity but have concentrated on general features and principles.

2　My thanks to Giampietro Gobo for suggesting this parallel.

3　There are over 1000 qualitative research practitioner members of the Association for Qualitative Research in the UK (and a similar number in the US equivalent QRCA). Although difficult to size accurately, the qualitative business accounts for around $2 billion of a total market research industry $15 billion (Imms and Ereaut, 2002).

4　Interestingly, both these parallel universes adopt the generic description 'qualitative research' for their own practice, and each excludes the other. Denzin and Lincoln's *Handbook of Qualitative Research* (2000), for example, is vast and comprehensive but barely mentions qualitative market research. At the same time, the British qualitative market research industry body calls itself simply the 'Association for Qualitative Research' and makes very little reference to a qualitative research world outside market research.

5　I have referred often to this series, because the preceding literature is limited and often unavailable. A few experienced researchers have set down a personal view of practice (Gordon and Langmaid, 1988; Robson and Foster, 1989; Gordon, 1999). Qualitative papers occasionally appear in the UK Market Research Society (MRS) journal and annual conference proceedings. The international market research body ESOMAR publishes biennial qualitative conference proceedings, but these are not widely accessible to academics. Miriam Catterall's analysis (2001) of the focus group in qualitative market research provides an unusually complete and informed picture of current British practice, though unfortunately this work is also not widely accessible.

6　Imms and Ereaut (2002) and the series of which it is part (Ereaut et al., 2002) give a more thorough introduction to the UK industry. Langer (2001) and Mariampolski (2001) provide details of the business in the US. Aspects of practice from Europe and elsewhere are described in Cooper (1999) and in the range of ESOMAR qualitative conference proceedings and monographs (e.g. Sampson, 1987).

7　There are of course critical debates in qualitative research concerning ideas of 'objectivity', the role of the researcher and issues of representation. I am using 'neutral' here to mean impartiality as to the outcome of the research.

8　There are in-house qualitative researchers within certain client organizations, notably account planners in some advertising agencies. The difficulty in credibly maintaining the balance of the 'dual role' in such a situation is evident in that, for certain work or for certain clients, research is still out-sourced to independent practitioners.

9　See www.mrs.org.uk and www.aqr.org.uk for codes of conduct relevant to the UK.

10　Group moderation has, in my view, gained excessive status with clients and the importance of analysis and interpretation needs active promotion (see Ereaut, 2002). It is, nevertheless, highly visible to clients and may unfortunately be used to judge the overall quality of the research.

11　Commercial researchers naturally also have their prejudices; they tend to assume that academics are highly cautious in their approach to research, are utterly detached from the 'real world', have unlimited time and freedom to research what they will, and write in incomprehensible jargon. This clearly does not fairly reflect the current realities of academic teaching, research and funding.

REFERENCES

Barbour, R. and Kitzinger, J. (eds) (1999) *Developing Focus Group Research*. London: Sage.

Barker, A., Nancarrow, C. and Spackman, N. (2001) 'Informed eclecticism: a research paradigm for the twenty-first century', *International Journal of Market Research*, 43(1): 3–27.

Bloor, M., Frankland, J., Thomas, M. and Robson, K. (2001) *Focus Groups in Social Research*. London: Sage.

Bourdieu, P. (1984) *Distinction*. London: Routledge.

Catterall, M. (1998) 'Academics, practitioners and qualitative market research', *Qualitative Market Research: An International Journal*, 1(2): 69–76.

Catterall, M. (2001) 'Focus groups in market research: theory, method and practice'. PhD dissertation, University of Ulster.

Catterall, M. and Maclaran, P. (1997) 'Focus group data and qualitative analysis programs: coding the moving picture as well as the snapshots', *Sociological Research Online*, 2(1), http://www.socresonline.org.uk/socresonline/2/1/6.html

Chandler, J. and Owen, M. (1989) 'Genesis to revelations: the evolution of qualitative philosophy', *Proceedings of the Market Research Society Conference*. London: MRS, pp. 295–305.

Chandler, J. and Owen, M. (2002) *Developing Brands with Qualitative Market Research*. Book 5 in G. Ereaut, M. Imms and M. Callingham (eds), *Qualitative Market Research* (7 vols). London: Sage.

Chrzanowska, J. (2002) *Interviewing Groups and Individuals in Qualitative Market Research*. Book 2 in G. Ereaut, M. Imms and M. Callingham (eds), *Qualitative Market Research* (7 vols). London: Sage.

Colwell, J. (1990) 'Qualitative market research: a conceptual analysis and review of practitioner criteria', *Journal of the Market Research Society*, 32(1): 13–36.

Cooper, P. (1989) 'Comparison between the UK and the US: the qualitative dimension', *Journal of the Market Research Society*, 31(4): 509–20.

Cooper, P. (1999) (ed.), 'Qualitative research for the 21st century', special issue, *Journal of the Market Research Society*, 41(1).

Cooper, P. and Patterson, S. (1995) 'The future of qualitative research', *Looking Through the Kaleidoscope: What is the Qualitative Mission?* Proceedings of Paris seminar. Amsterdam: ESOMAR, pp. 205–21.

Denny, R. (1995) 'Inspiring details: the role of ethnography in a kaleidoscope age', *Looking Through the Kaleidoscope: What is the Qualitative Mission?* Proceedings of Paris seminar. Amsterdam: ESOMAR, pp. 113–21.

Denzin, N. and Lincoln, Y. (eds) (2000) *Handbook of Qualitative Research* (2nd ed.). Thousand Oaks, CA: Sage.

Desai, P. (2002) *Methods Beyond Interviewing in Qualitative Market Research*. Book 3 in G. Ereaut, M. Imms and M. Callingham (eds), *Qualitative Market Research* (7 vols). London: Sage.

Drew, P. and Heritage, J. (eds) (1992) *Talk at Work*. Cambridge: Cambridge University Press.

Ereaut, G. (2002) *Analysis and Interpretation in Qualitative Market Research*. Book 4 in G. Ereaut, M. Imms and M. Callingham (eds), *Qualitative Market Research* (7 vols). London: Sage.

Ereaut, G. and Imms, M. (2002) 'Bricolage: qualitative market research re-defined', *Admap*, issue 434, December. Henley-on-Thames: NTC.

Ereaut, G., Imms, M. and Callingham, M. (eds) (2002) *Qualitative Market Research: Principle and Practice* (7-volume set). London, Sage.

Fern, E. (1983) 'Focus groups: a review of some contradictory evidence; implications and suggestions for further research', in R. Bagozzi and A. Tybout (eds), *Advances in Consumer Research*, 10: 121–6.

Fielding, N. and Lee, R. (2002) 'New patterns in the adoption and use of qualitative software', *Field Methods*, 14(2): 206–25.

Gabriel, C. (1990) 'The validity of qualitative market research', *Journal of the Market Research Society*, 32(4): 507–19.

Garfinkel, H. (1967) *Studies in Ethnomethodology*. Cambridge: Polity.

Geertz, C. (1973) *The Interpretation of Cultures*. London: Fontana.

Gofton, L. (1998) 'British market-research data on food: a note on their use for the academic study of food', in

A. Murcott (ed.), *The Nation's Diet*. London and New York: Longman, pp. 302–10.

Goodyear, M. (1998) 'Qualitative research', in *ESOMAR Handbook of Market and Opinion Research* (4th ed.). Amsterdam: ESOMAR, pp. 177–239.

Gordon, W. (1999) *Goodthinking: A Guide to Qualitative Research*. Henley-on-Thames: Admap.

Gordon, W. and Langmaid, R. (1988) *Qualitative Market Research: A Practitioner's and User's Guide*. Aldershot: Gower.

Imms, M. (1999) 'A reassessment of the roots and theoretical basis of qualitative market research in the UK', *Proceedings of the Market Research Society Conference*. London: MRS, pp. 203–21.

Imms, M. and Ereaut, G. (2002) *An Introduction to Qualitative Market Research*. Book 1 in G. Ereaut, M. Imms and M. Callingham (eds), *Qualitative Market Research* (7 vols). London: Sage.

Langer, J. (2001) *The Mirrored Window: Focus Groups from a Moderator's Point of View*. Ithaca, NY: Paramount Market Publishing.

Lillis, G. (2002) *Delivering Results in Qualitative Market Research*. Book 7 in G. Ereaut, M. Imms and M. Callingham (eds), *Qualitative Market Research* (7 vols). London: Sage.

McDonald, C. and King, S. (1996) *Sampling the Universe: The Growth, Development and Influence of Market Research in Britain Since 1945*. Henley-on-Thames: NTC.

McEnally, M. and de Chernatony, L. (1999). 'The evolving nature of branding: consumer and managerial considerations', *Academy of Marketing Science Review* [Online], 99(02), http://www.amsreview.org/amsrev/theory/mcenally02-99.html

Mariampolski, H. (1999) 'The power of ethnography', *Journal of the Market Research Society*, 41(1): 75–86.

Marks, L. (ed.) (2000) *Qualitative Research in Context*. Henley-on-Thames: Admap/AQR.

Marshall, H. (2000) 'Avoiding wrecked heads with magic and machinery: strategies for the coding phase of qualitative analysis', in S. Oakley, J. Pudsey, J. Henderson, D. King and R. Boyd (eds), *Sociological Sites/Sights*. Adelaide: The Australian Sociological Association and Flinders University.

Mason, J. (1996) *Qualitative Researching*. London: Sage.

Mason, J. (2002) 'Qualitative interviewing: asking, listening and interpreting' in T. May (ed.), *Qualitative Research in Action*. London: Sage, pp. 225–41.

May, T. (ed.) (2002) *Qualitative Research in Action*. London: Sage.

Mick, D.G. (1996) 'Consumer research and semiotics: exploring the morphology of signs, symbols and significance', *Journal of Consumer Research*, 13(Sept.): 196–213.

Miller, D. (ed.) (1995) *Acknowledging Consumption: A Review of New Studies*. London and New York: Routledge.

Morgan, D. (1997) *Focus Groups as Qualitative Research* (2nd ed.). Thousand Oaks, CA: Sage.

Morgan, D. and Krueger, R. (1997) *The Focus Group Kit* (6 vols). Thousand Oaks, CA: Sage.

Murcott, A. (1999) 'Scarcity in abundance: food and non-food', *Social Research*, 66(1): 305–39.

Myers, G. (1998) 'Displaying opinions: topic and disagreement in focus groups', *Language in Society,* 27: 85–111.

Patton, M. Quinn (1990) *Qualitative Evaluation and Research Methods* (2nd ed.). Newbury Park, CA: Sage.

Puchta, C. and Potter, J. (2003) *Focus Group Practice.* London: Sage.

Robson, S. and Foster, A. (eds) (1989) *Qualitative Research in Action.* London: Edward Arnold.

Sampson, P. (ed.) (1987) *Qualitative Research: The 'New', the 'Old' and a Question Mark.* ESOMAR Marketing Research Monograph Series, vol. 2. Amsterdam: ESOMAR.

Seale, C. (1999) *The Quality of Qualitative Research.* London: Sage.

Silverman, D. (1993) *Interpreting Qualitative Data: Analyzing Text, Talk and Interaction.* London: Sage.

Silverman, D (ed.) (1997) *Qualitative Research: Theory, Method and Practice.* London: Sage.

Smith, D. and Fletcher, J. (2001) *Inside Information: Making Sense of Marketing Data.* Chichester: Wiley.

Thorpe, M. (2003) Virtual connections; representation and commercial qualitative research, *Qualitative Market Research: An International Journal*, 6(3): 184–93.

Valentine, V. (1995) 'Opening up the black box: switching the paradigm of qualitative research', *Looking Through the Kaleidoscope: What is the Qualitative Mission?* ESOMAR Proceedings of Paris seminar. Amsterdam: ESOMAR, pp. 25–47.

Valentine, V. and Evans, M. (1993) 'The dark side of the onion: rethinking the meanings of "rational" and "emotional" responses', *Journal of the Market Research Society*, 35(2): 125–44.

Wardle, J. (2002) *Developing Advertising with Qualitative Market Research.* Book 6 in G. Ereaut, M. Imms and M. Callingham (eds), *Qualitative Market Research* (7 vols). London: Sage.

Wolcott, H. (1994) *Transforming Qualitative Data: Description, Analysis and Interpretation.* Thousand Oaks, CA: Sage.

Yelland, F. and Varty, C. (1997) 'DIY: consumer-driven research', *Proceedings of the Market Research Society Conference.* London: MRS, pp. 89–100.

33

Qualitative evaluation research

Moira J. Kelly

As members of the general public we encounter and engage in evaluation on a daily basis. Making assessments is part of participating in social activities (Pomerantz, 1984). It is so much a part of our lives that we are not usually consciously aware of it. As well as our informal interactions with others, the media provide us with evaluations of a whole range of things, from film reviews to reports about the outcomes of government-sponsored initiatives to improve education or reduce crime. Dissemination of research reports through the news media is now standard practice. For example, most days we will hear stories about topics like how a new scheme has helped to reduce homelessness, or how rates of teenage illegal drug use are increasing. These are examples of 'evaluation research' filtering through to our domestic lives via the television and newspapers.

Evaluation research is carried out in a range of settings across both the public and private sectors. One of the reasons for carrying out evaluation research is the increasing public accountability of those initiating and carrying out (expensive) activities to address social problems and improve the quality of public-sector services. This means that the majority of public-sector interventions carried out these days will be formally evaluated in some way. It is considered important to find out about what does and does not work, and (crucially) *how* things work, so that lessons can be learned and taken forward in future attempts to improve the social world in which we live. Developing knowledge of how things work is where qualitative research comes into its own in evaluation. However, in order to describe qualitative evaluation research practice it is necessary to consider the nature and position of evaluation as a particular form of social research.

Evaluation research draws on the same pool of methods as other social research, and consequently there are many similarities. A study can only be understood as an 'evaluation' in the context of its use. There is no specific set of methods that makes a research project an evaluation, or a qualitative evaluation. There are, however, a number of conceptual and pragmatic factors that differentiate evaluation from other forms of social research. Rossi and Freeman (1993) distinguish between 'basic' (or 'academic') and 'applied' (or 'evaluation') research. Applied research is considered here to be the same as evaluation research (though it may not be labelled as evaluation), so I will refer to evaluation throughout to avoid confusion. Although the distinction between basic and evaluation research is not always clear and there are many overlaps, there are some defining features which are summarized in Table 33.1.

This distinction implies that for a research project to be called an evaluation it has to be set up as such at the start, and that basic and evaluation research are carried out by separate groups of people. This is not the case, as research projects that may not be initially set up as evaluations can be drawn upon for evaluative purposes. The distinction also implies an active distancing between those who do evaluation research and those who do basic or academic research, leading to perceptions of a research hierarchy, with evaluation research 'often regarded less highly than "pure" or "basic" research' (Rossi and Freeman, 1993: 434). However, although researchers may not consider themselves 'evaluators', they may have carried out research that can be considered

Table 33.1   *Differences between 'basic' and 'evaluation' research*

Basic research	Evaluation research
• Carried out in areas of substantive interest to the investigator, and will contribute to such a knowledge base	• Aims to contribute to solving a practical problem
• Standards are set by intellectual peers	• Standards are pragmatic. Evaluations need to be 'good enough' to answer the questions of interest
• Researchers generally trained in a single disciplinary orientation to which they remain committed	• Researchers move around different programme areas
• Narrow group of methodological procedures used	• Diverse methods
• Utilization is assessed by peers (other academics)	• Utilization is assessed by peers (other evaluators), sponsors, and also in terms of the usefulness of the research in resolving policy and practice development, and ultimately the resolution of social problems

Source: Adapted from Rossi and Freeman (1993: 405).

in terms of its evaluative contribution. This will be explored later in the chapter.

My experience as both a researcher undertaking studies, and as a research manager who has developed and commissioned evaluation research in health, has highlighted a number of pragmatic issues that have particular significance for those engaged in evaluation. Evaluations will usually be commissioned to shed light on a particular activity or policy, meaning that the research commissioners may be more directly involved in the study aims and design than in basic research. However, in an area about which little is known, this may mean that the people who want the research done are not clear about what they really want, which makes it difficult all round, or they may want the research done to provide support for a particular scheme or initiative. It is also sometimes like trying to track a moving target (Peers and Johnston, 1994), given that priorities of funders can change and what was once a central project becomes peripheral. Alternatively it may suddenly become highly sensitive. There is also often the constraint of tight and unrealistic time-scales, meaning that the data analysis may not be as detailed as basic research.

An important difference between evaluation and basic research is that until recently evaluation research reports have been relatively inaccessible to a wider research community as they are often not formally published. The Internet has changed this dramatically, so that many reports of evaluations (certainly in public-sector evaluation) are now relatively easy to track down. In fact the tables have turned somewhat in that evaluation reports are often disseminated through websites over the course of the research, rather than just at the end as with most basic research.

This has led to much greater transparency regarding research methods and process. It has allowed access to reports at different stages of projects. Some of the examples used in this chapter are available for access through websites. Dissemination of research reports early on is important as although the project may not progress through all the stages initially envisaged or may be significantly changed, there may still be lessons that can be learned. The Internet has also opened up much greater international communication of evaluation projects and methodologies.

Another change in evaluation practice is that the profile of qualitative research, which has been relatively under-utilized in evaluation until recently, is increasing. There is still a strong emphasis on quantitative methods, especially from policy-makers. Some qualitative researchers have reacted against the quantitative orthodoxy, arguing that evaluation is best done through qualitative research (Shaw, 1999). However, it is proposed here that qualitative research is of equal status as an important part of the armoury of social research that can be used to do evaluation, rather than a better approach. Qualitative evaluation is therefore considered here as a particular form of research enterprise against the backdrop of a range of issues that arise when conducting an evaluation. Given that this chapter is about qualitative research *practice,* the emphasis is on describing the contexts in which qualitative evaluation is commissioned and conducted. This means that although the examples provided are qualitative, I shall also discuss some general issues arising in evaluation research that apply to both qualitative and quantitative research. This is especially relevant in evaluation where qualitative and quantitative studies may be carried out in conjunction with one another as components of a larger evaluation project.

OVERVIEW OF THE CHAPTER

The chapter is not intended to be either a comprehensive review of qualitative evaluation or of qualitative methods as these are more adequately covered elsewhere. The reader is referred to other chapters in this volume for discussion of methods such as interviews and ethnography, and texts that provide more detailed overviews of qualitative evaluation research (Shaw, 1999; Patton, 2002), and evaluation research in general (Rossi and Freeman, 1993; Pawson and Tilley, 1997). The aim of this chapter is to present the reader with an understanding of the contexts in which qualitative evaluation research is carried out and how it is applied in practice. This includes its relationship both with evaluation in general and with social research. I present a number of examples of qualitative research drawn both from projects I have worked on, and also from studies conducted by others. The examples given are biased towards health as that is my area of research practice.

This chapter will not describe how to do the perfect qualitative evaluation project as it is debatable whether such a thing is possible and it would leave the reader ill-prepared for understanding how such research is done in the real world, which is both where it takes place, and where it (hopefully) ends up. I hope to get across some of the tricky issues qualitative 'evaluators' have to deal with in getting their research done, as well as the rewards that can be gained. This includes discussion of qualitative research that is formally labelled 'evaluation', and studies that are set up as basic research but that can be considered to be 'evaluative'. A broad view of qualitative evaluation is taken, considering the role of basic research in evaluation as well as studies that are formally set up as evaluation research.

The chapter consists of five main sections. Examples are presented as short 'case studies' within these sections. The following section is an overview of evaluation research, including different types of evaluation, and study design. The second section examines the role of theory. The third section discusses the application of qualitative methodology in evaluation research. The fourth section considers practical issues in evaluation including setting projects up, the use of evaluation frameworks, and participatory research. The final section concludes by reviewing the current state of play in qualitative evaluation research.

EVALUATION RESEARCH

What is evaluation research?

Evaluation research carried out in the social sciences is about appraising human activities in a formal, systematic way. In line with a modernist agenda underwritten by the notion of progress, it is also about appraising activities that aim to 'better the lot of humankind' (Rossi and Freeman, 1993: 3). Patton provides a comprehensive definition:

> I use the term *evaluation* quite broadly to include any effort to increase human effectiveness through systematic data-based inquiry. Human beings are engaged in all kinds of efforts to make the world a better place. These efforts include assessing needs, formulating policies, passing laws, delivering programs, managing people and resources, providing therapy, developing communities, changing organizational culture, educating students, intervening in conflicts, and solving problems. In these and other efforts to make the world a better place, the question of whether the people involved are accomplishing what they want to accomplish arises. When one examines and judges accomplishments and effectiveness, one is engaged in evaluation. When this examination of effectiveness is conducted systematically and empirically through careful data collection and thoughtful analysis, one is engaged in evaluation *research.* (Patton, 1990: 11)

To begin to see what an evaluation research design might look like, let us take a hypothetical example of a neighbourhood experiencing a high level of crime. The government has allocated some funds to reduce crime in the neighbourhood and a decision needs to be made about how best to use them. The first stage in setting up an activity to reduce crime would be to assess the nature of the problem (evaluation) and consider suitable ways of dealing with it (interventions). Our initial evaluation (needs assessment) indicates that the local community would like the money to be spent on more police 'on the beat', believing that this will reduce crime in the neighbourhood. Three extra police officers are made available for a six-month period. We now need to decide how to judge the success of the scheme (outcomes), and decide what will indicate to us that it has worked (indicators). This raises questions like: How can we tell that there is a reduction in crime? What crimes will be included in our analysis? How much would crime levels need to reduce for us to say that the project is a success? Could the scheme be usefully applied in other communities? (generalizability). Would community perceptions of criminal activity and safety be assessed? Has the investment of resources been worth it? (cost-effectiveness). What research methods would we use? (qualitative, quantitative or both).

The example above is an illustration of how an evaluation research study might be set up around an intervention. Some of the terms used in evaluation research are included in parentheses. Despite the relative simplicity of the example, we can obtain a sense of how things begin to get complicated quite quickly once we start to consider the decisions to be made in setting up our evaluation. Despite starting off with a clear purpose, such as reducing the level of crime in a neighbourhood, evaluation can take a number of different paths. There are a lot of ways of categorizing the problem, which means that different methodologies can be used to explore and assess it. Until relatively recently funders of the type of study outlined above would have focused on 'levels' of crime before and after. However, in recent years the emphasis is shifting to a desire for more detailed evaluations of community experiences and views which qualitative research can contribute.

All applied research can be said to be 'evaluation' in that it is producing an assessment of some phenomenon. This may be in terms of describing things so that recommendations can be made about whether some kind of intervention is needed, or in terms of whether an intervention works or not. An intervention is a specified, but not necessarily specific, activity. It may be something that is already in place, or be a new type of activity. Evaluations are often set up when new interventions are being initiated, or when unexpected problems arise. For example, the HIV/AIDS epidemic stimulated a massive programme of scientific, clinical and social research in the late 1980s and 1990s. Evaluation research aimed both to understand the nature of the problem in its different manifestations and to evaluate interventions to prevent and manage it. An additional emphasis was on developing appropriate evaluation research methodologies (see, e.g., Aggleton et al., 1992; Boulton, 1994; Silverman, 1997; Power, 1998).

There are many contexts in which evaluation takes place. Different conceptual frameworks for evaluation emerge in part from the field of interest of researchers. Two prominent forms of contextual framework, 'programme evaluation' and 'organizational evaluation', are considered here.

Programme evaluation

Programme evaluation is applied to intervention programmes primarily carried out to address social problems in a population, or in a community setting: 'Program evaluation is the use of social research procedures to systematically investigate the effectiveness of social intervention programs that are adapted to their political and organizational environments and designed to inform social action in ways that improve social conditions' (Rossi et al., 1999: 20). Most methods texts explicitly labelled 'evaluation' are about programme evaluation. Depending upon the scale of the programmes to be evaluated, considerable resources may be required. Both the programmes themselves and the evaluations can become complex and at times unwieldy, and multiple evaluation studies may be conducted in parallel.

The widespread use of systematic programme evaluations came about in the twentieth century. Early evaluations were carried out in the areas of education and public health. The post-war period of the late 1940s and 1950s saw the development of extensive public programmes to meet the needs for housing, employment and health promotion. These were very expensive, and funders required information as to their effectiveness in addressing the social problems they aimed to improve (Rossi and Freeman, 1993). This contributed to the establishment of evaluation research as an important part of public-sector programme development. In addition, developments in research methods, particularly applied statistics, meant that more sophisticated research designs were made available, which increased the scope for evaluation. Arguably recent developments in qualitative methodology are poised to produce a similar impact on contemporary evaluation research.

Case study 1: Community-based alcohol programme

An example of a programme evaluation is a project I was involved in as a research manager at a national health promotion agency in England. Following earlier studies in countries such as Finland (Holmila, 1995) and Australia (Midford et al., 1995), the aim was to develop a research project to set up and evaluate a multi-component programme of community-level activities to reduce alcohol-related harms. Our conception of alcohol as a 'public health' issue took social and environmental factors into consideration, as well as the effects of alcohol on individual health. We were interested in the influence of drinking styles and contextual factors that lead to problems such as violence, accidents, vandalism, and absenteeism from work. Harm reduction activities might include banning the drinking of alcohol at football matches, schemes to prevent children buying alcohol, occupational health advice on alcohol, and health education in schools.

The first part of the evaluation was to write a detailed proposal. This required a literature review and audit of local alcohol projects (Thom et al., 1997). We then conducted a rapid appraisal of alcohol-related harms in two communities in South-East England (Oppenheimer, 1998; Sutcliffe, 1998). The rapid appraisal incorporated a range of research methods, including qualitative interviews with local key informants (e.g. police, teachers, public health specialists), observation, and surveys with the local public and those coming into contact with drinkers (e.g. taxi drivers). We were then ready to develop a framework of indicators and methods (qualitative and quantitative) that could be used in our community demonstration project or by local communities when setting up and evaluating such programmes. This was developed through a series of consultation workshops with professionals with an interest in alcohol-related harms across England (Kelly, 1999; Thom et al., 1999). Unfortunately, despite all our preparatory work we were unable to secure funding for our large-scale project, a problem that is not uncommon in evaluation research.

Organizational evaluation

The main difference between programme and organizational evaluation is the contexts in which they are carried out. At the same time as the development of programme evaluation, research was being carried out in organizations to examine the factors that influence the production and delivery of goods and services. Organizational evaluation research came about through the emphasis on measurement of performance outcome through statistically based quality control systems developed in the UK and the US during the Second World War (Prior, 1989). The focus of both the intervention and evaluation in organizations is on performance and productivity, rather than aiming to improve the social fabric of the world we live in (though of course this may be an indirect goal). For example, organizational evaluation in health takes the delivery of health services as its focus. Attention is directed to how the delivery of services can be improved regarding organizational outputs and quality of care.

Case study 2: Comparative study of terminal cancer care in hospice and hospital

An example of organizational evaluation is a study that compared the quality of inpatient hospice and hospital care for patients with terminal cancer and their spouses which was carried out by Seale and Kelly (1997a, 1997b). Qualitative and quantitative data were collected through semi-structured interviews with bereaved spouses. Interviews covered topics such as symptom control, communication with health professionals, and the provision of bereavement care for the surviving spouse. The study found that whereas treatments for

symptoms such as pain and nausea provided relief in both institutions, the psychosocial climate favoured the hospice as a place in which to die. It was concluded that the busy public atmosphere of some hospital wards may not be conducive to the good care of dying people. Including qualitative data allowed us to describe the nature of the interventions being evaluated, making it possible to describe (retrospectively) the process of care in greater detail and to provide guidance on how it could be improved.

A prominent feature of both programme and organizational research up to now has been the use of experimental method, and it is necessary to appreciate the role it has played in evaluation research to understand how things are evolving to widen the scope for using qualitative methods.

Experimental design and realistic evaluation

Accountability for the success of publicly funded initiatives has led to an emphasis on outcomes, or the question 'does it work?' The randomized controlled trial (RCT) is set as the gold standard for producing evidence that interventions work. Based on experimental method, an 'intervention' site or population will be compared with a 'control'. Taking the 'police on the beat' example described above, a simple RCT might involve a neighbourhood with increased police on the beat for a six-month period (intervention site), and one with no change (control site). The aim is then to see if after the six-month period reported crime had fallen, risen or remained the same. The hope would be that there would be a statistically significant reduction in crime in the area with more police.

Even as qualitative researchers, we might feel that this approach on the surface of things seems like a logical way of seeing if something works. However, evaluation (in social research) is about social problems and service delivery. These phenomena exist in the real world rather than laboratory contexts and the variables are very difficult to control. This has very real consequences, in that RCTs conducted in the social arena often demonstrate little or no difference between intervention and control groups. As Pawson and Tilley (1997) comment, Martinson's (1974) review of evaluation studies on attempts at the rehabilitation of offenders is the most cited paper in the history of evaluation research, but it is also the most derided as it concludes that 'nothing works'. As one can imagine, such a conclusion has major implications for those involved in the rehabilitation of offenders.

Pawson and Tilley present a hard-hitting and challenging appraisal of evaluation based on experimental method. Their critique 'is both a stock-taking exercise and a manifesto concerning evaluation's quest for scientific status' (1997: xi). They argue that 'experimentalists have pursued single-mindedly the question of whether a program works at the expense of knowing why it works' (1997: xv). Rather than trying to seek better ways of addressing the question of 'does it work?', the question itself is being refocused to 'how does it work (or not)?' Pawson and Tilley propose a new research paradigm, 'realistic evaluation'. This model is deliberately based in the terminology of traditional evaluation, but attention is given to 'what it is about a program which works for whom in what circumstances' (1997: 217). They suggest examining phenomena in relation to how the 'context-mechanism-outcome' pattern is configured. This pattern forms the basis for their model of realistic evaluation and it is argued that it will enable 'transferable and cumulative lessons' to be learned from research (1997: 217).

Pawson and Tilley's approach has proved to be popular with evaluators. They do not privilege the use of either quantitative or qualitative methods and provide examples of the application of both. In this sense realistic evaluation entails a level of pluralism, or fitting methods to research problems. However, it also requires a theory- rather than data-driven approach in which theory can be built and tested. This means that pluralism is not the goal of the research, and that choice about data collection and analytic method should always be explicitly influenced by theory.

THE ROLE OF THEORY

Evaluation research has been criticized for being atheoretical, or as a 'value-free way of measuring efficiency, effectiveness, organizational outcomes and process' (Prior, 1989: 134). This raises issues regarding how the research will be carried out and used as the social scientist 'will be encouraged to ignore most of the wider social and moral issues which impinge upon the problem at hand and to concentrate solely upon the technical problems of causation' (1989: 146). These are valid concerns and highlight important issues for the conduct of evaluation research.

All research, whether qualitative or quantitative, has a theoretical basis. It influences decisions both about the methodology and the frameworks used for conceptualizing the problem under study. For example, methodological decisions are made at an early stage about qualitative or quantitative research designs. The

disciplinary background and interest of the researcher will also mean that a particular theoretical approach is taken. For example, for a sociologist, theory may mean applying 'either a sociological framework (e.g. "feminist theory") or substantive theoretical knowledge of a sociological kind (e.g. risk, or stigma)' (Shaw, 1999: 87). The problem is therefore, not that evaluation is theory-free, but rather that it is not always made explicit in the way data are collected, analysed and interpreted. As Boulton comments, 'implicit in a research design is a theoretical model which defines the variables of interest and the expected relationships among them' (1994: 4).

Reports of evaluations may contain limited discussion of theory due to time and space pressures and the interests of the audiences at which reports are aimed. However, it is important that evaluation researchers, basic researchers and those at whom the research is aimed recognize that theory has played an important part and that there are alternative ways of understanding the problem. Taking up the example of alcohol-related harms discussed in case study 2, there are a number of possible ways of theorizing alcohol consumption that need to be considered in the design of such an evaluation study. Theorizing alcohol consumption in relation to the *amount* people drink, *drinking habits,* or the *social context* of drinking will all lead to different types of intervention (and consequently type of evaluation methodology) to reduce alcohol-related harms (Thom et al., 1999).

It is becoming increasingly common for evaluations to identify a theoretical model in the study design. This will be used in conjunction with the methodological approach and will influence the collection of data and the analysis and interpretation of the findings. A currently popular theory in evaluations linked to community development programmes to address issues such as health, crime and citizenship across the world is 'social capital' (Putnam, 1993; Kawachi, 1999; World Bank, n.d.). Social capital has been used as the theoretical basis for a programme of recent research that aims to contribute to the reduction of health inequalities in England.

Case study 3: Social capital and health

The mid-1990s started to see a shift in policy and research away from health education aimed at individuals. Interventions such as public health campaigns to reduce smoking were found to be ineffective in lower socio-demographic groups (Acheson, 1998) and therefore such campaigns were considered inconsistent with a central goal of the new Labour government, to reduce social inequalities. The policy goal shifted towards improving health by changing the contexts in which people live, i.e., communities (Department of Health, 1999). A problem with the new push for community-based initiatives was that the methods available to evaluate them were limited (Hancock, 1993). In my post as research manager in a national health promotion agency I was asked with a colleague to develop a tender document for a project that would contribute to the development of 'social indicators'. These indicators would eventually be used to see if changes in communities could be assessed and the relationship between community change and health outcomes evaluated. The theoretical model used as the basis for this study was 'social capital' (Putnam, 1993, 1995).

Putnam's twenty-year study of regional government in Italy demonstrated that such institutions were more effective in 'civic communities', which are marked by 'an active, public-spirited citizenry, by egalitarian political relations, by a social fabric of trust and co-operation' (1993: 15). It was proposed that the model used by Putnam could provide the basis for the development of a series of indicators that could be used to evaluate community development projects to reduce health inequalities in England. The first stage of the research was to see whether social capital as described by Putnam could be identified in UK communities. We commissioned a study that contained both qualitative and quantitative elements. This initial research can be regarded as a form of 'strategic research', conducted in order to explore the possibilities for using social capital as a model for further research and intervention.

The qualitative study involved interviews and focus groups with residents of two neighbourhoods, covering the issues central to Putnam's definition of social capital, i.e., civic engagement, social networks, social trust, and reciprocity. The qualitative study produced a rich and detailed analysis of social capital in the two communities (Campbell et al., 1999). A key finding was that relationships of trust and reciprocity were located overwhelmingly within informal face-to-face networks of friends, neighbours and relatives. This differed from Putnam's study in which a central role was played by more formal network types, such as membership of social clubs and societies, in the formation of social capital. Whereas the findings from the quantitative survey were inconclusive, the qualitative study concluded that the concept of social capital had the potential to contribute to understandings of what constitutes a 'health enabling community'. It also led to an extended programme of qualitative research on social capital (Swann and Morgan, 2002), covering ethnicity (Campbell and McLean, 2002), gender (Boneham and Sixsmith, 2002) and generation (Cattell and Herring, 2002).

This exploratory qualitative research has also contributed to the development of a social action research project (SARP) to improve health in two communities in England that includes a qualitative and quantitative programme evaluation (Social Action Research Project, n.d.). This project has explicitly drawn on the theory of social capital and its relationship to community health and wellbeing (Ong et al., n.d.). An important part of the evaluation of the project is an independent qualitative 'process evaluation'. This is conducted over the course of a project or programme and aims to describe in detail, usually through multiple qualitative methods, the processes through which an intervention is set up and carried out. The SARP process evaluation made it possible to describe the experiences of the two sites as the SARP developed, and its longitudinal nature allowed a number of 'tracer' issues to be identified and 'tracked' throughout the project (Ong et al., n.d.). Applying the principles of realistic evaluation, the process evaluation therefore considered *how* things were working (or not), as the case may be.

Evaluation research requires the application of theory in order to focus and prioritize inquiry (Pawson and Tilley, 1997). Theory can be considered in relation to how the issue is conceived. As Pawson and Tilley argue, 'data collection priorities are set within theory' (1997: 159). Theory building and testing are important if lessons are to be learned. In the example above, the initial study aimed to explore the value of social capital as a theoretical framework for community development initiatives in public health. Having identified its potential value, it was used as a basis for guiding and assessing the programme activities in the intervention study.

THE QUALITATIVE CONTRIBUTION

Qualitative evaluation

As with all research, a key criterion of quality is to use the most appropriate method to address your research problem. Evaluation research can make use of the full range of qualitative methods available. Data collected includes interviews, focus groups, observation, documents, video and tape recordings, and other media. However, as seen in the three case studies described so far, interviews are frequently used methods, reflecting their use in qualitative research in general. The wide range of analytic approaches now available to qualitative researchers can also be applied. These include grounded theory, critical discourse analysis, conversation analysis, ethnography and narrative analysis. However, a note of caution is to be sounded regarding the level of analysis carried out in evaluation studies. The possibility of carrying out intensive data analysis may be impeded by pragmatic factors, in particular the time available, and the priorities of the funders. There are ways around this, though, such as applying for additional funding to undertake separate analysis of some of the data at a later stage. This may not be included in the evaluation report but could be fed back at a later date and the insights used in future programme planning. It is common for evaluators to submit a report on the evaluation and then (time permitting) write papers for peer-reviewed journals. In this way dissemination is aimed at both policy and practice, and at disciplinary audiences (e.g. sociology, psychology, anthropology).

Can qualitative methods be used to assess whether something works?

This is a potential minefield and detailed debate of this issue is beyond the scope of this chapter. However, it is unlikely at the present point in time that qualitative methods would be used as the sole way of finding out whether a large-scale intervention works or not. Rossi and Freeman (1993) argue that both qualitative and quantitative methods have utility, but go on to say that qualitative methods are unlikely to hold up on their own in the political contexts in which evaluations take place. They cite Chelimsky's observation, 'It is rarely prudent to enter a burning political debate armed only with a case study' (1987: 27; cf. Rossi and Freeman, 1993: 437). In addition they argue that qualitative research is not a cheap option and that the costs may be prohibitive. Given the scale of some programme evaluations, and the potential fall-out from such studies, it seems unlikely that a totally qualitative design would be chosen, or that qualitative researchers would feel it was appropriate to take on the task of deciding upon programme outcomes. Some qualitative researchers such as Shaw (1999) argue that qualitative evaluation will usually be *the* design of choice for evaluation research. My view is that it depends what you are setting out to do, and that a major contribution of qualitative research to evaluation at the present time is its potential to describe in detail the processes through which social activities come about.

A crucial difference between basic and evaluation research is the emphasis on social or organizational change. Attention in evaluation research is on 'formulating a model purposefully to *alter* a phenomenon, as opposed to developing a causal model to *explain* the phenomenon' (Rossi and Freeman, 1993: 427). Rossi and Freeman argue that social scientists often do not grasp this difference. This can be seen in the way that social science has shown how much of the criminal behaviour in young men can be explained by the extent of such behaviour in other males in their social network. As interesting as such analyses are, they do not provide insights into practical and ethical ways of addressing the problem, short of

'yanking young males out of their setting and putting them into other environments' (1993: 428). An implication of this is that providing detailed, theoretically informed description (qualitative and quantitative) does not go far enough for the purposes of evaluation research. Can qualitative evaluation research studies suggest purposeful alterations in phenomena?

The extensive critiques and debates regarding theory and methodology in qualitative research have crystallized over the last ten years or so, producing clear standards of quality and rigour for the conduct and assessment of qualitative studies (see Gubrium and Holstein, 1997; Seale, 1999). A particular strength of qualitative methodology is that, through providing detailed description of what happens when interventions are carried out, as Pawson and Tilley suggest, we can begin to look more closely at how things work (or do not work). This can later lead to improved understandings of causal mechanisms. In examining how things work we can see more clearly why they do, or do not do, the things we intend them to, for example reduce crime or improve health. To come back to Chelimsky's point above, the ability to enter a political debate 'armed only with a case study' depends upon the quality of the analysis of that case study.

Qualitative research is currently in a good position to really enter into the arena and show what it can offer, especially given the acknowledged limitations of quantitative methodology in evaluation research, and the refocusing of the concerns of evaluation. Critiques of experimental method demonstrate that answering the big question of 'does it work?' requires a slower, more considered approach. Detailed qualitative analyses have much to contribute here. This includes studies carried out in the early stages of intervention projects such as the social capital and health study described above where the data were collected through interviews and focus groups (case study 3).

Basic research as evaluation

Qualitative studies can also be considered in terms of their evaluative implications. The evaluative implications of a series of studies of therapeutic communities for practitioners (as opposed to policy-makers) are discussed by Bloor and McKeganey (1989).

Case study 4: Therapeutic communities: an observational study

A series of participant observation studies carried out in eight different therapeutic communities by Bloor et al. (1988) made it possible to undertake a retrospective comparison across a range of practices. Bloor and McKeganey argue that comparative data makes it possible to 'imply an evaluative judgement between one set of contrasting practices and another: comparative description implies evaluation and promotes alterations in practice' (1989: 197). They use evaluation in a broad sense, making the evaluative judgements implicit in their study (as in all qualitative studies) explicit. It was observed that practitioners form judgements about the relative success of different treatment approaches in relation to individual clients or patients. They 'evaluate' in the broad sense of the term as part of their everyday work.

Drawing on their comparative materials, Bloor and McKeganey list a number of practices that appeared to promote therapy in the settings studied. These evaluations were presented to practitioners so that they could be used to inform the evaluations they make in their everyday work. This was viewed as a role for field research, 'to provide descriptive materials which can function as comparative or contrasting settings for practitioners to assess, and perhaps modify, their own practices' (1989: 200). Bloor and McKeganey's research indicates how qualitative studies can be evaluative: 'These *everyday* evaluative decisions cannot be replaced by a technical procedure, expropriated by a controlled design: these delicate, balanced disputatious, and sometimes arbitrary judgements occur on an everyday basis as a necessary part of service provision. But research can inform these judgements, can contribute to evaluation in this broad sense' (1989: 199).

Taking research findings back to practitioners is a way of taking up Rossi and Freeman's (1993) point about going beyond explaining to contributing ideas for change in social phenomena.

The contribution of ethnomethodology

Ethnomethodological approaches, developed by Garfinkel (1967) and Sacks (1992), with their emphasis on the social practices people engage in to produce phenomena, are increasingly used as methods of evaluation research (though they will rarely be referred to as evaluation). For example, they have been used extensively to evaluate the use of new technologies in the workplace (see Heath and Luff, 2000). The relevance of such analyses to evaluation is described by Silverman:

My underlying theme is simple: the relevance to practice of rigorous micro work informed by analytical issues rather than by social problems. Practically, it is usually necessary to refuse to allow our research topics to be defined in terms of the conceptions of social problems as recognized by either professional

or community groups. Ironically, by beginning from a clearly defined sociological perspective, I show how we can later address such social problems with, I believe, considerable force and persuasiveness. (1994: 69)

Detailed studies of HIV counselling by Silverman (1997) demonstrate how conversation analysis (CA) and membership categorization device analysis (MCDA) can be used to evaluate the practices of counsellors. While the analyses are not taken to assess the therapeutic value of the counselling outside the sessions, implications can be drawn regarding the effectiveness of certain interactive techniques used by counsellors. The analyses were fed back to counsellors via workshops that involved presentation of detailed transcripts of counselling sessions. In a different health area, a recent study by Heritage et al. (2001) used a multi-method approach, including CA and quantitative analysis, to evaluate rationing decisions in the financing of tympanostomy surgery. The study examines some of the practices physicians use to 'perpetuate a particular medical myth' (a history of prior surgery was treated as a sufficient reason for justifying current surgery) (2001: 725). This enabled the researchers to demonstrate the complexities and some of the difficulties involved in attempts to ration health care.

These studies were set up as basic rather than evaluation research, but are clear examples of research that is 'evaluative', and arguably can contribute to the understanding of causal mechanisms involved in social phenomena. Consequently, to take up Rossi and Freeman's point discussed above, such detailed analyses of *how* things work can help produce more informed decisions about how phenomena can be *altered*. However, rather than seeing explanation as too limited a goal for evaluation research, ethnomethodologists argue that there has been a rush to explain, meaning that limited time is spent 'trying to understand how the phenomenon works' (Silverman, 1994: 70). In a sense we are talking here about taking a step back in order to move forward. This is in line with Pawson and Tilley's 'context-mechanism-outcome' model, in which 'focusing is a process of learning more and more about less and less' (1997: 198). Referring particularly to evaluation aimed at practitioners, Silverman (1994) argues that we can organize research in a way that seeks to satisfy three ends:

1 A focus on how a particular phenomenon is constituted, looking at what people are actually doing in real-life situations.

2 A search for explanations grounded in data drawn from these situations, so that we can address 'why?' because we have secure knowledge of 'how'.

3 An invitation to a dialogue with practitioners based on a sound knowledge of what they are doing in situ.

The following case study is based on analysis of qualitative data drawn from the study described in case study 2 above. It demonstrates how ethnomethodology can provide a different analytic perspective on evaluation, by describing the practices through which assessments of health-care experience are produced by interview participants.

Case study 5: Producing lay evaluations of health care

Qualitative interview accounts of the death of a spouse from cancer were collected as part of a larger evaluation study (Seale and Kelly, 1997a, 1997b). A separate analysis was undertaken in which the accounts were treated as the 'topic' of analysis (Garfinkel and Sacks, 1970) using MCDA and CA (Kelly, 2003). The focus on the accounting practices of interview participants led to the examination of three related issues in the data: criticism of health professionals, assessment work, and doing interview talk. The analysis demonstrates the way in which the interview accounts are collaboratively produced by the interviewee and interviewer as evaluations of health-care experience. In order to make assessments the interviewees set up lay and professional identities with associated roles and responsibilities. A feature of the detailed assessment work undertaken in the accounts is the setting up of entitlements to certain experiences by interviewees, such as being with a spouse when they dic.

The analysis goes some way to demonstrating the aspects of care made relevant by carers when producing a 'consumer' evaluation. We can therefore begin to see what criteria consumers set up and use in this type of evaluation. Through examining the resources used in their accounts, such as entitlements to experience, and lay and professional roles and responsibilities, the standards lay people set up for assessing their health-care experience can begin to be described. The structural form of lay models of evaluation needs to be more fully explicated if the current trend for participatory models of health-care delivery is to be successful. This study also indicates that the lay–professional model set up by lay people in their accounts has functions that need to be taken into account when developing policy. Lay-people play a significant part in setting up professional–lay models of care. A more informed understanding of the relative functions of professional and lay expertise for both groups is required which considers the role of lay (and professional) practices in doing evaluation.

QUALITATIVE EVALUATION RESEARCH IN PRACTICE

Setting up an evaluation study

Evaluation research involves the same issues at set-up as other research projects. However, we have started to see that a number of additional factors may come into play in evaluation research studies. Evaluation is not 'ivory tower' research. It is hands-on and often entails a high level of responsibility to the funders and a group of people who each have a 'stake' in the conduct and outcomes of the research. Project and research goals will usually have to be negotiated with these stakeholders. Evaluation researchers need to take this into account in the way they set up their studies. As Peers and Johnston comment: 'The evaluation team set out to work in a way that was appropriate to the structure and purpose of the project, and that would be useful both to participants within its life-time and to those undertaking similar work after it was completed. This however, was no easy undertaking' (1994: 180).

There will usually be a research project team and a wider project team. The wider team will include people with an interest in the process and outcomes of the evaluation. Often this will include representatives from all sorts of areas, including lay people. It can make evaluation work daunting as research goals need to be communicated and/or negotiated with people who have a stake in the project, but perhaps no knowledge of research methodology. It is not uncommon that there will be differences between stakeholders as to what the project goals are (making things even more complex). For example, stakeholders in an evaluation of the social and environmental impact of a new airport runway may include representatives of local environmental groups and the construction industry, leading to a potentially explosive situation.

The research team will need to be clear about their goals and methods. Attention to issues of analytic rigour are vital if researchers are to stand their ground in sometimes rocky waters. Rossi (1987; cf. Rossi and Freeman, 1993: 413) provides a salutary example of the need to be able to stand by one's analysis when challenged. He describes a study to develop ways of enumerating homelessness in Chicago in the mid-1980s. Local homelessness organizations estimated that there were in excess of 20,000 homeless people in the city. However, Rossi's study produced much smaller estimates, of fewer than 3000 homeless people. This did not go down well with the stakeholders. He describes how he became 'persona non grata' overnight in circles of homelessness advocates, and suffered abuse at a meeting he was invited to: 'Those two hours were the longest stretch of personal abuse I have suffered since basic training in the Army during World War II. It was particularly galling to have to defend our carefully and responsibly derived estimates against a set of estimates whose empirical footings were located in a filmy cloud of sheer speculation' (1987: 413).

Silverman and Gubrium comment that 'organizations that give access to the researcher are likely to want some kind of return in terms of theory-free, usually quantified, "facts", as well as support for their current goals' (1989: 2). However, they might not like the facts when they get them. As Peers and Johnston comment: 'Evaluators set out to be objective. This is not likely to be entirely compatible with giving people what they want. It is normal to want good reports about oneself and objective information about other people' (1994: 193). The important point to be taken from Rossi's experience is that having attended to issues of quality in his research, he was able to defend his findings. Although he refers to a quantitative study, his experience is equally if not more pertinent to those undertaking qualitative evaluation.

Evaluation research, sometimes framed as 'value-neutral', is at times a highly politicized activity (Prior, 1989). A central concern is how involved the researchers should get in making suggestions about altering the phenomena under study. Basic researchers tend to steer clear of such involvement, not seeing it as their role, or something that they are suitably qualified to engage in. This is influenced by potential criticisms, for example in the form of the rhetorical question, 'Whose side are we on?' (Bloor and McKeganey, 1989: 210). There is no simple answer to how involved researchers should get. However, it is clear that considerable attention needs to be given to producing rigorous research that can contribute to future decision-making. Peer review is an important part of this process.

There are of course many positive benefits to be derived from developing collaborative relationships with stakeholders. For example, access to the 'field', and legitimation of the research by those at whom it is aimed, will make it more likely that the findings are taken up and used. Developing collaborative relationships can take time, depending upon the stakeholders, and the sensitivities surrounding the project.

The benefits of building up a good working relationship with stakeholders is demonstrated in the 'social capital and health' study described earlier in case study 3.

Case study 6: Social capital and health: engaging with stakeholders

After the initial study was commissioned, considerable discussion and preliminary research was undertaken in order to decide where the study should be based. We needed a 'community' that was accessible to the research team who were based in London. A town was decided upon, and the local Director of Public Health was written to about the study. He was happy for the research team to conduct the study in the town. He suggested that the project research officer made contact with local health promotion professionals. However, they were initially very wary of the research team coming to undertake the research in their town. They suggested setting up a meeting between the researchers and a larger group of local professionals with an interest in public health to discuss the study. The meeting went well, although people were still wary of what the research was about and how it would benefit the town. It was decided that we would meet as a group on a regular basis over the course of the project.

A good working relationship was built up that was mutually beneficial. The local professionals could advise on useful contacts, and provide information about the area. During the course of the research, a government initiative was set up to improve the health of disadvantaged communities (Health Action Zones). The local members of our group became part of the local Health Action Zone, and were able to use the study findings in setting up local initiatives to improve health. In my experience qualitative research, with its emphasis on detailed descriptions of social activities, has the capacity to really engage stakeholders. Discussions in our meetings were often vibrant, with people going away interested and motivated. Such was the success of our collaborative working that a one-day local seminar was held to present both the research findings from the social capital research, and the local Health Action Zone initiative.

Evaluation frameworks

Many of the decisions that have to be made in setting up an evaluation have already been highlighted. Evaluation designs need to be tailored to their purpose but also need to be flexible. Peers and Johnston remark, regarding their HIV peer education study, that one of the strengths of the study design was that 'it enabled us to track a moving target and tailor our activities to the projects as they developed, not as they intended to develop' (1994: 195). Evaluation research can be carried out at all levels of a

Table 33.2   *Evaluation design (a simple model)*

• Informative/strategic	• Describes the social system and changes taking place within it
• Process	• Describes what happens in the course of policy and programme implementation
• Outcome	• Measures the results achieved by interventions
• Impact	• Long-term use of outcome measures to assess the impact of intervention programmes on a given population (what happens *after* the intervention has finished, e.g. are the results maintained)

Source: Adapted from Thom et al. (1999).

programme or project, or just a part of it. It may be included from the start, 'tacked on', or conducted retrospectively.

Some evaluations can be complex and may involve 'strategic research' to be carried out first, in order to assess the nature of the issue or problem, how it can be conceptualized and, if appropriate, measured. The first stage of the social capital and health study (case study 3) was to see whether social capital could be observed in communities in England in the form identified by Putnam in Italy. The research demonstrated this was the case and that there was scope for building and measuring social capital in communities in England.

If the strategic research has been carried out in a site other than that where the intervention takes place, an additional piece of research may be required. This is referred to as a 'needs assessment' and will aim to produce a programme design appropriate to the context in which the intervention and research will be carried out. It will also influence the evaluation framework. Therefore evaluation may begin with a description of the area in which the project or programme will take place. Once the programme has been designed, research may be carried out at a number of 'levels' in order to evaluate it. These levels often involve the identification of evaluation criteria, or 'indicators' (Carlisle, 1972; Thom et al., 1999). A simple model of evaluation design can be seen in Table 33.2.

In most evaluations of large-scale programmes, an evaluation framework will be designed that will include assessment criteria related to the project aims at different stages. These are generally referred to as indicators. Qualitative studies tend to be undertaken at the informative and process levels and may involve collecting and analysing a number of forms of data, including interviews, observation, and analysis of documents. The 'informative' level

includes strategic research and needs assessment. Qualitative research may be carried out at this level in order to develop indicators, which can later be assessed through quantitative or qualitative methods. Going back to our 'police on the beat' example again, an outcome indicator, 'number of reported crimes', may be set up. Qualitative research would not be useful to measure this. However, an additional indicator may be 'perceptions of community safety'. A qualitative study could provide a useful assessment here. However, such a study will ideally have an explicit theoretical basis, rather than be a few qualitative questions thrown in that are quickly thematically analysed and reported back.

As seen in case study 3, a qualitative process evaluation may be carried out to describe how the project progresses. Outcome and impact evaluations are likely to be of most interest to the funders, but these are traditionally less likely to involve the selection of qualitative methods. However, given the problems with RCTs, qualitative process evaluations are assuming greater significance in understanding the contexts and mechanisms that influence the outcomes and impact of interventions.

Participatory research

A central theme in contemporary evaluation research is the notion of 'participation'. The increasing emphasis on 'lay' or 'user' involvement in all aspects of public service provision has led to evaluation research that includes the perspectives of consumers. In programme evaluation, the participation is usually by the 'community', and in organizational evaluation, by 'consumers'. The move towards consumer or community involvement may well have served to promote the value of qualitative methods in evaluation. For example, Boulton and Fitzpatrick comment in relation to health services: 'The growing demand in recent years for research which gives the consumer a "voice" in developing services has served to increase interest in qualitative research' (1994: 19).

However, as well as conducting studies that elicit views of services, there is a push to involve those under study in the research process. This is partly seen as an appropriate way to develop and deliver public-sector services, based on a democratic model of decision-making. Depending upon what you are researching, participation might mean involving representatives of different populations, such as members of the local community, patients, relatives, school teachers and school pupils.

Participatory research creates a number of additional audiences for the research findings. This may involve regular meetings 'in the field' during the research. It can be hard work, but can also be valuable in terms of producing a useful evaluation that has utility for those at whom the interventions are aimed. Feedback along the way may act as a form of informal review process, and may stimulate different ways of interpreting the data. It is no good producing an amazing piece of research about community development on paper if it does not tie in with local community perspectives. For some researchers, participatory methods mean collaborative relationships with those researched:

> Participatory research attempts to negotiate a balance between developing valid generalizable knowledge and benefiting the community that is being researched and to improve research protocols by incorporating the knowledge and expertise of community members. For many types of research in specific communities, these goals can best be met by the community and researcher collaborating in the research as equals. (Macauley et al., 1999: 774)

Participatory research also has the aim of getting people involved. If communities are involved in setting up the research, i.e., if they have a 'stake' in it, then in theory at least they will be more likely to invest in it in terms of time and support.

CONCLUSION

This chapter has reviewed some of the central issues involved in conducting qualitative evaluation research. The definitive qualitative evaluation research study has not been identified as a discrete form of research. Rather, it looks like other qualitative research studies, but is embedded in a potentially complex range of pragmatic and political issues that make each project different. The main issues covered are in line with three principles identified by Peers and Johnston (1994: 181): (i) the interpretation of project *theory* must be an integral part of evaluation; (ii) considerations of *utility* must inform all evaluation initiatives; and (iii) implementation of these principles depends on the identification and involvement of *stakeholders*.

The difference between evaluation research and basic research is primarily related to the purpose of the study. Evaluation research is undertaken in order to solve some identified problem, whereas basic research sets out to describe or explore some topic or issue to add to a body of social science knowledge. Both forms of research can and do contribute to the solution of problems and bodies of social science knowledge. However, one or the other tends to be prioritized. But the distance between evaluation and academic researchers appears to be contracting. Qualitative researchers in general are becoming more confident in drawing implications for policy and practice from their analyses. Evaluation researchers are also looking for better methodological ways of assessing social issues. This is also in line with an emphasis from funders of basic research as well as evaluation, that dissemination to a range of audiences is required that includes suggested applications for policy and practice.

Limitations of the RCT as the gold standard of methodology in evaluation research, has led to a reconsideration of 'does it work?' There has been a shift of interest from 'matters of technical success or failure' to 'how does it work?' This has increased the scope for qualitative evaluation research. This research is increasingly theoretically informed, rather than atheoretical. Contemporary evaluation research requires perhaps greater attention to quality criteria, as researchers will need to be in a strong position to defend their research against possible challenges from those with vested interests in the findings (who may not like what is found). The use of participatory models and the consequent involvement of stakeholders that is part of evaluation research in both programmes and organizations also means that contextual factors have had to be taken into account much more in recent years.

Contextual factors have also had an influence on the content of this chapter in that the examples discussed are drawn from studies undertaken in the public sector. It is important to note that the contextual issues arising will differ according to setting, though the issues described will be applicable across different areas and topics. For example, organizational evaluation was initially developed in industrial settings and there is ongoing cross-fertilization of evaluation frameworks and methodologies in both the public and private sectors. The examples are also primarily drawn from studies conducted in the UK. However, the studies described were seen to draw on theoretical and methodological models developed in different countries.

Some of the issues discussed in this chapter may be off-putting to the would-be qualitative evaluator. It is difficult, messy, involves keeping lots of people happy, and will have unpredictable outcomes. However, it is also challenging, interesting, involves developing relationships with people outside the 'ivory tower', and can make a difference. Chances are too that you may be doing it anyway, and can have the best of both worlds. The key message is that qualitative evaluation research is not about compromising quality in order to produce research about real-world problems.

ACKNOWLEDGEMENT

I would like to thank Vicki Taylor for her help in discussing the issues explored in this chapter.

REFERENCES

Acheson, D. (1998) *Independent Inquiry into Inequalities in Health*. London: The Stationery Office.

Aggleton, P., Young, A., Moody, D., Kaplia, M. and Pye, M. (eds) (1992) *Does it Work? Perspectives on the Evaluation of HIV/AIDS Health Promotion*. London: Health Education Authority.

Bloor, M. and McKeganey, N. (1989) 'Ethnography addressing the practitioner', in J.F. Gubrium and D. Silverman (eds), *The Politics of Field Research: Sociology Beyond Enlightenment*. London: Sage, pp. 197–212.

Bloor, M., McKeganey, N. and Fonkert, D. (1988) *One Foot in Eden: A Sociological Study of the Range of Therapeutic Community Practice*. London: Routledge.

Boneham, J. and Sixsmith, M. (2002) 'Men and masculinities: accounts of health and social capital', in C. Swann and A. Morgan (eds), *Social Capital for Health: Insights from Qualitative Research*. London: Health Development Agency, pp. 47–60.

Boulton, M. (1994) Introduction, in M. Boulton (ed.), *Challenge and Innovation: Methodological Advances in Social Research on HIV/AIDS*. London: Taylor & Francis, pp. 1–22.

Boulton, M. and Fitzpatrick, R. (1994) '"Quality" in qualitative research', *Critical Public Health*, 5(3): 19–26.

Campbell, C. and McLean, C. (2002) 'Social capital, exclusion and health: factors shaping African-Caribbean participation in local community networks', in C. Swann and A. Morgan (eds), *Social Capital for Health: Insights from Qualitative Research*. London: Health Development Agency, pp. 29–46.

Campbell, C., Wood, R. and Kelly, M. (1999) *Social Capital and Health*. London: Health Education Authority.

Carlisle, E. (1972) 'The conceptual structure of social indicators', in A. Shonfield and S. Shaw (eds), *Social Indicators and Social Policy*. London: Heinemann, pp. 23–32.

Cattell, V. and Herring, R. (2002) 'Social capital, generations and health in East London', in C. Swann and A. Morgan (eds), *Social Capital for Health: Insights from Qualitative Research*. London: Health Development Agency, pp. 61–78.

Chelimsky, E. (1987) 'The politics of program evaluation', *Society*, 25(1): 24–32.

Department of Health (1999) *Saving Lives: Our Healthier Nation*. London: Department of Health, www.official-documents.co.uk/document/cm43/4386/4386.htm. Accessed 30 December 2002.

Garfinkel, H. (1967) *Studies in Ethnomethodology*. Englewood Cliffs, NJ: Prentice-Hall.

Garfinkel, H. and Sacks, H. (1970) 'On formal structures of practical actions', in J. McKinney and E.A. Tiryakian (eds), *Theoretical Sociology: Perspectives and Developments*. New York: Appleton-Century-Crofts, pp. 337–66.

Gubrium, J.F. and Holstein, J.A. (1997) *The New Language of Qualitative Method*. Oxford: Oxford University Press.

Hancock, T. (1993) 'The Healthy City from concept to application: implications for research', in: J.K. Davies and M.P. Kelly (eds), *Healthy Cities: Research and Practice*. London: Routledge, pp. 14–33.

Heath, C. and Luff, P. (2000) *Technology in Action*. Cambridge: Cambridge University Press.

Heritage, J., Boyd, E. and Kleinman, L. (2001) 'Subverting criteria: the role of precedent in decisions to finance surgery', *Sociology of Health and Illness*, 23(5): 701–28.

Holmila, M. (1995) 'Community action on alcohol: experiences of the Lahti project in Finland', *Health Promotion International*, 10(4): 283–91.

Kawachi, I. (1999) 'Social capital and community effects on population and individual health', *Annals of the New York Academy of Sciences*, 896(1): 120–30.

Kelly, M. (1999) 'Alcohol: assessing the impact of community initiatives', *Healthlines*, March: 8–9.

Kelly, M.J. (2003) 'Telling the story: the status of accounts describing the death of a spouse', unpublished PhD thesis, University of London.

Macauley, A.C., Commanda, L.E., Freeman, W.L., Gibson, N., McCabe, M., Robbins, M. and Twohig, P.L. (1999) 'Participatory research maximises community and lay involvement', *British Medical Journal*, 319: 774–8.

Martinson, R. (1974) 'What works? Questions and answers about prison reform', *Public Interest*, 35: 22–45.

Midford, R., Boots, K. and Cutmore, T. (1995) 'COM-PARI, a three-year community based alcohol harm reduction project in Australia: what was achieved and what was learned'. National Centre for Research into the Prevention of Drug Abuse, Perth, Australia: Curtin University of Technology.

Ong, P., Birch, K. and Cropper, S. Nottingham Social Action Research Project (SARP): process evaluation. First report, http://www.phel.gov.uk/sarpdocs/nott_eval.pdf. Accessed 30 December 2002.

Oppenheimer, E. (1998) 'Alcohol related harms in Guildford, Surrey: a rapid assessment and recommendations for future interventions'. Internal report to Health Education Authority.

Patton, M.Q. (1990) *Qualitative Evaluation and Research Methods* (2nd ed.). Thousand Oaks, CA: Sage.

Patton, M.Q. (2002) *Qualitative Research & Evaluation Methods* (3rd ed.). Thousand Oaks, CA: Sage.

Pawson, R. and Tilley, N. (1997) *Realistic Evaluation*. London: Sage.

Peers, I.S. and Johnston, M. (1994) 'Theory, utility and stakeholders: methodological issues in evaluating a community project on HIV/AIDS', in M. Boulton (ed.), *Challenge and Innovation: Methodological Advances in Social Research on HIV/AIDS*. London: Taylor & Francis, pp. 179–98.

Pomerantz, A. (1984) 'Agreeing and disagreeing with assessments: some features of preferred/dispreferred turn shapes', in J.M. Atkinson and J. Heritage (eds), *Structures of Social Action*. Cambridge: Cambridge University Press, pp. 57–101.

Power, R. (1998) 'The role of qualitative research in HIV/AIDS', *AIDS*, 12: 687–95.

Prior, L. (1989) 'Evaluation research and quality assurance', in J.F. Gubrium and D. Silverman (eds), *The Politics of Field Research: Sociology Beyond Enlightenment*. London: Sage, pp. 132–49.

Putnam, R. (1993) *Making Democracy Work: Civic Traditions in Modern Italy*. Princeton, NJ: Princeton University Press.

Putnam, R. (1995) 'Bowling alone: America's declining social capital', *Journal of Democracy*, 6(1): 65–79.

Rossi, P.H. (1987) 'No good applied research goes unpunished!', *Social Science and Modern Society*, 25(1): 74–9.

Rossi, P.H. and Freeman, H.E. (1993) *Evaluation: A Systematic Approach* (5th ed.). Newbury Park, CA: Sage.

Rossi, P.H., Freeman, H.E. and Lipsey, M.W. (1999) *Evaluation: A Systematic Approach* (6th ed.). Thousand Oaks, CA: Sage.

Sacks, H. (1992) *Lectures in Conversation*, vols 1 and 2. Oxford: Blackwell.

Seale, C. (1999) *The Quality of Qualitative Research*. London: Sage.

Seale, C. and Kelly, M. (1997a) 'A comparison of hospice and hospital care for people who die: views of the surviving spouse', *Palliative Medicine*, 11: 93–100.

Seale, C. and Kelly, M. (1997b) 'A comparison of hospice and hospital care for the spouses of people who die', *Palliative Medicine*, 11: 101–6.

Shaw, I. (1999) *Qualitative Evaluation*. London: Sage.

Silverman, D. (1994) 'Analysing naturally-occurring data on AIDS counselling: some methodological and practical issues', in M. Boulton (ed.), *Challenge and Innovation: Methodological Advances in Social Research on HIV/AIDS*. London: Taylor & Francis, pp. 69–93.

Silverman, D. (1997) *Discourses of Counselling: HIV Counselling as Social Interaction*. London: Sage.

Social Action Research Project. SARP website, www.social-action.org.uk/sarp/ Accessed 30 December 2002.

Sutcliffe, H. (1998) 'Alcohol related harms in Ilford, Redbridge: a rapid assessment and recommendations for future interventions'. Internal report to Health Education Authority.

Swann, C. and Morgan, A. (eds) (2002) *Social Capital for Health: Insights from Qualitative Research*. London: Health Development Agency.

Thom, B., Stimson, G., Harris, S. and Kelly, M. (1997) 'Local action on alcohol problems: ten years on', *Drugs: Education, Prevention and Policy*, 4(1): 27–38.

Thom, B., Kelly, M., Harris, S. and Holling, A. (1999) *Alcohol: Measuring the Impact of Community Initiatives*. London: Health Education Authority.

World Bank. Social capital for development, www.worldbank.org/poverty/scapital/ Accessed 30 December 2002.

34

Action research

Donna Ladkin

Action research is grounded in the belief that research with human beings should be participative and democratic. Researchers working within this frame are charged with being sensitive to issues of power, open to the plurality of meanings and interpretations, and able to take into account the emotional, social, spiritual and political dimensions of those with whom they interact. 'Purpose' is also central to these methods; as Reason and Bradbury state in their introduction to the *Handbook of Action Research* (2001: 2), 'A primary purpose of action research is to produce practical knowledge that is useful to people in the everyday conduct of their lives.'

Research methods that aspire to such lofty standards in theory have much to live up to in their implementation and practice. This chapter draws on accounts of researchers at the University of Bath's Centre for Action Research in Professional Practice who have engaged in MPhil and PhD programmes using action research. The chapter emerged from two one-day workshops in which researchers from the Centre met to discuss the reality of putting action research theory into practice.

After defining terms and presenting a brief overview of issues central to these methods, the chapter addresses four features that arose during the workshops as particularly perplexing or challenging in the actual 'doing' of action research. These are:

- The undertaking of cycles of action and reflection.
- The practice of collaboration, particularly considering issues of power and politics.
- Developing sensitivity to action research as an emergent process.
- Finding presentational form to represent action research inquiries.

The chapter offers points to 'bear in mind' for each of these aspects, based on the experience of researchers who have grappled with them. Finally, the chapter concludes with a brief discussion of the extent to which conducting action research might be an 'aspiration' rather than a 'possibility'.

ACTION RESEARCH: DEBATES AND DEFINITIONS

Even a cursory review of the literature reveals little agreement on a sole definition for research methods that claim the label of action research. This may have something to do with the term's evolution: the notion itself has been developed by practitioners and theorists in a number of different fields including education (Mills, 2000; Ahar et al., 2001), management and organizational change (McKernan, 1996; Toulmin and Gustavsen, 1996) and social theory (Fals Borda and Rahman, 1991; Whyte, 1991). There are those such as Stringer and Bannister (1979) who argue that action research is akin to positivist research in every way except that its focus is on changing a situation or a practical concern. Indeed, Kurt Lewin, often viewed as the prime pioneer of these approaches, 'associated the idea of action research with the idea of doing experiments, albeit in the field rather than the laboratory' (Gustavsen, 2001).

Writings and theories about action research, including contributions from critical theory (Habermas, 1979; Carr and Kemmis, 1986), have helped to place the term more easily within, or at least in sympathy with, a post-positivist social constructivist paradigm (Lincoln, 2001; Reason and Bradbury, 2001). But even within that broadly defined heading, there are arguments as to whether or not it is part of 'social science' or something more distinctive than that. This is put forward by Stephen Corey's work in the field of education, where action research has been used since the 1920s. Richard Pring (2000) emphasizes this view when he writes:

> The social sciences provide tools for the educational researcher; they offer generalized knowledge which such a researcher must take cognizance of; but they cannot be the model of educational research. Just as man is not the subject of science, so educational research at its core cannot be scientific. …
>
> Nothing I have said should undermine the perceived relevance of the social sciences, of the need for large-scale explanatory accounts of society and of how human beings operate in and are influenced by society. Such must be the backcloth to educational thinking. The professional, struggling with the particular, will benefit from an acquaintance with the general – so long as he or she does not look to it for conclusions rather than evidence. At the heart of educational practice must be professional judgement, and that judgement needs to be informed by whatever is relevant. Educational research – understanding educational practice, draws upon social science research. But it is something more. (pp. 158–9)

To complicate its definition further, the term 'action research' is also sometimes used interchangeably with 'action inquiry' and/or 'action science'. Argyris and Schön are most credited with work in the development of action science (1974, 1978; Schön, 1983) and Torbert (1991a, 1991b) has taken these ideas as a starting point for his work in action inquiry. Reason (1994) writes:

> The purpose of both [action inquiry and action science] practices is to engage with one's own action and with others in a self-reflective way, so that all become more aware of their behaviour and its underlying theories. Both practices base their work on the 'raw' data of accounts and recordings of practice (usually in the form of talk) gathered by the actors themselves, and both encourage public testing of one's own perceptions and the use of action experiments to test new theories of action and to develop new skills. (p. 332)

Torbert (1991b) elaborates this when he writes:

> Action science and action inquiry are forms of inquiry into practice; they are concerned with the development of effective action that may contribute to the transformation of organizations and communities toward greater effectiveness and justice. (p. 219)

Certainly there is great overlap and blurring between these definitions (although champions of a particular term would undoubtedly not see it that way). Within this chapter, both action inquiry and action science are seen as specific types of action research. Action inquiry is one way of conducting action research, with a particular emphasis on the researcher's role in a situation, and action science emphasizes the creation of theory from cycles of action and reflection.

This brief overview of the development of action research is aimed to demonstrate the lack of a definitive definition for it. Perhaps one step towards clarity is to suggest it is best understood as an *orientation* towards research, rather than a particular methodology (Reason and McArdle, 2003). This is an important realization for those hoping to engage with these practices. Repeatedly during the two workshops from which material for this chapter is drawn, the comment 'But I'm not sure what I was doing was "action research" ' was voiced. I believe this speaks, not to the inexperience of the researchers involved, but to the fact that there is no one right way of doing action research. Instead, there is the intention of the researcher, coupled with a commitment to rigorous reflection and experimentation with new understandings or behaviours, which are the hallmarks of this approach.

Definitions are, however, helpful as starting points, and here McKernan's (1996) is offered because it speaks to several aspects of action research that are taken to be essential in understanding its use in this chapter. He writes:

> … in a given problem area, where one wishes to improve practice or personal understanding, inquiry is carried out by practitioners, first to clearly define the problem, second, to specify a plan of action, including the testing of hypotheses by application of action to the problem. Evaluation is then undertaken to monitor and establish the effectiveness of the action taken. Finally, participants reflect upon, explain developments and communicate these results to the community of action researchers. Action research is the systematic self reflective scientific inquiry by practitioners to improve practice. (p. 5)

McKernan clearly attributes action research with two qualities: its focus on the practical, and its claim to be scientific. The definition also describes what this chapter refers to as 'cycles of inquiry': the disciplined review of action undertaken, the 'off-line' reflection on that action and the search for alternative ways of behaving or frames for understanding, experimentation with those alternative frames or behaviours, and the monitoring of subsequent outcomes. Other assumptions that inform the writing of this chapter are presented explicitly below, followed by assumptions about epistemology, research strategies, and criteria for validity appropriate to this approach.

WORKING DEFINITION AND ASSUMPTIONS FOR THIS CHAPTER

For the purposes of this chapter, the underlying assumptions about what constitutes action research are:

*   That there is on the part of the researcher an *intentionality* for the 'outcome' of the project, that it should have practical consequences in the bettering of, or deeper understanding of, a situation.
*   That it implies a way of inquiring into that situation that embraces multiple ways of understanding that situation, and not one right path that will result in a 'better' outcome.
*   That the process by which the project is undertaken is seen as important, if not more important, than the 'result' – that includes an orientation to working 'with' people, and seeing oneself as part of the research frame rather than outside of it.
*   To that end, it acknowledges that all observation is biased, all situations are 'framed', and that a large part of the research process itself is the unpicking and unearthing of those frames through which the researcher or co-researchers view the situation.

EPISTEMOLOGY

The very term 'action research' implies that the nature of knowing purported by these methods is rooted in the experience of doing. 'Knowing' is seen to be embedded within cycles of action and reflection. Knowledge is not derived from or solely within the province of theoretical propositions, but is the product of an extended epistemology that includes multiple ways of knowing. Heron (1981, 1992) suggests that as well as propositional knowing (that based on theories or 'received' wisdom), the epistemology of action research should include:

*   Experiential knowledge – knowledge gained through the direct encounter with persons, places or things.
*   Practical knowledge – knowledge gained through the doing of things, demonstrated through skill and competence.

*   Presentational knowledge – the knowledge gained by ordering our tacit experiential knowledge into patterns.

In fact, Reason and Bradbury (2001) suggest the inclusion of and exploration of multiple ways of knowing should be a key criterion for validity of action research-based studies.

RESEARCH STRATEGIES AND METHODS

One way of conceptualizing a strategy for conducting action research is in framing it as first-, second- or third-person inquiry (Torbert, 1998; Marshall and Reason, 1994). In fact, integrating these three approaches is an imperative in action research, suggest Reason and Torbert (2001): 'We argue that a complete vision of a transformational social science which generates quantitative, qualitative, and action research, which in turn supports full human flourishing in community and in the more-than-human world, needs to encompass and integrate first, second and third person research practice and concerns' (p. 16). A brief account of each of these foci is given here beginning with third-person inquiry. Fuller renderings are given in the previously cited works or in Torbert (2001) or Reason (1994).

According to Reason and Torbert (2001), third-person research aims to create a wider community of inquiry between people who may not have face-to-face contact, but who share a common interest. Through their collaboration they may seek to influence or transform an even wider community, but through 'mutually-enhancing exercises of power that invite third persons into first, second and third person practice'.

Participative action research (PAR) is a good example of a third-person research practice. Fals-Borda and Rahman (1991) write that the primary task of PAR is the 'enlightening and awakening of common peoples'. To that end, PAR has been used extensively in addressing issues of power and powerlessness in communities, particularly of poor or disadvantaged peoples, to provide a means by which individuals affected can have a voice in creating governing policies and decisions. (For accounts of PAR inquiries, see, e.g., Swantz and Vainio-Mattila, 1988; Kelly et al., 2001; Martin, 2001.)

'Traditional' forms of data collection may be used by action researchers involved in third-person inquiries, including questionnaires, interviews, quantitative data, etc., but they will not be used unilaterally. Instead, the community involved in completing these interviews or questionnaires would take part in the sense-making process and in generating the next steps for which such data might be used.

Second-person research focuses on face-to-face encounters between individuals and in small groups. The focus of interest might be on the 'here and now' experience of being in a group together, or it might focus on an issue of common concern or interest. Co-operative inquiry is one of the best-documented forms of second-person inquiry (Heron, 1971, 1996; Reason, 1999). Reason and Torbert (2001) suggest the 'basics' of co-operative inquiry as:

> In co-operative inquiry, all those involved in the research endeavour are both co-researchers, whose thinking and decision-making contributes to generating ideas, designing and managing the project, and drawing conclusions from the experience; and also co-subjects, participating in the activity which is being researched.… As co-researchers they participate in the thinking that goes into the research – framing the questions to be explored, agreeing on the methods to be employed, and together making sense of their experience. (p. 20)

But second-person inquiries do not have to be as elaborate as formalized co-operative inquiry groups. Torbert (2001) makes the point that the everyday conduct of friendship can be an important second-person inquiry in evaluating the effectiveness of one's day-to-day actions. Additionally, he writes of the importance of language in mediating second-person inquiries. In particular, he suggests paying attention to whether one is 'framing', advocating', 'illustrating' or 'inquiring' when in dialogue with another, and the effect each type of communication might have.

Both second- and third-person strategies must be rooted in first-person inquiry. This is inquiry into how the researcher her or himself makes choices, frames experience and behaves. As suggested earlier, the action researcher sees him or herself as within the research frame, and an important aspect of that frame will be their biases and constructions of experiences. First-person inquiry aims to unearth those biases and informing assumptions that will influence the researcher's sense-making capacity. Of course, it is virtually impossible to unearth all our underlying assumptions, but first-person inquiry is a commitment to rigorously question, examine and reduce one's own blindness to those biases.

Critical subjectivity is a key component of each of these strategies, but is perhaps most apparent in first-person inquiry. Reason (1988) describes it further as 'a quality of awareness in which we do not suppress our primary subjective experience; nor do we allow ourselves to be overwhelmed and swept along by it; rather we raise it to consciousness and use it as part of the inquiry process' (p. 12). This is difficult to do on one's own, and Reason and Marshall (1987) note the importance of interacting with 'friends willing to be enemies' in order to reveal the blind spots and unarticulated assumptions inherent in any inquiry.

Methods used to conduct first-person inquiries are varied and continually growing. They include journaling (Janesick, 1999), the use of story-telling and narrative (Winter et al., 1999) and, increasingly, through multi-media and the combination of text, music and art forms (Lykes, 2001).

VALIDITY

For action researchers, how is the validity and quality of their work determined without the more traditional criteria of lack of experimenter bias, control groups or statistical significance? As if to emphasize this conundrum, Styhre et al. (2002) write:

> One of the key criticisms raised against action research is that action researchers are not taking a detached position vis-à-vis the research objects but rather actively become involved in the process. Action researchers are thus criticized for accepting or even actively pursuing an involvement in organizational matters that may have consequences for the research findings. (p. 98)

Clearly, those undertaking action research and those reading accounts of action research need to be using a different 'measuring stick' for assessing the quality and trustworthiness of documented studies. Reason and Bradbury (2001: 5) suggest five such criteria:

- The extent to which the research demonstrates emergence and enduring consequences.
- The extent to which the research deals with pragmatic issues of practice and practising.
- The extent to which the inquiry demonstrates good qualities of relational practice, such as democracy and collaboration.
- The extent to which the research deals with questions of significance.
- The extent to which the research takes into account a number of different ways of knowing.

Perhaps ultimately, the final arbiter of validity is usefulness. For those engaged in action and reflection cycles to the betterment of a situation, whether they intend to 'write up' their 'results' or not, whether an action or method is improving things has to be the 'lived' test of validity.

RESEARCHING ACTION RESEARCH

The aim of this chapter is to provide some insight into how these theories of action research unfold in practice. Over thirty researchers associated with the Centre for Action Research in Professional Practice at the University of Bath, who have been or are currently engaged in action research projects, met over two different day-long workshops to discuss their experiences of doing action research. The workshops themselves were planned as action research events: they were designed to be collaborative, to respond to emerging process and to work in a cyclical manner. Out of the many layers of conversation that occurred over the two days, four aspects of action research in practice have been selected to examine in detail. Each is illustrated by the stories researchers told about how, given ambiguity and the realities of working in the moment, they put theory into practice.

CYCLES OF ACTION AND REFLECTION

A cornerstone of most action research processes is the notion of cycles of action and reflection. In further understanding a situation or event, the researcher must engage in both active and reflective processes, as suggested by Reason (1994): 'As methods of action inquiry, practitioners would emphasize that these constructions of reality become manifest not just through the "mind" but through reflective action of persons and communities' (p. 333).

In theory these cycles are discrete and well defined. A person or group of people takes action, together or alone they reflect on that action, consider a new action to try, and then engage in action again, and so the cycle continues. Certainly the researchers gathered for the workshop used these terms to talk about their experiences of inquiry. But there were different emphases and issues that were not so clearly addressed in anything they had read about the way of 'doing' them. In particular, nothing they had 'read' had prepared them for the whole-body experience of engaging in these cycles. For instance, Margaret reported:

This was not just an intellectual process. The whole of me was included, my body, my mind, my psyche and my feeling self. I got ill, I struggled with painful emotions in relation to certain individuals. Through reliving and reconceptualizing these experiences I moved through them and took up a different position in relation to them. It was as if I allowed a different and more vulnerable part of my subjectivity into my professional identity. Through this process of reliving experience and reflection I arrived in a place from where I could write down what was happening and find a form for doing so which no longer felt destructive.

Conducting cycles of inquiry is often very demanding, particularly when reflection on the self leading to change is involved. Researchers spoke of times in which they believed the conclusions they were drawing from a cycle of inquiry were correct, only to discover a complete reframing of a situation was needed. This is demonstrated by Gill's story:

I just knew I could use these models to change things into the way I wanted them to be. This was a way of getting people to do 'what's right'. I used Torbert's model of, frame, illustrate, advocate, inquire – but people still weren't doing what I thought they should. I had a tough couple of years. I kept thinking, I'm not doing this right, I'll read more, I'm not saying it right, if I could get it right, they'd see. Then I realised, it's crazy to think of Action Inquiry as a way to get people to do what you want them to do. I realised I needed to be 80% more understanding and loving, I had to be easier on myself about what I could do – I needed to lighten up.

When I was asked in my viva, 'But how did you DO it, how did you make that shift?' I said, 'The method is you ask– "what's going on?" ' You take seriously your thinking. I looked at all those transcripts, listened to all those tapes, and finally I thought, the only thing in this system I can change is me. What effect would changing me have? I remember I felt powerless, but not that I didn't have any power. I had to trust a different form of sensemaking, I had to rely on accumulation and accretion, I had to allow it to build. It wasn't a rational process from there to there. Now I know what to do, I trust my own wisdom. I trust my body. When I get anxiety in my gut, it's a signal to 'pay attention', rather than to discount it or try to make it go away.

Margaret, again, spoke of how she undertook these cycles, demonstrating something of the commitment to examining and re-examining herself required by them:

… This involved an intense cycling between action and reflection, reliving my experience, writing and rewriting my reflections, bringing these to my supervision group, conceptualizing and re-conceptualizing what was happening, going back to work and trying something different, writing about that, and so on. For instance, in one particular case, I had to work through my reaction to a colleague who continually interrupted me and ignored what I was saying when we were with clients. Over a period of time I worked at conceptualizing what was happening between us, using different frames. I began to seize opportunities as they arose to establish a much more equal relationship, I explored the relationship between the expectations and hopes that I had in relation to her and the conceptual frames I had chosen to use. I reframed what I wanted from her, from thinking that she 'had it all', the professional expertise, prestige, knowledge, client contacts, to realizing that I had my own expertise. I developed my own way of consulting. I gave up the idea that she should be providing a secure base for our work. Instead I thought, 'She's sick and tired of being expected to be nurturing, just because she's a woman, that's why she is not being so. I don't like it, but I can at least see where she is coming from.' I realized that the way she was behaving had no reflection on me. I engaged with her from this different place.

But the cycles that people engaged in did not always move them forward into ever increasing levels of clarity. Rupesh for example, described the cycling process as one between 'clarity' and 'fog':

> It wasn't always so easy to see where I was in the process. Sometimes I'd seem to move with clarity, I could see that I was testing out something I'd planned. But other times it would seem that I was in fog, I wasn't sure if I was doing what I'd planned to do, or even if what I was doing had anything to do with the inquiry. Certainly the two processes, action and reflection, were not discrete. And the boundaries between 'content' and 'process' also blurred, what I found was that 'content' was being lived out in the process of doing.

Another aspect of these cycles in practice, is that the reflections on a particular action do not necessarily happen in the same 'cycle' as the action. Researchers reported that action/reflection cycles are not necessarily linear. Often, people would have insights on a particular action several weeks or even months after the action to which it pertained was taken. Marie offered:

> I'd been feeling very frustrated about the material that was being generated in a collaborative inquiry. I was looking for stories from people about their experiences. I kept reflecting that I had designed the workshop incorrectly ... but then I listened to the tapes of the sessions (for the third time) and heard the questions that people were asking, and somehow the stories behind those questions appeared as well. But this was after many weeks of reflecting, without actually HEARING.

Another aspect that emerged very clearly as being valuable in undertaking these cycles was the presence of others with whom to share ideas,

but also from whom to obtain support and encouragement. Reason and Marshall (1987) write about the importance of having others to engage with around inquiry processes, 'friends who will be willing to act as enemies' (and friends who are willing to act as friends) in order to help the researcher identify blind spots in their thinking or unearth assumptions that are colouring their sense-making. This was certainly key to Fiona, who succeeded in making a change in her personal presentation:

> It was only through talking with my friends about what I was trying to achieve, what its meaning was for me that I was able to continue. I went through that cycle a number of times, going in, noticing the way I was received, re-engaging with my friends, until I was finally able to enter a room and say, 'This is me.'

These cycles did not necessarily 'stop' at the point at which the researcher thought the research was complete and began 'writing up'. In Margaret's case, for example, as she started writing she began to see that the core of her inquiry lay in a very different place from where she had imagined it, and other researchers spoke of similar experiences. This phenomenon will be explored in greater detail under the topic of 'emergence', but seems important in emphasizing that in reality, cycles of action and reflection do not necessarily end when the researcher believes they are complete!

To bear in mind

Cycles of action and reflection are a key aspect of undertaking action research; in fact they offer a template for conducting this kind of research. Experiences of researchers engaged in these cycles adds:

- Cycles of inquiry are whole-person events, and involve the researcher's physical, emotional and psychological capacities as well as their intellectual ones.
- Inquiry cycles are 'messy', and are not necessarily discrete or linear. They can move much more fluidly, double back on themselves, and take unpredictable routes.
- Moving from fog to clarity and back to fog can be part of the process. Just because the inquiry is making less sense does not necessarily mean you are going in the wrong direction.
- Having others to reflect with, both to challenge and to provide encouragement and support, is crucial.

COLLABORATION

Reason and Bradbury (2001) stress the centrality of the collaborative nature of action research in the very subtitle of their volume, 'Participative Inquiry and Practice'. In earlier writing, Reason (1988, 1994) makes the distinction that action research is research *with* people, rather than *on* people. But what does this kind of participative approach mean in practice? This is particularly paradoxical as the impetus to engage in inquiry is often born of a strong desire on the researcher's part to improve a situation or have a positive benefit for those involved. As one of the participants on the workshop asked, 'How do I remain participative when I'm so opinionated?'

Further to this question is that concerning the responsibility of the initiator of an action research process, particularly in the early stages of a project. I myself found this a challenge in the design of the workshops to elicit material for this chapter. The days were framed as a collaborative inquiry into action research in practice. I designed a day that I hoped would encourage people to tell their stories of the doing of action research. But how collaborative should one be to obtain the kind of 'output' one wants (or thinks they want) from such an event? My journal entry from the first day's workshop recounted:

> I suggested people pair off and share a specific story about their experience of doing action research. These pairs would join another pair, and the listener of the story in the previous dyad would tell her or his partner's story in the new quartet. From these foursomes, one story would be chosen to share in the large group, with issues and themes from other stories feeding into it.
>
> I asked for their response, and was met with protest. 'Many of us have only begun our inquiries, we're not really at the point of telling stories about them.' 'Can we move into fours first of all, without the pair work?' My heart sank. I was worried about losing the richness of the stories that get told in pairs rather than in quartets. I shared this concern with the group. 'We promise we'll still tell our stories.' A bit more negotiation, but it was clear the group preferred to work in 'fours'. All right. I did ask for their views, I did say I would be flexible, this is supposed to be a collaborative event.

In fact, the stories did not appear in the way I had hoped. Instead, people reported back general 'themes' and questions they had tussled with as they had engaged in their projects. Later, on listening to the tapes, I realized there was a stronger process going on that was affecting what actually could be disclosed in that day. This was a group dynamic process, something every action researcher involved in researching with more than two people should be aware of.

Group Dynamics

Second-person inquiries require some basic understanding of group processes and dynamics. In reflecting on my design choices for the first workshop, I probably did not account adequately for the dynamics that would be present in the group. In my haste to capture the grounded material I wanted for this chapter, I failed to take into account that such stories would make individuals feel vulnerable, especially in such a large group. E-mail correspondence after the event with Elizabeth, one of the participants, confirmed this: 'I think I remember feeling overwhelmed because my story seems so long and unformed, I'll only know it when I've written it up ... it brought out all the fears of being exposed as a fraud and all my anxieties about "is what I've done really Action Research?" '

Even taking into account the effects of group dynamics, there is still a requirement on the part of the action researcher to work sensitively between strong and shared ownership. In practice there seems to be no clear answer to how the dance between ownership and participation is done 'correctly'. However, there were certain sensitivities that emerged as being important in negotiating this dynamic, which includes aspects of power and politics, as well as speaking to issues of commitment and vision.

Movement between strong and shared ownership

A story told by Christine and Carole during the second workshop illustrates this point. Christine and Carole were committed to bringing issues of 'sustainability' to the attention of an influential organization with which they were involved. Although they were committed to the 'content' of 'sustainability', they were also keen to use collaborative processes:

> We went to the Chief Executive of the organization and said we wondered if he had considered the importance of issues of sustainability in his organization. 'What's sustainability?' he asked. Chris replied and he said, 'OK, well, go write me a paper about it.' We wrote a short paper and presented it to him. In the meantime, he'd been doing some homework, too. 'From what I'm reading in your paper and finding out in newspapers and magazines', he said, 'and from what people are saying,

this is all about ethics.' 'OK', we thought, 'if that's the way he's framing it, that's our entry point.'

From that point, they altered their approach to embrace the personal and political requirements of the situation. This included engaging a third (male) consultant to work with them, accommodating an unagreed 'Steering Committee' in their negotiations and planning, and altering the representation of their 'findings' to respond to the personal and political needs of the Chief Executive. In particular, they were sensitive to the differences in their own view of the project, and the personal and political realities of the organization:

> For us, the highlight of what we were selling was the *process* by which we would glean insights and information. We were committed to using a participative action inquiry approach as a way of discovering the actual concerns of people who were members of the organization, rather than their reactions to an imposed framework. Our client, however, was much more concerned with the *outcomes* we would formulate. He was also very concerned about how the project (and his endorsement of it) would be perceived in the wider industry sector and beyond. The two key words at the forefront of our discussions were 'caution', and 'credibility'.

Christine and Carole continually found ways of working collaboratively within the organization, being both responsive to its needs while forwarding their own initiative and way of working. Sometimes, however, the entire focus of an inquiry needs to change in order to take into account co-inquirers.

For example, Geoff, who works as a police officer, spoke of wanting to conduct a co-operative inquiry into 'masculinity within the police force' during one phase of his project. He gathered a group of men together to do this, and discovered that although they were willing to take part because they liked him and wanted to help him out, this wasn't an area of central concern to them. By thinking more broadly and aligning himself with political agendas within the organization, he refocused the inquiry into 'leadership' within the force. This met with much greater levels of interest from both individuals and policy-makers, and has led to further developments within the force itself.

Geoff's example speaks to the importance of the initiator of the inquiry being able to hold the broadest notion possible about the 'purpose' of the inquiry. Working collaboratively does not mean that there is no initiating, holding or leadership function required. It does call for a style of enacting that function that is sensitive to the emergent quality of inquiry, along with an ability to articulate perceptions of what is happening and openness to other interpretations of those perceptions. It also calls for a sensitivity to the political implications and processes involved.

Power and Politics

Christine and Carole's story illustrates how their flexibility enabled them to enter the system and incorporate organizational realities in their process. The story also illustrates the political nature of this kind of engagement and the importance of being able to respond to these realities without holding fast to a notion of 'purity' of method. It can be a challenge for the action researcher to frame the politics they encounter in their project as part of the content of the inquiry, rather than an annoying irritant that 'gets in the way'. For instance, Rupesh offered:

> Having a clear theoretical model, in this case, 'learning histories' was very useful in helping me gain access to the organization. But once I was inside the organization, the method started to unravel because of internal politics. I began to see that I needed to embrace the tensions in the system, see them as the actual content of my inquiry. The theories are clear – out there the world is messy.

To bear in mind

- Working in a collaborative manner still requires a leadership function, even if it is providing a 'holding space' for the inquiry to unfold.
- An awareness of group dynamics is important; groups have to reach a certain level of maturity before they are able to engage in certain levels of collaboration and responsibility.
- Political dynamics may require flexibility and willingness to embrace organizational realities as part of the research frame.
- There is no *right* way of 'being collaborative'. Instead, it is important that the researcher continually be aware of the choices he or she is making about the level of ownership he or she is exercising, and whether or not that is appropriate from a number of different perspectives.

EMERGENCE

'Emergence' is possibly one of the most slippery ideas with which the action researcher needs to grapple in practice. In theory, the action researcher is working with less deterministic hypotheses than those experimenting within a more positivist frame. She or he is invited to begin with an intention and some idea of method, and enable a process to unfold (Cook, 1998).

In reality, however, it is more difficult to be free of these predetermined views of what an outcome should be, or how the process should 'go'. This is true throughout the process, but during the workshops it was raised as an issue particularly at the point at which the researcher believes the work is 'done', and there is only 'writing up' to do. This was the case in Margaret's experience:

> I began writing at the point where the two major consultancy projects had finished, and with them the end of a major phase of my inquiry. I was fired up by successful final conferences and a sense of completion ... I felt excited at the idea of writing about the new methods I had developed through inquiry and felt it would also be affirming to colleagues who had worked with me. I planned to write case studies describing how I had introduced reflexive practices into my work and designed change interventions that involved inquiry groups.
>
> BUT as I began to write, something completely different began to happen, something I didn't want to have happen at all. As I wrote, different inner voices began to speak and demand attention, complaining, talking about the painful experiences I'd had in relation to colleagues and clients while I'd been involved in the inquiry. They spoke for example of my recurrent experience of not getting recognition and not being properly valued in these work-based relationships.
>
> Being confronted in this way was extremely uncomfortable. The more I wrote, the more they gained momentum and the more painful the process became. In the end, I had to ask myself, 'Am I going to put my money where my mouth is and inquire into what's happening here?' I remembered that what had driven me to take up the inquiry in the first place was my experience of the difficult aspect of work-based relationships with women. I'd conveniently forgotten this impetus as I sat down to write my success story. And so it was to this focus that I returned.

Margaret could have ignored the process, she could have persevered and written what she planned to write. But her story indicates that this kind of research process can seem to have its own volition, its own unfolding story to tell. When things are not going 'right', when the researcher is feeling frustrated or not understanding, that is perhaps the point where the researcher's predetermined idea of where an inquiry should go, and where it actually wants to go, have diverged. Recognizing this divergence

and paying attention to what it might be saying calls for a particular kind of sensitivity on the part of the researcher.

In putting together material for this chapter, I faced a similar point of frustration and lack of clarity. Once again I turned to the tapes of the two days we had spent together, but this time instead of carefully transcribing text, I listened to the flow of conversation, the points at which there was energy and excitement in the voices. I had held a predetermined outcome in mind; I wanted stories of practitioners' experiences that would illustrate key themes of the action research process. The previous two times when I'd listened to the tapes, I hadn't heard stories. But this time I began to hear, not the 'lack of what I wanted to hear', but the group asking a myriad of questions. And as I started to hear those questions, I also began to hear the stories behind the questions. It was like seeing the opposite image in a picture that contains both. This made me realize that my desired outcome for the inquiry – stories – was inhibiting my ability to hear, really hear, what was going on for the group. But the process was evolving despite my framing of it. In retrospect, my frustration could be explained by my trying to make an emergent process fit my expectation. Instead, I had to free myself of what I was looking for, in order that I could see what was emerging, rather than what I'd decided would emerge.

Paying particular attention to one's own emotional reaction to what is going on is helpful too. Judi told the story of her engagement with the 'women in management' literature:

> I was reading all this material in the library, and I noticed I was feeling completely bored by it. Here was the field I wanted to engage in, that I had spent much of my time thinking about, but the literature was putting me to sleep. I noticed this, and realized I needed to come at the area from another direction, there was another way of framing and exploring the reality of women's experiences at work. Out of that realization came the book 'Women Managers: Travellers in a Male World'.

Whereas traditional research methods would advise the researcher to be as 'detached' as possible, this experience seems to argue that in order to be sensitive to the emergent volition of a research project, one's own emotional reaction is important to notice and respond to.

To bear in mind

- Being sensitive to emergent processes requires a 'state of mind', an openness that can be difficult to maintain if the researcher is determined to 'improve' a situation. A component of that way of being is a deep belief on the part of the researcher that she or he does not know the answers before beginning.

- This openness of mind would ideally strive to find ways of taking into account aspects of a situation that seem unimportant or trivial. Co-researchers who are outside the situation can be useful in pointing to key features that the researcher may be ignoring.

- The emotional response a researcher is experiencing may be an important source of data about deeper understandings or new framings that lie below the surface of intellectual engagement.

- Emergence is an unfolding process subject to its own workings and time-frames. Sometimes a pattern cannot emerge until necessary parts of the 'puzzle' are present. Cultivating a respect for not-knowing is essential for working with emergent processes.

GOING 'PUBLIC'

Often the 'product' of action research is a change in the situation that has been under study, rather than a report about that change. However, the 'writing up' process can be part of formal study, or can be part of a contract with an involved organization or community. Two particular concerns were raised about 'presenting' action research as part of the workshops; these were finding form and transparency of accounts.

Finding form

One of the recurring questions that action researchers attending the workshop had grappled with was ways of 'presenting' their inquiries, which somehow captured the 'messiness' of the process, and the fact that it was ongoing rather than 'complete' while being understandable and of value to those outside the process. There was a view expressed by a number of researchers that they had to 'tidy up' their accounts in order to make them 'real research'. For instance, Wilhem offered: 'In the end my PhD ended up being very much about myself. I wondered at how I could have this accepted as "real" research ... I felt I had to tidy it up, explain things away to make it acceptable.'

This seems to express something of the tension between the researcher's experience of the process as being cyclical, unplanned, punctuated by flashes

of insight – 'messy' – and the expectations and needs of the reading audience that arguments be linear and clear, that conclusions should be reached. This is demonstrated by Christine and Carole's story, which is recounted here, along with the solution they found to providing their client with an output both parties could appreciate:

Our project was being enacted in parallel for the development of a 'body of knowledge' being researched and written about other aspects of the organization's work. When complete, this body of knowledge would sit on the organization's website, accessible to members wanting to gain knowledge on a range of topics. The other areas were being researched by desk researchers and completed by consulting firms with expertise in specific topic areas. Our contribution to the body of knowledge would be very different, it was created through the interaction of over two hundred members of the organization over a period of six to nine months. We anticipated that the nature of the knowledge produced by our project would also be different: emerging knowledge and questions rather than a clear set of principles and implications. We were confident that the richness of what we would discover would override the client's misgivings about the process we were using.

Following our second workshop we produced two large reports to be included in the organization's body of knowledge. The first included information about how we undertook the inquiry and what happened as the process unfolded. It contained a huge amount of dialogue, just about everything anyone had said during the two days of events was written up, along with all the virtual inputs. The document was loosely structured around recurrent issues and themes.

The Steering Committee members were concerned about including this largely unprocessed document as they saw it as 'just people talking'. They were keen to see clearly laid out arguments, tools that people could easily pick up and use rather than what they saw as people's opinions. So, we re-examined what we'd produced, looking at it particularly through the frame of sustainability and ethics. We created a structure which presented the paradoxes inherent within the field and illustrated these by bringing in real bits of dialogue from our workshops.

We further widened the debate by incorporating ideas from other experts and commentators working in the fields of sustainability and ethics. Around a given topic we would present differing views in the form, 'Here's what people are saying, here are some things you might think about, here are a few models to use, such as Triple Bottom Line accounting, there aren't any clear-cut answers but here are some things to try.'

We were very aware as we were writing the second document of our process of making choices. We'd say, 'That's a good quote, let's include that'; and then quiz ourselves – why did we see it as a good quote? Aware of our own bias and agenda, we were concerned to produce a 'balanced view'. We believed if we went too far down one track, we would put people off. One of the insights we'd had over the course of the project was that many times dissent about sustainability was actually born of lack of understanding of the issues. We wanted to create a document which would help people achieve a level of understanding around the issues that would enable them to reach their own conclusions.

The story illustrates the need for flexibility and responsiveness to the client organization, as well as holding on to a clear view of what it meant to be handling the project in a way congruent with the philosophy of action research. Another point that this story raises is the notion of a 'balanced view: what does it mean to have a 'balanced view' within a research paradigm that recognizes the subjectivity of the researcher? In conversation, Judi suggested: 'all research is biased in some way, it is about recognizing your bias, being as upfront about it as possible and recognizing how it will colour your interpretations. It is about understanding the choices you make, rather than not making them.' In other words, critical subjectivity must play a part in the awareness one brings to the form-finding process, as well as all the other parts of an action research project.

Transparency

Action researchers are encouraged to be as 'transparent' as possible in their use of methods and their engagement with co-inquirers. This can be understood in terms of 'relational practice', that the researcher works with his or her co-researchers and together they decide how to move forward and what is important for them to inquire into. In other words, in an ideal world, the 'wool is not pulled over the eyes' of co-researchers for the furtherance of some ideal of 'objective truth'. Transparency also means being as truthful as possible about the reasons behind choices taken in the research process, and in being committed to articulating biases that affect framings and interpretations. During the workshop, the extent to which being completely transparent is actually possible was discussed. The conversation circled around the idea that 'the opposite of deceitfulness is not necessary complete transparency'. Peter expressed the view that there is a different kind of complexity and subtlety involved here. He suggested: 'Being collaborative or participative doesn't mean you have to be transparent all of the time. You don't need to give away your own space, your own privacy. It's a much more complex quality than that.'

Instead of striving for 'complete transparency', which is never possible, it was seen as important to hold questions concerning the purpose of the project and the level of transparency that was appropriate given that purpose. Once again, the political implications of revelations were also seen as important to be considered.

Margaret coined something of the meaning of this when she spoke of 'integrated subjectivity'. Whereas we use the term 'critical subjectivity' to mean the ability to articulate the frames and biases from which you are perceiving, integrated subjectivity, for Margaret, meant being able to decide what level and form of subjectivity was appropriate to a given situation. Her study was largely a first-person inquiry into her working relationships with other women, and she chose not to disclose her research with them as she saw its purpose primarily about making changes to her own framings and subsequent behaviours. She reported:

> This is where I see it is important to recognize the different ways in which one goes public when doing research, and to be clear about the purpose and politics of how to frame one's findings to different audiences in the public arena. There is part of me that feels badly about not sharing my inquiry process more fully with those colleagues about the part they played in my research. I feel I should have shared more about my own inquiry process. But then I wonder what purpose would that serve, and would it cause more possible damage? These are questions I am still grappling with. I would have liked to have had an account that was less personal and more easily shared and affirming of our collective achievements. These accounts are what I am now developing – going public in a different way with parts of my inquiry that are more easily shared and which offer useful inquiry methods to others to strengthen collaborative relationships – my next phase of 'going public'.

To bear in mind

- Finding form to represent a study is as much a part of the action research process as the 'doing' part of the inquiry. The process of 'finding form' itself can create new insights and push the inquiry into different directions.
- Finding form is often a collaborative process, one that has to give according to organizational or community needs and politics. There is no one right way of negotiating these waters; clear intent (to remain collaborative and open to other viewpoints) should be a guiding principle.
- There are varying degrees of 'transparency' available in going public with a project.

Sensitivity to the political dimension and the ultimate purpose of the project is key in making choices about the level of transparency to reveal.

ACTION RESEARCH: POSSIBILITY OR ASPIRATION?

During the second workshop, at a point in the discussion that had turned towards the compromises researchers inevitably have to make in the undertaking of their inquiries, Peter suggested: 'Action research is an aspiration, rather than a possibility.'

One way of understanding this assertion is that the theory of action research suggests that it occurs in an ideal world. In this world, every member of a researcher's co-operative inquiry group attends every meeting (they usually can't), cycles of action and reflection move continually towards greater and greater clarity (they don't), the researcher knows the level of responsibility and ownership to take in every situation in order to be appropriately 'collaborative' (impossible), and at the very least, one's tape recorder always works and produces crystal-clear reproductions (probably not!).

Instead, real researchers engaged with these approaches must tussle with a range of 'confounding' factors, including various levels of commitment and engagement from co-inquirers who promised unerring support at the beginning of a project, political machinations within organizations that can turn an agreed-upon project topsy-turvy, the discovery that the focus of an inquiry that has taken up a considerable amount of time is completely wrong, or even internal battles within the researcher her or himself as she or he encounters the implications of new insight. Furthermore, the action researcher is encouraged not to see these as 'inconveniences' to be 'got round', but as key contributing factors within the research frame itself.

Even if an action research project proceeds smoothly, at the very least there is the impossibility of action researchers ever being completely aware of their own biases and frames, therefore always calling into question the veracity of their interpretations (but of course this is true for anyone engaged in any form of research).

But perhaps within this apparent paradox is a nugget at the heart of doing action research well. In striving towards an ideal of collaboration, working towards an articulation of the self's frame for perceiving, or committing to reflection and action, even though it is impossible to do any

of these perfectly, the researcher embraces something of the essence of what it is to be human working towards the betterment of human conditions. Perfect 'action research' cannot exist. At its root is the unpredictability and confounding nature of human beings and our systems. Taking authentic action itself is risky and has unpredictable consequences. The success of the action researcher must in some way be measured by his or her willingness to grapple with messiness and imperfections and the impossibility of ever getting it 'right' while still holding a notion of the possibility of a research method that contributes, as Reason and Bradbury (2001) suggest, to the 'flourishing of the human spirit'.

ACKNOWLEDGEMENTS

I should like to acknowledge and thank all those in the CARPP community who contributed their time and input to this chapter, and especially Peter Reason, Judi Marshall, Jack Whitehead and Steve Taylor who generously offered their comments on draft versions.

REFERENCES

Argyris, C. and Schön, D (1974) *Theory in Practice: Increasing Professional Effectiveness.* San Francisco: Jossey Bass.

Argyris, C. and Schön, D. (1978) *Organizational Learning.* Reading, MA: Addison-Wesley.

Arhar, J.M., Holly, M.L. and Kasten, W.C. (2001) *Action Research for Teachers: Traveling the Yellow Brick Road.* Englewood Cliffs, NJ: Merrill/Prentice-Hall.

Carr, W. and Kemmis, S. (1986) *Becoming Critical: Education, Knowledge and Action Research.* Geelong, Victoria: Deakin University Press.

Cook, T. (1998) 'The importance of mess in action research', *Educational Action Research,* 6: 93–109.

Fals Borda, O. and Rahman, M.A. (eds) (1991) *Action and Knowledge: Breaking the Monopoly with Participatory Action Research.* New York: Intermediate Technology/Apex.

Gustavsen, Bjorn (2001) 'Theory and practice: the mediating discourse', in P. Reason and H. Bradbury (eds), *Handbook of Action Research: Participative Inquiry and Practice.* London: Sage, pp. 17–26.

Habermas, J. (1979) *Communication and the Evolution of Society.* Boston: Beacon Press.

Heron, John (1971) 'Experience and method, an inquiry into the concept of experiential research'. Human Potential Research Project, University of Surrey.

Heron, John (1981) 'Philosophical basis for a new paradigm', in P. Reason and J. Rowan (eds), *Human Inquiry: A Sourcebook of New Paradigm Research.* Chichester: John Wiley, pp. 19–37.

Heron, John (1992) *Feeling and Personhood: Psychology in Another Key.* London: Sage.

Heron, John (1996) *Co-operative Inquiry: Research into the Human Condition.* London: Sage.

Janesick, Valerie (1999) 'A journal about journal writing as qualitative research technique, history issues and reflections', *Qualitative Inquiry,* 5(4): 505–24.

Kelly, James G., Mock, Lynne and Davies Tandem, S. (2001) 'Collaborative inquiry with African American community leaders: comments on participatory action research process', in P. Reason and H. Bradbury (eds), *Handbook of Action Research: Participative Inquiry and Practice.* London: Sage, pp. 348–56.

Lincoln, Yvonna (2001) 'Engaging sympathies: relationships between action research and social constructivism', in P. Reason and H. Bradbury (eds), *Handbook of Action Research: Participative Inquiry and Practice.* London: Sage, pp. 124–32.

Lykes, M. Brinton (2001) 'Creative arts and photography in participatory action research in Guatemala', in P. Reason and H. Bradbury (eds), *Handbook of Action Research: Participative Inquiry and Practice.* London: Sage, pp. 363–71.

McKernan, J. (1996) *Curriculum Action Research: A Handbook of Methods and Resources for the Reflective Practitioner* (2nd ed.). London: Kogan Page.

Marshall, Judi and Reason, Peter (1994) 'Adult learning in collaborative action research: reflections on the supervision process', *Studies in Continuing Education: Research and Scholarship in Adult Education,* 15(2): 117–32.

Martin, Anne (2001) 'Large group processes as action research', in P. Reason and H. Bradbury (eds), *Handbook of Action Research: Participative Inquiry and Practice.* London: Sage, pp. 200–8.

Mills, G. (2000) *Action Research: A Guide for the Teacher Researcher.* Englewood Cliffs, NJ: Prentice-Hall.

Pring, Richard (2000) *Philosophy of Educational Research.* London: Continuum.

Reason, Peter (1994) 'Three approaches to participatory inquiry', in N.K. Denzin and Y.S. Lincoln (eds), *Handbook of Qualitative Research.* London: Sage, pp. 324–39.

Reason, Peter (ed.) (1988) *Human Inquiry in Action: Developments in New Paradigm Research.* London: Sage.

Reason, Peter (1999) 'Integrating action and reflection through co-operative inquiry', *Management Learning* special issue: 'The Action Dimension in Management: Diverse Approaches to Research, Teaching and Development', 30(2): 207–27.

Reason, Peter and Bradbury, Hilary (eds) (2001) *Handbook of Action Research: Participative Inquiry and Practice.* London: Sage.

Reason, Peter and McArdle, Kate (2003) 'Brief notes on the theory and practice of action research', in Saul Becker and Alan Bryman (eds), *Understanding Research Methods for Social Policy and Practice.* London: Sage, in Press.

Reason, Peter and Marshall, Judi (1987) 'Research as personal process', in D. Boud and V. Griffen (eds), *Appreciating Adult Learning.* London: Kogan Page, pp. 112–26.

Reason, Peter and Torbert, William (2001) 'The action turn: toward a transformational action science', *Concepts and Transformation,* 6(1): 36–52.

Schön, D.A. (1993) *The Reflective Practitioner: How Professionals Think in Action.* New York: Basic Books.

Stringer, P. and Bannister, D. (eds) (1979) *Constructs of Sociality and Individuality.* New York: Academic Press.

Styhre, Alexander, Kohn, Kamilla and Sundgren, Mats (2002) 'Action research as theoretical practices', *Concepts and Transformation,* 7(1): 93–105.

Swantz, Marja-Liisa and Vainio-Mattila, Arja (1988) 'Participatory inquiry as an instrument of grass-roots development', in P. Reason (ed.), *Human Inquiry in Action: Developments in New Paradigm Research.* London: Sage, pp. 127–43.

Torbert, W.R. (1991a) *The Power of Balance: Transforming Self, Society and Scientific Inquiry.* Newbury Park, CA: Sage.

Torbert, W.R. (1991b) 'Teaching action inquiry', *Collaborative Inquiry,* 5: 217–32.

Torbert, W.R. (1998) 'Developing wisdom and courage in organizing and sciencing', in S. Srivastva and D. Cooperrinder (eds), *Organizational Wisdom and Executive Courage.* San Francisco: New Lexington Press, pp. 189–206.

Torbert, W.R. (2001) 'The practice of action inquiry', in P. Reason and H. Bradbury (eds), *Handbook of Action Research: Participative Inquiry and Practice.* London: Sage, pp. 250–60.

Toulmin, M. and Gustavsen, B. (eds) (1996) *Beyond Theory: Changing Organizations through Participation.* Amsterdam: John Benjamins.

Whyte, W.F. (ed.) (1991) *Participatory Action Research.* Newbury Park, CA: Sage.

Winter, R., Buck, A. and Sobiechowska, P. (1999) *Professional Experience and the Investigative Imagination: The Art of Reflective Writing.* London: Routledge.

35

Teaching qualitative method: craft, profession, or bricolage?

Martyn Hammersley

The teaching of qualitative research methodology is surrounded by a host of difficult issues today, so much so that one sometimes wonders whether the task is even possible; or, at least, whether it can be done well. Of course, it has long been viewed as a tricky enterprise. But now there are additional problems. For one thing, there is so much diversity in forms of qualitative inquiry, each contending with the others, that hard and controversial choices seem to be required – in terms of what can and cannot, should and should not, be covered.[1] At the same time, and perhaps most problematic of all, in Britain and no doubt elsewhere as well, there are external pressures for social research to be codified, and for students to be 'trained' in the necessary techniques. Quantitative method is often seen, quite wrongly, as a matter of simply following procedures.[2] And there are demands that this procedural or technical model be extended to qualitative inquiry as well. What this implies is that students need simply to be taught the range of available techniques, along with the rules about when these are – and are not – appropriate; as well as being given practice in their application. Yet, the very character of qualitative research is taken by most of its practitioners to be at odds with this procedural model; and with good reason.

The idea that research is a procedural matter implies that its course can, and *should*, be planned at the start, and the resulting research design then implemented. However, there are obvious practical reasons why much qualitative research cannot follow this pattern. As Everett Hughes noted: '… the situations and circumstances in which field observation of human behavior is done are so various that no manual of detailed rules would serve …'; though he insists that the basic problems faced by all field researchers are more or less the same (Hughes, 1960: x). Doing research in 'natural' settings – that is, under conditions that are not specifically designed for carrying out research – and often over relatively long periods of time, means that one must adapt the research process to the situation and to any significant changes in it. This may be necessary even just to 'survive' in the field. Of course there are also specifically methodological reasons why qualitative research cannot usually be a matter of following some pre-specified plan. For one thing, failure to adapt to the situation being studied is likely to maximize reactivity, and thereby to threaten the validity of the research findings. Furthermore, the open-ended approach to data analysis that is characteristic of qualitative research means that what data are required will change over time; they cannot be identified reliably at the beginning.

This is not to deny that there are approximations to procedural rules in qualitative research. One candidate today might be 'audio-record interviews'. And, generally speaking, this is good advice. However, it is not an absolute or unproblematic requirement. It is important to be prepared for the informant who refuses to have an interview recorded. The plans of one of my students were thrown into disarray when the school pupils he intended to interview refused to have their words tape-recorded; he had to learn very rapidly how to take notes while listening and asking questions. There are also cases where audio-recording interviews is likely to result in important issues or views not being mentioned. Another of my students, whose research topic was loneliness, decided (probably quite rightly) that the people she had recruited via an advert in newspapers and magazines would be inhibited by the presence of a tape recorder in talking about their experience. She also realized that, since the interviews were to take place in bars and cafés, there would probably be too much background noise for audio-recording to be of any value. And the point is not just that, as in these cases, 'normal practice' may be impossible or inappropriate. Assumptions about normal practice can actually restrict the options considered in planning or carrying out a piece of research. While audio-recording of formal interviews is now usual, ethnographers do not generally try to tape-record the occasional, unpredictable conversations they have with participants during the course of their work. Yet, as a colleague of mine found, in some contexts it may be possible to get permission to do this, carrying the tape recorder with you and switching it on whenever appropriate (see Scarth, 1986: 182, 195–8). So, even in relation to this specific issue, what is possible and desirable is to some extent a contingent matter.

In short, then, for both practical and methodological reasons, it is not desirable to try to plan and carry out qualitative research under the guidance of some fixed set of methodological rules; though it is advisable to try to anticipate possible difficulties. Rather, there is a need for sensitivity as regards both topic and context; and for adaptation in the field, including flexibility in exploring what *might* be possible in particular circumstances. A commitment to '*normal* practice' can get in the way of '*good* practice'.

Of course, *philosophical* arguments are also often used against applying the procedural model to qualitative research. It is sometimes suggested that because every person, including both researcher and researched, has a distinctive socio-cultural location, it is always necessary to *find one's way* towards any understanding of social situations; how to do this cannot be standardized, or specified beforehand. Equally, there may be an insistence on the importance of creativity in research, and in social life more generally. From this point of view, research can no more be reduced to following rules than can producing a work of art. Or, at least, any attempt at such a reduction will amount to pursuing an inauthentic form of human action – not exercising one's full powers but acting like a robot – and it will, as a result, misrepresent the nature of human social life. In this vein, Williams writes that, since human conduct 'is seen [by field researchers] to be the work of self-conscious creativity rather than the product of internal or external predispositions or forces which act to determine conduct', it is not surprising that for them research itself must partake of the same character. He therefore argues for '... a view of data creation practices as less the operation of

neutral techniques, and more the development and exploitation of intimate participation in the life of those under study' (Williams, 1981: 559).

The procedural model has also sometimes been rejected on the grounds that it is ideological: that it systematically obscures the fact that how research is done, and thereby what findings are produced, necessarily reflect the personal and social characteristics of the researcher. In light of this, the demand is often made that qualitative researchers be reflexive: that, throughout the course of inquiry, they continually subject their own practice to scrutiny, in both methodological and ethical terms; and that they make explicit for readers their own role in producing the findings. This is a line of argument that initially arose with the publication of 'natural histories' of research, was given particular emphasis by feminists, and is now widely accepted.[3]

Finally, from postmodernism and other sources may be drawn the idea that the path that any research project follows is necessarily both constitutive and contingent; that it is under the control of nothing and no one, and *represents* nothing and no one – certainly not Reality or Rationality. Instead, the research process must be seen as a matter of formally arbitrary 'decisions' among incommensurable possibilities. Here, we are as far as we could be from the idea that research involves following the procedures of scientific method.

There are, then, a variety of grounds on which qualitative researchers reject what I have called the procedural model of inquiry; and it is not difficult to see that these have implications for views about how (and whether) qualitative methodology can be taught. In the next section, I shall look at some alternative models of qualitative research, and at their implications for pedagogy.

ALTERNATIVES TO THE PROCEDURAL MODEL

There are many different ways in which qualitative inquiry can be conceptualized. Here, I shall focus on just three: as a craft, as a profession, and as bricolage. These seem to me to capture the most important variations that are relevant to the task we face today in trying to teach others how to do qualitative research.[4]

Craft work

The notion of a craft is, in some ways, the closest of the three alternatives to the procedural model.[5] Its advocates share an unwillingness to move very far in methodological terms from what is required in actually doing research. Despite this, there are some important differences between these two models. A craft involves learning something that is more tacit and elusive than a set of techniques. As a result, proponents of this model are sometimes antagonistic towards methodology as a specialized activity. Thus, C. Wright Mills, writing about 'intellectual craftmanship', begins his discussion by commenting that 'useful discussions of method and of theory usually arise as marginal notes on work-in-progress or work about to get under way' (Mills, 1959: 25). And he goes on to insist that each researcher must be his or her own methodologist (Mills, 1959: 26), a point that Becker later reinforced (Becker, 1970: ch. 1). Mills does not deny that codification of procedures can be worthwhile, but he insists that great caution must be exercised about this. He comments that 'Every craftsman can of course learn something from over-all attempts to codify methods, but it is often not much more than a general kind of awareness' (Mills, 1959: 26).

To a large extent, what is required for research competence from the point of view of the craft model is the building up of skills; and skills are by their nature practical rather than technical.[6] In other words, they cannot be codified in such a way as to be transmitted simply by explicit instruction from one person to another. As Leonard comments, research skills are 'learned by coaching: they are "caught" rather than taught' (Leonard, 2000: 187). Furthermore, in general terms, skills are flexible. The skill of riding a bike, for example, involves not only being able to stay on it but also to deal with various routine, and not so routine, contingencies that can arise in the course of the activity; including taking precautionary action against danger from other vehicles. So, the idea of research as a craft not only points to its practical character but also allows for variation in what has to be dealt with, and a consequent recognition that the course of inquiry cannot be pre-programmed or entirely anticipated. Mills captures this with his insistence that the researcher must master method, *not be mastered by it* (Mills, 1959: 25).

Equally important, the notion of research as a craft involves recognition that one will not always be sure about the exact nature of the problem one faces, and that it may be necessary to try out various strategies in order to find a solution. Relevant here are what Becker refers to as *Tricks of the Trade* (Becker, 1998). In this book he is concerned with the task of analysing data, but this concept can be extended to other aspects of the research process: to research design, data collection, and even to relations in the field.[7]

In some places Becker writes as if 'tricks' referred to ready-made solutions to standard problems. He comments: 'every trade has its tricks, its solutions to its own distinctive problems, easy ways of doing something lay people have a lot of trouble with. The social science trades, no less than plumbing or carpentry, have their tricks, designed to solve their peculiar problems. Some of these tricks are simple rules of thumb derived from experience, like the advice that putting colourful commemorative stamps on the return envelopes will get more people to send their questionnaires back' (Becker, 1998: 2–3). However, later he points out that some of the most important tricks are not simple, ready-made solutions:

> The word 'trick' usually suggests that the device or operation described will make things easier to do. In this case, that's misleading. To tell the truth, these tricks [the tricks discussed in *Tricks of the Trade*] probably make things harder for the researcher, in a special sense. Instead of making it easier to get a conventional piece of work done, they suggest ways of interfering with the comfortable thought routines academic life promotes and supports by making them the 'right' way to do things. This is a case where the 'right' is the enemy of the good. What the tricks do is suggest ways to turn things around, to see things differently, in order to create new problems for research, new possibilities for comparing cases and inventing new categories, and the like. All that is work. It's enjoyable, but it's more work than if you did things in a routine way that didn't make you think at all. (pp. 6–7)

Here we can see the divergence between the procedural and the craft models most clearly. Applied to the research process as a whole, Becker's notion of 'tricks of the trade' would recognize, first of all, that all situations are unique and involve contingent processes of interaction; so that there is always the possibility that what worked on one occasion may not suffice on others. Moreover, it is necessary already to have had some relevant experience in order even to recognize the likely value of particular 'tricks'. And knowing how to apply them to any specific case requires thought, it is not automatic. In this sense, tricks of the trade are *supplements* to practical experience; they are not algorithmic substitutes for it. Finally, some of them are concerned with disrupting normal, easy routines; they are designed to force the researcher to explore what is possible rather than making do with what is available.

The idea of research as a craft implies that what is involved in teaching methodology is initiating novitiates into an embodied tradition; in the sense of a set of skills and ways of thinking that has been built up collectively over time, and which marks out the expertise of members of the craft by comparison with those outside it. Researchers in a field are assumed to represent a community of practice engaged in distinct forms of 'situated cognition' (see Lave and Wenger, 1991; Chaiklin and Lave, 1993). And what is required of novitiates is not that they acquire a discrete body of abstract knowledge that they can then simply apply, but that they work their way into a certain form of *habitus*: an orientation and a range of skills that will enable them to pursue the craft well.

This implies that the emphasis in teaching should be on the practicalities of research, and on introducing students to these in concrete ways. Apprenticeship is the most obvious pedagogical relation in this context; or what Lave and Wenger refer to as 'legitimate peripheral participation', where the learner engages in the craft, but only to a limited extent and with limited responsibility for the outcome. And, indeed, Becker reports that he learned how to do sociological work from Everett Hughes, to a large extent 'by hanging around him and learning to use his tricks, the way apprentices learn craft skills by watching journeymen, who already know them, use them to solve real-life problems' (Becker, 1998: 3–4). Also important may be simulation of research tasks, so that students can acquire research skills through practice under the guidance of a teacher who is also a skilled researcher. Hughes was one of the pioneers here as well. He describes how it became a standard element of his introductory course in field research that 'Each student, alone or with another, made a series of observations in a Census Tract or other small area of Chicago outside his everyday experience and reported on these observations almost week by week' (Hughes, 1960: iv). And, of course, inclusion of a project element in courses that teach qualitative methodology has become very common today.[8]

As already noted, the emphasis in a craft is very much on doing the work; and interest in methodology is limited to what will be of more or less direct help in this. Mills, for example, argues that 'serious attention should be paid to general discussions of methodology only when they are in … reference to actual work…'. And he comments that if all social scientists followed this 'obvious and straightforward' practice 'at least all of us would then be at work on the problems of [social science]'. He claims that much methodological discussion simply 'disturb[s] people who are at work', as well as leading to 'methodological inhibition' (Mills, 1959: 27). In much the same spirit, Seale argues that 'intense methodological awareness, if engaged too seriously, can create anxieties that hinder practice', though (like Mills) he recognizes that 'if taken in small doses [methodology] can help to guard against more obvious errors' (Seale, 1999b: 475).

Mann has put forward an even more radical version of this argument. He claims that whatever theoretical or epistemological views researchers hold, they will do research in more or less the same way: that there is a common 'sociologic' that applies to all social scientific research. He comments: 'Now, students may wish to acquaint themselves with epistemological debates. Perhaps it is necessary for them to do this before they realize that only one philosophical choice is required: to do or not to do research. We would then teach epistemology to show that it doesn't matter. But as it bores most students stiff, there are strong grounds for regarding it as optional candy-floss in our courses' (Mann, 1981: 549).[9]

What this makes clear is that the idea of research as a craft carries the implication that there is no great need for students to be taught what we might call the philosophy of social research; indeed, that this may be counterproductive. After all, in the context of the craft model, few demands are made on researchers to justify what they do in terms that extend beyond pragmatic effectiveness. What is important is knowing what works, or what is likely to work, not necessarily why it works; and, even less, what philosophical justification could be provided for using one particular approach to inquiry rather than another. Moreover, while there is considerable flexibility in relation to means, the notion of a craft assumes that what is the intended product of inquiry is fixed and unproblematic; that there is little need for reflection on this. In these various ways, then, the craft model involves minimal reflexivity – and this is an important respect in which it contrasts with the remaining two models.

The researcher as professional

'Professionalism' is a concept that has become highly contested, both within the social sciences and beyond. To a large extent, the positive value previously attached to this label has been displaced, and even negated. Professionalism is now widely seen as no more than an occupational strategy designed to resist external accountability and/or as a restrictive practice that limits consumer choice. Moreover, the critical challenge to the notion of professionalism has come partly from qualitative researchers (see, e.g., Becker, 1970: ch. 6). Given all this, it might be thought that the notion of qualitative inquiry as a profession lacks plausibility. Nevertheless, it captures an important aspect of the way in which some qualitative researchers have conceptualized their work, even if the term itself is not always employed.[10]

I shall focus on just two elements often associated with professionalism. The first develops out of the notion of a craft. By its nature a craft is specialized: it is directed towards a particular task, and it draws on collective expertise built up in pursuing that task. What is involved here is 'dedication', in the sense in which some computers are dedicated to specific tasks. However, the moral sense of 'dedication' is also relevant: there is a commitment to put the occupational goal above all others, except perhaps *in extremis*.

Writing in the late 1960s in support of this commitment, Polsky notes what he describes as 'a retrograde development': that a number of sociologists have promoted 'extra-scientific goals in the name of science' (Polsky, 1971: 115). And this is a trend that has continued, albeit taking on new political colours: those of Marxism, anarchism, feminism, anti-racism and disability activism (see Hammersley, 2000). One effect of this has been that commitment to the professional model can generate sharp opposition, as one of my students discovered. He was hired as a research fellow on a project concerned with investigating the implementation of a multicultural and anti-racist policy in a secondary school, and he used this study as the basis for his PhD (see Foster, 1990). He was committed to providing an objective account of relevant practices in the school, but experienced considerable pressure to adopt a more partisan approach. This came not from the school but from other researchers. His report that there was little sign of systematic racism on the part of school personnel led to his being attacked as unable to recognize the racism that was allegedly taking place 'under his nose' (Connolly, 1992: 142); that his work was 'disabling rather than enabling' (Blair, 1993: 64); and that he was himself racist (Gillborn, 1995). Among other things, such reactions raise questions about what one's responsibilities are to students who adopt the professional model in areas where it is not generally supported.[11]

The other, closely associated, feature of the professional model is autonomy: that professionals must be able to exercise discretion in pursuing the occupational task. This should operate both at an individual and at a collective level. It is necessary for professionals to pursue their vocational goal in the way that they judge to be most effective, exercising a licence not just in terms of the selection of means but also in interpreting the meaning of the occupational task in particular cases. In these terms, the professional must have the autonomy to be a reflective practitioner (Schön, 1983).

At the same time, in the context of the professional model, this autonomy is properly limited, in both individual and collective terms. Above all, it is restricted to what can be justified as necessary for pursuit of the occupational task. This has interesting implications at the level of individual autonomy, in terms of what should and should not be tolerated by researchers on the part of one another; an issue that takes on further complexity in the context of teaching. Today, the tendency is for the boundaries of toleration to be set by general ethical and political principles; and an implication of my discussion of Foster's case is that this may unjustifiably restrict academic freedom. However, there will also be respects in which the distinctive character of professional autonomy restricts what is well within the boundaries of wider ethical and political legitimacy. In particular, what is open to proscription here is anything that is not justifiable as necessary for pursuit of the occupational goal; and, especially, anything that is *inimical* to pursuit of that goal.

These implications of the professional model can be illustrated by considering how to respond to a student who wishes to study childhood sexual abuse, approaching it from a constructionist point of view and suggesting that it is only constituted as a phenomenon in and through accounts given of it. While this approach is likely to be regarded in the wider political realm as ill-founded and insulting to those who have suffered such abuse, from the point of view of the professional model this is no reason to rule it out in an academic context. But doubts about its legitimacy *can* be raised on other grounds, to the extent that the student claims that whether childhood sexual abuse occurred in any particular instance is simply a matter of how the events concerned are narrated. This, it might be argued, denies some basic presuppositions of research: that there are phenomena independent of researchers' accounts of them, and that there cannot be contradictory truths about the world. Of course, on the basis of these presuppositions, the professional model would also rule out research applying such an extreme constructionist perspective to any other phenomenon, including sexual differences and ethnicity.[12]

I have never been faced with a case quite like this, but I *have* supervised a student whose project seemed initially to raise these problems. She did indeed set out to study the discursive structuring of an account of childhood sexual abuse. However, in her approach there was no suggestion that claims of abuse are simply fabrications, only 'true' if found persuasive; nor that the particular account she examined was untrue or fictitious. And what she produced was, in my view, a very illuminating analysis of how a particular case of childhood sexual abuse was discursively formulated (see Davies, 1995). Nevertheless, her research, and that of Foster, point to difficult issues associated with the professional model, and wider problems too. Is the teacher of qualitative method responsible for the ethics of students' work? And, if so, what ethical standards should be adopted in a context where there is a lack of consensus among researchers, and in the broader community?

The idea of qualitative research as a profession has some important pedagogical implications, then. First of all, we should note that, as with the craft model, it places considerable emphasis on the learning of practical skills; and so apprenticeship and simulation are likely to be a significant element of the education of researchers in qualitative methodology on this model as well. However, the two distinctive features of professions I have identified carry additional requirements. 'Dedication', for example, indicates the need to emphasize the ethical obligations of research. Yet, as I noted, the ethics of a profession are different from, and may even be in conflict with, what is believed to be ethical in other terms. The central emphasis must be on the duty of the researcher to try to ensure that what he or she produces is sound knowledge, not falsehood; though, of course, that goal should not be pursued at *any* cost – other ethical considerations will also have to be taken into account (see Hammersley, 2002b).

Another pedagogical implication stems from the fact that, by comparison with the craft model, the professional model involves the exercise of considerable reflexivity on the part of researchers, both individually and collectively, about how they pursue their work. This requires that new entrants acquire the cognitive resources necessary to engage in such reflection; they need to be introduced to literature on methodology, social theory, and philosophy that will facilitate this. Furthermore, they must learn to participate in communal discussion about these matters, even if only vicariously at first.

At the same time, though, this reflexivity is bounded: like autonomy, it is framed by commitment to the goal of pursuing knowledge. Professionals are not required to 'question all assumptions', nor allowed to be freely creative in rethinking the occupational task. The medical practitioner, as an individual, and medical practitioners collectively, cannot legitimately redefine the goal of medicine as, say, to maximize the economic productivity of the workforce, or to eliminate the sick in order to improve the average health of the population. Any such change in occupational task lies outside their realm of discretion; though attempts at change in these and other directions *are* open to legitimate resistance by them. Exactly the same is true of the researcher, according to the professional model. While professionalism implies considerable licence, it still involves a contract with lay people and their representatives about the goal of the activity, and this restricts researcher autonomy and the sort of reflexivity that is appropriate.

So while, in the terms used here, a profession requires more reflexivity on the part of its practitioners, and therefore on the part of those entering it, than does a craft, reflexivity is not valued for its own sake, only in so far as it serves the occupational goal. Indeed, new entrants must be socialized into a commitment to that goal, and to the ethics associated with it. And this is perhaps the sharpest point of conflict between the professional model and the view of qualitative research as bricolage, which I shall discuss in the next section.

Research as bricolage

The term 'bricolage' is used here to cover those views of research that treat it as an art – in a sense that extends beyond the notion of craft, and is quite opposed to the idea of a profession. In contemporary French usage, 'bricolage' refers to 'do it yourself', and 'bricoleur' is usually employed to refer to a 'handyman'. There is also a more specialized interpretation deriving from the work of the anthropologist Claude Lévi-Strauss. Here, bricolage, like craft, implies a pragmatic orientation, but it is distinctive in that it requires using creatively what is already at hand, rather than seeking out and applying specially designed, standard techniques:

> In its old sense the verb 'bricoler' applied to ball games and billiards, to hunting, shooting and riding. It was however always used with reference to some extraneous movement: a ball rebounding, a dog straying or a horse swerving from its direct course to avoid an obstacle. And in our own time the 'bricoleur' is still someone who works with his hands and uses devious means compared to those of a craftsman. (Lévi-Strauss, 1966: 16–17)

In craft and professional terms, this creativity could be interpreted negatively, as use of the wrong tools for the job. However, from the perspective of the bricoleur it is a positive feature.

Lévi-Strauss refers to intellectual as well as practical bricolage, focusing in the former case on the contrast that is often drawn between 'primitive' and 'civilized' thought, and the cognitive hierarchy that this involves. He contrasts mythical thinking, what he calls 'the science of the concrete', with modern science. While he does not see the former as simply inferior to the latter, he *does* regard them as different modes of thought: intellectual bricolage works with sensory appearances, whereas in his view science identifies underlying structural principles. He sees art as lying somewhere between bricolage and science, in its capacity to symbolize underlying structural determinants through the representation of concrete individual forms.

For Lévi-Strauss, anthropology is a science, and therefore anthropological research is not itself a form of bricolage or even of art. He emphasizes that, despite some similarities, there is a real difference between the scientist or engineer and the bricoleur, in that the former is 'always trying to make his way out of and go beyond the constraints imposed by a particular state of civilisation while the "bricoleur" by inclination or necessity always remains within them' (Lévi-Strauss, 1966: 19). However, some writers, notably Denzin and Lincoln, have argued that 'the multiple methodologies of qualitative research may be viewed as a bricolage, and the researcher as a *bricoleur*' (Denzin and Lincoln, 1994: 3). They take much of the meaning of these terms from Lévi-Strauss, though they also reformulate and elaborate on it, drawing on other sources as well. For example, they quote Nelson et al. (1992: 2) describing the methodology of cultural studies as bricolage, in that it is 'pragmatic, strategic and self-reflexive'.[13]

In some respects, what Denzin and Lincoln recommend under the heading of 'bricolage' is not at odds with the craft or professional models. At one point they describe it as 'the combination of multiple methods, empirical materials, perspectives and observers in a single study', this adding 'rigor, breadth, and depth to any investigation' (Denzin and Lincoln, 1994: 2). However, in other places it is quite clear that they have in mind a radical break with what has previously passed for qualitative research. In the second edition of their *Handbook*, they comment, 'We are all interpretive *bricoleurs* stuck in the present working against the past as we move into the future' (Denzin and Lincoln, 2000: xv). In this new edition, they describe the qualitative

researcher as 'bricoleur *and quiltmaker*' (Denzin and Lincoln, 2000: 4; emphasis added); and also draw an analogy with montage in films. They declare that 'the interpretive bricoleur produces a bricolage – that is, a pieced-together set of representations that are fitted to the specifics of a complex situation' (Denzin and Lincoln, 2000: 4). This is an 'emergent construction' which 'changes and takes new forms as different tools, methods, and techniques of representation and interpretation are added to the puzzle'.

It is fairly clear from this that for Denzin and Lincoln what bricolage produces is art; perhaps a kind of 'collage'. They comment that interpretive bricolage involves 'aesthetic issues, an aesthetics of representation that goes beyond the pragmatic, or the practical' (Denzin and Lincoln, 2000: 4); and there is also a political dimension. They write:

> In texts based on the metaphors of montage, quilt making, and jazz improvisation, many different things are going on at the same time – different voices, different perspectives, points of view, angles of vision. Like performance texts, works that use montage simultaneously create and enact moral meaning. They move from the personal to the political, the local to the historical and the cultural. These are dialogical texts. They presume an active audience. They create spaces for give-and-take between reader and writer. They do more than turn the other into the object of the social science gaze … . (Denzin and Lincoln, 2000: 5)

So, the bricolage model involves a significant move away from a scientific conception of qualitative inquiry – whether interpreted in terms of the procedural, craft, or professional models – and towards viewing it as a form of art. But it is worth noting a significant ambiguity in the meaning of 'art' here. In its older usage, the term was close in sense to 'craft'. In the twentieth century, however, 'art' has increasingly come to be applied only to what is creative, novel, surprising, or even shocking. Indeed, craft skill sometimes plays little or no role. What has become central to much contemporary art is personal expression and audience impact. Moreover, some art in the twentieth century has been precisely concerned with subverting the distinction between art and not-art, and with ironicizing the high status of art while yet capitalizing on it.

The meaning that Denzin and Lincoln give to 'bricolage' is close to this modern notion of art. Crudely speaking, such art is concerned with imaginative freedom, and to a large extent this means freedom from the constraints of 'reality'. Thus, in the case of impressionism, freedom took the form of a focus on the subjectivity of perception. In the case of cubism, it was a freeing of the artist from having to adopt a single perspective. With surrealism the preoccupation was freedom from censorship by the conscious mind, so that the task became exploration of the unconscious as a creative realm below, or beyond, the everyday world. And a similar search for freedom seems to underly the idea of qualitative research as bricolage.

What are the implications of thinking about qualitative research as bricolage, or as art, for whether and how it can be taught? It seems that almost by definition the bricoleur is self-taught – that is what leads to the ingenuity and novelty of what is produced.[14] Indeed, it might even be argued that bricoleurs are born, not made, and from this point of view too any attempt at teaching them would be counterproductive. Perhaps the only task for pedagogy here is to encourage students to question all assumptions, to abandon what they have come to take for granted in their lives. Here, reflexivity becomes an all-embracing, but essentially negative, task. Moreover, whereas in the professional model reflexivity required, as its fuel, a sound knowledge of relevant literatures, the orientation of the bricoleur to those literatures must presumably be the same as that towards any other resource: they should be approached in an ad hoc and selective way, being used for whatever purposes seem worthwhile at the time. Here, too, guidance is likely to be regarded as an obstruction, or at least as an irrelevance.

GENERIC PROBLEMS

I want to end by noting that whichever of these alternative models we select as a guide in teaching qualitative research methodology, we are faced with two generic problems. The first, mentioned earlier, is that there is considerable pressure today for qualitative inquiry to be proceduralized; and for students to be 'trained' in its techniques, in a manner that is at odds with good research of any kind. The emphasis here is on students being given 'access' to the various techniques that make up qualitative (and also quantitative) inquiry, and provided with practical instruction in using these techniques. This pressure leaves little scope for apprenticeship, for reflexivity, or for introducing students to the literatures that are required to feed this; even though the need for such things may be formally acknowledged. As a teacher, one is faced with a choice between having to present qualitative research simply as a set of techniques, or trying to challenge this model through one's teaching,

while yet recognizing that this may be to the disadvantage of one's students in career terms. So, there are difficult issues about how to react to this pressure – especially since some of it comes from students themselves.

Closely related is the problem of mass higher education, and its extension to the postgraduate level. Previously, postgraduate, and prior to that even undergraduate, courses could be directed primarily at the task of preparing a new generation of academics in the relevant discipline, even if a substantial proportion of students would not follow this path. Today, even more than before, it is difficult to defend such an approach, either by an appeal to the value of liberal education or through arguing that an academic education has the capacity to develop generic skills that are of value in other occupations. Even at postgraduate level, the pressure is more and more towards serving the occupational needs of students, which often seems to amount to meeting the demands of likely future employers. This is an increasingly common theme in the realm of methodology teaching. In Britain, the methodological training that the Economic and Social Research Council insists all research students in the social sciences should have is aimed not just at facilitating their own research, thereby potentially fitting them for work as academic researchers and teachers, but also at preparing them for the much wider range of jobs that involve a 'research' component, such as setting up and running accountability regimes within large organizations (Collinson, 1998). Yet, there are serious questions to be asked about the compatibility of these different 'missions'.[15]

The second generic problem is how to prepare students for participation in a research community that is riven by methodological, philosophical and even political disputes. Should one teach a range of different approaches within the field of qualitative research, presenting each as legitimate? Or should one teach the approach that one believes is most valuable, and refuse to teach any that one regards as unjustifiable? In support of the first position, it can be argued that students need to have an accurate sense of the full range of approaches to qualitative inquiry, and of the arguments for and against these, so that they can make a reasoned choice for themselves and engage in dialogue with those who adopt a different approach. In support of the second position, it can be proposed that it would be a disservice to students to introduce them to approaches that are valueless.[16] Or it might be suggested that since the different approaches are incommensurable, it is not possible or healthy for students to learn more than one.

The first position is clearly exemplified in a recent text, where a range of very different qualitative research traditions is presented and exemplified on equal terms (Travers, 2001). The approaches covered include grounded theorizing, ethnomethodology, conversation analysis, feminist methodology and postmodern ethnography. Travers argues that his book is 'democratic', empowering students in making their own choices about which approach to adopt in their own work (Travers, 2002: 458). He sees it as a text for courses that 'review a wide range of methodologies and approaches' and also as a 'self-help guide' for students who do not have access to such a course (Travers, 2001: viii). This might be seen as presenting 'packages of techniques for the student consumer', as if the choice were equivalent to using WordPerfect or Word to type one's thesis (Yates, 1997: 489). However, Travers provides discussion of the rationales for the different approaches as well as accounts of what they involve in practical terms.

The second approach has been advocated by Yvonna Lincoln. She argues that, given the way in which commitment to a particular paradigm 'permeates every act even tangentially associated with inquiry', 'we have to make a commitment as inquirers to one or the other [paradigm] and behave in a fashion congruent with its dictates until we choose another system. To do otherwise is not only to commit paradigmatic perjury, it is to invite psychological disaster' (Lincoln, 1990: 81). Thus, she claims that 'training in multiple paradigms (at least in more than a historical sense) is training for schizophrenia'. Instead, 'we probably ought to recognize the profound commitments people make to worldviews and create centers where such training can go on, much as there are centers where psychologists can train to be Freudians, or Jungians, or Adlerians …' (Lincoln, 1990: 87).[17] Of course, it might be argued that this position is even more likely to reify the different approaches than the first.

Needless to say, there are midway positions between these extremes, and the majority of teachers of qualitative method are probably at neither end of the spectrum. Presumably, even if one presents what is believed to be the best way of doing qualitative research, there is still an obligation to prepare students for participation in a situation where there are very different approaches. They need to know something of the alternatives, the issues that separate these, and the resulting debates. In short, we should encourage students to become neither ostriches nor fighting cocks.

However, there is a practical problem here. The issues separating different approaches to qualitative inquiry are, to a considerable extent, fundamental philosophical ones about which there is a considerable, and often quite difficult, literature. Thus, it is not uncommon for the work of various philosophers to be referred to in the methodological literature, some of whom are renowned for their obscurity.[18] Are we to try to introduce students to this philosophical literature so that they can properly understand the issues and the references that are included in contributions to the debates? And, if we believe that they need these background resources, how are we to enable them to acquire what is necessary while at the same time also giving them sufficient chance to develop and hone their research skills? There is surely not time, nor perhaps energy, to do both these things in full. So, some compromise position has to be reached, but it is not clear what would be an appropriate one in present circumstances.

CONCLUSION

As Williams has noted, 'there remains something comfortable about any style of research that is teachable and learnable by reference to a set of well articulated procedural rules adhered to amongst a community of researchers' (Williams, 1981: 558). It is not difficult to see the appeal of the procedural model, and it is an especially tempting mirage from the point of view of anyone charged with the responsibility of teaching research methodology. However, that model is at odds with some of the realities of qualitative inquiry (and of research more generally), and with the way in which most qualitative researchers think about their work today. In this chapter I have discussed three alternatives to the procedural model, organized around the notions of craft, profession, and bricolage; and I have sketched the pedagogical implications of these alternatives.

It is perhaps worth emphasizing that all these models capture at least some aspects of qualitative inquiry, and of what is involved in teaching it. There are parts of qualitative research practice that can be proceduralized, to a degree. For example, just as once one has decided which statistical technique to employ it is a matter of following the rules, similarly having decided what mode of transcription to employ in processing audio-recording data it is a matter of observing the conventions. And students do need to know what these conventions are, and to be encouraged to stick to them (unless there are very good reasons for not doing so). It is perhaps even less controversial to suggest that qualitative inquiry matches the craft model: that it involves skills, that these skills can be learned, and that learning them can be facilitated by a teacher providing an example of good practice and supplying helpful feedback on performance. Of course, many qualitative researchers would insist that rather more reflexivity is required than the craft model implies; though, as I have indicated, there is disagreement about the proper scope of reflexivity, and this has very significant implications for pedagogy. Finally, most qualitative researchers – even those who, like me, deny that qualitative research is a form of art, in anything like the contemporary sense of that term – would accept that it is creative in important respects and that the notion of bricolage has *some* value: making the best of what is available in order to gain some overall sense of a situation is an essential element of qualitative inquiry. One might also accept that while in teaching methodology one can reasonably hope to make students better at research, one cannot make all of them – or, actually, *make* any of them – good researchers.

In the final section I raised some generic problems that we have to face almost whichever model we adopt. The first is external pressure to proceduralize qualitative method and thereby to facilitate the efficient training of new researchers. And I suggested that this problem has been compounded by the rise of mass postgraduate education, where the likely destinations of students are diverse and – as a result – so also are the expected 'learning outcomes'. The second problem concerned preparing students for work in a research community that is not organized around a consensual view of the purpose of inquiry, and how it can best be pursued. Here the question is how much diversity to present to students, and in what depth to introduce different approaches and the issues that divide them; while yet also dealing with the more practical aspects of research education.

Given the existence of sharply different conceptions of qualitative inquiry within the research community, along with mounting external pressure to apply the procedural model, teaching qualitative method is far from straightforward today. It involves some difficult decisions, and there is probably no single form of 'best practice'; only a range of alternatives that may be evaluated very differently by competing perspectives. We live in 'interesting' times.

NOTES

1 The two editions of the *Handbook of Qualitative Research* (Denzin and Lincoln, 1994, 2000), and reviews of them (see Snow and Morrill, 1995; Walford, 2001; Haywood and Mac an Ghaill, 2001), give some sense of the diversity.

2 An interesting counter to this false view is Catherine Marsh's argument against the use of conventional examinations to assess methodological skills, in the course of which she stresses the importance of 'creativity' and 'methodological flair' in quantitative research (Marsh, 1981).

3 For a bibliographical guide to 'natural histories' of research, see Hammersley (2002c).

4 It may seem that I have neglected the two most obvious alternatives: qualitative research as science or as art. However, in complicated ways this contrast lies behind the typology I am employing. Rather misleadingly, the procedural model is often seen as exemplifying science, whereas many commentators have emphasized the centrality of creativity to scientific work (see Nisbet, 1963, 1976). Similarly, both science and art involve a craft element. In many, though not all, ways science can be seen as a profession; and some artists have seen their work in this way, while others have rejected that model. Bricolage, as we shall see, has links with technical problem-solving but is also close to certain kinds of modern art. Most discussions of whether social inquiry is a science or an art appear to assume too homogeneous a view of what is to be found on each side of this divide; even though they often recognize that there is some overlap. For a discussion of qualitative inquiry as science and art, see Wolcott (1995).

5 Seale (1999a) has recently argued in favour of the craft model, though he acknowledges the value of philosophical and methodological reflection, which is given much more emphasis in the other two alternatives I shall discuss. Research has often been referred to as a craft, but without much explication of what that entails: see, for example, Epstein (1967), Emerson (1987), Bourdieu et al. (1991), and Karp (1999).

6 For a discussion of this distinction, see Hammersley (2002a: ch. 1).

7 Elsewhere, Becker has outlined some 'tricks' involved in writing up research (see Becker, 1986).

8 What occurs may not always approximate closely to the pedagogic ideal, needless to say. The projects may be seen as research rather than as *simulation* of research. And, working on their own projects, students will not necessarily receive the kind of detailed feedback that would be required for the craft to be learned. Equally, the model and feedback provided may not be those of a skilled practitioner but rather those of what, in British parlance concerned with the practical trades, is referred to as a 'cowboy'! There is also the whole question of how far students should be let loose on the world simply to do projects for pedagogical purposes.

9 In the same issue of the journal in which Mann's article appears, Halfpenny provides a contrasting view. He argues that different sociological approaches involve radically different philosophical orientations: 'The consequence is that although different approaches employ what are nominally the same research

strategies and data handling techniques, the importance and meaning of a strategy or technique and its place in the research process – the very understanding of its nature – differs from approach to approach. Thus successful teaching demands more than a casual review of the different strategies and techniques that commonly form the chapter headings of research methods texts. Instead, the strategies and techniques must be located within the sociological approaches – the conceptions of data, explanation and theory – that form the context of their employment, for it is only relative to approaches that the merits and demerits of the various strategies and techniques can be assessed' (Halfpenny, 1981: 565). Here, perhaps, particular qualitative approaches constitute distinct craft traditions, though it seems likely that what Halfpenny has in mind goes beyond the craft model.

10 Ironically, Becker's (1967) 'Whose side are we on?' exemplifies one aspect of this orientation. While this article has generally been treated as an injunction to side with the 'underdog', that is not what Becker proposed. His position is actually close to Weber's principle of value neutrality (see Hammersley, 2000: ch. 3). Other examples of the treatment of research as a professional activity, in senses close to that used here, can be found in Weber's (1948) essay on 'Science as a vocation', in Polsky (1971) and in Berger and Kellner (1982). See also Webb and Glesne (1992).

11 On the case of Foster's work, see Hammersley (1992: ch. 4, 2000: ch. 5).

12 Consistency in the application of such a ruling would also be demanded by the professional model, as against the 'ontological gerrymandering' that frequently occurs (see Woolgar and Pawluch, 1985). It is important to note that the category 'childhood sexual abuse' is an evaluative one, so that there will be different value frameworks in terms of which it could be defined; and social researchers can make no authoritative choice among these. The point is, however, that – once a particular framework has been selected to define the phenomenon for the purposes of study – whether or not childhood sexual abuse occurred is independent of our accounts of it.

13 Interestingly, Derrida anticipates the notion of 'ethnographic bricolage'. He also argues that the distinction between engineer and bricoleur undermines itself, suggesting that the engineer may be a myth produced by the bricoleur (Derrida, 1978: 285).

14 Without using the term 'bricolage' or its associates, Wolcott sees qualitative inquiry as having an important artistic dimension and relegates to 'craft' those elements of fieldwork that can be inculcated. However, he is clear that these craft elements are very important.

15 In Britain, and some other places, the pressure for methodological 'training' of students along the lines of the procedural model has run in parallel with government attempts to reshape the character of social and educational research. The aim has been to make it serve 'evidence-based' policy-making and practice better (see Hammersley, 2002a).

16 This need not reflect an entirely intolerant attitude: one might accept that other approaches can legitimately be taught on other courses or in other institutions.

17 MacIntyre (1990: 232–4) seems to reach something like the same position as Lincoln in his discussion of 'rival versions of moral inquiry'. Pallas (2001: 11), while arguing for an approach closer to that of Travers, also recognizes the danger of 'dissociative identity'.

18 There are, for example, several references to the work of Heidegger even in the first edition of Denzin and Lincoln's *Handbook of Qualitative Research* (Denzin and Lincoln, 1994). An associated problem is that some of the discussions of philosophical issues and positions within the literature of social research methodology are themselves inaccurate and misleading.

REFERENCES

Becker, H.S. (1967) 'Whose side are we on?', *Social Problems*, 14: 239–47.

Becker, H.S. (1970) *Sociological Work*. Chicago: Aldine.

Becker, H.S. (1986) *Writing for Social Scientists*. Chicago: University of Chicago Press.

Becker, H.S. (1998) *Tricks of the Trade*, Chicago: University of Chicago Press.

Berger, P. and Kellner, H. (1982) *Sociology Reinterpreted: An Essay on Method and Vocation*. Harmondsworth: Penguin.

Blair, M. (1993) 'Review of Peter Foster: *Policy and Practice in Multicultural and Antiracist Education*', *European Journal of Intercultural Studies*, 2(3): 63–4.

Bourdieu, P., Chamboredon, J.-C. and Passeron, J.-C. (1991) *The Craft of Sociology: Epistemological Preliminaries*. Berlin: Walter de Gruyter.

Chaiklin, S. and Lave, J. (eds) (1993) *Understanding Practice: Perspectives on Activity and Context*. Cambridge: Cambridge University Press.

Collinson, J.A. (1998) 'Professionally trained researchers? Expectations of competence in social science doctoral research training', *Higher Education Review*, 31(1): 59–67.

Connolly, P. (1992) 'Playing it by the rules: the politics of research in "race" and education', *British Educational Research Journal*, 18(2): 133–48.

Davies, M. (1995) *Childhood Sexual Abuse and the Construction of Identity: Healing Sylvia*. London: Taylor & Francis.

Denzin, N.K. and Lincoln, Y.S. (eds) (1994) *Handbook of Qualitative Research*. Thousand Oaks, CA: Sage (first edition). Second edition published in 2000.

Derrida, J. (1978) *Writing and Difference*. Chicago: University of Chicago Press.

Emerson, R.M. (1987) 'Four ways to improve the craft of fieldwork', *Journal of Contemporary Ethnography*, 16(1): 69–89.

Epstein, A.L. (ed.) (1967) *The Craft of Social Anthropology*. London: Tavistock.

Foster, P. (1990) *Policy and Practice in Multicultural and Antiracist Education*. London: Routledge.

Gillborn, D. (1995) *Racism and Antiracism in Real Schools*. Buckingham: Open University Press.

Halfpenny, P. (1981) 'Teaching ethnographic data analysis on postgraduate courses in sociology', *Sociology*, 15(4): 564–70.

Hammersley, M. (1992) *The Politics of Social Research*. London: Sage.

Hammersley, M. (2000) *Taking Sides in Social Research*. London: Routledge.

Hammersley, M. (2002a) *Educational Research, Policymaking and Practice*. London: Paul Chapman.

Hammersley, M. (2002b) 'Research and the ethics of belief', unpublished paper.

Hammersley, M. (2002c) *A Guide to Natural Histories of Research*, www.cardiff.ac.uk/socs/capacity/Activities/Themes/In-depth/guide.pdf

Haywood, C. and Mac an Ghaill, M. (2001) 'Review of *Handbook of Qualitative Research*, 2nd edn', *Qualitative Research*, 1(3): 411–14.

Hughes, E.C. (1960) Introduction, in B.H. Junker, *Field Work: Introduction to the Social Sciences*. Chicago: University of Chicago Press, pp. iii–xiii.

Karp, D.A. (1999) 'Social science, progress, and the ethnographer's craft', *Journal of Contemporary Ethnography*, 28(6): 597–609.

Lave, J. and Wenger, E. (1991) *Situated Learning: Legitimate Peripheral Participation*. Cambridge: Cambridge University Press.

Leonard, D. (2000) 'Transforming doctoral studies: competencies and artistry', *Higher Education in Europe*, 15(2): 181–92.

Lévi-Strauss, C. (1966) *The Savage Mind*. London: Weidenfeld & Nicolson.

Lincoln, Y.S. (1990) 'The making of a constructivist: a remembrance of transformations past', in E.G. Guba (ed.), *The Paradigm Dialog*. Newbury Park, CA: Sage, pp. 67–87.

MacIntyre, A. (1990) *Three Rival Versions of Moral Inquiry*. London: Duckworth.

Mann, M. (1981) 'Socio-logic', *Sociology*, 15(4) 544–50.

Marsh, C. (1981) 'The assessment of skills in research methods', *Sociology*, 15(4): 519–25.

Mills, C. Wright (1959) 'On intellectual craftmanship', in L. Gross (ed.), *Symposium on Sociological Theory*, Evanston, IL: Row, Peterson & Co., pp. 25–53. (A slightly different version appears as an appendix to *The Sociological Imagination*. New York: Oxford University Press, 1959.)

Nelson, C., Treichler, P.A. and Grossberg, L. (1992) 'Cultural studies', in L. Grossberg, C. Nelson and P.A. Treichler (eds), *Cultural Studies*. New York: Routledge, pp. 1–22.

Nisbet, R. (1963) 'Sociology as an art form', in M. Stein and A.J. Vidich (eds), *Sociology on Trial*. Englewood Cliffs, NJ: Prentice-Hall, pp. 148–61.

Nisbet, R. (1976) *Sociology as an Art Form*. London: Heinemann.

Pallas, A.M. (2001) 'Preparing education doctoral students for epistemological diversity', *Educational Researcher*, 30(5): 6–11.

Polsky, N. (1971) 'Research method, morality and criminology', in N. Polsky, *Hustlers, Beats and Others*. Harmondsworth: Penguin, pp. 115–47.

Scarth, J. (1986) 'The influence of examinations on curriculum decision-making'. Unpublished PhD thesis, University of Lancaster.

Schön, D. (1983) *The Reflective Practitioner*. London: Temple Smith.

Seale, C. (1999a) *The Quality of Qualitative Research*. London: Sage.

Seale, C. (1999b) 'Quality in qualitative research', *Qualitative Inquiry*, 5(4): 465–78.

Snow, D.A. and Morrill, C. (1995) 'A revolutionary handbook or a handbook for revolution?', *Journal of Contemporary Ethnography*, 24(3): 341–8.

Travers, M. (2001) *Qualitative Research Through Case Studies*. London: Sage.

Travers, M. (2002) 'Response', *British Journal of Educational Psychology*, 72(3): 457–8.

Walford, G. (2001) 'Review of *Handbook of Qualitative Research*, 2nd edn', *Qualitative Research*, 1(3): 407–11.

Webb, R.B. and Glesne, C. (1992) 'Teaching qualitative research', in M. LeCompte, W. L. Millroy and J. Preissle (eds), *Handbook of Qualitative Research in Education*. San Diego: Academic Press, pp. 771–814.

Weber, M. (1948) 'Science as a vocation', in H.H. Gerth and C.W. Mills (eds), *From Max Weber*. London: Routledge, pp. 129–56. (First published in German in 1919.)

Williams, R. (1981) 'Learning to do field research: intimacy and inquiry in social life', *Sociology*, 15(4): 557–64.

Wolcott, H.F. (1995) *The Art of Fieldwork*. Walnut Creek, CA: AltaMira Press.

Woolgar, S. and Pawluch, D. (1985) 'Ontological gerrymandering: the anatomy of social problems' explanations', *Social Problems*, 32(3): 314–27.

Yates, L. (1997) 'Research methodology, education, and theoretical fashions: constructing a methodology course in an era of deconstruction', *Qualitative Studies in Education*, 10(4): 487–98.

36

Writing a social science monograph

Barbara Czarniawska

SCIENCE AND FICTION: A LONG STORY

The idea that scientific and non-scientific writing might have much in common is neither remarkable nor new. The very fact that so much effort has been invested in differentiating art from science since Plato's *Republic* would suggest a proximity that was disquieting – at least to some. At the same time, there were always voices like that of Giambattista Vico, intent on abolishing this difference. Different schools of thought were in ascendance at different times.

One period worth mentioning is the early eighteenth century, when natural sciences began to assume their present shape. Schaffer (1993) shows scientists such as Isaac Newton and Jeremy Bentham doing a tremendous 'cultural work', gaining legitimacy for their science through political writing and public spectacles. This part of history is relatively well known; what attracts less attention is the meta-activity of erasing the traces of artistry and politics from their work, the accomplishment of having established a philosophical position of scientific realism as 'sheer representation of nature', and '... the "amnesia" of realism, in which the work that establishes representations is forgotten' (Schaffer, 1993: 279).

The realistic style, accompanying the philosophical position of realism, has earned a legitimate place in both sciences and the novel. Some more work was thus needed to establish the difference between the two, especially between the realist novel and sociology, which both emerged at about the same time in the nineteenth century. This time around, the legitimizing efforts were directed not only at establishing each of them as genres in their own right, but also at distinguishing between things that initially looked very much alike.

Hemmings (1978) traces the earliest recorded use of the word 'realism' to *Le Mercure français* which, in 1826, wrote about 'a literary doctrine ... which would lead to the imitation not of artistic masterpieces but of the originals that nature offers us ... the literature of truth' (pp. 9–10). In April of the same year, Comte began a series of lectures on a 'system of positive philosophy'. Both doctrines aimed at a representation *corresponding* to the world as it was – undistorted by a subjective or partial vision. Both centred on developing – and hiding – the art of *mimesis*, of representing the world. Emplotment – introducing structure that will make sense of reported events – was left to Nature.

Within the world of literature, this Promethean task of representing the world was not seen as particularly formidable: the fear was that abandoning emplotment, the right and the duty of a writer, would result in dullness and boredom. However, when put into practice, the principle itself proved untenable:

> All through the 'age of realism' novelists will be faced with the same dilemma: social institutions, human relationships, the separate courses of individual lives, all these cannot be presented in a work of art without a certain measure of trimming and tailoring. ... However firm his allegiance to realism, a novelist has to impose his own peculiar vision on what he sees, partly because this vision is inseparable from his artistic consciousness, and partly because without it his work would lack shape and point and would finally prove unreadable. (Hemmings, 1978: 33)

This dilemma attracted the attention of social scientists much later: unused to reflecting upon their writing, they have only recently begun to ponder over the paradoxes of 'objectivity' and 'correspondence theory of truth'. But the novelists were not only ahead of the social scientists in their self-reflectivity, they were also ahead in reaching the wider public. Throughout the nineteenth century it was still the novelists and historians who were *describing* the formation of mature capitalism. The economists, like Smith and Malthus, were laying the foundation of a *normative* science, under the aegis of moral philosophy or causal laws. By the end of the century, however, the novel turned to romanticism and then to modernism, while social science embraced positivism.

The years 1950–1970, exploiting the scientific contributions to the Second World War, brought another wave of 'scientization' to social sciences (Lepenies, 1988). The late 1970s, however, witnessed what is often called a 'linguistic turn' in the social sciences, which was soon accompanied by a 'literary turn' (Atkinson, 1990). Examples abound: the rhetorical analysis in economics (McCloskey, 1986) and in most of the social sciences and humanities (Nelson et al., 1987), the reconstruction of the burnt bridges between sociology and literary theory (Richard H. Brown, 1977; Bruss, 1982; Lepenies, 1988; Agger, 1990), the knitting of close ties between anthropology and literary theory (Clifford and Marcus, 1986; Geertz, 1988) and the growing awareness of the importance of narrative knowledge (Bruner, 1990).

REALISM IN THE POST-POSITIVIST ERA

These developments were possible because a new kind of criticism emerged in the literary realm, a criticism that rejected both the objectivist determinism of positivism and the subjectivist humanism of romanticism.[1] Examples of frameworks that incorporated these literary developments are Brown's 'poetic for sociology' (1977) and Richard Rorty's new pragmatism (Rorty, 1982). Rorty's position has been designed for philosophy, but it is directly applicable to social science studies.

First, the realist ontology is moved into the realm of belief. It is sensible and convenient to *believe* in the world of causes 'out there'; after all, most social actors do. To act, to react, to interact – all this requires a faith that there is a world of causes and that people can be agents in that world. This does not mean, however, that there are ways of describing this world that correspond to it 'as it really is':

To say that the world is out there, that it is not our creation, is to say, with common sense, that most things in space and time are the effects of causes which do not include human mental states. To say that truth is not out there is simply to say that where there are no sentences there is no truth, that sentences are elements of human languages, and that human languages are human creations (Rorty, 1989: 4–5).

Secondly, the superior notion of *episteme* (knowledge) becomes identical with *doxa* (opinion), previously held in disrepute by science (Rorty, 1991). Social actors have opinions on all kinds of matters and test them in action. Pragmatism is a philosophy meant for people of action; it is a kind of theory that explores practices rather than explains principles.

Social science thus becomes a kind of writing, and its various disciplines can be best compared to literary sub-genres. Therefore it should be only natural that social science, as a genre (or rather family of genres), engages in a conversation with other genres.

Is there a danger of too close a rapprochement between social science and literature? Hardly. A social scientist is in many respects more of a literary critic than is a novelist. The social worlds that the researchers describe are only in a certain sense products of their minds (in the sense that they are responsible for their own texts); these worlds were originally written by other social actors. They, like the literary authors, have quite a lot to say about the critics' opinions of their production. Social scientists work on an uncertain footing, in so far as they undertake mediation between the 'social authors' and the academic theorists.

One question still remains: whether, with so many styles in existence, realism is a good example to learn from. There seems to exist a contradiction between pragmatism's refutation of the 'mirror of nature' metaphor of science (Rorty, 1980) and early literary realism's eager espousal of it. But these were two different mirrors. When Stendhal said 'a novel is a mirror riding along a highway' (Levin, 1973: 66), he could not have had in mind 'the notion of knowledge as inner representation' (Rorty, 1980: 46). Mirrors are also versions of worlds.

Although the debates on realism – in science and in literature – continue, there is a growing consensus on understanding the concept: not as a 'way of writing corresponding to reality' but a 'way of writing corresponding to the contemporary criteria of realist writing' (Levine, 1993). The main issue is then an institutionalized preference for one given style of writing over another.

Accordingly, realism is but one literary style that offers insights into social reality, but a sturdy one. A British writer and literary theorist, Malcolm Bradbury, in a discussion with the US writer Tom Wolfe, said that the reason for realism, or a form of it, had in his opinion never really gone away, and that 'our modernist, postmodernist and therefore presumably anti-realist century' enjoys it perhaps more than ever (Bradbury, 1992).

This claim can be extended beyond the novel and into the social sciences. One would think that with the arrival of constructivism, relativism and postmodernism, realism has been banned once and for all. Far from it – it proliferates as perhaps never before. Within philosophy, there is the scientific realism of Rom Harré and the critical realism of Mary Hesse and Roy Bhaskar, promising to reconcile constructivism and realism. Sociology is not left behind: there is the 'symbolic realism' of Richard H. Brown, the 'conventional realism' of Peter Manicas, the 'social-science realism' of Andrew Sayer, and the 'real-ism' of David Silverman and Brian Torode.

There are therefore many demands for realism in social science and they are serious, but not very specific. Stern (1973) listed three ways of understanding realism in literature and literary criticism: 'A way of depicting, describing the situation in a faithful, accurate, "life-like" manner; *or richly, abundantly, colourfully*; or again mechanically, photographically, imitatively' (p. 40, my italics). It is against the third and in favour of the second of these interpretations of realism that the present appeal is made. For social scientists, realism may be the most attractive style in which to present their knowledge, because it is both legitimate and expected. The question is then not 'Whether realism' but 'What kind of realism'?

Let me briefly summarize the main points I have attempted to make in this introductory section. First, literature and social science have much in common, and in spite of the social sciences' long flirtation with the natural sciences, they continue to share common problems, so there is no reason not to exchange solutions. These problems are also relatively stable: how to represent (mimesis) and how to make sense of a representation (emplotment). Secondly, the realistic style, under siege in both literature and social science, remains robust and legitimate, and although this is not a reason to abandon experimental writing, no forecast of realism's demise can be made for the foreseeable future. This chapter is therefore written with the aim of encouraging reflection over a skilful crafting of realist social science texts, hoping that the same reflection might facilitate non-realist experimentation.

FICTION OR SCIENCE?

No mention has as yet been made of a difference between *fact* and *fiction*, yet isn't this the most crucial difference between the genres? A novel contains a fictive description of a social world, a social science monograph a factual one. Science should keep to facts and logic, leaving metaphors to poetry and stories to fiction. Yet, as McCloskey (1990a) pointed out, contrary to this received wisdom, the sciences can be said to be using a whole tetrad of rhetorical figures: stories, metaphors, facts and formal logic. *Belle lettres* or 'folk theories' mainly use stories and metaphors, but quite often facts, and sometimes even formal logic.

On the other hand, social scientists seldom use formal logic – in the sense of a particular mode of reasoning, because everybody uses logic in the sense of syntactic rules. What I want to emphasize is that 'science' is not separated from 'literature' by an abyss; over and above the bookstores' classification, a work is attributed to a certain genre according to the frequency with which it uses certain rhetorical devices. Umberto Eco, who is a legitimate citizen in both worlds, put it as follows:

> I understand that, according to a current opinion, I have written some texts that can be labeled as scientific (or academic or theoretical), and some others which can be defined as creative. But I do not believe in such a straightforward distinction. I believe that Aristotle was as creative as Sophocles, and Kant as creative as Goethe. There is not some mysterious ontological difference between these two ways of writing. ... The differences stand, first of all, in the propositional attitude of the writer, even if though their propositional [attitude] is usually made evident by textual devices. ... (Eco, 1992: 140)

We recognize a scientific text not because of its intrinsic scientific qualities, but because the author claims it is scientific (and this claim can be contested) and because he or she uses textual devices that are conventionally considered scientific (and this convention is contested all the time). Following Latour (1992), one can try to distinguish between these two kinds of text by saying that stories evolve along the *syntagmatic* dimension grounded in association, while scientific models evolve along the *paradigmatic* dimension, based on substitution. A narrative thus adds various events one after another over time, while a scientific model substitutes a group of particulars by a more abstract concept that covers them all. Generalization, and consequently prediction, operate differently in the two modes. Syntagmatic construction uses *metonymy*, i.e. it operates on the sense of part and whole (how things hang together). Paradigmatic construction, on the other hand, uses *metaphor*, i.e. it operates on the sense of like and unlike (similarity, analogy).[2] Turning to the social scientific texts, one cannot help noticing that both constructions appear: there are elements of the syntagmatic and the paradigmatic, of metonymy and metaphor, of narrative and logic.

McCloskey's tetrad can be enriched by Latour's insight. Logic and stories can be put together on a syntagmatic dimension, as two modes of association, of establishing a connection – in actual time and space, hypothetically, or counterfactually. Facts and metaphors reside on a common paradigmatic dimension, as two kinds of substitution, a dimension extended between the two modes of name-giving. 'Facts' are names or assertions about which we tend to agree easily ('this is the recently acquired computer'), while metaphors indicate a stage of inquiry rather than consensus ('will it be a boost or a sinking stone to your finances?'). The extremes would be proper names and metaphors, with similes and analogies in between.

Seen in this way, 'science' is no longer a priori distinct from 'literature'. McCloskey's tetrad now denotes a space within which one could position various works, and it would be their proximity to other similar works that would establish their genre. For example, metaphors (or models) seem to be more frequent in economics than stories, which are very frequent, on the other hand, in the sub-genre known as economic history (McCloskey, 1990a, 1990b). Geertz (1988) stressed the obvious importance of stories in anthropology, but he also pointed out that there are more metaphors than one would expect.

Scientific style as a literary accomplishment

In this section I shall look at a well-known social science text, showing how it incorporates literary means in its production. The example (James D. Thompson, *Organizations in Action*, 1967) follows what is considered to be an ideal of scientific reasoning, attempting to form logical propositions. Short and concise, it aims at covering all relevant issues and formulating the proper science of organizations, combining the incompatible (the rational system versus natural open systems approaches), and embracing an impressive range of schools and sources. Thompson's work is a striking example of an attempt to achieve closure in an intellectual field, and if it were taken literally, there would be no need for further organization theory.

Proposition 4.1: Organizations under norms of rationality seek to place their boundaries around those activities which if left to the task environment would be crucial contingencies.

The implication of this proposition is that we should expect to find organizations including within their domains activities or competencies which, on a technological basis, could be performed by the task environment without damage to the *major mission* of the organization. For the hotel, for example, provision of rooms and meals would be the major mission, and the operation of a laundry would be excluded; yet we find hotels operating laundries. On the other hand, provision of rooms and meals would not be within the major mission of the hospital, although hospitals commonly include these activities within their domains.

The incorporation of subsidiary competencies along with major missions is commonplace in organizations of all types and is not a major discovery. But our proposition is not an announcement of the fact; rather it attempts to indicate the direction in which domains are expanding. ... (Thompson, 1967: 39–40)

In my reading, Thompson says that organizations incorporate those activities that may be crucial to them, in order to avoid dependence on their environment. This is stated in the form of a theorem, i.e. an idea 'accepted or proposed as a demonstrable truth often as a part of a general theory' (*Webster's*, 1981: 1200). Before turning to demonstration, let us stay awhile with the proposition itself. Its formulation follows the rules of logic, but it concerns not 'facts' but tropes, of which the two most important are 'organization' and 'environment'.

'Organization' is clearly a *synecdoche*: that which is organized becomes an entity named after its attribute. The use of organizations in the plural, indicating an entity, and an entity that became the main subject of organization theory, appeared as late as the 1960s, with the advent of systems theory in the social sciences (Waldo, 1961); in fact, Thompson still speaks of 'administration theory' (administration being the synonym of management, connected by usage with public authority rather than private enterprise). Even more interesting is 'environment': this central concept in organization theory is residual, meaning simply 'that which surrounds organizations'. As John W. Meyer (1996) put it succinctly, the environment is the Other to the Actor, as the environment of a modern organization consists of other organizations (see also Perrow, 1991).

Thus Thompson's proposition suggests a logical connection between tropes; let us see how this is demonstrated. According to the rules of the (scientific) game, the demonstration cannot happen within the language (as one might expect in this context), but by a reference to reality.

Thompson's demonstrations do not involve concrete facts: we learn nothing about an experiment conducted at laboratory X on date Y. The illustrations are formulated in a way that resembles and repeats propositions, but the abstract tropes are replaced by generic terms like 'hotels operating laundries', 'hospitals', 'rooms'. The verbs oscillate between the always-valid Simple Present in the proposition ('organizations seek to place'), and the Conditional in the 'implication'.

The excerpt also contains Thompson's comment on the status of the proposition: '... our [sic] proposition is not announcement of the fact: rather it attempts to indicate the direction....' By that, as the previous sentence indicates, he did not mean that this was a hypothetical move in a hypothetical model; he suggested that the proposition contained more than a mere fact (by now trite), it contained a prediction. Thompson used *prolepsis*: 'the representation or assumption of a future fact or development as if presently existing or accomplished' (*Webster's*, 1981: 913).

One could thus claim that Thompson's 'scientism' is but a stylization: the entities in question are in fact tropes, and could be connected only with one another; the postulated connections are achieved by the use of yet another rhetorical figure. It would be wrong, however, to conclude from this that Thompson failed to achieve the scientific status he aspired to; this is the way scientific texts tend to look in the social sciences. Few of them even try to achieve such a strict stylization – most authors allow the stories to creep directly into their texts.

The critique of fiction in scientific texts is often grounded in a confusion of two ways of understanding fiction: as that which does not

exist, and that which is not true (Lamarque, 1990). If we separate these two, it becomes obvious that we cannot check, on the basis of Thompson's text alone, whether hotels with laundries really exist. Yet everything that is said may be true in the sense that it is credible in the light of what we know about actual organizations.[3] Now, I have never seen a hotel with a laundry, and therefore my conclusion is that either Thompson is wrong, or else he refers to a context unknown to me (USA, the 1960s, etc.). Whatever the case, the text does not permit me to check its 'factuality'.

In my book on writing management texts (Czarniawska, 1999), I analysed three more texts and came to a general conclusion: facts were missing. One clue to this mysterious absence can be found in Knorr-Cetina (1981), who pointed out that etymologically 'facts' (from *facere*) are fabrications, and their production is a specialty of certain places such as natural science laboratories. Social scientists seem to be only marginally engaged in fact production; their attention is focused on *how the facts*, and the important societal fictions, *are produced* (Knorr-Cetina, 1994).

This would bring social science once more closer to literature, where the status of facts is quite clear: 'Once accepted as true, the factual judgment ... dies as such in order to generate a stipulation of a code. ... Successful judgments are remembered as such only when they become famous ("the famous discovery of Copernicus" ...)' (Eco, 1979/1983: 86). Facts, once successfully fabricated, are used in the production of further facts; their repetition does not bring any added value into a discourse. Metaphors, on the other hand, 'tend to resist acquisition. If they are inventive (and thus original) they cannot be easily accepted; the system tends not to absorb them' (Eco, 1979/1983: 86). Once accepted, they become redundant and lose their attraction. Stories, on the other hand, are allowed to be redundant: a narrative of a redundant nature, says Eco defending detective stories, offers a fastidious reader an opportunity to repose, to relax. Thus the combination of stories and metaphors seems to be invincible, but at the same time seemingly puts an end to the genre of social science, which vanishes into literature.

Where is the core of this genre?

The anthropologist Margery Wolf is one of many social scientists who worry about 'how one is to differentiate ethnography from fiction, other than in preface, footnotes, and other authorial devices' (1992: 56). I note this standing concern, but fail to appreciate its gravity, partly because I do not see how this question can be answered once and for all. It is a question that needs to be asked – and answered – again and again, in a communal reflection over the genre. The answers will necessarily differ over times and places.

Genre reflection is, however, also a genre construction, an institution-building, and as such it invites policing attempts: somebody always takes on the duty of 'protecting the core'. As genre analysis in literature has shown, such policing leads to the suffocation of a genre in the worst case and to the facilitation of genre blurring and crossing in the best – as Hühn (1987) pointed out, while recounting the history of the detective story. Neither paradoxicality nor conflict weakens a genre; on the contrary, both enhance its controlling power. The grey zones – blurred genres – host innovators, those who rejuvenate and reform genres.

What I therefore plead for here is not replacing one genre with another, but creative borrowing. 'To the few wooden tongues developed in academic journals, we should add the many genres and styles of narration invented by novelists, journalists, artists, cartoonists, scientists and philosophers. The reflexive character of our domain will be recognized in the future by the multiplicity of genres, not by the tedious presence of "reflexive loops"' (Latour, 1988: 173). What Margery Wolf says of anthropology could be applied to all social sciences: 'a discipline with very permeable borders, picking up methodologies, theories, and data from any source whatever that can provide the answers to our questions' (1992: 51). All these 'loans' arrive in packages typical of the genre from which they have come. Traditionally, however, social scientists tended to ignore 'the form', insisting that it is the 'pure contents' that are being tapped. Latour's advice amounts to suggesting making a virtue out of a vice, an art out of an unreflective behaviour.

Having tackled (with levity) the issue of the borders of social science as a genre, the question as to the contents of this genre still remain: how to represent? and how to emplot?

MIMESIS, OR HOW TO REPRESENT THE WORLD

In this text, the notion of mimesis, as representation of the world in a text, is related to two elements of 'the world': the field of theory and the field of practice under study. In other words, I shall make no distinction between writing a literature review and writing up a fieldwork.[4] Both need to represent scientific literature or inscriptions of everyday life, and both need to emplot their representations.

A common-sense answer to the question 'how to represent?' is 'faithfully'. Reality should be re-created in the text. A scientific text should reflect what it describes, hopefully in a one-to-one correspondence. This should not be any problem as 'facts speak for themselves', and texts can be rendered loyally to the intentions of the authors.

That this is possible at all was challenged by the Impressionists in art and by, among others, Jorge Luis Borges in literature,[5] and finally in human sciences.[6] The following problems emerged:

- The incompatibility of worlds and words (Rorty, 1980, 1989): how can words be compared to that which they (purportedly) describe? A one-to-one correspondence is impossible if media are different.[7] It is therefore sensible to think of representation of an object as involving *production* of another object 'which is intentionally related to the first by a certain coding convention which determines what counts as similar in the right way' (Van Fraassen and Sigman, 1993: 74). Representation does not reflect; it creates.

- The politics of representation (Latour, 1999): considering that there are always competing versions of the world in circulation, who, and by what criteria, has the right to judge them? This second problem is already a search for a solution to the first one: if facts do not speak for themselves, who will speak on their behalf? How do conventions of coding arise? Who has the right to judge what is 'the right way'?

As these are complex queries, let me begin from the opposite end and ask, what is the purpose of skilful mimesis in a social science text? The common (academic) sense answer is: in the case of field material, *to make readers feel as if they were there, in the field*; in the case of literature review, *to make readers feel as if they read the literature themselves*. How to achieve these effects, if facts refuse to speak for themselves, and a truly faithful rendering of somebody else's text is a plagiarism?

There can be no normative answer to this question (see the next section), only a descriptive one: I can tell my readers how authors try to achieve this effect. Words cannot be compared to non-words, only to other words. This means that, as Hayden White (1999) put it, all descriptions of historical objects (and social objects are historical) are necessarily *figurative*. In order to evoke in a reader an image of something they have not seen, this image must be connected to something that they have already seen, and *tropes* – figures of speech – are the linguistic means to achieve just this effect. The word *metaphor*, which in Greek means a transport from one place to another, means exactly that in authorial practice: the reader is moved from 'here' to 'there', be it another physical setting, or another book. Also, not for nothing are tropes *figures* of speech: they are the means to visualize, 'to paint with words'.

White speaks of 'figural realism', which, as I read it, is identical with what Richard H. Brown (1977) called 'symbolic realism', with one important difference. While Brown considered symbolic realism as *a kind of* realism, counterpoised to e.g. scientific realism, White points out that *all* realism is necessarily symbolic, that is, figurative. Realism differs from other literary styles by the preference for certain tropes and not others (understatement rather than overstatement, to take an obvious example).

Voices in the fields

While choosing your tropes is a matter of skill, or art, the second problem is more political in character. As the map must not be the same as the territory, it is necessary to silence some of the voices that form the polyphony of the world, and to give some more space than others.

Here the analogy between dealing with a field of theory and a field of practice is very clear. The problem is common: whom to include, whom to exclude, and who deserves which type of attention. In the field of theory we have a set of conventions to aid the writer, and a set of practices, more or less recommendable.[8]

In brief, there are two main ways of dealing with other authors' texts. One is *exegetic*, that is, aiming at an explanation or a critical interpretation of a text. In this mode, the focus is on the other author's text: as a model, or as an object of criticism. The main thing is then to represent the other text as well as possible (that is, choosing appropriate tropes to connect the monograph to the text it analyses), and then to take a stance: eulogical, apologetic, critical, a step beyond.

The other, much more common in practice but rarely mentioned in prudish how-to-write-science books, is an *inspirational* mode (Rorty, 1992, contrasts it with 'methodical' reading), very close to de Certeau's (1984) idea of reading as *poaching*. In this mode, the other's text is re-contextualized for the purposes of the present text. The author borrows (acknowledging the loan) notions and terms coined by others, to use them in the context of the thesis.

The observation that the inspirational mode of using other people's texts is more frequent than the exegetic mode is not a proof of lax customs in academe: unless exegesis is the topic of a monograph, the inspirational mode is much more relevant to the task at hand.

What, however, about the field of practice, with its infinite multiplicity of voices and of vocabularies, structured by power relations that include the social science writer?[9] The difficulty of representing the multiple voices in field studies[10] was perhaps most sharply focused in anthropology. After decades of all-knowing anthropological texts that explained the 'native ways of being' to the 'more developed civilization', a wave of political and ethical doubts pervaded the discipline (best summarized in the volumes edited by Clifford and Marcus, 1986, and Marcus and Fischer, 1986). Many contributors to these volumes opted for a different, polyphonic ethnography, in which people could speak in their own voices, which led to much discussion about whether it was in fact possible.

It is worth recalling that these anthropologists took inspiration from Mikhail Bakhtin (1981), who had in mind not a polyphony in which many people are speaking, but something called *heteroglossia* or 'variegated speech'. This is an *authorial strategy* consisting of the fact that the author speaks different languages (dialects, slangs, etc.) in the text. There is no need for the illusion that 'these people' speak for themselves; indeed they do not. But the author pays them a compliment by making the reader clearly aware of the fact that different languages *are* being spoken within one and the same linguistic tradition.

From this perspective it is easier to approach a suggestion coming from the sociology of science and technology: of meeting the duty of representation by giving voice even to non-humans (Woolgar, 1988; Latour, 1992). Latour (1996) put this suggestion into action in his study that I discuss at more length in the next section, where 'Aramis' (an automated train system) got a voice of his (?) own. At a certain point in this story, Master and Pupil (who study Aramis's 'life') have a heated exchange on the sensibility of such a move: 'Do you think I don't know', barks the Master at the doubting Pupil, 'that giving Aramis a voice is but an anthropomorphization, creating a puppet with a voice?' (p. 59).

Thus social science ends up with a staged conversation in which the goal of political representation must live side by side with the awareness that we are performing an act of ventriloquism.

This amounts to giving up the ambition of speaking on behalf of the Other in any literal sense, the ambition to be 'a tribune for the unheard, a representer of the unseen, a kenner of the misconstrued' (Geertz, 1988: 133). But the fictiveness of this polyphony, once revealed, relieves social scientists from the criticism of silencing the voices. Social scientists do most harm when they impose their interpretations on what they claim are 'authentic voices from the field'. If rendering these voices is the purpose, the way to go about it is to quit social science (silence one's own voice) and to engage in the political activity of creating speaking platforms for those who are not heard.

Painting with words

But even when objects are not given the voice, they are given a presence in social science texts; similarly, some people do not talk, and yet they appear in such texts. How are settings, persons, events introduced and presented?

The most frequent description of a setting for a social science study follows the theatrical convention: stage instructions plus the cast of characters (often collective rather than individual: a group of employees, a profession, a social stratum). The influence of television series brought in another descriptive element: 'the story-so-far' (a historical background).

Another kind of introduction to a setting is typical to sociological ethnographies, Chicago-style. The authors borrow from naturalist fiction, introducing the reader 'as if a stranger or an outsider, in the fashion of a guidebook' (Atkinson, 1990: 32):

> 'Welcome to Technology Region – Working on America's Future', proclaim the signs along Route 61, the region's main artery. It is early, but the nervous, impatient energy of high-tech is already pulsating through the spectacular countryside. Porsches, souped-up Chevies, Saabs, indeterminate old family station wagons, motorcycles, company vans, lots of Toyotas – the transportational variety is endless – edge their way toward the exit ramps and the clusters of 'corporate parks', engineering facilities, conference centers, and hotels that are the place of daily congregation for the region's residents. As their cars jerk along, some drivers appear engrossed in thought, a few may be observed speaking into tape recorders or reading documents from the corner of their eyes. In the 'region' the future is now; time is precious; and for many of the drivers work has already begun.
>
> The parking lot in front of High Technologies' Lyndsville engineering facility is rapidly filling. (Kunda, *Engineering Culture*, 1992: 1)

A great many details, but not a complete list. Neither fictive accounts nor ethnographic reports aim at 'a literal description or transcription of people, places or events' (Atkinson, 1990: 40). Such a description would appear absurd, and indeed has been used to create the effect of absurdity in fiction (by e.g. Alain Robbe-Grillet and Nicholas Baker). A skilful description depends heavily on metonymy and synecdoche, on deleting information in the hope that the readers will fill in the blanks, which should also increase their engagement in the reproduction of the text (Atkinson, 1990: 52). Kunda assumes that his readers are familiar with car types enough to picture them; he attempts to re-create an atmosphere, not to give instructions on how to get to Lyndsville by Route 61.

Yet another literary device used to describe the setting is throwing the reader into the midst of the events, creating a puzzle to be solved – by adding more material, and by the subsequent analysis:

> *5 min.* John enters and goes into his office. He says something very quietly about having made a bad mistake. He had sent the review of a paper. ... The rest of the sentence is inaudible. (Latour and Woolgar, *Laboratory Life,* 1979/1986: 15)

Both guide-like introductions and 'throwing the reader into the deep water' anecdotes often employ a rhetorical device known as *hypotyposis*, 'the use of a highly graphic passage of descriptive writing, which portrays a scene or action in a vivid and arresting manner' (Atkinson, 1990: 71). To repeat Stern (1973), they aim at a description that is rich, abundant and colourful, a 'thick description', in Geertz's (1973) terms. Mimesis aims at a description that is both vivid and credible (the two aid one another), that is, a description that persuades.

Mimesis is not the last problem to tackle when writing a monograph. It lies in the rhetorical tradition to differentiate between mimesis (a description) and emplotment (an arrangement). But this differentiation makes only analytical sense: it is obvious that each description must be arranged. This arrangement can be coherent with the arrangement of the whole text, or incoherent with it. In other words, mimesis can corroborate the plot, or oppose it. Although it is possible to think of a mimesis opposing the plot and therefore contributing to some kind of a meta-plot, it is safe to assume that, in a social science monograph, an attempt at coherence is still a virtue. I shall suggest further that description should be subordinated to the requirements of the plot, not least in its volume: the descriptive material that is not needed in this function can be saved in an appendix. From all this it is obvious that, in my eyes, emplotment is the crucial part of writing a social science text.

PLOT, OR HOW TO THEORIZE

Emplotment (a term introduced by Hayden White, 1973, who ventured to say that historians do not *find* plot in history but *put it in* themselves) means introducing structure, which allows making sense of the events reported. Traditionally, it responds to a question 'why?' where, in the positivist view, the answer should be formulated in terms of causal laws; in the romantic view, in terms of motives; in post-positivist, post-romantic discourse (Brown, 1989), it assumes a form of showing 'how come?' where laws of nature, human intentions and random events form a hybrid mixture.

Inherited structures

The easiest way of introducing a structure is by means of chronology. Still, there are several types of chronologies that might be used. Here is a classical form of a thesis (a formal oration in Greek rhetoric):

1   Exordium: catches the audience's interest while introducing the subject.
2   Narration: sets forth the facts.
3   Proposition (or Division): sets forth points stipulated and points to be contested (states the case).
4   Proof: sets forth the arguments in support of the case.
5   Refutation: refutes opponents' arguments.
6   Peroration: sums up arguments and stirs audience. (Lanham, 1991)

This is an interesting example of how a meaningful structure becomes mechanical, and a theory becomes pure chronology. The structure looks as it does, because it was considered to work best (in the sense of doing persuasion work); in time, however, it became simply a chronology of a speech. I am quoting it partly to show how close it is to what is considered a conventional structure of a thesis, but also how meaningful persuasive devices can become mechanical by the fact that they are often repeated.

This is a traditional structure of a thesis, shared by an article and a monograph alike (although an article has to cramp it into a much shorter space, and the reader has to 'unstuff' it, like a big file that arrives 'zipped'):

1   Problem/issue/aims (Exordium)
2   Literature review
3   Hypotheses (Proposition)
4   Method
5   Results (Narration)
6   Discussion (Proof)
7   Conclusion (Peroration)

The similarity is obvious, and it is no coincidence: the structure of a thesis has developed from the structure of an oration. But a thesis is written rather than spoken (the traditional structure is worth remembering when preparing an overhead presentation of a thesis!), and this partly explains differences. A contemporary thesis is grounded in forensic rhetoric, but has some addition of a deliberative rhetoric: thus a 'Literature review'. What was written before is important differently than precedents are important in court. The truly modern addition is the 'Method' – positivism's contribution to classical rhetoric.

Not all monographs comply with this structure. It can be called a structure of a deductive thesis. An inductive thesis, let us say, a thesis written in a spirit of grounded theory approach (Glaser and Strauss, 1967), might look as follows:

1   There is something strange going on in the world ... (Exordium).
2   Has somebody else explained it? (Literature review). If not:
3   I'd better go and learn more about it. But how? (Method).
4   Now that I have understood it, I shall try to explain it to the others. So, let me tell you a story ... (Narration).
5   Now, what does it remind me of? Is there somebody else who thinks similarly? (Proof).
6   This is the end (and the point) of my story (Peroration).

Clearly, another variation of both classical oration plus the modern addenda. Like their classical predecessors, these structures hope for the persuasion effect. Also like their classical predecessors, however, they follow chronology – not of the oration, but of research itself.

This kind of chronological structuring produces as many problems as it solves. First of all, novices in the craft of research (Booth et al., 1995) often suffer from its insincerity. It is well known that research seldom goes as planned. What to do? Report all moves back and forth, hesitations and mistakes? This can be turned into an art, but most often it is not. Lie, therefore, and suffer?

This problem (fact or fiction of research?) is nevertheless secondary. The main question is still the classic one: will it persuade? And although it is not a question that can ever be answered once and for all, a suggestion can be made: that this kind of mechanical structuring is rarely considered a successful emplotment. What, then, is considered a successful emplotment? I suggest that plot can be fruitfully regarded as the work's theory, which can then serve to structure a monograph substantially, rather than formally.

The plot

Aristotle differentiated between a simple story ('a narrative of events arranged in their time-sequence') and a plot that arranges them according to a sense of causality (*Encyclopaedia Britannica*, 1989: 523).

Donald Polkinghorne (1987) dedicated much attention to the role of the plot and its possible uses in the human sciences: 'The plot functions to transform a chronicle or listing of events into a schematic whole by highlighting and recognizing the contribution that certain events make to the development of the whole' (pp. 18–19). But not only that: a plot can weave into the story the historical and social context, information about physical laws and thoughts and feelings reported by people. 'A plot has the capacity to articulate and consolidate complex threads of multiple activities by means of the overlay of subplots' (p. 19). This is an important property from the point of view of social scientists, often faced with the fact that, as many things happen simultaneously, a simple chronology is not sufficient to tell a story. And this analogy is not accidental: 'The recognition or construction of a plot employs the kind of reasoning that Charles Peirce called "abduction", the process of suggesting a hypothesis that can serve to explain some puzzling phenomenon. Abduction produces a conjecture that is tested by fitting it over the "facts"' (p. 19). Lastly, but most importantly, '[m]ore than one plot can provide a meaningful constellation and integration for the same set of events, and different plot organizations change the meaning of the individual events as their roles are reinterpreted according to their functions in different plots' (p. 19) A lavish party has a different meaning in the story of a success than in the story of a bankruptcy.

The most quoted explanation of what constitutes a basic plot is that by Todorov (1977: 111):

> The minimal complete plot consists in the passage from one equilibrium to another. An 'ideal' narrative begins with a stable situation, which is disturbed by some power or force. There results a state of disequilibrium; by the action of a force directed in the opposite direction, the equilibrium is re-established; the second equilibrium is similar to the first, but the two are never identical.[11]

Most tales contain more than one plot, which must be connected to one another. Such a combination of plots is usually achieved, says Todorov (1977), by one of two strategies: *linking* (co-ordination), i.e., adding simple plots to one another so they fit, and *embedding* (subordination), i.e. setting one plot inside the other. One can add, referring to Hayden White (1973), that, like a historian, a social scientist confronts 'a veritable chaos of events *already constituted*, out of which he must choose the elements of the story he would tell' (p. 6, footnote 5). Thus a necessity of two additional tactics: *exclusion* and *emphasis* (also, embedding can serve both combination and selection).

A poor storyteller hopes that chronology will stand for causality; a clever storyteller sells chronology for causality (what happens earlier causes what happens next: see Bruner, 1990). But even a clever storyteller cannot make chronology pass for causality in stories whose elements are connected by *succession* only ('it rained on Monday, I bought a car on Tuesday'); to become a plotted story, they need to be also related by *transformation* (Todorov, 1990). This can be achieved only by adding a third element ('I have had enough of forever getting wet when biking') by which consequent events (that is, the two first elements of a plot, an – assumed – 'normal state' and a deviation) became a new state of affairs. A plotted story thus involves not only a syntagmatic dimension but also a paradigmatic one.

Before I embark on an attempt to read social science texts with what is clearly a set of structuralist devices, I need to make a caveat. My attempt is made in a post-structuralist spirit; that is, I am fully aware that I am placing the structures on to the texts rather than finding them there, and that my attempt in itself is nothing but an emplotment, which can be evaluated by the readers in the same manner.

A well-plotted story

I shall now examine a monograph that joins sequentiality and causality/intentionality, succession and transformation.

Aramis or the Love of Technology (Latour, 1996) is a story of an automated train system that was tried in Paris and then abandoned. It begins, innocently enough, as a combination of two classic plots, one a detective story – who killed Aramis? – and the other a *Bildungsroman*, a story of a pupil learning from the master. The first plot depends for its pull on curiosity: the readers know the effects, Aramis is dead and buried in the Museum of Technology, and the cause is looked for – who did it? The second plot, embedded in the first, depends on the push of (mild) suspense: given Pupil's hunger for knowledge and Master's abundance of it, the readers might fairly surely expect an enlightened Pupil in the end, but they may count on various complications in his way.

Complications, when they arrive, are not of the manageable kind that are the stuff of fairy tales. The obstacles stand in the way, not so much of the heroes, but of the plots. The main plot, that of detecting those guilty of killing an innovation, proves to be unfeasible. At a certain point there are twenty contradictory interpretations offered for the demise of the Aramis project (Latour himself counts them elsewhere), all of them correct. Just before the final report has to be produced, the Master vanishes, not because the Pupil has to learn autonomy, but because the Master has more important things to think about.

What was a detective story turns into a tragic love story. Aramis has not been killed; it is just that nobody loved him enough to keep him alive. His less attractive rival, the metro system VAL, is loved and lives happily in Lille, a new Aramis is being born in San Diego – will it live?

The *Bildungsroman* turns into its opposite, a tormented inner journey of the Master into self-reflection, doubt and fear. The Pupil gets his grade and tries to ignore the ramblings of his former Master, whose excessive reflection makes him turn against the sacred values of science. Hardly a conventional ending for social science study.

The device of changing horses mid-stream, that is, transforming the main plots of the story, is a tricky business. One danger is obvious: the author might drown. Aramis, Master and their author survive the journey very well, but it does take a masterly coachman.

Another danger lies with the readers: they may not like the play of plots. Bronwyn Davies (1989) read feminist fairy tales to pre-school children, where plot was intact but the functions of characters were reversed. It was the princess, for example, who saved the silly, pretty prince from the dragon and then left him. Davies's small listeners did interpretative wonders in order to save the proper plot: as the result of her efforts the princess became dirty and poor and therefore understood herself, they explained, not to be a proper wife for the prince. ... Readers might resort to murder in order to save 'their' plots, at least symbolically.

Latour saved himself by doing a revolutionary transformation of plots but landing with another set of recognizable and legitimate plots. Herein lies another complication to popularizing his kind of experiment in social science. It assumes a reader very familiar with all the variety of plots in both fiction and sociology. Such clever tricks may well be lost on many readers, but the main trick – emplotment – is exemplary even if not easily imitated.

What, then, is usually judged a successful plot? It is a plot that is coherent, that contains a basic plot structure, and then plays around it: by complicating it, by introducing sub-plots and counter-plots. In other words, plot equals a well-thought theory, which in social science monographs, unlike in novels, is explicitly articulated (at the end or at the beginning).

Does this mean that the conventional structure needs to be abandoned? Not necessarily. My plea is that writers understand the purpose of the conventional structure, and cease to treat it mechanically. Once understood, it can be followed, abandoned or circumvented: it may become a frame within which a well-plotted story is inserted.

This text is based on an assumption that the ways of emplotment go through either imitating attractive plots, or inventing new plots – and in such case it is easier to do so if one understands the moves. Neither of these, however, guarantees the desired response of the readers.

HOW IS A TEXT READ?

An author tries to anticipate the readers' reaction in part by projecting the past criteria of the 'goodness' of a scientific text on to the future. I say 'in part' because all innovative writing hopes to establish new criteria by defying earlier ones. To be followed or to be broken, evaluation criteria seem to be helpful to a writer. A constructionist view, however, reveals the impossibility of establishing such criteria a priori. There is only a pattern of conventional readers' responses (known only retrospectively) and a horde of institutionalized norms for writing that might be observed or broken in practice.

One traditional set of such norms refers to 'validity', the correspondence between the text and the world, and to 'reliability', the guarantee of repeated results with the use of the same method. These are supposedly ostensive traits: they characterize (or not) the study, and therefore can be demonstrated.

Validity as a correspondence criterion has attracted most criticism from recent theories of knowledge. Whether one claims to speak of a reality or a fantasy, the value of utterances cannot be established by comparing them to their object, but only by comparing them to other utterances. Words cannot be compared to worlds, and a look into actual validation practices reveals that they always consist in checking texts against other texts.

It could be argued that the same observation shows that there exists reliability understood as replication. From the perspective held here, however, it could be claimed that results are repeated not because the correct method has repeatedly been applied to the same object of study, but because institutionalized research practices tend to produce similar results. One can go even further and claim that results are as much part of practice as methods are. An excellent illustration of this phenomenon is the debate within AIDS research, which shows that studies which do not arrive at what is seen as the legitimate conclusion are not funded (Horton, 1996). It is perhaps more accurate to speak of 'conformity' rather than reliability; it is not the results that are reliable, but the researchers – who are conforming to dominant rules.

Dissatisfaction with positivist criteria for 'good scientific texts' and a desire for alternative guidelines led to a search for a new set of criteria – within the interpretative tradition. Thus, Guba (1981) spoke of 'trustworthiness' of naturalist studies (composed of truth value, applicability, consistency and neutrality); Fisher (1987) spoke of 'narrative probability' (coherence) and 'narrative fidelity' (truth value), constituting 'narrative rationality'; while Golden-Biddle and Locke (1993) suggested authenticity, plausibility and criticality as the ways in which ethnographic texts convince their audiences. Unfortunately, like the positivist criteria they criticize, these are again *ostensive* criteria of a text's success, i.e. the

attributes of a text that can be demonstrated and therefore applied a priori to determine a text's success.

Reader-response theory has counteracted such objectivist reading theories (Iser, 1978), but in turn it subjectivized the act of reading, neglecting the institutional effect. Yet there is a limited repertoire of texts and responses at any given time and place, there are more and less legitimate responses, and there is fashion as a selection mechanism. The pragmatist theory of reading to which I adhere (Rorty, 1992) gives preference to *performative* criteria. These are not rules that, when observed by a writer, will guarantee the positive reception of his or her work, but descriptions that summarize the typical justifications given when a positive reception occurs. Such descriptions do not concern the text but the responses of the readers as reported in the legitimate vocabulary of the day.

A social science writer who desires success might thus do well choosing postmodernism as his or her mantle, but texts written at the peak of fashion might become classical or obsolete, and no properties of the text can determine which is going to be their fate. Durkheim and Weber held for a century, but they now seem to be losing to their less successful competitors, Tarde and Simmel.

An aspiring author cannot count on readers to tell what they are going to like next, but might try to remember how they justified their past judgements, hoping that it will hold for a while. There are two common types of justifications: the *pragmatic* and the *aesthetic*. It is even possible to claim that the latter is included in the former and vice versa, if treated broadly enough. Something 'works' because it touches me, because it is beautiful, because it is a powerful metaphor, but one can also hear engineers say of machines, 'look how beautifully it works!' Rorty (1992) says that although 'usefulness' is decided according to a purpose at hand, the best readings are not those that serve such a purpose but that have changed it. This he calls an *edifying* discourse or a discourse that has the power 'to take us out of our old selves by the power of strangeness, to aid us in becoming new beings' (1980: 360). Edifying discourse is thus one that is both useful and beautiful.

Consequently objectivity, that high praise when addressed to scientific texts, can be seen as no more and no less than conformity to the norms of justification common in a relevant community (Rorty, 1980: 36): a difficult achievement and *therefore* praiseworthy.

Judgements on what is objective and what is edifying are rarely unanimous (there is a variety of opinions in each community) and they change over time. Therefore one can at best speak of a kind of writing, or rather kinds of writing, that are considered legitimate, and that are read in a given time and place. The debate on what is good and bad writing can thus be replaced or at least aided by a discussion of genres, i.e., institutionalized forms of writing. Achieving an inventory and a description of genres not only allows for probabilistic estimates of success, but also permits understanding deviations. Every avant-garde, every vibrant fringe, every edifying discourse feeds on the mainstream, on normal science, on systematizing discourse. By the same token, the 'canonical tradition' (MacIntyre, 1988) depends on deviations for its survival, and also owes its eventual demise to them.

Social science texts, as a genre or perhaps a family of sub-genres, might thus make a skilful use of tropes and narratives; they might also use the insights of literary theory as an aid to self-reflection. This can help us escape from the inherited image of social science as a (still) defective natural science. I do not suggest that it should become a defective fiction instead. I argue for a conscious and reflective creation of a family of genres, which recognizes its tradition without being paralysed by it, which seeks inspiration in other genres without imitating them, and which derives confidence from the importance of its topic and from its own growing skills.

This chapter, as should be obvious by now, is grounded in a belief that social science, in order to matter more in the life of contemporary societies,[12] needs to reach readers from outside its own circles. While the texts of disciplinary self-reflection will remain interesting and relevant for social scientists only (which does not mean that they should abandon any literary pretensions – social scientists love beautiful texts, too), the bulk of social science needs to be skillfuly crafted. And the questions – from inside and outside, such as: Is it valid? Is it reliable? Is it Science? – should be replaced by something like: Is it relevant (pragmatic)? Is it beautiful (aesthetic)? Is it moving (edifying)?

NOTES

1   See, e.g., Harrari (1979) and Eco (1992) for anthologies and Selden (1985) for an overview of the new trends in literary theory.

2   Although metaphor goes beyond analogy. Analogy assumes continuity, metaphor assumes rupture. In other words, analogy *reports* similarity, metaphor *creates* it.

3   For a more complete discussion of verisimilitude in social science texts, see Atkinson (1990).

4   There exist excellent sources that treat them separately: Becker (1986), Clifford and Marcus (1986) and Hart (1998).

5   In his 'Del rigor en la ciencia' (*Historia universal de la infamia*, 1935/1967) Borges tells a story of cartographers who created a map that was identical with the empire it represented. The next generation threw away the map and forgot cartography.

6   Three volumes that are especially recommended to an interested reader are Levine (1993), Richard H. Brown (1995) and Van Maanen (1995).

7   This is relevant also for pictorial representations of the world, but I shall avoid speaking about art in order to save space.

8   I review these in *A Narrative Approach to Organization Studies* (1998).

9   I am not suggesting that the field of theory is not politically structured, but it is usually easier to grasp its structure and choose one's strategy (joining the mainstream, joining the avant-garde, opposing the mainstream, etc.).

10 I develop this theme in *Narrating the Organization* (1997) and in *Writing Management* (1999). See also Atkinson (1990) for the discussion of polyphony in sociological ethnographies.

11 It may seem that this definition excludes texts where narrative does not play much role, for example, structural analyses. But, as McCloskey (1990b) pointed out, each theory *is* a narrative, as verbs such as 'to influence' or 'to determine' denote events. Syllogisms are kinds of plot.

12 See also Flyvbjerg's (2001) impassioned call for 'a social science that matters'.

REFERENCES

Agger, Ben (1990) *The Decline of Discourse*. New York: Falmer Press.

Atkinson, Paul (1990) *The Ethnographic Imagination: Textual Construction of Reality*. London: Routledge.

Bakhtin, Mikhail M. (1981) 'Discourse in the novel', in *The Dialogic Imagination: Four Essays*. Austin: University of Texas Press, pp. 259–422.

Becker, Howard S. (1986) *Writing for Social Scientists*. Chicago: University of Chicago Press.

Booth, Wayne C., Colomb, Gregory G. and Williams, Joseph M. (1995) *The Craft of Research*. Chicago: University of Chicago Press.

Borges, Jorge Luis (1935/1967) 'Del rigor en ciencia', in *Historia universal de la infamia*. Buenos Aires: Emecé Editores.

Bradbury, Malcolm (1992) 'Closer to chaos: American fiction in the 1980s', *Times Literary Supplement*, 22: 17.

Brown, Richard H. (1977) *A Poetic for Sociology: Toward a Logic of Discovery for the Human Sciences*. New York: Cambridge University Press.

Brown, Richard H. (1989) *Social Science as Civic Discourse*. Chicago: University of Chicago Press.

Brown, Richard H. (ed.) (1995) *Postmodern Representations*. Chicago: University of Illinois Press.

Bruner, Jerome (1990) *Acts of Meaning*. Cambridge, MA: Harvard University Press.

Bruss, Elisabeth W. (1982) *Beautiful Theories*. Baltimore: Johns Hopkins University Press.

Clifford, James and Marcus, George E. (eds) (1986) *Writing Culture*. Berkeley: University of California Press.

Czarniawska, Barbara (1997) *Narrating the Organization*. Chicago: University of Chicago Press.

Czarniawska, Barbara (1998) *A Narrative Approach to Organization Studies*. Thousand Oaks, CA: Sage.

Czarniawska, Barbara (1999) *Writing Management*. Oxford: Oxford University Press.

Davies, Bronwyn (1989) *Frogs and Snails and Feminist Tales*. North Sydney: Allen & Unwin.

de Certeau, Michel (1984) *The Practice of Everyday Life*. Berkeley: University of California Press.

Eco, Umberto (1979/1983) *The Role of the Reader*. London: Hutchinson.

Eco, Umberto (1992) *Interpretation and Overinterpretation*. Cambridge: Cambridge University Press.

Encyclopaedia Britannica (1989) Micropaedia, vol. 9: 523.

Fisher, Walter R. (1987) *Human Communication as Narration*. Columbia: University of South Carolina Press.

Flyvbjerg, Bent (2001) *Making Social Science Matter*. Cambridge: Cambridge University Press.

Geertz, Clifford (1973) *The Interpretation of Cultures*. New York: Basic Books.

Geertz, Clifford (1988) *Works and Lives: The Anthropologist as Author*. Stanford: Stanford University Press.

Glaser, Barney and Strauss, Anselm (1967) *The Discovery of Grounded Theory*. Chicago: Aldine.

Golden-Biddle, Karin and Locke, Karin (1993) 'Appealing work: an investigation of how ethnographic texts convince', *Organization Science*, 4(4): 595–616.

Guba, Edwin G. (1981) 'Criteria for assessing truthworthiness of naturalistic inquiries', *Educational Communication and Technology Journal*, 29(2): 75–91.

Harrari, Josue V. (ed.) (1979) *Textual Strategies: Perspectives in Post-structuralist Criticism*. Ithaca, NY: Methuen.

Hart, Chris (1998) *Doing a Literature Review*. London: Sage.

Hemmings, Fredrick W.J. (1978) 'Realism and the novel: the eighteenth-century beginnings', in Fredrick W.J. Hemmings (ed.), *The Age of Realism*. Sussex: Harvester Press, pp. 3–35.

Horton, Richard (1996) 'Truth and heresy about AIDS', *New York Review of Books*, 23 May: 14–20.

Hühn, Peter (1987) 'The detective as reader', *Modern Fiction Studies*, 33(3): 451–66.

Iser, Wolfgang (1978) *The Art of Reading*. Baltimore: Johns Hopkins University Press.

Knorr-Cetina, Karin (1981) *The Manufacture of Knowledge*. Oxford: Pergamon.

Knorr-Cetina, Karin (1994) 'Primitive classification and postmodernity', *Theory, Culture and Society*, 11: 1–22.

Kunda, Gideon (1992) *Engineering Culture*. Philadelphia: Temple University Press.

Lamarque, Peter (1990) 'Narrative and invention: the limits of fictionality', in Cristopher Nash (ed.), *Narrative in Culture*. London: Routledge, pp. 5–22.

Lanham, Richard A. (1991) *A Handlist of Rhetorical Terms*. Berkeley: University of California Press.

Latour, Bruno (1988) 'The politics of explanation: an alternative', in Steve Woolgar (ed.), *Knowledge and Reflexivity*. London: Sage, pp. 155–77.

Latour, Bruno (1992) 'The next turn after the social turn …', in Ernan McMullin (ed.), *The Social Dimensions of Science*. Notre Dame: University of Notre Dame Press, pp. 272–92.

Latour, Bruno (1996) *Aramis or the Love of Technology*. Cambridge, MA: Harvard University Press.

Latour, Bruno (1999) *Pandora's Hope*. Cambridge, MA: Harvard University Press.

Latour, Bruno and Woolgar, Steve (1979/1986) *Laboratory Life: The Construction of Scientific Facts*. Princeton, NJ: Princeton University Press.

Lepenies, Wolf (1988) *Between Literature and Science: The Rise of Sociology*. Cambridge: Cambridge University Press.

Levin, Harry (1973) 'Literature as an institution', in Elisabeth and Tom Burns (eds), *Sociology of Literature and Drama*. Harmondsworth: Penguin, pp. 56–70.

Levine, George (ed.) (1993) *Realism and Representation: Essays on the Problem of Realism in Relation to Science, Literature, and Culture*, Madison: University of Wisconsin Press.

MacIntyre, Alasdair (1988) *Whose Justice? Which Rationality?* London: Duckworth.

Marcus, George E. and Fischer, Michael M. (1986) *Anthropology as Cultural Critique*. Chicago: University of Chicago Press.

McCloskey, D.N. (1986) *The Rhetoric of Economics*. Madison: University of Wisconsin Press.

McCloskey, D.N. (1990a) *If You're So Smart: The Narrative of Economic Expertise*. Madison: University of Wisconsin Press.

McCloskey, D.N. (1990b) 'Storytelling in economics', in Cristopher Nash (ed.), *Narrative in Culture*. London: Routledge, pp. 5–22.

Meyer, John W. (1996) 'Otherhood: the promulgation and transmission of ideas in the modern organizational environment', in Barbara Czarniawska and Guje Sevón (eds), *Translating Organizational Change*. Berlin: de Gruyter, pp. 241–52.

Nelson, John S., Megill, Allan and McCloskey, D.N. (eds) (1987) *The Rhetoric of the Human Sciences*. Madison: University of Wisconsin Press.

Perrow, Charles (1991) 'A society of organizations', *Theory and Society*, 20: 725–62.

Polkinghorne, Donald (1987) *Narrative Knowing and the Human Sciences*. Albany, NY: SUNY Press.

Rorty, Richard (1980) *Philosophy and the Mirror of Nature*. Oxford: Blackwell.

Rorty, Richard (1982) *Consequences of Pragmatism*. Minneapolis: University of Minnesota Press.

Rorty, Richard (1989) *Contingency, Irony and Solidarity.* Cambridge: Cambridge University Press.

Rorty, Richard (1991) 'Inquiry as recontextualization: an anti-dualist account of interpretation', in *Objectivity, Relativism and Truth*, vol. 1. New York: Cambridge University Press, pp. 93–110.

Rorty, Richard (1992) 'The pragmatist's progress', in Umberto Eco, *Interpretation and Overinterpretation.* Cambridge: Cambridge University Press, pp. 89–108.

Schaffer, Simon (1993) 'Augustan realities', in George Levine (ed.), *Realism and Representation.* Madison: University of Wisconsin Press, pp. 279–318.

Selden, Raman (1985) *A Reader's Guide to Contemporary Literary Theory.* Brighton: Harvester Press.

Stern, J.P. (1973) *On Realism.* London: Routledge & Kegan Paul.

Thompson, James D. (1967) *Organizations in Action.* New York: McGraw-Hill.

Todorov, Tzvetan (1977) *The Poetics of Prose.* Oxford: Blackwell.

Todorov, Tzvetan (1990) *Genres in Discourse.* Cambridge: Cambridge University Press.

Van Fraassen, Bas C. and Sigman, Jill (1993) 'Interpretation in science and in the arts', in George Levine (ed.), *Realism and Representation.* Madison: University of Wisconsin Press, pp. 73–99.

Van Maanen, John (ed.) (1995) *Representation in Ethnography.* Thousand Oaks, CA: Sage.

Waldo, Dwight (1961) 'Organization theory: an elephantine problem', *Public Administration Review*, 21: 210–25.

Webster's New Collegiate Dictionary (1981) Springfield, MA: G. & C. Merriam Company.

White, Hayden (1973) *Metahistory.* Baltimore: Johns Hopkins University Press.

White, Hayden (1987) *The Content of the Form.* Baltimore: Johns Hopkins University Press.

White, Hayden (1999) *Figural Realism.* Baltimore: Johns Hopkins University Press.

Wolf, Margery (1992) *A Thrice-Told Tale.* Stanford: Stanford University Press.

Woolgar, Steve (1988) *Science: The Very Idea.* London: Tavistock.

37

Publishing qualitative manuscripts: lessons learned

Donileen R. Loseke and Spencer E. Cahill

In this chapter we explore the complex world of publishing qualitative research. We begin by considering the current publishing climate. We then discuss the specific characteristics of publishable manuscripts and conclude with an exploration of some of the seemingly mysterious characteristics of the publishing process. Throughout, we use examples from our own experiences as authors, reviewers, members of editorial boards, and past co-editors of the *Journal of Contemporary Ethnography*.

THE BEST OF TIMES, THE WORST OF TIMES

It is, so to speak, the best of times and the worst of times for authors wishing to publish manuscripts based on qualitative research. It is the best of times for finding publishing outlets for such work. Granted, the authority of positivistic science, with its deductive logic and statistical analysis, remains dominant in many parts of the academy and some of the most prestigious journals remain closed to all manuscripts not conforming to this natural science model of research.[1] At the same time, there are many publication sites clearly open to authors of manuscripts using qualitative techniques and data presentation. These include highly rated official journals such as *Communication Quarterly*, *The Sociological Quarterly*, *Social Problems*, *Revue Française de Sociologie*, and *Zeitschrift für Soziologie*. Beyond official journals, there are countless others that often publish qualitative work such as *International Sociology*, *Media, Culture and Society*, *Text and Performance Quarterly*, and *Social Studies of Science* (US), *Sexualities* and *Sociology of Health and Illness* (UK), *Discourse and Society* and *Discourse Studies* (The Netherlands), *Kölner Zeitschrift für Soziologie und Sozialpsychologie* and *Soziale Welt* (Germany), *Société Contemporaine*, *Sociologie du Travail* and *Actes de la Recherches en Sciences Sociales* (France).

In addition, we now live in a time when a number of journals are dedicated to publishing qualitative genres of research and explicitly *exclude* research conforming to the natural science model of deductive logic and statistical analysis. These include *Ethnography* and *Qualitative Research* (UK), *Terraines* (France), *Qualitative Health Research*, *Qualitative Inquiry*, *Qualitative Market Research*, *Qualitative Studies in Psychology*, *International Journal of Qualitative Studies in Education*, *Qualitative Sociology*, and the *Journal of Contemporary Ethnography* (US). Still further, top-ranked journals previously wed to publishing research conforming to the natural science model, such as the *American Educational Research Journal* (Smith, 1987) and *Social Psychology Quarterly* (Lawler, 1994; Molm and Smith-Lovin, 1997), have made explicit efforts to attract manuscripts based on qualitative research.

Our list of journals publishing research based on qualitative data and analysis is only exemplary and far from exhaustive. Yet it clearly reflects the growing acceptance of qualitative work in the social sciences. Only three decades ago, qualitative researchers in North America were forced to establish their own journal (*Urban Life and Culture*, later renamed *Urban Life* and still later the *Journal of Contemporary Ethnography*) because other journals would not accept their work (Fine, 1999). This is the good news for scholars wishing to publish manuscripts based on qualitative research.

Yet the news is not all good. As we step inside the circle of qualitative researchers, we confront confusion, disagreement, and conflict. The most fundamental dispute is about what qualifies as 'qualitative research'. Glibly, of course, qualitative research is *not* quantitative research. Such a basic distinction mirrors the formal editorial policy contained on the front page of the journal of *Qualitative Sociology* where potential authors are told that the journal publishes articles 'which do not rely primarily on numerical data'. Defining qualitative research as simply non-numerical encourages us to consider how these research paradigms differ in their questions, assumptions, and techniques (see, e.g., Becker, 2001). It also makes sense to define qualitative in opposition to quantitative because qualitative researchers often feel diminished by the academic, political, and public authority of the natural science model of research associated with quantitative analyses (Denzin and Lincoln, 2000).

Yet it is not sufficient simply to define qualitative research as non-quantitative. As Gubrium and Holstein (1997: 5) note, because qualitative research 'is typically counterposed with the contemporary monolith of quantitative sociology, qualitative method is often portrayed in broad strokes that blur differences'. As they so aptly demonstrate, there are remarkably diverse images of human social life, assumptions about the nature of reality, and multiple research strategies all huddled under the umbrella term of qualitative research. According to at least one sympathetic observer, qualitative research is so diverse as to be 'disorderly' (Smith, 1987: 173).

Aspiring authors of qualitative work therefore do not find agreement about what this research should do, be, or look like. Instead, there is a 'carnivalesque profusion of methods, perspectives, and theoretical justifications' (Atkinson et al., 2001: 2) with no 'single, unchallenged paradigm ... for deciding what does and does not comprise valid, useful, and significant knowledge' (Bochner, 2000: 268). Although some observers (e.g. Denzin and Lincoln, 2000:18) claim that proliferating methods and styles of qualitative research provide researchers many 'choices', others maintain that not all of these 'choices' are equal in their value. For example, Snow and Morrill (1995: 341) observe that there is a 'rather contentious debate within qualitative circles regarding the very foundations of ethnographic knowledge and the appropriate character of such research and writing'.

This brief sketch of the diverse and fragmented field called qualitative research is critical to understanding the process of publishing such work. Although there are an increasing number of possible publication venues, the undefined nature of the method and contentious debates among qualitative researchers pose problems for authors: the more disagreement in an area of inquiry, the higher the rate of manuscript *rejection* (Beyer, 1978; Bakanic et al., 1987; Clemens et al., 1995; Gilliland and Cortina, 1997). The lack of consensus about what qualitative research is – and should be – increases the likelihood of manuscript rejection.

An increasing number of possible publication sites but lack of consensus about what qualitative research should be and do are the current historical contexts of publishing such work. Given this context, what then distinguishes published manuscripts from those collecting dust in the back of file cabinets? It is no surprise that scholars whose careers depend on the answer to that question have given it considerable attention (Bakanic et al., 1987; Hargens, 1988; Fiske and Fogg, 1990; Orum, 1990; Stryker, 1990; Fiske, 1992; Beyer et al., 1995; Clemens et al., 1995; Gilliland and Cortina, 1997; McGinty, 1999). Also not surprisingly, that question has no easy answers. Some observers believe that manuscripts of highest quality are published; others believe that published manuscripts tend to be those by authors at prestigious institutions, and by those whose interests reflect the biases of editors; others believe published manuscripts simply are those available to editors when publication deadlines approach (Bakanic et al., 1987). All observers are correct: manuscript quality, politics, and luck are each implicated in publication decisions.

That has been our experience on both sides of the editorial decision-making process. Our comments here are organized into sections that separately consider the issues of quality, politics, and luck in the publication process. The first addresses issues of manuscript quality, the characteristics of manuscripts that editors and reviewers say matter and that manuscript reviewers most often mention in their reviews (see Gilliland and Cortina, 1997, for references). These include the issues of method, importance and significance of findings, and clarity of writing. While in a just world manuscript quality would be sufficient to ensure publication, the world of scholarly publication is not always just. We move on to consider the political and practical issues involved in the publishing process. In order to offer practical advice to authors about dealing with editors and reviewers, we conclude with reflections upon our own decision-making process while co-editors of the *Journal of Contemporary Ethnography* (*JCE*). We maintain that although both politics and luck most assuredly are involved in the publication process, there are things authors can do to increase the chances that their manuscripts will be accepted for publication. Although we have organized our comments into sections, it is important to recognize that quality, politics, and luck are hopelessly intertwined in the real world of scholarly publishing. Evaluations of quality *always* have political sources and implications even if these evaluations are not politically motivated. Politics or luck seldom will save a fatally flawed manuscript; luck can be made.

In what follows, we draw heavily upon reviews of manuscripts submitted to *JCE* during our editorship. Our own work (and therefore the biases we carried into evaluating manuscripts) flirts with the postmodern turn in qualitative research but remains grounded in somewhat traditional 'neorealist' (Hammersley, 2001) notions of qualitative research. Given this, we offer only the most general advice for authors of manuscripts employing the unconventional sources of information and representational styles associated with postmodernism.

MANUSCRIPT QUALITY

It is our experience that publication outlets (for all types of work) have proliferated to such an extent that journal editors sometimes find themselves facing a publication deadline without enough manuscripts to fill the forthcoming issue. At the same time, even when journal pages need to be filled, many – if not most – submitted manuscripts do not make it into those pages: many journals accept only around one in ten or one in twelve submitted manuscripts.[2] This rejection rate is remarkably stable over time and does not vary much in relation to the number of journal pages to be filled, the prestige of the journal, or the number of submissions received (Hargens, 1988). Here we examine characteristics of manuscripts that reviewers and editors for *all* types of academic journals claim are important. Yet because of the lack of consensus about qualitative research genres, discussing visions of manuscript 'quality' is problematic. Aptly described as 'pre-paradigmatic' (Beyer, 1978), there are few commonly accepted standards or 'rules of the craft' (Schwalbe, 1996) and therefore no single standard for judging manuscript quality (Bochner, 2000). Nonetheless, we follow the lead of others who have found that reviewers and editors judge manuscript quality on the grounds of investigative and analytic method, significance and importance of findings, and clarity of writing. The particular problem faced by qualitative researchers is that manuscript reviewers often define these criteria differently and/or weigh them differently in their overall evaluation of manuscripts (Gilliland and Cortina, 1997).

Investigative and analytic method

The most basic lesson of introductory research methods courses is that methods, of any variety, are *tools* to investigate social life. Tools, of course, have specific purposes – hammers, saws, pliers, and screwdrivers are not interchangeable. Deciding whether a particular tool is better or worse than another depends on the task at hand, as does the decision to use a particular research strategy. Yet the analogy between research methods and tools is somewhat misleading because the toolbox of research methods is weightier than a home toolkit: particular research techniques carry heavy philosophical and theoretical baggage (see, e.g., Gubrium and Holstein, 1997; Schwandt, 2000). These include varying images of important questions and goals of research; different conceptions of relationships between human actors and their social, political, and cultural environment; varied notions of preferred relationships between researchers and those researched; and appropriate styles of representation. Although we agree with Becker (2001: 320) that much time can be wasted 'hashing over philosophical details which often have little or nothing to do with what researchers actually do', it remains true that different philosophical and theoretical commitments require different methods of research.

Regardless of the author's professed theoretical or methodological allegiances, articles submitted for publication are evaluated, in part, on the goodness of fit between epistemological/ methodological frameworks authors claim and what they actually deliver. One mark of quality is the logical fit between method and theoretical assumptions. While we were editors of *JCE*, one reviewer criticized a manuscript for failing to meet this criterion: 'Conceptually, the paper represents a somewhat confused contradictory set of themes, an uneven mix of functionalist assumptions and ethnographic methodology'.

We often received submissions from authors who presented their works as traditional ethnography. In these instances, reviewers and we wanted to see the critical characteristic of this method: the 'thick description' (Geertz, 1973) of social life based on 'intimate familiarity with the lived experience of real people doing real things' (Sanders, 1996: 290). Manuscripts claiming the mantle of traditional ethnography often were challenged when they contained only the *author's summary* of what was seen and heard rather than detailed empirical descriptions of what people actually said and did.

In addition, the explicit theoretical ambitions of manuscripts could be evaluated as incompatible with the specific analytic method. One reviewer wrote about a manuscript claiming to be ethnography:

> The problem of the paper is that the author has not understood (or chooses not to address) one of the fundamental tenets of ethnography: to grasp the culture of a group of people. The [theoretical scheme used by the author] imposes a very general and therefore almost empty definition of what [the topics of the paper] consist of. … What ethnography brings into focus, usually, is not some general features of some assumedly universal group life, but the way specific people conduct their everyday affairs.

As another example, when authors framed their work as narrative analysis, reviewers expected the manuscript to focus on the meaning of social experience from the *actor's* perspective (Riessman, 1993), and objected when the *author's* perspective prevailed:

> Given the centrality of the concept of narrative to your text I'm surprised about the lack of reference to the literature on narratives. Some at least brief attention might help you avoid violating your own intentions, as the present version of your manuscript does. On page 3, for example, you state that 'it is not our intention to debunk [a particular group's] stories'. Yet you come dangerously close to doing so in repeatedly contrasting [these stories] to an ostensibly objective historical record.

Similarly, some authors claimed a postmodern framework, yet reviewers questioned whether the claimed framework was actually used. A reviewer of one such paper argued:

> It seems that the use of ethnography to discuss postmodern phenomena warrants some attention to the problematics of ethnography introduced by [string of authors' names]. It feels as if the author has applied 'postmodern concepts' as an afterthought; and this paper would be much strengthened were the author to address/apply these concepts in a more purposive and focused manner.

While perceived discrepancies between the epistemological/methodological framework and manuscript contents led reviewers to criticize manuscripts, perceived compatibilities brought praise. Reviewers of manuscripts claiming an ethnographic framework, for example, greatly appreciated works containing rich empirical description: 'I am delighted to read the voices of the most neglected of [a particular group]. The experiences of these people have too long been silenced or overlooked.' Reviewers of narrative analyses likewise praised manuscripts with appropriate frameworks: 'The paper seems solidly grounded in field observation plus very relevant secondary historical materials and census data. The analysis is convincing and valuable insofar as it combines narrative analysis with examination of structural and historical conditions.'

These examples illustrate that authors should carefully consider the assumptions underlying their theoretical and methodological framework and the relationship between the two. As Hammersley (2001: 102) argues, we cannot escape the philosophical assumptions underlying our methods and analytic frameworks. We must face them. While that does not preclude creative uses and marriages of methods and analytic frameworks, such creativity requires thoughtfulness.

Significance and importance

Reviewers and editors also evaluate manuscripts in terms of their significance and importance. Here again, though, qualitative researchers are not united in their visions of what constitutes significance and importance. Within academia, research traditionally has been most prized when it increases general theoretical understanding (Lofland and Lofland, 1995), yet applied research is significant when it leads to resolutions of practical problems (Lyon, 1997). In comparison, work guided by a postmodern vision is evaluated as significant and important when it encourages emancipation of an oppressed group (Kincheloe and McLaren, 2000), evokes emotional responses in readers (Richardson, 2000), or advances the researcher's and perhaps readers' self-understanding (Ellis and Bochner, 2000).

Regardless of the specific ways in which manuscripts are judged significant and important, it remains true that quality manuscripts are about 'something', and this 'something' must be recognizable to readers, including those who review them for possible publication. As one reviewer commented: 'This article is part essay, part journal/field notes, part travel account, part ethnography, part analysis … it seems to be about everything and nothing at the same time and rambles on.'

Although different images of qualitative methods lead to different images of what is – and what is not – important, high quality manuscripts, of whatever variety, instruct. They teach readers something *new* (Beyer et al., 1995). Quality manuscripts therefore achieve their significance and importance by entering into a dialogue with others. Within some postmodern visions of qualitative research, this is a dialogue with readers, the world, and its representations:

> I found this manuscript creatively written, engaging, and thought provoking. This is an excellent example of what we can learn from autoethnographic reflection, study, and representation; an excellent example of connecting the auto with the ethno; theory with practice; theory with story; literary writing with sociological analysis.

In comparison, more traditional conceptions of qualitative research require authors to locate their work within the academic dialogue taking place in the current literature. Failure to do so is, in the words of one reviewer, fatal:

> A central and probably fatal flaw in this paper is your apparent lack of familiarity with recent ethnographic work – 40 to 50 year old studies are used to exemplify anthropology, with the suggestion that ethnographers have done nothing on contemporary culture. You need only peruse the pages and book reviews of [several journals listed] to see that there has been a wealth of research in the past 20 years on [the topic matter].

Quality manuscripts therefore require authors to engage in the ongoing intellectual conversation and this means addressing existing literature. One reviewer said this explicitly: 'When one publishes the results of research, one is joining an ongoing conversation among those who have been working in the field.'

Achieving significance – newsworthiness – also requires manuscripts of all varieties to engage the types of questions currently in vogue within the relevant framework. Or, in the words of one *JCE* reviewer, 'this is an engaging story, but it's only one more in a long line of ethnographies showing us that Goffman had a lot to say. What's new here?' Another manuscript did not survive the review process for similar reasons. One reviewer said the topic of the manuscript had not been important for a decade, and the theoretical perspective of the manuscript had long since been superseded; the second reviewer wrote that the manuscript 'covers well-traveled ground' and that the 'writer seems unaware of the now considerable body of work [in four relevant areas]'.

Critically, reviewers expect more than mere citations to existing literature. Significance and importance are achieved by going beyond current understandings. Stated simply by one reviewer: 'The authors make some cursory references to the literature on [topic] but their discussion does not move the conversation forward.' Stated more completely by a reviewer of another manuscript:

> It seems to me that any adequate analysis of narratives would make use of previous empirical work on similar kinds of data. By merely citing [a particular author] and [another particular author] you missed an opportunity to show how what you found looks like, or differs from, previous analysis of [the topic matter]. There are lots of points of articulation between your work and [other authors'].

At the same time, reviewers applaud manuscripts that join ongoing conversations:

> The manuscript is well conceived, articulate, focused, appropriate in theory and method, well-written, and contains a vast understanding of the relevant symbolic interactionist literature on policy and policy implementation. An engrossing topic, too!

Finally, high quality manuscripts speak to the interests of the target audience. For example, manuscripts submitted to journals specializing in qualitative work do *not* need to convince readers that such methods are valid and informative. Manuscripts that do so are 'preaching to the choir' and do not fare well with editors or reviewers who are members of the choir and already know the sermon by heart. Conversely, the same manuscript might fare quite well with a journal whose readership is not yet convinced of the value of qualitative methods.

Clarity of presentation

So far, what we have said about the characteristics of high quality manuscripts pertains to manuscripts using any form of data analysis and presentation. Regardless of the style of data analysis and presentation, *all* manuscripts are evaluated in terms of the appropriateness of methods and the significance and importance of their contributions to our understanding. A third characteristic of quality manuscripts, excellent writing, is particularly important for qualitative work. Unlike quantitative researchers who can be persuasive by using a variety of rather well-accepted rhetorical strategies associated with the natural sciences (see, e.g., Gusfield, 1981; Hilgartner, 2000), there is no agreement on how persuasiveness is achieved in qualitative analysis. It is not surprising, as noted by Lofland and Lofland (1995: 217), that there has been a 'virtual explosion in "writing about writing" in social science'. This explosion in concern about writing has three primary sources.

First, and most simply, social scientists have long been renowned for our tortured prose.

Attempting to claim the mantle of science, our writing far too often can be aptly described as a 'wasteland of inert prose' (Erikson, 1990: 25). Given this reputation, it is not surprising that there is a cottage industry in the social sciences on how to write understandable prose.[3] From our experience as editors and reviewers we are painfully aware of the all too common problem of incomprehensible prose. At times, this is a fatal flaw leading to manuscript rejection. As editors of *JCE*, for example, we returned one manuscript without sending it for review because it contained five grammatical and six spelling errors in the first paragraph that was one sentence spanning eight lines. In another instance we sent a manuscript for review that all three reviewers found unintelligible. In confidential comments to the editor (not shared with the author) the first reviewer wrote: 'The writing is so clumsy that I see no likelihood that the author is capable of bringing it to a publishable level.' The second wrote: 'There is poor word choice, incorrect syntax, vague expression.' And the third wrote: 'the author should clean up the awkward syntax. It makes it impossible to understand the argument.' In comparison, reviewers appreciate prose that is both clear and powerful:

> This paper does a number of things very well and is informative in multiple ways. I enjoyed the clarity of the writing throughout. The authors did what good writers are supposed to do – they made it easy for me to read the paper without sacrificing sophisticated analysis of complex issues. It is remarkable how plainly they were able to discuss some of the critical but thorny epistemological and practical issues associated with [the topic of the paper].

Our students often complain when we 'take off points' for grammatical and spelling errors when grading their papers, but points *are* 'taken off' for such errors in the world of scholarly publication. Potentially insightful and important manuscripts may be rejected because editors and reviewers find their prose incomprehensible or just too painful to read. As a former editor of the *International Journal of Qualitative Studies in Education* advises, attention to writing increases the likelihood that a manuscript will be accepted for publication (Sherman, 1993).

A second reason why writing is critical for manuscript quality is that only carefully crafted writing can do justice to the complexities of qualitative data (Janessick, 2000: 388). The importance of good writing cannot be diminished because, as one observer has noted (Sherman, 1993), our work will be fully persuasive only when we become skilled and skillful writers.

Yet what does it mean to write skillfully? Unlike the rhetorical form of scientific writing characterized by a widely recognized and accepted style (impersonal pronouns, passive voice, and the like), there are no agreed-upon standards or models for presenting qualitative data and analysis (Moxley, 1992). Yet it is clear that literary considerations are central (Atkinson, 2001). Although traditional ethnographic texts use 'expository prose' (Lofland and Lofland, 1995), even the most traditionally presented ethnographies must rely on stylistic devices used by creative writers of all varieties (Moxley, 1992). These include writing vivid and arresting scenes (Atkinson, 2001) and using metaphors, figures of speech, and poetic language to enliven arguments and hold readers' attention (Fine and Martin, 1990). Manuscript reviewers applaud such writing: 'I found this article so gripping that, while reading it, I let my phone ring and didn't answer a knock on my door.'[4]

While qualitative research must be skillfully written in order to hold readers' attention while instructing them, there is a third reason for recent concern about writing. Despite the disagreements dividing the community of qualitative researchers, many agree that the history of this research is one of *decreasing authorial authority* (see Tedlock, 2000, for a review). In the not so distant past, academic researchers could assume their readers would believe them. That authority was achieved by properly referencing the accepted canons of the discipline (Atkinson, 2001) and simply asserting that 'I was there and this is what I saw and heard and this is what it means'. Today, disciplinary canons are in dispute (Behar, 1995), as are previously presumed correspondences between 'representations' and 'reality' (van Loon, 2001). Today, good writing of all varieties must persuade, and persuasion requires skillful use of language (Atkinson, 2001).

Before leaving the topic of writing, we offer a note of caution to authors wishing to publish their dissertations or classroom projects as books or journal articles. Rarely do dissertations easily translate into books; rarely do dissertation chapters or classroom papers easily translate into journal articles. Dissertations and term papers are written to convince sponsoring faculty that the author has mastered a body of knowledge and intellectual skills, while journal articles and books must entice a much larger audience to read and take them seriously (see Fox, 1985: 10–12, for a further discussion of differences). Editors and reviewers easily recognize the difference. To be publishable, dissertations and classroom projects must be transformed. As a very supportive reviewer of one such untransformed submission to *JCE* wrote:

> This manuscript appears to be a paper written for a graduate course, and a first rate paper at that. I probably would have given the author an 'A'. However, what constitutes an excellent term paper is not the same as that which constitutes a manuscript suitable for publication in a scholarly journal. Despite the author's obvious talents as both a writer and a sociologist in the making, this manuscript needs to undergo a significant transformation in terms of epistemological reflexivity, theoretical grounding, and analytical sophistication before it will be ready for publication.

In a just world, methodologically sound, analytically coherent, significant, and well-written manuscripts would be published, yet the world of publishing qualitative work is not so just. There is little agreement among reviewers of manuscripts submitted to social science journals (Hargens, 1988; Gilliland and Cortina, 1997) and perhaps even less agreement among reviewers of qualitative manuscripts submitted to those journals. Given the lack of consensus about what good qualitative research should be, any given qualitative manuscript likely will be subjected to different evaluative criteria and therefore is unlikely to be roundly 'rejected' or unanimously 'accepted'. It is in the vast region of publication decisions between those extremes that politics and luck come into play.

THE PRAGMATICS OF PUBLISHING

The first thing authors should consider when choosing among the myriad publication outlets for qualitative work is their intended audience. If they hope to address a large audience, then commercial presses that market their books to public retail bookstores (such as to Barnes and Noble in the US and Waterstone's in the UK) are the appropriate venues. Although such popular writing is vastly different from more scholarly prose, there is a market for 'cross-over writers' who translate academic research into manuscripts of general interest (see Persell, 1985, and Richardson, 1990, for discussions about this type of publishing). While we personally believe that qualitative researchers should seek larger audiences for our work, it remains true that academia generally does not reward popularized writing. Academic careers most often depend on the quantity and quality of publications in scholarly journals and by university-sponsored presses.

Authors must choose between scholarly journal articles and books. Which will best promote the author's academic reputation and career depends. For example, Clemens and her co-authors (1995) argue that elite private universities in the US prize books while scholars at public universities are more likely to publish journal articles. They also note that the natural sciences privilege articles over books, the discipline of history privileges books over articles, and disciplines such as anthropology, sociology, and communications value both.

Of course, not all books and journals are equal when it comes to participating in scholarly dialogue, achieving academic reputation, and advancing careers. In general, within academic circles, a book published by a university press carries more prestige than one published by a commercial press, and a book addressed to fellow academics carries more prestige than a textbook addressed to students. Likewise, academic journals often are ranked in one of two ways. The *impact factor* is a measure of how often articles in the journal are cited by other researchers in their published work. Journals containing articles that are frequently cited by others have a higher impact than journals whose articles are not cited. There is also a measure of the journal's *reputation* and this is determined by surveys of established scholars in the associated fields of study (Crewe and Norris, 1991).[5]

Deciding whether to publish research as a book or as a series of journal articles and where to submit manuscripts is complicated, but we agree with Pasco (1992: 95) that 'authors should learn something about the business of publishing'. We offer only a short primer on the major ways in which the process of publishing books and journal articles differs.

First, book publishing is about personal relationships, network ties, and patronage. It is a particularistic system in which decisions to publish are very much tied to the author's scholarly reputation and previous publication record (Gilliland and Cortina, 1997). Hence, the process of publishing books can be quite unkind to as yet undiscovered authors and very, if not overly, kind to authors with established reputations and publication records (see Powell, 1985; Clemens et al., 1995).

While reviewers of book proposals most often are told the author's identity, most journals in the social sciences use a 'blind review' process in which authors do not know the names of reviewers and reviewers do not know the names of authors.[6] Research has found very little evidence that particularistic characteristics such as author's age, race, gender, or academic affiliation affect reviewers' recommendations when this blind review process is used (see Gilliland and Cortina, 1997, for a review of these studies). Of course, 'blind' review can be a theoretical ideal but a practical fiction. Clearly, it cannot exist outside English-writing countries where the relevant academic communities capable of evaluating work can be quite small networks of people who each knows what the others are doing. In the same way, blind review is not possible when the topic matter is so highly specialized that few others, again likely known to one another, can evaluate the manuscript. While we were editors of *JCE* we also learned the fiction of blind review for well-established authors whose work has a recognizable 'voice' and therefore is easily identifiable. One of the lessons we learned was that we could not send a manuscript by a recognizable and respected author to more junior scholars. Such reviewers at times returned manuscripts without review saying they could not critique the work of such a notable scholar or their reviews were little more than gushing 'fan letters', lacking constructive criticisms needed to improve the manuscripts. We quickly defined this as a problem and learned that only reviewers who themselves had established scholarly reputations would honestly review the work of those with similar reputations.

In brief, the 'blind review' process can be a fiction, yet it remains true that for social science journals it is an important ideal that does not exist in book publication. An implication is that, at least in comparison to book publication, journals are much friendlier to authors who have not yet established a scholarly reputation. Indeed, our experience confirms the assessment of a former editor of both *Social Psychology Quarterly* and the *American Sociological Review* (Stryker, 1990) that, in comparison to more seasoned scholars, younger scholars tend to receive more chances and assistance during the editorial review process.

The standards and criteria used to judge the publishability of books and journal articles also differ. For books, only university presses publish manuscripts based on their perceived scholarly merit (Persell, 1985), and even those presses hope to sell enough copies to recover the costs of publication. Commercial presses primarily are concerned with 'marketability', so proposals or manuscripts are evaluated in terms of their potential success in attracting a large audience (Powell, 1985). In comparison, most scholarly journal editors are concerned with maintaining and enhancing the standing of the journal as measured by impact and reputation. Although editors have their tastes and biases, they nonetheless

must publish articles that likely will be cited by other scholars and that will enhance the academic reputation of their journal. Of course, this means editors will be delighted to publish the work of senior scholars because their work tends to be regularly cited by others, yet journals have many more pages to fill and manuscripts are judged as high quality regardless of the academic credentials, reputations, or affiliations of authors.

Once authors decide whether to submit a book proposal or a journal article, they must carefully decide where to submit it. Book publishing houses have 'personalities' (Powell, 1985). Submitting a manuscript – however brilliant – to a publisher that does not specialize in its topic is a waste of time. Conversely, gaining the support of an editor of a book series can greatly increase chances that a manuscript will be published because publishers commonly follow their recommendations (Powell, 1985). So, too, journals have personalities. Our experience as editors of *JCE* taught us that some authors should more carefully consider their decisions on where to submit their manuscripts because we received many that clearly did not qualify as ethnography, even as most broadly defined. Likewise, Miller and Perrucci (2001) report that *Social Problems* rejects a large number of submissions because some manuscripts do not even remotely concern 'social problems'. Aspiring authors would do well to read several issues of a journal to see what kind of articles the journal publishes, to become acquainted with its 'personality'.

Yet aspiring authors also should be aware that the personalities of scholarly journals routinely change. Most editors of these journals serve three- or four-year terms, and it is not uncommon for a new editor to bring with her or him a new vision of what the journal should be. For example, when we assumed the editorship of *JCE* we announced in print and by word of mouth that we wanted to publish more innovative manuscripts from scholars in disciplines other than sociology and by those outside the US. Our decision opened up the journal to a larger variety of scholars doing more diverse types of work, yet that simultaneously meant that American sociologists doing traditional ethnography now faced more competition for the pages of *JCE*.

In brief, journals, like book publishers, have 'personalities', but changing ones. That is not under the control of authors who may find themselves caught in an editorial shift between a supportive outgoing editor who strongly encouraged revision and resubmission and an unsupportive incoming editor who unceremoniously rejects the revised manuscript.[7] Like us, almost every author who has been around academic publishing for any length of time has had that experience at least once. In such a case, an author has little choice but to pick up the pieces of her or his manuscript and take it elsewhere.

Authors can be savvy about where they submit their manuscript but cannot so shrewdly decide *when* to do so. This is matter of sheer luck, sometimes good, sometimes bad. For example, book publishers often publish a certain number of manuscripts each year on particular topics, so a solid manuscript or proposal might be rejected simply because it was received after that topical quota was met. Also, small publishers do not publish many books on similar topics. In the interest of balance, they might publish a lesser quality manuscript on an uncovered topic rather than a higher quality manuscript on an already covered one (Powell, 1985). Timing also affects the fates of manuscripts submitted to scholarly journals. Authors submitting manuscripts cannot know if the journal editor currently lacks enough accepted manuscripts to fill an upcoming issue and is willing to reduce expectations to do so or, conversely, has a backlog of manuscripts waiting to be published and can afford to be choosy. Even though timing can matter, book publishers and journal editors do not advertise (or even acknowledge) when they are desperate for manuscripts, so it is almost impossible for authors to make their own luck by timing their submissions.

INSIDE EDITORIAL OFFICES

In this section we draw upon our personal experiences to offer advice, particularly to novice authors, about how to think about the journal review process and how to respond to it in ways that might increase the chances of publication. We provide this advice in response to a series of questions we once asked as novice authors ourselves and later found ourselves answering as reviewers, members of editorial boards, and editors.

How much power do editors have?

The simple answer to this question is straightforward: editors have a great deal of power. Acquisitions editors for publishers, for example, are the most essential and powerful actors in that industry (Powell, 1985). Likewise, editors of academic journals are the ultimate gatekeepers. They often have the power to reject manuscripts without sending them to others for review and commonly control the most critical decision of selecting external reviewers. Editors have the power – and responsibility – to read reviewers' comments, to discard specific comments (or all the comments) of individual reviewers, and to weigh differently the importance of reviewers' comments. Indeed, most editors are not obliged to follow reviewers' recommendations at all and have the final say over whether manuscripts are accepted or rejected for publication.

Although most journal editors theoretically could create their own little publishing fiefdom, relatively few do. Granted, as we already discussed, journals often change their personalities when editors change, yet only permanent editors can make a journal's personality more or less perfectly reflect their own. Editors of official journals of scholarly societies must convince elected editorial board members that the journal's prestige is being maintained or enhanced and its official mandate is being fulfilled. Editors of independent journals must answer to their publishers and maintain or enhance the number of paid subscriptions. Hence, to individual authors, editors are all-powerful, yet to authors in the aggregate, editors' power is limited by the need to maintain the journal's academic prestige, mission, and financial health.

Who are the reviewers?

The answer to that question depends on the type of manuscript and publishing venue involved. Academic book publishers send manuscripts to reviewers with established reputations in the general topical area of the manuscript while publishers of textbooks send manuscripts to instructors of appropriate courses (Powell, 1985). Most typically for journals publishing qualitative research, editors send a manuscript to two or three reviewers chosen for their expertise in the theory, methods, and/or substantive topic of the manuscript. While formally this is called a 'peer review' process, some argue that it is not about 'peers' at all: most frequently, reviewers already have an established record of publication and have published in the journals for which they now review. Because relatively few people publish on a regular basis, reviewers tend to be in the same social networks, and these often are not the networks of the authors whose work they review (Orum, 1990). Yet the process is 'blind', meaning that reviewers – at least in theory – do not know who authored the manuscript being reviewed.

While all editors seek reviewers with relevant expertise, editors use different models for choosing reviewers. Some deliberately send manuscripts to reviewers who they believe probably will challenge the theoretical, methodological, or substantive positions taken in the manuscript. Although this increases the chances that manuscripts will be negatively evaluated, it simultaneously yields hopefully constructive criticism that may be used to improve manuscripts. Other editors send manuscripts to reviewers who they believe will be sympathetic to its theory, methods, and topic. Although this increases the chances of manuscript acceptance, it often fails to generate the critical commentary necessary to make manuscripts as good as they might be (Stryker, 1990).

A good reviewer, from both an editor's and an author's perspective, is one who does the review within the requested time-frame, gives the manuscript a fair and thorough reading, and offers constructive advice in a collegial tone (Simpson, 1990; De George and Woodward, 1994). It is the job of reviewers to make manuscripts better, which is why excellent reviewers focus on what can be done to strengthen the manuscript (Fiske, 1992). From our experiences as authors, we have learned to appreciate such reviewers greatly because following their advice has made our own manuscripts better. For example, a few years ago Spencer wrote a paper that attempted to combine autoethnographic reflections and neorealist ethnographic description and analysis. One of the initial reviewers of the manuscript offered the following astute advice:

> You are here attempting – using a sometimes semi-literary, informal, personal writing style – to do a methodological piece about emotions in field research at the same time that you analyze how emotional neutrality is produced among mortuary students. In my judgment, you haven't pulled it off. Yet there is much potential here for both a first-rate piece of analysis and a first-rate methodological essay and my advice is to write two pieces, instead of one.

Spencer followed this advice and rewrote the manuscript, focusing on description and analyses of the emotional practices of mortuary sciences students, and, after two revisions, published it. Similarly, our experience as editors taught us that the quality of journals depends on conscientious reviewers. Yet as both authors and editors we know that not all reviewers are appropriate, good, or conscientious. Both of us have received unfair or unhelpful reviews of our own work and as editors we have seen instances of unfair and useless reviews.

Reviewers cannot easily be typified. We learned, as editors, that advanced graduate students can be excellent reviewers because they often know the latest trends and alert authors to new approaches; yet graduate students invariably

recommended that every manuscript be published. We also learned that some established scholars are incredibly supportive of methods and presentational styles other than their own and are remarkably supportive of aspiring scholars, while others attack anything that does not conform to their own preferred methods and presentational tastes. We also learned that reviewers are not always consistent in their comments to authors and their confidential comments to the editor that are not shared with authors. For example, some reviewers wrote very critical – sometimes brutal – reviews to the authors but recommended in their confidential comments to us that the manuscript eventually be published because of its considerable promise. Others wrote very supportive comments to authors yet nonetheless recommended to us that we reject the manuscript because it was fatally flawed. Finally, we learned that reviewers have different evaluative styles. Some write very supportive comments in an apparent attempt to 'coach' authors, while others are relentlessly critical (Beyer et al., 1995; Gilliland and Cortina, 1997).

Characteristics of reviewers can at least partially explain some of the mystery surrounding publishing. The social process of selecting reviewers and reviewers' evaluative styles are not communicated to authors. So, for example, we sometimes would select two reviewers likely to evaluate the manuscript very differently because we wanted to see the potential range of opinion. Yet in these instances, when reviews arrived we often discounted the criticism of the negative reviewer and discounted the praise of the positive reviewer. Also, with experience, we learned that some reviewers invariably recommend either rejection or publication. We continued to rely on such reviewers because we appreciated their helpful advice to authors. Simultaneously, we routinely discounted their recommendations. Finally, as with other editors, we took some reviews more seriously than others (Gilliland and Cortina, 1997; McGinty, 1999). We weighted more heavily reviews demonstrating a thorough reading of the manuscript and took less seriously reviews that were superficial in either praise or criticism. Within the editorial office this made perfect sense, yet we realize that at times our decisions seemed to contradict reviewers' comments to authors.

Why are manuscripts rejected?

The most painful form of rejection is when editors themselves reject a manuscript without external review.[8] Because both of us had personally had our own manuscripts rejected without review and knew how angry those decisions had made us, we started our editorship at *JCE* with the plan to send *everything* we received to external reviewers. That lasted about six months. By then we had lost one excellent reviewer who wrote us that (s)he would no longer review because we were sending 'hopeless' manuscripts and wasting her/his time; another excellent reviewer sent us an angry note advising us to 'take some editorial responsibility' and not send her/him manuscripts that clearly were unpublishable. Because journals depend on the goodwill of reviewers, we did not want to risk losing responsible reviewers by sending all submitted manuscripts for review. Over time, we developed two reasons for rejecting manuscripts without review.

First, we rejected manuscripts without external review that we would not publish, however favorably reviewed they might have been. These included manuscripts based on survey research, laboratory experimentation, or secondary analysis of quantitative data because we did not think they qualified as ethnography. Very commonly, we also returned 75 to 200-page manuscripts because the pages of *JCE* were too scarce to be hogged by such lengthy manuscripts. We also once received a manuscript with a letter from the author demanding that we review it and accept it for publication within a month because the publication was needed for tenure. We would not ask reviewers to respond so quickly nor would we ever guarantee acceptance, so we returned the manuscript to the author. We also returned manuscripts that violated our sense of scholarly ethics: two were blatantly libelous of people who could be identified, another was based on information about prostitutes that the author had covertly collected while using their services.

Second, as we gained editorial experience, we started returning manuscripts based on our experiential knowledge that they would not survive the review process. We returned some manuscripts without review because they were simply unreadable. We also returned without review some manuscripts that might have survived the review process at *other* journals or that of different editors of *JCE*. They included those claiming to be ethnographies but containing no empirical description, those without references, poetry, and one requiring readers to visit a website to view images discussed in the text. Our 'return without review' policy therefore reflected our personal understandings of the mission of *JCE*, scholarly ethics, and manuscripts' chances of surviving the review process.

The second type of rejection decision comes after external review. At *JCE*, as elsewhere, decisions are based on the editor's reading of reviewers' comments to the author (sent to the author), as well as reviewers' confidential comments and recommendations to the editor (not sent to the author). Here again there is considerable editorial power. In the easy cases of rejection decisions, all reviewers agreed that the manuscript was somehow fatally flawed and could not advise the author how to make it publishable. More commonly, none of the reviewers found 'fatal' flaws, but all found problems. One or more reviewer might evaluate these problems as easily correctable while one or more others might think that it would take considerable effort to address them. At times we followed the advice of whichever reviewer seemed to have given the manuscript the most careful reading. At other times we based our decision on our own estimate of how much work it would take to make the manuscript publishable. It was not uncommon for reviewers to write in their confidential comments to the editor that a manuscript had 'potential' but would require a lot of work to realize that potential. In all honesty, our decisions regarding these manuscripts often depended on whether one or the other of us currently had the time to nurture the manuscript through extensive revisions. At still other times our decision depended on our backlog of accepted manuscripts. If we had a large backlog, we would sometimes reject manuscripts requiring significant effort; if we were running low we would ask the author to 'revise and resubmit' it.

Certainly, our comments about rejection can – and should – be read as examples of editorial power. It is clear that we exercised considerable editorial discretion and that our decisions reflected our personal standards and editorial circumstances. Yet potential authors themselves can reduce their chances of having their manuscripts rejected by following journal guidelines, conducting ethical research, refraining from making unreasonable demands, submitting the kind of work the journal is known to publish, and submitting methodologically sound, theoretically coherent, newsworthy, well-written manuscripts. From the perspective of authors, the difference between a 'rejection' and a 'revise and resubmit' is sometimes a matter of luck, yet it remains true that manuscripts that are closer to being publishable have better luck.

Rejections are difficult to take. We know. We both have received our fair share and understand the hurt and anger they bring. Yet, as Pasco (1992: 100) observes, 'the only people who do not receive rejection letters are those who do not submit their writings'. Those who want to stay in the publishing game must learn to move on to other publishing outlets, to another project, or back to the drawing board.

What should be done with a 'revise and resubmit' decision?

Very few manuscripts are initially accepted by any journal (Gilliland and Cortina, 1997). As with social science journals in general, the most common decision at *JCE* was to advise the author to 'revise and resubmit'. This means that while the manuscript in its present form did not meet publishing standards, we and/or the reviewers nonetheless believed the manuscript had potential. It is not surprising that 'revise and resubmit' is the most common editorial decision. It is sometimes a compromise decision reconciling conflicting reviews (see Bakanic et al., 1987; Hargens, 1988; Gilliland and Cortina, 1997), but more often is a decision to give the author another chance with the benefit of collegial advice. Revise and resubmit decisions come in several forms that authors can learn to recognize. At best, authors will receive a letter with a sentence such as 'we strongly encourage you to revise and resubmit'; at the other extreme is a sentence implying that 'if you really persist we will give it another look'. Although the very positive letter is very close to an 'acceptance with revision' and the very hesitant is close to a 'rejection', *all* are invitations from editors to work on the manuscript, improve it, and resubmit it.

In these most typical cases, editors send the author a letter detailing how the manuscript should be revised as well as copies of reviews. When the process works – and it often does – editors, reviewers, and authors are all pleased: editors and reviewers because they can see the fruits of their earlier advice, and authors because they have a stronger manuscript and a forthcoming publication. This was our most enjoyable experience as editors because it showed how a community of scholars can work together to advance our collective enterprise.

Yet the process does not always work. Some of our least favorite experiences were the times when authors resubmitted a manuscript without seriously responding to the reviewers' earlier comments. In a few instances, postmarks indicated that the author had revised the manuscript in a day or two, clearly indicating that revisions had been superficial. Authors who do not take revisions seriously exasperate editors and reviewers. For example, one reviewer refused to write a formal review of a revised and resubmitted manuscript because 'the changes [in this version] are defensive, cosmetic, and superficial'. Another superficially revised and resubmitted manuscript insulted two of the initial reviewers. One wrote: 'I came away from this paper with a feeling that they didn't read my first review.' The second reviewer wrote in length in her/his comments to us:

> What's going on? I feel like we're busting our butts and the writers are in another world. They wrote [in the accompanying letter detailing revisions made] that they felt this was a better paper because of the reviewers but then they simply gloss the larger part of the reviewers' and editor's critique. It would be more than reasonable to say that they didn't agree with our comments, but convince me why you should not. GRUMP!

As this reviewer implied, it is *not* necessary for authors to respond to each and every comment and suggestion made by each and every reviewer. Yet authors who do not make an effort in good faith to respond to reviewers' and editors' suggestions invite their wrath.

Reviewers' suggestions for revisions on any one manuscript often are different; at times reviewers can even offer contradictory comments and advice. In such cases, editors must serve as mediators, advising authors of which advice and suggestions to follow most closely while making the revisions. However, busy editors do not always take the time to do so, leaving authors in the lurch. Authors receiving a revise and resubmit editorial decision but contradictory advice from reviewers have the right to expect the editor's guidance. It is quite acceptable to contact editors and ask for clarification when reviewers' advice is inconsistent and editorial guidance is insufficient.

In our editorial experience, far too many authors are discouraged by recommendations to revise and resubmit. Our strongest advice is to stick with the revise and resubmit process as long as reviewers' and editors' comments are helpful. In looking over the records from our editorship of *JCE*, we were struck by how many authors who received very strong invitations to revise and resubmit manuscripts failed to do so. Although some subsequently were published in other journals or volumes, our check of the authors' index of the *Social Science Citation Index* indicated that far too many of these potentially significant manuscripts remain unpublished. That is a shame. We appreciate that critical reviews of manuscripts can be hurtful – at times downright devastating – angering, frustrating, and discouraging. They still stir those feelings in us. Yet we have learned to read critical reviews, vent our feelings, and then get back to work. That is how scholarly manuscripts become published.

PUBLISHING QUALITATIVE MANUSCRIPTS

In many ways, writing this chapter has been difficult for us because we remember the early years of our academic careers when publishing was a mystery. We each remember times when cherished manuscripts were returned without review and times when reviewers found serious flaws in what we thought were magnificently crafted arguments. In the past – and present – we have received reviews that seem unfair and wrong-headed. That has been and continues to be our experience as authors. On the other hand, we have experience as reviewers, members of editorial boards, and editors and have tried to act ethically and professionally in those capacities. We have given countless hours of our time attempting to improve others' work and see it published. We have learned that many reviewers are great, most are good, and a few are horrid. We have learned that some authors take great care in crafting manuscripts while others seem to lack any sense of scholarly craft. We have come to appreciate the demanding standards of scholarly publishing and the necessity to our collective enterprise of upholding these standards.

The collective enterprise of studying human social life and experience is best served by informative, persuasive, and enticing publications. Authors contribute to that enterprise when they carefully craft manuscripts that tell an important and newsworthy story, address their target audience, and are pleasurable to read, whatever the presentational style. Editors and reviewers do so by honestly and fairly evaluating manuscripts and helping authors realize those manuscripts' promise or, when necessary, by encouraging authors to move on to more promising projects.

That is easier said than done. Our scholarly community of qualitative researchers is a contentious one today. In being honest and fair, we often disagree about the significance of topics, the appropriateness of different investigative methods and analytic frameworks, and the effectiveness of different presentational styles. Authors, including us, sometimes get caught in the webs of our conflicting assessments. Our disputes are political but most often they reflect the politics of intellectual substance, not petty particularisms. Our scholarly community has long welcomed a cacophony of voices: fresh and familiar, privileged and disadvantaged, exalted and despised. Our disputes are over how best to give expression to those discordant voices. Yes, our scholarly community can get rather disorderly, but that is the price we pay for our lively and stimulating conversations.

There is little authors can do to avoid getting caught in our domestic disputes, but authors nonetheless can be savvy. We conclude by offering a simple list of things authors can do to increase the chances that their manuscripts will be favorably reviewed and eventually published:

1 Produce quality manuscripts as quality is defined within a particular vision of qualitative research.
2 Circulate the manuscript to colleagues for their informal review. Remember that best friends are no friends if they simply praise the manuscript; worst enemies are friends if they point out how the manuscript can be improved.
3 Submit the manuscript to an appropriate publishing venue. Do not submit the manuscript to the 'most prestigious' journal if that journal does not publish similar types of work or if its readership is not the manuscript's targeted audience.
4 If the manuscript was rejected before external review, determine why. If it was because the publication outlet was inappropriate, go back to step 3. If it was judged 'fatally flawed', go back to step 1.
5 If the editorial decision is other than 'accept' (which is very rare), read the editor's letter and reviewers' comments and then put them into a drawer for at least two days. Let your hurt and anger subside. Read them again and put them back into the drawer for several more days. Do not make decisions about what to do with the manuscript until your emotional reactions subside.
6 If invited to 'revise and resubmit', consider if the requested revisions would make the manuscript better – even if they entail considerable work. If they would, then get to work on them because the chances of publication greatly increase for revised and resubmitted manuscripts. If revising the manuscript in ways suggested would make it into a 'different' manuscript than you want to publish, do whatever revisions make sense to improve the manuscript and go back to step 3.
7 Keep at it, even if that means moving on to another project. Some manuscripts never make it into print, and others do so only after years of reflection and radical transformation. In the meantime, go back to step 1.

ACKNOWLEDGEMENTS

We would like to thank the reviewers and editors for their helpful comments. We particularly want to thank our colleagues outside the US for their insights: Ken Plummer and Robert Dingwall (UK) and Daniel Cefai and Danny Trom (France) came to our rescue when it was obvious that we were hopelessly parochial North Americans in our knowledge of journals and the publication process.

NOTES

1 It has long been commented on, for example, that the flagship journal in US sociology, the *American Sociological Review (ASR),* is all but limited to quantitative research – particularly research displaying whatever state-of-the-art statistical techniques are fashionable at the moment (Bakanic et al., 1987; Clemens et al., 1995). Yet this dominance of research conforming to the natural science mode of inquiry might be at least partially a US phenomenon. Three of the most highly rated journals in political science in the US tend to publish manuscripts using formal, mathematical, and quantitative approaches while three of the most highly rated journals in the UK publish qualitative, reflective, and theoretical work (Crewe and Norris, 1991).

2 All editors want their journals to be perceived as both popular (as measured by the number of submissions) and rigorous (as measured by rejection rates). Editors therefore tend to use creative record-keeping. Including 'revised and resubmitted' manuscripts as 'new submissions', for example, can raise the number of submissions. In the same way, creative record-keeping can decrease the acceptance rate and make the journal seem very rigorous. For example, Clemens et al. (1995) observe that the *American Journal of Sociology* reported an acceptance rate of 12 per cent in 1993. Yet if resubmitted manuscripts were not considered as new submissions a more meaningful statistic would be that 18 per cent of submitted manuscripts ultimately were accepted. Bakanic et al. (1987) report that while only 9 per cent of manuscripts submitted to the *American Sociological Review* between 1977 and 1981 received an initial acceptance, nearly 29 per cent were eventually published.

3 This includes (but certainly is not limited to) works such as Becker, *Writing for Social Sciences* (1986); Emerson et al., *Writing Ethnographic Fieldnotes* (1995: ch. 7); Huff, *Writing for Scholarly Publication* (1999); Wolcott, *Writing Up Qualitative Research* (2001); Giarrusso et al., *A Guide to Writing Sociology Papers,* 5th ed. (2001); Cook, 'Loose, Baggy Sentences' (1992); and Fine, 'The Ten Commandments of Writing' (1988).

4 The varied and innovative presentational styles associated with the postmodern turn in qualitative research must meet still other literary and aesthetic standards associated with that genre. Aspiring authors of these types of presentational styles can consult issues of *Qualitative Inquiry,* the *International Journal of Critical Psychology,* or *Text and Performance Quarterly* for examples.

5 Different styles of research presentation can have unintended consequences on a journal's impact rating. When researchers tend to reference their manuscripts heavily (such as in the natural sciences), journals containing referenced articles will have a high impact because they are frequently cited. Conversely, qualitative researchers tend to do less heavy referencing and this, in and of itself, leads to lower impact ratings of journals publishing such articles. At the extreme, research in a postmodern genre tends to avoid referencing, thereby all but assuring that journals containing such research will have no impact because others doing similar work will not cite them. Individual qualitative researchers therefore could do a service to the larger qualitative community by being more explicit in their citations. Bluntly stated, every citation to a journal containing manuscripts based on qualitative inquiry increases the impact, and hence the academic prestige, of that journal.

6 In sharp contrast, journals in the natural sciences typically do *not* use a blind review process. The reputation and institutional affiliation of manuscript authors are considered important in evaluating manuscripts.

7 Often, editors coming to the end of their terms will notify selected authors with outstanding 'revise and resubmit' manuscripts of the date of the pending editorial change. Because such a letter often means that the editor would very much like to publish the revised manuscript, authors would do well to pay careful attention to these dates.

8 While we were editors of *JCE* we rejected without external review anywhere from 10 to 18 per cent of manuscripts. In comparison, *Social Problems* rejected without review 35 per cent of manuscripts submitted between 1993 and 1996 (Miller and Perrucci, 2001). While somewhat dated, Beyer (1978) found sociology journals reject without review an average of 12 per cent of submitted articles, over 25 per cent of articles submitted to journals of political science, but only 4 per cent of articles submitted to journals of physics. The higher rejection rate in the social sciences, as compared with natural sciences, may again reflect lack of theoretical and methodological consensus.

REFERENCES

Atkinson, Paul (2001) 'Ethnography and the representation of reality', in Robert M. Emerson (ed.), *Contemporary Field Research: Perspectives and Formulations* (2nd ed.). Prospect Heights, IL: Waveland Press, pp. 89–101.

Atkinson, Paul, Coffey, Amanda, Delamont, Sara, Lofland, John and Lofland, Lyn (2001) 'Editors introduction', in Paul Atkinson, Amanda Coffey, Sara Delamont, John Lofland and Lyn Lofland (eds), *Handbook of Ethnography.* London: Sage, pp. 1–8.

Bakanic, Von, McPhail, Clark and Simon, Rita J. (1987) 'The manuscript review and decision-making process', *American Sociological Review*, 52: 631–42.

Becker, Howard (1986) *Writing for Social Sciences*. Chicago: University of Chicago Press.

Becker, Howard (2001) 'The epistemology of qualitative research', in Robert M. Emerson (ed.), *Contemporary Field Research: Perspectives and Formulations* (2nd ed.). Prospect Heights, IL: Waveland Press, pp. 317–30.

Behar, Ruth (1995) 'Introduction: out of exile', in Ruth Behar and Deborah A. Gordon (eds), *Women Writing Culture*. Berkeley: University of California Press, pp. 1–29.

Beyer, Janice M. (1978). 'Editorial policies and practices among leading journals in four scientific fields', *Sociological Quarterly*, 19: 68–88.

Beyer, Janice M., Chanove, Roland G. and Fox, William B. (1995) 'The review process and the fates of manuscripts submitted to *AMJ*', *Academy of Management Journal*, 38: 1219–60.

Bochner, Arthur P. (2000) 'Criteria against ourselves', *Qualitative Inquiry*, 6: 266–72.

Clemens, Elizabeth S., Powell, Walter W., McIlwaine, Kris and Okamoto, Dina (1995) 'Careers in print: books, journals, and scholarly reputation', *American Journal of Sociology*, 101: 433–94.

Cook, Claire Kehrwald (1992) 'Loose, baggy sentences', in Joseph M. Moxley (ed.), *Writing and Publishing for Academic Authors*. New York: University Press of America, pp. 235–60.

Crewe, Ivor and Norris, Pippa (1991) 'British and American journal evaluation: divergence or convergence?', *PS: Political Science and Politics*, 24: 524–31.

De George, Richard T. and Woodward, Fred (1994) 'Ethics and manuscript reviewing', *Journal of Scholarly Publishing*, 25: 133–45.

Denzin, Norman K. and Lincoln, Yvonna S. (2000) 'Introduction: the discipline and practice of qualitative research', in Norman K. Denzin and Yvonna S. Lincoln (eds), *Handbook of Qualitative Research* (2nd ed.). Thousand Oaks, CA: Sage, pp. 1–29.

Ellis, Carolyn and Bochner, Arthur P. (2000) 'Autoethnography, personal narrative, reflexivity: researcher as subject', in Norman K. Denzin and Yvonna S. Lincoln (eds), *Handbook of Qualitative Research* (2nd ed.). Thousand Oaks, CA: Sage, pp. 733–68.

Emerson, Robert, Fretz, Rachel I. and Shaw, Linda L. (1995) *Writing Ethnographic Fieldnotes*. Chicago: University of Chicago Press.

Erikson, Kai (1990) 'On sociological prose', in Albert Hunter (ed.), *The Rhetoric of Social Research: Understood and Believed*. New Brunswick, NJ: Rutgers University Press, pp. 23–34.

Fine, Gary Alan (1988) 'The Ten Commandments of writing', *American Sociologist*, 19: 152–7.

Fine, Gary Alan (1999) 'Field labor and ethnographic reality', *Journal of Contemporary Ethnography*, 28: 532–9.

Fine, Gary Alan and Martin, Daniel D. (1990) 'Sarcasm, satire, and irony as voices in Erving Goffman's *Asylums*', *Journal of Contemporary Ethnography*, 19: 89–115.

Fiske, Donald (1992) 'Strategies for planning and revising research reports', in Joseph M. Moxley (ed.), *Writing and Publishing for Academic Authors*. New York: University Press of America, pp. 221–34.

Fiske, Donald W. and Fogg, Louis (1990) 'But the reviewers are making different criticisms of my paper!', *American Psychologist*, 45: 591–8.

Fox, Mary Frank (1985) 'The transition from dissertation student to publishing scholar and professional', in Mary Frank Fox (ed.), *Scholarly Writing and Publishing: Issues, Problems, and Solutions*. Boulder, CO: Westview Press, pp. 6–16.

Geertz, Clifford (1973) *The Interpretation of Cultures*. New York: Basic Books.

Giarrusso, Roseann, Richlin-Klonsky, Judith, Roy, William G. and Strenski, Ellen (2001) *A Guide to Writing Sociology Papers* (5th ed.). New York: Worth Publishers.

Gilliland, Stephen W. and Cortina, Jose M. (1997) 'Reviewer and editor decision making in the journal review process', *Personnel Psychology*, 50: 427–52.

Gubrium, Jaber F. and Holstein, James A. (1997) *The New Language of Qualitative Method*. New York: Oxford University Press.

Gusfield, Joseph R. (1981) *The Culture of Public Problems: Drinking-Driving and the Symbolic Order*. Chicago: University of Chicago Press.

Hammersley, Martyn (2001) 'Ethnography and realism', in Robert M. Emerson (ed.), *Contemporary Field Research: Perspectives and Formulations* (2nd ed.). Prospect Heights, IL: Waveland Press, pp. 102–50.

Hargens, Lowell L. (1988) 'Scholarly consensus and journal rejection rates', *American Sociological Review*, 53: 139–51.

Hilgartner, Stephen (2000) *Science on Stage: Expert Advice as Public Drama*. Stanford: Stanford University Press.

Huff, Anne Sigismund (1999) *Writing for Scholarly Publication*. Thousand Oaks, CA: Sage.

Janessick, Valerie J. (2000). 'The choreography of qualitative research design: minuets, improvisations, and crystallization', in Norman K. Denzin and Yvonna S. Lincoln (eds), *Handbook of Qualitative Research* (2nd ed.). Thousand Oaks, CA: Sage, pp. 379–400.

Kincheloe, Joe L. and McLaren, Peter (2000) 'Rethinking critical theory and qualitative research', in Norman K. Denzin and Yvonna S. Lincoln (eds), *Handbook of Qualitative Research* (2nd ed.). Thousand Oaks, CA: Sage, pp. 279–314.

Lawler, Edward (1994) 'Editor's encouragement of qualitative research', *Social Psychology Quarterly*, 57: v.

Lofland, John and Lofland, Lyn H. (1995) *Analyzing Social Settings: A Guide to Qualitative Observation and Analysis*. New York: Wadsworth.

Lyon, Eleanor (1997) 'Applying ethnography', *Journal of Contemporary Ethnography*, 26: 3–27.

McGinty, Stephen (1999) *Gatekeepers of Knowledge: Journal Editors in the Sciences and the Social Sciences*. Westport, CT: Bergin & Garvey.

Miller, Joann and Perrucci, Robert (2001) 'Back stage at *Social Problems*: an analysis of the editorial decision process, 1993–1996', *Social Problems*, 48: 93–110.

Molm, Linda and Smith-Lovin, Lynn (1997) 'Call for papers: special issue of *Social Psychology Quarterly* on qualitative contributions to social psychology', *Social Psychology Quarterly*, 60: iv.

Moxley, Joseph M. (1992) *Publish, Don't Perish: The Scholar's Guide to Academic Writing and Publishing*. Westport, CT: Greenwood Press.

Orum, Anthony M. (1990) 'Sociology's self-imposed moral dilemma', *American Sociologist*, 21: 72–5.

Pasco, Allan H. (1992) 'Basic advice for novice authors', *Scholarly Publishing*, 23: 95–104.

Persell, Caroline Hodges (1985) 'Scholars and book publishing', in Mary Frank Fox (ed.), *Scholarly Writing and Publishing: Issues, Problems, and Solutions*. Boulder, CO: Westview Press, pp. 33–50.

Powell, Walter W. (1985) *Getting into Print: The Decision-Making Process in Scholarly Publishing*. Chicago: University of Chicago Press.

Richardson, Laurel (1990) *Writing Strategies: Reaching Diverse Audiences*. Thousand Oaks, CA: Sage.

Richardson, Laurel (2000) 'Writing: a method of inquiry', in Norman K. Denzin and Yvonna S. Lincoln (eds), *Handbook of Qualitative Research* (2nd ed.). Thousand Oaks, CA: Sage, pp. 923–48.

Riessman, Catherine Kohler (1993) *Narrative Analysis*. Newbury Park, CA: Sage.

Sanders, Clinton (1996) 'Review essay: producing, presenting, and professing ethnography', *Journal of Contemporary Ethnography*, 25: 285–90.

Schwalbe, Michael (1996) 'Rejoinder: this is not a world', *Qualitative Sociology*, 19: 539–42.

Schwandt, Thomas A. (2000) 'Three epistemological stances for qualitative inquiry: interpretivism, hermeneutics, and social constructionism', in Norman K. Denzin and Yvonna S. Lincoln (eds), *Handbook of Qualitative Research* (2nd ed.). Thousand Oaks, CA: Sage, pp. 189–214.

Sherman, Robert R. (1993) 'Reflections on the editing experience: writing qualitative research', *Qualitative Studies in Education*, 6: 233–9.

Simpson, Richard L. (1990) 'The ethical responsibilities of referees', *The American Sociologist*, 21: 80–3.

Smith, Mary Lee (1987) 'Publishing qualitative research', *American Educational Research Journal*, 24: 173–83.

Snow, David A. and Morrill, Calvin (1995) 'A revolutionary handbook or a handbook for revolution?', *Journal of Contemporary Ethnography*, 24: 341–8.

Stryker, Sheldon (1990) 'Ethical issues in editing scholarly journals', *American Sociologist*, 21: 84–7.

Tedlock, Barbara (2000) 'Ethnography and ethnographic representation', in Norman K. Denzin and Yvonna S. Lincoln (eds), *Handbook of Qualitative Research* (2nd ed.). Thousand Oaks, CA: Sage, pp. 455–86.

van Loon, Joost (2001) 'Ethnography: a critical turn in cultural studies', in Paul, Atkinson, Amanda Coffey, Sara Delamont, John Lofland and Lyn Lofland (eds), *Handbook of Ethnography*. London: Sage, pp. 273–84

Wolcott, Harry F. (2001) *Writing Up Qualitative Research*. Thousand Oaks, CA: Sage.

Part 7

THE INTERNATIONAL CONTEXT

38

The globalization of qualitative research

Pertti Alasuutari

Doing qualitative research is a very data-driven process in the sense that most of the time one has to proceed inductively from empirical observations towards more general ideas regarding theory or methodology. When proving that our interpretation is valid, suggesting an interpretation, or weighing the pros and cons of different interpretations, we also typically give examples or take excerpts from the qualitative data, for instance from transcribed interviews or from video-recorded naturally occurring situations. Thus, even when we do want to make a point that we think holds not only in the material at hand but also more generally, we have to prove and illustrate it at a 'local' level. For the same reason, when at a more methodological level we want to show what kind of analyses can be made of qualitative data, we give a concrete research example.

This has certain consequences for the globalization of qualitative research. By globalization in its broadest sense we can refer to the process whereby a global network of interconnections and interdependences uniting different countries and regions is becoming increasingly dense, so that we create an ever stronger sense of the world as one place (Held et al., 1999: 16; Tomlinson, 1999: 2). Within qualitative research and methodology this process would mean that, irrespective of where one lives and does research, to an ever greater degree we share the same theories, methods and ideas about how to do qualitative research and how to make sense of human phenomena on the basis of empirical qualitative data. This is of course partly because we have read and consulted the same articles, studies and textbooks. But what if the 'international' (read: American- or British-based English-language) publishers think that their audiences do not understand too exotic examples?

That was one of the problems I ran into when preparing the English-language version of my qualitative methods textbook *Researching Culture: Qualitative Method and Cultural Studies*. My publisher expressed a concern about the fact that in the book there were plenty of references to studies that had been published in Finnish:

> At a basic level, the proportion of Finnish work cited in the text will not be helpful to British, American or other readers, to whom this literature will not be readily available or familiar. ... Would it be possible to rework the text as you go along so that references of this kind are replaced by references to examples which are fairly well-known in the English language literature? I am not asking you to completely empty the text of any Finnish connection, but to ensure that the overall balance makes the English language reader feel at ease with the presentation.

The request was quite understandable, and I did change several research examples into work that had appeared in 'internationally' published books or journals. In some cases, having to build my point around a new research example probably improved the text, in other cases I was not pleased with the quality of research I found and thought that the original research example was better and more interesting. Yet I grudgingly had to promote a piece of research basically only because it had been published in English.

I think this example illustrates remarkably some of the problems related to the globalization of qualitative research, and especially to the fact that the English language and therefore the big American and British markets have such a dominant position in social science publishing.

The formation of a truly global network of researchers can only take place if there is a global flow of ideas across borders and language barriers. It means that we have to have access to the work being done in different countries and regions and in different languages. Then, if and when we have read and consulted the same articles, studies and textbooks, any of us can make a contribution to the discussion by challenging a previous idea or applying a method in a new and innovative way. Despite the problems referred to above, it seems that such a global network of qualitative research is gradually developing, and to be realistic, it can only happen at the 'crossroads' or meeting point called the English language. However, just as in other forms of globalization, the process forms – or is conditioned by – a structure consisting of centres and peripheries.

In the globalization discussion, it is also often argued that globalization more or less equals 'westernization' or plainly Americanization. It is argued that the global spread of US standards – for instance via the global media industry and US-based companies and brands – gradually homogenizes world cultures. By browsing through the names and institutions of authors who have published books on qualitative methods, one gets the impression that the globalizing world of qualitative research is also very US and Anglo dominated.

We should not, however, combine the spatial metaphor behind the notion of 'globalization' with the temporal imagery of modernization or scientific progress narratives, as is done in the idea that globalization equals Americanization. Although the position of the English language and the American publishing market is strong, there are still other networks and flows of influence in the world. Even more importantly, we must bear in mind that the whole idea of one universal line of development towards truth is an ideological construct and highly questionable when talking about the development of qualitative research. Instead, there are several parallel developments and flows of influence going on, and where a school of thought heads next depends primarily on the local cultural trends and needs of qualitative research.

In this chapter I shall discuss the problems and challenges related to the globalization of qualitative research. I shall first discuss the Anglo-American dominance of the publishing market and how that dominance is reflected in the progress narrative of qualitative research. Thereafter, I shall discuss the implications and possibilities of the spatial metaphor of globalization. It does not mean that we disregard the Anglo-American dominance, but the globalization framework provides us with conceptual tools to analyse why that is, rather than fall for the easy solution that methodological development is driven by an inner-directed quest for the truth. I shall also point out an additional aspect of the development of qualitative research. That is, rather than a question of flow of ideas across regions, globalization of qualitative research can be seen as a growing flow of ideas across disciplines, especially from the humanities to the social sciences – and back. Therefore, we must bear in mind that most of the innovations we make or read of are rediscoveries from neighbouring disciplines and from the history of social sciences and humanities. From that viewpoint, the rapidly globalizing body of knowledge known as 'qualitative research' is not so much a new thing as a repackaged bricolage of existing wisdom.

THE ANGLO-AMERICAN DOMINANCE OF SOCIAL SCIENCES

It is quite obvious that, especially during the latter half of the twentieth century, the social sciences have seen a gradual reorganization of the networks of information flows within the global community of social sciences. On the one hand it is undoubtedly true that cross-border contacts have become easier and therefore also more common, but on the other hand the networks have increasingly often centred in North American scholars. One could assume that, along with globalization, a single-centre network model will give way to a multi-centre world, but it seems that the centre has simply changed its location. The continent that has the oldest universities, and was once the heart of the development of the social sciences, Europe has been decentred.

Consider Jean Baudrillard's world-famous book *America*, which can be compared to other travelogues Europeans have for long written about their journeys to foreign countries and continents. Alexis de Tocqueville's book *Democracy in America* is an obvious progenitor. Baudrillard continues the tradition of Europeans and particularly Frenchmen writing about this remote continent. However, since the days of de Tocqueville the structural position of the author has totally changed. De Tocqueville actually wrote about 'the other', about a foreign country at the outskirts of Western civilization. But Baudrillard, when writing his book, was a French philosopher in the late 1980s, somewhat famous because of his fashionable, daring, 'postmodern' thoughts and style, but still fairly unknown to the great

(American, or English-speaking) public. Most of all, he is French. He likes to write about contemporary phenomena, but as a Frenchman his examples of course deal with France. And that is not 'common knowledge' or a commonly known environment. As a Frenchman he is slightly disadvantaged in the 'international' market. That is why it was a good trick to write a book about America. 'Everybody' is supposed to know the Golden Gate Bridge, Burger King, Los Angeles. And most of us (who is us?) know these scenes because of all the American movies and television serials we have seen. To write cultural analyses about such places and phenomena is interesting, because 'everybody' knows what you are talking about. In this sense Baudrillard's *America* is a good example of the Anglo-American dominance in the human sciences.

One could of course argue that the Baudrillard case proves the opposite: no matter what country you come from, if you have important things to say, it will be published by international publishers in English, which has become the lingua franca of science. It could even be that this is especially the case with textbooks dealing with research methods, for instance with qualitative methodology. That is because, although it may be difficult to get empirical research dealing with a peripheral location published by international publishers, theory and method are universal: if you are innovative methodologically, you will get your ideas across to the international market.

To obtain a rough estimate as to how dominant the Americans and authors from other English-speaking countries are in the qualitative research publishing market, I went through the list of books classified under 'qualitative methodology' on the Sage Publications web page on 7 May 2002. Of the 217 books listed there, I checked the country of origin of the authors on the basis of their institutional affiliation.[1] If there was more than one author (or editor in the case of edited books) to a book, and if they represented more than one country, I marked a 'point' to each country. However, if the authors all came from the same country, I gave only one 'point' to that country. There were a handful of cases in which the institutional affiliation of the authors was not mentioned, in which case I omitted the book in question. Of the total number of 232 'points', the United States got 139, the United Kingdom 47, Australia 12, Canada 11, Israel 8, France 3, New Zealand, Germany, Denmark and Sweden 2, and Japan, Norway, Singapore and Switzerland 1 point.[2] In other words, the English-speaking countries held 91 per cent of the 'market', and the United States and United Kingdom alone had an 80 per cent market share.

The Sage case may well be biased and cannot be generalized to the whole English-language qualitative methodology literature. However, I have good reason to assume that the market share of the rest of the world as opposed to American and British authors would be even lower if we took into account all major publishers, because several others do not consciously try to reach the international market. They are content with the US or UK home market, which also means that you hardly find a foreign author in their lists. The best way to study the market shares would be to analyse the actual sales of the books, which I suspect would further sharpen the picture of Anglo-American dominance.

How can we then explain the Anglo-American dominance? Just consider the still very strong position of quantitative methodology in the US social sciences and compare it to many European countries where qualitative methods have more or less become the mainstream. You could easily assume that, for instance, European social scientists would have a much stronger position in teaching qualitative methods to the global academic community.

As already implied above, the reasons for the Anglo-American dominance of the qualitative methodology publishing market are obvious and manifold. For one thing, because of the great number of higher-level education students in the country of 281 million inhabitants, the United States is the biggest single textbook market, which means that to ensure global sales of any book it has to be made suitable for the US market. Textbooks by British authors easily fit in the US market because of the close cultural connections between the US and the UK. The 'biggest market advantage' in turn reflects the related fact that the United States is also the biggest academic education and research market. Therefore it is quite natural that it also produces a lot of publishing authors. Another important reason is the role the English language has inherited from Latin as the new lingua franca of science.

It could of course be argued that the big 'market share' of American and British authors in the qualitative methodology literature justly reflects the superiority of these scholars as compared with authors from other countries. Or, to the same effect, although qualitative methods are still a challenge to quantitative social research in the American academic scene, perhaps the strong position of Anglo-American authors in the market is due to more emphasis laid on empirical research methods in teaching social sciences. That is how the anonymous referee of the first version of this chapter saw the situation.

According to him, the first version of this chapter 'doesn't discuss all of the intellectual and market forces that may have contributed to that'. And he goes on:

> The English language is one obvious factor, but it is not the only one. The emphasis on training in empirical research methods and techniques in American programmes is a powerful influence on the marketing of methods texts – joined at a later date by the British market, also driven by research training (both operate mostly at graduate level). The incorporation of qualitative research methods into numerically powerful empirical fields (such as health research) has also helped to promote the circulation of methods texts – not least when such fields search for bases for research legitimacy.

Thus, if other countries would only put more emphasis on training in empirical research methods and techniques, according to my critic there would be more methodology authors entering the international publishing market from non-English-speaking countries. Following this line of thought, he assumes that the Anglo-American dominance in the methodology literature is an exceptional case. According to him, social theory has a very different appearance:

> Contemporary versions of grand theory are, for instance, dominated by European figures – not just Baudrillard, but Bourdieu, Foucault, Derrida, Deleuze, Latour, Gallon, to name just some of the Paris people. This is to say nothing of the reception of German social philosophy, or Russian formalism. Theory and method are relatively context-free while empirical research is context-specific. They both travel well, and commercial publishers find they can sell them widely; empirical research is not commercially viable on a global scale. But theory and methods have very different kinds of origins and their circulation is very different. They establish very different spheres of exchange, different hierarchies of esteem, and so on.

To find out whether that is indeed the case, I studied the Sage online catalogue listing of social theory as it appeared on 20 October 2002.[3] Compared with the qualitative methodology book market, the picture is admittedly somewhat different. According to my small sample, the UK is the leading country and the US only number two. Altogether, the market share of English-speaking countries seems to be only three-quarters, compared with 91 per cent in qualitative methodology.

However, despite the difference, and in spite of the general impression that many theorists come from elsewhere, the great majority of book authors come from English-speaking countries. Why is that? Is the 'mother tongue advantage' of English-speaking authors a sufficient explanation?

I suggest that there is another, more subtle reason for the Anglo-American dominance in the social science book market. One factor that subtly strengthens the Anglo-American dominance is the fuzzy but strangely persistent notion of 'modern society' or 'modernity' in the sociological vernacular. The Anglo-American dominance is unconsciously legitimated by an implicit definition of 'modern society' as the object of most sociological studies. 'Modern society' is mainly the United Kingdom and the United States – and perhaps France and Germany, because the whole sociological discussion about the advent of modern society originated there in the late nineteenth century. The discussion of other countries has to be redeemed by pointing out its role as a special example. So Finland used to be discussed as an example of a small Western country living next to the big bear, the Soviet Union. Sweden and other Nordic countries are often dealt with as examples of the welfare state and of considerable state intervention in a (semi-capitalist?) Western democracy. Maybe considerable gender equality is another theme. The cases have to be discussed, even by non-Anglo-American scholars, from the viewpoint of the centre (or 'normality', as opposed to extremes illustrated by 'others'), as somehow interesting examples of 'the other'. This creates a tricky situation for a non-American author wanting to discuss, for instance, insufficient social welfare systems or gender equality in these countries. To avoid the interpretation that insufficient equality or social security is a particular characteristic of the country being discussed, the writer easily ends up defending the existing achievements, although the author's original point was to analyse the reasons why the situation has stayed unsatisfactory.

The special trends and characteristics of the centre (i.e., particularly the US) tend to be considered from the point of view of 'modernization': as something one expects to happen in the periphery some time in the future. This leads into the phenomenon of fashions in social thought: when a phenomenon such as, say, political correctness, or a theoretical paradigm, is born and discussed in the centre, a non-American writer cannot help taking it into account in his or her writings. In that way the discourses of the centre structure the discourses of the 'others', no matter how ill-fitted they are to the trends and socio-political situations in other countries. We enter the 'international' discussions in terms of the conditions set by Anglo-American scholarship and social and cultural trends. If we say that a phenomenon, such as political correctness, does not exist in our country to any considerable extent, it is easily seen as a sign of 'backwardness', and we are expected to make an interpretation of the reasons for its non-existence. In the latter case we make a worthwhile contribution to the 'international' discussion, which shows how its function is, in fact, to make sense of the phenomena that take place in the centre.

This leads us to the related factor, already referred to in the Baudrillard example, that strengthens the Anglo-American dominance. It is the default assumption that we are all familiar with American and British places, celebrities and popular events. If we for instance analyse an American television series, pop star or film, or a British celebrity such as Princess Diana, it is quite acceptable in an international publication. In addition to the more theoretical points made, such objects of study in themselves represent phenomena 'of general interest', because 'everybody' is supposed to know them. The same is not the case if one analyses people, places or phenomena deemed peripheral from the centre position. The reason why the audience should read analyses of more remote objects has to be made explicit, and in doing so we often relate the object in question to related phenomena in the centre. In other words, whoever enters the 'international arena' necessarily contributes to reproducing the same structures. We have to make Anglo-American and other readers believe that everything worthwhile takes place in the Anglo-American countries, in the centre. In order to get our works published in the international market, we have to contribute to reproducing the centre–periphery structure, both by making our contribution to the development of a field of study, and by making it in such a way that it becomes part of the 'centre discourse'. We have to adopt the gaze of the people in the centre, looking at ourselves from afar or above.

Such distancing from one's own given perspective is by no means only a harmful thing. On the contrary, being able to take distance from familiar phenomena and thus show them from a new angle is one of the key gadgets of social scientists. However, the problem with Anglo-American dominance is that such distancing is one-sided: only outsiders are required to take another's perspective, whereas people located in the centre easily slip into ignorant ethnocentrism.

We cannot totally circumvent the structural determinants of international English-language publishing, but in my view our aim should be to avoid glaring Anglo-American ethnocentrism. For instance, as editors of the *European Journal of Cultural Studies* (*EJCS*), we – that is, Ann Gray, Joke Hermes and myself – have made the observation that especially British and American

scholars every now and then submit articles to us that address only a narrowly defined audience. Although we emphasize that *EJCS* is an international journal based in Europe, some authors either miss that or simply do not realize that not all our readers are familiar with, say, prominent politicians in the local-level London political scene, or that the point of the whole analysis has to be other than a remark aimed at the national political discussion.

THE PROGRESS NARRATIVE

Part of the cultural dynamics that tacitly contributes to the Anglo-American dominance of social science and qualitative research is the stubbornness of modernization and progress narrative within the 'western' sociological imagination. According to this line of thought, which stems from the Enlightenment philosophers (Pollard, 1968), the development of human societies can be best thought of in terms of an evolutionary process, within which primitive, technically and economically less developed societies gradually develop towards a more 'modern' model. Some critics may welcome modernization, others may be critical of it and long for the past, but within this progress or modernization discourse one tends to assume that social development, aided by social science, means that gradually all societies will look alike: the features of different primitive world cultures will eventually converge upon a single global 'culture of modernity'.

For instance, Saint-Simon argued that in the cultural evolution of mankind, there are 'organic' and 'critical', i.e., peaceful and revolutionary phases. According to him, the world has seen two organic phases, classical Hellenism and Medieval Catholicism. He named the third, coming phase 'positive' and 'industrial'. According to him, development is led by providential and inevitable divine guidance, but in the final phase its ideal realization requires from humankind conscious, enlightened co-operation, which is directed by the science of society. Later, Saint-Simon's disciple August Comte developed the same three-stage narrative and argued that humankind moves from the Theological or fictive phase to the Metaphysical or abstract phase and then to the Scientific or positive phase.

When we conceive of the development of human disciplines within this discourse, we tend to narrate it as a single story of scientific progress, within which old assumptions are every now and then questioned and challenged by a new paradigm, thus increasing our knowledge of society. For instance, in the influential *Handbook of Qualitative Research*, Denzin and Lincoln tell the development of qualitative research in terms of such a progress narrative (Denzin and Lincoln, 2000).[4]

According to them, the history of qualitative research in the human disciplines consists of seven moments, which are the traditional (1900–1950); the modernist or golden age (1950–1970); blurred genres (1970–1986); the crisis of representation (1986–1990); the post-modern, a period of experimental and new ethnographies (1990–1995); postexperimental inquiry (1995–2000); and the future (2000–).

Denzin and Lincoln associate the traditional moment to Malinowski's discussion of the scientific principles of objective ethnography and to the Chicago School urban ethnography. Malinowski's norms of classical ethnography established the image of the male 'lone Ethnographer' who first endures the ultimate ordeal of fieldwork in a strange, other culture, and after returning home with his data writes an objective account of the culture studied. The Chicago School added an emphasis on the life story and the 'slice of life' approach to ethnographic materials, seeking to develop an interpretative methodology that maintained the centrality of the narrated life-history approach (2000: 13).

In Denzin and Lincoln's narrative, the modernist phase, or second moment, is linked to the formalization of qualitative methods in several textbooks, such as Glaser and Strauss (1967) and Bogdan and Taylor (1975). They characterize this phase with an attempt to make qualitative research as rigorous as its quantitative counterpart. Thus, work in the modernist period clothed itself in the language and rhetoric of positivist and postpositivist discourse. Denzin and Lincoln mention Howard S. Becker's *Boys in White* (Becker et al., 1961) as a canonical text.

Denzin and Lincoln define the beginning and end of the third stage, the moment of blurred genres, by two books by Clifford S. Geertz, *The Interpretation of Cultures* (1973) and *Local Knowledge* (1983). In these works Geertz argued that the old approaches to the human disciplines were giving way to a more pluralistic, interpretative, open-ended perspective. According to him, the observer has no privileged voice in the interpretations that are written; the central task of theory is to make sense out of a local situation. According to Denzin and Lincoln, the naturalistic, postpositivist and constructionist paradigms gained power in this period.

The fourth stage, the crisis of representation, occurred according to Denzin and Lincoln with the appearance of five books, *Anthropology as Cultural Critique* (Marcus and Fischer, 1986), *The Anthropology of Experience* (Turner and Bruner, 1986), *Writing Culture* (Clifford and Marcus, 1986), *Works and Lives* (Geertz, 1988) and *The Predicament of Culture* (Clifford, 1988). According to Denzin and Lincoln, these books made research and writing more reflexive and called into question the issues of gender, class and race. They articulated and discussed ways out of the conclusion that the classic norms of objective ethnography can no longer be accepted or defended. Therefore, new models of truth, method and representation were sought.

Only four years after the beginning of the previous stage, Denzin and Lincoln distinguish the next moment, which they call 'the postmodern, a period of experimental and new ethnographies' (1990–1995). According to them, it struggled to make sense of the triple crisis of representation, legitimation and praxis. In this instance, Denzin and Lincoln make reference to only one book, *Composing Ethnography: Alternative Forms of Qualitative Writing* (Ellis and Bochner, 1996).

Five years from that stage, Denzin and Lincoln again distinguish a new stage or moment, this time called the postexperimental (1995–2000), immediately followed by the seventh and last moment, the future (2000–). When jointly discussing the last two moments, they write that fictional ethnographies, ethnographic poetry and multimedia texts are today taken for granted. And they continue: 'Postexperimental writers seek to connect their writings to the needs of a free democratic society. The demands of a moral and sacred qualitative social science are actively being explored by a host of new writers from many different disciplines.'

I have summarized Denzin and Lincoln's narrative of the development of qualitative research at considerable length because it quite carefully records the different major turns that qualitative methodology discussions have seen during the past decades. Therefore, I recommend reading that story and consulting the literature referred to therein to acquire an overall picture of the recent history of qualitative research.

However, that story also testifies to the problems and dangers of the progress narrative, which cannot be entirely avoided even if the storytellers are themselves aware of the pitfalls. Denzin and Lincoln do make many reservations to their story. For instance, when first introducing their model of the seven moments (2000: 2), they do define their scope by saying that they discuss the development of qualitative research in North America. In the same instance they emphasize that these seven moments overlap and operate simultaneously in the present. Furthermore, they say they are mindful that any history is always somewhat arbitrary and always at least partially a social construction (2000: 11). Finally, they emphasize that future researchers' interests in these moments are largely unpredictable: some are now out of fashion, but may again become fashionable in the future (Lincoln and Denzin, 2000: 1047).

Despite these reservations it is undeniable that their story, as an example of a progress narrative, also functions as a way to argue implicitly that what they describe as the last moments are where up-to-date, well-informed researchers should now be going if they are not there yet. Likewise, researchers and studies mentioned as examples of the most recent moments represent the avant-garde or cutting edge of present-day qualitative research. It is hardly a surprise that the authors of exemplary studies of these moments of qualitative research development are a very small and practically all-American group of people. And the closer to the present you get, the more frequently are there new stages, and the narrower is the group.

GLOBALIZATION: FROM A TEMPORAL TO A SPATIAL METAPHOR

Compared with the modernization and progress narrative, the globalization story is less akin to the ethnocentric bias, because it implies global spread and increasing mutual interconnectedness rather than unidirectional development. Within the spatial metaphor behind the concept of globalization, it is easier to investigate the multiple routes of influence in the world of scholars, books and scholarly institutions.

Moving over to the spatial metaphor does not mean that we entirely reject the temporal aspect. Some theories of globalization in fact present the modernization story in a new guise. In particular, discussions about the cultural aspects of globalization have circled around the thesis of homogenization, according to which increasing mutual interconnectedness of world cultures leads to a homogenized global culture. Thus, the globalization discussion has rejuvenated an older theory of cultural imperialism and Americanization (Holton, 1998: 166–72). According to the arguments presented in that debate, American companies have a predominant role in the ownership of 'the cultural industry'. The US has also been claimed to hold a role in constructing a regulatory framework within the culture and information industries that favours US interests. Moreover, it is argued that there is a deeper diffusion of (American-originated) cultural practices and social institutions throughout the world, referred to as 'McDonaldization' by George Ritzer (1993). All this is claimed to contribute to an ever more thorough homogenization of world cultures (e.g. Thussu, 1998), with the US as the model.

If such a homogenization thesis is applied to the development of qualitative research, one would argue that because the United States is such a strong market area of academic education and publishing, the views on methodology that gain a paradigmatic position there will eventually achieve dominance throughout the world. From this position, we can lament the prospect that the US dominance easily overrules the richness of multiple parallel scientific and methodological traditions. This variant of the modernization or progress narrative does not necessarily assume that the best and most advanced methodological views gain the upper hand, it is just that theories and methodologies formulated from a centre position are more easily heard and seen.

It seems that in some ways the homogenization thesis holds also in the field of qualitative research. For the reasons discussed above, there is a flow of influence from American authors to other parts of the world. English-language publishers form the global marketplace of ideas and thus strengthen the position of US-based publishers. Because English is the lingua franca of contemporary science, international publishing is often equated with English-language publishing.

For the same reasons, ideas stemming from elsewhere also enter the world market via American or 'major international' publishers. Scholars anywhere wanting to be heard internationally publish in American journals and books published by American or 'major' publishers. Similarly, books that have appeared in other languages get translated and thus enter the American market.

In that sense, what at first sight appears like increasing Anglo-American dominance, gradually leading into homogenization or 'Americanization' of qualitative research, is not that straightforward. The dynamics of international publishing in English also means that the American scholarly community is repeatedly influenced by people coming from elsewhere in the world.

That is one of the aspects of globalization. In the globalization discussion it is emphasized that not just money, products and ideas cross borders increasingly often; migration is one of the aspects and drivers of the process. The 'brain drain' from different parts of the world to US universities also contributes to the strong position of US-based publishers and the US academic scene. This is an old phenomenon. Just consider people like the founder of American anthropology, Franz Boas, a key figure in the development of survey methodology, Paul Lazarsfeld, or a key figure in the Chicago School of social research, Florian Znaniecki: they were migrants from non-English-speaking European countries who then made their career in the US.

Therefore, what seems to be increasing US dominance in the world of human science disciplines is in many ways based on a rich international cultural heritage. What now appears like the cutting edge of qualitative research is in countless ways the outcome of the accumulation of social science knowledge, much of which stems from elsewhere than just the English-speaking countries. To take just one example, in Denzin and Lincoln's story of the development of qualitative research, from the 1980s onwards new stages are almost regularly initiated by American anthropologists, but the points they make are mainly implications for ethnography drawn from the French discussion on postmodernity.

In the discussion about the cultural aspects of globalization, what is known as the 'hybridization' thesis challenges the homogenization thesis, and argues that because of globalization there are more and more 'hybrid' cultural forms on the globe. To apply that to the field of qualitative research, it can be argued that the increasingly strong position of English as a common language among world social researchers means that the shared cultural and scientific heritage, embodied in all the literature published in English, is constantly enriched. The American and other major English-language publishers do work as a kind of trading room of ideas in qualitative research and more generally in human disciplines. They work both ways: the US scholarly community gains influence from people abroad, and scholars working in different parts of the world can see what is going on elsewhere by reading English-language books.

In this instance we must, however, hasten to note the problems related to the Anglo-American dominance of the publishing field, discussed in the previous sections. As I said, the dominance of the big US market sets restrictions on what kind of work gets published. To interest the (American) audience and thus to get published, empirical research has somehow to address the American reality or political and cultural agenda. The same goes for innovations in social and cultural theory. To catch on in the English-language market, a new theory or theoretical framework

has to somehow speak to the current situation in the American reality. If that is not the case, it may be largely ignored and perhaps 'discovered' at a later stage. For that reason, it can be said that innovations made in academic communities speaking other languages form a resource of ideas, waiting for the right moment to be found in the centre – that is, in the English-language community.

Unlike natural science, whose development can be described as accumulation of knowledge about the laws of nature, human disciplines are quite different. They are more like a running commentary on the cultural and political turns that different societies or larger regions go through over the decades. Because there is no unidirectional progress in social development, different historical and cultural contexts have provided the world academic community with the conceptual and methodological tools with which to tackle almost anything that is possible in the human reality, seen from a plethora of viewpoints. However, such a collectively owned toolbox is never and cannot ever be at once utilized to the full. It is rather that the changes we see in the development of human disciplines in one country or region are due to the fact that some of those tools are in and others are out. Very rarely we witness a wholly new tool being developed, although each user leaves their marks on the tools they use.

The same goes for qualitative research as a special area. Instead of assuming the unidirectional progress of science, we should perceive the qualitative research scene as consisting of interconnected networks. Because human disciplines typically address locally important problems, theoretical and methodological ideas are either discovered from the global collective 'archive' or invented anew each time there has been a use for them. With all due respect to present-day and future innovative thinkers, in many respects it seems that the shared human cultural heritage and the potentials of the human mind provide us with the tools people use each time the conditions are suitable for them. For the same reason, similar development in different parts of the world creates similar lines of thought both in social life and in the realm of human disciplines.

International discussion about the origins of what is known as cultural studies – a school of thought also influential for the development of qualitative research – is a good example. According to the standard canonized version, cultural studies originated in the 1950s and 1960s in Britain, especially in the Centre for Contemporary Cultural Studies (CCCS) at the University of Birmingham. However, the 'school discourse', in terms of which there is a single tradition that has then spread around the world, has been challenged. For instance, Handel K. Wright (1998) has half seriously argued that cultural studies originates in Africa. In a similar vein, I have traced the formation of cultural studies scholarship in Finland to several different sources of influence, with the Birmingham School as only one of them.

Even when discussing the formation of cultural studies in the Birmingham School, it has been pointed out that it came into being as a fusion from several sources of influence. From the very outset the British roots of cultural studies represented at least literary studies, history and sociology. The Birmingham School was just as comfortable in borrowing terms and picking up influences from Lévi-Strauss's structuralism, and symbolic interactionism, as from the Marxist theorists Althusser and Gramsci. In a word, the Birmingham School cultural studies was an outcome of the intermeshing of influences at the time when the so-called 'linguistic turn' took place in the human disciplines.

In that sense, the ideas and sensibilities underlying the Birmingham School were sort of 'in the air', and therefore it is no wonder that similar formations of 'researching culture and society after the linguistic turn' took place in several places simultaneously. The 'spirit of the time' urged that culture be taken seriously and granted certain independence, but simultaneously several people realized that 'cultural matters', or meaning-making practices, need to be seen within the context of power and politics. Defined from this vantage point, it becomes clear that cultural studies actually has several independent histories. The researchers at CCCS and their 'godfathers' Richard Hoggart, E.P. Thompson and Raymond Williams were just one group who invented cultural studies among many others, such as Pierre Bourdieu (*Outline of a Theory of Practice*, 1977; *Distinction*, 1984), Clifford Geertz (*The Interpretation of Cultures*, 1973) and Marshall Sahlins (*Culture and Practical Reason*, 1976).

Thus it can be said that several groups of people invented cultural studies simultaneously, independently from each other – a phenomenon that is quite common in the history of science. However, in addition to that it is important to notice that cultural studies also spreads by association; that is, cultural studies has had a contagious effect on the writers quoted in its texts. Many of these writers have been drawn into cultural studies, and most have readily accepted the label. Janice Radway, for instance, had never as much as heard of the Birmingham School when she was told, after her book had been published,

that *Reading the Romance* (Radway, 1984) slotted into the category of cultural studies. Today, the book counts as one of the classical works of American cultural studies.

QUALITATIVE RESEARCH: A SHORT HISTORY OF THE CONSTRUCTION

Parallel with the story of the multiple and discursive formation of cultural studies as an academic movement and discipline, qualitative research can also be seen as a social construct, which spreads around the globe more by association than by exportation. One could argue even more strongly that in some ways and to a degree, 'cultural studies' and 'qualitative research' are competing social constructions, with which scholars can associate themselves, thus spreading the field by contagion. At least we can say that the development of qualitative research as a cross-disciplinary, firm body of knowledge is the outcome of a process by which the know-how or craft of doing empirical social research has been accumulated by borrowing from and consulting researchers from different disciplines in the social sciences and humanities. The accumulated knowledge has then been renamed as 'qualitative methodology', and scholars applying parts of that knowledge in their research have been renamed as or associated with 'qualitative research'.

From the viewpoint of sociology, behind that history is the methodological development by which the quantitative social survey acquired a dominant position within the discipline by the end of the 1950s. It gained such a strong position that the social survey became virtually a synonym for empirical social research. It was understood as *the* scientific method of studying social phenomena, and it also provided the model for other possible methods such as (quantitative) content analysis: you define your population, take a representative random sample, define variables, code the data and test your hypotheses by analysing statistical relations between the variables. In other words, in addition to a set of procedures it provided the whole language of empirical social research. Surrounding the survey language was a more diverse field labelled as 'social theory'. The idea was that after gaining inspiration from theories, researchers operationalize them into survey research designs and test them as hypotheses, thus giving at least circumstantial evidence to verify them.

By the 1970s there was growing dissatisfaction with the limitations of survey research.

Those who were particularly displeased with it either went back to the history of sociology or learned from other disciplines how to study social and cultural phenomena. Although a great deal of the skills that people acquired and procedures they adopted stemmed from the old stock of common knowledge of the craft of analysing and reflecting on social phenomena, in the new paradigmatic situation they were given a new meaning. The whole process of questioning and reasoning about social phenomena, making observations about them and coming up with empirical findings based on other research than an analysis of statistical relations between variables, was relabelled as 'qualitative research' or 'qualitative methodology'. This renaming of a great deal of the tricks of the trade of sociological reasoning effectively concealed the fact that, prior to the 1950s, practically everything that went by the name of sociology or empirical social research was other than survey research, and would in that sense represent 'qualitative research'.

Most of what goes by the name of qualitative methodology is just another name for the basic skills of social scientists. It is just that, due to the amnesia of sociology caused by the effects of the survey paradigm, these skills, the craft of social research, did not seem to have any space left. Instead of craft, the survey paradigm wanted so desperately to make sociology a science in the false model of natural science that people did not have much space in which to discuss or pass on the 'secret' that behind the clean, straightforward and elegant-looking front of a published social science research report is a process that involves and requires puzzlement, innovation and sociological imagination. We may argue that such uniqueness of each research process is characteristic of qualitative research, and we may even celebrate qualitative researchers for their innovativeness that defies all the rigid rules of science, but by doing so we contribute to reproducing a biased and harmful view of the methodological field of the social sciences and humanities as a two-party system.

Because qualitative research methods are more like a new package to a collection of old tools than a new developing area of scholarship, the picture of Anglo-American dominance we obtain by studying the list of textbook authors is actually an illusion. A great majority of the knowledge of human societies and behaviour, and of the logic followed in applying that knowledge to empirical research that is marketed as qualitative research methods, is borrowed from the common international heritage of the human sciences. Some of that knowledge dates back all the way to Ancient Greek philosophers, whereas later ingredients and spices of this pot of soup are fetched from many sources. Classical European sociology, social and cultural anthropology, symbolic interactionism, ethnomethodology, 1950s and 1960s French structuralism and post-structuralism, have probably had great influence, to name just a few examples. But more important than naming the geographically dispersed and cross-disciplinary sources of influence to present-day English language literature on qualitative methodology is to notice that interesting – or dull for that matter – mixtures of more or less the same ingredients, flavoured with some local components, can be found practically almost everywhere and in a number of languages. To a degree, wherever social scientists pause to reflect on the logics of their research on and reasoning about social phenomena, and write about such reflections to pass on the craft of doing empirical social research, they will tap the same sources.

HOW DOES ONE BECOME A QUALITATIVE RESEARCHER?

Given the nature of qualitative research as a social construction, at least during the formation of qualitative research as an area of scholarship 'in its own right', one did not necessarily become a qualitative researcher or an expert in qualitative methods by first taking courses in qualitative methods and then doing qualitative research. Instead, one learned by doing, by reflecting on what one did, and by trying to reconstruct the rules one followed by doing it. Then, becoming labelled as a qualitative researcher was the final seal. Such a process of entering the field was probably an inefficient way to learn the craft, because it certainly sometimes entailed reinventing the wheel, but it also meant that people brought with them their own educational and disciplinary backgrounds and thus enriched the array of discourses labelled as qualitative research.

My own entrance to the field from the early 1980s onwards is a case in point. It was a surprise to me to soon become labelled as an 'expert' in qualitative research, especially because, before starting to do empirical research and even before I had already started teaching courses in qualitative methods, I had hardly read a single book about qualitative methods from cover to cover, let alone taken courses in them.

During the time I studied sociology at the University of Tampere, from the late 1970s until

1983 when I completed my MA thesis, qualitative methods (or 'soft methods' as they were alternatively called) were not taught that much because our teachers' generation was trained to be modern scientific sociologists, whose methodological training mostly consisted in survey research. However, that era was marked by what was called positivism critique, which mostly stemmed from Marxian social thought, and the tide was just turning from an economic Marxist structural orientation to approaches that emphasized the importance of everyday life and people's own experience and sense-making. In that context, I became interested in the Birmingham School cultural studies and the way they studied youth or working-class subcultures (e.g. Willis, 1977, 1978; Hebdige, 1979). It was therefore logical that my student colleague Jorma Siltari and I did an ethnographic study of a group of men who played darts in an urban pub (Alasuutari and Siltari, 1983), and that study led to a larger research project that was completed in 1985 (for a later published English translation see Sulkunen et al., 1997).

By the time I conducted the first case study, my literacy in qualitative research methods was mostly restricted to the scarce methodological appendixes that appeared in some of the studies I had read as examples and models. The few textbooks I tried to read were in my view so boring and different from the approach I had adopted from the Birmingham School that I only skimmed them. However, my ignorance about qualitative methodology did not prevent me from starting to teach qualitative methods right after I had obtained my MA. The reason why they asked me to do it was obvious: only very few people had done an empirical study based on anything else than survey. Therefore, I just had to force myself into reading at least something, but I think that my first lectures consisted mostly in reflecting on and reconstructing my own fieldwork 'methods', and discussing theoretical and methodological frameworks such as semiotics.

At the time, my objects of interest within the social sciences and humanities certainly reflected the paradigm constellation within Finnish sociology. In addition to direct influence from researchers and theorists within the country, influences in the domestic field were filtered from several directions. Many older generation sociologists had studied at least for some time in the United States and become trained as survey researchers. However, in the 1970s economistic and purely theoretical, even philosophical Marxism, or the Scandinavian, especially Danish *Kapitallogiker* school[5] (together with the

more Soviet-influenced, explicitly political Marxism-Leninism), enjoyed a firm paradigmatic footing, especially among the younger generation. Marxism was a response to American 'behavioral science', and sought to account better for the structural determinants of society. By the late 1970s, however, researchers were beginning to look for 'softer' approaches that took account of people's everyday life. The solution was to be provided by the concept of way of life, adopted from Soviet and German Marxist sociology. Many articles by J.P. Roos (see Roos, 1985) were a particularly important influence in this regard. In addition to East and West German influences, such as Jürgen Habermas, the French cultural sociologist Pierre Bourdieu became early on very popular in Finland, and in addition to him there was a constant flow of influences from French philosophy and 'poststructuralist' social theory. Names like Michel Foucault, Roland Barthes, Jacques Lacan and Louis Althusser became known, read in French or in translations into Finnish or English. On top of all that, there were the old traditions of Finnish folklore and ethnology, which caught my interest when I later tried to relate my experience from fieldwork to those of others and to develop methods for analysing life stories.

Those were the main ingredients from which I cooked up an account of theories, methods and practices sold as a qualitative research textbook, but more or less the same texts could as legitimately be sold as 'cultural studies' (see Alasuutari, 1997) or simply as sociology. That very well illustrates the character of qualitative research as a construction. Therefore, I think my story shows that the same basic wisdom behind what is known as qualitative research can be independently acquired from several sources and traditions. That is because the main gist is the same as in all social research, informed by different traditions of social and cultural theory: to question and problematize everything you tend to take for granted.

On the other hand, the configurations of theoretical and methodological trends and influences peculiar to a particular country or region are also a strength for the development of empirical social research. For instance, had I been formally trained as a qualitative researcher before entering the field, I may not have looked elsewhere for ideas. Therefore, the professionalization of qualitative research as an independent field of scholarship brings with it the danger that the flow of influences from outside is diminished, especially if textbooks are primarily published by Anglo-American scholars.

TOWARDS GLOBALIZATION OF QUALITATIVE RESEARCH

Despite the dangers related to specialization and to conceiving of the development of qualitative research in terms of a progress narrative, it must be emphasized that qualitative research has certainly been a useful construction in the sense that nowadays students do not have to reinvent the wheel that often. Those of us who have assumed the identity of qualitative researchers and tried to pass on the craft of social research by reconstructing the fuzzy logics of doing empirical social research have helped to unravel an essential part of the profession. Although it was especially due to the positivist attitude prevailing in the social survey paradigm that created the amnesia of sociology, the tricks of the trade were never really thoroughly discussed or consciously thought through. Before qualitative research textbooks started teaching them, new generations of social researchers had to learn to master their profession by trial and error.

Given all this, wouldn't it then be fair to say that qualitative research has entered the stage where empirical researchers around the world no longer reinvent the wheel over and over again, in ignorance of each other? Doesn't the seven-moment story about the development of qualitative research told by Denzin and Lincoln tell exactly about the development ever since the first moment, when qualitative research was established as a field of scholarship?

I think it is certainly fair to acknowledge that we have come a long way since, say, Bronislaw Malinowski's (1961[1922]) guidelines for ethnographic research or Vladimir Propp's (1975[1928]) method of studying the narrative structure of folktales. As Denzin and Lincoln argue, the 1980s and 1990s alone included three historical moments.

However, there are important fallacies in the progress narrative at least as far as the global scene of qualitative research is concerned.

First, the temporal root metaphor of the progress narrative makes it difficult to account for several parallel developments going on in different human disciplines and in different regions. Although from a North American perspective it may seem that all major discoveries from neighbouring disciplines have already been made, even the story of seven moments referred to above can be said to testify to a different picture. The moments typically depict situations in which qualitative researchers draw implications from and react to challenges from new philosophical and theoretical trends in the human disciplines. In that sense, the moments come 'from outside' qualitative research as a field of inquiry in its own right. It is most likely that future changes in the field will take place under similar circumstances: somewhere in the human disciplines researchers come up with a new fresh idea and – sooner or later – an empirical researcher applies it to their research and writes about the innovation. Moreover, we have hardly exhausted ideas and discoveries about human reality that have already been made elsewhere on the globe. In fact, lessons from other cultures and from parallel traditions of social thought are a largely untapped and promising resource.

Second, the progress narrative easily guides us to conceive of the history of qualitative research as scientific development, within which outdated and antiquated modes of thought are now and again critiqued and rejected for better, more adequate and valid ways of conceiving of the human reality. As tempting as such a story is, I think it is wiser to be more humble and modest and to start from the assumption that qualitative research consists of a toolbox of approaches and practices aimed at a rational, entertaining and touching running commentary on social and cultural phenomena. The particular tools picked up and trimmed each time depend on the local historical and cultural context. At times, an entirely new tool may be developed, but it is foolish to think that there could be one tool that is applicable in any situation. From this viewpoint, true globalization of qualitative research does not mean that at any point in time there would be a global trend towards using a single tool or a set of latest design tools. There are such global trends and fashions, but hopefully globalization means that there is increasing knowledge and circulation of tools developed in different parts of the world. Truly global qualitative research could depict a trading point for different approaches and practices circulating within the global community of researchers.

NOTES

1   That was the quickest way to study the matter, although it is partly problematic. Some scholars may in fact be immigrants, i.e. 'legal aliens' as the US law calls them. But even if authors' nationality differs from their place of residence, it reflects the strong position of the country in which the author resides.

2   My own textbooks, *An Invitation to Social Research* (Sage, 1998) and *Researching Culture: Qualitative Method and Cultural Studies* (Sage, 1995) were not

classified as 'qualitative methodology' and are not therefore included in these figures.

3   It listed 272 books, from which I took a random sample of 42 books and checked the institutional affiliations of authors in a similar vein as I did in the case of qualitative methodology. However, to give due credit to books that introduce or discuss a theorist like Bourdieu, Durkheim, Giddens, Simmel or Weber, I also gave one point to the country of origin of the theorist mentioned in the book's title or subtitle. The fact that I studied only such a small sample of course means that chance plays a bigger role and that the results give only a very rough estimate of the actual situation. A bigger sample would, for instance, mean that there would be more countries that get a point or two. Anyway, the 42 books turned into 47 points, which were distributed in the following manner. Out of 47 points, the UK got 18, the US 8, Australia 5, France 5, Canada 4, Germany 3, India 2, Denmark 1, and the Netherlands 1 point.

4   In an earlier critique of Denzin and Lincoln's account of the development of qualitative research, Atkinson et al. (1999) also point out the teleological character of the Denzin and Lincoln scenario. As they put it, 'despite the postmodernist standpoint from which they survey the scene, a grand narrative of intellectual progress is reinvented' (1999: 468).

5   As a short introduction, see the Special Issue on the Critique of Political Economy, *Acta Sociologica*, 20(2), 1977.

REFERENCES

Alasuutari, Pertti (1997) 'The construction of cultural studies in Finland', *European Journal of Cultural Studies*, 2(1): 91–109.

Alasuutari, Pertti and Siltari, Jorma (1983) 'Miehisen vapauden valtakunta' ['The realm of male freedom']. *Tampereen yliopiston Yhteiskuntatieteiden Tutkimuslaitoksen Julkaisuja* [Research Reports of the Research Institute of the Social Sciences, University of Tampere], series B 37.

Atkinson, Paul, Coffey, Amanda and Delamont, Sara (1999) 'Ethnography: post, past, and present', *Journal of Contemporary Ethnography*, 28(5): 460–71.

Becker, H.S., Geer, B., Hughes, E.C. and Strauss, A.L. (1961) *Boys in White: Student Culture in Medical School*. Chicago: University of Chicago Press.

Bogdan, R.C. and Taylor, S.J. (1975) *Introduction to Qualitative Research Methods: A Phenomenological Approach to the Social Sciences*. New York: John Wiley.

Bourdieu, Pierre (1977) *Outline of a Theory of Practice*. Cambridge: Cambridge University Press.

Bourdieu, Pierre (1984) *Distinction: A Social Critique of the Judgement of Taste*. Cambridge, MA: Harvard University Press.

Clifford, J. (1988) *The Predicament of Culture: Twentieth-Century Ethnography, Literature, and Art*. Cambridge, MA: Harvard University Press.

Clifford, J. and Marcus, G.E. (eds) (1986) *Writing Culture: The Poetics and Politics of Ethnography*. Berkeley: University of California Press.

Denzin, Norman K. and Lincoln, Yvonna S. (2000) 'Introduction: the discipline and practice of qualitative research', in Norman K. Denzin and Yvonna S. Lincoln (eds), *Handbook of Qualitative Research* (2nd ed.). Thousand Oaks, CA: Sage, pp. 1–28.

Ellis, C. and Bochner, A.P. (eds) (1996) *Composing Ethnography: Alternative Forms of Qualitative Writing*. Walnut Creek, CA: AltaMira Press.

Geertz, Clifford (1973) *The Interpretation of Cultures*. New York: Basic Books.

Geertz, Clifford (1983) *Local Knowledge: Further Essays in Interpretive Anthropology*. New York: Basic Books.

Geertz, Clifford (1988) *Works and Lives: The Anthropologist as Author*. Cambridge: Polity Press.

Glaser, Barney G. and Strauss, Anselm L. (1967) *The Discovery of Grounded Theory: Strategies for Qualitative Research*. Chicago: Aldine.

Hebdige, Dick (1979) *Subculture: The Meaning of Style*. London: Routledge.

Held, David, McGrew, Anthony G., Goldblatt, David and Perraton, Jonathan (1999) *Global Transformations: Politics, Economics and Culture*. Cambridge: Polity Press.

Holton, Robert J. (1998) *Globalization and the Nation-State*. London: Macmillan Press.

Lincoln, Yvonna S. and Denzin, Norman K. (2000) 'The seventh moment: out of the past', in Norman K. Denzin and Yvonna S. Lincoln (eds), *Handbook of Qualitative Research* (2nd ed.). Thousand Oaks, CA: Sage, pp. 1047–65.

Malinowski, Bronislaw (1961 [1922]) *Argonauts of the Western Pacific*. New York: E.P. Dutton.

Marcus, G.E. and Fischer, M.M.J. (1986) *Anthropology as Cultural Critique: An Experimental Moment in the Human Sciences*. Chicago: University of Chicago Press.

Pollard, Sidney (1968) *The Idea of Progress: History and Society*. New York: Basic Books.

Propp, Vladimir (1975 [1928]) *Morphology of the Folktale*. Austin and London: University of Texas Press.

Radway, Janice A. (1984) *Reading the Romance: Women, Patriarchy, and Popular Literature*. Chapel Hill: University of North Carolina Press.

Ritzer, George (1993) *The McDonaldization of Society: An Investigation into the Changing Character of Contemporary Social Life*. Newbury Park, CA: Pine Forge Press.

Roos, J.P. (1985) *Elämäntapaa etsimässä [Searching for the Way of Life]*. Helsinki: Tutkijaliiton julkaisusarja 34.

Sahlins, Marshall (1976) *Culture and Practical Reason*. Chicago: University of Chicago Press.

Sulkunen, Pekka, Alasuutari, Pertti, Nätkin, Ritva and Kinnunen, Merja (1997) *The Urban Pub*. Helsinki: Stakes.

Thussu, Daya Kishan (ed.) (1998) *Electronic Empires: Global Media and Local Resistance*. London: Edward Arnold.

Tomlinson, John (1999) *Globalization and Culture.* Cambridge: Polity Press.

Turner, V. and Bruner, E. (eds) (1986) *The Anthropology of Experience.* Urbana: University of Illinois Press.

Willis, Paul (1977) *Learning to Labour: How Working Class Kids Get Working Class Jobs.* Farnborough: Gower.

Willis, Paul (1978) *Profane Culture.* London: Routledge & Kegan Paul.

Wright, Handel K. (1998) 'Dare we de-centre Birmingham? Troubling the "origin" and trajectories of cultural studies', *European Journal of Cultural Studies*, 1(1): 33–56.

Index